DICTIONARY OF
AFRICAN BIOGRAPHY
1971

DICTIONARY OF AFRICAN BIOGRAPHY

SENIOR PATRON:

HIS IMPERIAL MAJESTY HAILÉ SELASSIÉ I,
EMPEROR OF ETHIOPIA

PATRONS:

His Majesty Hassan II, King of Morocco; His Excellency Ahmadou Ahidjo, President of the Federated Republic of Cameroon; His Excellency General Etienne Eyadema, President of the Republic of Togo; His Excellency Major-General Yakubu Gowon, Head of the Federal Military Government of Nigeria; His Excellency Felix Houphouet-Boigny, President of the Republic of Ivory Coast; The Hon. Siaka P. Stevens, Prime Minister of Sierra Leone; His Excellency William V. S. Tubman, President of the Republic of Liberia.

HON. GENERAL EDITOR:

ERNEST KAY
Author of Biographical and Other Works;
Editor and Publisher of London

EXECUTIVE EDITOR:

Georgina A. Reynolds

EDITOR:

Elizabeth Bly

ASSISTANT EDITORS:

Jennifer Brittain-Catlin; Jean M. Bubbers; Rolf E. Gooderham; Andrea Hanfman; Richard A. Kay; Patricia Tierney; Marina Salandy.

All communications to: D.A.B., Artillery Mansions, Victoria Street, London, S.W.1, England

DICTIONARY
OF
AFRICAN BIOGRAPHY

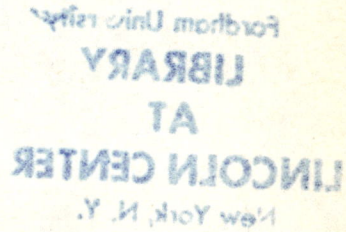

SECOND EDITION
1971

With the
**FULL TEXT OF THE CHARTER OF THE
ORGANIZATION OF AFRICAN UNITY**

MELROSE PRESS LTD., LONDON

©1971 by Melrose Press Ltd., London, England
ALL RIGHTS RESERVED

PRINTED OFFSET LITHO AND BOUND IN GREAT BRITAIN BY
COX AND WYMAN, LTD., FAKENHAM AND READING
COMPOSED BY PERIDON LTD., LONDON, N.W.9, ENGLAND

FOREWORD BY THE HON. GENERAL EDITOR

This Second Edition of the 'Dictionary of African Biography' is larger in scope than the First Edition which was published in 1970; it has taken sixteen months to prepare and includes biographical sketches of persons of achievement in all the nations in membership with the Organization of African Unity. Even though it is enlarged there are still omissions within its pages but, as each Edition is published, I hope that the omissions become fewer. Every effort has been made to have questionnaires returned to us. The eventual aim is for the 'Dictionary of African Biography' to include all men and women of achievement in the independent African countries.

Published again under the distinguished patronage of His Imperial Majesty Hailé Selassié, Emperor of Ethiopia, and of other Heads of State and Government in Africa, the 'Dictionary of African Biography' has aims which are common to those of the O.A.U. These are: To spread throughout the world information about persons of contemporary achievement in the countries within the O.A.U.; to bring these countries and peoples ever closer together; to promote the unity of the African nations and assist in their continued development.

We are honoured to include again in this Edition the full text of the Charter of the Organization of African Unity. This was printed in the First Edition of the 'Dictionary of African Biography' at the express request of the Emperor of Ethiopia and His Excellency Diallo Telli, Secretary-General of the O.A.U., both of whom I personally consulted in Addis Ababa. The decision to reprint the Charter in this Second Edition is at the request of leading Africans.

In my Foreword to the First Edition I made it clear that the 'Dictionary of African Biography' is a biographical reference work concerned with free Africa and that nowhere within its pages would be found any reference to the Republic of South Africa, Southern Rhodesia, or the Portuguese colonies in the Continent of Africa. We still stand—and will continue to do so—by this pledge and we will never assist the racialist regimes in Africa by promoting their citizens within our pages. We deeply regret that the rebellion in Southern Rhodesia continues at the time of writing and we hope that it will have been overcome by the time the Third Edition appears. We utterly repudiate those regimes which subjugate the vast majority of their populations.

My colleagues and I have been delighted to note the progress made in so many directions by the Organization of African Unity during the past year and we extend our warm congratulations to His Excellency Dr. Kenneth Kaunda, President of Zambia, on his dynamic leadership of the O.A.U. President Kaunda was in England in October 1970 and he made a deep impression on the majority of the British people. He will, we are sure, lead the O.A.U. to its rightful place as a unified world power alongside those which already exist.

I would like to express my warm thanks to all who have co-operated with us in the production of the Second Edition, including the O.A.U. and many Embassies and High Commissions in London.

Artillery Mansions,
Victoria Street,
London, S.W.1, England
January, 1971

CHARTER OF THE ORGANIZATION OF AFRICAN UNITY

We, the Heads of African States and Governments assembled in the City of Addis Ababa, Ethiopia;

CONVINCED that it is the inalienable right of all people to control their own destiny;

CONSCIOUS of the fact that freedom, equality, justice and dignity are essential objectives for the achievement of the legitimate aspirations of the African peoples;

CONSCIOUS of our responsibility to harness the natural and human resources of our continent for the total advancement of our peoples in spheres of human endeavour;

INSPIRED by a common determination to promote understanding among our peoples and co-operation among our States in response to the aspirations of our peoples for brotherhood and solidarity, in a larger unity transcending ethnic and national differences;

CONVINCED that, in order to translate this determination into a dynamic force in the cause of human progress, conditions for peace and security must be established and maintained;

DETERMINED to safeguard and consolidate the hard-won independence as well as the sovereignty and territorial integrity of our States, and to fight against neo-colonialism in all its forms;

DEDICATED to the general progress of Africa;

PERSUADED that the Charter of the United Nations and the Universal Declaration of Human Rights, to the principles of which we reaffirm our adherence, provide a solid foundation for peaceful and positive co-operation among States;

DESIROUS that all African States should henceforth unite so that the welfare and well-being of their peoples can be assured;

RESOLVED to reinforce the links between our states by establishing and strengthening common institutions;

HAVE agreed to the present Charter.

ESTABLISHMENT

Article I

1. The High Contracting Parties do by the present Charter establish an Organization to be known as the ORGANIZATION OF AFRICAN UNITY.
2. The Organization shall include the Continental African States, Madagascar and other Islands surrounding Africa.

PURPOSES

Article II

1. The Organization shall have the following purposes;
    a. to promote the unity and solidarity of the African States;
    b. to co-ordinate and intensify their co-operation and efforts to achieve a better life for the peoples of Africa;
    c. to defend their sovereignty, their territorial integrity and independence;
    d. to eradicate all forms of colonialism from Africa; and
    e. to promote international co-operation, having due regard to the Charter of the United Nations and the Universal Declaration of Human Rights.

2. To these ends, the Member States shall co-ordinate and harmonize their general policies, especially in the following fields;
   a. political and diplomatic co-operation;
   b. economic co-operation, including transport and communications;
   c. educational and cultural co-operation;
   d. health, sanitation, and nutritional co-operation;
   e. scientific and technical co-operation; and
   f. co-operation for defence and security.

PRINCIPLES

Article III

The Member States, in pursuit of the purposes stated in Article II, solemnly affirm and declare their adherence to the following principles:
1. the sovereign equality of all Member States;
2. non-interference in the internal affairs of States;
3. respect for the sovereignty and territorial integrity of each State and for its inalienable right to independent existence;
4. peaceful settlement of disputes by negotiation, mediation, conciliation or arbitration;
5. unreserved condemnation, in all its forms, of political assassination as well as of subversive activities on the part of neighbouring States or any other States;
6. absolute dedication to the total emancipation of the African territories which are still dependent;
7. affirmation of a policy of non-alignment with regard to all blocs.

MEMBERSHIP

Article IV

Each independent sovereign African State shall be entitled to become a Member of the Organization.

RIGHTS AND DUTIES OF MEMBER STATES

Article V

All Member States shall enjoy equal rights and have equal duties.

Article VI

The Member States pledge themselves to observe scrupulously the principles enumerated in Article III of the present Charter.

INSTITUTIONS

Article VII

The Organization shall accomplish its purpose through the following principle institutions:
1. the Assembly of Heads of State and Government;
2. the Council of Ministers;
3. the General Secretariat;
4. the Commission of Mediation, Conciliation and Arbitration.

THE ASSEMBLY OF HEADS OF STATE AND GOVERNMENT

Article VIII

The Assembly of Heads of State and Government shall be the supreme organ of the Organization. It shall, subject to the provisions of this Charter, discuss matters of common concern to Africa with a view to co-ordinating and harmonizing the general policy of the Organization. It may in addition review the structure, functions and acts of all the organs and any specialized agencies which may be created in accordance with the present Charter.

Article IX

The Assembly shall be composed of the Heads of State and Government or their duly accredited representatives and it shall meet at least once a year. At the request of any Member State and on approval by a two-thirds majority of the Member States, the Assembly shall meet in extraordinary session.

Article X

1. Each Member State shall have one vote.
2. All resolutions shall be determined by a two-thirds majority of the Members of the Organization.
3. Questions of procedure shall require a simple majority. Whether or not a question is one of procedure shall be determined by a simple majority of all Member States of the Organization.
4. Two-thirds of the total membership of the Organization shall form a quorum at any meeting of the Assembly.

Article XI

The Assembly shall have the power to determine its own rules of procedure.

THE COUNCIL OF MINISTERS

Article XII

1. The Council of Ministers shall consist of Foreign Ministers or such other Ministers as are designated by the Governments of Member States.
2. The Council of Ministers shall meet at least twice a year. When requested by any Member State and approved by two-thirds of all Member States, it shall meet in extraordinary session.

Article XIII

1. The Council of Ministers shall be responsible to the Assembly of Heads of State and Government. It shall be entrusted with the responsibility of preparing conferences of the Assembly.
2. It shall take cognisance of any matter referred to it by the Assembly. It shall be entrusted with the implementation of the decision of the Assembly of Heads of State and Government. It shall co-ordinate inter-African co-operation in accordance with the instructions of the Assembly and in conformity with Article II (2) of the present Charter.

Article XIV

1. Each Member State shall have one vote.
2. All resolutions shall be determined by a simple majority of the members of the Council of Ministers.
3. Two-thirds of the total membership of the Council of Ministers shall form a quorum for any meeting of the Council.

Article XV

The Council shall have the power to determine its own rules of procedure.

GENERAL SECRETARIAT

Article XVI

There shall be an Administrative Secretary-General of the Organization, who shall be appointed by the Assembly of Heads of State and Government. The Administrative Secreatry-General shall direct the affairs of the Secretariat.

Article XVII

There shall be one or more Assistant Secretaries-General of the Organization, who shall be appointed by the Assembly of Heads of State and Government.

Article XVIII

The functions and conditions of services of the Secretary-General, of the Assistant Secretaries-General and other employees of the Secretariat shall be governed by the provisions of this Charter and the regulations approved by the Assembly of Heads of State and Government.

1. In the performance of their duties the Administrative Secretary-General and the staff shall not seek or receive instructions from any government or from any other authority external to the Organization. They shall refrain trom any action which might reflect on their position as international officials responsible only to the Organization.

2. Each member of the Organization undertakes to respect the exclusive character of the responsibilities of the Administrative Secretary-General and the staff and not to seek to influence them in the discharge of their responsibilities.

COMMISSION OF MEDIATION, CONCILIATION AND ARBITRATION

Article XIX

Member States pledge to settle all disputes among themselves by peaceful means and, to this end decide to establish a Commission of Mediation, Conciliation and Arbitration, the composition of which and conditions of service shall be defined by a separate Protocol to be approved by the Assembly of Heads of State and Government. Said Protocol shall be regarded as forming an integral part of the present Charter.

SPECIALIZED COMMISSIONS

Article XX

The Assembly shall establish such Specialized Commissions as it may deem necessary, including the following;
1. Economic and Social Commission;
2. Educational and Cultural Commission;
3. Health, Sanitation and Nutrition Commission;
4. Defence Commission;
5. Scientific, Technical and Research Commission.

Article XXI

Each Specialized Commission referred to in Article XX shall be composed of the Ministers concerned or other Ministers or Plenipotentiaries designated by the Governments of the Member States.

Article XXII

The functions of the Specialized Commissions shall be carried out in accordance with the provisions of the present Charter and of the regulations approved by the Council of Ministers.

THE BUDGET

Article XXIII

The budget of the Organization prepared by the Administrative Secretary-General shall be approved by the Council of Ministers. The budget shall be provided by contributions from Member States in accordance with the scale of assessment of the United Nations; provided, however, that no Member States shall be assessed an amount exceeding twenty percent of the yearly regular budget of the Organization. The Member States agree to pay their respective contributions regularly.

SIGNATURE AND RATIFICATION OF CHARTER

Article XXIV

1. This Charter shall be open for signature to all independent sovereign African States and shall be ratified by the signatory States in accordance with their respective constitutional processes.
2. The original instrument, done, if possible in African languages, in English and French, all texts being equally authentic, shall be deposited with the Government of Ethiopia which shall transmit certified copies thereof to all independent sovereign African States.
3. Instruments of ratification shall be deposited with the Government of Ethiopia, which shall notify all signatories of each such deposit.

ENTRY INTO FORCE

Article XXV

This Charter shall enter into force immediately upon receipt by the Government of Ethiopia of the instruments of ratification from two thirds of the signatory States.

REGISTRATION OF THE CHARTER

Article XXVI

This Charter shall, after due ratification, be registered with the Secretariat of the United Nations through the Government of Ethiopia in conformity with Article 102 of the Charter of the United Nations.

INTERPRETATION OF THE CHARTER

Article XXVII

Any question which may arise concerning the interpretation of this Charter shall be decided by a vote of two-thirds of the Assembly of Heads of State and Government of the Organization.

ADHESION AND ACCESSION

Article XXVIII

1. Any independent sovereign African State may at any time notify the Administrative Secretary-General of its intention to adhere or accede to this Charter.
2. The Administrative Secretary-General shall, on receipt of such notification, communicate a copy of it to all the Member States. Admission shall be decided by a simple majority of the Member States. The decision of each Member State shall be transmitted to the Administrative Sectretary General, who shall, upon receipt of the required number of votes, communicate the decision to the State concerned.

MISCELLANEOUS

Article XXIX

The working languages of the Organization and all its institutions shall be, if possible African languages, English and French.

Article XXX

The Administrative Secretary-General may accept on behalf of the Organization gifts, bequests and other donations made to the Organization, provided that this is approved by the Council of Ministers.

Article XXXI

The Council of Ministers shall decide on the privileges and immunities to be accorded to the personnel of the Secretariat in the respective territories of the Member States.

CESSATION OF MEMBERSHIP

Article XXXII

Any State which desires to renounce its membership shall forward a written notification to the Administrative Secretary-General. At the end of one year from the date of such notification, if not withdrawn, the Charter shall cease to apply with respect to the renouncing State, which shall thereby cease to belong to the Organization.

AMENDMENT OF THE CHARTER

Article XXXIII

This Charter may be amended or revised if any Member State makes a written request to the Administrative Secretary-General to that effect; provided, however, that the proposed amendment is not submitted to the Assembly for consideration until all the Member States have been duly notified of it and a period of one year has elapsed. Such an amendment shall not be effective unless approved by at least two-thirds of all the Member States.

IN FAITH WHEREOF, We, the Heads of African State and Government have signed this Charter.

Done in the City of Addis Ababa, Ethiopia this 25th day of May, 1963.

ALGERIA	MALI
BURUNDI	MAURITANIA
CAMEROUN	MOROCCO
CENTRAL AFRICAN REPUBLIC	NIGER
CHAD	NIGERIA
CONGO (Brazzaville)	RWANDA
CONGO (Leopoldville)	SENEGAL
DAHOMEY	SIERRA LEONE
ETHIOPIA	SOMALIA
GABON	SUDAN
GHANA	TANGANYIKA
GUINEA	TOGO
IVORY COAST	TUNISIA
LIBERIA	UGANDA
LIBYA	UNITED ARAB REPUBLIC
MADAGASCAR	UPPER VOLTA

PROTOCOL OF THE COMMISSION OF MEDIATION CONCILIATION AND ARBITRATION

PART I
ESTABLISHMENT AND ORGANIZATION

Article I

The Commission of Mediation, Conciliation and Arbitration established by Article XIX of the Charter of the Organization of African Unity shall be governed by the provision of the present Protocol.

Article II

1. The Commission shall consist of twenty-one members elected by the Assembly of Heads of State and Government.
2. No two Members shall be nationals of the same State.
3. The Members of the Commission shall be persons with recognized professional qualifications.
4. Each Member State of the Organization of African Unity shall be entitled to nominate two candidates.
5. The Administrative Secretary-General shall prepare a list of the candidates nominated by Member States and shall submit it to the Assembly of Heads of State of Government.

Article III

1. Members of the Commission shall be elected for a term of five years and shall be eligible for re-election.
2. Members of the Commission whose terms of office have expired shall remain in office until the election of a new Commission.
3. Notwithstanding the expiry of their terms of office, Members shall complete any proceedings in which they are already engaged.

Article IV

Members of the Commission shall not be removed from office except by decision of the Assembly of Heads of State and Government, by a two-thirds majority of the total membership, on the grounds of inability to perform the functions of their office or of proved misconduct.

Article V

1. Whenever a vacancy occurs in the Commission, it shall be filled in conformity with the provisions of Article II.
2. A Member of the Commission elected to fill a vacancy shall hold office for the unexpired term of the Member he has replaced.

Article VI

1. A President and two Vice-Presidents shall be elected by the Assembly of Heads of State and Government from among the Members of the Commission who shall each hold office for five years. The President and the two Vice-Presidents shall not be eligible for re-election as such officers.
2. The President and the two Vice-Presidents shall be full-time members of the Commission, while the remaining eighteen shall be part-time Members.

Article VII

The President and the two Vice-Presidents shall constitute the Bureau of the Commission and shall have the responsibility of consulting with the parties as regards the appropriate mode of settling the dispute in accordance with this Protocol.

Article VIII

The salaries and allowances of the Members of the Bureau and the remuneration of the other Members of the Commission shall be determined in accordance with the provisions of the Charter of the Organization of African Unity.

Article IX

1. The Commission shall appoint a Registrar and may provide for such other officers as may be deemed necessary.
2. The terms and conditions of service of the Registrar and other administrative officers of the Commission shall be governed by the Commission's Staff Regulations.

Article X

The Administrative expenses of the Commission shall be borne by the Organization of African Unity. All other expenses incurred in connection with the proceedings before the Commission shall be met in accordance with the Rules of Procedure of the Commission.

Article XI

The Seat of the Commission shall be at Addis Ababa, Ethiopia.

PART II

GENERAL PROVISIONS

Article XII

The Commission shall have jurisdiction over disputes between States only.

Article XIII

1. A dispute may be referred to the Commission jointly by the parties concerned, by a party to the dispute, by the Council of Ministers or by the Assembly of Heads of State and Government.
2. Where a dispute has been referred to the Commission as provided in paragraph 1, and one or more of the parties have refused to submit to the jurisdiction of the Commission, the Bureau shall refer the matter to the Council of Ministers for consideration.

Article XIV

The consent of any party to a dispute to submit to the jurisdiction of the Commission may be evidenced by:
    (a)   a prior written undertaking by such party that there shall be recourse to Mediation, Conciliation or Arbitration;
    (b)   reference of a dispute by such party to the Commission; or
    (c)   submission by such party to the jurisdiction in respect of a

dispute referred to the Commission by another State, by the Council of Ministers, or by the Assembly of Heads of State and Government.

Article XV

Member States shall refrain from any act or omission that is likely to aggravate a situation which has been referred to the Commission.

Article XVI

Subject to the provisions of this Protocol and any special agreement between the parties, the Commission shall be entitled to adopt such working methods as it deems to be necessary and expedient and shall establish appropriate rules of procedure.

Article XVII

The Members of the Commission, when engaged in the business of the Commission, shall enjoy diplomatic privileges and immunities as provided for in the Convention on Privileges and Immunities of the Organization of African Unity.

Article XVIII

Where, in the course of Mediation, Conciliation or Arbitration, it is deemed necessary to conduct an investigation or inquiry for the purpose of elucidating facts or circumstances relating to a matter in dispute, the parties concerned and all other Member States shall extend to those engaged in any such proceedings the fullest co-operation in the conduct of such investigation or inquiry.

Article XIX

In case of a dispute between Member States, the parties may agree to resort to any one of these modes of settlement: Mediation, Conciliation and Arbitration.

PART III

MEDIATION

Article XX

When a dispute between Member States is referred to the Commission for Mediation the President shall with the consent of the parties, appoint one or more members of the Commission to mediate the dispute.

Article XXI

1. The role of the mediator shall be confined to reconciling the views and claims of the parties.
2. The mediator shall make written proposals to the parties as expeditiously as possible.
3. If the means of reconciliation proposed by the mediator are accepted, they shall become the basis of a protocol of arrangement between the parties.

PART IV

CONCILIATION

Article XXII

1. A request for the settlement of a dispute by conciliation may be submitted to the Commission by means of a petition addressed to the President by one or more of the parties to the dispute.
2. If the request is made by only one of the parties, that party shall indicee-that prior written notice has been given to the other party.
3. The petition shall include a summary explanation of the grounds of the dispute.

Article XXIII

1. Upon receipt of the petition, the President shall, in agreement with the parties, establish a Board of Conciliators, of whom three shall be appointed by the President from among the Members of the Commission, and one each by the parties.
2. The Chairman of the Board shall be a person designated by the President from among the three Members of the Commission.
3. In nominating persons to serve as Members of the Board, the parties to the dispute shall designate persons in such a way that no two Members of it shall be nationals of the same State.

Article XXIV

1. It shall be the duty of the Board of Conciliators to clarify the issues in dispute and to endeavour to bring about in agreement between the parties upon mutually acceptable terms.
2. The Board shall consider all questions submitted to it and may undertake any inquiry or hear any person capable of giving relevant information concerning the dispute.
3. In the absence of agreement between the parties, the Board shall determine its own procedure.

Article XXV

The parties shall be represented by agents, whose duty shall be to act as intermediaries between them and the Board. They may moreover be assisted by counsel and experts and may request that all persons whose evidence appears to the Board to be relevant shall be heard.

Article XXVI

1. At the close of the proceedings, the Board shall draw up a report stating either:
    (a) that the parties have come to an agreement and, if the need arises, the terms of the agreement and any recommendations for settlement made by the Board; or
    (b) that it has been impossible to effect a settlement.
2. The Report of the Board of Conciliators shall be communicated to the parties and to the President of the Commission without delay and may be published only with consent of the parties.

PART V

ARBITRATION

Article XXVII

1. Where it is agreed that arbitration should be resorted to, the Arbitral Tribunal shall be established in the following manner:
    (a) each party shall designate one arbitrator from among the Members of the Commission having legal qualifications;
    (b) the two arbitrators thus designated shall, by common agreement, designate from among the Members of the Commission a third person who shall act as Chairman of the Tribunal;
    (c) where the two arbitrators fail to agree, within one month of their appointments, in the choice of the person to be Chairman of the Tribunal, the Bureau shall designate the Chairman.
2. The President may, with the agreement of the parties, appoint to the Arbitral Tribunal two additional Members who need not be Members of the Commission but who shall have the same powers as the other Members of the Tribunal.
3. The arbitrators shall not be nationals of the parties, or have their domicile in the territories of the parties, or be employed in their service, or have served as mediators or conciliators in the same dispute. They shall be of different nationalities

Article XXVIII

Recourse to arbitration shall be regarded as submission in good faith to the award of the Arbitral Tribunal.

Article XXIX

1. The parties shall, in each case, conclude a *compromis* which shall specify:
    (a) the undertaking of the parties to go to arbitration, and to accept as legally binding, the decision of the Tribunal;
    (b) the subject matter of the controversy; and
    (c) the seat of the Tribunal.
2. The *compromis* may specify the law to be applied by the Tribunal and the power, if the parties so agree, to adjudicate *ex aequo et bono*, the time-limit within which the award of the arbitrators shall be given, and the appointment of agents and counsel to take part in the proceedings before the tribunal.

Article XXX

In the absence of any provision in the *compromis* regarding the applicable law, the Arbitral Tribunal shall decide the dispute according to treaties concluded between the parties, International Law, the Charter of the Organization of African Unity, the Charter of the United Nations and, if the parties agree, *ex aequo et bono*.

Article XXXI

1. Hearings shall be held in *camera* unless the arbitrators decide otherwise.
2. The record of the proceedings signed by the arbitrators and the Registrar shall alone be authoritative.

3. The arbitral award shall be in writing and shall, in respect of every point decided, state the reasons on which it is based.

PART VI

FINAL PROVISIONS

Article XXXII

The present Protocol shall, after approval by the Assembly of Heads of State and Government, be an integral part of the Charter of the Organization of African Unity.

Article XXXIII

This Protocol may be amended or revised in accordance with the provisions of Article XXXIII of the Charter of the Organization of African Unity.

IN FAITH WHEREOF, We the Heads of African State and Government, have signed this Protocol.

Done at Cairo, (United Arab Republic), on the 21st day of July, 1964.

ALGERIA	MALI
BURUNDI	MAURITANIA
CAMEROUN	MOROCCO
CENTRAL AFRICAN REPUBLIC	NIGER
CHAD	NIGERIA
CONGO (Brazzaville)	RWANDA
DAHOMEY	SENEGAL
ETHIOPIA	SIERRA LEONE
GABON	SOMALIA
GHANA	SUDAN
GUINEA	TOGO
IVORY COAST	TUNISIA
KENYA	UGANADA
LIBERIA	UNITED ARAB REPUBLIC
LIBYA	UNITED REPUBLIC OF TANGANYIKA AND ZANZIBAR
MADAGASCAR	
MALAWI	UPPER VOLTA

FUNCTIONS AND REGULATIONS OF THE GENERAL SECRETARIAT

PART I

Rule 1

The General Secretariat, as a central and permanent organ of the Organization of African Unity, shall carry out the functions assigned to it by the Charter of the Organization those that might be specified in other treaties and agreements among the Member States, and those that are established in these Regulations.

Rule 2

The General Administrative Secretariat shall supervise the implementation of decisions of the Council of Ministers concerning all economic, social, legal and cultural exchanges of Member States:

(i) keeps in custody the documents and files of the meetings of the Assembly, the Council of Ministers, of the Specialized Commissions and other organs of the Organization of African Unity;

(ii) within its possibilities, the General Secretariat shall place at the disposal of the Specialized Commissions the technical and administrative services that may be requested. In case a session of a Specialized Commission is held outside the Headquarters of the Organization, at the request of a Member State, the General Secretariat shall conclude agreements or contracts with the Government of the Member State on whose territory the Session of the Specialized Commission is being held, to guarantee adequate compensation of the disbursements incurred by the General Secretariat;

(iii) receives communications of ratifications of instruments of agreements entered into between Member States

(iv) prepares an Annual Report of the activities of the Organization;

(v) prepares for submission to the Council, a report of the activities carried out by the Specialized Commission;

(vi) prepares the Programme and Budget of the Organization for each Fiscal Year, to be submitted to the Council of Ministers, for its consideration and approval.

Rule 3

The General Secretariat of the Organization of African Unity is the Secretariat of the Assembly, of the Council of Ministers, of the Specialized Commissions and other organs of the Organization of African Unity.

Rule 4

The Organization of African Unity has its Headquarters in the City of Addis Ababa.

Rule 5

The Headquarters for the official use of the Organization, for objectives and purposes strictly compatible with the objectives and purposes set forth in the Charter of the Organization. The Administrative Secretary-General may authorize the celebration of meetings or social functions in the Headquarters of the Organization when such meetings or functions are closely linked, or are compatible with the objectives and purposes of the Organization.

PART II

THE ADMINISTRATIVE SECRETARY-GENERAL AND

THE ASSISTANT ADMINISTRATIVE SECRETARIES-GENERAL

The Administrative Secretary-General

Rule 6

The Administrative Secretary-General directs the activities of the General Secretariat and is its legal representative.

Rule 7

The Administrative Secretary-General is directly responsible to the Council of Ministers for the adequate discharge of all duties assigned to him.

Rule 8

The appointment, term of office and removal of the Administrative Secretary-General are governed by the provisions of Articles XVI and XVIII of the Charter and of the Rules of Procedure of the Assembly.

Rule 9

The participation of the Administrative Secretary-General in the deliberations of the Assembly, of the Council of Ministers, of the Specialized Commissions and other organs of the Organization shall be governed by the provisions of the Charter and by the respective Rules of Procedure of these bodies.

Rule 10

The Administrative Secretary-General shall submit reports requested by the Assembly, the Council of Ministers and the Commissions.

Rule 11

The Administrative Secretary-General shall furthermore:
(i) carry out the provisions of Article XVIII of the Charter, and submit Staff Rules to the Council of Ministers for approval;

(ii) transmit to Member States the Budget and Programme of Work at leastone month before the convocation of the sessions of the Assembly, of the Council of Ministers, of the Specialized Commissions and of other organs of the Organization;

(iii) receive the notification of adherence or accession to the Charter and communicate such notification to Member States, as provided in Article XXVIII of the Charter;

(iv) receive the notification of Member States which may desire to renounce their membership in the Organization as provided in Article XXXII of the Charter;
(v) communicate to Member States, and include in the Agenda of the Assembly, as provided in Article XXXIII of the Charter, written requests of Member States for amendments or revisions of the Charter;
(vi) establish, with the approval of the Council of Ministers, such branches and administrative and technical offices as may be necessary to achieve the objectives and purposes of the Organization;
(vii) abolish, with the approval of the Council of Ministers, such branches and administrative and technical offices as may be deemed necessary for the adequate functioning of the General Secretariat.

The Assistant Administrative Secretaries-General
Rule 12

The appointment, term of office and removal of the Assistant Administrative Secretaries-General are governed by the provisions of Articles XVI and XVII of the Charter and the Rules of Procedure of the Assembly.

Rule 13

The Administrative Secretary-General shall designate one of the Assistant Administrative Secretaries-General who will represent him in all matters assigned to him.

Rule 14

One of the Assistant Administrative Secretaries-General shall exercise the functions of the Administrative Secretary-General in his absence, or because of any temporary incapacity of the Administrative Secretary-General, and shall assume the office of the Administrative Secretary-General for the unexpired term in case of a definite vacancy. In case of definite vacancy, the Council will designate one of the Assistant Administrative Secretaries-General who will replace the Administrative Secretary-General provisionally.

PART III

ORGANIZATION OF THE GENERAL SECRETARIAT

Rule 15

The General Secretariat has the following departments:
(i) the Political, Legal and Defence Department;
(ii) the Economic and Social Department;
(iii) the Administrative, Conference and Information Department.

The Administrative Secretary-General shall create divisions and sub-divisions, as he may deem necessary, with the approval of the Council.

PART IV

FISCAL RULES

Rule 16

The Administrative Secretary-General shall prepare the Programme and Budget of the Organization as provided in Article XXIII of the Charter, and shall submit it to the Council of Ministers for scrutiny and approval during its first ordinary session.

Rule 17

The proposed Programme and Budget shall comprise the programme of activities of the General Secretariat of the Organization. It shall include the expenses of the Assembly, of the Council of Ministers, of the Specialized Commission and of other organs of the Organization.

Rule 18

In formulating the Programme and Budget of the Organization the Administrative Secretary-General shall consult the different Organs of the Organization of African Unity.
The proposed Programme and Budget shall include:
(i) a list of contributions made by Member States in accordance with the scale established by the Council of Ministers and by reference to the provisions of Article XXIII of the Charter;
(ii) an estimate of various incomes;
(iii) a description of the situation of the Working Fund.

FINANCIAL RESOURCES

Rule 19

Once the budget is approved by the Council of Ministers, the Administrative Secretary-General shall communicate it to the Member States, with all pertinent documents, at least three months before the first day of the Fiscal Year. The budget shall be accompanied by the list indicating the annual contributions assigned by the Council to each Member State. The annual contribution of each Member State becomes due on the first day of the Fiscal Year.

Rule 20

The Administrative Secretary-General is the Accounting Officer of the Organization and shall be responsible for the proper administration of the Budget.

Rule 21

The Administrative Secretary-General shall submit to Member States a quarterly statement on payments of contributions and outstanding contributions:

Rule 22

There shall be a General Fund, in which the following amounts will be entered.
(i) annual contribution of Member States;
(ii) miscellaneous income, unless the Council of Ministers determine otherwise;
(iii) advance from the Working Fund
From such General Fund all expenditures established in the budget shall be set.

Rule 23

The Administrative Secretary-General may establish fiduciary funds, reserve funds and special funds with approval of the Council of Ministers. The objectives and limitations of these funds shall be defined by the Council of Ministers. These funds shall be administered in separate accounts, as provided in special regulations approved by the Council of Ministers.

Rule 24

The Administrative Secretary-General, may accept, on behalf of the

Organization, gifts, bequests and other donations made to the Organization, provided that such donations are consistent with the objectives and purposes of the Organization, and are approved by the Council of Ministers.

Rule 25

In the case of monetary donations for specific purposes, these funds shall be treated as fiduciary or special funds, as provided in Rule 22. Monetary donations for no specific purposes shall be considered as miscellaneous income.

Rule 26

The Administrative Secretary-General shall designate the African Banks or Banking Institutions in which the funds of the Organization shall be deposited. The interests accrued by such funds, including the Working Fund, shall be entered as miscellaneous income.

ACCOUNTING

Rule 27

The accounts of the Organization shall be carried in the currency determined by the Council of Ministers.

FINANCIAL SUPERVISION

Rule 28

The Council of Ministers shall be responsible for the supervision of the finances of the Organization.

Rule 29

The Administrative Secretary-General shall submit to the Council of Ministers any matter relating to the financial situation of the Organization.

PART V

MISCELLANEOUS

Rule 30

The Administrative Secretary-General shall submit to the Council of Ministers for its approval, at the earliest possible moment, the complete Regulations governing the Accounting Method of the Organization, in accordance with established international accounting practices.

AMENDMENTS

Rule 31

These Regulations may be amended by the Council of Ministers by a simple majority subject to the approval of the Assembly.

DICTIONARY

OF

AFRICAN BIOGRAPHY

ABANDA-ESSOMBA, Aloys, born Nkoa-Ebè District of Bikok, Cameroon, 21st June 1921. Administrative Secretary. Education: C.E.P.E., Primary School of Catholic Mission of Bikop, 1928; Mvolye Boarding School & Petit Séminaire St. Joseph d'Akono, 1933-38. Married, 11 children. Appointments include: Secretary, Book-keeper, Equatorial Company of Mines (C.E.M.), Betare-Oya, Dept. of Lom & Djerem, 1941-46; Auxiliary Agent, 5th Class, Administrative Corps, 1947; Administrative Assistant, Civil & Financial Services, 1948; Administrative Deputy, ibid, 1952; Administrative Secretary, ibid, 1967; Head of Secretariat, District of Ayos, Dept. of Nyong & Mfoumou, 1960-62; Head, District of Ayos, Dept. of Nyong & Mfoumou, 1964; First Deputy Head, Nanga-Eboko, Dept. of la Haute-Sanaga, 1964-66; Head of Secretariat, under direction of Public Health Dept.; General Commissariat of Public Health & Population; Vice-President of the Republic, Yaoundé, 1966-70; Registrar, Civil Prison, Nkongsamba, 1970—. Honours include: Cameroon Order of Merit, 3rd Class, 1962; ibid, 2nd Class, 1969. Address: B.P. I, Prefecture Nkongsamba, Cameroun.

ABAYOMI (Chief Sir) Kofo, born 10th July 1896. Medical Eye Specialist. Education: Methodist Boys High School, Lagos, Nigeria; M.B., Ch.B., Edinburgh University, U.K., 1928; Coombe Hospital, Dublin, Ireland; Moorefield Eye Hospital, London, U.K.; D.T.M. & H., 1929; M.D., 1936; LL.D., Mount Allison, Canada, 1958; LL.D., Ibadan University, Nigeria, 1962. Personal details: Son of Chief Onashokun—Oyo & Chief Baba Isule, Lagos; Married. Appointments: Director of many firms; Vice-Chairman, Bata Shoe Co.; Chairman, Rediffusion, Nigeria. Memberships: Metropolitan Club, Lagos; Ikayi Club; Dining Club; Royal Commonwealth Soc: Honours: Knighthood, 1951; Rhodes Grant, Ophthalmology, 1941. Address: P.O. Box 300, Lagos, Nigeria.

ABBAS, Ashour Ali, born 1st June 1936. Civil Servant. Education: Senior Cambridge (Tanzania), 1958; B.A., Punjab Univ., Pakistan, 1963; M.B.A., Institute of Business Education, Karachi University, Pakistan, 1965. Married. Appointments: Assistant Commercial Officer, January 1965-June 1968; Commercial Officer, July 1968—. Address: Embassy of Tanzania, Ruychrocklaan 123, The Hague, Netherlands.

ABBOTT, Cyril Hartley, born 12th April 1931. Inspector of Weights & Measures. Education: Technical; Board of Trade Certificate as Inspector of Weights & Measures. Married, 2 children. Memberships: Institute of Weights & Measures Administration; Treasurer, Mbale Branch, Royal Society of St. George. Address: Weights & Measures Bureau, P.O. Box 358, Mbale, Uganda.

ABBOTT, Okra Jones, born 11th February, 1921. University Teacher; Researcher. Education: B.S., Agriculture, Berea College, U.S.A., 1949; M.S., Poultry Nutrition, University of Kentucky, 1952; Ph.D., Biochemistry-Nutrition, University of Wisconsin, 1956; Post Doctoral study as Visiting Senior Scientist in Pharmacology (germ-free animals), College of Medicine, University of Kentucky, 1964-65. Married. Appointments: Teacher, Vocational Agriculture, Pendleton County Schools, Butler, Kentucky, 1949-50; Graduate Teaching Assistant in Poultry, University of Kentucky, 1951; Graduate Research & Teaching Assistant in Poultry Nutrition, University of Wisconsin, 1952-55; Part-time Instructor, Poultry Science (correspondence course), U.S. Armed Forces Institute, 1954-55; Assistant Professor, Poultry Products Technology, University of Delaware, 1956-59; Associate Professor, Poultry Science, University of Kentucky, 1960-66; Associate Professor, Animal Science, ibid, 1966-67; Associate-Professor, Animal & Veterinary Science, West Virginia University, 1967—; Senior Lecturer, Animal Science & Production, Makerere University, Kampala, Uganda (West Virginia University—U.S.A.I.D.), 1967—. Memberships: Fellow, American Association for the Advancement of Science; American Institute of Biological Science; Society for Appplied Gnotobiotics; American Society of Animal Science; Poultry Science Association; World's Poultry Science Association; American Chemical

Society; New York Academy of Science; Sigma Xi. Contributor to professional journals. Address: Faculty of Agriculture, Makerere University, P.O. Box 7062; Kampala, Uganda.

ABDEL-RAHMAN, Aisha (Pen-name, Bint El Shati), born 6th November, 1913. Professor & Chairman of Arabic Literature & Islamic Studies. Education: Ph.D., Arabic Literature. Married. Appointments: Member, High Council of Literature & Science, Cairo, U.A.R.; Visiting Professor, Universities of Khartoum, Algeria & Fas, Morocco. Memberships: Society of Arabic Writers; Association of Afro-Asian Writers; Chancellor in Journal Al Ahrara, Cairo; Scientific Committee, Higher Council of U.A.R. Universities. Publications: Elucidation of the Elocution in the Koran, 1962, 1970; The Contemporary Arab Poetess, 1962; Alub'l Ala Al-Ma'ari, 1965; The Koran & Human Rights, 1968; New Values for Arabic Literature, 1968; Our Heritage Past & Present, 1968; An Essay on Man (A Koranic Study), 1969; Our Language & Life, 1969; Biographies of the Ladies of the Prophet's Household (5 vols: The Mother of Prophet; The Wives of the Prophet; The Daughters of the Prophet. Sayeda Zainab; Sukaina bint Al-Hussein); Risalet Al-Chofran: A Verified Text, 5 eds.; Al-Ghofram: A Critical Study; Al-Muhkam Dictionary by Ibn Seidah (A Verified Text); Human Life with Abu'l Ala'; Madinat el-Salam in the Life of Abu'l Ala'; Al-Khansa' (The Famous Arab Poetess); On the Bridge (Autobiography); The Return of Pharoah (An Egyptian Story); The Master of the Farm; Collections of Short Stories: Life—Portraits of Women: A Sinning Woman; The Secret of the Riverbank. Honours: Medallion of Thinkers, 1st Class, Morocco; 2 Prizes, Academy of Arabic Language, 1950, 1952; Prize of Government in Social Studies, Cairo. Address: Amier El Khoby Str., No. 13, Heliopolis, U.A.R.

ABDINASER, Abdalla, born 11th November 1932. University Professor; Head of Department. Education: National Diploma in E. Engineering, Enfield College of Technology, U.K., 1952; D.Sc., University of Paris, France, 1959. Married, 3 children. Appointments: Superintendent, Production Engineer, Ethiopian Electric Light & Power Authority, Ethiopia, 1954-57; Associate Professor, Head of Electrical Engineering Department, Hailé Selassié I University, 1960—. Memberships: A.M.I.E.E., U.K.; Electrical Engineering Society, France; Civil Engineering Society, France; Associate Mbr., I.E.S., U.S.A.; Ethiopian Association of Engineers & Architects. Publications: The Art & Science of Illumination, 1967; also several articles in technical journals. Honours: Distinction, Doctorial Thesis; 'Tenure', Board of Governors, Hailé Selassié I University, 1969. Address: Electrical Engineering Department, Faculty of Technology, Hailé Selassié I University, P.O. Box 385, Addis Ababa, Ethiopia.

ABDULKADER, Adamali, born Tanzania, 20th November, 1925. Company Secretary. Education: Qualified Stenographer-Typist, 1942; Diploma in Economics & Social Philosophy, U.S.A., 1957; Qualified Lecturer in First Aid, 1963. Married, 1 son. Appointments include: Secretary, The International Motor Mart Ltd., Dar es Salaam, 1942—; Scout-master, 7th Dar es Salaam Scouts Group, 1947—; Cadet Officer, St. John Ambulance Brigade, Dar es Salaam, 1960; Divisional Officer, ibid, 1961; Divisional Superintendent, 1965; currently, Divisional Superintendent-in-Charge, Azania Division; Honorary Lecturer, First Aid, supervising First Aid Instruction & Training Classes. Memberships include: Fellow, International Academy, Canada, 1962; Magical Youths International, U.S.A., 1965—; International Brotherhood of Magicians, U.S.A., 1961—; Management Committee, Dawoodi Bohra Education Board, 1957—; Bohra Religious Classes, 1955—; Military Police, Honorary Service, 1939-45. Author of over 300 articles, stories & poems in English & Gujrati, published in Nasim-E-Sahar of Poona, B.Y.O. magazine of Karachi, Oogto Sooraj of Ujjain & Zahabiyah of Nairobi. Honours include: War Medal, 1939-45; Title of Gold Leaguer & recipient of Gold Medal, Health & Strength League, London, U.K., 1957; Long Service Decoration & numerous medals, Scout Headquarters, London, U.K.; Long Service Medal, St. John Ambulance Assn., London. Address: P.O. Box 648, Dar es Salaam, Tanzania.

ABELES, Norbert, born Vienna, Austria, 17th September 1923. Educator & Mechanical Engineer. Education: Erzherzog-Rainer Bundes-Real Gymnasium, Vienna 11; Associate, Royal Technical College for Science & Technology, Glasgow, U.K.; B.Sc., Engineering, University of London; Technical Teachers Certificate. Married, 2 children. Appointments include: misc. positions in industry in U.K. till 1951; Assistant Lecturer, Constantine College of Technology, 1951-55; H.M. Overseas Civil Service, 1956-64; from 1955-64: Lecturer-Sr. Lecturer-Head of Engineering Department, College of Technology, Yaba, Lagos, Nigeria; Acting Vice-Principal-Principal, ibid; Lecturer i/c Mechanical Engineering, South Australian Institute of Technology, Whyalla, Australia, 1965-66; Contract Officer, Govt. of Kenya, 1969—; Head, Engineering Department & Acting Principal, Kenya Polytechnic, Nairobi, 1967-68; Principal, Mombasa Technical Institute, 1969—. Memberships include: Fellow, Nairobi Branch, East African Institution of Engineers; East African Examination Council; Institution of Mechanical Engineers, London, U.K.; Companion, Royal Aeronautical Society, London. Address: c/o Mombasa Technical Institute, Mombasa, Kenya.

ABERRA JEMBERE (His Excellency), born 2nd September 1928. Administrator: Lawyer. Education: B.A., LL.B., Hailé Selassié I University, Ethiopia. Married, 1 son. Appointments: Head of Section, Private Secretariat, H.I.M. the Emperor of Ethiopia, 1946-48; Executive Secretary, Boy Scout Association of Ethiopia, 1948-52; Secretary-General, Ethiopian Orthodox Church Head Office, 1953-56; Vice-Administrator, Hailé Selassié I, Welfare Trust, 1957; Secretary-General to the Council of Ministers, 1958; Acting Administrator-General, Hailé Selassié I Foundation, 1959-61; Secretary-General to the Council of Ministers, 1961—. Memberships: Honorary Secretary-General, Ethiopian Red Cross Society; Chairman, Executive Committee, National

Literacy Campaign Organization; Vice-Chairman, Ethiopian Literary (Writers) Association; Honorary Treasurer, Fund for the Disabled Association; Board of Managers, Y.M.C.A.; National Board, Scout Association of Ethiopia; Executive Council, Ethiopian National Commission for UNESCO. Author of 3 monographs in Amharic on social topics, also an article published in the 'Journal of Ethiopian Law'. Honours: Rank of Vice-Minister; Officer of the Order of Menilik II, 1966. Address: P.O. Box 550, Addis Ababa, Ethiopia.

ABIRI, John Omoniyi Alayioye, born 9th June 1938. University Lecturer. Education: St. Philip's School, Ile-Ife, Nigeria; Oduduwa College, Ile-Ife; B.A., University College, Ibadan; M.Ed., University of Birmingham, U.K.; Dip.Ed., Ph.D., University of Ibadan, Nigeria. Personal details: Son of Late Abraham Abiri & Marian Aramide Abiri; married to Dorcas Adunni Abiri, daughter of Chief S. J. Awoyemi, the Jagunosin of Ife, & the late Emilia Adebimpe Awoyemi; 2 sons, 3 daughters. Appointments: Clerk, Federal Audit Department, Lagos, 1965; Teacher, Ife Grammar School, Ile-Ife, 1956-57, 1961-62, 1963; Research Fellow, Institute of Education, University of Ibadan, 1965-67; Lecturer, Department of Education, ibid, 1967—. Memberships: Graduate Mbr., British Psychological Society; International Association of Applied Psychology; Honorary General Secretary, Nigerian Psychological Society; United Kingdom Reading Association; Yoruba Studies Association of Nigeria. Honours: Irving & Bonnar Graduate Prize, University College, Ibadan, 1961; George Cadbury Prize in Education, University of Birmingham, U.K., 1965. Address: Department of Education, University of Ibadan, Ibadan, Nigeria.

ABLIZA III (Togbe) Kwasi, Fiaga of Volo Traditional Area, born 1917. Education: Elementary, Somanya Wesleyan Mission Primary School, 1923-27; Kpong Weslyan Senior School, Accra, Ghana, 1931-35; Kibi Government Technical School, 1934-37; English, Union College, Johannesburg, South-Africa, 1953-55; Advanced Certificate & Diploma, Religion (U.S.A.), 1956-60. Personal details: installed on ancestral Paramount Stool under Stool name, Togbe Kwasi Abliza III, Fiaga of Volo Traditional Area. As Fiaga of Volo initiated: Primary & Middle Schools; Volo Rest House; Evangelical Presbyterian Church; Volo Agricultural Nursing Station Office & Store; Volo Clinic; Volo Post Office; Volo Health Office; Volo Veterinary Officer; 21 miles of Volo-Podoe road; Middle School Examinations Centre. Memberships include: Regional House of Chiefs, Ho, Volta Region; National House of Chiefs; Sogakofe Secondary School Board of Governors; Chairman, Tongu District Association of Towns & Villages Committees; Patron, Tongu Scholars Union, Sogakofe; Saint Francis Training College Board of Governors, Hohoe, 1958-65; Chairman, Dzodze Training College Board of Governors, 1964-66; Volta Region Scholarships Selection Board, 1956-61; President, Tongu Confederacy Native Authority, 1945-60. Honours include: invited to Ghana Independence Celebrations, 1957; ibid, Ghana Republic Celebrations, 1960; ibid, Queen of England's visit to Ghana, 1961. Address: P.O. Box 1, Volo via Akuse, Tongu District, Volta Region, Ghana.

ABOAGYE-da-COSTA (Hon.) Alexander Apeatu, born 18th September 1933. Barrister-at-Law. Education: Mfantsipim School, Cape Coast, 1948-51; LL.B., University of Hull, U.K., 1958; LL.M., University of Manchester, 1960; B.L., Middle Temple; called to the Bar, November 1961. Appointments: Legal Practitioner, 1961-66; District Magistrate, 1966-69; Member of Parliament, Asamankese Constituency, Ministerial Secretary Ministry of Youth & Rural Development, Member of the Constituent Assembly, 1968-69. Memberships: President, Metropolitan Club, Accra, Ghana. Author of thesis on Alien Control in the United Kingdom. Address: The Constituent Assembly, Accra, Ghana.

ABOLARIN, Michael Olajide, born 18th October 1937. Parasitologist. Education: Government College, Keffi, 1954-59; Nigerian College, Zaria, 1960-62; B.Sc., University of Ibadan, 1962-65; M.Sc., University of Liverpool, U.K., 1966-67. Married, 2 children. Appointments: Parasitologist, Northern Nigerian Ministry of Animal & Forest Resources, 1965-67; Lecturer, Parasitology, Department of Biological Sciences, Ahmadu Bello University, Zaria, 1967-69; Project Co-Manager, Kainji Lake Research Project, 1969—. Memberships: Fellow, Royal Microscopical Society; Science Association of Nigeria. Publications: Comparative Studies of Freshwater Fish Protozoam Parasites from East & West Africa; First Observations of Some Limmogical Factors of River Oli; The Snail Populations in the Newly Formed Kainji Lake & its Riverine Surroundings. Address: Project Co-Manager, Kainji Lake Research Project, Box 95, New Bussa, Nigeria.

ABOU-IBADALLAH (Hadj) M'Hammed, born 1918. Vice-President of the Regional Tribunal of Casablanca. Education: Diploma, University of Karaouine. Married, 9 children. Appointments: Lawyer, 11 years; Judge, 1 year; President of the Tribunal of Chraa, 7 years; Council Member to the Regional Tribunal of Casablanca, 1 year; Attorney-at-Law, 1 year; Vice-President, Regional Tribunal, Casablanca, Morocco. Memberships: Judges' Association of Morocco, 'Rabitat al Koudat'. Address: 3 rue Chemin, Fleuri-Hermitage, Casablanca, Morocco.

ABOYADE, Ojetunji, born Awe, Oyo, Nigeria, 9th September 1931. Economist; University Professor. Education: Baptist Boys' High School, Abeokuta, Nigeria; B.Sc.(Econ.), Hull University, U.K., 1957; Ph.D., Pembroke College, Cambridge, 1960. Married, 1 son, 2 daughters. Appointments: Professor of Economics, University of Ibadan, Nigeria; Member, Governing Council, UN Institute of Development & Planning, Dakar, Senegal; Editor, Nigerian Journal of Economics & Social Studies. Publications: Foundation of an African Economy—A Study of Investment & Growth in Nigeria; The Economy of Nigeria, 1968. Address: Department of Economics, University of Ibadan, Nigeria.

ABRAHAM, Acha Grace, born 28th May 1935. University Teacher. Education: M.Sc., Botany, Kerala, India. Married to Dr. Abraham Thomas. Appointments: Lecturer, St. Teresa's College, Ernakulam, Kerala; ibid, St. Augustine's College, Cape Coast, Ghana; Opoku Ware School, Kumasi, Ghana; University of Science & Technology, Kumasi. Address: c/o University of Science & Technology, Kumasi, Ghana.

ABUBAKAR, Iya, born Belel, Sardauna Province, Nigeria, 14th December 1934. University Professor. Educated: Elementary School, Belel, Nigeria, 1940-44; Middle School, Yola, 1944-48; Government College, Zaria, 1948-52; Nigerian College of Arts, Science & Technology, Zaria, 1952-55; B.Sc., University of Ibadan, 1958; Ph.D., Cambridge University, U.K., 1962. Appointments: Research Assistant, California Institute of Technology, U.S.A., 1960-61; Lecturer in Mathematics, Ahmadu Bello University, Zaria, 1962-64; Senior Lecturer, ibid, 1964-65, 1966-67; Visiting Assistant Professor, University of Michigan, U.S.A., 1965-66; Professor, Head of Department of Mathematics, Ahmadu Bello University, Zaria, 1967-68; Dean, Faculty of Science, ibid, 1968-69. Memberships: Special Mbr., Northern House of Assembly, 1963-66; Northern Nigeria Public Accounts Committee, 1964-66; Advisory Committee on Atomic Energy Commission, 1964—; Federal Government's Working Parties on Technical Education & Vocational Training & on Economic Planning, 1966; Northern Nigeria Scholarship Board, 1967-68; National Universities Commission, 1968—; North-Eastern State Scholarship Board, 1968—; Interim Common Services Agency Scholarship Committee, 1968—; North-Eastern State Public Accounts Committee, 1969—; various ad hoc committees set up by State Governments to advise on specific issues. Leader of Nigerian delegations to: Tenth Congress of the International Union of Geodesy & Geophysics in Berkeley, U.S.A., 1963; General Assembly of the International Atomic Energy Agency in Vienna, Austria, 1964; ibid, Tokyo, Japan, 1965. Address: Faculty of Science, Ahmadu Bello University, Zaria, Nigeria.

ABUNGU, Alex Peter Kwadi, born 12th January 1940. Auditor. Education: Cambridge Overseas School Certificate; R.S.A., Intermediate; Association of International Accountants, Intermediate; A.C.C.A., Intermediate. Appointments: Surveyor (land), Kenya Government, 1960-61; Audit Assistant, 1961-63; Senior Examiner of Accounts, 1963-68; Auditor, 1968-69; Senior Auditor, East African Community, 1969—. Memberships: Dambusters Club, Nairobi, Kenya. Honours: Award for outstanding classwork, Thurrock Technical College, Essex, 1967. Address: East African Community, Nairobi, Kenya.

ABU SHADI, Mohamed, born 15th August 1913. Bank Chairman. Education: B.Comm., A.C.I.P.; Cairo University, U.A.R.; American University, Washington, D.C., U.S.A. Appointments: Controller-General, Insurance Department, Ministry of Finance, 1949-52; Director-General, Government Insurance & Provident Funds, 1953; Chairman & Managing Director, Development & Popular Housing Co., 1954-55; Sub-Governor, National Bank of Egypt, 1955-60; Chairman, ibid, 1961—; currently, Chairman, Union de Banque Arabes et Francaises. Memberships: U.A.R. Club of Commerce; Deputy Chairman, Societe d'Economie Politique de Statistique et de Legislation d'Egypte: Associate, Chartered Institution Patent Agents, London, 1946; Heliopolis & National Bank of Egypt Sporting Clubs. Publications: The Art of Central Banking & Its Application in Egypt, 1952; Central Banking in Egypt, 1952. Recipient of the El Gamhoureya Order II, 1955. Address: Chairman, National Bank of Egypt, Cairo, U.A.R.

ACKAH, Christian Abraham, born Cape Coast, Ghana, 2nd June 1908. Educationist. Education: Adisadel College, Cape Coast, Ghana; B.A.(Hons.), M.A., Ph.D.(Lond.), University of London, The London School of Economics, U.K. Married, 6 sons, 2 daughters. Appointments include: Teacher, Adisadel College, 1926; Senior Geography Master, ibid, 1931-36; Senior Officer, Ghana Government Treasury, 1937-51; Headmaster, Aggrey College, 1952; ibid, Ghana National College, Cape Coast, 1953-56; Supervisor of Ghana Students in U.K. & Ireland, 1956-58; Senior Research Fellow, University of Ghana, 1961; First Principal, University College of Cape Coast, 1962-64; Principal, ibid, 1966-68. Memberships include: Life Fellow, The Royal Geographical Society, London, U.K.; Life Member, Royal Institute of Philosophy, ibid; British Sociological Association; Fellow, Ghana Academy of Arts & Sciences. Publications include: West Africa, A General Certificate Geography. Address: Baffoa Lodge, P.O. Box 264, Cape Coast, Ghana.

ACQUAYE, Ebenezer, born 5th June 1931. University Lecturer; Chartered Surveyor. Education: B.Sc.(Estate Management), London University. Married, 3 daughters. Appointments: Estate Officer, Tema Development Corporation, Tema, Ghana; Senior Lands Officer, Lands Department, Ghana; Senior Lecturer, Acting Head, Department of Land Economy & Estate Management, University of Science & Technology, Kumasi, Ghana. Memberships: Fellow, Ghana Institute of Surveyors; F.R.I.C.S. Address: Department of Land Economy & Estate Management, University of Science & Technology, Kumasi, Ghana.

ADADE (Honourable) Nicholas Yaw Boafo, born Wenchi, Ashanti Akim, Ghana, 1927. Barrister-at-Law; Attorney-General; Minister of Justice. Education: Accra Academy, 1944-46; B.Sc.(Econ.), University College of the Gold Coast, 1953; B.Com.(Lond.); LL.B.(Lond.); enrolled at Lincoln's Inn, London, U.K., 1954. Personal details: Married, 2 children. President, National Union of Gold Coast Students, Ghana, 1952-53; enrolled at Ghana Bar, 1957. Appointments: Practised in Kumasi, 1957-64; Editor, Ghana Law Reports, 1964-67; Part-time Lecturer, Faculty of Law, University of Ghana, 1965-67; Director, Ghana News Agency, 1967-68; ibid, Ghana Commercial Bank, 1968-69; Appointed Attorney-General in April 1969 in an N.L.C. Cabinet Reshuffle, resigned in July 1969; Member of Parliament for Ashanti Akim South Constituency. Memberships:

National Liberation Council Legal Committee, 1966-67; Chairman, National Liberation Council Committee on Management Agreements, 1966-68; Secretary, Ghana Bar Association, 1966-69; General Legal Council, 1966—. Address: P.O. Box M.60, Accra, Ghana.

ADADEVOH, Babatunde Kwaku, born Lagos, Nigeria, 4th October 1933. University Professor & Physician. Education: Igbodi College, Yaba, University of Ibadan; Birmingham Medical School; England; Postgraduate Medical School, London, England; Harvard Medical School, Boston, U.S.A. Married. Appointments include: House Officer, Professorial Unit, Birmingham, U.K., 1960; House Officer, Hammersmith Hospital, London, 1960-61; Lecturer, University of Ibadan, Nigeria, 1962; Research Fellow, Harvard Medical School & Massachusetts General Hospital, Boston, U.S.A., 1962-64; Lecturer in Medicine, University of Lagos, Nigeria, 1964-67; Senior Lecturer in Medicine, University of Lagos, 1967-68; Professor, Department of Chemical Pathology, University of Ibadan. Memberships include: Royal College of Physicians, London; Secretary, Association of Physicians of West Africa; Member of Council, Science Association of Nigeria; International Society of Endocrinology. Publications: Mode of Action of Androgenic Hormones; Adrenocortical Functions in Africans; Papers on Endrocrinology & Human Reproduction, especially as related to Africa. Honours, Prizes, etc.: Cricket Colours, Igbobi College & University of Ibadan; Nigeria Cricket Team. Address: Department of Chemical Pathology, University of Ibadan, Ibadan, Nigeria.

ADAH, Moses Egene, born 23rd August 1939. University Lecturer. Education: Provincial Secondary School, Okene, Nigeria, 1955-60; Government College, Keffi, 1961-62; B.Sc., 1966, M.Sc., 1968, Ahmadu Bello University, Zaria, 1963-68. Married, 2 children. Appointments: Assistant Lecturer (Abu), 1967-69; Lecturer, 1969—. Memberships: American Geophysical Union; The American Physical Union; Science Association of Nigeria. Address: Department of Physics, A.B.U., Zaria, Nigeria.

ADAM, Assi Camille, born 18th July 1922. Advocate to the Court of Appeal. Education: Secondary studies, Seminary, Bingerville, Ivory Coast; ibid, Dakar & St. Louis, Senegal; Baccalaureat, Perigeux, Dordogne-France; Lic. Law, Diploma, E.S.P., Paris, France. Married, 5 children. Appointments: First Magistrate to serve in his own country, Ivory Coast, 1952-55; Advocate to the Court of Appeal, Abidjan, Ivory Coast. Memberships: Founder, 3rd President, Association of Ivory Coast Students in France. Address: B.P. 698, Abidjan, Ivory Coast.

ADANDE, Senou Alexandre, born Port Novo, Dahomey, 12th March 1913. F.A.O. Inter-States Representative. Education: Diploma, L'Ecole Normale William Ponty de Goree, Senegal; L'Institut d'Ethnologie, Paris, France; L'Ecole du Louvre. Married, 9 children. Appointments include: Librarian, Archivist, Museum Worker, 1936-48; Head, Ethnology Department, French Institute of Black Africa (IFAN), Dakar, Senegal, 1948-60; Minister of Agriculture & of Farmers; Minister of Agriculture & Rural Development, 1958-59; Minister of Finance, 1960-62; Minister of Agriculture, 1962-63; Keeper of the Seals & Minister of Justice, 1963-65; President, Director-General, Sodak, 1966-67; currently, F.A.O. Inter-States Representative. Memberships: Commissioner-General, Negro Arts Exhibition, First World Festival of Negro Arts, Dakar, 1966. Publications include: Le mais et ses usages dans le Bas-Dahomey; Les masques et leur role dans les societes africaines; Imperieuse necessite des Musees africaines; Les recades des Rois du Dahomey. Honours include: Laureate, l'AOF, 1946; Special Mention, First World Festival of Negro Art, for his work Les recades, 1966; Grand Officier de l'Ordre National du Dahomey; Commandeur de l'Ordre National du Senegal; Grand Cordon de l'Etoile Brillant, China; Chevalier de l'Ordre National de la Legion d'Honneur; Chevalier des Palmes academiques; Medaille Civil, France. Address: B.P. 256, Niamey, Niger.

ADAPOE, Benjamin Kodzo, born Adina, Ghana, 18th February 1929. Agriculturist. Education: Elementary, Ghana, 1935-45; Secondary, Private Night School, 1946-47; Primary Agricultural, Ministry of Agriculture, Ghana, 1948-49; Post-secondary Agricultural, Agricultural Training College, Ghana, 1951-53; Farm Management, East German Ministry of Education, Berlin, 1962-63. Married, 5 sons, 2 daughters. Appointments: Agricultural Assistant, Ministry of Agriculture, Ghana, 1954-56; Foreman i/c, Pest Destruction (West Africa) Ltd., 1957-58; Senior Laboratory Assistant, Agronomy, University of Ghana Agriculture Research Station, Kade, 1958-61; Agricultural Technician, ibid, 1964-65; Assistant Farm Manager, 1965-68; Assistant Farm Manager, Crop Science Department, University of Ghana, Legon, 1969—. Memberships: Studenten-Komitees, Berlin, German Democratic Republic; Deutscher Turn-und Sportbund, Gotha; Faculty of Agriculture Senior Staff, University of Ghana, Legon; C.A.S.T. Senior Staff Club, Akwatia, Ghana; Thrift Kan, Accra. Publications: Farm Management Annual Reports (Univ. of Ghana Agric. Rsch. Stn. (Kade) Annual Reports), 1964-65, 1965-66, 1966-67; Faculty of Agriculture Farm—Legon—Special Report, 1968-69; Farm Management Principles in Economic Harmony with Agricultural Research & Extension in Ghana. Prizes, awards, etc: Book Prize & Silver Cup, Lawn Tennis Championship, A.R.S. Kade, Ghana, 1960; 1st Prize, Silver Cup, Table Tennis Championship, ibid, 1960; 3rd Prize, Bonze Medal, Table Tennis Competition, Potsdam, East Germany, 1963. Address: Crop Science Department, Faculty of Agriculture, University of Ghana, Legon, Ghana.

ADDAE, Stephen Kojo, born 31st July 1936. Lecturer in Medicine. Education: Achimota School, Ghana, 1950-56; M.B., B.Sc., University College, Ibadan, Nigeria, 1962; M.Sc., Ph.D.(Physiology), University of Rochester, Rochester, U.S.A., 1967. Appointments: House Officer, University Teaching Hospital, Ibadan, Nigeria; Postgraduate Fellow, Rockefeller Foundation, Rochester, U.S.A., 1964-67; Post-doctoral Fellow, University of Rochester,

1967-68; Lecturer in Physiology, Ghana Medical School, Accra, Ghana, 1968-69; Lecturer, Acting Head, Department of Physiology, ibid, 1970—. Memberships: American Association for Advancement of Science; Association for Tropical Biology; West African & Ghana Science Association; Secretary, Ghana Medical Association, 1969-70. Author of numerous articles on his subject published in medical journals. Honours: Best Clinical Student Award, University of Ibadan, 1959. Address: Ghana Medical School, P.O. Box 4236, Accra, Ghana.

ADDO, Nelson Otu, born 4th November 1933. Demographer; Sociologist. Education: B.Sc.(Sociology); M.Sc.(Econ., Lond.); Ph.D.(Lond.). Married, 2 children. Appointments: University Lecturer & Research Fellow in Demography, University of Ghana. Memberships: International Union for the Scientific Study of Population; Ghana Sociological Association. Author of numerous works in his field. Address: Demographic Unit, Department of Sociology, University of Ghana, Legon, Ghana.

ADDY, Hutton Ayikwei, born 26th November 1930. Paediatrician. Education: Primary, 1936-45; Accra Academy, Ghana, 1946-50; University of the Gold Coast, 1951-54; Queen's University, Belfast, U.K., 1954-59; Institute of Child Health, University of London, 1964-65; London School of Hygiene & Tropical Medicine, 1967. Married, 3 sons. Appointments: House appointments, Belfast City Hospital & Musgrave Park Hospital, Belfast, 1960-61; Medical Officer, Ministry of Health, Ghana, 1961-68; Senior Medical Officer, ibid, 1968—. Contributor to Ghana Medical Journal. Address: Princess Marie Louise Hospital (Children's), P.O. Box 122, Accra, Ghana.

ADEBAYO (Prince) Isaac Adepoju, born Ila Orangun, Nigeria, 21st November 1929. Public Relations Practitioner. Education: N.A. School, Ila Orangun, 1934-44; Boys' High School, Ibadan, 1946-51; Yaba Technical Institute, 1951-54; University College, Achimota, Gold Coast (Ghana), 1954-58; B.Sc.(Hons., Econ.) of the University of London, 1958. Personal details: a Prince by birth, married, 3 children. Appointments include: Teacher, 1945; Civil Engineering Assistant, Federal Republic Service, 1952-54; Administrative Officer, Public Service of Western Nigeria, 1958-62; Marketing Representative, Nigerian Tobacco Company Ltd., 1962-64; Public Relations Officer, Nigerian Tobacco Company Ltd., 1964-69; Public Relations Manager, ibid, 1969—. Memberships: President, Ibadan Junior Chamber of Commerce; President, Public Relations Committee of Y.M.C.A. of Nigeria; Patron, Ila Orangun Elements, Society of Great Britain & Ireland; Chairman, Ila Grammar School Board of Governors; President, Ibadan Boys' High School Old Boys' Association. Address: Nigerian Tobacco Company Limited, P.O. Box 6, Ibadan, Nigeria.

ADEBIYI, Samuel Durojaiye, born 10th February 1928. Judge. Education: Yaba Methodist School, Nigeria, 1932-36; Igbobi College, 1937-43; Middle Temple, King's College, London, U.K., 1951-53. Married, 5 children. Appointments: Crown Counsel, Nigeria, 1954-58; Legal Adviser, Ministry of Finance, 1959-61; Deputy Solicitor-General, 1962-64; Director of Public Prosecutions, 1964-67; Judge, High Court, 1967—. Memberships: Junior Circuit Steward, Ereko Circuit, Methodist Church of Nigeria, 1968—. Publications: Fundamental Human Rights in Nigeria—Some Decided Cases & Future Problems (Nigerian Law—Some Recent Developments), 1964. Address: High Court, Lagos, Nigeria.

ADEBO, Simeon Ola, born Abeo-kuta, Nigeria, 5th October 1913. International Official; Barrister-at-Law. Education: Abeo-kuta Grammar School; King's College, Lagos, Nigeria; B.A.(Hons.), London, U.K.; LL.B.(Hons.), ibid; Barrister-at-Law, Gray's Inn, London. Married, 3 sons, 1 daughter. Appointments include: Senior Administrative Officer, Government of Nigeria, 1943-57; Chief Secretary & Head of the Civil Service, Western Nigeria, 1957-62; Ambassador & Permanent Representative of Nigeria at the United Nations, New York, U.S.A., 1962-67; Under Secretary-General of the United Nations & Executive Director, United Nations Institute for Training & Research, 1968—. Memberships: President, Society for International Development, 1966-68; International Co-Chairman, Institute on Man & Science; International Co-Chairman, Adlai Stevenson Memorial Fund; Trustee, Nigerian Institute of International Affairs. Honours: LL.D., Western Mich. University, 1963; University of Nigeria, 1965; Fordham University, 1966; Lincoln University, 1966; Beaver College, Pa., 1966; D.C.L., Union College, Schenectady, 1965; C.M.G. (Companion of the most distinguished Order of St. Michael & St. George). Address: c/o U.N. Institute of Training & Research, 801 U.N. Plaza, New York, N.Y. 10017, U.S.A.

ADEDOYIN, Adegboyega Folaranmi, born 11th September 1922. Specialist Gynaecologist. Education: Methodist Boys' High School (Senior Cambridge—Grade I with exemption for London Matriculation); M.B., Ch.B., B.A.O., Queen's University, Belfast, U.K. Personal details: Prince, Son of the late Akarigbo of the Igeba Remo, Western Nigeria. Appointments: Senior Specialist, Obstetrics & Gynaecology in the Western State, Nigeria. Memberships: The Royal College of Physicians of Ireland; D.R.C.O.G., London; D.T.M. & H., U.K. Author of Review of the Treatment of Eclampsia. Honours: British Universities Record Holder in the High Jump, 1946; Long Jump, 1947; British Champion in High Jump; Irish Champion, High Jump, Long Jump & Hop, Step & Jump, 4 years; 5th, High Jump, Olympic Games, 1948. Address: c/o State Hospital, Abeokuta, Nigeria.

ADEGBENRO (Reverend) Samuel Oni, born Ile-Ife, Nigeria, 10th APril 1916. Clergyman. Education: Methodist School, Otapete, Ilesha, Nigeria; Methodist School, Agbeni, Ibadan; Wesley College, Ibadan. Married. Headmaster of various schools for 17 years; Catechist; Clergyman, Christ Apostolic Church, Ibadan. Memberships: Young Men's Christian Association, Christ Apostolic Church, More, Ile-Ife, 1950—. Address: Christ Apostolic Church, P.O. Box 530, Ibadan, Nigeria.

ADEGBESAN (Honourable) Anthony Bolaji Wilson, born Ijebu, Western State, Nigeria, 6th September 1896. Technician. Education: Roman Catholic Mission, Obonwon, 1908-12; St. Gregory's Grammar School, Lagos, 1912-14. Married, 1 son, 3 daughters, retired. Appointments: Teacher, 1915-18; Clerical Accounting Clerk, 1919-21; Agricultural Technologist, 1922-57; Zoologist, University of Ibadan, 1957-64. Memberships include: President, St. Anthony's Guild, St. Mary Cathedral, Ibadan; ibid, Holder of Church Wardens, Ibid; Treasurer, Ijebu Group; Treasurer, Diocesan Council; Treasurer, Ibadan Boy Scouts. Honours: Queen's Coronation Medal, 1953; K.S.G., His Holiness Pope John XXIII; Member of the Order of Niger, 1965. Address: 26 Araromi St., Oke Padre, Ibadan, Nigeria.

ADEGBOYE, Joseph Oladokun Durojaiye, born 24th April 1943. University Lecturer. Education: St. Mark's Primary School, Offa, Nigeria, 1951-56; St. Paul's College, Zaria, 1957-61; Boys' High School, Gindiri-Jos, 1962-63; B.Sc.(Hons.), Ahmadu Bello University, Zaria, 1967. Appointments: Science Teacher, St. Paul's College, 1964; Assistant Lecturer, Ahmadu Bello University, 1968–. Memberships: Nigerian Field Society; Senior Adviser, Fellowship of Christian Students; University Gospel Singers; Patrol Leader, Boy Scouts; Editor, Cultural & Debating Society. Co-author of article 'River Fisheries Surveys in Northern Nigeria', published in The Nigerian Field. Honours: Graduate Award, Ahmadu Bello University, 1968; African-American Graduate Fellowship, 1970. Address: Department of Zoology, University of North Carolina, Chapel Hill, North Carolina 27514, U.S.A.

ADEJUNMOBI, Sam. A., born 17th April 1926. Lecturer. Education: B.A., Va. Union University, Richmond, Va., U.S.A.; M.A., Harvard University, Cambridge, Mass.; Academic Diploma in Education, London University. Appointments: Lecturer, History Teaching & Comparative Education, University of Nigeria, Nsukka; ibid, University of Ibadan. Memberships: Historical Society of Nigeria; Association of University Teachers; Alpha Kappa Mu, 1956. Publications: The Nigerian Situation—A Lesson from History, Nigerian Opinion, 1967; Student Teachers & Practical Teaching, West African Journal of Education, 1967; The Role of the Universities & A.T.T.C.'s in Respect of In-Service Training of Secondary & Primary School Teachers, Proceedings of the Conference on High-Level Teacher Training, 1969. Honours: included in Who's Who in American Universities & Colleges, 1956; Danforth Fellow, 1956-57. Address: University of Ibadan, Ibadan, Nigeria.

ADEKOGBE, Elizabeth Adeyemi, born Ijebu-Ife, Ijebu Province, Western Nigeria, 24th October 1919, deceased 1968. Teacher; Feminist; Politician; Chief. Education: St. Louis Roman Catholic Mission School, Ijebu-Ife, 1924-28; St. Augustine's R.C. Mission School, Ijebu-Ode, 1929-32; St. Agnes's R.C. Teacher Training College, Yaba, 1933-35. Married to Prince L. A. G. Adekogbe, H.R.H. Oba Akija of Ikija-Ijebu, 2 daughters. Appointments included: Member, Board of Management, Co-operative Bank of Western Nigeria, mid 1950s; Exco Member, Co-operative Union of W. Nigeria, mid 1950s; Councillor, Ijebu Eastern District Council, 1956-64; variously, Chairman, Education Committee, ibid; ibid, Tax Assessment Committee; General Purposes Committee; Councillor, Ijebu Divisional Council, 1956-63; Chairman, Judiciary Committee, ibid; Nominee Director, W. Nigeria Development Corporation (W.N.D.C.), Ilushin Estates Ltd. (Government's Subsidiary Co.), 1963-66; Member, University of Ife Provisional Council, 1963-66. Memberships included: Founder & Life President, Women's Movement of Nigeria, 1952-68; ibid, Ibadan Dugbe Women's Co-operative Society, 1953-68; Chairman, Nigeria National Democratic Party Women's Wing, 1963-66; Treasurer, National Council of Women's Societies, late 1950s; West Regional Treasurer, National Council of Nigeria & the Cameroons, 1953; West Regional Financial Secretary, Action Group Women's Wing, 1955. Publications included: Articles on Women's Affairs. Broadcaster & Lecturer. Honours included: Installation as the Iyalaje of Ikija-Ijebu, Chieftaincy Title, 1953. Address: P.O. Box 348, Ibadan, Nigeria.

ADELEYE II (Oba) Adetunla, The Elekole of Ikole, born Ikole Ekiti, Western Nigeria, 14th August 1938. Education: Teacher Training, Wesley College, Ibadan; Nigerian College of Arts, Science & Technology, Zaria. Personal details: Son of Adeleye I, a former Elekole; married to Queen Ayo Adeleye, 7 children. Appointments include: Teacher, Primary School & Teacher Training Institution; installed as Elekole (king), 1958; President, Ikole Grade 'B' Customary Court, 1958-59; Member, Western Nigerian Finance Corporation, 1959-60; ibid, Western House of Chiefs, 1960-65; Minister Without Portfolio, 1963-65. Memberships include: Secretary-General, Ekiti Students' Union, 1959; President, Wesley College Branch, ibid, 1960; Secretary, Western Nigeria Obas, 1960. Address: The Elekole's Palace, P.O. Box 1, Ikole Ekiti, Nigeria.

ADEMOLA (Chief) Olori Gladys Wuraola, born 28th October 1909. Trader. Received Arabic education. Married to Oba Ademola Alake, 1925, 2 daughters. Descended from the Moslem, Balogun Ikija. Memberships: Women's Guild of Methodist Church, Ogbe Abeokuta; Seriki of Church Women, Ogbe Abeokuta. Honours: Olori of Ademola's wife, 1928; Iyalode Oloris of Ake Abeokute, 1947; Iyalode Ikija of Abeokuta, 1960. Address: No. 1 Oke-Ilewo St., Ibara, Abeokuta, Western State, Nigeria.

ADENIYI (Chief) Joseph Adedotun, born Oka Akoko, Nigeria, 6th November 1931. Teacher. Education: St. John's School, Oka, 1937-43; Jubilee Central School, Ikare, 1944; Ondo Boys' High School, Ondo, 1947-51; Fourah Bay College, Freetown, Sierra Leone, 1955-59, 1960-61. Married, 4 children. Appointments include: Railway clerk, 1952-55; Teacher, A.C. Grammar School, Oka, 1959-64; Principal, ibid, 1964–. Memberships: President, Nigerian Union of Students, Sierra Leone, 1960-61; Chairman, Nigerian Union of Teachers,

Oka Branch; Akoko Divisional Self-Help Committee; one time member, Western Nigeria Regional Board of Education. Publications: Religious denominations in Oka. Honours: Chief Ojomo of Ewu-Ikanmu, Oka, 1967. Address: P.O. Box 24, Oka Akoko, Nigeria.

ADE-ONOJOBI (Chief) Olusola, Base of Itoku born, Lagos, Nigeria, 16th September, 1933. Gynaecologist & Obstetrician. Education: Primary, Lagos Government School, 1941-45; Secondary, King's College, Lagos, 1946-52; Trinity College, Dublin, Ireland, 1953-59; Postgraduate, Ronkswood Hospital, Worcester, U.K. Personal details: Made an Ogboni Chief by the Alake of Abeskuta, Oba Gbadebo II; Married. Appointments: House Surgeon & House Physician, General Hospital, Lagos, Nigeria, 1959-60; Medical Officer, Western State of Nigeria, 1960-63; Senior Medical Officer, 1964-69; Acting Specialist Obstetrician & Gynaecologist, 1970. Memberships: Secretary, Kings College Society, 1950; Editor, 'Spectator', Panes House, Kings College, 1950-51; College Organist, 1951-52; Editor, 'K.C. Exponent' (College Weekly Paper), 1952; Assistant Organist, St. Davids Church, Lagos, 1952-53; Treasurer, Dublin University Boxing & Gymnastic Club, 1955-57; Social Secretary, Association of Students of African Descent, Dublin, 1958; Boxing Team Manager, Western Nigeria Boxing Team, 1964; Assistant Organist, St. Thomas's Church, Badagey, 1965-66. Contributor, Journal of Obstetrics & Gynaecologists, 1970. Honours: Kenneth Marchant Memorial Prize for Biology, Kings College, 1952; Kenneth Moore Prize, Dublin University Medical School, 1954; Irish & Scottish Universities Welterweight Boxing Champion, 1955; Came 1st & was 'Respondent', B.A. exam for Professional Students, Trinity College, Dublin, 1957. Address: Ministry of Health, Western State, Nigeria.

ADEREMI, Ademula Oyeranmi, born 4th December 1929. Medical Practitioner. Education: Government College, Ibadan, Nigeria, 1941-47; Norwich City College, U.K., 1948-49; Edinburgh University, Scotland, 1949-55. Personal details: Eldest son of His Highness Sir Adesoji Ackremi, The Oni of Ife; Married, 4 children. Appointments: Medical Officer, Western Nigeria, 1955-59; Senior Medical Officer, ibid, 1959-66; General Practitioner & Proprietor, Marian Clinics & Nursing Home, Lagos, 1966–. Member of the Rotary Club, Ibeja, Nigeria. Address: 32 Oba Akrer Avenue, Ikeja, Lagos State, Nigeria.

ADESIDA (Chief) Adebola Asake, born Awe-Oyo, Western Nigeria, 27th May 1933. Nurse; Social Worker. Education: Primary & Secondary Education, Nigeria; Dip., Ophthalmic Nursing, Moorefields Eye Hospital, London, England; State Registered Nurse, Royal Free Hospital, London; Simpson Memorial Maternity Pavilion, Edinburgh, Scotland. Personal details: daughter of the late Chief J. A. Ajao, the Otun of Oyo, Balogun of Awe; wife of His Highness The Deji of Akure. Appointments include: Nursing Sister, Specialist Hospital, Akure, 1957; The Eyesorun of Akure, 1957; Voluntary Social Worker. Memberships include: President, Akure Branch, National Council of Women's Societies; Vice-President, Western Nigeria Branch, ibid; Director, Akure Branch, Red Cross Society; Member, Akure Branch, Council of Social Services; Akure Branch, Old Age Relief Services; Akure Branch, Leprous Patients Comfort Committee. Honours include: Chieftaincy Title, 1957. Address: Deji's Palace, P.O. Box 1, Akure, W. Nigeria.

ADESIDA II (His Highness Desi of Akureland), Ademuagun, born Akure, Western State, Nigeria, 8th November 1925. Solicitor & Advocate. Education: St. David's School, Akure; King's College, Lagos; M.A.(Hons.), Trinity College, University of Dublin, Ireland; LL.B., ibid; B.L., Middle Temple, London, U.K. Personal details: succeeded father as Desi of Akure, Nigeria, 1957; married, 6 children. Appointments include: Member, Western House of Chiefs; Vice-Chairman, Committee for Law Revision, Western State; Vice-Chairman, Council of Obas & Chiefs, Western State; Minister Without Portfolio during civilian regime, Western State; Chairman, Nigerian Council of World Affairs. Memberships include: Trinity College Historical Society; 400 Club, Nigeria; Patron, various organizations. Honours, Prizes, etc.: Commander of the Federal Republic of Nigeria, 1965; Justice of the Peace. Address: P.O. Box 1, Akure, Western State, Nigeria.

ADESOGAN, Ezekiel Kayode, born 1st October 1939. Lecturer. Education: B.Sc., Chemistry (Special), London, 1964; Ph.D., Ibadan University, Nigeria, 1968. Married, 2 children. Appointments: Postdoctoral Research Fellow, Chemistry Department, University of Ibadan, 1968-69; Leverhulme Research Fellow, The Robert Robinson Labs., University of Liverpool, U.K., 1968-70; Lecturer, University of Ibadan, Nigeria, 1970–. Memberships: Scripture Union; Chemical Society of London; Royal Institute of Chemistry. Co-author of some 12 research papers in Journal of Chemical Society, & Chemistry & Industry. Address: Chemistry Department, University of Ibadan, Ibadan, Nigeria.

ADESOJI II (Sir) Aderemi, The Oni of Ife, born Ife, Nigeria, 15th November 1889. Education: C.M.S. School, Ife, Nigeria. Personal details: member of Royal House of Ile-Ife. Appointments include: Clerk, Railway Construction, 1909; Clerk, Railway Civil Service, 1910; Trader, 1921; Member, Western House of Assembly, 1946; Member, Legislative Council, Nigeria, 1947; Director & Member, Nigeria Produce Marketing Company, 1947; Member, House of Representatives, 1951-54; Central Minister without Portfolio, 1951-55; led Delegation to Coronation of Queen Elizabeth, 1953; Delegate to Conference for revision of Nigerian Constitution, London, Lagos, 1954, London, 1957 & 1958, P.C. (W.R.) 1954; President, House of Chiefs, 1954-60; Governor, Western Region, 1960-62. Honours, Prizes, etc.: C.M.G., 1943; K.B.E., 1950; K.C.M.G., 1962; LL.D.(Hons.), University of Ife, 1967. Address: The Afin, Ile-Ife, Western State of Nigeria.

ADESOLA, Akinpelu Oludele, born 6th November 1930. Surgeon. Education: M.B., B.Ch., B.A.O.(Belfast), 1956; F.R.C.S.(Eng.),

1960; M.Ch.(Belfast). Appointments: Surgical Tutor, Queen's University of Belfast, 1959-61; Senior Registrar, Surgery, U.C.H., Ibadan, 1961-62; Lecturer, Surgery, University of Lagos, 1962-64; Senior Lecturer, Surgery, ibid, 1964-65; Associate Professor, Surgery, 1965-67; Professor, ibid, 1967—; currently, Deputy Provost, College of Medicine. Memberships: President, West African Society of Gastroenterology, 1968—; Surgical Research Society of Gt. Britain; Secretary, Association of Surgeons of West Africa, 1964-66. Publications: Author of papers on hyperparathyroidism, experimental ascites, hepatic lymph production, gastric functions in Nigerian Children, diverticulitis, peptic ulceration in Nigerians, adult intussusception, thyroiditis, etc. Editor, Tropical Surgery, 1970; Editor-in-Chief, Journal of the Nigeria Medical Association. Honours: Smyth Prize, Surgery, Queen's University of Belfast, U.K., 1956; Senior Buswell Fellow, University of Rochester, N.Y., U.S.A., 1963-64; External Examiner in Surgery, University of Ibadan, 1969—. Address: Professor of Surgery & Deputy Provost, College of Medicine of the University of Lagos, P.M.B. 12003, Lagos, Nigeria.

ADESUYI, Samuel Lawrence, born Ileoluji, Nigeria, 30th November 1923. Medical Practitioner; Chief Medical Adviser to the Federal Government of Nigeria. Education: St. Peter's School, Ile-Oluji; Government College, Ibadan; Higher College, Yaba; Achimota College, Accra, Ghana; School of Medicine, Yaba, Nigeria; Medical School, University College, Ibadan; West London Hospital Medical School, U.K.; Royal Institute of Public Health & Hygiene, London; London School of Hygiene & Tropical Medicine; L.S.M.(Nig.); M.R.C.S.(Eng.); L.R.C.P.(Lond.); D.P.H.(Eng.); F.M.C.P.H.(Nig.); Certificate in Medical Statistics & Epidemiology(Lond.). Married, 2 children. Appointments: House Physician & Surgeon, Adeiyo Hospital, Ibadan, 1950-51; Medical Officer, Ministry of Health, Nigeria, 1951-59; Specialist Medical Statistician, Ministry of Health, 1959-65; Deputy Chief Medical Adviser to the Federal Government, 1965-69; Chief Medical Adviser, 1969—; Associate Lecturer, Biostatistics, Lagos University College of Medicine, 1963—; Member, WHO Advisory Board on Health Statistics, 1968—. Memberships: President-elect, World Federation of Public Health Associations, 1970; President, 1970—, & Life Fellow, Society of Health, Nigeria; Secretary-General, Nigeria Medical Association, 1960-62; Life Fellow, Royal Institute of Public Health & Hygiene, London, U.K.; Fellow, Royal Society of Tropical Medicine; Former Vice-Chairman, Lagos Island Club, Nigeria; Patron, Lagos Amateur Volleyball Association; Vice-President, Nigerian Olympic Association; President, Nigeria Medical Council; Secretary-General, National Council on Health; Chairman, West African Examinations Board, Royal Society of Health; Chairman, Medical Research Council of Nigeria; President, Institute of Medical Laboratory Technology of Nigeria; Chairman, Board, Federal School of Medical Laboratory Technology; Chairman, Board, Federal Schools of Dental Hygiene & Dental Technology; Chairman, Board, Federal School of Radiography; Chairman, Midwives Board of Nigeria; Court of Governors, College of Medicine, University of Lagos; Vice-Chairman, St. John Council of Nigeria; Board of Management, Lagos University Teaching Hospital; Board of Management, University College Hospital, Ibadan; Board of Governors, Institute of Administration, University of Ife. Author of various papers & articles in professional publications. Honours: Sir Walter Johnson's Prize in Anatomy, 1946, in Physiology, 1946, & in Public Health & Forensic Medicine, 1950; Blair Aitken's Memorial Prize in Medicine, 1950; May & Baker Prize in Surgery, 1950; Tanner Memorial Prize, 1958. Address: Federal Ministry of Health, Lagos, Nigeria.

ADEYI, Margaret Modupeola, born 6th April 1931. Research Nurse. Education: Senior Cambridge Examination; State Registered Nurse; State Certified Midwife; Food Science & Applied Nutrition Course, Ibadan University, Nigeria. Married, 1953, 6 children. Appointments: Staff Midwife, University College Hospital, Ibadan; Research Nursing Sister, Ibadan University. Memberships: Society of Health. Address: P.O. Box 612, Ibadan, Nigeria.

ADEYINKA, Adebayo. Business Executive; Politician. Education: Onitsha Baptist School, Issele, Uku, Nigeria; New African High School, Onitsha; Signals Army Corps. Training College, Accra, Ghana, 1942. Married with children; War veteran of World War II, 1939-45. Appointments: Member of House of Representatives, Nigeria, 1955-59; Member, U.N.O. Delegation 17th Session, General Assembly, New York, U.S.A., 1962; Executive Director, W.N.M.B., 1963-66; Member, Nigeria Ports Authority, 1964-66; Director, Nigeria National Bank, 1963-66; Director, Wema Board Estate Ltd., & Chairman, Board of Directors Lapal Properties Co. Ltd., 1963-66. Memberships: Banned National Democratic Party; Banned N.C.N.C.; Zonal Chairman, Banned Zikist Movement, & N.N.D.P. Youth Vanguard. Honours: War Medal, 1945; Gold Medal, Nigerian Ports Authority, 1964. Address: P.O. Box 2074, Ibadan, Western State, Nigeria.

ADIKPETO, Bernard Coovi, born 9th March 1939. Rural Engineer. Education: Baccalaureat, General Mathematics & Physics; Agronomy Engineer (INA); Rural Engineer (Lakes & Forests). Married, 3 children. Appointments: Economic Engineer, 1967-68; Chief Engineer of Public Works, 1968; Director, Rural Engineering Service & Land Improvements, 1969—. Memberships: Council of Administration of the SNAFOR (National Society for Forest Development); President, Council of Administration of the Rizie-Coop de Dume (Agricultural & Horticultural Society). Address: Director, Genie Rural et des Ameliorations Foncieres, B.P. 268, Porto-Novo, Dahomey.

ADJEI, Kwame Efah, born 23rd December 1933. Lecturer; Managing Director. Education: B.Sc.(Econ.), University of Pennsylvania, U.S.A., 1958; M.B.A., Temple University, Philadelphia, 1960; Ph.D., New York University, 1967. Married, 3 children. Appointments: Lecturer, School of Administration, University of Ghana, 1961-67; Managing Director, State

Fishing Corporation, Teme, Ghana, 1967-70; Acting Director, School of Administration, University of Ghana, 1970–. Memberships: Ghana Association for the Advancement of Management; Legon Society of National Affairs. Publications: Proposed Programme of Social Security for Ghana; Occupational Choice & Organizational Selection of Ghanaian Executives in the Civil Service, State Corporations and Private Foreign Corporations in Ghana (Ph.D., N.Y. Univ.). Honours: Founders Day Award, New York University, 1967. Address: School of Administration, University of Ghana, Legon, Ghana.

ADJETEY ADJEVI, Nicolas, born 27th December 1920. Civil Servant. Education: Admissibility to E.N.F.O.M. Appointments: Director of Personnel, Fonction Publique Togolaise, –1963; General Secretary, National School of Administration, 1963–. Memberships: President, Counsellor, Sporting Society ESSOR, Lome; Central Togo Red Cross Committee; President, Financial Commission of the Togo Football Federation; ibid, Financial Commission of the Togo Red Cross; Vice-President, Local Section of the CRT. Address: B.P. 64, Lome, Togo.

ADOLLO, John Jemine, born 27th December 1939. Journalist; Editor. Education: Hussey College, Warri, Nigeria, 1956-60; South-East Technical College, London, U.K., 1962-63; Kennington College, London, 1963-64; Diploma in Journalism, College of Journalism, London, 1966. Appointments: Sub-Editor, Nigerian Daily Times, 1967-68; Assistant Editor, Magazine Annuals & Periodicals, 1968-69; Editor, Magazine Annuals, Daily Times of Nigeria Ltd., 1969–. Memberships: Nigerian Union of Journalists. Editor of Nigerian Year Book; Who's Who in Nigeria; Diaries etc. Address: 3/7 Kakawa Street, Lagos, Nigeria.

ADOTEVI, Stanislas, born 4th February 1934. Professor of Philosophy. Director. Education: Ecole Normale Superieure; Ph.D. Married, 2 children. Appointments include: Professor of Philosophy; Director of Cabinet, Ministry of Foreign Affairs; Secretary-General to the Government; Commissioner for Information, Ministry of Information; Director, Institut de Recherches Appliquees du Dahomey (IRAD); Commissioner-General for Culture. Author of various articles and revues. Address: B.P. 88, Porto-Novo, Dahomey.

ADU-AMPOMA, Samuel Maxwell, born Yonso, Ashanti, Ghana, 15th July 1928. Educationalist & Author. Education: Presbyterian & Government Schools; Achimota School, Accra, Ghana, 1943-46; Certificate 'A' Teacher, Achimota Teacher Training College, 1948-49; B.Sc.(Lond.), University College of the Gold Coast, 1954; Postgraduate Diploma in Education,(Lond.), ibid, 1955; M.Sc., Educational Administration, Bowling Green State University, Ohio, U.S.A., 1959-60. Appointments include: Teacher, Sunyani Government School, Ghana, 1950; Chemistry Teacher, Education Officer, Government Secondary Technical School, 1955-59; Headmaster, ibid; Principal Education Officer, Ministry of Education, 1961-68; currently, Principal Education Officer, in charge of Science Education, ibid, Accra. Memberships include: President, Ghana Association of Science Teachers, 1967-69. Publications include: A Qualitative Analysis for School Certificate; A First Handbook of Science Activities; Experimental Science for Elementary Schools Books 1-4; Teachers' Books for Books 1, 2, 3, & 4. Address: Ministry of Education, P.O. Box M 45, Accra, Ghana.

AFEWERK TEKLE, born 22nd October 1932. Painter; Sculptor; Designer. Education: Elementary School, Ethiopia; Leighton Park School, Reading, U.K.; Central School of Arts & Crafts, London, 1947; Slade Faculty of Fine Arts, University of London; various European academies for 2 yrs. Given studio in National Library of Ethiopia, Addis Ababa, by H.I.M. Haile Selassié I. Exhibitions include: Addis Ababa Municipal Hall (one-man), 1954 (1st significant art exhibition of post-war Ethiopia, opened by H.I.M. Haile Selassié I); Retrospective, Addis Ababa, 1961; Moscow, U.S.S.R., 1964 (followed by U.S.S.R. lecture tour); One-man show, Washington & New York, U.S.A., 1964 (followed by lecture tour); Lecture tour, Dakar, Senegal, Turkey, Congo & Egypt. Commissions: Decoration of St. George's Cathedral, Addis Ababa; Monumental stained glass windows, Military Academy, Harar, Ethiopia; Stained glass windows, Africa Hall (H.Q. of U.N. Commission for Africa). Memberships: Past President & Treasurer, Toastmasters Club; International Fencers Club; Judge, Horticultural Club. Subject of many critical appreciations. Honours: Prix de Rome, 1955; National Painting Prize, 1959; Hailé Selassié I Award for Fine Arts, 1964; Commander of the Order of Merit, Senegal, 1966; Officer of Arts & Letters, France, 1966. Address: Villa Alpha, P.O. Box 717, Addis Ababa, Ethiopia.

AFFOYON, Didier, born Porto-Novo, Dahomey, 1937. Director, Agricultural Service. Education: Primary School, St. Michel, Cotonou, 1944-50; CEPE, 1950; BREVET, College Victor Ballot, Porto-Novo, 1954; BAC, ibid, 1957; Ecole Nationale Superieure Agronomique, Toulouse, France, 1957-61; Overseas Bureau of Scientific Research & Technology (ORSTOM), 1961-63. Married, 4 children. Appointments include: Deputy Director, E.A.-R.A., 1964; Director, ibid, 1964; Technical Adviser, Ministry of Rural Development Co-operation, 1967; Deputy Director of Agricultural Information & Agronomy Research; Director, The Agricultural Service, 1965-69; Chief of Grouping, OCLALAV of Niger, 1970. Address: B.P. 113, Zinder, Niger.

AFOLABI, Paul Fehintola, born Ilero, Nigeria, 8th December 1930. Teacher. Education: Ilero Baptist School, 1940-47; Teacher Training Course, Baptist College, Iwo, 1950-53; Fourah Bay College, Freetown, Sierra Leone, 1958-61; B.A. in Economic Studies (Dunelm). Married, 5 children. Appointments include: Pupil Teacher, Baptist School, Iganna, 1948-49; Teacher, Baptist School, Tede, 1954-55; Headmaster, ibid, 1956-57; Teacher,.

Baptist Academy, Lagos, 1958; Graduate Teacher, Oranyan Grammar School, Oyo, 1961-66; Senior Tutor, ibid, 1962-66; Principal, Ansar-Ud-Deen High School, Shaki, 1967—. Memberships include: Board of Governors, St. Bernardine's Girls' Grammar School, Oyo; Shaki Recreation Club; Oke Oro Baptist Church, Shaki. Address: Ansar-Ud-Deen High School, P.O. Box 28, Shaki, Nigeria.

AFOLALU, Ogidiolu Raphael, born Ilawe-Ekiti, Western Nigeria, 24th October 1934. Educator. Education: St. John's Primary School, Ilawe, 1942-48; Teacher Training, St. Leo's College, Abeokuta, 1949-52; Nigerian College of Arts, Sciences & Technology, 1956-58; B.A., University College, Ibadan, 1958-61. Married, 5 children. Appointments: Teacher, Primary School, 1953-54; Teacher, Aquinas College, Akure, 1955-56; Senior African Tutor, Annunciation School, Ikere-Ekiti, 1961-65; Principal, Notre Dame College, Ushi Ekiti, 1966-69; Principal, St. Charles' Grammar School, Oshogbo, 1970—. Memberships: Federation of Catholic Teachers; President, Ilawe Students' Union, 1959-60; Secretary, Ilawe Progressive Union, 1963-64; Pax Romana Student Organization; Historical Society of Nigeria; Nigerian Union of Teachers. Publications: A Textbook History of West Africa; Africa Since 1800 (to be published); Task for Laymen in Contemporary Africa, 1961; Enemies of Peace, 1967; The Catholic Church in Nigeria (African Missionary Mag.), 1970, etc. Honours: 3rd Prize, Essay Competition, The Significance of Abraham Lincoln, U.S. Information Service, 1960. Address: St. Charles' Grammar School, P.O. Box 125, Oshogbo, Nigeria.

AGANBI (Chief) Titus Obogariemu, born 1st January 1930. Teacher. Education: Baptist Primary School, Eku, Nigeria, 1938-45; Baptist College, Benin City, 1949-50; Baptist College, Iwo, 1953-54; B.A., St. David's University College, Lampeter, Cardiganshire, U.K., 1963. Married, 9 children. Appointments: Assistant Headmaster, Baptist Secondary Modern School, Eku, Nigeria, 1955-56; Tutor, Baptist College, Iwo, 1957-60; Vice-Principal, Baptist Boys' High School, Abeokuta, 1964; Principal, Baptist College, Benin City, 1965-67; ibid, Baptist High School, Eku, 1968—; Education Secretary, N.B.C. Schools, Mid-west, 1968-69. Memberships: Chairman, Mid-west Association of Teachers of English, 1966-67. Address: Baptist High School, P.O. Box 8, Eku, via Sapele, Nigeria.

AGBLEMAGNON, Ferdinand N'sougan, born Ahepe, Togo, 30th May 1929. Diplomat. Education: Primary Schools, Ahepe, Anecho & Lome; former pupil of Higher Technical School, Bamako, Niger; attended, Modern College of Die; Lycée Champollion, Grenoble, France; Lycée Lakanal, Paris; studied at the Faculty of Sciences & Humanities, Paris; Faculty of Law, University of Paris; Practical School of Higher Studies, ibid; Faculty of Sciences, ibid; Institute of Psychology; Institute of Ethnology. Appointments: Representative of the International Movement for Brotherly Union between races & peoples, 1962—; President, UNESCO group in charge of the O.N.G. Committee of school education in Africa, 1962-64; Delegate to the Togo General Conference (13th Conference), 1964; ibid, Special Intergovernmental Conference connected with UNESCO, 1966; Head of the Togo Delegation to the 14th General Conference of UNESCO, 1966; Vice-President of the UNESCO Expects Re-union on Education Planning, 1967; President, World Congress of Rural Sociology, Drinerlo, 1968; Vice-President, 9th International Congress on Science, Anthropology & Ethnology, Tokyo-Kyoto, Japan, 1968; Delegate, then Head of the Togo Delegation to the 15th General UNESCO Conference, 1968; Ambassador, Permanent Togo Delegate to UNESCO, France. Memberships include: Africanists' International Society; African Culture Society; Committee Member, Director of the International Association of Sociologist of the French Language; Vice-President, Federation for Respect for Man & Humanity (F.R.H.); International Association of Political Sciences. Representative at numerous Conferences, & Delegations both for UNESCO & other Internation Organizations; Visiting Professor to many foreign Universities, including Montreal, 1964 & Mexico, 1965. Address: 5, rue de la Roseraie, 92-Meudon La Foret, France.

AGBODEKA, Francis, born 31st December 1931. University Dean. Education: Achimota School, Ghana, 1947-52; B.A.(Lond.), University College of the Gold Coast, 1956; Ph.D.(Ghana), 1968. Married, 3 children. Appointments: Acting Head, Department of History, University College of Cape Coast, 1962—; Acting Dean, Faculty of Arts, ibid, 1969—. Memberships: Fellow, Historical Society of Ghana. Publications: The Rise of the Nation States (A history of West African Peoples), 1965. Address: Faculty of Arts, University College of Cape Coast, Cape Coast, Ghana.

AGBOTON, Damien-Gilbert, born 4th April 1925. Teacher; Public School Director. Married, 8 children. Member of the A.M.O.R.C. Address: Directeur d'Ecole Publique, B.P. 320, Porto-Novo, Dahomey.

AGBOTON, Padonou Ambroise, Minister of Public Works & Affairs, born Zinvie, Dahomey, 20th December 1923. Education: Primary studies, Dahomey, 1929-37; Ecole Normale, Togo, 1944-47; Higher studies in France, 1962-64; Diploma, Institute of Higher Overseas Studies, 1964. Appointments: Administrator, Corps National, 1964; Head of the General Administration Section, Personnel Department attached to the Governor's Cabinet, Dahomey, 1954-57; Director, Head of Cabinet, Ministry of Justice, Legislation & Public Affairs, 1959; Head of Mission, Technical Councillor, Deputy Director, Cabinet within the Presidential Cabinet, 1964-66; duties in the Territorial Command, 1966-68; Deputy Prefect of Atlantic; Prefect of Atlantic. Memberships: Union Official, 1954-60; General Secretary, Union of General Administration (Dahomey section of the Federal Union); ibid, Administrative, Financial & Accountants' Agents' Service; Director, Youth Movement, 1954-60; President, Youth Council, Dahomey; ibid, National Defence against Alcoholism Committee; Vice-President, Youth of Africa; ibid, Youth of the French Union;

'WAY' (World gathering of Youth). Honours: Chamber of Commerce Half-Century Medal, 1959; Knight, National Order of Dahomey, 1964; ibid, National Order of Upper Volta, 1965; National Order of Dahomey, 1970. Address: Ministere de la Fonction Publique et du Travail, Porto Novo, Dahomey.

AGGARWAL, Arjan Dass, born 8th September, 1931. Physician; Provincial Medical Officer. Education: Cambridge School Certificate, 1948; Bachelor of Medicine & Bachelor of Surgery, University of Bombay, India, 1957; Diploma, Public Health, University of Liverpool, U.K., 1963. Married. Appointments: Medical Officer, Kenya Ministry of Health, 1957—; Medical Officer of Health, 1961—; Provincial Medical Officer, 1968—; Memberships: Director, Lions Club, Nyeri; Nyeri Club; Nyanza Club; Kenya Red Cross Society. Honours: World Health Organization Fellowship for Public Health Studies, 1962-63. Address: Provincial Medical Officer, Eastern Province, P.O. Box 273, Embu Kenya.

AGGARWAL, Gurparshad, born 17th November 1933. Accountant. Education: Senior Cambridge School Certificate. Appointments: Assistant Chief Accountant; Chief Accountant/ Secretary; Financial Controller. Associate Member, The Association of Certified & Corporate Accountants. Address: P.O. Box 4648, Nairobi, Kenya.

AGGARWAL, Hari, born Kisumu, Kenya, 19th October 1930. Civil Engineer. Education: Cambridge School Certificate, Duke of Gloucester School, Nairobi; Technical College, Bournemouth, U.K.; B.Sc.(Engineering), Royal Technical College, Salford. Married, 2 children. Appointments include: Trainee Engineer, 1953-54; Private Practice, Uganda, 1954-60; Engineer, Messrs. Ove Arup & Partners, Kampala, 1960-61; Assistant Engineer, Kisumu Municipality, Kenya, 1961; Acting Town Engineer, ibid, 1962-64; Town Engineer, 1964—. Memberships include: Board of Govenors, Sigalagala Technical School & Kisumu High School; President & Trustee, Cosmopolitana Club, Kisumu; Director, Kisumu Lions Club; Management Committee & President, Arya Samaj, Kisumu; Nyanza Club; A.M.I.Mun.E.; A.M.I.Sruct.E.; C.E.; Agriculture Society of Kenya; Chairman, Works & Building Committee, ibid. Address: Town Engineer, Municipality of Kisumu, P.O. Box 105, Kisumu, Kenya.

AGNEW, Swanzie, born 9th June 1916. Professor of Geography. Education: Edinburgh University, U.K., 1933-37; University of Montpellier, France, 1938-39. Personal details: Wife of Sir Fulque Agnew, Baronet. Appointments: Assistant Lecturer, University of Edinburgh, U.K., 1939-46; Visiting Lecturer, McMaster University, Canada, 1946-47; Acting Head of Department, University of Fort Hare, South Africa, 1953-59; Headmistress, Royal Ballet School, Richmond, U.K., 1960-65; Professor, University of Malawi, 1965—. Memberships: Chairman, The International Geographical Union National Committee of Malawi; Patron of the Association of Malawian Geographers. Publications: The Historical Geography of South Africa (co-author), 1963; Malawi-in-Maps (co-author), in press. Address: University of Malawi, Chancellor College, Box 5200 Limbe, Blantyre, Malawi.

AGNIHOTRI, Dev Raj, born Thane Wal, Gurdas Pur Punjab, India, 1st May 1919. Civil Servant; Interpreter of Indian Languages. Education: Government High School, Gurdas Pur, Punjab; Matriculation Examination, Punjab University, 1936; Qualified Steno-Typist, Oriental Commercial College, Lahore, 1937-38; Government Entrance Examination, ibid, 1942. Appointments: Clerk, Sugar Factory, Kichha, United Provinces, 1940-41; ibid, Military Field Accounts Department, Indian Civil Service, 1942-43; Steno-Typist, Executive Committee, Indian National Congress, Nairobi, Kenya, 1944; Trains Clerk-Chief Goods Clerk, East African Railways & Harbours, ibid, 1945; Clerk & Interpreter, Judicial Department, Kampala, Uganda, 1947; Special Constable (Hon.), Uganda Police, 1952; Senior Officer, District Registry, High Court, Jinja, Busoga District, 1953; Promoted to Executive Grade, 1954; Office Assistant, 1957; Higher Executive Officer attached to Chief Justice of Uganda in Chambers & Court, 1964; Senior Executive Officer, Civil Registries Superintendent, 1967. Memberships: Uganda Sports Club, Kampala; Sports Secretary, Sikh Union, ibid; Muslim Sports Club. Honours: Colonial Police Medal, for meritorious service in Special Constabulary of Police Force; Independence Medal, for long service in Uganda. Address: c/o High Court of Uganda, P.O. Box 7085, Kampala, Uganda.

AGOLA, Evan Jasper, born about 1907-08. Lower Primary Teacher; Clerk in Holy Orders. Education: Maseno Primary School, 1924-28. Married, 6 sons, 5 daughters. Appointments: Ordained Deacon, 1943; Priest, 1945; Rural Dean, 1955; made Canon, 1956; Consecrated Assistant Bishop of Maseno, Kenya, 1965; Bishop of Maseno South, 1970. Address: P.O. Box 115, Kisumu, Kenya.

AGOSSA HOMEVO, Antoine, born Athieme, Dahomey, 13th June 1936. Government Administrator. Education: Public Primary School, Athieme, 1943-48; Behanzin Secondary School (ex-College Victor Ballot), Porto-Novo, 1948-55; Faculty of Law & Economic Science, University of Dakar, Senegal, 1955-59; ibid, University of Paris, France, 1959-61; Overseas Institute of Higher Studies, Paris, 1959-61; Lic., Law & Economic Science; Diploma, I.H.E.O.M. Married, 4 children. Appointments: Director of Cabinet, Ministry of Commerce, Economy & Tourism, 1961-63; Assistant to the Prefect of the South (Atlantic), 1963; Deputy Prefect, Ouidah (Department of the Atlantic), 1963-66; Prefect, Department of Zou, 1966—. Honours: Merite du Benin (Medal of Vermeil). Address: Prefecture of Zou, Abomey, Dahomey.

AGUDA, Akinola, born 10th June 1923. Judge. Education: Government College, Ibadan, Nigeria, 1939-44; LL.B.(Hons.), LL.M., London School of Economics & Political Science, London, U.K., 1947-52; Ph.D., School of African & Oriental Studies. Appointments:

Senior Crown Counsel, Western Nigeria Ministry of Justice, 1955-59; Administrator-General & Public Trustee, Western Nigeria, 1960-65; Dean, Faculty of Law, University of Ife, 1965-66; Principal Legal Draftsman for Western Nigeria, 1966-67; Director of Public Prosecutions, 1967-68; Judge, High Court of Western State of Nigeria, 1968—. President, Nigerian Society of Criminology. Publications: Principles of Criminal Liability in Nigerian Law, 1965; Law of Evidence in Nigeria, 1966; Address: High Court of Justice, Ibadan, Nigeria.

AGYEI, Emmanuel Kenneth, born 15th August 1938. Physicist; Lecturer. Education: Presbyterian Primary School, Duayaw-Nkwanta, Ghana; Prempeh College; B.Sc.(Lond.), University of Ghana; M.Sc., Ph.D., McMaster University, Canada. Married, 1 son, 1 daughter. Appointments: Lecturer, Department of Physics, University of Ghana. Memberships: Associate, Canadian Association of Physicists; ibid, American Association for the Advancement of Science; Ghana Science Association. Author of A Study of the Isotopic Abundance of Boron from Various Sources, Canadian Journal of Earth Science, 1968. Address: c/o Department of Physics, University of Ghana, Ghana.

AGYEMAN, Albert Kofi, born Kumasi, Ghana, 2nd July 1926. Chartered Accountant. Education: Cambridge School Certificate, 1947; Achimota School, Ghana; Intermediate C.I.S.; Inter B. Commm. Part I; Associate of the Institute of Chartered Accountants in England & Wales and Member, Ghana Institute of Chartered Accountants. Appointments include: Probationer Manager, U.A.C. of Ghana Ltd., 1951-54; Lecturer in Accountancy and Allied Subjects, Kumasi College of Technology, & later School of Administration, Achimota, Ghana; Accountant, Volta River Authority, 1962-64; Partner in Amorin, Agyeman Ayew & Company, Chartered Accountants, 1965—. Memberships include: Kumasi Golf Club. Address: c/o Messrs. Amorin Agyeman Ayew & Co., Chartered Accountants, P.O. Box 1551, Kumasi, Ghana.

AGYEMAN-DICKSON, Yaw Duah, born Konongo, Ghana, 23rd November 1925. Educationalist. Education: Adisadel College, Cape Coast; Wilberforce State College, Xenia, Ohio, U.S.A.; Michigan University, Ann Arbor, Michigan; Maryland University Law School, Baltimore, Maryland; M.A.; B.Sc.(Hons.); Ph.D.; M.Sc. Appointments include: Founder, Headmaster, Ashanti Akim Secondary School, 1954; Tutor, Konongo Odumasi Secondary School, 1954-56; Mass Education Officer, 1956-61; Acting Headmaster, Navrongo Secondary School, 1961-62; Assistant Headmaster, Ghana Secondary School, Koforidua, 1962-63; Headmaster, Bawleu Secondary School, 1963-66; Headmaster, Asamankese Secondary School, 1966-70; ibid, Eden Educational Unit, 1970—. Memberships include: Fellow, American Geographical Society; Fellow, American Historical & Social Science Society. Publications include: West Africa on the March—A study & intimate survey of problems & potentialities, U.S.A., 1952. Address: P.O. Box 5108, Accra, Ghana.

AHADOU SABOURE (His Excellency), born Adigalla, Ethiopia, 25th September 1926. Diplomat; Consular General. Education: studied Amharic; attended School Alliance Française, Diré-Daoua, Ethiopia, 1934-35. Appointments: Collector of Taxes, Municipality of Diré-Daoua, 1941-42; Deputy Inspector, Province of Harar, 1942-43; Secretary, 1st Secretary, Imperial Ethiopian Consulate, Djibouti, French Somaliland; 1943-49; Journalist, Director of the Ethiopian Journal 'Aujourd'hui' for the Ministry of Information; Political Observer, Congo-Kinshasa, July to December, 1960; Ambassador Plenipotentiary & Representative Extraordinary to the Republic of Somalia, 1961-65; Ethiopian Consul General (with the rank of Ambassador) in the French Territory of Afars & Issas, 1966—. In his journalistc & diplomatic career has been sent on several special missions including the Ethiopian Economic Delegation to different parts of Italy, 1959. Honours: Grand Cross, Order of the Star of Ethiopia & several other foreign decorations. Address: Rue Clochette, B.P. 230, Djibouti, French Somaliland.

AHIDJO, (His Excellency) Ahmadou, President of the Cameroun Federal Republic & Head of Government, born Garoua, Cameroun, August 1924. Education: Diploma EPS, Yaounde, Cameroun. Appointments: Radio Operator, Head of Radio-Telegraphic Station, 1947; elected, First Assembly of the French Trust Territory of Eastern Cameroun, 1947; Councillor, Assembly of French Union, 1953; Secretary, ibid, 1954; President, Cameroun Assembly, 1957; Deputy Prime Minister, 1957-58; Prime Minister, 1958-60; President, Cameroun Republic, 1960-61; President, UAM, 1962; Founder, President, National Cameroun Union (UNC), 1966—; President & Head of Government (United East & West Camerouns), Cameroun Federal Republic, 1961—. Address: Yaounde, Cameroun.

AHIMIE, Humphrey Sunday Odekhoa, born 16th November 1930. Pathologist. Education: Government College, Ibadan, Nigeria, 1944-49; University College, Ibadan, 1949-53; King's College, Newcastle-upon-Tyne, U.K., 1954-58; MB.BS.(London); D.C.P.(London). Married, 3 children. Appointments: House Physician, Tynemouth Victoria Jubilee Infirmary, North Shields, U.K., 1959; Medical Officer, Federal Government, Nigeria, 1969; Specialist Pathologist i/c Blood Transfusion, Lagos State, Ministry of Health, 1966—. Address: Blood Transfusion Unit, Pathology Department, Lagos, Nigeria.

AHMAD, Naseem, born 10th January 1934. Lecturer in Economics. Education: M.A.(Economics), University of the Panjab, Lahore, India; Ph.D., ibid, Free University of Berlin, West Berlin, 1961. Personal Details: Married to Silvia Ahmad, Assistant Lecturer, Ghana Institute of Languages, Accra, Ghana. Appointments: Lecturer, Economics, University of Peshawar, West Pakistan, 1955-58; Research Economist, Ifo-Institute of Economic Research, Munich, 1961-63; Senior Lecturer, Economics, University of Ghana, Legon, 1963—; Acting Head of Department, ibid, 1970—. Memberships: Fellow & Council, Economic Society of Ghana, 1964; Editor, Economic Bulletin of Ghana,

1965-67. Publications: Sierra Leone—An Economic Survey, 1963; Development Banks & Corporations in Tropical Africa (with E. Becher), 1964; Deficit Financing, Inflation & Capital Formation—The Ghanaian Experience, 1960-65, 1970. Honours: A. Haque Gold Medal & Watson Silver Medal, Highest Economics M.A., University of the Panjab, 1954. Address: Department of Economics, University of Ghana, Legon, Ghana.

AHMED, Hussein Rajabali, born 14th March 1929, Barrister-at-Law; Advocate. Education: LL.B., University of London, U.K. Member, Supreme Council for Africa of the Aga Khan. Member, Lincoln's Inn Society, London, U.K. Address: P.O. Box 5275, Kampala, Uganda.

AHMED, Jamal M., born 17th April, 1917. Writer; Diplomat. Education: Gordon College, Sudan; University College of Southwest, Exeter, U.K., 1943-46; Balliol, Oxford. Married, 7 children Appointments: Sudan Ambassador to Arab Countries; ibid, Ethiopia; Sudan Permanent Delegate to United Nations; Sudan Ambassador to Court of St. James; Permanent Under Secretary, Ministry of Foreign Affairs, Sudan; Retired, 1970. Memberships: President, Debating Society, Gordon College, 1936; Secretary & President, Overseas Students, Exeter, 1943-46; Secretary, Sudan Cultural Centre, 1948-56; Editorial Board, Journal Modern African History. Publications: Translated into Arabic, Federalist Papers, 1959; ibid, Africa Rediscovered, 1963; Intellectual Origins of Egyptian Nationalism, 1961, 1968; Readings in African Affairs, 1969; Sali Fu Hamar, 1970. Honours: Decorated by the following: Late King Faisal of Iraq, 1956; King Hussein of Jordan, 1957; President Quatly of Syria, 1958; Emperor Hailé Selassié of Ethiopia, 1963; President Dion Hamani of Niger, 1967; President Mobutu of Congo, 1969. Address: P.O. Box 83, Khartoum, Sudan.

AHMED KHAWAJA, Tanwir, born 13th November, 1936. Physician. Education: F.Sc. (Pre-Medical); M.B., B.S., Punjab University, Lahore, West Pakistan. Currently practising medicine in Tabora, Tanzania. Memberships: Charter Member & third Vice-President, Lions Club, Tabora; Tanganyika Medical Association; Social Clubs, Tabora. Address: P.O. Box 132, Tabora, Tanzania.

AHN, Peter Martin, born 8th October, 1928. Soil Scientist. Education: Cambridge University, U.K., 1948-50. Appointments: Soil Survey Officer-Scientific Officer, Gold Coast-Ghana Soil & Land-Use Survey, 1954-62; Research Fellow, Faculty of Agriculture, University of Ghana, Legon, Accra, Ghana; Senior Lecturer, Soil Science, ibid, 1964—. Memberships: British Ghana & International Societies of Soil Science. Publications: Soils of the Lower Tano Basin, South-Western Ghana, 1960; West African Soils, 1970; numerous journal articles & papers. Address: Department of Crop Science, University of Ghana, Legon, Accra, Ghana.

AHONLONSOU, Andre, born Porto-Novo, Dahomey, 21st April 1920. Posts, Telephones & Telecommunication's Inspector. Married, 8 children. Appointments: Postmaster, Posts, Telephones & Communications, LABE, Guinea, 1949-57; Chief Accountant, Agence Comptable, Posts, Telephones & Telecommunications, Dakar, Senegal, 1958-59; Accounts Agent, Savings Bank, Ptale, Dahomey, 1961-62; Assistant Delegate, Porto-Novo Government, 1963-64; Inspector, Ptaux, Cotonou, Dahomey, 1965—. Honours: Commander of Merit of Benin. Address: Centre de Cheques Postaux, Cotonou, Dahomey.

AHOUDJI, Segandji Joseph, born 3rd February, 1924. Posts, Telephones & Telecommunication's Inspector. Education: Studied at the Overseas High School of Posts & Telecommunications, Toulouse, France. Appointments: Former expert, U.I.T., 1969-70; Technical Adviser, Telegraphic Development, Congo-Kinshasa; Instructor, Professional Teaching Centre, Posts, Telephones & Telecommunications of Conakry, Cotonou, Dahomey. Address: P.T.T. Cotonou, Dahomey.

AIDOO, Augustine Kofi, born 27th July, 1924. Bookseller; Business & Commercial Administrator. Education: Elementary, 1932-40; London Polytechnic School, U.K., 1959-61. Personal details: Related to present Asantehene; married, one child. Appointments: Chief Clerk, Assistant Manager, Egremont & Company, Bekwai, 1947-52; General Storekeeper, U.S.T., Kumasi, Ghana, 1952-59; Senior Storekeeper, Bookshop, University College Cape Coast, ibid, 1962-65; Administrative Assistant, ibid, 1966-67; Assistant Bookshop Manager, 1967—; Acting Bookshop Manager, 1967-69. Memberships: Committee Secretary, Anglican Church, Bekwai; Central & Local Executive, Sacred Order of Silent Brotherhood. Honours: Presented to Rotary International Party by the President of the Booksellers Association during a British Council Bursary, Leeds, U.K., 1966. Address: University College Cape Coast, Ghana.

AIMAKHU, Vincent Esonseriubo, born 23rd March 1935. Medical Practitioner. Education: St. Patrick's College, Asaba, Nigeria, 1950-54; University College, Ibadan, 1955-63; University College Hospital, Ibadan, 1964-67; University of Newcastle-upon-Tyne, U.K., 1967-68. Married. Appointments: Medical Registrar, University College Hospital, Ibadan, Nigeria, 1965-67; Medical Registrar, General Hospital, Newcastle, U.K., 1967-68; Senior Registrar, University College Hospital Ibadan, Nigeria, 1968-69; Consultant Obstetrician & Gynaecologist, ibid, 1969—; Lecturer in Obstetrics & Gynaecology, University of Ibadan, 1969—. Member, Royal College of Obstetricians & Gynaecologists. Author of scientific articles in medical journals. Honours: Commonwealth Scholar, 1967-68. Address: Department of Obstetrics & Gynaecology, University College Hospital, Ibadan, Nigeria.

AINA, Samuel Abiodun, born 1st January 1937. Librarian. Education: Elco Boys' High School, Mushin, 1951-54; 4 subjects, 'A' Level G.C.E. (Private Tutor); Postgraduate Diploma, Librarianship, University of Ibadan, Nigeria. Married, 2 sons, 1 daughter. Appointments: Accounts Supervisor, U.A.C., 1958-63; Senior

Library Assistant, Ahmadu Bello University, 1963-66; Assistant Librarian, ibid, 1966—. Memberships: Honorary Secretary/Treasurer, Northern States Division, Nigerian Library Association, 1969—. Address: c/o Kashim Ibrahim Library, Ahmadu Bello University, Zaria, Nigeria.

AINSWORTH, Frederic John, born 14th July 1913. Teacher. Education: Whitgift School, Croydon, U.K., 1924-32; B.A.(Hons.), University College, London, 1932-35; Dip. Ed., Kings College, London, 1937-38. Married. Appointments: Head, Teacher Training Department, Maseno School, Kenya, 1939-48; Principal, Chadwick College, Butere, 1949-56; Principal, St. Mark's College, Kigari, 1957-64; Administrative Secretary, C.M.S. Language School, 1965—. Memberships: Chairman, Kenya Mission, Church Missionary Society, 1963-67; Secretary, Luo Old Testament Translation Committee, 1945-56; Co-Chairman, Luyia Old Testament Translation Committee, 1951-70; Language Association of East Africa; Kenya Language Association. Publications: Khweche Okhusoma (First Luyia Reader); Tiko gi Rosa (First Luo Reader); Luo Basic Course; Kikuyu Basic Course. Honours: Rosa Marison Scholar, University College, London, 1932-35. Address: C.M.S. Language & Orientation School, P.O. Box 9849, Nairobi, Kenya.

AINSWORTH, Sybil Marjorie, born 21st May 1914. Teacher. Education: Board of Education Teacher's Diploma, London, U.K. Married to C. J. Ainsworth, Maseno, 1941. Appointments: Teacher, Maseno School, Nyanza, Kenya; ibid, Teacher Training, Chadwick College, Butere; ibid, St. Mark's College, Kijari, Emhr; Teacher, C.M.S. Language School, Nairobi. Memberships include: Church Missionary Society, 1941—. Address: C.M.S. Language & Orientation School, Nairobi, Kenya.

AIRY, Michael William Burnside, born 16th October 1930. Chartered Engineer. Education: Marlborough College; Stroud Technical College. Appointments: Technical Manager, Hydraulics, Gailey & Roberts, Ltd.; Resident Partner, Cook & Airy. Memberships: Institution of Mechanical Engineers, London, U.K.; Associate, East African Institution of Engineers. Address: P.O. Box 615, Nairobi, Kenya.

AISSI, Jose Raymond, born 20th September 1922. Police Commissioner. Education: C.E.P.E.; Diploma, Federal Police School, Dakar, Senegal; Diploma, National High School, St. Cyr-au-Mont-d'Or, France. Married, 8 children. Appointments: Head of the Public Security Service, Dahomey, 1962; Head of Studies & Regulations, 1963; in charge of Personnel Administration, Administrative Service, National Security, Dahomey, 1964-66; appointed Director, National Instruction Centre for Police & Personnel, 1966—. Honours: Commander of Merit, Benin. Address: Commissariat Central, Porto Novo, Dahomey.

AJAEGBU, Hyacinth Iheanyichuku, born 7th January 1937. University Lecturer. Education: B.A.(London), University of Ibadan, Nigeria; Ph.D., ibid. Married, 1 son, 1 daughter. Appointments: Lecturer, Geography, University of Ibadan, 1967—. Memberships: Treasurer, Nigerian Geographical Association, 1969-70; West African Science Association; Nigerian Economic Society; Association of Commonwealth Geographers. Author of journal articles on: Rural Development, Population & Migrations; Medical & Geographical Studies; Population & Rural Economic Development; & Regional Planning. Honours: University of Ibadan Postgraduate Scholar, 1964-67; Ford Foundation Travel Study Award, 1969; Commonwealth Academic Fellowship, 1970-71. Address: Department of Geography, University of Ibadan, Ibadan, Nigeria.

AJAYI, Ekundayo, born Shagamu, Nigeria, 1st March 1909. Civil Engineer & Land Surveyor. Education: Eko Boys' High School, Lagos, Nigeria, King's College, Lagos, Nigeria, Merchant Venturers Technical College; Bristol University, England. Appointments include: Teacher, Methodist Boys' High School, Lagos; Clerk, Nigerian Secretariat; Senor Building Inspector, Accra, Ghana; Deputy Town Engineer, Lagos City Council; Chief Engineer, Western Nigeria Development Corporation; Managing Director, E. Ajayi & Co., Land Surveyors & Estate Agents; Managing Director, The Nigerian Mapping Co. Ltd. Memberships include: Foundation Member, First Secretary, Child Care Society, Accra; Lagos Chamber of Commerce and represented Chamber on The Lagos Executive Development Board & Lagos City Council Caretaker Committee; Member, Lagos State Boxing Board of Control; Vice-President, Nigerian Institution of Surveyors. Address: 22 Moor Road, Yaba, Nigeria.

AJAYI, Jacob Festus Ade, born 26th May 1929. Historian. Education: St. Paul's School, Ikole, Ekiti, Nigeria, 1934-39; Christ's School, Ado-Ekiti, 1940; Igbobi College, Lagos, 1941-46; Higher College, Yaba, 1947; University College, Ibadan, 1948, 1949-51; B.A.(1st Class Hons.), Lond., University College, Leicester, U.K., 1952-55; Ph.D., University of London, 1955-58. Married, 5 children. Appointments: Lecturer in History, University of Ibadan, Nigeria, 1958-63; Professor, ibid, 1963—; Dean, Faculty of Arts, 1964-66; Assistant to the Vice-Chancellor, 1966-68; Head, History Department, 1966-69; Fellow, Centre for Advanced Study in the Behavioral Sciences, Stanford, Calif., U.S.A., 1970-71. Memberships: Vice-President, Historical Society of Nigeria; Chairman, Ibadan University Press; Councillor, West African Examinations Council; National Antiquities Commission; National Committee on Archives; Editorial Advisory Boards, Journal of the Historical Society of Nigeria, Ibadan, Journal of African History & Journal of Developing Areas; UNESCO National Commission. Publications: Milestones in Nigerian History, 1963; Yoruba Warfare in the Nineteenth Century (w. R. S. Smith), 1964; Christian Missions in Nigeria, 1841-91: the Making of a New Elite, 1965; A Thousand Years of West African History (ed.), 1965. Address: University of Ibadan, Ibadan, Nigeria.

AJAYI, John Olayiwola, born Fiditi, Oyo, Western Nigeria, 18th February 1940. Teacher.

Education: St. Patrick's Catholic School, Fiditi, 1947-54; L.A. Secondary Modern School, ibid, 1955-57; Blessed Murumba Teacher Training College, Ile-Ife, 1960-61; St. Leo's College, Abeokuta, 1964-65. Personal details: First son of James Ajayi Adegbite & Adunola Adegbite; married to the former Miss Folake Odegbaro (nurse), 1 son. Appointments include: School Teacher, 1958-59, 1962-63; Senior Prefect, St. Leo's College, Aleokala, 1965; Headmaster, St. Thomas's Catholic School, Ejigbo, 1966-67; ibid, St. Ferdinand's Catholic Secondary Modern School, Ogbomoso, 1968—. Memberships include: Fiditi Student's Union; St. Leo's College Dramatic Society. Publications: Contributes regularly to 'Ajowa', the annual Journal of the Fiditi Students' Union. Address: Catholic Mission, Fiditi, Ibadan, Western State, Nigeria.

A.KEINO, Moses Kiprono, born 25th September 1937. Economist. Education: Primary School, Ketaruet, 1946-51; Intermediate School, Kabianga, 1952-54; Secondary School, Kapenguria, 1955-56; Bible College, Kijabe, 1958-59; Karl Marx University, Leipzig, Germany, 1962-63; B.Sc., M.Sc., Karlshorst Hochschule für Ökonomie, Berlin, 1963-67. Married, 1 son, 1 daughter. Appointments: Teacher, 1957; Statistical Officer, East African Railways & Harbours, Kenya, 1960-62; ibid, Ministry of Economic Planning & Development, Nairobi, Kenya, 1967-69; Member of Parliament, 1969—. Memberships: President, Kenya Students Union, German Democratic Republic; Kenya African National Union; Commonwealth Parliamentary Association.

AKEREDOLU (Chief) Justus Dojuma, born Owo, Nigeria, 17th July 1915. Higher Technical Officer, Antiquities. Education: Professional Certificates, University of London; Museum & Archaeological Technology; Technical Drawing & Photography. Married, many children and grandchildren. Appointments include: Art Instructor, Govt. School, Owo, Nigeria, 1933-37; Art Instructor, Methodist High Schools, Lagos, Nigeria, 1940-44; Technical Instructor, Federal Ministry of Education, Museums, Lagos, Nigeria, 1954-57; Higher Technical Officer, Federal Department of Antiquities, Nigeria. Memberships include: Museums Association of Great Britain; Associate, International Council of Museums; International Institute for The Conservation of Museums Objects, London; Royal Photographic Society, London; Fellow, Royal Anthropological Institute, London. Publications: Art publicity exhibitions of art works in Europe and America. Honours, Prizes, etc.: Traditional Chieftaincy Award by His Highness, The Olowo of Owo, Nigeria, in recognition of humble contribution to Art Education in Nigeria, 1959. Address: Perseverance Lodge, 11 King's Terrace, P.O. Box 88, Owo, Nigeria.

AKINGBA, Joseph Bandele, born 7th June 1924. Obstetrician & Gynaecologist. Education: Government College, Ibadan, Nigeria, 1940-45; Higher College, Yaba, 1946-48; University College, Ibadan, 1951-52; King's College Hospital Medical School, London, U.K., 1952-55. Personal details: One of 24 surviving children; Christian upbringing; Married to a Christian nurse, 1 son, 2 daughters. Appointments: House Jobs, University College Hospital, Ibadan, 1956-59; ibid & Register, Kent & Canterbury Hospital & the Combined Boston Hospitals, Lincs., U.K., respectively, 1959-63; Senior Registrar, Lagos University Teaching Hospital, 1963; Lecturer, Obstetrics & Gynaecology, Lagos University College of Medicine, 1963-66; Senior Lecturer, ibid, 1966—. Memberships: British Medical Association; Nigeria Medical Association; Association of Surgeons of West Africa; Society of Obstetrics & Gynaecology of Nigeria; Scripture Union, Nigeria; Vice-President & currently, President, Gideons International Lagos Camp; Christian Laity of Nigeria. Publications include: Pattern of Haemoglobin Concentration in 1401 Indigenous Nigerian Gynaecological In-patients, 1968; Some Aspects of Menstruation in Nigerian Females, 1968; Procured Abortion—Counting the Cost, 1970. Address: College of Medicine, University of Lagos, P.M.S. 12003, Lagos, Nigeria.

AKINJOGBIN, Isaac Adeagbo, born 12th January 1930. University Professor. Education: Ijebu-Ode Grammar School, Nigeria, 1946-50; St. Cuthbert's Society, University of Durham, U.K., 1954-57; School of African & Oriental Studies, University of London, U.K., 1960-63. Married, 1 son, 3 daughters. Junior Research Fellow, 1957-60; Lecturer in History, University of Ife, Nigeria, 1963-68; Director, Institute of African Studies, University of Ife, 1965-68; Professor, Head of Department, ibid, 1968—. Memberships: Secretary, Historical Society of Nigeria; Executive Mbr., Yoruba Language Studies Association. Publications: Dahomey & its Neighbours 1708-1818, 1967; Ewi Iwogyi, 1969; A Short History of Ede (translations), 1961; also various articles in his field. Honours: Commonwealth Scholar, 1960-63. Address: University of Ife, Ile-Ife, Nigeria.

AKINKUGBE, Ajibayo, born 3rd February 1929. Doctor of Medicine. Education: Ondo Boys' High School, 1936-47; Portsmouth Municipal College, U.K., 1950-51; Aberdeen University, 1950-57. Married. Appointments: Medical Officer, Western Nigeria, 1958-62; Registrar, Aberdeen Maternity Hospital, U.K., 1962-64; Specialist, Senior Specialist, Obstetrics & Gynaecology, 1966—; Senior Principal Medical Officer, Ife-Ilesha Zone, 1969—. Memberships: Royal College of Obstetricians & Gynaecologists; Nigerian Medical Association; Fellow, Association of West African Surgeons; Society of Obstetricians & Gynaecologists of Nigeria. Author of various articles in medical journals. Address: State Hospital, Ile-Ife, Nigeria.

AKINKUGBE, Oladipo Olujimi, born Ondo, Nigeria, 17th July 1933. Physician. Education: Government College, Ibadan, 1946-50; University of Ibadan, Nigeria, 1951-55; University of London, U.K., 1955-58; University of Liverpool, 1959; University of Oxford, 1962-64. Personal details: son of Chief & Mrs. D. A. Akinkugbe; married to Dr. F. M. Dina, eldest daughter of Chief & Mrs. I. O. Dina of Ibadan; 2 sons. Appointments include: House Physician, King's College Hospital, London, U.K., 1958; House Surgeon, The London Hospital, 1959; Clinical Assistant, Medical Unit, ibid, 1959-60; Medical

Officer (Special Grade), Ministry of Health, Western Nigeria, 1961-62; Commonwealth Physician Research Fellow, Balliol College, Oxford & Regius Professor of Medicine, 1962-64; Consultant Physician, University College Hospital, Ibadan; Lecturer, Medicine, University of Ibadan, 1964; Senior Lecturer, ibid, 1967; Professor, 1968—; Dean of Faculty of Medicine, 1970. Memberships include: Secretary, Association of Physicians of Nigeria, 1966—; International Society of Nephrology; Medical Research Society of Gt. Britain; University College Hospital Medical Society; Nigeria Medical Council; Nigeria Council for Medical Research; Rotary International. Publications: papers on Hypertension & Renal Diseases. Honours: M.B., B.S.(Lond.); L.R.C.P.(Lond.); M.R.C.S.(Eng.), 1958; D.T.M. & H.(Liverpool), 1960; M.R.C.P.(Ed.), 1961; D.Phil.(Oxon), 1965; F.R.C.P.(Ed.), 1968; M.D.(Lond.), 1969. Address: Dean, Faculty of Medicine, University of Ibadan, Nigeria.

AKINKURO, Michael Adenugba, born Irele, Ondo, Nigeria, 7th November 1936. Teacher. Education: Methodist School, Irele, Ondo Province, Nigeria, 1942-49; Grade III, Ifaki T.T. College, 1952-53; Grade II, Wesley College, Ibadan, Nigeria, 1959-60. Married, 2 sons, 1 daughter. Appointments include: Headmaster, Methodist Secondary Modern School, Idanre, Ondo Province, 1965. Memberships include: fully accredited Local Preacher in Methodist Church; Class Leader & Member of Choir of Methodist Church, Ondo, Nigeria. Address: P.M.B. 3, Idanre, via Akure, Nigeria.

AKINLA, Oladele, born 28th April 1926. Obstetrician & Gynaecologist. Education: Government College, Ibadan, Nigeria; University College, Ibadan; St. Bartholomew's Hospital Medical College, University of London, U.K. Married to the former Miss Oluyemi Adedeji, 4 children. Appointments: House Officer, University College Hospital, Ibadan; Senior House Officer, Leeds Maternity & Women's Hospital: Obstetric Registrar, Hackney Hospital, London, U.K.; Senior Lecturer, Obstetrics & Gynaecology, University of Lagos, & Consultant, ibid, Lagos University Teaching Hospital. Memberships: British Medical Association; Past Chairman, Family Planning Council of Nigeria; Fellow, Royal Society of Medicine; Island Club, Lagos. Publications: Experience with the Plastic Intra-Uterine Device in Lagos, 1968; Social Obstetrics in Africa, 1969; Abdominal Emergencies in Obstetric Practice, 1969; Abortion—A Medico-social Problem, 1969. Address: Coll. of Medicine, University of Lagos, P.M.B. 12003, Lagos, Nigeria.

AKINOSI, Joel Oyekunle, born 3rd July 1934. Oral Surgeon. Education: Abeokuta Grammar School, 1947-52; Norwich City College, U.K., 1956-57; B.D.S., University of London, 1957-61. Married, 2 sons, 2 daughters. Appointments: Resident Dental Surgeon, The London Hospital, 1962; Senior Resident, West Middlesex Hospital, 1963-64; Clinical Assistant, Institute of Dental Surgery, London, 1964-65; Lecturer & Consultant Oral Surgeon, University of Ibadan, Nigeria, 1966-69; Senior Lecturer & Consultant Surgeon, University of Lagos, Nigeria, 1969—. Memberships: Fellow, Association of Surgeons of West Africa; Nigeria Medical Association; Associate, British Association of Oral Surgeons; L.D.S.R.C.S.(Eng.), 1962; F.D.S.R.C.S.(Eng.), 1965; ibid (Ed.), 1965; F.M.C.D.S.(Nig.), 1970. Publications: Adamantinoma in Ibadan, Nigeria; Craniofacial Fibrons Dysplasia in Nigerian Africans: High Velocity Missile Injuries of the Jaws; African Histoplasmosis Presenting as a Dental Problem. Address: Department of Dental Surgery, Lagos University Teaching Hospital, P.M.B. 12003, Lagos, Nigeria.

AKINSANYA, Marian Olaniwun, born 8th March 1913. Nurse; Midwife. Education: Sagamu Girls' School; S.R.N.; S.C.M.; Hospital Administration Certificate. Personal details: member Royal Family of Erikikunsa Ewusi; married, 4 children. Appointments: Midwife, Nigeria; Represented PATNON, Australia, at I.C.N., 1961; ibid, Germany, 1966; Nursing Sister-Matron-Senior, Lagos Island Maternity Hospital. Memberships: Life Member, Nigerian Red Cross; National Council of Women Societies; International Council of Women Society; Foundation Member, PATNON; church organizations. Address: 39 Oyekan Road, Suru Lere, Lagos, Nigeria.

AKINYEMI, Gabriel Ojo, born Ibadan, Nigeria, 20th July 1913. Civil Engineer. Education: Primary, St. Paul's School, Gbongon, 1924-26; St. Peter's School, Aremo, Ibadan, 1927-29; Government College, Ibadan, 1930-32; Yaba Higher College, 1934-37; A.M.I.C.E., City & Guilds Engineering College, London, U.K., 1945-48. Married, 8 children. Appointments include: School Prefect, 1932-33, 1936-37; Captain, School Tug-of-War Team, 1933; Leader of School Agricultural Group, 1933; District Engineer for Roads, Buildings & Works, 1938-45; Executive Engineer, ibid, 1950-58; Senior, ibid, 1958-60; Chief Civil Engineer, 1960-67; Administrative Officer, Staff Grade, 1967—; Permanent Secretary, 1967-68; Chairman, Western Nigeria Housing Corporation, 1968—. Memberships: Fellow, British Institution of Civil Engineers; West African Joint Group of Engineers; Nigerian Society of Engineers; Council of Christian Laity. Honours: School Book Prize for Good Conduct, 1928; School Book Prize for Proficiency, 1933; Member of the Federal Republic of Nigeria, 1965. Address: c/o W.N. Housing Corporation, P.M. Bag 5214, Ibadan, Nigeria.

AKINYEMI, Philip Adebisi, born Ikire, Western Nigeria, 12th February 1925. Teacher. Education: Nigerian Teachers' Higher Elementary Certificate, 1949; B.Sc.(Econ., Lond.), London School of Economics, U.K., 1959. Married, 6 children. Appointments include: Principal, Egbado Training College, Ilaro, 1962-64; Headmaster, George Burton Memorial College, Ilesha, 1965; Headmaster, Okeho-Iganna Grammar School, Iseyin, 1966—. Memberships include: Scoutmaster, Boy Scouts of Nigeria, 1948-52; District Commissioner, 1960—. Publications include: An Economic Analysis of Government Scholarships to Mecca, 1965; The New Forty-Hour Working Week, 1965. Honours include: Certificate of Honour,

Boy Scouts Association of Nigeria, 1968. Address: Private Mail Bag, Iseyin, Nigeria.

AKLILU LEMMA, born Jigjiga, Harar, Ethiopia, 18th September 1932. Professor of Parasitology; University Dean. Education: Ras Makonnen Elementary School, Harar, Ethiopia, 1942-50; General Wingate School, Addis Ababa, 1950-55; Certificate in Biology, University College of Addis Ababa, 1959; North Western University, Chicago, Illinois, U.S.A., 1958-59; B.Sc.(Zoology), University of Wisconsin, Madison, Wisconsin, 1960; D.Sc., Johns Hopkins University, School of Hygiene & Public Health, Baltimore, Maryland, 1964. Appointments include: Research Assistant, Marine Biological Laboratory, Woodshole, Massachusetts, U.S.A., 1961; Teaching Assistant, Johns Hopkins University, Baltimore, 1962-63; Assistant Professor of Parasitology, Hailé Selassié I University, Addis Ababa, Ethiopia, 1964-65; Assistant Dean & Professor, ibid, 1965-66; Dean, Faculty of Science, Director, Institute of Pathobiology, Associate Professor of Biology, ibid, 1966-70; Vice-Chairman, Chief Organizer, National Committee for National Scientific & Technical Research Council of Ethiopia; Visiting Scientist, Stanford Research Institute, Menlo Park, California, U.S.A., 1970—. Memberships include: Council for the International Cell Research Organization, Paris, 1969—; American Society of Parasitologists; Scientific Council for Africa; Ethiopian National Education Committee; Ethiopian Medical Association. Recipient of Fellowships including: Johns Hopkins University Training, 1960-64; W.H.O. Research to the United Arab Republic & Sudan, U.S. Naval Medical Research Unit No. 3, 1962; ibid, Travelling Fellowship, 1965; International Atomic Energy Agency Travelling Fellowship, 1969; Imperial Ethiopian Government Scholarship. Author of numerous works in his field; also of various papers delivered at International Congresses & Conferences. Honours: Recipient of Hailé Selassié I Gold Medal for Scientific Research in Ethiopia. Address: Life Sciences Division, Stanford Research Institute, Menlo Park, California 94025, U.S.A.

AKOI AHIZI, Paul, born 30th June 1941. Government Official; Technical Counsellor. Education: LL.D., Polit. Sci., Diploma, Higher Studies of Public Law. Married, 2 children. Appointments: Inspector of Work & Social Affairs; Technical Counsellor, Cabinet of the Ministry of Work & Social Affairs, Abidjan, Ivory Coast. Address: B.P. 1714, Abidjan, Ivory Coast.

AKOL, George James Obed Cayes, born 28th April 1935. Electrical Engineer. Education: Ngora Primary School & Secondary School, 1952; Nabumali High School, 1955; Makere University College, Uganda, 1959; Brighton College of Technology, 1965. Personal details: second son of Ejulierei & Nebu Ikopit of Kumi, Teso. Married, 1 son. Appointments: Assistant Engineer (electrical), Kampala City Council, Uganda, 1965-68; Senior Assistant Engineer, ibid, 1968—. Address: P.O. Box 417, Kampala, Uganda.

AKOLO, Fred Andayi, born Lukohe Village, Kakamega District, Kenya, 28th December 1945. Engineer. Education: Kwwisero Primary School, 1953-60; Kakamega Secondary School, 1961-64; Kenyatta College, 1965-67; studying Engineering Diploma, Kenya Polytechnic, Nairobi, 1968—. Appointments: President, Kenyatta College Students' Council, 1966-67; with Ministry of Works, Kenya, 1968—; Interpreter, Court of Appeal for East Africa, 1969; Chairman, Kenyatta College Old Students' Association, 1969-70. Memberships: Chairman, Kenyatta College Mathematics Club, 1965-66; Vice-Chairman, Kenyatta College Current Affairs Club, 1966; Adviser, Kenyatta College Senior Debating Society, 1967; International Order of Good Templars Popular Debating Society, Nairobi, 1968. Honours: Prize for Debating, Kakamega Secondary School, 1964. Address: P.O. Box 2267, Nairobi, Kenya.

AKOLO, Jimo Bola, born 21st September 1935. Lecturer; Artist. Education: Diploma in Fine Arts, Zaria, Nigeria; M.Sc., Education, Indiana, U.S.A. Appointments: Freelance Artist, 1961-63; Education Officer, 1963-64; Lecturer/ Artist, 1966—. Memberships: Society of Nigerian Artists; The Nigerian Audio-Visual Association; Nigerian Arts Council. Exhibitions: Solo Show, Lagos, 1962; ibid, Ibadan, 1964; Commonwealth Institute, London, U.K., 1964; Joint Exhibition, London, 1965; ibid, U.S.A., 1965; London, 1968; Moscow, U.S.S.R., 1968; Warsaw, Poland, 1965; Lagos, Nigeria, 1970. Honours: Mention of Honour, Sao Paulo Biennale, 1961; Nigerian Cultural Award, 1962. Address: Institute of Education, A.B.U., Zaria, Nigeria.

AKOTO, Vao Francois, born Sakassou, Abidjan, Ivory Coast, 1913. Secretary-General of the P.D.C.I. Personal details: Son of Kouassi Akoto & Anougbre N'Guessan; married, 21 children. Appointments: Monitor & Catechizer, 1933-34; Secretary, Head Office of Baoules; Member, African Agricultural Syndicate; Secretary-General, P.D.C.I., 1946—; Counsellor-General, 1960—; Member, Directorial Committee, P.D.C.I. Honours: Chevalier de l'Etoile Noire du Benin; Officier de l'Ordre National de la Côte d'Ivoire. Address: B.P. 2, Sakassou, Abidjan, Ivory Coast.

AKPOMUDJERE, Emmanuel, born Eku, Nigeria 22nd May 1938. Legal Practitioner. Education: Baptist Primary School, Eku, Nigeria, 1946-53; West African School Certificate, Government College, Ughelli, 1954-59; Ahmadu Bello University, Zaria, 1964-65; LL.B., University of Ife, 1967; B.L., Nigerian Law School, 1968. Personal details: descended from a family of Chiefs at Eku, Chief Emagono, Chief Erhijakpon & Chief Akpomudjere. Married, 2 children. Appointments: Editor-in-Chief, Quarterly Journal of Yaba Baptist Church, Yaba; Secretary, Eku Progress Union, Lagos Branch, 1963-70. Memberships: Nigerian Bar Association, Lagos Branch; Secretary, Midwest Fellowship in Christ, 1968-70. Address: c/o Mr. M. A. Emagono, Ideal Public Relations Ltd., 14/16 Abibu Oki Street, Lagos, Nigeria.

AKPOTOWHO (Chief) Isaiah Ojugba, born Obiaruku, Nigeria, 6th June 1924. Merchant. Education: passed Std. 6 Examination,

Government School, Sapele, and obtained the First School Leaving Certificate, 1944. Personal details: eldest son of late Chief John Onyelinisue Akpotowho of Obiaruku, Aboh Division, Mid-Western Nigeria; married, 12 children. Appointments include: Storekeeper & Clerk-in-charge, John Holt & Co., Ltd., Sapele, Obiaruku, 1945-59; Manager, First Baptist School, Obiaruku, 1957-64; Councillor, Ukwuani District Council, Amai, 1959-65; Member, Scholarship Board, Aboh Division, 1960-62; Moderator, Abbi Baptist Association of Nigerian Baptist Convention, 1965-67; Member, Education Board, N.B.C. Schools, Mid-West Nigeria, 1966-68; Member, Advisory Board, Baptist Hospital, Eku, 1967-70; Managing Proprietor, Sportslight Bar & Hotel, Obiaruku; Agent, Unity Life & Fire Insurance Co. Ltd., Nigeria, 1967—; Agent, Mercury Assurance Co. Ltd., for Motor Vehicles, Nigeria, 1968—. Memberships: Financial Secretary, Ethiope River Social Club, Obiaruku, Nigeria. Honours include: Chieftaincy Title, Onotu of Umuedede Obiaruku, Aboh Division, Nigeria, 1962. Address: Akpotowho's Villa, P.O. Box 4, Obiaruku, Mid-Western Nigeria.

AKWAWUAH, Kwadwo Asafo, born Kumasi, Ashanti, Ghana, 1st August 1929. Business Executive. Education: Certificate in Management Studies, Leicester College of Technology, U.K., 1957; Diploma in Management Studies, British Institute of Management, London, 1960; Fellowship Diploma, Institute of Commerce, London, 1961; M.B.A., University of Chicago, U.S.A., 1965. Married, 4 children. Appointments: Managing Director, A. Akowuah & Co. Ltd., 1961-62; Chairman, Board of AGA Investments Ltd.; Managing Director, Amalcos Ltd., 1968-69; Chairman of the Board, Managing Director, Tropical Imports & Exports Ltd.; Managing Consultant, Task Force-Food Distribution, Ministry of Agriculture, 1970. Memberships: Kumasi City Council, 1968-69; Ashanti Regional Planning Committee; Chairman, ibid, Trade & Industry Sub-Committee, 1968—; Kumasi City Statutory Planning Committee, 1968-69. Publications: Prelude to Ghana's Industrialization; Introduction to Familiar Economy (to be published). Honours: Ford Foundation Scholar, University of Chicago, U.S.A., 1962-65. Address: P.O. Box 1566, Kumasi, Ghana.

AKWEI, Richard Mabuo, born 22nd September 1897. Headmaster. Education: Government School; Accra Training College for Teachers, Ghana, 1910-15. Married, 3 children. Appointments include: Founder & Headmaster, Ghana National School, Accra. Memberships: Chairman & Founder, Gold Coast Football Association, now GAFA; Chairman, Gold Coast Boxing Board of Control; Lawn Tennis Champion & International Player; Foundation Member & Past Chairman, Ghana Red Cross Society; Past Chief Scout Commissioner of Ghana. Honours, Prizes, etc.: Coronation Medal, 1953; Silver Wolf, 1960; Grand Medal of Ghana for public services, 1968. Address: Ghana National School, P.O. Box 246, Accra, Ghana.

AKYEAMPONG, Daniel Afedzi, born 24th November 1938. Theoretical Physicist. Education: Senya Beraku Local Council School, 1943-53; Mfantispim School, 1954-59; B.Sc.(Hons.), Mathematics, University of Ghana, 1963; Ph.D., Imperial College of Science & Technology, University of London, U.K., 1966. Married. Appointments: Lecturer, Mathematics, University of Ghana, Legon, 1966—. Member, American Physical Society. Publications: Articles on theoretical high energy physics & elementary particle physics in Physical Review, Journal of Mathematical Physics, Nuovo Cimento, Nuclear Physics, etc. Honours: Associate, International Centre for Theoretical Physics, Trieste, Italy, 1966; Fellow, Ghana Academy of Arts & Sciences, 1969. Address: Department of Mathematics, University of Ghana, P.O. Box 62, Legon, Ghana.

ALDRIDGE, Clive Bruce, born 19th August 1936. Valuation Surveyor. Education: public school, U.K.; Upper Latymer College, West London. Personal details: Interested in youth training, former instructor for Duke of Edinburgh Award in judo, canoeing, hiking & pioneering. Currently, Government Valuer. Associate, Institute of Chartered Surveyors. Address: Box 2795, Dar es Salaam, Tanzania.

ALDRIDGE, Hugh Edward John, born India, 5th March 1942. Lecturer in Physics. Education: Wellesley Scholar, Wellington College, U.K., 1956-60; B.A., Worcester College, Oxford, 1961-64; Diploma of Education, Makerere University College, Uganda, 1964-65. Personal details: son of Lt.-Col. G. E. Aldridge, O.B.E., & grandson of Edward Aldrdige, medical missionary in China; married to the former Jacqueline Anne Hetherington, 1969. Appointments: Teacher, Physics & Mathematics, Kololo Senior Secondary School, Kampala, 1965-67; Lecturer, Physics, National Teachers' College, 1967—. Memberships: M.C.C.; First Hon. Sec., Uganda Schools Cricket Association, 1968-70; Fixtures Secretary, Uganda Cricket Association, 1968; Honorary Secretary, Uganda Kobs, 1968-70; Cricket Captain, Kampala Sports Club, 1969; Founder & Captain, Teamakers Cricket Club, 1964-70; ibid, Uganda Gypsies Cricket Club, 1966-70. Publications: Editor, The Young Uganda Cricketer, 1968; Assistant Editor, Uganda Science Teachers' Journal, 1969-70. Address: c/o National Westminster Bank Ltd., 2 Eastcheap, London, E.C.3, U.K.

ALELE, Christian Oritsetimeyin, born Warri, Nigeria, 31st October 1929. Physician. Education: Government College, Ibadan, 1943-48; University College, Ibadan, 1948-52; Welsh National School of Medicine, Cardiff, South Wales, U.K., 1952-55. Personal details: Second son of Mr. & Mrs. Alele; married the former Mavis Fay Anderson, 1 son & 1 daughter. Appointments: Consultant Physician, Lagos University Teaching Hospital, 1963-66; Senior Lecturer, Medicine, University of Lagos Medical School, 1965-66; Physician, Ministry of Health, Jamaica, 1966-71; Director-Designate, Division of Nuclear Medicine, University Hospital, Mona 7, Jamaica. Member, Constant Spring Golf Club, Kingston, Jamaica. Publications: Amoebiasis in Lagos, West African Medical Journal, 1966; Studies in Hypertension (co-author), ibid, 1960. Address: c/o Ministry of Health, Kingston, Jamaica.

ALETOR, Gabriel Akhuemokhan, born 24th December, 1936. Medical Practitioner. Education: Government School, Irma, Midwest Nigeria, 1944-51; Government College, Benin City, 1952-56; King's College, Lagos, 1959; M.B., B.S., (Lond.), University College, Ibadan, 1959-61; University College Hospital, Ibadan, 1961-64. Married, 1 son. Appointments: Medical Officer of Health, Benin City, 1966; Medical Officer, 1966-69; Senior Medical Officer, Auchi, 1969-70; Major, Nigerian Army, C.O., Base Hospital, Auchi, 1969-70. Memberships: Provincial Scout Commissioner; Scout Master; Cub Scoutmaster; Leader of Nigerian Scouts to 2 world jamborees, Marathon, Greece, 1963 & Idaho, U.S.A., 1967. Publications: A Handbook for House Surgeons in Obstetrics & Gynaecology, etc. Honours: Academic Awards in Science in Secondary School; Prize & Hons. in Public Health, Final M,B., B.S. (Lond.); Chieftaincy title of Chief Oruwako of Akoko-Edo, Midwest State, given him by the Chiefs & Obas for useful services rendered, 1970. Address: Department of Obstetrics & Gynaecology, University College Hospital, Ibadan, Nigeria.

ALEXANDER, Reginald Stanley, born 14th November 1914. Chartered Accountant; Director of Companies; Tour Operator. Education: Nairobi School, Kenya, 1920-23; Nakuru School, ibid, 1923-30; Prince of Wales School, 1931. Personal Details: Son of Douglas Alexander, deceased, 1930, & Gertrude Alexander; married Maree Pollok, 1941. Appointments: Founder, Senior Partner, Alexander, MacLennan, Trundell & Co., Chartered Accountants, Nairobi, 1946-62; Founder & Chairman, Kenya Oil Co., 1959—; Founder & Managing Director, Bruce Travel & Funga Safari Ltd. Memberships: Councillor & Alderman, Nairobi City Council, 1948-56; Mayor, ibid, 1954-55; Kenya Parliament, 1956-69. Address: c/o Bruce Travel & Funga Safari Ltd., Kenya.

ALHASSAN, Idirisu, born 19th September, 1941. Teacher; Principal. Education: Junior Primary School, Mokwa, Nigeria, 1949-52; Senior Primary School, Bida, 1953-55; Secondary School, 1956-61; Post-Secondary, Kano, 1962-64; History, English & Arabic, University, Kano & Zaria, 1964-68; B.A. (Hons.), History. Personal Details: Grandfather was a Mallam; Father is Imam of Kpaki. Appointments: Graduate in Training & Archivist of Department under Professor H. F. C. Smith; School Teacher; currently Principal, Secondary School, Sokoto. Memberships: Muslim Student Society of Nigeria; Historical Society of Nigeria. Address: c/o Ministry of Education, North-Western State, Sokoto, Nigeria.

ALI (Alhadji) Ali, born 12th October 1911. Deputy Mayor. Commercial & Economic Education. Married, three wives, 20 children. Appointments: Economic & Social Adviser; Deputy Mayor, Yaoundé Town, Cameroun. Address: B.P. 366, Yaoundé, Cameroun.

ALIO (El Hadj) Aboubakar Yenikoye, born 26th September 1920. Civil Servant; Deputy Prefect. Education: Diploma, Ecole Primaire Supérieure. Appointments: Secretary to the Tribunal, 1940-57; Member of the Niger Territorial Assembly, 1952-57; President, Niamey Civil Tribunal, Niger, 1957-59; Assistant to the Commander, Commander, Tillabery Circuit, 1959-62; Commander, Madaoua Circuit, 1962-64; Head of Personnel, Ministry of T.P., 1964-65; Director, Collectivités Territoriales, 1965-66; Deputy Prefect, Tahoua, 1966-68; ibid, Dogondoutchi, 1968—. Honours: Knight, Black Star of Benin; Knight, Nichan El-Annouar; Officer, National Order of Niger. Address: Sous Prefet Dogondoutchi, Republic of Niger.

ALIYU, Yahya Dogara, born 30th November 1938. Secretary, Institute of Education. Education: Primary School, Zangon Katab, 1946-50; Middle School, Zaria, 1951; Government College, 1952-57; Nigerian College of Arts, Science & Technology, Zaria, 1958-60; B.A. (Hons.), University of Ibadan, 1960-63; Diploma, Moray House College of Education, Edinburgh, U.K., 1965-66. Married, 2 children. Appointments: Education Officer, Advanced Teachers College, Zaria, 1963-66; Senior Education Officer & Head of the Department of English, ibid, 1966-68; Vice-Principal & Head, Department of English. 1968-69; Lecturer, English Language, Ahmadu Bello University, Institute of Education, Zaria, 1969; Secretary, ibid, 1970—. Memberships: President, Rotary Club of Zaria; Executive Member, Zaria, Province Education Development Fund. Publications: Modern Hansa Reader (w. A. H. M. Kirk-Greene); Introduction to Hansa Poetry (w. D. Scharfe). Address: Institute of Education, Ahmadu Bello University, Zaria, Nigeria.

ALKALI, Hamidu Hama-Gabdo, born Yola, Northern Nigeria, 25th October 1927. Teacher & Administrator. Education: Yola Primary School, 1936-39; Yola Middle School, 1939-44; N.P. Law School, Kano, 1944-48; School for Arabic Studies, Kano, 1949-50; Dip. O.A.S., School of Oriental & African Studies, University of London, England, 1954-55; B.A., ibid, 1959-62; M.A.(Lond.), 1969. Married, 8 children. Appointments include: Secretary to Legal Adviser, Adamawa N.A., 1953-55; Master, Grade II, Ministry of Education, North, 1956-57; Assistant Education Officer, North Regional Government, 1957-59; Education Officer, ibid, 1959-63; Inspector of Education, & Principal, Teachers College, ibid, 1963-66; Deputy Chief Education Officer (Teacher Training), 1966-69; Provost of Abdullahi Bayero College, Amadu Bello University, 1966-69; Dean of Faculty of Arts & Islamic Studies, Amadu Bello University, 1966-69. Director, Institute of Education, ibid, 1970—; Visiting Professor, African Languages & Literature, University of Wisconsin, Madison, U.S.A., 1969. Memberships include: Historical Society of Nigeria; Secretary, Muslim Students' Union of Great Britain & N. Ireland, 1961; United Nations Association Britain; East & West Friendship Council, Britain; Nigerian National Educational Research Council; Joint Consultative Committee on Education; Association for Teacher Education in Africa; West African Council for Teacher Education. Contributor to journals of Kano studies. Address: Institute of Education, Ahmadu Bello University, Zaria, Nigeria.

ALLANGBA, Koffi, born 19th January 1925. Professor of Surgery. Education: Diploma, William Ponty School, 1945; ibid, School of Medicine, Dakar; Aggregate in Surgery, 1970. Married, 1 child. Appointments: Director of Medicine, 1949; Assistant Surgeon, Abidjan, Ivory Coast, 1964. Secretary General, Medical Society of the Ivory Coast; ibid, Medical Review, ibid; President, International Association for Medical Research & Cultural Exchange, Ivory Coast; French Association of Surgeons; Medical Correspondent of Black Africa. Author of articles in his field. Honours: Officer, Public Health Decoration; ibid, National Order of Ivory Coast; Knight, Academic Palms of France. Address: B.P. 20, 950 Abidjan, Ivory Coast.

ALLEN, Charles Dudley, born Dublin, Ireland, 26th October 1918. Government Chemist. Education: B.A.(Hons.), Experimental Science, Dublin University, Ireland, 1940. Appointments include: Senior Physics Master, Campbell College, Northern Ireland, 1940-41; Plant Superintendent, I.C.I. Explosives, 1941-45; Major, R.I.A.S.C. Directorate of Food Inspection, India, 1945-46; Sales, May & Baker, India, 1947-48; Lecturer, Chemistry, Scottish Church College, Calcutta, 1948-58; Lecturer, Science Subjects, Kampala Technical Institute, Uganda, 1958-60; Government Chemist, Ministry of Internal Affairs, Uganda Government, 1960–. Memberships include: Associate, The Royal Institute of Chemistry; Society of Chemical Industry. Address: Analytical Laboratory, P.O. Box 2174, Kampala, Uganda.

ALLEN, Hubert John Brooke, born Tanga, Tanganyika, 26th December 1931. University Lecturer in Local Government Studies. Education: Schools in Kenya & England, U.K.; B.A., St. John's College, Oxford, 1954; M.A., ibid, 1958; Dip. Educ., U.C. North 1966; M.Soc.Sci., Birmingham University, 1970; Bar Exams (Pt. I). Personal details: Son of J. W. T. Allen, Swahili scholar; Married to Phoebe Catherine Vesey (nee Stoney); 2 sons, 1 daughter. Appointments: w. H.M. Overseas Civil Service (Uganda Protectorate Administration), 1955-62; Oversea Service College, Farnham Castle, Surrey, U.K., 1962-65; Institute of Local Government Studies, Birmingham University, 1966–; currently on secondment to Ahmadu Bello University, Zaria, Nigeria, 1967-70. Memberships: Associate, Centre for West African Studies; Royal Commonwealth Society; African Studies Association of the U.K.; The Uganda Society; Past Secretary, The Uganda Club; Institute of Public Administration, Dublin; Churchwarden, St. Andrew's Church, Zaria. Publications: Editor/Compiler, 'Work Overseas': a Guide to Opportunities in Developing Countries, 1963-65; Contributor of articles for e.g. Quarterly Journal of Administration, 'Frontier', etc. Address: c/o Institute of Local Government Studies, P.O. Box 363, Birmingham, U.K.

ALLEN, John Willoughby Tarleton, born 14th November 1904. Swahili Scholar. Education: Westminster School; B.A., St. John's College, Oxford, 1926; M.A., ibid, 1931. Personal details: Married Winifred Emma (nee Brooke), 1929; 1 son & 2 daughters. Appointments: w. Tanganyika Territory Education & Administrative Services, 1929-58; Aden Protectorate, 1947-58; University Hall, Makerere University College, 1958-64; Rockefeller Swahili Research Fellow, 1965–; Director, Institute of Swahili Research, Dar es Salaam University College, 1966-69. Founder Member, Tanganyika Society. Publications: Founder Editor, Tanganyika Notes & Records; Author of Arabic Script for Students of Swahili; numerous translations & critical commentaries on Swahili 'tenzi' & other poetry; articles in T.N.R., Swahili, etc. Address: Halford, Boults Lane, Old Marston, Oxford, U.K.

ALLERTON, John, born 13th April 1917. Chief Engineer. Education: Normanton Grammar School, U.K.; Royal Naval Signal School. Married. Appointments: Wireless Section, R.N., 1939-47; South African Broadcasting Corporation, 1947-53; Central African Broadcasting Services, Northern Rhodesia, 1954, through successor organizations to Senior Maintainance Superintendent & Chief Engineer, Zambia Broadcasting Services. Member, Institute of Electrical & Electronics Engineers, U.S.A. Address: P.O. Box R.W.15, Ridgeway, Lusaka, Zambia.

ALLI, Ambrose Folorunso, born 22nd September 1929. Medical Pathologist. Education: S.P.C., Asaba, Nigeria, 1944-48; University of Ibadan, 1953-60; Post Graduate, London Hospital Medical College, U.K.; Post Graduate Medicine, Hammersmith; M.B.B.S. (London), D.C.P., D.Path., 1962-66. Married, 2 sons. Appointments: Assistant in Forensic Medicine to Professor F. E Camps, London Hospital Medical College, 1962-63; Registrar, Pathology, Herts. & Essex General Hóspital, Bishops Stortford, Herts, 1963-65; Lecturer, Consultant, Pathology, University of Ibadan, Nigeria, 1966-68; Senior Lecturer, Pathology, Abu, Zaria, 1969–. Memberships: Forensic Science Society; Academy of Forensic Science; Nigerian Medical Association; British Medical Association; Pathological Society of Great Britain. Publications: Pulmonary Emphysema in Ibadan; Joint Author of following: Rhabdomyosarcoma of Upper Respiratory Tract in Ibadan; Liver in Sickle Cell Disease; Goiter in Western Nigeria; Superficial Cancer in Ibadan; Anergilloma in Nose in Ibadan, etc. Address: Department of Pathology, Abu Hospital, Zaria, Nigeria.

ALLOTEY, Francis Kofi Ampenyin, born 9th August 1932. Mathematical Physicist. Education: University Tutorial College, London, U.K.; Borough Polytechnic, London; Imperial College, London University; M.A., Princeton Univerity, U.S.A.; D.I.C. (London); M.A. Married, 2 sons. Appointments: Lecturer, University of Science & Technology, Kumasi, Ghana, 1961-68; Senior Lecturer, ibid, 1968–; Associate, International Centre for Theoretical Physics, International Atomic Energy Agency, UNESCO, Trieste, Italy. Memberships: Fellow, Royal Astronomical Society, U.K.; Author of several papers in European & U.S. scientific journals. Address: University of Science & Technology, Kumasi, Ghana.

ALLOTEY-PAPPOE (Rev.), Ebenezer, born 31st December 1916. Minister of Religion; School Superintendent. Education: 1923-33: Peki Wesleyan School; Accra, ibid; Dodowah; Aburi Kemp Wesleyan Boarding School, 1933; Mfantsipim School, Cape Coast, 1934-35; Teacher Training, Wesley College, Kumasi, 1936-39; Joint Theological College (now Trinity College), Kumasi, 1944-46; St. Andrew's College, Selly Oak, Birmingham, U.K., 1961-62. Personal Details: Son of the Rev. J. E. Allotey-Pappoe of Accra; 4th child of 10 children; married the former Miss Violet Abigail Cofie, Staff Midwife, 1947; 3 boys & 3 girls. Appointments: Class Prefect, Elementary School; Accra Inter Schools Referee, 1940-43; Air Raid Precaution Sergeant, Wartime; Ministerial: Acting Manager, Schools, & Superintendent in Asikuma & Shama Circuits, 1947-54; Manager of Schools & Superintendent, Volta Mission Circuit, 1955. Memberships: SRA Prison Committee, 1955-58; Tarkwa Prison Visiting Committee; Chairman, Accra Ridge Hospital Visiting Committee, 1970; Convenor, Ghana Methodist Church Nominations Committee & Methodist Conference Precentor, 1965-70; Tutor, Freeman College, 1962. Lyricist & Translator. Honours: Special Award for Special Service as Assistant College Dispenser, Wesley College, 1937; Recipient of Ghana Methodist Church Deed of Foundation for Autonomy, Methodist Conference, Bradford, U.K. Address: Methodist Church, P.O. Box 1875, Adabraka, Accra, Ghana.

ALLOTEY-PAPPOE (Rev.), Joseph Emmanuel, born Accra, Ghana, 10th September 1887. Methodist Minister. Education: Wesleyan Higher Grade School, Accra; passed Civil Service Exam., 1904, & Candidates' Entrance Exam., Meth. Ch. Ministry, 1919; Fourah Bay College, Freetown, Sierra Leone, 1919-21; St. Andrew's College, Birmingham, U.K., 1964. Married, 10 children. Appointments include: Post & Telegraphs Dept., Gold Coast Civil Service, 1904-19; Gold Coast Rifle Volunteer Force, 1906-9; 1st Minister, Oeki, Trans-Volta District, by British Meth. Ch. Conf., 1919-23; transferred to Accra, 1924; Methodist Religious Lecturer & Examiner, Government Training College for Teachers, 1924-28; Superintendent Minister, Dodowa, Prampram (twice), Aburi, Mampong, Volta Mission, Accra, Nsawam, & Adabraka Circuits, 1928-64; Chairman, Accra District, 1964-68; Manager, Primary & Middle Meth. Schools, 47 yrs.; retired from active ministry, 1968; Meth. Chaplain, Nurses' Training Coll., Korle-Bu Hospital, 1951-54, & for Prisons, Accra, 1924-28, 1944-54; Lay Magistrate, Juvenile Court, 1952-54; Member, Cinema Board of Control, 1951-54; Board of Governors, Korle-Bu Hosp., 1951-53, Ghanata Secondary School, 1961-64; Chairman, Board of Governors, Aburi Methodist Training College for Teachers, 1964-68; 1st Chaplain, Boys' Brigade, Accra, 1953-54; Chaplain, Achimota College, 1944-54; Ghana Methodist Church Ministerial Representative, British Methodist Church Confs., Sheffield, U.K., 1964. Memberships include: Red Cross Committee, 1944-45; Christian Council of the Gold Coast, 1944-48; Assoc. Member, Boy Scouts, 1944—; Executive Member, Friends of Lepers Society, 1953-54; Board of Prisons, Nsawam Medium Security Prisons, 1962; African Liberal Council, 1967—. Composer of hymn tunes, chants, vespers, songs & dances, including songs for the 'Ghana Methodist Church Women's Fellowship', a booklet entitled 'Compositions', the anthem 'Bless the Lord, O my Soul' and the Drivers Round, 'If you drink don't drive, If you drive don't drink'. Honours: Associate, 1912, Licentiate, 1917, & Fellow, 1919, The Victoria College of Music, U.K.; Ghana Boy Scout Badge; Assistant Organist, Wesley Church, Cape Coast, 1911; Church Organist & Choirmaster, Wharton Freeman Chapels Accra, 1902-19; Honorary Organist, Varick Memorial Chapel, A.M.E. Zion Church, Cape Coast, 1912; recipient of Ghana Methodist Church Conference U.K. Scholarship, 1964; represented Ghana Methodist Church Conference, Sheffield, Yorkshire, U.K., 1964. Address: c/o Methodist Church, P.O. Box 1875, Accra, Ghana.

ALUKO, Samuel Adepoju, born Ode Ekiti, Western Nigeria, 18th August 1929. Educator; Economist. Education: St. Mary's School, Ode Ekiti, 1936-40; Emmanuel School, Ado Ekiti, 1941; Christ's School, Ado Ekiti, 1942-45; B.Sc.(Econ.) London (private study in Nigeria), 1954; M.Sc., London School of Economics, London University, 1957; Ph.D., Economics, 1959. Personal details: Son of Chief Fagbohun Aluko & Omolu Aluko; married to Joyce Ofuya, from Midwestern Nigeria, graduate of L.S.E. & now Assistant Registrar, University of Ife; 5 children. Appointments: Principal, Zik's College of Commerce, Nigeria, 1952-53; Vice-Principal, Lagos City College, 1954; Principal, National High School, Ebute wetta, 1955; Acting Head, Department of Economics, University of Ife, 1962-64; Head, Department of Economics, University of Nigeria, Nsukka, 1964-66; Professor & Head, Department of Economics, University of Ife, 1967—; Dean, Faculty of Social Sciences, University of Ife, 1967-68, 1968-69. Memberships: Foundation President, Nigerian Economic Society; Associate Editor, ibid; American Association of Public Finance; Canadian Economic Association; Special Committee on Society, Development & Peace, & Consultant, Advisory Committee on Technical Services, World Council of Churches. Publications: Problems of Self-Government in Nigeria, 1956; Joint Author, Economic Growth in World Perspective, 1966; Financing Education in Nigeria, 1966; Fiscal Incentives for Industrial Development in Nigeria, 1967; Incentives for Commercial Development in Nigeria, 1969; Effects of Tariff on Development in Nigeria, 1970; also numerous journal articles. Honours: Studentship, London School of Economics, University of London, 1957-59. Address: Department of Economics, University of Ife, Ile-Ife, Nigeria.

AMADI, Eugene George Uzoma, born Akabo-Ikeduru Owerri Province, 24th May 1935. Teacher. Education: C.M.S. School, Mbieri, Nigeria; T.T.C. Irete; St. Mark's College, Awka; B.A., Harden College of Education, University of Nigeria, Nsukka, 1965. Married, 5 sons, 1 daughter. Appointments: Headmaster, C.M.S. School, Amankuta-Mbieri, 1958-61; Head of Geography Department, Iheme Grammar School, Arondizuofu; Teacher,

Vice-Principal, acting-Principal, Egbu Girl's Secondary School, Nigeria, 1965—. Memberships: Chairman, Education Committee, Ikeduru County Council; Lay Reader, Anglican Church, Egbu Parish; Auditor, Adabo Parish; Secretary, Kingmakers, Akabo, & took active part during the enthronement of Chief J. N. Nwansi Ike II of Ikeduru, 1958. Author of 'Introducing Comprehensive Secondary School in Ikeduru'. Address: Egbu Girls' Secondary School, P.O. Box 198, Owerri, Nigeria.

AMANKWATIA, Osafroadu, born Kumasi, Ashanti, Ghana, 12th November 1917. Legal Practitioner. Education: Mfantsipim School, Cape Coast, Ghana; King's College, Newcastle, U.K.; Durham University and London University, U.K.; Barrister-at-Law of the Inner Temple Inns of Court, London. Married. Appointments include: Founder & Principal of Division Schools, Suame, Kumasi, 1942-45; Legal Adviser to the Gold Coast Marketing Association Limited, 1957-60; Secretary (Ashanti Branch), Gold Coast Youth Conference, 1943-45; Gold Coast Delegate to the World Youth Conference, 1945; appointed Regional Adviser to Students intending to study Overseas, Ministry of Education, Ghana, 1967. Memberships include: Commissioner, Boy Scouts' Association of Kumasi, Educational District, Ashanti; Local Preacher, Methodist Church, Ashanti Circuit, 1944. Freemason, Lodge Morality 1362 S.C., Kumasi, Ghana; ibid, Lodge Kumasi, 1472, S.C., Kumasi; O.D.D., Garden City Lodge, 11593. Address: Pinanko Chambers, P.O. Box 1422, Kumasi, Ashanti, Ghana.

AMAR, Jacques, born 11th July 1927. Doctor of Medicine; Cardiologist. Education: M.D., Faculty of Medicine, Paris, France; Diploma, specializing in Cardiology. Married, 3 children. Appointments: former Cardiologist, Averros Hospital, Casablanca, Morocco. Address: c/o Averros Hospital, Casablanca, Morocco.

AMARA, Taieb, born 5th March 1930. Pacha of the Town of Safi. Appointments: Head of the Territorial Bureau of Kenitra, 1956-57; Head of the Economic & Administrative Services, Province of Rabat, Morocco, 1957-58; Pacha, Head of the Social & Economic Service, Ministry of the Interior, 1958; Pacha, Head of the Department of Ouezzane, 1958; Pacha of the Town of Oujda, 1962; Deputy Director of General Affairs, Cabinet of the Ministry of the Interior, 1963-65; Pacha of the Town of Safi, 1965—. Honours: Ouissam 'Errida', 1st class. Address: Pacha, Ville de Safi, Morocco.

AMBOGA, George Mark, born 20th July 1923. Librarian. Education: Kaimosi, Maseno, Alliance High School Kikuyu; Makere University College, Kampala, Uganda. Personal details: 2nd son of Stephano Atsinwa, founder Jeanes School, Inspector of Schools also founder of 100 schools in North Maragoli, Kenya. Appointments: Warden, African Community Centre, British Overseas Food Corporation, Kongwa, Tanganyika, 1945-51; Library Assistant, Makerere University College, Kampala, Uganda, 1953-61; Librarian, East African Industrial Research Organization, East African Community, 1962—. Memberships: former mbr., London Library Association. Address: P.O Box 30650, Nairobi, Kenya.

AMBROSE, David Percy, born 27th March 1939. University Lecturer in Mathematics. Education: Primary School, Loughton, Essex, U.K., 1944-50; Harsnetts Scholar, Chigwell School, Essex, 1950-57; B.A.(Hons.), Hertford College, Oxford University, 1959-62; M.A., University of Colorado, 1962-64. Appointments: Senior Mathematics Master, Harecroft Hall School, Gosforth, Cumberland, U.K., 1958-59; Teaching Associate, University of Colorado, U.S.A., 1962-64; Lecturer, Mathematics, University of Botswana, Lesotho & Swaziland, 1965-70; Senior Lecturer, ibid & Head of Department, ibid, 1967-70. Memberships: Mathematical Association, U.K.; Mathematical Association of America; Association of Teachers of Mathematics, U.K.; National Council of Teachers of Mathematics, U.S.A. Publications: Three 'Eight Point' Circles of a Cyclic Quadrilateral, 1966; Mathematics Teaching in Botswana, Lesotho & Swaziland, 1968; Romathe International University in Lesotho, 1969; Riding High in Colorado, 1965. Address: Head, Department of Mathematics, University of Botswana, Lesotho & Swaziland, P.O. Roma, Lesotho.

AMBROSOLI, Guiseppe, born 25th July 1923. Missionary Doctor. Education: M.D., Medicine & Surgery, Milan University, Italy, 1949; Diploma, Tropical Medicine & Hygiene, 1951; Ordained Catholic Priest, Verona Fathers Society, 1955. Personal details: Grandfather was member of Italian Parliament, 1899-1904; Father was founder of the Ambrosoli Italian Factory for honey & sweets. Appointments: Missionary Doctor, Kalongo Hospital, Catholic Church Kalongo, Lira, Uganda. Life Fellow, Society of Tropical Medicine & Hygiene, London, U.K. Honours: Prize 'Missione del Medico' Angelo De Gasperis, Foundazione Carlo Erba, Milan, 1963. Address: Kalongo Hospital, Catholic Church Kalongo, Private Bag, Lira, Uganda.

AMEDEGNATO, Patrice, born Dayes, Kakpa, Togo, 2nd March 1929. Agricultural Engineer. Education: Agricultural Secondary School, 1947; Preparatory Class, French National School of Agriculture, 1951; Diploma Engineering, College of Agriculture, Tunis, Tunisia, 1954; Diploma, College of Tropical Agronomy, Paris, France, 1955; Certificate, National Centre of Agricultural Co-operation, Paris; Diploma of Social Sciences, Paris. Married, 3 children. Appointments include: Head, Division of Agriculture, Dapamgo, 1957; ibid, Abakpami, 1958; Assistant Director, Fonds Commun des SP, 1960; Professor of Co-operation, Togo National School of Administration, 1960; Director-General, Federation of Public Societies for Rural Action, 1961; Professor, Centre for Social Formation of Togo, 1963; Head, Service de la Co-operation et de la Mutualité Agricoles, 1967. Memberships include: President, UNICITO, Togo; President, Caisse populaire des Agents, Ministry of Rural Economy; Vice-President, Association of the

Inhabitants of the City of Tokoin. Address: B.P. 341, Lome, Togo.

AMEGA, Louis-Koffi, born 22nd March 1932. Magistrate. Education: Lic. en Droit; Higher Studies Diploma in Private Law, Roman Law & the History of Law; Brevet, French Overseas National School. Married, 5 children. Appointments: Juge d'Instruction, Brazzaville, Congo, 1960; President, The Tribuna of Brazzaville-Congo, 1962—; Vice-President, Tribunal of Lome-Togo, 1965; Councillor, Supreme Court of Togo, 1967; President, Judicial Chamber of the Supreme Court of Togo, 1968—. Memberships: Corresponding Member, National Centre for Juvenile Delinquency, U.S.A.; President, Committee of Banks & Finance Houses; National Correspondent, United Nations Institute of Researches on Social Defense. Publications: Situation Juridique de la Veuve in Revue PENANT, 1962. Honours: Chevalier de l'Ordre du Mono. Address: Supreme Court of Togo, Lome, Togo.

AMENECHI, Patrick Iloba, born 29th June 1933. Secretary, Nigerian Council for Science & Technology. Education: B.Sc., 1st Class, Chemistry, London, 1957; M.Sc., London, 1962; Ph.D., Manchester, 1968; Diploma, Imperial College, 1961. Married, 4 children. Appointments: Chemist, Federal Ministry of Health, 1957; Assistant Government Chemist, 1959; Senior Chemist, 1963; Deputy Government Chemist, 1965; Federal Government Chemist, 1969; Secretary, Nigerian Council for Science & Technology, 1970. Memberships: Nigerian Science Association; Associate, Royal Institute of Chemistry. Contributor of many articles—to scientific journals. Honours: University College Scholarship, 1955. Address: Secretary, Nigerian Council for Science & Technology, Nigeria.

AMICHIA, René, born Sassandra, Ivory Coast, 18 September 1931. Director General of Credit Development Bank. Education: Lycée de Ginglo. Ivory Coast; Lycée Technique of Dakar, Senegal; Centre of Economic, Financial & Banking Studies, Paris, France. Married to Bobin Raymonde, 8 children. Appointments: Chief Constable, Credit Côte d'Ivoire, 1956-58; Assistant Administrator, ibid, 1958-61; Directeur, d'afence (Bonaki), 1961-63; Première Fondé de Pouvoir, 1963-67; Director General, 1967—. Memberships: President, Junior Chamber of Economic Affairs, 1969-71; Première Vice-President, Lions Club, 1970-71. Address: c/o Credit de la Côte d'Ivoire, Ivory Coast.

AMIN, Ambalal Vaghjibhaz, born 1st January 1919. Medical Practitioner. Education: M.B., B.S., Bombay University, India, 1945. Member of the St. John Ambulance Brigade & Association. Honours: Associate Serving Brother, Medal awarded by St. John Ambulance, 1965; Long Service Medal up to 1959, awarded by St. John Ambulance, 1968. Address: P.O. Box 1574, Nairobi, Kenya.

AMIN, Chandubhaz Vaghjibhaz, born 18th July 1921. Medical Practitioner. Education: M.B., B.S., Bombay University, India, 1948. Member of the St. John Ambulance Brigade & Association. Honours: Associate Serving Brother, Medal awarded by St. John Ambulance, 1965; Long Service Medal, ibid, 1968. Address: P.O. Box 1574, Nairobi Kenya.

AMIN, Jashbhai Raojibhai, born Virsad, India, 1st April 1926. Businessman & Financier. Education: Inter-Science of Bombay University; Passed Ordinary Examination, Accountancy, Banking & Insurance. Personal Details: Member of the 'House of Raoamin' in East Africa & India. Appointments: Chairman, Kenya Trading Corporation Ltd.; Managing Director, Mutual Investors' Ltd. & holder of directorships in a number of companies of East Africa. Memberships include: Patel Samaj; Mombasa Social Service League; Premier Club; Patel Brotherhood; Rotary Club; Freemason Temple. Address: P.O. Box 933, Mombasa, Kenya.

AMIN, Jayantkumar V., born 11th August 1927. Specialist Eye Surgeon. Education: M.B., B.S.; M.S.; D.O.M.S. Personal details: one of a family of doctors. Appointments: Honorary Eye Specialist, Civil Hospital & B.J. Medical College, Ahmrdabad, India. Past Committee Member, Uganda Medical Society. Address: P.O. Box 1628, Kampala, Uganda.

AMIN, Raojibhai Chhotabhai, born 31st March 1914. Business Executive. Education: B.A., History & Economics, Bombay University, India, 1937. Appointments: Depot Manager, Central Province Office, Kenya Farmers Association (Co-op) Ltd., 1940-41; Branch Manager, Central & Nyanza Provinces Offices of Maize & Produce Controls, Kenya, 1942-46; Manager, Africa Produce Co. (Kenya) Ltd., & Maida Ltd. at Kenya & Uganda Offices, 1946-62; General Manager, Uganda Maize Industries Ltd., 1962—. Address: General Manager, Uganda Maize Industries Ltd., P.O. Box 767, Kampala, Uganda.

AMIN, Suresh A., born Kampala, Uganda, 20th March 1943. Architect. Education: B.Arch. Appointments: Assistant Architect, N.H.C. (three years); Architect in private practice, Kampala, Uganda. Memberships: Uganda Society of Architects; Indian Institute of Architects. Address: P.O. Box 6531, Kampala, Uganda.

AMISSAH, Austin Neearbeohe Evans, born 3rd October 1930. Judge; Educator. Education: Government Boys' School, Accra, Ghana, 1935-40; Achimota School, 1941-49; St. Bees School, 1949-50; B.A., Oxford University, U.K., 1954; M.A., ibid, 1959; Barrister-at-Law, Lincoln's Inn, London. Married, 1 son, 2 daughters. Appointments: Crown Counsel, 1955-60; Senior State Attorney, 1960-61; Principal State Attorney, 1961-62; Director of Public Prosecutions, 1962-66; Justice of Appeal, 1966—; Dean, Law Faculty, University of Ghana, 1969--. Author of articles in the University of Ghana Law Journal & the Ghana Law Review. Address: Court of Appeal, P.O. Box 119, Accra, Ghana.

AMISSAH (The Most Reverend) John Kodwo, born 17th November, 1922. Catholic Archbishop. Education: St. Peter's School,

Kumasi, Ghana; St. Teresa's Seminary, Amisano; St. Augustine's College, Cape Coast; Pontifical Urban University, Rome, Italy. Appointments: Ordained Priest, 1949; Teacher, St. Teresa's Minor & Major Seminary, 1950-51, 1954-57; Auxiliary Bishop, 1957; Elected Archbishop of Cape Coast & Metropolitan of Ghana, 1959; Took charge of Diocese, 1960. Memberships: Chairman, First Pan African Symposium of Catholic Episcopal Conferences, Kampala, 1969; First Councillor of Standing Committee, SECAM (Symposium of Episcopal Conferences of Africa & Madagascar; Chairman, University College Cape Coast; Member, Council of State. Recipient, Grand Medal. Address: Archbishop's House, P.O. Box 112, Cape Coast, Ghana.

AMLESU YOSEPH, born Khartoum, Sudan, 17th March 1938. Editor. Education: American Mission Girls' School, Khartoum North, Sudan, 1941-55; Unity High School, Khartoum, 1955-57; B.A., Hailé Selassié I University, Addis Ababa, Ethiopia, 1961; The New School For Social Research, New York, N.Y., U.S.A., 1962-64; M.A., 1965. Married, 3 children. Appointments: Guide, United Nations Headquarters, New York, 1963-64; News Reporter & Editor, Radio, Ministry of Information Addis Ababa, Ethiopia, 1965-1967; Editor, Addis Ababa, Chamber of Commerce. Memberships: Ethiopian Women's Welfare Association. Address: P.O. Box 517, Addis Ababa, Ethiopia.

AMMAR, Abbas Moustafa, born Egypt, 10th December 1907. International Civil Servant. Education: B.A., M.A.(Distinction), Cairo University U.A.R.; Ph.D., Manchester University, U.K.; Higher Diploma in Pedagogy & Social Studies, Higher Training College, U.A.R.; Higher Studies Diploma, Social Anthroplogy, Cambridge, U.K. Married, 1 son. Appointments include: Lecturer, Socio-Economics, Intermediate College of Commerce, Cairo, U.A.R., 1931-37; Research Work in Social & Cultural Anthropology, Manchester & Cambridge Universities, U.K., 1937-42; Lecturer & Assistant Professor, Social Anthropology & Socio-Economics, Cairo University, U.A.R., 1942-47; Head, Petitions Division, Trusteeship Department, U.N., 1948-50, 1951-52; Director-General, Rural Welfare Department, Ministry of Social Affairs, U.A.R., 1950-51; Minister of Social Affairs, 1952-54; Minister of Education, 1954; Assistant Director-General, International Labour Office, Geneva, Switzerland, 1954-64; Deputy Director-General, ibid, 1964—. Publications include: (Arabic) Anthropological Study of the Arabs, 1946; Report on Adult Education & People's University for Workers, 1947; Report on Population Situation in Egypt, 1953; Re-organization of the Egyptian Village in a Decentralised Administration, 1954; (English) The Peoples of Sharquia; An Anthropo-Socio-Economic Study of the Eastern Province of the Nile Delta (2 vols.), 1946. Address: 2 rue Crespin, 1206 Geneva, Switzerland.

AMOAH, Emmanuel Ankoma, born 6th July, 1937. Businessman. Education: Middle School Leaving Certificate, Nyakrom Methodist Middle School, 1952; West African School Certificate (Grade II), Kibi Abuakwa State College, 1953-57; Associate Member, Corporation of Certified Secretaries, University of Science & Technology, Kumasi, Ghana, 1958-60. Appointments: Branch Manager, S.C.O.A. Motors, 1960-67; Regional Representative, WYETH International, 1968—. Address: WYETH International, P.O. Box 5230, Accra Ghana.

AMOAH, James Kwame, born 3rd July, 1943. Ceramist. Education: Elementary School, Nsuta, Ashanti, Ghana, 1949-57; Secondary, Prempeh College, Kumasi, 1958-62; B.A., Art with 2nd Class Upper Division, University of Science & Technology, ibid, 1962-66. Widower Appointments: Assistant Research Fellow, Department of Ceramics, University of Science & Technology, 1966—; Study Leave on Deutsche Akademische Austauschdienst Scholarship, Kunst Hochschule, Kassel, West Germany, 1969; Exhibited in Germany, Austria, Mexico, U.S.A. Member, Ghanaian Contemporaries, a group of young Ghanaian artists. Honours: Invited by Austrian Government to Ceramist Symposium, 1967; Certificate of Honour, 'Made in Ghana Goods' Exhibition, Art Council of Ghana, 1967; ibid, Art Contest organised by Mobil Oil, Ghana Ltd. & Art Council of Ghana. Address: Kunst Hochschule, 35 Kassel, Federal Republic of Germany.

AMOBI, Benedict Obiora, born 13th July 1920. Consultant Obstetrician & Gynaecologist. Education: Practicing School, Akwa, Nigeria, 1933-36; Igbobi College, Lagos, 1937-41; University College, Dublin, 1943-49; Postgraduate School in Obstetrics & Gynaecology, London, U.K. 1959. Personal details: son of Chief B.O.E. Amobi, Igwe of Ogidi; married, 2 sons, 2 daughters. Appointments: Medical Officer, General Hospital, Lagos, Nigeria, 1951; ibid, General Hospital Dozema, 1951-52; Port-Harcourt, 1952-53; Umuchia, 1953-56; Owerri, 1956; Calabar, 1956-59; Senior Medical Officer i/c, Anang Province, 1959-60; ibid, Aba Province, 1960-62; Consultant Obstetrician & Gynaecologist, General Hospital, Enugu, 1962-66; Acting Chief Medical Officer, East Central State, 1970. Memberships: West African Association of Surgeons, Chairman, Eastern Branch, 1964-67; Nigerian Medical Council, 1964-67; Enugu Chamber of Commerce. Address: P.O. Box 343, Enugu, Nigeria.

AMODE, Joseph Olorunfemi, born 26th April 1936. University Lecturer; Education: Native Authority Primary School, Okene, Nigeria, 1945-49; Middle School, Okene, 1950; West African Senior Certificate, Grade I, Government College, Keffi, 1951-56; G.C.E. (A level) Nigerian College of Technology, Zaria, 1957-59; B.Sc.(Eng.), M.Sc., University of New Mexico, Albuquerque, U.S.A., 1960-65; Osaka University, Japan, 1968-70. Married. Appointments: Survey Draughtsman, Grade II, 1957; Pupil Mechanical Engineer, M.O.W., Kaduna, 1965; Assistant Lecturer, Mechanical Engineering Department, Ahmadu Bello University, Zaria, 1966-67; Lecturer, ibid, 1967—. Memberships: Associate Mbr., American Society of Mechanical Engineers; National Honorary Mechanical Engineering Fraternity, U.S.A.; Senior Staff Club, Ahmadu Bello University, Nigeria; former General-Secretary, Foreign Students' Association, Kansai (Senri), Japan.

Honours: Hockey & Soccer Colours, Government College, Keffi, 1956. Address: Ahmadu Bello University Zaria, Nigeria.

AMOO, Enoch, born 27 June 1931. Medical Practitioner. Education: Sir John Cass College, London, U.K.; Zurich University, Switzerland; Hamburg University, Germany; Medical Academy Dusseldorf; M.D., University of Bonn, 1962. Married, 4 children. In private medical practice, Ghana, Chairman, United Nationalist Party, Western Region, Ghana. Address: Ahanta Clinic, Bekwai Road 109/1, P.O. Box 217, Takoradi, Ghana.

AMORAW WUBENEH TESSEMA, Ras, born Gondar, Ethiopia, born 7th July, 1897. Crown Councillor. Education: Amharic & Geaze. Married, 7 children. Appointments: Member of the Senate, Ethiopia, 1942-45; Deputy Governor of Gondar, 1945-49; Senator, 1949-69; Crown Councillor, 1969—. Member, Patriotic Association. Honours: Patriots' Medal & St. George Medal, 1942; Honorary Medal of Ethiopia, 1951; Victory Medal of Star, 1956; Grand Medal of Minelk II & Ethiopian Honorary Star Cordon, 1969; British Medals & African Star, 1939-45. Address: P.O. Box 5031, Addis Ababa, Ethiopia.

AMPEH II, (Nana) Kwame, Tapa Hene, born 1870. Farmer. Education: Primary, Class 3. Married, 5 wives, 35 children. Paramount Chief of Tapa for 78 years. President, Akan Kadjebi local council, 8 years. Honours: George V medal. Address: P.O. Box 1, Tapa Abotoase, via Worawora, Volta Region, Ghana.

AMPOFO, Samuel Twum, born Asiakwa, Akyem Abuakwa, Ghana, 1st August 1925. Teacher. Education: Primary School, Kwaso, Nkwatia & Asiakwa, 1932-37; Middle School, Abetifi & Begoro Presbyterian Boarding Schools, 1938-41; Akropong Presbyterian Training College, 1942-46; B.A.(Hons.), History, University of Ghana, 1957, Postgraduate Certificate of Education, ibid, 1959-60. Personal details: Son of Daniel R. Dakwa, a Presbyt Catechist, & Ellen C. Badua; married to Margaret Lily Ampofo, 3 daughters. Appointments: Headmaster, Abetifi Training College, 1957-59; ibid, Swedru Secondary School, 1960-61; Senior History Master, Swedru Secondary School, 1962; Assistant Headmaster, ibid, 1963; Headmaster, Ofori Panin Secondary School, 1963—. Memberships: Secretary, Kwahu Elementary School Teachers Union, 1949-51; Chairman, Schools & Colleges Sports Federation, Eastern Region, 1965-68; Chairman, Public Secondary Schools Sports Association, 1968—; Fellow, Historical Society of Ghana; Vice-Chairman, Okyeman Scholarship Board, 1965-68; Chairman, Ghana Association of History Teachers, 1965-69; Ghana Amateur Athletic Association; Eastern Region Representative, ibid, 1968—; Vice-Chairman, National Executive of Schools & Colleges Sports Federation. Honours: University Colours, Lawn Tennis, 1960. Address: Headmaster, Ofori Panin Secondary School, P.O. Box 11, New Tafo, Akyem Abuakwa, Ghana.

AMSALU AKLILU, born 4th September 1931. University Professor; Head of Department. Education: B.D., Cairo, U.A.R.; B.A., ibid; Ph.D. Tübingen, Germany. Married, 2 sons. Appointments: Lecturer in Ethiopian Languages, Hailé Selassié I University, Addis Ababa, Ethiopia, 1963-65; Assistant Professor, ibid, 1965-69; Head of Department, Ethiopian Languages & Literature, ibid, 1979—. Memberships: Executive Secretary, Language Study Group of Ethiopia; Member Executive Committee, Language Association of East Africa. Publications: English-Amharic Dictionary (co-author); in preparation Amharic-English Dictionary. Address: Hailé Selassié I University, P.O. Box 1176, Addis Ababa, Ethiopia.

ANA, James Robert, born 22nd February 1923. Dental Practitioner. Education: Cambridge School Certificate, 1942; Chemist & Druggist Diploma, 1946; Bachelor of Dental Surgery, 1960. Married, 6 children. Appointments: Hospital Pharmacist, 1946-52; Dental Surgeon, Government, 1960-63; Principal, Schools of Hygiene & Dental Technology, 1963-70; University Lecturer, Periodontology, 1970—. Memberships: Fellow, Dental Surgery, Royal College of Surgeons, U.K., 1963; Associate, British Association of Oral Surgeons; Fellow, West African Association of Surgeons; Secretary, Nigerian Dental Association; Executive Member, Nigeria Medical Association; Vice-Chairman, Calabar Education Foundation. Publications: Maxillo-Facial Injuries in War, 1968; Nutrition & Dentistry, 1969. Honours: Hon. Fellowship, Nigeria Medical Council in Dental Surgery, 1970. Address: Dental Department, College of Medicine, University of Lagos, Nigeria.

ANANE-TABURY, Enoch Kwasi Wye, born 7th December 1913. Public Administrator. Education: Presbyterian Junior School, Duayaw-Nkwanta, Ghana; Presbyterian Senior School, Kumasi, Ashanti; Achimota College, Accra; Leicester University College, U.K.; various attachments for practical training to Winchester City Council, Hampshire County Council, Ministry of Housing & Local Government, U.K. Married. Appointments: Clerk, 2nd Division, Ashanti Political Administration, Ghana; Senior Executive Officer, ibid; Administrative Officer; Senior Assistant Secretary, Ministry of Transport & Communications; Principal Assistant Secretary; Principal (Permanent) Secretary i/c Ministry of Transport & Communications. Memberships: Senior Civil Service Association, Ghana; Corporation of Certified Secretaries. Address: P.O. Box M.38, Accra, Ghana.

ANDERSON, Colin, born Argentina, 10th August, 1931. Medical Practitioner. Education: St. Andrews Scots School, Buenos Aires, Argentina; Colegio Nacional de San Isidro, ibid; M.D., Facultad de Medicina, Universidad Nacional de Buenos Aires. Married. Appointments: Registrar, Pathology, Glasgow, Royal Infirmary, U.K.; Senior Registrar, ibid; Consultant Pathologist, Ministry of Health, Tanzania. Memberships: Royal College of Pathologists; Pathological Society of Great Britian & Ireland; Association of Clinical Pathologists; International Society of Geographical Pathology, Switzerland; East African Leprosy Association. Publications: Mixed

Mesodermal Tumours of the Ovary (J. Path. Bact.), 1967; The J.G. Apparatus in Hypertensive Patients with Coarctation of the Aorta of the Adult Type (J. Path.), 1969; Carotico-Cavernous Sinus Aneurysm (D.S.M. Med. J.), 1969; Malignancies in Tanzania (Acta Tropica), 1970. Address: Central Pathology Laboratory, P.O. Box 9073, Dar es Salaam, Tanzania.

ANDERSON, Janet Watson, born 5th May 1923. Medical Practitioner. Education: Huntly Gordon School; Aberdeen University; London School of Hygiene & Tropical Medicine, U.K. Appointments: Medical Officer, Uganda Government, 1956-64; ibid, Maternal & Child Health Section, Nairobi City, Council Public Health Department, 1965—. Address: Box 8438, Nairobi, Kenya.

ANDERSON, Theodore Farnworth, born England, 22nd October 1901. Physician. Education: Rugby School; Trinity Hall, Cambridge; University College Hospital, London, U.K. Married to the former Isobel Cecily Downey, 1925; 2 daughters. Appointments: Gen. Practice, Nairobi, Kenya, 1925; Medical Officer, Colonial Medical Service, 1928; Commission RAMC, 1939; Retired, as Colonel, 1945; Director of Medical Services, Somaliland Protectorate (now Somalia), 1945-49: Director of Medical Services, Kenya, 1950-57; Member, Legislative Council of Kenya, 1950-57. Memberships include: Royal Commonwealth Society, U.K.; British Medical Association; East India Sports Club, London; Rye Golf Club; Nairobi Club; Limuru Club, Kenya. Publications include: numerous articles in medical press. Honours include: Mention in Despatches, 1943; O.B.E. (military), 1944; C.M.G., 1958. Address: P.O. Box 10, Limuru, Kenya.

ANDOH, Thomas, born Beyin, via Axim, Ghana, 22nd November, 1915. Teacher and Agriculturalist. Education: Wesley College, Kumasi, Ghana; School of Agriculture, Ibadan, Nigeria; Agriculture Course in United Kingdom. Personal details: grand uncle, Enoh Bilay, was a General in one of the Western Nzima Wars, also a great grandson of King Kweku Ackah, one of the important Nzima Kings. Appointments include: Leader of the Western Nzima Chiefs in the political crisis of 1936; Headmaster of the Atuabo School, 1937; Leader of Western Nzima Farmers and represented them in the Cocoa Hold-up Conference, 1938; Head of the Seed Multiplication Division, 1965-67. Memberships include: Chairman, Western Nzima Youth Association, 1956. Publications include: was a regular contributor to African World and West African Review. Address: c/o P.O. Box M. 37, Accra, Ghana.

ANDREWS, Eric Keith (Rev.), born London, England, U.K., 10th February 1911. Anglican Minister of Religion. Education: University College School, Hampstead; Tyndale Hall, Clifton, Bristol. Married, 1 son & 1 daughter. Appointments include: Deacon, 1938; Priest, 1939; Assistant Curate, St. Mary, Fulham, London, 1938-40; Priest-in-charge, St. Thomas, N. Kensington, London, 1940-42; St. Matthew, Worthing, 1942-47; Rector, Newick, Sussex, 1947-56; ibid, Pembridge, Herefordshire, 1956-66; exchanged one year with Vicar of Margate, Natal, 1961-62; led Party to the Holy Land, Israel & Jordan, 1962; Vicar of Kiambu & Limuru Diocese of Mount Kenya & Chaplain of Limuru Girls' School, 1966—. Memberships: Royal Commonwealth Society; Kaimbu Country Club; Limuru Country Club. Honours: Protestant Reformation Society Prize, 1937; Tyndale Hall Bible Diploma (cum laude), 1938. Address: The Vicarage, P.O. Box 116, Kiambu, Kenya.

ANDRIAMANANTENA, Célestin, born 19th February 1918. Journalist. Education: College Paul Minault; Diploma, International Centre of Higher Journalistic Studies, Strasbourg, France. Married, 2 daughters & 2 sons. Appointments: Secretary-General, Christian Youth Centre, Tananarive, Malagasey Republic, 1946-47; Journalist, 1947-70. Memberships: Union of Malagasy Poets & Writers; President, Malagasy Press Syndicate, 1960—; Elected Member, Municipal Council of Tananarive. Publications: Founder & Director, Humorous Journal, HEHY; Author of Several Artistic & Literary Works, e.g. Bitsilla, Vavahady Vaovao, Rasalama, etc. Address: Director-General, HEHY, B.P. 1648, Tananarive, The Malagasy Republic.

ANDRIAMANJATO, Richard Mahitsison, born Mahitsy, Madagascar, 31st July 1930. Pastor; Director of a Secondary School. Education: Secondary Galliéni School; Baccalauréat, 1950; Higher Studies, Montpellier, France, 1950; Degree in Theology & Philosophy, University of Strasbourg, 1957. Married, 3 boys, 1 girl. Appointments include: Pastor, Protestant Parish of Ambohitantely, Madagascar, 1957; Participant, Independence Congress, Madagascar, 1958 & elected President of 10 united political parties; First President, Antokon'ny Kongresin'ny Fahaleovantenan'i Madagasikara (A.K.F.M.), 1958—; elected Mayor, Tananarive, 1959; elected Deputy, National Assembly & Speaker for the Opposition, 1960; President, Municipal Council, Tananarive, participating in founding of Federation Mondiale des Villes Jumelées of which he a Member of the Executive Council, 1960; Committee President, All Africa Conference of Churches, 1969. Other activities include: Director, Grand Collége Rasalama, 1959; Vice-President, 1963, President, 1965, Union of Protestant Schools in Tananarive; Member, National Council of Protestant Churches in Madagascar, 1963, '68; Executive Committee, All Africa Conference of Churches, 1963; Vice-President, Christian Conference for Peace, 1964; Mbr. de la Présidence, World Council for Peace, 1967; Member of Ecumenical Commission, Ecumenical Council of Churches, 1968. Author of collections of poetry, a theatrical play and of the article 'Le Tsiny et le Tody' dans la pensée malgache, 1957. Honours: Recipient of The Joliot Curie Medal for World Council of Peace, 1968. Address: 1 Rue de General Léon André, Tananarive, Malagasey Republic.

ANDRIANASOLO, Robin, born Tananarive, Madagascar, 28th October 1934. Statistician. Education: C.E.P.E.; C.E.S.D., B.E., Baccalauréat Maths.; Diploma, National School of Statistics & Economic Administration (ENSAE) Paris, France. Married, 2 children. Appointments include: Statistician, Division of Studies, Analysis and Research, National Institute of Statistics & Economic Research (INSRE), Tananarive, 1961-65; Head of Department of Statistics, Organisation Commune Africaine et Malgache (OCAM), 1965—. Memberships include: Association of Malgaches Engineers (AIM); Association of African Statisticians. Publications include: Enquête sur les Budgets familieuse en milieu urban malgache. In collaboration with the statistics staff of OCAM: Bulletin Statistique de l'OCAM; Notes techniques sur la méthodologie en matière de statistiques africaines. Address: Chef du Service de la Statistique OCAM, B.P. 437, Yaoundé, Cameroon.

ANEIZI, Aly Nureddin, born 24th March 1904. Banker; Economist. Education: Coranic & Elementary School, Benghazi, Libya, 1910-14; Graduated, Secondary Agricultural School, Pescia, Italy, 1915-21; Diploma, Agronomical Institute, Florence, 1921-24; Laureate, Faculty of Economics & Commercial Sciences, University of Naples, Faculty of Arab-Islamic Studies, Oriental Institute, Naples; Institut Francais, University of Grenoble, Naples. Married, 3 sons, 1 daughter. Appointments: Secretary, Real Estate Registry Office, Benghazi, Libya, 1931-33; Officer, Civil Affairs Office, Government of Cyrenaica, 1933-35; Director, 'Aukaf', Benghazi Province, 1935-41; Councillor, Province of Benghazi, 1937-41; with the National Movement in fight for independence of Libya, 1941-44; Official of the Arab League in Eygpt, participated in meetings of U.N.O., 1945-51; Represented Cyrenaica in the U.N.O. Council for Libya, 1951-52; Elected Representative, Soluk Area, Benghazi, House of Representatives; Vice-President, House of Representatives; President, Finance Committee; Minister, Finance & National Economy, 1953-55; Minister of Finance & Economics. 1954-55; Governor, National Bank of Lybia, 1955-61; Ambassador to Lebanon & Jordan, 1961-63; Minister of Petroleum Affairs, 1963-64; Chairman, Sahara Bank, Libya Insurance Co. & National Navigation Co., 1964—; Chairman, Libyan Olympic Committee, 1967-69. Memberships: Life Mbr., Tripoli Golf Club; President, Intellectual Society of Libya, 1965. Publications: Libya Today. Honours: First Class Order of Libyan Independence, 1954; First Class Order, Cedar of Lebanon, 1962; First Class Crown of Jordan, 1962. Address: c/o Sahara Bank, P.O. Box 270, Tripoli, Libya.

ANGLIN, Douglas George, born Toronto, Canada, 16th December 1923. Professor of Political Science. Education: B.A. Toronto, Canada, 1948; M.A., D.Phil.(Oxon.), England, 1955-56. Married, 2 daughters. Appointments include: Assistant Professor, subsequently Associate Professor, Political Science & International Relations, University of Manitoba, Winnipeg, Manitoba, Canada, 1951-58; Associate Professor, subsequently Professor, Political Science, Carleton University, Ottawa, Canada, since 1958; Associate Research Fellow, Nigerian Institute for Social and Economic Research, University of Ibadan, Nigeria, 1962-63; Vice-Chancellor, University of Zambia, Lusaka, Zambia, 1965-69; Research Associate, Center of International Studies, Princeton, U.S.A., 1969-70. Publications include: The St. Pierre and Miguelon Affaire of 1941, 1966; numerous journal articles on African and international affairs. Honours, Prizes, etc.: Rhodes Scholarship, (Ontario), 1948. Address: Dept. of Political Science, Carleton University, Ottawa, Canada.

ANGMORTEY-KWAMI, Evans John, born 22nd February 1926. Judicial Officer. Education: Presbyterian Mission Primary & Middle Schools, Odumase Krobo, Eastern Region, Ghana, 1936-44. Married, 3 sons, 1 daughter. Appointments: Dispensary Attendant, Konongo Gold Mines Ltd., 1945-46; School Teacher, Methodist & Presbyterian Mission Primary Schools, 1947-48; Native Court Registrar, 1949-59; Local Court Registrar, 1959-64; Local Court Magistrate, 1964-66; District Magistrate Grade II, 1966—. Past Secretary, Grand United Order of Odd Fellows. Honours: Native Courts (Colony) Registrars Certificate of Proficiency, 1950. Address: Ghana Judicial Service, P.O. Box 87, Suhum, Ghana.

ANGO, Ehilet-Basile, born 25th April 1927. Printer; Director. Education: studied at the Lycee Technique Estienne, Paris, France, 1957-61. Married. Appointments: Compositor-Typographer, 1946-56; Head of Service, Director of Official Papers, Republic of the Ivory Coast. The two official papers printed are JORCI & JODAN. Address: B.P. 4354, Abidjan, Ivory Coast.

ANGOUNOU MVELE, Jeremie, born 21st November 1920. Educator: Author: Director. Education: Primary School, American Presbyterian Mission School, Foulassi, Sangmelima, Cameroun. Appointments: Schoolmaster, Primary School, Olama, Cameroun, 1939-40; Shorthand-Typist, Momjepom, Yokadouma, 1940-41; Primary Schoolmaster, Nkolmvolan, Abong-Mbang, 1941-42; ibid, Elat, Ebolowa, 1945-49; Accountant, Director, SIP, Prefecture of Ebolowa, 1949-50; Founder of Primary Secular School, Ebolakoun, 1951; Director-Founder, Head of Establishment, Cours Normal, Angounou; President of ASTEM, Ebolowa (Centre). Memberships include: General Vice-President, Legal Suppliant, National Representant of Private Secular Instruction, Cameroun, 1962-64; Deputy General Secretary Bantou Tribal Union, 1951-56; General President, Scholarly Association, Ntem, 1957—; Secretary General of the Cultural Centre, Ebolowa, 1964—. Publications: Je ne peux pas manger; Mon voyage a'Port-Harcourt, 1952; La Dot; Caracteres generaux des races du Cameroun; (In Boulou) Nkobo Nkul; Minkana; Mvondo Mongo; (Musical compositions & songs) L'Hymne de la Paix; Voici le nouveau Jour; La Maison qui marche; Fin d'Année; Welcome Brothers; My Loving Father & Mother. Honours: Recipient of several literary prizes; Cameroun Decoration, 3rd Class, 1968. Address: B.P. 152, Ebolowa, Cameroun.

ANGURA, Samuel Baker, born 28th August 1941. Public Officer; Civil Servant. Education:

Malera Primary School, 1949-52; Bukedea Primary School, 1953-54; Tesso College, Aloet, 1955-56; Cambridge School Certificate, Nyakasura School, 1960; B.Sc., Washington & Jefferson College, Pittsburgh Penna, U.S.A., 1961-62, 1964-65; Law Course for Administrative Officer, Nsamizi Training Centre, Uganda, 1967; Master Electronics Practical Course (Current) 1968; Electronic Diploma Engineering Course (Current), 1968; Training Course for Administrative Officers, Institute of Public Administration. Married. Appointments: Assistant Secretary, Ministry of Education, 1966—; Secretary, Uganda National Commission for UNESCO, 1966—, in this capacity attended numerous Conferences and Congresses; Senior Assistant Secretary, ibid, 1970—. Address: Ministry of Education, Crested Towers Buildings, P.O. Box 7063, Kampala, Uganda.

ANGWENYI, Charles Peter, born 1st January 1939. Economist. Education: B.A., Colby College, U.S.A.; M.A., University of Massachusetts; Ph.D. cand. Appointments: Planning Officer, Ministry of Economic Planning & Development, Kenya, 1968; Lecturer in Economics, University College, Nairobi, 1968-69; Management, Standard Bank Ltd., 1970; Memberships: American Economic Association; Institute of Bankers; United Kenya Club. Publications: Shakespeare's Othello— Two-Tone; American Economic Problems; The Effect of Population Growth on Economic Development in Kenya; Monetary Policy & Credit Availability in Kenya. Honours: Blue Hill Foundation Award, Colby College, 1963; International Tuition Fellowship, University of Massachusetts, 1966-68; Institute of. International Education Fellowship, 1967-68. Address: The Standard Bank Ltd., P.O. Box 30001, Nairobi, Kenya.

ANIEROBI, Clement Udenna, born Amawa Ogbunike, Onitsha, 29th April 1916. Teacher. Education: STD VI, 2 years Niger Diocese, 1923-30. Married, 4 sons, 1 daughter. Appointments: Teacher, 1931—; C/S Teacher, 1942-55; Higher Elementary Teacher, Grade II, 1956—; Headmaster, Ikoya School, Nigeria; St. Christophers, Ode Aye; Central School, Western State; Headmaster, St. Paul's Anglican School, Okitipupa, 1954—. Memberships: (former) Chairman, National Union of Teachers, Okitipupa branch; Treasurer, ibid. Honours: Recipient of Native title, Ogbueffi, Udenna Ikenma Anierobi. Address: No. 7 Olagbegi Street, Okitipupa, Nigeria.

ANIKHINDI, Vasudeo Bhimrao, born 6th January 1936. Medical Practitioner. Education: S.S.C., Poona, India, 1953; I.Sc., Karnatak University, Dharwar, India, 1956; M.B., B.S., Kasturba Medical College, Mangalore, S. India. Personal Details: Son of a business family; married the former Miss Vijaya Laxaman Rao Nadgir, Arts Graduate of Karnatak University. Appointments: House Surgeon, Welock Hospital, Mangalore; Assistant Civil Surgeon, Government Civil Hospital, Belgium, 4 years; Medical Officer, M/s. Sangobay Sugar Estates Ltd., Uganda; M/s. Madhvani Sugar Works Ltd., Uganda. Address: Resident Medical Officer, Madhvani Sugar Works Ltd., P.O. Box 54, Jinja, Uganda.

ANNAN, Joseph Samuel, born Sekondi, Ghana, 1st January 1914. International Civil Servant. Education: Methodist Primary School, Sekondi; Mfantispim School, Cape Coast; Achimota College, Accra; Heriot-Watt College, Edinburgh, U.K. Married. Appointments include: Electrical Engineer, Gold Coast Railway, 1940-45; Labour Officer, 1945-46; Senior Labour Officer, 1947-48; Senior Assistant Secretary, 1951-55; Principal Assistant Secretary, 1956; Permanent Secretary, 1957-60; Liason Officer for Africa, Food & Agricultural Organisation, 1960-62; Deputy Director, Project Management Division, UN/FAO World Food Programme, Rome, Italy, 1962—. Memberships: Committee, World Council of Churches, (Advisory Comm. on Technical Services); World Methodist Council; Chairman, Staff Co-operative, F.A.O.; Vice-Chairman, Credit Union, ibid. Publications: Co-operatives in Madras State; Co-operatives in Ceylon; Co-operation—a Way of Life. Address: c/o UN/FAO World Food Programme, Food & Agricultural Organization, Rome, Italy.

ANOKBONGGO, Willy W., born 18th November 1937. Doctor of Medicine. Education: Cambridge Overseas School Certificate, Uganda; M.D., Hungary. Married, 3 children. Appointments: Medical Officer in various hospitals, Uganda Ministry of Health; Research Worker, Makerere University College Medical School, Kampala, Uganda. Memberships: Olympic Doctors Association. Author of several papers on pharmacological subjects. Honours: Selected as Ugandan Team's physician during 1968 Olympics; Uganda Government Fellow. Address: P.O. Box 270, Lira, Uganda.

ANSAH-TWUM, Kwadwo Abrefa, born Wenchi, Ghana, 23rd February 1932. Lawyer; Judge. Education: Wenchi Methodist School, 1941-46; Cambridge School Certificate, Grade II, Mfantsipim Secondary School, 1950; London Matric Exam, 1951; 'A' Levels, University Tutorial College, U.K., 1954; LL.B., Nottingham University, 1958; B.L., Middle Temple, 1959. Personal Details: Mother, Yaa Ahwene was last child of the Queenmother of Wenchi in Brong Ahafo Region of Ghana, therefore member of Ahemfi Yefri Royal House of Wenchi to which the Paramount Stool & the Queenmother's Stool belong; Married, 4 children. Appointments: Teacher, Wenchi Methodist School, 1951-54; Private Legal Practitioner, Ghana, 1960-67; Circuit Judge, 1967—. Memberships: Chaplain, Freemason Lodge; Vice-Grand, Noble Grand & Council Master, Grand United Order of Oddfellows. Address: Circuit Court, P.O. Box, 119, Accra, Ghana.

ANTELME, Joseph Gustave Robert, born 20th February 1922. Company Managing Director. Education: Royal College, Curepipe, Mauritius; University of Witwatersrand, Johannesburg, South Africa. Appointments: Managing Director, Vain-Lug Mts. Ltd.; Managing Director, Retreaders Ltd.; Chairman, Cecilant Investment Pty. Ltd.; Chairman, Esperance Investment Ltd.; Managing Director, Dry Cleaning & Steam Laundry Ltd. Memberships: Rotary Club of Port Louis; Dodo Club of Curepipe; Grand Baie Yacht Club; Le

Morne Angler's Club. Address: P.O. Box 399, Port Louis, Mauritius.

ANTIA, Asuquo Udo, born 8th September 1927. Doctor of Medicine; University Professor. Education: Hope Waddell Training Institute, Calabar, Nigeria; University College, Ibadan; M.B.Ch.B., Sheffield University, U.K.; D.T.M. & H., Liverpool University, U.K.; The John Hopkins University, Baltimore, U.S.A. Married, 5 sons. Appointments: President Physician in General Medicine, Surgery, & Paediatrics, U.K., 1957-61; Medical Officer (Special Grade), Nigerian Civil Service, 1961-62; Senior Registrar, in Paediatrics, University College Hospital, Ibadan, Nigeria, 1962-63; Assistant Physician (Paediatrics), The John Hopkins Hospital, Baltimore, U.S.A., 1963-65; Lecturer, Senior Lecturer, Professor, University of Ibadan, Nigeria, 1965—. Memberships: Correspondence Mbr., Association of European Paediatric Cardiologists; Council Mbr., Paediatric Cardiology Section, Internation Society of Cardiology; Treasurer, Paediatric Association of Nigeria; Association of Physicians of West Africa. Author of several papers in medical journals. Honours: Commonwealth Fund Fellowship, 1963-65. Address: Department of Paediatrics, University College Hospital, Ibadan, Nigeria.

ANTOINE, Joseph Robert, born 10th March 1920. Director of Mauritius Sugar Industry Research Institute. Education: Royal College, Mauritius; Dip. Agric., College of Agriculture, Mauritius, 1943; B.Sc.(Hons.), Imperial College of Science & Technology, University of London, U.K.; Dip.Agric.Sci., Gonville & Caius College, Cambridge University, U.K. Personal Details: Son of the late Gaston Antoine, M.B.E.; married Edna, daughter of the late Edwin Cure; 1 son & 3 daughters. Appointments: Assistant Plant Pathologist, Department of Agriculture, Mauritius, 1951-54; Senior Agricultural Officer, Department of Agriculture, Mauritius, 1954-55; Plant Pathologist, Mauritius Sugar Industry Research Institute, 1955-56; Chief Pathologist, ibid, 1966-68; Director, 1968—; Lecturer, College of Agriculture, Mauritius, 1951-68. Memberships: A.R.C.S.; Chairman, Standing Committee on Sugar Cane Diseases of International Society of Sugar Cane Technologists, 1962-68; Regional Vice-Chairman, ibid, 1969; President, Association of Former Agricultural Students, 1958, 1961, 1962; President, Society of Agricultural & Sugar Technology, 1963-64; ibid, Royal Society of Arts & Sciences, Mauritius, 1969; Rotary Club of Port Louis. Author of various scientific papers dealing with sugar cane pathology. Address: Mauritius Sugar Industry Research Institute, Reduit, Mauritius.

ANTWI-AGYEI, Kwadwo, born 13th May, 1941. Manager. Education: Middle School Leaving Certificate (with distinction), Trebuom Catholic Middle School, 1948-56; Grade I, Opoku Ware Secondary School, Kumasi, Ghana, 1957-61; Grade D, Grade C G.C.E. Advanced Level Certificate, ibid, 1961-63; B.A.(Hons.), Political Science, University of Ghana Legon, 1963-66. Appointments: Teacher, Asanteman Secondary School, Ministry of Education, Government of Ghana, 1966-69; Farmer, 1969; Currently Trainee Manager to head Branch Office, G.C.H.C. Teme; Seconded to Ministry of Agriculture to Organise Purchasing Section of 'Task Force' for buying of foodstuffs. Address: P.O. Box 3669, Kumasi, Ghana.

ANYAFULU, Okwuchukwu Lawrence, born 30th June 1934. Pharmacist. Education, 1939-47; Secondary Education, 1948-53; Ph.C., School of Pharmacy, 1954-59. Married, 5 children. Appointments: Pharmacist, Government Dispensary, 1964-65; Manager, West African Drug Co. Ltd., 1965—. Memberships: Pharmaceutical Society of Nigeria; Secretary-General, Nigerian Union of Pharmacists, 1962-65; Pharmacy Board of Nigeria, 1963-65. Address: P.O. Box 529, Lagos, Nigeria.

ANYONYI, Cosmas James, born Imasaba Idakho, Kakamega, Kenya, 1902. Retired Police Inspector. Education: Shyamusinqiri Primary School; Upper Primary, Mukumu Mission School, 1921; Training Centre, Kenya Police Depot, 1924. Married, 11 children; Eldest son, Permanent Secretary, Kenya Government. Appointments include: Third Constable, Kenya Police, 1925; Second Constable, ibid, 1926; First Constable, Criminal Investigating Department, 1928; Corporal; Third Sergeant, 1936; First Sergeant, 1949; Transferred to Government House, & to U.K. to broaden experience, 1949; Senior Chief Sergeant Major, Kenya, 1950; Inspector, 1950; Retired, 1957; Driver for Duke of Gloucester & the then Princess Elizabeth on visits to the country; Member, General Service United Special Branch. Memberships include: athletic & football associations; Past Chairman, Abaluhyer Association, Nairobi, Kenya. Honours include: Africa Star, 1939; War Medal, 1939-45; Colonial Police Forces Award for Long Service & Good Conduct; Certificate of Honour, 1952; Coronation Medal, 1953. Recently toured Kenya & shot a Lion & Leopard. Address: Masaba Shyamusinqiri, Shiseso Sub-Location, Idakho Location, P.O. Box 16, Kakamega, Kenya.

APEA I, Nana Kusi (Paramount Chief), born Wenchi, Brong Ahafo, Ghana, 26th August 1926. Education: Passed Std. 7, 1943; self-trained & took G.C.E. Level, correspondence course, Wolsey Hall, Oxford, U.K., 1944-49; trained in Ministry of Labour (Britain) & Industrial Welfare Society (London) & qualified as Training Within Industry (T.W.I.) Trainer, 1959-60. Personal details: youngest Paramount Chief when installed in 1950 & 10th Paramount Chief of the ruling Sofoase Yefre Royal line in Wenchi Traditional Area & 17th Paramount Chief on the Ohene Gyan Stool. Married, 13 children. Appointments include: Sales Clerk, 1946; Elected Paramount Chief, 1950; Industry Training Officer, 1960-63; Administrative Manager, Vice-Principal & Lecturer, U.A.C. Group Training College, Lagos, 1963-66; re-installed as Paramount Chief of Wenchi Traditional Area, 1966. Memberships include: Scout & Patrol Leader, Troop Leader, District Scout Association, Wenchi; Red Cross, Wenchi; Patron, Wenchi Youth Association; Patron; Brong Ahafo Sports Association. Honours: 'Thanks Badge', World Boy Scout Association. Address: Omanhene's Palace, P.O. Box 6, Wenchi Brong Ahafo, Ghana.

APPASSAMY, Joseph Freddy, born 24th January 1926. Local Government Official. Education: Secondary, Royal College of Port Louis, Mauritius; Local government studies, U.K.; Member, Institute of Public Relations, 1970. Married, 1 son, 2 daughters. Appointments: Joined local government, Port Louis, 1944; Deputy Town Clerk, ibid, 1960; Secretary, Association of Urban Authorities, 1960; Acting Chief Public Relations & Welfare Officer, 1965; Mauritian Correspondent, International Union of Local Authorities. Memberships: Racing Club of Mauritius; Port Louis Tennis Club; Mauritius Music Society. Author of A Handbook for Councillors, 1969. Awarded, Medal of City of Port Louis for meritorious service in local government, 1966. Address: 9 Max Rohan Avenue, Beau Bassin, Mauritius.

APPIAH-MENKA, Akenten, born Aboabogya, near Kumasi, Ghana, 3rd July 1934. Barrister & Solicitor. Education: LL.B.(Hons.), University of Manchester, U.K., 1959; Barrister-at-Law, Lincoln's Inn, 1960. Married, 5 children. Appointments include: Member of the Ashanti Regional Planning Committee, Ashanti, Ghana; Member of the Ghana Constituent Assembly, charged with the duty of drawing up a constitution for Ghana; Elected to Parliament, Second Republic of Ghana, 1969; Parliamentary Secretary to the Ministry of Trade, Industries & Tourism; Leader, Trade Delegation to the Soviet Union, Poland, Hungary, Czechoslovakia, Bulgaria, Rumania & the U.A.R., 1970. Memberships: Chairman, Ghana Second International Trade Fair Committee; Secretary, Ghana Students' Union of Gt. Britain & Ireland, 1959-60; Secretary, Ashanti Branch, Ghana Bar Association, 1967—. Address: P.O. Box 664, Kumasi, Ghana.

ARABA, Adekunle Babatunde, born 27th September 1936. Doctor of Medicine; Physiologist; University Lecturer. Education: Igbobi College, Lagos, Nigeria, 1951-55; Nottingham Technical College, U.K., 1956-58; B.Sc., Kings College, London, 1958-61; Westminster Medical School, 1961-64. Married, 3 daughters. Appointments: Tutor, Demonstrator in Pharmacology, King's College, London, U.K., 1961-65; House Surgeon, Queen Mary's Hospital, Roehampton, 1964-65; House Physician, Hackney Hospital, London, 1965; Senior House Officer, Lagos University Teaching Hospital, 1965-66; Part-time Junior Lecturer in Physiology, University of Lagos Medical School, 1966-67; Registrar in Medicine, Lagos University Teaching Hospital, 1967; Lecturer in Physiology, College of Medicine, University of Lagos, 1967—; Honorary part-time Physician, Department of Medicine, Lagos University Teaching Hospital. Memberships: Nigerian Society of Neurological Sciences; West African Society of Gastroenterologists; British Medical Association; Nigerian Medical Association. Author of papers in medical journals. Honours: Scholarship to Westminster Medical School, 1961; Scholarship for Clinical Study, Federal Government of Nigeria, 1962; Fellowship of Norwegian Agency for International Development, 1970. Address: Department of Physiological Sciences, College of Medicine, University of Lagos, P.M.B., 12003, Lagos, Nigeria.

ARADAMIS SAHLE, born 16th April 1936. Governor of Shire-Endaslasie, Ethiopia. Education: Diploma, Commercial School; Certificate, H.S. School; Local Administrations Training, Germany. Appointments: Director, Tigrai Development Organisation; Manager, Harar Taidl Co.; Chief of P. in Water Resources. Address: Shire-Endaslasie, P.O. Box 50, Tigre, Ethiopia.

ARAOYE, Theophilus Olufemi, born Ilawe-Ekiti, Western State of Nigeria, 4th April 1934. School Principal. Education: Holy Trinity Anglican School, Ilawe-Ekiti & St. Paul's School, Igbara Oke, Nigeria; Ilesha Grammar School, Nigeria; Teacher Training, St. Andrew's College, Oyo, Nigeria; B.A., The University of Nigeria, Nsukka, Nigeria, 1963. Married, 4 children. Appointments include: Music Master, St. Andrew's College, Oyo, 1955-56; Organist, St. Peter's Church, Iremo Ife, 1959-60; University Students' Organist, Nsukka, 1960-63; Vice-Principal, Iragbiji Grammar School, Iragbiji, 1964; Principal, Timi Agbale Grammar School, Ede, 1965; Principal, Ebenezer Grammar School, Abeokuta, 1966-67; Assistant Organist, St. John's Church, Igbein Abeokuta, 1967; Principal, Ode-Ekiti High School, Ode-Ekiti, 1968—; Organist, St. Mary's Church, Ode-Ekiti, 1968—. Memberships include: Executive Member of Dramatic Society, University of Nigeria, Nsukka, 1960; Auditor of Lawn Tennis Club, University of Nigeria, Nsukka; in charge of Dramatic Society in Ilesha Grammar School, Ilesha, 1963; led the Youth Club of Ebenezer Grammar School, Abeokuta, to win first place in Western Nigeria Junior Festival of the Arts in Drama; Mbr., Nigerian Careers Council; Leader, Civic Voluntary Group for Raising Funds. Honours: 2nd place in Original Music Composition, Senior Festival of the Arts of Western Nigeria, 1956. Address: Ode-Ekiti High School, Ode-Ekiti, Western Nigeria, Nigeria.

ARCHAMPONG, Emmanuel Quaye, born 12th October 1933. Surgeon. Education: Accra Academy, 1948-51; University College of the Gold Coast, Achimota, Ghana, 1952-55; B.Sc., University College, London, U.K., 1955-58; L.R.C.P., M.B.B.S.(Hons.), University College Hospital, London, 1958-61. Appointments: House Physician, Medical Unit, University College Hospital, London, U.K., 1961-62; House Surgeon, Surgical Unit, ibid, 1962-63; Senior House Surgeon, Leicester Royal Infirmary & General Hospital, U.K., 1964-65; Surgical Registrar, Queen Elizabeth II Hospital, Herts; Lecturer in Surgery, Ghana Medical School, Legon, Ghana. Memberships: Fellow, Royal College of Surgeons, England; Fellow, Royal College of Surgeons, Edinburgh; Fellow, West African Science Association. Author of numerous papers published in medical journals. Honours: Cluff Memorial University College, London, 1957; Prize in Obstetrics & Gynaecology, University College Hospital, London, 1960. Address: University of Ghana Medical School, P.O. Box 4236, Accra, Ghana.

AREMU, Olaleye, born 24th November 1930. Dental Surgeon. Education: B.Sc.; Dr. of Dental Surgery. Personal Details: Son of Olawale Aremu, Farmer, & Tolani; married, 5 children.

Appointments: Prefect, High School, Baptist Academy, Lagos; Superintendent, Baptist Dental Care Centre, Ibadan; Acting Medical Secretary, Nigerian Baptist Convention. Memberships: American Dental Association; American Society of Oral Medicine; Nigerian Medical Council. Honours: Certificate of Merit, American Society of Oral Medicine. Address: Baptist Dental Centre, P.M.B. 5113, Ibadan, Nigeria.

ARMSTRONG, Christopher Wyborne, born Armagh, Northern Ireland, 9th May 1899. Farmer. Education: Winchester College, Winchester, U.K.; Trinity College, Cambridge. Personal details: Son of the Rt. Hon. H. B. Armstrong of Dean's Hill, Armagh; married Hilde, daughter of Hans Kolz of Lubeck; 1 son & 1 daughter. Appointments include: Lt., RFA, BEF, France, 1918; Burma Oil Co., Burna, 1922-39; Royal Engineers, BEF, France, 1939-40; Burma Oil Co., 1940-42; Controller of Petroleum Industry. Burma, 1942; A.Q.M.G., MEF, Egypt, 1942-43; GHQ, Army in India, 1944-45; Commissioner, MAGWE Division, Burma, 1945-46; Member of Parliament, Armagh, Northern Ireland, 1954-59; Farmer, Kenya, 1960—; Memberships include: Carlton Club, London, U.K.; Ulster Club, Belfast, U.K.; Multhaiga Club, Nairobi, Kenya. Honours: O.B.E. (military), 1943. Address: Kwetu Farm, Box 49, Gilgil, Kenya.

ARMSTRONG-SMITH, G., born Hull, U.K., 5th June 1912. Chemist; Metallurgist. Education: B.Sc. (Distinction in Chemistry, Physics & Pure Mathematics); M.Sc. (1st Class Hons. in Chemistry); Ph.D. Married, 1 daughter. Appointments include: Research Chemist, Fuel Research Institute of South Africa; Chief Chemist, Ammunition Department, South African Department of War Supplies; Chief Chemist & Metallurgist, South African Mint; Laboratory Chief, Rhokana Corporation Ltd., Zambia; Superintendent of Metallurgical Control, Nehanga Consolidated Copper Mines, Ltd. Memberships include: Institute of Metals; Fellow, South African Institute of Mining & Metallurgy; Institute of Mining & Metallurgy, London, U.K.; Fellow, Royal Institute of Chemistry. Publications include: Hydrogen, oxygen & nitrogen in cobalt metal, 1969; Origin & control of sulphur in electrowon cobalt metal, 1970; Primary Copper: A review of methods of production & quality control, & many other articles in professional journals. Honours: Gold Medal, S. African Institute of Mining & Metallurgy, 1942; Goldfields Premium Award, Institute of Mining & Metallurgy, London, 1963. Address: P.O. Box 2000, Kitwe, Zambia.

ARO, Theophilus Olatunde, born 18th February 1937. Lecturer in Physics. Education: W.A.S.C., Government College, Keffi, 1950-55; A.L., G.C.E., Nigerian College of Arts, Science & Technology, Zaria, 1956-58; B.Sc., University College, Ibadan, 1958-61; D.Phil., Oriel College, University of Oxford, 1961-64. Married to Mary Ibidun Aro, 1 son & daughter. Appointments: Lecturer, Physics, Ahmadu Bello University, Zaria, Nigeria, 1965—. Memberships: Assiciate, Institute of Physics & Physical Society, London, U.K.; Science Association of Nigeria. Publications: Microwave Interference Method of Measuring Shock Velocity in a Shock Tube (co-author), 1966; Attempted Microwave Measurement of Temperature of a Shock-heated Plasma (ibid), 1967; Skin-depth Effect of a Cylindrical Shock-Produced Plasma, 1968; Measurement of Plasma Temperature Using a Waregnide Probe, 1968. Address: Department of Physics, Ahmadu Bello University, Zaria, Nigeria.

ARSHAD, Muhammad, born 18th June 1936. Civil Engineer. Education: B.Sc., Edwardes College, Peshawar, Pakistan, 1954; B.Sc.(Engrng.), Northampton College of Avanced Technology (now the City University), 1963. Married to Pauline, 5 children. Appointments: Senior Engineering Assistant, British Railways, now on secondment to East African Railways; Assistant Engineer, Unganda Engineering District, 1966-68; Deputy District Civil Engineer, Nairobi Engineering District, 1968—. Memberships: Institution of Civil Engineers. Chartered Engineer; East African Institution of Engineers; Fellow, Permanent Way Instutution. Address: East African Railways, P.O. Box 30536, Nairobi, Kenya.

ARYA, Om Prakash, born 8th October 1930. Medical Practitioner. Education: M.B.B.S., Punjab, India; D.T.M. & H., U.K.; D.P.H., London, U.K.; D.I.H., Soc. Apoth., London, U.K.; Dip. Ven., Liverpool, U.K. Appointments: Medical Officer, Army Medical Corps, India; ibid, District Medical Officer &, Medical Officer (Special Grade), Ministry of Health, Uganda; Senior Medical Officer & Honorary Lecturer, Department of Preventative Medicine, Makerere University, Kampala, Uganda. Memberships: International Union against the Venereal Diseases & the Treponematoses; British Medical Association; Associate, Association of Physicians of E. Africa; Medical Protection Society, London, U.K. Contributor of many articles to medical journals. Honours: Scholarship— Vernacular Final Exam., 1943; several prizes in sport while at school & college. Address: Senior Med. Officer, University Health Serv., Makere University, Kampala, Uganda.

ARYEE, Isaac Okine-Quarshie, born 4th August 1918. Banker. Education: Prince of Wales School, Freetown, Sierra Leone. Married, 4 sons, 1 daughter. Appointments: Sub-Accountant, Barclays Bank DCO, Freetown, Sierra Leone, 1958-60; Sub-Manager, ibid, Tepa, Ghana, 1960-62; Manager, ibid, Bekwai, Ghana, 1962-65; ibid, Dunkwa, 1965-67; ibid, Takoradi, 1967—. Memberships: Grand United Order of Oddfellows; Takoradi Tennis Club. Address: P.O. Box 0100, Takoradi, Ghana.

ASANTE, George Stephen, born 3rd October 1930. University Professor. Education: Presbyterian School, Mpraeso, Ghana, 1936-45; Grade I Certificate, Adisadel College, Cape Coast, 1946-49; Certificate, Agricultural Training College, Kumasi, 1950-52; B.S.A. (Biochemistry), Purdue University, U.S.A., 1956-69; Ph.D., Cornell University, U.S.A., 1959-63. Married, 5 children. Appointments: Research Assistant, Cornell University, U.S.A., 1959-63; Lecturer, Senior Lecturer, University of Science & Technology, Kumasi, Ghana, 1963-65;

Associate Professor, Acting Head, Department of Biochemistry, ibid. Memberships: Biochemical Society, London. U.K.; Ghana Science Association; Management Board, Food Research Institute, Ghana; President, Mpraeso Youth Association. Author of papers in his field. Address: University of Science & Technology, Kumasi, Ghana.

ASARE, Jacob Kwame, born 29th September 1929. Engineer. Education: University College, Gold Coast, 1949-51; University of Southampton, 1951-54; University of Ghana, 1967-70; B.Sc.,(Engrng.) & LL.B.(Hons.). Married, 3 children. Appointments: Assistant Engineer, Broadcasting; Engineer, ibid; Deputy Chief Engineer; Director of Engineering. Memberships: Institution of Electrical Engineers; Fellow, Ghana Institution of Engineers; Chartered Engineer. Publications: Wired Broadcasting Service in Ghana. Address: Ghana Broadcasting Corporation, P.O. Box 1633, Accra, Ghana.

ASEFA, Kapanda, born 17th October 1937. Diplomat. Education: B.A.(Pub. Admin.) HSIU. Married, 3 children. Appointments: Registry Clerk, Department of Forestry, Limbe, Malawi, 1958; Soapmaker, Lever Bros. Ltd., Limbe, 1958-61; Administrative Officer, Malawi Government, 1965—; currently, Second Secretary, Malawi Embassy, Addis Ababa, Ethiopia. Rosicrucian. Address: Malawi Embassy, P.O. Box 2316, Addis Ababa, Ethiopia.

ASFAHA CAHSAI (Kegnezmatch), born Adi Ugri, 19th September 1919. High Court Judge. General Education. Married, 5 children. Appointments: Teacher; Inspector of Schools; Establishment Officer; Director of Labour; Director General of Education; High Court Judge, Asmara, Ethiopia. Memberships: Chairman, Blin School of Asmara; ibid, Asmara Officers' Club; Eritrean Welfare Society of Asmara. Publications: School Books. Honours: Awarded title of Kegnezmatch by H.I.M. Hailé Selassié I. Address: High Court, Asmara, Ethiopia.

ASHIWAJU, M. Garba, born 16th December 1935. University Lecturer. Education: Primary & Secondary Education in Nigeria; Polytechnic & University Education in England & Germany respectively; specialized in African Languages & History. Appointments: Lecturer, Nigerian Languages, Department of Languages, African Institute, University of Leipzig, 1964-68; Lecturer, History, Ahmadu Bello University, Zaria, 1968-69; Lecturer, ibid, Abdullahi Bayero College, Ahmadu Bello University, Kano, 1969—; Editor (Languages) of Kano Studies. Member & North-Western Area Secretary of the Historical Society of Nigeria. Publications: Ashiwaju/Brauner: Lehrbuch der Hausasprache, 1965/66; Ashiwaju: Lehrbuch der Yorubasprache, Leipzig, 1968; Forms & Methods of Colonial conquest in Africa during the 19th century, 1965; Some forms of plural building in Hausa, ibid. Recipient of Leipzig University Prize for Excellent work, 1967. Address: c/o Department of History, Ahmadu Bello University, Zaria, Nigeria.

ASHONG, Daniel Cobblah, born 16th January 1902. Retired Civil Servant; Magistrate. Education: Elementary School, 1920-24; Accra Royal School, Ghana, 1924-27; Several external university courses, 1929-36. Widower, 10 children. Appointments: Entered Civil Service, 1928; Promoted, 1st Division, superceding 26 seniors, 1947; Senior Executive Officer, Gold Coast Political Administration; Sec. Local Government Service Commission, Local Government Service, Gold Coast, 1956-58; District Magistrate, 1960—. Member, Rodger Club (now defunct), Accra. Honours: Book Prizes & Badge of Merit awarded by late Sir James Maxwell, then Governor of Gold Coast, Accra Royal School, 1927. Address: District Court, Bechem, B/A. 10, Bechem, Brong-Ahafe, Ghana.

ASHUN, Joseph Enimil, born 6th December 1929. Medical Practitioner. Education: B.Sc., London; U.K.; M.B., Ch.B., Aberdeen; M.R.C.P., Edinburgh; D.T.M. & H., Liverpool. Appointments: Physician, Ministry of Health, Ghana; Physician Specialist in Private Practice. Address: West-End Clinic, P.O. Box 0560, Takoradi, Ghana.

ASKE, Sigurd, born 20th July 1914. Missiologist; Mass Communications Expert. Education: Primary, secondary & theological education, Norway; studies in U.K., 1935-36, China, 1936-38, Yale University Divinity School, U.S.A., 1947, Columbia University, 1948, & Japan, 1951-52; B.A., Augustana College, Sioux Falls, S.D., U.S.A.; M.A., Chinese Religion, Kennedy School of Missions; Ph.D., Missiology, Chinese Religion, Hartford Seminary Foundation, Conn. Appointments: Assistant China Director, Lutheran World Convention, Chungking, China, 1945; National Student Secretary, Lutheran Church of China, Hankow, 1946; Superintendent, Japan Mission, Evangelical Lutheran Free Church of Norway, Kobe, Japan, 1950-57; Consultant, Sei Bun Sha (literature), 1954-57; Associate Director, Department of World Missions, Lutheran World Federation, Geneva, Switzerland, 1958-67; Director, ibid, 1967-68; General Director, Broadcasting Services, ibid, 1960—; Executive Director, World Association for Christian Broadcasters, 1961-63. Memberships: Ecumenical Satellite Commission, 1970—; Christian Literature Fund; Fellow, Royal Asiatic Society; Central Committee, World Association for Christian Communication, 1968—. Author of numerous articles in secular, professional & religious press & publications, on missiological, communication & development issues, in several languages. Co-editor of several books, among them: The 75 year History of the Evangelical Lutheran Free Church of Norway, 1952. Honours, prizes: Centennial Award, Augustana College, Sioux Falls, S.D., U.S.A., 1961. Address: General Director, Lutheran World Federation Broadcasting Service, 150 route de Ferney, 1211 Geneva 20, Switzerland.

ASLAM, Syed Ali, born 11th February 1911. Physician; Pathologist. Education: M.B.B.S., K.E. Medical College, India; Ajmal College, Delhi. Married. Appointments: Captain, Indian Army, 1940-51; Reached rank of Lieutenant-Colonel; Research on Diabetes Mellitus, Nairobi,

Kenya, 1951—. Memberships: Youth Freedom League, India; Muslim Brothers, Egypt; British Medical Association; Kenya Medical Association; United Kenya Club; President, Islamic Cultural Society. Publications: Republican System of Islam. Discoverer of Eugenin Compound. Honours: 8th Army Star; Italian Star Service Medal; War Medal; Certificate of Devotion to Duty of Highest Order, 1949. Address: P.O. Box 3285, Nairobi, Kenya.

ASSIMENG, John Maxwell, born 15th November 1939. University Lecturer. Education: B.A.(Hons.), Sociology, University of Shana, Legon, 1961-64; D.Phil., University of Oxford, U.K., 1964-68. Currently with Department of Sociology, University of Ghana, Legon. Memberships: Assistant Editor, Ghana Sociological Association; Society of African Church History; Editor, Legon Observer, Legon Society on National Affairs. Publications: Status Anxiety & Cultural Revival (Ghana J. Sociol.), 1969; Religious & Secular Messianism in Africa (Research Review, Legon), 1969; Dynamics of Religious Sects (Ghana Bull. Theol.), 1970; Sectarian Allegiance & Political Authority (J. Mod. African Studies), 1970. Address: Department of Sociology, University of Ghana, Legon, Ghana.

ASUNI, Tolani, born 6th January 1924. Medical Practitioner. Education: Igbobi College, Lagos, Nigeria, 1937-42; B.A., M.B., B.Ch., B.A.O., Trinity College, Dublin University, Ireland, 1945-51; D.P.M., M.D., M.A., London University, U.K., 1957-60. Appointments: Senior Specialist Psychiatrist & Medical Superintendent, Neuro-Psychiatric Hospital, Abeokuta, Nigeria; Associate Lecturer, Universities of Ibadan & Lagos. Memberships: Expert Committee, World Health Organization; President, Association of Psychiatrists in Africa; Vice-President, Association of Psychiatrists in Nigeria; General Secretary, Nigerian Criminological Society; Scientific Commission, International Society of Criminology; Preparatory Committee for Forensic Psychiatry, World Psychiatric Association. Publications: Suicide in Western Nigeria (B.M.J.), 1962; Community Development & Public Health By-Product of Soc. Psychiatry (W.A. Med. J.), 1964; Attempted Suicide in W. Nigeria (ibid), 1967; Homicide in Western Nigeria (Brit. J. Psych.), 1969. Address: Aro Neuro-Psychiatric Hospital, Abeokuta, Nigeria.

ATANG, Protus George, born 15th September 1933. Veterinary Surgeon. Education: Class I Veterinary Assistant Certificate, Veterinary School, Vom, Nigeria, 1955; B.V.M.S., University of Glasgow Veterinary School, U.K., 1961; Diploma in Tropical Veterinary Medicine (D.T.V.M.), The Royal (Dick) School of Veterinary Medicine, Edinburgh), 1964; Member of the Royal College of Veterinary Surgeons. Appointments: Commissioned 2nd Lieutenant, British Army, 1959; Veterinary Practitioner, U.K., 1961; Veterinary Officer, Cameroon Government Service, 1962; Director, Veterinary Services, Cameroon, 1962-66; External Examiner, Medicine, Veterinary School, Vom, Nigeria, 1962-65; Deputy Director, Inter-African Bureau for Animal Health, O.A.U., 1966-69; Diriector, ibid, 1969—; International Co-ordinator, Joint Project Against Contagious Bovine Pleuropneumonia, 1970; Board of Governors, College of African Wildlife Management, Tanzania. Memberships: Kenya Veterinary Association; Donovan Maule Theatre, Nairobi. Author & co-author of papers in professional publications. Honours: Prize, Scholar of the Year, Veterinary School, Vom, Nigeria, 1955; Certificate of Merit (2nd Class) in Medicine, University of Glasgow Veterinary School, 1961. Address: O.A.U./I.B.A.H., P.O. Box 30786, Nairobi, Kenya.

ATANGANA, Valentin, born 4th December 1932. Mayor. Education: C.E.P.E. Married, 10 children. Appointments: Secretary, Tribunal of 1st degree, S.A.A., 1956; Mayor, C.M.R., S.A.A., 1963; President, Sub-section National Union of Cameroun (U.N.C.), S.A.A., 1966; President, Section U.N.C., Lekie, 1969; Member, National Political Bureau, U.N.C., 1969. Honours: Order of Merit, 2nd Class, Cameroun. Address: B.P. 85, Cameroun.

ATHIYO, Edward Lorika, born 29th August 1929. Administrative Officer. Education: Lotome Primary School, Uganda; Agora High School; Administration Course on Local Government, U.K., 1961. Personal details: Father served in Colonial Government. Appointments: Veterinary Learner, 1953; Accounts Clerk, Karamoja, D.A.; Clerk to Council, ibid; Executive Officer; Secretary, Karamoja, D.A.; Secretary-General, ibid, 1953-63; District Commissioner; Senior Administrative Officer, Grade I. Memberships: Uganda Club; Y.M.C.A. Attended Uganda Constitutional Conference, 1961-62. Address: P.O. Box 1, Mbarara, Uganda.

ATITSOGBUI, Ayawovi Godwin, born 1910. Magistrate. Education: Elementary School, Keta, Ghana, 1921-28; New African University College, Anloga, 1938-42; Local Government Training School, Accra, 1952; reading law, School of Careers, Accra, 1968—. Appointments: Personal Secretary to Togbui Sri II, Awomefia of Anlo, O.B.E., C.B.E., 1st Traditional Chief, Volta Region, Gold Coast Legislative Council, Accra, & Member, Joint Provincial Council of Chiefs, Dodoma; Personal & Travelling Secretary to Togbui Katsriku Awusu II, Awadada (Field-Marshal) of Anlo; Assistant State Secretary, Anlo State, Anloga, 1929-38; Certified Registrar, 1930-38; Clerk-Treasurer, 1952 (Certified); Magistracy, 1967—. Memberships: Regional Chairman, Volta Region, Local Government Workers Union; National Chairman, ibid; Odd Fellow. Honours: Prizes awarded by Local Government Workers Union, Accra, 1965. Address: P.O. Box 22, Nkonya Ahenkro, Ghana.

ATSYOR, John Olympio Kwesi Ekudi, born 9th March 1933. Psychiatrist. Education: Roman Catholic Primary School, Likpe-Mate, Volta Region, Ghana; Roman Catholic Middle School, Kpando, Volta Region; St. Augustine's College, Cape Coast, 1948-54; M.B., Ch.B., B.A.O., Queen's University Medical School, Belfast, U.K., 1957-63; Institute of Psychiatry,

Maudsley St., London, 1965-66; Paddington Day Hospital, London, 1966-67; D.P.M., Horton Hospital, Epsom, Surrey, 1967-68. Married, 3 children. Appointments: Teacher, Bishop Herman Secondary School, 1954-56; Houseman, Mater Hospital, Belfast, 1963-64; Medical Officer, Korle-Bu & Mental Hospital, Accra, Ghana, 1964-65; Medical Officer (Psychiatry), Ankaful Mental Hospital, Cape Coast, 1968—. Memberships: British Medical Association; Royal Medico-Psychological Association; Ghana Mental Health Association. Publications: The Doctor & Witchcraft (Med. Jrnl. of Queen's Univ.). Address: Ankaful Mental Hospital, P.O. Box 412, Cape Coast, Ghana.

ATTA AGYEMAN IV (Nana), Sanwuabra, Omanhene of Sefwi Bekwai, born 1st January 1908. Farmer. Education: 7th Standard Examination, Roman Catholic School, Kumasi, Ghana, 1925. Married, 5 wives, 33 children. Appointments: Clerk, the Omanhene's Native Court, 1926-30; Law Clerk, with C.E.M. Abbensetts of the Supreme Court, 1932; Army, 1941-43; Elected & installed as Omanhene of Sefwi Bekwai, 1943-45; Abdicated, 1945; Licensed Letter Writer, 1945-51; Re-elected, Omanhene, 1957; Destooled by C.P.P. Government, —1967; Reinstated by N.L.C., 1967. Address: P.O. Box 28, Sefwi Bekwai, Ghana.

ATTAL, Victor, born 26th February 1916. Director of Society, Maison Zagdoun. Address: 23 Rue Massicault, Tunis, Tunisia.

ATTAL, Victor, born 14th December 1924. Dental Surgeon. Education: D.D.S.(Paris), France; French Certificate of Physiology, Paris; French M.S. of Endodontics, Paris. Appointments: Odontologiste, Expert Consultant to Courts of Justice. Address: Expert pres les Tribunaux, 15 Avenue de Paris, Tunis, Tunisia.

ATTOH, Julius Nathan Aryeetey, born 1st June 1943. Architect. Education: James Town Methodist School, Accra, Ghana, 1950-58; W.A.S.C. Grade I, G.C.E., Government Secondary Technical School, Takoradi, 1959-63; B.Sc.(Tech.), Design, University of Science & Technology, Kumasi, 1963-67; M.Sc., Architecture, ibid, 1967-69. Appointments: Architect, Keneth Scott Associates, 1969; ibid, P.W.D., Accra, 1969—. Address: P.W.D. (Architects Branch), P.O. Box 136, Accra, Ghana.

ATUMRASE, James Olaitan, born 6th June 1924. Medical Practitioner (Orthopaedic Surgeon). Education: King's College, Lagos, Nigeria, 1939-43; University College, Ibadan, 1949-52; M.B., B.S., St. George's Hospital Medical School, London, U.K., 1952-55. Appointments: House Surgeon, Whipps Cross Hospital, London, 1955-56; House Physician, Coventry, 1956; House Surgeon, University College Hospital, Ibadan, Nigeria, 1957-58; Medical Officer, Federal Ministry of Health, Lagos, 1958-69; Specialist Surgeon, Ministry of Health, Lagos State, 1969—. Memberships: Island Club, Lagos; Fellow, Royal College of Surgeons, Glasgow. Contributor to professional journals. Address: Royal Orthopaedic Hospital, Igbobi, Lagos, Nigeria.

AUDU, Ishaya Sha'aibu, born 1st March 1927. Physician; Paediatrician; University Vice-Chancellor. Education: Primary & Secondary Education, St. Bartholomew's Schools, Wusasa, Zaria, 1933-44; University Education, Ibadan, Nigeria, & London, U.K., 1946-54; ibid, U.S.A., 1964-65; M.B., B.S. & D.C.H.(Lond.); M.R.C.P.(Edin.); D.T.M. & H.(Liv.). Personal details: married Victoria Abosede Ohiorhe, S.R.N. & S.C.M.; 1 son & 5 daughters. Appointments: House Officer, Senior House Officer, Registrar, Ibadan, 1955-58; Consultant Physician-Paediatrician, Government of Northern Nigeria & Personal Physician to the Premier, 1960-62; Lecturer-Associate Professor, Paediatrics, University of Lagos, 1962-66; Vice-Chancellor, Abu, Zaria, 1966—. Memberships: Nigeria Medical Association; Royal Society of Medicine, London, U.K.; Association of West African Physicians; Paediatric Association of Nigeria. Publications: Author of over 20 articles in Medical Journals; Medical Education in Nigeria, 1969. Honours: Ware Prize in Pathology, London University, 1952; Hon. L.H.D., Ohio University, 1968; Hon. F.M.C.(Paed.), Nigeria, 1969. Address: Vice-Chancellor, Ahmadu Bello University, Zaria, Nigeria.

AUGE, Leon, born 1st November 1929. Magistrate; President de Chambre a la Cour Supreme. Education: Lic. en droit; Diploma d'eleve titulaire de l'Ecole Pratique des Hautes Etudes (Economic & Social Science Section). Appointments: Chargé, Cultural Affairs, Ministry of Labour, 1958; Director, Social Affairs, 1959—; Assistant to the Procurer of the Republic, 1963; Councillor to the Supreme Court, 1966; Member, Higher Council of Resort, l'Office Africain et Malgache de la proprieti industrielle. Memberships: President, Association of the Students of Gabon, 1947-53; President, du Conseil de Surveillance de l'Iuprimerie Gabonaise. Publications: Le Gabon (International Encyclopaedia of Comparative Law); L'Evolution Constitutionelle du Gabon, Revue Senegalaise de droit. Honours: Chevalier de l'Etoile Equationale. Address: President de Chambre a la Cour Supreme, B.P. 775, Libreville, Gabon.

AUSTARA, Oystein, born 16th October 1931. Forest Entomologist. Education: State Forestry School, Kongsberg, Norway, 1956-58; M.F., Faculty of Forestry, Agricultural University of Norway, 1959-62. Appointments: Forest Entomologist, Norwegian Forest Research Institute, 1432 Vollebekk, 1962—; Forest Entomologist, Seconded to East African Agriculture & Forestry Research Organization, Nairobi, Kenya, 1966-70. Memberships: Society of Norwegian Foresters; Norwegian Entomological Society. Author of several papers published in agricultural journals. Address: Norwegian Forest Research Institute, 1432 Vollebekk, Norway.

AUSTEN PETERS (Brigadier, Chief) Adeniyi Olumuyiwa, Bajito of Joga Orile Egbado, Akogun Ejiwa of Iddo, Akogun Olofin of Lagos, born 2nd April 1924. Orthopaedic Surgeon; Director-General, Armed Forces Medical Services, Nigeria. Education: Grammar School,

Abeokuta, Nigeria; King's College, Lagos; Prince of Wales' College (University Section), Achimota, Ghana; Trinity College, Cambridge, U.K.; B.A., 1945; M.B.B.Chir., 1952; M.A., 1956; Medical College, London Hospital; Institute of Orthopaedics, London University (Royal National Orthopaedic Hospital), London; attended various orthopaedics courses & demonstrations in 1954, 1955, & 1957. Appointments: House Surgeon & Casualty, St. Mary's Hospital for Women & Children, London, U.K.; House Physician & Casualty, St. Alfege's Hospital; House Surgeon, Beckenham General Hospital; ibid, Brighton General Hospital, 1950-52; Assistant to General Practitioner, London, 1951-52; Senior House Officer in Orthopaedics, Lewisham General Hospital, London, 1952-53; ibid, Royal National Orthopaedic Hospital, Stanmore, 1953; Group Registrar in Orthopaedics, Croydon Group of Hospitals, 1953-54; Junior Registrar & Lecturer, Department of Venereal Disease, London Hospital, 1954-55; Group Registrar in Orthopaedics, West & East Ham Group of Hospitals, St. Mary's Hospital for Women, Plaistow Hospital, & others, 1955-58; Medical Officer, Royal Orthopaedic Hospital, Igbobi, Yaba, Nigeria, 1958-61; Commanding Officer, Military Hospital, Yaba, 1961-64; Senior Medical Officer, 2 Brigade, Royal Nigerian Army; Acting Orthopaedic Surgeon, Military Hospital, Yaba, 1961—; Director, Medical Services, Nigerian Army, 1964; Acting Director-General, Armed Forces Medical Services of Nigeria, 1966—. Memberships include: Royal College of Surgeons; Licentiate, Royal College of Physicians; Fellow, Royal Society of Medicine, 1957; Associate Mbr., British Orthopaedic Association, 1959; Chairman, Ikeja Division, Amateur Boxing Association; Executive Board, International Council of Sport & Physical Education (advisory body to UNESCO), 1960; Minister's Nominee, National Sports Council of Nigeria, 1962; Nominated Military Member, ex Officio, of: Nigerian Medical Council; Board of the University College Hospital, Ibadan; Board of the University Teaching Hospital, Lagos; Pharmacy Board of Nigeria; The Nursing Council of Nigeria; The Midwives Board of Nigeria. Attended numerous conferences & congresses of a medical or military nature including: International Committee of Military Medicine & Pharmacy, Athens, 1961; 2nd International Advance Course for Military Surgeons, Florence, 1962; International Red Cross Centenary, Geneva, Switzerland, 1963; Association of Military Surgeons of the U.S.A., Washington, U.S.A., 1966. Keen sportsman, awarded colours for Cricket & Football, King's College, Lagos, 1938-39; ibid, Trinity College, Cambridge, U.K., 1943-45; London Hospital Medical College, 1946-50. Address: Armed Forces Medical Services, Ministry of Defence, Lagos, Nigeria.

AVA AVA, Jean-Louis, born 18th October 1922. Teacher; Politician. Education: Primary Certificate; Elementary Diploma. Married, 11 children. Appointments: Director, various primary schools; Member of Legislative Assembly, 1965-67 (re-elected, 1970-75); President, Parliamentary Group, National Cameroun Union (U.N.C.), Alcamor. Composer of (words & music) several religious & patriotic hymns. Cameroun Representative at the 14th July Celebrations, Paris, France. Honours: Cameroun Title of Merit, 3rd Class; Knight, Cameroun Order of Valour. Address: B.P. 110, Akonolinga, Cameroun.

AVAFIA, Kwami Emmanuel, born Amedzofe, Volta Region, Ghana, 27th July 1940. Librarian; Sociologist. Education: Secondary: Mawuli School, 1955-60; Library training in Ghana Library School, 1961-62; Honours Degree, Sociology, University of Ghana, Legon, 1963-66. Personal details: son of a Presbyterian Priest. Appointments: Assistant Librarian, Parliament House Library; Cataloguer, University of Ghana Library; Elected Fellow, Legon Hall, 1966; Documents Librarian, University of Zambia, 1968-70. Memberships: Ghana Libarary Association; British Library Association; Ghana Sociological Association. Currently working on indigenous African Religions. Undertook a study of attitudes of the educated toward indigenous Ghanaian beliefs. Comparative study in Zambia (Urbarn Lusaka). Honours: Toured a number of libraries in Africa & Europe, 1969; Student Leader, Legon Hall, 1964. Address: c/o The University of Zambia.

AWOLOWO, Obafemi (Chief), born Ikenne, Ijebu Remo, Nigeria, 6th March 1909. Statesman & Politician. Education: Wesley College, Ibadan, Nigeria; London University, London, England. Married, 2 sons, 2 daughters. Appointments include: Teacher, 1928-29; Stenographer, 1930-34; Newspaper Reporter, 1934-35; Motor Transporter & Produce Buyer, 1936-44; Solicitor & Advocate, Supreme Court of Nigeria, 1947-51; Minister of Local Government & Leader of Government Business, Western Region, 1952-54; Co-founder & First General Secretary of Egbe Omo Oduduwa, a Yoruba Cultural Movement; Founder & Federal President of the Action Group of Nigeria; Premier, Government of Western Region of Nigeria, 1954-59; Leader of the Opposition in Federal Parliament, 1960-62; Leader of Yorubas, 1966—; Chancellor of University of Ife, Nigeria, 1967—; Vice-Chairman, Federal Executive Council & Federal Commissioner for Finance, 1967—. Memberships include: Fellow of the Royal Economic Society; Associate of the Institute of Journalists. Publications include: Path to Nigerian Freedom; Awo (Autobiography); Thoughts on Nigerian Constitution; My Early Life; The People's Republic; & various pamphlets. Honours, Prizes, etc.: B.Com.(Hons., Lond.), 1944; LL.B.(Lond.), 1946; B.L.(Hons.), 1946; LL.D., 1961; D.Sc.(Econ.), 1967; D.Litt., 1968; Ashiwaju of Ijebu Remo; Losi of Ikenne; Lisa of Ijeun; Apesin of Oshogbo; Odole of Ife; Ajagunla of Ado Ekiti; Odofin of Owo; Obong Ikpan Isong og Ibibioland. Address: P.O. Box 136, Ibadan, Western State, Nigeria, W.A.

AWOONOR-WILLIAMS, Juliana Angel, born 24th June 1924. Teacher. Education: Accra Government Girls' School, Ghana, 1937-40; Teachers Certificate A, Svhimoys College, Accra, 1941-44; Associate Certificate in Education, University College of Ghana, 1951-52; Social Studies, New School for Social Research, New York, U.S.A., 1961. Personal details: member of Royal Family of Lante Dzanwe, AGA division of Ussher Town; married, 2 sons. Appointments:

Headmistress, Sra Middle Girls' School, 1950-51; Tutor, Aburi Girls' Secondary School & Teacher Training Colleges, Aburi & Odumase-Krobo, 1953-57; National Organizing Secretary, Ghana Red Cross Society, 1957-67; Secretary-General, ibid, 1967-69; Headmistress, Presbyterian Girls' Vocational Training Centre, Accra, 1969—. Memberships: Vice-President, United Nations Association of Ghana; Gahan Womens' Association. Honours: Grand Medal, State of Ghana, 1968; Title of Humanitarian, Ancient & Mystical Order Rosaecrusis, 1969. Address: Presbyterian Girls' Vocational Training Centre, Accra, Ghana.

AWUKU, Kwabena Anakwa, born 12th March 1929. University Lecturer. Education: Achimota Secondary School, Ghana, 1945-48; Achimota Training College, 1949-50; B.Sc., Agriculture(London), University of Ghana, 1952-57; M.S., Agricultural Education, Cornell University, U.S.A., 1960-61; M.A., Biology, University of Northern Iowa, 1966-68. Married, 2 sons. Appointments: Junior Teacher, Grade I, Ministry of Education, Ghana, 1951-52; Education Officer, ibid, 1957-62; Senior Education Officer, 1962-63; Lecturer, Animal Science, University of Ghana, 1963-66; Lecturer, Science Teaching, University College of Cape Coast, 1966—. Memberships: Ghana Association of Science Teachers; Convener, Training College Panel, 1964-66; General Secretary, 1969—; Chairman, Curriculum Development Committee, 1969—. Address: Department of Curriculum Studies, Faculty of Education, University College, Cape Coast, Ghana.

AWUKU-ASABRE, Timothy, born 14th November 1919. Medical Practitioner. Education: Mfantsipim, Ghana, 1935-39; Achimota, Ghana, 1941-43; Edinburgh University, Scotland, 1944-50. Appointments include: National Health Service, England; House Officer, 1952-53; Ministry of Health, Ghana, 1954-57; Genral Practice, 1957—. Memberships include: Royal Medical Society, Edinburgh. Address: P.O. Box 458, Kumasi, Ghana.

AWUMEE, Jenkins Kwame, born Achito, Volta Region, Ghana, 27th December 1936. Sales Representative. Education: Alakple Roman Catholic School, Ghana, 1946-54; Anloga Secondary School, Ghana, 1954-58; Diploma Courses, National School of Salesmanship, Manchester, U.K., 1967. Married. Appointments: Managing Director, J. K. Awumee Ltd., a company registered in The Gambia & representing office machinery & equipment. Memberships: Institution of Works Managers, London, U.K.; Associate, All The Grand Lodges of Amorci of the World. Address: P.O. Box 574, Bathurst, The Gambia.

AWUTE, D. Pascal, born 16th May 1937. Agricultural Engineer; Agronomist. Education: Lycée Bonnecaniere, Lome Togo; Regional School of Agriculture, France; Higher School of Tropical Agriculture, France; Utah State University, Logan, U.S.A.; Madison University, ibid; Institut Agronomique Mediterranean, France; Institut Padagogique d'Agronome, France. Married, 1 son & 1 daughter. Appointments: Deputy Director, Semnard, Dapango, Togo; Director, Agricultural Modernization, Est, Mono, Togo; Chief, Agriculture, Loma Kara, Togo; ibid, Dapango; Deputy Director, Agricultural Services, Lome, Togo. Address: Agricultural Engineer, Direction Services Agricoles, Lome, Togo.

AYENI, John Peter, born 11th February 1941. Physician. Education: Bar Primary School, 1947-51; Aloi Primary School, 1952-54; Boroboro Junior Secondary School, 1955-56; Sir Samuel Baker Senior Secondary School, 1957-60; Higher School Certificate, Ntare School, 1961-62; B.M., B.S., Makerere University College, Kampala, 1963-68. Married. Appointments: Houseman, Mulago Hospital, 1968-69; Medical Officer, Masaka Hospital, 1969-70; Postgraduate course in Surgery, Makerere University, Kampala, 1970—. Memberships: Uganda Medical Association; The Medical Protection Society Ltd., London, U.K. Address: Department of Surgery, Mulago Hospital, P.O. Box 7051, Kampala, Uganda.

AYISI, Christian Harry, born Ghana, 14th September 1928. Educator. Education: Teacher's Training, Wesley College, Kumasi, Ghana, 1943-46; B.A. (London External), University College of Ghana, 1957-60; Self educated for London External Academic Diploma in Education, 1965; Educational Psychology, University of London Institute of Education, 1966; M.A., 1967; Ph.D., 1969. Appointments: Teacher, Methodist Middle Boarding Schools, 1947-54; ibid, Prempeh College, Kumasi, 1954-57; ibid, 1960-66; Assistant Headmaster, ibid, 1963-66; currently Lecturer in Educational Psychology, University College of Cape Coast, Ghana. Memberships: Ghana Mental Health Association; Textbooks & Publications Committee, Ghana Ministry of Education; Wesley College Board of Governors; Ghana Methodist Conference. Contributor of entries on Psychology & Mental Health to African Encyclopedia. Address: Faculty of Education, University College of Cape Coast, Cape Coast, Ghana.

AYOOLA, Ebenezer Olufemi, born 24th July 1928. Nigeria High Court Judge. Education: Saint Peter's College, Oxford University, U.K.; Inner Temple, London; University of Durham. Degrees: M.A.B.C.L.(Dunelm); B.Sc.(Econ.); LL.M.(London);Dip.Educ.(Oxon.); Barrister-at-Law. Appointments: Judge, High Court, Western State, Nigeria, 1967—. Formerly Chairman, Editorial Board of Nigerian Monthly Law Report. Address: P.O. Box 1268, Ibadan, Nigeria.

AYOUNE, Jean-Remy, born 5th June 1914. Civil Administrator. Education: Certificate of Final Secondary Studies. Married, 10 children. Appointments: Editor, Press & Information Service in the Cabinet of the High Commissioner General for France, Brazzaville, Congo; Counsellor, French Embassy in West Germany; First Gabon Ambassador to West Germany; First Secretary General of the Gabon Government; Ministry of Public Affairs; Chief Civil Administrator, Ministry of Foreign Affairs & Co-operation. Memberships: Founder, Secretary of the Gabon Mutual Society; ibid, Union for educating young Africans, Brazzaville; Gabon Official's Union; Political Bureau of the Gabon Democratic Party. Author of several articles on sociological studies. Honours: Commander, Equatorial Star; ibid, Legion of Honour; Grand Officer, Camerounian Order of Distinction; ibid, Central African Republic Order of Distinction; Mauritanian Order of Distinction; Grand Cross, German Order of Distinction; Knight of the Academic Palms; ibid, Black Star of Benin; Commander of the Order of the Leopards. Address: B.P. 389, Libreville, Gabon.

AZADJI, Prosper, born 1915. Civil Servant Retired. Education: Diploma from the William Ponty School. Married, 5 children. Head of the Cabinet, Ministry of Finances, 1959-60; Deputy, National Dahomey Assembly, 1964-66; Principal Administrative Secretary to the C.E. Address: Hinvi-Dovo, via Attogon, Dahomey.

AZANTINLOW (Sir) Ayieta, Paramount Chief of Builsa, born 1903. Personal details: Self-educated; Married, 11 wives, 30 children. Appointments: Paramount Chief, installed, 1931-; Vice-President, Acting President, 1966; President, Upper Region House of Chiefs, Upper Region, Ghana, 1968–. Memberships: Farmers Association; Civic Education. Honours: Recipient of following medals: King George V; King George V & Queen Mary; King George VI & Queen Mary, 1937; Queen Elizabeth II & Grand Medal awarded by N.L.C. Address: Box 31, Sandema via Navrongo, Upper Region, Ghana.

AZIKE, Anyaegbuna, born 9th February 1928. Medical Practitioner. Education: St. Gregory's College, Lagos, Nigeria, 1941-46; University College Dublin, 1947-53. Married, 7 children. Appointments: Medical Officer, Government of Eastern Region, Nigeria, 1955-63; Medical Superintendent, Oji River Leper Settlement, Nigeria; Senior Medical Officer, Onitsha, East Central State, Nigeria, 1965–. Address: 'Wigan House', 57 Tasia Road, Onitsha, East Central State, Nigeria.

AZINGE, Nicholas Olisajindu, born 29th March 1930. Medical Practitioner; Consultant. Education: Government College, Umahia, Nigeria, 1944-49; M.B., B.Ch., B.A.O., University College, Dublin, Ireland, 1957; Postgraduate training, London & Edinburgh, U.K., 1963-64; M.R.C.P., Ireland; D.T.M.&H., Liverpool. Married, 5 children. Appointments: House Surgeon, St. Luke's, Bradford, 1957; House Physician, Royal City of Dublin Hospital, 1958; Medical Officer, Adeoyo Hospital, Ibadan, 1959; Senior Medical Officer, General Hospital, Auchi, 1961-62; Specialist Physician, General Hospital, Benin, 1965–. Memberships: Royal College of Physicians in Ireland; Benin Club. Publications; Anatomy & Physiology Scholarship Prize, 1953; Honours pathology, 1955. Address: Specialist Physician, c/o General Hospital, Benin, Nigeria.

AZU, Diana Gladys Afarley, born 21st January 1943. Social Anthropologist. Education: Secondary O Level, St. Monica's Secondary School, Mampong-Ashanti, Ghana, 1959; A Level, Holy Child Secondary School, Cape Coast, 1960-61; B.A.(Hons.), Sociology, University of Ghana, Legon, 1962-65; M.A., African Studies, ibid, 1965-67; Workshop in Family Planning Communication, Bangkok, Thailand, 1968. Married. Currently Senior Co-ordinator, Planned Parenthood Association of Ghana. Memberships: Y.W.C.A., Accra Branch; Ghanaian Association of University Women; Ghana Sociological Society. Address: Planned Parenthood Association of Ghana, P.O. Box 5756, Accra North, Ghana.

B

BAALLAWY, Said Suleiman, born 4th December 1938. Scientific Research Officer. Education: completed secondary education, 1960; B.Sc.(Hons.), Delhi University, India, 1965; M.Sc., London University, U.K., 1969; Certificate in Malacology, Copenhagen, Denmark, 1967. Appointments: Scientific Research Officer, 1965–. Member, British Society of Parasitology. Publications: Contributor of many articles to medical journals. Honours; Science Prize, Secondary School, 1957; Science Prize, Department of Zoology, Delhi University, India, 1963 & 64. Address: Scientific Research Officer, P.O. Box 1462, Mwanza, Tanzania.

BABALOLA, Adebimpe, born 30th October 1929. Teacher; Manageress. Education: Baptist Day School, Ogbomosho, Nigeria; Baptist Academy, Lagos; Methodist Girls' High School, Lagos; Baptist Women's Teacher Training College, Idi-aba, Abeokuta, 1944-48; Battersea Polytechnic & Northern Polytechnic, London, U.K., 1956-59. Married. Appointments: Teacher, Nigeria, 1949-55; Assistant Domestic Warden, University of Ibadan, 1961-63; Domestic Warden, International School, Ibd, 1963-67; Manageress, Domestic Services, ibid, 1968–. Memberships: Institutional Management Association, London; Hotel & Catering Institute, London. Address: International School, University of Ibadan, Ibadan, Nigeria.

BABALOLA (Chief) Elijah Are, born Oye-Ekiti, Nigeria, 1900. Teacher. Education: All Saint's School, Oshogbo, 1918-21; St. Andrew's College, Oyo, 1922-26; B.A.(Durham), Fourah Bay College, University College, Sierra Leone, 1940-44. Personal details: paternally of high chieftaincies, maternally, royal; married, 10 children; now a High Chief in father's line. Appointments include: Student Teacher, St. Paul's School, Owo, Nigeria, 1924; Headmaster, St. Stephen's Central School, Ikare, 1927-30; Headmaster, St. Philip's Central School, Ile-Ife, 1931-32; Headmaster, St. Stephen's Primary School, Ondo, 1933-34; Headmaster, St. Saviour's Primary School, Ijebu-Ode, 1935-39; Organizer, founder & 1st Proprietor, Ekiti Parapo College, 1937-56; Senior Theological Course for L.Th., St. Andrew's College, Oyo, 1940; Senior Student, Fourah Bay College, Sierra Leone, 1944; Latin Tutor, Ijebu-Ode Grammar School, Nigeria, 1944; English & Method Master, St. Andrew's College, Oyo, 1945-46; Acting Principal, Christ's School, Ado Ekiti, 1947; Principal, Ibadan Boys' High School, 1948-51; Minister of Public Works, Western

Region, 1952-56; Member, House of Representatives, 1952-54; Principal & Founder, Islamic High School, Ibadan, 1957-59; Chairman, Western Nigeria Finance Corporation, 1960-62. Memberships: Scouting Patrol Leader, 2nd Oyo, 1922-26; 1st Ondo, 1924; Rover Scout, 1925; Vice-President, Ife Literary Society, 1931-32; President, Ekiti Progressive Union, 1933-39, 1945-56; Vice-President, Torch Bearers' Association, St. James's Cathedral Church, Ibadan; Local Leader, St. Andrew's College Old Boy's Association; Vice-President, Nigerian Union of Teachers, Ile-Ife District, 1931-32; Treasurer, Ondo District, ibid, 1933-34; Financial Secretary, Ijebu-Ode District, 1935-39; Treasurer, Scripture Union, Ijebu-Ode Church District Council, 1935-39; Secretary, Nigerian Youth Movement, Ijebu-Ode Branch, 1938-39; Leader, Young Men's Christian Association, St. Saviour's Church, Ijebu-Ode, 1937-39; Organizer & Secretary, Abyssinian War Relief Fund, Ijebuland, 1935; Councillor for Oye District, Ekiti Divisional Council, 1947-56. Mover in urbanization in Ekitiland—e.g. Oye town moved to new site, 1928-30 & 1945-49, & 11 other towns & villages moved to Ikole on his advice, 1933. Hobbies: walking, cycling, lawn tennis, reading. Honours, prizes, etc: Grade A Teachers' Certificate, 1928; Iru Ileke (Royal Beaded Emblem), using only by Yoruba Obas, presented to him by Oloye of Oye-Ekiti & his chiefs, 1961. Address: Ososami Road, Obe-Ado, P.O. Box 603, Ibadan, Nigeria.

BABALOLA, S. Adeboye Oladele, born 17th December 1926. University Teacher; Researcher. Education: Christ Church School, Ipetumodu, Nigeria, 1931-37; Iabobi College, Lagos, 1938-43; Achimota College, Accra, 1944-46; Queen's College, Cambridge University, U.K., 1948-51; S.O.A.S., University of London. Appointments: Assistant Master, Igbobi College; Principal, ibid; Lecturer, University of Ife, Nigeria, 1962-4; ibid, University of Lagos, 1964-65; Senior Lecturer, ibid, 1965-67; Professor, African Languages & Literature, 1969—. Memberships: President, Egbe Ijinle Yoruba; ibid, Yoruba Studies Association; West African Linguistic Society. Publications: The Content & Form of Yoruba Ijala, 1966; Awon Oriki Orile, 1967; Iwe Ede Yoruba, 1964/5. Honours: Amamy Talbot Prize, 1966. Address: School of African & Asian Studies, University of Lagos, Nigeria.

BABIIHA (His Excellency) John Kabwimukya, born Toro, Uganda, 1913. Vice-President of the Republic of Uganda; Minister of Animal Industry, Game & Fisheries. Education: St. Leo's High School, Virika; St. Joseph's Secondary School, Mbarara; St. Mary's College, Kisubi; Diploma in Veterinary Science, Makerere College, Uganda, 1933-38; Diploma in Parliamentary Procedure & Practice, Westminster & Belfast Schools, Commonwealth Parliamentary Associations of Great Britain & Northern Irland, 1956; Certificate for Agric., Forestry, Fisheries & Home Econs., W. Va. University, U.S.A., Certificate in Vet. Med., Iowa State Univ. of Sci. & Tech., U.S.A., Cert. in Vet. Med., Colo. State University, U.S.A., & Cert. in Vet. Med., A & M Tex. University System, College Town, U.S.A., under USAID auspices, 1963. Married, with children. Appointments: Assistant Veterinary Officer, Veterinary Department, Uganda, 1939, working at Mbarara Stock Farm, Ankole & East Mengo; Posted to Teso District, 1941; in charge, Acholi District, Northern Region, 1942-43; Bunyoro District, 1943-44; Masaka District, 1944-45; Deputy Treasurer, Government of Toro District, 1945-54; Nominated to Uganda Legislative Council, 1954-58; Elected, ibid, 1958-62; Specially Elected to National Assembly & Appointed Minister of Animal Industry, Game & Fisheries, 1962; Vice-President, Republic of Uganda, 1966—; Founder Member, Uganda People's Congress, & Chairman since its inception; Vice-President, ibid. Memberships: Agricultural Productivity Committee, 1956; Economic Development Council, 1956-57; Direct Election Committee, 1958; District Councils Bills Committee, 1954-55; Uganda Cooperative Development Council, 1955-58; Toro Rukurato (Toro District Council), 1954-60; President, Catholic Schools Association, Toro, 1951-53; Board of Governors, Kichwamba Technical School, Toro; Board of Governors, St. Scholastic's Teacher Training School, Toro; Board of Governors, St. Leo's College, Toro; Buhinga Hospital Advisory Board, Fort Portal; Virika Hospital Advisory Board. Catholic Mission, Virika; Uganda Society; East African Social Research Institute, Makerere; Toro Round Table Society; Ex-Director, Uganda Fish Marketing Corporation; Lions' Club; American Veterinary Medical Association, U.S.A. & Canada, 1963; Chairman, East African Council of Veterinary Education; Uganda Delegate, FAO Conference, Addis Ababa, 1963 & FAO Biennial Conference, Rome, 1965; Leader, Uganda Delegation, Closing Ceremony, Ecumenical Council, Vatican, 1965. President, Good Samaritan Fund; Patron, Uganda Veterinary Association; Uganda Society for Prevention of Cruelty to Animals. Represented Uganda at several international conferences. Publications: The Bayaga Clan in Western Uganda (Uganda Jrnl.), 1957. Honours: Knight, Order of the Stars of Queen Sheba of Ethiopia, Ethiopia, 1962; Pope Paul VI's Gold Medal & Distinguished Diploma as Uganda Delegate to closing of Ecumenical Council, 1965; Order of the Leopard, Democratic Republic of the Congo, 1966; Knight, Order of the Grand Cross of Pius IX, Pope Paul VI, 1970; Head of State Medal & Certificate, International Order of the Lions, 1970. Address: P.O. Box 7003, Kampala, Uganda.

BABOLOLA, Jokotoye, born Ogbomosho, Nigeria, 22nd January, 1927. Chemist & Druggist; Ophthalmic Optician. Education: Baptist School, Abeokuta, 1934-38; Baptist Boys' High School, Abeokuta, 1939-46; School of Pharmacy, Yaba, 1950-53; City University, London University, U.K., 1955-58. Married, 2 children. Appointments: Postal Clerk & Telegraphist, Posts & Tels., Lagos, 1947-49; Personnel Clerk & Typist, Printing & Stationery Department, Secretariat, ibid, 1949-50; Pharmacist, Kingsway Chemists, 1954; Pharmacist, African Timber & Plywood Ltd., Sapele, 1954-55; Research Assistant, Northampton College (now City Univ.), London, U.K. & Assistant Refractionist, London Refraction

Hospital, 1959; Ophthalmic Optician to Government of Northern Nigeria, 1960-63; Managing Director, Western Chemists-Opticians Ltd., 1963—; Managing Director, Allied Enterprises & Distributors Ltd. Memberships: Deacon, Union Baptist Church, Ekotedo, Treasurer, ibid; Ibadan; Past President, Y.M.C.A.; ibid; Ogbomosho Recreation Club. Publications include: Ocular Characteristics in West Africans & Europeans: A Comparison of Two Groups (Brit. J. Physiol. Optics), 1960; The Facilitation of Reading by Partially Blinded Persons (ibid), 1961; A Summary of Refractions in Northern Nigeria (J. Inst. Optical Sci.), 1962. Address: Western Chemists-Opticians Ltd., NW4/348 Dugbe St., Box 150 Ekotedo, Ibadan, Nigeria.

BACCOUCHE, Hedi, born 15th January 1930. Professor. Education: Secondary Education: L. es L., Sorbonne, Paris, France; Institute of Political Sciences, Paris. Appointments: President, Federation of Neo-Destour, France & Europe; Secretary-General of the Tunisien Youth; Deputy Director, Destourienne Socialist Party; Governor of Bizerta; ibid, Sfax; Gabes. President, Director, Social Security in Tunis. Honours: Recipient of distinctions from Morocco, Niger, Finland, Roumania, Jordan, Lebanon & Tunisia. Address: Cité St. Exupéry, Immeuble Mermoz, Tunis, Tunisia.

BACKHOUSE, Mary Joan, born 8th January 1915. Missionary Teacher of the Church Missionary Society. Education: Shrewsbury High School, U.K., 1927-34; B.A.(History), Somerville College, Oxford University, 1934-36; Diploma of Education, ibid, 1937. Personal details: Daughter of Henry Onions Backhouse of Calgary near Salisbury, Rhodesia. Appointments: Assistant Mistress, Romford County High School, 1937-42; ibid, A.C.M.G.S. Elelenwa, 1944-56; Principal, ibid, 1956-57; Assistant Mistress, St. Anne's Ibadan, 1958-61; Principal & Founder, Asaba G.G.S., 1962-67, 1969-70; Diocesan Women's Worker, Benin Anglican Diocese, 1970. Member & Treasurer, Mid-West Principals Conference, 1965. Honours: O.B.E., 1969. Address: 54 Haygate Road, Wellington Salop, U.K.

BADIANI, Vasantrai Nagji Kanji, born Kampala, Uganda, 11th February 1935. Salesman. Education: B.Sc.(Hons.); M.Sc., Inorganic Chemistry. Married, 1 daughter. Education: Teacher, 1960-66; Commonwealth Scholarship, 1966-69; Salesman, Glass Factory, 1969—. Address: P.O. Box 814, Kampala, Uganda.

BADOE, Emmanuel Augustus, born Asokore-Ashanti, Ghana, 17th February 1923. Surgeon. Education: Achimota College; M.B., Ch.B., Sheffield University, U.K.; F.R.C.S., U.K.; D.T.M.&H. Appointments include: House Officer, Infirmary, Wigan, U.K., 1950; Senior House Officer, Kingston General Hospital, Hull, U.K., 1951-53; Medical Officer, Ghana Government, Ghana, 1953; Surgical Specialist, ibid, 1956; Senior Lecturer, Department of Surgery, Ghana Medical School, Accra, Ghana, 1965—; Associate Professor, Department of Surgery, ibid. Memberships include: Secretary, Ghana Medical Association, 1965-68; Association of Surgeons of West Africa; Royal Society of Medicine, London, U.K. Contributor of numerous papers to medical journals. Smith & Nephew Fellow, 1962; Eisenhower Exchange Fellow, 1968. Address: Department of Surgery, Ghana Medical School, P.O. Box 4236, Accra, Ghana.

BADRU, Comfort Ibironke, born Lagos, Nigeria, 13th August 1922. Teacher. Education: St. Peter's School, Lagos; Christ Church Cathedral School, Lagos; Teachers' Grade II Certificate, United Missionary College, Ibadan, 1940-42; Diploma in Nursery Education, Darlington Training College, U.K., 1951-52; Teachers' Intermediate Grade, 1966. Widow, 1 son, 2 daughters. Appointments: Class Teacher, Girls' School, Benin, Nigeria, 1943-44; Class Teacher, Holy Trinity School, Ebute Ero, Lagos, 1945-49; Headmistress, Infant & Junior Section, Christ Church Cathedral School, Lagos, 1950-51; Sectional Head in following Anglican schools, 1953-68: Holy Trinity, Ebute Ero, Lagos; St. Paul's, Breadfruit, Lagos; Headmistress, Bishop Adelakun Howells Memorial School, Suru Lere, Lagos, 1969—. Memberships: Headquarters Commissioner for Cubs, Boy Scout Movement of Nigeria; Akela Leader, ibid; Management Committee; Management Committee, Citizenship & Leadership Training Centre. Honours: Scout Medal of Merit, 1966. Address: Bishop Adelakun Howells Memorial School, Hogan Bassey Crescent, Suru Lere, Lagos, Nigeria.

BADU, Isaac Kwaku, born 16th December 1933. Dental & Oral Surgeon. Education: Prempeh College, Ghana; University of Edinburgh, U.K.; Fellow in Dental Surgery, Royal College of Physicians & Surgeons of Glasgow, Postgraduate Institute of Dental Surgery, Glasgow, 1969. Married, 3 children. Appointments: Houseman, West Middlesex Hospital, 1961; Senior Houseman, Nottingham General Hospital, 1961; Dental Surgeon, Ministry of Health, Ghana; Senior Dental Surgeon, ibid, 1967—. Memberships: British Association of Oral Surgery; Chairman, Ashanti & Brong-Ahafo Division, Ghana Medical Association, 1970-71. Address: Komfo Anokyi Hospital, P.O. Box 1934, Kumasi, Ghana.

BAETA, Amesika Barbara Rose, born 28th May 1937. Managing Director of Flair Catering Services. Education: Achimoa School, Ghana; Heyton College for Girls, Heyton near Liverpool, U.K.; Glasgow & West of Scotland College of Domestic Service, U.K. Personal details: Daughter of the Rev. Professor C. G. Baeta, Head, Department of Religions, University of Ghana, Lagos. Appointments: Catering Officer, Ministry of Health, Ghana; Assistant Director, Y.W.C.A. Hostel, Accra; Director, Y.W.C.A. Hostels & Food Services, Ghana; Owner & Managing Director, Flair Catering Service, Accra. Memberships: Institutional Management Association, U.K.; Zonta International; Y.W.C.A.; Home Science Association, Ghana. Address: c/o Flair Catering Service, Accra, Ghana.

BAETA, Christian Gongalves, born 23rd May 1908. Presbyterian Minister; University

Professor. Education: B.A., B.D., Evangelisches Missionsseminar, Basle, Switzerland; Ph.D., University of London, U.K. Married, 3 sons, 2 daughters. Appointments: Tutor, Presbyterian Training College, Akropong, Ghana; Principal, Evangelical Presbyterian Seminary, Ho; Synod Clerk, Evangelical Presbyterian Church; Senior Lecturer, then Professor, University of Ghana, Legon. Memberships: British Old Testament Society; Ghana Academy of Arts & Sciences. Publications: Prophetism in Ghana; Christianity in Tropical Africa (ed.). Honours: Hon. D.D.; D.Theol.; O.B.E.; Grand Medal of Ghana. Address: Department for the Study of Religions, University of Ghana, Legon, Ghana.

BAGSHAWE, Antonia Frances, born 11th November 1938. Medical Practitioner. Education: Msengari Convent, Nairobi, Kenya, 1945-53; Rye St. Anthony, Oxford, U.K., 1954-56; King's College, London, 1956-58; St. George's Hospital, London, 1958-61. Appointments: Resident Physician & Surgeon, St. George's Hospital, London, 1962-63; Medical Registrar, Kenyatta National Hospital, Nairobi, Kenya, 1964-66; Lecturer in Medicine, University College, Nairobi, 1967–. Memberships: Hon. Secretary, Association of Physicians of East Africa, 1969-70; Hon. Secretary, Kenya Association of University Women, 1968; Hon. Treasurer, ibid, 1966. Address: The Medical School, P.O. Box 30588, Nairobi, Kenya.

BAHIZI (His Excellency) Gervais Protais, born 19th June 1924. Diplomat; Ambassador. Education: Primary Studies, Catholic Mission, Jomba, 1932-39; Distinction in Humanities, Official School of Nya-Gezi, 1939-44. Customary Head of the Group Busanza-Binza, 1945-60; President, Political Party, Progressive Rural Party of Kivu, 1958-60; Vice-President, of the Territorial Council of Rutshuru, 1959-60; participated in the Political Round Table Conference, Brussels, 1960; ibid, Work Group, Brussels; Deputy, Kivu Province, 1960–; Member of the Congolese Delegation to the 15th Session of the United Nations Organization, 1960; Permanent Representative of the Republic of the Congo to the U.N., 1961; Charge d'Affaires, U.N.O., 1961; Representative of the Republic of the Congo, Extraordinary General Assembly, U.N.O, 1961; Charge d'Affaires, ibid, Nigeria, 1962-64; Ambassador Extraordinary & Plenipotentiary to the Democratic Republic of the Congo, ibid, 1964-68; ibid, United Kingdom & Northern Ireland, 1969–. Memberships: Permanent Commission for the protection of the indigenous, 1956-60; Permanent College of C.I. Bwsha, 1959-60; Anglo-Belgium Club. Honours: Knight, Civil Order of Merit, Democratic Republic of the Congo; Commander, National Congolese Order of the Leopard. Address: 26 Chesham Place, London S.W.1.

BAHTA GHEBREYOHANNES, born 24th July 1931. Insurance Executive. Education: High School, Addis Ababa, Ethiopia; LL.B. Married, 2 sons. Appointments: Director-General of Civil Aviation, Imperial Ethiopian Government, Asmara; Chairman & General Manager, International Insurance Company, Asmara. Memberships: Chartered Insurance Institute, London; Vice-President, Rotary Club; World Peace Through Law Centre, Geneva, Switzerland. Honours: Title of Kegnezmatch conferred by Emperor for services to the state. Address: International Insurance Company, P.O. Box 288, Asmara, Ethiopia.

BAILLY-CHOUMARA, Helene, born 18th January 1928. Medical Entomologist. Education: M.D.; Maitre de Recherches de l'Office de la Recherche Scientific et Technique Outre Mer. Appointments: Head, Entomological Laboratory, Institut Scientifique Cherifien. Memberships: Deputy Secretary, Society of Natural Sciences & Physics, Morocco. Author of publications on medical entomology. Address: c/o Institut Scientifiqu Cherifien, Rabat, Morocco.

BAKASHABARUHANGA, Paul, born Bwizibwera, Kashari, Ankole, 6th July 1940. Land Surveyor. Education: Mbarara High School; Nyakasura School, Fort Portal; B.Sc.(Lond.), Maths. & Physics, Makerere University, Kampala, 1965; Parts I & II, Army Survey Course, School of Military Survey, Newbury, U.K.; Certified Land Surveyor, East Africa, 1970. Appointments: Staff Surveyor, District Surveyor, Kigezi, Uganda, 1967; Senior Staff Surveyor, Regional Lands & Survey Officer, Mbale, 1968-69; Assistant Commissioner for Lands & Surveys (Uganda), 1970–. Memberships: Professional Association of Uganda; Association of Surveyors of Uganda; Outward Bound Mountain School, Loitokitok, Kenya. Recipient of University athletics awards. Address: c/o Lands & Surveys Department, P.O. Box 7061, Kampala, Uganda.

BAKELE GAYID, born 13th December 1936. Assistant Minister, Imperial Ethiopian Government. Education: Elementary, Debre Berhan; Secondary, Teferi Makonnen; B.A., University College, Addis Ababa; M.Ed., Administration, Haward University. Appointments: Chief of Administration, Municipality of Addis Ababa, Technical Department, 1958; Secretary-General, Municipality of Addis Ababa, 1958-61; Director-General for Administration, Ministry of Education, 1961-63; Assistant Minister for Administration, ibid, 1963–. Member, Hailé Selassié University Alumni Association. Address: Ministry of Education & Fine Arts, P.O. Box 1367, Addis Ababa, Ethiopia.

BAKER, Samuel John Kenneth, born Keighley, Yorkshire, U.K., 8th May 1907. Professor Emeritus. Education: University of Liverpool, 1924-28; B.A., 1927; M.A., 1931. Appointments include: Lecturer in Geography, University of Liverpool, 1930-46; ibid, Makerere College, 1946-48; Professor of Geography, Makerere University College, 1946-67; Vice-Principal, ibid, 1965-67; Adviser, Academic Administration, ibid, 1967-68; Professor, Emeritus, ibid, 1967–; Honorary Lecturer, University of Leicester, U.K., 1968–. Memberships: Life Member, Ugandan Society; President, ibid, 1966-67; President, Uganda Geographical Society, 1962; Chairman, ibid, 1963-66; Honorary Vice-President, ibid, 1968–; Fellow, Royal Geographical Society; Royal Commonwealth Society. Contributor of articles on the East African Countries to Encyclopaedia

Britannica & Chambers's Encyclopaedia. Honours include: Uganda Independence Medal, 1964; O.B.E., 1966. Address: 79 Springroyd Terrace, Bradford, Yorkshire, BD8 9SN, U.K.

BAKEWELL, Christabel Mary, born 4th October 1903. Missionary Wife; Mother; Semi-trained Teacher; Women's Social & Christian Welfare Worker; Amateur Medical Dresser; Secretary; Language School Teacher. Education: Melbourne Church of England Grammar School to University Entrance Standard. Personal details: Daughter of the Reverend W. T. C. Storrs, M.A.(Cantab.) & Adelaide Laura Storrs; married to John Bakewell, M.A.(Melb.), 1936; 1 son, 2 daughters. Appointments: from 1922-35: Secretary to Woman Journalist, Melbourne Argus, 5 years; Office Secretary, Mission to Lepers, 5 years; Librarian, 1 year; Women's Work as wife of Principal of Katoke Teachers Training College, Bukoba, Tanzania, 1936—; Language School Teacher, CMS Language School, Nairobi, Kenya. Memberships: Life Member, Old Girls' Society, M.C.E.G.G.S.; Mothers' Union, C. of E.; Church Missionary Society; Australian-New Zealand Society, Nairobi; Christian Hostels Fellowship, ibid; British & Foreign Bible Society. Address: Church Missionary Society Language School, P.O. Box 9849, Nairobi, Kenya.

BAKEWELL, Lionel John, born 14th November 1902. Clerk in Holy Orders; Missionary; Teacher. Education: Melbourne Church of England Grammar School, Australia, 1916-21; B.A., Trinity College, University of Melbourne, 1922-25; M.A., ibid, 1927; Th.L. (1st Class), 1927; Primary Teachers' Certificate, Melbourne Teachers' College, 1942. Married, 1 son, 2 daughters. Appointments: Curate, St. Stephen's, 1927; Travelling Sec., A.S.C.M., 1928; C.M.S. Missionary, Diocese of Central Tanganyika, 1929-65; Headmaster, Katoke Teachers' Training School, 1933-34, 1936-40; Archdeacon of Bugufi (later Western Tanganyika), 1949-60; Chancellor, ibid, 1949-63; Registrar, 1961-63; Archdeacon without territorial jurisdiction, 1960-63; Examining Chaplain to Bishop of Central Tanganyika, 1951—; Bible Society Translator, 1960-63; Hon. Canon, Dodoma Cathedral, 1963; Principal, C.M.S. Language School, Nairobi, Kenya, 1965—. Memberships: Old Melburnians; Union of the Fleur-de-Lys; Church Missionary Society; Kenya Language Association; Australia & New Zealand Society; British & Foreign Bible Society; Scripture Union. Co-translator: Prayer Book in Ha, 1959; St. Mark's Gospel in Ha, 1962. Honours: Bromby Prize in Biblical Greek, 1925. Address: C.M.S. Language School, Box 9849, Nairobi, Kenya.

BAKO, Mamadou, born Garoua, Cameroun, 1933. Controller of Post & Telecommunications. Education: Correspondence courses, Centre d'Enseignement Superieur des Postes et Telecommunications d'Outre-Mer, Paris. Married, 4 children. Appointments include: Chef du Bureau Central Radio, 1959—. Memberships: Founder, Union Camerounaise (which became Union Nationale Camerounaise—the U.N.C.) Directorial Committee, Commissaire aux Comptes, 1958-62; Assistant Secretary, La Jeunesse du Parti, 1962-65; President, Departmental Section, U.N.C. Bénoue; Municipal Councillor, Garoua, 1958—; Mayor, ibid, 1960—; President, Cameroun Development Bank, 1962-65; Economic & Social Council (C.E.S); Secretary, Bureau of C.E.S.; Administrator, Cameroun International Bank for Commerce & Industry (B.I.C.I. Cameroun); Society de la Cimentarie du Nord Cameroun (CIMENCAM); Society Cotonniere Industrielle du Cameroun (CICAM). Honours: Commander of l'Ordre de la Valeur Camerounaise & holder of several other foreign decorations. Address: c/o Office of Post & Telecommunications, Garoua, Cameroun.

BAKOH, Ncho Jacob, born 1927. Certified Accountant. Education: Basel Mission & Government Schools, Kumba, 1938-45; St. Paul's Commercial College, Aba, Nigeria, 1946-50; College of Technology, Kumasi, Ghana, 1959; College of Administration, Accra, 1960. Married, 2 wives, 8 children. Appointments: Teacher, Commercial College, 1950-52; Accounts Clerk, C.D.C., 1952-58; Accountant, C.D.C., 1961; Chief Accountant, Cameroon Bank Ltd., 1962-66; Practising Accountant, 1968—. Memberships: Associate, Association of Certified & Corporate Accountants; Cameroon Association of Certified Accountants. Address: P.O. Box 20, Victoria, West Cameroon.

BALANCY, Pierre Guy Girald, born 8th April, 1924. Ambassador of Mauritius to the U.S.A. & High Commissioner to Canada. Education: Student, Royal College, Port-Louis & Bhujoharry College, Port-Louis, Mauritius. Married to Therese Louis. Appointments: Local Government Officer, 1946-63; Founder, Chief Editor, l'Express (daily newspaper), 1963-64; joined Diplomatic Service, 1968; Ambassador of Mauritius, 1968; Member, Mauritius Legislative Council, 1963-68; Municipal Councillor, 1963-64; Parliamentary Secretary, Ministry of Education & Cultural Affairs, 1963-65; Minister of Information, Posts & Telegraphs, 1965-67; Minister of Works, 1967-68. Memberships: Secretary, Cercle Litteraire de Port-Louis, 1962; Cercle Remy Ollier, 1955-59; Action Sociale, 1959-60; Comm. Direction Centre Culturel Francaise, 1967-68; Exec. Comm., Labour Party, 1961-68. Publications: Human Brotherhood in a Modern Multi-Racial Society, 1956. Honours: C.B.E. Address: 2308 Wyoming Avenue, N.W., Washington, D.C. 20008, U.S.A.

BALBAA, Shafik I., born 13 February 1920. Professor of the Chemistry of Crude Drugs. Education: B.Sc.(Agr.); B.PH.; PH.CH.; M.Pharm.; Ph.D. Appointments: Lecturer, Pharmacognosy, 1951; Assistant Professor, ibid, 1958; Professor of Crude Drugs, 1964; Head, Pharmacognosy Department, Cairo University, U.A.R.; Dean, Faculty of Pharmacy, ibid, 1966. Memberships: Sigma Xi; Rho Chi; Phi Sigma; Gamma Sigma Epsilon; Egyptian Pharmaceutical Society; Egyptian Chemical Society; Egyptian Botanical Society; Tewfekieh Tennis Club; Cairo University Staff Club. Publications: Medicinal Plant Constituents & 65 papers in the field of Pharmacognosy & Phytochemistry. Honours: Holder of the Newcomb Memorial Award for the best research paper published in 1954 in the U.S.A. in the field of pharmacognosy. Address: Dean, Faculty of Pharmacy, Kasr El-Eini Street, Cairo, U.A.R.

BALCAR, Oldrych, born 12th July 1906. Chartered Surveyor. Education: Lvov, Poland, 1912-24; B.Sc., M.Sc., University of Lvov, Poland, 1925-31; Army Cadet, Poland, 1931-32. Personal details: Son of Civil Engineer; Married to Doreen A. Saward, 1 son, 1 daughter. Appointments: Head of Survey Department, Poland, 1934-39; First Line Officer, Polish Army & P.P.C.s, 1939-44; Head & Regional Head of Survey Departments, New Hebrides, Pacific & Gold Coast, Ghana, 1949-52; Senior Lecturer, University of Nigeria, Nsukka, 1962-63; Director, Lands & Survey's, Cameroun Federal Republic, 1963-65; Senior Lecturer, U.S.T., Kumasi, 1966—. Fellow of Royal Inst. of Chartered Surveyors. Memberships: Ghana Inst. of Surveyors; Past Vice-Chairman & Past Chairman, Ghana Branch, R.J.C.S. Publications include: Photogrammetry (joint author), 1945; Cadastre, 1946; Surveying in the New Hebrides (Journal of R.J.C.S.); The use & advantages of aerial photography in developing countries (paper read at Biennial Conference, University of Ibadan, Nigeria), 1970. Address: c/o, U.S.T., Kumasi, Ghana.

BALIDDAWA, Zephaniah Mugeere, born December 1939. Director-General of Civil Aviation, East African Community. Education: B.Sc.(Lond.), Physics & Maths., Makerere University College, 1964; Commercial Pilot's Licence; Air Traffic Control Certificate. Appointments: Operations Officer; Principal Operations Officer; Chief Operations Officer; Deputy Director-General; Director-General. Member, Institute of Transport. Address: Directorate of Civil Aviation, East Africa, P.O. Box 30163, Nairobi, Kenya.

BALL, Kenneth James, born 23rd June 1915. Chartered Architect; Chartered Surveyor. Education: Chesterfield School; Sheffield University, U.K. Appointments: Architect, Derbyshire County Council; ibid, P.W.D., Kuala Lumpur, Malaysia; State Architect, Perak, ibid; Senior Architect, P.W.D., Singapore; Chief Architect, ibid, Chief Architect, National Housing Corporation, Kenya. Memberships: Hon. Secretary, Ipoh Rotary Club. Address: National Housing Corporation, P.O. Box 30257, Nairobi, Kenya.

BALOGUN, David Ayodele, born 11th November 1932. Lecturer. Education: B.A., English & History, Ahmadu Bello University, Nigeria; M.Sc., Education, Indiana University, U.S.A.; Teachers' Certificates III & II; N.C.E.; Graduate Certificate in Education; Diploma in Audio Visual Comm. Married, 3 sons. Appointments: Primary School Headmaster, Nigeria, 1955-57; History & Literature Master, 1961-62; Audio-Visual Specialist, 1966-68; Head of Instructional System, 1969—; Member, Chieftaincy Commission, Kwara State, 1969; Chairman, LEA Review Committee, Kwara State, 1970. Memberships: Vice-President, Nigeria Audio Visual Association; National Education Association; Higher Education Association; Historical Society of Nigeria; Fellowship of Christian Students. Author of various papers. Address: Education Department, Ahmadu Bello University, Zaria, Nigeria.

BALOGUN, Ismail Ayinla Babatunde, born 24th January 1930. Lecturer in Arabic & Islamic Studies. Education: B.A.(Hons.), Classical Arabic, University of London, U.K., 1963; Ph.D., Arabic & Islamic Studies, University of London, 1967. Married, 4 sons, 1 daughter. Appointments: Headmaster, Fazl-i-Omar Ahmadiyyā Schools, Lagos & Ilaro, Nigeria, 1949-53; Principal, Ansar-ud-Deen Secondary Commercial School, Surulere, Lagos, 1963-64; Lecturer in Arabic & Islamic Studies, University of Ibadan, 1967—. Memberships: Secretary, Conference of Muslim Lecturers & Administrative Staff of Nigerian Universities; Historical Society of Nigeria. Publications: The Penetration of Islam into Nigeria (African Studies Seminar Paper 7, University of Khartoum, Sudan), 1969; Training of Arabic Teachers for Schools & Colleges (W. African Jrnl. of Educ.), 1969. Address: Department of Arabic & Islamic Studies, University of Ibadan, Ibadan, Nigeria.

BALOGUN, Kolaisole (Chief Balogun of Otan), born 1926. Barrister at Law. Education: LL.B., London, U.K., 1950; B.L., Lincoln's Inn, 1951. Appointments: Federal Minister of Information & Research, Nigeria, 1955-58; Commissioner to Ghana, 1959-61; Chairman, National Shipping Line, 1962-65; Member, Western Nigerian Government, 1967-70. Memberships: Royal Commonwealth Society; President, Nigerian Arts Council; Nigerian Institute of International Affairs. Publications: My Country Nigeria; Mission to Ghana; Africa Forgives; Village Boy. Address: P.O. Box 20, Ibadan, Nigeria.

BALOGUN, Mosiudi Olatunde Ademola, born Ijebu-Ode, Nigeria, 12th December 1928. Bank Manager. Education Cambridge School Certificate Grade II; Managers' Training Course, London, U.K., 1963. Married; 3 sons, 3 daughters. Appointments: Sub-Manager, Barclays Bank DCO, Mallam Maduri, Kano Province, Nigeria, 1963-64; Manager, Barclays Bank DCO, Gombe, Bauchi Province, 1965-67; Manager, Barclays Bank of Nigeria, Akure, Western State, 1967—. Member, Akure Club. Address: Barclays Bank of Nigeria, Ltd., Akure, Western State, Nigeria.

BAMPOE, David Opare, born 2nd January 1926. Librarian. Education: Teacher Presbyterian Training College, Akropong, 1942-46; B.A.(Lond.), University, College of the Gold Coast, 1950-54; A.L.A., North-Western Polytechnic, London, U.K., 1959-60; F.L.A., 1967. Personal details: Son of Senior Presbyter, Presbyterian Church, Akropong; married, 5 children. Appointments: Assistant Librarian, University College of South Wales & Monmouthshire, 1960-61; ibid, University of Ghana, Legon, 1961-64; Deputy University Librarian, University of Science & Technology, Kumasi, Ghana, 1964—. Memberships: Fellow, Library Association; Member, Several Boards of Governors, Secondary Schools, Kumasi. Publications: A Guide to the Despatches from &

to the Gold Coast of the British Administration, 1850-1902; Official Publications of Ghana, 1600-1966 (in prep.) Honours: Carnegie Award, 1968. Address: Deputy University Librarian, University Library, University of Science & Technology, Kumasi, Ghana.

BANAGE, William Bazeterra, born 27th September 1933. Professor of Zoology. Education: B.Sc.(London), 1st class honours in zoology, botany & geography, Makerere University College, Uganda, 1957; Ph.D. (Dunelm), Zoology, University of Durham, 1957-60. Married, 1962, 3 sons & 1 daughter. Appointments: Research Fellow/Demonstrator, Zoology & Agricultural Biology, 1960-62; Lecturer, Agricultural Zoology, 1962-65; Rockefeller Research Fellow, 1966-67; Reader in Agricultural Zoology, 1968-69; Reader, Zoology, 1968-69; Professor of Zoology, Makerere University, Kampala, Uganda, 1969; research carried out at University of Durham, 1957-60; Rothamsted Experimental Station, 1956-59; E.A.A.F.R.O., Muguga, Kenya, 1961; Imperial College, London Univ., U.K., 1966-67; The Nature Conservancy, Merlewood Research Station, 1966-67; Royal Holloway College, Univ. of London. Memberships: Founder Member & Secretary, Uganda Branch, East African Academy, 1963-64; Exec. Council Member, ibid, 1963-66; Editor & Librarian, 1964-65; Chairman, IBP Comm., 1967—; Convenor, Biological Comm., 1967; Vice-President, Uganda Society, 1964-65; President, ibid, 1965-66; Comm. Member, 1963—; Life Member, European Society of Nematologists; British Ecological Society; British Ornithologists Union; East African Natural History Society; East African Wild Life Society; Fauna Preservation Society; East African Research Working Party, 1969-70. Author of many papers & articles in scientific journals; Editor, East African Academy Proceedings, 1964. Honours: include: Swynnerton Burtt Prize, Natural History, 1952; Swynnerton Memorial Prize, Biology, 1954; Shell Company Prize, Science, 1957. Address: Department of Zoology, Makerere University, Kampala, Uganda.

BANCIL, Manmohan Singh, born Moshi, Tanzania 17th May 1938. Chartered Civil & Municipal Engineer. Education: Cambridge Overseas School Certificate, First Division (6 distinctions, 2 credits), 1955; University Preliminary Course, Battersea College of Technology, London, U.K., 1956-57; B.Sc.(Engrng, Hons.), London University, 1962. Married, twin sons, 1 daughter. Appointments: Assistant Engineer, M/s Square Grip Reinforcement (Ltd.), London, 1959-61; Executive Engineer, Ministry of Communications & Works, Tanzania, 1962-65; Deputy County Engineer (& Acting County Engineer for several months), County Council of Kipsigis, Keriche, Kenya, 1965-68; Town Engineer, Arusha Town Council, Tanzania, 1968—. Memberships: Associate, Institution of Civil Engineers; ibid, Institution of Municipal Engineers; Director, Lions Club. Address: Town Engineer, P.O. Box 3013, Arusha, Tanzania.

BANDA (The Honorable) Aleke Kadonaphani, born Livingstone, N. Rhodesia, 19th September 1939. Politician. Education: United Missionary School, Rhodesia; Inyati School, ibid. Appointments: Editor, Malawi News, Malawi, 1959-66; Director-General, Malawi Broadcasting Corporation, ibid, 1964-66; Director, Reserve Bank of Malawi, 1965; Minister of Development & Planning, 1966-67: Minister of Economic Affairs, 1967-68; Minister of Trade & Industry, 1968—. Memberships: M.C.P.'s Founder Member & Secretary General; ibid, Secretary General & Co-Commander, 1966. Address: Box 453, Blantyre, Malawi.

BANDA (His Excellency) Hastings Kamuzu, President of the Republic of Malawi, born Kasungu District, Nyasaland, 1906. Education: Ph.B., Chicago, U.S.A., 1931; M.D., Mecheray Medical College, Tennessee, U.S.A., 1937. Appointments: General Practitioner, Liverpool, North Shields, Kilburn, U.K., 1953; General Practitioner, Kumasi, Ghana, 1955-58; President-General, African National Congress, Nyasaland, 1958; Leader, Malawi Congress Party, 1960; Minister of Natural Resources, 1961-64; Prime Minister, Malawi, 1964-66; President, 1966—. Memberships: L.R.C.P., Edinburgh, U.K. Address: State House, Zomba, Malawi.

BANGERT, Ida Gunhilda, born 1st October 1909. Missionary Doctor. Education: M.D., University of Copenhagen, Denmark, 1936. Appointments: Missionary Doctor, Sudan United Mission Hospital, Numan, N.E. Nigeria, 1947—. Memberships: Royal Society of Tropical Medicine & Hygiene, London, U.K. Address: c/o The Sudan United Mission Hospital, Numan, N.E. Nigeria.

BANGUDU, Ezekiel Adeniyi, born 7th July 1938. Lecturer. Education: Gindiri Boys' Secondary School, 1950-55; Nigerian College of Arts, Science & Technology, Zaria, 1956-58; B.Sc.(London), upper Second Honours, University College, Ibadan, 1958-62; D.Phil., Mathematical Institute, Oxford University, U.K., 1966. Married, 1 son. Appointments: Lecturer, Mathematics, Ahmadu Bello University, Zaria. Member, Balliol College Society. Publications: Hypervirial Theorems & Expectation Values for Helium (w. P. D. Robinson), 1965. Address: Department of Mathematics, Ahmadu Bello University, Zaria, Nigeria.

BANJO, Ladipo Ayodeji, born 2nd May 1934. Lecturer. Education: Igbobi College, Lagos, Nigeria, 1948-51; M.A.(English), University of Glasgow, U.K., 1955-59; Dip.Ed., Dip.E.S., University of Leeds, 1959-60, 1964-65; M.A., Linguistics, University of California, Los Angeles, U.S.A., 1965-66; Ph.D.(English), University of Ibadan, Nigeria, 1969. Appointments: Education Officer, Western Nigeria, 1960-64; Lecturer in English Language, University of Ibadan, 1966—. Memberships: President, Nigeria English Studies Association; West African Linguistic Society; Yoruba Studies Association of Nigeria. Publications: Oral English for School Certificate (co-author), 1970; several articles in learned journals. Address: Department of English, University of Ibadan, Ibadan, Nigeria.

BANJO, Olumide Adebayo, born Western Nigeria, 12th November 1931. Medical Practitioner. Education: St. Andrew's Infant School, Oyo, 1936-38; St. Andrew's Primary School, Oyo, 1939-42; C.M.S. Grammar School, Lagos, 1943-48; Norwich City College, Norwich, U.K., 1951-52; King's College Medical School, Newcastle upon Tyne, 1952-57; Bristol University, Bristol, 1960-62; School of Tropical Medicine, Liverpool, 1963. Married. Appointments include: Clerk, Ministry of Lands & Surveys, Lagos, 1949-50; Laboratory Technician, General Hospital, Lagos, 1950-51; House Surgeon, Royal Victoria Infirmary, 1957-58; Medical Officer, Ministry of Health, Ibadan, 1958-61; Senior Medical Officer, ibid, 1961-66; Specialist Radiologist, Ministry of Health, 1966—; currently, Senior Consultant Radiologist, in charge of Adeoyo State Hospital, Ibadan, Nigeria. Memberships include: Fellow, Royal Society of Medicine, U.K.; British Medical Association; Past Secretary, West Branch, Nigeria Medical Association; Chairman, Examining Board in Radiology for the Nigeria Medical Council; Ibadan Tennis Club. Publications include: An Introduction to Tropical Diseases, 1965; I Was a 'Locum', 1967. Honours include: M.B.B.S.(Dunelm), 1957; D.M.R.D.(RCS(Eng.), RCP(Lond.)), 1962; D.T.M.H.(Liverpool), 1963; first indigenous Western Nigerian Radiologist. Address: Adeoyo Hospital, Ibadan, Nigeria.

BANNERMAN, Charles James, born 17th December 1909. Educationist. Education: Mfantsipim School, Cape Coast, Ghana; London University Institute of Education. Married, 7 sons, 1 daughter. Appointments: Assistant Headmaster, Prempeh College, 1949-52; Headmaster, Abuakwa State College, 1952-58; Principal, Methodist Training College, 1960-61; Principal, Winneba Training College, 1961-65; Senior Assistant Registrar, University College, Cape Coast, Ghana, 1965—. Publications: A Ga Grammar of Function. Address: University College, Cape Coast, Ghana.

BANNERMAN, E. W. Q., born 19th April 1912. Medical Practitioner. Education: Mfantsipim, Cape Coast, Ghana, 1926-29; Edinburgh University, U.K., 1930-35; London School of Hygiene & Tropical Medicine, 1936. Appointments: Deputy Chief Medical Officer, Ghana, 1955-60; Resident Medical Officer, University of Science & Technology, Kumasi, 1962—. Honours: Officer, Order of St. John of Jerusalem, 1960. Address: University of Science & Technology, Kumasi, Ghana.

BANNERMAN, Henry Satorius, born Accra, Ghana, 5th July 1918. Medical Practitioner; Member of Parliament, Ghana. Education: Mfantsipim School, Ghana, 1932-36; Achimota School, 1937-39; Edinburgh University, U.K., 1942-47; London School of Tropical Medicine, 1949. Married, 5 children. Appointments: Casualty Officer, House Surgeon, Bradford Royal Infirmary, 1947-49; Medical Officer, Gold Coast Medical Service, 1949-52; Former Member, Accra & Tema City Council Management Committee; Chairman, Public Health & Transport Sub-Committee, ibid; Member, Constituent Assembly; Member of Parliament for Accra Central. Memberships: National Chairman, United Nationalist Party; President, Ghana Medical Association; Ghana Press Council; Parochial Church Council, Holy Trinity Cathedral, Accra; Board of Governors, O'Reilly Secondary School; Board of Trustees, Centre for Civic Education; National Vice-Chairman, Ghana Y.M.C.A., 1966; Accra Hospitals Management Board, 1969; Delegate, World Medical Assembly, 1965, 1970; Hon. Medical Officer & Steward, Gold Coast Boxing Board of Control, 1956; Central Midwives Board, 1956-70. Address: P.O. 1189, Accra, Ghana.

BANSE, Bokousi Alfred, born 1937. Head of Commercial Interior Service. Education: Diploma, National School of Administration, Upper Volta; Diploma, National Centre of Agricultural Co-operation, Paris, France; Diploma, Rural Polytechnic Institute of Katihangau, Mali. Appointments: Shareholder in MAVOCI (Cigarette Manufacturers); Head of Commercial Interior Service. Publications: article on the National Development Bank of Upper Volta.

BANTURAKI, James, born 28th October 1937. Civil Servant. Education: Junior Sec. III, Mbarara High School, Uganda, 1957; Uganda Civil Service Clerical Entrance Exam, 1962; East African Certificate of Education Exam., 1968. Married, 2 sons, 1 daughter. Appointments: Junior Clerk, Ankole District Administration, 1959-63; Clerical Officer, ibid, 1964-65; Senior Clerical Officer, Ministry of Public Service & Cabinet Affairs, Uganda Government, 1966-67; Executive Officer, ibid, 1968—. Memberships: Uganda YMCA Central Executive Committee & Central Council; Secretary, Board of Directors, Mbarara YMCA Branch; Secretary, Mbarara Branch, National Union of Youth Organizations; Executive Committee, Ankole Branch, Save the Children Fund; Treasurer, Mbarara Town Parish Church. Honours: Uganda Order of Procedure YMCA Certificate, 1965. Address: P.O. Box 243, Mbarara, Uganda.

BANUGIRE, Firimooni Rweere, born 1941. Economist. Education: B.A.Econ., University of East Africa; M.Sc.(Econ.), London School of Economics, U.K.; Ph.D.(student, external), London University. Appointments: Economist, Ministry of Planning & Economic Development, Uganda, 1966-70; Marketing Adviser, Export Promotion Council, 1970—. Memberships: Executive Committee, Uganda Economics Association, 1970-71; Editorial Board, ibid, 1970-71. Author of several papers & various poems. Address: P.O. Box 6368, Kampala, Uganda.

BANYANGA, Angelino, born 18th December 1932. Personnel Manager. Education: Grade II Cambridge School Certificate, St. Leo's College, Fort Portal, Uganda, 1953; Certificate in Personnel Management, Glasgow School of Management Studies, U.K., 1963; Certificate of Graduate Membership, Institute of Personnel Management, London, 1963. Married, 7 children. Appointments: Accounts

Clerk, Accountant-General, Uganda Protectorate, 1956; Accountancy Apprentice, Uganda Electricity Board, 1956-57; Cost Accounts Clerk, East African Tobacco Co. Ltd., Jinja, 1957; Secretary-General, Uganda Trades Union Congress, 1959-60; Industrial Relations Officer, then Assistant Personnel Manager, Uganda Sugar Factory, 1961-64; Executive Secretary, EAAFRO & EAVRO, 1964-66; East African Representative, European Economic Community, Brussels, Belgium, 1966-67; Headquarters, East African Common Services Organization, 1967-68; Labour & Welfare Officer, Coffee Marketing Board, 1968-69; Personnel Manager, ibid, 1969—. Chairman, Disciplinary Committee, Coffee Sports Club. Address: Coffee Marketing Board, P.O. Box 7154, Kampala, Uganda.

BARAKAT, Gamal Eldin, born 18th February 1921. Diplomat; Ambassador. Education: LL.B., Cairo University, U.A.R., 1940; Higher Diploma in Economics, ibid, 1944; Diploma, International Law Academy, The Hague, Netherlands, 1948; B.Litt., Oriel College, Oxford University, U.K., 1949. Married, 1 son, 2 daughters. Appointments: Third Secretary, London, U.K., 1950-52; Political Department, Foreign Ministry, Cairo, U.A.R., 1953-55; Consul-General, Aleppo, 1955-58; Counsellor, Washington, U.S.A., 1958-60; Head, Training Department, Foreign Ministry, Cairo, U.A.R., 1961-63; Member, OAU Expert Comm., Addis Ababa, Ethiopia, 1963-64; Ambassador to Uganda, 1964-68; ibid, Burundi, 1968; ibid, Finland, 1968—. Publications: Status of Aliens in Egypt, 1949; Lectures in Diplomacy & Diplomatic Terminology (Arabic), 1962. Honours: Order of Merit, 4th Grade; Order of the Republic, 2nd Grade, Egypt; Order of Merit, Syria. Address: U.A.R. Embassy, Stenbackinkatu 22, Helsinki, 25, Finland.

BARANGO-TARIAH (Chief) Godfrey Goldie Francis, born Buguma, Kalaberi, Degema Division, Rivers State, Nigeria, 24th April 1927. Educationist; Certified Practitioner in Commercial Subjects. Education: St. Michael's School, Buguma, Rivers State; Kalabari National College, Buguma, 1943; External Student, Wolsey Hall, Oxford, U.K.; Nigerian Railway Correspondence Training; Barclays Bank training; M.C.P., A.C.P.(Lond.); F.S.C.T., inter-B.A.(Lond.); Diploma in Commerce, 1st Class; R.S.A.; F.R.G.S.; F.R.Econ.S.; Higher Cert. of Commercial Education (L.C.C;); Senior Teachers' Cert. Personal details: Appointed as head, Tariah family of Bugama, Rivers State, holding a traditional chieftaincy title in the Kalabari Clan, Rivers State, 1955—; Married, 8 children. Appointments: English & Maths. Master, K.N.C., Buguma, 1943; Accounting Officer, Barclays Bank, Port Harcourt, 1944; Correspondence Officer, Nigeria Railways, Enugu, 1944-46; Principal, Oguta National College of Commerce, 1946, 1956; Principal, Zik's Institute, Onitsha, 1950-55; Manager, King's College of Commerce, Buguma, 1957; Manager & Principal, ibid, 1967-68; Census Supervisor, Eastern Nigeria Service, 1953; Joint Manager, Premier College, Onitsha & King's College of Commerce, 1957-66; Senior English Master, Holy Rosary Secondary School, Port Harcourt, 1969, engaged in establishing Secondary Commercial School, Rivers State. Memberships: College of Preceptors, London; Vice-President, Onitsha Branch, British Council, Eastern Nigeria, 1952-55; Secretary, Association of Proprietors of Eastern Nigeria Secondary Commercial Schools, 1957-67; General Research Inc., Philadelphia, U.S.A.; Chairman, Development Committee, Kolaberi County Council; Chairman, Education Committee, ibid, 1960-61; Fellow, Society of Commercial Teachers, U.K.; Fellow, Royal Geographical Society; Fellow, Royal Economic Society; Team Manager, Rivers State Football Association. Author of speeches, addresses, articles, & memoranda on political & educational topics, 1953-66; author of pamphlets & poetry. Recipient of several prizes & awards, including Certificate of Merit for College, University of African Arts, East Africa, 1964. Address: c/o King's College of Commerce, P.O. Box 4, Buguma, Rivers State, Nigeria.

BARD, Michel Henry, born 18th October 1929. Director. Education: Baccalaureat; studied Law. Married, 2 children. Appointments: various posts in marketing; Assistant Departmental Director; Society Director; Departmental Director. Address: B.P. 997, Abidjan, Ivory Coast.

BARGON, Robert Campbell, born 24th April 1931. Auditor. Education: Boroughmuir Secondary School, Edinburgh, U.K. Appointments: Auditor, Federal Government of Rhodesia & Nyasaland, 1957-63; Senior Auditor, Government of Malawi, 1964-66; Principal Auditor, ibid, 1966-68; Assistant Auditor General, 1968—. Memberships: Zomba Gymkhana Club; Chartered Institute of Secretaries. Address: P.O. Box 33, Zomba, Malawi.

BARIBWEGURE, Joachim, born 15th August 1923. Functionary of Burundi. Education: Primary, unable to complete secondary education; Personal details: son of a peasant family; married to Charlotte Nzirubusa, 6 children. Appointments: Editor, Ndongozi, the first journal of Burgundi, 1948-60; Founder, the Parti Du Peuple in opposition to the extremist Royalist party, UPRONA, 1960; Minister of Work & Social Affairs, 1965-66; travelled in Belgium & France as member of various political & socio-educative commissions. Memberships: Founding Comm., la Legion de Marie & des Ligues du Sacre-Coeur; 1st Burgundi President, Comitium Legio Mariae; Founding Comm., Mutualites Chretiennes, Syndicat Chretien et des Classes Moyennes; 1st Counselor General, Mutualites au Burgundi; Vice-President, Syndicat Chretien et Secretaire General des Classes Moyennes; Elected Member, Conseil des Centres Extra-Coutumiers. Address: c/o Conseil des Centres Extra-Coutumiers, Burundi.

BARIGYE, John Patrick, born 10th January 1940. Civil Servant. Education: King's College, Budo, Uganda; M.A., Economics, King's

College, Cambridge, U.K. Personal details: son of Sir Charles & Lady Gasyonga; married. Appointments: Assistant Secretary, Ministry of Commerce & Industry, Uganda, 1962; Foreign Service Officer, 1963; Third Secretary, Uganda High Commission, London, U.K., 1964; Second Secretary, ibid, 1965; Senior Assistant Secretary, Ministry of Foreign Affairs, Uganda, 1966; Principal Assistant Secretary, ibid, 1967; Under-Secretary, 1968; Secretary for Foreign Affairs, 1969. Represented Uganda at many international conferences. Honours: Knight Commander of the Order of St. Sylvester, awarded by His Holiness the Pope, 1969. Address: Ministry of Foreign Affairs, P.O. Box 7048, Kampala, Uganda.

BARKHAM, David William, born 23rd April 1931. Physician. Education: City of London School; Downing College, Cambridge; St. Thomas's Hospital, London, U.K. Appointments: Senior Consultant Physician, New Mulago Hospital, Kampala, Uganda; Honorary Lecturer, Medicine, Makerere Medical School, Kampala. Address: Department of Medicine, New Mulago Hospital, P.O. Box 7051, Kampala, Uganda.

BARLOW, Margaret Maria, born April 1942. Librarian. Education: Gayara High School; Makerere College School; B.A.(Hons.), Makerere University College, 1967; A.L.A. Certificate, Ealing Technical College, London, U.K. Married, 1 son. Appointments: Foreign Service Officer, 1967; Assistant Librarian, Makerere University, Kampala, Uganda, 1968—. Memberships: Secretary, Uganda Branch, East African Library Association; Makerere Swimming Club. Address: Makerere University, P.O. Box 7062, Kampala, Uganda.

BARNABO, Raphael Nangboh, born 20th April 1943. Banking Agent. Education: Commercial Studies, Accountancy & Banking; Brevet d'etudes Bancais; Professional qualification, Banking & Accountancy; Diploma of Higher Studies in Accountancy; Economics & Social Studies Diploma. Appointments: Banking Agent since 1964. Memberships: ex-Member, Directorial Bureau, National Union of Workers of Togo; ex-Secretary-General, Syndicat des Cadres et Employes de Banques et Etablissements Financiers du Togo; Vice-President, Administrative Council, Caisse Nationale de Securite Sociale du Togo; ibid, Association of Old Pupils of Technical Colleges of Togo; Economic & Social Council of Togo, Togo.

BARNETT, Patricia Ann, born 30th May 1938. Missionary Teacher. Education: Cowley Girls' Grammar School, St. Helens, Lancashire, U.K.; Teacher Training Course, Whitelands College, Putney, London. Appointments: Two Teaching Posts in Junior Schools in Lancashire; Tutor, St. Mark's Teachers' College, Kigari, Embu, Kenya, 1964—. Memberships: Church Missionary Society; Honorary Area Representative, Embu & Kirinyaga Districts, Kenya Students Christian Fellowship. Publications: Collaborator, Religious Education Teachers' Handbook, 1971. Address: St, Mark's Teachers' College, Kigari, P.O. Embu, Kenya.

BARNOR, Matthew Anam, born 15th September 1917. Medical Practitioner. Education: Accra Government Boys' School, Ghana, 1923-32; Mfantisipim School, 1933-37; Achimota College, 1937-40; Edinburgh University, U.K., 1942-47; University of London School of Tropical Medicine, 1947-49. Married. Appointments: Medical Officer, Ghana Medical Service, 1949-58; General Practice, 1958—. Memberships: Hon. Secretary, Ghana Medical Association, 1959-62; Past President, ibid, 1963-66; Founding Member, Planned Parenthood Association of Ghana; Past Vice-President, 1967-69. Author, History of Medical Societies in Ghana (Ghana Med. J.). Address: Link Road Clinic, P.O. Box 1135, Accra, Ghana.

BAROUM (The Honourable) Jacques, Foreign Minister of Chad, born Laye, 13th July 1932. Education: Primary School, Chad; Secondary School, Brazzaville, Congo; M.D., Faculty of Medicine, Paris, France; Diploma in Tropical Medicine, ibid. Appointments: Member, Chad Ruling Party; Minister of Health & Social Service; Minister of Foreign Affairs, 1965—. Chad's first African Doctor of Medicine. Address: Ministry of Foreign Affairs, Fort Lamy, Chad.

BARRETT, David Brian, born 30th August, 1927. Anglican Missionary; Researcher; Lecturer. Education: B.A., M.A., Aeronautical Engineering, Cambridge University; B.D., Theology, ibid; S.T.M., magna cum laude, Union Theological Seminary, New York, U.S.A.; Ph.D., Sociology of Religion, Columbia University. Appointments: Scientific Officer, Royal Aircraft Establishment, Farnborough, U.K., 1948-52; post in Church of England, Church of the Province of East Africa, Episcopal Church, U.S.A., 1952-65; Secretary for Research, Church of the Province of East Africa, 1965-68; Adjunct Professor, Religion, Columbia University, U.S.A., 1968—; Research Secretary, Anglican Conservative Council, 1970—. Member of theological, missionary & Africanist societies. Publications: Schism & Renewal in Africa, 1968; African Initiatives in Religion, 1970; Co-editor of editions in 4 languages, World Christian Handbook; over 40 articles in dictionaries, journals & reviews. Address: Box 230, Nairobi, Kenya.

BARRETT-STONE, Herbert, born 27th November 1920. Life Assurance Agent. Married, 1 son. Appointments: Manager for U.K., American Life insurance Co., Wilmington, Delaware, U.S.A.; Regional Secretary, ibid, Europe & Africa; Agency Director, West Africa. Fellowships: Chartered Insurance Institute, U.K.; Institute of Arbitrators, U.K. Address: Agency Director, West Africa, American Life Insurance Company (NIG) Ltd., P.O. Box 2577, Lagos, Nigeria.

BARUWA, Abraham Babatunde, born Lagos, Nigeria, 18th October 1923. Accountant. Education: C.M.S. Primary School, Lokoja, Nigeria; Bethel African Primary School, Lagos; Saint Patricks Primary School, Lagos; Abeokuta Grammar School; Norwood Technical College, London, U.K. Personal details: descendant of

Chief Olusi of Lagos; Married, 4 children. Appointments: Managing Proprietor, Bluebells Group of Companies, Bluebells Commerce & Services, Bluebells Brokers (Policies) Co., Bluebells Commercial & Industrial Co. Memberships: Fellow, Royal Economic Society; Fellow, British Society of Commerce; International Commission of Jurists. Address: 3 Isale-Agbede Street, P.O. Box 2122, Lagos, Nigeria.

BASANT RAI (Hon.) Dayanundlall, born La Rosa, Mauritius, 2nd November 1923. Minister of Social Security, Mauritius. Education: Mare d'Albert & Mahebourg Government Schools. Married. Appointments: Principal, La Rosa High School, 1943-63; in charge, free Hindi School (part-time), 1943—; Member, Public Assistance Advisory Committee, 1948-60; Elected Member & Chairman, New Grove Village Council, 1952-67; District Councillor, 1953-67, 1968-69; Chairman, District Council South, 1962-67, 1968-69; Chairman, Association of District Councils, Mauritius, 1962-67, 1968-69; Elected Member, Legislative Council for Vieux Grand Port, 1959, re-elected 1963; Elected Member for Vieux Grand Port & Rose Belle, Legislative Assembly, 1967, as Member of Independence Party; Parliamentary Secretary, Ministry of Works & Internal Communications, 1967; Minister of Social Security, 1969—. Memberships: President, Hindu Maha Sabha, 1965-70; Secretary, Mauritius Sanatan Dharma Temples Federation (Hindi speaking), 1964-70; Sugar Industry Labour Welfare Fund Committee, 1965-66; President, La Rose C.C.S., 1965-69; President, Social Welfare Centre, 1960-69; President, La Rosa Temple, 1959-70; M.B.C. Advisory Council, 1966-69; C.H.A., 1960-63, 1967-69; Town & Country Planning Board, 1965-67, 1968-69; London Constitutional Conference, 1965; Commonwealth Parliamentary Conference, Uganda, 1967. Honours: O.B.E., 1968. Address: La Rosa, New Grove, Mauritius.

BASAZA, James Wilson Bizoza Karuhije, born 28th November 1936. Public Administrator; Teacher. Education: Primary, 1945-59; Junior Secondary, 1949-52; Senior Secondary, 1953-55; B.A.(London), Makerere University College, 1956-60; Dip. Ed. (East Africa), 1961. Married, 4 sons, 2 daughters. Appointments: Graduate Teacher & Housemaster, 1961-64; Assistant Secretary, 1964-68; Principal Assistant Secretary, 1968-70. Memberships: Christ Church Council; Arusha Amateur Theatrical Arts Society. Honours: The Dina Waligo Science Prize, 1954. Address: c/o Finance & Administration Secretariat, P.O. Box 3081, Arusha, Tanzania.

BASHEER, Sheikh Mohammad, born 22nd December, 1934. Physician. Education: Primary & Secondary, Uganda; Graduated with honours, Royal College of Surgeons, Ireland, 1961; L.M., Dublin, 1962; D.Obst.R.C.O.G., London, 1964; D.C.H. (R.C.P. & S.I.), 1964. Personal details: Father recipient, M.B.E., 1961; Married. Appointments: Medical Officer, New Mulago Hospital, Kampala, Uganda, 1964; 1st Paediatric Registrar, Rotunda Hospital, Dublin, Ireland, 1965; Medical Registrar, National Children's Hospital, ibid, 1966-68; Clinical Tutor, Paediatrics, Trinity College, 1966-68; Clinical Tutor, Neonatal Paediatrics, ibid, 1969—; Senior Paediatric Registrar, Rotunda Hospital, 1969—. Memberships: British Medical Association; Irish Medical Association; Elm Park Golf & Tennis Club, Dublin; Royal College of Physicians, Ireland. Author of articles awaiting publication. Honours: E.C.F.M.G., 1967. Address: Shalimar, 26 Ard Na Mara Park, Malahide, Co. Dublin, Ireland.

BASIRU DUTSE, A. M. S., born Dutse, Kano, Nigeria, 15th January 1940. Headmaster. Education: Dutse J.P.S., 1947-50; Birnin Kudu S.P.S., 1951-53; Wudil Teachers' College, 1956-60. Personal details: son of Alhaji Mohemmed Sunusi, Village Head of Gurduba, Dutse, & member of Royal Family of Dutse; Married, 3 children. Appointments: Pupil Teacher, Kibiya J.P.S., 1954-55; Assistant Headmaster, Birnin Kudu Senior Primary School, 1960-63; Headmaster, Makafi Primary School, Kano City, 1964-65; Headmaster, Kofar Naise Primary School, Kano City, 1966—. Memberships include: Scoutmaster, 2nd Kano Troop; Young Farmers' Club. Honours: Prize in Rural Science, Wudil Training College, 1960. Address: Kofar Haise Primary School, c/o Local Education Authority Office, Kano State, Nigeria.

BASSI, Paul, born Marama, Biu, Nigeria, 27th October 1934. Educator. Education: C.B.M. Primary Schools, Marama & Garkida, 1944-50; C.B.M. Training College, Waka, Biu, 1952-54; Mayflower Correspondence College of Practical English, London, 1956-57; S.U.M. Higher Elementary Training College, Gindiri, 1957-58; G.C.E., 'O' Levels, 1967-68. Married, 4 sons. Appointments include: Students' Hostel Chairman, Gindiri Training College, 1958; President, College Literary & Debating Society, 1958; Sports Captain, College Athletic Team, 1958; Headmaster, Garkida Senior Primary School, 1959-61; N.E.P.U. Candidate, N. Regional Parliamentary Elections, 1961; Secretary, Divisional Branch, N.E.P.U., 1962; Clerk, National HQ, Publicity & Information & Legal Defence Offices, ibid, 1962; N.E.P.U./N.P.F. Candidate, Federal Parliamentary Elections for House of Representatives, Lagos, 1964; Headmaster, Methodist Transferred School, Zaria, 1967-69. Memberships include: Provincial President, Nigerian Union of Teachers, 1969-70; Provincial Secretary, ibid, 1968. Address: Methodist Transferred School, P.O. Box 222, Zaria, N.C. State, Nigeria.

BATCHELOR, Edward Martin, born 27th November 1924. Teacher. Education: The Judd School, Tonbridge, U.K., 1933-42; M.A.(Oxon), Exeter College, Oxford University, 1942-43, 1946-48; Diploma of Education, ibid. Married, 2 children. Appointments: War Service, Brigade of Gurkhas, South-East Asia Command; Assistant Master, Hove County Grammar School, 1948-49; ibid, Wadi Seidna Secondary School, Imdurman, Sudan, 1949-58; ibid & Deputy Headmaster, Sir Samuel Baker School, Gulu, Uganda, 1958-62; Acting Headmaster, Masindi Senior Secondary School, 1962-63; Headmaster, Jinja Senior Secondary School, 1963-65; Headmaster, Nyakasura School, 1965—. Publications: English for African Students; The Approach to School Certificate English (w. J. O. 'C. Morgan). Address: Nyakasura School, P.O. Box 16, Fort Portal, Uganda.

BATCHELOR, Raymond Harold Walter, born 24th June 1924. Civil Servant; Professional Sports Coach & Administrator. Education: Gainsborough School, U.K.; South East Essex Technical College; London University School of Oriental Languages; F.A. Coaching Certificate; A.A.A. Coaching Certificate; A.A.A. of England Official Track & Field Certificate; F.A. Trainers' Certificate; A.B.A. Judge & Referee; M.C.C. Coaching Certificate; Certificate of Physical Education. Appointments: British Army, 1942-49; B.B.C. Publications, 1950-54; Regional Sports Officer, Kenya, 1954-60; Athletics Coach, Coast Province, 1955-62; Athletics Coach, Rift Valley Province, 1962-65; National Soccer Coach, Kenya, 1960-66; Games Tutor, Boxing Coach, Aquinas Boys' High School & Alliance Boys' High School, 1966-67; Director of Sport & Coaching, Malawi Government, 1967—. Memberships: Secretary, Coast Province Sports Association, 1955-62; Secretary, Rift Valley Sports Association & Boxing Clubs, 1962-65; Founder & Chairman, A.B.A. of Malawi, 1967-69; Founder & Chairman, A.A.A. of Malawi, 1967-69; Technical Officer, Chief Coach, Olympic & Commonwealth Games Team of Malawi, 1970; Special Member, A.A.A. of Kenya, 1956-65; Elected Member, F.A. of Kenya, 1956-65; A.B.A. of Kenya, 1959-67; Chairman, Secondary Schools F.A. of Kenya, 1962-67; Secretary, Olympic & Commonwealth Games Association of Malawi; Advisory Council of Sport, Malawi; National Football League of Kenya. Publications: An Introduction to Progressive Resistance Exercises, 1956; The Side Benefits of Physical Education (Univ. of Uganda), 1969; Common Sports Injuries & Their Treatments; Soccer Coaching for Africa (in prep.); Athletic Coaching for Africa (in prep.). Address: P.O. Box 452, Blantyre, Malawi.

BATENGA, K. L., born 1st January 1927. Administrative Officer. Secondary School Education. Appointments: Mines Assistant; Market Master; Administrative Officer, Local Government. Address: P.O. Box 5, Singida, Tanzania.

BAUEROCHSE (Rev.) Ernst, born 7th June 1925. Missionary Pastor; Radio Station Director. Education: Hermannsburg, Mission Seminary, Germany; University of Hamburg; University of Durham, U.K. Appointments: Missionary, Western Ethiopia, 1954-57; Field Director, German Hermannsburg Mission, Ethiopia, 1957-67; Assistant Station Director, Radio Voice of the Gospel, Addis Ababa, 1967-70; Station Director, ibid, 1970. Publications: Die offene Tur, 1957; Sum Hirten berufen, 1959; Confirmation (in Amharic), 1963. Address: Radio Voice of the Gospel, Addis Ababa, P.O. Box 654, Ethiopia.

BAXI, Shantilal Chuntlal, born Jamnagar, Saurastrah, India, 22nd February 1909. Advocate; Commissioner for Oaths; Notary Public; Secretary; Attorney Agent. Education: Nawanagar High School, Jamnagar; B.A., French, Gujerate College, Ahmedabad; LL.B., Bombay University. Settled in Jinja, Uganda, 1935; Married, 8 children. Appointments: Hon. Secretary: Indian Association (Jinja), Central Council of Indian Associations in Uganda, Jinja Indian Education Society, Jinja Parents Association, Indar Singh Gill Nursery School, Busoga Tenants Association, Indian Retail Traders Association, Indian Merchants Chamber, 1953-70; Jinja Chamber of Commerce & Industry; Hindu Sabha; President, Nile Brahma Samaj Busoga, Jinja; Practise of law, Jinja, 1938-70; Hon. Superintendent, Nile Education Society N.P. Patel Boarding House, Jinja. Memberships: Township Authority, Jinja; Busoga District Education Board; Probation Committee; Hospital Committee. Honours: Independence Medal, Uganda Government, 1967. Address: Flat no. 5, Saraswati Building, Saraswati Road, near Podar School, Santa Cruz West, Bombay 54, India.

BAXTER-GRILLO, Dorothea Lilian, born 3rd June, 1931.. Physician. Education; St. Andrew's High School for Girls, Kingston, Jamaica; L.R.C.P.I., L.R.C.S.I., LM., D.C.H., Royal College of Surgeons, Ireland; Stanford University, U.S.A.; Ph.D., University of Ibadan, Nigeria. Married. Appointments: Medical Paediatric & Surgical Internship, 1955-56; Fellow, Paediatrics, Stanford, University, 1960; Registrar, Paediatrics, Ibadan University, Nigeria, 1961; Lecturer, Anatomy, ibid, 1962; currently Senior Lecturer, Anatomy. Memberships: Fellow, International Academy of Law & Science; Anatomical Society of Great Britain & Ireland. Contributor to scientific journals. Address: Department of Anatomy, University of Ibadan, Ibadan, Nigeria.

BAYERO (Alhaji) Ado, Emir of Kano, born Kano, Nigeria, 1st June 1930. Education: Kano Secondary School, Institute of Administration of the Ahmadu Bello University, Nigeria. Appointments include: Clerk, Standard Bank; Accountant, Local Authority; Clerk, Kano City Council; Member, House of Assembly, 1955-57; Chief of Police, Local Authority; Nigerian Ambassador to Senegal, 1962-63; Emir of Kano, 1963—; Chancellor, University of Nigeria, 1966. Memberships: President, Nigeria Society for The Welfare of The Disabled. Honours, prizes, etc.: C.F.R., 1965. Address: The Emir's Palace, P.M.B. 3002, Kano, Nigeria.

BAYONNE, Nicolas-Abel, born 25th November 1938. Professor; Magistrate. Education: Lic. Law., Lovanium; D.E.S. Private Law, ibid; studied at the National Centre of Judicial Studies, Paris, France; LL.D. Appointments: Deputy Attorney-at-Law, Democratic Republic of the Congo, 1964-65; District Tribunal Judge, 1965; High Court Judge, 1966; Head of the Cabinet to the Ministry of Justice, 1966;

Counsellor to the Court of Appeal, 1966-67; Counsellor, Court of Supreme Justice, 1968—. Assistant Professor, Faculty of Law, Lovanium, 1965-69; Professor, ibid, 1969-70; Dean, 1970—. Memberships: Vice-President, A.E.D.; Criminologists International Society, 1966—. Author of several articles on judicial Law. Address: B.P. 204, Kinshasa, Democratic Republic of the Congo.

BDLIYA, Daniel M., born Kidang, Nigeria, 1933. Teacher. Education: Marama Primary School. Nigeria, 1947-51; Garkida S. Primary School, Nigeria, 1952-53; Waka T.T.C., Nigeria, 1955-57, 1963-64. Married, 4 children. Appointments include: Headmaster, Bilatum Primary School, 1958-62, and again, 1966-69. Address: Bilatum Primary School, P.A. Biu, via Yola, North Eastern State, Nigeria, W.A.

BEAN, Leslie Hugh, born 2nd February 1906. Association Executive. Education: Sherborne School, U.K.; Royal Military College, Sandhurst. Appointments: Somerset Light Infantry, British Army, 1926; Served in Royal West African Frontier Force, commanding 2nd Battalion The Sierra Leone Regiment; Colonel, General Staff G.H.Q., West Africa Command, 1945; Seconded to Gold Coast as Resettlement Officer, 1946-47; General Manager, Ghana Chamber of Mines, 1948; currently Director, ibid; Member, Legislative Assembly, 1951-54. Memberships: M.C.C.; I. Zingari; Free Foresters; Rotary Club of Accra. Honours: M.B.E., 1945; O.B.E., 1956. Address: Ghana Chamber of Mines, P.O. Box 991, Accra, Ghana.

BECHEUR, Mohamed, born 11th July 1909. Advocate. Education: Lic. en droit; Brevete d'Arabe. Married, 7 children. Appointments: Advocate of the Court of Appeal, Sousse; ibid, Supreme Court of Appeal, Tunis; Former member, the Order of Advocates of Sousse. Former Municipal Counsellor, the the Town of Sousse. Address: Rue d'Algerie a Sousse, Tunisia.

BECHRAOUI, Mohamed Tahar, born 18th October, 1925. Educator. Education: Arabic Elementary Diploma; Certificate of Proficiency in Education; Arabic Higher Diploma; Grade of Teacher. Married, 7 children. Appointments: Teacher, 1948-64; attached to the Central Administration, Ministry of National Education, 1964—; Social Service, ibid; Office Education, ibid; Foreign Relations, ibid. Memberships: Tunisien Teachers' Union. Destourien Socialist Party of Tunis. Author of numerous poems, published in journals and broadcast over the radio; also poems in the Arab language entitled 'Cri du Coeur' (as yet unpublished). Address: 3, Rue Pasteur Le Bardo, Tunisia.

BECHRAOUI, Moktar, born 10th January, 1926. Inspector of Technical Instruction. Married, 5 children. Appointments: P.T.A., Mechanical Manufacture, 1946-59; Head of Works, Technical Lycée, 1959-63; Inspector of Technical Instruction, 1963—. Memberships: collaborator with B.I.T. & BIRD, Tunis; Expert Consultant, UNESCO; member of many organizations, programmes & experiments of Technical Instruction, Tunis. Recipient of many distinctions from the above-named organizations. Address: 22 Rue d'Angleterre, Tunis, Tunisia.

BECKLEY, Anthony Olubunmi, born 5th July 1933. Civil Engineer. Education: B.Sc.(C.E.), Howard University, Washington, D.C., U.S.A.; M.Sc.(C.E.), Carnegie-Mellon University, Pittsburgh, Pa. Married. Appointments: Senior Partner, Olubunmi Beckley & Associates Consulting Engineers/Architects. Memberships: American Society of Civil Engineers; Nigerian Society of Engineers. Publications: Flow of Air/Water Mixtures in Closed Conduits. Honours: Senior Award, Department of Civil Engineering, Howard University, 1958. Address: Olubunmi Beckley & Associates, P.O. Box 3415, 78 Yakubu Gowon Street, Lagos, Nigeria.

BEECHER, Gladys Sybil Bazett, born 9 August 1901. Teacher; Housewife. Education: Cheltenham Ladies' College, U.K., 1922-24; B.A., University College, London, 1924-26; London Day Training College, 1926-27. Married. Appointments: Missionary School Teacher, Kabete, 1927-30; Bible Translation, 1941-48. Memberships: Mothers' Union; Y.W.C.A. Address: P.O Box 21066, Nairobi, Kenya.

BEECHER, Leonard James, born 21 May 1906. Archbishop Emeritus. Education: St. Olave's Grammar School, Southwark, U.K., 1917-24; A.R.C.S., Imperial College, London, 1926; B.Sc., Institute of Education, 1926-27; M.A., ibid, 1936; D.D., Lambeth, 1961. Married. Appointments: Assistant Master, Alliance High School, Kikuyu, 1927-30; Missionary Priest, Diocese of Mombasa, 1930-45; Archdeacon, ibid, 1945; Assistant Bishop, 1950-52; Bishop of Mombasa, 1953; Archbishop of East Africa, 1960-70. Honours: Royal African Society Medal for distinguished service to Africa, 1969; C.M.G. Address: P.O. Box 21066, Nairobi, Kenya.

BEERAJ, David Robert, born 29th August 1938. University Lecturer. Education: Secondary, Royal College, Port Louis, Mauritius; B.Sc., (1st Class Honours), University of Wales, Cardiff, U.K., 1964. Personal details: Married to Marie-Ange Genevieve Pascal, 1965, 2 children. Appointments: Education Officer, Royal College, Port-Louis, Ministry of Education, Mauritius, 1965; Lecturer, Mauritius College of Agriculture, Ministry of Agriculture, 1965-68; Lecturer, School of Agriculture, University of Mauritius, 1968—. Address: School of Agriculture, University of Mauritius, Reduit, Mauritius.

BEGASHAW ASHINE, born 8th August 1938. Airline Pilot. Education: Abeye Elementary School; General Wingate Secondary School; Diploma Aircraft & Aero Engine Repair; Dimploma as Commercial Pilot. Appointments: Junior First Officer; First Officer; Senior First

Officer, Boeing 720B/707 Airplane International Routes. Memberships: Founder Member, Ethiopian Airline Pilot Association; Advisory Body, ibid. Address: c/o Ethiopian Airline s.c., P.O. Box 1755, Addis Ababa, Ethiopia.

BEH, Konan, born 1935. Professor. Education: L. es L., L. es Lettres; Studied at the Institute of Administrative Undertakings; Institute of Juridic Sciences & Finance; National College of Administration, 1966-68. Married, 2 children. Appointments: with the Central Bank of the Western States of Africa, 1962-66; Head of Mission to the Ministry of National Education, 1968-69; Professor, Modern College of Katiola, Ivory Coast. Memberships: National Union of Teachers, 2nd Degree, Ivory Coast (SYNESCI). Address: B.P. 122, Katiola, Ivory Coast.

BEKELE ASFAW, born 14th May 1931. Dentist & Oral Surgeon. Education: High School Leaving Certificate, Hailé Selassié I Secondary School, Ethiopia, 1952; Intermediate Diploma, University College of Addis Ababa, 1955; B.Sc., Chemistry & Maths., The American University, Washington, D.C., U.S.A., 1957; D.D.S., Howard University, Washington, D.C., 1963. Married, 1 son. Appointments: Menelik II Hospital, Ethiopia; Police Hospital; Army Hospital. Memberships: Ethiopian Medical Association; Howard University Alumni Association. Address: c/o Abubeker Mohamed Shek, P.O. Box 816, Addis Ababa, Ethiopia.

BEKELE WENDE, born 1st March 1931. Public Servant; Post Office Employee. Education: Hailé Selassié I University, Addis Ababa, Ethiopia; Fil. Kand. (Pol. Mag.), Stockholm University, Sweden, 1957-63. Appointments: Administrator, Ministry of Education; Lecturer, Hailé Selassié I University; Executive Secretary, Board of Directors, Imperial Board of Telecommunication; Director, General Posts, Post Office Department. Address: Director-General of Posts, Department of Posts, Ministry of Communications, Telecommunications & Posts, Ethiopia.

BELABO, Paul Richard Vekaa, born 5th January 1941. Legal Practitioner. Education: Government Colleges, Keffi & Zaria, Nigeria, 1957-63; LL.B., Ahmadu Bello University, 1967; LL.M., Columbia University, New York City, U.S.A., 1968; Barrister & Solicitor, The Supreme Court of Nigeria, Lagos, 1970. Appointments: Chemistry Master, W. M. Bristow Secondary School, Nigeria, 1964; Lecturer in Law, Ahmadu Bello University, Zaria, 1969-70. Memberships: Ahmadu Bello University Staff Club; Nigerian Law Teacher's Association; Nigeria Bar Association. Author of articles in legal journals. Preparing 2-vol. casebook on commercial law: Business Organization; Commercial Transactions. Address: Faculty of Law, Ahmadu Bello University, Zaria, Nigeria.

BELINGA, Marc, born Ekoum-Doum, Mfou, Cameroon, in 1920. First Deputy Prefect, Yabassi, Cameroon. Education: titulaire du C.E.P.E. and of D.E.G. Married, 9 children. Appointments include: Head of Department, Personnel Guidance, 1946-53; Department Head & Head of Office, Ministry of Finance, 1953-60; Head, District of Minta and Akom, 1960-66; Sub-Prefect, Dibombari, 1966-68; Assistant Prefect, 1968-69; Sub-Prefect, & President of the Tribunal, Bengbis, 1969—; First Deputy Prefect, Yabassi. Honours include: Cameroon Decoration of Merit, 3rd class, 1961; ibid, 2nd class, 1967. Address: Sub-Prefect, p,i, de Bengbis, Cameroon.

BELL, Edward Darroch, born Greenock, Scotland, U.K., 7th January 1932. Chartered Electrical Engineer. Education: Higher National Certificate, Paisley Technical College and Contantine Technical College, Middlesbrough. Married. Appointments include: Assistant Engineer, South of Scotland Electricity Board, 1955-58; Mains Engineer, 1958-62, Distribution Engineer, Coast, 1962-63; Coast Area Manager, 1963-65, Chief Commercial Engineer, 1965-68, all at East African Power and Lighting Co. Ltd. Memberships include: Muthaiga Country Club; Mombasa Club; Muthaiga Golf Club. Address: c/o East African Power & Lighting Co. Ltd., P.O. Box 30099, Nairobi, Kenya.

BELL, Fairfax, born 17th February 1904. Retired Medical Officer; Tea & Coffee Planter. Education: Winchester College, U.K., 1917-22; B.M., B.Ch., M.A., Corpus Christi College, Oxford, 1922-27; Resident House Physician to Children's Department, St. Thomas' Hospital, 1927-32; M.R.C.S.; L.R.C.P.; D.P.H.; D.T.M. & H. Married. Appointments: Resident House Physician, West London Hospital, 1933; Resident House Physician, Brompton Chest Hospital, 1934; Colonial Medical Service, 1935-53; Medical Officer of Health, Kampala, Uganda, 1953; Medical Officer of Health, Mombasa, Kenya, 1954; Medical Officer of Health, Nakùru County Council, Kenya, 1956-57; Planter, Kenya, 1957—. Memberships: Royal College of Medicine; British Medical Association. Author of various journal articles. Honours: Natural History Prize, Winchester College, 1921. Address: Sirwa Farm, P.O. Kaimosi, Kenya.

BELL, Ross Harvey, born 19th May 1918. Medical Doctor. Education: M.D., University of Toronto, Canada; D.T.M.H., London School of Tropical Medicine, U.K. Married, 3 children. Appointments: Medical Superintendent, U.M.S. Memorial Hospital, Tungan Magajiya, via Koutagora, Nigeria. Honours: Coronation Medal, 1952. Address: U.M.S. Memorial Hospital, Tungan Magajiya, via Koutagora, Nigeria.

BEN ALI, Mohamed, born 17th February 1932. Acteur a la R.T.T. Appointments: Journalist, 1950-55; Actor, Radio & Theatre, then Television, 1955—; Cinema, 1966—. Memberships: Troupe de l'Unite Theatricale, 1948; Troupe du Theatre Populaire, 1954; La Troupe du Nouveau Theatre, 1955; La Troupe des Etoiles de l'Art, 1960; Troupe du Theatre Populaire, 1968; Troupe du Theatre Republicaine. Author of 17 theatrical pieces, 25 television pieces & 35 radio pieces; Publisher, Art Review, 1955. Honours: 2nd Prize,

Cinematographic Interpretation, Ministry of Culture, 1966. Address: 9 immeuble Leroud Escellier 2, Cite El Menzah, Tunis, Tunisia.

BEN CHEIKH, Abdelkader, born 11th June 1929. Professor. Education: Educational Research, Institute of Sciences & Education, Tunis; Technical Research Bureau. Married, 4 children. Appointments: Teacher, 1956-63; responsible for the Educational Bulletin for secondary teaching, 1963-68; Educational Research on Reading, 1968-70; Editor of 'Et ma part de l'Horizon', 1970. Author of editional articles in intructional educational bulletins. Address: Villa 4-2, Rue de la Justice, Khaznadar, Tunis, Tunisia.

BENCHENEB, Rachid, born 9th January 1915. Inspector-General of Administration, Ministry of the Interior. Education: Secondary Studies, Alger, Algeria; Higher Studies, Alger & Paris, France; Diploma of Higher Studies, Doctor of Letters, The Sorbonne; Brevette de l'Ecole in living oriental languages; Centre for Higher Administrative Studies for Africa & Modern Asia, Paris, France. Married, 3 children. Appointments: Charge de Mission, Governor General's Council Algeria, 1944-45; Sub-Prefect, & Chateau-Chinon, 1946; Attaché, Council of the Interior, 1948-54; Secretary General of Laws, 1955-59; Inspector-General of Administration, Ministry of the Interior, Tunis, 1959—. Author of publications on the theatre. Honours include: Knight, Legion of Honour; Cross of War; Officer of the National Order of Merit; Officer, Palmes Academiques. Address: Inspector-General of Administration, Ministry of the Interior, Tunis, Tunisia.

BENDELAC, David, born 13th May 1920. Accountant. Education: Secondary school studies in accountancy and calculation. Appointments: Head Accountant, 1938-42; Head Accountant, Director of the Company, 1942-60; Expert Accountant officially registered in Morocco, 1960—. Memberships: National Association of Judiciary Experts in Morocco. Address: 5 Avenue de l'Armée Royale, Casablanca, Morocco.

BENIS, Mohamed, born Fes, Morocco, 6th August, 1932. Engineer. Education; Baccalureats, 1st & 2nd parts; M.P.C., Certificate, General Chemistry; Diploma, Chemical Engineering, E.S.C.M. Appointments: with the Cabinet to the Ministry of E.N., 1957-58; ibid, Ministry of A.E., 1958-59; Economic Counsellor, Mobil Oil, 1959-64; Research, O.N.E., 1966; Chemical Laboratory Official, 1969-70. Memberships; former Member of the International Chamber of Commerce. Recipient of distinguished mention for Diploma in Chemical Engineering, 1955. Address: 8 Rue de Belgrade, Casablanca, Morocco.

BENKHEDDA, Benyoucef, born 23rd February 1920. Pharmacist. Education: Lycée de Blida; University of Algers. Personal details: Married, 3 children; became an Algerian Military Prisoner for 8 months in 1943 for refusing to rejoin the French Army; detained in the Civil Prison of Algers, 1954-55. Memberships: Algerian People's Party, 1943; M.T.L.O., 1946-54; President, Provisional Government of Algerian Republic, 1961-69; decreed the Cease-Fire, March, 1962; Established the French-Algerian Agreement of Evian for Co-operation between Algeria & France. Address: Place El Louds, Hydra, Algeria.

BENKIRANE, Abdelkader, born 27th June 1930. Film Producer & Distributor. Education: Commercial & Cinematographic studies. Appointments: participated in the production of the following films: Marie Chantal Contre le Dr. Kah; Requiem pour un Agent Secret; Mission Apocalypse; Bob Flemin Mission Casablanca; Attentat Contre les 3 Grands; Producer, La Route du Kif. Memberships: Societé de Distribution la plus importante au Maroc, groupant un circuit de salles aussi très important. Address: 10 Avenue des F.A.R., Casablanca, Morocco.

BEN MOUSSA, Naima, born 31st October 1937. Schoolteacher. Appointments: Teacher, Private Convent School, run in conjunction with the Tunisian Government. Memberships: Socialist Party, 1951; Tunisien Women's Union, 1956 (former Secretary-General). Address: 10 Rue El Jormau, Tunis, Tunisia.

BENNANI, Ahmed, born 12th December 1926. Banker; Vice-Governor of the Bank of Morocco. Education: Diploma of Higher Commercial Instruction; Lic. Law, Faculty of Paris, France. Appointments: Director-General, Depot Funds & Administration; Secretary-General, Ministry of Finance, Morocco, 1963; Secretary of State, Ministry of Commerce, Industry, Mines & Merchant Marine, 1964; Secretary of State for Economic Affairs to the Prime Minister, 1967-68; Vice-Governor, Bank of Morocco, Rabat, 1968—. Memberships: Administrator, National Bank of Economic Development; ibid, Moroccan Bank of Foreign Commerce; Moroccan Market Funds; Union of French & Arab Banks; Moroccan Navigation Company. Honours: Officer, Order of the Throne, 1970. Address: B.P. 445, 277 Avenue Mohammed V, Rabat, Morocco.

BENNEH, George, born 6th June 1935. Lecturer. Education: Achimota School, Ghana, 1950-56; B.A.(Hons., Geography), University of Ghana, 1957-60; Ph.D., London School of Economics, U.K., 1961-64. Appointments: Lecturer in Geography, University of Ghana, 1964—; Visiting Lecturer, Department of Geography, Copenhagen University, Denmark, 1966; Editor, Bulletin of the Ghana Geographical Association, 1965—. Memberships: Ghana Geographical Association; American Association for the Advancement of Science; Management Committee, Commonwealth Geographical Bureau, 1968—; International Geographical Union Commission on Humid Tropics. Publications: A New Geography of Ghana (co-author), 1970; also contributor to professional publications. Address: Department of Geography, University of Ghana, Legon, Accra, Ghana.

BENNETT, Gordon David, born 2nd December 1928. Consulting Engineer.

Education: B.Sc.(Eng.), Birmingham College of Technology (now the University of Aston in Birmingham). Appointments: trained with Cadbury Bros. & North Eastern Electricity Board, U.K.; joined Kennedy & Donkin, 1954, Rural Electrification, Main Transmission & Hydroelectric Schemes in North Scotland; with Kennedy & Donkin (Africa), 1957-8, 1965—; Rural Electrification in Uganda & Ivory Coast Completion of Owen Falls Hydroelectric Scheme in Uganda. Memberships: Institution of Electrical Engineers; East African Instition of Engineers; Association of Consulting Engineers of Kenya; Associate, College of Advanced Technology, Birmingham, U.K. Address: Messrs Kennedy & Donkin (Africa), P.O. Box 2825, Kampala, Uganda.

BENNETT, Kenneth Geoffrey, born Somerset, U.K., 11th January 1911. Barrister-at-Law. Education: Clifton College. Appointments: Called to Bar, Middle Temple, 1932; Practice, English Bar, 1932-36; Advocate, Tanganyika Bar, 1937-38; Resident Magistrate, Tanganyika, 1938; Crown Counsel, ibid, 1946; Solicitor-General, Nyasaland, 1948; Puisne Judge, Uganda, 1953; frequently acted as Chief Justice; Governor-General, 1962; Retired, 1967. Memberships include: East India Sports Club; Kampala Club. Honours include: Coronation Medal, 1953; Uganda Independence Medal, 1962; C.M.G., 1966. Address: c/o The High Court, P.O. Box 126, Kisumu, Kenya.

BENNIS, Abdellatif, born 20th July 1932. Director of Agricultural Instruction. Education: B.Sc., 1952; National School of Agriculture, Maison Carre, 1954-55; ibid, Grignon, 1955-57; Diploma of Agricultural Engineering, ibid, 1957; Specialization in Education, ORSTOM, Paris, France, 1957-58. Appointments: Engineering Instructor, Agronomic Research Department, Rabat, Morocco, 1958-60; Deputy Director, ibid, Secretary-General, National Institute of Agronomic Research, 1960-65; General Director, Mission Valeur Agricole, 1965-66; Director, Agricultural Instruction & Professional Formation, 1967—. Memberships: Treasurer, Moroccàn Association of the Friends of Science; Society of Natural Sciences & Global Physics; Honorary Vice-President, Association of former Engineers of the National School of Agriculture, Meknes. Honours: Decoré du Wissam Errida, 1969. Address: Avenue de la Victoire, B.P. 415, Rabat, Morocco.

BENNOUNA, Mehdi, born 22nd February 1919. Journalist. Education: Primary School, Tetouan, Morocco; Secondary School, Nablus, Palestine; School of Law, University of Fouad I, Cairo, Egypt, 1940; B.A., Journalism, American University, Cairo, 1941. Married, 4 children. Appointments: Chief Editor, Arabic daily Al-Hurriyah, Tetouan, Morocco, 1945-47; Founder & Director, Morocco Office of Information, New York, U.S.A., 1947-53; Chief Editor, Arabic daily Al-Oummah, organ of the National Reformist Party, Tetouan, Morocco, 1954-56; Administrative Secretary-General, 1st Moroccan Parliament (Assemblee Nationale Consultative), 1957-58; Counsellor for Press & Public Relations to H.M. King Mohammad V, 1958-59; President & General Manager, Maghreb Arab Press News Agency (M.A.P.), & Publisher & Director, La Depeche (in French), Casablanca, 1959—. Member, Moroccan Reformist Party until 1956. Numerous newspaper & magazine articles, & author of all material published by Moroccan Office of Information, 1947-53. Publications: Our Morocco, a true story of a Just Cause (printed clandestinely in English in Morocco), 1951. Honours: Knight, Order of the Throne, Morocco, 1969; Decoration d'Honneur et Valliance for service in the Congo, Morocco, 1962; UN decoration for service in the Congo, 1962; various decorations from Tunisia, U.A.R., Hashemite Kingdom of Jordan, Lebanon, Iraq & Iran. Address: Maghreb Arab Press News Agency, 10 rue Ibn Aicha, Rabat, Morocco.

BEN SAID, Abdesselem, born 10th November 1928. Architect D.P.L.G.; Urban Planner. Education: Diploma, Higher National School of Fine Arts, Paris, France. Married, 3 children. Member, Permanent Commission of Civil Buildings of Tunis & Carthage. Address: 12 Av. Des Etats Unis D'Amerique, Tunis, Tunisia.

BENTAIEB, Mohamed Athomed Larbi, born 31st January 1903. Functionary, Ministry of Youth Sports & Social Affairs. Education: Brevet d'arabe; certificate du fin d'Etudes. Married, 7 children. Appointments: Clerk, then Secretary, Bureau of Judicial Assistance to the Ministry of Justice, 1929-56; Retired to the Ministry of Youth Sports & Social Affairs. Memberships: Vice-President, French Federation of Baseball; President, The Tunisian League of Baseball; ibid, Union of Moslem Sports Societies; Federation of Tunisian Scouts; National Commissioner of Tunisian Scouts; President, Moslem Sports Union; Deputy Treasurer, Syndicate of Justice. Publications: Conferences on Scouting & Sports. Honours: Gold Medal, Baseball, 1948; ibid, Football, 1957; Medal of Sporting Merit; Medal of the Tunisian Republic. Address: c/o Ministry of Youth Sports & Social Affairs, Tunisia.

BENTOUDJA, Ahmed, born 5th March 1905. Army Officer; Colonel. Education: Holder of BEPC, 1919; Pupil Officer, Military School of Meknes, Morocco. Married, 13 children. Appointments: Sub-Lieutenant, 1925; Operation Pacification, Morocco, 1925-1935; Officer in the War (where he was wounded & taken Prisoner), 1939-45. Honours include: Officer, Legion of Honour; Croix de Guerre (Army Corps citation), 1939-45; Croix de Guerre T.O.E. (Army Corps citation, Brigade Division); Commander, Order of the Throne. Address: 4 Rue Raphael Carela, Rabat, Morocco.

BENTSI—ENCHILL, Kwesi Kobea Ogue, born 22nd September 1902. Obstetrician-Gynaecologist. Education: Achimota School & College; M.A., M.B., B.Ch., Trinity College, Dublin University, Ireland; Queen's University, Belfast, U.K.; University College Hospital, London. Married, 4 children. Appointments:

Medical Officer, Gold Coast Government; ibid, Ghana Government; Obstetrician-Gynaecologist, Ghana Government; Professor & Head of Department of Obstetrics & Gynaecology, Ghana Medical School. Memberships: Freemason; Achimota Golf Club. Publications include: The Changing Face of Obstetric Practice in Ghana. Address: Ghana Medical School, P.O. Box 4236, Accra, Ghana.

BENZAQUEN, Georges, born 19th May 1934. Lawyer. Education: Diploma, Polytechnic Insurance School; Lic. Law; Diploma in Higher Studies of Private Law. Married, 2 children. Appointments: General Secretary to the Contingency Insurance Company Ltd., until 1956; Registered as a Lawyer, Casablanca, 1956—; Defender, Supreme Court, 1965—. Memberships: Association of Lawyers. Address: 48 Rue du Prince Moulay Abdellah, Casablanca, Morocco.

BERGER, Vincent, born 14th October 1925. Mining Engineer. Education: Baccalaureats & Diploma, Higher National School of Mining, Saint-Etienne, France. Married to Colette Chaussy, 4 children. Appointments: Engineer, Intercolonial Mining Society (Rep. Centrafricaine), 1950-56; Directeur de la Centramine (ibid), 1956-65; Directeur de la Cie Togolaise des Mines du Benin, Lome, Togo, 1966-70. Member, Lions Club. Address: P.O. Box 362, Lome, Togo.

BERNARD, Samuel Adolphus Taiwo, born Morlane Town, Kassipoto Section, Bumpe Chiefdom, Moyamba District, Sierra Leone, 16th February 1903. Retired Civil Servant; Assessor; Chiefdom Councillor. Education: Countess of Huntingdon School, Waterloo; United Brethren in Christ School, Rotifunk; Cathedral Model Boys' School, Freetown; Railway Traffic Training Schools, Freetown & Ebutu Metta, Lagos, Nigeria. Appointments: Passed Civil Service & Promotion Exams., Sierra Leone Government Railway Department, retired through ill-health, 1922-41; Justice of the Peace; Assessor of Magistrate & Supreme Courts of Sierra Leone; Expert Adviser, Customary Law, Moyamba District; Chiefdom Councillor, Bumpo Chiefdom; President, Deputy President, & member of many committees, Moyamba District Council, 1950-67; Member, Bo Town Council Management Committee, 1966—; Management Committee, Moyamba District Council, 1969-; Past Assistant Registration Officer & Supervisor, Elections Department, Moyamba District; represented Moyamba District in proposed Committee on Democratic One Party System, & various other committees of government. Memberships: President, Waterloo Melrose Circle & Black Fifteen Club; Committee of Gentlemen Social Club, Moyamba. Address: Rotifunk, Sierra Leone.

BERNAT, Edwin Plato, born 28th March 1913. Professor of Mechanical Engineering. Education: Grammar School, Czortkow, Poland, 1923-31; Faculty of Mechanical Engineering, Technical University of Lwow, ibid, 1931-37; B.Eng., 1935; M.Eng., 1939. Married. Appointments: Assistant Lecturer & Lecturer, Technical University of Lwow, 1935-39; Flying Officer, Technical Branch, Royal Air Force, 1943-47; Lecturer, Assistant Professor, Mechanical Engineering, Polish University College, London, U.K., 1947-53; Lecturer, Mechanical Engineering, University of Sheffield, 1953-62; Professor & Head, Mechanical Engineering Department, Ahmadu Bello University, Zaria, Nigeria. Memberships: Associate, Royal Aeronautical Society, 1946; American Institute of Aeronautics & Astronautics, 1950; Institution of Mechanical Engineers, 1965; Fellow, Royal Society of Arts. Publications: Mechanics of Flight, Textbook for Pilots (Polish); Theory of Beams (Application of Laplace Transformation Method to problems in deflection of beams); contributions to vols. 3 & 4, Dictionary of Physics. Address: Department of Mechanical Engineering, Ahmadu Bello University, Zaria, Nigeria.

BERNOUSSI, Mohamed, born 20th June 1927. Director-General. Education: D.L., L. es L.; National School of Administration, Paris, France. Appointments: Comptroller, Defence Engagements, 1960-61; Deputy Secretary-General, Ministry of Finance, 1961; Director, General Treasury, Morocco, 1961-70; Director of Cabinet, Ministry of Finance, 1955-56; Professor, Moroccan School of Administration; Professor, Faculty of Law; Deputy, National Assembly; President, Provincial Assembly; Director-General, National Social Security, Morocco. Memberships: President, Lions Club, Rabat, 1970. Author of 2 publications. Honours: Knight, Order of the Throne. Address: Avenue Mohamed V, Rabat, Morocco.

BERRIE, Geoffrey Kenneth, born 4th September 1928. University Teacher. Education: Manchester Grammar School, U.K., 1939-46; B.Sc.(Botany), University of Manchester, 1946-49; Ph.D.(Botany), University of London, 1958. Married, 5 sons. Appointments: Lecturer, Botany, University College, Ibadan, Nigeria, 1952-59; Lecturer-Senior Lecturer, Botany, University of Sydney, Australia, 1959-64; Professor of Biology, University of Lagos, Nigeria, 1964; ibid, University of Malawi, 1965-69; Head, Department of Science, Cambridgeshire College of Arts & Technology, U.K., 1969-70; Professor of Botany, Fourah Bay College, University of Sierra Leone, 1971—. Memberships: Society for Experimental Biology; British Bryological Society; American Bryological Society; Nigerian Field Society; Science Association of Malawi. Author of about 15 publications in chromosome cytology of lower plants (mostly liverworts) & liverwort taxonomy & phylogeny. Address: Botany Department, Fourah Bay College, University of Sierra Leone, Freetown, Sierra Leone.

BERRY, Mohinder, born Mauran, Punjab, India, 3rd July 1935. Senior Auditor, East African Community; Auditor of Income Tax, General Fund Services of the Community in Kenya, Uganda, & Tanzania. Education: Matriculated, 1952; Intermediate Degree Exam., Punjab University, 1956; Final Examination, Auditing & Accounting, 1963; Final Examination of the Corporation of

Secretaries, 1966; studying for I.C.W.A. Personal details: son of a large family; married Snah Lata, 1955; 2 sons, 1 daughter; athletic interests. Appointments: Audit Assistant, 1958-63; Trainee Examiner of Accounts, 1963-64; Examiner of Accounts, 1964-66; Trainee Auditor, 1967; Auditor, 1967-69; Senior Auditor, 1970—; Part-time Teacher, Institute of Adult Studies, University College, Nairobi, Kenya, & British Tutorial College. Memberships: Treasurer, Arya Samaj; Treasurer of the Sports Club; Associate, Chartered Institute of Secretaries, London, U.K. Address: P.O. Box 30468, Nairobi, Kenya.

BERTHIER, Andre, born 18th March 1907. Archaeologist; Museum Curator. Education: Ecole des Chartes, Paris, France. Married Suzanne Trognee, 3 children. Appointments: Deputy, Constantine, Algeria, 1947-48. Memberships include: Correspondent, Institute of France; Vice-President, Archaeological Society of Constantine, Algeria. Author of various publications. Honours: Officer of the Legion of Honour; Military & War Medals. Address: Museum of Constantine, Algeria.

BERTOLI, E. Luciano, born Casteggio, 10th October 1925. Building Engineer & Architect. Education: Polytechnic, Milan; Graduated, Pisa University, Italy, 1955. Married, 2 children. Appointments: Free-lance professional, 1955—. Memberships: Order of Engineers, Milan, Italy; International Union of Architects; Commission for Works, Carthage; Architectural Adviser to the Tunisien Bank; Vice-President to the Italian Club in Tunis. Honours: Knight, Officer of the Order of Merit, Italy; recipient of the title Dr. Ing from the Bureau d'Etudes. Address: 66 ru Nahas Pacha, Tunis, Tunisia.

BETBEDER (Rev.) Paul, born Biarritz, France, 17th August 1906. Missionary; White Father. Education: Secondary Education, Baccalaureat, France; Seminary, Bayonne; French Seminary (Rome), Gregorian University; Doctor in Divinity, 1930. Appointments include: The White Fathers, 1931; Curate, France, 1930-31; Curate, Tanzania, 1934-38; Parish Priest, ibid, 1938-44; Religious Superior, Provincial White Fathers, Tanzania, 1944-46; Secretary to Bishop, Bukoba, ibid, 1946-47; Parish Priest, ibid, 1947-60; Curate, ibid, 1960-68. Memberships include: Uganda Society; West Lake Branch, Society of History, Tanzania. Publications include: Kihaya Grammar, 1949. Address: The White Fathers, Private Bag, P.O. Bukoba, Tanzania.

BEUNDE, John Harris, born Bwanmbe, Kribi, 15th May 1908. Teacher. Education: Elementary, Standard VI; Secondary, Class II; Book-keeping & Accountancy by correspondence, Bennett College, Sheffield. Personal details: member of evangelist family; married, 10 children. Appointments: Schoolmaster, Native Administration, West Cameroon, 1926-34; Account Clerk, Stores Supervisor, John Holt, Kribi & Ebolowa, 1935-40; Produce & Goods Storekeeper & Branch Office Manager, R. & W. King, Kribi, Ebolowa, & Douala, 1940.49; currently with CITEC as Wholesale Storekeeper, Attaché de Direction & Deputy Sales Manager, 1949—. Memberships: President, Association Fraternelle Kribienese (now defunct); Vice-President, French-speaking West African Countries for Declaration of Interdependence (ibid); Cameroon National Union. Publications: Manager, Espoir Camerounais; Contributor to column, Opinion Camerounaise in La Presse de Cameroon under name of Njuk a Beunde. Honours: Merite Camerounaise, 3rd Class; Medaille d'Honneur du Travail en Or. Address: CITEC, B.P. 5492, Douala, Federal Republic of Cameroon.

BEWES, Peter, born 21st September 1932. Surgeon. Education: Nairobi School; Marlborough College; M.A., M.B., M.Chir., Emmanuel College, Cambridge University, U.K.; St. Thomas's Hospital, London. Personal details: son of the Rev. T. F. C. Bewes, Canon of Mt. Kenya Diocese. Appointments: Senior Registrar, Surgery & Hon. Lecturer, Surgery, Mulago Hospital & Makerere University College. Fellowships: Royal College of Surgeons, U.K.; D.(Obst.)R.C.O.G.; Association of Surgeons of East Africa; Royal Society of Medicine. Honours: Albert Hopkinson Prize, Anatomy, Emmanuel College, Cambridge, 1953. Address: Dept. of Surgery, Malago Hospital, P.O. Box 7051, Kampala, Uganda.

BHANGOO, Kulwant Singh, born 25th February 1943. Physician; Lecturer. Education: Mbale Senior Secondary School, Uganda, 1954-61; M.B., Ch.B., Makerere University College; Matriculated, Punjab University, India, 1957; Passed 1st Part (Primary) F.R.C.S., U.K., 1969; submitted thesis to University of East Africa for Degree of M.D., 1970. Married. Appointments: Junior House Officer, Mulago Hospital, Uganda, 1967-68; Assistant Lecturer, Anatomy Department, Makerere Medical School, 1968; Lecturer in Anatomy, ibid, 1968—. Memberships: President, Mbale Students' Union, 1960-61; Secretary, Literary & Debating Society, Mbale, 1959; Makerere University College Squash Champion, 1965 & 1966, etc. Co-author: The Fruit Bat. Author of several articles submitted for publication. Honours: Uganda Government Scholar, 1956; British Council Prize for Elocution, 1959; Makerere College Exhibition Prize, 1966; Mujibhai Madhvani Prize, ibid, 1967. Address: Department of Surgery, Lusaka Central Hospital, P.O. Box 2379, Lusaka, Zambia.

BHARDWAJ, Bharat, born 20th March 1934. Optician. Education: Duke of Gloucester School, Nairobi, Kenya: Northampton College, U.K. Appointments: Managing Director, M/S Lens (MSA) Ltd., Kenya, & M/S Optica. Memberships: Chairman, Nairobi Motor Club; Committee, East African Safari; Vice-Chairman, K.R.D. Club; Committee, Kenya Bridge Association; Committee, Arya Samaj; Committee, S.V.I.G. Club. Honours: Motor Sportsman of the Year, 1967; Runner-up, ibid, 1968. Address: P.O. Box 1625, Nairobi, Kenya.

BHASIN, Satya Prakash, born Nairobi, Kenya, 3rd October 1921. Medical Practitioner. Education: Wadia College, Poona, India; graduated in medicine from Lucknow University, India, 1955. Memberships include:

S.V.I. Gymkhana, Nairobi, Kenya. Address: P.O. Box 4966, Nairobi, Kenya.

BHATT, Charoovadan, born India, 23rd September 1934. Dental Surgeon; Orthodontist. Education: B.Sc., Otujarat University, India; B.D.S., Bombay University; D.M.D., ibid; Dr.med.dent., Albert Ludwig University, Freiburg, Germany. Appointments: Dental Surgeon in Charge, Otuiu Hospital, Uganda, 1965-66; ibid, Jinja Hospital, ibid, 1966-69; Entebbe Hospital, Uganda, 1969-70. Memberships: Uganda Dental Association; Lions Club of Entebbe. Address: P.O. Box 8, Entebbe, Uganda.

BHATT, Gunvantraj Jayantilal, born 9th January 1935. Medical Practitioner. Education: M.B., Ch.B., Birmingham University Medical School, U.K., 1962. Currently practising medicine, Fort Portal, Uganda. Memberships: President, Lions Club, Fort Portal; President, Asian Education Society. Address: P.O. Box 54, Fort Portal, Uganda.

BHEENICK, Rundheersing, born 1st October 1944. Economist. Education: Roman Catholic School, Bon Accueil, Mauritius; Cambridge School Certificate, 1st Division, Royal College, Port Louis, 1961; Cambridge Higher School Certificate, ibid, 1963; B.A.(Hons.), Merton College, Oxford, U.K., 1964-67; Postgraduate study, ibid, 1967-68. Married. Appointments: Lecturer, Development Economics, University of Mauritius, 1968-69; Economist, Economic Planning Unit, Prime Minister's Office, then Ministry of Planning & Development, 1969-70; Industrial Development Officer, U.N. Industrial Development Organization, Vienna, Austria, 1970—. Author of several government reports, including first annual survey of economy of Mauritius—Report on the Economy of Mauritius in 1967, 1969. Honours: Primary School Scholarship, 1956; Laureate & English Scholarship, Royal College, 1963. Address: Bon Accueil, Brisee Verdiere, Mauritius.

BHIMA, Samuel Valla, born 15th June 1924. Medical Practitioner; Obstetrician & Gynaecologist. Education: Makerere University College, Kampala, Uganda; Mulago Medical School, Kampala. Appointments: Government Medical Officer, Zombe, Malawi, 1953-54; District Medical Officer, Nchen, 1954-57; Government Medical Officer, Blantyre, 1958-59; District Medical Officer, Nchen, 1959-63; Medical Superintendent, Zombe, 1963-64; Registrar, Obstetrics & Gynaecology, 1965-69. Memberships: British Medical Association; Malawi Medical Association; Hospital Advisory Board. Author of various medical articles. Address: Box 95, Blantyre, Malawi.

BHUCKORY, Somdath, born 1st November 1921. Town Clerk. Education: Primary, Long Mountain; Second-class Teachers' Examination; Barrister-at-Law, Middle Temple. Appointments: Primary School Teacher, 1943-49; Practised at Local Bar, 1954-60; Town Clerk, Municipality of Port Louis, 1960—. Memberships: Vice-President, Hindi Pracharini Sabha; President, Port Louis Hindi Parishad; ibid, Hindi Parishad Central Committee; The Triveni; Beau Bassin; Rotary Club of Port Louis; Amicale Ile Maurice-France. Publications: Local Government in Mauritius; Hindi in Mauritius; An Outline of Local Government; in Hindi: Hindi Sahitya kiek jhanki (A Glimpse of Hindi Literature); a collection of poems: Mujhe kuch kahna Hai (I have to say something). Address: Town Clerk, City Hall, Port Louis, Mauritius.

BHUVA, Bhupendra Shantilal, born 18th June 1935. Medical Practitioner specializing in Radiology. Education: M.B., Ch.B. (with commendation), Glasgow University, U.K., 1962; D.Obs.R.C.O.G., 1964; D.M.R.D., 1965. Appointments: Resident House Physician, Stobhill General Hospital, Glasgow; Resident House Surgeon, Royal Infirmary, ibid; Resident, Gynaecology & Obstetrics, Stobhill General Hospital; Registrar, Western Infirmary; Radiologist in Charge, Social Service League Group of Hospitals, Nairobi, Kenya; Specialist Radiologist, Ministry of Health & Housing, Muhimbili Hospital, Dar es Salaam, Tanzania; Consultant Radiologist, Aga Khan Hospital, ibid; Honorary Lecturer, Radio Diagnosis, Faculty of Medicine, University College, University of East Africa. Memberships: Assistant Treasurer, Medical Association of Tanzania; British Medical Association; Board of Directors, Lions Club, Dar es Salaam; Chairman, Lions Club Blood Transfusion Service Project. Honours: William Rainy Bursary for highest aggregate marks in pre-medical subjects, Glasgow University, 1958; John Hunter Medal in Systematic Anatomy, ibid. Address: P.O. Box 21166, Dar es Salaam, Tanzania.

BIDAUT, Jean, born 12th July 1919. Assistant Director-General, Société Française D'Etudes et de Realisations D'Equipements de Telecommunications (SOFRECOM). Education: Engineering Diploma, Polytechnic School, Paris, France; ibid, Higher National School of Telecommunications, Paris. Married, 2 children. Appointments: Former Director, Office of Posts & Telecommunications of French Equatorial Africa, 1951-56; ibid, French West Africa, 1956-60. Honours include: Chevalier de la Legion d'Honneur. Address: SOFRECOM, 8 rue de Berri, Paris, France.

BIGIRWENKYA, Zernbaberi Hosea Kwamya, born Masindi, Uganda, 24th May 1927. Secretary-General of the East African Community. Education: B.A.(Lond.), Makerere University College, 1953; Postgrad. Course, Institute of Education, London University, U.K., 1956-57. Married, 5 children. Appointments include: Permanent Secretary, Ministry of Animal Industry, 1962; Permanent Secretary, Foreign Affairs, 1963-68; Secretary-General, E. African Community, 1968—. Memberships include: President, East African Management Institute; Hon. Member, Arusha Chamber of Commerce; Chairman, E. African Leprosy Association; Rotary Club of Arusha. Honours: Star of Menelek II, awarded by H.I.M. Emperor of Ethiopia. Address: Secretary-General's Office, East African Community, P.O. Box 1001, Arusha, Tanzania.

BILLATA WOLDE GIORGIS WOLDE YOHANNIS, born 6th May 1895. Journalist. Attended all the famous schools & monasteries in

Ethiopia at the highest level—mastered Ethiopian literature. Married, 5 sons, 2 daughters. Appointments: Assistant Editor, Berhanena Selam (Amharic paper), 1925-53; Editor, Addis Zemen & Sendeq Alamachen (Amharic), 1940-60; Head, Amharic Publications Department with rank of Assistant Minister, & a Special Consultant, Minister of Information, Imperial Ethiopian Government. Memberships: Literary Association; Founding Member, Patriotic Association. Assisted in translating 'Fitha Negest', ancient Canon, Civil & Criminal Law. Publications (all in Amharic): Aggazi (The Liberator); Biltsigna Begibrina (Prosperity Through Agriculture); Sene-Migbar (Morale & Etiquette); Ye Alem tebay Hassetena Bikay (The Nature of the World, Happiness & Sorrow); Kesira Behwala (Leisure Time); Attesrek (The Eight Commandment); Ye-ismael kutquato (Ismael's Bush); Tarik Aymut indiachawet (The Immortality of History); Addisitu Ethiopia (Modern Ethiopia); Yebalina Yemist Chewata inca-Selantia (Family Leisure Time Jokes); Ye Nebr Jirat (The Tigers' Tail); Ye Wonde lij kurat Sele Agar mamot (Man's Pride in Patriotism). All these books are included in the elementary & high school curriculum. Honours: Hailé Sellassié I Gold Medal; Knight, Order of the Star of Honour of Ethiopia; Commander, Order of Menelik II; Winner, Poetry Contest organized by Ethiopian Literary Association. Address: Ministry of Information, Addis Ababa, Ethiopia.

BILLING, Ralph Thomas, born 10th June 1938. Education Officer. Education: B.A. (Hons.), University of Nottingham, U.K., 1959; Dip. Ed., University of Sheffield, 1960. Married, 4 children. Appointments: Teacher, Leicestershire, 1960-64; Assistant Education Officer, Island of St. Helena, 1965-68; Education Officer, ibid, 1968—. Honours: Revis Open Scholarship, University of Nottingham, 1956. Address: Education Department, Jamestown, Island of St. Helena, South Atlantic Ocean.

BILLINGHURST, John Robert, born London, U.K., 17th April 1927. Medical Practitioner; Physician; Surgeon. Education: Epsom College; St. John's College, Oxford; The London Hospital; B.A., 1948; M.A., 1952; B.M., B.Ch.(Oxon.), 1952; D.Obstr., R.C.O.G., 1953; M.R.C.P.(London), 1960. Married, 2 children. Appointments include: House Physician, Medical Unit, The London Hospital, U.K.; House Surgeon, Surgical Unit, ibid; Resident Accoucheu, ibid; Service with R.A.M.C. in Ghana & Nigeria; Junior Registrar, Cardiac Department, ibid; Medical Registrar, Hillingdon Hospital, Middlesex, U.K.; ibid, Whittington Hospital, University College Hospital, London, U.K.; Lecturer in Medicine, Makerere University College Medical School, Uganda; Senior Lecturer in Medicine, ibid; Hon. Physician, Mulago Hospital, Kampala, Uganda. Memberships include: Chairman, Board of Governors, Mulago Hospital, Kampala; President, Uganda Medical Association; Member, Association of Physicians of East Africa; Chairman, Uganda Music Society. Contributor to numerous professional journals, including: British Medical Journal, Lancet, East African Medical Journal, & Journal of Applied Physiology. Editor, new edition of 'jowell's Diagnosis & Treatment of Diseases in the Tropics', 1968; Author of Epilepsy Challenged, 1970. Awards include: Frederich Treve Prize in Surgery, The London Hospital, 1951. Address: Department of Medicine, Makerere Medical School, Box 7072, Kampala, Uganda.

BILLINGTON, William Roy, born England, 18th November 1908. Medical Missionary. Education: Shrewsbury School, U.K.; Trinity College, Cambridge; Birmingham University; M.A.; M.D.; B.Chir. Married, 2 sons. Appointments: House Surgeon, General Hospital, Birmingham; Mengo Hospital, Kampala, Uganda, 1936—; Medical Superintendent, ibid, 1951-70; currently, Health & Welfare Adviser, Church of Uganda. Member, Church Missionary Society, 1936—. Honours: M.R.C.S.(Eng.); L.R.C.P., 1933; O.B.E., 1953. Address: Mengo Hospital, P.O. Box 14051, Kampala, Uganda.

BILSON, John, born 12th June, 1928. Physician. Education: Senior Cambridge School Certificate, St. Augustine's Secondary School, Cape Coast, Ghana, 1947; B.Sc., Western Michigan University, Kalamazoo, U.S.A., 1954; M.D., Howard University, Washington, D.C., 1959. Married, 4 children. Appointments: one of four founders & first Registrar-Treasurer, Labone Secondary School, Accra, Ghana, 1949; Science Teacher, College of West Africa, Monrovia, Liberia, 1950-51; Medical Officer, Komfo Anokye Hospital, 1959; Medical Officer in Charge, Allen Clinic, Kumasi, Ghana. Memberships: President, All-African Students' Union, Ann Arbor, Michigan Branch., 1956-57; President, All-African Students' Union, Washington, D.C. Branch, 1958-59; Medical Officer in Charge, Red Cross Society, Ashanti Branch, 1960-61. Address: Allen Clinic, P.O. Box 1879, Kumasi, Ghana.

BINOCHE, Bernard, born 10th January, 1923. Deputy Director-General in charge of the direction of the African Branches of the OPTORL Company. Education: Diploma, H.E.C., Higher Commercial Studies, Paris, France; Licensed in Law. Address: c/o The OPTORL Company, 5 rue Bellini, Puteaux, France.

BINOUS, Mohsem, born 18th October, 1932. Inspector at the Ministry of Finance. Education: College Diploma, Tunis, Tunisia; Former Pupil of the Tunisian School of Administration. Writer & Translator, Journal 'Tunis-Soi', 1952-54; Special Correspondent, Moroccan Magazine 'Houna Koulou Chei'; Editor, Magazines 'El Feu', 'L'Art', 1953; Chronicler, Journal 'Le Petit Malin', 1967—. Memberships include: Past President, Association of Scholastic Youth. Address: 27 Rue de la Hafsia, Tunis, Tunisia.

BINT-EL-SHATI, See Abdel-Rahman, Aisha.

BIOBAKU, Saburi Oladeni, born Abeokuta, Nigeria, 16th June 1918. Historian. Education: Government College, Ibadan; Higher College, Yaba; University College, Exeter, U.K.; Trinity College, Cambridge; Institute of Historical Research; University of London. Personal details: married daughter of Chief Imam L. B. Agusto, Q.C., of Lagos, 1 son. Appointments include: Master, Government College, Ibadan 1941-44; Education Officer, Government College, Umuahia, 1947-49; Assistant Liaison Officer for Nigerian Students in U.K., 1951-53; Registrar, University College, Ibadan, 1953-57; Director, Yoruba Historical Research Scheme, 1956—; Secretary to Premier & Executive Council, Western Nigeria, 1957-61; Pro-Vice-Chancellor, University of Ife, Nigeria, 1961-65; Director, Institute of African Studies, ibid, 1961-65; Director, Institute of Administration, ibid, 1963-65; Vice-Chancellor, University of Lagos, & Professor & Director of African Studies, 1965—. Memberships include: Antiquities Commission & Archives Committee; Vice-Chairman, Editorial Board, Encyclopaedia Africana; Chairman, Committee of Vice-Chancellors of Nigerian Universities; Executive Board, Association of African Universities; President, Historical Society of Nigeria; Chairman, Nigerian Society for Public Administration; Member of Council, Nigerian Institute of International Affairs; Member of Council, University of Science & Technology, Kumasi, Ghana. Publications include: The Origin of the Yorubas; The Egba and Their Neighbours (1842-72). Honours include: created the Are of Iddo, Abeokuta by the Alake of Abeokuta, Nigeria, 1958; C.M.G. 1961. Address: University of Lagos, Lagos, Nigeria, W.A.

BIRDSALL, Byron, born 18th December, 1937. Artist; Teacher. Education: B.A., Seattle Pacific College, Washington, U.S.A.; M.A., Stanford University, California. Married. Appointments: Teacher, Mt. View—Los Altos High School District, Mt. View California, 1960-66; Education Officer, Ministry of Education, Uganda, 1966-69; Full-time Artist, Mombasa, Kenya, 1970—. Exhibitions: various in U.S.A.; Three One-man Shows, Nommo Gallery, Kampala, Uganda; One-man Show, Uganda Museum; One-man Show, Gallery Watatu, Nairobi, Kenya. Member, East African Philatelic Society. Address: P.O. Box 20012, Kampala, Uganda.

BIRKBECK, Alexander Charles Wyatt, born Malawi, 21st June 1943. Company Director. Education: Hydrage House, Hastings, Sussex, U.K., 1952-57; Oundle School, Northants., 1957-61. Personal details: eldest son of Major-General T. H. Birkbeck, C.B., C.B.E., D.S.O., J.P., & Mrs. R. E. W. Birkbeck. Farmer & Businessman, 1961—; various directorships. Memberships: Carpenters' Company, London; Annabels, London; Muthaiga Country Club, Nairobi, Kenya. Address: P.O. Box 9909, Nairobi, Kenya.

BISALLA, Abdullahi, born 28th December 1935. Banker. Education: Elementary School, Abuja, Nigeria, 1943-47; Government Secondary School, Bida, 1948-52. Married, 3 children. Appointments: Clerk, Northern Nigerian Government, 1954-58; Clerk, Barclays Bank DCO (now Barclays Bank of Nigeria Ltd.), 1958-63; Accountant, ibid, 1963-65; Manager, Birnin Kebbi, 1966; Gombe, 1967-68; Minna, 1968—. Memberships: Insitute of Bankers; Associate, Nigerian Institute of Management; Treasurer, Minna Club. Contributor to bankers' magazines. Address: Barclays Bank of Nigeria Ltd., Minna, Nigeria.

BISHAKA, Barnabas Rushago Sinamenye, born Nyalutembe Village, Bufunbira County, Uganda, 15th July 1945. Agriculturist. Education: Nyalutembe Primary School, 1954-55; Primary Leaving Certificate, Kaburasazi Primary School, 1956-59; Junior Leaving Certificate, Mutolene Junior Secondary School, 1960-61; Cambridge School Certificate, Kigezi College, Butobere, 1962-65; East African Diploma in Agriculture (University of East Africa), Arapai Agricultural College, 1966-68. Appointments: Assistant Agricultural Officer, Bugumbira County, Kigezi South West, 1969—. Member, Uganda Agricultural Society. Address: Department of Agriculture, P.O. Box 1028, Kisoro, Kabale, Uganda.

BISSONNET, Henri Charles Andre, born 22nd November 1913. Chief Counsellor, Cour des Comptes. Education: Doctor of Law; Diploma, Free School of Political Science. Personal details: son of Paul Bissonnet, Engineer & Berthe Liesse; second marriage to Marie Henriette Trouffier; 1 daughter of 1st marriage. Appointments: Deputy Director of the Treasury, 1956; Head of Service, Central Administration of Finances, 1962; Chief Counsellor, Cour des Comptes, 1965—. Memberships: Administrator of the Central Bank of West African States. Honours: Officer of the Legion of Honour; Cross of War; Officer of the National Order of the Ivory Coast Republic; ibid, the Malagasy Republic; Islamic Republic of Mauritania; Chevalier of the National Order of the Republic of Chad. Address: c/o La Cour des Comptes, 27 rue de Constantine VIIe.

BISSOONDOYAL, Basdeo, born Tyack Village, Mauritius, 15th April 1906. Author. Education: Villiers René School, Port Louis, Mauritius, 1913-20; Boys' Scholarship Examination, 1920; B.A.(Hons.), Punjab University, India, 1937; M.A., Calcutta University, 1939. Appointments include: Teacher, Primary School, Port Louis, Mauritius, 1921-26; ibid, Reetoo School, Saint Julien Village, Flacq, Mauritius, 1926-32; Honorary Professor, Gurukula University, Hardwar, India, 1936. Memberships include: Arya Samaj, Mauritius, 1926-32; Indian National Congress, 1936-39; Librarian, Bhardwaj Library, Dayan and Dharmshala, Port Louis, Mauritius. Publications include: Hindu Scriptures, 1960; India in French Literature, 1964; Deux Indiens Illustres, 1968; The Truth About Mauritius; Essence of the Vedas; L'Essence du Vedisme, 1969; The Message of the Four Vedes, 1970. Honours include: Sahitya Vachaspati, awarded by the Indian Academy, Hindi Sahitya Sammelan, 1969. (Frist author outside India to receive this title.) Address: 14 Vallonville Street, Port Louis, Mauritius.

BISSOONDOYAL, Sookdeo, born 25th December 1908. Teacher; Journalist. Education: 1st Class Teachers' Certificate; Proficiency in English, French, Hindi & Latin. Married, 2 sons, 2 daughters. Appointments: Government Service till 1945; M.L.A., 1948—; Minister & Government Member, 1963-69; currently Leader of the Opposition. Publications: Concise History of Mauritius; The Truth about the Sugar Industry & the Workers; Relations de Voyages. Address: Port Louis, Mauritius.

BJÖRNESJÖ, Karl Birger Yngve, born 11th February 1915. Physician; Biochemist; Educator. Education: Med. Kand., University of Uppsala, Sweden, 1938; Med. lic., ibid, 1943; Med.dr., 1953. Married. Appointments: Research Fellow, Department of Medical Chemistry, University of Uppsala, 1948-52; various assignments as Physician, mainly in international medicine, 1943-48; Associate Professor, Clinical Chemistry, University Hospital, Uppsala, 1953-54; Head, Department of Clinical Chemistry, Central County Hospital, Karlstad, 1955-66; Director, Children's Nutrition Unit, Addis Ababa, Ethiopia, 1962-64; WHO Professor of Biochemistry, & Director, Clinical Pathology Unit, Medical Faculty, Hailé Selassié I University, Addis Ababa, 1966—. Memberships: New York Academy of Sciences; Swedish Medical Association; Swedish Biochemical Society; Swedish Association of Clinical Chemistry; Ethiopian Medical Association. Author of some 60 publications in fields of medicine & biochemistry. Honours: External Exaniner, Medical Faculty, University College, Dar Es Salaam, Tanzania, 1969 & Medical Faculty, University of Ibadan, Nigeria, 1970; Knight, Northern Star Order. Address: Medical Faculty, Hailé Selassié I University, P.O. Box 1176, Addis Ababa, Ethiopia.

BLACKWOOD, Michael Hill, born 31st May 1917. Solicitor: Notary Public. Education: Croxton Preparatory School; Ormskirk Grammar School, U.K.; LL.M.(Hons.), Liverpool University, 1939. Married Iris France, 1 son, 1 daughter. Appointments: Solicitor, Partner, Firm of Wilson & Morgan, Legal Practitioners, Blantyre, Malawi; served in Royal Artillery, with 11(EA) Div. as Major in U.K., East Africa, Madagascar (now the Malagasy Republic), Ceylon, India, Burma, 1940-46; Town Councillor, Blantyre, 1950-52; Mayor, Blantyre, 1951-52; Blantyre Town Planning Comm., 1950-52; Blantyre Water Board, 1950-52; Chairman, ibid, 1951-52; Director, Blantyre Sports Club, 1949-52; Vice-President, 1951-52; Chairman, Nyasaland Public Library, 1951; Jundicial Assistance Comm., International Bar Council, 1951; President, Nyasaland Society for the Blind, 1955-62; President, Convention of Association, 1955-56; ibid, Nyasaland Association, 1955-59; Nyasaland Legislative Council, 1954-56; Elected Member of Parliament for Blantyre & Lomba, 1956-65; Nominated Member of Parliament for Blantyre, 1966-70; Nyasaland Executive Council, 1956-61; Registrar of the Diocese of Malawi, 1957-62; Chancellor, ibid, 1962-69; Director of 33 companies, Malawi; Chairman, Public Accounts, Select Comm. of Malawi Parliament, 1966-70. Memberships: Blantyre Sports Club; Country Club, Limbe. Honours: C.B.E. & mentioned in War Despatches., 1939-45. Address: Box 9, Blantyre, Malawi.

BLAGDEN, John Ramsay, born Davas, Switzerland, 25th July 1908. Barrister-at-Law. Education: Hawtreys School, U.K., 1917-22; Marlborough College, 1922-27; M.A., Emmanuel College, Cambridge University, 1927-30; Barrister-at-Law, Lincoln's Inn, London, 1930-34. Married, 3 daughters. Appointments: Practice at the Bar, 1934-39; Territorial Army & War Service, to rank of Lieutenant-Colonel, 1928-47, 1948-50; Permanent President, Military Government Courts, BAOR (rank of Colonel), 1945-47; Judge, Control Commission High Court, West Germany, 1947-50; Senior Magistrate, Sarawak, 1950-56; Puisne Judge, Trinidad & Tobago, 1956-60; Puisne Judge, Northern Rhodesia, 1960-64; Judge of Appeal, Northern Rhodesia & Zambia, 1964-65; Chief Justice, Zambia, 1965-69; currently Regional Chairman of Industrial Tribunals. Memberships: Ski Club of Great Britain; Special Forces Club; International Law Association; World Peace Through Law Association. Honours: O.B.E., 1945; T.D., 1943; Grand Cordon of the Order of the Star of Ethiopia, 1965. Address: The White House, Finningham, Stowmarket, Suffolk, U.K.

BLAKE, Eileen Florence, born 21st May 1911. Lecturer in History. Education: University of London, U.K. Married to J. W. Blake, 3 children. Appointments: Lecturer, History, University of Botswana, Lesotho & Swaziland, Roma, Lesotho. Publications: From Stone Axe to Space Age (with G. M. Haliburton), a history textbook for the secondary schools of Botswana, Lesotho & Swaziland. Address: Vice-Chancellor's Lodge, University of Botswana, Lesotho & Swaziland, P.O. Roma, Lesotho.

BLANCHE, Jacques Roland, born Paris, France, 28th September 1913. Company Manager. Education: Lycée Jansen de Sailly, Paris, France. Personal details: married Solange Samat from Reunion Island, 1936. Appòintments: General Manager, Consortium Cinematographique, Mauritius, 1936-52; General Manager, Blanche Bizgor Ltd., Port Louis, Mauritius, 1953-70. Memberships: Honorary Member, Racing Club de France, Paris. Address: c/o Blanche Bizgor Ltd., Port Louis, Mauritius.

BLANKSON, Oman Ghan, born 17th November, 1899. Retired. Education: Primary, Wesley Methodist, Winneba, Ghana, 1905-17; Certificate of College of Preceptors, 1917; Teachers' Certificate, Schedule H; Associate of Music, A.Mus.V.C.M., London. Married. Appointments: School-teacher, 1918-22; Junior Clerk, Miller Brothers, 1923-30; Book-keeper, ibid, 1930-36; Cheif Clerk, U.A.C. of Ghana Ltd., 1937-43; Storekeeper & Local Representative, 1944-52. Memberships: Violinist, Winneba Dance Orchestra, 1920s; Choirmaster, Organist, Winneba Methodist Church, 1919-58; Patron, Winneba Students' Union, 1948-54. Publications: Robertsville Hymnal containing hymns, chants, & anniversary songs, 1949. Honours: Certificate for long service (15 years), U.A.C. of Ghana, 1938; Retiring Award, gold watch, ibid, for 29 years' service. Address: Anamoaba Fie, P.O. Box, Winneba, Ghana.

BLIGNAUT, Christiaan Johannes, born Barkley East, Cape Province, South Africa, 7th December 1931. Physician. Education: M.B., Ch.B., University of Cape Town Medical School, 1954; D.O., London, 1965. Personal details: ancestors came from France with the Huguenots in 1688; married Delene Naude, 1958, 4 children. Appointments: Intern, General Medicine & Surgery, Groofe Schuur Hospital, Cape Town, 1955; General Medical Officer,

Nkhoma, D.R.C. Mission Hospital, Malawi, 1956-58; Surgical Resident, Pennsylvania Hospital, Philadelphia, U.S.A., 1958-59; Medical Suprintendent, Nkhoma Mission Hospital, Malawi, 1959—. Memberships: Medical Association of South Africa, 1955; Malawi Nurses & Midwives Council; Christian Council of Malawi; First Chairman, Private Hospital Association, Malawi; Board Member, ibid; Brown Memorial Trust; General Administration Committee, Nkhoma Synod, Church of Central Africa Presbyterian. Publications: The Danger of Intraperitoneal Neomycin, 1962. Address: c/o Nkhoma Mission Hospital, Malawi.

BLOMGREN, Robert Milton, born 16th March 1938. Mathematician. Education: B.S., North Park College, 1960; M.S., University of Minnesota, 1963; Ph.D., ibid, 1968. Appointments: Lecturer, Mathematics, University College, Nairobi. Memberships: American Mathematical Society; Mathematical Association of America. Address: P.O. Box 30197, Nairobi, Kenya.

BOAITEY, Stephen Asamoah, born Mampong-Akrofoso, Ashanti, Ghana, 5th December 1912. Land Surveyor, Education: Presbyterian Mission Boarding School, Mampong, 1929; Gold Coast Survey School, 1930-32; Photogrammetry, Directorate of Colonial Surveys, Teddington, U.K., 1949-50; Evening Classes, Twickenham Technical College; Advanced Studies, Imperial College, London University. Married, 2 children. Appointments include: Land Surveyor, Gold Coast Survey Dept., Civil Service, 1930-64; retired from Senior Service, 1964; seconded to Gold Coast Regiment, RWAFF Survey Unit, served with rank of Sergeant, 1939-44; served as Military Servey Instructor, Teshie Camp, Accra; Principal Assistant Surveyor, Ghana Water Supplies Division, 1964; Principal Survey Officer, WHO/UN Special Fund Project, Water Supplies Division; helped to establish Ghana Water & Sewerage Corporation, 1965; currently in private practice as Ghana Licensed Surveyor. Memberships include: Communicant Member, Presbyterian Mission; Ghana Legion; The Ghana Ex-Servicemen's Union; President, Mampong-Akrofoso Welfare Association; Ghana Licensed Surveyors' Association; Ashanti Youth Association. Honours, prizes, etc: elected Fellow, Royal Geographical Society, 1950. Address: P.O. Box 1485, Kumasi, Ashanti, Ghana.

BOATENG, Ernest Amano, born 30th November 1920. Educator. Education: Achimota College, 1929-41; B.A.(Hons., Geography), Oxford University, U.K., 1946-50; M.A., 1953; B.Litt., 1954. Married, 3 daughters. Appointments: Lecturer, Geography, University College of Ghana, 1950-57; Senior Lecturer, ibid, 1957-61; Visiting Assistant Professor, University of Pittsburgh & University of California, Los Angeles, U.S.A., 1960-61; Professor, Geography, University of Ghana, 1961—; Dean, Faculty of Social Studies, 1962-69; Principal, University College of Cape Coast, 1969—. Memberships: UNESCO International Advisory Committee on Humid Tropics Research, 1961-63; National Planning Commission, Ghana, 1961-64; Scientific Council for Africa, 1963—; Smuts Visiting Fellow, University of Cambridge, 1965-66; Council for Scientific & Industrial Reasearch, Ghana, 1967—. Publications: A Geography of Ghana, 1959; various articles on geography in Encyclopaedia Britannica & learned journals. Honours: Henry Oliver Beckit Memorial Prize, Oxford, 1949; Grand Medal, Ghana, 1968. Address: University College of Cape Coast, Cape Coast, Ghana.

BOB-LAMPTEY, Jacob, born 16th June 1916. Cinematographer. Education: Presbyterian Junior School, Asuboi, Ghana, 1923-27; Anglican Mission School, Nsawam, 1928-31; Achimota College, 1932-38; Men's Institute, Birmingham, U.K., 1950-53; University of Southern California, Los Angeles, U.S.A., 1962. Married, 5 sons, 3 daughters. Appointments: Cashier, Messrs Lamant Co., Ghana, 1940-48; Assistant Paying Officer, Cocoa Rehabilitation Scheme, Koforidua, 1949; Special Front-page Photographer, Sunday Mirror, Ghana, 1953; U.S.I.S. Cinematographer, West Africa, 1958; TV Cameraman, CBS, N.B.C. ABC & Hearst Metrotone News, New York. Associate Member, Society of Motion Picture & Television Engineers, U.S.A. Address: P.O. Box 440, Accra, Ghana.

BOCK, Kenneth Russell, born 11th February 1930. Plant Pathologist; Virologist. Education: B.Sc., Ph.D., A.R.C.S., Imperial College of Science, London University, U.K. Appointments: Senior Scientific Officer, Coffee Berry Disease Research Unit, Kaidi, Kenya; Head, Division of Plant Pathology, Nematology & Quarantine Services, EAAFRO (East African Community). Memberships include: Chairman, East African Standing Technical Committee on Plant Import & Export; ibid, East African Comm. on Sugar Cane Research; Association of Applied Biologists. Author of publications on coffee berry disease, virus diseases of hops, diseases of sugar cane & coconut, etc. Address: EAAFRO, East African Agriculture & Forestry Research Organization, P.O. Box 30148, Nairobi, Kenya.

BOCOMBA, Michel, born 18th May 1922. Deputy Administrator, Administrative & Financial Services. Education: Diploma, l'Ecole Superieure Edouard Renard. Appointments: Deputy Head, External Commerce Service, 1956; Head, Administration Control, 1960; Assistant Prefect, 1960; Head, External Commerce Service, 1961—. Member, Treasurer & Secretary, African Touring Club. Honours: Knight, Black Star of Benin; Knight, Star of Anjouan; Knight, Congolese Merit.

BOFFEY, Thomas Brian, born 3rd July, 1939. University Lecturer. Education: Sandbach School, 1949-57; B.Sc., Liverpool University, U.K., 1957-60; M.Sc., ibid, 1960-62; Ph.D., London University, 1962-67. Married, 3 children. Appointments: Lecturer, Mathematics, Northern Polytechnic, London, 1965-67; ibid, Chancellor College, University of Malawi, 1967-69; Lecturer, Computing & Operational Research, Liverpool University, 1969—. Publications: Elastic Constants of Metallic Lithium (J. Phys. C.), 1968; Comment on Toya's Method for

Obtaining the Phonon Frequencies in Monovalent Metals (Phys. Letters A), 1969. Address: Department of Computational & Statistical Science, Liverpool University, Liverpool, U.K.

BOGA, Ramzan Kassamali, born Zanzibar, 21st December 1935. Civil Engineer. Education: Agakhan School, Zanzibar, 1940-42; Government Boys' Secondary School, Zanzibar, 1948-52; First Grade Senior Cambridge School Certificate, 1952; Bachelor Degree (E.E.) Victoria Jubilee Technical Institute of Bombay University, 1959; Postgraduate Diploma in Concrete Technology, University of Leeds, England, 1961; Research Work, University of Leeds, leading to Master's Degree (M.Sc.), financed partly by the Agakhan Scholarship Funds, and partly by the University of Leeds, 1962-64. Personal details: wife of Swiss nationalaity. Appointments include: Designer, Civil Engineering Offices of a variety of structures, including buildings, power stations, heavy foundations, etc., with the following firms: Mr. D. P. Sachania, Architect, Zanzibar, 1959-60; M/s Constructors John Brown, London, 1961-62; M/s Frutiger und Sohne, Ag., Thun, Switzerland, 1964-65; M/s P. E. Malmstrom Copenhagen, Denmark, 1965-67; Mr. R. A. Sutcliffe, M.I. Struct. E., Nairobi, 1967—. Memberships include: Secretary, International Society, Leeds University and Foreign Students' Representative in the Leeds University Union, 1962-64; Member of the Foreign Students' Council at the International Student Centre, Copenhagen, Denmark, 1965-67; also at the International Student Centre, Chairman of Debating Society; Chairman of the Dramatic Group; one of the Editors of the International Newsletter; one of the founders and first Joint Secretary of Elphinstone College Overseas Student Union, 1954-55. Address: P.O. Box 4136, Nairobi, Kenya.

BOGOHE, Lameck Makaranga, born Bukabile Nassa Mwanza District, Tanganyika, Tanzania. Businessman. Education: Kabita Primary School, 1940; Ikizu Day School, 1942-43; Ujiji Training School, 1948-50; Cape Town voice of prophecy Bible School; Junior & Senior Certificate in Religion, 1951-53. Appointments: General Secretary, Sukuma Union, 1953-54; Assistant Treasurer, Tanganyika African Association, 1953-54; elected Representative, ibid annual conference for Lake Province; Joint Founder, TANU, 1954; Training Course, Poultry Industry, Government Central Breeding Station, Mpwapwa, 1955; elected Councillor, Mwanza African Advisory District Council, 1955-60; ibid, Sukumaland Federal Council, Malya, 1956-59; Comm. Mbr., Solima Growers Cooperative Society, 1956-63; ibid, Kigunabahabi Growers Coop. Union, Ltd., 1957-59; Rep., Victoria Fed. of Coop. Unions Ltd., 1957-59; Sub-Chiefdom Council & Chiefdom Council, 1962-64; Councillor & Vice-Chairman, Mwanza District Council, 1966-69; Sec., M.P. for Mwanza East, 1965-69. Address: Mwanza District Council, P.O. Box 770, Mwanza, Tanzania.

BOJUWOYE, Michael F., born 12th January 1935. Medical Practitioner. Education: St. Leo's College, Abeokuta, Nigeria, 1951-54; GCE 'A' Level, Nigerian College of Technology, 1957-60; M.B., B.S.(Lond.), University College, Ibadan, 1965. Married, 2 children. Appointments: Senior Hospital Officer, Obstetrics & Gynaecology, Lagos Island Maternity Hospital, 1966; Senior Hospital Officer, Surgery, Lagos University Teaching Hospital, 1966-67; Staff Medical Officer, ibid, 1967—. Member, Nigeria Medical Association. Address: Lagos University Teaching Hospital, Lagos, Nigeria.

BOKWANGO, Andre-Romain, born Ngiri, Democratic Republic of the Congo, 2nd February 1927. Editor; Journalist; Novelist. Education: School Prefect; took correspondence course. Personal details: youngest of 9 children. Appointments: Army Service, 7 years; visited U.S.A. & Germany in connection with his Editorial responsibilities; Founder, National Council of Women of the Congo. Publications: Les Contes des Bangalas; Presence Congolaise; Coup d'oeil sur le passe Ancestral; L'Enfant Inconnu; Eva (a review for the modern woman). Address: c/o Eva, B.P. 8546, Kinshasa, 79 rue Nzobe, Bandalungwa, Kinshasa, Democratic Republic of the Congo.

BOLTON, Kenneth Ewart, born Worcestershire, U.K., 15th March 1914. Journalist. Education: King Edward's, Stourbridge, U.K. Married, 1 son, 1 daughter. Appointments include: Lt.-Col., 11th (H.A.C.) Regiment, R.H.A., Western Desert, Sicily, & Italy; Reporter, County Express, Daily Mail, News Chronicle, U.K.; News Editor, Birmingham Gazette & Evening Dispatch; Deputy Editor, Evening Dispatch; Editor & Director, East African Standard, Nairobi, Kenya. Memberships include: Fellow, Royal Society of Arts; Fellow, Royal Commonwealth Society; Nairobi Club. Publications include: The Lion and the Lily; The Saturday Essays; Harambee Country. Honours include: O.B.E., 1963; M.C., 1943; Commonwealth Award in Journalism, 1968; Silver Medal for Editorials, 1969. Address: East African Standard, P.O. Box 30080, Nairobi, Kenya.

BONA, Dudu Bentis, born 20th December 1920. Administrator; Natural Ruler; Paramount Chief. Education: Jaiana Primary School, then U.B.C., 1932-36; Bo Government Secondary School, 1937-42. Married, many children. Appointments: Member of Parliamanet, 1957-67; elected Paramount Chief, Jaiama Nimikoro, 1953. Member, Farmers' Society. Honours: Justice of the Peace, 1955; Certificate of Honour, 1958. Address: c/o N.A. Office, Jaiama Nimikoro, P.O. Box 190, via Koidu, Kono District, Sierra Leone.

BONAVERO, Pierre Paul Marius, born 27th September 1921. Director. Education: studied at the Free School of Political Science. Appointments: Founder, Society of Emyrne, Tananarive, Malagasy (Export Business); Treasurer, Trade Union for Cameroun Import & Export; Vice-President (Agricultural Section for raising Forests & Fisheries), Inter-professional Group for the Study & Co-ordination of the Cameroun Economic Interests; Director, Daniel Ancel & Fils, Douala, Cameroun. Memberships: Chamber of Commerce; Member of the

Management Committee for the cash stabilisation of Café Robusta. Address: Daniel Ancel & Fils, Douala, Cameroun.

BOND, Margaret Hester, born Trowbridge, England, 3rd June 1905. State Registered Nurse; Certified Midwife; Missionary. Education: Trowbridge Girls' High School; Uplands School, St. Leonards-on-Sea, to Matriculation; Westminster Hospital, General Nursing Training 1929-32; Kingston-on-Thames Hospital, Midwifery Training, 1932. Appointments include: following Nursing and Midwifery training, was accepted for training by the Church Missionary Society and sent to Mengo Hospital in Kampala, Uganda, as a Nursing Sister in October, 1933; Matron, Ngora Hospital, 1953-56; Matron, Mengo Hospital, 1956-64; retired from Mengo Hospital, January 1964; appointed as first Travelling Secretary to the Uganda Hospitals Christian Fellowship, 1965. Memberships include: Overseas Club, Uganda Music Society; Uganda Nurses & Midwives Council, 1956-64. Publications include: Notes on Surgical Nursing—lecture notes in Luganda for student nurses (before they were taught in English). Honours, prizes, etc. New Year's Honours M.B.E., 1959, Investiture Buckingham Palace, July 1959; Uganda Independence Medal, 1962. Address: Uganda Hospitals Christian Fellowship, P.O. Box 14020, Kampala, Uganda.

BONGO (His Excellency) Albert-Bernard, President of Republic of Gabon, born Lewai, District of Léconi, Haut-Ogooué, Gabon, 30th December 1935. Education: Official School, Bacongo, Brazzaville; Technical College, ibid; Commercial Diploma. Married, 2 children. Appointments include: entered Civil Service, 1958; assigned to Ministry of Foreign Affairs, 1960; Deputy Director, Presidential Cabinet, 1962; Director, ibid, 1962; at Ministry of Information & Tourism, 1963-64; at Ministry of National Defense, 1964-65; Government Commissioner, Court of State Security, 1964-65; entered Government as Delegate Minister to President of Republic, i/c of National Defense & Coordination; Minister of Information & Toursim, 1966; Vice-President, Republic of Gabon, Republic of Gabon, 1967; President & Head of Government, ibid, 1967; Founder, P.D.G., Democratic Party of Gabon. Honours include: Grand Chanceller, National Order of Equatorial Star; Grand Cross of National Order of Ivory Coast and of National Order of Niger; Grand Officer, National Central African Order; Commander, National French Order of Merit; Combattant Officer of Merit; Colonel in the Reserves. Address: Officer of the President, B.P. 546, Libreville, Gabon.

BONONGWE, Richard Peterson, born 3rd March 1922. Medical Assistant. Education: Standard 8, Bandawe Mission, Chintheche Boma, Malawi, 1942. Married, 6 children. Appointments: Military Service, 1942-45; Medical Assistant, 1945—. Memberships: Past Treasurer, Nyasaland Student Association; Vice-Secretary, Malawi Congress Party; Sports Organizer, Mbabzi Estate Club; Secretary, ibid; Member, Wages Advisory Board, Wages Advisory Council. Honours include: Military Defence Medal. Address: Mbabzi Estate Ltd., Lilongwe, Malawi.

BOROKINI-DADA, Akinsanya, born 4th June 1930. Medical Practitioner. Education: St. Jude's School, Ebute Metta, 1939-43; C.M.S. Grammar School, Lagos, Nigeria, 1944-49; Glasgow University, U.K., 1961-63. Appointments: Medical Officer, Nigeria, 1962-67; Senior Medical Officer, 1967. Memberships: Vice-Patron, Young Fellows Christian Union; Committee, Holy Trinity Church, Ikorodu. Address: P.O. Box 903, Lagos, Nigeria.

BOROTA, Jan, born 17th September 1925. Silviculturist. Education: High School, 1946; M.Sc., Forestry Faculty, University of Prague, Czechoslovakia, 1950; D.Ph., ibid, 1957; Habilitation, Lvolen, 1965. Appointments: Lecturer, Forestry Faculty, University of Prague, 1950-65; Study Tour, India, 1963; Forest Research Officer, Mensuration, Tanzania, 1965-67; Professor, Forestry & Timber Products Colleges, Department of World Forestry, Lvolen, Czechoslovakia, 1968-69; Silviculturist, Tanzania, 1969—. Author of some 48 papers in various Slovak, Czech & English journals. Address: P.O. Box 2066, Dar es Salaam, Tanzania.

BOT BA NJOCK, Henri Marcel, born Lolodorf, Cameroun, 3rd December 1925. University Professor. Education: Primary School, Cameroun, —1942; Secondary Instruction, 1940-50; Higher Instruction, France, 1960-63; L. es L., Sorbonne, Paris, France; Diploma, School of Living Oriental Languages, Paris; Doctorat d'Etat ès Lettres et Sciences Humaines, Sorbonne, Paris, 1970. Married, 6 children. Appointments: Professor at a Private College, Cameroun, 1946; Police Inspector, Cameroun, 1950-52; School-teacher, ibid, 1952-54; Assistant, School of Oriental Languages, Paris, 1958-62; Lecturer, Federal Cameroun University, Yaoundé, 1962; Foreign Assistant, Sorbonne, Paris, 1967-70; Lecturer, School of Oriental Languages, Paris, 1968-70; Professor, Federal Cameroun Universtiy, Head of the Department, African Languages & Linguistics, 1970—. Memberships: Africanists' Society, Paris; Linguistic Society, ibid; Councillor, Linguistic Society of West Africa. Author of numerous works in his field. Address: B.P. 337, Yaoundé, Cameroun.

BOTCHWAY, Christian Ayebeng, born Accra, Ghana, 4th December 1934. Dental Surgeon. Education: Accra Government Boys' School, 1939-48; Achimota Secondary School, 1949-55; B.D.S., King's College Dental School, University of London, U.K., 1956-61; M.Sc.D., Graduate Dental School, University of Toronto, Canada, 1965-67; L.D.S., R.C.S.Eng., 1961. Married, 1 son, 2 daughters. Appointments: Dental House Surgeon, King's College Hospital, London, U.K., 1961; Senior House Surgeon, ibid, 1962; Dental Surgeon, Ministry of Health, Ghana, 1962-67; Senior Dental Surgeon, ibid, 1968—. Memberships: Toastmasters International, Skondi/Takoradi Branch; Sekondi Tennis Club; Takoradi Cricket Club. Publications: Pedodontics in Ghana (Am. J. Childrens Dent.), 1964. Address: Effia Nkwanta Hospital, P.O. Box 229, Sekondi, Ghana.

BOUAZIZ, Naceur, born 31st March 1937. Producer; Director. Education: Al Ahlia, Zeitounien instruction; pupil of Professor Agrebi in the Theatre. Personal details: son of Cheikh Mohamed El Nouldi Bouaziz, Magistrate. Appointments: Typographer, 1950-53; Editor of artistic themes in periodicals; Collaborator in the following Reviews: Flambeau de l'Art; Noujoum El Fann; Koul Chai Bil Makchouf, 1953-57; Director, Administrator, journal of Pr. Hamadi Dsaziri known under the pen-name of Es-Sitar, 1960-62; Founder, 3rd Folklore Ballet of Tunis, 'Ranet Kholkhal', 1960-62; Founder, 'Theatre Africain', troup of dramatic artists, dancers & musicians, 1962—; Founder, Film Society, Maghreb Films; Director, Adahoua El Madina (weekly paper); Founder, General Union of Arts & Culture, 1969—. Composer of over 100 melodies; Author of several plays broadcast on the Arab Radio, also of articles in the Army journal. Address: 23 Rue Albert Samain, 23, 'El Omrane', Tunisia.

BOUBAKEUR, Hamza, born 15th June 1912. University Professor; Rector of the Moslim Institute of the Mosque of Tunis. Education: Maitre-Chancelier des ordres de Chevalerie de l'Islam Sunnite. Personal details: descendant of the 1st Calife de l'Islam, AbuBakr as-Siddiq. Appointments: Professor; Rector; Former Deputy to the Vice-President, the Commission of Foreign Affairs, Paris, France. Memberships: Corresponding Member, several cultural institutions & religious associations of Africa, Europe & Asia. Honours: Grand Cross & several Orders of Knighthood, e.g. Legion of Honour; Palmes Academiques; Merite Agricole, etc. Publications include: Folklore ALgerian; Le Coran—traduction francaise et commentaire; Le psalmode Coranique. Address: 47 rue G. Sauir Hilani, Tunis, Tunisia.

BOUCHERLE, Pierre, born Tunis, 11th April 1894. Artist. Appointments: Professor, Tunis Lycée, Fine Arts' School, Tunis. Memberships: Autumn Salon, Paris; Founder of the group, 'L'Ecole de Tunis'. Edited Commemorative Plaque for the Grand Exhibition, Paris, 1935, Texts of Georges Dumhamel, Academie Francaise, Andre Salmon, Poet & Art Critic; Lugne-Pöe, Director of the Theatre de l'oeuvre, Paris. Honours: First recipient of the Tunisien Governments' Artistic Travelling Scholarship; Knight, Legion of Honour. Address: 10 Rue Es-Sadikia, Tunis, Tunisia.

BOUCHOUCHA, Sadok, born 30th November 1925. Pharmacist. Education: Pharmacist's Diploma in Serology, Biological Chemistry & Clinical Biochemistry, Faculty of Montpellier, France. Married, 6 children. Appointments: Pharmacist, Bizerta, Tunisia, 1953. Memberships: Vice-President, Municipality of Bizerta, 1957-60; Municipal Counsellor, Bizerta, 1960-63. Honours: Recipient of distinction in Serology, 1953. Address: 1 Bis Square Commandant Bijaoui, Bizerta, Tunisia.

BOUIC, Joseph, born 9th February 1909. Company Director. Education: Cambridge School Certificate; Associate, Association of Certified & Corporate Accountants. Appointments: Managing Director, Ireland Fraser & Co. Ltd., 1950—. Memberships: Mauritius Turf Club; Dodo Club. Address: P.O. Box 58, Port-Louis, Mauritius.

BOUMEDIENNE (His Excellency, Colonel) Houari, President of the Algerian Republic, born Guelma, 1925. Education: Zaitouna University, Tunisia; Al Azhar University, U.A.R.; Military School of Paris, France. Appointments: received Military Training in Cairo; Commandant, Wilaya 5, Oran, Algiers, 1955; Chief of Staff, National Liberation Forces, 1960; Minister of National Defence, 1962; First Vice-President, Ministerial Council, 1963-65; President of the Algerian Republic, 1965—. Address: The Presidency Palace, Algiers, Algéria.

BOUMIE, Emmanuel, born 17th March 1930. Member of Parliament. Married, 10 children. Appointments: Deputy, Chad, 1962; Municipal Councillor, DOBA; Re-elected Deputy, 1964; Chad Delegate to the U.N.O., 20th, 21st, 22nd, & 23rd Sessions, New York, U.S.A., 1965-68; First Federal Secretary, Longone-oriental of PTT, DOBA, 1967; Re-elected Deputy, Legislative elections; Member, Quaestor, National Assembly, 1969—; Chief Technical Agent, Public Health Scale, 1969. Memberships: Chad Progressive Party Honours: Officer of Civil Merit; Officer, National Order of Chad. Address: Questeur a l'Assemblée Nationale du Chad, Fort Lamy, Chad.

BOUMNACK, Preni Henri, born Boumnkok, Cameroon, 30th September 1919. Secretary of State for Public Works. Education: Graduation Diploma, Ecole Normale, Foulassi, 1938. Married, 10 children. Appointments include: Master of Education, 1939-43; Customs Officer, 1944-54; Head, Administrative Post, 1955-56; Customs Officer, 1957-65; Deputy, Legislative Assembly, 1965—; Secretary of State for Public Works, 1965—; concurrently Chef Supérieur, Dmala, 1958—. Secretary-General, Friendly Association of Ban Tribe; Hon. Member, Union Nationale Cameroun. Honours include: Cameroon Order of Merit, 3rd class, 1955; ibid, 2nd class, 1964; Knight, National Order of Merit, 1965. Address: B.P. 1060, Yaoundé, Cameroun.

BOURGADE, Eugene, born 9th May 1908. Dealer in Livestock & Meat. Education: Secondary Studies, Paris, France. Appointments: Meat Dealer, 1930-39; Breeder & Dealer, Livestock, 1943-45; Meat Dealer, 1945-53; Administrator of Societies in Africa, 1953-60; Technical Advisor to the Ministry of Agriculture of Chad, 1960-70; Delegate to F.A.O. & P.A.M. Director of Council Ministry of Agriculture, 1960-65; Vice-President, Territorial Assembly of Chad, 1958-59; President, ibid, 1959. Membership: President, Rotary Club of Fort Lamy. Honours: Officer of the National Order of Chad, 1961. Address: Ministry of Agriculture, Fort Lamy, Chad.

BOURGES, Maurice, born Marseille, France, 4th January 1936. Director-General; Engineer. Education: studied at Polytechnical School; National School of Ports & Roads; Engineer of

Ports & Roads. Married, 4 children. Appointments: Head of the 4th Sector, Public Works Department, Ivory Coast, 1961-62; Head of the 2nd Sector, ibid, 1962-64; Director-General, Bureau National d'Etudes Techniques de Developpement de la Côte d'Ivoire (B.N.E.T.D.), 1967—. Author of several publications on Roadways and works within the Ivory Coast. Address: B.P. 1556, Abidjan, Ivory Coast.

BOURGUIBA (His Excellency) Habib, President of the Republic of Tunisia, born Monastir, 3rd August 1903. Education: Diploma, Literature, Pol. Sci. & Law; Lic. Law, Free School of Political Science, University of Paris, France. Appointments: Member, Destour Party, 1921; Founder, Neo-Destour Party, 1934; arrested for political reasons, 1934-36 & again, 1952-54; returned to Tunisia, 1955; President Tunisian National Assembly, Prime Minister & President of the Council, 1956-59; Minister of Foreign Affairs & Defence, 1959; President of Destour Socialist Party & Republic of Tunisia, 1957—. Author of 'Le Destour et ia France', 1937; 'La Tunisie et la France', 1954; Honours: Ordre du Sang; Order of the Confiance (diamond). Address: The Presidency, Palace, Tunis, Tunisia.

BOURGUIBA, Habib, Jr., born 9th April 1927. Lawyer; Diplomat. Education: Diplome fin etudes, College Sadiki, Tunis, Tunisia; Baccalaureat, 2nd Part, Dijon, France; Law Schools, Paris & Grenoble; Licence en droit, Grenoble. Married, 3 children. Appointments: Ambassador of Tunisia to Rome, 1957-58; Ambassador to Paris, 1958-61; Ambassador to Washington, D.C., 1961-63; Secretary-General, Government of Tunisia, 1963; Foreign Minister, 1964-70; Minister of Justice, 1970—. Honours: Grand Cordon de l'Independence et de la Republique Tunisienne; numerous foreign decorations. Address: Al Mahroussa, Ave. Salambo, Tunis, Tunisia.

BOURKOU, Louise, born 5th July 1934. Teacher; Deputy, National Assembly. Married, 6 children. Appointments: Teacher, 1950-62; Deputy, 1962-70. Memberships include: Association des femmes du Parti, 1962. Honours; Chevalier, l'Ordre National Tchadion. Address: B.P. no. I, Assembly Nationale, Fort Lamy, Chad.

BOUTROS-GHALI, Boutros-Youssef, Born 14th November 1922. Editor; Educator. Education: Licence in Law, Cairo University, Egypt, 1946; Diploma, Political Science Institute, Paris University, France, 1947; Ph.D., Paris, 1949. Appointments: Professor of International Law & International Organizations, Cairo University, Egypt; Head, Department of Political Sciences, ibid; Editor, Al Siassa Dawlya. Memberships: Egyptian Society of International Law; Egyptian Society of Political Science; Coptic Society of Archaeology; International Law Association. Author of more than 60 articles & essays in Arabic, French & English. Author of 10 books on International Relations & International Law. Address: Al-Ahram, Galla Street, Cairo, Egypt.

BOUVET DE LA MAISONNEUVE (Count) Guy, born 1919. Judicial Adviser. Education: Baccalaureat, Latin, Greek, Philosophy; Lic. en Droit. Married Henriette de Billeheust d'Argenton. Practised in Morocco & France. Honours: Cross of War. Address: Casablanca, Morocco.

BOUYAHIA, Chedly, born 20th October 1918. University Professor. Education: Agreg. d'Arabe, 1949; Doctorat es lettres d'Etat, Paris, France, 1969. Appointments: Professor, Faculty of Letters, University of Tunis, Tunisia. Publications: various articles in literary reviews in Arabian & French; La vie litteraire en Ifrigiya sous les Zirides; Ibu Rasiq, Quradat ad-dahab. Address: 1 rue d'Ajaccis, Tunis, Tunisia.

BOWA, Allan Chisekele, born Fonkofouko Village, Chinsali District, North Province, Zambia, 27th December 1926. Teacher. Education: Standard 6, Lubwa Mission School, 1946; Teachers' Course, Practical & Theoretical Agriculture, Senga Agricultural Training School, 1946-48. Married. Appointments: Assistant Head Teacher, Chinsali School, 1948-53; Head Teacher, ibid, 1953-55; Mikomfwa Housing Area Board & Representative, African Affairs Committee, 1958-63; Councillor, Municipal Council, Luanshya, 1963-70; Deputy Major, ibid, twice; Member, Urban African Services Committee of Enquiry, 1960; Local Time Office, Roan Mines Ltd., 1968—. Memberships: African National Congress, 1953-58; Zambia African National Congress, 1959; United Churches of Zambia; Chairman, United National Independence Party, 1963-65; Constituency Secretary, ibid, 1965-66; Youth Regional Secretary, 1966-67; Main Regional Secretary, 1967; Chairman, Parent-Teachers' Association, 1959-65; Luanshya Local Council of Education, 1965-70; Official Visitor, Luanshya Prison, 1965-68. Address: P.O. Box 457, Luanshya, Zambia.

BOWESMAN, Charles, born 26th June 1907. Surgeon. Education: M.B., B.Ch., B.A.O., Trinity College, Dublin, Ireland, 1931; M.D., 1933; D.T.M. & H., Edinburgh, 1935; F.R.C.S. Ed., 1938; F.A.C.S., 1956. Married. Appointments: joined Colonial Service, 1934; Surgical Specialist (Gold Coast), now Ghana, Ministry of Health; retired from Government, 1957; Private Surgical Practice, Ghana, 1960-70. Fellowships: Royal Society of Medicine; Royal Society of Tropical Medicine. Publications: Surgery & Clinical Pathology in the Tropics, 1960. Honours include: O.B.E. Address: Ellis Avenue Private Clinic, P.O. Box 1494, Kumasi, Ghana.

BOYDE, Tom Robin Caine, born 31st August 1932. Professor of Biochemistry. Education: City of London School, U.K., 1947-50; M.B., B.S., University College, London, 1950-55; Kings College, Newcastle, 1959-62; B.Sc., 1st Class Hons., Durham. Appointments: Flight Lieutenant Medical Branch, Royal Air Force, 1956-59; Registrar & Lecturer, Department of Clinical Biochemistry, University of Newcastle, 1959-68; Wolfson Lecturer, Royal College of Surgeons of England, 1968-69; Professor, Biochemistry,

Makerere University, Kampala, Uganda, 1969—. Memberships: Biochemical Society; Association of Clinical Biologists. Publications include: Biotodynamics, 1965. Address: P.O. Box 7072, Kampala, Uganda.

BRADFIELD, Brian Norton, born 4th September 1921. Farmer. Education: N.S.C.I., Republic of South Africa. Address: P.O. Box 168, Manzini, Swaziland.

BRADLEY, David John, born 12th January 1937. Research Worker in Tropical Diseases. Education: Wyggeston Boys' School, Leicester, U.K.; Selwyn College, Cambridge; University College Hospital, London; M.A., B.Ch.(Cantab.); M.I.(Biol.). Married, 1 son, 1 daughter. Appointments: Medical Research Officer, Ross Institute, Bilharzia Research Unit, Mwanza, Tanzania, 1961-63; Lecturer in Medical Microbiology, Makerere Medical School, Kampala, Uganda, 1964-66; Senior Lecturer, Preventive Medicine (Parasite Ecology), Makerere Medical School, 1966-69; Tropical Research Fellow, Royal Society, Oxford, U.K., 1969—. Memberships: Royal Society of Tropical Medicine & Hygiene; British Econological Society; Freshwater Biological Association. Author of papers on various subjects in field. Joint author: Drawers of Water (in press). Address: Sir William Dunn School of Pathology, University of Oxford, South Parks Road, Oxford, OX1 3RE, U.K.

BRADLEY, Michael John, born Belfast, Ireland, U.K., 11th June 1933. Legal Draftsman. Education: St. Malachy's College, Belfast, 1945-51; LL.B.(Hons.), Queen's University, Belfast, 1951-54, 1959-61; Trinity College, Dublin University, Ireland, 1959-61; Incorporated Law Society of Northern Ireland, 1961-64. Married. Appointments: Solicitor, Belfast, 1964-67; State Counsel, Government of the Republic of Malawi, Zomba, 1967-69; Acting Assistant Registrar-General, Malawi, 1968; Legal Draftsman, Government of the Republic of Botswana, 1970—. Memberships: Incorporated Law Society of Northern Ireland; Malawi Law Society; Botswana Society; Royal Commonwealth Society. Malawi & Botswana Correspondent, African Law Reports, 1967—. Address: Attorney-General's Chambers, Private Bag 9, Gaberones, Botswana.

BRAEMER, Pierre, born 29th March 1916. Directeur de la Banque Centrale des Etats de l'Afrique de l'Ouest, Nouakchott (Rim). Education: Secondary Studies in Law, Hanoi, Tonkin. Married to Jacqueline Duport, 1947, 2 sons, 2 daughters. Appointments: Sous les drapeaux de 1937-46; Bank of Indochina, 1946-56; Institut d'Emission de l'AOF et du Togo, became Banque Centrale des Etats de l'afrique de l'Ouest; Dakar, 1956-59; Quagadougou, 1959-65; Nouakchott, 1965—. Memberships: Gouverneur suppleant du F.M.I.; Administrater, Banque Mauritanienne de Developpement; Administrateur de l'Office des Postes de Mauritanie; Lion Club de Haute Volta. Honours: Chevalier de l'Ordre National du Merite Francais; Officier de l'Order National de Merite Voltaique; Crois de Guerre. Address: c/o Banque Centrale Des Etats de l'Afrique de l'Ouest, B.P. 227, Nouakchott (Rep. Islamique de Mauritanien), Mauritania.

BRAMLEY, John Ewart Dawson, born 1st February 1928. Surgeon. Education: Shebbear College, North Devon, U.K., 1938-40; Ledbury Grammar School, 1941-45; B.D.S. (2nd Class Hons.), University of Birmingham, 1945-51; M.B., Ch.B., University of Sheffield, 1955-59. Appointments: House Surgeon, Royal Hospital, Sheffield, 1959-60; Resident Surgeon, Methodist Hospital, Ituk Mbang, Uyo, South East State, Nigeria, 1961-67; Registrar, Orthopaedic Surgery, Coventry, U.K., 1969-70. Fellow, Royal College of Surgeons, Edinburgh, U.K., 1968; ibid, England, 1970. Address: Green Mount, Hollington Lane, Stramshall, Near Uttoxeter, Staffordshire, U.K.

BRANSBY-WILLIAMS, Walter Rowland, born 29th March 1918. Entomologist. Education: Preparatory School, Heatherdown, Ascot, U.K.; Secondary School, Clifton College, Bristol, U.K.; B.A.(Cantab.), 1939; D.A.P. & E. (London), 1957; M.Sc.(East Africa), 1969. Married, 1 son. Appointments: Captain, East African Army Medical Corps, 1946; Field Officer, Ross Institute, Tanga, Tanganyika, 1946-50; ibid, Research Officer, Tropical Pesticides Research Institute, Arusha, Tanzania, 1951—. Memberships: Institute of Biology; Fellow, Royal Society of Health. Author or Co-author of 12 scientific papers. Address: P.O. Box 3024, Arusha, Tanzania.

BRAY, Margaret Anne, born 12th September 1933. Teacher. Education: University of London Teachers' Certificate, St. Gabriel's College, London, U.K. Appointments: Tutor, Canon Lawrence Teachers' Training College, Lira, Uganda, 1960; Principal, St. Hilda's Supplementary Teachers' Training College, Gulu, ibid, 1961-65; Tutor, Bishop Kitching College, Ngora, 1966—. Member & Missionary, Church Missionary Society. Address: Bishop Kitching College, P.O. Box 20, Ngora, Uganda.

BRESCHI, Bruno, born 23rd May 1932. Physician. Education: M.D., University of Modena, Italy, 1957; Specialist Diploma, Obstetrics & Gynaecology, University of Padua, Italy, 1967. Appointments: Medical Officer in Charge, St. Mary's Hospital, Ogwashi Uku, 1960-62; ibid, St. Francis Hospital, Okpara Inland Nigeria, 1963—. Publications: Malattie Tropicali (w. F. Canova), 1966. Address: St. Francis Hospital, Okpara Inland, Via Sapele, Nigeria.

BREW, Ebenezer Emmanuel Abraham, born Elmina, Ghana, 8th June, 1912. Administrative Officer. Education: Elementary Leaving Certificate, 1927; Cambridge School Certificate, 1933; Self-improvement Correspondence Courses, 1940—. Married, 3 sons, 7 daughters. Appointments: Clerical Grade, Shorthand Typist, Court Registrar, Sub-Accountant, 1935-49; Finance Officer, 1950-52; Senior Executive Officer, 1953-58; Administrative Officer, Grade IV, 1959-60; ibid, Grade III, 1961-62; ibid, Grade II, 1963-67; Grade I, 1968-70; Administrative Secretary, Ghana National Service Corps, 1970—. Memberships:

Ghana Delegations to World Health Assembly, 1959—; Past Vice-President & Executive Member, Ghana Society for Prevention of Tuberculosis; Past Executive Member, Society of Friends of Lepers; Life Member, Ghana Red. Cross Society; African Liberal Council. Honours: Appointed Honorary Staff Member, National Communicable Disease Center, Atlanta, Ga., U.S.A., 1969; Member, Ghana Delegation, World Health Assembly, Boston, Mass., 1969. Address: National Service Corps, Office of the Prime Minister, P.O. Box 1627, Accra, Ghana.

BREWIN, David Richard, born England, 16th March 1927. College Principal; Agricultural Education Specialist. Education: B.Sc.(Agric.), Durham University D.T.A. (Trinidad); Certificate in Education. Appointments include: Agricultural Officer, Extension, Tanzania; Editor, Ukulima wa Kisasa, Tanzania. Producer, various agricultural radio programmes; Principal, Ministry of Agriculture Training Institute, Ukirigum, Tanzania; Assistant Director, Training, Ministry of Agriculture, Tanzania; Principal, Swaziland Agricultural College and University Centre, Swaziland, 1966-69; Agricultural Education Specialist, World Bank, 1970—. Memberships include: Agricultural Education Association, U.K.; University of Newcastle Agricultural Society. Publications include: The Agriculture of Ukara Island (with Luman), Empire Cotton Growing Review, 1956; Agricultural Education in Africa, Overseas Education, Vol. XXXIV, 1, 1962; The Agriculture of Kilimanjaro, Tanganyika, Notes & Records. Address: Education Projects Department, World Bank, Washington, D.C., U.S.A.

BRIDGE, Turner Donovan, born 14th March 1924. Publisher; Company Director. Education: Haberdashers School, U.K. Married, 1 son, 2 daughters. Appointments: served with H.M. Forces, Infantry; Staff Officer, Malaya; Major, RIF; Director, various British Publishing Companies. Memberships: Middle East Association; Royal Asian Society; Kampala Club. Publications: Kuwait Today, A Welfare State; Tanzania Today; Ethiopia; Mombasa; Kampala; Welcome To Aden (2 edits.); Homes For Kenya; E.A. Architects Jubilee Handbook: Tanga; Malindi; Zambia Farming Today; Commerce & Industry in Tanganyika; Tea in Africa; Tea in Malawi; Welcome to Jeddam, Kilimanjaro Country. Address: University Press of Africa, 1 West Street, Tavistock, Devon, U.K. & Bank House, Government Road, Nairobi, Kenya.

BRIGHT, John R. H., born 10th October 1931. Accountant. Education: Babson College; Syracuse University, U.S.A. Widower, 4 children. Appointments: Accountant, Bureau of Audits, Republic of Liberia; Assistant Secretary & Under-Secretary, Department of Commerce & Industry. Member, Institute of Certified Public Accountants of Liberia. Contributor to the Journal of Commerce & Industry. Honours: Knight Official, 1960. Address: Department of Commerce & Industry, Monrovia, Liberia.

BRIGNON, Jean, born 16th August 1931. University Professor. Education: University Graduate. Married, 4 children. Appointments: Tutor, Professor, Faculty of Arts, Rabat, Morocco; Inspector of History Instruction in Morocco. Publications (joint author): Histoire du Maroc, 1967; also a number of historical handbooks for secondary education. Address: Faculté des Lettres, Rabat, Morocco.

BROADBENT, Marcus Stanley Reuss, born 29th July 1899. Medical Practitioner. Education: Dulwich College, London, U.K.; M.A., Peterhouse College, Cambridge; St. Bartholomew's Hospital, London, qualified, 1928; M.R.C.S.(Eng.); L.R.C.P.(Lond.). Appointments: Senior House Surgeon, Mildmay Mission Hospital, London, 1928-29; Medical Officer, East African Medical Service, 1930; Area Superintendent, St. John Ambulance, Kenya. Memberships: Hon. Member, St. John Ambulance, Kenya; District Grand Lodge, East Africa. Author, Some Unusual Symptoms Associated with Malaria (E.A. Med. J.), 1943. Honours: Serving Brother of the Order of St. John of Jerusalem, 1968. Address: c/o Brooke Bond Leibig Tanzania Ltd., P.O. Box 14, Mufindi, Tanzania.

BROCK, Andrew, born 28th November 1934. Physicist. Education: M.A., Ph.D., Gonville & Cauis College, University of Cambridge, U.K., 1953-56; Cavendish Laboratory, ibid, 1956-60. Appointments: Lecturer, Physics, University College of Rhodesia & Nyasaland, 1960-67; ibid, University College, Nairobi, 1967-70; Senior Lecturer, University College, Nairobi, 1970—. Memberships: Fellow, Royal Astronomical Society; ibid, Royal Meteorological Society; Associate, Institute of Physics; American Geophysical Union. Author of scientific papers on geophysical topics, especially palaeomagnetism. Address: University College, Nairobi, P.O. Box 30197, Nairobi, Kenya.

BRODIE, William, born 12th October 1923. Orthopaedic Surgeon. Education: Kilmarnock Academy, U.K., 1929-41; M.B., Ch.B., University of Glasgow, 1941-46. Married, 5 children. Appointments: House Surgeon, Glasgow Royal Infirmary; Surgeon, British Army Medical Service; Lecturer in Anatomy, University of Glasgow; Surgical & Orthopaedic Registrar, Glasgow Royal Infirmary; Senior Registrar, Orthopaedic Surgery, Leeds & Bradford; Consultant Orthopaedic Surgeon & Surgical Teacher, University of Glasgow, U.K.; Senior Lecturer, Orthopaedic Surgery, & Head of Department, University College, Nairobi, 1968—. Memberships: Fellow, Royal College of Surgeons, Glasgow, 1962. Author of medical papers. Address: Medical School, University College, Nairobi, P.O. Box 30588, Nairobi, Kenya.

BRODIE-MENDS, Zaccheus Dougan Ekwow, born 20th November 1926. Medical Officer. Education: C.M.S. Central School, Onitsha, East Central State, Nigeria, 1933-40; Dennis Memorial Grammar School, Onitsha, East Central State, 1941-44; Cambridge School Certificate, 1944; M.B., Ch.B., Medical Faculty, University of Glasgow, U.K., 1947-52; Associate of Hospital Administration, Columbia University, U.S.A., 1967. Personal details: son of T. D. Brodie-Mends, M.B.E. (deceased) & Chief (Mrs.) Eleanor N. Brodie-Mends, Chief Iya Alaje of Lagos; Married with children. Appointments: House Officer, Blackburn Royal Infirmary, 1953-54; Medical Officer, Ministry of Health, Nigeria, 1955—; currently, Principal Medical Officer, i/c Lagos Island Maternity Hospital. Memberships: British Medical Association; Nigeria Medical Association; Freemason; Order of Shepherd; Patron, Onitsha Youths League, Lagos Branch; Vice-Patron, Nigeria National Musics; Lay Reader, Lagos Anglican Church. Honours include: WHO Fellowship, 1967. Address: 8 Kugbuyi Street, Idi-Oro, Yaba, Lagos, Nigeria.

BROOKS, Joseph Warren, born 30th June 1917. Professor of Civil Engineering. Education: B.Sc.(Civil Engineering), Queen's University, Kingston, Canada, 1939; M.A.Sc., University of Toronto, 1951. Married, 1 daughter. Appointments: Visiting Professor (Canadian International Development Agency), Ahmadu Bello University, Zaria, Nigeria. Memberships: Former President, Kingston Branch, Engineering Institute of Canada; Professional Engineers of Ontario; Rotary Club of Zaria. Publications: Stresses in Beams with Circular Holes (Eng. Inst. of Can. Trans.), 1967. Honours: Department Medal in Civil Engineering, Queen's University, 1939; UNESCO Technical Assistance Expert, Middle East University, Ankara, Turkey, 1958-60. Address: Department of Civil Engineering, Ahmadu Bello University, Zaria, Nigeria.

BROUGH, Anthony Thomas, born Britain, 25th August 1932. Statistician. Education: M.A.(Economics), St. Catharine's College, Cambridge. Appointments include: Statistician, East Africa High Commission, 1956-61; Senior Economist Statistician, Kenya Government, 1961-63; Chief Statistician, Kenya, 1963-70; Financial Advisor, Kenya Treasury, 1970—. Memberships: International Statistical Institute; Past President, Economics Club of Kenya. Publications: Past Editor, E.A. Economic Review. Address: The Treasury, P.O. Box 30007, Nairobi, Kenya.

BROWN (Canon) Albert Mack, born 25th June 1929. Clergyman. Education: St. John's College, York, U.K.; Hatfield College, Durham; Ridley Hall, Cambridge. Personal details: Ordained, June, 1955; married Joan L. Middleton, July, 1955. Appointments: CMS Missionary, 1959—; Principal, Diocesan Theological College, Rwanda, 1963-69; Vicar, Kigali, Rwanda, 1969—; Canon, Anglican Diocese of Rwanda, 1965—. Address: B.P. 61, Kigali, Rwanda.

BROWN, Eric Septimus, born 26th May 1912. Entomologist. Education: Magdalen College School, Oxford, U.K., 1922-31; B.A., Zoology, St. Peter's College, Oxford University, 1931-34. Married Jacqueline Florence Burton, 1938. Appointments: Schoolmaster, Biology, Raileybury & Imperial Service College, Hertford, 1934; Liaison Officer, Middle East, Anti-Locust Unit, Cairo, U.A.R., 1946; Commonwealth Pool of Entomologists, Commonwealth Institute of Entomology, 1951; Secondments: Research on Coconut Pests, Seychelles Islands, 1951-52; ibid, British Solomon Islands Protectorate, 1954-56; Research on Wheat Pests, Middle East, 1957-60; East African Agriculture & Forestry Research Organization, Maguga, Nairobi, Kenya, 1962—. Memberships: Royal Entomological Society of London; Society of British Entomology. Publications: numerous works on insect systematics & Economic Entomology. Address: c/o Commonwealth Institute of Entomology, 56 Queen's Gate, London, S.W.7, U.K. or East African Agriculture & Forestry Research Organization, P.O. Box 30148, Nairobi, Kenya.

BROWN, James Arthur Kinnear, born 2nd September 1902. Physician. Education: Hymers College, Hull, U.K.; Manchester & Liverpool Universities. Appointments: Senior Consultant for Leprosy, Founder of the Uzuakoli Leprosy Centre of Southern Nigeria, 1930-37; Clinical Practice in England, 1937-51; Senior Consultant, Uganda, 1951—. Memberships: British Medical Association, U.K.; Uganda Branch, ibid; Fellow, Royal Society of Hygiene & Tropical Medicine. Publications: numerous papers dealing with Vitamin B in Leprosy & Police in Nigeria; also various papers dealing with epidemiology of leprosy, in Uganda, the Lepromin test, Immunology & the trial of B.C.G. vaccination against leprosy. Honours: C.M.G., 1967. Address: Sonning, 10 Leicester Road, Hale, Altrincham, Cheshire, U.K. & P.O. 39, Kumi, Uganda.

BROWN, Roland George MacCormack, born London, U.K., 27th December 1924. Lawyer. Education: Trinity College, Cambridge; Called to the Bar, Gray's Inn, 1949. Married, 1 son, 1 daughter. Appointments include: Practised at the Bar, 1949-61; Attorney-General, Tanzania, 1961-66; Legal Consultant on International & Commercial Affairs, Tanzania, 1966—. Publications include: The Law of Defamation (with Richard O'Sullivan, Q.C.). Address: Attorney-General's Chamber, P.O. Box 4050, Dar as Salaam, Tanzania.

BROWN, Tom Whittingham, born Hull, U.K., 19th August 1915. Teacher. Education: Westminster School, London, U.K., 1928-33; B.A., M.A., Peterhouse College, Cambridge, 1933-36. Appointments include: Assistant Master, Dunchurch Hall, Rugby, U.K., 1936-38; ibid, Catgilfield, Edinburgh, 1938-39; Radio Officer, Merchant Navy, 1940-43; Radar Officer, Royal Navy, 1943-45; ibid, Royal Indian Navy, 1945-46; Housemaster, Clifton College, Bristol, 1947-51; Headmaster, King's School, Gloucester, 1951-65; ibid, Duke of York School, Nairobi, Kenya, 1965—; Senior Education Officer, Kenya Institute of Education, 1969—. Memberships include: Teaching Commission, International Geographic Union; Founder Chairman, Society of Headmasters of Independent Schools in the U.K.; former Council Member, Headmasters Association, U.K.; Treasurer, Kenya Heads Association; Institute of British Geographers; British Association for the Advancement of Science; President, Geological Club of Nairobi; Chairman, International Services Comm., Rotary Club. Author of chapters in UNESCO Source Book for Geography Teachers & I.A.A.M. Handbook for Teachers. Honours: R.N.V.R. Decoration, 1962. Address: Kenya Institute of Education, Box 30231, Nairobi, Kenya.

BRUBAKER (Rev.) Allen Graybill, born Mt. Joy, Pennsylvania, U.S.A., 27th August 1927. Clergyman; Missionary Teacher. Education: B.A., Upland College, Upland, California; further studies, Juniatta College, Huntingdon, Pennsylvania. Married, 3 sons. Appointments: Pastor, Brethren in Christ Church, Altoona, Pa., 1949-53; Superintendent, Sikalongo Mission, Choma, Zambia, 1953-56; Education Secretary, Brethren in Christ Church, Zambia, 1956-59; Supt., Macha Mission, Choma, 1961-62; Principal, Choma Bible Institute, 1968; National Organizing Secretary, New Life for All, Zambia, 1970. Memberships: Brethren in Christ Church, ordained Minister since 1951. Address: Brethren in Christ Church, Box 115, Choma, Zambia.

BRUNO-GASTON, Albert Philip, born Freetown. Sierra Leone, 17th May 1922. Retired Chartered Electrical & Mechanical Engineer. Education: Prince of Wales Secondary School, Freetown; Lagos Technical Institute, Nigeria; Huddersfield College of Technology, U.K.; Leeds College of Commerce & Management Studies. Personal details: Father half-French, half-Nigerian, Mother, Sierra Leonean. Appointments: Lecturer, Lagos Technical Institute, Nigeria, 1943-44; Engineer, British Electricity Authority, Yorkshire Division, U.K., 1947-51; Electrical Engineer, Installations, Government of Sierra Leone, 1951-53; Electrical Engineer, Northern Province, Government of Sierra Leone, 1953-54; Electrical Engineer, Construction, Government of Sierra Leone, 1954-55; Assistant Engineer in Chief, ibid, 1955-57; Engineer in Chief, Electricity Department, 1957-64; General Manager & Chief Executive, Sierra Leone Electric Corporation, 1964-70; Retired, 1970. Memberships: Fellow, Institute of Electrical Engineers, Great Britain; Associate, Huddersfield Technical College, Dip.Eng.(Mech.); Dip.Eng. (Elect.); President, Sierra Leone Institute of Management; Fellowship, Institute of Economic Development, U.S.A. Publications include: Thesis on the Steam Cycle, 1948, for Ass. Huddersfield Technical College. Honours: J.P. Address: P.O. Box 1177, Freetown, Sierra Leone.

BUBAKAR, Iya, born Belel, 14th December 1934. University Professor. Education: Elementary School, Belel, Nigeria, 1940-44; Middle School, Yola, 1944-48; Government College, Zaria, 1948-52; Nigerian College of Arts, Science & Technology, Zaria, 1952-55; B.Sc.(Lond.), University of Ibadan, 1955-58; Ph.D.(Cantab), Cambridge University, U.K. Appointments: Research Assistant, California Institute of Technology, U.S.A., 1960-61; Lecturer in Mathematics, Ahmadu Bello University, Zaria, Nigeria, 1962-64; Senior Lecturer, ibid, 1964-65, 1966-67; Visiting Assistant Professor, University of Michigan, U.S.A., 1965-66; Professor, Head of Department of Mathematics, Ahmadu Bello University, Zaria, Nigeria, 1967—; Dean, Faculty of Science, ibid, 1968-69. Memberships: Special Member, Northern House of Assembly, Nigeria, 1963-66; Member, Northern Nigeria Public Accounts Committee, 1964-66; ibid, Advisory Committee on Atomic Energy Commission, 1964—; Federal Government's Working Party on Economic Planning, 1966; ibid Technical Education & Vocational Training, 1966; Northern Nigeria Scholarship Board, 1967-68; National Universities Commission, 1968—; Interim Common Services Agency Scholarship Committee, 1968—; North-Eastern State Public Accounts Committee, 1969—. Also various ad hoc committees set up by State Governments to advise on specific issues. Leader of Nigerian delegations to: 10th Congress of the International Union of Geodesy & Geophysics, Berkeley, U.S.A., 1963; General Assembly of the International Atomic Energy Agency, Vienna, Austria, 1964; ibid, Tokyo, Japan, 1965. Also attended the Nigerian delegation to the Commonwealth Conference on Defence Science, India, 1963 & several conferences on educational, scientific & university matters held in Africa, Australia, Europe, & U.S.A. Author of numerous papers on mathematics & other subjects in various international journals. Address: Ahmadu Bello University, Zaria, Nigeria.

BUCKLEY, Robert Milton, born 27th January 1931. Physician. Education: Matriculated (1st Class), Helderberg College, Somerset West, Cape Province; M.B., Ch.B., University of Cape Town, South Africa, 1954; D.T.M.&H. (Conjoint), London, U.K., 1962; M.R.C.O.G., 1970. Personal details: 3rd generation missionary; Father descended from British 1820 settlers; married Lilian Emma Guy, Missionary nurse. Appointments: Medical Officer, Maluti Hospital, Lesotho; ibid, Kanye Hospital, Botswana; Malamulo Hospital, Malawi; Yuka Hospital, Zambia; Kendu Hospital, Kenya; Ishaka Hospital, Uganda; Medical Director, Yuka & Ishaka Hospitals. Affiliate Alumnus, Loma Linda Medical School, California. Author of Patterns of Cancer at Ishaka Hospital in Uganda, 1967. Address: P.O. Box 8629, Nairobi, Kenya.

BUGEMBE, John Baptist, born 28th September 1930. Teacher. Education: Primary, 1940-45; Secondary, 1946-49; Primary Teacher Education, 1951-52; Junior Secondary Teacher Education, 1959; Certificate of Associateship, Makerere University Institute of Education, Uganda, 1962-63; Diploma in Teaching English as a Second Language, Leeds University, U.K., 1965-66. Married, 2 sons, 3 daughters. Appointments: Tutor of English, Ggaba Teacher Training College, 1953-54; Headmaster, Primary School, 1955-58; Headmaster, Junior Secondary School, 1960; Senior Tutor, i/c English & Education, Ggaba Teachers' College, 1961-67; Assistant Schools Broadcasting Officer, Ministry of Education, 1967-69; Acting Principal, Ggaba Teachers' College, 1968; Assistant Inspector of Schools, Primary English, at present seconded to Buloba Language Unit, doing research & producing language material for use in primary schools. Memberships: President, Uganda Catholic Teachers' Guild, 1963-66; Hon. Secretary, Uganda Education Association, 1968—; Uganda Language Society; Ngoma Players. Co-author, The Nile English Course, Books Five, Six, & Seven. Address: Buloba

Language Unit, P.O. Boc 5256, Kampala, Uganda.

BUKOVSZKY, Ferenc, born 1st July 1908. Associate Professor of Physics. Education: Secondary School, Mezotur, Hungary, 1918-26; Faculty of Science, University of Szeged, 1926-31; Dr.Phil., ibid, 1935; Dipl. Maths.- Physics Teacher, Szeged, 1931; Candidate, Physical Sciences, Budapest, 1963. Married, 2 sons. Appointments: Assistant-Professor, Physics, University of Szeged, 1929-37; Headmaster, Teacher, Maths. & Physics, Koszeg & Nagykanizsa, 1937-53; Associate Professor, Physics, University of Technical Sciences, Budapest, 1953—; Head, Department of Physics, Federal Advanced Teachers' College, Lagos, Nigeria, 1963-67; Lecturer, Physics, University College of Cape Coast, Ghana, 1968-69. Publications: papers on Crystal Physics (Acta Physica Hungarica), 1957-65; various papers in Physical Review, Budapest & Journal of Math. Association of Nigeria. Address: University of Technology, Budafoki ut 8, Budapest XI, Hungary.

BULCHA DEMEKSA, born Bodgi, Wollega, Ethiopia, 9th July 1930. Vice-Minister of Finance of Ethiopia. Education: B.A. (Economics), University College, Addis Ababa, 1955-59; M.A.(Economics), Maxwell Graduate School, Syracuse University, U.S.A., 1959-60; LL.B., extra-mural studies, Hailé Selassié I University Law School, 1962-67. Married, 5 children. Appointments: Teacher, Addis Ababa, 1947-55; Director of Finance, Credit & Investment Department, Ministry of Finance, Imperial Ethiopian Government, 1960; Director-General, Budget Department, ibid, 1962; Assistant Minister, 1965; Vice-Minister of Finance, 1967—; Part-time Lecturer, Economics, Hailé Selassié I University, Addis Ababa, 1960-62; Alternate Governor for Ethiopia, IBRD, 1961-63; Alternate Governor for Ethiopia, African Development Bank, assisting Committee of Nine in ADB's formation, 1964-66; Member, National Investment Committee, 1964-65; Member, Board of Commissioners, Imperial Highway Authority, 1964—; Director of following: Ethiopian Investment Corporation S.C., 1962-69; Chairman, Ethiopian Grain Corporation, 1965-69; Imperial Board of Telecommunications of Ethiopia, 1965-69; Development Bank of Ethiopia, 1967-69; Ethiopian Shipping Lines S.C., 1964—; Ethiopian Air Lines S.C., 1966—; National Resources Development Corporation S.C., 1968—; Imperial Home Ownership & Savings Association, 1969—. Address: Ministry of Finance, Addis Ababa, Ethiopia.

BULENGO, Anthony Paschal, born 14th April 1931. Medical Practitioner. Education: Primary, Ussongo, Nzega, Tanzania, 1938-41; Secondary, St. Mary's School, Tabora, 1942-50; L.M.S.(E.A.), M.B., Ch.B.(U.E.Afr.), Makerere University College, Kampala, Uganda, 1951-58; D.P.H., 1963-64; D.I.H.(U. St. And.), 1966. Married, 3 children. Appointments: Pre-registration Intern, Dar es Salaam, 1958-59; Government Medical Officer, 1959-60; District Medical Officer, 1960-62; Senior Medical Registrar/Assistant Medical Superintendent, Dar es Salaam Hospitals Group, 1962-63; S.M.O. i/c Industrial Health, Tanzania Government, 1965-68; Specialist Industrial Health, 1968—; Assistant Chief Medical Officer, i/c Public Health, 1969—; S.M.O./Company Doctor, East African Cargo Handling Services Ltd., Dar es Salaam & Tanzania Ports, 1970—. Memberships: Executive Council Member, Medical Association of Tanzania; Executive Committee Member, East African Academy, Tanzania Branch; Former Council & Executive Committee Member, Dar es Salaam Group Occupational Health Service Association; Dar es Salaam Cultural Society; WHO Expert Advisory Panel on Occupational Health, 1968-73. Contributor to medical publications. Recipient WHO Fellowship, St. Andrew's University, Chadwick Gold Medal Prize, 1966. Address: Medical Department, E. A. Cargo Handling Services Ltd., P.O. Box 9072, Dar es Salaam, Tanzania.

BULWA, Frederick Mukasa, born Kampala, Uganda, 20th March 1920. Medical Practitioner. Education: St. Henry's, Kitouu, Uganda, 1933-36; St. Mary's College, 1937-40; L.M.S.(E.A.), Makerere University College, 1941-47; M.B., Ch.B., ibid, 1964. Married with children. Appointments: Medical Officer, Arua Hospital, 1949-50; Medical Officer, Mulago Hospital, 1951-60; L.M. (R.O.T.), 1955; Consultant Gynaecologist & Obstetrician, 1962-65; Senior Consultant, ibid, 1965-67; Senior Lecturer, Obstetrics & Gynaecology, 1967—. Memberships: Royal College of Obstetrics & Gynaecology, 1962; Past President, Uganda Medical Association; Hon. Treasurer, Association of Surgeons of East Africa; Hon. Treasurer, Makerere Medical Graduates Association; Chairman, Midwifery Training Committee. Honours: Archer Prize, 1943. Address: Mulago Hospital, P.O. Box 7051, Kampala, Uganda.

BUNDHUN, Abdool Raouf, born 14th January 1937. Parliamentary Secretary. Education: Cambridge School Certificate; Higher School Certificate. Appointments: Public Assistance Officer, 1958-61: Secondary School Teacher, 1961-69; Elected Member, Mauritius Legislative Assembly, 1967; Elected Municipal Councillor for City of Port Louis, 1969; Parliamentary Secretary to Minister of Youth & Sports, 1969—. Memberships: Secretary-General, Mauritius National Youth Council, 1966-69; Treasurer, Mauritius Council of Social Services, 1965-69; President, Port Louis Youth Federation, 1961; Attended 7th General Assembly of the World Assembly of Youth, Liege, Belgium, 1969. Honours: UNESCO Travel Grant, Britain, Denmark, & West Germany, 1966. Address: 33 Jawaharlal Nehru Street, Port Louis, Mauritius.

BUNJORO, Sebastian, born 25th June 1934. Administrative Officer. Education: Ihungo Secondary School, Bukoba, 1948-53; Government Commercial College, 1954. Married, 8 children. Appointments: District Officer, 1960-63; Senior Assistant Secretary, 1964-66; Acting Principal Secretary, 1967; Administrative Secretary, 1967-69; Principal Assistant Secretary, 1970—. Member, Tanganyika Library Service. Address: Ministry of Home Affairs, P.O. Box 9223, Dar es Salaam, Tanzania.

BUONOCORE, Domenico, born Vico Equense, Sorrento, Italy, 16th February 1895. Naval Engineer; Naval Architect. Education: Diplomato e Patentato Construttore Navale, Nautical Institute Nino Bixio, Sorrento; Dr. of Naval Engineering, Navy High School, Genoa; Aeronotic & Ship Engineering, Naval Academy, Livorno. Married, 2 children. Appointments: Inspector, Italian Naval Registry for naval classification; Technological Officer of own property; Expert, Tribunale di Mogadiscio, Somalia; Consulting Naval Architect, hulls & engines; Lecturer, Maritime & Naval Matters, Maritime School of Mogadiscio; Assistant Director, Volo della Somalia, 18 years. Memberships: Casa d'Italia, Mogadiscio; Aereo Club della Somalia. Publications: Cavi; La Vela Come Propulsore; Timone & Curva di Evoluzione; Constużione Navale Mercantile; articles in various journals. Honours include: Cavaliere per merito della Repubb. Italiana. Address: P.O. Box 621, Mogadiscio, Somalia.

BURACZEWSKI, Adam, born 14th April 1926. Mathematician. Education: M.Sc., Warsaw University, Poland, 1953; Ph.D., Mathematical Institute of the Polish Academy of Sciences, Warsaw, 1961. Appointments: Lecturer & Senior Lecturer, Warsaw Technical University, 1953-62; Senior Lecturer & Associate Professor, ibid, 1962—; Professor of Mathematics & Head of Department, University of Science & Technology, Kumasi, Ghana, 1965—. Memberships: American Mathematical Society; Polish Mathematical Society; American Association for the Advancement of Science; Ghana Science Association. Author of research papers in the field of functional analysis. Address: c/o University of Science & Technology, Kumasi, Ghana.

BURGESS, Henry Jacques Leslie, born 11th August 1930. Physician. Education: Secondary, Edinburgh Academy, U.K.; M.B., Ch.B., University of St. Andrews, 1956; D.T.M.&H., University of Liverpool, 1958; D.P.H., London School of Hygiene & Tropical Medicine, 1961. Married, 3 sons. Appointments: Medical Officer, Ministry of Health, Uganda, 1958-59; Nutrition Officer, ibid, 1960-64; Intercountry Nutrition Consultant, East & Southern Africa, World Health Organization, 1965—. Memberships: Fellow, Royal Society of Tropical Medicine & Hygiene; Nutrition Society. Address: World Health Organization, P.O. Box 351, Blantyre, Malawi.

BURKS, Edgar H., born 17th March 1921. Missionary. Education: A.B., Baylor University, U.S.A., 1945; B.D., Southern Baptist Theological Seminary, 1948; Th.D., ibid, 1951; M.R.E., 1963. Married to Linnie Jane Joslin Burks, 1 daughter. Appointments: Professor, Christian Ethics, Nigerian Baptist Theological Seminary, Ogbomosho, Nigeria, 1956-65; Vice-Principal, ibid, 1964-65; Executive Secretary, Baptist Mission of Nigeria, 1965—. Author of The Early Church, Ibadan, Nigeria, 1962. Honours: Life Service Award, Southwest Baptist College, Bolivar, Missouri, U.S.A., 1959. Address: Executive Secretary, Baptist Mission of Nigeria, P.M.B. 5113, Ibadan, Nigeria.

BURIIRO KAHIGIRIZA, Jacob, born 25th August 1921. Surveyor. Education: Bweranyangi Primary School, Uganda, 1932-34; Mbarara High School, 1935-40; King's College, Budo, 1941-43; Survey School, 1944-48. Married, 1 son, 3 daughters. Appointments: Surveyor, 1944-57; Assistant Enganzi (Assistant Chief Minister), Kingdom of Ankole, Uganda, 1957-61; County Chief (Nyabushozi), 1961-63; Chief Minister, 1963-67; Retired, 1967; Director, Bank of Uganda, 1969. Memberships: Chairman, Mbarara Branch, YMCA, 1965-68; Trustee, Uganda YMCA, 1968—; Trustee, Uganda Independence Scholarship Fund, 1965—; Board of Governors, Ntare Senior Secondary School, Mbarara High School, Mary Hill High School, Bweranyangi Girls' Senior Secondary School, & Bishop Stuart Teacher Training College. Address: P.O. Box 227, Mbarara, Uganda.

BURNETT, Donald Frank, born 9th March 1936. Schoolmaster. Education: Exeter School, Exeter, U.K.; Honours degree, Modern History, St. Peter's Hall, Oxford University. Married Pauline Muthoni Munyi, 1970. Appointments: at Midhurst Grammar School, 1959-60; St. Albans School, Abbey Gateway, St. Albans, 1960-64; Kangaru School, Embu, Kenya, 1964-66; The City School, Lincoln, U.K., 1966-67; Maseno School, Kenya, 1967—. Address: P.O. 120, Maseno, Kenya.

BURNEY (Sir) Cecil Denniston, born 8th January 1923. Company Director. Education: Eton College, U.K.; Trinity College, Cambridge University; Mechanical Sciences Tripos. Married, 2 children. Appointments: M.L.C., Northern Rhodesia, 1959-64; M.P., Zambia, 1964-68; Chairman, Public Accounts Committee, Zambia; Managing Director, Northern Motors Ltd.; Director, Security Building Society. Memberships: Ndola Club; Carlton Club; Bath Club; Leander Club. Address: P.O. Box 672, Ndola, Zambia.

BURNHILL, Charles Sykes, born Leeds, U.K., 11th November 1921. Architect; Planner. Education: A.R.I.B.A., Associate, Royal Institute of British Architects; Dip. T.P., Diploma in Town Planning, Ledds, U.K.; A.M.T.P.I., Associate, Town Planning Institute; A.I.A.S.(QS), Associate, Incorporated Association of Architects & Surveyors. Married, 2 children. Appointments: Senior Architect, Wakefield, U.K., 1949-54; ibid, Leeds, 1954-57; Principal Architect, Salisbury, 1957-68; Regional Planning Officer, Lilongwe, Malawi, 1968-69; Chief Town Planning Officer, Malawi, 1969—. Member & Past Chairman, Lilongwe Rotary Club, 1969-70. Publications: Revised Master Plan, New Capital City, Lilongwe; New City Centre, New Capital City, Lilongwe. Address: Chief Town Planning Officer, Malawi Government, P.O. Box 279, Lilongwe, Malawi.

BURZONI, Francois Jean Matteo, born 18th July 1921. Doctor of Medicine; Specialist in Tuberculosis. Education: studied at the Faculty of Medicine, Paris, France. Married, 3 children. Appointments: General Practitioner, various hospitals in Paris; Chief Doctor, Tubercular Centre, 1951—; Founder, Anti-tubercular Dispensary, Marrakesh; created & installed, Tubercular Centre, El Razi Hospital, Marrakesh; organised the B.C.G. vaccination of nearly one million people, 1951-53; founded Anti-tubercular Dispensaries at Safi & Mogador; organized Mobile X-Ray Units to tour Marrakesh; created & organized Radiology Service, El Razi Hospital; founded Centre for Chest Surgery, 1960; founded a Tuberculosis Laboratory, 1964; founded Anti-tubercular Dispensary, El Kelaa; also smaller units in the surrounding district, 1966; Medical Director, El Razi Hospital; Regional Medical Consultant on Tuberculosis. Memberships: Vice-President, Alliance Française; ibid, Friends of the Theatre, France; Vice-President, Founder-Member, Association équestre de l'Atlas; Past President, Founder-Member, 'Poisson d'Or', a literary & artistic group; French Society of Public Health; British Tuberculosis Association. Participated in numerous conferences & international congresses including: Principal Recorder at a Symposium on Tuberculosis in developing countries, London, U.K., 1967; Participant, Principal Recorder, Congress of International Union, Amsterdam, Netherlands, 1968; ibid, New York, U.S.A., 1969; Moroccan Representative at the 6-day Tunisienne Maghrebines & the National Congress of Bordeaux, France, 1970. Author of numerous articles in his field. Honours: Knight, Order of Public Health. Address: Hôpital El Razi, Marrakesh, Morocco.

BUSIA (The Rt. Honourable) Kofi Abrefa, born 11th July 1913. Prime Minister. Education: Teacher Training: Wesley College, Kumasi, Ghana, 1931-32; Achimota College, 1935-36; B.A., Medieval & Modern History(London), 1939; B.A., P.P.E., Oxford University, 1941; M.A., ibid, 1946; D.Phil., Social Anthropology, 1947. Appointments: Staff, Wesley College, Kumasi, Ghana, 1932-34; ibid, Achimota College, Accra, 1936-39; Administrative Officer, Government of the Gold Coast, 1942-49; Officer i/c, Sociological Surveys, Gold Coast Government, 1947-49; Research Lecturer, African Studies, University College, Gold Coast, 1949-51; Senior Lecturer, Sociology, ibid, 1952-54; Professor, ibid, University of the Gold Coast, 1954-59; ibid, Institute of Social Studies, The Hague, Netherlands, 1959-54; Sociology & Culture of Africa, University of Leiden, ibid, 1960-62; Director of Studies for World Council of Churches, Birmingham, U.K., 1962-64; Professor, Sociology, Research on African Problems, Senior Associate Member, St. Anthony's College, Oxford, U.K., 1964—; various visiting professorships. Memberships: Exec. Comm., International Sociological Association, 1953-59; International Social Science Council, UNESCO, Paris, France, 1955-64; National Assembly of Ghana, 1951-59; Leader, Parliamentary Opposition, Ghana Parliament, 1956-59; Chairman, National Advisory Comm. N.L.C., 1967; ibid, Centre for Civic Education, 1967; Prime Minister of Ghana, P.M., 1969—. Publications include: The Challenge of Africa, 1962; Purposeful Education for Africa, 1964; Urban Churches in Britain, 1966; Africa in Search of Democracy, 1967. Address: P.O. Box 6161, Accra North, Ghana.

BUTLER, Alan John, born Poole, England, 19th June 1930. Minister of Religion. Education: Poole Grammar School; Kelham Theological College. Married, 1 son. Appointments include: Mission Priest, Orange Free State, Union of S. Africa, 1957-59; Curate, Kimberley Cathedral, 1960; Rector of Kuruman, 1961-65; Rector of Gaberones, Botswana, 1965—; elected to Gaberones Town Council, 1967; Deputy Mayor of Gaberones, 1968. Memberships include: President, Gaberones Co-operative Society, 1965-68; Treasurer, Botswana Scouts' Association, 1966—; Vice-Chairman, Botswana Christian Council, 1967-68; Chairman, Christian Council Action Committee, 1968. Address: The Rectory, P.O. Box 59, Gaberones, Botswana, S.A.

BWANGAMOI, Okot, born 1st December 1933. Veterinary Pathologist. Education: Gulu Primary School, 1940-48; Gulu High School, Uganda, 1949-51; St. Leo's College, Fort Portal, 1953-55; Makerere University, 1956-62; Colorado State University, U.S.A., 1963-66. Personal details: son of Chief Lacito Okech & Julaina Auma. Appointments: Office Boy, 1952; Petrol Boy, 1952; Assistant Veterinary Officer, 1962-63; Veterinary Research Officer, 1966; Lecturer, University College, Nairobi, Kenya, 1966-70. Publications include: A Survey of skin diseases of domestic animals & defects which down-grade hides & skins in East Africa, 1970; Pathological observation of Gazellostrongylus (Paracooperia) infection in gazelles in Kenya, 1970. Honours: Victor Ludorum, Gulu High School, 1950; Uganda Discus Record, 1954; Makerere Discus Record, 1958. Address: Faculty of Veterinary Science, University College, Nairobi, P.O. Kabete, Kenya.

BYABATO, Francis, born Bukoba, Tanzania, 25th March 1935. Public Servant. Education: St. Thomas More's Secondary School, Bukoba; St. Francis College, Dar es Salaam; University of Wisconsin, Madison, U.S.A. Married 1 son, 3 daughters. Appointments: Tanzania Government Service, 1957-64; E.A. Community Service, 1964—. Address: c/o East African Community Service, Arusha, Tanzania.

BYARUGABA, Paul Atwoki, born 5th August 1940. Mathematician; Meteorologist. Education: B.Sc.(Special) Hons. Mathematics (London); WMO Class I Diploma, Meteorology. Appointments: Director, Meteorological Services, Uganda, 1969—. Address: E.A. Meteorological Department, P.O. Box 7025, Kampala, Uganda.

BYATIKE, Thomas Byuma, born 10th September 1936. Public Servant. Education: B.A., Economics, Politics, & History, Makerere University, Kampala, Uganda, 1956-60; M.A., Economics, Williams College, Williamstown, Mass., U.S.A., 1962-63. Appointments: Trade Officer, Ministry of Commerce, Kampala, 1960-63; Executive, Uganda Development Corporation, 1964-65; Tutor, Economics, Kivukoni College, D.S.M., 1965-67; Research Secretary, Makerere University, 1967—. Address: c/o Makerere University, Kampala, Uganda.

C

CALDER, Marion Taylor, born 28th September, 1944. Editor. Education: Scottish Certificate of Education, Higher Level; Diploma in Commerce with distinction, Modern Languages, Strathclyde University, U.K. Married. Appointments: Administration, IBM (United Kingdom) Ltd., Glasgow, 1965-68; Editor, Hansard, National Assembly, Malawi, 1969-70; Member, Business & Professional Women's Association. Address: P.O. Box 80, Zomba, Malawi.

CAMERON, Hector Macdonald, born 20th December 1922. Pathologist. Education: M.B., B.Ch.(Belfast), 1945; D.Path., 1952; M.D. (Belfast), 1959. Appointments: Professor of Pathology, University of Nairobi, Kenya; Editor, East African Medical Journal. Memberships: Fellow, Royal College of Pathologists; Pathological Society of Gt. Britain & Ireland; Association of Clinical Pathologists; Kenya Medical Association Contributor of scientific articles to medical journals. Address: University of Nairobi, P.O. Box 30588, Nairobi, Kenya.

CAMILLE, Henri Lewis, born 13th August 1915. Lecturer in Comparative Studies. Education: Royal College, Curepipe, Mauritius; Diploma in Co-operation, Co-operative College, Loughborough, U.K., 1951-52, 1962-63; languages: English, French & Spanish. Appointments: Clerk, Poor Law & Labour Departments, Mauritius Government Clerical Service, 1936-46; Co-operative Officer, Mauritius Department of Co-operation, 1947-61; Assistant Registrar, Co-operative Societies, Mauritius, 1962-63; Deputy Registrar, ibid, 1963-64; Registrar of Co-operative Societies, Mauritius, 1964-66. Memberships: President, Mauritius Co-operative Union, 1964-66; Chairman, Mauritius Co-operative Wholesale Society, 1965. Address: School of Administration, University of Mauritius, Mauritius.

CAMPBELL, Colin Moffat, born Charing, Kent, U.K., 4th August 1925. Business Executive. Education: Stowe, 1939-43. Married, 2 sons, 1 daughter. Appointments include: Captain, Scots Guards, 1943-47; employed with James Finlay, 1947—; Calcutta, 1948-58; Nairobi, Kenya, 19458—; President, East Africa Tea Trade Association, 1960-61, 1962-63, 1966-67; Chairman, Tea Board of Kenya, 1960—; President, Federation of Kenya Employers, 1962—; member, Labour Advisory Board, Kenya, 1962—. Honours include: M.C., 1945. Address: Box 12244, Nairobi, Kenya.

CAPUCCI, Ronald, born Manchester, U.K., 24th May 1919. Catering Advisor; Lecturer on Business Administration; Personnel Manager. Education: High School; External B.Sc. & Ph.D., Business Administration & Economics; Diplomas in Accounts & Book-keeping, & Personnel Management. Married, 2 sons. Appointments: served RAF, Middle & Far East, World War II; Senior Management positions, Tennants Brewery, British Drug House, Government Communications H.Q., & Cadbury Bros. Ltd. in various parts of Africa; administration appointments & Adviser on catering & student feeding, farm co-operatives, etc.; Lecturer on Business Administration, University of Botswana, Lesotho & Swaziland, Lesotho. Memberships: Fellow, Hotel & Catering Institute; Fellow, Cookery & Food Association; Fellow, Royal Society of Health; Royal Institution of Public Health & Hygiene; British Institute of Management. Recipient of several honours from Ghana, including Honorary Chieftaincy. Address: University of Botswana, Lesotho, & Swaziland, P.O. Roma, Maseru, Lesotho.

CARDOZO, Lavoisier Joseph, born 2nd January 1940. Physician. Education: St. Mary's College, Kisubi, Uganda; M.B., B.Ch., Makerere University College, 1957-64; Postgraduate training & specialization in Internal Medicine & Neurology, London & Edinburgh, U.K., Leading to M.R.C.P.(Edinburgh). Appointments: Intern, Mulago Hospital, 1964-65; Medical Superintendent, Masindi Hospital, 1965; Senior House Officer, Mulago Hospital, 1965-67; Clinical Assistant, Hospitals in London, Edinburgh & Glasgow, U.K., 1967-68; Specialist Physician, Ministry of Health, Government of Uganda, 1968—. Memberships: Association of Physicians of East Africa; Uganda Medical Association. Contributor to professional journals. Honours: Special Commonwealth Scholarship, 1967. Address: Box 299, Jinja, Uganda.

CAREN, Hazel Elisabeth Eaves, born 5th October 1921. Nurse. Education: Private Schools. Newcastle-under-Lyme, U.K. & Highbury, London; Felixstowe College for Girls 1931-32; Bottom High School, Lancashire, 1931-38; Neasden, London, 1939-41; General Certificate, Royal Hospital, Wolverhampton, 1942-45; Midwife, Barrett Maternity Home, Northampton, 1945-47; Staff Nurse, Children's Ward Sister, Manchester, 1953-54; with C.E.Z.M.S., East Pakistan, 1955-57; Assistant Matron, the Matron, C.M.S. Hospital, Omdurman, Sudan, 1967; work concentrated in leprosy field— resigned as Matron to further studies in this work. Memberships: Royal College of Nursing; Cowdray Club. Address: The Mission Hospital, Omdurman, Sudan.

CARLES, Alan Blake, born 14th October 1932. Veterinarian. Education: Cambridge University, U.K., 1951-57. Appointments: Private Practitioner, Nakuru, Kenya, 1957-61; Lecturer, Animal Production, University of Nairobi, Kenya. Memberships: M.R.C.V.S.; Inaugural President, Animal Production Society of Kenya; Kenya Veterinary Association; British Veterinary Association; E. African Academy; Sheep Veterinary Society; Ecological Society of Australia; Subcomm., Agricultural Society of Kenya. Author of Reproductive Disorders in Sheep, 1969. Address: Faculty of Veterinary Science, University of Nairobi, P.O. Kabete, Kenya.

CARLIN, Murray Melles, born 31st August 1921. Writer. Education: B.A., Rhodes

University, South Africa; M.A., Emmanuel College, Cambridge, U.K. Widower, 4 children. Appointments: South African Infantry, Western Desert & Prisoner-of-War, World War II; Office-boy; Librarian; Advertising Copywriter; Schoolteacher; Lecturer in English, Kumasi College of Technology, Ghana; Senior Lecturer, Makerere University, Uganda. Member, Oxford & Cambridge Club, London, U.K. Publications: Not Now, Sweet Desdemona (play); The Thousand (play) (both these performed by Tower Theatre, London, April 1970); also poems & articles in various journals, principally Transition. Address: Box 7062, Kampala, Uganda.

CARLING, David, born 5th November 1932. Physician. Education: Kendal Grammar School, U.K., 1943-48; Royal Grammar School, Lancaster, 1948-51; University of Birmingham, 1951-56; University of Liverpool, 1957. Married to Gwenyth Mary, 2 children. Appointments: House Surgeon, Royal Lancaster Infirmary, 1956-57; Medical Superintendent, Bornu Leprosy Settlement, Maiduguri, 1958—. Address: Sudan United Mission, Maiduguri, N.E. State, Nigeria.

CARNEIRO, John G., born Entebbe, Uganda, 1st September 1926. Teacher. Education: Matriculated from St. Joseph's High School, Arpora, Goa; B.A.(Hons.), Bombay University, India; B.Ed., Karnatak University, India. Married, 5 children. Appointments: Teacher, Uganda Civil Service; Headmaster, Old Kampala Primary School, 1961; ibid, Nakivubu Primary School, 1963; Norman Godinho School, 1963—. Memberships: Chairman, Kampala Schools, AAA, 1962-64; ibid, Kampala Schools Head Teachers' Association, 1966-68; Kampala Kindergarten Association, 1970. Author of a paper on Dynamics of Indian Population Problems, 1949. Address: Headmaster, Norman Godinho School, Kampala, Uganda.

CAROSIN, Marie Francois Maurice Piërre (Brother Remi), born Curepipe, Mauritius, 26th May 1917. Religious Teacher; Member of the Order of the Brothers of the Christian Schools, the De La Salle Brothers. Education: Loreto Convent, Curepipe; Secondary: St. Joseph's College, Curepipe; Brothers Scolasticate, Tananarive, Malagasy Republic; Universite Catholique, Lille, France; Brevet Elementaire; Matriculation of London University; Lic. en Lettres Modernes; Diplome de Pedagogie Generale; Diplome de Psychologie de l'Enfant. Personal details: son of Aurel Maurice Carosin & Marie Monique Louise Adam. Appointments: Teacher, St. Joseph's College, Curepipe, 1937-59; Director & Housemaster, St. Mary's College, Rose-Hill, 1959-69; Founder, Director & Headmaster, College de la Confiance, Beau-Bassin, Mauritius. Memberships: Educational Advisory Board, Government of Mauritius; Ex-member, Mauritius Sports Association; Founder & 1st President, Volley-Ball & Basket-Ball Comm., ibid. Address: Rev. Brother Remi Carosin, College de La Confiance, Dr. Reid Street, Beau-Bassin, Mauritius.

CARR, Anne Doris Gordon, born 16th May 1929. Agricultural Missionary. Education: St. Helen's School, Northwood, Middlesex, U.K.; B.Sc., Wye College, Kent. Married to S. J. Carr, 1954, 2 children. Appointments: Teacher, Yei Teacher Training College, 1954-57; assisted establishment of Undukori Training Farm, Equatoria, Sudan, 1957-62; ibid, Nyakashaka & Wambabya Development Schemes in Western Uganda. Address: Wambabya Development Scheme, P.O. Box 4, Hoima, Uganda.

CARR, Arthur Thomas, born 11th May 1939. Administrative Tutor. Education: Workington Grammar School, Cumberland, U.K., 1952-57; Workington College of Further Education, 1957-63; Teaching Diploma, Manchester University, 1964-65; Associate, Chartered Institute of Secretaries. Married, 1 son. Appointments: Administrative Officer, College of Further Education, Workington, 1957-60; Accounting Officer, Atomic Energy Commission, 1960-62; Finance Officer, Education Authority, 1962-64; Lecturer, The College, Swindon, Wiltshire, 1965-67; Tutor & Administrator, Institute of Development Management, Morogoro, Tanzania, 1967—. Memberships: Swindon & District Society, Chartered Institute of Secretaries; Local Examinations Board, Tanzania; Secretary, Morogoro Golf Club. Honours: Senior Prize Winner, Workington College, 1963. Address: P.O. Box 604, Morogoro, Tanzania.

CARR, Stephen John, born 22nd May 1928. Agricultural Missionary. Education: St. Albans College, Lomas de Zamota, Argentina; B.Sc., Wye College, Ashford, Kent, U.K. Married Anne Grant, 2 sons. Appointments: Lecturer, Agriculture, Awka College, E. Nigeria, 1952-54; Responsible for Agricultural Education in Primary Schools, Western Equatoria, Sudan, 1954-57; Founder & Manager, Undukori Training Farm, Equatoria, Sudan, 1957-62; ibid, Nyakashaka & Wambabya Development Schemes in Western Uganda. Memberships: Uganda Agricultural Society; Agricola Club; Lions. Author of Down to Earth. Address: Wombabya Development Scheme, Box 4, Hoima, Uganda.

CARSWELL, John Wilson, born 13th August 1937. Surgeon. Education: M.B.B.S., Westminster Medical School, U.K., 1961; M.R.C.S., 1961; L.R.C.P., 1961; F.R.C.S., 1967. Married, 3 daughters. Appointments: Registrar, Mayday Hospital, U.K., 1966-68; Medical Officer (Special Grade), Mulago Hospital, Kampala, Uganda, 1968—. Memberships: Uganda Medical Society; Uganda Society. Address: Department of Surgery, P.O. Box 7051, Kampala, Uganda.

CARSWELL, Margaret Jane, born 20th February, 1937. Physician. Education: M.B., B.S., University College, London, U.K., 1962; Westminster Hospital Medical School; M.R.C.S., L.R.C.P., 1962; D.A., 1965. Married, 3 daughters. Appointments: S.H.O., Anaesthetics, Chase Farm Hospital, London, 1965; Medical Officer, Nsambya Mission Hospital & Medical Adviser, Nsambya Babies Home, Uganda. Memberships: Uganda Medical Association;

Uganda Society. Address: P.O. Box 7146, Kampala, Uganda.

CARTER, Betty Joyce, born Bryan, Texas, U.S.A., 8th October 1926. Businesswoman. Education: Kemp High School, Bryan, Tex.; Bennett College; B.A., Howard University, Washington, D.C.; Samuel Houston College, Austin, Tex. Married to Hon. Joseph Boayoo, 3 sons, 3 daughters. Appointments include: Low-cost Housing; built duxplexs & cottages; Fishing Company Founder; founded first garbage disposal company in Liberia, then asked by President Tubman to start the City Better Cleaners company with W. Thomas Bernard. Address: P.O. Box 672, Monrovia, Liberia.

CARTER, James Roger, born 11th October 1911. Adviser on Educational Planning. Education: Rugby School, U.K., 1928-30; M.A., St. John's College, University of Cambridge, 1930-33. Married, 2 sons, 1 daughter. Appointments: Adult Education, various posts, 1933-44; Official, U.N. Relief & Rehabilitation Administration, 1944-47; Administrative Civil Servant, British Civil Service, 1947-60; First Secretary & Education Officer, British Embassy, Washington, U.S.A., 1949-52; Principal, Kaimosi Training College, Kenya, 1960-62; Administrative Education Officer, Kenya Government, 1963-67; Ford Foundation Adviser on Educational Planning, Government of Tanzania, 1967-70. Secretary, Kenya Education Commission, 1964-68. Publications: The Legal Framework of Educational Planning & Administration in East Africa, 1966. Address: Ministry of National Education, P.O. Box 9121, Dar es Salaam, Tanzania.

CARVER, John Christian Niven, born 28th September 1928. Civil Servant. Education: Ruzawi School, Marandellas; Michaelhouse, Natal, South Africa; B.A., Rhodes University, Grahamstown; M.A., Oxford University, U.K. Married, one son, one daughter. Currently, Capital City Liaison Officer, Lilongwe, Malawi. Member, Rotary Club. Address: P.O. Box 211, Lilongwe, Malawi.

CAUKWELL, Robert Arthur, born 19th November 1928. University Lecturer in Land Surveying. Education: Kingham School, 1936-45; Professional Associate, Royal Institution of Chartered Surveyors, 1964; Licensed Land Surveyor, Kenya, 1963; Member, Institution of Surveyors of Kenya, 1969; Certified Land Surveyor, E. Africa, 1968. Married. Appointments: Surveyor, Kenya Government, 1949-68; Lecturer, University of East Africa, University College, Nairobi, 1968-70; University of Nairobi, 1970—. Memberships: Secretary, Kenya Branch, Royal Institution off Chartered Surveyors, 1970; Alpine Club. Address: University of Nairobi, P.O. Box 30197, Nairobi, Kenya.

CAUVIN, Francis, born 28th December 1905. Doctor of Medicine; Director of Moroccan Social Services. Education: Secondary School, Toulon, France; Lauréat, Faculty of Medicine, Bordeaux, France. Married, 2 children. Appointments: Military Doctor, 1929-39; Doctor, Public Health Service, Morocco, 1933-46; Public Health Inspector, 1947-50; Director, Medical Social Services, Morocco, 1951-58. Memberships: Councillor, Executive Committee of the International Union for Sanitary Education, 1952-57; President, French Association in Rabat, 1961-64; Councillor, Director, Union of French people overseas, 1962-66. Honours: Lauréat, Académie de Médicine; Knight, Legion of Honour; Croix de Guerre, T.O.E.; Moroccan Colonial Medal; Commander, Ouissam Alaouite. Address: 5 Rue Beaumier, Rabat, Morocco.

CAUWE, Andre, born Ypres, Belgium, 29th November 1913. Jesuit. Education: Cand. en philologie Classiqqu, Belgium; Lic. Philosophic, Fac. Jesuits of Louvain; Lic. Theologie, Rome, Italy. Appointments: Professor, College Notre Dame, Anvers, Belgium, 1938-39; ibid, Ecole Assistants Medicaux, Kisantu, Congo, 1939-40; Petit Seminaire, LemFu, 1940-42; College, Note Dame de la Victoire, Bukavu, 1942-45; Gerant Co-operative des Agriculteurs, Kisantu, 1950-60; Director, Des Oeuvres Medicales Catholiques de Congo, Kinshasa, Democratic Republic of the Congo, & Secretary General, Caritas-Congo, 1960-60. Publications: various articles in journals & reviews on Congolese problems; Les Co-operatives, solution pour l'Afrique?; Les Co-operatives et leur conditions de reussite, 1969; Monographie sur l'union des Co-operatives du Bas-Fleuve. Address: Secretary General de Caritas—Congo, B.P. 3176, Kinshasa, Democratic Republic of the Congo.

CAYER, (Right Reverend) John Aime, born 17th April 1900. Bishop. Education: Sherbrooke, Montreal & Quebec Colleges, Canada; D.D., Innsbruck University, Austria. Appointments: Entered Franciscan Order, 1919—; Ordained Priest, 1926; Chaplain, St. Mary's Hospital, Montreal, Canada, 1926; Teacher, St. Anthony's College, Edmonton, 1927-36; Rector, ibid, 1930; Professor of Theology, Roman Catholic Seminary, Regina, Sask., 1940-45; Franciscan Fathers Commissary, 1945; Minister Provincial for the Order in Canada, 1948; Bishop of Alexandria & Vicar Apostolic of Egypt, 1949—. Knight of Columbus. Address: 10 Sidi Metwalli, Vicariat Apostolique, Alexandria, U.A.R.

CAZENAVE, Robert, born Orthez, Basses-Pyrénées, France, 28th February 1913. Patent & Trade Mark Attorney. Education: Baccalauréats, Latin, Greek, Philosophy, Maths; LL.D. Married, 1 child. Appointments include: Lawyer, Court of Appeal, Toulouse, France, 1935-50; Lawyer, Yaoundé, Cameroon, 1951-68; Patent & Trade Mark Attorney, O.A.M.P.I. & other African countries, 1964—. Former French memberships: President, Conseil de la Resistance, Toulouse, Central Committee, Young Lawyers of France & French Community, Paris; Vice-President, War Veterans: Organization, Toulouse; Vice-President, Union of Associated Family Organizations, Toulouse; President, Mountaineering Club 'Escagarol', Toulouse. Former Cameroon memberships: President, Rotary

Club, Yaoundé; President, League for Human Rights, Yaoundé; President, League of Education, Yaoundé. Current Cameroon memberships: Hon. President, Amicale des Français au Cameroon; Vice-President, International Association for the Protection of Industrial Property, Zurich, Switzerland; President, Association for the Protection of Industrial Property in Africa & Madagascar; Deputy President, Golf Club, Yaoundé; Professor, National School of Administration & Magistracy, Yaoundé. Publications include: Numerous articles in Gazette du Palais et des Tribunaux, Paris; Le Conseiller du Commerce Exterieur, Paris; La Propriété Industrielle, & Industrial Property, Geneva; Revue de Droit Intellectuel, Brussels, etc. Honours include: Medal of the French Resistance, 1945; Combattant's Cross, 1946; Cross of Voluntary Combattant of the Resistance, 1946; Knight, Cameroon National Order of Valour, 1959; Officer, ibid, 1970. Address: B.P. 500, Yaoundé, Cameroon.

CEDILE, Jean Henry, born 8th January 1908. Gouverneur de la France d'Outre Mer (retired). Education: Lycée d'Auxene(Youne); Ecole National de la France d'Outremer; Lic. en Droit. Appointments: Administrateur de la France d'Outre Mer, Cameroun, 1932-39; Governor, Togo, 1948-51; Secretary-General, French Equatorial Africa, 1951-59; President, Electrical Energy of Cameroun, 1960—. Honours: Grand Officer of the Legion of Honour; Companion of the Liberation; Cross of War, 1939-45. Address: c/o Energie Electrique du Cameroun, Cameroun.

CHABAANE, Mahmoud, born 15th April 1928. Regional Supervisor of Primary Schools; Author. Education: Sadiki College, Tunis; Ecole Normale d'Instituteurs; High School; University of Southern California, U.S.A. Appointments: Teacher; Schools' Director; Inspector of Primary Schools, Tunis; Regional Inspector of Primary Schools, Tunis. Memberships: Scoutmaster, Tunisien Scouts; Tunisien Nationalist Party; Secretary-General, Young Scholars; President, Modern Co-operative Teaching; Secretary-General, Association of School Inspectors. Author of numerous books on education, children's stories & various articles. Honours: Knight, Order of the Tunisien Republic. Address: 2 bis Rue de Cronstadt, Montfleury, Tunis, Tunisia.

CHABI, Mama, born 4th December 1923. Minister of Rural Development. Education: Diploma, Victor Ballot School. Married with children. Appointments: Deputy, 1957-63; Senator, 1959-61; Minister of Justice & Foreign Affairs, 1963-66; Minister of National Education, 1968-69; Minister of Rural Development, 1970—; Director of the Paper 'Sa Nation', political paper of the P.D.U. Memberships: President, Dahomey Association for the Defence & Interests of Islam, 1967—; Geberal Secretary, P.D.U., 1960-63. Honours: Commander, National Order of Senegal, 1962; Commander, National Order of Dahomey, 1967. Address: Minister of Rural Development & Co-operation, Porto-Novo, Dahomey.

CHACO, Mavelil Chaco, born 4th May 1927. Teacher; Researcher. Education: B.Sc.; M.Sc.; Ph.D.; A.R.I.C. Married, 2 children. Appointments: Teacher; Postdoctoral Research Fellow; Research Associate; Lecturer; Senior Lecturer. Memberships: Fellow, Chemical Society; Associate, Royal Institute of Chemistry. Author of numerous scientific publications. Honours: National Research Fellowship of India, 1957-59; Medal for one publication, 1964. Department of Chemistry, University of Ghana, Legon, Ghana.

CHAGGAR, Mohinder Singh, born 10th March 1936. Architect. Education: Grammar School, Mombassa, Kenya; Arechitectural Training, School of Architecture & Engineering, Mainz, West Germany. Appointments: Acting Chief Architect, State Hotel (Apolo Hotel), Kampala, Uganda; own practice as Techno Haus chartered architects. Memberships: Lions Club of Kampala; Uganda Society of Architects. Address: P.O. Box 4243, Kampala, Uganda.

CHAHALI, Bernard, born February 1938. Administrator. Education: Standard I-VIII, 1945-54; IX-X, 1955-56; XI-XII (Cambridge School Certificate), 1957-59; XIII-XIV (Higher School Certificate), 1960-61; B.A.(General), Makerere University College, Uganda, 1962-65. Married, 2 daughters. Appointments: Assistant Secretary, Ministry of Education, Tanzania, 1965; Assistant Secretary, Treasury, 1966-70, firstly dealing with formulation of National Budget, but now working in the External Finance & Technical Co-operation Division. Memberships: Scoutmaster, St. Francis Secondary School, Dar es Salaam, 1960-61; Dramatic Society, ibid. Honours: Presented with cup by Governor, Sir Richard Turnbull, as best actor in play 'The Valiant'. Address: Ministry of Finance, P.O. Box 9111, Dar es Salaam, Tanzania.

CHAKER, Moncef, born 11th July 1935. Engineer. Education: Primary School, Sfax, Tunisia; Certificate of Studies & Baccalaureat 2nd part, Tunis; University studies at Bordeaux, France; Engineering Diploma of the Techniques of Rural Equipment, National Engineering School for Rural Works & Sanitary Techniques. Married, 3 children. Appointments: Head of the Subdivision of Industrial Agriculture; Director, Rural Spirit Centre of Research. Memberships: Treasurer, Destourienne Cell, Strasbourg; ibid, Destourienne Cell of Agronomic Research; Secretary-General, ibid; Treasurer, General Union of Tunisien Students (Sadiki College Section); Third Commission of the International Institute of Refrigeration. Address: Boulevard Hedi Saidi, Immeuble Printemps No. 4, Apt. No. 16, Tunis, Tunisia.

CHAKKOUCH, Driss, born 25th July 1943. Officer of the Royal Marines. Appointments: Career in the Royal Marines, promoted to Lieutenant of his ship. Address: Marine Royale, Casablanca, Morocco.

CHAKROUN, Mohamed, born 11th June 1914. Advocate of the Supreme Court of Appeal. Education: Lic. Law. Appointments: Deputy, Constituent Assembly, then National Assembly, 1956-64; Minister of Social Affairs, 1956-57;

Secretary of State for Social Affairs, 1957-58; National Order of Advocates, 1965-67. Address: 1 Rue Mustapha, Mebarek, Tunis.

CHAMBRIER, Rahandi Eloi, born Libreville, Gabon, 1st December 1933. Doctor of Medicine. Education: Secondary studies, Lycée Michelet Vauve; Higher studies, Faculty of Medicine, Paris, France; Diploma, Tropical Medicine. Married, 6 children. Appointments: Resident Doctor, various hospitals, Paris, France; Head, Medical Paediatrics' Service, General Hospital, Libreville, Gabon; Founder & Head, Maternity & Surgical Clinic, Libreville; Deputy Mayor, Libreville. Memberships: President, National Order of Doctors, Gabon; Responsible for Party Information for the Political Bureau, Gabon. Author of various medical papers. Address: B.P. 1320, Libreville, Gabon.

CHANDARANA, Pravin Chhotalal, born 23rd May 1933. Secretary; Accountant. Education: B.Com.(Bombay); A.A.C.C.A. Married to Sharda, 1 son, 2 daughters. Appointments: Group Chief Accountant with a Shipping Company. Memberships: Health Committee, Lions Club, Nairobi; Examination Committee, Association of Accountants in East Africa. Address: P.O. Box 1209, Nairobi, Kenya.

CHANDE, Jayantilal Keshavji, born 27th August 1929. Business Executive; Company Director. Married, 3 sons. Appointments— General Manager: National Milling Corp., Tanzania; Chairman: Tanganyika Standard (Newspapers) Limited; Management Supply Company Ltd.; Fourways Travel Service (Tanganyika) Ltd.; Director: National Bank of Commerce, Tanzania; Tanzania Electric Supply Company Ltd.; Tanzania Tourist Corp.; East Africa Harbours Corp.; International Computers & Tabulators (Tanzania) Ltd.; Tanganyika Portland Cement Company; International School of Tanganyika Ltd.; National Distributors Ltd.; Mtibwa Sugar Estates Ltd.; Tanzania Distilleries Ltd. Memberships—President: World Council of Young Men's Service Clubs; Red Cross Society, Dar es Salaam, 1961-64; Dar es Salaam Chamber of Commerce & Agriculture, 1961-62; Association of Chambers of Commerce & Industries in Eastern Africa, 1963-64; Tanganyika Association of Chambers of Commerce, 1964-68; Association of Round Tables in Eastern Africa (Kenya, Uganda, Tanganyika, Ethiopia, Aden, & Mauritius), 1966-67; The Tanganyika Society, 1963-68; Vice-Chairman: The Dar es Salaam Secondary Education Society; Chairman: Board of Examiners, College of Business Education, Tanzania; Board of Governors, Shaaban Robert Secondary School, Dar es Salaam; Tanzania Management Committee, Automobile Association of East Africa; Dar es Salaam Round Table, 1958; Vice-President: Tanganyika Red Cross Society; Executive Council in Tanganyika; Round Table, 1959-61; National Assembly, ibid, 1959-61; Survey Panel, International Industrial Conference Board, New York; Trustee, East African Gandhi Memorial Academy Society; Upanga Sports Club, Dar es Salaam; Lohana Education Trust, East Africa; Acting Chairman: Board of Trustees, National Museum of Tanzania; Royal Commonwealth Society; Fellow, Institute of Directors; Donovan Maule Theatre Club, London; The Company of Veteran Motorists; Dormer Masonic Study Circle. Address: P.O. Box 9251, Dar es Salaam, Tanzania.

CHANDERLI, Abdelkader, born 1st March 1915. Economist; President, Directeur-General de CAMEL. Education: University of Paris, France; School of Political Sciences. Married, 3 children. Appointments: Public Relations Director, UNESCO; Representative of the FLN to the United States; Ambassador of Algeria to the United Nations; Director-General of the Ministry of Foreign Affairs, Algeria. Memberships: Vice-President, Economic & Social Council of the UN, 1964-65. Publications: Education & Development; Terres Saintes; Geographie de l'ignorance. Address: Dar Al Alou, II Rue Buffon, El Biar, Algeria.

CHANTLER, Anthony John Clyde, born 15th March 1937. Lecturer. Education: King William's College, Isle of Man, U.K., 1946-55; Sidney Sussex College, Cambridge, 1957-60; Leeds University, 1963-64. Appointments: English Master, St. Augustine's College, Cape Coast, Ghana, 1960-63; Lecturer in English & African Literature, University College of Cape Coast, 1964—. Address: Faculty of Arts, University College of Cape Coast, Cape Coast, Ghana.

CHAPMAN NYAHO, Daniel Ahmling, born Keta, Ghana, 5th July 1909. Business Executive. Education: Bremen Mission Schools, Keta & Lome; Achimota College, Ghana; St. Peter's Hall, Oxford University, U.K.; Postgraduate Courses: International Law, International Relations, International Organization, Columbia University & New York University, U.S.A.; Postgraduate Course, Prehistoric Archaeology, Oxford University, U.K. Married, 2 sons, 4 daughters. Appointments include: Teacher, Government Senior Boys' School, Accra, Ghana, 1930; Master, Achimota College, 1930-33; Senior Geography Master, ibid, 1937-46; Area Specialist, Department of Trusteeship & Information from Non-Self-Governing Territories, United Nations Secretariat, New York, U.S.A., 1946-54; Secretary to the Prime Minister & to the Cabinet, Gold Coast, Ghana, 1954-57; Head of Ghana Civil Service, 1957; First Ambassador of Ghana to the U.S.A., & Permanent Representative at the United Nations, 1957-59; Chairman, Mission of Independent African States to Cuba, Dominican Republic, Haiti,· Venezuela, Bolivia, Paraguay, Urugay, Brazil, Argentina, & Chile, 1957-59; First Vice-Chairman, Governing Council of United Nations Special Fund, 1959; Headmaster, Achimota School, Ghana, 1959-63; Director, United Nations Division of Narcotic Drugs, Geneva, 1963-66; Ambassador (Special Duties), Ministry of External Affairs, Ghana, 1967; Executive Director, Pioneer Tobacco Company, Ghana, 1967—. Memberships include: General Secretary, All-Ewe Conference, 1944-46; Vice-Chairman, Commission on University Education in Ghana, 1960-61; Member, Board of Management of the United Nations International School, 1950-54, 1958-59; United Nations Middle East & North Africa Technical Assistance

Mission on Narcotics Control, 1963; Political Committee of the National Council, Ghana, 1967; Chairman, Arts Council of Ghana, 1968-69; Board of Trustees, General Kotoko Trust Fund; Chairman, Volta Union, 1968-69; Fellow, Ghana Academy of Arts & Sciences. Publications include: The Human Geography of Eweland, 1946; Natural Resources of the Gold Coast, 1938; Our Homeland—Book I, South-East Gold Coast, 1945. Honours include: C.B.E., 1961; Hon. LL.D., Greenboro Agricultural & Technical College, U.S.A. Address: P.O. Box 11, Accra, Ghana.

CHARLES, Georges, born 26th December 1926. University Professor. Education: D.es Sc., French University, 1963. Married, 7 children. Appointments: Assistant, Faculty of Science, Poitiers, France, 1953; Head Assistant, ibid; Lecturer, Faculty of Sciences, Yaoundé, Cameroun, 1964; Head of the Department of Chemistry, ibid, 1964-69; Professor, ibid, 1969—. Memberships: West African Science Association; Chemical Society of France. Publications: Chimie des Substances Naturelles (joint author); Alcoloides Steroidiques XCIV (joint author), etc., published in C.R. Acad. Sc. Address: B.P. 812, Yaoundé, Cameroun.

CHATSIKAH, Lewis Alexander, born 18th November 1934. Lawyer. Education: Henry Henderson Institute, Blantyre, Malawi; Dedza Secondary School, Dedza; Goromonzi School, Salisbury, Rhodesia; Lincoln's Inn, London, U.K. Personal details: son of A. Gray Chatsikah, Soldier, Civil Servant, Farmer & Preacher. Appointments: State Counsel, 1965-67; Legal Aid Counsel & Local Courts Commissioner, 1967-68; Director of Public Prosecutions, 1968-70; Puisne Judge, High Court, 1970—. Address: High Court, Blantyre, Malawi.

CHATTOPADHYAYA, Gouriprasad, born 27th December 1919. Medical Administrator. Education: M.B., B.S., P.W. Medical College, Patna, India, 1943; Diploma in Public Health, All-India Institute of Health & Hygiene, Calcutta, India, 1954; Diploma in TB Diseases, Delhi, 1957. Appointments: Resident Surgical Officer, P.W. Medical College, Patna, 1944-46; Assistant Medical Officer, Railway Service, Government of India, 1947-58; Medical Officer of Health, Central & Western Regions, Government of Ghana, 1959-61; Port Health Officer, Takoradi, Ghana, 1962-66; Principal Medical Officer, Government of Ghana, 1966—. Address: Ministry of Health, P.O. Box 63, Cape Coast, Central Region, Ghana.

CHAUDHRY, Mohamed Ijaz, born 10th August 1936. Surgeon. Education: Primary & Secondary Schooling at Mombassa, 1955; B.Sc., Zoology & Botany, Punjab University, Lahore, Pakistan; M.B., B.S., ibid, 1964; F.R.C.S., Royal College of Surgeons, Edinburgh, U.K., 1969. Personal details: one of 8 brothers & sisters from middle-class family; obtained F.R.C.S. Scholarship by Ministry of Overseas Development, U.K. Appointments: Medical Officer in Charge, District Hospital, Kilifi, Kenya, 1965-66; Surgical Registrar, Kenyatta National Hospital, Nairobi, 1967-69; Surgical Specialist, District Hospital, Meru, Kenya, 1970—. Memberships: Local Sports Club; Captain, Tennis Club. Address: P.O. Box 8, Meru, Kenya.

CHAUDHURY, Debadi Saran, born 1st February 1932. Physician. Education: M.D., Calcutta University, India, 1954; Postgrad. training, Leprology, Madras, 1955; Diploma, Tropical Medicine & Hygiene, Liverpool University, U.K., 1967. Personal details: son of an Educationalist & Scholar; Married to Dr. M. Chaudhury, also a Leprologist. Appointments: Medical Officer, Gandhi Foundation, 1956-61; Leprologist, Ministry of Health, Ghana, 1962-70. Memberships: Ghana Medical Association; International Leprosy Association; Life Fellow, Royal Society of Tropical Medicine & Hygiene. Author of numerous technical papers in international medical journals. Honours: Gandhi Foundation Fellowship, 1951. Address: Senior Medical Officer i/c, Leprosy Service, P.O. Box 26, Elmina, Ghana.

CHAUDHURY, Maitreyi, born 4th April 1937. Physician. Education: M.D., Calcutta University, India, 1961. Personal details: daughter of a Metallurgical Engineer; married to Dr. D. S. Chaudhury, Leprologist, Ministry of Health, Ghana. Appointments: Medical Officer, Diara Centre, Singur Rural Health Project, All-India Institute of Health, 1962-63; ibid, Leprosy Service, Ministry of Health, Government of Ghana, 1964—. Member, Ghana Medical Association. Publications: A case report of gangrenous balanitis in progressive reaction in leprosy (with Dr. D. B. Chaudhury), 1966. Address: Medical Officer, Leprosy Service, Post Box 26, Elmina, Ghana.

CHEGE, Onesimus Simon, born 19th July 1929. Civil Engineer. Education: Cambridge School Certificate, Alliance High School, 1947; B.E., Civil Engineering, Banaras Hindu University, India, 1955; D.I.C. (Public Health Engineering), London University, U.K., 1962. Married, 4 children. Appointments: Engineer, Ministry of Works, Kenya Government, 1957-63; Provincial Engineer, ibid, 1963; Assistant Director, Water Development Department, 1965-67; Director, ibid, 1967—. Memberships: Associate, East African Institution of Engineers. Address: Box 30521, Nairobi, Kenya.

CHEIKH, Abdelhamid, born 3rd May 1945. Air Traffic Controller. Education: Civil Aviation School, Tunis, Tunisia; Federal Aviation Agency School, Oklahoma, U.S.A. Owner of orange plantation with brothers. Appointments: Air Traffic Controller, Control Tower, Tunis Airport, Tunisia, 1966—. Member, Tunisian Air Traffic Controller's Association. Address: 13 rue des Eparges, La Cagna, Tunisia.

CHESSON, Joseph Jefferson Francis, born 20th April 1919. Lawyer; Advocate; Solicitor; Counsellor-at-Law. Education: American Lutheran Mission, Liberia, 1935; College of West Africa, Monrovia, 1939; B.A., Liberia College (now University of Liberia), 1943; Certificate of Accountancy, London School of Commerce, U.K., 1940; LL.B., American University, Washington, D.C., U.S.A., 1953; Hon. LL.D., Monrovia College, 1959; D.J., American University School of Law, Washington, D.C., U.S.A., 1968. Married, 10 children. Appointments: Cadet, Treasury Department, Liberia, 1935-37; Book-keeper, ibid, 1937-40; Accountant, Civil Service Provident Fund, 1940-42; Assistant Clerk, Supreme Court of Liberia, 1942-43; . Clerk, ibid, 1943-48; Assistant Attorney-General of Liberia, Tax Division, 1953-54; Senior Assistant Attorney General for Prosecutions & Other Litigations, 1954-56; Chairman, Joint Security Commission, Republic of Liberia, 1954-63; Associate Auditor, Interpol, Paris, France, 1954-55; Chief, Liberian Central Bureau, ibid, 1954-57; Executive Committee (rep. Africa & Asia), 1957-59; Solicitor-General of Liberia, 1957-61; Attorney-General of Liberia, 1961-63; Professor of Law, University of Liberia, 1954-60; Liberian Economic Special Commission, 1954-55; Chairman, Liberian Elections Claims Commission, 1954-56; Vice-President, Interpol, Paris, France, 1959-63. Memberships: President, 1st International Criminal Police Organization's Regional Conference in Africa, South of the Sahara, 1962; International Organization of Chiefs of Police, U.S.A.; Hon. Member, Supreme Court Bar, Haiti, 1963—; International Society of Lawyers, U.S.A., 1954—; Vice-President, Liberian Olympic Committee, 1957—; Hon. Member, Club Africian-Fiesta, Kinshasha, Congo, 1965—; Past Noble Father, Most Worthy Grand Lodge of Odd Fellows, Republic of Liberia; Past Master, Most Worthy Grand Lodge of IOGT; Past Master, Most Worshipful Grand Lodge of Free & Accepted Masons of Liberia; Past Grand Master, United Brothers of Friendship & Sisters of the Mysterious Ten of the Republic of Liberia & the Federation of Nigeria; Pan American Clipper Club, N.Y., U.S.A.; President, African Students Association of the U.S.A. & Canada, 1949-52; Club 91, London, U.K.; Amondo Ross Club, London; The Waves Club, Monrovia, Liberia; First President, Les Amis, Inc., Monrovia; Board of Directors, Monrovia College; Former Member, Board of Directors, Y.M.C.A. of Liberia; Former Member, Board of Directors, Boy Scouts Council of Liberia; Former Director-General, National Sports & Athletics Commission, Liberia; Patron, National Federation of Women Lawyers, Liberia; Patron, National Federation of Liberian Women's Associations; Patron, Merry-Makers Club of Liberia; Patron, Liberian Athletic Club; Secretary, Liberia Press Association, 1943-48; Trinity Pro-Cathedral, Monrovia; Former Superintendent, ibid; Liberian National Football Team, 1934-48; Liberian National Tennis Team (twice holder of Singles Trophy), 1938-48; Vice-President, Liberian Football Association, 1954-57; President, ibid, 1957-65; Liberian Sports Delegation, All African Games, Dakar, Senegal; Chairman, Liberian Sports Delegation, Ivory Coast, 1962-65; Chairman, Liberian Sports Delegation, Guinea, 1960-65; Chairman, Liberian Sports Delegation to Sierra Leone, 1951-63; Chairman, Liberian Sports Delegation, Ghana 1960-65; Chairman, Liberian Sports Delegation, Organizing Committee, First All African Games, Brazzaville, Congo, 1965; President, Zone 3, First All African Games, 1964-65; Chairman, Liberian Sports Delegation, ibid, 1965; Supreme Council of Sports for Africa, 1965; Chairman, Liberian Sports Delegation, Tokyo Olympic Games, 1964; Representative of Liberia, Mexico Olympic Games, 1968; Liberian Sports Commission, Monrovia; President, Western Defenders Football Association, Monrovia, 1958-62; Liberian Tennis Association; Liberian Inter-Schools Sports Association; Liberian Boxing Association; Liberian Track & Field Association; Liberian Volley-Ball Association; Liberian Basket-Ball Association; Liberian Referees Association; Supreme Court of Liberia (Lawyers) Association; Former Leader, National Bar Association, Liberia; Ad hoc Judge, International Court of Justice, Hague, Holland, in case of Liberia & Ethiopia vs. South West Africa, 1961; Senior Counsellor-at-Law, Republic of Liberia; Grievance Committee, Montserrado County Bar Association. Represented Liberian Government at: Sanniquellie Conference of Heads of African States & Governments, Liberia; Liberian Boundary Commission to the Governments of France, Paris, 1958; Liberian Delegation to the U.N. General Assembly, 1949, 1963; Liberian Delegation to I.L.O., Geneva, Switzerland, 1953; Liberian Delegation to W.H.O., Geneva, 1953; Liberian Delegations to Interpol Congresses, 1954-63; Liberian Delegation, Law of the Seas Convention, Vienna, Austria, 1962; Liberian Delegation, I.L.O. Special Labour Investigation Regarding Forced Labour, Geneva, Switzerland, 1963. Honours: Knight Grand Commander, Star of Africa, Liberia; Knight Grand Commander, Star of African Redemption, Liberia; Knight Commander, House of Orange-Nassau, Netherlands; Knight Grand Commander, Federal German Eagle, Federal Republic of Germany; Grand Commander, Grand Cross, Haitian Order of Toussaint L'Ouverture; Knight Grand Commander of the Cedars of Lebanon; Commander of the Order of the Elephant Ivory Coast; Grand Commander, Order of Merit, Malagasy Republic; Grand Official, Order of the People's Republic of Yugoslavia, etc. Address: P.O. Box 1625, Monrovia, Liberia.

CHEVILLARD, Henri Louis Jean, born 12th February 1930. Principal Administrator of Maritime Affairs. Education: Baccalauriats; Lic., Law; Diploma, Centre of Higher Administrative Studies for Africa & Modern Asia. Married, 3 children. Appointments include: Head of Maritime Circonscription, Oran, Algeria, 1962-64; Deputy Head, Personnel Secretariat, Merchant Marine, Paris, France, 1964-67; Head, Merchant Marine Services, Secondary Ports & River Transport of Senegal, 1967—. Honours include: Chevalier de l'Ordre National du Merite Francais; Commemorative Medal, etc. Address: B.P. 4032, Dakar, Senegal.

CHHATRISHA, Gajendrarai Zaverchand, born Kenya, 22nd June 1936. Dental Surgeon. Education: B.D.S., University of Bombay, India; L.D.S.R.C.S., Royal College of Surgeons, U.K. Married, 2 daughters. Appointments include: Private Practice, Nakuru, Kenya, as a dental surgeon, 7 years; attached to Provincial General Hospital, Nakuru, as a Consultant Dental Surgeon. Memberships; East African Dental Association; Secretary, Lions Club of Nakuru, 1969-70; Nakuru Athletic Club. Honours: 100% Secretary Award, Lions Club of Nakura, 1970. Address: P.O. Box 120, Nakuru, Kenya.

CHIBUMBA, Mela Monde Muyeke, born 5th June 1940. Social Worker; Teacher; Bookkeeper. Education: G.C.E. O-Level; Diploma in Social Welfare; Part 3 Book-keeping, Institute of Book-keepers. Married, 4 children. Appointments: Senior Caseworker; Groups Organizer; Industrial Teacher. Memberships: 1st African Woman Councillor in Zambia, Luanshya Municipal Council, 1963—; Executive Committee, Zambia Social Service Council; Natuisinge Nutrition Committee & Chairlady, Publicity & Fund Raising, Ibenga Girls School; Founder member, Luanshya Branch, YWCA; Vice-Chairman, Luanshya Youth Development Scheme; Advisory Committee, Nindolo Ecumencial Foundation; Family Planning Committee, Luanshya; Voluntary family caseworker, etc. Address: P.O. Box 405, Luanshya, Zambia.

CHIBWANA, Phillip, born 14th August 1940. Farmer. Education: Msumba School; Chithebwe Mission School; Kayoyo School; Mtandire School; Junior Certificate, by correspondence, 1967. Married, 4 children. Appointments: Secretary, local branch, M.C.P., 1959; Organizing Secretary, ibid, 1960; Vice-Chairman, 1961; Secretary, Area Branch, 1962; Member, Assessment Board, 1965; Member, Malawi Development Corporation, 1967. Ntchisi Cooperative Society; Secretary, Msumba Farmers Club. Address: Malawi Development Corporation, Box 566, Blantyre, Malawi.

CHIDUME, Eusebius Nwankwo, born 24th December 1933. Medical Practitioner. Education: B.Sc., Anatomy, Queen's University, Belfast, U.K., 1958; M.B.B.Ch., B.A.O., ibid, 1961; F.R.C.S.Edin., 1964. Married, 4 daughters. Appointments: Demonstrator in Anatomy, Queen's University, Belfast, 1962-63; House Officer, Royal Victoria Hospital, Belfast, 1961-62; Senior House Officer, Surgical, ibid, 1963-64; Surgical Registrar, Mater Infirmorium Hospital, Belfast, 1964; Surgical Specialist, Ministry of Health, East Central State, Nigeria, 1964—. Member, Sports Club, Abekaliki, East Central State. Honours: University Scholarship, Queen's University, 1957-58. Address: Ministry of Health, General Hospital, Abekaliki, East Central State, Nigeria.

CHIDZERO, Bernard T. G., born Salisbury, Rhodesia, 1st July 1927. Political Scientist; Official, United Nations. Education: Primary School, Southern Rhodesia, 1939-45; Secondary School, Matriculation, St. Francis College, Mariannhill, Natal, South Africa, 1946-49; Pius XII University College (now University of Botswana, Lesotho & Swaziland), 1950-52; B.A. (with distinction in Psychology), Ottawa University, Canada, 1953-55; M.A.(cum laude) in Political Science; McGill University, Montreal, Canada, 1955-58; Ph.D., Political Science. Married, 4 children. Appointments include: Lecturer, Pius XII University College, 1953; Teaching Assistant, Comparative Government, McGill University, 1957-58; Research, Economic & Political Aspects of British Policy in Central Africa, as a Factor in the Formation of the Federation of Rhodesia & Nyasaland, Nuffield College, Oxford, U.K., 1958-60; Economic Affairs Officer, U.N. Economic Commission for Africa, 1960-63; Representative of the U.N. Technical Assistance Board, & Director of Special Fund Programmes in Kenya, 1963-65; Resident Representative of the U.N. Development Programme in Kenya, 1966-68; Director, Commodities Division, U.N. Conference on Trade & Devel., 1968—. Memberships include: SODEPAX; Agricultural Society of Kenya; Editorial Board, Journal of Modern African Studies; Special Lectureship Committee, University of East Africa. Publications include: Tanganyika and International Trusteeship, 1961; Nzvengamutsvairo (novel, written in Shona, African language spoken in Rhodesia); numerous papers on economic & political problems of East Africa & Central Africa. Awards include: Alexander Mackenzie Fellowship In Political Science, McGill University, Canada, 1957-58; Canadian Social Science Research Council (grant), 1958; Canada Council (grant), 1958-59; Nuffield Studentship, 1958-60; Ford Travel and Study Program, 1959. Address: c/o UNCTAD, Palais des Nations, H 1211, Geneva, Switzerland.

CHILIVUMBO, Alifeyo Bartholomew, born 24th August 1939. Lecturer. Education: Linga Primary School, Malawi, 1947-53; Blantyre & Dedza Secondary Schools, 1954-59; B.A. Sociology, Makarere University, Uganda, 1960-63; Ph.D. Sociology, University of California at Los Angeles, U.S.A., 1964-68. Appointments: Lecturer in Sociology, Chancellor College, University of Malawi, 1968-70. Memberships: American Sociological Association; Black Students Union, UCLA, 1966-68. Author of various papers in professional publications, & of Chitwara Cotton Development Project: A Sociological Survey, 1970. Honours: Research Prize, Faculty of Arts, Makerere University College, 1963. Address: P.O. Box 5200, Limba, Malawi.

CHILVERS, Roy Michael, born 21st March 1934. Fisheries Biologist. Education: City of Norwich School, U.K.; B.Sc.(Hons.), Zoology, Sheffield University, U.K. Married, 1958, 2 children. Appointments: Assistant Scientist, F.R.B.C., St. John's, Newfoundland, 1956-58; Scientific Officer, M.A.F.F., Radiobiological Lab., Lowestoft, U.K., 1959-66; Senior Scientific Officer, E.A.F.F.O., Jinja, Uganda, 1966-70. Memberships: Fellow, International Academy of Fisheries Scientists; British Ecological Society; Freshwater Biological Association; Uganda Society; Board of Managers, Victoria Nile School, Jinja. Publications include: Tagging Experiments on Aquaria kept fish; A note on gross fish output from Lake Victoria since 1958. Address: Beggars Close, Prospect Road, Oulton Broad, E. Suffolk, U.K.

CHIMPHAMBA, Brown Beswick, born Ncheu District, Malawi, 16th December 1937. Lecturer. Education: Lake View & Gowa Mission, Malawi, 1944-53; Blantyre & Dedza Secondary Schools, 1953-60; University College of Rhodesia & Nyasaland, 1961; B.Sc.(Hons.) Durham, Fourah Bay College, Sierra Leone, 1962-66; M.Sc., Biology, Malawi University, 1966-68; Research for Ph.D. Botany, University College, London, U.K., 1968—. Married, 1 son, 1 daughter. Appointments: Research Associate,

Biology, University of Malawi, 1966-68; Senior Assistant Lecturer, ibid, 1968—. Memberships include: President, Malawi, Students Association, Fourah Bay College, Sierra Leone; Secretary, African Students Association, ibid; Vice-President, Tea Club; Sigma Club; High Society Club; Biology Association of Malawi. Publications include: Conservation in Malawi (Malawi Sci. Mag.), 1967. Honours: Awarded Commonwealth Scholarship to study at University College, London, U.K., 1968. Address: Chancellor College, University of Malawi, Malawi.

CHIMPHANJE, Ashan Samu, born 17th January 1934. Teacher; Member of Parliament. Education: Chitsime Village, N.A. Chitukula, Lilongwe, Malawi; Chikhutu Primary School; Standard 8, Kongwe, Dowa District, 1953; Teacher Training College, Nkhoma, 1953-55;T3, Domesi Government Teacher Training College, 1960; Junior Certificate, Transafrica Correspondence College; G.C.E. O-Level, British School of Careers. Married, 4 children. Appointments: Teacher, Kalolo Senior Primary School, 1955-59; Headmaster, Kabuthu Senior Primary School, 1960-63; Headmaster, Chimoko, 1963-64; Member of Parliament, 1964—. Memberships include: Commonwealth Parliamentary Association. Honours: Independence Medal, 1964; Republic Medal, 1966. Address: P.O. Box 283, Lilongwe, Malawi.

CHINE, Mustapha, born 16th February 1933. Engineer. Education: L. es Sc. Diploma of Atomic Engineering. Appointments: Deputy Commissioner, Atomic Energy; Head of the Scientific Research Division, Minister of Education, Youth & Sport. Memberships: Association of Atomic Engineers. Author of several papers in his field. Address: 43 Rue Akhtal El Manzah, Tunis, Tunisia.

CHINTALI (Rev.) Frederick Sande, born about 1910. Minister, Church of Central Africa Presbyterian. Education: Primary, Domasi, 1921-24; Teacher Training, 3rd Grade, Jeannes School, Domasi, 1942; Theological Course, Mlanje, three years, 1944; Private Studies by correspondence, Barington House, Cambridge & Wolsely Hall, Oxford, U.K. Married, 6 children. Appointments: Minister, Blantyre, Malawi, 1944-52; Minister, Zomba, 1952—; Chairman, Public Services Commission, Malawi Government, 1961—. Address: C.C.A.P. Mission, P.O. Box 70, Zomba, Malawi.

CHIPETA, Wedson, born 30th August 1939. Lecturer in Economics. Education: B.Sc. (Econ.), 1st Class Honours, Makerere College, Uganda, 1965; M.A., Yale University, U.S.A., 1966; Licentiate, Institute of Book-Keepers. Personal details: Son of a peasant family. Appointments: Administrative Officer, Malawi Government, 1965; Lecturer, Economics, University of Malawi, 1967—. Memberships: Vice-Chairman, Agricultural Industry Wages Advisory Council; Treasurer, Chancellor College Cultural Society. Publications: The Role of Customary & Modern Money in the Rural Exchange Economy of Malawi; The Nature & Significance of Resources Used in Malawian Peasant Agriculture: Some Case Studies, 1969; Land Tenure & Problems in Malawi, 1971. Honours: Book Prize, Department of Economics, Makerere University, College, 1963; Honours Degree Prize, ibid, 1965. Address: Chancellor College, University of Malawi, P.O. Box 5200, Limbe, Malawi.

CHIPMAN (Rev.) Alfred Charles, born Geeveston, Tasmania, 27th April 1942. Clerk in Holy Orders. Education: Liscentiate of Theology, Australia. Appointments: Head Prefect, Hobart Technical High School, 1960; Senior Student, Ridley College, Melbourne, 1965; Assistant Curate, St. John's, Launceston, 1966-68; Assistant Youth Organiser, Diocese of Mt. Kenya, 1969—. Memberships: C.M.S. Australia; Mountain Club of Kenya. Address: P.O. Box 48, Kerugoya, Kenya.

CHIPWAYA, Saul, born 3rd March 1932. Civil Servant; Manager. Education: Munali High School, Zambia; Diploma in Public Administration, Exeter University, U.K. Married, 3 children. Appointments: Administrative Assistant, District Administration, Zambia, 1954-57; District Assistant, 1958-59; District Officer, 1960-61; Assistant Secretary, Ministry Headquarters Administration, 1964-65; Under Secretary, Refugee Commissioner, 1965-66, serving in various ministries; Permanent Secretary, Home Affairs, Provincial & Local Government, Local Government & Housing, & Lands & Mines Ministries, 1967-69; Permanent Secretary, East African Affairs, Zambia Government Liaison Officer in East Africa, & Trade Commissioner, East Africa, 1968; General Manager, National Agricultural Marketing Board. Memberships: Institute of Public Administration; Rotary Club; Many government boards & cooperatives. Address: National Agricultural Marketing Board, Box 122, Lusaka, Zambia.

CHIRWA, Fleetfort N., born 20th April 1941. Teacher; Secretary. Education: Form II; Primary Teacher's Course; Studying C.I.S. Married, 4 children. Appointments: Teacher; Deputy Headteacher; Headteacher; Councillor; Deputy Mayor; Mayor, Lusaka City Council; Chairman, Handicapped Council of Zambia. Memberships: National Secretary, Red Cross of Zambia; Road Safety Committee; Committee, Agricultural Society; Zambia Council of Social Services; Local Government Association of Zambia. Address: Zambia Red Cross, Box RW.1, Lusaka, Zambia.

CHIRWA, Orton Edgar Ching'oli, born 30th January 1919. Politician; Barrister-at-Law. Education: St. Francis' College, Natal, South Africa, 1944; B.A., Fort Hare, South Africa, 1947-50; B.Ed., ibid, 1951; Called to the Bar (1st Malawi African to be called), Lincoln's Inn, London, U.K., 1958; Ph.D. student, University of London, 1969—. Married. Appointments: 1st African Legal Practitioner, Limbe & Blantyre, Malawi, 1958-64; Founder & 1st President, Malawi Congress Party, 1959-60; M.P. & Minister of Justice & Attorney General, Malawi Government, 1961-64; Assistant Commissioner for Lands, Tanzania Government, Dar es Salaam, 1965-69. Honours: Q.C., Malawi, 1963. Address: P.O. Box 23042, Oyster Bay, Dar es Salaam, Tanzania.

CHISONGA, Gayo Hilary, born October 1906. Priest in Holy Orders. Education: St. Andrew's, Zanzibar (then Minaki), 1922-27; St. Cyprian's, Namasakata, 1945-47, 1949-50; St. Augustine's, Canterbury, U.K., 1964-65. Appointments: Curate, Luatala, 1950-56; Priest in Charge, Nakarara, 1956-63; Archdeacon of Luatala, 1965-68; Bishop of Masasi, 1963—. Address: Bishop's House, K.J.T. Mtandi, P.O. Masasi, Mtwara Region, Tanzania.

CHITAMBALA, Frank Macharious, born Zambia, 28th September 1930. Administrator. Education: Form II, Malole Secondary School; Studied Public Administration, India & Political Science, Soviet Union; Diploma in Youth, Political Parties & Industrial Organizations. Married, 4 sons, 2 daughters. Appointments: Provincial Clerk, Political Party, Zambia, 1954; Chief Clerk, ibid, 1955-56; Provincial General Secretary, 1956-58; Acting National Secretary, UNIP, 1959-60; Divisional President, Political Party, & Private Secretary to Party President Kaunda, now President of Zambia, 1960-61; Regional Secretary, 1963-64; Parliamentary Secretary, Ministry of Transport, Power & Communications, 1964; Parliamentary Secretary, Ministry of Home Affairs, 1964-66; Minister of State for Land Resettlement, 1966-68; Provincial Minister of State i/c of the Province, 1968-69; Cabinet Minister i/c of Province, 1969; Member of Parliament, Zambia, 1964-69; Lecturer, Institute of Rural Development, Denmark, 1967; Secretary, National Convention of 4-year Development Plan of Zambia, Committee on the Role of Youth in Zambia, 1967. Publications: Guideline to Party Leadership, 1964; The Party & the People, 1965; The Secret True Leadership, 1968; The Guideline to Party Organization, 1968. Member, UNIP Constitutional Committee, 1955-66. Attended several youth & student conferences overseas. Introduced method of political education through seminars to UNIP, 1963. Address: P.O. Box 3171, Lusaka, Zambia.

CHITTICK, Hubert Neville, born Hove, England, U.K., 18th September 1923. Archaeologist. Education: Rugby School & Cambridge University (intervening War Service, Intelligence Corps, graduated, 1949); Called to the Bar & took Postgraduate Diploma in Archaeology. Appointments include: assisted on various excavations, Middle East, 1951-52; Curator of Museums, Republic of Sudan, 1952-56; appointed to set up Antiquities Department, Tanganyika, 1957; . currently, Director, British Institute of History & Archaeology, 1961—. Memberships include: Fellow, Society of Antiquaries. Publications include: Ghazali, A Monastery in the Northern Sudan (w. P. L. Shinnie), 1961; Kisimani Mafia, Excavations at an Islamic Settlement on the East African Coast, 1961; numerous reports & articles in journals; Editor of Azania. Address: P.O. Box 7680, Nairobi, Kenya.

CHIWAULA, Leonard Winfred, born 12th December 1924. Public Servant; Depot Supervisor. Education; Mission School & private study. Married, 8 children. Appointments: Councillor; Deputy-Mayor, Lilongwe Municipal Council; Depot Supervisor, M.L.O. (Wenela) Ltd., Malawi. Memberships: Town & Country Planning Committee; former Chairman, Lilonge Football League; Church Elder of S.D.A. Address: P.O. Box 145, Lilongwe, Malawi.

CHOKSHI, Nalinikant Chimanlal, born 1st June 1933. Physician. Education: Primary & Secondary in Jinja (Uganda) up to Senior Cambridge & London Matric., 1949; Premedical Science Course, Wilson College, Bombay University, India, 1950-52; M.B., B.S., Grant Medical College, J.J. Groups Hospitals, 1952-57; Diploma, Obstetrics & Gynaecology, D.G.O., 1959. Personal details: son of Physician & Midwife; married Urmila Shah, 1969. Appointments: House Officer, Obstetrics & Gynaecology, J.J. Groups of Hospitals, Bombay, 1958; House Officer, Pediatrics, 1958-59; ibid, King George VI Hospital (now Kenyatta), Nairobi, Kenya, 1959-60; Gen. Medical Practice, Jinja, Uganda, 1960—. Memberships: Round Table, 1960; Council, ibid, 1960-69; Treasurer, 1964; Chairman, 1966; Secretary, Uganda Medical Society, 1963-67, 1970; Board, College of General Practitioners, 1965—; Jinja Club; Sailing Club, etc. Address: 10 Clive Road East, Box 267, Jinja, Uganda.

CHOTAI, Popatlal Nathalal, born 26th February, 1934. Physician. Education: M.B., B.S., Bombay, India. Married, 3 children. Currently in private general practice, Nairobi, Kenya. Memberships: Park Road Primary School Committee; Represented Nairobi, Lohana Supreme Council. Address: P.O. Box 8777, Nairobi, Kenya.

CHOUFANI, Abdelmajid, born 12th February, 1938. Vice-President of the Regional Tribunal of Casablanca. Education: Diploma, National Institute of Judicial Studies, French Language Section, Rabat, Morocco. Married, 4 children. appointments: Teacher, Public Education; Magistrate, since Moroccan Independence, 1957—; Memberships: President of the Association & Safeguard of Children in Casablanca. Publications: Une Etude sur le Regime des Associations au Maroc & Une Etude sur la Police Judiciaire Morocaine, published by the Royal Police Review. Address: Regional Tribunal, Casablanca, Morocco.

CHRISTIAN, Edward Clifford, born 27th November 1930. Pathologist. Education: M.B., B.Ch. B.A.O., University College, Cork, Ireland, 1957; Diploma in Pathology, Royal College of Physicians, 1960; Diploma in Clinical Pathology, London University, 1960; Member, College of Pathologists, U.K., 1964; M.D., National University of Ireland, 1964. Appointments: House Physician, St. Finbarrs Teaching Hospital, Cork; House Surgeon, ibid, 1957-58; Resident Clinical Pathologist, Crumpsall Hospital, 1958-59; ibid, 1960-61; Special Grade Medical Officer, Pathology, Kumasi Central Hospital, Ministry of Health, Ghana, 1961-62; Visiting Pathologist, Tempole University Hospital, Philadelphia, Pa., U.S.A., 1962-64; Researcher, Ghana National Institute of Health, 1965-66; Senior Lecturer Pathology, Ghana Medical School, 1966—. Publications include: Three Cases of Rhinosporidiosis in Ghana, 1966; Infant & Child Mortality in Ghana; Congenital

Fibroelastosis; Preparation of Atlas of Histopathology in the Tropics (w. Dr. Laing). Recipient of honours. Address: c/o Ghana Medical School, Ghana.

CHURCH, David Edward, born 21st July 1932. Architect. Education: Prince of Wales School, Nairobi, Kenya, 1944-46; St. Lawrence College, Kent, U.K., 1946-50; Oxford School of Architecture, 1952-57. Personal details: son of Dr. J. E. Church, Missionary Doctor, Uganda & Ruanda; married Judith Church, 1959, 5 daughters. Appointments: Assistant Architect, Messrs Norman & Dawbarn, 1957-61; ibid, H. R. Hughes, Nairobi, 1961-63; Partner, Messrs. Hughes & Polkinghorne, Kampala, Uganda, 1963-70. Memberships: Fellow, Royal Institute of British Architects; Rotary International. Author of Chapter on The Architecture of Hospitals & Health Centres, in the book: Medical Care in Developing Countries, M. King. Honours: 1st Prize, Architectural Competition for Bank of Uganda Headquarters, Kampala, 1967; 1st Prize, Architectural Competition for Uganda High Court Building, Kampala, 1969. Address: P.O. Box 3044, Kampala, Uganda.

CHURCH, John C. T., born Kabale, Kigezi, Uganda, 3rd March 1931. Orthopaedic Surgeon. Education: Prince of Wales School, Nairobi, Kenya; St. Lawrence College, Ramsgate, U.K.; M.B., B.Ch. & M.D., Emmanuel College, Cambridge University, 1956, 1968; St. Bartholomew's Hospital, London; D.T.M. & H. (Antwerp), 1958. Personal details: son of 2 medical missionaries in Uganda & Rwanda. Appointments: House Physician, St. Bartholomew's Hospital, 1955; House Surgeon, ibid, 1955-56; Orthopaedic H.S., Chase Farm Hopsital, London, 1956; Obstetrician & Gynaecologist, H.S., Lewisham Hospital, London, 1957; Surgical Registrar, Luton & Dunstable Hospital, 1958-59; Doctor-in-charge, Medical Mission Hospital, Rwanda, 1959-63; Lecturer, Anatomy, Makerere University College, Medical School, Uganda, 1964-68; Senior Lecturer, ibid, 1968–. Memberships: D.Obstet. R.C.O.G., 1957; F.R.C.S.(Edinburgh), 1968. Publications include: Satellite Cells & Myogenesis: a Study of the Fruit Bat Web (in press); A Study of Tissue Regeneration in the East African Fruit Bat, 1965 (for which gained prize from the Association of Surgeons of E.A.); Cell Populations in skeletal muscle after regeneration, 1970. Honours: Raymond Horton-Smith Prize for best M.D. thesis, University of Cambridge, 1967-68. Address: Department of Surgery, Kenyatta National Hospital, P.O. Box 30588, Nairobi, Kenya.

CISSE, Boubacar Amadou, born 1930. Deputy Administrator; Head of the sub-division of Kiembara, Tougan. Education: Primary studies, Doriet Fada, 1937-44; Secondary studies, Niamey Niger, 1945-48. Married, 7 children. Appointments: Secretary, Health Department, 1949-59; Secretary, Yako & Sapone, 1960-61; Head of Administrative Posts, Tougouri; ibid, Pissili, 1962; Deputy Commander, Dedougou, 1962-63; Head, Administrative Post, Meguet, 1963; Head P.A., Bagassi, 1964-66; Head of subdivision, Koumbri, 1966-67; Deputy Commander, Kaya, 1967; Head Mayoral Subdivision, 1968-70; Head, Sub-division, Kiembara, 1970–. Address: Chef Sub-division de Kiembara, Tougan, Upper Volta.

CLARK (Reverend), Eric Douglas Colbatch, born 13th July 1908. Missionary. Education: Bradfield College, Berks., U.K., 1921-26; B.A., St. John's College, Oxford University, 1926-29; Dip. Educ., Institute of Education, London, 1929-30; Wycliffe Hall, Oxford, 1939-40. Appointments: Master, Achimota College, Ghana, 1930-37; Principal, Dennis Memorial Grammar School, Onitsha, 1937-50; ibid, Sierra Leone Grammar School, Freetown, 1951-52; Rural Training Centre, ASABA, Nigeria, 1952-66. Honours: M.B.E., 1963; O.B.E., 1966. Address: c/o Church Missionary Society, 157 Waterloo Road, London, S.E.1, U.K.

CLARKE, Lilian M., born 23rd January 1909. Educational Missionary. Education: London School Certificate, 1927; National Froebel Foundation Certificate & Ministry of Education Certificate, 1930. Personal details: daughter of a London Accountant. Appointments: Teacher, Richmond High School, 1930-31; Lecturer, Zoology & Hygiene, Maria Grey Training College, 1931-32; Teacher & Lecturer, Northfield, Watford, 1932-40; Headmistress, Kabale Girls' Boarding School, 1941-47; Principal, Kigezi Girls' Teacher Training College, Uganda, 1947-55; Schools Supervisor, Kigezi, 1956-61; Representative of Rwanda Mission in Uganda & Supervisor, Church Schools, Kigezi, 1962–. Memberships: Uganada Red Cross Association; Uganda Federation for the Blind; Chairman, Kigezi Christian Teachers' Association. Address: P.O. Box 114, Kabale, Kigezi, Uganda.

CLARKSON, Thomas Herbert, born Yorkshire, U.K., 19th May 1938. Electrical Engineer. Education: Goole Grammar School, Yorkshire, U.K.; Rotherham College of Technology, Yorks.; Student Apprenticeship with Electricity Board, 6½ years. Married, 2 sons. Appointments: Various postions, U.K., till 1968; 2nd Assistant Engineer, East African Power & Lighting, 1968-69; Engineer in Charge, Nairobi District, Kenya., 1970–. Carried out first ever Insulator Change on 132,00 volt Power Line with line alive in East & Central Africa, 1970; trained 1st 'Hot Line Team' to carry out works on live power lines. Memberships: Institution of Electrical Engineers; East African Institution of Engineers; Associate, Kenya Institute of Management. Address: P.O. Box 30177, Nairobi, Kenya.

CLASSEN, Geogre Augustus, born Moscow, Russia, 3rd May 1915. Mining Engineer. Education: Private Schools in Cyprus; Diploma, The English Commercial College, Cyprus; High School, Hamburg, Germany; The Royal School of Mines Imperial College U.K.; Associate Member, Institution of Mining & Metallurgy; Chartered Engineer. Married, 2 children. Appointments include: Trainee Surveyor, Department of Surveys, Cyprus, 1932-33; Surveyor & Draughtsman, Cyprus Mines Corporation, 1933-36; Surveyor and Geophysical Assistant to A. B. Broughton Edge, Geophysical and Mining Consultant of London,

Mysore and Hyderabad, South India, and also in North Wales, U.K., 1937-38; Mine Surveyor and Geologist, The Ooregum Gold Mining Co. of India Ltd., Mysore, South India, 1939-48; Engineer Geologist, African Land Development Board, Ministry of Agriculture, Kenya, 1948-53; Executive Engineer, ibid, 1953-64; Adviser for Rural Water Supplies, Water Development Department, Kenya, 1964-68; Assistant Director, ibid., 1968—. Memberships include: Fellow, Geological Society of London; The Mining Club, London; Nairobi Club, Nairobi; President, The Geological Club of Kenya, 1965-66; Deputy President, The Kenya Horticultural Society; The Agricultural Society of Kenya. Publications include: Papers on Geophysical Prospecting, The Kolar Gold Field Mining & Metallurgical Society; Chapter on Range Water Development for the East African Range Management Handbook (in preparation); Contributor on Water Supplies in African Land Development in Kenya, 1946-62'. Honours, Prizes, etc.; M.B.E. for services to Rural Water Development in Kenya, 1963. Address: Water Development Department, P.O. Box 30521, Nairobi, Kenya.

CLOSEL, J. A. Regis, born 7th June, 1922. Mechanical Engineer. Education: St. Joseph's College, Curepipe; Dip. Agriculture (Hons.), Mauritius College of Agriculture; B.Sc. (Hons.), Engineering, University of the Witwatersrand, Johannesburg, South Africa; C.Eng. Married, 2 sons, 2 daughters. Appointments: Works Manager, Mauritius Government Railway; General Manager, ibid; Mechanical Engineer & Station Superintendent, Fort Victoria Power Station, Central Electricity Board, Mauritius. Memberships: Institution of Mechanical Engineers, England; Engineers Association, Mauritius. Recipient, Coronation Medal, 1953. Address: Fort Victoria Power Station, Cassis, Mauritius.

COCHAIN, Jean-Pierre, born 24th August, 1935. Plastic Surgeon. Education: M.D.; Diploma, Faculty of Medicine, Paris, France. Appointments: Resident Doctor, various Hospitals, Morocco; Head of the Plastic Surgery Service, Central Hospital, Casablanca, Morocco. Memberships: Moroccan Society of Surgery; Editorial Committee of the 'Moroccan Medical' & 'Journal of Medicine'. Author of numerous medical publications on plastic & aesthetic surgery. Address: 2 Boulevard Perrault, Casablanca, Morocco.

COE, Graham Emblen Beverley, born 14th April, 1933. British Council Officer. Education: Brentwood School, 1945-51; Jesus College, Cambridge, U.K., 1953-56; Leeds University, 1961-62; Married, 1 son, 1 daughter. Appointsments: Lecturer, Kuwait; Associate Professor, Allahabad, India; Director, English Language Centre, Malawi; Director, British Council, Isfahan, Iran. Publications: Practical English Prose; Co-Author, English by Degrees; English by Heart. Address: c/o Personnel Records, The British Council, 65 Davies St., London, W.1, U.K.

COFFIN, Henry Douglas Gordon, born 16th December 1914. Optician; Civil Servant. Education: Shoreham Grammar School, Sussex, U.K., 1923-25; Technical College, Gosport, Hants., 1925-27; Shoreham Grammar School, 1927-31; Professional Diploma of Worshipful Company of Spectacle Makers, School of Optics, Stockwell, 1931-33; Fellow, ibid, 1935. Married, 2 children. Appointments: Consulting Optician, England & Northern Ireland, 1933-39; Leprosy Relief, Church of Scotland Mission Leper Colony, Itu, Eastern Nigeria, 1939-51; Seconded to Nyasaland Government to build & establish Government Leprosarium, Kochirira, Nyasaland, 1951-54; Leprosy Settlement Supervisor, ibid, H.M. Overseas Civil Service, 1954-58; Leprosy Superintendent, Federal Public Service, Federation of Rhodesia & Nyasaland, 1958-60; Higher Executive Officer, Federal Ministry of Works Liaison Officer, Nyasaland, 1960-63; Medical Adviser, Nyasaland Government, Ministry of Health, 1963-64; Senior Executive Officer, & Personal Assistant, Secretary for Health, Nyasaland, also Secretary, National Blood Donor Committee & Ministry of Health Press Offcer, 1964-66; Chief Executive Officer (General Duties), Ministry of Health, 1966-68; Senior Establishments Officer, Ministry of Health, 1968-70, also Secretary, Brown Memorial Fund. Memberships: Toc H; British Leprosy Relief Association (now Leprosy Relief Association); Committee, Nyasaland Branch, Federal Public Service Association, 1963-64; Secretary, Nyasaland Overseas Officers' Association, 1963-64; Committee, Nyasaland Angling Society, 1963-66; Trustee, New Theatre Group, 1963-68. Honours: M.B.E., 1970. Address: 'Garth', Hillside Road, Verwood, Wimborne, Dorset, BH21 6HE, U.K.

COHEN, David, born 1st November 1905. Solicitor-General. Education: B.A., LL.B., Capetown University, South Africa. Married, 1 daughter. Appointments: Practised as Barrister, Kimberley, 1928-38; ibid, Attorney, 1938-47; Barrister, Capetown, 1947-67; joined Attorney-General's Chambers, Mbabane, Swaziland, 1968; promoted to Solicitor-General. Memberships: Chairman, Mbabane Bowling Club; Vice-President, Swaziland Sub-district Bowling Association; Mbabane Club & Theatre Club. Author of law book & Editor, sev. law reports. Honours: Senior Counsel, S. Africa, 1965. Address: P.O. Box 139, Mbabane, Swaziland.

COIGNET, André Noël, born 5th December 1905. Assurance Company Director. Education: Christian Brothers School, Mauritius. Appointments: Mauritius Fire Insurance Company; Managing Director, The Mauritius Union Assurance Company, first local insurance company to underwrite life assurance business as general insurance business coupled with treaty reinsurances. Memberships: Hon. Treasurer, Mauritius Mental Health Association; l'Amicale des Aveugles; Unofficial visitor to H.M. Prisons; Probation Committee. Address: The Mauritius Union Assurance Co. Ltd., 13 Sir William Newton Street, Port Louis, Mauritius.

COKER, Rachel Patience Naomi, born 9th April 1903. Retired Teacher; Justice of the Peace. Education: Cathedral Day School,

Freetown, Sierra Leone; Annie Walsh Memorial School, ibid. Personal details: member of Caulker family of Shenge-Kagboro Chiefdom, Sierra Leone; married, 2 daughters. Memberships: Past President, Young Womens' Christian Association; ibid, Ladies' Missionary Guild; Deaf & Dumb Society; Vice-President, Association of Justices of the Peace.

COKER, William Zacheus, born 14th June 1929. Scientist. Education: B.Sc.(Hons., London), Special Zoology, University College of Cape Coast, Ghana, 1955; M.Sc., London School of Hygiene & Tropical Medicine, U.K., 1957; Ph.D., Liverpool School of Tropical Medicine, 1964. Married, 2 sons, 2 daughters. Appointments: Medical Entomologist, Ministry of Health, 1957-64; Senior Research Officer, Ghana Academy of Science, 1964-67; University Lecturer, University of Ghana, Legon, 1967–. Memberships: Honorary Secretary, Ghana Science Association; World Health Organization, Expert Advisory Panel on Insecticides, 1962-67, 1967-72. Author of a number of papers on mosquito genetics, including insecticide resistance in Annals of Tropical Medicine & Bulletin of World Health Organization. Honours: Fellow Commoner, Churchill College, University of Cambridge, 1970. Address: Zoology Department, University of Ghana, Legon, Ghana.

COLE, Metcalfe Ajadi, born 4th May 1888. Retired Businessman. Education: Methodist Boys' High School; C.M.S. Grammar School. Married, 5 children. Appointments: served to level of Chief Draughtsman, Sierra Leone Railways, 36 years; Operator & Founder, Agagayi Stores East & West, Freetown; Councillor, City of Freetown, 1947; Member, Legislative Assembly, Freetown, 1948; Justice of the Peace. Memberships: Sidesman, Member of Parochial Committee, Treasurer of the Synod, & People's Warden, Holy Trinity Church, Freetown; Founder, Sierra Leone Political Group; Founder & President, Association of Justices of the Piece of Sierra Leone; Life Associate, Commonwealth Parliamentary Association. Took a number of trips to U.K. & other West African States to broaden his knowledge & discover ways of improving the Sierra Leone economy. Instrumental in development of agriculture & industry, most noticeably with the foundation of the Sierra Leone weaving industry, which foundered later through lack of home-produced cotton. Honours: M.B.E., 1970. Address: 4 Bishop Street, Freetown, Sierra Leone.

COLEMAN, William Frank, born 21st March 1922. Engineer. Education: B.Sc.(Eng.), London, U.K.; Postgrad. Diploma in Electronics, Southampton University; Chartered Engineer, U.K. Married to Aba Quashie, 1950, 4 children. Appointments: Lecturer, Achimota College, Ghana, 1947-48; Chief Engineer, Ghana Broadcasting Corporation, 1958-60; Director/ Director-General, Ghana Broadcasting Corporation, 1960-70. Memberships: Fellow, Institution of Electrical Engineers, U.K.; ibid, Ghana Institute of Engineers; Vice-President, ibid; Director, International Council of The National Academy of Television Arts & Sciences, U.S. Honours: M.B.E., U.K., 1960; G.M., Grand Medal of Ghana, 1968. Address: P.O. Box 7670, Accra North, Ghana.

COLERIDGE, Hugh C. C., born 14th January 1942. Physician. Education: Monkton Combe Junior School, 1952-55; ibid, Senior School, Bath, Somerset, U.K., 1955-60; M.B., B.S.(London), St. Bartholomew's Hospital Medical School, London, 1960-65. Personal details: Grandfather & Father, long service in Tanzania Government Service & British Colonial Service respectively; married, 1968. Appointments: House Surgeon, Windsor, 1966; House Physician, St. Helier Hospital, Carshalton, 1966, 1967; Obstetric House Surgeon, ibid, 1968; Medical Officer, Apac Hospital, Lango, Uganda, 1968-70; Medical Officer, Kabale Hospital, Uganda, 1970–. Member: British Medical Association. Address: Kabale Hospital, Kabale, Uganda.

COLLIN (Honourable) Jean Baptiste, born 19th September 1924. Minister of Finance & Economic Affairs. Education: Lic., Law & Oriental Languages. Appointments: Head, Department of Diourbel, 1947; Head, Information Service, Director, Radio Dakar, Senegal, 1948; with Government Pilgrimage to Mecca, 1946; Head of Mission, French Overseas Ministry, 1949-50; Head of Conscription, Cameroun, 1951-54; Head, Department of Commune & Director of Political Affairs, Cameroun, 1955; Director, Modernization Section, North Cameroun, 1956; Cabinet Director, Senegal Government, Senegal, 1957-58; Deputy Head, Cap-Vert Province; Governor, ibid, 1960; Government General Secretary & Commissioner to the High Court, 1960; Permanent Secretary to the Higher Council of the Magistrature, 1961-62; Government General Secretary, Secretary-General to the Presidency of the Republic, 1963-64; Minister for Finance & Economic Affairs, 1964–; Elected Deputy, National Assembly, 1968–; Mayor, Joal-Fadiouth, 1968–; Decreed Minister for Finance, 1968-70; Re-confirmed Minister for Finance & Economic Affairs, 1970–. Honours: Commander, National Order of Senegal; Grand Officer, German Order of Merit; ibid, National Order of Tunis; National Order of the Camerouns; Liberian Order of Redemption; Commander, Order of the Leopard (Congo); ibid, National Order of the Ivory Coast; National Order of Togo; Officer, National Order of Guinea; ibid, National Order of Dahomey. Address: Assemblé Nationale, B.P. 86, Dakar, Senegal.

COLLINS, Edmond B., born 7th January 1934. Agricultural Engineer. Education: B.S.Ag.E., West Virginia University, U.S.A., 1957; M.S.Ag.E., ibid, 1961. Married, 2 children. Appointments: Research Assistant, West Virginia University, 1959-61; Assistant Professor, Agricultural Engineering, ibid, 1962-65; Lecturer, Agricultural Engineering, Egerton College, Kenya, 1965-67; Head, Agricultural Engineering Department, ibid, 1967–; Chief of Party, USAID/WVU Contract, Kenya, 1967–. Memberships: American Society of Agricultural Engineers; East African Institute of Engineers; Intermediate Technology Development Group; American Association for the Advancement of

Science; Agricultural Society of Kenya; Chairman, Cambridge Examination Development Committee, Agriculture, 1968–; Tau Beta Pi. Publications: Automation of Burley Tobacco Barn Ventilation Doors (co-author), 1961; Factors Affecting Sirption Isotherms of Alfalfa (co-author), 1966; Fences, 1966; The Affect of Density, Initial Moisture Content, and Spontaneous Heating on Drying Isotherms (co-author), 1967; Agricultural Engineering Diploma Programme, 1968. Address: Agricultural Engineering Department, Egerton Agricultural College, Njoro, Kenya.

CONNELL, Johanna (Sister M. Eugene), born 27th August 1925. Physician. Education: National University of Ireland, Cork Branch, 1950-56. Member, Franciscan Missionary Sisters for Africa, 1949–. Appointments: Intern, Obstetric Department, St. Finbans Hospital, Cork, Ireland, 1956; Intern, Surgical Department, Our Lady's Hospital, Cashel, Ireland, 1957; House Surgeon, Royal Hospital, Wolverhampton, U.K., 1957; Senior Hospital Officer, Obstetrics, National Maternity Hospital, Holles St., Dublin, Ireland, 1958; Missionary Doctor, Nsambyan Hospital, Kampala, Uganda, 1959-63; Missionary Doctor, Kamuli Mission Hospital, 1963–. Address: Kamoli Mission Hospital, P.O. Box 99, Kamoli, Uganda.

CONRADIE, Frans Willem, born Brits, Transvaal, South Africa, 5th May 1928. Mechanical Engineer. Education: South African Government Engineer's Certificate of Competency. Married. Appointments: South African Air Force, World War II; Mechanical Draughtsman, various firms; Power Station Shift Engineer; Plant Engineer, Langeberg Co-op.; Manager/Engineer, Suid Kunene Fisheries, 1964–.. Member, Institute of Certificated Engineers, South Africa. Address: P.O. Box 44, Walvis Bay, South West Africa.

COOK (Sir) James (Wilfred), born 10th December, 1900. University Administrator. Education: Sloane School, Chelsea, London, U.K.; Tuffnell Scholar, University College, London; D.Sc., Ph.D.(Lond.). Married, 3 sons. Appointments include: Lecturer in Organic Chemistry, The Sir John Cass Technical Institute, 1920-28; Research Chemist, Department of Scientific & Industrial Research, 1928-29; Reader in Pathological Chemistry, University of London, 1932-35; Professor of Chemistry, University of London, 1935-39; Research Chemist, The Royal Cancer Hospital (Free), 1929-39; Professorial Lecturer in Chemistry, University of Chicago, U.S.A., 1938; Regious Professor of Chemistry, University of Glasgow, U.K., 1939-54; Pedler Lecturer, Chemical Society, 1950; Principal, University College of the South West, Exeter, 1954-55; Vice-Chancellor, University of Exeter, 1955-66; Council Member, University College of Rhodesia & Nyasaland, 1955-66; currently, Vice-Chancellor, The University of East Africa, Kampala, Uganda. Memberships include: Chairman, Chemical Council, 1959-63; Hon. Director, M.R.C. Carcinogenic Substances Research Unit, 1956-66; Member, Council, D.S.I.R., & Chairman, Postgraduate Training Awards Committee, 1960-65; President, Royal Institute of Chemistry, 1949-51; President, Section B, British Association, 1957; Fellow, University College, London; Member, University Grants Committee, 1950-54; Committee on Cost of National Health Service, 1953-56; Committee of Enquiry into Pharmaceutical Industry, 1965–; Chairman, Committee on Composition of Milk, 1958-60; Advisory Committee on Pesticides & other Toxic Chemicals, 1962–; Advisory Committee on Scientific & Technical Information, 1965–; Hon. Member, Polish Chemical Society; Hon. Member, Chilean Chemical Society; Corresponding Member, National Academy of Exact Sciences of Buenos Aires. Publications include: Editor, Progress in Organic Chemistry, Vols. I-VI; numerous papers on organic chemistry, especially in relation to cancer, hormones, polycuclic compounds, bile acids, etc. Honours & Awards include: Kt., 1963; Hon. Sc.D.(Dublin); Hon. D.Sc.(Nigeria); Hon. D. de l'U'(Rennes); Davy Medallist, Royal Society, 1954; Prize of Union Internationale Contre le Cancer (awarded jointly with Professor Sir Ernest Kennaway), 1936; Part Recipient of first award of Anna Fuller Memorial Prize, 1939; Recipient of Katherine Berkan Judd Prize, Memorial Hospital, New York, U.S.A., 1940; Officier de l'Ordre de Léopold. Address: University of East Africa, P.O. Box 7110, Kampala, Uganda.

COOPER, Samuel Spriggs Payne, born 30th June 1930. Civil Servant. Education: College of West Africa, Liberia; Tuskegee Institute, U.S.A.; College of Agriculture, Cornell University; B.Sc., College of Agriculture & Economics, ibid; M.P.A., Cornell University Graduate School of Business & Public Administration. Appointments: General Manager, Agricultural & Industrial Credit Corporation; Chief, Budget Finance & Material Control, & at intervals Acting Director, Central Experiment Station; Director of Research, C.A.E.S.; Special Assistant to Secretary of Agriculture & Commerce; Under-Secretary of Agriculture. Memberships: Official Board, 1st Methodist Church; President, Alpha Phi Alpha; National Council, National Board, & Local Board, YMCA; Worshipful Master, St. Paul Lodge, Ancient Free & Accepted Masons; Special Representative of Grand Master, United Brothers of Friendship. Honours: Grand Commander, Humane Order of African Redemption, Liberia, 1964; Knight Offical, ibid, 1968. Address: c/o Department of Agriculture, Monrovia, Liberia.

COPPIETERS é WALLANT, Renaud, born 23rd September 1935. Lawyer; Judge. Education: D.L., Louvain University, Belgium, 1960. Appointments: Childrens' Judge, Kinshasa, Congo, 1964-69; Judge, Tribunal of the 1st instance, Kinshasa, Congo, 1969–. Address: B.P: 693, Kinshasa, Congo.

CORCORAN, Anthony, born England, 3rd November 1933. Marketing Consultant. Education: St. Anselm's College, Birkenhead, U.K. Married. Appointments include: Resident Representative, Nestlé, Uganda; Marketing Manager, Nestlé, East Africa; Marketing Director, Rothmans of Pall Mall (Kenya) Ltd., Sales Promotion Manager, British American Tobacco, Kenya, Ltd.; Partner, Corcoran &

Tyrrell, Marketing Consultants. Memberships include: Institute of Marketing; Associate, British Institute of Management; Nairobi Club; Nyari Club. Honours: A.M.E.A.M.F., 1967. Address: P.O. Box 4365, Nairobi, Kenya.

COULIBALY, Augustin Sondé, born Tin-Orodara, Upper Volta, 1933. Journalist; Novelist; Poet. Education: Primary, Orodara, 1942; Secondary, Abidjan, Ivory Coast, 1946; Advanced Studies in Journalism, Centre International d'Enseignement Supérieur de Journalisme, University of Strasbourg, France, 1962. Married, 4 children. Appointments include: Head, Cabinet of Minister of Justice, Ouagadougou; Founder & Director, Le Cercle d'Activités littéraires et artistiques de Haute-Volta, 1967—; collaborator on several journals including Encres Vives, Poesie Vivante, Dialogue et Colture. Publications include: (novels) Les rives du Tontombili, 1955; Enfer lune de miel, 1956; Les saintes erreurs, 1958; Les dieux délinquants, 1968; (poems) Minuit-Soleil, 1960 (awarded prix Encres Vives, 1965); Paradis noir, 1965; Quand chante le Nègre, 1966. (eesays) Problèmes culturels du monde noir et réponses africaines, 1963. Poems published in Encres Vives, Afrique, etc. Address: Directeur de Cabinet au Ministère de la Justice, Ouagadougou, Upper Volta.

COWIE, Mervyn Hugh, born Nairobi, Kenya, 13th April 1909. Director. Education: Brighton College; Brasenose College, Oxford University, U.K. Married, 3 sons, 2 daughters. Appointments include: Hon. Game Warden, Kenya, 1932; K.A.R. Reserve of Officers, 1932-38; War Service, 1939-45; Founder & Director, Royal National Parks of Kenya, 1946-66. Member, Kenya Legilative-Council, 1951-60; Director of Manpower, 1953-66. Memberships include: Fellow, Institute of Chartered Accountants; ibid, Zoological Society, London; Vice-President, Fauna Preservation Society, London, U.K.; Vice-President, E.A. Wild Life Society. Publications: Fly Vulture, 1961; I Walk With Lions, 1964; African Lion, 1965. Honours: C.B.E., 1960; E.D., 1954. Address: P.O. Box 505, Nairobi, Kenya.

COX, Anthony Philip, born 22nd March 1933. Broadcaster. Education: G.C.E. 'A' Level. Married, 2 sons. Appointments: various positions, B.B.C., 1951-62; Specialist Studio Manager to B.B.C. African Service, 1963; Broadcasting Adviser, Government of The Gambia, 1963-65; Producer, B.B.C. African Service, 1966-70; Head of Programmes, Malawi Broadcasting Corporation, 1970—. Memberships: B.B.C. Club; Life Member, Wig & Pen Club, Fleet Street, London, U.K. Editor, The Gambia News Bulletin, 1965. Devised & produced radio programmes on many of Africa's leading musicians, & also responsible for a major musicological series under the title 'Africa's Music & the World', all broadcast by B.B.C. African Service. Address: Head of Programmes, Malawi Broadcasting Corporation, P.O. Box 453, Blantyre, Malawi.

CRAMPTON, Edmund Patrick Thurman, born Blackpool, U.K., 30th April 1929. Educator; Principal. Education: Blackpool Grammar School; B.A.(Hons.), Geography, Cambridge University, 1952; P.G.C.E., ibid, 1953; M.A., 1956; M.A., Trinity College, Dublin, Ireland, 1961; B.D., ibid, 1969. Married, 3 children. Appointments: Principal, Benue Provincial Secondary School, Nigeria, 1960-64; Principal, Birnin Kudu Secondary School, 1965-66; Principal, Sokoto Provincial Secondary School, 1966-67; Principal, Government Secondary School, Katsina, 1967—. Memberships: Cambridge Union; President, Cambridge University Liberal Club, 1951; Fellow, Royal Commonwealth Society; St. Catherine's Society; Licensed Lay Reader, Ondo Benin Diocese, 1959. Publications include: The Growth of Christian Communities in Northern Nigeria. Address: Government Secondary School, Katsina, Nigeria.

CREPET, H. R. H., born 29th November 1924. General Manager of Shell Gabon. Education: E.M.I.A., Secondary School, Rheims, France & Tunis. Appointments: Commissioned Artillery Officer, 1944-49; joined Shell Group, 1949; held various positions in Algeria, France, Venzuela, The Netherlands & Iran; Technical Manager, Shell Company, Algiers, 1963-65; General Manager & Senior Executive, ibid, 1965-68; Personnel Assistant, Shell Group, Explorative & Productions Coordinates, The Hague, 1968; General Manager, Shell Gabon, 1969—. Memberships: Rotary Club, Port Gentil. Honours: Knight, Legion of Honour; Croix de Guerre & T O E. Address: B.P. 146, Port Gentil, Gabon.

CROWLEY, Mary Christina, born 25th December 1915. Teacher. Education: Kilcolman Primary School, Enniskean, Co. Cork, Ireland, 1929; Loreto Convent, Co. Cork, 1929-33; B.A.(Hons.), Dip. Educ., University College, Cork, 1933-37. Personal details: Eldest of family of seven. Appointments: Various appointments teaching in England & Wales Secondary & Primary Schools, 1942—; Tutor, Muslim Girls' High School, 1964-67; Acting Principal, Girls' High School, Gibu Egbo, 1967-68; Tutor, Adeola Odutola College, Ljebu-Ode, Nigeria, 1968—. Member & Secretary, Polyglot Society. Address: Adeola Odutola College, Ljebu, Nigeria.

CRUZ FERNANDEZ, Manuel, born 1st September 1938. Journalist. Education: Bachelor of Journalism. Married, 3 children. Appointments: Writer, 1958; Editor, 1967; Director of Publication, Journal Espana, 1969; OPI Correspondant, 1966; Editor, Agency AMEX, Madrid, Spain, 1969. Memberships: International Press Association of Tangier. Address: Inm., Hospital Espagnol, Tangier.

CUDJOE, Seth Dzifanu, born 7th February 1910. Physician. Education: Medicine, University of Edinburgh, U.K., Royal College of Physicians & Surgeons, Edin.; Psychiatry, Edinburgh, London, Marburg, Germany; Modelling & History of Art, Edinburgh College of Art & Birbeck College, London University; Pianoforte, George Forrest Neillands, Edinburgh; African Drumming, Phillip Gbeho, Accra, Ghana. Personal details: Great great grandfather, Nuku Gbenyo, founder & first Chief of Adina, Ghana; Great grandfather, Yevugah,

2nd Chief; father, Gbenyo, 5th Chief. Appointments: General Practice, London, U.K., 1940-55; Senior Medical Officer, Ministry of Health, Ghana, 1968–; Socio-medical Research Officer on the patterns of mother/child relationships in Ghana, 1968–. Memberships: One time Fellow, Royal Anthropological Institute of Great Britain & Ireland; Founder & First President, West African Arts Club, London (now absorbed into Ghana High Commission), 1950. Honorary Positions: President, Ghana Society of Writers; Vice-President, Ghana Society of Artists; Committee Member, Ghana Society of Music; Ghana National Monuments Board; Ghana Broadcasting Advisory Board; Chairman, Arts Council of Ghana, 1959-61; Member, ibid, 1969–; Board of Directors, Ghana Film Industry Corporation, 1969–. Address: Ministry of Health, Ho, Volta Region, Ghana.

CUNDY, Henry Martyn, born 23rd December 1913. University Professor of Mathematics. Education: Monkton Coombe School, 1927-32; B.A. (1st Class Honours), Maths. Tripos, Trinity College, Cambridge University, U.K., 1935; Ph.D., 1938. Personal details: Married Kathleen Ethel Hemmings, B.A.(Cantab.), 1939; 3 sons, all B.A.(Cantab.). Appointments: Head, Mathematics Department, Sherbourne School, Dorset, 1956-66; Assistant Director, School Mathematics Project, 1966-68; Professor of Mathematics, University of Malawi, 1968–. Memberships: Fellow, Institute of Mathematics & its Applications; Past Assistant Editor, Mathematical Association; Association of Teachers of Mathematics; National Council of Teachers of Mathematics; Traduate's Fellowship, English Folk Dance & Song Society; Mlanje Mountain Club. Publications: Mathematical Models (w. A. P. Rollet); The Faith of a Christian; Editor, S.M.P. Advanced Mathematics. Recipient of the Rayleigh Prize, 1938. Address: Chancellor College, P.O. Box 5200, Limbe, Malawi.

CUNNINGHAM, Griffiths Laurence, born 11th July 1930. Adult Educationalist; Rural Developer. Education: B.A., Geography, Toronto, Canada; M.A., ibid; Ph.D., Agricultural History (uncompleted). Appointments: Vice-Principal, Kivukoni College, Dsm, 1962-63; Principal, ibid, 1964-69; Adviser, Rural Development to Government of Tanzania, 1969-70. Memberships: Agricultural Economic Society of East Africa; Fabian Society; Economic Society of Tanzania. Publications: some journalistic pieces, 'Socialism & Rural Development in Tanzania' East Africa Journal of Rural Development, 1969; The Politics of Rural Development in Africa (a chapter with L. Cliffe). Address: Ministry of Regional Administration & Rural Development, Box 2676, Dar es Salaam, Tanzania.

CUNNINGHAM, Matthew Paton, born Ayrshire, Scotland, U.K., 10th September 1926. Veterinary Surgeon. Education: Girvan High School; Glasgow University, U.K. Married, 3 sons. Appointments include: Lecturer, Department of Veterinary Medicine, University of Glasgow Veterinary School, 1952-58; Principal Veterinary Research Officer, E.A. Trypanosomiasis Research Organization, 1958-67; Project Manager, F.A.O. Immunological Research on Tick-borne Diseases & Tick Control Project 300, 1967–. Memberships: Society of Cryobiology; Society for Protozoology. Publications include: numerous professional articles & papers. Address: c/o East African Veterinary Research Organization, Muguga, P.O. Kabete, Kenya.

CURTIS, Ernest Edwin, born Stalbridge, Dorset, U.K., 24th December 1906. Bishop of Mauritius. Education: Foster's School, Sherbourne, U.K.; B.Sc., University of London; Royal College of Science, Institute of Education; Wells Theological College; A.R.C.Sc. Widower. Appointments include: Senior Mathematics Master, Lindisfarne College, 1928; Principal, St. Paul's Theological College, Mauritius, 1937; Vicar, All Saints, Portsmouth, U.K., 1947; Vicar, St. John Baptist, Locks Heath, Southampton, 1956; Bishop of Mauritius & the Seychelles, 1966. Memberships include: Royal Commonwealth Society, London. Address: Bishop's House, Phoenix, Mauritius.

D

DADA, Gilbert Ladele, born Agbowa Ikosi, Nigeria, 28th December 1908. Retired Civil Servant. Education: Tinubu Methodist School; St. John's Anglican Aroloya School; C.M.S. Grammar School; Igbodi College, Yaba. Married, 2 wives, 12 children. Appointments include: Temporary Clerk, Marine Department, Civil Service, 1932; 1st Class Clerk, ibid, 1953; Assistant Chief Clerk, Nigerian Ports Authority, 1955; Assistant Stores Officer, ibid, 1956; Stores Officer, 1960; Senior Stores Officer, 1961-66; Retired, 1966. Memberships: Boy Scout, 1930; Patrol Leader, 1931; Rover Scout, 1935; Secretary, Agbowa Ikosi Progressive Union, 1938-40; Church Warden, Committee Member, 1941-44; Choirmaster, 1946-47; Chairman, Building Committee, 1967-68; Patron, Wesley Guild, 1967-68; Elders Union, F.B.M.M. Church, Ikate; Board of Governors, Methodist High School, Agbowa; Kosi Club, Agbowa; Old Students' Association, Ikosi High School. Address: 4 Ladele Dada Street, Ikate, Surulere, Nigeria.

DADA, Mofolorunso Olutola, born 12th August 1922. Civil Servant. Education: Ijebu-Ode Grammar School, Nigeria; Industrial Welfare Society, London, U.K., 1961; Industrial Relations Course, Ibadan University, 1957-58; Advanced Course, Industrial Relations, N.E.C.A. & University of Lagos, 1969. Married. Appointments: Administrative Assistant, Kingsway Stores, Lagos, 1949-54; Labour & Staff Officer, Western Nigeria Production Board, 1955-57; Acting Personnel Secretary, ibid, 1957-58; Personnel Officer, Nigerian Ports Authority, 1948-61; Senior Personnel Officer, ibid, 1961-68; Acting Deputy Chief Industrial Relations Officer, 1968-70. Memberships: Life President-General, Auxiliary Society, Wesley Church, Lagos; Apena Iledi, Ikeja, R.O.F.; Chief Ranger, Ancient Order of Foresters, 1960, 1968; Grand Chief Templar, Nigeria I.O.G.T., 1954-70; Ijebu Northern District Council, 1956-65; Ijebu Divisional Council, 1958-61; Commanding

Officer, Lagos Battalion, Boys' Brigade, 1967—; Methodist District Synod, Lagos, 1963—; Captain, 2nd Lagos Company, Boys' Brigade, 1964—; Board of Governors, Igbobi College, Lagos, 1965—; National Council, Nigeria Boys' Brigade, 1965—; Deputy President, Amalgamated Union of U.A.C. Workers, 1949-50; Government Labour Advisory Board, 1947-50; Trade Union Congree of Nigeria, 1946-54. Address: Nigerian Ports Authority, 26-28 Marina, Lagos, Nigeria.

DADA, Timothy Ekunday, born 18th February 1924. Medical Practitioner; Obstetrician & Gynaecologist. Education: St. John's School, Aroloya, Lagos, Nigeria; C.M.S. Grammar School, Lagos; M.B., Ch.B., University of Bristol Medical School, U.K.; University of London Postgraduate Medical School; M.R.C.S.(Eng.); L.R.C.P.(Lond.); D.(Obst.) R.C.O.G.; M.M.S.A.(Lond.); M.R.C.O.G.; F.M.C.O.G.(Nig.). Married. Appointments: Casualty Officer, Southmead Hospital, Bristol; House Officer, Obstetrics & Gynaecology, St. Luke's Hospital, Bradford; Registrar, Obstetrics & Gynaecology, Leicester Royal Infirmary; Specialist, ibid, Ministry of Health, Lagos, Nigeria; Senior Specialist, ibid. Memberships: 400 Club; Metropolitan Club; Ikoyi Club; Island Club; Nigerian Medical Association; Society of Obstetrics & Gynaecology, Nigeria; Royal Society of Medicine, London. Publications: Investigation of Infertility. Address: Lagos Island Maternity Hospital, Campbell St., Lagos, Nigeria.

DADEY, Christian Ayesu, born 28th September 1915. Chief Agricultural Officer. Education: Primary, 1924-31; Secondary, 1932-35; Cambridge School Certificate Examination, Mfantsipim School, Ghana; Intermediate B.Sc., London, Achimota College, 1936-39; Diploma Course, Agriculture, School of Agriculture, Ibadan, Nigeria, 1942-44; B.A., School of Agriculture, Cambridge University, U.K., 1948-52; Postgraduate course in Agriculture, ibid, 1951-52; M.A., 1955; Diploma in Tropical Agriculture, Imperial College of Tropical Agriculture, Trinidad, W.I., 1954-55; Danish University, Copenhagen, Denmark; Afforestation Course, Arnhem, Netherlands, 1950; State College University, Pa. & Cornell University, Ithaca, N.Y., U.S.A., 1959; Michigan University, 1959; University of California, Berkeley, 1959. Married, 4 sons, 2 daughters. Appointments: Clerical, 1939-44; Assistant Agricultural Officer, 1944-52; Agricultural Officer, 1952-58; Senior Agricultural Officer, 1958-59; Chief Agricultural Officer, 1959; Principal Secretary, Ministry of Agriculture, 1964-66; Principal Secretary, i/c Agricultural Planning, Ministry of Economic Affairs, 1966-67; seconded to Volta River Authority, i/c of all agricultural activities, 1967; retired from Civil Service, 1968; Chief Agricultural Officer, Volta River Authority, 1968—. Represented Ghana as follows: One-man Delegation, 10th World Poultry Congress, Edinburgh, U.K., 1954; One-man Delegation, FAO/ECA Agricultural Statistics Conference, Lagos, Nigeria, 1960; Leader, Delegation to Agriculture Statistics Conference, Addis Ababa, Ethiopia, 1964; Technical Leader, Delegations to FAO Conferences, 1964, 1965; Inter-Governmental Committee, WFP, Rome, Italy, 1965, 1967; Leader, Delegation to U.K., France, Holland, Germany, & U.S.S.R. to purchase machinery, 1961; Rep. of Ghana on Rice Research Committee, Rokupr, Sierra Leone, & Oil Palm Research Committee, Benin, Nigeria; Rep. Ministries of Agriculture & Economic Affairs, Research Committee, Academy of Sciences (now Council for Scientific & Industrial Research). Memberships: National Advisory Committee, Volta River Resettlement Agriculture & Related Activities; Social, Agricultural, & Economic Sub-Committee, Volta Lake Research Project; Management Board, Institute of Aquatic Biology, Council for Scientific & Industrial Research, Ghana; Accra Ridge Church Council, 1970-71; Freemason. Publication: Rice Extension Scheme in Dagomba District, Northern Ghana (Ghana Farmer), 1958. Honours: Principal Scholarship, Achimota; Government Scholarship for Diploma Course, Ibadan, Nigeria; Government Scholarship, 1948-52; Government Scholarship for 1 year's Academic Course in Tropical Agriculture, Trinidad; USAID Participant Programme, 1959. Address: Volta River Authority, P.O. Box M. 77, Accra, Ghana.

DADSON, Banyan Acquaye, born 20th July 1938. Chemistry Lecturer. Education: B.Sc.(Special, Chemistry), University of Ghana, 1964; M.Sc.(Chemistry), ibid, 1965; Ph.D., University of Cambridge, U.K., 1969. Married, 2 children. Appointments: Assistant Lecturer, University of Ghana, 1965-66; Lecturer, ibid, 1966—. Memberships: Ghana Science Association; Science Teachers' Association; Chemical Society, U.K. Publications: Alkaloids of Fagara Xanthoxyloides, 1966; Total Synthesis of Tubifoline etc., 1968; Total Synthesis of Tubotaiwine, 1969; Total Synthesis of Geissoschizaline, 1969. Honours: Science Teachers' Association Research Medal, 1958; Achimota Scholar, 1960; University Scholar, 1964; Ghana Elder Dempster Independence Trust Award, 1966; Commonwealth Scholar, 1966. Address: Department of Chemistry, University College, Cape Coast, Ghana.

DAHLAB, Saad, born 18th April 1918. Statesman; Diplomat; Industrialist. Studied Journalism, Political & Social Sciences. Bhola College, Algeria. Appointments: Foreign Minister, Provisional Government of the Algerian Republic, Tunisia, 1958-61; Ambassador to Morocco, 1962-64; Director-General, Berliet Algeria, 1965—. Memberships include: Co-ordination & Executive Committee; National Liberation Front; Algerian People's Party; Movement for the Triumph of Democratic Liberty. Address: Berliet Algerie, P.O. Box 15, Rouiba, Algiers, Algeria.

DAKE, Jonas Mawuse Kwaku, born 12th February 1936. Civil Engineer; University Lecturer. Education: Mawuli Secondary School, Ho., Ghana, 1952-55; University of Science & Technology, Kumasi, 1956-61; University of Manchester, Institute of Science & Technology, U.K., 1962-63; Massachusetts Institute of Science & Technology, U.S.A., 1963-66; B.Sc.(London); M.Sc.,(Tech., Manchester); Sc.D., M.I.T. Married, 5 children. Appointments:

Assistant Lecturer, U.S.T., 1963-64; Lecturer in Civil Engineering, U.S.T., 1965-68; Senior Lecturer in Civil Engineering, ibid, 1968-70; Senior Lecturer in Civil Engineering, University of Zambia, 1970—. Memberships: Education & Training Committee, Ghana Institution of Engineers; American Geophysical Union; Ghana Institution of Management & Public Administration; U.S.T.Council, 1968-69. Publications: Essentials of Engineering Hydraulics (a textbook directed towards African Civil Engineering Students); many technical & professional papers in international journals; newspapers articles. Address: University of Zambia, Lusaka, Zambia.

DALFOVO (Reverend Father), Albert Titus, born Las Heras, Argentina, S.A., 27th November 1933. Missionary Priest. Education: Primary School, Trent, Italy; Gymnasium, Brescia, Italy; Intermediate & Philosophy, Sunningdale, U.K.; Theology, Milan, Italy; Mass Media, Rome, Italy; Philosophy, Makerere University, Kampala, Uganda. Appointments: School Supervisor; Parish Priest; Director, Arua Catholic Centre, Uganda; Visiting Justice, Arua Government Prisons, Uganda. Memberships: Missionary Society of the Verona Fathers (Sons of the Sacred Heart, F.S.C.J.). Editor of the Nile Gazette. Address: Nile Gazette, P.O. Box 264, Arua, Uganda.

DALTON, Derek James, born 2nd January 1923. Electrical Engineer. Education: Rugawi School; St. George's College; Faraday House. Appointments: Project Engineer, Nkula Falls, Electricity Supply Commission of Malawi; Assistant General Manager, ibid; General Manager. Memberships: Fellow, Institution of Electrical Engineers. Address: Electricity Supply Commission of Malawi, P.O. Box 186, Blantyre, Malawi.

DAMAGUM, Bulama Ali, born Damagum, Nigeria, 1943. Teacher. Education: Damagum Junior Primary School, 1954-58; Yerwa Senior Primary School, 1958-61; Borwu Teacher Training College, 1961-65. Appointments include: Class Teacher, Borwu Local Education Authority, 1966; Teacher, Damagum Primary School, 1967; Headmaster, Jafere Primary School, 1968—. Address: Jafere Primary School, Jafere, E.P.A. Damagum, Nigeria.

DANA, Henri, born 14th July 1924. Counsel to the Supreme Court of Appeal. Education: Secondary School, Carnot Lycée, Tunis, Tunisia. B.Phil., LL.B., Diploma of Higher studies in Private Law, Roman Law & the History of Law, Faculty of Law, Paris, France. Address: 6 Rue d'Angleterre, Tunis, Tunisia.

DANEE, Asha, Medical Practitioner. Education: M.B.B.S., Amritsar, Punjab University, India; D.C.H., Glasgow University, U.K. Married to Mr. Krishan Gopal Danee, 1 son, 1 daughter. Appointments: Internee, Kenyatta National Hospital, Nairobi, Kenya, 1960-61; Med. Officer, Dispensaries, Maternity & Child Welfare, City Council of Nairobi, 1961—. Member of the British Medical Association. Address: P.O. Box 9161, Nairobi, Kenya.

DANEE, Krishan Gopal, born 19th May 1932. Chartered Civil & Structural Engineer. Education: B.S.(Eng.), Civil Engrng., London, U.K.; M.Sc.(Eng.), Highway & Traffic Engrng., Birmingham; P.Engr., Province of Ontario, Canada. Married to Dr. Asha Danee, 1 son, 1 daughter. Appointments: Structural Designer w. Mr. Z. Pick, London, U.K., 1956-57; Structural Designer w. Mr. R. A. Sutcliffe, Nairobi, Kenya, 1957-58; Asst. Lecturer in Civil Engrng., University College (formerly Royal College), 1958-61; Principal Asst. Engr., Nairobi City Council, 1961—. Memberships: Inst. of Civil Engrs., London; Inst. of Structural Engrs.; Inst. of Municipal Engrs.; Orient Lodge (Masonic), Nairobi; Central Lions Club, Nairobi. Address: P.O. Box 9161, Nairobi, Kenya.

DANIELS, Ebenezer Coleman, born 16th May 1932. Medical Practitioner. Education: Mfantsipim Secondary School, 1947-50; B.Sc., University of Ghana, 1952-56; M.B., Ch.B., University of Liverpool, 1956-61. Personal details married to Eva Ata-Amonco, 5 daughters. Appointments: House Officer, St. Catherine's Hospital, Cheshire U.K.; Senior House Officer, Bootle Hospital; Medical Officer, Ministry of Health, Ghana; Non-Medical Administrator, St. Paul's Hospital, Tamole. Member of the Society of General Practitioners. Address: St. Paul's Hospital, P.O. Box 291, Tamale, Ghana.

DANJOUX, Guy Edmond Mathieu, born 15th August 1926. Architect; Civil Servant. Education: Diploma in Architecture, London, U.K., Diploma in Tropical Architecture, London; Diploma in Town & Country Planning, Birmingham; Diploma in Comprehensive Planning, The Hague, Netherlands. Appointments: Architect, London, U.K., 1958-60; Architect, Ministry of Works, Mauritius, 1960-62; Town Planner, Ministry of Housing, London, U.K., 1963-64; Assistant, Town & Country Planning Officer, Mauritius. Memberships: Associate Mbr., R.I.B.A.; ibid, Town Planning Institute, U.K.; Central Committee of the Mauritius Racing Club. Honours: 1st Prize Design, A.A. Tropical School in Architecture, 1958; 1st Prize, Best Report on Cross Ventilation in Tropical Countries, 1958. Address: Ministry of Housing, Lands, Town & Country Planning, Port Louis, Mauritius.

DANKYI, Richard Isaac, born 11th December 1925. Medical Practitioner. Education: Middle School, 1930-39; Mfantsipim School, Cape Coast, 1940-44; Medical School, Trinity College, Dublin, Ireland, 1948-54; M.B.; B.C.L.; B.A.O.; L.A.H.; B.A. Married, 1 son, 1 daughter. Appointments: House Surgeon, City & County Hospital, Londonderry, 1954-56; Medical Officer, Ministry of Health, Ghana, 1956-60; Medical Officer, Dunkwa, Goldfields, 1960-69; C.A.S.T., Akwatic, 1969-70; Private Medical Practitioner, 1970—. Memberships: General Medical Assn., England; General Medical Assn., Ghana. Address: Samaritan Clinic, P.O. Box 5223, Accra, Ghana.

DANTAS, Kenny Alexander, born 11th October 1942. Electrical Engineer. Education: Cambridge 'O' Levels, 1957; 'A' Levels, 1959; B.Sc.(Electrical Engineering), St. Andrew's University, Scotland, 1963. Married to Maria-Luz née Cardozo, 1 son. Appointments:

Graduate Trainee, Central Electricity Generating Board, 1963; General Assistant Engineer, ibid, 1965; Assistant Engineer (Generation) with Uganda Electricity Board, Owen Falls Power Station, Jinja, 1966; Electrical Maintenance Engineer, ibid, 1969 Memberships: Associate Member of the Institution of Electrical Engineers, London; Associate, East African Institute of Engineers. Address: Owen Falls Power Station, P.O. Box 1101, Jinja, Uganda.

DANVERS (Lt.-Colonel) Alexander Antony John, born 10th July 1909. Airline Executive; Retired Army Official. Education: Ampleforth College, Yorkshire, U.K., 1918-27; Royal Military College, Sandhurst, 1927-29; Staff College, Quetta, India, 1942. Married, 4 children. Appointments: Prince Albert Victors Own Cavalry, Indian Army, 1929-49; Comptroller to H.E. the Governor of Kenya, 1952-57; Assistant General Manager, Sabena Belgian Airlines, Nairobi, Kenya, 1957–. Memberships: Cavalry Club, London, U.K.; Mount Kenya Safari Club, Kenya; Muthaiga Country Club, Kenya. Honours: Military Cross, 1942. Address: Box 3708, Nairobi, Kenya.

D'ARBELA, Paul George, born 4th July 1934. Medical Practitioner. Education: Chiefly in Uganda; M.B., Ch.B., Makerere University College Medical School, Kampala, Uganda, 1960; Postgraduate Education in U.K. Appointments: Internship, Mulago Hospital, Kampala, Uganda, 1961-62; Research Fellow, Dept. of Medicine, Makerere Univ. Medical School, 1962-64; Research Fellow in Cardiology, Royal Postgraduate Medical School, Ducane Rd., London, U.K., 1965-66; Registrar, Central Middlesex Hospital, ibid, 1966-67; Government Physician, Jinja Hospital, Uganda, 1967-68; Lecturer in Medicine, Makerere University College School, 1968-70; Senior Lecturer in Medicine, ibid, 1970. Memberships: Royal College of Physicians, London; Royal College of Physicians, Edinburgh; National Secretary, Uganda Association of Physicians of East Africa; Uganda Medical Association; Hon. Editor, The Uganda Practitioner; Eisenhower Fellow, Uganda, 1969; Hon. Chairman, ibid, 1969. Publications include: contributor of numerous articles to: Mulago Medical Journal; East African Medical Journal; Journal of Endocrin.; British Heart Journal; American Heart Journal; British J. Radiol.; Uganda Practitioner; Trans. Roy. Soc. Trop. Med. & Hygiene. Honours: Leimann Prize in Medicine, Makerere University College Medical School, 1960; Shell Company Prize for Best Student, ibid, 1960; Gold Medal in Medicine, 1960. Address: Dept. of Medicine, Makerere University Medical School, P.O. Box 7072, Kampala, Uganda.

D'ARBOUSSIER (His Excellency) Gabriel, born Djenne, Mali, 14th January 1908. Diplomat. Education: Studied in France for LL.B. & also at the Colonial School. Married, 4 children. Appointments: Colonial Administrator, 1938-45; Co-Founder, Democratic African Assembly, 1946; French Parliamentarian, 1945-60; President, French West African Counsel, 1957-59; Minister of Justice, Senegal, 1960-63; Ambassador to France, 1963-65; Under-Secretary-General, O.N.U., 1965-68; Ambassador to the Federal Republic of Germany, Austria, & Switzerland, 1968–. Editor of l'Afrique vers l'Unité, 1961. Honours: Hammarskjöld Prize, 1967; Dr.h.c., University Seaton Hall, Newark, U.S.A.; Grand Cross, National Order of Senegal; Grand Cross of Merit, Federal Republic of Germany; Grand Cross, National Order of the Cedar of Lebanon; Commander, Legion of Honour. Address: Embassy of Senegal, 53 Bonn, Bonn-Center 1204, Federal Republic of Germany.

DARE, Joseph Olawuyi, born Gbongan, Nigeria, 22nd April 1938. Teacher. Education: 1st School Leaving Certificate, 1952; Grade 3 Teachers' Certificate, 1958; Grade 2 Teachers' Certificate, 1962. Married, 1 child. Appointments include: Class Teacher, St. David's Anglican Secondary Modern School, Ode-Omu, 1963-67; Principal, ibid., 1967–. Memberships include: Christian Fellowship Society. Address: St. David's Anglican Seconday Modern School, Ode-Omu, via Ede, Western Nigeria.

d'ARGENT, Joseph Noel Alfred, born 14th December 1922, Deputy Accountant General; University Lecturer. Education: Cambridge School Certificate; London Matriculation; Inter-B.Sc., London, U.K. Appointments: Examiner of Accounts, Audit Department, 1942-57; Finance Officer, Ministry of Finance, 1957-64; Chief Finance Officer, Ministry of Finance, 1965-67; Deputy Accountant General of Mauritius, 1967–; Lecturer, University of Mauritius, 1969–. Memberships: Chairman, Widows & Children's Pension Scheme, Mauritius. Address: Deputy Accountant General, Treasury, Mauritius.

DARWISH, Ali Hussein, born Zanzibar, 12th August 1936. Lecturer in Fine Art. Education: D.F.A., University of East Africa; D.F.A., Slade School of Art, University of London, U.K.; Ph.D., History of Islamic Art & Architecture, University of East Africa. Personal details: Married, 1 son, 1 daughter. Appointments: Assistant Lecturer, 1963-65; Lecturer, 1965–. Group Exhibitions include: The London Contemporaries; The Graven Image Exhibitions; Commonwealth Artists, London, 1963; Recently held a 3-man show in Nairobi, Kenya (similar show in U.S.A. Planned for approx. 1971). Work in private collections in U.S.A., Europe, Asia, & Africa. Publications: Contributor to articles on Islamic & Oriental Art; African Encyclopaedia; An Examination of Islamic Influence on Certain Aspects of Decorative Arts in Selected Areas of the Offshore Islands & Coasts of East Africa, Ph.D. Thesis, 1972. Honours: awarded a number of prizes in painting. Address: Makerere University, P.O. Box 7062, Kampala, Uganda.

DATE-BA, Lawrence Memsa, born 12th November 1904. School Teacher; District Magistrate. Education: B.A., Akropong Presbyterian Training College, 1922-25. Personal details: stood for election as N.L.M. Candidate, General Elections, 1956. Appointments: Schoolmaster; Assistant Supervisor of Schools: Assistant Education Officer; District Magistrate. Memberships: Oddfellows; Freemasons; General President, Presbyterian Teacher's Union, 1942-52; Address: P.O. Box 145, Winneba 142, Ghana.

DICTIONARY OF AFRICAN BIOGRAPHY

DAUDU, Patrick Cyrús Adamola, born 28th December 1932. Lecturer. Education: Primary School, Okene, 1942-45; Middle School Okene, 1946-49; Teacher Training Centre, Okene, 1950-51; Teacher Training College, Kátsina, 1955-56; Nigerian College of Technology, Zaria, 1957-60; University College, Ibadan, 1960-63; University of Pittsburgh, U.S.A., 1964-65. Personal details: Daudu family of Magongo. Married, 3 sons, 2 daughters. Appointments: Primary School Teacher, 1952-54; Temporary Executive Officer, Northern Regional Govt., Kaduna, 1963; Education Officer, Northern Regional Govt., ibid, 1963-64; Lecturer in Public Administration, A.B.U., Zaria, 1966—. Memberships: Graduate School of Public & International Affairs Alumni; Former President, Zaria Chapter, ibid. Publications: The Strategy of Motivating Participation in Development at the Local Level in Northern Nigeria, Institute, Zaria, 1968; Administrative Stocktaking in North-Western, North-Central, & Kano States of Nigeria (in Administration), 1968. Honours: Master of Hall, Tafawa Balewa Hall, Institute of Administration, A.B.U., Zaria. Address: Institute of Administration, A.B.U., Zaria, Nigeria.

DAURA, Muhammad Bello, born 15th February 1935. Research Fellow, Centre of Islamic Legal Studies. Education: Dutsi Elementary School, 1945-48; Sandamu Elementary School, 1948-49; Katsina Middle School, 1949-52; Government College, Zaria, 1952-57; SOAS, University of London, U.K., 1958-60; University of Ibadan, Nigeria, 1961-63; B.A.(Hons.), Classical Arabic, SOAS, Univ. of London, 1965. Married to Maoiya Zangi & Ladi Madake, 5 children. Appointments: Senior Library Assistant, 1963-65; Assistant Librarian, 1966-67; Assistant Research Fellow, 1967-69; Research Fellow, 1969—. Memberships: Conference of Muslim Lecturers & Administrators, Staff of Nigerian Universities; Vice-President, Old Boys' Assn. Zaria Branch, Barewa Government College, Zaria. Publications include: Hausa Customs (co-author), 1968; Introduction to Classical Hausa; The Limit of Polygamy in Islam (Journal of Islamic & Comparative Law, Journal of the Centre of Islamic Legal Studies). Address: Faculty of Law, Inst. of Administration, A.B.U., Zaria, Nigeria.

DAVEY-HAYFORD, Mark, born Ghana 21st February 1902. Medical Practitioner. Education: S.P.G. Grammar School, Cape Coast, Ghana; Queen's University, Belfast, Northern Ireland, U.K.; Edinburgh University; Licentiate, Royal College of Physicians & Surgeons; Licentiate, Royal Faculty of Physicians & Surgeons; Diploma, Tropical Medicine & Hygiene; Member of Royal College of General Practitioners, London. Personal details: Son of Rev. Mark Christian Hayford, M.A., D.D., F.R.C.S.; Married, 4 children. Appointments: Retired Medical Superintendent, Ministry of Health, Ghana; Ex-President, Eastern Division, Ghana Medical Association; Ex-National Chairman, Society of General Medical Practitioners, Ghana; Former President, Toastmasters International, Ghana. Memberships: Achimota Golf Club; Major, Ghana Volunteer Force, Accra, Ghana; Tesano Club, Accra; National Geographers Society, Ghana & Columbia, U.S.A. Publications: editorials & articles, late Gold Coast Observer; poems in various publications; Columnist, The Guardian, Ghana. Address: P.O. Box 1657, Accra, Ghana.

DAVIES, David Saunders, born 18th April, 1927. Bank Official. Education at Oldham, U.K. Married, 1966. Bank Clerk, U.K., 1943; Commissioned in H.M. Forces (Army), 1946; Bank Clerk, Kenya, Sudan & Nigeria, 1951-69; Assistant General Manager, United Bank for Africa Ltd., Lagos, Nigeria, 1969—. Address: United Bank for Africa Ltd., P.O.B. 2406, Lagos, Nigeria.

DAVIES, John Howard, born 2nd November 1927. Agricultural Research Worker. Education: Lewis's School for Boys, Pengam, Glam., U.K.; B.Sc., University College of Wales, Aberystwyth. Married, 2 sons, 1 daughter. Appointments: Pasture Research Officer, Sudan Veterinary Service, Sudan, 1950-54; Officer-in-charge, Agricultural Research Station, Mokya, Nigeria, 1958-61; ibid & Head of Grassland Section, Shika Research Station, 1961-67; Deputy Director, Institute for Agricultural Research, Samaru, 1967-70. Address: Institute for Agricultural Research, Ahmadu Bello University, Samaru, Zaria, Nigeria.

DAVIES, Patience Elizabeth, born 28th July 1911. Paediatrician. Education: London University, U.K.; Royal Free Hospital Medical School, London; M.B.; D.C.H. Married, 2 children. Appointments: Honorary Consultant Paediatrician, Kenyatta National Hospital, Nairobi, Kenya; Consultant Paediatrician, Aga Khan Hospital, Nairobi. Member, Royal College of Physicians, London, 1970. Address: Box 317, Nairobi, Kenya.

DAVIS, Edwin Casral, born in 1903. Engineer; Company Director. Education: Warwick School, U.K. Personal details: Father, A. Davis, journalist & author, founded first newspaper in Nairobi, the 'Leader', now absorbed into the 'Standard'. Appointments: Managing Director, Davis & Shirtliff Ltd., Hydraulics & Water Supply Engineers (Firm founded in 1928). Memberships: Fellow, East African Institute of Engineers. Address: Davis & Shirtliff Ltd., P.O. Box 1762, Nairobi, Kenya.

DAVIES-MA'AYE, Isaac Emerson, born end April 1896. Retired Schoolteacher. Education: Urban Secondary School; Fourah Bay College, University of Sierra Leone; M.A.(Durham). Appointments: Assistant Master in several Secondary Schools, 1916-48; Lecturer, Teacher Training Colleges, Freetown & Bo, 1964-67; Principal, Rokel Secondary School, Freetown, 1968-69. Memberships: Hon. Sec., West Ward, Ratepayers' Association & Ratepayers' Association, 1945-48. Publications (in preparation): Sierra Leone's Historical Background. Honours: J.P., Sierra Leone Police District. Address: Ia Ascension Town Road, Freetown, Sierra Leone.

DAVRAINVILLE, Jacques, born 10th November 1929. Technical Advisor. Appointments: Controller, P.T.T., France, 1952; Deputy

Inspector, P.T.T. Alger Bourse, Algeria, 1954; Postmaster, Michelet, Algeria, 1956; Fort National, 1957; Laghouat, 1957; Inspector, Alger Bourse, 1958; Principal Deputy Inspector, P.T.T., Direction Genérale, 1959; Chief, Postal & Financial Services Division, Libreville, Gabon, 1966; Technical Advisor, P.T.T., Libreville, 1968. Address: Direction des Services Postaux et Financiers, Libreville, Gabon.

DAVY, Edwin George, born 17th September 1917. Meteorologist. Education: Stowmarket Grammar School, U.K., 1929-36; Queen Mary College, University of London, 1937-39; Kings College, ibid, 1940. Married, 1 son, 4 daughters. Appointments: Royal Engineers, H.M. Forces, 1940; Royal Artillery, 1941; Royal Air Force, 1942-46; Statistician, Rothamsted Agricultural Station, U.K., 1946; Director, Meteorological Services, Mauritius; Assistant Director of Observatory, Mauritius. Memberships: Fellow, Royal Statistical Society. Author of several papers in his field. Honours: O.B.E., 1963. Address: The Observatory, Vacoas, Mauritius.

DAWIT GABRU, born 6th January 1913. Senator. Education: Teferi Mekonen School, 1925; German Agricultural Institute, Bersheba, Israel, 1930; Diploma in Law, University College, Addis Ababa, Ethiopia, 1954; Aba Dina Police Staff College Certificate, 1954; Certificate, Police Administration Course, Perdu University, 1955. Married, 2 sons, 4 daughters. Appointments: Director of Veterinary Dept., Ministry of Agriculture, 1934-36; with Ethiopian Police Force in various capacities including Chief, C.I.D.; Secretary-General for Arrus Provincial Governatorate, 1943; Supt. of Prisons, 1944; Director of Ministry of Interior, 1945; Chief of Provincial Police, Begemdir Gondar, 1946; transferred to Shoa Province, 1948; Liaison Officer, Aba Dina Police Staff College, 1949; Chief of Aba Dina Staff College, 1958; Chief of Crime Prevention & Training Dept., Police Headquarters. Memberships include: International Assn. Chief of Police; Inter-parliamentary Union: Board of Directors, Y.M.C.A. Honours & Titles include: Colonel, 1958; Assistant Minister, 1964; Senator, 1965; Hailé Selassié I Golden Medal, 1970. Decorations: Ethiopian Star Knight Order; Menelik II Knight Order; Menelik II, Officer Order; The Royal Order of Swords, Sweden, 1953; The St. George Commander Order, Greece, 1958. Address: P.O. Box 566, Addis Ababa, Ethiopia.

DAWODU (Alhagi) Ganiyu Olawale, born Lagos, Nigeria, 13th March 1933. Commissioner for Agriculture, Natural Resources, Trade & Industry, Lagos State. Education: Ansar-un-Deen School, Ahmadiyah High School, St. Gregory's College, Lagos; G.C.E., 1955. Married, 4 children. Appointments include: Member, Lagos City Council, 1957-66; Chairman, Establishment Committee, 1962-65; Member, Lagos City Transport Services, 1963-65; Chairman, Lagos City Council, 1965-66; Company Director, 1966-68; Commissioner, Ministry of Trade etc.; ibid, Health & Social Welfare, 1968—. Memberships: Bd. of Governors, St. Gregory's School, 1960-67; Bd. of Governors, Achmadiyah High School, 1959-62; Organizing Secretary, Action Group of Nigeria, 1958-66; Muslim Association of Nigeria; Island Club, Lagos. Address: Ministry of Agriculture, Natural Resources, Trade & Industry, P.M.B. 1028, Ikeja, Lagos State, Nigeria.

DEAN, Pauline Mary, born 16th April 1921. Missionary Doctor. Education: M.B., Ch.B., Liverpool, U.K., 1945; Board Certified Paediatrician, U.S.A., 1966. Personal details: Became Medical Missionary of Mary, 1953. Appointments: Residency, Children's Hospital, Columbus, Ohio, U.S.A., 1950-53; Residency, Obstetrics, Our Lady of Lourdes Hospital, Drogheda, Ireland, 1955-56; Paediatrician, 1957-60; Paediatrician, St. Luke's Hospital, Nigeria, 1961-67; Medical Superintendent, Drogheda, Ireland, 1968-69. Memberships: Irish & America Paediatric Association; B.M.A.; I.M.A.; Nigerian Medical Association. Address: St. Luke's Hospital, Aunua-Uyo, South-eastern State, Nigeria.

DEARSLEY, Geoffrey Wallis, born 4th August 1924. Aeronautical Engineer; Teacher & Missionary. Education: Haberdashers Askes, New Cross, London, U.K., 1936-41; Kingston Technical College, Surrey, 1941-43; B.Sc.(Eng.), Northampton College, University of London, 1944; London Bible College, 1949-50. Personal details: Married, 4 children. After personal dedication to Jesus Christ went to Nigeria with the Sudan United Mission. Appointments: Scientific Officer, Aeronautical & Armament Experimental Establishment, Boscombe Down, Wilts., U.K., 1944-49; Teacher, Principal, Secondary School, Gindiri, Nigeria, 1950-60; Foundation Member, Scripture Union Council, 1957—; Warden, Gindiri Teachers' College & Schools, 1960-62; General Secretary, Fellowships of Christian Students, 1960-66; Superintendent, British Branch, Sudan United Mission, 1963—; Secretary, 5 Branches Sudan United Mission, 1965—; Secretary, Council of Evangelical Churches, N. State of Nigeria, 1968—; President, Theological College, 1969—. Honours: O.B.E. Address: Sudan United Mission, P.O. Box 643, Jos, Nigeria.

DEBARD, Roland, born 7th November 1926. Social Administrator. Married, 4 children. Appointments: Head of Depot, Head of Ste. Achats, A.P.T., Dakar, Senegal; Director, Dakar; Director, ETAPERU Co., Abidjan, Ivory Coast; Foreign Administrator, Bamako Mali; ibid, Bobo Dioulasso, Upper Volta; Administrative Delegate, SADIA, Abidjan, Ivory Coast. Memberships: Lions Club, Abidjan; Royal Ocean Racing Club, London, U.K. Address: SADIA, B.P. 1810, Abidjan, Ivory Coast.

DEBEBE HABTE YOHANNES, born 26th December 1926. Banker; Business Executive. Education: Ras Mekonnen School, Harrar, Ethiopia, 1942-45; Hailé Selassié 1st Secondary School, Addis Ababa, 1945-47; Rosenberg College, St. Gallen, Switzerland, 1947-48; St. Christopher's College, London, U.K., 1948-49; Guildford Technical College, Surrey, 1949-50; London School of Economics, 1960-61. Personal details: Married, 2 children. Appointments include: with State Bank of Ethiopia, 1947; Exchange Control Department, ibid, 1950-55;

Deputy Exchange Controller, 1955-60; Supervisor, Foreign Branch, 1961-63; Secretary, Investment Committee, former State Bank of Ethiopia, 1956-63; Founder, Promoter, Managing Director, & Alternate Chairman, Addis Ababa Bank S.C., 1963—; Director, Blue Nile Insurance Corporation, S.C.; ibid, Addis Shekla S.C.; Steel Company of Ethiopia, S.C.; Addis Ababa Chamber of Commerce, Vice-President, 1968-69; 1969-70; ibid, Ethiopian Bankers' Association; National Textiles, S.C.; Honorary Consul-General of Denmark in Ethiopia, 1969. Memberships include: Addis Ababa Rotary Club; Director, ibid, 1967-68, 1970-71. Honours: Chevalier, Order of the Danebrog.

DE CORGNOL, Patrice Roger, born 22nd April 1912. Social Administrator. Education: LL.B., Diploma of the School of Political Science. Memberships: French Automobile Club; French Racing Club. Author of articles on economics in numerous publications. Honours: Chevalier, Legion of Honour; Commander, Order of the Ivory Coast.

DEDEKE, Jenuola Adesiyau, born 2nd June 1906. School Principal. Education: African Church School, Ifaka; Secondary Girls' Seminary, 1918-22; Teacher Training, 1922-23. Personal details: daughter of The Most Rev. J. A. & Mrs. Lakeru; married to Nathaniel Dedeke, Nigerian Secretariat. Appointments: Teacher at: Anglican Girls' School; Methodist Girls' High School; Founder of Princess School & Ideal Girls' School. Memberships: Annual Anglican Diocesan Synod, Lagos Province, Nigeria; President, National Council of Women, Lagos Branch, Nigeria; President, Ladies: Progressive Society; President, Ladies' Guild African Church; Board of Governors, Ideal Girls' School, New Era Secondary Girls'; Anglican Sec. Girls'; Sisalis Girls' School. Address: P.O. Box 6, Yaba, Lagos, Nigeria.

DEEKS, Elizabeth Catherine Jane, born 8th November 1937. Teacher. Education: B.Sc. (Special), Leicester, U.K.; P.G.C.E., Leicester. Personal details: Father, a teacher in St. Andrews' College, Oyo, Nigeria, 1-934-49; Mother, a nurse in Ado Ekih, Nigeria. Appointments: Assistant Teacher, Tottenham High School, London, U.K.; Vice-Principal, Head of Geography Department, Dispensary Mistress, St. Monica's Grammar School, Ondo, Nigeria, 1965—. Memberships: Church Missionary Society; Secretary, S.C.M., Western Region, Nigeria, 1970; Nigerian Geographical Association. Address: St. Monica's Grammar School, P.O. Box 84, Ondo, Nigeria.

De FOULHIAC de PADIRAC, Raymond, born 23rd April 1915. Director: Rubber Manufacturer. Education: Baccalauréats, Collège Saint Louis de Gonzague; Diploma, Free School of Political Science. Married, 4 children. Appointments: General Director, French Rubber Institute, 1945—; General Director, African Institute of Rubber Research. Memberships: Counsellor, International Rubber Research Board; ibid, l'Association Nationale de la Recherche Technique (A.N.R.T.); President, Commission de Cooperation Technique de l'A.N.R.T. Honours: Knight, Legion of Honour; Officer, National Order of Merit; ibid, National Order of the Ivory Coast; Order of Merit of the Central African Republic. Address: Bureau 42, rue Scheffer, Paris 16, France.

DEGANO (Rev.) Giocondo, born 13th November 1934. Editor of Leadership Magazine. Education: D.D., Milan, Italy. Personal details: Priest, Member of the Verona Fathers' Institute. Appointments: Editor, Lobo Mewa (fortnightly in the Lwo language); Editor, Leadership Magazine (English). Member of the Uganda Social Communications Committee. Address: P.O. Box 3872, Kampala, Uganda.

DE GRAFT-HAYFORD (Air Commodore) John Ebenezer Samuel, born London, U.K., 24th November 1914. National Organizer, Ghana Workers' Brigade. Education: Bellahouston Academy; Diploma in Public Administration, London University; Inter-B.Sc., ibid, O.T.C., Derby; Officer Training Wing, Aldershot; F.R.Econ. Soc. Married, 5 children. Appointments: Commissioned Lieutenant; Secretary-Accountant, State Cocoa Marketing Board, Ghana, 1948-53; Shipping Manager, ibid, 1953-57; Acting General Manager, 1958; Secretary, Board of Legal Education, 1958-59: Commander, Air Volunteer Force (as Lt.—Col.), 1960-61; Chief of Air Staff & Commander, Ghana Air Force, 1961-63; Defence Adviser, Ghana, U.K., 1963-64; Voluntary Exile, 1964-66. Memberships: Chairman, Ghana Legion, 1960; Vice-President, Ex-Servicemen's Union, 1957-58; Chairman, Ghana Boxing Board of Control, 1968; Child Care Society; Patron, Professional Boxers' Welfare Association, 1968; Member & Committee Chairman, Constituent Assembly, 1969; Chairman, Ghana Management Association; Fellow, Ghana Economic Society; Chairman, Food Supply Committee. Publications: With the Devil on the Gold Coast; Forbidden Fruit; Among the Denizens of Mars; Divided House (W.A. Review); Democracy (Economist); Problems of Indebtedness; Training of African Soldiers; also numerous short stories & poems. Territorial Decoration, 1946; War Medals, 1939-45; 1939-45 Star; Coronation Medal, 1953; Republic Medal, 1960; Welterweight & Middleweight Boxing Champion of West Africa, 1941 (retired undefeated); Coronation Cycle Champion, W. Province. Address: Ghana Workers' Brigade, P.O. Box 1853, Accra, Ghana.

De GRAFT-JOHNSON, John Coleman, born Accra, Ghana, 21st March 1919. Economic Historian; Educator; Diplomat. Education: Schools in Accra & Saltpond; Mfantsipim School, Cape Coast; B.Com., Edinburgh University, U.K., 1942; M.A.(Hons.), Economic Science, ibid, 1944; Ph.D.(Econs.), 1946. Married, 4 children. Appointments include: Head Office Staff, Commercial Bank of Scotland, Edinburgh, 1942-44; Joint Treasurer, Scottish National Union of Students, 1942-43; one of Organizers, Pan-African Congress, Manchester, 1945; Vice-President, Pan-African Federation; 1st Division Civil Servant, Economic Department, Colonial Office, London, 1946-48; President, Gold Coast Union of G.B. & Ireland, 1948-49; Assistant Controller of Commerce & Industry, Department of Commerce & Industry,

Gold Coast Government, & Secretary-Accountant, Agricultural Produce Marketing Bd., 1950; Resident Tutor, Institute of Extra-Mural Studies, University of the Gold Coast, 1950-56; Member, 1st National Committee on the Volta River Project & Member, Government Delegation to Canada, 1953; Member, National Food Board, Ghana, 1952-56; Deputy Chairman, Retail Trade Workers' Wages Board, 1952-56, 1958-61; Professor of Economics, Department of African Studies, University of Delhi, India, 1956-58; External Examiner for the M.A. in Economics, ibid, 1958-61; Senior Resident Tutor, Insitute of Extra-Mural Studies, University of Ghana, 1958-62; Associate Professor, ibid, 1962; Acting Director, 1962; Director & Professor, Institute of Public Education (ex-Inst. of Extra-Mural Studies), 1962-65; Research Unit, Economics Department, 1965-67; Joint-Secretary, Preparatory Committee, Africanist Congress, Commonwealth Hall, University of Ghana, 1962; Member, General Purposes Committee (Executive Committee), Praesidium, Ghana Academy of Sciences, 1963-64; Chairman, Finance Committee, ibid, & Co-opted Member, General Purposes Committee, 1965-66; Master, Commonwealth Hall, Univ. of Ghana, 1961-65; Chairman, Committee on the Local Purchasing of Cocoa, 1966; Director, Ghana Commercial Bank, 1966-67; Chairman, Bd. of Directors, State Insurance Corporation, 1966-67; Examiner for M.A. in Political Science, University of Ghana, 1966; seconded to Ghana Ministry of External Affairs, 1967; Ambassador of Ghana to Netherlands & Belgium, 1967--; concurrently accredited to the E.E.C. & to Luxembourg, 1968-70; Programme Organizer, Economic History & History of Economic Thought, University of Ghana, 1970—; Editor, Economic Bulletin of Ghana, 1970—. Memberships include: Fellow, Royal Commonwealth Society; Fellow, Royal Economic Society; Fellow, Nigerian Field Society, U.K.; Associate, Institute of Management, London; Fellow, Historical Society of Ghana; President, ibid, 1961-67; Associate, Institute of Bankers, London; Fellow, Economic Society of Ghana; Scottish Economic Society, Glasgow; Fellow, Ghana Academy of Arts & Sciences. Publications include: African Glory: The Story of Vanished Negro Civilizations, 1954, 1955, 1966 (translated into Czech & Italian); African Experiment: Co-operative Agriculture in British West Africa, 1958; An Introduction to the African Economy, 1959; Report of the Committee of Enquiry on the Local Purchasing of Cocoa, 1966 (with K. B. Ntim, F. R. Kankam-Boadu, J. W. Jordan); Gold Coast In Perspective (monograph); Background to the Volta River Projects (booklet); other monographs & contributions to numerous learned journals, magazines, & newspapers. Honours: Grand Cross of the Order of Merit, Grand Duchy of Luxembourg. Address: Department of Economics, University of Ghana, Legon, Accra, Ghana.

DEGRAFT-JOHNSON, Joseph William Swain, born 6th October 1933. Civil Engineer. Education: B.Sc.(Hons.), University of Leeds, U.K., 1958; M.Sc., University of Birmingham, 1959; Ph.D., University of California, U.S.A., 1965. Married, 4 children. Appointments: Lecturer, Senior Lecturer, Assoc. Professor, University of Science & Technology, 1961-69; Director, Building & Road Research Institute, CSIR, 1969—. Memberships: Institution of Civil Engineers, U.K.; Inst. of Highway Engineers; American Society of Civil Engineers; U.N. Technical Committee on Housing, Building, & Planning. Author of 20 publications on soil mechanics, highway engineering, & housing in various national & international journals. Address: Building & Road Research Inst., University P.O. Box 40, Kumasi, Ghana.

de HEER, Nicholas Andrew, born 15th September 1930. Physician; Nutritionist. Education: Adisadel College, 1943-48; Achumista School, 1949-50; Cambridge School Certificate, 1948; London Matriculation, 1949; B.Sc.(Inter); University of the Gold Coast, 1951-53; M.B.B.S., King's College & Westminster Hospital Medical School, U.K., 1953-58; L.R.C.P., M.R.C.S.(Eng.), 1958; D.P.H., D.T.M.&H., School of Public Health & School of Tropical Medicine & Hygiene, Liverpool, 1961; Dip. Nutr., Dept. of Nutrition, London School of Tropical Medicine, 1968. Personal details: son of Sir Tsibu Darku, Kt., O.B.E., Paramount Chief of Asin State; married, 2 sons, 3 daughters. Appointments: Casualty House Officer, Westminster Hospital, London, 1958-59; Medical Officer, Ministry of Health, Ghana, 1959-60; Research Officer, National Research Council, ibid, 1962-64; Epidemiologist i/c Medical Field Units, Volta Region, 1962-65; Regional Medical Officer, 1964-67; Medical Nutritionist, i/c Nutrition Division, Ministry of Health, 1968-70; Executive Secretary, Nutrition Advisory Committee. Memberships: Royal Society of Health, England; British Society for International Health Education; Society of Friends of Friendless Churches; Editor, Society for Prevention of Tuberculosis, Ghana. Publications include: A Tuberculosis & Diabetic Survey, Ho, Ghana, 1962; Health in Ghana—Waterborne Diseases, 1969; The Role of Nutrition in the Control of Communicable Diseases, 1970. Honours include: Vice-Chairman, Codex Alimentarius Commission, WHO/FAO, 1970. Address: Nutrition Division, Ministry of Health, P.O. Box M78, Accra, Ghana.

De la MOUREYRE, Raymond, The Very Reverend, born St. Flour, France, 8th March 1911. Bishop. Appointments: Missionary, Brazzaville, Congo, 1936-59; Bishop of Mouila, Gabon, 1959—. Publications include: Dieu est Bon; also other educational & scientific books. Address: Le Val Marie, B.P. 95, Mouila, Gabon.

DEM, Tidiane, born 8th June 1908. Businessman. Primary School, Bingerville, Ivory Coast; Accountancy Correspondence Course from Paris. Married, 10 children. Appointments: Accountant, C.F.C.I., U.A.C., 1926-30; Korhogo District Agent, C.F.C.I., 1930-38; Member, Privy Council, Ivory Coast, 1949-56; Member, General Council of the Territorial Assembly & Deputy, National Assembly, 1957-59; Secretary of State for Animal Husbandry, 1959-61; Minister of Animal Husbandry, 1961-63. Memberships: Foundrer-Mbr., Ivory Coast Progressive Party, 1945-46; Deputy Secretary-General, P.P.C.I. Author of several historical works. Honours:

Knight, Black Star of Benin, 1956. Address: B.P. 15, 121 Korhogo, Ivory Coast.

DE MBELE, Michel, born 1920. Chief Civil Administrator. Education: Diploma, I.H.E.O.M., Paris, France; ibid, I.R.F.E.D., Paris. Appointments: Deputy to the Director of Finances; ibid, Planning Director; Cabinet Director to the Ministry of Commerce, Industry, & Crafts; Technical Counsellor to the Cabinet of the President of the Republic. Memberships: President, Administrative Council, O.C.A.S.; ibid, Administrative Council S.D.R.S.; Administrator, U.S.B. Honours: Officer, National Order of Senegal. Address: Villa 2776, SICAP Dieppeul III, Dakar-Liberte, Senegal.

DEME, Aliou, born 1919. Appointments: Chief Clerk of the Court to the Territories of the French Community, 1957-59; Examining Magistrate, Tribunal de Prèmiere Instance, Mopti, Mali, 1959; President, ibid, 1960; Councellor, Supreme Court, 1961; Attorney, Supreme Court, 1962—. Honours: Knight, National Order, 1967.

DEMISSEW ASSAYE, born 1st May 1929. Civil Servant. Education: Graduated, Teacher Training College, Addis Ababa, Ethiopia, 1949; B.A., Public Administration, American University of Beirut, 1959. Personal details: married to Sister Bisrate Melak Mengesha, 2 sons. Appointments: School-teacher, 1949-55; Acting Director, General Ministry of the Interior, 1959-62; Director-General, ibid, 1962-66; Assistant Minister, Ministry of Land Reform & Administration, 1966—. Publications: contributor to Amharic newspapers in Addis Ababa. Address: Ministry of Land Reform & Administration, P.O. Box 206, Addis Ababa, Ethiopia.

DENDY, David A. V., born 20th November 1933. Industrial & Food Technologist. Education: B.Sc., Ph. D., Liverpool, University, U.K. Personal details: married, 2 children. formerly Conductor, Nairobi Orchestra & Vice-President, Lions Club, Nairobi. Appointments: Research Scientists, East African Industrial Research Organization, 1963-68; Head, Food Processing Section, Tropical Products Institute, 1968—. Memberships: Fellow, Royal Institute of Chemistry. Author of numerous articles in his field. Address: c/o Tropical Products Institute, Culham, Abingdon, Berks, U.K.

DENNIS, C. (Charles) Cecil, Jr., born 21st February 1931. Lawyer; Counsellor-at-Law. Education: High School; College of West Africa, Monrovia; B.A., Lincoln University, Pa., U.S.A., 1954; LL.B., Georgetown University, Washington, D.C., 1957. Personal details: son of Charles Cecil Dennis, Sr. Member, House of Representatives, Republic of Liberia; Publisher, Daily Listener. Married to Agnes Cooper Dennis—Chairman, Dept. of Science, University of Liberia. Appointments: Attorney-at-Law, 1957; Legal Counsel of the Liberian Senate & Director, Legislative Drafting Service, 1957—; Professor, Louis Arthur Grimes School of Law, University of Liberia, 1958-62; Counsellor-at-Law, 1960; Hon. Consul-General, Republic of South Korea, Monrovia, 1970. Memberships: The Montserrado Bar Assn.; Liberian National Bar Assn.; Bar Assn. of the City of New York; Freemason: Y.M.C.A. Honours: Knight Commander, Human Order of African Redemption, Republic of Liberia. Address: Chase Manhattan Bank Building, P.O. Box 1179, Monrovia, Liberia.

DENNIS (Hon. Mr. Justice), John Africanus, born 27th February 1920. Resident Circuit Judge. Education: Graduate of Cape Palmas High School; Diploma, 1941. Appointments: Counsellor-at-Law; Resident Circuit Judge, 4th Judicial Circuit, Harper, Maryland Co., Republic of Liberia. Memberships: Vice-President, National Bar Association; Actual Past Master, Ancient Free & Accepted Masons, Grand Lodge of Liberia; Actual Past Master, Morning Star Lodge, No. 6, Ancient Free & Accepted Masons, Harper City, Liberia; District Deputy Grand Patron, Order of Eastern Star, Grand Chapter of Liberia; Past Patron, Golden Sheaf Chapter, No. 2, O.E.S. Harper City; Past District Deputy Grand Master, U.B.F. District; Deputy Grand Master, Grand United Order of Odd Fellows, Liberia; Former President, Crowd 16, Harper City. Honours: Liberian Age & Liberian Star, Monrovia, Liberia; Grand Commander of the Star of Africa, for distinguished service to Government. Address: Gregory Street, Harper, Cape Palmas, Liberia.

DE PAU, Diane, born Brussels, 10th December 1900. Artist; Portrait Painter. Education: studied at the Polytechnic School of Art, London, U.K., 1916. First Art Exhibition, Brussels, 1933; since then has exhibited in many places including Paris, Nice, Algeria, Tangiers, Rabat. Her works are permanently represented in the Museum of Art & History, Brussels, Belguim; ibid, Algiers, Algeria. Portraits commissioned by King Albert I of Belgium, 1923, also by ex-King Mohamed V of Morocco, 1956. Address: 28 Rue d'Esnes, Casablanca, Morocco.

DERDERIAN, Armand, born 2nd August, 1930. Educator. Education: L. es Sc., Diploma, Higher Studies in Geometry, 1956. Appointments: Professor, Lycée Lyantey, 1956—. Memberships: USM-TCC Moroccan (Sports Union & Casablanca Tennis Club); President, Bridge Club. Honours: Bridge Champion, 1966-67. Address: 2 Rue Neuf-Brisach, Casablanca, Morocco.

de REEPER, John, The Very Reverend, born Hertogenbosch; Holland, 19th November 1902. Bishop. Education: Secondary School, Philosophical & Theological Studies. Appointments include: Teacher at College, Hoorn, Holland, 1927-33; Missionary in Kenya, of which 4 years in various missions; Founder and Rector of St. Peter's Seminary, Kakamega, 1933-47; Assistant to the Superior General of Mill Hill Missionary Society, London, 1947-60; Prefect Apostolic of the Masai Missions in Kenya, 1960-64; Bishop of the Diocese of Kisumu, Kenya, 1964—. Memberships include: St. Joseph's Society for the Foreign Missions, Mill Hill, London N.W.7; Government Commission of Kenya for Marriage and Divorce. Publications include: numerous articles on Canon Law; 'A Missionary

Companion' (book); 'The Sacraments on the Missions' (book). Honours include: Officer in the Order of Orange Nassau (a Dutch knighthood distinction). Address: Bishop's House, P.O. Box 150, Kakamega, Kenya.

DEREGOWSKI, Jan Bronislaw, born 1st March 1933. University Lecturer. Education: B.Sc.(Eng.), Civil Engrng., London, U.K.; B.A., Psychology; Ph.D., Psychology. Married, 2 children. Appointments: various posts in Industry in Engineering, -1965; Research Fellow, University of Zambia, 1965; University Lecturer, 1969. Consulting Editor, Journal of Cross-Cultural Psychol. Member of Institution of Mechanical Engineers. Author of various articles on cross-cultural studies in: Journal of Exp. Psychol., Brit. Journal Psychol., International Journal of Psychol., Acta Psychlogica, Psycologia Africana, Brit. Journal Soc. & Clinical Psychol, etc. Address: c/o Dept. of Psychology, King's College, Aberdeen, U.K.

DESAI, Maganlal Dahyabhai, born Talangpur, Surat District, India, 22nd July 1907. Civil Servant. Education: B.A.(Hons.), Bombay University, India. Married, 8 sons. Appointments include: Senior Clerical Interpreter, High Court of Tanganyika, 1930-42; ibid., Supreme Court of Kenya, 1942-46; Clerk of Court of Appeal for Eastern Africa, 1946-50; Associate Registrar, ibid., 1951-63; Registrar, ibid., 1964-67; Registrar of Common Market Tribunal, East African Community, 1968—. Memberships include: President, Founder Member, Surat Jilla Sera Samaj, Dar es Salaam, Tanganyika; Secretary, Founder Member, Dar es Salaam Cultural Society; Committee Member, Devkunvar Arya Girls' School Board, Dar es Salaam; Committee Member, Surat District Association, Nairobi, Kenya; Secretary, Highridge Primary School Parents' Association, Nairobi. Author of literary articles in Gujerati & English in various magazines. Honours include: M.B.E., New Year's Honours List, 1962. Address: Box 30371 Nairobi, Kenya.

De SAIBULL, Solomon Alexander, born 9th February 1935. Conservationist; Administrator. Education: Tabora Secondary School, Tanzania, 1955-56; B.A., Makerere University College, Kampala, Uganda, 1957-61; Exeter University, Devon, U.K., 1961-63; Middle Temple Inns, London. Personal details: 1st son of large, polygamous family. Appointments: Assistant Secretary, Ministry of Lands, Forests & Wildlife, 1963-64; Assistant Conservator, Ngorongoro, Ministry of Agriculture, Forests & Wildlife, 1964-65; Sr. Assistant Conservator, ibid, 1965; Conservator, Ngorongoro, Ministry of Agriculture, Food & Co-operatives, 1965—. Memberships: East African Academy; Tanzania Society; Fabian Society, U.K.; East African Wildlife Society; Institute of Advanced Motorists. Author of several articles on nature conservation. Address: Ngorongoro Conservation Unit, P.O. Box 6000, Ngorongoro Crater, via Arusha, Tanzania.

de SAINT ANTOINE, Jacques D. de R., born 29th November 1923. Sugar Technologist. Education: Honours Diploma & Student Scholarship for overseas studies, Mauritius College of Agriculture, 1945; B.S.(Chem. Engrg.), Louisiana State University, U.S.A. Married, 3 children. Appointments: Chemist, Rose Belle Sugar Factory, 1945-46; Lecturer, Sugar Technology, Mauritius College of Agriculture, 1950-54; Assistant, Acting Registrar, Central Control & Administration Board, ibid; Sugar Technologist, Chief Sugar Technologist, Assistant Director, Mauritius Sugar Industry Research Institute, 1956—; Technical Adviser to the Mauritius Sugar Syndicate. Memberships include: President, Mauritius Society of Agricultural & Sugar Technology, 1956 & 1970; The Royal Society of Arts & Sciences; The International Society of Sugar Cane Technologists. Author of numerous scientific papers including publications in the 'Revue Agricole et Sucriere de l'Ile Maurice' and also in the Annual Reports of the Mauritius Sugar Industry Research Institute. Address: Sugar Industry Research Institute, Reduit, Mauritius.

DESALU, Ayodele B. O., born 19th May 1932. Medical Practitioner. Education: Igbobi College, Yaba, Nigeria, 1947-51; Norwood Technical College, London, U.K., 1954-56; M.B.; Ch.B., University of Bristol, 1956-61; M.S., Yale University, New Haven, Conn., U.S.A., 1963-65. Appointments: House Surgeon, House Physician, Bristol Royal Infirmary, 1961-62; Post Registration House Officer, Paediatrics, University College Hospital, Ibadan, Nigeria, 1962-63; Temporary Lecturer in Anatomy, University of Ibadan, 1963; Lecturer in Anatomy, ibid, 1963—; Rockefeller Foundation Fellow, Yale University, 1963-65. Memberships: Anatomical Society of Britain; Science Assn. of Nigeria; Treasurer, Nigeria Medical Assn., Western State. Publications: Correlation of Localization of Alkaline & Acid Phosphatases with Morphological Development of the Rat Kidney (Anatomical Records), 1966; Development of Acid & Alkaline Phosphatases in the Rat Kidney (M.S. Thesis, Yale), 1965. Address: Dept. of Anatomy, University of Ibadan, Ibadan, Nigeria.

DESHIELD (Hon.) Leonard T., born 24th November 1934. Lawyer; Diplomat. Education: B.A., North Carolina State University, U.S.A.; M.A., International Relations & Organizations, American University, Washington, D.C. Married, 2 sons, 2 daughters. Appointments: Research Assistant, Bureau of African-Asian Affairs, Dept. of State, Republic of Liberia, 1960-65; Director, Bureau of African-Asian Affairs, 1965—; President, Liberia Football Association, 1964—. Memberships: Rotary Club International; Alpha Phi Alpha Fraternity; Y.M.C.A.; Crowd 18 Inc.; Master Mason. Honours: K.C. Address: Bureau of African-Asian Affairs, Dept. of State, Republic of Liberia.

De SOUZA, James E., born 14th December 1915. Accountant. Education: Matriculation, Bombay University, 1935; studied Economics at Makerere College, Extra-mural Course; Diplomas in Typewriting, Shorthand & Accountancy at Indian Institutions. Personal details: married, 2 sons, 3 daughters; served in Uganda Defence Force, Second World War, 1940-43. Appointments: Office Superintendent; Higher Executive Officer, Accounts; Senior Executive Officer, ibid; Chief Executive Officer; Chief Accountant, Ministry of Finance. Honours: Queen Elizabeth's Coronation Medal; Uganda Independence Medal. Address: Ministry of Finance, Treasury Department, Kampala, Uganda.

DESTOPPELEIRE, André, born Marles-les-Mines, France, 22nd June 1924. Corporation Executive. Education: Baccalaureat; Certificat de Mathématiques Génerales; Ingénieur des Arts et Manufacture. Married, 5 children. Appointments Include: Permanent Way Inspector, Mali Railways, 1949-57; Chief Permanent Way Engineer, Senegal Railways, 1958; ibid, Ivory Coast Railway, 1959-63; Assistant to the General Manager, Cameroon Railways Corporation, 1964-65; General Manager, ibid. 1965—; Member, Board of Directors, Energie Electrique du Cameroon; Managing Director, Cameroonian Timber Impregnation Co. Ltd.; Lions Club. Honours: Knight, Cameroon Order of Valour. Address: P.O. Box 304, Douala, Cameroon.

DEVGAN, Manju, born 15th November 1943. Physician. Education: Primary School, Kenya; M.B., Ch.B., Makerere University College Medical School, Kampala, Uganda. Personal details: both parents Doctors in Kenya. Married to Mr. B. K. Devgan, F.R.C.S., Ear, Nose, & Throat Surgeon. Appointments: Resident House Surgeon, Mulago Hospital, Kampala, Uganda, 1966-67; Resident Pathologist, King's College Hospital, London, U.K., 1967-68; General Practice, Ndola, 1968—. Member of Business & Professional Women's Club of Ndola. Honours: Best Medical Graduate & Gold Medalist, University of East Africa, 1965-66; Ladkin Memorial Prize in Preventive Medicine, University of East Africa, 1965-66. Address: P.O. Box 6075, Ndola, Zambia.

DEVOUGE, Robert Raymond, born 19th May 1914. Engineer; Director. Education: Polytechnic & National School of Bridges & Roads. Appointments: Director, Abidjan-Niger Railway, Ivory Coast, 1947-50; Director, Congo-Olean Railway, Congo-Brazzaville, 1951-54; Deputy Director, Cameroun Railway Administration, 1954-57; Deputy Director, Central Railway Office, Outre Mer, Paris, 1958-69; Director-General, ibid, 1970—. Honours: Knight, Legion of Honour. Address: 38 Rue de la Bruyere, Paris, 9, France.

DEWAR, Robert James, born 13th January 1923. Forester. Education: High School, Glasgow, Scotland, U.K.; B.Sc.(Forestry), Edinburgh University; Wadham College, Oxford. Personal details: married to Christina Marianne Ljungberger of Stockholm, 2 sons, 1 daughter. Appointments: Assistant Conservator of Forests, Nigeria & Nyasaland (Malawi), 1944-55; Deputy Chief Conservator, later Chief Conservator, 1955-64; Permanent Secretary various ministries, 1964-69; Staff Member, World Bank, Washington, D.C., U.S.A., 1969—. Memberships: Traveller's; Royal Commonwealth Society; Fauna Preservation Society. Honours: C.B.E., 1964; C.M.G., 1969. Address: 7612, Edenwood Court, Bethesda, Maryland 20034, U.S.A.

DEZUARI, Ernest, born Tunis, Tunisia, 25th November 1932. Architect. Education: French Primary School, Tunis; Secondary Studies in Switzerland, 1949-58. Architectural achievements include: Civil Hospital, Kef, Tunisia; Primary Schools, Tunis, Borolo; Scientific Building, Boys' Secondary School & Technical School, Sousse; Technical College, Rodes; numerous other schools, hotels, industrial buildings, & institutions. Participated in many international competitions & prizes and honours include, 1st Prix de Roma (co-architect); 2nd Prize, Sousse Festival, 1959; Diploma, Advanced Technical School, State of Berne, Switzerland, 1956; government appointment as architect of civic buildings in Tunisia, 1959. Address: 18 rue Caton, Tunis, Tunisia.

DIA, Ibrahima Malick, born 28th August 1934. Doctor of Veterinary Sciences; Expert in Marine Biology & Oceanography. Education: Diploma, Faculty of Medicine, Paris, France; studied at the French Institute of Industrial Refrigeration; Diploma, Biological Oceanograpy, ORSTOM. Married, 2 children. Appointments: Director of Fisheries, Senegal, 1958; President of the FAO Committee for the East-central Atlantic; Counsellor Extraordinary to the Supreme Court, 1969. Memberships: Rotary Club. Publications: La Rôle du Poisson dans l'Alimentation et l'Economie Senegalaise, 1963. Address: 1 Rue Joris, Dakar, Senegal.

DIADHIOU, Pierrre Cledor, born 21st September 1929. Civil Servant; Tax Inspector. Appointments: Registration Receiver, 3rd Bureau, Dakar, Senegal; 1961-70; Inspector, Verifier, Brigade of Verification Research, Dakar, 1970—. Memberships: Treasurer-General, Amicale des Impots et des Domaines, Senegal. Honours: Knight, National Order of Senegal. Address: B.P. 258, Dakar, Senegal.

DIALLO, Mamadou Souleymane, born 21st May 1933. Veterinary Surgeon. Education: National Veterinary School, Alfort, France, Diploma, in Veterinary Surgery, Faculty of Medicine, Paris; Diploma I.E.M.V.T., Maisons-Alfort; Certificate in Higher Studies of Aviculture, National Institute of Husbandry, Paris. Appointments: Director, Research Centre Zootechniques of DAHRA, Senegal, 1960-67; Deputy Director, Animal Breeding & Husbandry, Senegal, 1967-68; Director, ibid, 1968—.

DIALLO, Youssoupha, born 9th January 1938. Aeronautical & Civil Engineer; Diplomatic Representative. Education: B.E.P.C., Dakar, Senegal, 1955; Baccalaureat in Mathematics, 1958; General Mathematics, 1959; Higher Mathematics; Diploma, National School of Civil Aviation, Paris, France, 1962; Married, 4 children. Appointments: Deputy Chief, Aerial Navigation, 1962-63; Deputy Director, Civil Aviation, 1963-64; Director, Senegal Civil Aviation & Merchant Marine, 1964-68; Senegal Representative, O.A.C.I. Council, Montreal, Canada, 1968—; President, Special Committee to combat the capture of illicit aeroplanes, 1969—. Memberships: Alpha Etha Rho. Publications: L'Infrastructure Aeronautique, 1962; L'Aviation Civile Senégalaise, 1966. Honours: Honorary Doctor, University of Aeronautical Technology, St. Louis, Missouri, U.S.A., 1970; Address: 1080 University Street, Suite 814, Montreal PQ, Canada.

DIAMANT, Ben Zion, born Jerusalem, Israel, 19th October 1925. Public Health Engineer. Education: Teachers' Training College, Jerusalem, 1939-43; College of Engineering, Haifa, 1945-50; School of Public Health, University of California, Berkeley, U.S.A., 1956-58. Married, 2 children. Appointments: Sr. Public Health Engineer, Ministry of Health, Israel, 1954-61; Public Health Engineer Adviser, World Health Organization, Nigeria, 1961-65; ibid, F.A.O. irrigation projects, Ghana, Uganda, Ceylon, 1966-67; ibid, W.H.O., Kenya, 1967—; Honorary Lecturer, Public Health Engineering, School of Medicine, Nairobi, 1967—. Memberships: American Public Health Association; Israeli Institute of Engineers & Architects; East-African Institute of Engineers; Israel Public Health Association. Author of numerous articles on environmental sanitation. Address: World Health Organization, P.O. Box 30016, Nairobi, Kenya.

DIAROUMEYE, Ali, born 1916. Veterinary; Economic & Technical Adviser. Married, 10 children. Appointments: Veterinary, F.O.M., 1939-57; Economist, Technical Adviser, Responsible for Trade Fairs, Ministry of Economic Affairs, 1963—. Honours: Knight, National Order of Niger. Address: Ministère des Affairs Economiques, B.P. 480, Niamey, Niger.

DICKSON (Hon. Mr. Justice) Arthur Richard Franklin, born 13th January 1913. Barrister-at-Law; High Court Judge. Education: Ruseas Secondary School, Jamaica, W.I.; Cornwall College; Lincoln's Inn, London, U.K. Married, 4 sons. Appointments: w. Colonial Legal Service, 1941-62 as: Magistrate, Turks & Caicos Islands; Asst. to Attorney General & Legal Draughtsman, Barbados; Stipendiary Magistrate, Guyana; Magistrate, Nigeria; Chief Magistrate; Chief Registrar, High Court of Lagos; Pusine Judge, High Court, Lagos, Retired 1962; Resident Magistrate, Zambia, Pusine Judge, High Court, Uganda. Memberships: Royal Commonwealth Society; Inst. of International & Comparative Law; Kampala Club. Publications: Revision of Ordinances (1908-1941), Turks & Caicos Islands. Address: High Court, Kampala, Uganda.

DICKSON, Kwamina Busumafi, born 16th July 1932. University Professor. Education: B.A., University College, Gold Coast, 1956; Ph.D., University College, London, U.K., 1960. Married. Lecturer in Geography, University of Ghana, 1960-65; Visiting Professor, Columbia University, U.S.A., summer, 1965; Sr. Lecturer, University of Ghana, 1965-70; Professor of Geography, ibid, 1970—. Memberships: President, Ghana Geographical Association; Fellow, Ghana Academy of Arts & Sciences; American Geographical Society. Author of numerous papers, including 20 major articles and 2 books on the geography of Ghana. Address: Dept. of Geography, University of Ghana, Legon, Ghana.

DIENG, Diakha, born 16th August 1933. Diplomat. Education: Baccalaureat, Faidherbe de St. Louis; LL.L., Dakar & Paris, 1955-59; Ecole des Impots, Paris, 1958-60. Appointments: Inspector of Taxes, France, 1960-61; Counsellor, then 1st Counsellor, Embassy of Senegal to Brussels, Belgium, 1961-63; 1st Counsellor, Embassy of Senegal to Paris, France, 1963-64; Secretary-General, U.A.M.C.E., ibid, O.C.A.M., 1964-68; Ambassador of Senegal to Cairo, U.A.R., 1968-70; Cabinet Director, Ministry of Foreign Affairs, Senegal, 1970-. Honours: Officer, National Order of Senegal; Commander, National Order of Madagascar; ibid, National Order of Niger; National Order of the Ivory Coast; Valiant Order of the Camerouns. Address: Ministère des Affaires Etrangères, Dakar, Senegal.

DILJORE, Mahmood, born 15th September 1930. Accountant. Education: Matriculation, 1950; A.C.C.A., 1967; passed Inst. of Taxation Exams., 1967. Married, 5 children. Appointments: Examiner of Accounts, Government Audit Department, 1950-68; Lecturer in Accountancy, University of Mauritius, 1968-69; Accountant, ibid, 1969—. Address: 7 Impasse Vinah Sawiny, Beau-Bassin, Mauritius.

DIOP, Babacar, born 4th August 1928. Veterinarian; Marine Biologist. Education: D.V.M., Maisons-Alfort, France, 1960; Doctor in Biological Oceanography, Marseille, 1961. Married, 5 children. Appointments: Deputy Director, Oceanography & Maritime Fisheries, 1962-66; President, Director-General, S.O.S.A.P., 1962—. Memberships: President, Inter-Governmental Committee of Fisheries, F.A.O., 1968-69; President, National Association Veterinaries in Senegal. Publications: La pêche Maritime au Senegal, 1963; Ses Pêcheries de l'ouest Africain, 1967. Address: S.O.S.A.P., 3 rue Joris, B.P. 289, Dakar, Senegal.

DIOP, Fadilou, born 14th May 1919. Advocate. Association of Juridic Studies & Research (A.S.E.R.J.); responsible for the popularization of Senegal Law. Memberships: Editorial Committee of 'Revue Sénégalaise de Droit'. Author of articles in 'Revue Sénégalaise de Droit', also of several conference papers. Address: 26 Rue Thiers, B.P. 1385, Dakar, Senegal.

DIOP, Sogobri Kara, born 13th November 1914. Businessman; Magistrate. Education: studies included Law, Finance, Commerce & Administration. Personal details: married with several children; wife: Director of Primary School in Niamey, Niger. Appointments: Clerk to the Court, Bailiff, Lawyer, Magistrate, Counsellor to the Court of Appeal. Memberships: Secretary, Société Anonyme la Nigerienne participation Niger 51% et Canada 49% siege Social Niamey. Honours: Medal, Ancien Combattant, 1939-45; Commander, National Order of Dahomey. Address: B.P. 2134, Niamey, Niger.

DIOUF, Mathurin Ibrahim, born September 1937. Engineer in Civil Aviation. Education: Catholic Primary School, Bouake, Ivory Coast, 1942-49; Technical School, Abidjan, 1949-55; School of Public Works, Bamako, Mali, 1955-58; studied in Paris, France, 1958-60; National School of Civil Aviation, Paris, 1960-62. Married, 7 children. Appointments: Commander of the Abidjan Airport, Ivory Coast, 1965—. Memberships: Vice-President, Abidjan Aeroclub.

DIOUF, Ousmane, born 7th September 1926. Technical Counsellor for Youth & Sport. Education: studied Law, Faculty of Law, Toulouse, France. Married, 5 children. Appointments: Head of the Service for Youth & Sport, Chad; Technical Counsellor to the Ministry of Work, Youth & Sport, Chad; Honorary Consul of Senegal to Chad. Memberships: International Basketball Referee; Technical Commission for the African Federation of Basketball; Archaeological Society of GERS; French Champion, U.S.F.E.N. of Basketball. Publications: Education Physique et Sports dans les Nouveaux Etats Africans; another book in preparation. Honours: Bronze Medal for Physical Education, 1955; Chad Independence Medal, 1959; Knight, Order of d'Artagnan, 1964; Knight, National Order of Chad. Address: B.P. 496, Fort-Lamy, Chad.

DIPOKO, Jasper E., born 18th May 1917. Accountant. Education: High School, Yaoundé, Cameroun. Studies in Accountancy. Married, 5, sons, 2 daughters. Appointments: Chief Accountant, Agricultural Centre; Deputy Head of Administration & Finance, Cameroun Broadcasting Service; Budgeting Administration, General Centre of Information; Head of Administration & Finance, Cameroun Broadcasting Service. Address: Radiodiffusion du Cameroun, B.P. 281, Yaoundé, Cameroun.

DITTRICH, Ronald Leslie, born 18th March 1933. Bank Manager. Education: B.A.(Hons.), University of Birmingham, U.K., 1954. Married, 2 children. Appointments: Manager, Barclays Bank of Nigeria Ltd., Kaduna South, Nigeria, 1969—. Memberships: Warwickshire County Cricket Club; Associate, Institute of Bankers with Diploma in Investment. Author of Local Government in Worcestershire in 13th Century. Honours: Baxter Prize in Local History, 1954. Address: Barclays Bank of Nigeria Ltd., P.M.B. 2112, Kaduna South, Nigeria.

DIXON, Henry Wickham, born 22nd January 1914. Chartered Mechanical Engineer. Education: Merchant Taylors' School, Crosby, U.K.; Technical School, Horwich, RMI. Appointments: Major & Lt.-Col., Royal Engineers; Sr. Official, Mechanical Department, Sudan Railways; General Manager, Director, Sudan Portland Cement Co. Ltd.; Managing Director, East African Portland Cement Co. Ltd. to date. Memberships: Fellow, Institute of Mechanical Engineers; Royal Automobile Club, London, U.K., Muthaiga Country Club, Nairobi, Kenya; Nairobi Club. Honours: M.B.E. Address: P.O. Box 101, Nairobi, Kenya.

DIXON, John Lindley, born Leeds, U.K., 12th March 1930. Estates Officer, Church of Uganda. Education: Primary Schools, Leeds, 1935-40; Leeds Grammar School, 1940-43; S.C. & H.S.C., Mill Hill School, London, 1943-47; B.A.(Maths.), M.A., Cambridge University, 1952, 1955. Appointments include: Sergeant, R.A.E.C., 1948-49; Computer, Lands & Surveys Department, Uganda, 1952-62; became Citizen of Uganda, 1963; Administrative Assistant, Church of Uganda, 1963-66; Estates Officer, ibid, 1966—. Memberships include: Committee, Uganda Society, 1964—; President, ibid, 1968; Committee & Chairman of Managing Committee, Uganda Students' Christian Hostels Association: Treasurer, Namirembe Music Festival Organization; Founder-Treasurer, Uganda Organists' Association; Uganda Music Society; Royal College of Organists; Kampala Amateur Theatrical Society; Organist, St. John's Church, Entebbe, 1954-62; Assistant Organist, Namirembe Cathedral, 1963—. Publications include: Papers on Tellurometer Computations, Empire Survey Review, 1959, Survey Review, 1964. Honours include: Uganda Independence Medal, 1963. Address: P.O. Box 14029, Mengo, Kampala, Uganda.

DIXON, Samuel R. Ebenezer, born 20th March 1921. Christian Minister. Education: B.S., University of Liberia; B.D., Gammon Theological Seminary, Interdenominational Theological Centre, Atlanta, Ga., U.S.A.; D.D., University of Liberia, 1969. Appointments: Self-employed, 1944-52; Clerk, then Office Personnel & Liaison Officer, Liberia Company, 1952-62; Ordained Deacon, Methodist Church, 1960; Ordained Elder, ibid, 1962. Memberships: Past Master, United Brothers of Friendship; Master Mason, St. Paul Lodge No. 2, Clay-Ashland; Atlanta Consistory A.A.S.R.; United Supreme Council, ibid; Freemasonry 33rd degree, Washington, D.C., U.S.A.; National President, Christian Ministers' Association of Liberia, Inc.; Executive Committee, Social Services Association of Liberia, Inc.; Rotary International, Monrovia, Liberia; Board of Directors, Family Planning Association, Liberia; YMCA; Order of Eastern Star; Board of Trustees, College of West Africa, Liberia. Honours: Knight Grand Commander, Humane Order of African Redemption, 1969. Address: First United Methodist Church, Ashmun Street, P.O. Box 1160, Monrovia, Liberia.

DJAIT, Michem, born 6th December 1935. University Professor. Education: Sadiki College, Tunis, 1940-54; Studies in Paris, High School & Sorbonne, France, 1954-62; History Graduate, Sorbonne, Paris, France, 1959; History Aggregate, 1962. Married, 2 children. Appointments: Professor, Faculty of Theology, Tunis, 1962-67; ibid, Faculty of Arts, Tunis, 1962-70; Lecturer, Sorbonne, Paris, France, 1970. Memberships: Fellow, Middle East Studies, Association of North America. Author of numerous articles in 'Al-Foke'; textbooks on Islamic studies & Tunisien history. Address: University of Tunis, Tunisia.

DLAMINI, Benjamin Ndzabankulu, born 12th June 1936. Teacher. Education: B.Sc., University of South Africa, 1962; Postgraduate Certificate of Education, University of Botswana, Lesotho, & Swaziland, 1965. Married to Gugu Treasure Shongwe, 1 son, 3 daughters. Appointments: Teacher, 1963-67; Headmaster, 1967-69; Under-Secretary (Training), 1970; Clerk to Parliament, 1970. Memberships: Secretary, Shiselweni District, Swaziland National Union of Teachers, 1963; General Secretary, ibid, 1966-68; President, 1968-70; Secretary, United Nations Associations of the Kingdom of Swaziland, 1069-70; Chairman, Baha'i Youth Committee, 1959-60; Assistant Secretary, Past Recording Secretary, National

Spiritual Assembly of the Baha'is of Swaziland, Lesotho, & Mozambique. Publications: Educational Planning in Swaziland 1966-76 (mimeographed dissertation), 1965; Possibilities & Impossibilities of Introducing Modern Mathematics in our Schools, U.B.L.S. Science Newsletter; Iron & Sulphur, Experiment U.B.L.S. Science Newsletter, 1967; Introduction of a Local School Certificate, U.B.L.S. Bulletin of Sec. Schools, 1968; Education for Self-reliance, U.B.L.S. Bulletin of Sec. Schools, 1969. Address: Dept. of Establishment & Training, P.O. Box 170, Mbabane, Swaziland.

DODIYI-MANUEL, Ikriko, born 1st August 1914. Surgeon, Medical Hypnotist & Physiologist. Education: Bishop Crowther Memorial School, Abonnema, Nigeria; Hope Waddell Institute, Calabar; Govt. College, Umuahia; Higher College, Yaba & School of Medicine, Nigeria; Charles University, Prague, Czechoslovakia; M.D., 1951; D.Tb.C., WHO, 1962. Personal details: son of Chief Tom West (Dodo) & Princess Doku Bob Manuel of Kalabari, Rivers State of Nigeria; married, 5 children. Appointments: Surgeon, University & State Hospital, Vinohrady, Prague, Czechoslovakia, 1952; Medical Officer, Ministry of Health, Eastern Nigeria, 1954-61; Senior Medical Officer, ibid, 1962-66, 1968-69; Physiologist, in charge of T.B. Control Service, Ministry of Health, Port Harcourt, 1967-68; Director (S.M.Q. i/c), General Hospital, Port Harcourt, R.S. of Nigeria, 1970. Address: Ministry of Health, General Hospital, Port Harcourt, Nigeria.

DODOO, Emmanuel Ofei, born 30th October 1929. Deputy University Registrar. Education: B.A.(Lond., History), University of the Gold Coast, 1953; LL.B.(Hons., Lond.), External Student, 1966. Married, 2 sons. Appointments: Assistant Inspector of Taxes, 1954-58; Inspector of Taxes, 1958-60; Senior Inspector of Taxes, 1960-61; Assistant Registrar, University of Ghana, Legon, 1961-62; Senior Assistant Registrar, ibid, 1962-69; Deputy Registrar, 1969–. Memberships: Ghana Historical Society; Ghana Hockey Federation; Ghana Cricket Association. Address: The Registry, University of Ghana, P.O. Box 25, Legon, Ghana.

DODU, Silas Rofino Amu, born 11th December 1924. Doctor of Medicine: University Professor. Education: Achimota School; University of Sheffield, U.K.; School of Tropical Medicine, London; Postgraduate Medical School, London. Married, 4 daughters. Appointments: Special Grade Medical Officer, Ghana, 1953-57; Physician Specialist, 1957-65; Professor of Medicine, 1965–. Memberships: Fellow, Royal College of Physicians, London; ibid, Ghana Academy of Arts & Sciences; President, Ghana Science Association, 1961-62; ibid, Ghana Medical Association, 1966-68. Publications: Editor, Ghana Medical Journal, 1960-66; also author of articles on diabetes & hypertension. Honours: Walter S. Kay Prize, University of Sheffield, U.K., 1950; Medal for Final M.B., Ch.B., University of Sheffield, 1951; Eisenhower Exchange Fellow for Ghana, 1957-58; Commonwealth Senior Fellowship, 1969; Overseas Fellow, Churchill College, Cambridge, 1971. Address: Department of Medicine, P.O. Box 4236, Accra, Ghana.

DOLLET, Robert A. A., born 21st April 1920. Engineer; Director. Education: Diploma, French National Professional School; Engineer, Higher National School of Arts & Trades: Marine Engineer, 1st Class. Married, 4 children. Appointments: Engineer, Works' Organizer, France–Senegal, 1947-54; Agency Chief, Ste. de Forages, SASIF, Ivory Coast, 1954-60; Director & Director-General, ibid, 1960-69; ibid, Ste. Senégalaise, SASIF, Senegal, 1969–. Memberships: Vice-President, Engineering Group 'Arts & Metiers', Ivory Coast; Rotary International; French Society of Civil Engineers. Honours: Lieutenant de Vaisseau Honoraire. Address: SASIF, B.P. 1811, Abidjan, Ivory Coast.

DONKOR; Fabian Kodjoe, born 26th February 1935. Administrator; Assistant Registrar. Education: Primary School Leaving Certificate, 1950; Cambridge School Certificate, 1954; Cambridge Higher School Certificate, 1956; B.A., London University, U.K., 1960; Postgraduate Certificate in Education, 1962; Certificat d'Etudes Françaises, Bordeaux, France, 1963. Married, 5 children. Appointments: Graduate Teacher, 1960-61, 1963-64, 1964-65; Senior French Master, Acting Assistant Headmaster, 1965-66; Assistant Headmaster, 1966-67; Junior Assistant Registrar, 1967-68; Assistant Registrar, 1968–; Examiner in French, West African Examinations Council. Memberships: Associate Mbr., Ghana Association of French Teachers; Lt., Officer Training Corps, Ghana Armed Forces–Cadet Corps. Author of essays on Psychology. Address: Registrar's Department, University College of Cape Coast, Ghana.

DONKOR, Samuel Appah, born 2nd September 1930. Bank Manager. Education: Accra Academy, 1946-50; Achimota Training College, 1951; Kumasi College of Technology, 1952; Government Secondary Technical School, 1956-58; B.Sc.(Econ.), London School of Economics & Political Science, London, U.K., 1963; Associate of the Institute of Bankers, 1969. Appointments: Manager, Barclays Bank, D.C.O., Dunkwa, 1967-70; Manager, Kejetia Kumasi Branch, 1970–. Member of the Board of Governors, Dunkwa Secondary School, 1970–. Address: Barclays Bank, D.C.O., Kejetia Branch, P.O. Box 874, Kumasi, Ghana.

DONTOH, Robert Johnson Ghartey, born 19th October 1929. Army Officer (Retired) & Accountancy Student. Education: Articled Accountancy Clerk, Messrs. G. B. Olivant Ltd., 1949-52; Regular Officers' Special Training School, Military Academy, Teshie, Accra, Ghana, 1957; Officers' Training School, Eaton Hall, Chester, U.K.; D.S.C., Defence Services Staff College, Wellington, India; currently studying Cost Accountancy, Leeds College of Commerce, Leeds, U.K. Personal details: married, 3 sons, 1 daughter. Appointments: with Royal Scots Fusiliers, nr. Folkestone, U.K.; Lieut., 2nd Battalion of Infantry, Ghana, 1958; Captain, ibid, 1959; served in the Congo, 1960; Seconded, Liaison Officer, United Nations Peace-keeping Force in the Congo; A.D.C. to the Forces Commander, U.N. Forces in the Congo, 1960; with Ghana Recce Squadron, Ghana, 1961; with British Tank Regiment, North Africa;

Qualified as Squadron Leader, Course in Armoured Warfare, Armoured Corps Training Centre, Bovington, Dorset, U.K.; Major, with command of Recce Squadron, 1961-62; Commanding Officer, Recce Regiment, 1963; Junior Staff College, Defence College, Teshie, Accra, 1964; Promoted Lieut.-Colonel, 1966; Chairman, Central Region Committee of Administration, N.C.L. Government; Staff Officer, Grade 1, Army H.Q.; Retired, 1969. Honours include: Grand Medal, for courage during 1966 Coup, 1968. Publications: Contributor to General Ocran's 'The Myth is Broken' (Ghana Coup), 1966. Address: Leeds College of Commerce, 43 Woodhouse Lane, Leeds 2, U.K.

DOSSEH, Benjamin, born 14th August 1915. Retired Director of Posts, Telephones, & Telecommunications (P.T.T.). Education: Primary Studies Certificate, 1931; Federal School of the National Marine, 1931-36; Baccalaureat, Federal School of Posts, Telephones, & Telecommunications, 1937-38; Lic. Law., Institute of Political & Economic Higher Studies. Appointments: Deputy Director, P.T.T., Dahomey, 1952-58; ibid, Togo, 1958-61; Cabinet Director, Ministry of Public Works, 1963; Technical Counsellor, ibid, 1964-67. Memberships: President, Association of Former Combattants of Togo; Vice-President, Togolese Red Cross. Honours: Croix de Guerre, 1939-45; Officer, Black Star; Medal of Honour of the P.T.T. of the F.O.M.; C.V.R. Medal; European Fighting Cross; Knight, French National Order of Merit. Address: P.O. Box 838, Lomé, Togo.

DOSSOU, Setondji Félix, born Porto-Novo, Dahomey, 4th August 1939. Occupational Psychologist. Education: Licencié de Psychologie; Diplomate, Industrial Psychology Division, Institute of Psychology of Paris; Doctorat de 3rd cycle en cours (2nd year). Married, 4 children. Appointments include: Research Assistant, African Centre for Applied Human Sciences (C.A.S.H.A.), Aix-en-Provence, France, 1962-66; Director of Studies, Expert, Ministry of Planning for the Ivory Coast, Department of Productivity, 1966-68; Research Assistant, Expert, National Office of Professional Training, 1968—. Memberships include: African Centre for Applied Human Sciences; Engineer, Ste. André Vidal et Associés IA.U.A.); African & French Psychology Societies. Publications include: Les cadres supérieures de l'entreprise en Côte d'Ivoire, 1965; La maitrise industrielle, 1968; Eléments pour pour une Africanisation de l'emplois et de l'economie, 1968. Address: c/o André Vidal et Associés, 15 rue Henri-Heine, Paris 16e, France, Box 8475, Abidjan, Ivory Coast.

DOVI-AKUE, Paul Adote, born 16th June 1916. Civil Servant. Education: Higher Studies in Commerce & Economy. Appointments: Commercial Agent responsible for Ets. R. Eychenne-Unicomer, North Togo, Dahomey, 1945-53; Director of Import-Export Society, 1954-58; Director, Economic Affairs, Togo Government, 1959-64; Representative of Togo Government, Washington, U.S.A., 1960-61; Director-General, Agricultural Products Office, Togo, 1965; Commercial Technical Counsellor, ibid, 1966-69; Technical Counsellor, Ministry of Commerce, Industry & Tourism, 1970—. Memberships: National Monetary Committee of Togo; Vice-President, Golf Club; Tennis Club; Vice-President, Riding Club. Honours: Officer, Order of Mono (National Togo Order), 1964; Das Grosse Verdienstkreuz; Mit Stern Der Verdienstordens Bundes Republik Deutschland, 1961. Address: B.P. 396, Lomé, Togo.

DOVLO, Moses, born at Keta, Volta Region, Ghana, 15th November 1934. Civil Servant; Public Relations Officer. Education: Ewe Presbyterian Junior School, Agata, Volta Region, 1940-44; Cambridge University Overseas School Certificate, Ewe Presbyterian Senior School, Keta, 1945-48; G.C.E.(London), Presbyterian Secondary School, Odumase-Krobe, Eastern Region, 1949-52; Certificate in Business Administration, Collegé des Sciences Sociales et Economiques, Paris, France, 1966-67. Married. Appointments: Teacher, Odorgonne Secondary School, Adabraka, Accra, Ghana, 1953-57; News Reporter, Ghana Broadcasting System, Ministry of Information, 1958-60; Assistant Editor, ibid, 1960-63; Journalist, Research Writer, Research & Publications Division, Ministry of Information, 1963-65; Public Relations Officer, Capital Investments Board, Government of Ghana, 1965-69; 1st Public Relations Officer, now Head of the Department, Ghana Commercial Bank, 1968. Address: Ghana Commercial Bank, Head Officer, P.O. Box 134, Accra, Ghana.

DOYLE (Sister) Mary, born 3rd August 1912. Doctor of Medicine. Education: M.D., 1937 & Postgraduate Education, Ireland. Personal details: joined Medical Missionary Congregation in Ireland, 1954. Appointments: Resident Physician, various positions, Ireland; General Practitioner, U.K., 1940-45; ibid, Ireland, 1947-54; Head, Mission Hospital, Uganda, 1957-67; Secretary, Uganda Catholic Medical Bureau, 1967—. Memberships: British Medical Association; Irish Medical Association; Uganda Medical Association & Council. Address: Uganda Catholic Medical Bureau, P.O. Box 2886, Kampala, Uganda.

DRANI, Chas Origa Okuni Futo, born 16th February 1928. Customs & Excise Officer. Education: Seminary Education, 1939-46; Teacher Training, 1947-50; Cambridge University Overseas Examination (private candidate), 1953; passed Laws of Uganda Exam. & other exams. in Administration & Man Management. Personal details: descendant of Clan Chieftainship, Palanywa, East Madi, Uganda. Appointments: Teacher, 1950-53; Sub-Inspector, Uganda Police Force, 1954, rising to rank of Senior Superintendent of Police; Chief Investigation Officer, Custom & Excise Department, East African Community, 1967. Member, Middle Temple Inn of Court, studying Law as a hobby. Address: P.O. Box 9945, Mombasa, Kenya.

DREW, George Reuben Hughes, born 2nd August 1916. Doctor of Medicine. Education: B.A., Manchester University, U.K., 1938; M.B., Ch.B., Edinburgh University, 1943. Appointments: Medical Officer, Nigeria, 1944-53; Senior

Medical Officer, 1953-58; Chief Health Officer, Western Nigeria, 1958-60. Memberships: The Organ Club, London; Nigerian Medical Association. Honours: O.B.E., 1965. Address: Private Mail Bag, 5026, Ibadan, Nigeria.

DREW, John Desmond Currey, born Derby, U.K., 19th April 1933. Archivist. Education: Sedbergh School, Yorkshire, 1946-51; The Queen's College, Oxford, 1954-58; B.A.(Oxon.), 1958; M.A.(Oxon), 1962. Appointments: Research Officer, National Archives of Rhodesia & Nyasaland, 1958-62; Records Management Officer of National Archives of Rhodesia & Nyasaland, 1962-63; Director, National Archives of Malawi, 1963—. Memberships: Secretary-General, East & Central African Branch, International Council on Archives, 1969—; Malawi Government Representative for Inter-Governmental Committee on Federal Records, 1964—. Publications: Malawi National Bibliography (annually from 1967); various articles of a professional & historical nature in sundry African journals, 1963—. Address: National Archives of Malawi, P.O. Box 62, Zomba, Malawi.

DRNOVSEK, Janko, born Trbovlje, Yugoslavia, 8th January 1923. Engineer; Professor. Education: Dip.Eng., Ljubljana, Yugoslavia; Dr. of Tech. Sciences, Karlsruhe. Appointments: Consulting Engineer, Ljubljana; Associate Research Professor, Ljubljana; UNESCO Expert on Soil Mechanics & Foundation Engineering, University of Nairobi, Kenya. Memberships: International Society on Soil Mechanics & Foundation Engineering; Institute of Yugoslav Engineers; East African Institution of Engineers. Publications: 'Rupture Line in a Two-Layer Non-Cohesive Medium'; Soils & Foundation, The Japanese Society of Soil Mechanics & Foundation Engineering, 1970. Address: University of Nairobi, P.O. Box 30197, Nairobi, Kenya.

DUGGAN, Raymond Trevor, born 18th December 1940. Personnel officer. Education: Matriculated, South Africa; Studying for B.Comm. Degree, University of South Africa. Appointments: Instructor, South African Police, 1961-62; Mill Personnel Officer, Ubombo Ranches Ltd., 1962-64; Assistant to Labour Controller, Ubombo Ranches Ltd., 1964-66; Welfare Manager, ibid, 1966-67; Assistant Personnel Manager, 1967-68; Assistant Labour Controller in charge of Security, 1968—. Memberships: include: Chairman, Swaziland Rugby Sub-Union, 1965-67; Associate, South African Institute of Personnel Management; Committee Member, Ubombo Ranches Rugby Club, 1963-66; Rifle Club, ibid, 1966-68, 1970; Committee Member, Swaziland Rifle Assn., 1966-68, 1970. Address: c/o Ubombo Ranches Ltd., Big Bend, Swaziland.

DUNCAN, Josbert Thomas Kofi, born Lagos, Nigeria, 2nd October 1931. Medical Practitioner; Radiotherapist. Education: Holy Cross School; Lagos Government School; King's College, Lagos; University College, Ibadan, 1951-55; St. Mary's Hospital Medical School, London, U.K., 1958; Darwin College, Cambridge, 1965-68; M.B.B.S., 1959; L.R.C.P., M.R.C.S., 1958; D.M.R.T., R.C.S., 1963; F.F.R.,R.C.S., 1967. Married, 4 daughters. Appointments: House appointments, Amersham General Hospital, Bucks., U.K., 1958-60; Senior House Officer, General Hospital, Lagos, Nigeria, 1960-61; Senior House Officer, Registrar & Surgical Registrar, Addenbrooke's Hospital, Cambridge, U.K., 1961-65; Surgical Registrar, Lagos University Teaching Hospital, Nigeria, 1965-66; Assistant Radiotherapist, St. Thomas' Hospital, London, U.K., 1966-67; Lecturer in Radiotherapy, College of Medicine, University of Lagos, Nigeria, 1968—; WHO Consultant in Radiology. Memberships: Treasurer, Nigerian Cancer Society; British Institute of Radiology; Ikoyi Golf Club, Lagos. Publications: The Scope of Radiology in Nigeria—A Preliminary Assessment (W.A.Med.J.), 1960; Cancer Problems in Lagos (W.A.Med.J.), 1968. Honours: Commonwealth Scholar, Cambridge, 1966. Address: College of Medicine, P.M.B. 12003, Lagos, Nigeria.

DUNN, Vernard Joseph, born 11th January 1936. Motor Mechanic; Poultry Farmer. Education: Matriculation. Personal details: ancestors were Sugar Growers in Mangete of Mtunzini District of Zululand. Married to Sybil Susan Dryding of Cape Town, South Africa, 3 sons, 1 daughter. Appointments: Foreman, Poultry Farm, Cape Town; Tory Kiln Operator, Smoked Haddock Dept., Irun & Johnson; Manager, Sugar Cane Plantation, Zululand; Fleet Maintenance, Pineapple Plantation in Swaziland; General Farm Manager, Swaziland; Motor Mechanic, various garages in Swaziland; Self-employed Poultry Farmer, Swaziland. Address: P.O. Box 295, Manzini, Swaziland.

DURAND-REVILLE, Luc, born 12th April 1904. Economist. Education: School of Higher Commericial Studies; Faculty of Law & Economic Science, Paris, France. Appointments: with the Society for Economic Development of the Eastern Countries 1924; National City Bank of New York, France, 1929; President, Societe du Haut Ogooue, 1935; Ibid, Ets. Ch. Peryrissac, 1955; Ets. Gonfreville, 1942; Vice-President, Cie. Optang, 1950, Senator, 1946-58. Memberships include: Honorary President, Academy of Sciences Overseas; ibid, Academy of Commercial Sciences; President, French Association of Friends of Albert Schweitzer; Publications: L'Empire de la Civilisation; Linéaments d'une politique de coopération au developpement; La Formation de l'Epargne en Afrique; L'Investissement privé au Service du Tiers-Monde; also author of numerous articles on the problems of economic development in Africa. Honours: Knight, Legion of Honour; Commander, National Order of Merit; K.B.E. Address: 5 rue Bellini 92 Puteaux, France.

DUTHIE, Alan Stewart, born 19th May 1938. University Lecturer. Education: High School of Dundee, 1943-56; M.A., University of St. Andrews, 1956-60; Diploma General Linguistics, University of Edinburgh, 1960-62; Ph.D., University of Manchester, 1964; B.D.(External), London, 1969. Appointments: Lecturer, Department of Linguistics, University of Ghana, 1964—. Memberships: Linguistic Association of Great Britain; West African

Linguistic Society; Linguistic Circle of Accra; Tyndale Fellowship for Biblical Research. Author of articles on Theology. Address: Department of Linguistics, P.O. Box 61, Legon, Ghana.

DUTTA, Chitta Ranjan, born 1st September 1929. University Professor. Education: Matriculation, Dasani, India, 1945; B,Sc., Bagerat P.C. College, 1947; L.M.F., Calcutta Medical School, 1951; M.B.B.S., ibid, 1953; M.Sc.(Med.) in Anatomy, Queen's University, Kingston, Ontario, Canada, 1960. Appointments: Demonstrator of Anatomy, Calcutta National Medical College, India, 1954-58; Teaching Fellow, Queen's University, Canada, 1959-60; National Research Fellow of Canada, Queen's University, 1960-61; Assistant Professor of Anatomy, Marquette University, U.S.A., 1961-62; Associate Professor, ibid, 1962-64; Associate Professor, Calcutta National Medical College, India, 1964-65; Acting Head, Associate Professor, Ghana Medical School, 1965-70. Memberships: Indian Medical Association; Ghana Medical Association. Author of several works in his field. Honours: Silver & Gold Medals for highest marks in examinations, 1951; Address: Ghana Medical School, Box 4236, Accra, Ghana.

DUVAL (His Eminence) Lèon Etienne, born Chênex, Haute Savoie, France, 9th November 1903. Roman Catholic Archbishop. Education: Junior Seminary, La Roche-sur-Foron, Haute Savoie, France; Senior Seminary, Annecy, 1921-26; Gregorian University, Rome, Italy, 1926-28. Ordained Priest, Rome, 1918; ordained Bishop of Constantine & l'Hippone, 1947; transferred to Archdiocese of Algiers, 1954; created Cardinal, 1969. Appointments include: Curate, St. Gervais-les-Bains, 1928-29; Professor, Grand Séminaire d'Annecy, 1930-42; Vicar-General, Annecy, 1942-46; Bishop of Constantine, 1946-54; Archbishop of Algiers, 1954—; Cardinal of St. Balbine, 1969—. Publications include: Paroles de Paix, 1955; Messages de Paix, 1961; Laïcs, Prêtres, religieux dans l'Eglise, 1967. Honours include: Officer of Legion of Honour, 1963. Address: Avenue Ali Ourak, Bologhine, Alger, Algeria.

DYSON, William Garth, born 6th October 1926. Forestry Research Officer. Education: Manchester Grammar School, U.K., 1940-44; B.A., St. John's College, Oxford, 1948; M.A., ibid, 1951; Ph.D., University of East Africa, Nairobi, Kenya, 1969. Married, 3 children. Appointments: Assistant Conservator of Forests, Kenya Forest Department, 1948-60; Research Officer, Silviculturist, Kenya Forest Department, 1960-63; Principal Scientific Officer, Tree Breeder, East African Agriculture & Forestry Research Organization, 1963—. Memberships: Commonwealth Forestry Association; Society of British Foresters; East African Natural History Society; Nairobi Scientific & Philosophical Society; Kenya Fly Fishers' Club. Author of several articles in forestry & other scientific journals. Honours: Colonial Forestry Scholarship, 1947. Address: East African Agriculture & Forestry Research Organization, P.O. Box 30148, Nairobi, Kenya.

DYVORNE, Denise. Journalist. Received an education in the arts, Paris, France. One son. Appointments: Editor, 'La Vigil Marocaine' 1951—; writes chiefly on art subjects, social & women's problems. Officially recognized as a Journalist & Publicist by the Casablanca Tribunal Address: 6 Rue de Blida, Casablanca, Morocco.

DZOBO (Reverend) Noah Komla, born 12th January 1926. University Lecturer; Minister of Religion. Education: Presbyterian Training College, Akropong Akwapim, Ghana, 1945-48; B.D., Lancaster Theological Seminary, Pa., U.S.A.; M.A., University of Wisconsin, 1969; Ph.D., University of Edinburgh, U.K. Personal details: married, 3 children; wife is Senior Tutor in College of Education. Appointments: Teacher, Chaplain Presbyterian Training College, Akropong, Ghana, 1962-65; Principal, Anfoega Training College, 1965-66; Lecturer, University College, Cape Coast, 1966-69; Lecturer, Institute of Education, University of Keele, Staffs., U.K., 1969-70. Memberships: President, S.C.M., Ghana, 1966—; ibid, Ghana Association of Religious Knowledge Teachers, 1969-70. Author of several articles on Educational Theology in the 'Ghana Journal of Education' & 'The Ghana Bulletin of Theology'.

E

EBRAHIM, Gulamabbas J., born 2nd April 1932. Senior Lecturer in Paediatrics; Consultant Physician. Education: Tanga, Tanzania & Dar es Salaam; Undergraduate Medical Education, University of Poona, India; Postgraduate Medical Education, Edinburgh & London, U.K. Appointments: Special Grade Medical Officer, Ministry of Health, Tanzania, 1961-63; Consultant Paediatrician & Director of Paediatric Studies, Dar es Salaam School of Medicine, 1964-68; Senior Lecturer & Acting Head, Dept. of Paediatrics, Faculty of Medicine, University College of Dar es Salaam, University of E.A., 1968-70. Memberships: Secretary, Association of Physicians of East Africa, 1968; East African Academy. Publications: Practical Maternal & Child Health Problems in Tropical Africa, 1968; The Newborn in Tropical Africa, 1970; Child Care for the Tropical Mother; 20 scientific papers on various aspects of tropical child health. Address: Institute of Child Health, 30 Guilford Street, London, W.C.1, U.K.

EBRAHIM, Murtaza Jaffer, born Zanzibar, 29th May 1941. Mechanical Engineer. Education: University College, Nairobi, Kenya; University of East Africa. Personal details: ancestors from India. Married. Appointments: Industrial Engineer, Industrial Studies & Development Centre (U.N. sponsored project), Ministry of Commerce & Industries, 1966—. Attended 23rd International Course on Management for Small-scale Industries, Research Institute for Management Science (RVB), Delft, Netherlands. Memberships: Graduate Member of Institute of Mechanical Engineers, U.K.; Small Industry Club, Delft, Netherlands. Address: c/o IND Centre, P.O. Box 2650, Dar es Salaam, Tanzania.

ECOOKIT, Stephen John, born Aketta, Teso, Uganda, 11th May 1940. Physician. Education: Ngora High School; First-class School Certificate, Teso College, Aloet; King's College,

Budo; M.B., Ch.B. (Credits in Surgery & Public Health), Faculty of Medicine, Makerere College, 1967; currently studying for M.Med.Surg., University of East Africa. Appointments: various positions as Senior House Officer. Memberships: Uganda Medical Society; Medical Defence Union; Lay-Lecturer's Certificate, St. John Ambulance Brigade. Address: P.O. Box 7051, Kampala, Uganda.

EDINGTON, George M., born 18th April 1916. Pathologist. Education: High School of Glasgow, Scotland, 1927-35; M.D., University of Glasgow, 1935-39. Married. Appointments: R.A.M.C., 1941-46; Specialist Pathologist in charge of Medical Research, Institute & Laboratory Services, Ghana, 1957; Consultant Pathologist, Liverpool, U.K., 1958; Professor & Head of Dept. of Pathology, University of Ibadan, Nigeria, 1958—; Dpty. Vice-Chancellor, ibid, 1968—. Memberships: F.R.C.P.; Chmn., Comm. on Geographical Pathol., International Union Against Cancer; Council, International Soc. of Geographical Pathol.; Expert Adviser, W.H.O. Panel on Cancer. Publications: Pathology in the Tropics (co-author), 1969; Numerous publs. on tropical haematology & pathology. Honours: Life Member, British Red Cross Society, 1957; M.B.E., 1958; C.B.E., 1969. Address: Dept. of Pathology, University of Ibadan, Ibadan, Nigeria.

EDO, Antoine, born 30th June 1940. Ministerial Appointments. Education: Secondary School, Commercial Technical Lycée for Boys, Yaoundé, Cameroun; National Academy of Arts & Crafts, Technical, Economical, & Financial Institute, Paris, France; Higher Certificate in Commercial Studies; Diploma in Technical Finance. Married, 3 children. Appointments: Head of the Product & Exportation Service, Ministry of Commerce & Industry, Yaoundé, Cameroun. Address: B.P. 1180, Yaoundé, Cameroun.

EDOBOR, Enomhamidobo Vincent, born Ogwa-Ishan, Nigeria, 22nd November 1934. Teacher. Education: Std. VI Cert., 1954; Teachers' Cert. Grade III, 1957; Teachers' Cert. Grade II, 1961; Diploma of Journalism & TV, School of Journalism & TV, Berks, U.K., 1968; G.C.E., 1967. Married, 3 sons, 2 daughters. Appointments include: Probationary Teacher, 1955; Secretary, Ogwa Youths' Association, 1962; Master, Catholic Modern School, Ebelle, 1962; Headmaster, 1964; currently, St. John's Catholic School, 1964; Secretary, Ogwa Community Development Committee, 1968. Memberships include: Vice-Chairman, Lawn Tennis Club; Secretary, Ogwa Community Development Committee; Secretary, .Ogwa •Youths' Association; Table Tennis Club; Vice-Chairman, Primary School Sports Council; Committee Member, Ishan East Co-operative Societies Union; Member, Ishan Branch Delegation, Midwest Co-operation Federated Union, Benin, 1969. Address: c/o St. John's Catholic School, Ogwa-Ishan, via Ubiaja, Midwestern State, Nigeria.

EDOO, Ben Bonsu, born 30th October 1928. Physician; Neurologist; Electroencephalographer. Education: Achimota School, Ghana, 1944-47; B.Sc.(Lond.), B.A., University College of the Gold Coast, 1948-52; M.B., B. Chir., University of Cambridge, U.K., 1952-55; West London Hospital Medical School, 1956-59; University of Oslo, Norway, 1967-68; M.R.C.P.(Edin.); D.T.M.&H.(Liverpool). Married, 4 children. Appointments: Registrar in Psychiatry & Electroencephalography, St. Francis Hospital, Haywards Heath, Sussex, 1964-65; Lecturer in Medicine, University of Ghana Medical School, 1966—. Member, British E.E.G. Society. Contributor to professional publications. Honours: All Schools ¼-mile Champion, 1948; Ghana National ¼-mile Champion, 1951, 1952; Swinford-Edwards Prize in Surgery, West London Hospital Medical School, 1959. Address: Department of Medicine, University of Ghana Medical School, Korle-Bu, Accra, Ghana.

EDOO, Hossenjee, born 26th July 1934. Teacher & Journalist. Education: St. Joseph's College; Graduated in English(Hons.), Scottish Church College; M.A.(Enlish), Calcutta University, India; Studied for LL.B., ibid; Certificate in Social Science, Berlin. Married, 2 daughters. Appointments: Founder & Editor, of M. Blitz, 1966-70; Executive Member, Muslim Committee of Action; Secretary, Mauritius Islamic Centre, 1970; Principal, St. Francois Xavier College, P. Louis, 1970; Political Adviser, Mauritius Federation of Trade Unions, 1966-70. Member of I.O.J., Prague, Czechoslovakia. Publications: Apsara (Impressions on India); Subhas (a social & political novel on Indian labourers); A Study in Socialism. Address: Principal Street, Francois Xavier College, Port Louis, Mauritius.

EDUKUGHO (Chief) Reece Degbeyin, born Warri, Nigeria, 21st February 1915. Merchant. Education: Warri Government School, Nigeria, 1923-30; King's College, Lagos, Nigeria, 1930-34. Personal details: third son of Chief Degbeyin Edukugho, Timber Merchant of Koko Fame Warri Division, 1900-27, & Princess Alero Egbe of Ugbuwangue, Warri great-granddaughter of Akengbuwa I, the Olu of Warri; father of 1st Mid-West Lady Barrister, Mrs. Grace B. Ogbemi, called to the Bar, Middle Temple, London, U.K., September, 1958. Appointments include: Hon. Member & Deputy Speaker, Western House of Assembly, Western Region, 1956-60; Member, Nigeria Constitutional Conference Delegation to London, 1957, 1958; Chairman, Mid-West State Licence Buying Agents' Association; Chairman Warri Area Planning Authority; Chairman, Warri Urban District Council Management Committee, 1961-62; Managing Director, R.D.E. Limited (Ofile Saw-Mill), Warri & Peju Guest House, Warri. Memberships: Mid-West State Bendel Development & Planning Authority; Mid-West State Produce Inspection Board; Warri Club. Address: 28 Cemetery Road, P.O. Box 329, Warri, Mid-Western State, Nigeria.

EFALE EDANG, Solomon, born 1922. Civil Administrator. Education: Diploma, High School, Yaoundé, Cameroun. Married, 12 children. Prefect, Haut-Nyong, Cameroun; Director, Public Accounts Service, Cameroun Oriental; Central Director of Pay & Pensions to the Ministry of Finance; Director, Ministry of Cadastre, Cameroun Oriental; Civil Administrator, S.C.F., Cameroun. Memberships: Union Nationale Camerounaise (UNC). Honours: Knight, Black Star of Benin; Knight, Order of Valour; Cameroun distinctions, 3rd, 2nd, & 1st Class. Address: B.P. 794, Yaoundé, Cameroun.

EFOBI, Christopher Ugwuchukwu, born 1st July 1925. Pharmacist; Company Director. Education: Dennis Memorial Grammar School, Onitsha; Cambridge School Xertificate, Grade I; B.Sc.(Hons., Pharmacy), University of Iowa, Iowa City, U.S.A.; Ph.C., Technical College, Dundee, Scotland, U.K. Married, 4 children. Appointments: Officer, Customs & Excise, Lagos, Nigeria; Field Secretary, African Academy of Arts & Research, Nigeria; Manager, Kingsway Chemists of Nigeria Ltd.; Director, ibid. Memberships: Pharmaceutical Societies of U.K. & Iowa, U.S.A.; Secretary, Onitsha Council of Social Services; Chairman, Onitsha District Amateur Football Assn. Address: Kingsway Chemists of Nigeria Ltd., P.O. Box 559, Lagos, Nigeria.

EFURHIEVWE, Samuel Oghenekohwo, born Ekrejeta Abraka, Nigeria, 19th April 1933. Educator. Education: C.M.S. School, Abraka, 1947-53; Provincial Grade III Teachers' Training College, Warri, 1956-57; Benin Delta Grade II Teachers' Training College, Benin City, 1962-63. Personal details: son of Chief Efurhievwe Ofowinor. Married, 2 daughters. Headmaster of the following schools: Western Urhobo District Schools, 1958; Egborode-Okpe, 1959-60; Urhuorie-Abraka, 1961; Ikwewu-Amukpe, Sapele, 1964-66; Ijomi-Oghasa, Sapele, 1967—. Memberships include: Patron, Ekrejeta Youth Club, Abraka; General Secretary, Ekrejeta Welfare Association: Ekrejeta Conference, Abraka, 1961—. Address: Local Authority School, Ijomi, P.O. Box 10, Oghara P.A., via Sapele, Nigeria.

EGBOH, Adu Andrew, born 30th November 1924. Pharmacist. Education: St. Gregory's College, Lagos, Nigeria; Christ the King College, Onitsha; Diploma in Pharmacy, School of Pharmacy, Yaba, 1948. Personal details: from the Royal Family. Ekpoma, Benin Province; married, 7 children. Appointments: Hospital Pharmacist, 1948-63; Pharmaceutical Registrar/Secretary to the Pharmacists Board of Nigeria, 1963—; Commissioner for African International Pharmaceutical Federation, 1960-64; Editor-in-Chief, Pharmaceutical Journal of Nigeria, 1960-64; Editor, Pharmakon, 1956-57; Editorial Panel, West African Pharmacists; Secretary, Quality Control & Advertisement Committees, Federal Government. Memberships: President, General Nigerian Union of Pharmacists; Council, Pharmaceutical Society of Nigeria; Council, Society of Health, Nigeria; formerly Round Table, Lagos Branch; Cheshire Home, Lagos. Publications: Quality Control in Pharmaceutical Preparations, 1966; Pharmacy in Nigeria, Past & Present, 1966; Drugs Used During Pregnancy, 1967; Hospital Pharmacy in Nigeria, 1970. Honours: 1st Nigerian to receive WHO Fellowship, courses on hosp. pharmacy admin. & quality control, 1966. Address: Private Box 456, Lagos, Nigeria.

EGBUEZE, Nwolisa Chuka Laurence, born 2nd November 1924. Trade Unionist; Industrialist. Education: General Certificate of Education; Local Diplomas in Trade Unionism, Industrial Relations & Salesmanship. Personal details: grandson of Chief Obi Egbueze; married, 2 sons, 2 daughters. Appointments: Teacher, 1941-42; Locomotive Engineer, 1942-56; Petroleum Marketing Executive, 1957-67; Industrialist & Business Director, 1968—; Director, Jibros Estate Agents, Nigeria; Northern Nigeria Regional Secretary, Association of Locomotive Drivers & Allied Workers, Nigerian Government Railway, 1950-56; President, Council of Labour, Zaria, Nigeria, 1955-56. Memberships include: Secretary, Zikist (Pre-independence Natìonalist) Movement, Kanfanchan, Nigeria, 1947-50; Financial Secretary, National Council of Nigerian Citizens (political union), Lagos, 1963-64; President, Ibusa Cultural Union, Ebute-Metta, 1961-62; President, Ibusa Youth Assn., Ibusa Club, 1961-65; President, Onyenwe Cultural Dance Society, 1961-70. Honours: International Lawn Tennis Championship Trophy, British Petroleum, West Africa, Ltd., Accra, Ghana, 1963. Address: P.O. Box 1935, Lagos, Nigeria.

EGDELL, Henry George, born 14th May 1932. Psychiatrist. Education: M.B., Ch.B., University of Leeds, U.K., 1956; D.P.M., University of Newcastle upon Tyne, 1965. Appointments: Medical Officer, Uganda Army, 1957-60 & Uganda Government, 1960-62; Psychiatric Registrar, St. Luke's Hosp., Middlesbrough, U.K., 1962-65; Sr. Registrar Psychiatrist, Royal Victoria Infirmary, Newcastle upon Tyne, 1965-68; Lecturer & Sr. Registrar, Makerere University Coll., Uganda, 1968-70. Memberships: Royal Coll. of Physicians; Royal Medico, Psychol. Assn.; Soc. of Clinical Psychiatrists. Publications: The Medical Assistant & Psychiatric Care; Development of Child Psychiatric Services in Uganda; Up-Country Psychiatric Services in Psychopathologie Africaine. Address: Dept. of Psychological Medicine, Royal Victoria Infirmary, Newcastle upon Tyne, U.K.

EKAME-BULU, Victor-Marcel-Paul, born Mbonjo II, Cameroun, 9th July 1909. Teacher. Education: Primary School, Dibombari; C.E.P.E., Douala, 1927; Diploma de Moniteur Indigene, Foulassi (Sangmelima), 1930; Appointments: Instruction Monitor, French Protestant Mission, Ntolo, then Douala, 1930-32; ibid, Official School, Loum, 1933-35; Commercial Clerk, F.A.O., Douala, 1937-47; Founder-Secretary-General, Employers' Union, Wouri, 1944-47; Founder-Director-Manager, Société Commissionnaire Africaine (SOCOMA), 1948-58; Head of the Emplcyment Agency, Main D'Oeuvre, Douala, 1958-59; Bursar, Teaching School, N. Kongsamba, 1960-62; ibid, Regional Centre of Physical Education & Sport, Dschang, 1963-64; Coastal Representative, Eastern Cameroun National Assembly (ALCAMOR), 1965-70. Memberships: President, Social & Cultural Studies Section, Cameroun Economic & Social Council, 1961-65; Secretary, Sub-Section, U.C., Dibombari; former Vice-President, Mungo Department Section; Mbr. Elect, Departmental Section U.N.C.,

Mungo. Recipient of Cameroun distinctions, 2nd & 3rd Class. Address: B.P. 5478, Douala-Akwa, Cameroun.

EKEMU, Richard Epalu, born 7th September 1943. Agriculturist. Education: Kamuda Primary School, 1951-52; Madera Primary School, 1956-59; Soroti College, 1960-61; Tororo College, 1962-65; Arapai Agricultural College, 1966-69; College Diploma in Agriculture, 1968; University Diploma in Agriculture, 1969. Personal details: married to Bennie Ekemu, an Assistant Agricultural Officer. Appointments: Teacher, Farm Institute, 1969—. Member of Professional Centre of Uganda (Agricultural Society of Uganda). Address: P.O. Box 47, Moroto, Uganda.

EKONG, John Utip, born 18th October 1930. Physician. Education: M.B., Ch.B., St. Andrew's University, Scotland, U.K.; M.R.C.P., Edinburgh; M.R.C.P., Glasgow; D.T.M.&H., Liverpool. Personal details: married, 1 son. Appointments: Senior Consultant Physician (Rank of Colonel) to the Armed Forces of Nigeria. Memberships: Board of Management, Lagos University Teaching Hospital; Court of Governors, College of Medicine, Lagos University. Address: Military Hospital, Yaba, Lagos, Nigeria.

EKONGOLO NLATE, Albert, born Nyengue, Cameroon, 27th April 1922. Administrator. Education: Acienne Ecole Supérieure, Yaoundé, Cameroon. Married, 15 children. Appointments include: Acctng. Sec., S.A.P., North Cameroon; Sec., North Cameroon Region; ibid, Djoum Sub-division; Prefecturate of Ebolowa; ibid, Batouri; Asst., Bertoua District; Sub-Prefect, Djoum; ibid, Ndikinimeki; Bot-Makak, 1965—. Honours include: Merite Camerounais, 3rd class; ibid, 2nd class; Chevalier, Ordre de la Valeur. Address: B.P. 44, Bot-Makak, Cameroon.

EKUBAN, Ebenezer Emmanuel, born 21st October 1931. University Lecturer. Education: B.A.(London), 1956; M.Ed.(Toronto), 1964; M.A.(London), 1968; Completing Ph.D. Course (London), 1970. Married, 3 sons. Appointments: Education Officer, Ghana, 1957-62; Senior Education Officer, ibid, 1963-64; Area Inspector of Secondary Schools & Training Colleges in the Central & Western Regions of Ghana, 1965; University Lecturer in Education, University College of Cape Coast, Ghana, 1965—. Member of the British Section, Comparative Education Society in Europe. Publications: The Headmaster & Supervisor (Ghana Teachers' Journal), 1965; Curriculum Reforms in Developing Countries (Proceedings of the British Section, Comparative Education Society in Europe), 1968; Education in Cities; Cape Coast; The World Year Book of Education, 1970. Recipient of several scholarships. Address: University College of Cape Coast, Faculty of Education, Cape Coast, Ghana.

EL-ABD, Hamed A., born Gunzur, Nile Delta, 28th November 1928. Professor of Educational Psychology. Education: B.Sc., B.Ed., Ain Shams, University of Cairo, U.A.R., 1952; M.A., Institute of Education, London University, U.K., 1961; Ph.D., ibid, 1964. Personal details: married to Dr. N. Seif, Associate Professor of Education, Cairo Teachers' Training College, U.A.R. Appointments: Teacher of Mathematics in Secondary Schools, Egypt, U.A.R., 1952-57; Psychology Scholarship, W. Germany & U.K., 1957-63; Research Investigator, Institute of Education, London University, U.K., 1964; Associate Professor of Psychology, Assiout Teachers' Training College, Egypt; Professor of Educational Psychology, Makerere University, Kampala, Uganda, 1965-71. Memberships: Associate, British Psychological Association; Foreign Affiliate of the American Psych. Assn.; East African Academy; Egyptian Psychological Society. Author of various articles, abstracts, & research reports, inclng. contbrns. to The E.T.S. International Newsletter, Princeton, 1968, 1969, 1970 & J. of Multivariate Analysis of Behavior, 1970. Awards: Carnegie Travel Grant, 1967; Commonwealth Foundation Grant, 1969; NUFFIC Grant, 1970. Address: Makerere University, P.O. Box 7062, Kampala, Uganda.

EL-ALLAM (Chief) Abdulgader Ali, born 15th October 1919. Diplomatist. Education: Specialized in Languages, High School. Appointments: President. Construction & Materials Co., Benghazi, Libya; Libyan Ambassador to Iraq & Morocco; Former Adviser, Esso Standard Libya Inc.; Mudir of Gubba (Libya), Minister of Agriculture, Communications, Defense, National Economy & Minister of Foreign Affairs, Government of Libya. Address: P.O. 1982, Benghazi, Libya.

ELAYED, Ahmed, born Sousse, Tunisia, 7th April 1934. Professor. Education: Agregation d'Arabe, Paris, France, 1961; currently preparing doctorate on bilingualism & dev. of modern Arabic in Tunisia. Married, 2 children. Appointments include: Tchr., High Schl., 1961-65; currently, Prof., Ecole Normale Supérieure & Bourguiba Inst. of Languages, Tunis, Tunisia; Educ. Adviser in Sec. Educ.; Assoc. Prof., Linguistics Section, Ctr. of Econ. & Social Rsch. Publications include: Cours Elementaires d'Arabe. Also contbr. of articles to prof. jrnls. & mags. Address: 23 Rue d'Espagne, Tunis, Tunisia.

EL BARI CHEIKH, Mohamed, born 22nd January 1912. School Director; Journalist. Education: Primary School, 1925; Secondary Arabic Schooling, Grand Mosque Zitouna, 1928. Married, 7 children; eldest son a professor at the age of 30. Appointments: Director of School, Curé (Imam), 1936—; Journalist on the following papers: Ezzohra, 1936; Ennahda, 1938; El-Irada, 1945; El-Amal (presently published). Memberships: President, Red Cross Society; Sign of Religious Institutions (Islam); Charitable Societies. Imprisoned for the National Cause, 1952; took part in Pilgrimage to Islam, 1963. Recipient of Independence Medal, 1953. Address: Hammam, Sousse, Tunisia.

ELEBUTE, Emmanuel Adeyemo, born 15th September 1932. Surgeon. Education: B.A., Trinity College, University of Dublin, Ireland, 1954; M.B., B.Ch., B.A.O., ibid, 1956; M.A., 1967. Personal details: father, Mr. E. F. Elebute, was the first African to be manager of an insurance company in Nigeria. Married. Appointments include: Senior House Surgeon, Royal National Orthopaedic Hospital, Stanmore, U.K., 1959-60; Registrar, Professorial Unit, Dept. of Surgery, University College Hospital, Ibadan, Nigeria, 1961-62; Senior Registrar, ibid, 1962; Senior Registrar, Dept. of Surgery, Lagos University Teaching Hospital, Lagos, 1962-63; Lecturer in Surgery, University of Lagos Medical School, & Consultant Surgeon, Lagos University Teaching Hospital, 1963-66; Senior Lecturer in Surgery, ibid, 1966-67; Associate Professor in Surgery, College of Medicine, University of Lagos, 1969—. Fellowships: Royal College of Edinburgh, 1960; Royal College of England, 1960. Memberships include: National President, Nigeria Medical Association, 1968-70; Assistant Editor, N.M.A. Journal, 1964-68; Progress & Development Committee, International Federation of Surgical Colleges, 1969—; Hon. Secretary, Association of Surgeons of West Africa, 1967—; Official Delegate, World Council Meeting, International Federation of Surgical Colleges, ibid, 1968; active member of many other profl. socs. Publications: articles in many internationally circulated medical journals; Tropical Surgery (Co-Editor). Many awards at Dublin University. Address: Department of Surgery, College of Medicine, University of Lagos, P.M.B. 12003, Lagos, Nigeria.

EL FDILI, Nezha, born Fes, Morocco, 1939. Teacher. Appointments: Teacher of the Arab Language at a Primary School in Casablanca. Address: Quartier la Gironde, 11 Rue d'Auros, Casablanca, Morocco.

EL-FELLOUSSE, Rachio. born 30th July 1937. Head of Primary Instruction to the Ministry of Cultural Affairs. Education: Primary Certificate; Secondary Certificate of Studies; Diploma, Moroccan School of Administration; Lic. Law; Higher Studies at the Moroccan School of Administration. Married, 2 children. Appointments: Teacher; Professor at Regional School of Instructors; Head of the Paedagogy Bureau to the Delegation of the Ministry of National Education; Head of the Paedagogy Organization to the Ministry of National Education; in charge of the Instruction Division, ibid. Memberships: Treasurer, Higher Council of Popular Culture; ibid, Association of Old Pupils of the Moroccan School of Administration; National Council of the Party of Istiglahal; Secretary-General, Association of Young Arabs. Author of several plays & novels published in journals & broadcast on the R.T.M. Address: 4 Rue Marassa, Boulevard Amar Ibn Yassir, Rabat, Morocco.

EL-HASSOUMI, Ali, born 4th September 1933. Teacher. of History & Geography. Education: L'Ecole Franco-Arab, Rue Sidi, Ali Azouz; Baccalaureat, Lycée Carnot; Lic., History & Geography, L'Ecole Normale Superieure, Tunis. Married, 1 child. Appointments: Teacher, Secondary Schools, Tunis; Director, I.E.A. Economic Journal I.E.A. (African economic information). Address: 116 Bd. du 20 Mars, Bardo, Tunisia.

EL-KINDY, Zahor Nassor, born Tabora Region, Tanzania, 16th May 1937. Lawyer; Magistrate. Education: Tabora Secondary School, Tanzania LL.B., University College, Dar es Salaam, 1964; School of Oriental & African Studies, University of London, U.K. Married, 1 son, 1 daughter. Appointments include: with Attorney-General's Chambers; District Magistrate, District Court, Dar es Salaam, Tanzania, 1964; ibid, Bukoba District Court; Resident Magistrate, Res. Magistrate's Court, Mwanza, 1964; District Court, Shinyanga, 1965; ibid., Iringa, 1965; Mtwara, 1966; Bukoba, 1966; Sr. Res. Magistrate, ibid, High Court & District Res. Magistrate's Court, Arusha, 1967; District Registrar, High Court; Senior Resident Magistrate, Resident Magistrate's Court, Dar es Salaam, 1969-70; Judge, High Court of Tanzania, ibid, 1970—. Address: High Court of Tanzania, P.O. Box 9004, Dar es Salaam, Tanzania.

ELLE NTONGA, Francois-Xavier, born 1933. Registrar; Clerk of the Court. Education: Primary Studies, Catholic Mission School, Doume, Cameroun; Little Seminary of Akono, 1947-52; Studied Philosophy, Grand Seminary of St. Frances de Sales, 1952-54. Appointments: Teacher, 1957-58; Director, College d'Etourdi, 1958-60; Deputy Clerk to the Court, Court of Appeal, Dschang, 1961-63; Head of the Personnel Service, Ministry of Justice, 1964—. Memberships: Director, Classic Chorale, Church of Our Lady of Victory, Yaoundé, Cameroun. Honours: Recipient of Cameroun distinction, 3rd class. Address: B.P. 1126, Yaoundé, Cameroun.

ELLIS, Jeffrey Oliver, born 9th February, 1922. Professor of Linguistics. Education: Universities of Manchester & London, U.K.; University of Prague, Czechoslovakia; B.A. (Hons., German), 1944; Ph.D., Comparative Slavonic Philology, 1948. Appointments: Lecturer in German, University of Hull, U.K., 1955-61; Lecturer in General Linguistics, University of Edinburgh, 1961-65; Fellow in General Linguistics & Director of Contemporary Russian Language Analysis Project, University of Essex, 1965-66; Professor of Linguistics, University of Ghana, 1967—. Memberships: Chairman, Linguistics Association, Great Britain, 1959-62; Philological Society; West African Linguistic Society; Linguistic Circle of Accra. Publications include: Towards a General Comparative Linguistics, 1966; To Be in Twi, The Verb 'Be' and Its Synonyms (co-author), 1969; Linguistics in a Multilingual Society, 1970. Address: Dept. of Linguistics, University of Ghana, Legon, Ghana.

ELLMAN, Antony Oliver, born 5th December 1939. Agricultural Economist. Education: B.A., Oxford University, U.K., 1962; London School of Economics, 1965-67. Married. Appointments: Manager, Co-operative Farm Settlent, Tanzania, 1962-65; Agricultural Economist, Ministry of Rural. Development, Tanzania, 1967-70. Publications: Kitete, a Land Settlement Scheme in Northern Tanzania in Land Reform, Land Settlement & Co-operatives, No. 1, 1967; The Introduction of Agricultural Innovations Through Co-operative Farming, East African Journal of Rural Development, Vol. 3, No. 1, 1970; Progress, Problems & Prospects in Ujamaa Village, Programme in Tanzania

Economics Research Bureau, Dar es Salaam, 1970. Address: 3 Mickleham Hall, Dorking, Surrey, U.K.

ELLS, Peter Ronald, born 10th January, 1918. Accountant. Education: Solihull School, Warwickshire, U.K.; College of Accountancy. Married. Appointments: Auditor, Windward Islands, W. Indies; Chief Accountant, Com. Dev. Corp., W. Indies; Company Secretary, Messrs Stevenson & Rush, London, U.K.; Financial Secretary, W. Indies; Principal Assistant Secretary, Government of Lesotho. Memberships: W. India Committee, London, U.K.; W. India Club, London; Royal Commonwealth Society, London. Honours: O.B.E., 1967. Address: Financial Controller, Uganda Coffee Marketing Board, Amber House, P.O. Box 7154, Kampala, Uganda.

ELMANDJRA, Mahdi born Rabat, Morocco, 13th March 1933. Professor. Education: Lycée Lyautey, Casablanca; B.A., Political Science, Cornell University, New York, U.S.A.; Ph.D.(Econ.) in International Relations, London School of Economics, London University, U.K. Married, 2 daughters Appointments include: Assistant Professor, Faculté de Droit Rabat, Morocco, 1957-58; Counsellor, Moroccan Permanent Mission to the U.N., 1958-59; Director-General Moroccan Broadcasting & Television System, 1959-60; Chief, Africa Division, UNESCO, Paris, 1961-63; Director Executive Office of the Director-General UNESCO, 1963-66; Assistant Director-General for the Social Sciences, Human Sciences & Culture, UNESCO, 1966-69; Visiting Fellow, Centre for International Studies, L.S.E., U.K. Honours: Knight, Order of Arts & Letters. Address: 9 Bis Rue Michel Ange, Paris 16, France.

EMMETT, Ronald Robert, born 25th April, 1930. Pharmacist. Education: Matriculated, Durban High School, Natal; Dip. Pharm., University of Natal; M.P.S.; M.S.P.A., Married. Appointments: Owner, Manzini Pharmacy, President St., Manzini, Swaziland. Memberships: Past President, Manzini Rotary Club; President, Swaziland Pharmaceutical Society; South African Pharmaceutical Society; Foundation Member, Manzini Town Board; Past Financial Committee Chairman, ibid; Chairman, Swaziland Racing Pigeon Association. Address: President St., P.O. Box 661, Manzini, Swaziland.

EMUCHAY, Dick Waobianyi, born 5th August 1919. Physician. Education: Government School, Azumini, 1927-31; Government College, Lagos, Nigeria, 1932-35; King's College, Lagos, 1936-37; Higher College, Yaba, Lagos, 1938-42; University of St. Andrew's, Scotland, U.K., 1945-49; Liverpool School of Tropical Medicine, 1952-53. Married, 5 sons, 2 daughters. Appointments: Senior Science Master, Igbobi College, Lagos, 1943; General Medical Practice, Lancs., U.K., 1949; House Surgeon, Leigh Infirmary, ibid, 1950; Senior House Surgeon, 1951; Gynaecological House Surgeon, 1952; Medical Officer, i/c Rural Areas, Aba, 1955, Medical Officer, i/c General Hospital, Degema, 1958; Medical Officer, i/c Maternity Hospital, Aba, 1959; Medical Superintendent, Cottage Hospital, Azumini, 1961—. Memberships: Manchester Medical Society; President, Ndoki Union; President, Azumini Welfare Association. Publications: 'Tetanus' (Eastern Nigeria Medical Bulletin), 1967. Address: Cottage Hospital, Azumini, Ndoki, East Central State, Nigeria.

ENDALKACHEW MAKONNEN, born Addis Ababa, 1927. Minister of Communications, Telecommunications, & Posts, Ethiopia. Education: Hailé Selassié I Secondary School, Addis Ababa; Exeter University & Oxford University, U.K.; M.A.(Hons.,, Political Economy), 1950. Married, 2 sons, 4 daughters. Appointments: Attaché, Ministry of Foreign Affairs, Ethiopian Foreign Service, 1951; Chief of Protocol, ibid, 1952; Director-General in Charge of Political Affairs, 1953; Vice-Minister for Foreign Affairs, 1954; Member, Ethiopian Delegation, Bandung Conference, 1955; Ethiopian Delegation, London Conference on the Suez Canal, 1956; Menzies Committee, ibid, Cairo, 1956; Vice-Minister of Social Affairs & Education, 1957-58; Ethiopian Ambassador to the Court of St. James, London, 1959-60; Minister of Commerce & Industry & Chairman of Ethiopia's National Coffee Board, 1961-66; Permanent Representative of Ethiopia to the U.N. with Cabinet Minister rank, 1966-69; subsequently Member of the Security Council, 1967-69; served twice as President of the Security Council; Minister of Communications, Telecommunications & Posts, 1969—. Headed numerous Ethiopian Delegations, notably Vice-President, Trade & Development Conference, Geneva & Chairman, Economic Commission for Africa (sessions held at Addis Ababa). Memberships include: Vice-President, Alliance of the Y.M.C.A.; active participant in many social & cultural organizations. Address: P.O. Box 4774, Addis Ababa, Ethiopia.

ENDELEY, Emmanuel Mbela Lifaffe, born Buea, Cameroon, 10th April 1916. Medical Practitioner; Politician. Education: Government School, Buea; Roman Catholic School, Bonjongo; Government College, Umuahia, Nigeria; Government Scholarship to Nigeria School of Medicine, Higher College, Yaba, 1934-43. Personal details: son of Chief Mathias Lifaffe Endeley, who became Chief of the Bakweri Tribe in succession to his father, Chief Endeley Likenye, who had led his tribesmen against German entry in 1891. Appointments include: Assistant Medical Officer, Nigeria Government Medical Service, 1943-46; Secretary of the 20,000-strong Cameroon Development Corporation Workers' Union, 1947-49; President-General, ibid, 1949-50; Director, Management Board, Cameroon Development Corporation, 1950-52; Minister without Portfolio & subsequently Minister of Labour, Council of Ministers, Nigeria Federal Government, 1952-54; Leader of Government Business, Government of Southern Cameroon, 1954-58; Premier, Southern Cameroon Government, 1958-59; Leader of Opposition West Cameroon Govt., Cameroon Federation, 1959-65; Leader of the House & Parliamentary Group of Cameroon National Union, West Cameroon Legislature, 1965—. Memberships include: President, Bakweri Co-operative Union of Farmers; President, West Cameroon Co-operative

Banana Growers' Association. Honours include: O.B.E., 1956. Address: P.O. Box 5, Buea, West Cameroon, Federal Republic of Cameroon.

ENGMANN, Helen Maude, born 11th October 1935. Medical Practitioner. Education: Achimota School; King's College, Newcastle upon Tyne, U.K. Married, 2 children. Appointments at Polyclinics in Accra, Ghana. Address: Kaneshie Polyclinic, Accra, Ghana.

EPERU, Michael, born 5th March 1937. Broadcaster. Education: Soroti College, 1952-53; Tororo College, 1954-56; Kyambogo T.T.C., 1957; B.B.C. Staff Training College, London, U.K., 1961. Married, 13 children. Appointments: Programme Assistant, 1957; Programme Assistant Grade 1, 1962; Senior Programme Assistant, 1962; Programme Organizer, 1966; Head of Programmes, Radio Uganda, 1968. Member of B.B.C. Club. Address: Radio Uganda, P.O. Box 2038, Kampala, Uganda.

ERLICH, Julius, born 5th November 1902. Mechanical Engineer. Education: B.Sc., Technical Engineering, University of Liege, Belgium; 1st Class Ship's Engineer's Certificate; Proficiency in English Diploma, Cambridge University, U.K. Married, 1 son. Appointments: Managing Director, S.A. Radcielina, Poland, 1929-39; Lt.-Commander (Engineer), Polish Navy, 1939-47; Managing Director, Klepriver Lime Wks., Ltd., 1947-50; Works Manager, Coedmore Quarries, Anglo-Transvaal Corp., Durban, South Africa, 1950-63; Sales Administrator, Illings (Pty.), Ltd., Anglo-American Corp., Durban, 1963—. Memberships: Past Vice-Chairman, S.A. Institute of Mechanical Engineers; Institute of Certificated Engineers, South Africa; Institute of Quarrying, London; Durban Country Club. Recip. 6 war campaign medals, 1939-45. Address: Messrs. Illings (Pty.), Ltd., P.O. Box 991, Durban, Natal, South Africa.

ERUCHALU, Raphael Chukudile Okoye, born 1st January 1927. Medical Practitioner; Surgeon. Education: D.M.G.S., Onitscha, 1942-46; Higher College, Yaba, 1947-48; University College, Ibadan, Nigeria, 1948-51; University College Hospital Medical School, London, U.K., 1951-55; Royal College of Surgeons, England, 1959; L.R.C.P.(Lond.); M.R.C.S.(Eng.), M.B., B.S.(Hons., Eng.), 1954. Personal details: son of Chief D. U. Eruchalu of Nnobi, Onitsha Province. Married, 5 children. Appointments: House Physician, U.C.H., London, U.K., 1954-55; House Surgeon, ibid, 1955; Senior House Surgeon, U.C.H., Ibadan, Nigeria, 1956-57; Registrar, Surgery, ibid, 1957-58; Senior Registrar, Surgery, 1960-62; Specialist Surgeon, Ministry of Health, Enugu, 1962-67; Senior Lecturer in Surgery, U.N.N., 1967—; Fellow of Royal College of Surgeons (Eng.) 1959. Publications: The Problem of Acute Appendicitis in our Society (paper), 1962; The Acute Pyogenic Abscess in the Differential Diagnosis of Acute Appendicitis(paper), 1964. Awarded O.F.R., Nigerian National Honour, 1953. Address: University of Nigeria, Nsukka, Enugu Campus, Nigeria.

ESAN, Victor Owolabi, born 30th November 1906. Legal Practitioner. Education: St. James's Anglican Church School; Ibadan Grammar School, Nigeria; University College, London, U.K.; Barrister-at-Law, Lincoln's Inn, 1948. Married, 2 sons, 6 daughters. Appointments: enrolled at Nigerian Bar as Barrister & Solicitor, 1948; First Secretary (Town Clerk), Ibadan District Council, 1953-57; Commissioner for Finance, Emergency Administration, Western Region, May to December 1962; First Commissioner, Public Service Commission, Western State, 1967—. Memberships: Co-founder & First Secretary, Ibanda Progressive Union, 1930; Co-founder & First President, Oke 'Badah Union, Lagos, 1940—; Ikoyi Club, Lagos; First Chancellor, Ibadan Diocese, Anglican Church of the Province of West Africa, 1952-62. Address: P.O. Box 283, Ibadan, Nigeria.

ESIEN, Efiong Esien, born Calabar, 12th April 1919. Businessman. Education: Class 11 (Middle). Personal details: head of family of 32; father of 13 children. Appointments: served in Signal Unit; Royal West African Frontier Force; served, East Africa, India, Burma, 1940-46; Civil Servant, 1946-49; with Richard Costain for 9 months; Own Business, Importation, Exportation, Clearing, Forwarding, & Transport Building. Memberships: Chairman & Patron, The Mysterious Rovers of Calabar (Football Club); African Club, Calabar. Address: 8 Akinhanmi Street, Suru-Lere, Yaba, Nigeria.

ESSIEN, Daniel Paul, born 7th February 1933. Physician. Education: Ikot Edong High School, Abak, S.E. State; Ibibio State College, Ikot Ekpene; St. Patrick's College, Calabar; M.B., B.S.(Lond.), University College Hospital Medical School, Ibadan, Nigeria; M.R.C.O.G. Personal details: detained by the former Rebel Govt. in Biafra, 1968, for supporting the Federal Military Govt., liberated by Federal Troops, 1969. Appointments: Resident Post, University College Hospital, Ibadan, Nigeria, 1961-64; Registrar in Obstetrics & Gynaecology, Teaching Hospitals, Birmingham & Oxford, U.K., 1965-66; Medical Officer, Obstetrics & Gynaecology, Govt. Hospitals in former Eastern Nigeria, 1967—. Address: Methodist Hospital, Ituk Mbang, Uyo, S.E. State, Nigeria.

ESSIEN, Ephraim Udofia, born 27th December 1927. Occupational Physician; Industrial Medical Officer. Education: Methodist College, Uzuakoli, Nigeria; City College, Norwich U.K.; Kings College, London; St. George's Hospital Medical School; M.B.B.S. (Hons.), Applied Pharmacology & Therapeutics, London, 1959; M.R.C.S.(Eng.) & L.R.C.P. (Lond.), 1959; D.T.M.&H., Liverpool, 1960; L.M., Dublin, 1961; D.I.H., London, 1966. Personal details: 2nd son of late Chief Udofia Essien, Ikot Ekpene, Nigeria; Married, 3 daughters. Appointments: Medical Officer, Shell BP Petroleum Development Co. of Nigeria Ltd., 1961; Senior Medical Officer, ibid, 1967—. Memberships: Fellow, Royal Society of Tropical Medicine & Hygiene, London; Society of Occupational Medicine, London; Occupational Health Subcommittee, National Industrial Safety Council, Lagos. Address: Medical Department, Shell-BP Ltd., Private Mail Bag 2418, Lagos, Nigeria.

ESSIEN, Okon Etim, born 10th January, 1942. University Lecturer. Education: Primary, Ibiono, 1950-53; Secondary, Hope Waddell, Calabar, S.E. State, Nigeria, 1954-58; B.A., University of Nigeria, Nsukka, 1962-65; M.A., Dip. in TESL, University of California, Los Angeles, U.S.A., 1967-68. Appointments: Graduate Teacher, English, Holy Child College, Ifuho, Ikot, Ekpene, 1965-66; Lecturer, English Language & Lingistics, Ahmadu Bello University, Kano, 1968—. Memberships: Kano Club; Secretary, University Staff Club. Publications: English as our Common Language (Nigerian Outlook), 1964; Nigerian English (Insight), 1969; What is Grammar (ibid), 1970; The English Language & the Nigerian Teacher (forthcoming). Address: Abdullahi Bayero College, Ahmadu Bello University, P.M.B. 3011, Kano, Nigeria.

ESUMAN-GWIRA, John Buckman, born 30th September 1937. Medical Officer. Education: Adisadel College, Cape Coast, 1951-57; Kasr-el-Aini Hospital, Cairo University, 1959-66. Personal details: son of W. E. Esuman-Gwira, a Land Surveyor; Married, 1 child. Memberships: Ghana Medical Association; Gymkana Club, Tamale. Fellow of the Student Leadership Programme, African-American Institute, U.S.A., 1963. Honorary Citizen of the City of El-Paso, State of Texas, U.S.A., 1963. Address: Medical Officer, Ministry of Health, P.O. Box M.44, Accra, Ghana.

ETIENNE, Marcel Jospeh René, born 7th September 1919. Director of Statistics. Education: Royal College, Mauritius; The Polytechnic, London, U.K.; London School of Economics. Appointments: Assistant Statistician, Central Statistical Office, 1947; Statistician, ibid, 1952; Assistant Director of Statistics, 1959; Director of Statistics, 1969—. Fellow of the Institute of Statisticians. Memberships: Associate of the Institute of Statisticians; member of many local social & philanthropic societies. Editor of the Bi-annual Digest of Statistics. Address: Central Statistical Office, Rose Hill, Mauritius.

ETIM-BASSEY, Ernest, born 24th September 1936. Journalist. Education: Akim Qua Town School, Calabar; Hope Waddel Training Institute; West African People's Institute, Calabar; Diploma in Journalism(Lond.); Atteste in Journalism, University of Strasbourg; Diploma in Journalism, Moscow State University; M.I.J., London. Personal details: descended from Royal Family of King Eyamba IV & King Eyo V of Creek Town, Calabar; Married, 1 son. Appointments: Civil Service, 1953-54; Translator, 1954-57; Broadcaster, 1957-59; Public Relations Practitioner, 1958-60; Public Relations & Publicity Officer, 1960-66; Editor (Magazine); Editorial Adviser (Newspaper & Publications); Press Secretary to the Military Governor, South-Eastern State of Nigeria; Senior Information Officer, Ministry of Home Affairs & Information, Calabar, Nigeria; Features Editor, Federal Information Service, Lagos. Memberships: Secretary, Boy Scouts Assn., Eastern Nigeria, 1955-58; Social Secretary, Nigerian Broadcasting Corporation Sports Club; British Institute of Journalists; Secretary, The African Club, Calabar; Secretary, Calabar Community, Lagos. Publications: Evolution of Nigerian Press 1859-60. Honours: 1st Class Certificate (Literature), Eastern Nigeria Festival of Arts, 1956; Certificate of Merit (Literature), 1956; Silver Medal, 1957. Address: P.O. Box 131, Calabar, Nigeria.

ETUKUDO, Efiong Saul, born Mbioto, Nigeria, 15th December 1920. Teacher. Education: Mbioto Town School, Etinan Institute, Uyo; St. Edward's Seminary, Accra, Ghana; Nigerian Teachers' Certificate, 1946; B.A.(Hons., London), 1951. Married, 6 children. Appointments include: Headmaster, Ibibio State College, Ikot Ekpene, Nigeria, 1948-51; Principal, Emmanuel College, Owerri, 1952-55; Principal, Teacher Training College, Opobo, 1956; Onna T.T.C., 1964-65; Efa T.T.C., 1965-69; Chief Examiner in History, Teachers' Certificate Examinations, Eastern Nigeria Government, 1957-67; Principal, Government Secondary School, Eket, 1970. Memberships include: Secretary, Ibibio State Union; Accra, 1942. Publications include: Pioneers of Civilzation. Address: Government Secondary School, P.M. Bag 7, Eket, Nigeria.

EVANS, Richard Llewellyn, born 18th July 1941. Obstetrician; Gynaecologist. Education: St. Peter's School, York, U.K., 1953-59; King's College, University of London, 1959-62; King's College Hospital Medical School, 1962-65; M.B., B.S., 1965; M.R.C.S.; L.R.C.P.; A.KC., 1965; D.R.C.O.G., 1967. Appointments: House Officer in General Surgery & Medicine, Plymouth General Hospital, Devon; Senior House Officer in Obstetrics, ibid; Senior House Officer in Surgery; Registrar in Obstetrics & Gynaecology, King's College Hospital; due to take up appointment as Obstetrician & Gynaecologist, Regional Teaching Centre, Mwanza, Tanzania, 1972. Fellowships: Royal Society of Medicine; Royal College of Surgeons. Memberships: Association of Surgeons of East Africa; Royal College of Obstetricians & Gynaecologists. Publications: Large Vaginal Papilloma, Proceedings of the Royal Society of Medicine; Vaginal Condyloma (article), Journal. Obstet. Gynaec., British Commonwealth. Address: P.O. Box 413, Kitovu Hospital, Masaka, Uganda.

EYA, Jean Christian, born 11th April 1937. Civil Servant. Education: Studied at Koum, Sanguelime, 1944; Official School of Kipwe, 1952; Certificate in Primary Studies, 1955; 1st part Baccalaureat, 1961. Married, 1 child. Appointments: with the Ministry of Foreign Affairs, 1966; joined an Administration Course, 1966—. Memberships: football club & other sporting activities. Recipient of prize for French Recitation, 1968. Address: B.P. 2479, Messa Yaoundé, Cameroun.

EYADEMA (General) Etienne, President of the Republic of Togo, born Lama-Kara, 1937. Joined French Army & was sent to Indo-China, 1953-55; later stationed in Algeria, Dahomey, & Niger; promoted Captain after elections 1963; Major, 1964; Chief of General Staff, Togo Armed Forces, 1965; Lieutenant-Colonel, 1965; President of the Republic, Minister of National Defence, 1967—; Brigade General, 1967. Address: Lome, Togo.

EYAKUZE, Valentine Mukono, born 21st October 1930. Physician. Education: Bukoba & Tabora, Tanzania; M.B., Ch.B., Makerere Medical School, Kampala, Uganda; M.R.C.P., Edinburgh, U.K. Married, 2 sons. Appointments: Medical Officer, Tanzania Government, 1958-63; Medical Specialist, ibid, 1964-66; Director, East African Institute for Medical Research. Memberships: East African Academy; Council, Association of Physicians of East Africa. Author & Co-author of articles in East African Med. Jrnl. & other professional publications. Address: East African Institute for Medical Research, Mwanza, Tanzania.

EYO, Ekpo Edet, born Calabar, Nigeria, 7th February 1929. Specialist Physician (Internal Medicine) & Specialist in Diagnostic Radiology. Education: Duke Town School, Calabar, Nigeria, 1935-41; King's College, Lagos, Nigeria, 1942-47; Univ. College, Ibadan, Nigeria, 1948-52; Oxford Univ. Medical School & Univ. of Oxford, U.K., 1952-55; Univ. of Bristol, 1961-63. Personal details: son of Chief & Mrs. Edet Eyo of Calabar. Married 2 sons, 1 daughter. Appointments include: Pre-registration House Surgeon, Southampton General Hospital, 1955; House Officer & Medical Registrar, University College Hospital, Ibadan, 1957-59; Specialist Physician & Consultant, General Hospital, Lagos, 1965; Associate Lecturer & Consultant in Medical Radio-Diagnosis, Lagos University Teaching Hospital, 1965; Personal Physician to the Federal Nigeria Head of State, 1967. Memberships include: Fellow, Royal Society of Tropical Medicine & Hygiene; Nigerian Medical Association; National Treasurer & General Secretary, Lagos Branch, ibid; Association of Radiologists of West Africa; Association of Physicians of West Africa; West Africa Society of Gastroenterologists; Nigerian Cancer Society; Science Association of Nigeria. Author of miscellaneous publications in professional journals. Honours, prizes etc.: M.B., B.S.(Lond.), 1955; M.R.C.S.(Eng.); L.R.C.P.(Lond.), 1955; D.J.M.&H.(L'pool), 1957; M.R.C.P.(Edin.), 1960; D.M.R.D.(Eng.), 1963. Address: 51 Campbell St., P.O. Box 1342, Lagos, Nigeria.

F

FABAMWO, Elijah Adetola, born Aparaki, Ijebu-Ode, Nigeria, 26th September 1918. Teacher. Education: Emmanuel School, Isonyin, 1925-31; St. Andrew's College, Oyo, 1937-40; OU/ICA Teacher Training Course, Ibadan, 1959-60; University of Oxford, Institute of Education, Teacher Training & Educational Administration, U.K., 1963-64. Married, 2 sons, 3 daughters. Appointments include: Pupil Teacher, St. Paul's School, Gbongan, 1932-35; Class Teacher, Christ Church Porogun School, Ijebu-Ode, 1940-51; Headmaster, ibid, 1952-59; English & Geography Master, St. Matthew's Teacher Training College, Ljebu-Ode, 1960-64; Headmaster, Christ Church Cathedral School, Lagos, 1965—. Memberships include: Secretary, British Council Group, Ijebu-Ode, 1945-59; Patron, Youth Christian Association, Christ Church, Porogun; Guild of Stewards, Cathedral Church of Christ, Lagos; Treasurer, Head- teachers' Association, Lagos; Chairman, Nigeria Union of Teachers, Lagos Island; Board of Governors, St. Matthew's College, Ikoto, Ijebu-Ode, 1957-59; Chairman, Ijebu-Ogbo District Education Committee, 1957-59; Secretary, Board of Governors, Anglican Girls' Grammar School, Ijebu-Ode, 1956-59. Publications: Measures for Improving Primary Education in Nigeria, 1964. Address: Christ Church Cathedral School, P.O. Box 3416, Lagos, Nigeria.

FABUNMI (Chief) Michael Ajayi, Odole Atunobase of Ife, born Ile-Ife, Western Nigeria, 3rd January 1906. Retired Civil Servant. Education: St. Phillip's Primary School, Aiyetoro, Ile-Ife, 1912-17; Ibadan Grammar School, 1918-20; Roman Catholic Higher Elementary Teacher Training College, Oke Are, Ibadan, 1921-23. Personal details: installed as Chief Odole Atunobase of Ife, 1965; married, several children. Appointments: Schoolmaster, Catholic Training College, Oke Are, Ibadan, 1924-27; Senior Tutor, St. Gregory's College, Ikoyi, Lagos, 1928; Stenographer, United Africa Co. Ltd., 1929; First-Class Clerk, Agriculture Department, 1930-41; Assistant Chief Clerk, Provincial Administration, W. Region, Nigeria, 1942-47; Chief Clerk, Provincial Administration, E. Region, 1948-50; Secretary, Class 2, Ife Divisional Council, 1951-60; Secretary, Ife Town Planning Authority, 1961-63; Memberships: Secretary, Ife Union, Ibadan, 1924-27; President General, Union of Local Government Staffs, Western Region, 1958; Chairman, Ife Hospital Visiting Committee, 1965; Research Associate, Institute of African Studies, University of Ife, 1968. Publications: Ife Shrines; Yoruba Idioms. Honours: Coronation Medal, 1953; M.B.E., 1961; J.P., 1964; M.O.N., 1964. Address: 8 Ogbon Oya St., Ile-Ife, Nigeria.

FADIGA, Abdoulaye, born Touba, Ivory Coast, 10th March 1935. Business Executive; Director-General. Education: Bac., Lycée de Troyes, 1948-54; LL.D.; D.E.S., Political Economics; D.E.S., Economic Science; D.E.S., Public Law. Married. Appointments include: Secretary-General de l'O.I.A.C., 1960-61; Assistant Director, Price Control Office for Agricultural Production, 1961-68; currently, Director-General, ibid, Abidjan, Ivory Coast. Memberships: O.C.P.; B.N.D.A.; COMAFRICA; SODEPALM; SACO; SONAFI. Address: Caisse de Stabilisation et de Soutien des Priz des Productions Agricole, B.P. 1835, Abidjan, Ivory Coast.

FADUGBA, Akinbode Olumuyiwa, born 27th January 1932. Legal Practitioner. Education: Ilesha Grammar School, Nigeria; Ibadan Boys' High School; Birmingham College of Commerce, U.K.; University College, London; Council of Legal Education Law School, London. Personal details: father from Arapate Segilaoke family of Ilesha & leader of Egbe omo Ibile Ijesha; grandfather was a chief at Ife; grandmother from Olobgenla family of Agbedegbede Ruling House of More, Ife; married, 4 sons, 1 daughter. Appointments: Publicity Secretary, National Council of Nigeria & Cameroons (now banned), Ife; Publicity Secretary, Nigeria National Democratic Party; Member, Western State Electoral Commission.

Memberships: Ife Tennis Club; Social Secretary, Ife Recreation Club; Ilesha Social Club. Address: 7 Lagere Road, P.O. Box 54, Ile-Ife, Nigeria.

FAGBE (Chief) Williams, The Olobunodo of Ijare, born 10th November 1908. Managing Director of Fagbe BRS. Education: Primary. Appointments: Member, Akure Divisional Council, Nigeria, 1955-59; made Traditional Chief, the Ologunodo of Ijare, 1961. Address: 9 Broad St., P.O. Box 75, Akure, Western State, Nigeria.

FAKIH, Omar Ahmed, born 5th November 1932. Diplomat, Kenya Foreign Service. Education: B.A., University of London, U.K.; Dip. Ed. (E.A.). Married, 4 children. Appointments: Education Officer, Kenya, 1958-64; Diplomat, 1964—. Address: Counsellor, Kenya High Commission, 45 Portland Place, London, W.1, U.K.

FAKIRA (The Hon.) Abdool Monaf, born Port-Louis, Mauritius, 10th August 1929. Social Worker; Politician. Education: Government Primary School; Private Secondary College. Appointments include: Founder-President, Jeunesse Social-Democrate (1st Political Youth Organization in Mauritius), 1955-66; Secretary, Social Democratic Party, 1956-63; General Secretary, ibid, 1963-67; City Councillor, Port Louis, Deputy Mayor of Port Louis, 1962; Mayor, ibid, 1964; Vice-President, International Union of Socialist Youth, Vienna, Austria, 1965—; elected Member of Parliament, 1967; joined ruling Independence Party & C.A.M., 1968; attended meetings World Assembly of Youth, Ghana & Denmark, 1960, 1962. Memberships include: Commercial & Other Workers' Union; Executive, Union Culturelle Francaise, 1963-65; Executive, Mauritius Sports Assn., 1962-66; President, Muslim Scouts' Sports Club, 1959-67; President, Port Louis Youth Federation, 1958; Treasurer, Mauritius National Youth Council, 1959-62; Amicale Mamice, Malagasy Republic; Executive, Mauritius Branch, Commonwealth Parliamentary Assn., etc. Address: 2 St. Francois Xavier St., Port Louis, Mauritius.

FAKUNLE, Timothy Adetunji, born Esa-Oke, Nigeria, 7th January 1920. Teacher. Education: First School Leaving Cert., 1937; Wesley College, Ibadan, 1939-43; Grade II Teachers' Cert., 1942. Married, 4 sons, 3 daughters. Appointments include: Pupil Teacher, 1938; Teacher, Methodist Girls' School, Imo Abeokuta, 1943; Organist, All Saints' Church, Abeokuta, 1944; Supervizing Teacher, Abeokuta Circuit & Egbado Mission, 1944; Teacher, All Saints' Primary School, Oshogbo, 1948-51; Headmaster with African Church Organization, 1951-53; Captain, African Lads' & Lasses' Brigade Co., African School, 1952; started as printer of own works, 1952; full-time Printer & Publisher, 1953—; started an Orchestra, 1953; Hotelier, Oshogbo; Manager & Proprietor, Major Commercial Training College, Oshogbo, 1965—. Memberships include: Officer, Boys' Brigade; President, Total Abstinence Society, All Saints' School; Captain, Boys' Brigade 1st Oshogbo Company, 1956; Councillor, Ijesha Northern District Council, 1961-62; Education Committees, Oshogbo District & Ijesha Northern District Councils; Chairman, Oshogbo Group Council, Boys' Brigade, 1963; Local Preacher, Methodist Church, 1963; Circuit Steward, ibid, Oshogbo, 1964; Civil Defence Committee, 1967-68. Author & Publisher of Elementary & New Era Books, Model Questions & Answers, & General Knowledge Books for Primary & Secondary Schools, numbering over 70. Address: 3-7 Fakunle Street, P.M.B. 326, Oshogbo, Nigeria.

FALAYI, Samual Oladele, born 6th May 1925. Medical Librarian. Education: St. Peter's School, Ile-Oluji, Nigeria, 1932-39; Igbobi College, Yaba, 1941-48; School of Agriculture, Ibadan, 1947-48; Loughborough College, Leics., U.K., 1956-57; Columbia University, N.Y., U.S.A., 1963. Appointments: Treasury Clerk, 1946; Agricultural Assistant, 1947-49; Marine Clerk, 1950; Library Assistant, Federal Ministry of Health, 1950-60; Medical Librarian, ibid, 1960-64; Medical Librarian, College of Medicine, University of Lagos, 1964—. Memberships: Secretary, Lagos Division, Nigerian Library Association, 1961-62; Chairman, ibid, 1964-65; Councillor of the Association, 1964-65; pro tem Vice-President of the Association, 1965; Committee on Library Resources, 1966; Fellow, U.S. Medical Library Association, 1962-63; Committee on International Co-operation, 1969, 1970; Chairman, 6th Session, 2nd International Congress of Medical Librarianship, Washington, D.C., U.S.A., 1963; International Liaison Committee, 3rd ibid, 1969; Current Organizing Committee, 4th ibid. Publications: History of Medical Organization in Nigeria, 1959; Book Acquisition Problems in Nigeria, 1963; Problems of Medical Information Systems & Centres in the developing Countries of Africa, 1969 Address: The Library, College of Medicine, University of Lagos, P.M.B. 12003, Lagos, Nigeria.

FALEMI, Gabriel Olayanju, born 3rd November 1930. Trader. Married, 3 sons, 1 daughter. Appointments: Proprietor & Managing Director, Falemi Pharmaceutical Chemists Ltd., Lagos, 1968—. Memberships: Committee, Pharmaceutical Industrial Association of Nigeria. Address: Falemi Pharmaceutical Chemicals Ltd., P.O. Box 3084, Lagos, Nigeria.

FANIRAN, Adetoye, born 1st August 1938. University Lecturer. Education: B.A.(Hons.), London; University of Ibadan, Nigeria, 1964; Ph.D., University of Sydney, N.S.W., Australia. Married. Appointments: Lecturer in Geography, University of Ibadan, Nigeria, 1968—. Memberships: Nigerian Geographical Assn.; Geographical Society of N.S.W. & Australian Geography Teachers' Assn.; Nigerian Science Assn.; Corporate Member, Nigerian Mining, Geological & Metallurgical Society. Publications: Creating a commerical dairying industry in a nomadic pastoral economy, The Australian Geographer; The index of drainage intensity: a provisional new drainage factor, The Australian Journal of Science; Duricrust, relief & slope populations in the Sydney District, N.S.W., Nigerian Geog. Journal; Slope measurement & aerial photographs, ibid, Examples of Landform from Nigeria; Maghemite in the Sydney duricrust, American Mineralogist. Address: Dept. of Geography, University of Ibadan, Ibadan, Nigeria.

FANSHAWE, Peter Evelyn, born 13th September 1911. Retired Naval Officer; Representative in Ghana of the West African Committee. Education: Royal Naval College, Dartmouth, 1925-28. Married, 1 son, 1 daughter. Appointments: from Cadet to Captain, Royal Navy, 1929-66; joined West Africa Committee, 1967. Memberships: Army & Navy Club; Hurlingham Club; Royal Naval Sailing Association; Naval Member, Royal Yacht Squadron, Honours: O.B.E., 1945; D.S.C., 1952; C.B.E., 1966. Address: Royal Navy, P.O. Box 3408, Accra, Ghana.

FAQUIR, Mohammed, born 5th October 1904. General Medical Practitioner. Education: L.S.M.F.(Pb, Hons.), 1925; Licentiate, State Medical Faculty, Punjab, India; British Postgraduate Medical Federation, University of London. Married, 3 sons. Appointments: Sub-Assistant Surgeon, Uganda Medical Department, 1925; subsequently Medical Officer (East Africa) & District Medical Officer in charge of Medical Services, Teso & Karamoja. Fellow of Royal Society of Medicine, London, 1960. Memberships: Royal College of General Practitioners, London, U.K.; Councillor, Soroti Town Council; Chairman of Education Committee, ibid; Hospital Advisory Committee, Soroti Hospital; Visiting Justice, Central Government Prison, Soroti. Address: P.O. Box, 239 Soroti, Uganda.

FARGHALY, Mohamed Ahmed, born 21st March 1903. Counsellor. Education: Oxford & Cambridge Universities, U.K.; Victoria College. Appointments: Senator, Municipal Counsellor; President, Alexandria Cotton Exporters Association; President, Commission Bourse de Minet El Banal; Chairman and/or Director of 37 companies, industrial & commercial, including National Bank of Egypt, Farghaly Cotton & Investment Co. Member of many clubs & Steward of Jockey Club of Egypt. Honours: Title of Pacha; German & Italian decorations (Grand Officiale). Address: c/o National Bank of Egypt, Cairo, U.A.R.

FARRELL, Ronald Bertram, born Ireland, 7th June 1914. Technical Buyer. Education: Bournemouth School, U.K.; Technical College, Bournemouth. Appointments: Buyer to Sir Hubert Scott Paine, Southampton; with Imperial Airways, served France, The Belgian Congo, South Africa, Nigeria, Persian Gulf, India, Burma, & Ceylon; Special Duties, R.A.F., Burma Campaign, World War II; Chief Buyer, Mobil Oil Refinery, South Africa; Chief Buyer, Swaziland Electricity Board, Mbabane. Memberships: Mbabane Club; Secretary, Swaziland Golf Union. Address: 2 Ansell Crescent, Mbabane, Swaziland.

FARSEY, Suleiman Jabir, born 19th June 1930. Medical Practitioner; University Lecturer. Education: Primary & Secondary, Zanzibar, 1938-49; L.M.S. E.A., University, Kampala, Uganda, 1950-56; M.B., Ch.B. (E.A.), 1964; D.P.H., St. Andrews University, U.K.; Health Education & Community Development, North Carolina University, Chapel Hill, U.S.A., 1963. Personal details: family, noted Moslem theologians; nephew, present Chief Kadhi (Moslem Judge), Kenya—Sheik Abdulla Saleh Farsey; Married. Appointments: Medical Officer, Zanzibar Protectorate Government, 1958; District Medical Officer, Pemba, ibid, 1959; Medical Superintendent, Chake Hospital, 1961; Medical Officer of Health, Zanzibar, 1962; Senior Medical Officer, Pemba, 1964; Lecturer, Makerere University College, Kampala, Uganda, 1965; Senior Lecturer, ibid, 1968. Memberships: Association of Physicians of East Africa; Uganda Medical Association. Contributor to scientific journals. Recipient, college & university prizes. Address: P.O. Box 7072, Kampala, Uganda.

FASEHUN, Bandele Odunayo, born 1st October 1930. Medical Practitioner; Surgeon. Education: M.B., Ch.B., University of Leeds, U.K., 1956; F.F.A., College of Surgeons, Ireland, 1963. Appointments: House Physician, Bootle Hospital, Liverpool, 1957; House Surgeon, Blackburn Royal Infirmary, 1956-57; Medical Officer, Western Nigeria, 1957-61; Specialist, Anaesthetist, Western Nigeria, 1963-64; Specialist Surgeon, 1967—. Memberships: Fellow, Royal College of Surgeons, Edinburgh, 1967; Oshogbo Sports Club; Akure Recreation Club. Address: State Hospital, Akure, Nigeria.

FAUBEAU, Adrien Jean, born Cai-be, South Vietnam, 4th January 1925. Economist; Director. Appointments include: Head of Campaign, The National Life, Cie. d'Assurances, 1951-53; Head, Shipping Service, A.E.F.I., Saigon, 1953-55; Actionnaire and Fondé de Pouvoirs, Cong Ty Van Tai Vietnam, Saigon (S.U.N.), 1955-61; Actionnaire and Commercial Director, S.T.I.C., Paris, France, 1962-63; Economics Manager, I.F.O., C.E.G.I., Paris, 1963-67 (on leave from Ministry of Planning for Ivory Coast); Founder & Technical Director, Ste. Finuma, 1967—. Memberships include: General Secretary, Amicale des Anciens de l'Indochine, Abidjan, Ivory Coast. Partjcipant in Conference on le Nuocmam, Abidjan, 1965. Address: Ste. Finuma, B.P. 20. 874, Abidjan, Ivory Coast.

FAULKNER, Montfort Clement Arnold d'Alves, born Sao Thome, 20th March 1913. Civil Servant; Accountant-General of the Government of Sierra Leone. Education: Ebenezer, Bathurst Street, Model Schools, & Methodist Boys' High School, Sierra Leone; passed Junior Cambridge & Cambridge School Certificate Examinations. Personal details: grandfather, Enoch Faulkner, was 1st African District Commissioner, & father, James Newton Faulkner, was Supervisor of Cable & Wireless; Married, 1 son, 4 daughters. Appointments: Telephone Operator, G.B. Olivant Ltd., 1935; Clerk, Freetown City Council, 1936; Third Grade Clerk, Government of Sierra Leone, 1938; Second Grade Clerk, 1948; First Grade Clerk, 1950; Sub-Accountant, 1953; Accountant, 1958; Senior Accountant, 1962; Principal Accountant (Financial Controller), 1962; Deputy Accountant-General, 1963; Acting Accountant-General, 1964; Accountant-General (2nd African to hold this post), 1966—; on secondment to the Sierra Leone Royal West African Frontier Force, 1939-40, on civil duties. Memberships: Young Men's Christian Association, Sierra Leone; President, Parent-Teacher Association, Freetown Secondary School for Girls; President, Parent-Teacher Association,

Methodist Boys' High School; Treasurer, Parent-Teacher Association, Annie Walsh Memorial School; Meliora Literary Society; Methodist Boys' High School Old Boys Association; Whitley Council (Staff Side); British Council; British Council Photographic Club; Founder Member, Freetown Reform Club; Wesley Methodist Church & Senior Society Steward; Past Master in Freemasonry, Scottish Constitution; Mackay Commission of Inquiry, March 1968; Sole Commissioner inquiring into the administration & finance of the Transport & General Workers Union for the period 1st January 1963 to 31st December 1968, 1969; Treasurer, Nursery Schools Association of Sierra Leone; Boy Scouts Movement. Honours, Prizes, etc: School Prize for General Proficiency, 1930. Hobbies: Photography (cine, still & colour); Reading; Gardening; Motoring. Address: 'Chrismont', 13 Brookfields Motor Road (lower end of King Harman Road), Freetown, Sierra Leone.

FAYALA, Mohamed, born 20th August 1927. College Professor. Education: Secondary Studies, Sadiki College, Tunis; Higher Studies, University of Bordeaux, France. Married, 2 children. Appointments: Schoolmaster; Headmaster, Lycee de Garcons, Sousse, Tunisia; Headmaster & School Inspector. Memberships: Tunisien Association of Mathematical Sciences; Tunisien Commission for the advancement of the teaching of Mathematics (UNESCO); Sporting Association of Sousse, 1958; Municipal Counsellor, Sousse, 1969—. Author of several books on mathematics. Honours: Officer, Order of the Republic. Address: Lycee de Garcons, Sousse, Tunisia.

FAYE, John Colley, born Bathurst, Gambia, 25th February 1908. Clerk in Holy Orders, Politician. Education: St. Mary's Anglican School, 1913-21; Methodist Boys' High School, 1921-25; S.C., 1926; 1st Class Teachers' Certificate, 1927; Southampton University, U.K., 1938; Theology, 1936-38. Married, 1 daughter. Appointments include: Pupil Teacher, Methodist Boys' School, 1925-27; Tutor, ibid, 1927-31; Headmaster, Methodist Central School, 1932-34; Assistant Headmaster, St. Mary's Anglican School, 1934-37; Scoutmaster & Headmaster, ibid, 1938-42; Town Councillor, Bathurst Advisory Town Council, 1940-42; Headmaster, Transfiguration School, Kristi-Kunda, 1942-48; Supervisor of Schools (Anglican), 1942-48; Scoutmaster & Founder, Bishop's Own Troop, 1945-48; Inaugurator & Manager, Kantora Producers' Co-ops., 1945-48; Deacon of the Anglican Communion, 1947; Member, Legislative & Executive Council, 1947-51; Member of Government without Portfolio (Agriculture & Education), 1951-53; Minister of Works & Communications, 1954-60; Party Leader, Gambia Democratic Party, 1957-60; ibid, Democratic Congress Alliance (an amalgam of the Democratic Party & Muslim Congress), 1960-65; Commissioner for the Gambia in U.K., 1963-64; Hon. Curate, Holy Trinity, Hampstead, 1963-64; Hon. Curate, St. Mary's Pro-Cathedral, 1965—. Memberships include: Commonwealth Parliamentary Association, 1947—; Overseas Club, U.K., 1948-50; Royal Commonwealth Society, 1963—; Vice-President, Gambia Horticultural Society, 1958—. Publications include: Gambia—A Song for Gambian Youth, words & music published 1964. Honours include: British Council Bursar, Southampton University, U.K., 1938; M.B.E., 1947; Member of Gambian Delegation, African Congress, London, 1948; Representative from Gambia, Colonial Conference, Festival of Britain, 1951; ibid, Parliamentary Conference, Ottawa, Canada, 1952. Address: P.O. Box 74, 46 Gloucester Street, Bathurst, The Gambia,

FAYEMI, J. Bolarin, born 24th January, 1936. Businessman. Education: Government Class VI. Married, 4 children. Currently, Managing Director, Goodwill Brothers Co. Member, Ibadan Tennis Club. Address: P.O. Box 1374, Ibadan, Nigeria.

FELIHO, Isidore Vincent, born 8th July 1933. Administrator; Librarian. Education: B.E.P.C.; C.A.P. Libraire; Baccalaureat; Married, 2 children. Appointments: Teacher, 1959-61; Librarian, Centre of Higher Education, Porto Novo, Dahomey, 1963-64; Head of Mission to the National Ministry of Education, 1964-65; Director of the National Library, 1965—. Address: Librairie Nationale, Porto-Novo, Dahomey.

FELIX, Jean Eliel, born Beau Bassin, Mauritius, 4th April, 1913. Printer. Education: Royal College of Mauritius; I.C. School, London, U.K. Married 3 sons, 3 daughters. Appointments include: joined Government Service, 1933; Assistant Government Printer, 1945-47; Government Printer, 1947-68; Memberships include: General Purposes, Minor Grade & Trade Test Committee; Committee to Elaborate the Constitution of the Whitley Council for the Civil Service; The Mauritius Senior Professional Civil Servants Association; Chairman, Government Printing Department, Whitley Council; Chairman, Widows & Orphans Pension Fund; Hon. President, Government Printing Sport Association; Board of Film Censors; Saint John Kirk Session; Life Member, Cercle de Rose-Hill; Hon., The Mauritius Turf Club. Recip: Companion of the Imperial Service Order, 1957. Address: 14 Shand Street, Beau Bassin, Mauritius.

FERREIRA (Major) A. A. Jorge, born 1st August, 1938. Medical Practitioner, Nigerian Army Medical Corps. Education: St. Paul's School, Lagos, 1944-51; Christ's School, Ado Ekiti, 1952-56; University of Ibadan, 1957-65. Married. Appointments: Medical Officer, Federal Ministry of Health, 1966-67; ibid, 2 Field Ambulance, Nigerian Army, 1967; Assistant Director, Medical Service, Commanding Officer, 3 Field Ambulance & Divisional Surgeon to 3 Marine Commando Divs., 1968-70; currently, Commanding Officer, 78 Armed Forces Hospital, Lagos. Memberships: Director, African Affairs, National Union of Nigerian Students, 1963-65; Assistant General Secretary, Nigerian Youth Congress, 1965; General Secretary, Nigeria-Soviet Friendship Society. Awarded Soviet Medal in commemoration of centenary of birth of V.I. Lenin, 1970. Address: P.O. Box 2303, Lagos, Nigeria.

FERREIRA, Jose Xavier, born Goa, India, 29th September 1930. Police Officer.

Education: Matric., St. Anthony's High School, Assolna, Goa, 1941-48; P.S.I. Course, Police Training School; Inspectorates Law Examination, 1955; Gazetted Officers' Law & Administrative Exam., 1961; Specialist Courses. Appointments: Customs Officer, Tanganyika, 1949-51; Sub-Inspector of Police, ibid, 1951-55; Inspector of Police, 1955-57; Senior Inspector of Police, 1957-58; Chief Inspector of Poice, 1958-60; Assistant Superintendent of Police, 1960—; in charge of Tanzanian Identification Bureau, 1955—. Memberships: various positions with the Red Cross; Police Exhibition; Police Mess; Police Journal Committees, etc.; Business & Advertising Manager, Tanzania Police Journal. Author of various articles in the Tanzania Police Journal. Address: Tanzania Identification Bureau, Criminal Investigation Department, P.O. Box. 9094, Dar es Salaam, Tanzania.

FETUR ABRAHAM, born Saganeti, 29th October, 1910. Member of the Imperial Ethiopian Senate. Education: St. Micael School, Saganeiti, Eritrea. Appointments: Secretary to Consulate, former British Colony of Aden, 1954; Consul, Yemen, 1958-59; Consul-General, Somalia, 1959-61; Member of the Imperial Ethiopian Senate, 1962—. Publications: Fascist Cruelty in Ethiopia, Immediately after World War II, The New Times & Ethiopian News, 1947. Recip: Official Order of the Star of Honor, Ethiopia. Address: c/o The Imperial Ethiopian Senate, Addis Ababa, Ethiopia.

FIBERESIMA (Chief) Isaac John Sikikiri, born 29th March, 1906. Physician. Education: Primary School, Okrika & Bonny, St. Peter's & St. Stephen's; CMS Grammar School, Lagos, Nigeria, 1923-25; King's College, ibid, 1926-27; Pharmacy School, 1928-31; Qualified, Royal College of Surgeons, Dublin, Ireland. Personal details: Chief & natural ruler; Father, ibid; married, 3 children. Appointments: Government Medical Officer, 1956-61; Legislator, Eastern Nigeria House of Assembly, 1961-66; Private Practice, 1962—; President, Rivers State Movement, 1962-67; arrested & detained, 1967-70; currently, Chairman, Rivers State Development Corporation. Memberships: Fellow, Royal Empire Society; Master Mason, Scottish Lodge. Address: 7 Freetown St., Port Harcourt, Rivers State, Nigeria.

FIDDES, Patricia M. See under LARBY.

FIELDER, Peter Wyatt, born 1st July 1932. Electrical Engineer. Education: Prince of Wales School (now Nairobi School), Nairobi, Kenya; Dauntseys School, Wiltshire, U.K.; B.Sc.(Hons.), University College, London University. Appointments: Protection Engineer, E.A.P.&L.; Electrical Engineer, ibid; Generation Superintendent; Chief Engineer, Generation. Memberships: Chartered Engineer; M.I.E.E.; M.E.A.I.E. Address: c/o E.A.P.L., Nairobi, Kenya.

FIERLINGER, Peter Stewart, born Japan, 5th September 1934. Lecturer in Horticulture. Education: Primary School, U.S.A.; B.Sc., University of Agriculture, Prague, Czechoslovakia; M.Sc., Horticulture, University of Brno, ibid. Appointments: Plant Breeder, 1958-68; Head, Department of Vegetable Crops, Main Station for Mutation Breeding, Stupice, Czechoslovakia, 1962—; Lecturer, Department of Horticulture, University of Science & Technology, Kumasi, Ghana, 1968—. Member of TGC, University of California, Davis, U.S.A. Publications: Possibility of Utilizing Mutation Processes in Breeding Leguminous; Mutation Breeding in Tomatoes, Sweet Pepper; Utilization of Induced Mutation, 1968; Seasonal Trend in some introduced vegetables in the Tropical Forest Zone; Cultivation Practice in Onions, 1970. Address: Dept. of Horticulture, University of Science & Technology, Kumasi, Ghana.

FIFCHES, William Rodney, born 30th July 1943. Geologist; University Lecturer. Education: Bexhill Country Grammar School, U.K., 1954-61; Leeds University, 1961-65; Research Inst. of African Geology, ibid, 1965-68. Married, 1 daughter. Appointments: Lecturer in Geology, University of Ghana, Accra, Ghana; currently Lecturer in Geology, University College of Wales, Aberystwyth, U.K. Member of the Geological Society of London. Author of reports and papers on African Geology. Address: Department of Geology, University College of Wales, Aberystwyth, U.K.

FINDLEY, Joseph Patrick Henry, born 24th September 1927. Lawyer. Education: Secondary Education Certificate, Bassa High School, 1947; B.A., University of Liberia, 1951; Attorney-at-Law, Second Judicial Circuit Court Bar, Bassa County, 1952. Married, 4 sons, 4 daughters. Appointments: 1st Magistrate of Elections, Liberia, 1955; Director of International Conferences, State Department, Liberia, 1956; Resident Circuit Judge, Second Circuit, Bass, Liberia, 1956; Private Practice, 1967—. Memberships: International Bar Association; First Vice-President, National Bar Association of Liberia; former Senior Warden, St. John's Episcopal Church, Bassa County. Honours: Knight Commander, Humane Order of African Redemption. Liberia, 1956; Knight Grand Commander, ibid, 1964. Address: Postbox 21, Buchanan, Grand Bassa County, Liberia.

FISHWICK, Wilfred, born 1st October 1918. Electrical Engineer; Technical Adviser. Education: M.A., Mechanical Sciences, Pembroke College, Cambridge, U.K., 1938-40; Ph.D., Research in Electrical Engineering, 1946-48. Appointments: I.C.I. Ltd., Manchester, 1948-50; Lecturer, Edinburgh University, 1950-55; Professor & Head, Department of Electrical Engineering, University of Wales, Swansea, 1955-68; Chief Technical Adviser, Faculty of Engineering, UNESCO Project, University of Nairobi, Kenya, 1967—. Memberships: Fellow, Institution of Electrical Engineers, London; Senior Member, Institution of Electrical & Electronic Engineers, New York; Institute of Measurement & Control, London; Fellow, Cambridge, Philosophical Society. Author of professional publications. Recipient, Blackall Award, American Society of Mechanical Engineers, 1958. Address: UNESCO Project (Engineering), Box 30197, Nairobi, Kenya.

FLEUREAU, Maurice, born 7th November 1906. Director; Insurance Executive. Education: D.L. Married, 2 children. Appointments: with

Paris Insurance Union, 1930—; Inspector, Paris Insurance Union Algiers & Oran; Inspector General, Paris Insurance Union, Casablanca; Controller, General, Director, ibid, Morocco; Director-General, Entente (UAP); Memberships: Vice-President, Moroccan Federation of Insurance Societies: Honourary President, Union of Fire Insurance Companies in Morocco. Address: 17 Avenue de Boulogne, Casablanca, Morocco.

FLOWERDEW, Frank Digby Mackworth, born Pakistan, 1st October 1913. Medical Practitioner. Education: Framlingham College, 1927-31; St. Thomas's Hospital, U.K., 1931-37; M.R.C.S.; L.R.C.P. Married, 2 sons, 1 daughter. Appointments: Children's Home Physician, St. Thomas's Hospital, 1937; R.A.M.C., 1939-45; Medical Practitioner, Nairobi, Kenya, 1946—. Memberships: Nairobi Club; Jesters Club. Address: P.O. Box 832, Nairobi, Kenya.

FODEN (Commander) Thomas Howarth, born Bristol, U.K., 24th September, 1914. Commander, Ghana Navy. Education: Wellington School, U.K. Married. Appointments: Royal Navy, 1940-62; Ghana Navy, 1962-70. Memberships: Royal Commonwealth; Royal Naval Sailing Association. Address: P.O. Box 2665, Accra, Ghana.

FOKAM-KAMGA, Paul, born 1930. Principal Inspector of Labour. Education: Baccalaureat, 1953; Licence en Droit, 1956; Diploma, Institute of Political Sciences, Paris, France, 1959; Diploma ENFOM, Inspection du Travail. Appointments: Chief of Technical Services, Central Ministry of Labour, 1960-61; Director, Cabinet Minister of Justice & Minister of the Interior, 1961-62; Director of Labour, 1962; Deputy Government Commissioner, State Tribunal, 1963; Secretary-General, Ministry of Labour & Social Law, 1965; Professor of Labour Law, l'ENAM et au Centre Perfectionnement des Cadres de l'Administration du BIT Yde; Member of Council, d'Administration de l'ENAM; Minister of Information & Tourism, President, Organization for Developing African Tourism, 1967. Honours: Merite Camerounais de 2nd Class, 1966; Chevalier de l'Ordre de la Valeur, 1967; Officier de l'Ordre de la Valeur, 1970.

FOLENG, John Isidore Akongnwi, born 10th July, 1936. Accountant. Education: West African School Certificate, St. Joseph's College, Sasse, Buea, West Cameroon, 1951-56; Diploma, Book-keeping & Accountancy, R.S.A. Book-keeping, Stage II, Privately, 1957-58; A.A.C.C.A., F.C.I.S., South London College, U.K., 1959-60, 1962-63; Inland Revenue Training College, Stanmore & attachment in a District Inspector's Office. Appointments: Accounts Clerk, Treasury Department, Buea, West Cameroon, 1957-59; Accountant, ibid, 1963; Acting Senior Accountant, 1963-65; Assistant to Administrator of Income Tax, Victoria, 1965; Acting Administrator of Income Tax, West Cameroon, 1965; Study Leave, U.K., 1966-67; Director of Taxes, West Cameroon, 1967—. Member, Senior Service Staff Club, Bota. Address: Inland Revenue Department Headquarters, Victoria, West Cameroon.

FORD, Stanley Oswald, born 22 June 1926. Economic Geologist. Education: Dr. Challoner's Grammar School, Amersham, U.K., 1936-41; Taunton School, 1942-44; B.Sc.(Geology), University of Bristol, 1949-52; Ph.D., University of Durham, 1954-57. Married, 2 sons, 2 daughters. Appointments: Resident Geologist, Sinai Mining Co., Egypt, U.A.R., 1952-54; Senior Geologist, Gold & Base Metal Mines, Nigeria, 1958-61; Resident Consultant Geologist, Sinai Manganese Co., U.A.R., 1961-63; Geologist, 1963-66; Chief Mining Geologist, Ministry of Commerce & Industry, Government of Tanzania, 1966-70; Fellow of the Geological Society of London, 1958. Memberships: Institution of Mining & Metallurgy; Society of Economic Geologists; The Mining Club, London; Hon. Treas., Dodoma Club, 1969-70. Publications: The Ferruginous Manganese Ores of Om Bogma, Sinai, Egypt (co-author), International Geol. Congress, Mexico, 1956. Address: Mineral Resources Division, P.O. Box 903, Dodoma, Tanzania.

FORGET, Guy Joseph, born Mauritius, 6th August 1902. Ambassador for Mauritius in France. Education: Attorney-at-Law, Supreme Court of Mauritius, 1927. Married, 4 sons, 2 daughters. Appointments: elected Member Municipal Council, Port Louis, 1940; Nom., ibid, Rose Hill, 1945; elected, Rose Hill, 1950; Chairman, Rose Hill, 1952; Member, Port Louis, 1956; Deputy Mayor, ibid, 1958; Mayor, 1959; elected Member of Council, Mauritius, 1948-68; Minister of Health, 1957; Minister of Works & Communications, 1965; Minister of Finance, 1967; Deputy Prime Minister, 1961-68; Ambassador to France, 1968—; Ambassador to Italy, 1970—. Memberships: President, Literary Circle, Port Louis; Founder Member, Cercle de Rose Hill; Founder Member, Stella Clarisque Club; Associate, Racing Club. Recip. C.B.E., 1969. Address: c/o Mauritian Delegation to France, Paris, France.

FORREST, Stanley, born Castle of Auchry, Aberdeenshire, Scotland, 24th July 1895. Farmer & Medical Practitioner (retired). Education: Robert Gordon's College, 1909-13; M.A., Aberdeen Univ., 1920; M.B., Ch.B., 1924. War Service, Gordon Highlanders, 1914-19. Appointments include: East African Medical Service: Medical Officer, Uganda, 1925-29; Medical Specialist, Tanganyika, 1939; Ag. D.D.M.S., 1944; A.D.M.S., 1945; D.D.M.S., 1945; retired, 1946. Fellowships: R.S.T.M.&H., 1926; Royal Commonwealth Society, 1928. Memberships include: Nairobi Club, 1947; Makuyu Club, 1946. Honours, Prizes, etc: Coronation Medal, 1937. Address: Craig Elvan, Makuyu, Kenya.

FORSTER, Edward Bani, born Bathurst, Gambia, 17th December 1917. Psychiatrist. Education: St. Mary's Day School, Bathurst; L.M.S. Grammar School, Freetown, Sierra Leone; M.A., M.D., D.R.M.(R.C.P.), Trinity College, Dublin, Ireland. Married, 2 sons, 1 daughter. Appointments: House Surgeon, Birmingham Accident Hospital, U.K.; House Physician, Warlingham Park Mental Hospital; Assistant Medical Officer, Central Mental Hospital, nr. Warwick; Medical Officer, Colonial Medical Service, Gambia; Consultant Psychiatrist, Ghana Medical Service; Asst. Professor of Psychiatry, Ghana Med. School, Legon. Memberships: Fellow of Royal Society of Arts; R.M.P.A.; B.M.A.; Ghana Medical Association; American Association for the Advancement of Psychotherapy. Publications: A longitudinal ecological study of 100 consecutive admissions to the Accra Mental Hospital; A Study of Thioridazine HCl. in Chronic Schziophrenia; The Theory & Practice of Psychiatry in Ghana; Depressions in West Africa; Schizophrenia as Seen in Ghana; Clinical Trial on Istonic (Dimetharine). Address: Ghana Medical School, P.O. Box 1305, Accra, Ghana.

FORSTER, Essi Matilda, born Sekondi, Ghana, 12th September 1922. Barrister-at-Law. Education: La Sagesse Convent, Romsey, Hampshire, U.K.; Called to the English Bar, 1945; Called to the Ghana Bar (first woman Barrister-at-Law), 1947; Called to the Gambian Bar, 1947. Married, 3 children. Appointments include: Registrar-General, Ghana, 1956; Legal Adviser, Mobil Oil Ghana, Ltd., 1957. Memberships include: Executive Council, Ghana Girl Guides' Association; National Council, Y.W.C.A., Ghana; former Vice-President & Chairman of the Constitution Committee, ibid; Secretary, Ridge Church Sunday School; Secretary International Federation of Women Lawyers, Ghana; Executive Committee, Inner Wheel Club of Accra; Past President, ibid. Address: Mobil Oil Ghana Ltd., P.O. Box 450, Accra, Ghana.

FOSS, Eric Francis, born Perros-Guitec, France, 8th February 1918. Schoolmaster. Education: Elizabeth College, Guernsey, U.K.; Pembroke Dock Grammar School; Sandown Grammar School; B.A.(Hons., Geography), University College, London; Teachers' Certificate, Teachers' Diploma, Westminster College, London. Married, 2 sons. Appointments include: Teacher, Shebbear College, Devon, U.K.; Head of Geography & French Departments, Kingsholme School, Weston-super-Mare; Head of Geography & Religious Knowledge Departments, Shebbear College; Deputy Head, ibid, 1960; Principal, Gambia High School, Bathurst, The Gambia, 1966. Memberships include: Royal Life Saving Society; Incorporated Association of Headmasters. Address: Gambia High School, Bathurst, The Gambia.

FOSTER, Stanley Owens, born 16th December 1933. Physician. Education: A.B., William College, 1955; M.D., University of Rochester School of Medicine, 1960. Appointments: Epidemiologist, Division of Indian Health, Phoenix, Arizona; Teaching Fellow in Chest Diseases, San Francisco, Calif.; Medical Epidemiologist, Nigerian Smallpox Measles Programme. Memberships: Am. Public Health Association; Alpha Omega Alpha, 1960. Address: Ministry of Health, Lagos, Nigeria.

FOUCHARD, Philippe, born 5th February 1937. University Professor. Education: Lic. Law; D.L., Aggregate of Private Law. Married, 3 children. Appointments: Advocate to the Court of Appeal, Dijon, France; Assistant, Lecturer, Faculty of Law, Dijon; Senior Lecturer, Professor, Faculty of Law, Abidjan, Ivory Coast; Director, 'Revue de l'Arbitrage:. Memberships: French Branch of the International Law Association; French Committee of Private International Law; Association of Professors of the Faculty of Law for development & co-operation. Author of several papers published on law. Honours: Officer, National Education Order of Merit, Ivory Coast. Address: 51 bis Boulevard de Troyes, 21- Talant, Dijon, France.

FOUYAS, Methodios, born Corinth, 14th September 1925. Archbishop of Aksum, Ethiopia. Education: B.D., Athens, Greece: Ph.D., Manchester, U.K.; D.D.(Hon.), Edinburgh. Appointments: Secretary-General of the Patriarchate of Alexandria; First Secretary of the Holy Synod of the Church of Greece. Member of many societies & clubs. Publications include: History of the Church of Corinth; The Social Message of St. John Chysostom; Kanonica kai Poimantika Parerga, I-IV; Editor of: Abba Salama, a review of the Association of Ethio-Hellenic Studies and of Ekklesiastikos Pharos, a quarterly theol. review. Honours: Gordon of Holy Trinity, Ethiopian Lambeth Cross, Gold Cross of Greek Red Cross, St. Vladimir of the Patriarchate of Moscow. Address: P.O. Box 571, Addis Ababa, Ethiopia.

FOWLER, John Payce, born 22nd October 1937. Rural Development Worker. Education: Cambridge Overseas School Certificate, Kenya, 1955; National Certificate of Agriculture, Dorset, U.K. & Dorset County Certificate of Agriculture, 1959; London Bible College Short Course Diploma, 1960; Church Missionary Society Training College, 1963. Married, 1962. Appointments: District Officer (Emergency), Land Consolidation, Kikuyu Country, Kenya, 1956-58; Farm Manager, 1960-62; Manager, Church Farm, Nakuru,. 1964-68; Leader, Christian Rural Extension Service, Nakuru, 1968-70. Memberships: Hon. Sec., Christian Rural Fellowship of East Africa; Agricultural Missions, Inc., U.S.A.; Institute of Rural Life at Home & Overseas. Address: c/o Berea Farm & Mission, Private Bag, Nakuru, Kenya.

FOWLER (Rev.), John Sims, born Wembley, England, 24th February 1925. Minister of Religion. Education: Wolverhampton Grammar School, 1935-43; Trinity College, Cambridge, 1943-46; B.A., 1946; M.A., 1950; 1,st Class Mechanical Sciences Tripos; Clifton Theological College, Bristol, 1948-52; B.D., London University (1st Class), 1952. Married. Ordained Deacon, 1952, Priest, 1953, Anglican Church. Appointments include: Undergraduate Demonstrator & Research, Engineering Lab., Cambridge Univ., 1945-46; Graduate Apprentice, English Electric Co. Ltd., Rugby, 1946-48; Asst. Curate, Rodboorne Cheney, Bristol, 1952-55; Missionary of Church Missionary Society, 1956; Chaplain to Bishop of Lagos, 1956-60; Tutor, C.M.S., Training College, U.K., 1961; Oyo, Western Nigeria, 1961-62; Director, Christian Council of Nigeria Institute of Church & Society, Ibadan, 1962—. Publications include: a study by a double regraction method of the development of turbulence in a long circular tube (co-author), 1947; A Faith to Live By, 1965; Towards a Better Life, 1966; The Role of the Church in Rural Development. Honours, Prizes, etc: Rex

Noir Prize in Mechanical Science, Univ. of Cambridge, 1945; Ricardo Prize in Thermodynamics, Univ. of Cambridge, 1945; Senior Scholar, Trinity College, Cambridge, 1945-46. Address: Institute of Church & Society, P.O. Box 4020, Ibadan, Nigeria.

FOWLER, Sally Margaret, born 30th June 1936. Educator. Education: Walthamstow Hall School, Sevenoaks, Kent, U.K., 1943-54; Teachers' Certificate of Education, 1957; Church Missionary Society Training College, 1963. Married to John P. Fowler, 3 children. Appointments: Assistant Matron & Housemistress, Walthamstow Hall School, 1954-55; Teacher, Cranbrook, 1958-59; Teacher, St. Andrew's School, Turi, Kenya, 1959-62. Address: Berea Farm & Mission, Private Bag, Nakuru, Kenya.

FOX, John Henry Malcolm, born 8th January 1936. Warden, University of Nottingham Adult Education Centre. Education: Boston Grammar School; B.A.(Hons.), English, University of Nottingham, U.K. Married. Appointments: Lecturer in English Literature, University of Nottingham, Department of Adult Education, 1965-67; Lecturer in English, Adult Studies Centre, Kikuyu Institute of Adult Education Studies, University College, Nairobi, Kenya, 1967-69; Warden, University Adult Centre, Nottingham, U.K., 1969—. Publications: occasional papers in adult education & studies in adult education. Address: University Adult Centre, 14-22 Shakespeare Street, Nottingham, U.K.

FRAISSE, Andre Paul Fernand, born 21st February 1929. Education: Studied Engineering, National High School of Agronomy, Toulouse, France; 3 Certificates, L. es Sc. Married, 3 children. Research Assistant, Research Institute on Oil & Oily Substances (IRHO); Principal, Station La Me, Ivory Coast, 1954-56; Director, ibid, 1956-63; Director-General, SODEPALM (Society for the Development & Exploitation of Palm Oil), Abidjan, 1963-68; ibid, Group of Societies, SODEPALM, PALIVOIRE, PALM-INDUSTRIE, 1969-70. Memberships: Lions Club, Abidjan, Ivory Coast. Author of articles in the Revue Oleagineux. Honours: Knight, National Order of Merit, France; Officer, National Order of the Ivory Coast; ibid, Agricultural Decoration, Ivory Coast. Address: B.P. 2049, Abidjan, Ivory Coast.

FRANCIS, John Henry, born Derby, U.K., 15th February 1938. University Lecturer in Ceramics. Eeucation: Derby & District College of Art, 1953-58; School of Ceramics, Royal College of Art, London, 1960-63. Married. Appointments: Director, Mirac Ltd., Ceramic Engineers Design Consultants & Mangement Consultants, Somerset; Free-lance Designer & Ceramic Consultant; Lecturer, Ceramics, School of Fine Art, Makerere University, Kampala, Uganda. Various commissions, mainly architectural, decorative ceramic wall surfaces, & ceramic mural work, Kampala. Honours: Associate, Royal College of Art, London, 1963; Silver Medallist, ibid, 1963. Address: p.O. Box 7062, Kampala, Uganda.

FRASER, Marionette Aina, born Freetown, Sierra Leone, 3rd April 1927. Nurse. Education: St. Joseph's Convent Secondary School, Sierra Leone, 1934-46; Hope Hospital, Salford, Lancs., England, 1947-51; South London Hospital, Clapham Common, London, England, June-December 1951; Battersea Polytechnic, Battersea, London, England, January-December 1952. Personal details: great granddaughter of Thomas Peters of Sierra Leone (history re-freed slaves); married, A. K. Fraser, Manager of Sierra Leone Ext. Telecoms. Ltd.; 3 children. Appointments include: Nursing Sister, General Hospital, Freetown, Sierra Leone, 1953-56; Sister-in-Charge, Maternity Hospital, Freetown, Sierra Leone, January-August 1956; Sister-in-Charge, Schools Clinic, Freetown, Sierra Leone, 1958-59; Matron, Netland Maternity Home, Freetown, Sierra Leone, 1959— (own Private Home). Memberships include: Midwives' Examination Board, Sierra Leone; Vice-President, Sierra Leone Nurses' Association; Executive Member, Planned Parenthood Association, Sierra Leone. Honours, Prizes, etc: Credit Cert. in Nursing, Hope Hospital, 1950; S.R.N. Cert., General Nursing Council for England & Wales; Health Visitor/School Nurse Cert. of Royal Sanitary Institute, London, 1952. Address: P.O. Box 254, Freetown, Sierra Leone.

FREEMAN, Ifan Charles Harold, born 11th September 1910. Educationist. Education: Friars School, Bangor, Wales; M.A., University of Wales. Married, 2 daughters. Appointments: Major, Royal Artillery, 1939-46; Education Service Kenya, 1946-58; Assistant Director, ibid, 1953-58; Director of Education, Nyasaland, 1958-61; Permanent Secretary, Ministry of Education, Malawi, 1961-64; Registrar, University of Malawi, 1965—. Honours: C.M.G., 1964; T.D., 1961. Address: University of Malawi, P.O. Box 5097, Limbe, Malawi.

FRENCH, Sarah Anne, born 31st May 1940. Lecturer. Education: B.A.(Hons., Physics), Oxford University, U.K., 1961; Dip. Ed., London University, 1962: M.Phil., Physics, ibid, 1966. Appointments: Teacher, Ursulin High School, Brentwood, Essex, 1962-63; Assistant in Physics, University of Lovanium, Kinshasa, Democratic Republic of the Congo, 1966-68; Lecturer, University College, Cape Coast, Ghana, 1968-70. Memberships: Ghana Association of Science Teachers; Ghana Science Association; Association for Science Education. Publications: An Approach to the Teaching of MKS Magnetism & Electrics (G.A.S.T. Occasional Publication No. 4). Address: University College, Cape Coast, Ghana.

FRÈRE, Guy, born Montigny, Sambre, Senegal, 22nd January 1924. Industrialist. Education: Baccalaureat, Elementary Maths.; Specialized Maths., Lycée St. Louis, Paris, France; Professional Civil & Mining Engineer. Married, 1 child. Appointments include: Chief Engineer, Division of Symetain, Kinshasa (Congo); Assistant, then Director, Ste. Mines, Bou Azzer, & of Graara, Morocco; Director of Works, Sechiney St. Gobain (mines), Tananarive, Madagascar; Director, Phosphates of Thiés, Dakar, Senegal, & of Somirema (Mines de Terres Zares), Mauritania, & of African Silicates

Company, Dakar. Memberships include: Social & Economic Council of Senegal; Director, autonomous port of Dakar; Lions Club, Dakar. Honours: National Order, Senegal. Address: B.P. 241, Dakar, Senegal.

FRIEDLANDER, James Stuart, born 25th March 1942. Lawyer. Education: B.A., University of Wisconsin, U.S.A., 1963; J.D., Harvard University, 1966. Married. Appointments: U.S. Peace Corps Volunteer, Malawi, 1967-68; Treaties Officer, Ministry of External Affairs, Blantyre, 1969-70. Memberships: Sec., Olympic & Commonwealth Games Assn. of Malawi; Sec., Amateur Athletic Assn. of Malawi; World Peace Through Law Center; Alpha Epsilon Pi; Phi Kappa Phi; Lawn Tennis Association of Malawi; U.S. Professional Tennis Registry. Publications: Malawi Treaty Series (1964-69). Address: P.O. Box 943, Blantyre, Malawi.

FRIEDMAN, Fanny, born 25th March 1926. Doctor of Medicine. Education: Lovedale Alice, Cape Province, S. Africa; Wm. Pescon High, Kimberley; M.B., Ch.B., Capetown. Married, 1 son. Appointments: Private Practice in Kimberley & New Castle, Natal, 1952-58; Medical Officer, Swaziland Government, 1958-68; Permanent Secretary, Ministry of Health, Swaziland, 1968—. Awarded M.B.E., 1967. Address: P.O. Box 5, Mbanane, Swaziland.

FROST, Richard Aylmer, born London, U.K., 29th May 1905. Officer of the British Council (retired, 1965). Education: Westminster School; Christ Church, Oxford; Harvard University, U.S.A. Married, 2 sons, 2 daughters. Appointments included: before the war, on the Historical Staff of The Times; during the war, in Royal Air Force Volunteer Reserve; Head of Empire Information Service, Central Office of Information, 1946; joined The British Council as Representative, East Africa, to start the work of the Council, 1947; retired from The British Council, 1965. Memberships include: The Athenaeum, London; Nairobi Club, Kenya; Agricultural Society of Kenya. Publications include: The British Commonwealth & the World; The British Commonwealth & World Society. Honours, Prizes, etc: Stanhope Historical Essay Prize, Oxford Univ., 1926; Dixon Research Scholarship, Christ Church, 1928; University Fellowship, Harvard University, 1928-29; M.B.E. (Military), 1944; O.B.E. (Civil), 1952. Address: Kaprachoge, P.O. Box 63, Nandi Hills, Kenya.

FULTON, William Francis Monteith, born Aberdeen, Scotland, 12th December 1919. Medical Practitioner. Education: B.Sc., University of Glasgow, 1941; M.B., Ch.B. (Commend.), ibid, 1945; M.D.(Hons.), 1961; M.R.C.P.(London), 1949; ibid (Edin.), 1962; ibid, Glasgow, 1966; F.R.C.P., 1968. Married, 2 children. Appointments include: Accident Physician, Resident Surgeon, Western Infirmary, Glasgow; Surgeon, Merchant Navy; Medical Registrar, Western District Hospital, Glasgow; Research Assistant in Cardiology, University of Edinburgh; Senior Registrar in Medicine, Stobhill General Hospital, Glasgow, & Lecturer in Materia Medica & Therapeutics, University of Glasgow; subsequently, Consultant Physician & Senior Lecturer, ibid; Senior Fellow, Johns Hopkins Hospital, Baltimore, U.S.A.; Professor of Medicine, University College, Nairobi, Kenya. Memberships include: British Society for Experimental Medicine; Assn. of Physicians of Great Britain & Northern Ireland; British Cardiac Society; Scottish Assn. of Physicians; East African Assn. of Physicians. Publications include: The Coronary Arteries, 1965; Modern Trends in Pharmacology & Therapeutics, 1967. Address: University College, Nairobi, & Kenyatta National Hospital, P.O. Box 30588, Nairobi, Kenya.

FURLEY, Oliver Willis, born 11 July 1927. University Teacher. Education: M.A., St. Andrews University, Scotland, 1950; B.Litt., Oxford University, U.K., 1952. Appointments: Lecturer in History, St. Andrews University; ibid, Makerere University College, Uganda; University College of the West Indies; Edinburgh University; currently, Senior Lecturer in History, Makerere University, & Chairman of the Joint Board of Graduate Studies. Memberships: African Studies Association of the U.K. Publications: articles on E. African & West Indian History; a chapter in 'Britain Pre-Eminent'; History of Education in East Africa (co-author). Address: Makerere University, Box 7,062, Kampala, Uganda.

G

GABDOU, Mahamat, born 19 June 1934. Director of Commerce, Industry & Transport. Education: Diploma, Institut des Hautes d'Outre-Mer (I.H.E.O.M.), Paris; Economic & Financial Administration, 1960 & 1963. Married, 2 sons, 2 daughters. Appointments: Assistant Director of Economic Affairs, Ministry of Economics & Transport, 1964-65; Director of Commerce, Industry & Transport, ibid. Memberships: President, Cine Club, Fort Lamy; Executive Committee, U.N. Economic Commission for Africa. Recip. Chevalier de l'Ordre National du Tchad, 1965. Address: Ministry of Economics, Finance & Transport, B.P. No 424, Fort Lamy, Tchad.

GADDE, Carl-Frederick Olof, born 26 February 1918. Trade Promotion Adviser. Education: B.A., University of Lund, Sweden, 1941; B.L., ibid, 1946. Married. Appointments: Secretary, National Industry Commission, Sweden, 1946; Assistant Manager, General Export Association of Sweden, 1946; Deputy General Manager, 1962; Trade Promotion Adviser (U.N.) in Tanzania, 1968. Address: U.N.D.P., P.O. Box 9182, Dar es Salaam, Tanzania.

GAGLI, Kodjo Emmanuel, born Atatkpame, Togo, 22nd December 1913. Doctor of Medicine. Certificate of Primary Studies, Lome, Togo, 1928; Ponty School, Senegal, 1934; Diploma, School of Medicine, Dakar, 1938; Diploma, Doctor of Medicine, Paris, 1960; Diploma, Administrator of Public Health, Paris. Appointments: Doctor, Health Service, Togo, 1938-53; ibid, Dakar, Senegal, 1954-56; Director, Health Service, Togo, 1960;

Vice-President, National Assembly of Togo, 1965-66; Minister of Health & Justice, 1966-67. Honours: Medal of Honour for Epidemics; Officer, Order of Mono, Togo; German Grand Cross of Merti; Commander, National Order of Liberia. Address: B.P. 15, Lome, Togo.

GAISIE, Samuel Kwesi, born 28th January, 1938. University Lecturer. Education: Bekwai Methodistt School, Ghana, 1941-51; Mfantsipim Secondary School, 1951-55; B.A.(Hons., Sociology), London, Second Class Upper, University of Ghana, 1961; M.A., London School of Economics, 1964. Married, 3 children. Research Fellow in Charge, Demographic Unit, University of Ghana, Legon, 1968—. Member, International Union for the Scientific Study of Population. Publications: Dynamics of Population Growth in Ghana, 1969; Co-Author, Some New Results on Sampling of Vital Rates (in print); various papers in field. Honours: Ghana Government Bursary, 1956-57; Ghana Government University Scholarship, 1958-61; University of Ghana Postgraduate Fellowship, 1961-64. Address: Demographic Unit, University of Ghana, P.O. Box 96, Legon, Ghana.

GALAMBOS, Janos, born 1st September, 1940. Mathematician. Education: Primary & Secondary School, Hungary; Doctor Degree, Mathematics, L. Eotvos University, Budapest, 1958-63. Married. Appointments: Assistant Professor, L. Eotvos University, Budapest, 1963-64; Lecturer, University of Ghana, Legon 1965-69; Lecturer, University of Ibadan, Nigeria, 1969-70; Senior Lecturer, ibid, 1970. Memberships: Bolyai Math. Association; Institute of Mathematical Statistics. Author of 23 papers in professional publications. Address: Department of Maths., Temple University, Philadelphia, Pa. 19122, U.S.A.

GALBA-BRIGHT, Jacob, born Freetown, Sierra Leone, 3rd September 1898. Director of Companies. Education: Mays Memorial High School; Cathedral Boys' School; Collegiate School. Personal details: grandson of late Geo. A. Williams of Lagos; married with children. Appointments: Headmaster, Jordan Day School, Murray Town; Lay Preacher, United Methodist Church, Wilberforce Circuit; Tradesman & Newsagent, Gerihun, 1918; Founder, Import & Export Business, Freetown, 1919; spent 20 years in Nigeria & Ghana; Councillor, Central Ward, Freetown City Council, Sierra Leone; served on following committees: Fourah Bay College; Cost of Living; Joint Industrial Council; Railway Advisory; elected Alderman & Member for East Ward, Freetown City Council; Director, Sierra Leone Produce Marketing Board; Director, Sierra Leone Port Authority; Justice of the Peace; Commissioner for Oaths; Director, Sierra Leone Road Transport Corporation; Committee of Management, Freetown City Council; Board of Governors, Sierra Leone Grammar School; Hon. Consul for Japan in Sierra Leone, 1964. Memberships: Past Hon. Secretary, African Chamber of Commerce; Foundation Member, Chamber of Commerce of Sierra Leone; 1st Vice-President, ibid, 1964; Fellow, Institute of Directors; Churchman of the Anglican Communion & Lay Reader, Holy Trinity Parish; District Grand Master, all Scottish Lodges in Sierra Leone; Institute of Journalists, London, U.K.; F.N.C.M. Publications: History of Freemasonry in West Africa (Northern Freemason). Address: 3 Trelawney Street, P.O. Box 121, Freetown, Sierra Leone.

GALPIN (The Reverend), Alan Roy Clews, born 6th June 1933. Clerk in Holy Orders: Educationist. Education: Cranbrook School, Kent, U.K.; M.A., Classics & Theology, Cambridge University; Clifton Theological College; Postgraduate Certificate in Education, University of London. Married. Appointments: Assistant Curate, St. Paul's Church, Onslow Sq., London, 1959-62; Tutor & Chaplain at a Teacher Training College for Primary School Teachers; Educationist, employed by Government of Uganda. Memberships: Missionary, with the Church Missionary Society. Address: Canon Lawrence College, P.O. Box 81, Lira, Uganda.

GALPIN, Catharine Mary (née Arden-Clarke), born 23 June 1935. Housewife; formerly State Registered Nurse. Education: Sherborne School for Girls, Sherborne, Dorset, U.K., 1948-52; O.N.C., Wingfield Orthopaedic Hospital, 1953-55; S.R.N., St. Thomas' Hospital, London, 1955-59; R.S.C.N., Great Ormond St. Hospital for Sick Children, 1961-62. Personal details: Father Sir Charles Arden-Clarke was the last Governor of the Gold Coast & first Governor-General of Ghana. Appointments: Staff Nurse, Norfolk & Norwich Hospital, 1962. Memberships: Missionary with the Church Missionary Society. Recip. Gold Medal, St. Thomas's Hospital, 1959. Address: Canon Lawrence College, Box 81, Lira, N. Uganda.

GAMA, Mialama Lawrence, born 1st January, 1932. Director of National Service. Education: Certificate, Law, University of Dar es Salaam, Tanzania. Appointments: Administrative Assistant, 1954; Employment Assistant, 1954-55; Inspector, Police, 1956-60; Gazetted Police Officer, 1961-63; Chief of Personnel, National Service, 1963; Assistant Director, ibid, 1964-70; Director, 1970. Memberships: Tanu; Chairman, Tanu Study Group. Address: P.O. Box 1674, Dar es Salaam, Tanzania.

GAMLEN, Godfrey Loraine, born 11 March 1898. Engineer. Education: Marlborough College. Appointments: Served France, R.G.A., 1914-17; Surveyor, Persian Gulf Survey; District Engineer, Bengal Nagar Railway, India; Supervisory Engineer, Nyasaland Railways; Director & Engineer, Industrial Equipment, Kenya Railways. Memberships: F.R.G.S.; A.M.Int.T.; F. Pway Inst.; F.E.A. Inst. Engineers; Nairobi Club. Publications: Transport on River Shive, Nyasaland, R.G.S., Vol. 86 No. 5, 1935. Address: P.O. Box 51, Kisumu, Kenya.

GAMOR, Martha Schlinkmann, born Wabash, Ind., U.S.A., 28th November, 1928. Nursing Tutor. Education: R.N., Deaconess Hospital School of Nursing, Evansville, Ind., 1951; B.Sc., Nursing, University of Evansville, 1952. Married, 2 sons, 1 daughter. Appointments include: Instructor of Nursing, Deaconess Hospital, Evansville, 1952; Missionary Nurse, San José, Costa Rica, 1953; ibid, San Pedro Sula, Honduras, 1953-56; Missionary Nurse, Adidome,

Ghana, 1957-59; Nursing Tutor, Ministry of Health, Accra, Ho, Worawora, Ghana, 1960—. Memberships include: American Red Cross; Indiana State Nurses' Association; American National League of Nurses. Address: P.O. Box 1778, Accra, Ghana.

GANGE-HARRIS, Edward John, born 21st June 1917. Soldier; Civil Servant. Education: Bristol Cathedral School, U.K. Appointments: Major, R.A. (Retired); Officer in Charge of British Administration, Pakistan Army Headquarters, 1949-58; Executive Officer & District Commissioner, Nyasaland & Malawi, Central Africa, 1960—. Memberships: Pakistan Society in London; National Fauna Society of Malawi; The Wild Life Conservation & Preservation Society of South Africa. Editor, Volunteer Magazine of British Forces in Pakistan, 1949-53. Honours: Territorial Efficiency Medal; M.B.E., 1952. Address: P.O. Box 1, Mlanje, Malawi.

GARBA (Alhaji), Mallan Toulon, born 1918. Attached to the Cabinet, in charge of Missions at the Ministry of Public Works. Recip. of Medals, Honours, & Prizes from Niger, Upper Volta, Ivory Coast, Western Germany, & Tunisia. Address: c/o Vice-President of the Political Party in Power, Niamey, Niger.

GARBER, Eudora Lionetta, born Nigeria. Teacher. Education: Annie Walsh Memorial School, Freetown, Sierra Leone, 1932-35; Women Teachers' Training College, Freetown, 1936-38; Lincoln Teachers' Training College, Lincoln, U.K., 1948-50. Married. Appointments include: Assistant Teacher, Annie Walsh Memorial School, Freetown, Sierra Leone, 1939; Senior Assistant Teacher, ibid; Co-opted Member, Freetown City Council Education & Publicity Committee, 1959-66. Memberships include: active, Girl Guides' Association, 1934—; Deputy Chief Commissioner of Sierra Leone, 1964; Chief Commissioner, 1966—; Certified Girl Guide Trainer, 1955; attended West African Regional Girl Guide Conferences in Nigeria, 1955, 1964, & All-Africa Conf., Salisbury, Rhodesia, 1956. Honours, Prizes, etc.: Medal of Merit, Girl Guides Association, 1956; awarded Palm Leaf Medal by Sierra Leone Boy Scouts Association for special distinguished service in Girl Guides Association, 1970. Address: 148A Circular Road, Freetown, Sierra Leone.

GARDINER, Robert K. A., born Kumasi, Ghana, 29th September 1914. Executive Secretary, United Nations Economic Commission for Africa. Education: B.A.(Econ.), Cambridge University, U.K., 1941; M.A., Oxford University, 1942. Married, 1 son, 2 daughters. Appointments: Lectr., Economics, Fourah Bay College, Sierra Leone, 1943-46; Mbr., Trusteeship Dept., United Nations, N.Y., U.S.A., 1947-49; Dir., Extramural Studies, University College, Ibadan, Nigeria, 1949-53; Dir., Social Welfare & Community Development, Government of Ghana, 1953-55; Permanent Secretary, Ministry of Housing, Government of Ghana, 1955-57; Head, Ghana Civil Serive, 1957-59; Deputy Executive Sec., U.N. Economic Commn. for Africa, Addis Ababa, Ethiopia, 1959-60; Mbr., U.N. Mission to the Congo, 1961; Dir., Div. of Public Administration, U.N., N.Y., U.S.A., 1961-62; Officer-in-Charge, U.N. Operations in the Congo, 1962-63; Executive Sec., U.N. Economic Commn. for Africa, Addis Ababa, 1962—; Reith Lectr., B.B.C., 1965; Gilbert Murray Memorial Lectr., Oxfam, Oxford, 1969; J. B. Danquah Mem. Lectr., Ghana, 1970. Mbr. of various professional societies & activities in international affairs. Publications: The Development of Social Administration, w. H. O. Judd, 2nd edn., 1959; A World of Peoples, 2nd edn., 1965. Recipient of nine honorary doctorates. Address: c/o U.N. Economic Commission for Africa, Addis Ababa, Ethiopia.

GARDNER (Reverend) Geoffrey Maurice, born 12th February 1928. Ordained Minister. Education: B.A.(Hons.), London, U.K., 1951; P.G.C.E., London, 1952; Dip.Th.(Dunelm), 1959. Married, 2 children. Appointments: Tutor, St. Peter's College, Zaria, 1953-57; Curate, Bradford, U.K., 1959-61; Teacher, Christ's School, Ado-Ekiti, 1961-68; Tutor, Immanuel College, Ibadan, Nigeria, 1968—; Principal, ibid, 1970—. Chairman, Association of Bible Knowledge Teachers of Nigeria. Address: Immanuel College, P.O. Box 515, Ibadan, Nigeria.

GARDNER, Phyllis Annette, born 29th October 1928. Medical Practitioner. Education: M.B.B.S., London, 1953; D.R.C.O.G., 1955; A.K.C.; King's College & St. George's Hospital, London, U.K. Married to Mr. Geoffrey Gardner, 2 sons. Appointments: House Officer, Bristol, 2 years; in training, Church Missionary Society, 1 year; Medical Missionary, Wusasa Hosp., Zaria, Nigeria, 1956-57; Medical Officer in Charge, Ile Abiye Hospital, Ado Ekiti, 1961; Locum M.O., University of Ibadan Health Service, 1968—. Memberships: Christian Medical Fellowship; Inter Varsity Fellowship of Evangelical Unions; C.M.S. Address: Immanuel College, Box 515, Ibadan, Nigeria & Glenfern Hemyock, Devon, U.K.

GARVEY-WILLIAMS, Frank Henry, born 18th December 1921. Educator. Education: Teignmouth Grammar School, U.K.; Durham University. Appointments: Master, Nyakasura School, Uganda, 1952-56; Master, Ntare School, 1956-57; Headmaster, Sir Samuel Baker School, 1958-63; Sr. Inspector of Secondary Schools, 1963-70; Asst. Chief Inspector of Schools, 1970—. Fellow, Royal Geographical Society; Member, Uganda Society. Address: Central Inspectorate, Ministry of Education, P.O. Box 3568, Kampala, Uganda.

GATHANI, Bachulal Tribhovan, born Gondal, Saurastra, India, 16th July 1910. Company Director. Education: Grassia College, India. Married. Appointments: Managing Director, Gathani Group of Companies in East Africa, United Kingdon & India; Acting Member, Legislative Council of Kenya, 1954; served on numerous Government & Public Boards & Committees; former member of Board of Commerce & Industry, Labour Advisory Board, Development Committee, Trade Licensing Board, Education Committee, Immigration Board, etc. Fellowships: British Society of Commerce; Institute of Chartered Secretaries.

Memberships: Past-President, East African Indian National Congress; President, Indian Association, Nairobi, Kenya; President, Federation of Chambers of Commerce & Industry of Eastern Africa, 1950-53, 1954-58; twice President of Indian Chamber of Commerce, Nairobi; Trustee of several institutions. Address: c/o Gathani Ltd., P.O. Box 329, Nairobi, Kenya.

GAVA, Ramadhan Kasule Kizito, born Entebbe, 20th February, 1910. Retired Assistant Education Officer. Education: Kibuli Central School; Teachers' Certificate, Kampala T. T. College, Uganda; 30 Extramural Courses, Makerere. Widower, 7 sons, 6 daughters; Remarried, 2 sons. Appointments: Teacher, 1928-39; Education Secretary-General, Muslim Schools, Uganda, 1940-64; Assistant Education Officer, Uganda Government, 1965-68; Retired, 1969. Memberships: Secretary, Uganda Muslim Education Association, 15 years; ibid, Young Men's Association, 20 years; ibid, Uganda Muslim Community, 22 years; ibid, East African Muslim Welfare Society, 5 years; Chairman, Probation Case Committee, 5 years. Publications: Eddiini Busiramu; Okugungula Abato Muddiini. Recipient, Independence Medal by H.M. The Queen of England, 1962. Address: P.O. Box 374, Kampala, Uganda.

GEBREMIKAEL, G. SELASSIÉ, born Asmara, Ethiopia, 19th June 1932. Permanent Representative of Pan-African Workers Congress & World Confederation of Labour. Education: Catholic Mission of Saganeite Elementary School, 1947-50; Catholic Mission Middle School, Adi Ugri, 1950-52; B.Phil., University of Propoganda Fide, Rome, Italy, 1955; License, Philosophy, ibid, 1956; 1 vear Law, Asmara, 1956; Faculty of Law, Turin, 1957; Diploma, Postgraduate Course (I.P.S.O.A.), 1960; LL.D., University of Rome, 1964. Appointments: Inspector of Labour, Asmara, Ethiopia, 1956-57; Legal Experience, Turin, Italy, 1958-60; Social Studies of Pro Deo, Rome, 1961-62; i/c African Problems, World Committee, U.I.J.D.C., 1963-64; Permanent Representative, Pan African Workers Congress & World Confederation of Labour by E.C.A., I.L.O., O.U.A., Addis Ababa, Ethiopia, 1965-69. Participant in numerous international conferences. Address: P.O. Box 2783, Addis Ababa, Ethiopia.

GEKONYO, James Mbogo, born 27th March, 1928. Medical Practitioner; University Lecturer. Education: Science & Education, Makerere College, Kampala, Uganda; M.B.B.S., St. Mary's Hospital, London, U.K., 1958; D.P.H., University of Liverpool, 1962. Appointments: Intern Posts, London suburban hospitals; M.O.H., District Hospitals, Kenya Government Medical Service: Medical Officer i/c Training; Senior Lecturer, Department of Preventive Medicine-Dean, Faculty of Medicine, University of Nairobi, 1968—. Memberships: Council, Kenya Medical Association; Expert Committee on Professional & Technical Education of Medical & Auxiliary Personnel, WHO, 1967. Address: University of Nairobi, P.O. Box 30588, Nairobi, Kenya.

GEMIN, Gerard, born 22nd March, 1936. Travel Agent. St. Sulpice College, Paris, France.

Married. Appointments: Assistant Manager, Havas Travel Service, London, U.K.; Manager, Havas Exprinter, Abidjan, Ivory Coast; ibid, Ivoire Voyages, ibid; ibid, I.C.T.A./Ivoire Voyages; Memberships: Vice-President, Skal Club, Abidjan; Treasurer, Syndivoyages, Abidjan; ibid, Aeroclub des Lagunes, Abidjan. Honours: Chevalier de L'ordre National Ivoireiu. Address: P.O. Box 2636, Abidjan, Ivory Coast.

GEORGIADIS, Byron Nicholas, born Tanzania, 29th April 1927. Barrister-at-Law. Education: Prince of Wales School, Nairobi, Kenya, 1940-45; M.A.(Hons.), Brasenose College, Oxford, U.K., 1946-50. Married, 2 sons, 1 daughter. Appointments include: Advocate of the High Court of Kenya, 1952; Advocate of the High Court of Tanzania, 1959. Memberships: Board of Governors, Prince of Wales School, Kenya; President, Kenya Fly Fishers Club; Limura Hunt; Malindi Sea Fishing Club; Nairobi Club; Old Cambrian Society. Address: P.O. Box 2851, Nairobi, Kenya.

GERMAN, Gordon Allen, born Aberdeen, Scotland, U.K., 12th May 1935. Physician; Professor of Psychiatry. Education: M.B., Ch.B.(Commend.), University of Aberdeen Faculty of Medicine, 1958; D.P.M., Royal College of Physicians & Surgeons, London, 1962. Appointments include: Senior House Officer, Ross Clinic, Aberdeen, 1959-60; Psychiatric Registrar, ibid, 1960-63; Senior Registrar, 1963-64; Psychiatric Registrar, The Maudsley Hospital, London, 1964-65; Senior Registrar, Psychiatry, ibid, 1965-66; Professor & Head, Department of Psychiatry, Makerere University College Medical School, Uganda; Consultant Psychiatrist, Uganda Government, 1966—. Memberships include: Royal College of Physicians, Edinburgh, 1963; Chairman, Uganda Mental Health Advisory Committee, 1966—; Founder Member, Uganda Child Development Group, 1967—; Chairman, Steering Committee for African Assn. of Psychiatrists, 1968; Vice-Chairman, Uganda National Association for Mental Health, 1969; Council Member, African Assn. of Psychiatrists, 1969—; East African Assn. of Physicians. Author of numerous publications in field including: Madness & Its Myths, East African Medical Journal, 1959; Effects of Serum from Schizophrenics on Evoked Cortical Potentials in the Rat, Brit. Journal of Psych., 1963. Recip. of many prizes & awards including: Herman Goldman Lecturer, New York Medical Centre, New York, U.S.A., 1970. Address: P.O. Box 7072, Kampala, Uganda.

GETAHUN TAFESSE, born 2nd April 1927. Cabinet Minister. Education: 12th Grade, H.S.I.S.S., Ethiopia, 1950; Law, by correspondence, La Salle; Economics, by correspondence, Bennett College. Widower, 1 daughter. Appointments: Teacher, Hailé Selassié 1st Secondary School; Assistant Personnel Manager, Telecommunication Board; Director, Security Department; Director General, His Imperial Majesty's Private Cabinet; Assistant Minister, ibid. Honours: H.I.M.'s Hailé Selassié War Medal with Five Palm Tree Leaves, Ministry of PEN, Addis Ababa; Victory Star Medal, ibid; Royal Victory Medal by H.M. Queen Elizabeth; Dr. Nkrumah Medal, Ghana. Address: His

Imperial Majesty's Private Cabinet, Special Branch, P.O. Box 511, Addis Ababa, Ethiopia.

GHAI, Dharam, born 29th June 1936. Economist. Education: B.A., University of Oxford, U.K., 1958; B.Phil.(Econs.), ibid, 1959; Ph.D.(Econs.), Yale University, U.S.A., 1961. Appointments: Lecturer in Economics, Makerere University College, 1961-65; Research Fellow, Economic Growth Centre, Yale University, U.S.A., 1965-66; Senior Research Fellow, Institute for Development Studies, University College, Nairobi, Kenya, 1966-67; Research Professor & Director of Economic Research, Institute for Development Studies, University College, Nairobi, 1967—. Publications: Taxation for Development: A Case Study of Uganda; 40 articles on development possibilities of E. African Countries. Editor of: Portrait of a Minority: Asians in E. Africa. Address: I.D.S., University of Nairobi, Box 30197, Nairobi, Kenya.

GHAIDAN, Usam Isa, born 5th February 1936. Architect. Education: Diploma in Architecture, Hammersmith, U.K. Appointments: 7 years of private practice as an Architect; currently, Lecturer in Architecture, University College, Nairobi, Kenya.

GHALIOUNGUI, Paul, born 18th September 1908. Physician. Education: M.B., B.Ch., Cairo, U.A.R., 1929; M.D., ibid, 1933; M.R.C.P., London, U.K., 1934; F.R.C.P., 1964; (Corr.) F.A.C.P., 1969; Kaiserin Elisabeth Spital, Vienna, Austria; London Hospital. Married, 2 sons. Appointments: Professor & Chairman, Internal Medicine, Ain Shams University, Cairo, U.A.R.; Consultant Endocrinologist, Director of Laboratories, Ministry of Public Health, Kuwait. Memberships: Honorary Life President, Egyptian Endocrinological Society; General Secretary, Institut d'Egypte & Egyptian Society of the History of Medicine; Board, Egyptian Society of the History of Science; Vice-President, Egyptian Society of Rheumatic Diseases; National Research Centre; Fellow, Faculty of History of Medicine, L.S.M., London; ibid, Royal Society of Medicine, Sections of History of Medicine & Endocrinology; corresponding member of various other scientific societies. Publications (in English): Magic & Medical Science in Ancient Egypt, 1963; Health & Healing in Ancient Egypt, 1965; Thyroid Enlargement in Africa with Special Reference to the Nile Basin, 1965; Endocrines, Gout & Vitamins; (in Arabic): The Medicine of the Ancient Egyptians, 1958; Medicine & Magic, 1960; Health & Healing in Ancient Egypt, 1965; Ibn an Nafis, 1970; Contributor to books & encyclopaedias; Author of 150 papers. Honours: invited to lecture in numerous countries. Address: P.O.B. 8808, Personal, Sabah Hospital, Kuwait.

GHARTEY-SAM, Kweku, born Winneba, Ghana, 12th April 1933. Diplomat. Education: Teachers' Certificate 'A'; Intermediate B.Sc. (Econ.), London; Branch 'A' Foreign Service Examination. Married, 1 son, 4 daughters. Appointments: Teacher, Methodist Boys' School, Winneba, 1953-58; Higher Executive Officer, Ministry of External Affairs, Accra, 1959-60; 3rd Secretary, Embassy of Ghana, Tokyo, Japan, 1960-62; 2nd Secretary, ibid, 1962-63; Desk Officer, East European Affairs, Legal Division, Administration, etc., Ghana Ministry of Foreign Affairs, 1963-66; Charge d'Affaires, Embassy of Ghana, Bamako, Mali, 1966-68; Head of Chancery, ibid, 1968-70; Chief Passport Officer, Ministry of External Affairs, 1970. Memberships: President, Winneba Branch, Methodist Youth Fellowship; Executive Member, Ghana Youth Association; Workcamp Association of Ghana; Peoples Education Association of Ghana. Address: Chief Passport Officer, Ministry of Foreign Affairs, P.O. Box M 53, Accra, Ghana.

GHATAK, Jagadananda, born 2nd January 1928. Senior Lecturer in Botany. Education: B.Sc.(Hons.), Calcutta University, India, 1949; M.Sc., ibid, 1951; Ph.D., Leeds University, U.K., 1959. Appointments: Lecturer in Botany, City College, Calcutta, India, 1952; Lecturer, Surendranath College, Calcutta, 1953-57; Ph.D. Student, Leeds University, 1957-59; Lecturer in Botany, Surendranath College, 1959-61; Systematic Botanist, Botanical Survey of India, 1961-65; Senior Lecturer in Botany, University College, Cape Coast, 1965—. Memberships: Life Member, Linnaean Society, London, 1967—; F.L.S., London; Ghana Science Association, 1970—; Past Member, Botanical Society of Bengal, India, & the Indian Science Congress Association. Publications include: Contbr. to research pubIs. on Cytotaxonomy of Tropical Pteridophytes & Cytoembryology of Bignoniaceae in Journal of Linnaean Society, London; Nucleus; Bull. Bot. Surv. India; Bulletin Botanical Society, Bengal; Proceedings of Indian Academy of Science; Proceedings Indian Science Congress; Journal University College, Cape Coast. Address: Department of Botany University College, P.O. Box 021, U.C.C.C., Cape Coast, Ghana.

GHEBREMEDHIN ASSIEL (Col.), born 15th March 1919. Superior Police Officer. Education: Secondary, Italian Recruits' Course; Police N.C.O.s' Course; Police Inspectors' Course; Senior Police Officer Course. Personal details: member of noble family of Zazzega Hamasien Eritrea, direct descendent of Princess Sebenegherghis, Emperor Adiam Seghed Yasu, Emperor Fasilidos of Gondar. Appointments: Member, Imperial Federal Council, 1952-54; Superintendent of Police, various districts of Eritrea Police Force, 1954-63; Assistant Commissioner of Police, Eritrea, 1963-65; Deputy Chief Police Officer, Kaffa Province, 1965-68; ibid, Tigrai Province, 1968—. Memberships: President, Kaffa Prov. Football Federation, 1965-68; Vice-President, Lions Club, Jimma, 1965-68; Board of Directors, Y.M.C.A., Jimma, 1966-68; ibid, Tigrai, 1968-70; President, Tigrai Prov. Football Federation, 1968-70. Author, Chi e' dell'Eritrea. Honours: Officer of the Order of the Ethiopia Star; H.S. First Silver Medal; H.S. First Gold Medal. Address: 20 Aba Mechial Sefer 133/A, Asmara, Ethiopia.

GHOSH, Asok Kumar, born 21st November 1922. Obstetrician & Gynaecologist. Education: Matriculation, Calcutta, India, 1937; Inter.

Science, Calcutta, 1939; M.B., B.S., Carmichael Medical College, Calcutta, 1945. Married. Appointments: House Appointments & Registrarship, 1945-51; Gynaecologist, Sindri Fertilizers & Chemicals Ltd., 1951-59; Medical Officer, Ghana Medical Service, 1959-65; Senior Medical Officer, Gynae, Ghana Medical Service, 1965-70. Memberships: Indian Medical Association; Ghana Medical Association. Publications: Prenatal Observations on Bengali Women (I.M.A.&R.) 1948; The Aged & the General Practitioner (I.M.A.&R.), 1950; Stress Incontinence in Women (I.M.A.&R.), 1960; Ganglion Block as a Method of Analgesia in Operations on Cervix Uterii (I.M.A.&R.), 1956. Address: Cape Coast Central Hospital, P.O. Box 174, Cape Coast, Ghana.

GHOUHAN, Nagindas Ranchhod, born 15th April 1935. Bank Official. Education: B.Com. Appointments: Accountant; Acting Bank Manager, Nanyuki, Kenya. Memberships: Treasurer, Lions Club International; Committee Member, Nanyuki Sports Club; Trustee, Indian Association, Nanyuki. Address: P.O. Box 214, Nanyuki, Kenya.

GIBSON, Ian Alexander Scott, born 14th February 1922. Plant Pathologist. Education: Tonbridge School, U.K., 1935-39; M.A., Sidney Sussex College, University of Cambridge, 1939-41, 1945-47; Ph.D., ibid, 1951-53, 1955. Married, 1 son. Appointments: Reconnaissance Pilot, R.A.F., S.E. Asia, 1941-45; Plant Pathologist, Overseas Food Corporation, Urambo, Tanganyika, 1948-51; Forest Pathologist, Kenya Forest Department, 1953-66; Forest Pathologist, East African Agriculture & Forestry Research Organization, 1966-70. Memberships: Association of Applied Biologists; British Mycological Society; American Phytopathological Society; Institute of Biology. Author of some 40 scientific papers. Address: P.O. Box 30148, Nairobi, Kenya.

GIBSON (Colonel) R. Henri, born Harper City, Cape Palmas, Maryland County, Liberia, 14th October 1927. Professional Soldier. Education: St. Mark's Parish Day School, Cape Palmas; St. John High School, Cape Mount; U.S. Army Ordnance School, Aberdeen, Md., U.S.A. Married, 4 children. Appointments: Mail Clerk, local Post Office, Liberia, 1947-48; Provate, Liberian Frontier Force, 1950; commissioned as Justice of the Peace, 1968; served as Aide-de-Camp to President of Liberia, 3 months, 1968; rose to rank of full Colonel, 1970, with special assignment of Commander of the President of Liberia's Special Guard (Mansion Guard). Memberships: Trinity Cathedral Episcopal Church; Ancient Free & Accepted Masons; United Brothers of Friendship; Odd Fellows; Elks of Liberia; Army Officers Club. Honours: The Liberian Order of Distinguished Service; Knight Official, Liberian Humane Order of African Redemption; Good Conduct Medal; Long Service (15 yrs.) Medal; Commander, Star of Africa, Liberia; Royal Victorian Order, U.K.; Commander, National Order of the Central African Republic; Order of the Republic of West Germany; Order of National Merit, Mauritania; Member of President of Liberia's Suite on State visits to U.S.A., Italy, Israel, U.K. & Ghana, 1958-62. Address: Tubman Apartment Hall, c/o Executive Mansion, Monrovia, Liberia.

GIHA, Omer Hassan, born 1st January 1933. University Lecturer; Research Worker. Education: Primary, Intermediate & Secondary Education in the Sudan; Diploma in Agriculture, Faculty of Agriculture, University of Khartoum, Sudan; M.Sc., ibid; Ph.D., University of Nottingham, U.K. Appointments: Inspector of Agriculture, Ministry of Agriculture, Republic of the Sudan; Demonstrator, Department of Crop Protection, Faculty of Agriculture, University of Khartoum; Lecturer, Dept. of Crop Protection, ibid; Lecturer & Research Worker, Dept. of Crop Protection, Faculty of Agriculture, Institute for Agricultural Research, Samaru, Nigeria. Memberships: Sudan Philosophical Society; Sudan Agricultural Society. Publications: Epidemiology of Cotton leaf curl virus in the Sudan, Cotton Gr. Review, 1969; Fusarium wilt of Cotton in the Sudan, Cotton Gr. Review, 1969. Address: Dept. of Crop Protection, Institute for Agricultural Research, P.M.B. 1044, Zaria, Nigeria.

GILBEY, John Edward Mortimer. Missionary, Congregational Council for World Mission. Education: Silcoates School, Nr. Wakefield, Yorks., U.K.; The Queen's College, Oxford. Married, 5 children. Appointments: Headmaster, Ambatonakanga Boys' High School, Tananarive, Madagascar, 1949-54; Treasurer, London Missionary Society, Tananarive, 1955-66; Administrative Secretary, Church of Jesus Christ in Madagascar, 1967-69; General Secretary, Yorkshire Congregational Union, 1970—. Address: 12 Westfield Terrace, Wakefield, Yorks., U.K.

GILLE, Alain Henri Gerard, born 3rd November 1922. International Civil Servant (UNESCO). Education: Lycée Saint-Louis & Institut National Agronomique, Paris, France; University of Montreal, Canada; Cornell University, U.S.A. Married, 2 children. Appointments: Research Engineer, Laboratoire des Agriculteurs de France, 1946; Head of Research, Laboratoire de Biogeographie, Montreal, 1947-48; Charge des questions de conservation, UNESCO, 1949-58; Science Officer for Africa, UNESCO, 1959-63; Director, UNESCO Field Science Office for Africa, 1964-70. Memberships include: Soc. de Biogeographie, France; Soc. pour la Protection de la Nature et d'Acclimatation de France; Association des Ecrivains Scientifiques de France. Comite Scientifique du Parc National de la Vanoise, France; East African Wildlife Society, Kenya. Publication: Ecologie des principaux types de paturage de la region de Granby, 1948; Ecologie du Spiraea tomentosa, 1950; Conservation Education, 1949; Survey of the Natural Resources of the African Continent, 1953; Our African Heritage, 1953; Survey of the Scientific & Technical Potential of the Countries of Africa. Address: UNESCO/FSOA, P.O. Box 30592, Nairobi, Kenya.

GILLETT, Jan Bevington, born 28th May 1911. Taxonomic Botanist. Education: Leighton Park School, Reading, U.K., 1925-29; King's College, Cambridge, 1930-34. Appointments:

Biology Master, Cheadle Hulme School, 1936-40; War Service, Burma, 1940-46; Botanist, Deft Agriculture, Baghdad, Iraq, 1946-49; Flora of Tropical East Africa, Royal Botanic Gardens, Kew, 1949-64; Botanist in Charge, East African Herbarium, Nairobi, Kenya, 1964-70. Fellow of Linnaean Society, London. Member of International Association of Plant Taxonomy. Publications: The Plant Formations of Western British Somaliland & the Harar Province of Abyssinia, 1941; Indigofera (Microbair) in Tropical Africa, 1958; various taxonomic papers mainly on African Papilicroceae; Pest Pressure, an underestimated factor in Evolution, 1962. Address: East African Herbarium, Box 5166, Nairobi, Kenya.

GILLOUX, Paul Jean Marie, born 4th January 1922. Director of Bank. Education: Licencie en Droit. Married, 4 children. Appointments: Director, B.N.C.I., Basseterre, Guadeloupe; S/Director, B.I.C.I., Douala, Cameroun; Director, B.N.P., Cotonou, Dahomey. Memberships: Rotary Club. Awarded: Chevalier de l'ordre National du Merite. Address: Banque Nationale de Paris, B.P. 75, Cotonou, Dahomey.

GILMOUR, Andrew Winter, born 29th October 1931. Company Director. Trinity College, Glenalmond, Scotland, U.K. Married, 3 sons. Appointments: Chairman, Blyth Brothers & Co. Ltd.; Director, Mauritius Commercial Bank Ltd. Memberships: Mauritius Naval & Military Gymkhana Club; Grand Bay Yacht Club. Address: Blyth Brothers & Co. Ltd., P.O. Box 56, Port Louis, Mauritius.

GINGYERA-PINYCWA, A. G. G., born 22nd January 1938. University Lecturer. Education: Senior Secondary School, Nyapea College, West Nile; B.A., Makerere University, Kampala, Uganda; M.A., University of Chicago, U.S.A.; currently, doctral candidate. Married, 2 children. Appointments: Assistant District Commissioner, Karamota & Teso Districts, Uganda; Acting Town Clerk, Soroti; Lecturer, Makerere University, Kampala. Author of several articles in learned journals. Address: Department of Political Science, Makerere University, P.O. Box 7062, Kampala, Uganda.

GIRMA W. GIORGIS, born 12th December, 1925. Civil Servant; Businessman. Education: Taferi Mekonnen School, Ethiopia, 1932-35; Scuola Principe Pipiemote, 1937-40; studied in Canada, Sweden & Netherlands. Married, 5 children. Appointments include: Signal Corps, Ethiopian Army, 1941; commissioned Signals Officer, 1943; transferred to Imperial Ethiopian Air Force, 1946; Chief, ATCS & Ground Service Division, Civil Aviation Department, 1950; Chief, Federal Civil Aviation Department, Asmara, 1956; elected Vice-President, ICAO, 1958; Director-General, Ministry of Public Works & Communications, 1959; ibid, Ministry of Commerce, Industry & Planning, 1959; elected Member of Parliament & President of House of Deputies, 1960; Member, Municipal Council, Addis Ababa; Director, Kaffa & Illubabor Wood Industry S.C.; Managing Director, Commerce & Development Activities, S.C.; Australian Trade Correspondent; Head, Ethiopian delegations to numerous international conferences. Memberships: Board of Directors, Addis Ababa Chamber of Commerce; Lions International Addis Ababa Club; Social Service Society, Addis Ababa; Member & Adviser of several co-operative organizations. Author, Air & Men—General Knowledge of Aviation. Honours: Halié Seiassié Star Medal Cavalery; Menilik II Service Medal Cavalery; City Council Gold Medal for Community Service & Leaderships. Address: P.O. Box 377, Addis Ababa, Ethiopia.

GITATHA, Samuel Kinyanjui. Parasitologist. Education: B.Sc., M.Sc., Columbia University, New York, U.S.A. Appointments: Senior Scientific Officer (Protozoologist), East African Trypanosomiasis Research Organization, 1964-69. Member of East African Academy. Publications: Lack of Influence of Sex and Post Weaning age on Susceptibility of Mice to Trypanosome Infection, I.S.C.T.R., Nairobi, 1966; Some Investigations on the Effect of Berenil in Cattle Trypanosomiasis, I.S.C.T.R., Bangui, 1968; Treatment of dogs experimentally infected with T.brucei sub-group organisms.

GLEDHILL, David, born 31st July 1929. University Lecturer. Education: Heath Grammar School, Halifax, Yorks., U.K.; Durham University. Memberships: Institute of Biology; Linnean Society of London; British Ecological Society; International Society of Plant Morphologists; Association pour l'Etude Taxonomique de la Flore d'Afrique Tropilale. Author of articles & papers in prof. jrnls. Address: Department of Botany, University of Bristol, Bristol BS8 1U9, U.K.

GLOVER, Immanuel Ablade, born 1st August 1934. Lecturer; Artist. Education: Art Teachers' Certificate, Kumasi College of Technology, Ghana, 1957-58; Diploma of Art, Central & National Diploma in Design, L.C.C. Central School of Art & Design, London, U.K., 1959-62; Art Teachers' Diploma, Newcastle University, 1964-65. Married, 3 children. Appointments: Art Tutor, Winneba Specialists' Traning College, 1963; Poster Artist, Ghana Information Services, Accra, Ghana, 1964; Lecturer, Fabric Design & Printing, University of Science & Technology, Kumasi, 1965—; Owner, Glo Art Gallery (Ghana's first & only art gallery). Memberships: Secretary/Organizer, Ghanaian Contemporaries (artist group); Fellow, Royal Society of Arts. Publications: Adinkra Symbolism, a chart of Adinkra symbols, 1969. Six one-man exhibitions of textiles, drawings & paintings, 1963, 1964, 1967, 1968, 1969, 1970. Brush name: nee glo. Address: Faculty of Art, University of Science & Technology, Kumasi, Ghana.

GODFREY, Victor Nigel, born London, U.K., 18th February 1917. Social Administrator. Education: King Edward VI's School, Chelmsford; London School of Economics, University of London. Married, 1 son, 1 daughter. Appointments: Major, British Army, 1940-46; Senior Probation Officer, Essex Probation Service, 1946-53; Principal Probation Officer, Zambia, 1954-57; Chief Social Welfare Officer, Zambia, 1957-61; Director, Welfare & Probation

Services, Zambia, 1962-64; Assistant Secretary, Housing, 1964-65, & Social Development, 1965-66; Secretary, Zambia National Provident Fund, 1966—. Memberships: Fellow, Royal Society of Arts; British Institute of Management; Royal Institute of Public Administration; Institute of Office Management; Institute of Personnel Management; Associate, Institue of Directors; Past President, Rotary Club of Lusaka; Chainama Hills Hospital Advisory Committee; Workmen's Compensation Control Board; Chairman, Chelston Township Council, 1965-70; Founder & Chairman, Zambia Society for the Care of the Aged. Honours: Territorial Decoration; Impala Award for services to Scouting, 1946-68. Address: P.O. Box R.W. 99, Lusaka, Zambia.

GODINHO, Carlo Placido, born 4th November, 1926. Businessman; Hotelier. Education: M.A., Cambridge University, U.K.; Law degree, ibid. Appointments: Managing Director, Norman Godinho & Sons Ltd.; ibid, Speke Hotel Ltd.; ibid, Kampala Playhouse Ltd., Uganda. Memberships: Chairman, Income Tax Local Committee, ibid, Board of Governors, Hirnomi Teacher Training College; Norman Godinho Primary School; Member, 2 Secondary School Boards of Governors; Past Deputy District Governor, Lions Clubs, District 411 E.A. Recipient, Medal from Pope Paul, 'Pro Ecclesia et Pontifice', 1969. Address: P.O. Box 159, Kampala, Uganda.

GOMA, Lameck Kazembe Haza, born Lundazi, Zambia, 4th August 1930. Zoologist; Educator; University Administrator. Education: Lubwa Mission, 1942-45; Munali Secondary School, 1945-49; B.Sc.(Rhodes), Fort Hare University College, South Afria, 1950-52; B.A.(Zoology), Cambridge University, U.K., 1953-55; M.A., ibid., 1959; Ph.D.(Zoology), London University. Personal details: born of Ruling House, Goma Clan & Kambombo Royal Family; married, 2 sons, 1 daughter. Appointments include: Research Entomologist, Department of Agriculture, Northern Rhodesia, 1952-53; Nuffield Research Fellow in Zoology, Makerere University College, Uganda, 1955-60; Research Fellow, Ross Institute, London School of Hygiene & Tropical Medicine, London University, U.K., 1960-62; The Entomologist, E. African Virus Research Institute, Entebbe, Uganda, & Hon. Lecturer in Entomology, Makerere, 1962-64; Lecturer in Zoology, University of Ghana, Legon, Accra, 1964-65; Professor & Head of Zoology, University of Zambia, 1965-69; Pro-Vice-Chancellor, ibid, 1966-68; Vice-Chancellor, 1969—. Memberships include: 1st Chairman, Uganda Branch, & a Vice-President, E. African Academy, 1962-64; Executive Committee, E. African Society for Biological Research; Chairman, Zambia's National Food & Nutrition Commission; National Council for Scientific Research, Zambia; National Commission for UNESCO; Official Representative of Zambia, Scientific Council of Africa, O.A.U.; ibid, Commonwealth Scientific Committee; Chairman, Bd. of Governors, Zambia 64 Foundation. Publications include: Ngoza na Kasiwa, 1962; The Mosquito, 1966; also author of scientific & conference papers. Address: The University of Zambia, P.O. Box 2379, Lusaka, Zambia.

GOMEZ, Robert-Michel, born 20th April 1934. Primary School Inspector. Education: Primary Studies, Cotonou, & Abomey, Dahomey, 1942-47; C.E.P.E., Victor Ballot College, Porto-Novo, 1947-52; B.E.P.C., Dabou, Ivory Coast, 1952-54; Baccalaureat, William Ponty School, Senegal, 1954-55; C.F.E.N., University of Dakar, Senegal, 1960-62; C.E.L.G., C.E.S., High School, St. Cloud, France. Married, 3 children. Appointments: Teacher, 1955-60; Director of College of General Instruction, 1961-66; Technical Counsellor, Ministry of National Education, 1967-70; Inspector of Primary Schools, 1970—. Publications: 'Mon Premier Livre de Vocabulaire' (elementary educational book). Address: Inspector of Primary Education, Parakou, Dahomey.

GONDWE, Goodall Edward, born 1st Decmber, 1936. Banker. Education: Cambridge Overseas School Certificate, 1st Division Certificate, Blantyre Secondary School, Malawi, 1957; Cambridge Overseas Higher School Certificate, Biology, Chemistry & General Paper, Dedza Secondary School, 1959; University College of Rhodesia, 1960-62; University College of Makerere, Kampala, Uganda, 1962; B.Sc.(Econ.), London. Personal details: brother & father in diplomatic service. Appointments: Estate Manager, Vipya Tung Estates; Teacher, Blantyre Secondary School; Assistant, United Nations Economic Priorities Team, 1963; Assistant to Economic Adviser to the Prime Minister, 1964; Exchange Control Assistant, Reserve Bank of Malawi, 1965; Banking Operations & Accounts Section, ibid, 1966; Started Economic Research & Statistics, 1966, Assistant to the General Manager, 1967; Assistant Research & Statistics Adviser, appointed Malawi I.M.F. Correspondent, 1968; Exchange Control Adviser, Head of Department, 1968; Head, Banking Operations, appointed Secretary, Decimal Currency Board, 1969; Deputy General Manager, 1970; General Manager, 1970. Memberships: Lions Club, Blantyre; Chairman, Blantyre Jaycees. Address: Reserve Bank of Malawi, P.O. Box 565, Blantyre, Malawi.

GONDWE, Herbert Smith, born 7th July, 1919. Principal Assistant Secretary. Education: completed secondary, Livingstonia Mission, Malawi, 1938. Married, 14 children. Appointments: Boma Cashier, 1941; District Officer, 1956; District Commissioner, 1961; Principal Assistant Secretary, 1963. Address: District Officer, Handeni, Tanzania.

GONI, Ibrahim Alkali, born 1937. Educator. Education: Nguru Elementary School, 1944-47; Yerwa Central Primary School, 1948; Bornu Middle School, 1949-53; Ilorin Teachers' College, 1954-57; Advanced Teachers' College, Zaria, Nigeria, 1962-65; Commonwealth Bursar, U.K., 1970-71. Personal details: father & grandfather acclaimed 'Goni', a title given to persons who can recite all the verses of the Koran. Appointments: Teacher, Bama Senior Primary School, 1958-59; Headmaster, Senior Primary School, Gwoza, 1960-61; Ibid, Yerwa Central School, 1961-62; Assistant Education Officer, 1965—. Memberships: Sokoto Club; Bar-Secretary, Gombe Club. Address: Arabic Teachers' College, Gombe, N.E. State, Nigeria.

GONZALES, Pierre-Isidore, born 4th April 1917. Advocate; Magistrate. Education: Greek & Latin Humanities, College of Our Lady of Perpetual Succour, Cap-Haitien, Haiti; Saint-Martial College, Port-au-Prince; Lic. Law, Free Law School, Cap-Haitien, University of Haiti. Appointments: with the Engineering Corporation of J. G. White & SHADA, 1940-45; Professor of Arts, College of Our Lady of Perpetual Succour, Cap-Haitien, 1944-46; ibid, Lycée Philippe Guerrier, Cap-Haitien, 1947-52; Lawyer, 1952-62 Professor of Civil Law, Free Law School, Cap-Haitien, 1952-56; recruited by the UNO & sent to the Congo; Judge, Kikwit District, 1962-63; President of the Primary Court of Claims, Coquilhatville, Mbandaka, 1962-64; ibid, Leopoldsville, Kinshasa, 1965-68; Counsellor to the Court of Appeal, Kinshasa, 1968; First President, Court of Appeal, Lubumbashi, 1968—. Memberships: Vice-President, Committee of the Society of Juridic Studies of Katanga. Publications: Annotated Civil Code of Procedure, 1959. Honours: Officer, National Order of the Leopard, 1969. Address: B.P. 330, Lubumbashi, Democratic Republic of the Congo.

GONZALEZ, Claude, born 21st August, 1928. Inspector of National Education. Education: L. es L. (Phil.), University of Nancy, France. Married, 2 children. Appointments: Education Counsellor, Department of Vosges, France, 1960-61; Inspector of National Education, Bizerta, Tunisia, 1962—. Author of Audio-visual Teaching Methods. Honours: Knight, Order of the Academic Palms, 1966. Address: 56 Rue R. Poincarre, 88-Mirecourt, France.

GOODAY, David Oliver Malcolm, born 27th May 1936. Lecturer in Agricultural Economics. Education: Dulwich College, London, U.K.; B.Sc., Agriculture, Wye College, University of London; Postgraduate Certificate in Education, Exeter University. Appointments: Lecturer, Ministry of Agriculture, Training Institute, Tanzania; Training Officer, Ministry of Agriculture, ibid; Lecturer in Agriculture, Natural Resources Development College, Zambia; Lecturer in Agricultural Economics & Head Dept. of Economics & Extension, Swaziland Agricultural College & University Centre. Memberships: The Agricultural Economics Society; Royal Commonwealth Society. Address: Swaziland Agricultural College & University Centre, P.O. Luyengo, Swaziland.

GOODMAN, John David, born 8th April 1920. Zoologist-Parasitologist. Education: B.Sc., Parsons College, 1942; M.A., University of Michigan, U.S.A., 1947; Ph.D., ibid, 1952. Appointments: Associate Professor, Mercer University, Georgia, 1948-49; Assistant Professor, then Professor, University of Redlands, California, 1951-66; Visiting Professor, Faculty of Science, Makerere University, Uganda, 1958-59; Faculty of Agriculture, 1966-70. Memberships: American Society of Parasitologists; American Microscopical Soc.; Wildlife Disease Association; Am. Soc. of Ichthyologists & Herpetologists; Herpetologists League; Am. Ornithologist's Union; Cooper Ornithology Soc.; Wilson Ornithol. Soc.; Iowa Ornithol. Union; Western Society of Naturalists; Soc. of Systematic Zoology. Author of publications in field of parasitology, tropical ecology, wildlife diseases, desert biology, field studies on montane birds, schistosomiasis, herpetology, tropical malacology and freshwater biology. Address: Laboratory of Zoology-Parasitology, Dept. of Animal Science & Production, Faculty of Agriculture, Makerere University, P.O. Box 7062, Kampala, Uganda.

GORMAN, Thomas Patrick, born 4th December 1938. University Lecturer. Education: Oxford University, U.K., 1959-62; Leeds University, 1962-63. Married, 2 daughters. Appointments: Lectr. in charge of Dept. of English, Kenya Inst. of Administration, 1963-65; Lectr. in Language & Literature, Dept. of English, University College Nairobi, Univ. of East Africa, 1965—. Memberships: Council of the Survey of Language Use & Language Teaching in Eastern Africa (representing Univ. College Nairobi), 1968-70; Chmn., Kenya Language Association, 1968-69; Council, Language Association of Eastern Africa; Chmn., Edit. Bd., ibid. Publications include: Language in Education in Eastern Africa, 1970; Glossary in English, Swahili, Kikuyu, & Dholuo, 1970; Ed., Jrnl. of the Language Assn. of Eastern Africa, 1970. Address: Faculty of Arts, Univeristy of Nairobi, Box 30197, Nairobi, Kenya.

GOUINDEN, Vele, born 4th February 1895. Former Member, Civil Service of Mauritius. Education: Cambridge Certificate for Senior Students, Royal College, Curepipe, 1911. Married. Appointments: joined Civil Service of Mauritius, 1914; retired as Assistant Postmaster General, 1956; Temporary Minister of Education, 1961; Chairman, Development Bank of Mauritius, 1967—; Member, Legislature of Mauritius, 1959-63, 1964-67. Memberships: Tea Control Board; Triveni Club. Awarded M.B.E., 1955. Address: Development Bank of Mauritius, Chaussee, Port Louis, Mauritius.

GOUNDIAM, Ousmane, born Diourbel, Senegal, 23rd April 1922. General Prosecutor, Supreme Court of Dakar, Senegal. Education: Diploma, Ecole primaire superieure, 1942; Ecole Normale, 1942-45; Lycée de Montpellier, 1947; Baccalaureat, Philosophy, 1947-49; LL.D., University of Montpellier, 1949-52; graduated as Magistrate, Ecole Natiohale de la France d'Outre-Mer, Paris, 1957. Appointments include: Teacher, Dakar, 1945-47; Police Court Magistrate, Ivory Coast & Mali, 1953-57; Judge, Kayes, Mali, 1960-62; concurrently, Public Prosecutor, Segou; Barrister, Court of Appeal, Bamako; General Prosecutor; Supreme Court of Mali; Councillor, Supreme Court of Dakar, Senegal, 1962; President, High Court of Justice; President of Branch of Supreme Court of Dakar; Judicial Adviser, Ministry of Foreign Affairs; functions of Procureur General, Supreme Court, Dakar. Member, Arbitration & Conciliation Commission of OAU; Senegal Representative to Commission on Algerian-Moroccan Conflict; Member, Superior Council of Magistrature; Member, Bureau of Senegal Association of Judicial Studies & Research; President, National Senegal Committee of International Year for Human Rights; General Prosecutor, Supreme

Court of Senegal; Director, Legal Division, Officer of the High Commissioner for Refugees, U.N., 1969. Publications include: Droits de l'homme dans les pays en voie de developpement (revue Afrique Documents); Bilan de l'acte de Stockholm sur la propriete artistique et litteraire (revue Senegalaise d'etudes et de recherches juridiques); Regime foncier du Senegal (revue Civilisations). Theatre Plays: Femmes d'hier, Femmes d'aujourd'hui; L'ombre de Dinga; Il etait autrefois. Honours include: Officer, National Order of Senegal. Address: Haut Commissariat des Nations Unies pour les Refugies, Palais des Nations, 1211 Geneva, Switzerland.

GOWON (Major-General), Yakubu, born 19th October 1934. Head of State; Commander-in-Chief of the Armed Forces of the Federal Republic of Nigeria. Education: Senior School Certificate, Government College, Zaria, 1953; Regular Officers' Special Training School, Teshie, Ghana, 1954; Royal Military Academy, Sandhurst, U.K., 1955-56; Eaton Hall Officer Cadet Training School, Cheshire, 1955. Married, 1 son. Appointments include: Young Officers' Course, Hythe & Warminster, U.K., 1957; 2nd Lieutenant, 4th Battalion (the 1st Nigerian Officer to be appointed Adjutant of the 4th Battalion), 1960; served with the U.N. Forces in the Congo, 1960-61; Staff College, Camberley, Surrey, U.K., 1962; Lieutenant-Colonel, Adjutant-General, Nigerian Army, 1963; served in the Congo, 1963; Joint Service Staff College, Latimer, Chesham, U.K., 1965; Commander, 2nd Battalion, Nigeria, January, 1966; Chief of Staff, Nigerian Army Headquarters, January 1966; Head of the Federal Military Government, & Commander-in-Chief, of the Armed Forces, Federal Republic of Nigeria. August, 1966. Address: Supreme Headquarters, Lagos, Nigeria.

GRANT, A. Cameron, born 9th December 1929. University Lecturer. Education: Scottish Schools; Universities in U.S.A., Canada, & U.K.; awarded Doctorate. Married, 2 children. Appointments: Research Assistant, University of Edinburgh, U.K. Author of various journal publications in U.K. & U.S.A. Address: Department of History, University College of Cape Coast, Cape Coast, Ghana.

GRECH, Edwin Saviour, born 27th September 1928. Obstetrician & Gynaecologist. Education: St. Aloysius' College, Malta; M.D., St. Luke's Medical School, Royal University of Malta, 1955; D.Obst.R.CO9, 1959; M.R.C.O.G., 1963. Married, 2 children. Appointments: Postgraduate Studies, various house appointments & residencies, U.K., 1958-63; Lecturer, Makerere University College, Kampala, Uganda, 1964-66; Senior Lecturer, ibid, 1967-69; Reader, 1969–. Hon. Consultant Obstetrician & Gynaecologist, Mulago Hospital; Hon. Visiting Gynaecologist, Mengo Mission Hospital, Kampala. Memberships: Vice-President, Uganda Medical Association, 1970–; Fellow, Association of Surgeons of East Africa; Kampala Club, Uganda; Casino Maltese, Malta. Contributor of scientific papers to professional journals. Honours: Carnegie Corporation of New York Travelling Scholarship, 1968; Visiting Professor; School of Public Health, University of California, Berkeley, U.S.A., 1968; Adgar Travelling Research Fellowship, 1969. Address: Department of Gynaecology & Obstetrics, Medical School, P.O. Box 7072, Kampala, Uganda.

GREEN, Frederick Norman, born Birkenhead, Cheshire, U.K., 2nd April 1895. Medical Practitioner. Education: Birkenhead School, Cheshire, 1906-14; Exhibition in Classics, Magdalene College, Cambridge University, 1914; Medical Education, Magdalene College, Cambridge, & Liverpool United Hospitals, 1919-25; M.A.(Cantab.); M.B., B.Ch. (Cantab.), 1925; M.R.C.S., L.R.C.P., 1925; D.T.M.(Liverpool), 1925. Married. Appointments include: served in the First World War, 1914-18; with B.E.F., France, 1918-19; Medical Superintendent, Kijabe Hospital, Kenya (African Inland Mission), 1926-27; ibid, Nyakach Hospital, 1927-29; ibid, Maseno Hospital, Kenya (Church Missionary Society), 1930-44; General Practitioner, Chelmsford, Essex, U.K., 1946-61; Medical Superintendent, Amudat Hospital, Kitale, Kenya, 1961-62; ibid, Shyira Hospital, Ruhengeri Rwanda, 1962-63; ibid, Lake Bunyoni Leprosy Settlement, 1965-68. Memberships include: East African Medical Association; British Medical Association; Anglican Lay Reader, Diocese of Mombasa, Kenya; ibid, Diocese of Chichester, U.K. Contributor to East African Medical Journal. Address: Mirembe, West Broyle Drive, Chichester, Sussex, U.K.

GREEN, Reginald Herbold, born Walla Walla, Wash., U.S.A., 4th May 1935. Economist. Education: A.B.(Highest Hons.), Whitman College, Walla Walla, Wash., 1955; M.A., Harvard University, Mass., 1957; Ph.D., ibid, 1961. Appointments: Teaching & Research Fellow, Harvard University, 1959-60; Postdoctoral Fellow, University of Ghana, 1960-61; Assistant Professor, Yale University, 1961-65; Visiting Lecturer, University of Ghana, 1963-65; Research Fellow, Makerere University, 1965-66; Consultant, Uganda Ministry of Planning, 1965; Consultant, Tanzania Ministry of Finance, 1965-66; Economic Adviser, Tanzania Treasury, 1966–; Hon. Professor, Economics, University of Dar es Salaam, 1969–. Memberships: Economic Society of Tanzania; African Studies Association; Asian Studies Association; American Association of University Professors; American Civil Liberties Union. Publications include: Unity or Poverty: Economics of Pan-Africanism (co-author), 1968; Stages in Economic Development: Changes in the Structure of Production, Demand & International Trade, 1968; also papers in field. Honours: Wells Prize, Harvard University, 1961. Listed: American Men of Science. Address: Treasury Box 9111, Dar es Salaam, Tanzania.

GREENOUGH, Robert, born Blackburn, U.K., 22nd July 1932. Headmaster. Education: Kirkham Grammar School, Lancashire, U.K.; B.A.(Hons., History), Dip. Ed., Univ. of Durham. Personal details: married to Muriel (née Hamilton) who was Founder and Headmistress of Soroti Infant School & District Guide Commissioner, Teso, Uganda, 4 sons (one Robert, winner of Area Science Award by British Council in Teso, 1968). Appointments include: Flying Officer, Royal Air Force, 1954-57;

Assistant Master, Leicestershire, 1957-63; Adult Tutor, Wigston, Leicestershire, 1963-64; Education Officer, Uganda, 1965; Headmaster, Senior Secondary School, Soroti, Uganda, 1966-68. Memberships include: National Association for Mental Health; Association for Programmed Learning; Treasurer, Teso District Athletic Union; Teso District Adult Education Committee (Supervisor of Classes & Organizer of first local correspondence study project in Uganda); Captain, Soroti Star F.C. Publications include: Contributor to 'Uganda Goes Ahead', 1969, by arrangement of the Vice-President of Uganda; Commerce for G.C.E., Correspondence Course (Makerere Univ. College). Honours, Prizes, etc.: Robson Shield, Univ. of Durham, 1953. Address: Senior Secondary School, P.O. Box 174, Soroti, Uganda.

GREEN-WILKINSON, Francis Oliver, born Aston, U.K. 7th May 1913. Anglican Archbishop in Central Africa and Bishop in Zambia. Education: Eton College, U.K.; M.A., Magdalen College, Oxford, 1946; Westcott House, Cambridge. Appointments include: served in British Army during World War II, in Tunisia, Egypt, Libya, Italy, & France, 1939-46; Major, ibid; ordained in Anglican Church, 1946; Curate, St. Mary's, Southampton, 1946-50; Curate, Pretoria Cathedral, South Africa, 1950-51; Bishop of Northern Rhodesia (now Zambia), 1951—; also Archbishop of Central Africa, 1962—. Awards include: Military Cross, 1943; C.B.E., 1958. Address: Bishop's Lodge, Box 183, Lusaka, Zambia.

GRETTEN MWAIJANDE, A., born November 1915. Accountant. Education: Central School, Rungwe Moravian School, 1932-35; Central School, Government School, Malangali, 1936; Clerical Class Government Secondary School, Tabora, Tanzia, 1938-39; Accounting Course, Dar es Salaam, 1958, Married, 9 children. Appointments: Clerk & Provincial Treasury Staff, 1940-58; Upper Division Clerk, 1958-62; Assistant Accountant, Grade II, 1962-65; Assistant Accountant Grade I, 1965-68; Accountant, 1968—. Member, T.A.N.U. Awarded 2 books as 1st in class, 1938. Address: c/o Second Vice-President's Office, P.O. Box 3021, Dar es Salaam, Tanzania.

GRIFFIN, Geoffrey William, born Eldoret, Kenya, 13th June 1933. Civil Servant. Education: Prince of Wales School, Nairobi. Appointments: Army Service, 1952-55; Deputy Commandant, Wamumu Youth Camp, 1955-57; Youth adviser, Kenya Government, 1957-64; Director, National Youth Service, Kenya, 1964—; founded Starehe Boys' Centre, Nairobi, for care & education of 900 orphaned & needy boys, 1959; Honorary Director, ibid; Honorary Administrator, Commonwealth Save the Children Funds in Kenya, 1963. Memberships: Chairman, Standing Committee on Children & Young Persons; Central Probation Committee of Kenya. Created a Moran of the Kenya Order of the Burning Spear, 1969. Address: P.O. Box 9089, Nairobi, Kenya.

GRILLO, T. Adesanya Ige, born 29th January 1927. Physician; Professor of Anatomy. Education: Hope Waddell Training Institute, Calabar, Nigeria; L.R.C.P.I. & L.R.C.S.I., Royal College of Surgeons, Dublin, Ireland; M.A., Ph.D., St. John's College, Cambridge University, U.K. Married. Appointments: Supervisor, Anatomy, St. John's College, Cambridge University, 1955-60; Lecturer, Anatomy, St. Mary's Hospital Medical School, London University, 1960; Assistant Professor, Stanford University, California, U.S.A., 1960-61; Senior Lecturer, University of Ibadan, Nigeria, 1962-65; Professor, Anatomy, ibid, 1966—; Senior Research Associate, Division of Research, Sinai Hospital, Detroit, Michigan, U.S.A., 1965; Visiting Professor, University of Khartoum, Sudan, 1969. Memberships include: Anatomical Society of Great Britain & Ireland; Biochemical Society of Great Britain; Histochemical Society, U.S.A.; Fellow, Zoological Society, London; ibid, Philosophical Society, Cambridge; New York Academy of Science; Fellow, Royal Microscopical Society; ibid, Member, Board of Regents, International Academy of Law & Science; Fellow, Association of Physicians of West Africa; Fellow, Nigerian Medical Council. Author of numerous publications in scientific journals. Honours: French-O'Carroll Medal, Biological Society, Royal College of Surgeons, Ireland, 1954; Irish Medical Association Prize for best essay by medical student, 1955. Address: Department of Anatomy, University of Ibadan, Ibadan, Nigeria.

GRIMES, Llewellyn George, born Cardiff, U.K., 3rd October 1933. Physics Lecturer. Education: B.Sc., Bristol University, 1955; Ph.D., ibid, 1958. Married, 2 sons. Appointments: Research Assoc., University of Pennsylvania, Pa., U.S.A., 1958-60; Sr. Lecturer, University of Ghana, 1960—. Memberships: Associate, Institute of Physics, London; British Ornithological Union. Author of articles in Ibis and Nature. Address: Dept. of Physics, University of Ghana, Legon, Ghana.

GROVE, Hazel Margaret, born Cheam, Surrey, U.K., 17th October 1932. Lecturer in History. Education: Rosebery Grammar School, Epsom, Surrey; B.A.(Hons., History), Nottingham University; Postgraduate Certificate in Education, London University. Appointments: Senior History Mistress, Holy Child School, Cape Coast, Ghana, 1958-64; Lecturer in History, National Teachers' College, Kampala, Uganda, 1964-70; Member, History Panel which advises on syllabus for Secondary Schools for Uganda Government, 1966-70. Committee Member, Women's Association, Uganda University. Editor, The History Teacher, Journal of Uganda History Teachers' Association. Address: National Teachers' College, P.O. Box 20012, Kampala, Uganda.

GRUNDY, Robert, born 30th October 1941. Physician. Education: Blackpool Grammar School, Lancashire, U.K.; University of London Medical School; St. George's Hospital Medical School. Married. Lecturer in Medicine, Makerere University College, Kampala, Uganda, 1968-70. Member of Royal College of Physicians, London, 1968. Publications: Amoebic Meningoencephalitis in Uganda, East African Medical Journal, 1970; Schistosaniasis in W. Nile, Uganda (in preparation). Address: The Coach House, Glencairn, St. Columb, Cornwall, U.K.

GUERTAOUI, Abdelaziz Ahmed, born 11th November 1925. Teacher. Education: Primary, Secondary, & Technical Schools. Married, 5 children. Appointments: Teacher, French Language, 1943-55; with the Ministry of Education, Division of Technical Instruction, 1955-60; Director, Technical Agricultural College, 1960-63; with the Ministry of Equipment, 1963-67; School Director, Rabat, 1967-69; ibid, 1969—. Memberships: Scoutmaster, French Scouts Association, 1945-55; attended an International Scout Rally in Berkhampstead, U.K., 1950. Recipient of Certificate of Merit for Teaching & Agriculture; distinguished by a Royal Decoration. Address: Directeur de l'Ecole, Ouad el Makhazine Bouitat, Rabat, Morocco.

GUIEYSSE, Pierre, born 22nd January 1899. Industrialist, Education: General Certificate in Mathematics. Appointments: President, Director-General, Automobile Societies of the African Coast; ibid, Senegal Transport Co.; ibid, Ets. Guieysse. Memberships: Chamber of Commerce, Dakar, Senegal. Honours: Legion of Honour; Croix de Guerre (French); Officer, National Order of Senegal. Address: Ets Guieysse, Dakar, Senegal.

GUIRMA, Frederic-Fernand, born Ouagadougou, Upper Volta, 27th April 1931. United Nations Political Affairs Official. Education: Primary, Ecole Soeurs Blanches Notre Dame d'Afrique, Ouagaduogou; Secondary, Lower Seminary of Pabre, ibid; M.A.(History), Loyola University, Los Angeles, U.S.A. Appointments: Secretary-General, Syndicates, C.A.T.C., Upper Volta, 1954-58; President, ibid, 1958-60; Secretary to Ambassador & Vice-Consulate, Kumasi, Ghana, 1960—; Ambassador of the Upper Volta to Washington, U.S.A. & Permanent Representative to the O.N.U., 1960-62; Official, Political Affairs Office, United National, 1967—. Publications: Children's books: The Princess of the Full Moon, 1970; The Story of Wisdom, 1971. Honours: Commander, National Order of the Upper Volta; Grand Cross, Order of St. Sylvester, Vatican; Commander, National Order of Mauritania; Knight, National Order of Cameroun; ibid, National Order of the Congo, Brazzaville. Address: 7 Serpentine Drive, New Rochelle, New York 10801, U.S.A.

GUREME, Francis Drake Rammes, born 19th September 1926. Administrative Officer. Education: Mborara High School, Uganda, 1939-43; King's College, Budo, 1944-46; Makerere College, Kampala, 1947-48; E.A. School of Cooperation, 1953; Course in Public Administration, Entebbe, 1960. Married, 4 sons, 2 daughters. Appointed Coop. Manager, Produce Marketing Board, 1970. Vice-President, Uganda Civil Service Association. Recipient, Independence Medal, 1962. Address: P.O. Box 5705, Kampala, Uganda.

GWENGWE, John Williams, born 21st April 1930. Member of Parliament; Teacher; Education Officer. Education: Primary & Secondary, Malawi; University of London, U.K. Appointments: Teacher; Education Officer; Junior Minister of Education: Junior Minister of Trade & Industry; Minister of Trade & Industry, Malawi. Publications: Sulizo Achieves Greatness; English in Malawi; Heroes of Old Malawi; Chichewa Series for Primary Schools; Chichewa Series for Secondary Schools. Address: Ministry of Trade & Industry, P.O. Box 944, Blantyre, Malawi.

GWIRA, Kobina Daniel, born Sekondi, Ghana, 2nd January, 1923. Barrister; Diplomat. Education: St. Peter's School, Sekondi; Adisadel College, Cape Coast; Law, Public Administration, Trinity College Dublin, Ireland; Called to Bar, King's Inns, Dublin. Married, 5 children. Appointments: Private Law Practice with father, 1954-61; High Commissioner to Sierra Leone; Ambassador to Yugoslavia; Ambassador to Bulgaria; Ambassador to Rumania; Judge of the High Court of Ghana. Memberships: Secretary, Western Regional Bar Association; Sekondi Golf Club; Secretary, Arden International Club; Accra Club; Freetown Golf Club. Address: 82 South Park Road, Wimbledon, London, S.W.19, U.K.

GYAMFI, Charles Kumi, born 4th December, 1929. National Soccer Coach. Education: School Leaving Certificate. Appointments: Regional Soccer Coach, Ghana, 1960; Deputy National Coach, ibid, 1961; National Soccer Coach, 1962. Memberships: Trainer, Asante Kotoko Football Club, 1951-54; Captain, Great Ashanti Football Club, 1954-56; ibid, Ghana National Soccer Team, 1958-60. Author, The Twelve Commandments of Football. Honours: The Sportsman of the Year, 1953; Grand Medal, 1968. Address: c/o Sports Council of Ghana, P.O. Box 1272, Accra, Ghana.

GYANDOH, Maysel Stella, born Cape Coast, Ghana, 27th May 1933. Barrister-at-Law; Banker. Education: Primary Education in Ghana & Lagos, Nigeria; Holy Child College, Cape Coast, Ghana, 1947-50; Kumasi College of Technology; Woolwich Polytechnic, London, U.K.; LL.B., London School of Economics & Political Science, University of London, 1956-59; Called to the Bar, Inner Temple, London, 1960; Banking & Government Control of Business, New Haven, Connecticut, U.S.A., 1964-65. Personal details: daughter of Ex-Paramount Chief of Asebu, Ghana; Married, 5 children. Appointments: Private Law Practice, 18 months; Officer Grade I, Exchange Control Department, Bank of Ghana, 1961; Deputy Manager, ibid, 1963; Manager, with responsibility for setting up new department, Exchange Control Audit Department, 1967; Deputy Exchange Controller & Head, Exchange Control Department, 1968-70; Deputy Chief, Bank of Ghana (only woman to be appointed to this grade), 1970; currently Head, Training Office, Bank of Ghana, & Secretary to a Cabinet Committee. Memberships: International Federation of Women Lawyers; Ghana Consumers' Association; Associate Fellow, Volta Hall, University of Ghana; Patron (& keen player), Bank of Ghana Netball Club. Address: Deputy Chief, Bank of Ghana, P.O. Box 2674, Accra, Ghana.

H

HADDAD, Mohamed, born 10th November 1928. Surgeon; Gynaecologist. Appointments: Ancien Externe, Hospital of Paris, France, 1952-56; Chef des Service, Surgery & Obstetrics, Gafsa, Tunisia, 1960-62; Gynaecologist, Aziza, Othuana, Tunis. Address: 15 Rue Essaoikia, Tunis.

HADDOCK, David Robert Wigston, born Southport, U.K., 22nd June 1927. Physician. Education: King George V School, Southport, 1937-44; Liverpool University, 1944-50; M.D., Liverpool; M.R.C.P., London; D.T.M.&.H., Liverpool. Married, 2 children. Appointments include: Medical Officer, Liverpool Hospitals, 1950-56; Special Grade Medical Officer, Tanzania, 1956-61; Medical Specialist, & subsequently Consultant Physician, Tanzania, 1961-65; Senior Lecturer in Tropical Medicine, Liverpool School of Tropical Medicine, 1965; currently, Associate Professor of Medicine, Ghana Medical School, Ghana. Memberships include: Fellow, Royal Society of Tropical Medicine & Hygiene; Member, Ghana Medical Association; British Medical Association. Contributor to journals of medicine. Awards include: Milne Medal in Tropical Medicine, Liverpool, 1959. Address: Ghana Medical School, P.O. Box 4236, Accra, Ghana.

HADDON, Arthur John Charles, born 11th April 1925. Chartered Civil Engineer; Chartered Town Planner. Education: Berkhamsted School, Herts., U.K.; B.Sc.(Engineering), London University; Dip.T.P., ibid. Appointments: Deputy City Engineer, Nairobi, Kenya, 1958-66; General Manager & Director, Lyford Cay Company, Nassau, Bahamas, 1966-70; Vice-President, Galbreath-Ruffin Corporation, New York, U.S.A.; General Managing Director, Mei Foo Investments Ltd., Hong Kong, 1970. Fellowships: Institution of Civil Engineers, G.B.; Institution of Municipal Engineers Memberships: Town Planning Institute; East African Institute of Engineers. Responsible for many modern town planning & highway networks, Nairobi, Kenya. Address: Mei Foo Investments Ltd., Room 305, Realty Building, P.O. Box 977, Hong Kong.

HAFIDH, Ali Salim, born Zanzibar, 19th November 1940. Journalist. Education: Primary & Higher Secondary Education in Zanzibar; Studied Arts & Humanities, C.W. Post College, Long Island, New York, U.S.A. Personal details: married to Farida Hafidh. Appointments: Information Officer, 1967—; Features Editor, Maelezo Features Service, 1968—. Memberships: Committee Member, Tanzania Press Club; Afro-Shirazi Party; Afro-Shirazi Youth League. Publications: various articles & book reviews in East Africa & overseas journals. Address: Tanzania Information Services, P.O. Box 9142, Dar es Salaam, Tanzania.

HAGOOD, Martha, born 15th October 1923. Physician; Missionary; Obstetrician; Gynaecologist. Education: A.B., Samford University, Birmingham, Alabama, U.S.A., 1944; M.D., Medical College, Birmingham, Alabama, 1947; Diplomate, American Board of Obstetricians & Gynaecologists. Appointments: Intern, University Hospital, Birmingham, Alabama, 1947-48; Resident, Baptist Hospital, ibid, 1948-49; Staff Physician, Attending Surgeon's Office, Army Civilian Department, Ft. Knox, Kentucky, U.S.A., 1949-50; Resident Obstetrician-Gynaecologist, University Hospital, Birmingham, Alabama, 1950-53; Obstetrician-Gynaecologist, Japan Baptist Hospital, Kyoto, Japan, 1953-66; Staff Physician, Eku Baptist Hospital, 1966—. Memberships: American College of Surgeons; Phi Mu. Address: P.M.B. 4040, Eku Baptist Hospital, Eku via Sapete, Nigeria.

HAGYARD, John, born Wolverhampton, U.K., 14th April 1926. Bookshop Manager. Education: Tettenhall College, Staffs., 1933-44; B.A., Nottingham University, 1948-51. Married, 4 sons. Appointments include: Assistant Manager, W. H. Smith & Sons Ltd., England, 1953; Supplies Officer, London Missionary Society, London, 1958; Bookshop Manager, Gaberones, Botswana, 1966. Memberships: include: Congregational Church, England, Deacon: Union Church, Trinity Church, Gaberones, Elder. Address: P.O. Box 91, Gaberones, Botswana.

HAILE BERRA (Kegnezmatch), born 30th April 1917. Governor, Ghimbi District, Wollega Province. Education: H.S.I. Secondary School, Lekempte, Wollega; Matriculation, General Wingate School, Addis Ababa, Ethiopia; Diplomate in Local Administration from German Government. Personal details: father, Negadherez Berra Wondtha, mother, Wolleth Yohannes Tebe. Married Miss Belainesh Haile, children. Active member of 'Drive Italian Campaign', imprisoned for two years. Speaks 6 languages. Appointments include: Vice--Provincial Education Officer, Lekempte, Wollega Province, 1956-57; Member of Ethiopian Parliament, 1957-61; Governor, Assosa District, Wollega Province, 1961-63; Governor, Arjo District, Wollega Province, 1964-65; Governor, Lekempte District, 1966; Governor of a District in Gojjam Province, 1967-68; Governor, Ghimbi District, Wollega Province, 1969—. Memberships: Patron of many welfare organisations in various districts; Chairman, Parliamentary Foreign Relations Committee, Study Tour of U.S.A., 1959. Address: Ghimbi, Wollega Province, Ethiopia.

HAILE MINASSE (His Excellency), born 12th February 1930. Diplomat; Lawyer. Education: B.A.(Econ.), University of Wisconsin, U.S.A.; LL.B., Columbia University Law School; M.A., Columbia University International Law; Ph.D., Columbia University. Married, 4 children. Appointments: Legal Adviser, Ministry of Foreign Affairs; Civil Service Commissioner; Chief of Political Affairs, H.I.M. Private Cabinet; Minister of State for Information; Ethiopian Ambassador to the United States. Publications: Domestic Jurisdiction: U.N. Consideration of Domestic Questions and their International Effects. Address: 2209, Wyoming Avenue N.W., Washington, D.C. 20008, U.S.A.

HAILOU DESTA KASSA (Lij), born January 1930. Government Official. Education: College De Frere, Palestine; Hailé Selassié Secondary School, Ethiopia; General Wingate Secondary School, ibid; Bible College, Swansea, Wales, U.K. Married to Woizero Atseda Bellay, 2 daughters. Appointments: Secretary-General, Federal Secretariat, 1952; Director, Department of Federal Affairs, Ministry of Pen, 1953; Special Secretary to the Vice-Minister of Interior for Land Contracts & Municipal Affairs, 1955; Chief of the Plan & Policy Dept., Ministry of National Defence, 1957; Director-General, Military Production Plan & Policy, 1959; Assistant Minister, Ministry of National Defence for Military Training Education & Health, 1966—. Memberships: National Scholarship Committee; National Literacy Campaign Organizations Executive Committee; National Malaria Eradication Planning Committee; Senior Member, Board of Directors, Ethiopian National Red Cross; Chief Executive & Coordinator, Ethiopian Voluntary Service; Executive Committe, International Christian Fellowship of Ethiopia; Ethiopian Philatelic Assn.; Imperial Racing Club. Honours: The Refugee Medal with 5 palmettes, 1959; Victory Star Medal, 1959; Hailé Selassié 1st Gold Medal, 1960; Emperor Hailé Selassié 1st Grand Gold Medal of the Ethiopian Red Cross, 1961; Cavalier of the High Order of Menelek II, 1961; Officer of the High Order of Menelek II, 1965. Foreign Awards: 1st Class Gold Cross, Greek National Red Cross, 1959; Medal of Distinguished Humanitarian Service, U.S.S.R. Red Cross & Red Crescent, 1961; Citation of Honour, for Services to Humanity, American National Red Cross. Address: c/o Ministry of National Defence for Military Training Education & Health, Ethiopia.

HAINAUT, Jean-Pierre, born 9th September 1920. Industrialist. Education: Licence es Lettres. Married. 2 children. Memberships: Administrator of various societies; President, French Chamber of Commerce & Industry of Morocco; Past President, Rotary. Address: 17 Zenkat Okba Ben Nafaa, Meknes, Morocco.

HAIZEL, Emmanuel Aidoo, born 24th January, 1928. University Lecturer; Senior Resident Tutor. Education: Achimota School, 1937-47; B.A.(Hons.), History, 2nd Class, Upper Division, University of Ghana, 1948-53; Postgraduate Certificate, Education, ibid, 1956-57. Married, 2 sons, 3 daughters. Appointments: Teacher, History, Achimota School; History Tutor, Winneba Post Secondary Training College; Assistant Headmaster, Swedru Secondary School; Headmaster, Half Assini Secondary School; Lecturer, Education, University of Ghana; Senior Resident Tutor, Institue of Adult Education, ibid. Memberships: Executive Member, African Adult Education; ibid, Ghana Hockey Federation. Contributor to professional publications; Address: Institute of Adult Education, University of Ghana, P.O. Box 31, Legon, Ghana.

HAJI, Hussein, born 20th October 1939. Public Administrator. Education: Primary School, Ujiji, 1945-50; Mwanhala Middle School, Nzega, 1951-52; Tabora Boys' Secondary School, Tabora, 1953-60; Universitá di Napoli, Naples, Italy, 1961; Attorney Generals Chambers, Dar es Salaam, Tanzania, 1962; B.A.(Geography & Political Science), Makerere University College, Kampala, Uganda, 1966. Personal details: married, 1 daughter. Appointments: Law Assistant, Attorney General's Chambers, D.S.M., 1962; Librarian, Kivukoni College, Dar es Salaam, 1966; Administrative Officer, Grade VI, Central Establishment Division, President's Office, 1966—. Address: P.O. Box 2483, Dar es Salaam, Tanzania.

HAJJI, Mekki, born 7th April, 1922. Educator; Cultural Administrator. Married, 6 children. Appointments: Teacher for 14 years of French & Arabic in Primary Schools in Morocco before Independence; in charge of Primary, Secondary, & Higher Education for Juvenile Delinquents after Moroccan Independence. Memberships: Parent-Pupil Association in Lycées & Colleges. Attended the first Africa-Regional Training Course on Institutional Treatment of Juvenile Offenders, sponsored by the U.N. Economic Commission for Africa & U.A.R. National. Honours: Recipient of Decoration of Ouissam Er-Riola, 1969. Address: 35 Rue de Souche, Casablanca, Morocco.

HALBE, Vinayak Narayan, born 29th May 1918. Sugar Technologist; Agronomist. Education: B.Sc.(Hons., Agriculture), Bombay University, India; Diploma in Co-operation. Personal details: son of N. S. Halbe, Magistrate (India). Appointments: Agricultural Officer, Bombay Govt., India, 1939; Farm Superintendent, Deccan Factories, 1940-47; Plantation Manager, Sugar Factories, 1947-58; Plantation Manager, Pioneer Sugar Company, Uganda Sugar Factory, Uganda, 1958; Plantation Adviser, Muhoroni Sugar Company & Uganda Tea Estates; General Manager, Nyando Sugar Co. & Agricultural Services Ltd., Muhoroni, Kenya, 1967-70; Development Manager, National Sugar Works, Kinyala Ltd., The Republic of Uganda, 1970. Memberships: Charter Member, Lions Club of Lugazi, Uganda; 1st Vice-President, Lions Club, Masinsi; International Society of Sugar Technologists. Publications: articles on Sugar Cane Technology in the journals of the Deccan-Sugar Technologists Assn., India. Address: National Sugar Works (Kinyala), Ltd., P.O. Box 179, Masindi, Uganda.

HALIBURTON, Gordon MacKay, born 28th March 1928. University Lecturer. Education: B.A., Acadia University, N.S., Canada, 1948; B.Ed., ibid, 1951; M.A., Dalhousie University, 1955; Ph.D., University of London, U.K., 1966. Married, 2 children. Appointments: Education Officer, Sierra Leone, 1957-60; Member, Staff, Mfantsipim School, Ghana, 1963-65; Head of History, University of Botswana, Lesotho, & Swaziland, 1968—. Address: University of Botswana, Lesotho, & Swaziland, P.O. Roma, via Maseru, Lesotho.

HALIMOJA, Yusuf, born 19th March 1934. Information & Education Officer, Family Planning Association of Tanzania. Education: Nambuta Primary & Lulindi Central Schools, 1944-49; Chidya Secondary School, 1950-53; Minaki Teachers' College, 1954-55; attended course on Textbook Writing, Production & Distribution, Institute of Education, London University, U.K., 1964-65. Married, 5 children. Appointments: Teacher, 1956-67; Headmaster, 1961-67; Book Production Officer, Ministry of National Education, 1967-70; First Information & Education Officer of the Family Planning Association of Tanzania, 1970. Memberships: Tanganyika African National Union (TANU); National Union of Tanganyika (NUTA), Family Planning Association of Tanzania. Publications: Author of a book on The Story of the Tanzania National Assembley, September, 1970. Recip. of many prizes in story writing & poem competitions. Presented with second prize, Expo 70 poem competition, by President Nyerere, 1970. Address: Dar es Salaam, Tanzania.

HALL, Stuart, born 28th May 1929. Physician. Education: U.C.H. Medical School, London, U.K.; M.B., B.S., D.P.H., D.I.H., D.O.Hyg., (London). Appointments: Medical Officer, Kilembe Mines, Uganda, 1959-60; Ross Institute, E.A.G. Branch, 1961-67; Senior Lecturer in Preventive Medicine, Makerere Medical School, Kampala, 1967-69; Publications: Uganda Atlas of Disease Distribution (co-editor), 1968. Address: TUC Centenary Institute, London School of Hygiene & Tropical Medicine, Keppel Street, London, WC1E 7HT, U.K.

HAMILTON, George Nathaniel, born 27th November 1898. Retired Senior Surveyor. Education: Trinity Wesleyan School, 1904-10; Wesleyan Boys' High School, 1911-13; Eko Boys' High School, Lagos, Nigeria, 1914-15; Seventh-Day Adventist Mission, 1916-17. Appointments: Trainee, Religious Ministry, 1916-17; Probationer Postal Clerk & Telegraphist, 1917-18; 3rd Class, ibid, 1918-20; 2nd Class, 1920-23; 1st Class, 1923-39; Chief Superintendent, Posts & Telegraphs, Nigeria, 1939-43; Assistant Surveyor, 1943-51; Senior Surveyor, 1951-54; Divisional Surveyor, 1953-54. Memberships: Past Master, Ancient Free & Accepted Masons; Past Master, Ancient & Mystical Order of Rosy Cross. Honours: M.B.E., 1955. Address: 182A Clifford Street, P.O. Box 275, Yaba, Lagos, Nigeria.

HAMMOND-QUAYE, Neils Frederick, born 20th July 1929. Medical Practitioner. Education: Government Boys' School, Accra, Ghana; Mfantsipim, Cape Coast; M.Sc., L.R.C.P.&S., University of Edinburgh, U.K.; L.R.F.P.S.(Glasgow); D.P.H., University of Toronto, Canada. Personal details: married to Margaret Rebecca Asbayomi, 4 children. Appointments: Medical Officer, Ghana, 1960; District Medical Officer of Health, 1967; Chief Planning Officer, Ministry of Health, 1968. Memberships: Ghana Medical Association; British Medical Association. Publications: The Pattern of Disease in Ghana, Ghana Medical Journal, 1969. Address: Ministry of Health, P.O. Box M 44, Accra, Ghana.

HAMWEMBA, Bennie Sinamanjolo, born Bwengwa, June 1927. Teacher. Education: Standard VI, Form 11, Rusangu Mission School & Solusi Missionary College, 1946-48; Teachers' Course for 2 years. Appointments: School-master, 1949-59; Freedom Fighter on Provincial Level, Finance Section, 1960-63; elected Councillor, 1964-70; Member of Parliament, Monze Central Constituency, Zambia, 1968—. Memberships: Commonwealth Parliamentary Association; African National Congress; Opposition Party in Zambia; S.D.A. Address: P.O. Box 116, Monze, Zambia.

HAMZAOUI, Abdelaziz, born Tunisia, 17th May 1935. Ambassador of the Tunisian Republic to Canada. Education: Sadiki College, Tunis; B.A., Sorbonne, Paris, France; M.A., School of Political Science, Paris; M.A., Ph.D., Fletcher School of Law & Diplomacy; Harvard Business School, U.S.A.; International Teachers' Programme. Married, 1 son. Appointments: Faculty Associate, Harvard Business School, Cambridge, Mass., U.S.A.; Director of Studies, National School of Administration of Tunisia; Minister Plenipotentiary; Director, Administrative & Consular Affairs; Ambassador, Director, Secretariat of State for Foreign Affairs, Tunisia; Ambassador of the Tunisian Republic to Canada. Honours: Commander, Order of the Republic of Tunisia, 1967; Grosses Ver Dienstkreuz Mit Stern(PRG); Commander, National Order of Ivory Coast; Grand Officer of the Hamayoun of Iran. Address: 515 O'Connor Street, Ottawa 4, Ontario, Canada.

HANDA, Sarjitkumar, born 4th May 1941. Medical Practitioner. Education: M.B., B.S., G.R. Medical College, Gwalior, M.P., India, 1966. Appointments: in General Practice. Memberships: Mwanza Gymkhana Club; Mwanza Yacht Club. Awarded Distinction in Forensic Medicine, 1965. Address: P.O. Box 96, Mwanza, Tanzania.

HANSON, John Orleans Degraft, born 7th October 1932. University Lecturer. Education: Mfantsipim Secondary School, 1947-50; Adisadel College, 1951; B.A.(Lond.), University College, Gold Coast, 1951-56; B.A., M.Litt., King's College, Cambridge University, U.K., 1957-60. Married, 4 sons, 2 daughters. Appointments: Secretary, Ghana Classical Association, 1962-68; Senior Tutor, Legon Hall, University of Ghana, 1964-68; Acting Head, Dept. of Classics, ibid, 1966—. Memberships: Editorial Board, Okyeame, Journal of Ghana Writer's Association, 1964-66. Publications: A Reconstruction of Euripides 'Alexandros'— Hermes, 1964; 'The Secret of Medea's Success', Greece & Rome, 1965; The Curse of Theseus: A Euripidean Innovation, Merops, 1966; The Secret of Opokuwa (a children's novelette), 1967. Awards include: First-Class Degree Prize, Legon Hall, University of Ghana, 1956; Stephen Behrens-Cohen Travel Exhibition, Kings College, Cambridge, 1959. Address: Dept. of Classics, Univ. of Ghana, Legon, Ghana.

HARAWA, Bernard Anderton, born 1st June 1938. Education Secretary-General. Education: Teachers' Certificate, Domasi, Malawi, 1960; Diploma in Education, Strammillis College, Belfast, Ireland, U.K., 1961; B.Sc.(Ed.), University of Dayton, Ohio, U.S.A., 1965; M.Sc.(Ed.), ibid, 1967; B.A. Harawa; Dip. Ed. Personal details: married to Carol Jean Miller, B.A., University of Dayton, Ohio. Appointments: Assistant, Special Sessions Office, Dayton, U.S.A., 1963-65; Graduate Assistant in Education Psych. & Health Science, 1966-67; Education Secretary-General, 1968—. Memberships: Phi Delta Kappa; National Catholic Education Assn.; Christian Service Committee of Malawi; Museum Board of Malawi; Examination Council; National Library Service Board. Publications: Analysis of the Philosophy Underlying Principles of Secondary Education in Malawi (Thesis); How Break-Up Marriages can be Avoided or Solved (article in Moni magazine). Address: Catholic Secretariat, P.O. Box 5368, Limbe, Malawi.

HARRAGIN, William Lee, born 2nd November 1925. Advocate; Company Director. Education: Town House Close Preparatory School, Norwich, U.K., 1934-39; Marlborough College, Wiltshire, 1939-43; B.A., 2nd Class Honours Degree (Part 1 Economics, Part 11 Law), Trinity Hall, Cambridge, 1949; M.A., ibid, 1954; Barrister-at-Law, Gray's Inn, 1950. Personal details: father, Sir Walter Harragin, C.M.G., Q.C. (deceased), formerly Colonial Legal Service, Chief Justice, Gold Coast. Last appointment President Court of Appeal, Bechuanaland, Basutoland, & Swaziland. Mother, Lady Marjorie Howard Harragin (née Hardy). Appointments: Partner, Hamilton, Harrison, & Mathews, 1954-68; Area Administration Manager, Coca-Cola (Mid Africa) Limited, 1969—. Memberships: Muthaiga Country Club, Nairobi; Muthaiga Golf Club, Nairobi; Karen Country Club; Limura Country Club; Mombasa Sea Angling Club; Malindi Sea Fishing Club; Junior Carlton Club, London. Address: P.O. Box 30134, Nairobi, Kenya.

HARRIES, James R., born 26th June 1919. Physician (Internist). Education: Porth Grammar School; King's College Hospital, London, U.K.; Charing Cross Hospital, London; M.D.; D.C.H.; D.T.M.&H.; F.R.C.P. Married, 2 children. Appointments include: Senior Specialist, King George VI Hospital, Nairobi, Kenya, 1962-64; Consultant Physician in General Medicine, H.H. The Aga Khan Platinum Jubilee Hospital, Nairobi, 1958-64; Hon. Lecturer in Medicine, Makerere College, Kampala, Uganda, 1961—; External Examiner in Medicine, University College of East Africa, 1960; Consultant Neurologist, Kenyatta National Hospital (ex-K.G. VI), 1964—; Senior Physician, H.H. The Aga Khan Platinum Jubilee Hospital, Nairobi, 1964—; Hon. Lecturer in Medicine, University of East Africa, 1964—; Part-time Medical Adviser to Pfizer Corporation for the African Area, 1964—; Private Consultant Practice; Kenya Representative to IVth International Poliomyelitis Conference, Geneva, 1957; Physician-in-Waiting, H.R.H. The Princess Margaret, during East African Tour, 1958. Memberships: The British Cardiac Soc.; New York Academy of Science; Assn. of Physicians of East Africa; British Medical Assn.; Royal Society of Tropical Medicine; Royal Commonwealth Soc. Author of numerous publications in various professional journals including The Lancet, British Medical Journal, & East African Medical Journal. Honours include: O.B.E. (Civil), 1969. Address: 3rd Floor, Agip House, Haillé Selassié Ave., Box 20406, Nairobi, Kenya.

HARRIS, William John, born Oamaru, New Zealand, 1st September 1903. Librarian; Educator. Education: Canterbury University College, N.Z.; B.A., University College, Oxford, U.K.; School of. Librarianship, University College, London. Married. Appointments include: Assistant Master, Christ's College, N.Z., 1923-25, 1930-31; Librarian & Lecturer in Bibliography, Otago University, 1935-48; Librarian, Ibadan University, Nigeria, 1948-68; Director, University Press, 1950-68; Director, Institute of Librarianship, 1960-64; Deputy Vice-Chancellor, 1964-66; Acting Vice-Chancellor, 1966-68; Professor of Library Studies, University of Ghana, 1968-70; Librarian, University of Technology, Benin, Nigeria, 1970—. Memberships: President, N.Z. Library Association, 1946-47; President, West African Library Association, 1954-59; Editor, ibid, 1954-63; Vice-President, Nigerian Library Association, 1963; Ghana Library Association; Hon. Fellow, Library Association, London; Vice-President, Historical Society of Nigeria, 1966-69. Publications include: Guide to New Zealand Reference Material, 2nd ed., 1950; Books About Nigeria, 5th ed., 1969; Robert Gibbings, a Bibliography (joint compiler), 1962; Co-operation Between Universities in Printing & Publishing (W. African Intellectual Community, ed. Saunders & Dowouna), 1962; Ibadan University Library: Its Birth & Growth, 1968; National Bibliography in Nigeria (Proc. of Int. Conf. on African Bibliog.), 1969, & numerous other publications in prof. journals on bibliography & librarianship. Editor: Wala News, bulletin of W. African Library Association, 1954-63; Nigerian Libraries, 1964-66. Honours: D.Litt., University of Ibadan, Nigeria, 1969. Address: University of Technology, Benin City, Nigeria.

HARRISON, Charles Ernest, born 3rd February 1921. Journalist; Public Relations Consultant. Education: Schools in Manchester, U.K. Appointments: News Editor, Uganda Argus, 1955-59; Editor, ibid, 1959-70; Public Relations Consultant, 1970—. President Kampala Rotary Club, 1966-67. Address: P.O. Box 2986, Kampala, Uganda.

HARTFIELD, Vincent Jonathan, born London, U.K., 25th September, 1932. Doctor of Medicine; Gynaecologist. Education: St. George's School, Harpenden, U.K.; M.B., B.S., Kings College, University of London; St. George's Hospital, London, 1957; Selly Oak Colleges, Birmingham; M.R.C.S.; L.R.C.P.; D.A.; M.R.C.O.G. Married, 4 children. Appointments: Medical Officer, Anaesthetist, Wesley Guild Hospital, Ilesha, Western State, Nigeria, 1961; Obstetrician-Gynaecologist, ibid, 1966; Deputy Medical Superintendent, 1966; Member, Midwives Board of Nigeria, 1966; National Executive, Family Planning Council of Nigeria, 1968; Education Committee, Midwives Board of Nigeria, 1968. Fellowships: Eugenics Society; Fellowship of Reconciliation. Memberships: Methodist Missionary Society; Soc. of Gynaecologists & Obstetricians of Nigeria; Association of Surgeons of West Africa; Delius Society; British Medical Association; Medical Association for Prevention of War. Recip. of: Annual Award for Research, Association of West

African Surgeons, 1968. Address: Wesley Guild Hospital, Ilesha, Western State, Nigeria.

HARTHOORN, Antonie Marinus, born Holland 26th August 1923. Physiologist; Pharmacologist; Veterinarian. Education: King's School, Harrow, U.K.; Royal Veterinary College, London; State College of Utrecht, Netherlands; Pharmacological Institute, Hanover, Germany; London University, U.K. Married, 3 children, 2 step-children. 5 years' war service. Appointments: Fellow of the Royal College of Veterinary Surgeons, London. Memberships: Physiological Society; British Veterinary Association; Veterinarians Union; Extraordinary Member of the Netherlands Veterinary Association. Publications: Application of Physiological & Pharmacological Principles to Animal Capture (monograph), Wildlife Soc., N.Y.; The Flying Syringe; sections of two textbooks on anaesthesia & pharmacology; 80 scientific articles.

HARZALLAH, Ahmed, born Monastir, Tunisia, 27th January 1938. Producer, Cinema & TV. Education: Centre Experimental de Cinema, Rome, Italy. Appointments: Producer, attached to SATDEC, 1960-64; Chief of Production & Programmes, Educational TV, Institut de l'enseignement pour Adultes, 1966-68; Producer, 1968—. Especially interested in the theoretical & practical problems of applying audio-visual techniques in education & development. Memberships: Vice-President, l'Association des Jeunes Cineastes Tunisiens; Jury, International Film Festival, Salerno, Italy; Jury, International Amateur Film Festival, Kelibia, Tunisia. Contributor to professional journals. Films include: le Pur Sang Arabe; Vers la connaissance; Nattiers de Nabeul; Sogicot; Gamoudi Films include: le Pur Sang Arabe, 1963; Gamoudi, 1964; El Fouladh, 1966; Sogicot, 1966; Vers la connaissance, 1967; Pelerinagea la Mecque, 1964; le propos des Nattiers de Nabeul, 1964-68; Tazerka. Honours: Special Prize, Japon Prize, 1968. Address: 8 rue de Sicile, Sousse, Tunisia.

HASKINS, James George, born Bulawayo, 24th April 1914. Director of Companies; Minister of Works & Communications. Education: Plumtree School, Plumtree. Married, 1 son, 2 daughters. Appointments include: Minister of Commerce, Industry & Water Affairs, 1966-69; Minister of Finance, 1969-70; Minister of Works & Communications, 1970. Honours include, O.B.E.; J.P. Address: c/o Ministry of Works & Communications, P. Bag 7, Gaberones, Botswana.

HASSAN, Mohamed, born 10th January, 1919. Police Officer; Senior Assistant Commissioner, Head of C.I.D. Education: Matriculation, Punjab University, India, 1935. Married to Ishrat Begum, 2 sons, 1 daughter. Appointments: W.O.I, East African Army, World War II, 1939-48; Q.M. Stores, Kenya Police, 1949-51; Uganda Police Force, 1952—; Senior Assistant Commissioner, Head of C.I.D. 1965—. Awards: Colonial Police Medal for Meritorious Service, 1961; Uganada Independence Medal, 1962; recip. of several medals for World War II.

HASSAN II (His Majesty) Mohammad, King of Morocco, born Rabat, 9th July 1929. Education: studied Civil Law, University of Bordeaux, France. Appointments: exiled with his father, the late King Mohammad V, to Corsica & Madagascar, 1953; returned to Morocco to Command Royal Armed Forces, 1955; assumed Royal Power, 1957; Vice-President, Royal Government Council, 1960; Prime Minister, 1960; proclaimed King of Morocco, 1961—. Leader of Sherifian Delegation of Franco-Moroccan Military, 1957; Head of Moroccan Delegation to UN Assembly, 1960. Address: Royal Palace, Rabat, Morocco.

HASSOUNA, Mohamed Abdel-Khalek, born 28th October 1898. Secretary-General, League of Arab States. Education: University of Cairo, U.A.R. & Cambridge University, U.K. Appointments: Lawyer, 1921; subsequently, Egyptian Diplomatic Corps.; served in Berlin, Germany, 1926; Prague, Czechoslovakia, 1928; Brussels, Belgium, 1929; Rome, Italy, 1930; Ministry of Foreign Affairs, Cairo, U.A.R., 1932-39; Under-Secretary of State, Ministry for Social Affairs, 1939; Governor of Alexandria, 1942; Minister of Social Affairs, 1949; Minister of Education, 1952; Minister for Foreign Affairs, 1952; Secretary-General, League of Arab States, 1952. Honours: Grand Cordon of the Order of the Nile; Legion d'Honneur; decorations conferred by Belgium, Ethiopia, Italy, The Holy See, Syria, etc.

HAWKINS, Leonard Arthur Wyon, born Ilford, Essex, U.K. 19th November, 1909. Chartered Accountant. Education: Chigwell School, Essex. Married, 1 son. Appointments include: Partner, Spain Bros. Batchelor & Co., Southampton, Portsmouth, London, 1935-42; Auxiliary Air Force, 1939-42; Assistant Chief Accountant, Rhodesia Railways, 1946; Chief Accounts & Finance Officer, Rhodesia Railways, 1950; Principal Executive Officer (Technical), Rhodesia Railways, 1956; Assistant General Manager (Operations), Rhodesia Railways, 1961; Chairman & Chief Executive Officer, Swaziland Railways, 1961—. Memberships include: Fellow of the Institute of Chartered Accountants, England & Wales; President, Rhodesia Society of Accountants, 1959; Member of the Institute of Transport; Royal Commonwealth Society; Bulawayo Club; Mbabane Club; Rotary Club, Mbabane; Bulawayo Country Club. Honours, Prizes, etc. C.B.E. New Years List, 1966; Swaziland Independence Medal. Address: Swaziland Railway, Box 475, Mbabane, Swaziland.

HAWKINS, Michael Oliver Slade, born 11th May 1928. Civil Servant. Education: School Certificate, Higher Certificate, Wycliffe College, Stonehouse, Glos., U.K.; B.A.(Econs.), St. John's College, Cambridge University. Married, 2 sons, 1 daughter. Served in Royal Navy, 1946-48. Appointments: Administrative Officer, Kenya, 1951-62; Administrative Officer, Bechuanaland, 1962-66; Permanent Secretary, Botswana, 1966—. Memberships: Marylebone Cricket Club (M.C.C.); Nairobi Club. Address: Ministry of Works & Communications, Private Bag 7, Gaborone, Botswana.

HAYDEN, Rosemary Juliet, born 14th May 1923. Medical Practitioner. Education: M.B.B.S., London, U.K., 1946; M.R.C.S., L.R.C.P., 1945; D.C.H., 1948; University of Nottingham; London School of Medicine (Royal Free Hospital). Married, 3 daughters. Appointments: various, Royal Free Hospital, 1946 & North Middx. Hospital, 1948; Med. Registrar, Nottingham General Hospital, 1949; Med. Officer, Sudan Medical Service, 1951; Med. Officer, Nairobi City Council, 1959; Sr. Med. Officer, Maternal & Child Health, Nairobi City Council, 1964—. Memberships: Vice-Chmn., Association for Physically Disabled of Kenya; Vice-Pres., Society for Deaf Children, Kenya; Nurses, Midwives & Health Visitors Council of Kenya (nominated by Soc. of Med. Officers of Health); Kenya Med. Assn.; Kenya Paediatric Assn.; Kenya Geological Soc. Address: P.O. Box 2761, Nairobi, Kenya.

HAYFRON, George Duker, born 26th April 1926. Circuit Judge. Education: Adisade College, Cape Coast; Barrister-at-Law, Middle Temple, 1960. Personal details: second son of late Robert John Hayfrou, Barrister-at-Law; Married to Yvonne Euralie Graham of Worthing, Barbados, 7 children. Appointments: Circuit Judge, Judicial Service, Ghana. Address: Circuit Court, P.O. Box 153, Sunyani, Ghana.

HAZAREESINGH, Kissoonsingh, born 24th October 1909. Principal Private Secretary to Prime Minister of Mauritius. Education: Cert. in Social Science, London School of Economics, University of London, U.K., 1943-45; 2nd Devonshire Course, Inst. of Educ., 1950-51; Course on Community Dev., ibid, 1955-56; Docteur-es-Lettres, Sorbonne, Paris, France, 1961-62. Married, 3 children. Appointments: Labour Officer, 1938; Assistant National Service Officer, 1939-53; Poor Law Supervisor, 1946-48; Deputy Public Assistance Commissioner, 1948-53; Social Welfare Commissioner, 1953-59; Dir., Central Information Office, 1959-66; current position, 1966—. Memberships: Indian Cultural Association; Royal India Society. Publications include: Chroniques du Lundi, 1962; Undying Values, 2nd edn., 1963; Tagore et l'Ile Maurice, 1962 (ed. Maisonneuve a Paris, 1969). Address: Prime Minister's Office, Government House, Port Louis, Mauritius.

HAZELDINE, Gordon David, born Cape Town, S. Africa, 18th December 1930. Librarian. Education: Diocesan College, Cape, South Africa; University of Cape Town, 1946-50; University of Florence, Italy; B.A., Lib. Dip. Appointments: Deputy Archivist, Central African Archives, 1951-52; Librarian, Command Library (R.A.F.), Middlesex, U.K.; Chief Librarian, McMillan Memorial Library, Nairobi, Kenya, 1954-60; Chief Librarian, Nairobi City Council Libraries, 1961-65; Deputy Librarian, University of Malawi, 1965-70. Memberships: Past Chairman, East African Library Association; Kenya Horticultural Society; Life Member & Past Chairman, Nairobi Music Society; Chairman, University of Malawi Staff Association; Chairman, Blantyre City Garden Club. Publications: Articles for East African Library Association Bulletin & SCAUL newsletter; Travel in East Africa, past & present, (Compiler & Editor), Shell Co. of E.A. Ltd.; Bibliographies etc. Recip. Carnegie Corporation of New York Travel Award, 1963. Address: Chancellor College Library, University of Malawi, P.O. Box 5200, Limbe, Malawi.

HEATHCOTE, Arthur Cyril, born 16th April 1922. Director of Posts & Telecommunications. Education: Buxton College. Married, 2 daughters. Appointments: Postal Surveyor, Malawi, 1951-56; Head of Postal Services, Nigeria, 1956-62; Director of Posts, Telecommunications, & Civil Aviation, Lesotho, 1964-70. Fellow of the Royal Commonwealth Society. Awarded O.B.E., for distinguished service in the improvement & development of postal & telecommunications services in Lesotho, 1969. Address: P.O. Box 413, Maseru, Lesotho.

HEGER, Erhardt A., born Czechoslovakia, 29th August 1931. College Principal. Education: Dipl.rer.pol., Universities of Innsbruck, Austria & Munich, Germany; Degree in Education, University of Stuttgart. Appointments: Tutor, Commercial High Schools & Vocational Training Institutions, Germany, 1955-63; Tutor i/c, 1964-65 & Principal, 1966—, College of Business Education, Dar es Salaam, Tanzania. Address: P.O. Box 1968, Dar es Salaam, Tanzania.

HEIN, Raymond Charles Henry, born 26th September 1901. Barrister-at-Law (Middle Temple). Education: Royal College, Mauritius; B.A.(Hons.), Wadham College, Oxford, U.K. Appointments: Member of Legislative Council, 1936-48; Mayor of Port Louis, 1948; Chairman; Mauritius Commercial Bank, Ltd.; Swan Insurance Co. Ltd.; New Mauritius Dock Co. Ltd.; Mauritius Life Assurance Co. Ltd. Memberships: former President, Mauritius Turf Club; former President, Alliance Française. Honours: Chevalier de la Legion D'Honneur; Queen's Counsel. Address: Cathedral Square, Port Louis, Mauritius.

HENDRICKSE, Ralph George, born 5th November 1926. Paediatrician. Education: Battswood School, Wesley College, & Livingstone High School, Cape, South Africa; M.B. Ch.B., University of Cape Town, 1943-48; M.D., ibid, 1957; Postgraduate Studies to M.R.C.P.(Edin.), Edinburgh & Glasgow, U.K., 1955; Postgraduate Studies, U.K. & U.S.A., 1961-62. Married. Appointments: Medical Officer & Senior Hospital Officer, McCord Zulu Hospital, Durban, South Africa, 1949-54; Medical Officer i/c, Willis F. Pierce Memorial Hospital, Southern Rhodesia, 1951 (on secondment); Senior Registrar, University College Hospital, Ibadan, Nigeria, 1955-57; Consultant Paediatrician, 1957-69; Lecturer, University of Ibadan, 1957-59; Senior Lecturer, ibid, 1959-62; Professor & Head of Department of Paediatrics, 1962-69; Director, Institue of Child Health, 1964-69; Senate Representative, University Council, 1966-69; Senate Representative, Board of Management, University College Hospital, 1966-69; Director, University Bookshop, Ibadan, representing University Council, 1967-69; Senate Representative, Board of Management, Wesley Guild Hospital, Ilesha, 1963-69; Member, Advisory & Executive

Committee, Institute of African Studies, University of Ibadan, 1964-79; Adviser on Africa, International Foundation for Child Health, New York, U.S.A., 1965—; Adviser, Federal Nigerian Government, Ministry of Health, on child health problems, 1965-69, Consultant Editor, Clinical Paediatrics, 1965—, & African Journal of Clinical Science, Government, Ministry of Health, on child health problems, 1965-69; Consultant Editor, Clinical Paediatrics, 1965—, & African Journal of Clincal Science, 1969—; Co-opted Member, Education Committee, Nigerian Medical Council, 1967-69; Senior Lecturer, Special Appointment, Tropical Child Health, School of Tropical Medicine & Department of Child Health, Liverpool University, & Hon. Consultant Physician, Alder Hey Children's Hospital, Liverpool, U.K., 1969—. Memberships: Fellow, Royal College of Physicians of Edinburgh; Royal College of Physicians, London; Fellow, Royal Society of Medicine; Fellow, New York Academy of Sciences; Life Member, Paediatric Association of Nigeria; British Paediatric Association; British Medical Association; Nigerian Medical Association; Fellow, Royal Society of Tropical Medicine & Hygiene; Association of Physicians of West Africa, etc. Author of more than 50 papers in professional journals, & chapters in various books. Producer of a film on Single Cell Anaemia & participant in radio & TV broadcasts. Invited participant at a number of scientific conferences in Africa, Europe, & U.S. Honours: Heinz Fellow, British Paediatric Association, 1961; Rockefeller Fellow, 1961-62. Address: School of Tropical Medicine, Pembroke Place, Liverpool, L3 5QA, U.K.

HENDRICKSON, Duane Luther, born Seattle, Washington, U.S.A., 27th December 1931. Teacher. Education: B.A., Pacific Lutheran University, Parkland, Washington, 1957; Teaching Qualifications completed from University of Washington, Seattle, 1961. Married, 3 children. Appointments include: Teacher, Teachers' College, Numan, Nigeria, 1962-63; Principal, Bronnum Secondary School, 1964—; Education Secretary, Danish Branch of the Sudan United Mission, Nigeria, 1967—. Address: Sudan United Mission, Numan via Jos, Nigeria.

HENDRY, Ernest John William, born London, U.K., 2nd October 1914. Civil Servant. Education: Polehampton School Preparatory, 1919-25; Reading School, 1926-32. Married, 1 son, 1 daughter. Appointments: w. Royal Navy (war service N. Atlantic & Far East), 1933-55; Establishment Officer, H.M. Overseas Colonial Service, Nyasaland, 1955-63; Principal Personnel Officer to Malawi Government, 1964—. Member of the Zomba Gymkhana Club. Associate, Adu Report on Localization of the Civil Service, Nyasaland, 1961. Secretary, Skinner Commission for the Malawi Civil Service, 1963. Honours: M.B.E., 1967. Address: c/o Office of the President & Cabinet, P.O. Box 309, Zomba, Malawi.

HENRIES (Hon.) George Edward, born 25th June 1935. Lawyer (Counsellor-at-Law). Education: College of West Africa, 1952; B.A., Carleton University, Ottawa, Canada, 1958; J.D., Cornell University Law School, Ithaca, New York, U.S.A., 1962. Personal details: married to Marjorie K. Phelps, 3 daughters. Appointments: Assistant Attorney-General of Liberia, 1962-70; Solicitor-General of Liberia, 1970—. Memberships: Assistant General Superintendent, Providence Baptist Sunday School; Worshipful Master, Oriental Lodge, No. 1, A.F. & A.M., Monrovia; Liberian National Bar Assn.; American Society of International Law; International Society for the Study of Comparative Public Law; Y.M.C.A.; International African Law Assn. Publications: Measures to Combat Recidivism (Liberian Law Journal), 1966; Alternatives to Imprisonment & Their Impact on the Implementation of the Standard Minimum Rules for the Treatment of Prisoners (International Review of Criminal Policy). Honours: Knight Grand Commander, Humane Order of African Redemption (Liberian Decoration), 1964. Address: Department of Justice, Monrovia, Liberia.

HENRIES, Richard Abrom, born Monrovia, Liberia, 16th September 1908. Counsellor-at-Law. Education: College of West Africa (High School); B.A., Liberia College (now University of Liberia), 1931; LL.D., University of Liberia, 1949; D.C.L., 1952. Married to Doris A. Banks, 9 children. Appointments: Associate Professor of Mathematics, Liberia College, 1932; Chief Clerk, Commonwealth District of Monrovia, 1932-34; Chief Clerk, Treasury Dept., 1934-38; Supervisor of Schools, Sinoe & Maryland Counties, 1938-43; Member, House of Representatives, Liberia Legislature, 1943-51; Speaker, House of Representatives, R.L., 1951—; President, Board of Trustees, Univ. of Liberia, 1951—; President, National Bar Association, R.L., 1958—; President, Inter-Parliamentary Union (Liberian Group), 1959—. Memberships include: Charter Member, Liberian Scholastic Honour Society, 1950; The American Society of International Law, 1965; Grand Order of Lebanon, 1965; The United Supreme Council, U.S.A., 1948; Past Grand Master, Ancient Free & Accepted Masons of Liberia; Sublime Prince of the Royal Secret; United Supreme Council of the Southern Jurisdiction. Author of Liberia, The West African Republic; The Liberian Nation. Recipient of all Liberian Decorations including the highest: Grand Cordon, Most Venerable Order of Knighthood of the Pioneers, R.L., 1955; Foreign High Decorations received from: Ivory Coast, Dahomey, Togo, Senegal, Vatican, U.K., France, Italy, Greece, Yugoslavia, Haiti, Nationalist China, Senegal, Holland, etc. Address: The Capitol, Monrovia, Liberia.

HEPP, Bernard Francois, born 20th March 1919. Director; Administrator. Education: Diploma, French Overseas National School; D.L.; Diploma, Muslim Centre of Higher Studies, Paris. Appointments: French Administrator Overseas; Member, General Secretariat, United Nations; interim Governor of Dahomey; Under-Director of Credit Lyonnais. Publications: Les Conditions du developpement économique de la Côte d'Ivoire, 1953; Monnaie et Credit en Afrique Noire francophone, 1967. Honours: Knight, Legion of Honour, Address: 14 Rue de Remusat, Paris 16, France.

HEREWARD, Daphne, born Croydon, Surrey, U.K., 28th November 1922. Lecturer in Classics. Education: Eothen School, Caterham, Surrey, 1928-41; M.A., Somerville College, Oxford University; 1st Cl. Literae Humaniores, ibid, 1947; British School of Archaeology, Athens, Greece, 1947-48; Research Assistant, Institute for Advanced Study, Princeton, New Jersey, 1948-50; Staff Member, Lexicon of Patristic Greek, New Bodleian, Oxford, 1950-51; Assistant Lecturer in Classics, Royal Holloway College, London, 1953-58; Classical Specialist, Notre Dame High School, Norwich, 1959; Sir James Knott Fellow, University of Durham, 1959-60; Lecturer in Classics, Auckland University, New Zealand, 1960-62; Lecturer in Classics, The University of Ghana, Legon, Accra, Ghana, 1965—. Memberships: The Classical Association; Hellenic Society. Author of numerous publications including contributions to Classical Review. Awarded Woolley Scholarship for Archaeological Research, Somerville College, 1947. Address: The University, Legon, Accra, Ghana.

HERMANS, Christopher L., born 23rd December 1936. Civil Servant. Education: B.A.(Hons., Geography), Oxford University, U.K., 1959; M.A., Sociology, Howard University, Washington, D.C., U.S.A., 1961; M.A.(Econ.), Vanderbilt University, Nashville, Tennessee, 1967. Married, 4 children. Appointments: Assistant Development Secretary, Bechuanaland Government, 1961-67; Permanent Secretary, Ministry of Development Planning, Botswana Government, 1967-70; Permanent Secretary, Ministry of Finance & Development Planning, 1970—. Memberships: American Academy of Political & Social Science; Am. Society of Public Administration; Vice-Chairman, Botswana National Lawn Tennis Association. Publications: Poetry in 'Transition'. Address: Permanent Secretary, Ministry of Finance & Development Planning, Private Bag 8, Gaborone, Botswana.

HEUSCH, Bernard, born 24th January 1930. Engineer; United Nations Expert. Education: Agronomical Engineer, E.N.S.A.T.; Engineer, O.R.S.T.O.M.; Dr. Ing. Married, 3 children. Appointments: Agronomical Engineer, SOGETIM, Rabat, Morocco, 1957-60; Head of Laboratory Analysis of Soil, Somet, Rabat, 1960-63; Engineer, Sebou Project, Rabat, 1963-65; Head of Erosion Section, D.R.S., Forest Research Station, Rabat, 1965-70. Memberships: President, Alpine Club of Rabat; Vice-president, Royal Moroccan Federation of Mountain Skiing; Yacht Club, Morocco. Author of numerous works in his field Published in engineering & geographic journals. Address: B.P. 763, Rabat, Morocco.

HEWARD-MILLS, Nathaniel Neelanquaye, born Accra, Ghana, 12th July 1931. Legal Practitioner. Education: Sierra Leone Grammar School, Freetown; B.A., University of Durham, U.K., 1956; LL.B., University of Hull, 1960; Called to the Bar, Middle Temple, 1962. Married, 3 children. Appointments include: Assistant State Attorney, Ministry of Justice, Ghana, 1963-64; took over father's practice, 1964—; defended Lutze Herold, 1965; Counsel, Railways & Ports Authority, Commission of Enquiry into the Ghana Cargo Handling Company. Memberships include: Accra Turf Club; Chairman, Accra Horseman's Club. Address: Agbado Chambers, P.O. Box 4225, Accra, Ghana.

HEWITT, Bernard Robert, born Australia, 11th February 1927. Chemist. Education: B.Sc., Sydney, Australia; M.Sc., N.S.W., ibid; B.A., Queensland. Appointments: served in Royal Australian Navy, 1945-46; University Teacher; Industrial Lab. Management & Agricultural Research, in Australia; Lecturer in Chemistry, University of Malaya, 1965-68; Senior Lecturer in Chemistry,ibid, 1968—. Memberships include: Royal Australian Chemical Institute; Associate Member, Institute of Fuel, U.K. Publications: Author of 20 publications on soils & plant physiology; co-author of a book on tropical agriculture. Recipient of Pacific Star War Medal. Address: Box 5200, Limbe, Malawi.

HEYMAN, Maurice Druce, born 17th March 1926. Medical Missionary. Education: M.A., M.B., B.Ch., Cambridge University, U.K.; M.R.C.S., L.R.C.P., D.P.H., D.T.M.&H., D.Obs.R.C.O.G., St. Thomas's Hospital, London. Appointments: Medical Officer, Mission Hospitals in Tanzania, 1959-67; Medical Officer of Health, Maralal & Marsabit Districts, N. Kenya. Member of Bible Churchmen's Missionary Society (Protestant, Anglican). Address: BCMS Marsabit, P.O. Marsabit, E. Province, Kenya.

HICKS, Andrew Charles, born Longreach, Australia, 25th November 1918. Medical Practitioner. Education: Westminster School, London, U.K.; Middlesex Hospital Medical School, University of London. Memberships include: Fellow, Royal College of Surgeons, England, 1951; Fellow, International College of Surgeons, 1952; Fellow, Association of Surgeons of East Africa, 1952; Founder President & Honorary Secretary for a number of years of Medical Association of Kenya. Publications include: The Importance of Potassium Metabolism in Surgery, East African Medical Journal, 1953; Coral Ulcer, East African Medical Journal, 1957; Haustro-Caecal Invagination as a Cause of Intussusception, Journal of the International College of Surgeons, 1960; One Serpent or Two, An excursion into the Ancient Medical World, First Presidential Address, Medical Association of Kenya, East African Medical Journal, 1965. Honours include: Fellow, British Medical Association, 1960. Address: Cargen House, City Square, P.O. Box 20022, Nairobi, Kenya.

HINCHEY, Herbert John, born 13th February 1908. Civil Servant. Education: Sydney Grammar School, Australia; Sydney University; London School of Economics, U.K. Married. Appointments: Bank of New South Wales, Australia, 1932-39; Colonial Administrative Service, 1940-65; Financial Secretary, W.P.H.C., 1948-52; Financial Secretary, Mauritius, 1952-57; Financial Secretary, E.A.H.C. & East African Common Services Organization, 1957-65; Financial Adviser, Mauritius, 1967—. Memberships: Royal

Commonwealth Society; The Corona Club; The Nairobi Club; The East India & Sports Club. Honours: C.B.E., 1957; C.M.G., 1966. Address: Ministry of Finance, Government House, Port Louis, Mauritius.

HINGHONDO, Elijah Augustine, born 12th December 1941. Assistant Agricultural Officer. Education: Senior Secondary Four. Personal details: married, 2 daughters. Appointments: Assistant Agricultural Officer, Uganda. Address: P.O. Kapchorwa, Sebei, Uganda.

HIRST, Jack, born 13th August 1924. Chemist. Education: B.Sc. 1st Cl. Hons. (Chemistry), University College, London University, U.K., 1945; Ph.D., ibid, 1950. Married. Appointments: Assistant Lecturer, University College, London, 1948-49; Lecturer, University of Ibadan, Nigeria, 1949-56; Senior Lecturer, ibid, 1956-62; Professor, 1962—; Head of Chemistry Department, 1966-69. Memberships: Chemical Society, England; Science Association of Nigeria; Non-political Member, National Liberal Club; Royal Overseas League. Author of various publications in chemical journals. Address: Dept. of Chemistry, University of Ibadan, Ibadan, Nigeria.

HITCH, Barbara Mary, born 6th April 1923. Medical Practitioner. Education: St. Helen's School, Northwood, Middx.; Howell's School, Denbigh; S.R.N., Nurses' Training School, Royal Infirmary, Liverpool, 1941-45; University of Liverpool Medical School, 1946-52; Qualified M.B., Ch.B., 1952; D.Obs.R.C.O.G., 1954. Appointments: House Surgeon, Walton Hospital, Liverpool; Doctor CMS Hospital, Ado-Ekiti, W. Nigeria; ibid, Iyi Enu Hospital, Onitsha, E. Nigeria; CMS Hospital, Omdurman, Republic of the Sudan; as Missionary of the Church Missionary Society, visited Nigeria, 1955-66, Transferred to the Sudan, 1967. Recip. Gold Medal, 1945. Address: 3 Cromptons Lane, Liverpool, L18 3EU, U.K.

HIZA, Philip Robert, born 19th February 1938. Surgeon; Lecturer in Surgery. Education: M.B., Ch.B., University of East Africa, 1964; F.R.C.S., Edinburgh, 1968. Personal details: married to Eileen Elizabeth Hiza, 4 children. Appointments: Medical Officer, Tanzania, 1965-66; Fellowship Studies, Edinburgh, 1967-68; Surgical Specialist, Tanzania, 1968-70; Lecturer in Surgery, University of Dar es Salaam, 1970. Memberships: Tanganyika African National Union; Royal College of Surgeons (Edinburgh); Association of Surgeons of East Africa. Recipient of Abhyankar Prize, 1964. Address: Box 3054, Moshi, Tanzania.

HOBBS, Elisabeth Anne Birkby, born 14th May 1936. Nurse. Education: St. Christopher School, Letchworth, Herts.; Medway Technical College, Chatham, Kent; Bristol University; Battersea College of Technology, London; Hammersmith Hospital, B.Sc., 1957; S.R.N., 1960; Q.I.D.N.S., 1961; Pt. 1 Midwifery, 1961; H.V. Cert., 1961. Married to Dr. G. A. Hobbs. Address: c/o 14 Hillcrest Avenue, Chertsey, Surrey, U.K.

HOBBS, George Anthony, born 26th May 1935. Medical Missionary. Education: St. Edmund's School, Hindhead, U.K.; Sherborne School; Sidney Sussex College, Cambridge; St. Thomas's Hospital, London. D.R.C.O.G., 1962; D.C.H., 1968. Married. Appointments: Medical Officer, Wusasa Hospital, Northern Nigeria, 1963-64; Medical Superintendent, Ile Abiye Hospital, Ado Ekiti, Western Nigeria, 1965-70; Area Medical Adviser, Nigeria Red Cross Relief Operation, Enugu, 1970-71. Address: c/o 14 Hillcrest Ave., Chertsey, Surrey, U.K.

HOBSON, Brian Hugh, born 15th May 1915. Breweries Executive. Educated: Rugby School, U.K.; Cambridge University. Married, 3 children. Appointments: Managing Director, E.A. Breweries Ltd. Group, 1963—; Chairman, Kenya Export Promotion Council, 1966—; Chairman, E.A. Breweries Association, 1960—; Kenya nomination as Conciliator of the International Settlement of Industrial Disputes. Memberships: President, Kenya Bridge Association; A Governor of the World Bridge Association; Jockey Club of Kenya. Address: Londesborough House, Loresto Ridge, P.O. Box 30161, Nairobi, Kenya.

HOBSON, Percival Alfred, born 9th June 1926. English Tutor. Education: B.A., University of Durham, U.K., 1951; Diploma in Education, ibid, 1952; M.A. (Research into the Writings of the Pilgrim Fathers), 1957. Personal details: married to Patricia Jackson, 2 sons, 2 daughters. Appointments: Senior English Tutor, College Librarian, Wesley College, Ibadan, Nigeria, 1961-63; Examiner, Ministry of Education, W. Nigeria; Head of English Department, Nakuru Secondary School, Nakuru, Kenya, 1964-66; Examiner in Oral English, Cambridge School Certificate; Head of English Department, National Teachers' College, Kyambogo, Kampala, Uganda, 1966—. Memberships: Association of Teachers of English as a Foreign Language; British Council Register of Teachers of English as a Foreign Language. Publications: following Poetry published in East Africa Journal: Charter Flight London-Nairobi, 1967; Lightning at Night, 1967; Genesis—Leakey's Version, 1969; Mombasa—the Afternoon Land, 1970; Eschatos, 1970. Address: National Teachers' College, P.O. Box 20012, Kampala, Uganda.

HOCKENHULL, Tony Darlington, born 25th July 1924. University Lecturer in Engineering. Education: Adam's Grammar School, Newport, Shropshire, U.K.; B.A., St. Catharine's College, Cambridge, 1945; M.A., ibid, 1951. Married to Lucy Elizabeth Lees. Appointments: Sub-Lieutenant, Royal Naval Volunteer Reserve, 1945-47; Assistant Engineer, Anglo-Iranian Oil Co. Ltd., 1947-48; Instructor Lieutenant, Royal Navy, 1948-53; Captain, Major, 1953-65; Education Officer, Malawi Government (seondment to University of Malawi), 1965-68; Senior Lecturer in Engineering, Polytechnic University of Malawi, 1968; Head of Department of Engineering, ibid, 1969. Fellow, Institute of Mechanical Engineers. Memberships: Chartered Engineer; The Naval Club, London. Address: University of Malawi, The Polytechnic, Private Bag 14, Blantyre, Malawi.

HODGSON, Walter Henry, born 18th September 1925. Automobile Engineer. Married, 5 children. Current Appointment, Mayor, Chingola Municipality, Zambia, 1968—. Memberships: British Empire Commonwealth League; Kitwe Club. Address: 2317, Chingola, Zambia.

HODOMOU, Sylvestre Agbamahou, born Ovidah, Dahomey, 31st December 1940. Artillery Officer. Education: Ecole Militaire, Ovagadovgou (Ecole Primain), 1955; l'Ecole Militaire de St. Louis, Senegal, 1956; Baccalaureat, 1963; St. Cyr Coetquidan, l'ecole Militaire Inter-Arme, France; l'ecole d'Application d'Artillerie de Chalone sur Marne; Sub-Lieutenant of Artillery, 1967. Married. Appointments: Officer Assistant to the Lieutenant Commanding Support Company, Support Group of Ovidah, Dahomey, 1967; Officer Commanding, ibid, 1968; Minister of National Education, Youth, & Sports, 1968; President, Commission of Verification & Control, Ministry of Public Works; General Staff, Dahomey Army. Address: Etat-Major des FAD, Cotonou, Dahomey.

HOETS, Amy Elizabeth, born Knights, South Africa, 12th July 1906. Teacher. Education: Malmesbury Girls' High School; Cape Town Teachers' Training College. Married to Athol Taylor Hoets. Appointments: Assistant Teacher, Junior School; later Teacher of English in the only Native High School & Training College in S.W. Africa; Senior Assistant in charge of English, Augustineum Native Training College, Windhoek; Acting Principal, ibid. Memberships: Women's Auxiliary Agriculture Society; Executive Member, S.W.A. Federation of Business & Professional Women's Clubs; Vice-President, Windhoek B.P.W. Club; S.W.A. Arts Association; served on Town Council, Okahandja, for 8 years; Deputy Mayor & Mayor, ibid. Member, Little Theatre. Publications: Contributor to South-West Africa Journal. Address: The Augustineum Government Training College, Private Bag 13227, Windhoek, S.W.A.

HOFFACKER, Lewis, born 11th February 1923. Diplomat. Education: B.A., George Washington University, Washington, D.C., 1948; M.A., Fletcher School of Law & Diplomacy, Boston, 1949; Devonshire Course, Oxford University, 1960-61. Appointments: 3rd Secretary, American Embassy, Tehran, 1951-53; Vice-Consul, American Consulate-General, Istanbul, 1953-55; Egyptian & Sudanese Desk Officer, Dept. of State, 1955-58; 2nd Secretary, American Embassy, Paris, 1958-60; American Consul, Elizabethville, Congo, 1960-62; 1st Secretary, American Embassy, Leopoldville, 1962-63; National War College, 1963-64; Director, Operations Centre, State Dept., 1964-65; Counsellor, American Embassy, Algiers, 1965-67; Chief, U.S. Interests Section, Swiss Embassy, Algiers, 1967-69; American Ambassador to Cameroun & Equatorial Guinea, 1969—. Memberships: African Studies Association; Phi Beta Kappa. Address: Yaoundé, Cameroun.

HOFFMAN, Charles Siegfried, born 27th March 1915. Physician. Education: University of Heidelberg, Germany; University of Glasgow, U.K. Appointments include: Regional Medical Officer of Health, Ministry of Health, Ghana, 1960—; Surgeon-Lt.-Commander (Reserve). Honours: Grand Medal, Ghana, 1969. Address: Ministry of Health, P.O. Box 63, Cape Coast, Ghana.

HOLLIDAY, Robert, born 21st March 1912. Agronomist. Education: 1st Cl. Hons. (Agricultural Botany & Bacteriology), University of Leeds, U.K., 1934. Appointments: Lecturer in Agricultural Botany, Royal Agricultural College, Cirencester, Glos, 1935-39; District Agric. Officer, Worcestershire, U.K., 1939-43; County Agric. Officer, Yorkshire, E.R., 1943-46; Regional Crop Advisory Officer, Eastern Counties, 1946-50; Senior Lecturer, Agronomy, University of Leeds, 1950-68; Professor of Agronomy, Makerere University College, Uganda, 1968—. Memberships: British Society for Advancement of Science; Agricultural Education Association. Publications: Contributor to many professional journals & publications including: Chemistry & Industry; Journal of British Gasslands Society; Agricultural Progress; Journal of Agriculture; Agricultural Engineering Symposium; Restoration of P.F. Ash Covered Land, Final Research Report, University of Leeds; a Synopsis of the Leeds University Research on the Value of Fertilizers in Solution, ibid; Elements of Agriculture (book), revisions of chapters dealing with cereal, root, & fodder crops.

HOLST-RONESS, June Matilda Bernice, born Freetown, Sierra Leone, 10th June 1929. Doctor of Medicine. Education: Freetown Secondary School for Girls; Skerry's College, Edinburgh, U.K., 1946-48; Robert Gordon's College, Aberdeen, 1948-49; St. Andrew's University, 1949-55; Edinburgh Western General Hospital, 1957. Personal details: family Creole; father descendant son of Canon Spain, one of founders of Bishop Crowther Memorial Church, Cline Town, Freetown; married a Norwegian dentist resident in Sierra Leone, 1956, 2 sons. Appointments: Houseman to Professor M. Fairlie, Gynaecology & Obstetrics Department, University of St. Andrew's, 1956; Houseman to Professor Ian Hill, Consultant Cardiologist, Physician to H.M. the Queen in Scotland, Department of Medicine, ibid; Medical Officer i/c, Princess Christian Mission Hospital, Freetown, Sierra Leone, 1959-63; Doctor i/c, Netland Nursing Home, 1959—; General Practitioner, Freetown, 1963—. Memberships: Founder President, Inner Wheel Club of Freetown (International Organization); Secretary, Medical Practitioners' Union, 1964—; Executive Member, Family Planning Association, Freetown; Medical Adviser, Sierra Leone Women's Federation, 1959-61; Member, Board of Trustees, Freetown Secondary School for Girls, 1962—. Contributor to the Medical Practitioners' Union Magazine. Address: P.O. Box 1432, 8a Howe Street, Freetown, Sierra Leone.

HONORE, Louis Elric, born 1st September 1907. Senior Lecturer in Statistics. Education:

Royal College, Curepepe, Mauritius; B.Sc. (Econs.), London School of Economics, U.K. Married, 3 sons, 5 daughters. Appointments: Statistician, 1945; Assistant Director, Central Statistical Office, 1951; Director, ibid, 1960; retired from Government Service & appointed Senior Lecturer, University of Mauritius. Fellow of the Institute of Statisticians. Awarded O.B.E., 1964. Address: The University of Mauritius, Rose Hill, Mauritius.

HORI, Hiroshi, born Japan, 10th December 1919. Planning (Civil) Engineer. Education: M.S., Civil Engineering, Tokyo Imperial University, Japan, 1944; Graduate School, University of Illinois, U.S.A., 1955-56. Married to Toyoko Hori. Appointments: Technical Officer, Japanese Navy, 1944-45; Staff Member, Nissan Construction Co., Japan, 1945-55; Engineer Staff, Electric Power Development Company, Japan, 1955-64; Senior Planning Engineer, Mekong Committee, United Nationas in Thailand, 1964-68; Planning Director, National Water Resources Council, Tanzanian Government, 1969–. Memberships: Institute of Civil Engineers, Japan; Assn. for International Technical Co-operation, Japan; President, Japanese Association in Tanzania; Rotary International, Dar es Salaam, Tanzania. Publications: Development Potential of Major Tributaries of the Mekong River (Japanese Government Publication), 1961; Research on Flood Control in U.S.A. (Electric Power Development Company of Japan), 1962; Development of Electric Power in Developing Countries (Overseas Technical Co-operation Agency of Japan), 1959. Honoured by the Mekong Committee, U.N., as prominent engineer of planning, Bangkok, Thailand, 1969. Address: National Water Resources Council, P.O. Box 9, 242, Dar es Salaam, Tanzania.

HORNSBY, Cyril Ronald, born Newcastle upon Tyne, U.K., 4th December 1930. Academic Accountant. Education: Wallsend Grammar School; B.A.(Econ), Kings College, University of Durham, 1956; Associate, Institute of Chartered Accountants in England & Wales, 1965. Married, 2 children. Appointments: National Service, R.A.F., 1949-51; Working in Industry & Commerce, U.K., Singapore, & Pakistan, 1948-59; Accountant, Auditor, Professional Accounting Offices, London, U.K., 1959-65; Lecturer, Department of Accounting, University College, Nairobi, Kenya, 1965; Head of Department, ibid, 1966-70; Senior Lecturer, 1967; Reader, 1969. Memberships: Council, Association of Accountants in East Africa, 1967–; Council, Kenya Institute of Management, 1966–; Chairman, Finance Committee, All Saints' Cathedral, Nairobi, 1965–; President, Senior Common Room, University College, Nairobi, 1965–; President, King's College (Univ. of Durham) S.R.C., 1955-56; Vice-President, National Union of Students of England, Wales, & Northern Ireland, 1956-57. Author of numerous technical & administrative papers & articles, mostly connected with the promotion of accounting in developing countries. Address: Department of Accounting, University of Nairobi, P.O. Box 30197, Nairobi, Kenya.

HORROBIN, David Frederick, born 6th October 1939. Doctor; Medical Research Worker; University Professor. Education: K.C.S., Wimbledon, U.K.; Balliol College, Oxford; St. Mary's Hospital, London; M.A., D.Phil., B.M., B.Ch. Married to Nafisa Mahmoud, 2 children. Appointments: Fellow, Magdalen College, Oxford, 1963-68; Professor of Medical Physiology, Nairobi Medical School, Kenya, 1969–. Fellowships: Royal Society of Medicine; American Association for the Advancement of Science; British Medical Association. Publications: Communication Systems of the Body, 1964; The Human Organism, 1966; Medical Physiology & Biochemistry, 1968; Science is God, 1969; Principles of Biological Control, 1970; International Handbook of Medical Science, 1970. Author of various papers on neurophysiology, reproductive physiology, pre-eclampsia & hypertension in: Quart. Jrnl. Exper. Physiol.; Brain Research; Lancet; Jrnl. Theoret. Biol.; & Jrnl. of Obs. & Gyn.; Br. Commonwealth. Address: Dept. of Medical Physiology, University of Nairobi, Box 30197, Nairobi, Kenya.

HORTON, Alexander Romeo, born 20th August 1923. Banker. Education: Booker T. Washington Institute, Liberia; College of West Africa; B.A.(Econ.), LL.D., Morehouse College, Atlanta, Ga., U.S.A.; M.B.A., Wharton School of Finance & Commerce; University of Pennsylvania. Personal details: son of Rev. Dr. D. R. Horton, D.D. & Mrs. Ora Milner Horton (Dr. of Education); married to Mary Eliza Cooper, 1 son, 1 daughter. Appointments: Assistant Economic Adviser to the President of Liberia, 1955-63; President, Bank of Liberia, 1955–; Secretary of Commerce & Industry, Republic of Liberia, 1964-68; First Chairman, Economic Commission for Africa; Committee of Nine, Establishment Development Bank for Africa. Memberships: Chairman, Y.M.C.A. Hungry Club (A Businessman's Luncheon Club); Chairman, Banker's Association of Liberia. Publications: The Development of Industrial Institutions in West Africa through International Co-operation; How to Improve the Climate for Private Foreign Investment; Free Enterprise in West Africa, etc. Honours: LL.D., Morehouse College, 1968; Grand Cross, Order of Orange-Nassau, Netherlands, 1964; Grand Band, Order of Star of Africa, Liberia, 1964; Grand Commander, Order of Star of Africa, ibid, 1965; Decoration, Government of Mauritania, 1967; Knight Commander, Order of African Redemption, Liberia, 1959; Officer, National Order of the Ivory Coast, 1962; Decoration, Government of Togo, 1963; Decoration, Government of Tunisia, 1963. Address: Bank of Liberia, P.O. Box 131, Monrovia, Liberia.

HOUMØLLER-JØRGENSEN, Martin, born 1st June 1928. Doctor of Medicine. Education: M.B., B.S., Copenhagen, Denmark, 1955; D.T.M.&H., London, U.K., 1960. Married to Dr. Else Houmøller-Jørgensen. Appointments: Medical Officer, Denmark, 1955-57; Medical Officer, Medical Missionary, Numan Christian Hospital, Nigeria, 1957-65, 1967-68; Medical Superintendent, ibid, 1965-67, 1968-70. Memberships: Field Superintendent, Danish Branch, Sudan United Mission. Address: Danish

Branch, Sudan United Mission, Numan via Jos, Nigeria.

HOUPHOUET-BOIGNY (His Excellency) Felix, President of the Republic of the Ivory Coast, born Yamoussokro, Ivory Coast, 18th October, 1905. Education: M.D., Medical School, Dakar, Senegal. Appointments include: Head of his District, 1940; Founder, Honorary President, African Agricultural Union, 1944; Founder, President, African Democratic Rally (RDA), 1946; Mayor, Abidjan, Ivory Coast, 1956-60; elected to the French Constituent Assembly, 1945-52; President, Grand Council, French West Africa, 1957-58; Prime Minister, 1958—; President, 1958. Honours: Recipient of Honorary Doctorate, University of Pennsylvania, U.S.A.; ibid, Rennes, France; Tel-Aviv, Israel. Address: B.P. 1354, Abidjan, Ivory Coast.

HOVINE, Andre-Rene Jacques, born 4th September 1931. Bank Director. Education: Lic. Law; D. es Sc. Economic; Certificate, French National Overseas School. Married, 2 children. Appointments: Head of Economic & Planning Section, Financial Control AEF, 1957-59; Deputy Planning Commissionaire, Congo-Brazzaville, 1960-62; Director, Caisse d'Atonome d'Amortissement, Ivory Coast, 1963—. Memberships: various state societies; Ivory Coast Credit; Electric Energy of the Ivory Coast; Society for the Exploitation of Palm Oil; National Bureau of Technical Studies & Development, Financial Administration Society of Habitat. Honours: Knight, National Order of Merit; Military Cross of Valour. Address: B.P. 670, Abidjan, Ivory Coast.

HOWARD, Philip, born Cambridgeshire, U.K., 17th August 1913. Business Executive. Education: H.M.S. Conway, U.K. Married, 3 children. Appointments include: Branch Manager, Managing Director, Chairman, Bookers (Malawi), Ltd., Trading Company now 51% owned by the Malawi Government as the National Trading Co. Ltd.; Executive Director, National Trading Co. Ltd.; Managing Director, London & Blantyre Supply Co. Ltd., 1952; Chairman, ibid, 1954; Chairman, Air Malawi; Chairman, Cold Storage Co. Ltd.; Chairman, Nzeru Radio Co. Ltd.; Director, Reserve Bank of Malawi; Director, B.A.T. (Malawi), Ltd.; Board Member, Malawi Housing Corporation, Director, Agrimal (Malawi) Ltd.; Member, National Tourism Board. Memberships include: Chairman, Chisiza-Makata Memorial Trust (scholarship fund); Society of Malawi (Scientific & Historial); National Fauna Preservation Society. Honours, Prizes, etc: O.B.E., 1963; Malawi Independence Medal, 1965. Address: P.O. Box 34, Blantyre, Malawi.

HUDDA, Zulfikar Ali K., born 7th July 1942. Physician. Education: M.B., B.S. Personal details: married. Appointments: Junior House Officer, Mulago Hospital, Kampala, Uganda, 1968; Medical Officer, Toro, Kahuna Hospital, E.A. Tea Estates, Ltd., Fort Portal, 1969—. Memberships: Lions Club, Fort Portal. Address: P.O. Box 1785, Kampala, Uganda.

HUGHAN, David Selwyn, born Richmond, U.K., 26th September 1931. Agronomist. Education: B.Sc.(Agric.), Reading University, U.K. Married, 3 children. Appointments include: Research Manager, Chirundu Sugar Estates, Federation of Rhodesia & Nyasaland, 1957; Cultivation/Research Manager, ibid, 1960; Project Manager, Nakambala Sugar Estate, Zambia, 1964; General Manager, Nakambala Estate, Mazabuku, Zambia, 1968. Memberships include: Royal Agricultural Society, U.L.; Wild Life Conservation Society of Zambia. Author of various papers on irrigation, weed control, etc. Address: Nakambala Estate Ltd., P.O. Box 240, Mazabuka, Zambia.

HUGHES, H. Richard, born London, U.K., 4th July 1926. Architect. Education: Kenton College, Nairobi, Kenya; Hilton College, Natal, South Africa; Architectural Association, London, U.K. Married, 2 daughters. Appointments include: Assistant Architect, Connecticut, U.S.A., 1953-55; ibid, Nairobi, Kenya, 1955-57; Private Practice, Architecture, East Africa, 1957—. Memberships include: Chairman, Kenya Branch, Capricorn Africa Society, 1959-61; Vice-President, Kenya Arts Society, 1965—; Governor, Hospital Hill School, 1963—; ibid, Limuru Girls' School, 1967—; Naivasha Yacht Club, 1968; United Kenya Club, 1951—; Nairobi Club; Royal Insitute of British Architects; Architectural Association; Friends of the Tate Gallery. Contributor to the following publications: Modern Churches of the World, 1965; New Buildings in the Commonwealth, 1961; New Architecture of Africa, 1964. Address: P.O. Box 14390, Nairobi, Kenya.

HUGHES, Roland, born Aberffraw, Wales, 29th November 1912. Schoolteacher; Missionary. Education: Kingswood School, Bath, U.K., 1924-31; University College of North Wales, Bangor, 1931-37; B.A.(Wales), 1934; M.A., ibid, 1935; Diploma in Education, 1935. Appointments include: Tutor, Wesley College, Ibadan, Nigeria, 1937-46; Principal, ibid, 1947-54; Education Secretary (West), Methodist Church of Nigeria, 1954-62; Principal, Jesus College, Oturkpo, 1963—; Education Secretary (North), Methodist Church of Nigeria, 1963—. Memberships include: Member, Advisory Board of Education, Western Nigeria, 1954-62; Member, Advisory Board of Education, Northern Nigeria, 1964-66. Honours, Prizes, etc: Gladstone Research Student, University of Wales, 1935-37; M.B.E. Address: Jesus College, Oturkpo, Benue, Plateau State, Nigeria.

HUNTER-SMITH, John David, born 30th March 1923. Agriculturalist. Education: St. Albans School, U.K., 1931-39; B.Sc.(Agric.), Reading University, 1940-43; A.I.C.T.A., Imperial College of Tropical Agriculture, 1944-45. Married to Kathleen Jeane Turner. Father, J. Hunter-Smith, M.B.E., Principal, Herts. College of Agriculture. Appointments: Agricultural Officer, Tanganyika, 1945-55; Provincial Agric. Officer, ibid, 1955-56; Principal Agric. Officer, Deputy Director, Under-Secretary, Swaziland, 1956—. Honours: S.I.M., Swaziland Independence Medal, 1970; O.B.E., 1970. Address: P.O. Box 162, Mbabane, Swaziland.

HUTCHINGS, Geoffrey Justin Mackay, born 16th August 1937. Lecturer. Education: King Edward VII School, Johannesburg, South Africa; B.A., University of Witwatersrand; Dip. Ed., University College of North Wales, U.K.; Postgraduate work in Linguistics, University of Reading. Married to Anne Damant, 4 children. Appointments include: various teaching & lecturing posts in Britain & West Africa; Head of English, Malawi Polytechnic, 1969—. Member of Mlanje Mountain Club. Publications: various papers in professional journals. Address: The Polytechnic, Private Bag 14, Blantyre, Malawi.

HUTT, Michael Stewart Rees, born 1st October 1922. Professor of Pathology. Education: St. Thomas' Hospital Medical School, London, U.K.; M.D.(Lond.); F.R.C.P.; F.R.C.Path. Married, 4 children. Appointments: Senior Lecturer & Consultant Pathologist, St. Thomas' Hospital & Medical School, London, 1958-62; Professor of Pathology, The Medical School, Makerere University, Kampala, Uganda, 1962-70; Professor of Geographical Pathology, St. Thomas' Hospital Medical School, London, U.K., 1970. Memberships: East African Academy; East African Association of Surgeons; East African Association of Physicians; International Academy of Pathologists; Association of Clinical Pathologists; Pathology Society of Great Britain; International Society of Epidemiology; International Society of Geographical Pathology. Author of over 50 publications on geographical aspects of disease in Africa, w. special reference to cancer, cardiovascular disease, renal disease & splenomegaly. Address: St. Thomas' Hospital Medical School, London, S.E.1, U.K.

HUTTON, Frederick George, born 18th December 1921. Chartered Civil Engineer. Education: Amersham College, Amersham, Bucks, U.K.; Christ's College, Finchley, London. Married to Cecile Anne Mecredy, granddaughter of R. J. Mecredy, pioneer cyclist of Dublin; 2 sons, 2 daughters. Appointments: Municipal Engineer, Eldoret, Kenya; County Engineer, Naivasha County Council; Chief Assistant Engineer, City Council of Nairobi. Memberships: Institute of Civil Engineers; Associate Member, Institute of Water Engineers; East African Institute of Engineers; Life Member, Royal Scottish Country Dance Society. Publications: The City of Nairobi Reel, a Scottish Country Dance. Address: Ceilidhe Corner, P.O. Box 20036, Nairobi, Kenya.

HUXLEY, Peter Arthur, born London, U.K., 26th September 1926. Crop Physiologist & Horticulturist. Education: Alleyn's School, Dulwich, London; B.Sc.; Ph.D.; F.I.Biol. Married, 4 children. Appointments include: Assistant Lecturer, Senior Lecturer, Horticultural Botany, Faculty of Agriculture, Makerere University College, Uganda, 1954-64; Director of Research, Coffee Research Foundation, Kenya, 1965-69; Professor of Horticulture, Reading University, U.K., 1969—. Publications include: various scientific papers. Address: Reading University, Reading, U.K.

HYLAND, Anthony David Charles, born 8th August 1935. Architect. Education: Whitgift School; University College, London University (Bartlett School of Architecture), U.K. Married to Vivien Denzille Risdon, 2 children. Appointments: Chief Architect, Ghana Architectural & Civil Engineering Co., Accra, 1964-67; Lecturer, later Senior Lecturer in Architecture, University of Science & Technology, Kumasi. Memberships: Associate, Royal Institute of British Architects; Associate, Ghana Institute of Architects: Hon. Secretary, Ghana Committee of I.C.O.M.O.S. Publications: Imperial Valhalla (Journal of the Society of Architectural Historians), 1962. Address: University of Science & Technology, Kumasi, Ghana.

HYND, David, born Perth, U.K., 25th October 1895. Medical Practitioner & Medical Missionary. Education: Lanark Grammar School; M.A., Glasgow University, 1919; B.Sc., ibid, 1920; M.B., Ch.B.(Hons.), 1924; D.T.M.&H., London, 1925. Married, 1 son, 2 daughters. Appointments: Research Worker, Physiology Department, Glasgow University; House Surgeon, Beckett's Hospital, Barnsley, Yorks; Medical Superintendent & Founder, Raleigh Fitkin Memorial Hospital, Church of the Nazarene, Manzini, Swaziland; Medical Superintendent, Mbuluzi Leprosarium. Memberships: 1st Director, Red Cross of Swaziland, 1932-68; Past President, Swaziland Medical Association; British Medical Association; Royal Society of Tropical Medicine & Hygiene; President, Swaziland Conference of Churches; Central Advisory Board of Education; Past Vice-President, Manzini Rotary Club; Constitutional Conference to consider Independence Constitution for Swaziland, London, 1963; Justice of the Peace, Swaziland; Past Chairman, Swaziland Council of Social Services; Chairman, Swaziland Bible Society; Vice-Chairman, Waterford Inter-Racial School; 1st President, Holiness Association of South Africa; Swaziland Branch, British Red Cross Society; Medical Association of South Africa; Antislavery Society, London. Publications include: Disease of Heart (British Med. J.); Importance & Results of Medical Missions in Africa (pamphlet); Africa Emerging, 1959. Honours, Prizes, etc: King George V Silver Jubilee Medal for Service in Swaziland, 1935; Coronation Medal, 1953; O.B.E., 1938; C.B.E., 1947; Independence Medal, Swaziland, 1970. Address: P.O. Box 333, Mbabane, Swaziland.

I

IBRAHIM, Hassan, born Alexandria, Egypt, U.A.R., 7th February, 1917. Politician, retired. Education: Military College, Cairo, U.A.R.; Air Force College, Cairo. Married. Appointments included: Officer, Flight Officer, Squadron Leader, Wing Commander, Egyptian Air Force, 1940-52; Member of the Revolution Supreme Council, 1952-56; Chairman, National Production Council & the High Dam Committee, 1954-56; Minister of State for the United Arab Republic Presidency Affairs, 1954-56; Minister of State for Planning & Chairman of the Planning Committee, 1954-56; President, El-Nasr Company for the Manufacture of Pencils & Graphite Products, 1957-61; President, Paints &

Chemical Industries Company, 1957-61; President, Economic Development Organization, 1957-59, 1961-62; Member, United Arab Republic Presidency Supreme Council, 1962-64; Vice-President of the United Arab Republic, 1964-66; Memberships include: Honorary Member, El-Tahreer Club, Cairo; Honorary President, Union Athletic Club of Alexandria, until 1954; Honorary member of all Egyptian Clubs, & all the Athletic Clubs of the United Arab Republic. Honours include: The Nile Collar of the U.A.R., 1956; The Syrian Grand Ribbon of Merit Order, 1948; The Libyan Grand Ribbon of the Independence High Standing Order, 1952; The Yugoslavic Flag Order of First Grade, 1955; Le Grade d'Officier de l'Ordre de la Valeur du Cameroun, 1963; Le Grade de Grand Officier de l'Ordre National du Niger, 1964; Le Grade de Grand Officier de Grand Ribbon de Ma'rab Order, 1964; The Bulgarian People's Order of First Grade, 1965; The Polish Grand Ribbon of 'Polonia Restituta' Order, 1965; The Grand Ribbon of the Yugoslavic Star Order, 1965; The Grand Ribbon of the Libanese Honorary Order of Merit, 1965; The German Democratic Republic Golden Star of Nations Friendship, 1965; The Moroccan Throne Order of Distinguished Grade, 1965; The Malaysian Collar of 'Defender of State', 1965. Address: Khartoum Street, No 6, Heliopolis, Cairo, U.A.R.

IBUKUN (Chief) Olu, born 11th January, 1932. Engineer; Scientist; International Civil Servant. Education: Government College, Ibadan, Nigeria; University College, ibid; University of London, U.K.; British Broadcasting Corporation, London; B.Sc.(Eng.); D.I.C.; Ph.D.(Lond.); M.I.E.E.; A.M.I.E.R.E.; C.Eng.; A.Inst.P. Personal details: Hereditary Chief Ajagunna of Ogbagi, Nigeria. Appointments: Lecturer, Physics, University of Ibadan, 1957-61; Managing Director, West Nigeria Radiovision Service Ltd., Ibadan, 1961-63; Research Fellow, Ibadan University, 1963-65; Deputy Director, UNESCO Regional Centre for Science & Technology for Africa, Nairobi, Kenya, 1965-67; Programme Specialist, Africa Section, Department of Application of Science to Development, UNESCO Headquarters, Paris, France, 1967-70; Director, UNESCO Field Science Office for Africa, Nairobi, Kenya, 1970—. Member, Western Nigeria Parliament, Action Group Member, Owo Central, 1959-60; Member, Nigeria Federal Parliament, ibid, Owo North, 1964-66. Memberships: Fellow, Physical Society; Nigerian Society of Engineers; Science Association of Nigeria; Hon., East African Academy. Contributor of scientific papers to learned journals; Author, The Return (fiction), 1970. Honours: Sylvanus Thompson Graduate Scholar, British Institution of Electrical Engineers, Imperial College of Science & Technology, London, 1957. Address: UNESCO Field Science Office for Africa, P.O. Box 30592, Nairobi, Kenya.

IGA, Samson Mutekanga, born Namutamba, Singo, Uganda, 14th April, 1914. Engineer. Education: Mityana Central School; Nyanjaeradde Government School; King's College, Budo; Dip. Engineering, Makerere University College; Brixton School of Building Engineering, U.K. Appointments include: joined Dept. of Public Works, Uganda, 1938; Engineering Assistant, ibid; Assistant Road Surveyor; Lecturer, Engineering School, Kampala; Lecturer, Uganda Technical College; Assistant Librarian, ibid, Uganda National Football Coach. Memberships include: Buganda & Uganda Football Associations; Uganda Sports Association. Honours, Prizes, etc: M.B.E., 1956. Address: Uganda Technical College, P.O. Box 7181, Kampala, Uganda.

IGE, Samuel Oladele, born 6th September 1930. Barrister-at-Law; Lawyer. Education: LL.B., London School of Economics, University of London, U.K.; Barrister-at-Law, Lincoln's Inn, London; Research on Land Tenure, University of Chicago, U.S.A., 1960; International Seminar, Harvard University, 1969. Personal details: married, 6 children. Appointments: Clerk, John Holt & Co. Ltd., 1951-53; Trainee Executive, Shell Company of West Africa, Ltd., 1957-58; Private Legal Practice, 1959—. Publications: Race Problems in the U.S.; Problems of Land Tenure in Western Nigeria. Address: 2 Araromi St., P.O. Box 1437, Ibadan, Nigeria.

IGHODARO, Samuel Osarogie, born Benin City, Nigeria, 21st March, 1911. High Court Judge. Education: St. Andrew's College, Oyo, 1928-31; Fourah Bay College, Sierra Leone, 1935-40; LL.B., University College, London, U.K., 1945-49; B.L., Gray's Inn, 1949; B.C.L.(Durham), 1948; M.A.(Durham), 1944; B.A.(Durham), 1938; B.A.(London), 1938; Diplomas in Education & Theology(Durham). Married, 3 sons, 1 daughter. Appointments include: Housemaster, Igbobi College, Lagos, Nigeria, 1940-45; Legal Practitioner, Benin, 1950-51; Minister of Health, Western Region, 1952-56; Legal Practitioner, Ibadan, 1956-58; Executive Director, Development Corporation, 1958-59; Attorney-General & Minister of Justice, Western Region, 1959-63; Senior Lecturer & Acting Dean, School of African Studies, University of Lagos, 1966-67; High Court of Judge, Midwest State, 1967—. Memberships include: Vice-President, Red Cross Society, Western State, 1963-64; Legal Adviser, ibid, 1959-63; Chancellor, Anglican Diocese, Midwest. Publications include: Justice Amongst the Edo Ethnic Group in Midwestern Nigeria (Staff Seminar Papers, 1966-67). Honours, Prizes, etc.: Queen's Counsel, 1962. Address: High Court of Justice, P.O. Box 499, Benin City, Midwest State, Nigeria.

IGWE, Jacob Ezenwa, born 3rd May 1933. Surgeon. Education: Government School, Ikot (Elementary); Ekpene; C.M.S. Grammar School, Lagos, Nigeria; University College, Ibadan, 1952-56; St. Mary's Hospital Medical School, University of London, U.K., 1956-59; Royal College of Surgeons, London, 1963-66; L.M.S.S.A.(London), 1969; M.B., B.S. (London), 1960; F.R.C.S.(Edinburgh), 1966. Personal details: married. Appointments: Pre-registration, Edgware General Hospital, London; Battle Hospital, Reading, Berks., 1959-60; Medical Officer, General Hospital, Enugu, 1961-63; Consultant Orthopaedic Surgeon, Specialist Hospital, Enugu, East Central State, Nigeria. Memberships: Sports Club,

Enugu; Recreation Club, ibid. Address: Specialist Hospital, Enugu, East Central State, Nigeria.

IGWEBE, Benson Okeke, born Aro-Ndi, Izuogu, 1st September 1918. Physician. Education: Infant & Primary, 1928-30; Secondary Forms, 1931-32; Private Tuition, Wolsey Hall, Oxford, 1933-35; Cambridge School Certificate; M.B., C.H., University of St. Andrew's, Scotland, U.K., 1950; M.D., ibid, 1954. Married, 7 children. Appointments: Pupil Teacher, Ekenobizi, Umuahia, 1933-35; Custom's Officer, 1936-45; Medical House Officer, South Shields, Co. Durham, 1950-51; Casualty Officer, Oldham, Boston, U.K., 1952; Medical Officer, Government of Nigeria, 1953-55; Medical Superintendent & Proprietor, St. Andrew's Hospital, Onigivi, 1956—. Fellow, of the Royal Society, London. Memberships: Nigerian Medical Association; Founder, St. Andrew's Hospital, Okigwi (built in honour of the University of St. Andrew's, Scotland, U.K.). Publications: River Blindness (thesis), Tropical Ulcers (thesis), 1955. Honours: D.T. M.&H. (England). Address: St. Andrew's Hospital, Okigwi, Nigeria.

IJAGBEMI, Elisah Adeleye, born 24th May 1939. University Lecturer. Education: B.A. (Hons.), Kings College, University of Durham, U.K., 1961-64; Ph.D., University of Edinburgh, Scotland, 1964-68. Married, 2 children. Appointments: Assistant Lecturer in African History, University of Sierra Leone, 1965-67; Lecturer in History, Ahmadu Bello University, Zaina, Nigeria, 1968—. Member of the Historical Society of Nigeria. Publications include: Gbanka of Yoni; A Biography of Gbandegowa (in preparation); articles in scholarly journals. Address: Department of History, Ahmadu Bello University, Zaria, Nigeria.

IKOMI, Ebenezer Aboyowa, born 18th February, 1930. Obstetrician & Gynaecologist. Education: Kings College, Lagos, Nigeria; University College, Ibadan; M.B., B.S., London Hospital Medical College, London University, U.K.; L.R.C.P.(Lond.); M.R.C.S.(Eng.); M.R.C.O.G. Married, 2 sons, 1 daughter. Appointments: House Surgeon, Obstetrics, Churchill Hospital, Oxford; Registrar, Obstetrics & Gynaecology, St. Albans Hospital, Herts; Consultant Obstetrician & Gynaecologist, Island Maternity Hospital, Lagos, Nigeria. Contributor to scientific journals. Honours: Fellow, Population Control, 1966; Bio-Medical Fellow, Sloan Hospital for Women, Columbia University, U.S.A.; SCAAP Fellow, Toronto General Hospital, Toronto University, Canada, 1966; Ford Foundation Fellow, Mt. Sinai Hospital, N.Y., 1970. Address: 4b Force Road, Onikan, Lagos, Nigeria.

IKPEME, Bassey James, born 7th May 1918. Medical Practitioner. Education: Hop Waddell Institution, Calabar; King's College, Lagos, Nigeria; School of Medicine, Yaba, Nigeria; Westminster Hospital Medical School, London, U.K.; Guy's Hospital Medical School, London. Personal details: married, 4 children. Appointments: Medical Officer, Nigerian Medical Service; Senior Medical Officer, Acting Deputy Director, Medical Services, East Nigeria; Medical Directo, Ikpeme Clinic, Calabar. Fellow, Royal Commonwealth Society, London. Memberships: Commissioner, S.E.S. Public Service Commission; President, Nigerian Red Cross Society, Calabar; President, S.E. State Medical Association. Publications: Paludrine in the treatment of Malaria, 1946; Okrika Conjoined Twins (British Journal of Surgery), 1954. Honours: International Caps in Cricket & Football (Nigeria). Address: Medical Director, Ikpeme Clinic, Calabar, Nigeria.

IMAM, M. M., born 1st January 1932. Lecturer. Education: D.Sc.(Bonn.); M.Sc.(Sind); B.Sc.(Sind). Personal details: married to Rehana Imam, 3 children. Appointments: Assistant Cotton Botanist; Economic Botanist; Research Fellow, German Academic Exchange; Lecturer, University of Cape Coast, Ghana. Memberships: F.L.S.(London). Author of 22 publications in the field of applied & pure botany. Honours: Gold Medallist, University of Sind, 1959. Address: University College, Cape Coast. Ghana.

IMMERDAUER, Bernard, born 26th December 1910. Economist. Education. Graduated in Economics & Law, University of Jan Casimir, Poland, 1931-33; Master of Social Science, The Graduate Faculty of Political & Social Science, New School for Social Research, New York, U.S.A., 1942; M.A., English, Columbia University, 1943; Graduate, Industrial College of the Armed Forces, 1961. Appointments: Foreign Correspondent of leading Polish Daily, 1934-39; Economic Analyst, Departments of Commerce & Agriculture, Washington, D.C., U.S.A., 1943-44; Economic Analyst, Petroleum Reserves Corporation (joined with Petroleum Administration for War), later Oil & Gas Division of the Department of the Interior, 1944-47; Assistant Professor of Economics, University of Oklahoma, 1947-51; Economic Analyst, Petroleum Administration for Defense, Dept. of the Interior, and the Petroleum Branch, Office of Price Stabilization, 1951-53; Writer, 1953-57; Full-time Student, Ph.D. Course in Economics, 1957-58; Economic Analyst, Program Office, USAID Mission in Haiti, 1958-63; Program Office, USAID Mission in Haiti, 1958-63; Program Economist, USAID Mission in Recife, Brazil, 1963-66; Regional Economist, with U.S. Army Corps of Engineers, 1966-68; Senior Economist, United Nations Development Programme, Uganda Ministry of Planning & Economic Development, 1968—. Publications: Contributor to: Government Financing, a chapter in the 'History of Petroleum Administration for War', 1947; 'Transportation of Oil', 1951; approx. 130 articles in the Polish Press. Address: Ministry of Planning, P.O. Box 13, Entebbe, Uganda.

IMOKE, Samuel Efem, born 26th January 1912. Medical Practitioner. Education: Presbyterian School, Itigidi, S.E. State, Nigeria, 1918-26; Government College, Umuahia E.C. State, Nigeria, 1929-32; Higher College, Yaba, Lagos, 1932-34; School of Medicine, Nigeria, 1934-41. Personal details: married to Comfort Agbonibuan Imoukhuede, Nursing Sister, S.R.N., B.H.M.B., B.M.H., C.S.M. Appointments: Medical Officer, Nigerian Civil Service,

1941-52; Private Medical Practitioner, 1952-54; Minister of Labour, Eastern Nigeria, 1954-56; Minister of Finance, ibid, 1956-62; Minister of Education, 1962-66; Founder & Medical Officer, Eja Memorial Joint Hospital, Itigidi, 1966-68; Medical Superintendent, Eja Memorial Joint Hospital, Itigidi, 1966-68. Honours: 1st Prize (Public Health), School of Medicine, Nigeria, 1938. Address: Eja Memorial Hospital, Itigidi, Obubra, South Eastern State, Nigeria.

INYA-AGHA, Sam. Ayo., born 16th March 1934. Pharmaceutical Chemist. Education: Lagos Anglican Boys' Grammar School, 1949-54; Ibadan Campus, University of Ife, 1955-59; Ph.C.(London), Dip. Pharm. Married, 3 sons, 1 daughter. Appointments: Government Pharmacist, 1960; Manager, Retail Pharmacy, 1960-62; Proprietor & Founder, Manufacturing, Wholesale, & Retail Pharmacy, 1962-70. Memberships: Executive Member, Central Sports Council; Chairman, Enugu Amateur Athletics Club; Secretary-General, Nzuko Unwana (Cultural); Enugu Sports Club; Enugu Recreatives Club. Address: Oscar Pharmacy, Ltd., 117 Zik Avenue, Enugu, Nigeria.

INYANG, Robert Asuquo Etim, born 31st March 1930. Dental Surgeon. Education: Cambridge Senior School Certificate, Grade 1, 1947; B.Sc., Howard University, U.S.A., 1952; D.D.S., University of Alberta, Canada, 1957. Personal details: son of A. E. Inyang, Barrister-at-Law & Mrs. N. E. Inyang, M.B.E., Principal of Edgerley Memorial School, Calabar, Nigeria, until 1968; married, 5 children. Appointments: Dental Surgeon, 1957; Dental Surgeon, Grade 1, 1964; Senior Clinical Dental Surgeon, 1965; Principal Dental Surgeon, 1969. Fellow, Medical Council in Dental Surgery. Memberships: International College of Dentists, 1970; Medical Council of Nigeria; W.H.O. Inter-Regional Seminar on the Training & Utilization of Dental Personnel in Developing Countries, New Delhi, India, 1967; Nigerian Delegation, 2nd Commonwealth Medical Conference, Kampala, Uganda, 1968; W.H.O. Travelling Scholar, 1968; Nigerian Delegation, 20th Regional Meeting, W.H.O. Conference, Nairobi, Kenya, 1968; Scottish Freemasonry 1150 S.C.; Calabar Improvement League; Island Club, Lagos. Publications: The Proposed Training of Dental Auxiliaries at the University of Lagos Medical School (Journal of the Nigerian Medical Association), 1966. Address: P.M.B. 12562, 1 Yakubu Gowon St., Lagos, Nigeria.

IRUMBA, Nathan, born 27th December 1944. Personal Assistant to the Minister of Foreign Affairs, Uganda. Education: Duhaga Boys' School, 1951-56; Duhaga Junior Secondary, 1957-58; Ntare School, Mbarara, 1959-62; H.S.C., Makerere College School, 1963-64; B.A.(Hons.), Makerere University College, 1965-68. Appointments: Assistant Chief Editor, Makererean, 1966-67; Assistant Secretary (Foreign Service Officer) & Personal Assistant to the Minister of Foreign Affairs, Uganda, 1968-70; Uganda Representative, U.N. General Assembly, 1968, 1969 & U.A.R. Summit, 1969. Memberships: Secretary, Debating Club, Makerere College; Students' Representative Council, Makerere University College. Address: Ministry of Foreign Affairs, P.O. Box 7048, Kampala, Uganda.

ISAACS, Ebinu John Stephen Kink, born 23rd December 1944. Assistant Agricultural Officer. Education: 1st Class, Primary, 1959; 1st Class, Junior Secondary, Kaberemaido; Nabumali High School, 1965; Diploma in Agriculture, Bukalasa Agricultural College, 1968. Appointments: Assistant Agricultural Officer, Kaberemaido. Member of Uganda Agricultural Society. Address: Department of Agriculture, P.O. Box 94, Kaberemaido, Uganda.

ISHAGARA, Emmanuel Erasmus, born Fort Portal, 27th March 1935. Public Transport Manager. Education: Namilvango Junior Boys' School; St. Peter's Primary School, Virika; St. Leo's College, Virika, Fort Portal; Public Passenger Transport Course, U.K. Personal details: married to Catherine Sebabi, 1 son, 1 daughter. Appointments: with Uganda Transport Co. Ltd., 1961–; Traffic Manager, ibid, 1968–. Chairman of Kampala Round Table, 1970-71. Address: P.O. Box 7038, Kampala, Uganda.

ISHANI, Anil, born 26th October 1937. Lawyer. Education: Barrister-at-Law, Middle Temple, London, U.K. Appointments: Secretary, Agakhan Supreme Council for Africa. Memberships: City of Nairobi Round Table No 21; Nairobi Club. Address: c/o Nairobi Club, Kenya.

ISICHEI, Francis Okoafo, born Umuezeafadia, Umuaji, Asaba, Nigeria, about 1903. Teacher. Education: Asaba Government School, 1908-16; passed Grade 7; Pupil Teachers' Exams., 1916-17; Teachers' 3rd Class Certificate, Warri Normal College, 1918-19; 2nd Class Certificate, 1920; Teachers' Agricultural Certificate, 1922; 1st Class Teachers' Certificate, 1925; London Matriculation, 1948. Personal details: 13th in order of descent from Nnebisi, founder of Asaba Town, on father's side, & 10th in order of descent from Nnebisi, on mother's side; married, with children. Appointments: Assistant Teacher, Illah Government School, 1920-36; Teacher, Ogwashi-Uku Government School, 1927-32; Teacher, Asaba Government School, 1932-34; Headmaster, ibid, 1934-36; Headmaster, Issele-Uku Government School, 1937-40; Headmaster, Uromi Government School, 1940-41; Headmaster, Ahoada Government School, 1941-45; made to serve as a subordinate teacher as victimization for activities as President of Association of Government Teachers & Masters, Owo Government School, 1946; Bonny Government School, 1946-48; Senior Tutor, Teachers' Training College, Uyo, 1949-53; Tutor, Umuahia Government College, 1954; Supervising Teacher, Education Offices, Port Harcourt & Umuahia (supervising & inspecting schools), 1953-57; retired, 1958; President, Asaba Grade B Customary Court, w. 3 Associate Judges, 1959; Tutor, St. Patrick's College, Asaba, 1960-66. Memberships: President, Eastern Region, Association of Government Teachers & Masters, 1943-44; Federal President, ibid, 1944-45; Secretary, Pensioners' Association, Asabu, 1959-69; President, ibid, 1969; Member of Asaba local

Parliament or Oturaza, 1966—; Adviser, Executive Committee, ibid, 1968-69; Member of Panel, ochendo-Asaba or Regency, 1969—; Hon. Treasurer, Asaba Urban Development Committee; Rehabilitation & Reconstruction Committee, 1970—. Publications include: Several newspaper articles & addresses, published in Nigerian Advertiser, The Comet, & Eastern Nigeria Guardian; The Cable Point Land Dispute & Its Administrative Repercussions, 1943; Treatise on the New Ibo Orthography. Honours include: 1st Prize in Open Competition, with treatise regarding the position of the New Ibo Orthography in Ibo literature; Coronation Medal, 1953. Address: 17 Umuaji Street, Asaba, Mid-West, Nigeria.

ISMAIL, Ahmed Ismail, born Erigavo, 9th November, 1925. Public Servant. Education: St. Joseph's High School, Aden, Arabia; Assistant Prison Governors' Course, Wakefield, U.K.; Studied Penology & Correction, Southern Illinois University, U.S.A. Address: Commandant of the Custodial Corps., P.O. Box 721, Mogadishu, Somalia.

ISMAIL, Firoz Rajabali, born 20th April 1941. Industrial Economist: Education: B.A.(Hons.), Economics, East Africa, Makerere University College, Kampala, Uganda, 1963-66; Postgraduate Diploma in Industrial Development Programming, The Hague, Netherlands, 1967-68; Certificate in Project Analysis (arranged by The World Bank), Nairobi, Kenya. Appointments: Industrial Economist, 1966—; Alternate Directorship of following public companies: Friendship Textile Mills Ltd.; Mwanza Textiles Ltd. Representative for the Ministry of Commerce & Industries on the following: Tanzania Investment & Industrial Promotion Committee; Industrial Coordination Committee; Working Party on Manufacturing & Processing Industries. Official Member of Tanzania Delegation to the following conferences: International Conference on Problems of Development Banks & Development Conferences, West German Govt.; Study Group Meeting on Industrial Data Programming, UNIDO; Conference on Industrialization & Shipping, East African Community. Memberships: Economic Society of Tanzania; Tanzania Products Promotion Council; National Price Control Advisory Board; Economic Committee of TANU Youth League. Publications: Author of papers (restricted). Address: Industrial Studies & Development Centre, P.O. Box 2650, Dar es Salaam, Tanzania.

ITA, Nduntuei Otu, born 22nd November 1936. Librarian. Education: University of Ibadan, Nigeria; A.L.A.; F.L.A.; LL.B.(London). Married. Appointments: Senior Cataloguer, Regional Library, Enugu, Nigeria, 1961-63; Sub-Librarian, University of Nigeria, 1965-67; Librarian, Institute of Administration, Zaria, 1968—. Memberships: Hon. Treasurer, Nigerian Library Association; Chairman, Northern States Division, ibid, Convener, Standing Committee on Cataloguing & Classification. Publications: Anthropological & Linguistic Bibliography of Nigeria; A Survey of Writings from the Earliest Times to 1966; Educational Planning & School Library Development in Nigeria, International Library Review, 1969. Address: Institute of Administration, P.M.B. 1013, Zaria, Nigeria.

ITEBA, Sylvanus Douglas, born January 1940. Science Laboratory Technician. Education: Cambridge Overseas School Certificate (G.C.E.); Ordinary & Advanced Certificate, Institute of Science Technology (Science Laboratory Technicians Course). Married. Appointments: Laboratory Assistant, 1961-64; Laboratory Technician, 1964-69; Senior Laboratory Technician, 1969. Address: East African Industrial Research Organization, P.O. Box 30650, Nairobi, Kenya.

IWE, Agori, born 1906. Bishop. Education: St. Andrew's C.M.S. School, Warri, until 1922; St. Andrew's College, Oyo, 1924; St. Paul's Training College, Awka, 1937; Birkenhead, Liverpool, U.K., 1949. Personal details: married, 7 children. Appointments: School Teacher, Catechist; Pastor; Archdeacon; Bishop; Councillor, Central Urhobo District Council; Appeal Court Judge; Mid-West Advisory Council. Publications: Published the Prayer Book in Urhobo language with the Gospel according to St. John. Editor the New Testament in Urhobo. Honours: J.P., 1959; M.B.E., 1957; C.F.R., 1965. Address: Bishopscourt, P.O. Box 82, Benin City, Nigeria.

IYANDA, Eman Aremu, born Ogbomoso, Nigeria, 23rd November 1923. Teacher. Education: Ogbomoso Baptist Day School, 1938-34; Teacher Training College, Baptist College, Ogbomoso & Iwo, 1937-40; B.A., University of Ibadan, 1948-52; Diploma in Education, London Institute of Education, UK., 1952-53. Married, 3 sons, 2 daughters. Appointments: Teacher, Baptist Primary Schools, Northern State, Nigeria, 1941-48; Vice-Principal, Oyo Baptist Boys' High School, 1954-55; Principal, ibid, Baptist Boys' High School, Shaki, & Baptist High School, Ejigbo; currently Headmaster, Ogbomoso Girls' High School. Memberships: Director, Central Bank of Nigeria, 3 yrs.; Rubber Panel, Western Region; Tax Appeal Panel, Oshun Division; Census Officer, Oshun Division, 2 yrs.; Electoral Officer, ibid, 2 yrs.; Christian Workers' Board, Nigerian Baptist Convention; Board of Governors, 2 Secondary Grammar Schools; Chairman, Board of Governors, Igede Baptist High School; Central Board, Nigeria. Address: Ogbomoso Girls' High School, P.O. Box 136, Ogbomoso, Nigeria.

IYER, Venkiteswar-Rama, born 15th November 1914. Chemical Engineer. Education: B.Sc., Annamalai University, India, 1934; M.Sc., Banaras University, India, 1937; Research Scholar in Chemistry, Institute of Science, Bangalore, India, 1937-39. Married, 3 children. Appointments: Technical Officer, Indian Ordnance Factories, 1939-48; Chemical Process Officer, Fertilisers & Chemicals, SINDRI, India, 1948-54; Development Officer, Ministry of Commerce & Industry, New Delhi, 1954-62; Technical Adviser, Indian Investment Centre, New Delhi, 1962-65; Deputy Project Manager & Chemical Engineer, UNIDO Industrial Studies & Development Centre, Dar es Salaam, Tanzania, 1965—. Member of American Institute of Chemical Engineers, New York, U.S.A.

Publications: Fertiliser Industry in the ECAFE Region. Address: U.N. Industrial Studies & Development Centre, P.O. Box 2650, Dar es Salaam, Tanzania.

IZAMA, Angelo Abdalla, born 15th August 1924. District Commissioner (Administrative Officer). Education: St. Aloysius College, Nyapea, 1942-49. Personal details: descendant of Chief Kongoro. Appointments: Clerk-Interpreter, D.C.'s Office, Moyo, 1950-54; Medical Service, 1955-63; elected Secretary-General, Madi, & Constitutional Head (Lopirigo) of Madi, 1963-67; District Commissioner, 1967—. Memberships: Uganda Club, 1964—; Director, Lions Club, Tororo, 1969-70; E.A.A.A., 1962-70. Address: P.O. Box 1, Tororo, Uganda.

IZZET, Abdullah, born 26th November 1901. Agricultural Engineer. Education: Private Tutors; Federal Polytechnic School, Zurich, Switzerland, 1923. Personal details: son of former Egyptian Ambassador to London. Appointments: Vice-President, Banque Italo Egiziano, Cairo, Egypt, 1933; Owner, Import-Export Society; Representative, M.A.N. Farbwerke Hoechst. Memberships: Automobile Club of Cairo; Guezira Sporting Club, ibid; Aero Club of France; Grasshoppers of Zurich, Switzerland. Honours: Bey sous le Royaume D'Egypte; Commander, Crown of Italy, 1938. Address: Tengstrasse, 36 Munich 13, German Federal Republic.

J

JABBAL, Hindpal Singh, born 15th February 1937. Electrical Engineer. Education: B.E.; M.Sc.; M.E.A.I.E. Appointments: Protection Engineer, East African Power & Lighting Co. Ltd., Nairobi, Kenya. Member of the E.A. Institute of Engineers. Awarded British Commonwealth Scholarship, 1965. Address: c/o E.A. P. & L. Co. Ltd., P.O. Box 30177, Nairobi, Kenya.

JACKSON, Osborne A. Y., born 7th July 1938. University Teacher. Education: B.Sc., Maths., University of Ghana, 1959-62; M.Sc., Statistics, University of Birmingham, U.K., 1963-64; Ph.D., Statistics, London University, 1964-67; D.I.C., ibid. Appointments: Lecturer, University of Science & Technology, Ghana, 1962-63; Lecturer, Kingston College of Technology, U.K., 1966-67; Lecturer, University of Science & Technology, Kumasi, Ghana, 1967—. Fellow of Royal Statistical Society, 1964—. Publications: Author of articles in British statistical journals including: Testing for the Exponential Distribution, Journal of the Royal Statistical Society, 1967; Tests of Separate Families of Hypotheses, Biometrika, 1968; Fitting Distributions to Wool Fibre Diameters, Journal of the Royal Statistical Society, 1969. Address: Dept. of Mathematics, University of Science & Technology, Kumasi, Ghana.

JACOBS, Alan H., born 4th November 1929. Social Anthropologist. Education: M.A., University of Chicago, U.S.A., 1953; D.Phil., Oxford University, U.K., 1965. Married, 3 children. Appointments: Acting Government Sociologist, Kenya, 1961-62; Assistant-Associate Professor, University of Illinois, U.S.A. 1962-68; Chairman, African Studies Comm., ibid, 1966-68; Research Director & Senior Research Fellow, Cultural Division, University College, Nairobi, Kenya. Fellowships: American Anthropological Association; African Studies Association, U.S.A. Memberships: Life Member, Historical Association of Kenya; British Institute of History & Archaeology in East Africa. Publications: The Pastoral Maasai of Kenya: A Report of Anthropological Field Research, Ministry of Overseas Development, London, 1963; African Pastoralists, Anthropological Quarterly, 1965; A Chronology of the Pastoral Maasai, Hadith I, 1968; Maasai Marriage & Bridewealth, 1970. Recip. of Awards & Grants from: National Science Foundation, 1967-68; Ford Foundation Fellowship, 1956-58; Colonial Social Science Research Council Grant, 1961-62. Address: Cultural Division, I.D.S., University College, P.O. Box 30197, Nairobi, Kenya.

JACOBSEN, Einer, born 29th April 1907. Industrialist; Consul-General of Denmark in Senegal. Education: Studied in Denmark. Appointments: Director-General, Ets. V. Q. Petersen & Co., Dakar, Senegal, 1930-50; Administrator-Elect, ibid, 1950—. Memberships: Royal Danish Yacht Club, Copenhagen, Denmark; Automobile Club of France; International Sporting Club of Cannes. Honours: Officer, the Order of Denmark; Knight of the Legion of Honour; Officer, National Order of Senegal; ibid, Order of St. Olaf, Norwegian; Order of Vasa, Sweden; The Black Star of Benin. Address: 51 Bld. Roosevelt, Dakar, Senegal.

JADEJA, Shyamsinh Jalemsinh, born Dar es Salaam, Tanzania, 3rd November 1938. Barrister. Education: Primary, India; Secondary, Dar es Salaam, Tanzania; Law, Mathematics & Journalism, U.K.; Called to the English Bar, 1961. Personal details: family member of Morvi, the former Indian Princely State of Jadejas; married to Miss Rasika Gambhirsingh Jhala of the Royal Family of Lakhtar, Gujarat State. Appointments include: Legal Aid Counsel, Legal Aid Committee, Tanganyika Law Society; Secretary-General, Hindu Mandal, Dar es Salaam, 1966; Honorary Lecturer of Law to National Insurance Corporation Trainees, Dar es Salaam, 1968—. Member of the Standing Law Committee, 1969-70, & 1970-71 & the Law Reform Committee, 1969. Memberships include: former Council Member, Tanganyika Law Society. Address: S. J. Jadeja & Co., Advocates, P.O. Box 1370, Dar es Salaam, Tanzania.

JAJA, Millar Oboada Adafe, born 21st June 1929. Orthopaedic & Traumatic Surgeon. Education: King's College, Lagos, Nigeria, 1943-48; University College, Ibadan, Nigeria, 1948-52; Oriel College, University of Oxford, U.K., 1952-55; University of Birmingham, 1960-61; University of Liverpool, 1962; M.B., M.Ch. Orth.; F.R.C.S. Married to Annette Esuku, 3 sons, 2 daughters. Appointments: House Physician & Surgeon, Radcliffe Infirmary,

Oxford, 1956-57; Senior House Surgeon, Registrar, University College Hospital, Ibadan, Nigeria, 1957-60; Registrar, Queen Elizabeth Hospital, Birmingham, 1961; Registrar, Agnes Hunt & Robert Jones Orthopaedic Hospital, Oswestry, 1963; Lecturer in Surgery & Consultant Orthopaedic Surgeon, University of Ibadan & University College Hospital, 1963-65; Senior Lecturer in Surgery, ibid, 1965-66; Senior Lecturer in Surgery, University of Nigeria, Nsukka, 1967-69; Consultant Orthopaedic Surgeon, Military Hospital, Port Harcourt, 1970; Senior Lecturer in Surgery, College of Medicine, University of Lagos, 1970—. Fellow of Association of Surgeons of West Africa. Memberships: British Orthopaedic Association; Nigerian Medical Association; British Medical Association. Publications include: Perthes Disease & Sickle-Cell Disease of the Hip, Report of the Sixth Annual Conference of ASWA, 1966. Address: College of Medicine, University of Lagos, P.M.B. 12003, Lagos, Nigeria.

JAKUSKO (Alhaji) Ahmed Diori, born Jakusko, Bedde Division, Bornu Province, April, 1942. Teacher. Education: Jakusko Elementary School, 1950-52; Gashua Elementary School, 1953-55; Potiskum Senior Primary School, 1956-58; Bornu Provincial Secondary School, Maiduguri, 1959-60; Higher Elementary Teachers' Certificate Grade II, 1961-64; Senior Teachers' Grade I Certificate, Rural Education College, Minna, 1966-67. Married, 1 child. Appointments include: Headmaster Bizi Primary School, 1965; Headmaster, Gashua Central Primary School, 1967—. Memberships include: Patron, Gashua Central Primary School Branch, Young Farmers' Club; Nigerian Union of Teachers; Gashua Branch, Jama'tu Nasril Islam. Address: Bedde Local Education Authority, Education Office, Gashua via Nguru, North-Eastern State, Nigeria.

JAMAL, Amir Habib, born Dar es Salaam, Tanzania, 26th January 1922. Minister for Finance; Member of Parliament for Morojoso North. Education: Bachelor of Commerce (with Economics), University of Calcutta, India. Married, 4 children. Appointments: Member of Legislative Council, elected 1958; Minister for Urban Local Government, 1959; Minister for Communications & Power, 1960-64; Minister of State, President's Office, Directorate of Developments, 1964-65; Minister for Finance, 1965—.

JAMANI, Rahemtulla, born Mombasa, Kenya, 25th February 1924. Medical Practitioner. Education: Bachelor of Medicine & Surgery. Memberships: Uganda Medical Association; College of General Practitioners; Uganda Medical Society.

JAMES, Michel Henri, born 20th August 1936. Teacher. Education: Primary & Secondary school, Lycée Lyantey, Casablanca, Morocco; studied at the National School of Horticulture, Versailles, France; L. es Sc., Diploma, Faculty of Science, Rabat, Morocco. Married, 2 children. Appointments: Teacher, Rabat, 1962-63; Science Teacher, Boys' School, Sousse, 1965-68; Teacher, Ecole Normale d'Instituteurs, Sousse, 1969—. Address: Ecole Normale d'Instituteurs, Sousse, Morocco.

JANDO, Gurbachan Singh, born 1921. Architect. Memberships: A.M.I.S.E.; A.E.A.I.A.; F.I.A.A.; Uganda Society of Architects; Kenya Association of Architects; Host, Lions Club of Kampala; 1st Year Director, Lions Club Kla.; Trustee, Ramgarhia Sikh Sports Club. Address: P.O. Box 282, Kampala, Uganda.

JANTUAH, Kwame Sanaa-Poku, born 21st December 1922. Barrister-at-Law. Education: Teacher Training, St. Augustine Training College, Cape Coast; Politics & Economics, Plater College, Oxford, U.K., 1946-48; The College of Law, London, 1964-66; Called to the Bar, Lincoln's Inn, 1966; LL.B.(Hons.), London University. Personal details: member of the ruling Oyoko Royal Family of Ashanti; 1st marriage (dissolved) to Matilda (née Owusu) of the Royal Family of Agona; 2nd marriage to Astrid Margit (née Andersson) of Bodsjo, Sweden. Appointments: House Prefect, St. Augustine College, 1944; Teacher, 1945-46; Assistant Secretary-General, Asanteman Council of Chiefs, 1948-50; Editor of 'The Sentinel', Kumasi, 1950-51; Councillor, Kumasi Municipal Council, 1950-51; Member of Legislative Assembly, 1951-56; Minister of Agriculture, 1954-56; Deputy High Commissioner in London, U.K., 1957-59; Ambassador to Paris, France, 1959-62; Ambassador to Brazil, 1962-64; Representative at U.N. General Assembly; Member of Special Political, Economic, & Social Committees, 1958-59, 1961-63. Memberships: General Council of the English Bar; Ghana Bar Association. Address: City Chambers, P.O. Box 6467, Accra, Ghana.

JANVIER, Jacques Jean Pierre, born 12th October 1927. Professor; Cultural Adviser to the French Ambassador in Yaoundé, Federal Republic of Cameroun. Education: Agreg. Geography. Married to Genevieve Misset, 1 son, 1 daughter. Appointments: Teacher, Van Vollenhoven & Delafosse Lycées, Dakar, Senegal, 1952-58; Technical Adviser, to the Minister of Information, Senegal, 1958-67; ibid, French Ambassador in Cameroun, 1967—. Author of diverse articles on African History & Geography, etc. Honours: Knight of the National Order of Senegal, 1961. Address: Cultural Service to the French Embassy, Cameroun, B.P. 666, Yaoundé, Cameroun.

JARIKRE, Francis Uduoghoronyo Sunday, born 1st December 1933. Bank Manager. Education: Catholic Schools, Egbo-Ide, Sapele, & Warri; St. Thomas' Training College, Ibusa, 1950-54; City of London College, Moorgate, London, U.K., 1959-60; Institute of Administration, Ahmadu Bello University, Zaria, Nigeria, 1966. Married, 5 daughters. Appointments: Schoolmaster, 1955-57; Bank Accountant, 1961-64; Bank Manager, 1968—. Address: Barclays Bank of Nigeria Ltd., Sapele, Nigeria.

JAWARA (Sir) Dawda Kairaba, born Barajally, MacCarthy Island Div., 1924. Member of Parliament, The Gambia. Education: Muslim Primary School; Methodist Boys' Grammar School, Bathurst, The Gambia; Achimota College Veterinary School, Ghana; Glasgow University, U.K. Married. Appointments include: Veterinary Officer, Kombo St. Mary,

1954-60; Diploma in Tropical Veterinary Medicine, Edinburgh, U.K., 1957; Leader, People's Progressive Party, The Gambia, 1960; Minister of Education, 1960-61; Premier, 1962-63; Prime Minister, 1963-70; President of the Republic of The Gambia, 1970—. Memberships include: The Bathurst Club; Bathurst Reform Club; President, Gambia Veterinary Association. Honours, Prizes, etc.: Knight Bachelor, 1966; Grand Cross of the Order of the Cedars of Lebanon, 1966; Grand Cross of the National Order of the Republic of Senegal, 1967; Grand Officer of the Order of the Islamic Republic of Mauritania, 1967; Grand Cross of the Order of the Propitious Clouds of China, Taiwan, 1968; Grand Cordon of the Most Venerable Star of Knighthood of the Pioneers of Liberia, 1968. Address: State House, Bathurst, The Gambia.

JAYARAJAN, Chennancade Krishnan, born India, 15th July 1938. Town Planner. Education: B.Eng., University of Madras, India, 1960; Master of Technology in Town Planning, Indian Institute of Technology, Kharagpur, India, 1963. Appointments: Assistant Lecturer in Civil Engineering, 1960-61; Technical Teacher Trainee, India, 1961-63; Lecturer in Town Planning, 1963-67; Town Planning Officer, Tanzania, 1967—. Memberships: Associate of Institute of Town Planners, India; East Asia Regional Organization for Planning & Housing. Publications: approx. 10 articles on town planning in various journals in India. Address: P.O. Box 20671, Dar es Salaam, Tanzania.

JEAN-FRANCOIS, Louis Sydney, born 9th November 1929. Librarian. Education: St. Jean Baptiste de la Salle School, Port-Louis, Mauritius; Royal College School, Port Louis; Royal College, Curepipe; Higher School Certificates; B.A.(London); Associateship of the British Library Association (A.L.A.). Married, 3 daughters. Appointments: Assistant Librarian, Mauritius Institute, from 1955-59; Librarian, ibid, 1959—. Member of Racing Club of Mauritius. Awarded several prizes for Classics at Secondary School. Address: Mauritius Institute, Port-Louis, Mauritius.

JEANTOU, Maurice Emmanuel, born 29th December 1917. Deputy Commissioner of Income Tax. Education: English Scholarship Examination, Royal College of Mauritius, 1937; London University Intermediate Examination in Arts, ibid, 1938; Course of Training, Income Tax Law & Practice, Overseas Territories Income Tax Office, London, U.K., 1955. Married, 6 children. Appointments: joined Mauritius Civil Service, 1938; II Grade Clerk, Registrar General's Department, 1939; Assistant Commissioner of Income, 1965; Deputy Commissioner, Income Tax, 1968; Acting Commissioner, Income Tax, 1970. Member, Fabrique de la Cathedrale St. Louis. Address: Income Tax Office, Chaussee, Port Louis, Mauritius.

JEBB, Sheilagh May, born 31st January 1923. Missionary; Nurse. Education: St. Michael's, Limpsfield, U.K., 1927-40; Mothercraft Training, Cromwell House, Highgate, 1940-41; Nursing Training, Addenbrooke's Hospital, Cambridge, 1943-46; Midwifery Training, Edgware & Luton, 1947; S.R.N.; S.C.M. Personal details: parents were pioneer missionaries in W. Nigeria, 1910-33. Appointments: Extra Nursing Sister, Wesley Guild Hospital, 1951; Extra Nursing Sister, C.N.S. Hospital, 1952; Nursing Sister Tutor, Ile Abiye, Ado Ekite, 1953-64; Matron, ibid, 1964-69; Leader, Rural Health Gospel Team, 1969—. Missionary, with Church Missionary Society, 1950—.

JEETAH, Ramnath, born Riche Mare, Central Flacq, Mauritius, 13th June 1930. Government Minister. Education: Central Flacq Government School; Private Studies for Secondary Education. Married, 6 children. Appointments include: Manager, Eastern College, 1956-67; Flacq Girls' College, 1963-67; Minister of Information & Broadcasting, 1967 & 1968. Memberships include: Member of Legislative Assembly; Federation of Sanathan Hindi Temples; Chairman, Moka Flacq Small Planters Association; Chairman, Parasparik Sahayak Society. Address: Central Flacq, Mauritius.

JEWELL, John Hugh Auchinleck, born Seychelles, 11th June 1912. Surgeon. Education: St. Piran's School, Maidenhead, U.K.; Oundle School; B.A., M.B., B.Ch., Trinity College, Dublin University, Ireland; F.R.C.S.L. Appointments: Surgeon-Lt.-Commander, R.N.V.R., 1939-46; Surgeon, St. Joseph's Mercy Hospital, Georgetown, Guyana, 1946-56; Surgeon, consulting practice, Mombasa, Kenya, 1957—. Memberships include: Past Chairman, Mombasa Photographic Society; Association of Surgeons of East Africa; Past President, Lions Club of Mombasa; Mombasa Sports Club; Mombasa Club. Publications: Dhows at Mombasa, 1970. Address: P.O. Box 762, Mombasa, Kenya.

JIAGGE (The Honourable Mrs. Justice) Annie Ruth Baeta, born Lome, Togo. Judge of the Appeal Court, Ghana. Education: Keta Presbyterian School; Achimota Training College, Accra, Ghana; LL.B., London School of Economics & Political Science, U.K.; Lincoln's Inn. Appointments: Headmistress, Keta Presbyterian Senior Girls' School for 5 years; admitted to Bar, Ghana, 1950; practised Law, Ghana, 1950-55; appointed District Magistrate, 1955; Senior Magistrate, 1957; Judge, Circuit Court of Ghana, 1959; Judge, High Court of Ghana, 1961; Ghana Representative, U.N. Commission on the Status of Women, 1961; Chairman, Commission on Investigation of Assets, 1966; Judge, Court of Appeal, 1969; Chairman, 21st Session, U.N. Commission on the Status of Women (the 1st African to be elected to this office), 1968. Memberships: Past President, Y.M.C.A., Ghana; Executive Committee, World Y.W.C.A.; Past Vice-President, ibid; Actie Volunteer, World Council of Churches, 1956-70; Chairman, Seminar on the Political & Civic Education of Women, Accra, 1968. Publications: contributor to U.N. Declaration on the Elimination of Discrimination Against Women, 1966. Honours, Prizes, etc.: Gimbles International Award for contributions towards international understanding, 1969; Grand Medal, Ghana Government, 1969. Address: c/o Court of Appeal, Ghana.

JOBANPUTRA, Mansukhlal Vanmali, born 23rd February 1929. Advocate. Education: Barrister-at-Law, Lincoln's Inn, London, U.K. Memberships: Uganda Club; Kampala Sport Club. Address: P.O. Box 989, Kampala, Uganda.

JOHANSSON, Barbro Cecilia, born Malmö, Sweden, 25th September 1912. Headmistress. Education: B.A., University of Lund. Appointments include: Educationist, Church of Sweden Mission, Tanzania, 1946—; Teacher, Kigarma Teachers' College for Men, 1946-48; ibid., Kashasha Girls' Middle School, 1948-60; ibid, Kahororo Boys' Secondary School, 1960-61; Headmistress, Tabora Government Girls' Secondary School, 1965—; Member of Parliament, Tanzania Parliament, 1959-65; Adult Education Officer, Bukoba, 1970—. Memberships include: Regional Executive Committee, National Council of Tanzania Women; Tabora Region, Branch Committee, National Union of Tanzania Workers; Vice-Chairman, Tabora Region, Red Cross. Publications include: Fresh Start in Forgotten Area; The Church in the Age of Conflict: Africa in Focus. Honours include: Doctor of Philosophy (honoris causa), University of Gothenburg, Sweden, 1968. Address: Box 98, Bukoba, Tanzania.

JOHN, David Michael, born 3rd April 1942. Lecturer in Botany. Education: Llanelli Boys' Grammar Technical School, U.K., 1958-61; 1st Class Hons. Degree in Botany, Durham University, 1965; Ph.D., ibid, 1968. Married. Member of the British Phycological Society. Author of prof. papers. Address: Botany Department, University of Ghana, P.O. Box 55, Legon, Ghana.

JOHN, Nsame, born, Ndu Town, Donga & Mantung Division, Cameroon, about 1927. Teacher; Representative of West Cameroon House of Assembly. Education: Standard 4, Ndu Baptist Mission School, 1932-37; 1st School Leaving Certificate, Cameroon Baptist Mission School, Great Soppo, Buea, Fako Division, 1938-39; Grade II Teacher, Baptist Teachers' Training College, Iwo, Ibadan, Nigeria, 1943-47. Personal details: member of Royal Family, Donga & Mantung Division, father Chief Nfor Nongnibiri. Appointments: Pupil Teacher, Cameroon Baptist Mission School, Great Soppo, Buea, Fako Division, 1940-41; opened Infant School, Bai-Sombe, Meme Division, 1942; Head, Cameroon Baptist Mission School, Mbem, Nwa Sub-District, Donga & Mantung Division, 1947; Tutor, Baptist Pupils Teacher Training Centre, Bamenda, Mezam Division, 1951; Headmaster, Binka Cameroon Baptist Mission School., 1952-58; Teacher, ibid, Ndu, 1959; Representative, Eastern House of Assembly, Enugu, Nigeria, 1954-59; Deputy, Federal House of Assembly, Yaoundé, 1962; Chairman, Social & Cultural Affairs Committee & Member, Legislature & Constitutional Law Committee; West Cameroon Secretary of State for Forestry & Veterinary Services, 1965-68; Administrative & Legislative Affairs Committee, West Cameroon House of Assembly, 1968-69; currently, Assistant Secretary, Social Affairs Committee. Awarded, Ordre de la Valeur by President of the Federal Republic of Cameroon, 1969. Address: Ndu Market Square, Ndu, Donga & Mantung Division, West Cameroon.

JOHNSON, Solomon Obafemi, born 4th December 1926. Medical Photographer. Education: St. John School, Aroloya, Lagos, Nigeria, 1935-36; St. Jude's School, Ebute-Metta, Lagos, 1937-39; Holy Cross Cathedral, Lagos, 1939-41; St. Saviour Boys' High School, 1942-45; London School of Printing & Graphic Art, London, U.K., 1954-57. Appointments: Part-time Assistant, Cinematographer-Photographer, Hatherly Photographic Co., London, 1953-58; Private Practice, Nigeria, 1958-59; Photographer, National Archives, Ibadan, 1959; Senior Asst. Med. Photographer, University of Ibadan, 1959-62; Med. Photographer, Head of Medical Illustration Dept., College of Medicine, University of Lagos, 1962—. Memberships: Royal Photographic Society of U.K.; Incorporated Photographer, I.I.P., U.K.; Associate Member, Society of Motion Picture & Television Engineers, U.S.A. Publications: Need for the establishment of audiovisual facility centres in developing countries (in preparation). Awards: Fellowship Award, Public Health Service Audiovisual Facility, Dept. of Health, Education & Welfare, 1966. Address: College of Medicine, University of Lagos, Nigeria.

JOHO, Kalata Paul Christopher, born 22nd December 1933. Accountant. Education: St. Paul's Primary School, Lewa, Korogwe, Tanzania; St. Andrew's College, Minaki, Dar es Salaam, Tanzania. Appointments: Accountant, Ministry of Works, Tanzania, 1963; Bursar, Ministry of Education, Tanzania, 1965; Secretary, Village Settlement Commission, 1966; Senior Accountant, University of Zambia, Lusaka, Zambia, 1968. Address: c/o F.Z. Mnkande, P.O. Box 1322, Dar es Salaam, Tanzania.

JONES, Cecil Reginald Howard, born 2nd September 1926. Chartered Secretary. Education: Matriculated, Grammar School, London, U.K. Appointments: Employed, East Africa, 1948—; Area Accountant, East African Power & Lighting Co. Ltd., Nairobi, Kenya, 1960; Chief Accountant/Company Secretary, Kilembe Mines Ltd., Uganda, 1968—. Memberships: Fellow, Chartered Institute of Secretaries; ibid, Institute of Company Accountants. Address: P.O. Box 235, Kilembe, Uganda.

JONES (Sir) Glyn Smallwood, born 9th January 1908. Civil Servant (retired). Education: King's School, Chester, U.K.; B.A.(Hons.), St. Catherine's College, Oxford University, U.K. Married to Nancy Madoc Featherstone, 1 son (deceased), 1 daughter. Appointments: Provincial Administration, Northern Rhodesia; Minister of Native Affairs, ibid; Chief Secretary, Nyasaland; Governor, ibid; Governor-General, Malawi. Memberships: Athenaeum; Royal Commonwealth Society; Chester City Club. Honours: G.C.M.G., 1966; M.B.E., 1944.

JONES, John, born 17th June 1941. Lecturer in Physics. Education: Mountain Ash Grammar School, U.K.; B.Sc., University of Wales, 1962; Ph.D., ibid, 1966. Married, 1 child. Appointments: Research Fellow, University of

Wales, 1965-67; Lecturer in Physics, University of Malawi, 1967—. Currently working on the problem of the prediction of ability in the physical sciences for University of Malawi entrants for M.A.(Education) Degree. Memberships: Institute of Physics & Physical Society; National Committee, A.A.A. of Malawi; Malawi S.C.E. Committee. Author of articles in prof. journals. Address: Chancellor College, P.O. Box 5200, Limbe, Malawi.

JONES, Olive, born 9th July 1929. Civil Servant. Education: Llangollen Grammar School, Wales; B.A.(Hons., Economics), University of North Wales, Bangor, 1949; Postgraduate Studies, ibid, 1950. Appointments: Assistant Statistician, Admiralty, U.K., 1956-60; Statistician, East African Statistical Department, 1960-68; currently Principal Statistician, Common Market & Economic Affairs Secretariat, East African Community, 1968—. Memberships: East Africa Natural History Society; East Africa Wild Life Society. Address: C.M.E.A.S., Box 1003, Arusha, Tanzania.

JONES, Peter Anthony, born 27th September 1923. Agricultural Scientist. Education: Epsom College, Surrey, U.K.; M.A., Pembroke College, Cambridge University. Married, 3 children. Appointments: Research Agronomist, Department of Agriculture, Kenya; Senior Research Officer, ibid; Director, Coffee Research Service, Kenya; Chief Research Officer, Ministry of Agriculture, Swaziland. Member of Hawks Club, Cambridge. Publications: research & technical papers in various African & overseas journals. Awarded O.B.E., 1965. Address: Malkerns Research Station, P.O. Box 4; Malkerns, Swaziland.

JONES, Raymond Peter, born 14th February 1933. Inspector of Schools. Education: Manchester University, U.K. Married, 1 son, 2 daughters. Appointments: Teacher, U.K. & Uganda, 1956-63; Deputy Headmaster, Kitante Hill School, Kampala, 1964-65; Headmaster, Old Kampala Secondary School, 1965-69; Inspector of Schools & Chief Adviser to the Ministry of Education on Libraries, 1969—. Contributor to: East African Library Bulletin & The School Librarian. Editor, Manchester University Bulletin & The School Librarian. Editor, Manchester University Poetry, 1954; Jazz, Methuen, 1963. Address: Central Inspectorate, Ministry of Education. Box 3568, Kampala, Uganda.

JONES (Sir) Samuel Bankole, born Lagos, Nigeria, 23rd August, 1911. President, Sierra Leone Court of Appeal. Education: Methodist Boys' High School, Freetown, Sierrá Leone; Fourah Bay College; University College, Sierra Leone; M.A., B.C.L., Dip. Ed., Durham University, U.K.; Middle Temple, London. Married, 3 sons, 2 daughters. Appointments: Chairman, Fourah Bay College Council; Council Member, University of Sierra Leone; Chairman, Court of the University; Chief Justice, Sierra Leone, 1963; Acting Governor-General, August-November, 1965; President, Court of Appeal, Sierra Leone, 1965—. Memberships: Reform Club, Freetown; Fellow, Royal Commonwealth Society, London; President, Society for the Deaf, 1964; President, National Association for the Societies for the Handicapped, 1969; Fellow, International Society for the Study of Comparative Public Law, 1969. Honours: D.C.L.(honoris causa), Durham University, 1965; Knighted, 1965. Address: Office of the President of the Court of Appeal, Roxy Building, Walpole St., Freetown, Sierra Leone.

JOUANELLE, Felix Edmond, born Martinique, 20th November 1926. Administrator-in-Chief of Overseas Affairs; Inspector-General of State with responsibility for Co-ordination. Education: Lycée Schoelcher, Aime Cesaire; Lycée Ionis le Grand, Paris, France; Faculties of Letters & Law, Paris, E.N.F.O.M. Appointments: Head of Subdivision, Seguela, Ivory Coast, 1953-55; ibid, Issia, ibid, 1956-58; Prefect, Bafoulabe, Sudan, 1958-59; ibid, Jegou, Mali, Sudan, 1959-61; Inspector of Administrative Affairs, Bamako, Vice-President of the Supreme Court of Mali, 1961-62; Director of Council to the Minister of Commerce & Transport of Mali; Vice-President, National Commission for State Security, 1962-64; currently, Inspector General of State to the Presidency of the Republic of Senegal. Address: c/o The Presidency of the Republic of Senegal, Dakar, Senegal.

JOUDIOU, Christian, born 3rd December 1920. Deputy Director-General, Central Bank, Equatorial Africa & Cameroun. Honours: Knight of the Legion of Honour Address: 29 rue du Colisee, Paris, France.

JUMA (Hon.) Waziri, born 31st December 1931. Politician, Education: Tanga School, 1939-49; Nkrumah College, Zanzibar, 1949-50; Makerere College, Uganda, 1951-53. Appointments: Education Officer, 1954-57; Administrative Officer, 1957-60; District Commissioner, 1961-62; Regional Commissioner, 1963-65; Tanzanian Ambassador to Peking, People's Republic of China, 1965-66; Census Administrator, 1967; Secretary, Social Cultural & Women Affairs, 1968; Regional Commissioner & Member of Parliament, 1969. Address: P.O. Box 25, Tabor, Tanzania.

JUMAA (Rt. Rev.) Yohana Samwil, born 18th March, 1905. Bishop of Zanzibar & Tanga. Education: Magila Upper Primary School, Tanzania, 1918-21; St. Andrew's Teacher Training College, Zanzibar, then Minaki, ibid, 1921-26; Theological College, Hegongo, 1942-48. Married, 2 sons, 7 daughters, 17 grandchildren. Appointments: Teacher, Mlingoti, Magila, 1926; ibid, Sega & Mkuzi, 1927; Minaki Secondary School, 1928; Kiwanda Upper Primary School, 1932; Mkuzi Lower Primary School, 1935; Catechist, Tanga, 1937-42; Deacon, Ntalawanda, Mombo, 1945-46; Assistant Priest, Tongwe, 1948-53; ibid, Korogwe, 1954-59; Priest in Charge, Korogwe, 1959-60; ibid, Amani, 1960-63; Archdeacon of Korogwe, 1963-68; Bishop, Diocese of Zanzibar & Tanga, 1968—. Member, Guild of the Holy Name. Address: P.O. Box 35, Korogwe, Tanga, Tanzania.

JUNOD, Violaine Idelette, born 11th May, 1923. Social Work Educator. Education: B.A.(Social Studies), University of the

Witwatersrand, South Africa, 1944; M.A. (Anthropology), London School of Economics, U.K., 1954. Personal details: daughter of H. P. Junod, Author of Bantu Heritage & Initiator & Organizer, Penal Reform League in South Africa; granddaughter, H. A. Junod, Author of The Life of a South African Tribe. Appointments: Director, Entokozweni (Community Centre), Alexandra Township, Johannesburg, 1945-49; Research Assistant, Anthropology Department, Edinburgh University, U.K., 1951-52; Lecturer, African Administration, Natal University, South Africa, 1953-61; Research Associate, Center for Development Research & Training, African Studies Program, Boston University, U.S.A., 1961-62; Programme Co-ordinator, Peace Corps Project, Ghana & Nigeria, & Associate Specialist, African Studies Center, University of California, Los Angeles, 1962-63; Lecturer, Community Development & Group Work, Social Work & Social Administration Unit, Makerere University College, Kampala, Uganda, 1963-67; Reader & Head, Department of Social Work & Social Administration, ibid, 1967—. Memberships: Associate, African Studies Association; Council of Social Work Education. Publications: Editor, The Handbook of Africa, 1963; contributor to professional journals. Honours: British Council Scholar, 1949-52. Address: P.O. Box 7-62, Makerere University, Kampala, Uganda.

JUSTE, Albert Pierre, born 8th May, 1930. Interpreter. Education: Primary, College of Port-au-Prince, Haiti American School; Secondary, Lycée Alexandre Petion, Haite; B.S., 1950; M.S., 1952; Civil Eng., 1955. Appointments: Civil Engineer, Reynolds Metal Co., Haiti, 1955-60; French & Physics Instructor, College of West Africa, Monrovia, Liberia; French Broadcaster & Instructor, Radio & Television; Official French Interpreter. Memberships: Y.M.C.A., Monrovia; Liberian Football Association, ibid; National Sports & Athletic Commission, ibid; President, Liberia Track & Field Federation, 1965-69; Monrovia Bridge Club; Board Member, Liberia Bridge Federation; St. Paul Lodge, No. 2, AF&AM. Honours: Officer, Order of the Star of Africa; Knight Commander, Humane Order of African Redemption; Grand Commander, Star of Africa; Grand Officier, Ordre National of Mauritania, Cameroon & Central African Republic; Commandeur, Ordre National of Ivory Coast; Dahomey; Upper Volta; Tunisia, Togo & Mauritania. Address: P.O. Box 1245, Monrovia, Liberia.

K

KABASUBABO, Paul Louis, born Lusambo, born 1st July, 1927. Government Official. Education; Primary & Secondary, Boma. Appointments: with the Territorial Administration, 1945; Territorial Agent, 1957; Director, Ministry of Public works, 1960; Secretary-General, Ministry of Transport, 1961-64; President, Office of Exploitation of Transport, Congo. Publications: Reflexion sur la destinee de l'Otraco, 1970. Honours: Officer, Ordre National du Leopard; Officer, Madaille de la Reconnaisance Centrafricaine; Medaille d'argent du Merite civique; Medaille d'argent du Merite sportif. Address: President de l'Otraco, P.B. 98, Kinshasa, Congo.

KABBAJ, Mohamed, born 13th September 1936. Engineer. Education: Imperial College, Rabat, Morocco; Lycée Mixte, Fes; Higher Studies, Lycée Janson de Sailly, Paris, France; Lycée Saint Louis; Engineering Diploma, Higher School of Industrial Physics & Chemistry, Paris; Lic., Physical Sciences, Faculty of Sciences, Paris. Appointments: Engineer, Research Laboratory, Sari, Paris; Head of Service, Treatment of Phosphate, O.C.P., Rabat, Morocco; Technical-Commercial Head of Service, ibid. Memberships: Fertiliser Society. Address: Office Cherifien des Phosphates, 305 Avenue Mohamed V, Rabat, Morocco.

KABIR, Abba Kura, born 20th November 1939. Local Government Official. Education: Kara Elementary School, 1945-48; Bama Central School, 1948-50; Bornu Middle School, 1950-55; Bornu Secondary School, 1955-59; British Council Course, Kano, Nigeria, 1961; Diploma, Public & Social Administration, Torquay, U.K., 1964; Intermediate Local Government Course, Zaria, Nigeria, 1966. Personal details' son of Village Head, Abba Kabir; 2 wives, 2 children. Appointments: Local Government Supervisor & Local Authority Revenue Officer, Bama, N.E. State. Memberships: Vice-President, Dikwa Social Club; Secretary, Bama Social Club; Dikwa Divisional Red Cross Society; Secretary, Dikwa Football Association. Address: Dikwa Local Authority, Central Office, Bama via Maidugori, N.E. State, Nigeria.

KABORE, Lamoussa Alassane, born Sourgou, Kondougou, Upper Volta, 1923. District Administrator. Education: Primary, Ecole Regionale, Kondougou; C.E.P.E.; Secondary, Ecole Clozel, Abidjan; Diploma, E.N.A., National School of Administration. Personal details: member of a noble family of the Chiefdom of Sourgou; married, 4 sons, 5 daughters. Appointments include: Chief, Secretariat, High Commission, Opagadougou Community, 1958-59; Chief, Central Subdivision, Kondougou, 1960-61; ibid & Commandant, Safane Region, 1961-65; Commandant, Zorgbo Region, 1965-66; Chief Administrator, Dalpelogo, 1966-67; Chief, Subdivision of Sindou, 1967—. Actionnaire de la Societe des Grandes Moulins Voltaiques (Siege a Banfora). Publications include: Memoire sur l'Elevage. Honours: Chevalier de l'Ordre National, 1964: Officer, ibid, 1969; Medaille d'Argent a Bobo Dionlasso, 1970. Address: Sindou via Banfora, Upper Volta.

KABORE, Zirimgniga, born 22nd January 1922. Prefect. Education: Certificate of Primary Studies; Higher Studies, Higher Primary School of Treich-Laplene de Bingerville, Ivory Coast. Personal details: Prince of Thyou, decendant of Naba Koumdoumye 8e Moro-Naba of the Royal Dynasty of Ouagadougou, Upper Volta; married. Appointments: Section Head, Governor's Council, Upper Volta, Ouagadougou, 1949; Cabinet Head, Minister of Labour & Public Work, Upper Volta, 1958; Sub-Prefect, Ouargaye, ibid,

1959; Prefect, Kombissiri, Kassoum, Zorgo & Garango, 1960—. Honours: Knight of the National Order of the Upper Volta, 1962: Officer, ibid, 1968. Address: Commandant de Cercle, Kombissiri, etc., Upper Volta.

KABUYE, Christine Sophie, born 21st November 1938. Taxonomic Botanist. Education: Cambridge School Certificate, Gayaza High School, 1958; B.Sc., Botany & Zoology, Makerere University College, Kampala, Uganda, 1964. Appointments: Botanist, East African Herbarium, Nairobi, Kenya, 1964—. Member, A.E.T.F.A.T. Publications: Joint Author, A First Record of Multicellular Glandular Hairs in the Gramineae (Bot. J. Linn. Soc.); A New Species of Biophytum DC (Oxalidaceae) (Kew Bull.), 1969. Address: East African Herbarium, P.O. Box 5166, Nairobi, Kenya.

KADDU, Nuru Kintu, born 24th September 1933. Chartered Architect. Education: Preparatory School, Tanganyika; D.F.A., Sculpture & Design, School of Fine Art, Makerere University, Kampala, Uganda, 1953-57; Diploma, Bartlett School of Architecture, London University, U.K., 1958-64. Personal details: member of Muganda Tribe; married, 1 son, 2 daughters. Appointments: Practised Architecture, London, U.K.; Private Practice, Uganda, 1966—. Memberships: Council Member, Uganda Society of Architects (U.S.A.), 1966—; Vice-President, ibid, 1967; currently, President; 1st Uganda Representative, 2nd CAA Conference, New Delhi, 1967; Town & Country Planning Board, Uganda, 1967—; Executive Committee, EAIA, 1968—; Board of Architectural Education, University College, Nairobi, 1968—; Councillor, Kampala City Council, 1968—; Executive Member, CAA for Africa Region, 1969—; A.R.I.B.A. Address: P.O. Box 4847, Kampala, Uganda.

KADUMA, Godwin Zilaoneka, born 10th March 1938. Dancer; Actor. Education: St. Andrew's College, Minaki, 1961; Preparatory Course, Dartington College of Arts, Totnes, Devon, U.K., 1963; Central School of Speech & Drama, 1963-66; Dramatic Art Teachers' Diploma. Married. Appointments: Promoter of Theatre, Tanzania Government Division of Culture, 1966-67; Research Assistant, Tutorial Assistant, University College, Dar es Salaam, 1967-69; Assistant Lecturer, ibid, 1969—; with The National Dance Troupe of Tanzania, 1967; Choreographer, Frelimo Dance Co., African Arts Festival, Algiers, 1969; Choreographer, Leader & participator in The Tanzania Dance Company, Africa Week Festival, World Exhibition, Osaka, Japan, 1970; currently, Choreographer for the University Dance Ensemble, Dar es Salaam. Address: Department of the Theatre Arts, University of Dar es Salaam, P.O. Box 35044, Dar es Salaam, Tanzania.

KADZAMIRA, Zimani David, born 1st July 1941. Assistant University Lecturer. Education: Elementary, Highfield North School, Salisbury; Secondary, Kongwe, Blantyre, & Dedza Schools, Malawi; B.A., Politics, Princeton University, New Jersey, U.S.A., 1966; currently reading for M.A.(Econ.), University of Manchester, U.K. Married, 1 daughter. Appointments: Assistant Lecturer, Government, University of Malawi, 1966—; Member, Board of Directors, Malawi Broadcasting Corporation. Memberships: Committee Member, Society of Malawi (Historical & Scientific), 1968-69; Representative of University of Malawi, Governing Body of the International African Institute. Recipient, ASPAU Student Achievement Award (African Scholarship Program in American Universities), 1965. Address: 7A Elms Road, Heaton Moor, Stockport, Cheshire, U.K.

KAFE, Joseph Kofi Thompson, born 20th January 1933. Librarian. Education: B.A. (Hons.), University of London, U.K., 1960; Dip. Lib., ibid, 1964. Married, 2 children. Appointments: Library Clerk, St. Augustine's College, Cape Coast, Ghana, 1957; Junior Assistant Librarian, Legon, 1960-62; Assistant Librarian, 1962—. Memberships: Associate, British Library Association; Bellow, Legon Hall, University of Ghana; Hall Librarian, ibid, 1963-66; Hall Tutor, 1964-67; 1968—. Publications: European Contacts with West African in 15th & 16th Centuries (thesis-bibliography), 1964; Balme Library Thesis, an annotated list of these held in Balme Library, 1969. Recipient, Book Prize, General Proficiency as Library Clerk, St. Augustine's College, 1960. Address: Balme Library, University of Ghana, P.O. Box 24, Legon, Ghana.

KAGWA-NYANZI, Juanita Alice, born 8th September 1935. Paediatrician. Education: M.Sc.; M.D.; L.M.C.C. Married. Appointments: Special Lecturer; Lecturer; Senior Lecturer, Makerere Medical School, Kampala, Uganda. Memberships: Beta Kappa Chi, 1956; Fellow, American Academy of Paediatrics; University Women Association; Uganda Medical Association. Publications: Studies in Sickle Cell Anaemia—Clinical Observations on Progress & Outlook Beyond Childhood; Is Marriage Counselling Feasible in Africa to Prevent Sickle Cell Anaemia; Chemoprophylaxis of Homozygous Sickleas; Causes of Ophthalma Neonatorum in Uganda; Prematurity Diagnosed by Ossification Centres; Typhoid Fever in Childhood in Uganda. Address: Makerere Medical School, P.O. Box 7072, Kampala, Uganda.

KAHARA, Christopher, born Nairobi, Kenya, 30th November 1937. Under-Secretary, Kenya Treasury. Education: B.A.(Philosophy), Brooklyn College, New York, U.S.A., 1963. Married, 3 children. Appointments include: District Officer, Kenya, 1964; Under-Secretary, Kenya Treasury, 1968—. Memberships include: Executive Committee, African Club, Nairobi; Director, Sigona Golf Club; Secretary, Tubogo Golf Association; Treasurer, Africa Club; Board of Governors, Uthiru Secondary School; Secretary, Uthiru Self-Help Projects. Address: c/o P.O. Box 30007, Nairobi, Kenya.

KAHUMBU, John Francis, born 24th September 1933. Civil Engineer. Education: Alliance High School, Kikuyu, Kenya; Makerere College, Uganda; Leicester College of Technology, U.K.; Portsmouth College of Technology. Appointments: worked with construction firms, East Africa & England;

Deputy City Engineer, Nairobi, Kenya, 1964-67; Chairman & Managing Director of own firm, Schemes Ltd. (pioneer African engineering firm in Kenya), 1968—; Director, several firms. Memberships: Institution of Engineers, England; Fellow, East African Institution of Engineers; President, ibid, 1969-70; Chairman, Kenya Division, 1966-69. Author of various papers on engineering conferences on engineering education & training, East Africa & Europe. Address: P.O. Box 24786, Nairobi, Kenya.

KAI (Paramount Chief), Bartholomew Aloysius Foday, born Telu, Sierra Leone, 21st January 1910. Education: School for Sons of Chiefs (now Bo Government Secondary), Bo District, 1915-17. Personal details; grandson of Paramount Chief vandi Kai, 1st recognized chief of Bongor Chiefdom, amalgamated to Jaiama Chiefdom, 1951; married. Appointments: elected Paramount Chief, Jaiama-Bongor Chiefdom, Bo District, 1952; President, Bo District Council, 1955-59; Director, National Construction Company, 1962-66; Member, Fourah Bay College Council, 1969. Honours: Justice of the Peace, 1955; Certificate of Honour (Queen's), 1962; O.B.E., 1970. Address: Telu via Bo, Sierra Leone.

KAITANO, Wilson, born Malawi, 4th April 1935. Stores Clerk. Education: J.C. Form II; Studying G.C.E. O Levels. Married, 6 children. Currently with Sugar Corporation of Malawi. Memberships: Leader, P.A.W.U. Trade Union & Branch Secretary; Football Club; Welfare Club. Address: Sugar Corporation of Malawi, P.O. Box 5598, Limbe, Malawi.

KAJUBI, Samuel Kulumbaru, born June 1935. Senior Lecturer. Education: King's College, Budo; Makerere University & Mulago Hospital; Hammersmith Hospital, London, U.K.; University of Edinburgh; M.B.; M.R.C.P.E.; M.R.C.P.G. Appointments: Medical Officer, Uganda Government, 1963-64; Special Lecturer, Makerere University, 1965-67; Lecturer in Medicine, 1967-68; Senior Lecturer in Applied Physiology, Department of Internal Medicine, Makerere University, Kampala, 1969—. Memberships: E.A. Association of Physicians; Uganda Medical Association. Publications include: On Alcohol & Alcoholic Coma; Lactase Deficiency in Uganda; Acid Secretion in Ugandans; Pancreatic Disease in Ugandans; The Thyroid in Ugandans. Prizes include: Student's Prize in Pharmacology, 1961; Exhibition Prize, 1961. Address: Makerere University, P.O. Box 7072, Kampala, Uganda.

KAKOOZA (KAK) George Patrick Kagaba, born Kampala, Uganda, 24th November 1936. Fine Artist. Education: Primary Education Certificate; Secondary Education Certificate; Cambridge School Certificate; Certificate, Fine Art; Diploma, Fine Art (E.A.); Postgraduate Diploma, Fine Art (E.A.); Postgraduate Work Certificate, Ecole des Beaux Artes, Paris, France. Personal details: father, retired Gombolola Chief, Buganda Government; married, 1 son, 1 daughter. Appointments: Special Lecturer, Fine Arts, Makerere University, Uganda, 1965-66; Lecturer, ibid, 1966—. Exhibitions; One-man Show, Paris, France, 1964; 2 One-man Shows, Kampala (paintings, sculptures & drawings); participant in several group shows, East Africa & elsewhere. Several sculptures in public places in East Africa. Memberships: Vice-President, Alliance Française, K'la Branch; Secretary, Academic Staff Association, Makerere University; East African Academy; Makerere Staff Cricket Team. Contributor of articles on African art to African Encyclopaedia, Oxford. Honours: Disipline & Arithmetic Prize, 1946; Head Monitors' Prize, 1950; Design Prize (Project) & Modelling Prize, 1960; Margaret Trowell & Mod. Prize, 1962; several project prizes including Group Sculpture for Dar University, Uganda Expo 70 Pavilion. Address: Makerere University, P.O. Box 7062, Kampala, Uganda.

KALANDA, Mabika, born Mikalayi (Luluabourg) Democratic Republic of the Congo, 26th November 1932. Professor, Official University of the Congo (E.N.D.A.). Education: Primary, Mikalayi, 1940-46; Secondary, Kamponde, 1947-53; University of Levanium, 1954-58. Married, 2 sons, 5 daughters. Appointments include: Administrator, District Head of Region, 1959-60; District Commissioner, 1960; Commissioner General, Public Service, 1960-61; Professor, National School of Administration, 1961-63; Minister of Foreign Affairs, 1963; Rector, National School of Administration, 1966—; Professor, Official University of the Congo. Publications include: Baluba et Lulua, 1959; Tabalayi, 1962; La Remise en Question, Base de la Décolonisation mentale, 1965. Honours: Officer of the Chinese Nationalist Order, 1963. Address: B.P. 3357, Kinshasa/Kalina, Democratic Republic of the Congo.

KALANZI, Ernest Mulyambuzi, born Kampala, Uganda, 16th April 1920. Educator; Civil Servant. Education: Mengo Secondary School, 1935-39; King's College, Budo, 1940-43; Makerere University College, 1944-46; M.A., Edinburgh University, U.K., 1962. Married to Christine Nakitto, 3 sons, 2 daughters. Appointments include: Assistant Master, C.M.S. Mbarara High School, 1947-48; Assistant Master, Kibuli Secondary School, 1947-57; Headmaster, Kibuli Junior Secondary School, 1957-58; Assistant Secretary in: Ministry of Education, 1962-63; Ministry of Mineral & Water Resources, 1963-64; Ministry of Public Service & Cabinet Affairs, 1964-70; Senior Assistant Secretary, ibid, 1970—. Member of Uganda Society. Address: Ministry of Public Service & Cabinet Affairs, P.O. Box 27, Entebbe, Uganda.

KALANZI, George Albert, born 25th March 1920. Administrator; Dairy Farmer. Education: Mityana Junior Secondary School, Uganda; King's College, Budo; Studied Local Government, South Devon Technical College, Torquay & Leeds Borough Council, U.K.; ibid, Nigeria, Netherlands, Germany, & Sweden; D.P.A. Personal details: son of a Gombolola Chief; Married, 8 children. Appointments: Army, Attained rank of Regimental Sergeant-Major, 1943-46; Assistant Accountant, Kabakas Goverment, Mengo, Uganda; appointed Gomolola Chief, 1952-61; 1st Town Clerk, Mengo Municipal Council, 1962-67; detained under Emergency Regulations, 1967-69; currently, Dairy Farmer, raising exotic cattle &

pigs. Treasurer & Member, Eyekaliriza Businzigo Growers' Co-operative Society Ltd. Address: P.O. Box 202, Mityana, Uganda.

KALE, Oladele Olusiji, born 19th November 1938. Medical Practitioner. Education: C.M.S. Seminary School, Lagos, Nigeria, 1944-47; C.M.S. Grammar School, Lagos, 1948-50; Anglican Grammar School, Ijebu-Ode, 1951-55; ibid, Abeokuta, 1956-57; Trinity College, Dublin, Ireland, 1957-63; B.A., M.B., B.Ch., B.A.O., D.T.M.&H. Personal details: son of Seth I. Kale, Bishop of Lagos; Married, 1 son. Appointments: House Physician, Teaching Hospital, Lagos, 1963-64; House Surgeon, ibid, 1964; Senior House Physician, ibid, 1964-66; Registrar, St. Pancras Hospital, London, U.K., 1967; Hon. Registrar, Guy's Hospital, ibid, 1968-70. Memberships: Scout Troop Leader, Ijebu-Ode Grammar School, 1955; Political Secretary, Nigerian Union of Students of Great Britain & Ireland, Dublin, 1960-62; Vice-President, Pan African Students' Union of Ireland, Dublin, 1962-63; Secretary, Lagos University Teaching Hospital Club, 1965-66. Address: c/o Bishopscourt, P.O. Box 13, Lagos, Nigeria.

KALE, Seth Irunsewe, born Mobalufon, Ijebu, Nigeria, 6th June 1904. Minister of Religion; Clerk in Holy Orders. Education: Ijebu Ode Grammar School, 1918-20; Fourah Bay College, Freetown, Sierra Leone, 1931-35; B.A., M.A., University of Durham, U.K.; Dip. Ed., Institute of Education, University of London, 1939-40. Married to Juliana Odukoya, 4 sons, 2 daughters. Appointments: Tutor, Ijebu Ode Grammar School, 1921-31; Tutor, Lagos (C.M.S.), Grammar School, 1936-40; Vice-Principal, ibid, 1940-43; Principal, 1944-49; Principal, St. Andrew's College, Oyo, 1951-63. Publications: T'ibi T'ire (International Africa Institute Essay Prize); A Book of Yoruba Greetings; Christian Responsibility in an Independent Nigeria (with Dr. H. Hogan); Invitation to Russia. Honours: D.D., University of Nigeria, Nsukka, 1966; O.O.N., 1964; M.B.E., 1952. Address: Bishopscourt, P.O. Box 13, Lagos, Nigeria.

KALEEM, James Samuel, born 10th March, 1908. Teacher. Education: Government Elementary School, Tamale, Ghana, 1914-23; Government Teacher Training College, Accra, 1924-26; London Institute of Education Associate Course, 1954. Personal details: son of Tumale Dakpo a Nsungnah, Chief of Tamale. Appointments: Headmaster, Boarding School, Yendi, 1936-48; Senior Housemaster, Government Teacher Training College, Tamale, 1949-53; District Education Officer, ibid, 1955-56; Acting Principal, Government Teacher Training College, Pusiga, 1957-58; Vernacular Language Tutor, Government Secondary School, Tamale, 1959; Senior Education Officer, Tamale, 1960; Regional Education Officer, Northern Region, 1961; Principal Education Officer; Retired, 1968. Memberships: Bureau of Ghana Languages; Chairman, Committee of Northern Languages; Ghana Library Board; Arts Council of Ghana; Chairman, Municipal Council, Tamale. Publications: First Primer in Dagbani for Primary Schools; Follow-up Reader, ibid; Animal & Bird Stories in Dagbani for Middle Schools; Traditional Stories in Dagbani; Little Rhymes & Verses in Dagbani. Honours: King George VI Birthday Honours, Certificate & Badge, 1946; Ghana Grand Medal, 1968. Address: Zobogo-NA, Tamale, Ghana.

KALEJAIYE (Chief) Alaba, born Ososa, Ijebu Province, Nigeria, 25 October 1917. Secretary. Education: Olowogbowo Methodist School, Lagos, Nigeria; William Wilberforce Academy, Lagos, Nigeria; Industrial Relations, Michigan State University, U.S.A.; Industrial Relations, Ministry of Labour, London, U.K.; Incomes Policy & Development Economics, University of Oxford. Married, 3 sons, 2 daughters. Appointments include: Clerk, United Africa Co. Ltd., Lagos, Nigeria; Secretary-General, Nigeria Civil Service Union. Memberships include: Member of the Board of Electricity Corporation of Nigeria; Member of the National Labour Advisory Council; Member of the Lagos Manpower Committee; Member of the Lagos Juvenile Employment Committee; General Secretary, Ososa United Society, Lagos; General Secretary, Odogbolu Golden Club, Lagos; Social Secretary, Young Christian Fellowship. Honours, Prizes, etc: Member of the Order of Niger, 1965. Address: 23 Tokunboh St., P.O. Box 862, Lagos, Nigeria.

KALMOGO, Ignace, born 14th March 1936. Civil Administrator; Regional Administrator. Education: Primary School, Bam, Upper Volta, 1951-59; Secondary School, Little Seminary at Pabre, 1959-66; University, 1959-66; Diploma A, International Institute of Public Administration, University of Paris, France, 1968. Appointments: Regional Administrator, Boulsa, Upper Volta. Represented the Volta State at the Supreme Court in the affairs of ex-President Maurice Yameogo. Memberships: Executive Committee, Federation of Black African Students in France, 1962-65; President (twice), Cultural Affairs, ibid. Author of several articles on African students in Europe. Address: Commandant de Cercle de Boulsa, Upper Volta.

KALSI, Swadesh Singh, born 10th April 1943. Statistician. Education: B.Sc.(Hons.) (Econ.), London School of Economics, University of London, U.K.; Barrister, Lincoln's Inn, London. Personal details: father, Advocate of the High Court of Kenya. Appointments: Statistician, E.A. Statistical Department, Common Market & Economic Affairs Secretariat, East African Community, 1965—. Memberships: Royal Economic Society & Economic History Society, U.K.; Convocation, University of London; Classical Association, Kenya; APS, Columbia University, U.S.A. Address: E.A. Statistical Department, P.O. Box 30462, Nairobi, Kenya.

KALU, Michael Iowe, born 20th December, 1929. Medical Practitioner; Consultant Surgeon. Education: Methodist College, Uzuakoli, 1944-46; Igbobi College, Yaba, Nigeria, 1947-48; University College, Ibadan, 1949-53; Queen's College, Oxford & Radcliffe Infirmary, U.K., 1953-56; Royal College of Surgeons, Edinburgh, 1960; ibid, England, 1961; Postgraduate Medical School, Hammersmith Hospital, London, 1962;

M.R.C.S., L.R.C.P., 1956; M.B.B.S.(Lond.), 1956. Married, 4 children. Appointments: House Surgeon, General Hospital, Southampton. 1957, 1959-60; House Physician, Paediatrics, University College Hospital, Ibadan, Nigeria, 1957-58; Medical Officer, Casualty, General Hospital, Lagos, 1959; Medical Officer, Department of Pathology, ibid, 1958-59; Senior House Officer, Accident Service, Radcliffe Infirmary, Oxford, U.K., 1960; ibid, Department of Orthopaedics, Kent & Sussex Hospital, Tunbridge Wells, 1961; ibid, Department of Surgery, Hammersmith Hospital, London, 1962; Registrar, Department of Surgery, University College Hospital, Ibadan, Nigeria, 1963; Senior Registrar, ibid, 1963-64; Specialist Surgeon, Ministry of Health, Eastern Region, 1964—. Memberships: F.R.C.S.(Edin.), 1962; F.R.C.S.(Eng.), 1962; F.I.C.S., 1965; British Medical Association; Nigeria Medical Association; West African Students' Club, University of Oxford. Awarded 1st Prize, Form V, Igbobi College, Yaba, 1947. Address: General Hospital, Enugu, Nigeria.

KALULU, Solomon, born 14th June 1924. Teacher; Government Minister. Education: Chipemer; Waddildve; Lyceum College. Appointments: Teacher; Manager, Plastics Industry; Founder Member, Ruling Party; National Chairman of Party for 9 years; Minister of Lands & Works; Minister of Transport Power & Communication; Minister of Lands & Natural Resources. Member of Royal Family Honour of Ethiopia, 1966. Address: Box 55, Lusaka, Zambia.

KAMALI, Sabih Ahmad, born 1st July, 1927. University Professor. Education: M.A., English, & LL.B., Aligarh Muslim University, India, 1947; M.A. & Ph.D., Islamic Studies, McGill University, Montreal, Canada, 1955 & 1959. Appointments at: Aligarh Muslim University, India, 1948, 1962-63; Calcutta University, 1961; University of Ghana, Legon, 1963—; University of Ibadan, Nigeria, 1967; Harvard University U.S.A., 1969-70. Memberships: American Historical Association; various Muslim societies, India, Canada, U.S.A., Nigeria, & Ghana. Publications: Incoherence of the Philosophers (an English Translation of al-Ghazali's Tahafut al-Falasifah), 1958; Types of Islamic Thought, 1965; various articles in periodicals. Address: Department for the Study of Religions, University of Ghana, Legon Ghana.

KAMAU, Gregory, born 1st January, 1938. Public Administrator. Education: K.I.S.A. Primary School, Gakarara, 1945-49; C.C.M. Intermediate School, Gaichanjiru, 1950-52; Nyeri High School, 1953-56; B.A., 2nd Division, (Lond.), Makerere University College, Kampala, Uganda, 1957-61; Certificate, Public Administration, Kenya Institute of Public Administration, Kabete, 1962; Diploma, Public Administration & General Management, American University, Washington, D.C., U.S.A., 1969; Certificate, Communication Science, Michigan State University Communications Centre, 1969. Married. Appointments: Assistant Secretary, External Affairs Division, Kenya Government, 1961; Ministry of Forests, Wildlife, & Tourism, 1961-62; District Officer, Provincial Administration, Samburur District, 1962-63; ibid, Muranga District, 1963-64; Clerk, Central Regional Assembly, Nyeri, 1964; Assistant Secretary, Ministry of Agriculture, 1964; ibid, Treasury & Economic Divisions, East African Community, 1965-66; Joint Services Executive Secretary, E.A. Agriculture & Forests Research Organization & E.A. Veterinary Research Organization, 1966—. Memberships: Society for Advancement of Management; East African Community's Senior Staff Association. Address: P.O. Box 30148, Nairobi, Kenya.

KAMDAR, Hasmukh Harilal, born Dumana, India, 3rd February 1931. Consulting Surgeon. Education: Andheri College, Bombay, India; National Medical College, Bombay; Postgraduate Training, U.K. Degrees: M.B., B.S.(Bom.), 1959; M.S.(Bom.), 1959; F.R.C.S.(Edin.), 1960; F.R.C.S.(Eng.), 1961. Married. Appointments include: House Surgeon & Surgical Registrar, Nair Hospital, Bombay, 1955-59; Surgical Registrar, Bedford General Hospital, U.K., 1961; ibid, London Chest Hospital, 1962-63; Assistant Hon. Surgeon, Nair Hospital, Bombay, India, 1963-64; Hon. Assistant Lecturer in Surgery, National Medical College, 1963-64; Consultant Surgeon, Private Practice, Nairobi, Kenya, 1965—. Fellow, Association of Surgeons of East Africa. Memberships: Kenya Medical Association; British Medical Association; Association of Surgeons of India; Kenya Heart Foundation; S.U.I.G. Club. Publications: approx. 6 contributions to medical journals. Address: P.O. Box 4266, Braidwood House, Tom Mboya St., Nairobi, Kenya.

KAMDAR, Nirmala Hasmuka, born Eldoret, Kenya, 3rd September 1929. Consulting Gynaecologist & Obstetrician. Education: Wilson College, Bombay, India; National Medical College, Bombay; Postgraduate Studies; Degrees: M.B., B.S., 1955; D.G.O., 1957; D.R.C.O.G. (Lond.), 1962; M.R.C.O.G.(Lond.), 1962. Married. Appointments include: House & Registrar positions, Nair Hospital, Bombay, India; House positions, Huddersfield Royal Infirmary, Huddersfield, U.K.; ibid, Moton General Hospital, Banbury; Registrar positions, Forest Gate Hospital, London; Currently in Private Practice, Nairobi, Kenya. Fellow, Association of Surgeons of East Africa. Memberships: Kenya Medical Association; British Medical Association; St. John Ambulance Assn., Kenya. Address: P.O. Box 4266, Nairobi, Kenya.

KAMENYA, Noel Evans, born 8th August, 1942. Civil Servant. Education: Form VI, 1962; Principal Level, Maths & Physics; Subsidiary Level, Geography. Married, 2 sons, 1 daughter. Appointments: Technical Officer, Trainee, Stanmore, U.K., 1962-64; Technical Officer, 1964; attended Advanced Forecasting Course, Stanmore, 1966; Technical Officer, Grade I, 1966; Senior Meteorological Officer, Dar es Salaam Airport, Tanzania. Address: P.O. Box 18004, Dar es Salaam Airport, Tanzania.

KAMWENDO, John Ginwala, born 27th April, 1936. Mayor, City of Blantyre, Malawi; Director of Companies. Education: Matriculation. Married, 4 children. Appointments:

Group General Manager, Press Holding Group of Companies; Mayor, City of Blantyre. Memberships: Rotary Club; Red Cross Society. Address: Press (Holding) Ltd., Hardeiec House, Victoria Ave., Blantyre, Malawi.

KANE, Falilou, born Joal, Senegal, 14th July 1938. Administrator; Diplomat. Education: Primary & Secondary, 1943-56; Baccalaureat Sciences Experimentales, University of Dakar, 1956-60; Prix d'ecellence en Iere Moderne; Premier au concours de Droit, 1958; Prix de Droit Civil; Licence en Droit et Science Economiques, 1960. Married, 3 children. Appointments: Chief, U.N. Division, Ministry of Foreign Affairs, 1960; Technical Counsellor, 1962; Technical Counsellor to Ministry of Justice & Cultural & Social Adviser, Plenipotentiary Minister, Senegalese Permanent Mission to U.N. & Senegalese Embassy, 1966-67; currently, General Administrative Secretary, Common African, Malagasy & Mauritius Organization, Yaondé, Cameroun. Honours: Commandeur de l'Ordre National du Royaume du Maroc, 1964; Chevalier de l'Ordre National de la Republique Voltairque, 1964; Officier de l'Ordre de la Valeur de la Republique du Federale du Cameroun, 1966; Officer de l'Odre National du Tchad, 1966; Officer, de l'Ordre du Leopard de la Republique Democratique du Congo, 1969. Address: O.C.A.M., Box 437, Yaoundé, Cameroun.

KANGWAMU, Frederick J. I., born 24th December 1930. Junior Secondary Teacher. Education: Primary School, St. Aloysius, Nyamitanga, 1940-43; Junior Secondary & Senior Secondary School, 1944-50; Ibanda Teachers' Training College, 1951; Kyambogo T.T.C., 1957. Married, 4 sons, 4 daughters. Appointments: Grade II Teacher, 1952-56; Grade III Teacher, 1958-60; Member, Uganda Parliament, 1961-64; Headmaster, various schools, Ankole, 1965—. Memberships: President, Democratic Party; ibid, Catholic Parents' Association; Founder, St. Kagwa Bushenyi High School, 1968. Address: P.O. Box 1084, Bushenyi, Mbarara, Uganda.

KANIMBA, Alexis, born 17th July 1932. Judge of the Tribunal of First Appeal, Bukavu. Education: Primary School, 6 years; Humanities, 6 years; Philosophy, Higher Seminary of Nyakibanda, Rwanda, 3 years; Theology, ibid, 3 years; Course of Sociology & Law. Married, 3 children. Appointments: Agent of Judicial Order, Court of the First Appeal, Bukavu, 1958-60; Functionary of the Second Grade, ibid, Goma, 1960-63; Judge of Police, the Town of Bukavu, Kivu, 1963; Auxiliary Judge to the Tribunal of First Appeal, Bukavu, 1964; Magistrate of the Grade of First Deputy, 1970. Address: c/o Tribunal of the First Appeal, of Kivu, Bukavu, B.P. 14 24, Democratic Republic of the Congo.

KANJARGA, Issa, born Sokode, Togo, 1897. District Magistrate. Education: German Government School, Lome, Togo, 1908-1914; British Government School, Tamale, Gold Coast, 1915. Married, 3 children. Appointments: Sergeant, Gold Coast Regiment RW.AFF, 1915-28; Assistant Superintendent, Gold Coast Police, 1928-61; Secondment to Sierra Leone, 1934-35; Security Officer, 1962-66; District Magistrate Grade II, Judicial Service, 1968—. Publications: East African Campaign, 1966; Photograph at Kumasi Military Museum, 1922; Annual Report on the Gold Coast, 1948; Achievement in the Gold Coast, 1951. Honours: Victory Medals, 1st World War; Colonial Police Long Service Medal, 1940; Colonial Police Medal for meritorious service in King's Birthday Honours, 1948. Address: District Magistrate Grade II, P.O. Box 14, Bimbilla, Gold Coast.

KANJI, Chhotalal Kalidas, born Mombasa, Kenya, 16th December 1929. Lawyer. Education: B.A.(Hons.), Bombay University, India, 1949; M.A.; LL.B. Married, 3 children. Appointments include: Partner, A. B. Patel & Patel, Advocates, 1954—. Memberships include: Hon. Secretary, Rotary Club, Mombasa Kenya; United Sports Club; Hon. Secretary, Coast Bridge Association; Past Secretary, Mombasa Law Society; Vice-President, Saturday Sports Club; W.M., Mombasa Masonic Lodge. Address: P.O. Box 274, Mombasa, Kenya.

KANYARI, Ezekeri Rwamafa, born Kabwohe, Ankole, Uganda, 31st December 1936. Agricultural Officer, Horticulturalist. Education: B.Sc., Agriculture, London. Married, 2 sons, 1 daughter. Appointments: District Agricultural Officer, Kigezi, 1964-65; Agricultural Officer, Agronomy, Kawanda, 1965-68; ibid, Horticulture, Buganda Region, 1968—. Memberships: Uganda Horticultural Society; Uganda Agricultural Society; International Horticultural Society. Author of monthly & annual reports. Address: Department of Agriculture, P.O. Box 62, Bombo, Uganda.

KANYEREZI, Bwogi Richard, born 13th September 1934. Physician. Education: M.B., B.Ch. (E. Africa); M.R.C.P.(London). Appointments: Research Fellow in Medicine, 1964; Lecturer in Medicine, Makerere College Medical School, 1967; Senior Lecturer in Medicine, ibid, 1969; Rockefeller Fellow, Harvard Medical School, Boston, U.S.A., Sept. 1969 to Sept. 1970. Memberships: Council Mbr., International Rehabilitation Medicine Association; Association of Physicians of East Africa; Uganda Medical Association; Chairman, Cheshire Home for Disabled, Uganda. Author of various publications in med. jrnls. Address: Makerere University Medical School, P.O. Box 7072, Kampala, Uganda.

KANYI-TOMETI, Teko, born 2nd June 1920. Pharmacist. Education: Buea Government School, Cameroun, 1932-37; Government College, Umuahia, Nigeria, 1938-40; Dennis Memorial Grammar School, Onitsha, Nigeria, 1941-42; Higher College, Yaba, 1943-44; School of Pharmacy, Yaba, 1945-47. Appointments: Managing Director, Myrone Chemists Ltd., 1948. Member, Pharmaceutical Society of Nigeria. Address: Myrone Chemists Ltd., 48 New Court Road, P.O. Box 415, Ibadan, Nigeria.

KANYUNGULU, Victor Ndumba Esau, born 24th April 1926. School-teacher. Education: Chitokolok Mission Station, Zambezi District of

Zambia; Teacher, various schools, including Ntambu School, 1952—; Transafrica Correspondence College, 1954. Personal details: descendant of the Royal Family of Great Chief Chokwe. Appointments: Head Teacher, Chiyengele, Chikonkwelo, & Chikenge Schools; Assistant Teacher, Loloma & Ntambu Schools; Class Teacher, Luanshya Mwinilunga & Roon School. Memberships: First Chairman, UNIP, 1959-62; Secretary, UNIP Constituency, 1966-67; Regional Secretary, ibid, 1967-68; M.P. for Kabompo Constituency, 1968-70. Address: P.O. Manyinga, Kabompo, Zambia.

KAPELINSKI, Franciszek Jozef, born 24th December, 1914. University Lecturer. Education: Mag.Pr., University of Warsaw, Poland, 1936; Cert. de dr. Français, Paris, France; Dipl. d'et.Fr., Hautes Etudes, Bordeaux-Toulouse, Pau; Wsp. PTNO, Polish Society of Arts & Science. Married. Appointments: War Service, Polish Army; Teacher, Head, Polish Secondary School & Inspector of English Language; Teacher, U.K. Lecturer, Nigerian College of Arts Science & Technology, 1958-62; Ahmadu Bello University, Zaria, 1962-64; Lecturer, French, ibid, 1964; Senior Lecturer, 1965; Acting Head, Department of Languages, 1965-69. Memberships include: Consultive Committee on Hausa Studies; Historical Society of Nigeria. Contributor to professional journals in French, English, & Polish. Address: Ahmadu Bello University, Zaria, Nigeria.

KAPLAN, Yehuda Shemariah, born 22nd November 1931. Medical Practitioner. Education: M.B., Ch.B., University of Cape Town, South Africa; D.T.C.D., University of Wales, U.K. Married, 3 children. Appointments: Interne, New Somerset Hospital, Cape Town, South Africa, 1955; Senior Houseman, Baragwanath Hospital, Johannesburg, 1956-59; various other hospitals, 1960-62; Registrar, Johannesburg General Hospital, 1962-63; Medical Officer, Swaziland, 1963-66; Tuberculosis Medical Officer for Swaziland, 1966—. Memberships: Swaziland Medical Association; British Medical Association; British Tuberculosis & Thoracic Association; International Union Against T.B. Publications: Craniotabes in the African Child, South African Medical Journal, 1964. Address: National Tuberculosis Control Centre, P.O. Box 54, Manzini, Swaziland.

KAPOOR, Krishan Chand, born 1st July 1907. Physician. Education: State Medical School, Punjab, India. Personal details: descendant of well-known Pashawaria Kapoor Family, formerly of Lahore. Memberships: President, Indian Association, Lira, 1938-63; ibid, V.H. Education Society, Lira; V.H. Public School, Lira, 1938-63; Indian Sports Club, Lira, 1938-62; Lira Township Authority, Town Council, 1938-63; President, Lira Loins Club, 1967-70. Honours: Coronation Medal, 1953; Civil Division, O.B.E., 1956. Address: P.O. Box 58, Lira, Uganda.

KAPUMPA, Mumba Sampson, born 22nd October 1918. Businessman. Education: Std. IV, Government Exams, 1938. Married, 10 sons. Appointments: First Chairman, Mufulira Municipal Workers' Union, 1949-51; Member, Area Housing Board, 1953-58; Branch Secretary, ibid; UNIP Region Trustee, 1962—; UNIP Councillor, 1966-70; Candidate, 1970-73. Memberships: Provincial Chairman, Traders' Association, Copper Belt Province. Address: P.O. Box 904, Mufulira, Zambia.

KARANDAWALA, Kapilarathe Senerat Bandara, born 8th October 1923. Analytical Chemist. Education: B.Sc.(Hons.), Ceylon. Married, 3 children. Appointments: Assistant Government Analyst, Ceylon, 1950-65; Senior Chemist, Government of Nigeria, 1966; Adj. Deputy Government Chemist, ibid, 1966-70; Deputy Federal Government Chemist, 1970—; Acting Government Chemist, Kaduna, Nigeria. Fellow of The Royal Institute of Chemistry. Memberships: Ceylon Association for the Advancement of Science; Chemical Society of Ceylon. Address: Chemistry Department, Federal Ministry of Health. P.M.B. 2059, Kaduna, Nigeria.

KARANTAO, Karamoko, born 1925. Administrator. Primary Education. Married, 4 children. Appointments: with P.T.T., 1948-54; Liaison Officer, Governor's Cabinet, Upper Volta, 1954-57; Head, Liaison Inter-ministerial Service, 1966—; Director, Government Journal, 1966—. Memberships: Treasurer, Association of Artists & Painters; Literary & Artistic Circle of Upper Volta; Treasurer, Parent-Pupil Association, Municipal Lycée, Ouagadougou. National Administration & Printing Council, Upper Volta. Knight, Upper Volta Order of Merit. Address: B.P. 513, Présidence de la République, Ouagadougou, Upper Volta.

KARSAN, Nurdin Zaver, born Dar es Salaam, Tanzania, 23rd March 1927. Barrister-at-Law. Education: London Matriculation; Barrister-at-Law, Lincoln's Inn, London, U.K. Personal details: third son of Zaver Karsan, Merchant and approminent Member of the Ismailia Community in Tanzania; married. Address: P.O. Box 2181, Dar es Salaam, Tanzania.

KASALIRWE, Stephen Paul, born 19th November 1940. Civil Servant. Education: Mengo Junior Secondary School, 1949-58; St. Peter's College, Agra, India, 1959-61; B.Com., University of Aligarh, Aligarh, India, 1961-64. Married. Appointments: Assistant Secretary, Ministry of Commerce & Industry, Uganda, 1964-68; Assistant Secretary, Ministry of Information, Broadcasting & Tourism, 1968-70; Senior Assistant Secretary, 1970—. Member, Commerce Graduates' Association, Uganda. Address: Ministry of Information, Broadcasting & Tourism, P.O. 7142, Kampala, Uganda.

KASCHIK, Ernst Guenter Erich, born 16th January 1932. Accountant. Education: High School & College, Germany; College & University, South Africa; B.Comm.; A.F.C.S. (Engl.); F.A.(S.A.). Appointments: Director, various investment & property co.'s; Branch Manager, Provincial Building Society of South Africa; City Councillor, City of Windhoek; Member, Management Committee, ibid. Memberships: Round Table No. 34; M.M. Lodge 1613 SC. Publications: S.W.A. Director. Sworn

Translator & Sworn Appraiser, Supreme Court of South Africa. Recip.: Diploma 2,000 Men. of Achievement, 1969. Address: P.O. Box 7, Windhoek, South-West Africa.

KASE, Japhet Zakaria, born 20th April 1939. Politician. Education: Cambridge School Certificate, 1959; Married, 4 children. Appointments: Headmaster, Primary School, Hola, 1962-63; Treasurer, Tana River Branch, Kenya African Democratic Union, 1963; Member, Kenya National Assembly, 1963; Member, Kenya's Central Road Authority, 1963-66; Chairman, Tana River Branch, Kenya African National Union, 1964-70; Assistant Minister, Economic Planning & Development, 1966-69; Assistant Minister, Information & Broadcasting, 1969—. Memberships: Coast Social Club; Tana River Club; Chairman, Road Safety in Kenya, 1970; ibid, Kenya Youth Hostels Association; Automobile Association of East Africa; Agricultural Society of Kenya. Honours: Elder of Burning Spear of Kenya presented by the President of Kenya, Mzee Jomo Kenyatta. Address: P.O. Boxes 30025 & 1842, Nairobi, Kenya.

KASENGE, Raphael, born May 1924. Civil Servant. Education: Junior Secondary School, Kitovu, 1940-42; St. Mary's College, Kisubi, 1943-45; Leeds College of Commerce, U.K., 1954-56. Married, 4 sons, 4 daughters. Appointments: Clerk Grade 4, Uganda Government, 1946; Clerk Grade 3, 1949; Clerk Grade 2, 1950; Executive Class Grade B, 1951; Accounts Assistant, 1955; High Executive Officer (Accounts), 1962; Senior Executive Officer, 1964—. Memberships: Treasurer, St. Mary's Old Boys' Association, 1965—; Asst. Treasurer, St. Henry's College Old Boys' Association, 1968—. Recipient, Uganda Independence Medal, 1963. Address: Kampala, Uganda.

KASONGO, Harrison Peter, born 27th June 1934. Politician. Education: Junior Certificate, South Africa; 2 subjects, G.C.E. 'O' level, Economics & British Constitution. Constituency Secretary, United National Independence Party —1970; Chairman, Zambia Council for the Handicapped, Copperbelt & North Area Board; Ndola City Councillor, 1963-70. Memberships: Insakwe/Mitanda Admission & Review Committee; Ndola Theatre Club; Copperbelt Probation Sub-Committee; Ndola Urban Local Council of Education. Address: P.O. Box 1336, Ndola, Zambia.

KASOZI, Heny D., born 7th July 1929. Civil Servant. Education: St. Peters School, Nsambya, Kampala, Uganda; Royal Institute of Public Administration, London, U.K. Appointments: Clerk/Telephone Operator, BEA Corporation, 1951; Clerk, Uganda Co., 1951-53; Clerical Assistant, Ministry of Information, 1953-55; Clerical Officer, ibid, 1955-57; Senior Clerical Officer, 1957-58; Junior Assistant Secretary, Public Service Commission, 1958-60; Assistant Secretary, ibid, 1960-63; Chief Executive Officer, 1963; Chief Executive Officer, Ministry of Education, 1963-64; ibid, Office of the Prime Minister, 1965; ibid, Ministry of Health, 1965-69; ibid, Public Service & C.A., 1969—. Memberships: Secretary, Outward Bound Trust of Uganda; President, Mountain Club of Uganda. Address: Ministry of Public Service & Cabinet Affairs, P.O. Box 27, Entebbe, Uganda.

KATAMBE, Garba, born 1938. Director; Teaching Inspector. Education: Primary School, Madaoua, Niger, 1945-51; Niamey Modern College, Niger, 1952-55; Katibougou, Mali, 1956; Baccalaureat, Senegal, 1957-59; C.I. University of Abidjan, Ivory Coast, 1960-61; General Geology Certificate, University of Caen, France, 1962-63; E.N.S., St. Cloud, France, 1964. Appointments: Professor of Science, Tahoua, 1960; Professor of Science, Lycée, Niamey, 1962; Inspector, Primary Education, Tahoua, later Niamey, 1965-68; Cabinet Director, Ministry of National Education, Niamey, Niger, 1968—. Memberships: Vice-President, National Anti-Tubercular Committee. Address: Ministry of National Education, Ministère d'Education Nationale, Niamey, Niger.

KATANGA, Yohanna Adamu De-Goshie, born Katanga Warji, Nigeria, 20th May 1948. Educator. Education: Ningi Bay Senior Primary School; Banchi Teachers' College; Institute of Education, Ahmadu Bello University, Zaria. Appointments include: Dispenser, Banchi College, 1964-67; Instructor, Red Cross Society, 1966-67; Headmaster, Katanga Primary School, 1968-69. Memberships include: Red Cross Society. Address: c/o E.C.W.A. Church, Katanga Warji, P.A. Ningi Via Banchi, North-Eastern State, Nigeria.

KATATUMBA, George William, born 19th July 1943. Architect. Education: Primary, Nyamitanga School, Mbarara, Uganda, 1948-55; Secondary, Ntare School, ibid, 1956-62; B.Arch., University of East Africa, 1963-69. Appointments: Associate Partner, Jackson Hill Covell Matthews & Partners, Architects & Planning Consultants; Council Member, Uganda Society of Architects. Memberships: Uganda Society of Architects; East African Academy; East African Institute of Architects; Uganda Club. Honours: Award of the East African Institute of Architects for the best performance in the final year of university. Address: P.O. Box 6313, Kampala, Uganda.

KATETA (Al-Haj) Idi Ali, born 7th April 1929. Civil Servant, East African Community, Commonwealth Research & Social Services. Education: Public Administration Course, Wisconsin University, U.S.A., 1963; Royal Institute of Public Administration, London, U.K., 1968. Married, 6 children. Appointments: Assistant Establishment Officer, 1961-62; Establishment Officer, 1963; Assistant Secretary, 1964; Principal Assistant Secretary, 1965—; Under-Secretary, 1966-67; Deputy Secretary, 1968—. Memberships: Boy Scout since 1945. Address: Deputy Secretary, Communications, Research & Social Services, P.O. Box 1002, Arusha, Tanzania.

KATHUMBA, Harold Moses Frank, born 21st November 1938. Secretary. Education: Secondary, Malawi Government; Diploma (Distinction) in Business Administration,

Waterloo Lutheran University, Ontario, Canada, 1967; currently studying for Chartered Institute of Secretaries Exam. Married to Irene Catherine, 2 sons, 2 daughters. Appointments: Accounts Clerk & Typist, Malawi Government, 1958-60; Stenographer with Wallace Ltd., 1960-61; Secretary/Accountant, East Asiatic Company, 1961-68; Team Secretary, Cotton Productivity Research Unit, Agricultural Research Council of Malawi, 1969—. Member, Agricultural Advisory Council of Malawi Government. Address: Agricultural Research Council of Malawi, Makoka Research Station, P/Bag 3, Ntonowe, Malawi.

KATIKAZA, Obed Mbogo, born 10th April 1935. Diplomat. Education: B.A.(Hons.), London University, U.K., 1962; Course in Diplomacy, Nairobi, Kenya, 1965. Personal details: married to Mipael Mchome, nurse/midwife, 1 son, 1 daughter. Appointments: District Officer, Mbeya District, 1962; Assistant Secretary, Prime Minister's Office, 1963-64; Senior Assistant Secretary, Foreign Office, 1964-65; Principal Assistant Secretary, ibid, 1965; Chief of Protocol, 1965-66; Ambassador of Tanzania to the French Republic, 1967-68; Principal Secretary & Administrative Head of Diplomatic Service, Tanzania, 1968—. Member, East African Academy. Publications include: Dodoma—The Changing Cultural & Physical Landscape, 1960. Honours: Shell Exhibition Prize, 1960. Address: Principal Secretary, Ministry of Foreign Affairs, Dar es Salaam, Tanzania.

KATOKE, Israel Kambuga, born April 1928. University Lecturer. Education: Lukajange & Kigarama Primary School, 1939-45; Iliboru Secondary School, 1946-50; Government Training College, Tabora, Grade A teacher, 1951-52; B.A., Hartwick College, Oneonta, N.Y., 1961-64; M.A., Boston University; Ph.D. History, ibid, 1969. Married, 3 children. Appointments: Headmaster, Kahororo Secondary School, 1967-68; Lecturer, History, University of Dar es Salaam, Tanganyika, 1968; Associate Dean, Faculty of Arts & Social Science, ibid, 1970—. Specialist in the Oral History of Tanzania. Memberships: Hon. Secretary, Historical Association of Tanzania; Executive Committee, Tanzania Society. Publications: The Making of the Karagwe Kingdom, 1970; The Karagwe Kingdom: A History of Anyambo of North-Western Tanzania, 1970; Pre-Colonial Societies in the Lake Victoria Region; contributor to a number of learned journals. Address: The University of Dar es Salaam, P.O. Box 35050, Dar es Salaam, Tanzania.

KATUMBA, Batwerinde Benjumin, born West Mengo, Uganda, 8th June 1916. Educator. Education: Namirembe Primary School; Bishop College, Muicono-E. Married, 10 children. Appointments include: former Headmaster of following: Bira Primary School; Masuuliita Primary School; Nazigo Primary School; Headmaster & Fndr., Kaabbi Primary School; former Member, Buganda's Great Lukiiko. Memberships include: Synod, Diocese of Namirembe; Radio Uganda Advisory Committee; Literacy Supervisor; Branch Leader, Bugerere Coffee Growers. Address: Ekaababbi-Busiro c/o Mr. Y. B. Sentongo, P.O. Kailiri, Kampala, Uganda.

KATURAMU, Metusera Tibigambwa, born Hoima, 26th February 1922. Educator. Education: Nyakasura Schl.; King's Coll., Budo; Makerere Univ. Coll.; Newland Park College, U.K. Married, 7 children. Appointments include: School-teacher, Kabalega Schl., 1946-49; ibid, Bishop's Schl., Mukono, 1950-52; Headmaster, Duhaga J.S. Schl., 1953-62; Katikiro of Bunyoro Kingdom, 1962-67; Sec.-Gen., Bunyoro District, 1967—; Deputy Chairman, Uganda Public Service Commission, 1969—. Memberships include: Synod, Rwenzori Diocese Church of Uganda; Pres., Football Assoc., Western Region; Trustee, Hoima Sports Club; ibid, Bunyoro Sports Club; Uganda Club; Exec. Council, Uganda People's Congress (UPC); Chmn., Parliamentary Constituency, South West Bunyoro. Honours: Essay Prize, Makerere Coll., 1945; Uganda Independence Medal, 1963. Address: P.O. Box 6, Hoima, Uganda.

KATZARSKI, Minko, born 13th May 1929. Lecturer, Ghana Medical School. Education: Middle & Secondary Schools, Bulgaria; Medical School, Sofia. Appointments: Lecturer, Ghana Medical School. Member of Current Anthropology, U.S.A. Publications: The Anatomical Basis for Inquinal Hernia in Ghanaians. Address: c/o Ghana Medical School, Ghana.

KAUNDA (His Excellency) Kenneth David, President of Zambia, born 28th April 1924. Education: Munali Secondary School, Lusaka, Zambia. Appointments include: Secretary-General, African National Congress, 1953; President, Zambia African National Congress, 1958; President, U.N.I.P., 1960; Prime Minister, Legislative Assembly of N. Rhodesia, 1964; President, 1964—. Honours: Recipient of Honorary Doctorate of Law, National University, Ireland; Freeman of the City of Lusaka. Address: State House, P.O. Box 135, Lusaka, Zambia.

KAWUKI, Joseph Nsanusi, born Kampala, Uganda, 2nd July, 1934. Administrator; Welfare Officer. Education: Makerere University College, Uganda, 1955-59; B.A.(Lond.), University of Wales, Swansea, U.K., 1961-62; Diploma in Social Administration. Married, 2 daughters. Appointments include: Probation and After-care Officer, 1959; Principal Welfare Officer, 1963; Deputy Director of Refugees, 1965; Commissioner for Community Development, Probation and Welfare Services, 1967; all at the Ministry of Culture & Community Development; U.N. Correspondent on Crime and Delinquency. Memberships include: Management Committee, Nakivubo Settlement Primary School; National Council of Social Service for Uganda; Board of Trustees, Uganda Foundation for the Blind; Supreme Council, Y.M.C.A., Uganda; Chairman, Karamoja Children's Emergency Relief Fund; Secretary, Uganda National Disablement Advisory Council. Honours: Knight of the Order of St. Gregory the Great. Address: P.O. Box 7136, Kampala, Uganda.

KAYANJA-LUBEGA, Byuma Aloyisius, born 15th December 1909. General Medical Practitioner. Education: Junior & Senior

Secondary, 7 years; Diploma, Medicine, Makerere University, Kampala, Uganda, 6 years. Married, 3 sons, 6 daughters. Currently, Medical Practitioner, Kalungu Trading Centre. Memberships: Uganda Medical Association; Uganda Club; East Africa Academic Association; Masaka Rifle Club. Address: P.O. Box 294, Masaka, Uganda.

KAYE, Albert Ernest, born 16th May 1905. Teacher; Adviser in Correspondence Education. Education: M.A.(Hons.), New Zealand; Diploma, Education & Teacher A Certificate, ibid. Married, 3 children. Appointments: Teacher, Primary & Secondary Schools, New Zealand; New Zealand Correspondence School, 12 years; Deputy Headmaster, ibid; Correspondence Education Expert under SCARP, New Zealand Government, 1963-70; 1st Principal, Malawi Correspondence College, 1964-67; Head, Correspondence Unit, Makerere University College, Uganda, 1967—. Author of numerous correspondence courses & articles on correspondence education. Recipient, James Clarke Prize, History, Otago University, New Zealand, 1938. Address: Centre for Continuing Education, Makerere University, P.O. Box 16196, Kampala, Uganda.

KAYODE (Rev.) Samuel Adeboun, born Abeokuta, 7th July 1928. Minister of Religion. Education: Oke Ona United Grammar School, 1950-53; Baptist Theological Seminary, Ogbomosho, Nigeria. Married. Appointments include: Minister, Araromi Baptist Church, Lagos, Nigeria, 1954-55; Baptist Sunday School Field Worker, Nigerian Baptist Convention, 1956-57; Sunday School Director, Northern States of Nigeria, Nigerian Baptist Convention, 1958—; Leader, Nigerian Baptist Convention Delegation, 6th Baptist Youth World Conference, Beirut, Lebanon, 1963; Chairman, ibid, 7th Baptist Youth World Congress, Berne, Switzerland, 1968; re-elected Chairman, Baptist Convention Youth Committee, 1967-69. Memberships include: Ambassador-in-Chief, George Green Chapter, Royal Ambassador; Counsellor, Adekunle Adejumobi Chapter, ibid. Publications include: Twelve Suggestions For Your Sunday School, 1966. Address: Baptist Building, P.O. Box 118, Kaduna, Nigeria.

KAYONDO, John Billy, born 10th October 1937. Inspector of Schools. Education: Primary; Secondary; Secondary Technical; Technical Schools Teacher Education; Vocation Teacher Trained, Japan. Married twice, 8 children. Appointments: Technical Schools Teacher, 1960-61; Technical Schools Tutor, 1961-64; Inspector of Schools, 1964—. Member, Scooters Wood-Badge. Honours: Best Final Student, Kampala Technical Institute, 1959. Address: Ministry of Education, P.O. Box 3568, Kampala, Uganda.

KAYUMBO, Hosea Yona, born 16th February 1935. Lecturer in Agricultural Entomology & Zoology. Education: Graduate, Zoology & Botany, Makerere University College, Uganda; Postgrad., Entomology, Imperial College of Science & Technology, London, U.K. Married, 3 children. Appointments: Entomologist, Ministry of Agriculture, Tanzania, 1964-68; Lecturer, Faculty of Agriculture, University College, Dar es Salaam, Tanganyika. Memberships: East African Entomological & Insecticide Specialist Committee; Subcomm. on Wildlife, National Scientific Research Council; Working Party on Research Priorities & Administration of the East African Community. Publications: Cotton Pest in Western Tanzania, 1965; Insecticide Use on cotton in the sucking pest areas of Western Tanzania, 1969; Cashew in Tanzania, 1970. Address: Faculty of Agriculture, University College, Dar es Salaam, Tanzania.

KEBBA, Nicholas Lot Kalanyi, born 1st December 1936. Senior Regional Inspector, Ministry of Regional Administrations. Education: Kanoro Primary School, 1945-48; Iki-Iki Primary School, 1949-50; Nabumali High School, 1951-56; B.Sc.(Gen.), Makerere University, Uganda, 1957-62; Loughborough Cooperative College, 1963-64; Birmingham University, 1969-70. Appointments: Cooperative Officer, 1962-65; Administrative Officer, 1965-68; Regional Inspector, 1968-70; Senior Regional Inspector, 1970—. Address: Senior Regional Inspector, Ministry of Regional Administrations, Uganda.

KEBBEDE ABBEBE, born 8th February 1926. Journalist; Diplomat. Education: Diploma, London School of Journalism; D.Litt., Wilberforce University, Ohio, U.S.A. Personal details: wife, granddaughter of H.M. King Mikael of Wollo; 1 daughter. Appointments: Proprietor & Editor, Nouro-Bexede, daily newspaper; 2nd Secretary, Ethiopian Legation, Stockholm, Sweden, 1948-52; ibid, Ethiopian Embassy, Rome, Italy, 1952-54; 1st Secretary, Ethiopian Embassy, Washington, D.C., 1954-57; Managing Editor, Ethiopia Today, quarterly review, ibid; Assistant Press Officer, His Imperial Majesty's State Visits, U.S.A., Canada, & Mexico, 1957; 1st Secretary, Press Affairs, Ethiopian Embassy, London, 1957-58; Managing Editor, Ethiopian Review, ibid; Chargé d'Affaires, Washington Embassy, 1958-59; Counsellor, London Embassy, 1959-60; Chargé d'Affaires, ibid, 1960; Ambassador Extraordinary & Plenipotentiary, Nigeria, 1960-63; General Manager & Chairman of Editors, Menen (monthly Amharic magazine), Voice of Ethiopia (monthly English Magazine), ibid (daily English newspaper), Yethiopia Dimtz (daily Amharic newspaper), 1963-64; Deputy Mayor, Addis Ababa, 1964-67; Ambassador Extraordinary & Plenipotentiary, Liberia, 1967—; Ambassador Designate, Guinea & Sierra Leone, 1968. Memberships: Rotary Club, Addis Ababa; Board of Directors, Municipality Employees' Association; President & Chairman, Board of Directors, Welfare Society of Harar Governorate. Honours include: Title, Miketile Kentiba; Grand Officer, Star of Honour of Ethiopia; Knight, Great Band of the Humane Order of African Redemption; Polonia Restitute 2nd Class with Star; Victory Medal, Patriot's Medal & Refugee Medal, Ethiopia; Africa Star, Great Britain. Address: P.O. Box 4964, Addis Ababa, Ethiopia.

KEBEDE GEBRE-MARIAM, born 15th March 1931. Public Servant. Education: B.A., Public Administration, 1961; LL.B., 1967. Married, 2 children. Appointments: Chief Registrar of the Supreme Court, 1956;

Director-General, Central Personnel Agency, 1963-66; Deputy Commissioner, ibid, 1967-70; Commissioner, 1970. Memberships: Patron, Journal of Ethiopian Law; Law School Association, Hailé Selassié I University; Programme Committee, Y.M.C.A. Publications: Contributor to Journal of Ethiopian Law; Public Personnel Review. Address: Commissioner, Central Personnel Agency, P.O. Box 3240, Addis Ababa, Ethiopia.

KEBEDE GOBENA, born June 1938. Electrical Engineer. Education: Primary, 4 years; Secondary, General Wingate School, 4 years; G.C.E. 'O' Level; Engineering College, Ethiopia; B.Sc., Electrical Engineering, 1964; African-American Graduate Scholarship; M.Sc., Rhode Island University, U.S.A., 1967. Personal details: youngest son of a family of 10. Appointments: Administrative Engineer, 1964-66; Acting Technical Director, 1967-69; Technical Director, 1969—. Member, Ethiopian Engineers' Association. Address: Radio Voice of the Gospel, P.O. Box 654, Addis Ababa, Ethiopia.

KEBEDE TESEMMA, born April 1912. Senator; Lieutenant-Colonel. Education: Elementary; self-educated. Married, 8 children. Appointments: joined Imperial Body-guard, 1935; 2nd in Command, 2nd Kagnew Battalion, U.N. Army in Korea, 1952; Lt.-Colonel, & retired, 1958; Governor, Maji, Governorate General of Kaffa, 1958-67; Senator, 1968—. Honours: Decorations awarded by governments of Great Britain, U.S.A., & Korea. Address: P.O. Box 1602, Parliament, Addis Ababa, Ethiopia.

KECHAOU, Abdelhamid, born 25th December 1929. Chemist. Education: 2nd Part Baccalaureat, Chemistry, Sfax; Pharmacy, Tunisia; Pharmaceutical Studies, Lausanne, Switzerland; Laboratory Studies in Bacteriology, Parasitology & Hygiene; Studied for Doctorate, Switzerland. Married, 2 sons, 1 daughter. Memberships include: Regional Economic Committee (Committee of Co-ordination); Regional Committee of Finances, ibid; Sports Clubs; Regional President, Association for the Blind; Regional President, Regional Cultural Committee; Political Party; General Union of Students in Switzerland; International Federation of Pharmacists. Publications: Les Bacteriophages, 1958. Address: 13 Avenue Farhat Hached, Sfax, Tunisia.

KEEBLE, Oliver John, born Birkenhead, U.K., 15th October 1920. Barrister-at-Law. Education: Prince of Wales School, Nairobi, Kenya, 1935-39; Trinity College, Oxford University, U.K., 1946-49. Married, 2 sons, 1 daughter. Appointments include: Service in Army, ending as D.A.A.G., G.H.Q., 1939-46; Partner in Hunter & Greig, Advocates, Kampala, 1949—. Memberships include: President, Uganda Law Society, 1966-67; Kampala Club. Honours, Prizes, etc.: Rhodes Scholar, 1941. Address: P.O. Box 7026, Kampala, Uganda.

KEITA, Abderamane, born 20th August 1932. Director of the First Stage of Education. Education: Bacc., Secondary Studies; CEL.G., Higher Studies; Pedagogy: Diploma of Primary Education Inspectors, St. Cloud, France, 1961. Married, 6 children. Appointments: Teacher; Professeur de Cours Normale; Inspector of Primary Education; Director of the First Stage of Education. Address: Ministry of Education, B.P. 234, Niamey, Niger.

KEITA, Layes, born 25th October 1939. Head of Subdivision. Education: Public Primary School, Nouna; Apprenticeship Centre, Ouagadougou, Upper Volta; National School of Administration, Ouagadougou. Married, 2 sons, 2 daughters. Appointments: Head, Military Bureau of the District of Nouna, 1961; Head, Civil State Bureau; Secretary of the Tribunal of the First Degree; Controleur des Prixe Stoks; Inspector ad-Hoc of Estates; Secretary to the Prefect; President to the Tribunal of First Degree. Address: Deputy Administrator 2nd Class, Head of Subdivision, Toussiana Cercle de Bob-Dioulasso, Upper Volta.

KEITH, Kenneth Bryan, born 9th June 1919, Barrister-at-Law; Advocate, High Court of Kenya, Education: Bedford School; St. Catharine's College, Cambridge University, U.K.; Gray's Inn, London. Married to Sheila Isobel Lewis, 2 sons, 1 daughter. Appointments: British Army, 1939-45; Colonial Administrator, Nigeria & Kenya, 1946-51. Memberships: President, Law Society of Kenya, 1967-68; Chairman, Nairobi Round Table No. 1, 1960-61.

KEKE ADJIGNON, Joseph, born Avromkou, 5th December 1927. Advocate. Education: Licensed in Law. Married, 8 children. Appointments: Deputy, National Assembly, 1960; re-elected at each election; President, Commissions of Finance & Legislation; Councillor & President, General Council of Oueme; ibid, Villuye; Keeper of the Seals, Minister of Justice & Legislation; Secretary-General, Porto Novo Section, 1960-63; Minister of Economy, Dahomey, 1970—. Memberships: President, Association of Dahomey Student in France, 1948-56; Treasurer, African Students' Association; President & Honorary President, numerous associations. Honours include: Commander of the Legion of Honour, France; Grand Officer, National Order of Dahomey; Commander, National Order of Senegal; Commander, Agricultural Merit. Address: c/o Ministry of Economy, Dahomey.

KELLEHER, Raymond, born London, U.K., 6th January 1937. Physicist. Education: Finchley Grammar School, London; 1st Class Honours B.A., Trinity College, Cambridge; Ph.D.(Cantab.), Cavendish Laboratory & Radio & Space Research Station, 1965. Married, 1 son, 1 daughter. Appointments include: Lecturer in Physics, University College, Nairobi, 1964; currently Senior Lecturer. Memberships include: Associate, Institute of Physics. Publications include: translator of 3 scientific books from the Russian, published by Pergamon Press; translator of numerous scientific papers from the Russian, published by Pergamon Press & Faraday Press; author & co-author of original scientific papers in Nature Journal of Atmospheric & Terrestial Physics, Annales de Geophysique, etc. Honours, Prizes, etc.: Scholar of Trinity College, 1960. Address: Physics Department, University College of Nairobi, P.O. Box 30197, Nairobi, Kenya.

KEMENY, Tibor, born 8th February 1925. Medical Doctor. Education: Medical Diploma, 1950; Expert, Med. Laboratory Investig., 1953; Expert, Public Health, 1958; Ph.D., 1959. Appointments: Asst. Professor, Institute of Experimental Pathology, University Medical School, Budapest, Hungary, 1950-62; Chief, Department of Physiology & Pathology, Institute of Nutrition, 1962-67; W.H.O. Med. Nutritionist, Tanzania, 1967-70; Scientific Adviser, Food & Drug Directorate, Ottawa, Ontario, Canada, 1970—. Memberships: Int. Union of Nutrition Scientists; Affiliate, Royal Society of Medicine, London. Author of 96 med. publs. Recipient, Dr. Willmar Schwabe Prize, 1969. Address: Food & Drug Directorate, Ottawa 3, Ontario, Canada.

KENNEDY, Beatrice Venetia, born 8th May 1920. Educator; Licensed Lay Worker. Education: Thornbank School, Malvern, Worcs., U.K., 1928-32; Worcester Girls' Grammar, 1932-38; Salisbury Diocesan Teacher Training College, 1938-40. Appointments: Teacher, Devon County Council, 1940-41; Teacher, Gt. Malvern Council School, Worcs., 1941-49; Member, Community Lee Abbey, Lynton, N. Devon, 1949-52; Licensed Lay Worker on Staff of Bradford Cathedral, Yorks., 1952-63; Member of Church Missionary Society, London, 1963—; Warden, Martyrs' Community Centre, Kampala, Uganda, 1965-70. Address: c/o Mr. J. Kennedy, Ashlea, 13 Highfield Road, Malvern Link, Worcs., U.K.

KENNEDY, Peter Alexander, born 23rd February 1935. Medical Practitioner. Education: B.A., St. John's College, Cambridge, U.K., 1956-59; M.B., Ch.B., Edinburgh University Medical School, 1959-62; D.C.H.(Glasgow). Appointments: Leader & Physician/Paediatrician, Child Medical Care Unit, Enugu, Eastern Nigeria, 1969-70; Medical Officer, Paediatrics, Swaziland Government, 1966-69, 1970—. Member of the Royal College of Physicians, Edinburgh. Address: Hlatikulu Hospital, P.O. Box 20, Hlatikulu, Swaziland.

KENYANJUI, Christine Bigala-, born 14th July 1939. Nurse. Education: Senior Secondary, Namagunga, 1954-56; Nsambya Hospital, 1957-60; S.R.N., Luton & Dunstable Hospital, U.K., 1961-63. Married, 3 sons, 1 daughter. Appointments: Nursing Sister, Trypanosomiasis Research Centre, 1964—. Member, Nurses, Midwives, & Medical Assistants Council, Entebbe, Uganda. Address: E.A.T.R.O., P.O. Box 96, Tororo, Uganda.

KENYATTA (His Excellency Mzee) Jomo, President of the Republic of Kenya, born Ichaweri, Kenya, 20th October, 1891. Education: Church of Scotland Mission School, Kikuyi, Kenya; Moscow University, U.S.S.R.; B.A., Postgraduate Diploma Anthropology, London School of Economics, U.K., 1936. Appointments include: Joint-Founder, Pan African Federation, 1945-53; President, Kenya African Union, Kenya; elected President, Kenya African National Union, 1960; Leader of the Opposition KANU, 1962-63; Prime Minister on Kenya's attaining Independence, 1963; President, Republic of Kenya, 1964—. Memberships: Joint-Founder, Organization of African Unity. Organizer & Chairman, Good Neighbours Conference of 11 Nations, Nairobi, 1966. Author of 'Facing Mount Kenya', 1939. Address: Office of the President, P.O. Box 30510, Nairobi, Kenya.

KEOHAN, Joseph A., born 21st July, 1926. Lecturer in Biology, Plant Pathology, Microbiology & Animal Physiology. Education: B.Sc., University of Massachusetts, U.S.A., 1965; M.Sc., ibid, 1967; Assoc. B.Adm., Boston Institute; Cert., Soil Fertility, Cornell University, N.Y. Married, 1 son, 2 daughters. Appointments: General Manager, Research & Development, Kerr-McGee Chemical Corp.; Lecturer, Biology, University of Massachusetts; ibid, University of Malawi. Memberships: Phi Beta Phi; Alpha Zeta; former Head, Biological Association of Malawi; Microbiological Society of America; Weed Society of America; Phytopathological Society of America; Malawi Agricultural & Natural Resources Comm. Author of scientific publications. Address: University of Malawi, Bunda College of Agriculture, Box 219, Lilongwe, Malawi.

KER, Andrew David Rivers, born 22nd June 1929. Lecturer in Agricultural Education. Education: M.A.(Cantab.); D.T.A.(Trin.), Diploma in Tropical Agriculture, Trinidad. Married, 2 children. Appointments: Agricultural Officer, Uganda Government, 1954-63; Lecturer, Arapai Agricultural College, Uganda, 1963-69; Lecturer in Agricultural Education, Makerere University, 1969-70. Publications: Agriculture in Bukedi District, Uganda, Arapai Agricultural College, 1967. Address: Makerere University, P.O. Box 7062, Kampala, Uganda.

KERR, Glennys Scott, born 25th June 1934. Medical Practitioner; Missionary. Education: Bristol University Medical School, U.K., 1952-59; M.B., Ch.B.; D.(Obs.); R.C.O.G. Married, 3 children. Appointments: Doctor in Charge, Medical Unit, Diocese of Central Tanganyika (Church of England), Dodoma, Tanzania. Memberships: British Medical Association; Church Missionary Society of Australia. Address: P.O. Box 164, Dodoma, Tanzania.

KERR, Stanley, born 20th August 1936. Pharmacist. Education: University of Sydney, N.S.W., Austrialia; Qualified as Pharmacist, 1957. Married, 3 children. Appointments: Pharmacist, Sydney; Pharmacist & Manager, Central Tanganyika Chemist, Dodoma, Tanzania. Memberships: Pharmaceutical Societies of N.S.W. & Great Britain; Church Missionary Society of N.S.W. Address: Box 164, Dodoma, Tanzania.

KERRY, (Rev.) Josiah Ofili, born Akwukwu, Midwestern Nigeria, 10th January 1907. Clergyman. Education: Anglican Central School, Akwukwu; Lic. Diploma, National College of Music & Arts, London, U.K., 1950; Lic. Diploma of Proficiency, National Academy of Music Ltd., 1951. Married, 2 sons, 3 daughters. Appointments include: Anglican Church Organist & Choirmaster, 1931-63; one of Leaders, Akwukwu, 1931-62; Licensed Lay

Reader, Anglican Church, 1939-63; Co-Founder, Asaba Divisional Union, Lagos, 1950; Philosopher, Family Adviser, Speaker on Ibo Tradition, News Translator from English to Ibo, Newsreader in Ibo, Ibo Programme, Nigerian Broadcasting Corporation, 1952-63; President-General, Izu Njiko Akwukwu, 1957-62; President-General, St. John's Christian Movement, 1962-69; Ordained, 1964. Memberships include: Literary Club, Kaduna, 1935; Social Club, Jos, 1942; Nigerian Association of Church Musicians, Lagos, 1959; Editorial Committee, ibid, 1960. Publications include: Composer & Publisher, Church Hymns in Traditional Ibo Music, 1949; ibid, Two Church Responses in Ibo Traditional Music, 1950 & 1960. Honours include: Certificate of Honour, H.M. Queen Elizabeth II, 1953; Coronation Medal, 1953. Address: c/o Mrs. Felicia Ada Azuekwu, Post Office Akwukwu, Via Issele-Uke, Midwestern Nigeria.

KESE, Adu Gyamfi, born 14th March 1934. Nutritionist; Lecturer. Education: D.T.A., University of Science & Technology, Kumasi, Ghana; B.S. & M.S., University of Rhode Island, Kingston, R.I., U.S.A. Married, with children. Appointments: Lecturer; Acting Head, Department of Animal Production, University of Science & Technology, Kumasi; Senior Tutor, Unity Hall. Memberships: American Society of Animal Science; Ghana Society of Animal Science; Ghana Agricultural Science Association; Regional Planning Committee, B/A, Ghana; Board of Governors, Sunyani Secondary School. Papers in field published in prof. jrnls. Address: Department of Animal Production, University of Science & Technology, Kumasi, Ghana.

KESIRO, Samuel Bolaji, born 16th November, 1914. Barrister; High Court Judge, Cameroons. Education: Igbobi College, Lagos, Nigeria; Inns of Court, School of Law, London, U.K.; Trinity College, Dublin, Ireland. Married, 3 children. Appointments: Magistrate, Nigeria & Cameroons, 1959-61; Chief Magistrate, Cameroons, 1961-62; Chief Registrar, ibid, 1962-66; High Court Judge, 1966—. Fellow, Chartered Corporation of Secretaries. Address: High Court, Buea, West Cameroon.

KESSEY, Kwadwo Ohemen, born 21st March 1932. Engineer. Education: Wesley College, Kumasi, Ghana, 1951; B.Sc. Engineering, University of Illinois, U.S.A., 1959; M.Sc., D.Sc. Engineering, Columbia University, N.Y., 1963. Married, 2 children. Appointments: Teacher, Kokofu Middle School, Ghana; Mathematics Tutor, Prempeh College; Lecturer, City University of New York, U.S.A.; Senior Lecturer & Associate Professor, Mechanical Engineering Department, University of Science & Technology, Ghana. Memberships: Sigma Xi; A.S.M.E. Author of research papers published in engineering and scientific journals. Address: University of Science & Technology, Kumasi, Ghana.

KGOPO, Mokwadi Tom Mokgabisi, born Kanye, Botswana, 5th August 1925. Civil Servant. Education: B.A., University of South Africa; Worcester College, Oxford University, U.K. Married, 2 daughters. Appointments: joined Botswana Public Service, 1948; Clerical Officer; Assistant Establishment Officer; District Officer; Assistant Secretary, Secretariat; Principal, Ministry of Education; Under-Secretary; Permanent Secretary at Ministry of Local Government & Lands & Ministry of Education, since 1966; Permanent Secretary, Ministry of Health, Labour, & Home Affairs, 1970—. Memberships: Notwane Club; Botswana Society. Honours: M.B.E., 1966. Address: c/o Ministry of Health, Labour, & Home Affairs, P/Bag 2, Gaborone, Botswana.

KHADER, Mohamed, born 1st August 1929. Teacher; Pedagogical Adviser. Married, 3 sons, 3 daughters. Appointments: Teacher, Lycée de Bizerte, 1952; Pedagogical Adviser, 1962—. Memberships: Deputy Mayor, Bizerte, 1957-60; Municipal Councillor, 1960-63; First Vice-President, Municipality of Bizerte, 1966-69; Municipal Councillor, ibid, 1969—. Author of various articles in Tunisian journals & reviews. Address: 39 rue de Tunis 39, Bizerte, Tunisia.

KHAMISI, Francis Joseph, born Rabai, Kilifi District, Kenya. Journalist; Editor. Education: School Certificate, Catholic Higher School, Kabaa, Kenya. Married, 11 children. Appointments include: Editor, Baraza, 1939 —; Member, Kenya Legislative Assembly, 1958-60; Member, Central Legislative Assembly, 1957-61; Member, Mombasa Municipal Council, 1950-61; Member, Nairobi Municipal Council, 1945-57. Memberships include: General Secretary, Kenya African Union, 1944-46; President, Mombasa African Democratic Union, 1956-60; Agricultural Society of Kenya; Chairman, Kenya Press Club; President, Nairobi Coast Social Club; I.P.I. Publications: Baraza. Address: P.O. Box 30080, Nairobi, Kenya.

KHAN, Ali Ahmad, born 17th September 1938. University Lecturer. Education: B.Sc. (Hons.), M.Sc., Dacca University, East Pakistan; Ph.D., Manchester University, U.K. Married. Appointments: Lecturer, Chemistry, M.C. Government College, E. Pakistan, 1960-62; Research Fellow, Pak-Atomic Energy Commission, 1962; CENTO Research Fellow, CENTO Institute of Nuclear Science, Tehran, Iran, 1962-63; Lecturer, Chemistry, University College, Cape Coast, Ghana, 1967—. Memberships: Ghana Science Association; Participant & Contributor of paper, 7th Biennial Conference, West African Science Association, Ibadan, Nigeria, 1970. Contributor to scientific journals. Address: Chemistry Department, University College, P.O. Box 013, Cape Coast, Ghana.

KHAN, Edward Joseph Aladad, born 15th January 1924. Soil Chemist. Education: Primary & Secondary Education in Guyana: B.Sc. (Chemistry), University of Edinburgh, U.K., 1949; M.Sc., Diploma in Agricultural Science, University of Wales, 1958. Appointments: served as a Voluntary Recruit in the Royal Air Force, World War II, 1944-46; Assistant Agricultural Chemist, British Guiana (now Guyana), 1950-56; Agricultural Chemist, British Guiana, 1958-61; Soil Chemist, Tanganyika Sisal Growers' Association, 1962; Research Officer, i/c Kpong Station, Ghana, 1963—. Memberships: British Soil Science Society; International Soil Science

Society; Ghana Soil Science Society. Publications include: Chemical studies of upland peat in North Wales & humic acid (joint Author), J. Sci. Food Agric., 1959; White Sands of the Berbice Formation, British Guiana (co-author), Journal of Soil Science, 1963; several papers related to rice production in Ghana at West African Rice Seminars in Ghana & Nigeria. Contributor to 'Ghana Farmer'. Recip. of British War Medal, World War II, 1939-45. Address: University of Ghana, Agricultural Research Station, P.O. Box 9, Kpong, Ghana.

KHAN, Shakir Husain, born 15th March 1930. District Medical Officer. Education: B.Sc.(Hons). Microbiology; M.B., B.S. Married, 3 children. Appointments: House Position, 1958-60; Medical Officer, Pakistan Government, 1960-63; Medical Officer, Northern Nigeria, 1963-67; District Medical Officer, Nigerian Railway Corporation, Zaria, 1967—. Fellow of Royal Society of Tropical Medicine & Hygiene, London. Memberships: British Medical Association; Pakistan Medical Association. Address: c/o Nigerian Railway Corporation, Zaria, Nigeria.

KHANIWA, Sabiano Jackson, Born Khanyizira V.H., 1920. Farmer. Education: Primary, Standard II. Appointments: Farmer, Tea Holding of 6½ acres; Brick Maker, Burnt & Concrete Blocks. Address: Smallholder Tea Authority, c/o Box 51, Mlanje, Malawi.

KHANNA, Dwarka Nath, born 25th December 1912. Advocate, High Court of Kenya. Education: Government Indian School, Nairobi, Kenya, 1918-29; Wembley School of Commerce, 1930; London School of Economics, U.K., 1931-34; Called to the Bar, Middle Temple, 1934. Appointments: Advocate, High Court of Kenya, 1935—; in practice as a Lawyer, Nairobi, Kenya. Address: P.O. Box 1197, Baring Arcade, Standard Street, Nairobi, Kenya.

KHIMJI, Nizar Shivji, born Masaka, Uganda, 10th February 1942. Electrical Engineer. Education: H.H. The Aga Khan School, Masaka, Uganda, 1948-54; Government Secondary School (Old), Kampala, 1955; Government Secondary School, Masaka, 1956-59; College of Technology, Portsmouth, U.K., 1960-62; G.C.E. O Level (11 subjects); A Level (4 subjects); Scholarship Level (1 subject); B.Sc.(Eng.), Imperial College of Science & Technology, University of London, U.K., 1962-65; Associateship of the City & Guilds, London Institute (A.C.G.I.). Appointments: Graduate Engineer in Training, Graduate Apprentice, Messrs Crompton Parkinson Ltd., Chelmsford, U.K., 1966-68; Assistant Engineer, Section Engineer, Ag. District Manager, Uganda Electricity Board, Kampala, Uganda, 1968—. Memberships include: Associate of the City & Guilds London Institute; Institute of Electrical & Electronics Engineers, U.S.A.; Assoc. Member, Institution of Electrical Engineers, U.K.; Engineering Institute of Canada; East African Institute of Engineers; Institution of Electrical & Electronics Technician Engineers, U.K. Honours, Prizes, etc: Joint 2nd Prize, Arthur Acland English Essay Competition, Imperial College, London, 1965. Address: Kampala District Office, Uganda Electricity Board, P.O. Box 7143, Kampala, Uganda.

KHOFI-PHIRIR, Gowoka Nobi Kalowamfumbi, born 26th September 1931. Businessman; Member of Parliament. Education: Lunga Chiboko Village School, Nkhota Kota; Class III, Dwambazi School, ibid; Standard III, Bandawe Senior Primary School, Chintheche, 1943-45; Standard IV-VI, Kongwe Senior Primary School, Dowa, 1945-48; Standard X, Catholic Secondary School, Zomba, 1948-52; Commercial Course, Dedza Government Secondary School, 1953-54. Married, 7 children. Appointments: Organizing Secretary, Nyasaland African Congress; Director, Nkhota Kota Produce & Trading Society; Acting Secretary-General, Malawi Congress Party, 1960; Manager, Nkhota Kota Rice Co-operative Society Ltd.; Secretary, Malawi Goodwill Mission to West African Countries, 1965; 3rd Secretary, Malawi Embassy, Washington, D.C., U.S.A.; Member, Malawi Delegation to UN, 1965, 1966; Leader, Malawi Delegation to A.D.B., Abidjan, 1967; Member of Parliament, Nkhota Kota; Parliamentary Secretary, Ministry of Trade & Industry; ibid, Ministry of Economic Affairs; Leader of various international delegations. Address: Kalowamfumbi Township, P.O. Box 9, Nkhota Kota, Malawi.

KHOLKHOLLE, Alex, born 1933. Member of Parliament. Education: Teachers' Training College, Kamwenja-Nieri, 1955-56. Married, 1 son. Appointments: Headmaster, Marsabit Primary School, 1959-60; Vice-President of Northern Province People's Progressive Party, 1961-62; elected to Parliament, 1969. Address: P.O. Box 1842, Nairobi, Kenya.

KIBEDI, Wanume, born 3rd August 1941. Advocate. Education: Busoga College, Mwiri, Jinja, Uganda, 1955-60; articled to Waterhouse & Co., Solicitors, London, U.K., 1961-66; admitted as Solicitor to Supreme Court, 1966; LL.B.(Hons), University of London, 1968. Appointments: Secretary, Uganda Students' Association, U.K. & Eire, 1964-65; Vice-President, ibid, 1965-66; Founder, Chairman, Uganda Radical Students' Union, U.K., 1967-68; Treasurer, Uganda People's Congress, U.K., 1965-68; Editor, Black Star (organ of Organization of Uganda Students & Youth in Europe), 1966-68. Member, Uganda Law Society. Contributor of pamphlets and articles to various journals. Recipient, Taylor Essay Prize, Busoga College, Mwiri. Address: 22 Kampala Road, P.O. Box 2750, Kampala, Uganda.

KIBIRA, Emmanuel Bigirwa, born 10th October 1923. Senior Education Officer. Education: Primary, 1933-36; Secondary, 1937-42; Teachers' College, 1943-44. Widower, 6 children. Appointments: Secondary School Teacher, Mpwapula-Bukoba, 1944-52; Middle School Headmaster, Musoma, 1953-57; District Education Officer, Kwimba-Maswa, 1957-61; Regional Education Officer, D.S.M., 1962-69; at Ministry of Education Headquarters, 1970. Memberships: Vice-Chairman, Society for the Blind; ibid, Rehabilitation Centre; International Commissioner, Scouting; Council, Tanzania Society for the Preservation & Care of Animals; Editorial Advisory Board for Target & Lengo;

Salvation Army Appeal Committee. Joint Author, Nyakato Song Book. Address: Ministry of National Education, Box 9121, Dar es Salaam, Tanzania.

KIBISU, Peter Frederic, born 15th March 1932. Senior Management Executive; Trade Unionist; Politician. Education: Government Secondary School, Kakamega, Kenya; Post Office Training School, Mbagathi, Nairobi; Graduate School of Business Administration, Harvard University, U.S.A. Married, 6 children. Appointments: Telecommunications Engineer, P. & T. Corporation, 1949-59; Lecturer, P. & T. Corporation School, Mbagathi, Nairobi; Full-time Trade Union Secretary, General Secretary, President, Post Officer Workers' Union; Secretary-General, Kenya Federation of Labour, 1960—63; Senior Management Executive, Personnel Relations Co-ordinator & later Administration Manager, Shell Companies in East Africa (Kenya & Uganda), 1963-67; Advertising Account Executive, 1968; Member for Vihiga Constituency, Kenya National Assembly, 1969; currently, Assistant Minister for Labour, Government of Kenya. Associate Member, Kenya Institute of Management. Address: P.O. Box 326, Nairobi, Kenya.

KIBUKA, Florence, born Buddo, Uganda, 15th August 1940. Nursing Sister. Education: King's College, Buddo; Pre-nursing Course, U.K. Appointments: General Nursing, obtained S.R.N., 1962-65; Staff Nurse, Weston super Mare, 1966; obtained Midwifery S.C.M., 1967; completed Premature Course, Derby, Certificate held, 1968. Memberships: Brownie Guider, 1958-61; Sunday School Teacher, Uganda. Recipient, Progress Prize, General Nursing, 1964. Address: Mengo Hospital, P.O. Box 7161, Kampala, Uganda.

KIBUKAMUSOKE, John William, born Kampala, Uganda, 11th July 1927. Consultant Physician. M.B., Ch.B., Makerere Univ. Coll., 1954; D.T.M.&H., Liverpool Univ., U.K., 1960; M.R.C.P., Edinburgh, 1961; M.D., Univ. of East Africa, 1966; F.R.C.P., Edinburgh, U.K., 1968. Married, 4 children. Appointments include: Internship in Med., 1955; House Officer, Ob.-Gyn., 1956; House Officer, Paediatrics, Med. Rsch. Council's Infantile Malnutrition Unit, Mulago, 1956; Casualty Off., Mulago Hosp., 1956; Gen. Duty Med Off., Mbarara District Hosp., 1957; Sr. House Off. in Med., Mulago Hosp., 1958; Med. Registrar, 1959; Clinical Attachment, London Hosp., London, U.K., 1960-61; Sr. Registrar & Med. Off., Mulago Hosp., 1961-62; Hon. Clinical Lectr., Makerere Univ. Coll. Med. Schl., Uganda, 1961-67; Cons. Physician, New Mulago Hosp., 1962-66; Sr. Cons. Physician, 1966-67; Chmn., East African Med Rsch. Council, 1963-66; Sr. Lectr. in Med., Dept. of Med., Makerere Univ. Coll. Med. Schl., 1967-68; Professor of Clinical Medicine, ibid, 1968—. Memberships include: Uganda Poisons & Pharmacy Bd., 1962—; Pres., Uganda Med. Assoc., 1963; Past Pres., Family Planning Assoc. of Uganda; Chmn., Med. Comm., ibid, 1963-67; Bd. Mbr., Fac. of Med., Makerere Coll. Med. Schl., 1964—; W.H.O. Expert Advisory Panel, Parasitic Diseases, 1965—; Gvrng. Council, New Int. Coll. of trop. Med.; Pres., East African Acad. Contbr. Author of 31 publications including 'The Nephrotic Syndrome of Quartan Malaria (book), 1970. Honours include: Arthur Storrock Prize, Makerere Univ., 1949; Louis Mitchell Prize for published work, 1965. Address: Makerere Coll. Medical Schl., P.O. Box 7072, Kampala, Uganda.

KIBUKAMUSOKE, Sanyu N., born Uganda, 24th March 1943. Housewife & Secretary. Education: Nabumali High School; Temple College, Nairobi; Paris, France. Married to Professor J. W. Kibukamusoke. Appointments: Personal Secretary, E.A. Tobacco, Nairobi, Kenya Dairy Board, & Uganda Electricity Board, Kampala. Member of Executive Committees of several voluntary organizations in Uganda. Address: P.O. Box 1555, Kampala, Uganda.

KIBWANA, Daudi, born 19th March 1920. Teacher. Education: Central School; St. Andrew's College, Minaki; Grade 1, Teachers' Certificate, 1943. Married. Appointments: Teacher, 1934-39; Army Service, 1944-46. Memberships: Scoutmaster, 1954-60; Tanzanian Society for Prevention of Cruelty to Animals; Tanganyika African National Union. Address: P.O. Box 9121, Dar es Salaam, Tanzania.

KIENTEGA, Joseph, born Tanonsgo Yako, 1928. Census Taker to the Ambassador. Married, 5 children. Appointments: Secretary-General, Free Workers' Union, Ouagadougou, Upper Volta, 1957; Vice-President, l'Association des Originaires du Cercle de Yako, Ouagadougou, 1957; Cabinet Attaché, Ministere de l'Elevage et des Eaux et Forets, 1959; Checker to the Mayor of Ouagadougou, 1959; assigned to the Ministry of Foreign Affairs, 1961; assigned to the Ambassador of the Upper Volta to Ghana, Accra, as Census Taker, 1961; assigned to the Consulate-General of the Upper Volta at Kumasi, 1962; assigned to the Embassy at Accra, 1963; nominated Official Attaché to the Ambassador of the Upper Volta at Accra, Ghana, 1964; attached to the Cabinet of the Ministry of Foreign Affairs. Memberships: President, Association for the Economic Development of the Upper Volta, 1958; ibid, Theatrical Group, Cultural & Sports Association for the Free Workers & Fishermen of Ouagadougou, 1957. Honours: Gold Medal, Awarded by the Chamber of Commerce & Agriculture. Address: c/o Ministry of Foreign Affairs, Ouagadougou, Upper Volta.

KIGONGO MUSITWA, Yozefu, born Mitala Maria, 28th February 1908. Farmer; Member of Parliament. Education: St. John's High School, Nandere, 1923-24; St. Mary's College, Kisubi, 1925-26; Makerere University College, Kampala, 1927-29; Diploma in Agriculture, 1937. Married, 10 children. Appointments: Assistant Agricultural Officer, Uganda, 1930-59; Member of Parliament, Uganda, 1962—; Mixed Farming; President, Kukula Kwa Buganda Growers' Co-op. Soc. Ltd., Mukono. Member of Commonwealth Parliamentary Association. Recipient, Independence Queen's Medal, 1962. Address: P.O. Box 14182, Mengo, Uganda.

KIHAMPA, Johnson Wallace, born 2nd October 1924. Educator. Education: Grade 1

Teachers' Certificate, 1944; Cambridge School Certificate, 1956; C.H.S. Certificate, 1958; Associate of London Institute of Education, 1960. Married, 10 children. Appointments: Headmaster, 1953-59; District Education Officer, 1961-63; Executive Officer, 1963-65; Junior Minister, 1967-68; Minister, 1968—. Memberships: Secretary, Tanganyika Students' Association in the United Kingdom, 1959-60; Secretary-General, Tanganyika Union of African Teachers, 1960-61; Secretary, Association of Local Rural Authorities of Tanganyika, 1963-65. Address: Ministry of Lands, Housing, & Urban Development, P.O. Box 9132, Dar es Salaam, Tanzania.

KIHUGURU, George Baziwe, born 24th August 1933. University Dean. Education: B.A.(London); Dip. Educ. (East Africa). Married, 5 children. Appointments: Teacher, Ntare Secondary School, 1959-63; Minister of Education, Ankole Kingdom Government, 1963-65; Minister of Health & Works, ibid, 1965-67; Warden, Mitchell Hall, 1968-69; Dean, Makerere University, Kampala, 1970—. Memberships: Chairman, Membership Committee, Mbarara Branch, Y.M.C.A., 1965-67; Chairman, Mbarara Branch, Save the Children Fund, 1964-67. Address: Makerere University, Kampala, P.O. Box 7062, Kampala, Uganda.

KIMAMBO, Immaneuel Ndelahiyosa, born 6th January 1943. Civil Engineer. Education: Primary Education, Moshi, Tanzania, 1950-54; Old Moshi Secondary School, Moshi, 1955-62; B.Sc.(Engrng.), University College, Nairobi, Kenya, 1966. Appointments: Assistant Executive Engineer, 1966-69; Resident Engineer, Mwanza Airport Reconstruction; Regional Engineer, Mwanza Region. Memberships: Institution of Civil Engineers; East African Institution of Engineers; Hisorical Association of Tanzania. Address: Ministry of Communications, Transport & Labour, P.O. Box 9144, Dar es Salaam, Tanzania.

KIMBUZI, Gabriel Yohana, born 27th February 1929. Marine, Plant & Mechanical Engineer. Education: Senior Cambridge Certificate, 1949; Higher National Diploma in Mechanical Engineering, 1956. Married, 5 children. Appointments: Assistant Engineer, Shell Company, 1959-62; Mechanical Engineer, Tanzania Government, 1962-68; Senior Mechanical Engineer, Tanzania Government, 1968—. Memberships: Institution of Plant Engineers; Institution of Mechanical Engineers; Associate, Institute of Marine Engineers; Associate, British Institute of Management. Address: P.O. Box 9144, Dar es Salaam, Tanzania.

KIMDE (Prince) Wilfred Kaunlu, born Guyuk, Nigeria, 1939. Teacher; Law Student. Education: Senior Primary School, 1951-57; Teachers' College, Numan, Nigeria, 1958-60; Higher Teachers' College, Numan, Nigeria, 1962-63; Rural Education College, Minna, 1966-67. Personal details: father is one of Guyuk Ruling Family. Appointments include: Assistant Headmaster, Yungur Pr. School, 1961—; Headmaster, Gurum Pr. School, 1965; ibid, Guyuk Pr. School, 1967-69; Law Student, Ahmadu Bello University, Zaria. Memberships include: when a Student, Chairman of Numan Debating Society; Sports Editor, T.C. Numan, 1963. Address: c/o Faculty of Law, Ahmadu Bello University, Zaria, Nigeria.

KINGDON, Jonathan, born Tabora, Tanzania, 1935. Artist; Mammalogist. Education: Oxford University Diploma in Fine Art; Associate of The Royal College of Art (A.R.C.A.), U.K. Appointments: Senior Lecturer, Makerere University, Uganda. Memberships: Founder of Young Commonwealth Artists' Group, 1958; Trustee, Uganda Museum; Committee Member, Uganda Society. Exhibitions: Uganda, Tanzania, Kenya, & U.K. Public Commissions include: bronzes, stained-glass windows, mosaics, & murals in Uganda, Tanzania, & Kenya. Publications: Book on mammalia evolution (in press); illustrations for books & educational publications; reviews on art education & visual perception. Address: Makerere University, Kampala, Uganda.

KINUNDA, Michael Joseph, born 5th May 1934. Assistant Director of National Education (Planning & Development). Education: St. Francis College, Pugu, Dar es Salaam, Tanzania, 1952-53; Makerere University College, Kampala, Uganda, 1954-58; B.Sc.(London), 1958; Dip. Ed.(E.A.), 1959; M.A., Mathematics, Boston College, Massachusetts, U.S.A., 1963; Montclair State College, 1963; Educational Testing Services, Princeton, 1965; International Institute for Educational Planning, UNESCO, Paris, France, 1967-68. Appointments: Teacher, St. Francis College, Pugu, Dar es Salaam, 1959-61; Assistant Headmaster, Mzumbe Secondary School, Morogno, 1963-64; Inspector of Schools, Responsible for Mathematics & Physics, Central Inspectorate, Ministry of Education Headquarters, 1964-67; Assistant Director & Head of Planning Unit, Ministry of Education, 1967—. Memberships: Science Teachers' Association, Tanzania; The Mathematical Association, Tanzania; The Tanganyika Society; Y.M.C.A.; Director, The Music Conservatoire of Tanzania, Ltd. Address: Ministry of National Education, P.O. Box 9121, Dar es Salaam, Tanzania.

KINYANJUI, Peter Erastus, born 2nd April 1940. University Lecturer; Assistant Director of Institute. Education: Alliance High School, Kikuyu, Kenya; B.A.(Hons.), London, Makerere University College, Uganda; M.A.(Educ.), Syracuse University, New York, U.S.A. Appointments: Lecturer, Radio/TV, University of Nairobi; Senior Lecturer, ibid; Assistant Director, Institute of Adult Studies. Memberships: Future Plans Committee, International Council on Correspondence Education, 1969-73; Hon. Sec., Academic Staff Association of University of Nairobi, 1968-69, 1969-70. Publications: The Geography of Kenya (w. P. Fordham), 1967; Third Party Insurance in Short East African Plays in English, 1968; Evaluation of First Dag Hammarskjold Seminar on Correspondence Instruction in adult Education, Uppsala, 1967. Address: Institute of Adult Studies, University of Nairobi, P.O. Box 30197, Nairobi, Kenya.

KIRANGWA, Simon M., born Masaka District, Uganda, 13th December 1940. Accountant. Education: General Certificate of Education. Appointments: Internal Auditor, Ministry of Works, Uganda Government, Entebbe; Financial Attaché, United Nations Development Project Jinja, Uganda; Accounts Officer, East African Common Services Organization; Accountant, East African Community, Nairobi, Kenya. Address: East African Community, P.O. Box 30462, Nairobi, Kenya.

KIRWAN-TAYLOR, Harold Timothy, born 14th August 1930. Civil Servant; Administrative Officer. Education: Eton College, U.K., 1943-48. Married, 1 son, 1 daughter. Appointments: Royal Horse Guards, 1948-54; Administrative Officer, N. Rhodesia/Zambia, 1955-65; District Commissioner, 1961-65; Principal, 1965; Principal Assistant Secretary, Cabinet Office, Government of Lesotho, 1968-70. Honours: Officer, Order of Menelik II, Ethiopia. Address: P.O. Box 527, Maseru, Lesotho

KISSEITH, Docia Angelina Naki, Born Odumase Krobo, Ghana, 13th August 1919. Nurse; Midwife. Education: Presbyterian Primary School, Odumase Krobo; Krobo Girls' School, ibid; Cambridge School Certificate, Achimeta College, Accra; S.R.N., St. Thomas' Hospital, London, U.K.; Midwifery Training, Maternity Hospital, Korle Bu, Accra, Ghana; S.C.M., Queen Charlotte's Maternity Hospital, London, U.K.; N.A.C., Royal College of Nursing, London. Personal details: Granddaughter of Princess Naki Sackitey of the Manya Krobo Royal Family. Appointments: Staff Midwife, Maternity Hospital, Accra, Ghana, 1943-48; Manya Krobo District Midwife, 1948-49; Senior Sister, 1953-58; Hospital Matron, Director, Hospital Nursing Service, 1958-59; Senior Matron, Senior Director, ibid, 1959-60; Deputy Chief Nursing Officer, Ministry of Health, Accra, 1960-61; Chief Nursing Officer, ibid, 1961–. Memberships include: Nurses Board, Ghana, 1960–; Midwives Board, Ghana, 1960–; Central Council, Ghana Red Cross Society, 1960–; National Executive Committee, ibid; Private Hospitals & Maternity Homes Board, 1960–; Expert Advisory Panel on Nursing, WHO, 1961; Director, St. John Ambulance Association, 1961–; Secondary School Board of Governors, 1964; President, Ghana Girl Guides Association, 1965-; National Health Planning Committee, Ministry of Health, 1967–. Contributor to nursing journals. Honours: Manya Krobe State Council's Meritorious Award, 1964; Ghana Registered Nurses' Association Meritorious Award, 1966. Address: Ministry of Health, P.O. Box M-44, Accra, Ghana.

KITAKA, George Edward Bell, born 5th November 1937. Limnologist. Education: Namilyango College, 1958; B.Sc.(London), Makerere University College, 1965; M.Sc., University of Southampton, 1967; currently working on Ph.D., Makerere University, Kampala. Current Appointment: Assistant Director, E.A.F.F.R.O. Memberships: Entertainments Chairman, University Hall, Makerere University College, 1961-62, 1962-63; President, Abaana ba Buganda, ibid, 1963-64; Asst. Treasurer, Uganda Students' Association, 1963-64. Address: E.A.F.F.R.O., P.O. Box 343, Jinja, Uganda.

KITAW AZENE (Kenyamach), born 13th February 1915. Civil Servant. Married, 8 children. Appointments: Assistant to Chief Secretary, Lemu & Kalale Courts, 1929-35; Personal Envoy from His Imperial Majesty to people of Gojjam Province; Chief Secretary of War in Insero, 1941; served w. Insero Battalion I; Chief Secretary, Bichena District, Gojjam Province, 1944-48; Chief Secretary for Mocha & Bichena, 1948-50; Co-ordinator, Office of the Governor of Gojjam, 1950-51; served in Kola & Dega, Damot District; Chief Secretary, Tegulet & Bulga District, 1951-56; transferred to Menz & Yifat, 1956-62; District Governor, Bere District, Bale Province, 1962; Assistant District Governor, Elkare District, 1963; District Governor of Horo-Gudro District, Wollega Province, 1966–. Memberships: Merha-Bete Development Organization; Wollega Province Development Organization; President, Gudru District Development Organization. Honours: Medal w. five stripes for service in war effort, Victory Medal, & Medal of High Honour, 1961. Address: Gudru Awraja, Welega, Ethiopia.

KITCHIN, Robert William Fox, born 24th December 1931. Civil Servant. Education: M.A.(Cantab.). Married to Alison M. Chambers. Appointments: District Commissioner, Nyasaland Protectorate; Senior Administrative Officer, Office of Prime Minister, Malawi; Under-Secretary, Ministry of Works & Supplies, Malawi. Awarded M.B.E., 1968. Address: Ministry of Works & Supplies, Private Bag 45, Zomba, Malawi.

KITITWA, Jean-Marie, born Kitutu, 25th July 1929. Journalist; Business Executive. Education: Modern Humanities; Diploma, Marist Brothers School of Pedagogy, Nya-Ngezi. Personal details: grandson of the Great Chief Wamuzimu Longangi Mpaga & the Great Kazuza Mugelya-wa-Kinkaga who were founders of the Lega-Muzimi House (Kivu). Appointments: Deputy, 1960-65; Senator, 1965; Minister of Planning & Industrial Development; Ministry of Industry; Ministry of Fundamental Affairs; Ministry of Foreign Trade; First Secretary, Member, Political Bureau, Popular Revolutionary Movement; Editor, Echos de l'Est (weekly paper). Memberships: Administrator, President, United Agencies Company; Representative, The Statesman Mining Company. Author of several articles. Honours: Commander, National Order of the Leopard, Congo; Commander of Merih, Central African Republic. Address: P.O. Box 3249, Kinshasa/Kalina, Democratic Republic of the Congo.

KITOYI (Lieutenant) Arcade Romuald, born 30th January 1942. Army Officer. Education: Catholic Mission Primary School, St. Anne, Attake, Porto-Novo, 1949-56; Bac I, Bac II, African Military School of St. Louis, 1956-63; Military School, Strasburg, Germany, 1963-65; Officer, Military School of St. Cyr, France, 1965-66; Practical School, Arme Blinée et de la Cavalerie, 1966-67; Army Officer, Dahomean Armed Force (DAO). Director of National

Security from the time of the Provisional Military Regime to the coming of the Civil Regime. Honoured by ex-President Emile Derling Zinzou for services rendered, 1968. Address: Etat-Major des F.A.D., Cotonou, B.P. 772, Dahomey.

KIVUITU, Samuel Mutua, born 16th February 1939. Lawyer. Education: LL.B., University of London, 1964; admitted as Advocate of the High Court of Kenya, 1968. Married, 3 children. Appointments: State Counsel, Attorney General's Office, 1964-66; Resident Magistrate, 1966-68; Practising Lawyer, 1968—; elected Member of Parliament, 1969—. Memberships: Chairman, Mahakar School Old Boys' Association; Secretary, Kenya Association for International Law. Address: P.O. Box 12458, Nairobi, Kenya.

KIWIA, Seki Raymond John, born Kilimanjaro, Tanzania, 30th April 1931. Director, National Institute For Productivity. Education: Cambridge School Certificate; Ruskin College, Oxford, U.K.; Pittsburgh University, U.S.A. Personal details: son of the Founder of the Kilimanjaro Native Co-operative Union Limited. Appointments include: Labour Inspector; Labour Officer; Senior Labour Officer; Assistant Principal Industrial Relations Officer, E.A.R.&H.; Consultant Supervisory Training, National Institute for Productivity; Acting Director, National Institute for Productivity; Director, East African Harbours Corporation. Memberships include: Tanganyika African National Union; Kilimanjaro Native Co-operative Union; Chairman, Tanzania Institute of Management; E.A. Management Institute. Publications include: translated A Job Relations Manual into Swahili. Address: c/o National Institute for Productivity, P.O. Box 2021, Dar es Salaam, Tanzania.

KI-ZERBO, Jacqueline, born 23rd September 1933. Teacher of English. Education: Higher Studies, University of Paris, Sorbonne, France. Appointments: Teacher of English, Dakar, Senegal, 1958; ibid, Conakry, Guinea, 1958-59, 1959-60; Guagadougou, Upper Volta, 1960; Director, Cours Normal de J.F., 1960—. Memberships: Press Secretary, African Educationalists of the Upper Volta, 5 years; Vice-President, Red Cross of Volta.

KIZITO, Edward Kizza, born 11th November 1935. Dental Surgeon. Education: King's College, Buddo; Makerere University College; B.Ch.D., L.D.S., Leeds University, U.K., 1960-65; D.D.P.H., Toronto University, Canada, 1968-69. Married, 1 son, 2 daughters. Appointments: Dental Surgeon, Masaka Hospital, 1966-69; Dental Surgeon (Special Grade), 1969-70; Senior Dental Surgeon, 1970—. Memberships: President, Masaka Medical Club; Secretary, Masaka District Football Association, 1968; Chairman, ibid, 1970; Director, Masaka Division, Uganda Red Cross, 1970. Address: 256 Alexander Road, P.O. Box 18, Masaka, Uganda.

KIZITO, John Ssebaana, born 12th September 1934. Insurance Executive. Education: King's College, Budo; B.A., Makerere University; M.Sc., University of Oregon, U.S.A. Appointments: General Manager, National Insurance Corporation; Director, Bank of Uganda; Member, East African Legislative Assembly. Member, Lions Club. Address: P.O. Box 1415, Kampala, Uganda.

KIZZA-SEKADDE, Daniel, born 24th January 1942. Engineer. Education: Diplomat in Mechanical & Electrical Engineering; Diploma Certificate in General Economics; Intermediate Certificate in Accountancy; Intermediate Certificate in Motor Vehicle Engineering. Appointments: Factory Engineer, Uganda Development Corporation; Technical Officer, East African External Telecommunications Company (Cable & Wireless); Trainee (in field of Cost & Works Accountancy), ibid. Memberships: East African Institution of Engineers; East African Association of Accountants. Address: P.O. Box 14142, Mengo, Uganda.

KLINKENBERG, Kees, born 14th August 1933. Soil Surveyor. Education: Degree in Physical Geography, University of Amsterdam, The Netherlands, 1950-57. Appointments: with Soil Survey, Northern Nigeria, 1957; Senior Soil Survey Officer, Institute of Agricultural Research. Ahmadu Bello University, 1967. Memberships: Royal Netherlands Geographical Society; Royal Netherlands Geol. & Mining Society; Science Association of Nigeria; Nigerian Geographical Assn. Address: Institute for Agricultural Research, P.M.B. 1044, Zaria, Nigeria.

KLOPPER, J. M. L., born 1st July 1928. Medical Administrator & Practitioner. Education: B.A., B.Sc., M.B., B.Ch., University of Witwatersrand, Johannesburg, South Africa; D.P.H., Royal Institute of Public Health, London, U.K. Appointments: Medical Officer, Swaziland Government, 1959; Deputy Director, Medical Services, 1966; Director, Medical Services, Swaziland Government, 1968. Memberships: Chairman, Swaziland, Medical & Dental Associations; Chairman, Swaziland Nursing Council; Member, Botswana, Lesotho, & Swaziland Nursing Examining Board; Chairman, Workmens' Compensation Board: Swaziland Military Pensions Board. Address: Ministry of Health, P.O. Box S, Mbabane, Swaziland.

KLUDZE, Anselmus Kodzo Paaku, born 12th March 1938. Barrister & Solicitor. Education: Roman Catholic Boys' School, Hohoe, Ghana; Adisadd College, Cape Coast, Ghana, 1950-54; B.A.(Hons.), University of Ghana, 1963; LL.B.(Hons.), ibid, 1965; Ph.D., University of London, U.K., 1969. Appointments: Executive Officer, Ghana Civil Service, 1955-59; Lecturer in Law, University of Ghana, Legon, Accra, 1965—. Fellow, Royal Society of Arts, London. Memberships' National President, United Nations Students' Association of Ghana, 1961-62; National President, National Union of Ghana Students, 1962-63; President, Confederation of West African Students, 1963-65; Vice-President, Ghana National Union of Great Britain & Ireland, 1966-69; President, Association of Commonwealth Students, 1967-70. Address: Faculty of Law, University of Ghana, Legon, Accra, Ghana.

KNELLER, Alister Arthur, born Nairobi, Kenya, 11th November, 1927. Barrister-at-Law. Education: The King's School, Canterbury, U.K.; M.A., LL.B., Corpus Christi College, Cambridge; Gray's Inn, London. Personal details: father Arthur Harry Kneller, O.B.E. (deceased). Appointments: Resident Magistrate, Kenya, 1955; Senior Resident Magistrate, 1962; Senior State Counsel, 1966; Registrar, 1967; Judge, The High Court of Kenya, 1969—. Address: The High Court of Kenya, Box 140, Mombasa, Kenya.

KNIGHT, Reginald Arthur, born 21st January 1929. Electrical Engineer. Education: B.Sc., Electrical Engineering, University of the Witwatersrand, South Africa. Appointments: Motor Design Engineer, First Electrical S.A.; Protection Engineer, R.C.B.P.C., Zambia; Planning Engineer, Electricity Trust of South Australia; CHief Engineer, ESCOM, Malawi; Assistant General Manager, ibid. Member of the Institution of Electrical Engineers. Address: P.O. Box 186, Blantyre, Malawi.

KNIGHT, William Arnold, born 14th June 1915. Civil Servant. Education: B.A.(Hons.), University College of North Wales, U.K. Appointments: entered Colonial Audit Department, 1938; Service in Kenya, 1938-46; Mauritius, 1946-49; Sierra Leone, 1949-52; Guyana, 1952-57; Uganda, 1957-68; Auditor General, Uganda, 1962-68; retired, 1968; Economy Commissioner, Uganda, 1969-70. Member of East India & Sports Clubs. Honours: O.B.E., 1954; C.M.G., 1966. Address: P.O. Box 2513, Kampala, Uganda, or Neopardy Mills, nr. Crediton, Devon, U.K.

KOBA, Henry, born 30th August 1936. Journalist. Education: Primary & Secondary Schooling, MBaiki at Bangui, Central African Republic; High Diploma of Journalism, Studio School OCORA (ORTF), Paris, France. Married, 7 children. Editor, Director, Central African Republic Radio Service; ibid, River & Maritime Transport; irector-General, Ministry of Information, Bangui, Central African Republic. Memberships: President, Association of Centrafrican Journalist. Author of a brochure; 'Les Etats—Unis a l'heure des Lois Civiques'. Honours: Knight, National Order of Merit of the Central African Republic. Address: Ministry of Information, Bangui, Central African Republic.

KODWAVWALA, Yusuf, born Bantwa, India, 13th September 1928. Consultant Surgeon. Education: L.C.P.S., Christian Mission Hospital, Miraj, India; M.B., B.S., Grant Medical College, Bombay; F.R.C.S., London, England. Appointments include: Consultant Surgeon; Aga Khan Platinum Jubilee Hospital, Nairobi, Kenya. Memberships include: Member, Rotary Club, Nairobi, Member, Council Medical Association, Kenya, President Elext, 1969; Fellow, East African Surgeons' Association. Publications of mainly surgical interest. Address: P.O. Box 8508, Nairobi, Kenya.

KOFI, Abraham Benjamin Bah, born 12th March 1918. Retired Diplomat. Education: B.A.(Gen.), History & Geography, University College of Southampton, U.K. Married, 5 children. Appointments: Assistant Postal Controller, 1950-53; District Postal Controller, 1953-55; Foreign Service Trainee, 1955-57; 1st Ghanaian Chargé d'Affaires, Monrovia, 1957; Deputy High Commissioner, London, U.K., 1959-60; Head of Foreign Service, 1960-62; Ghana High Commissioner, Pakistan, 1962-66; Ambassador to U.S.A., 1967. Memberships: Elder, National Presbyterian Church, Washington, D.C., U.S.A.; ibid, St. Ninian's Presbyterian Church, Karachi, Pakistan. Honours: Decorated by Nasser, Bourguiba, & Tubman. Address: P.O. Box 5218, Accra, Ghana.

KOFI, Amenu Jonathan. Food Storage Officer. Education: B.Sc.(Agric.), University of Ghana, 1962; Ph.D., Food Science, Nutrition, Food Chemistry, Biochemistry & Biometry, University of Nottingham, U.K., 1966; Postgraduate Studies, ibid, 1966-69; Tropical Stored Products Institute, Slough, 1966. Appointments: Registrar & Teacher, Peki Secondary School, 1959; Agric. Officer, Soil Surveys & Analysis, Irrigation & Reclamation Unit (UNDP), Ministry of Agriculture, 1962-64; Food Storage Officer, Food Research Institute, 1964-65. Address: Food Research Institute, P.O. Box M.20, Accra, Ghana.

KOFI-TSEKPO, Winfried Mawuli, born 25th February 1938. Pharmacist. Education: Kumasi College of Technology, Ghana, 1959-61; B.Pharm.(UST), University of Science & Technology, Kumasi, 1964; M.Pharm.(UST), ibid, 1966; Ph.D., Portsmouth Polytechnic, Portsmouth, U.K., 1970; Post-doctoral Fellow in Medicinal Chemistry, Ohio State University, U.S.A., 1970—. Fellow, Chemical Society (London). Author of papers published in professional journals. Address: College of Pharmacy, Ohio State University, 500 West 12th Avenue, Columbus, Ohio 43210, U.S.A.

KOHLER, Helmold, born 1st November 1924. Master Goldsmith & Jeweller. Education: High School, Germany; Professional High School, Schwabisch-Gmund. Honours, Prizes, etc.: Professional High School Award as Best Scholar of the Year, 1950, 1951. Address: P.O. Box 1720, Windhoek, South West Africa.

KOHLI (Sethi) Tej, born 25th November 1922. Ophthalmologist. Education: Matriculation, Government Girls' High School, Srinagar, India, 1938; F.Sc., Sri Partap College, Srinagar, 1940; M.B., B.S., L.H.M. College, New Delhi, 1946; D.O.(London), 1960. Personal details: from a family of Medical Doctors; married to Dr. J. D. S. Kohli, 2 sons. Appointments: Medical Officer, State Hospital, Srinager, 1947; Medical Officer, Kusukshetsa Medical Relief Camps, 1947; Medical Officer in Charge, Women's Hospital, Ghazrabad, 1949; R.M.O., Women's Hospital, Kampur, 1952; S.H.O., Ophthalmology, Royal Infirmary, Preston, 1955; S.H.O., Ophthalmology, Royal Infirmary, Stoke on Trent, 1956; Registrar, Royal Infirmary, Aberdeen, Scotland, 1957; S.H.O., General Hospital, Kidderminster, 1959; Special Grade Medical Officer, Ophthalmology, Ghana Medical Service, 1961; Specialist Ophthalmologist, Ministry of Health, Ibadan, Nigeria, 1963; Senior

Specialist Ophthalmologist, ibid; Past President, Indian Association.

KOLEY, Chinmoy, born 4th November 1937. Statistician. Education: M.Sc.(Statistics), Calcutta University, India, 1958; Advanced Training in Statistics, Indian Statistical Institute, Calcutta, 1960. Appointments: Statistician, Howrah Improvement Trust, West Bengal, 1960-64; Statistician, Bureau of Statistics, Ministry of Economic Affiars & Development Planning, 1964—. Member of the East African Agricultural Economics Society. Publications: Analysis & Uses of Agriculture Survey Data in Tanganyika (with G. Karmiloff), Directorate of Development Planning, 1965; A Report on the Estimation of Future Traffic on the Road-bridges of Howrah Gty. (with N. Bakshi), Howrah Improvement Trust, W. Bengal, India. Address: Bureau of Statistics, Ministry of Economic Affairs & Development Planning, P.O. Box 796, Dar es Salaam, Tanzania.

KOMAKEC, Leander, born Kitgum, 10th May 1935. Radio & Television Producer. Education: St. Joseph Gulu Junior Secondary School, 1950-51; St. Aloysius College, Nyapea, 1952-55; B.A.(London), Makerere University College, 1961; M.Sc.(Educ.), Indiana University, U.S.A., 1965. Married. Appointments: Radio Programme Organizer, 1961-63; Television Executive Producer, 1965-68; Head of Educational Television Programmes, 1968—. Memberships: Uganda Journalist Club; Ngoma Players; Associate, National Education Association, U.S.A. Address: Educational Television, P.O. Box 3568, Kampala, Uganda.

KOMBET, Jean Pierre, born 26th March 1935. Ambassador of the Central African Republic. Education: former Pupil, Emile Gentil College, Bangui, Central African Republic; ibid, Ecole Normale, Bambari. Married, 10 children. Appointments: Inspector of Education; President of the Cultural Centre, Berberati; Municipal Councillor, Commune of Berberati; Deputy Mayor, ibid; then Mayor; Stage Ecole Normale des Instituteurs de Toulouse, France; Ecole Normale Superieure de Sevres, Paris; Quai d'Orsay, Paris; the Embassy of France in Italy, Rome (Diplomatic Training); First Secretary of the Embassy of the Central African Republic to the Permanent Representation of the United Nations Organization, New York, U.S.A., 1961; Ambassador Extraordinary & Plenipotentiary of the Central African Republic to the U.S.A., 1962-65; Head of the Central African Delegation, 11th International Coffee Conference, Guatamala; Member, Central African Delegation, 15th, 16th, & 17th Sessions, U.N.O., New York, U.S.A.; Permanent Representative, U.N.O., 1963; Head of the Central African Delegation, 4th Session Extraordinary, ibid; Secretary-General to the Ministry of Foreign Affairs, 1965-67; Head, Central African Delegation to the Joint Commission responsible for the Rearrangement & Recognition of the Frontier Boundaries between Central Africa & the Cameroun, 1965; Member, Central African Delegation, Summit Conference, Organization of African Unity, Accra, Ghana, 1965; ibid, Central African Delegation to Afro-Asian Conference, Alger, Algeria, 1965; ibid, Conference de l'Organisation Commune Africaine et Malgache, Tananarive, Madagascar, 1966; Head, Central African Delegation to the Joint Commission of Central Africa & Chad responsible for the Rearrangement & Recognition of the Frontier Boundaries, Batangafo, 1966; 7th Ordinary Session, Council of Ministers, 3rd Summit Conference, Organization of African Unity, Addis Ababa, Ethiopia, 1966; Member, Joint Central African-Sudanese Commission, 1967; Ambassador Extraordinary & Plenipotentiary to the Sudan, 1967; Head, Delegation to the Conference on Industry & Finances, Addis Ababa, 1968; Member, Central African Mission of Good Will to the negotiations for a Commercial Agreement between Central Africa & the Sudan, 1969; Member, 13th Ordinary Session, Council of Ministers, Organization of African Unity, Ethiopia; Delegation Head, 14th Ordinary Session, ibid; Delegation Head, for the Application of the Financial Mechanism of the Central African-Sudanese Commercial Agreement. Honours: Knight of Central African Merit; Commander, the Order of Central African Merit; Knight, Palmes Academiques; Officer, Merit of Chad. Address: P.O. Box 1723, Khartoum, Sudan.

KOMIHA, David George, born 18th March 1932. Works Supervisor. Education: Standard Six. Appointments: Supervisor of tobacco labourers, in charge of curing, grading, & auctioning; also purchasing & treating for export to West African countries. Address: Makoka Valley Estate, P. Bag 2, Namadzi, Malawi.

KONATE, Seydou, born 14th May 1938. Inspector of Labour. Education: Diploma, d'Universite des Sciences du Travail, l'Universite of Paris, France; Diploma, International Institute of Public Administration, Paris. Married, 2 children. Appointments: Regional Inspector of Labour, Ouagadougou, & Eastern Region of Upper Volta; Member, Upper Volta Delegation, Conference of African Ministers of Labour, Zambia, 1970; Government Delegate, Conference de l'Oit, Geneva, 1970. Memberships: Secretary-General, Club de Jeunes; Secretary-General, de l'Association de Soutien pour la Formation Professionnelle en Milieu Rural. Address: B.P. 120, Ouagadougou, Upper Volta, Zambia.

KONDANI, Ferdinand, born 11th October 1925. Administrator. Education: Diploma, l'Ecole des Cadres Superieurs de l'ex-A.E.F., Brazzaville, Republic of the Congo; Diploma, l'Institut des Hautes Etudes d'Outre-Mer, Paris, France. Appointments: Sous-Prefet, 1958; Prefet, 1961; Inspector, Administration & Financial Service, Congo, 1962; Inspector-General, Administration & Financial Service, 1965; Secretaire General du Government, 1967; Administrator, Administration & Financial Service, Congo. Honours: Chevalier de l'Ordre du Merite Congolais. Address: B.P. 472, Brazzaville, Congo.

KONNING, George Henry Kwesi, born 23rd June 1938. Pharmacist. Education: Fijai Secondary School, Sekondi, Ghana; B.Pharm., University of Science & Technology, Kumasi, 1964; M.Pharm., 1966. Married, 1 daughter. Appointments: Demonstrator, Faculty of

Pharmacy, University of Science & Technology, Kumasi, 1965-66; Reader, Pharmaceutics, Chelsea College, University of London, U.K., 1966—. Co-author of publications on the preservation of Pharmaceutical, cosmetic, or industrial emulsions against biodeterioration in scientific journals. Address: Department of Pharmacy, University of Science & Technology, Kumasi, Ghana.

KONOTEY-AHULU, Felix Israel Domeno, born, Odumase-Krobo, 12th July 1930. Medical Practitioner; Senior University Lecturer. Education: Presbyterian Junior & Senior Schools; Presbyterian Secondary School, 1945-46; Achimota Secondary School, 1947-49; Pre-varsity Course, Mfantsipim School, 1950-51; University College, Legon, 1951-53; Norwood Technical College, London, U.K., 1953-54; University College, London, 1954-56; Westminster Hospital Medical School, 1956-59; M.B., B.S.(London), 1959; M.R.C.S., L.R.C.P., 1959; D.T.M.&H.(Liverpool), 1962; M.R.C.P.(Glasg.), 1964; M.R.C.P.(Lond.), 1965. Married, 3 children. Appointments: House Physician, Bethnal Green Hospital, London, 1959; House Surgeon, St. Albans City Hospital, Herts., 1960; Medical Officer, Ministry of Health, Korle Bu Hospital, Accra, Ghana, 1960, 1965, 1969; Clinical Attachment, Westminster Hospital, U.K., 1962; Research Fellow, Department of Medicine, Royal Free Hospital, 1964-65; Lecturer, Ghana Medical School, 1966-70; Senior Lecturer, ibid, 1970—. Memberships: Fellow, Royal Society of Tropical Medicine & Hygiene, 1962; ibid, Royal Society of Medicine, 1966; ibid, Ghana Academy of Arts & Sciences, 1970; Temporary Consultant in sickle cell diseases, WHO, 1968, 1969, 1970. Author of numerous publications in scientific journals. Honours: Commonwealth Scholar, 1963-64; Schofield Scholar, Christs College, Cambridge, 1970. Address: Christ's College, Cambridge, U.K.

KORAKPE, Counsel, born Urhobo, Mid-west Nigeria, 13th April 1934. Educator. Education: Salvation Army School, Enugu, 1945-46; Provincial Teacher Training College, Warri, 1959-60; ibid, Abudu, 1963-64. Married, 5 sons, 2 daughters. Appointments include: Teacher, Ometan Memorial School, Ughoton, Urhobo Division, 1947; Headmaster, ibid, 1961—; Member, Education & Assessment Committee, Western Urhobo District Council, 1965—; Member, Representative Committee, Sapele Land Trustee, 1965-66; Managing Director, C. Korakpe Rubber Estate & Varsity Farms. Memberships include: Chairman, Ughoton Youth Club; President-General of following clubs: Ughoton, Jeddo, Ugedicodo, Omadino, & Ekpa; General Sec., Ughoton Community. Address: Ometan Memorial School, Ughoton Warri, Nigeria.

KORAU, Lere Musa, born Lere, Nigeria, 30th March 1938. Teacher. Education: Junior Primary School, Lere, Nigeria, 1951-54; Senior Primary School, Nigeria, 1955-57; Katsina Teachers' College, Grade III, 1958-60; Katsina Teachers' College, Grade II, 1962-63. Married, 2 wives, 3 children. Appointments include: Headmaster, L.E.A. Primary School, Kauru, 1965-68; Headmaster, L.E.A. Primary School, Kaura, 1965-68; Headmaster, L.E.A. Primary School, Dutsin-Wai, 1969—. Memberships include: Boy Scouts, 1958—; Young Farmers' Club; Dramatizing Society of Northern Nigeria, Kaduna, 1960—. Address: Headmaster, L.E.A. Primary School, P.O. Dutsin-Wai, North Central State, Nigeria.

KORNER, Per, born Oslo, Norway, 26th April 1936. Minister of Religion. Education: Matriculation, 1956; Bachelor of Divinity, 1965. Married. Appointments: Minister in Charge, Hlatikulu Parish of the Evangelical Lutheran Church, 1968—. Address: P.O. Box 41, Hlatikulu, Swaziland.

KORSAH, K. G., born Saltpond, Ghana, 4th July 1928. Surgeon. Education: B.Sc.(Lond.), University of the Gold Coast (now University of Ghana), Legon, 1953; Guy's Hospital Medical School, London, U.K., 1953-58; M.R.C.S., L.R.C.P., M.B., B.S., 1958; F.R.C.S.(Eng.), 1963. Appointments: House Surgeon & Physician, Gravesend & North Kent Hospital, 1958; Medical Officer, Surgical Unit, Kumasi Central Hospital, Ghana, 1959-60; Medical Officer, Department of Ob.-Gyn., ibid, 1960; transferred to Military Hospital Orthopaedic Unit, Accra; Casualty Officer, St. Bartholomew's Hospital, Kent, U.K., 1962; w. Surgical Department, Guy's Hospital, London, 1962-63; Sr. House Officer, Hospital for Sick Children, Great Ormond St., 1963; Supernumerary S.H.O., Robert Jones & Agnes Hunt Orthopaedic Hospital, Oswestry, Shropshire, 1964; Medical Officer, Ghana, 1964-65; Senior Medical Officer in Orthopaedic Surgery, 1966—; Adviser, Ministry of Health; Medical Adviser, Cripples Aid Society. Corresponding Member, African Correspondence Club for Rehabilitation of the Disabled. Author of papers published in med. jrnls. Address: Korle-Bu/Military Hospital, Accra, Ghana.

KOSKE, Richard, born April 1924. Director in Charge of Kenya National Radio & T.V. Services. Education: African Inland Mission, Litein, 1939-40; Government African School, Kabianga, 1941-43; Alliance High School, Kikuyu, Kenya, 1944-47; Kagumo Teacher Training College, 1948; Reading University, U.K., 1961-62. Married, 4 sons, 2 daughters. Appointments: Schoolmaster, 1949-55; Assistant Education Officer, Administration, 1956-60; Education Officer in Charge of Primary & Higher Education, 1962-64; Director of Broadcasting, Kenya National Radio & T.V. Services, 1964—. Memberships: Senior Civil Servants Society; various local clubs. Address: Voice of Kenya, P.O. Box 30456, Nairobi, Kenya.

KOSSUT, Zygmunt Stefan, born 16th April 1922. Economist. Education: B.A., M.A., Ph.D., Warsaw, Poland. Appointments: in Practice, 1941-50; Reader, The Central School of Planning & Statistics, Warsaw, Poland, 1950-67; Reader & Head of Department of Management & Administration, University of Dar es Salaam, Tanzania (former University College, East African University, Dar es Salaam), 1967—. Associate Member, Tanzania Branch, East

African Academy. Publications: Accounting in Home Trade, Warsaw, Poland, 1957; Accounting as Science, Warsaw, 1959; The Comparative Analysis of Economic Activities of Home Trade Enterprises, Warsaw, 1962; Home Trade Economics (with Professor K. Bolzar), 1966, 2nd edn., 1970. Address: Box 35046, Dar es Salaam, Tanzania.

KOTECHA, Govind, born 7th April 1940. Mechanical Engineer. Education: Intermediate Science Exam., University of Bombay, India; B.E.(Mech.), University of Roorkee, India, 1964; Management Training Certificate, Management Training & Advisory Centre, Kampala, Uganda, 1968. Married. Appointments: Engineer (Trainee), Madhvani Sugar Works, Uganda, 1964; Assistant Engineer, ibid, 1965; Assistant to the Chief Engineer, Projects & Development, 1966; Group Project Engineer (Manager), Madhvani Group of Industries, E. Africa, 1968—. Memberships: Associate, Society of Engineers, London; East African Institution of Engineers; Professional Centre of Uganda. Recipient, Thompson Memorial Gold Medal for the Best Industrial Project Work. Address: P.O. Box 3062, Kakira, Uganda.

KOUKOUI, Valere, born 24th June 1927. Commissioner of Police. Education: Diploma, l'Ecole Federale de Police de l'ex A.O.F.; Diploma, l'Ecole Nationale Superieure de Police, Saint-Cyr-Au-Mont-D'or, France. Married, 5 children. Appointments: Central Commissioner, Cotonou, Dahomey, 1962-65; Commissioner, Ouidah, 1965-66; Central Commissioner, Cotonou, 1966-67; Head, Security Service, Ministry of the Interior, Dahomey, 1967-68; Commissioner of Police, Abomey, 1968-70; Director, National Centre of Police Instruction, Cotonou, 1970—. Honours: Commander, Star of Africa; Officer, Order of Benin; Police Medal of Honour, Dahomey. Address: c/o Sureté, Cotonou, Dahomey.

KOULE NJANGA, Theodore, born 10th September 1927. Lawyer; Director. Education: Baccalaureat, Paris, France; D.L., Postgraduate Studies, C.A.P.A. Appointments: Lawyer, Paris; with the Central Bank of Economic Co-operation, Abidjan, Ivory Coast; Director, Cameroun Credit Bank, Douala, Cameroun; ibid, Exchange Bureau, Cameroun; Cameroun Banana Organization. Memberships: President, 1953-54, Vice-President, Association of Camerounian Students in France. Recipient of Cameroun Distinction, 3rd Class. Address: B.P. 221, Douala, Cameroun.

KOZA, Constance Miriam Thokizile, born Benoni, 26th June 1926. Lecturer. Education: Bachelor of Science, South Africa; Diploma in Education, ibid. Married, 1 son, 1 daughter. Appointments: High School Science Teacher, J.H.B., Pretoria, South Africa, 1951-56; Principal, Higher Primary School, Pretoria, 1956-59; Research Worker, Ntn. Ins. Pers. Res. CSIR, 1959-65; Agricultural Officer, Home Economics, Swaziland Government, 1959-67; Lecturer, Swaziland Agricultural College & University Centre, 1967—. Memberships: Branch District Secretary, National Council of African Women; Secretary, Principal's Council; Pretoria District Secretary, Transvaal Teachers' Association; Committee for Higher Education, Y.W.C.A.; Represented Swaziland in Home Economics Seminar, Nairobi, Kenya, 1965 & 1st Conference for Women of S.A., Laurenco Marques, 1970. Publications include: National Council of Women of S.A. Newsletter, 1962; Pitte 'The Township Women'; Swazi Recipes. Address: Swaziland Agricultural College & University Centre, Swaziland.

KPEDEKPO, Gottlieb Mawulor Kwasi, born 25th December 1935. Statistician. Education: B.Sc.(London), 1961; Dip. Statistics, Aberdeen University, U.K., 1963; Ph.D., ibid, 1966. Married, 1 daughter. Appointments: Research Fellow, Isser, 1966-70; Senior Research Fellow, ibid, 1970—. Fellow of the Royal Statistical Society. Memberships: American Statistical Association; International Union for the Scientific Study of Populations; Biometric Society; American Population Associations. Publications: Contributor to: Journal of Royal Statistical Society; Journal of American Statistical Association; Journal of Demography, America; Sankhya. Address: Institute of Statistical, Social, & Economic Research, P.O. Box 74, University of Ghana, Legon, Ghana.

KRAUSS, Hartmut Hans, born 9th November 1932. Veterinarian. Education: Graduated, Munich University, Germany, 1957; Dr. Med. Vet., 1957; Habilitation, 1966. Appointments: Reader, Department of Pathology & Microbiology, Faculty of Vet. Science, University College, Nairobi, Kenya; Apl. Professor in Veterinaerited Fakultaet, Giessen, German Federal Republic. Memberships: World Vet. Poultry Association; German Vet. Med. Society. Author of 30 publications in fields of virology, microbiology, & poultry diseases. Address: Department of Pathology & Microbiology, Faculty of Vet. Science, University College, Nairobi, P.O. Kabete, Kenya.

KRISHNAMURTHY, Kanukollu Venkata, born 24th August 1922. Civil Engineer; Hydrologist. Education: B.C.E., Madras University, India, 1943. Married, 4 children. Appointments include: Resident Engineer, Department of Irrigation, Iraq, 1960-61; Field Manager, India Mekong Tonlesap Investigation Team (Barrage Project), 1961-63; Secretary, Committee of Ministers, Flood Control, Government of India, 1964; Director, Progress Recording, Central Water & Power Commission, 1965; Project Manager, UNDP/WMO, Hydrometeorological Survey of the Catchments of Lakes Victoria, Kyoga, & Albert, for the Governments of Uganda, Tanzania, Sudan, & the U.A.R.; Indian Delegate, numerous conferences & study teams. Fellow of the Institute of Engineers in East Africa. Memberships: American Society of Civil Engineers; Institution of Engineers, India; American Geophysical Union of the Society of International Development. Publications include: Flood Control Planning & Hydrological Studies in the United States. 2 vols.; A Brief Note on Drainage & Water-logging Problems in India; Feasibility Investigations of Water Development Studies (co-author), presented at conference organized by Institution of Civil Engineers, London, 1966.

Address: Hydrometeorological Survey of the Catchments of Lakes Victoria, Kyoga & Albert, P.O. Box 192, Entebbe, Uganda.

KUFUOR, Francis Addo, born 14th February 1926. Organic Chemist. Education: Government Boys' School, Kuamasi, 1931-36; Achimota College, Achimota, 1937-46; B.Sc., Ph.D., University of Bristol, 1947-54. Married, 3 sons, 1 daughter. Appointments: Lecturer, Kumasi College of Technology, Ghana, 1954-61; Professor of Chemistry, University of Science & Technology, 1962-64; Professor of Chemistry, Head of Department of Chemistry & Chemical Technology, ibid, 1966—; Dean, Faculty of Science, 1967—; Pro-Vice-Chancellor, 1967-69; Fellow, Chemical Society, London; Associate, Royal Institute of Chemistry, London. Publications include: various reports on science & technology. Address: Faculty of Science, University of Science & Technology, Kumasi, Ghana.

KULUBYA, Mukasa Joseph, born Rubaga, Uganda, 16th April 1921. Librarian. Education: St. Mary's Coll., Kisubi, 1939-42; Jeaves' Schl., Kabete, Nairobi, Kenya, 1942; Middle East Command Educ. Coll., Gaza, 1944-45; Makerere Univ. Coll., E.A. Schl. of Librarianship, 1965-66. Appointments include: Army Educ. Instr., 1942-46; Sec., Afros Ltd., 1946-48; Labour Insp., Uganda/Kenya, 1948-49; Clerk & Interpreter, Judicial Dept., Uganda Govt., 1950; Rsch. Asst., East African Inst. of Social Rsch., Makerere Univ. Coll., 1957-58; Librarian & Sec., High Court Lib., 1960—. Address: The High Court Library, P.O. Box 7085, Kampala, Uganda.

KUMAR, Dhananjay, born 1st January 1935. Educator. Education: B.Sc., B.H.U., India, 1954; M.Sc., Patna University, 1956; Ph.D., University of Wales, U.K., 1966. Married, 3 children. Appointments: Lecturer, Ranchi University, India, 1956-63; worked w. Professor P. F. Wareing, F.R.S. (U.K.), 1963-66; Teacher, Plant Physiology, University of Dar es Salaam, Tanzania, 1966—. Address: c/o University of Dar es Salaam, Tanzania.

KUMOJI, Victor Akrofi, born 30th August 1926. Consultant Gynaecologist-Obstetrician. Education: Presbyterian School, Ada Foah & Achimota School, Ghana; B.Sc.(Lond.), Physics, Chemistry, & Zoology, University College of Gold Coast, 1951 (1st Graduate in Physics of the University); M.B., B.S., London University, U.K., 1956. Married, 3 children. Appointments: Medical Officer, Metropolitan Hospital, 1956; Senior House Officer, Ashford Hospital, 1957; Registrar, Obstetrics & Gynaecology, Windsor Group of Hospitals, 1962; Consultant Obstetrician-Gynaecologist, Ghana Medical Service, 1965—. Memberships: Royal College of Obstetrics & Gynaecology, 1964; Secretary, Planned Parenthood Association, Kumasi. Honours: Ghana Medical Scholarship, 1951; Ghana Government Postgraduate Medical Scholarship, 1960. Address: P.O. Box 26, Mampong/Akwasim, Ghana.

KUNDYA, Hilda H. I. Mamlay. Information Officer. Education: Technical College; Journalism & Information Officers' Course, U.K. Married, 1 son. Appointments: Information Assistant; Senior Information Assistant; Sub-editor; Assistant Editor, 'Nchi Yetu'; Information Officer & Editor 'Nchi Yetu' and 'Kwetu'. Memberships: Hon. Secretary, Mpwapwa Branch, Trade Union of Government Workers, 1959-61; Chairman, Dor Branch, ibid, 1961-63; Young Women's Christian Association; Deputy Chairman, ibid, Dor; National Executive; on Committee, Tanzania Press Club; Publicity Committee, National Council of Tanzania Women; National Union of Tanganyika Workers. Address: Tanzania Information Services, P.O. Box 9142, Dar es Salaam, Tanzania.

KUNJE, Maxwell Bennett, born 6th June 1939. Government Administrative Officer. Education: University College of Cape Coast, Ghana, 1961; London G.C.E. Advanced Level, 1964; Malawi Institute of Public Administration, Blantyre, 1963-64; Development Course, Churchill College, Cambridge University, U.K., 1967-68; currently studying for 1st year B.A. with University of South Africa. Personal details: first African District Commissioner for Kasupe, Dedza, & Mzimba Districts; married, 3 daughters. Appointments: Acting Executive Officer, Malawi Civil Service, Cholo Boma, 1963; Administrative Officer & District Commissioner, Kasupe, 1964; District Commissioner, Dedza, 1964-66; Section Officer, Office of President in charge of District Administration, Vat Zomba, 1866-67 & 1968-69; District Commissioner, Mzimba, 1969-70; Traditional Courts Commissioner for the Central Region, Lilonswe, 1970—. Member of the Churchill Association. Address: P.O. Box 278, Lilonswe, Malawi.

KUNUNKA, Nyamayarwo Barnabas, born 19th July 1917. Physician. Education: Kabalega Primary School & Junior Secondary School, Masindi, 1926-32; King's College, Budo, 1933-35; D.M.(E.A.), Makerere University, Uganda, 1936-41; M.A.H.A., Columbia University, U.S.A., 1967. Married, 6 sons, 4 daughters. Appointments: Medical Officer, Uganda Government, 1942-51; Private Medical Practice, 1952-63; Member of Parliament, 1955-59; Leader of Opposition in Parliament, 1957-59. Memberships: Chairman, Commonwealth Parliamentary Association, 1957-58; President, Uganda Medical Association, 1958-59. Contributor to British Medical Journal. Honours: won scholarships from time entered school to end of university studies; won 1st prizes in Makerere Entrance Examination, 1935. Address: P.O. Box 16102, Kampala, Uganda.

KWADWO II (Nana) Twene, born at Suma-Ahenkro, 5th October 1898. Personal details: enstooled as the Omanhene of Suma Traditional Area in 1954; destooled by the Proscribed Convention People's Party, 1958; exiled to Ivory Coast, 1958; reinstated by the N.L.C. Government with Decree No. 112, 1967; married, 2 wives, 50 children. Memberships: Patron, Brong/Ahafo Suma Traditional Council; President, Suma Local Council. Address: P.O. Box 2, Suma-Ahenkro, via Bere Kum, Brong/Ahafo, Ghana.

KWALEYELA, Nnawa Amukena, born 14th August 1937. Publishers' Representative.

Education: Primary School Certificate, Sefula Mission, 1954; Cambridge Higher School Certificate, Muali School, 1960. Journalism Diploma, African Writing Centre, 1961; B.Sc.(Journalism), University of Oregon, 1965. Married, 2 children. Appointments: Chief Reporter, The Leader, Lusaka, 1961-62; Sub-Edictor, Radio Zambia, Lusaka, 1965; Press Officer, Zambia Information Services, 1965-66; Information Officer & Founding Editor, University Magazine, University of Zambia, 1966-69; Part-time Lecturer in Journalism, Evelyn Hone College of Further Education & University of Zambia, 1968-69; Publishers' Representative, Zambia & Malawi (based in Lusaka), 1969—. Address: Thomas Nelson & Sons Ltd., P.O. Box 27, Lusaka, Zambia.

KWAME II (Nana) Agyefi, born 2nd February 1942. Paramount Chief. Education: Wassaw Simpa Local Council School, 1948; Teachers' Certificate, Kwahu Abetifi Teacher Training College, 1964-68. Personal details: known in private life as Abraham Kojoe Fase; belongs to the Atwea Clan of Nsein; married, 3 children. Appointments: enstooled Paramount Chief, Nsein Traditional Area, 1969; elected Member of the Standing Committee of the Western Region House of Chiefs, 1969; elected Member of the National House of Chiefs, 1969; elected Member of the Management Committee of Axim Local Council, 1969. Address: Omanhene, Nsein Traditional Area, P.O. Box 24, Axim, Ghana.

KWARKO, Kwasi Assoku. Medical Practitioner. Education: Primary, Achimota, Ghana; Middle, Secondary, & Intermediate (London), Achimota School; Undergraduate, Medical Training, Glasgow University, U.K.; Postgraduate, London University. Married, 4 children. Appointments: Senior Medical Officer (Gynaecologist), Ministry of Health, Ghana; Medical Superintendent, Tamale, Central & West Hospitals. Member, Royal College of Obstetrics & Gynaecology, London. Address: Central Hospital, Box 16, Tamale, Ghana.

KWAW FRAIKU KU III (Nana) Kobina Atta Panyin, born 18th July 1919. Omanhene (Farmer). Education: Elementary Standard 6. Personal details: head of Nsona family. Married, 4 wives, 22 children. Appointments: Member of Standing Committee, Joint Provincial Council of Chiefs; Vice-President, Western & Central Houses of Chiefs; President, Western Region, House of Chiefs. Member of Methodist Church, Shama. Honours: Her Majesty's Coronation Medal, June, 1953. Address: Omanhene Shama Traditional Area, P.O. Box 6, Shama, Ghana.

KWENDE, George Mofor, born 31st December 1933. Accountant. Education: Bali College, West Cameroon, 1950-43; Co-operative College, Ibadan, Nigeria, 1955; University of Ghana, Accra, 1961-63; S.W. London College, U.K., 1964-66. Married, 4 children. Appointments: Government Co-operative Officer, West Cameroon, 1955-60; Accountant, Civil Service, 1967; seconded as Chief Accountant to Cameroon Bank Limited, 1968; appointed Secretary & Director, ibid, by P.M. of West Cameroon, 1968—; also Chief Accountant. Memberships: Executive Committee, Cameroon Society of Certified Accountants; President, Cameroon Society of Chartered Secretaries; Executive Committee, Anglo Cameroon Society, 1965-66; President, National Union of Cameroon Students in Britain, 1964-65; President, National Union of Cameroon Students in Ghana, 1963. Articles published in Cameroon Students' Magazines in Ghana & Britain on Economic Development in underdeveloped countries. Address: Cameroon Bank Limited, Victoria, West Cameroon.

KWENJE, Nophas Dinneck, born 3rd March 1907. Acting General Manager, Malawi Press. Education: Church of Scotland Mission, Blantyre. Married, 1 son, 3 daughters. Appointments: Head Teacher, Church of Scotland Mission, Blantyre, 3 years; Editor, Works Manager, African Newspapers Ltd., 19 years; Member, Legislative Council, Zomba, 1956-61; Storekeeper, 1959—; Acting General Manager, Malawi Press, 1968—. Memberships: President, Nyasaland African Congress in Rhodesia; Malawi National Library; Chairman, Museum of Malawi Trustees Board; Malawi Electoral Commission. Address: P.O. Box 891, Blantyre, Malawi.

KWIATKOWSKI, Katherina Zaleska, see ZALESKA-KWIATKOWSKI, Katherina.

KYABALONGO, Helen Judith, born at Rubaga, 7th July 1947. Assistant Agricultural Officer. Education: Rubaga Girls' School; Christ the King School; Diploma, Bukalasa Agricultural College, 1968. Member, Uganda Agricultural Society. Address: P.O. Box 219, Ania, Uganda.

KYAGAMBIDDWA, Joseph, born January-February 1922. Music Teacher; Composer. Education: Primary, Kitovu, Masaka, 1934-37; Secondary, Bukalasa Junior Seminary, Masaka, 1938-41; studied Music & musicology, research into African Music with Dr. Klaus P. Wachsmann, Kampala, Uganda, 1942-50; Xavier University, New Orleans, La., U.S.A., 1950-53; Pius X School of Liturgical Music, Manhattanville College, New York, 1953-55; Hochschulinstitut fur Musik, Trossingen/Wurttenberg, Germany, 1961-65. Personal details: Pioneer of African Church Music in East Africa. Appointments: Music master, Masaka Secondary Schools, Uganda, 1956-60; Conductor, Canonizational Choir during canonization of Ugandan Martyrs, Rome, Italy, 1964; Choirmaster, Church Oratorio Choir, Kiteredde, Masaka, 1965-: Tutor, Music, National Teachers' College, Kyambogo, Kampala, 1966—; Choirmaster, Pope Paul's visit to Africa, 1969. Publications: African Music From the Source of the Nile, 1955; Ten African Religious Hymns, 1963; Ugandan Martyrs African Oratorio (records), 1964. Honours: 2 medals, Music Xavier University, 1953; Citation from Morningside Community Centre, N.Y., 1955; Bronze & Silver Medals from Pope Paul IV, 1964 & 1965. Address: P.O. Box 20012, Kampala, Uganda.

KYAGULANYI-NTWATWA, David Johnson, born 11th July 1934. Quantity Surveyor. Education: King's College, Budo, Uganda; Civil Engineering School, Nakawa;

Leicester College of Art, U.K.; College of Estate Management, London University. Married, 4 children. Appointments: Engineering Assistant, Uganda Government, 1957; Quantity Surveyor, ibid, 1966; Senior Quantity Surveyor, 1968; Acting Chief Quantity Surveyor, 1969. Memberships: Associate, Institution of Chartered Surveyors; ibid, Institute of Quantity Surveyors; Fellow & Committee Member, Association of Surveyors, Uganda; Head Prefect, King's College, Budo, 1951; Football Captain, ibid, 1951. Address: P.O. Box 2027, Kampala, Uganda.

KYALWAZI, Sebastian Kakule, born 31st October 1919. Surgeon; Professor of Clinical Surgery. Education: Makerere University Medical School, Uganda, 1942-48; F.R.C.S. (Edinburgh), 1961. Married 4 sons, 2 daughters. Appointments: Medical Officer, Ministry of Health, Uganda, 1949-54; Medical Officer, Special Grade, 1961; Government Consultant in Surgery, 1961-63; Senior Government Consultant in Surgery, 1963-67; Senior Lecturer in Surgery, Makerere University, 1967-68; Reader in Surgery, ibid, 1968-69; Professor of Clinical Surgery, Makerere Medical School, 1969—. Memberships: Fellow, Assn. of Surgeons of East Africa; President, ibid, 1 year. Honours: Knight of St. Gregory the Great, 1968. Author of professional publs. Address: Makerere University Medical School, P.O. Box 7072, Kampala, Uganda.

KYANIKIRE, Akisoferi Dongo, born 20th December 1937. Meteorologist. Education: Primary & Secondary Education at Busaba, Budaka, & Nabumali; B.Sc.(London), Makerere University, Uganda; Postgraduate Diploma in Meteorology, University of Melbourne, Australia. Married. Appointments: Auditor, with Uganda Government; Meteorologist, with East African Community; Uganda Member, Commission for Climatology, World Meteorological Organization. Address: East African Meteorological Department, P.O. Box 30259, Nairobi, Kenya.

KYEJO, Anderson Kenan, born 19th February 1933. Teacher. Education: G.C.E. (London); Teachers: Certificate, Tanzania Ministry of Education; Certificate in Education, Manchester University, U.K. Married, 3 children. Appointments: Primary School Teacher, 1954-61; Lecturer in Teachers' College, 1962-68; Education Administrator, Ministry Headquarters, 1969—. Publications: Principles of Education (in Swahili). Address: P.O. Box 9121, Dar es Salaam, Tanzania.

KYEMBA, Henry Kisajja, born Masese, Jinja, December 1939. Civil Servant. Education: Primary & Secondary School, Busoga College, Mwiri; Cambridge School Certificate, Busoga College, Mwiri, 1956; B.A.(Hons., History) (London), Makerere University College. Personal details: son of former Chief of Busoga & related to the famous Chief, Luba of Busoga. Married. Appointments include: Administrative Officer Cadet, posted to the then Prime Minister's Office, 1962-63; appointed Private Secretary to the then Prime Minister & later President, 1963-66; appointed Principal Private Secretary to the President, 1966-68; appointed Permanent Secretary, Principal Private Secretary to H.E. The President, 1968—. Memberships include: Mwiri Old Boys' Club; Makerere University College Old Students' Union. Awarded: Honour of Knight of the Order of St. Silvester by His Holiness Pope Paul VI, 1969. Address: State House, P.O. Box 11, Entebbe, Uganda.

KYOMO, Martin Muther, born 3rd March 1936. University Lecturer. Education: B.Sc. (Agriculture), Makerere University College, Uganda, 1962; M.Sc., Colorado State University, U.S.A., 1966; Major Field: Animal Breeding & Genetics. Appointments: Research Officer, Animal Production, 1962-64; Research Officer in Charge, Livestock Research Station, 1966-68; Chief Research Officer, Animal Production, Dar es Salaam, Tanzania; currently, Lecturer, Animal Husbandry & Acting Head, Animal Science Department, Faculty of Agriculture, Morogoro. Member, American Society of Animal Science. Author, Milk Compostion & Yield Characteristics (E.A. Agric. & For. J.). Address: P.O. Box 643, Morogoro, Tanzania.

L

LABAZIEWICZ, Henryk, born Sumy, Poland, 29th December, 1930. University Lecturer. Education: M.Sc., University of Warsaw, 1960. Married, 3 sons. Appointments: Research Worker, Institute of Physics, Polish Academy of Science, Warsaw, 1960-62; ibid, Institute of General Chemistry, ibid, 1962-64; Lecturer, Organic Chemistry, University of Science & Technology, Kumasi, Ghana, 1964—. Member, American Association for the Advancement of Science. Address: University of Science & Technology, Kumasi, Ghana.

LABINJO, Gabriel Oladipo, born Lagos, Nigeria, 6th February 1897, deceased, 26th July 1966. Minister of Religion; Salvation Army Officer. Education: Duke Town Schl., Calabar; Hope Waddel Inst.; Salvation Army Training Coll., Mildmay, London, U.K., 1923. Was married, 5 surviving children. Appointments included: Headmaster, Methodist Schl., Agbeni, Ibadan; Cathecist & Headmaster, Iwo Western Nigeria; ibid, Ago Ijaiye Methodist Schl., Lagos; Headmaster, Salvation Army Schl., Ebute Metta; held ranks from Captain to Brigadier, Salvation Army. Memberships include: Gen. Sec., Salvation Army; Pioneer of Salvation Army in Eastern Nigeria, 1925-36; Treas., Fellowship of African Ministers, 1962-66. Honours include: Long Service Medal, Salvation Army, 1958. Address: P.O. Box 646, Lagos, Nigeria.

LABURTHE-TOLRA, Phillippe-Pierre-Marie, born 9th July 1929. University Professor. Education: Licence & Aggregate of Philosophy, Sorbonne, Paris, France, 1962. Appointments: Director, Higher Teaching Centre, Porto-Novo, Dahomey, 1962-64; Professor of Philosophy & African Sociology, Cameroun Federal University, Yaoundé, 1964—. Author of several articles and books including: Le Lion et la Perle (translation); Soyinka ou la Tigritude (essay), 1968; Yaoundé, d'apres Zenker, en 1895, 1970;

Initiation Africaine (co-author), 1970. Honours: Recipient of Cameroun Distinction, 3rd class, 1967. Address: Centre des Recherches Africanistes, Faculté des Lettres et Sciences Humaines, B.P. 755, Yaoundé, Cameroun.

LAFINHAN, Emmanuel Oladele, born Ogbomoso, Nigeria, 22nd February 1912. Retired Educational Administrator. Education: Teachers' Higher Elementary Certificate (now Grade II Teachers' Certificate), 1932; Teachers' Senior Certificate (now Grade I Teachers' Certificate), 1949. Married, 2 sons. Appointments: Class Teacher, 1930-35; Head Teacher & Class Teacher, 1936-50; Travelling Teacher, 1951-54; Supervisor of Schools, 1955-57; Administrative Assistant to the Education Secretary, 1958-68; retired, 1968. Publications: Komonwe Kimi, Komonwe Keji, & Komonwe Keta (Yoruba leaders for primary schools); Komonwe Kerin, Komonwe Karun. Address: P.O. Box 40, Oke Ola, Ogbomoso, Western State, Nigeria.

LAGESSE, Guy, born 17th July 1935. Company Director. Education: College du St. Esprit, Mauritius; City of London College, U.K.; Associate, Chartered Insurance Institute, U.K., 1961. Appointments: Fire & Accident Manager, Swan Insurance Co. Ltd., Port Louis, Mauritius, 1963-67; Managerial Assistant, Anglo-Ceylon General Estates Co. Ltd., 1967—; Managerial Assistant, Swaziland Sugar Milling Co. Ltd., 1967—; Manager, The Mauritius Development Trust Co. Ltd., 1967—; Chairman, Exotic Exports Ltd., 1967—; Director, Mauritius Advertising Bureau Ltd., 1967—; Sworn & Exchange Broker, 1967—; Director, Tourist Development Company, 1967—; Director, Art Festival of City of Port Louis, 1966; Director, Folklorique Group, French International Confolens Festival, 1969. Memberships: Committee, Lions International; Secretary, Societe des Metteurs en Scene; President, Mauritius Car Club; Grand Bay Yacht Club; Dodo Club; Mauritius Naval & Military Gymkhana Club. Leading theatrical producer in spare time. Address: Anglo-Mauritius House, Port Louis, Mauritius.

LAGESSE, Marie-Rita Marcelle, born February 1916. Novelist; Civil Servant. Descendant of an old French family established on Mauritius since 1753. Appointments: with Social Security Service, Mauritius Government. Publications (novels): D'un Carnet; Les Contes du Samdedi; Sa Diligence s'éloigne à l'Aube; Le 20 Floreal au Matin; (plays): Ville laque; Carolynn; Les Palmiers de la Source (adaptation of 'Paul et Virginie' by Bernadin de St. Pierre). Recipient of Robet Barques Prize, 1956. Address: 'Hurlevent-la-Ravine', Coromandel, Beau-Bassin, Mauritius.

LAGUNDOYE, Sulaiman Botsende, born Owo, Western Nigeria, 13th October 1935. Medical Practitioner. Education: Government College, Ibadan, 1948-52; Nigerian College of Arts, Science, & Technology (now University of Ife), 1953-55; M.B., B.S. (Lond.), University College, Ibadan (now University of Ibadan), 1955-61; D.M.R.D., University of Edinburgh, U.K., 1964-66. Married, 2 sons, 1 daughter.

Appointments: House Physician, University College Hospital, Ibadan, 1961; House Surgeon, Adeoyo Hospital, Ibadan, 1962; Medical Officer, Oyo General Hospital, 1961; Rural Medical Officer, Ughelli Rural Health Centre, 1962-63; Medical Officer, Government Chest Clinic, Ibadan, 1963-64; Trainee in Radiology, University of Edinburgh at the Royal Infirmary, Edinburgh, U.K., 1964-66; Senior Medical Officer (Radiologist), Akure General Hospital, 1966-67; Lecturer in Radiology, University of Ibadan, & Hon. Consulting Radiologist, University College Hospital, 1967-70; Senior Lecturer & Hon. Consulting Radiologist, ibid, 1970—. Memberships: Secretary, Association of Radiologists of West Africa, 1969, 1970; Treasurer, Ibadan University Medical School Alumni Association, 1970; Patron, Ibadan District Table Tennis Association, 1969, 1970; Executive Western State Table Tennis Association, 1968, 1969, 1970; Chairman, Table Tennis Committee, Ibadan Federation of Boys' & Girls' Clubs; West African Gastroenterology Association; Historical Society of Nigeria. Publs: Arteriography of Battle Casualties of the Nigerian Civil War (w. G. A. A. Oyemade), 1970; Petrous Tomography in Congenital Deafness in Nigerian Children. Honours: Fellow, Nigerian Medical Council in Radiology, 1970. Address: Radiology Department, University College Hospital, Ibadan, Nigeria.

LAKHANI, Vinodrai Bhagwanji, born 27th November 1939. Physician. Education: M.B., B.S., University of Bombay, India, 1963; Internship, Northeastern Hospital, Philadelphia, U.S.A., 1964-65. Appointments: Resident, Internal Medicine & Cardiology, 1965-67. Memberships: F.A.G.S., U.S.A. Address: P.O. Box 552, Mombasa, Kenya.

LAKSESVELA, Birger, born 10th October 1921. Reader in Animal Nutrition. Education: B.Sc.(Agric.), 1951; Ph.D.(Agric.), 1962; Course in Comparative Physiology, 1964; Human Nutrition Research Unit, National Institute for Medical Research, London, U.K., 1965-66. Married to Joan Hodges, 1 son 2 daughters. Appointments: Planner of Farm Buildings, County of Telemark, Norway, 1951-52; Research Assistant, Agricultural Faculty of Norway, 1952; Research Leader, S.S.F. Bergen, Norway, 1954-67; Lecturer, Faculty of Veterinary Science, University of Nairobi, Kenya, 1967—; Senior Lecturer, ibid, 1968—; Reader in Animal Nutrition. Memberships: Nutrition Society, U.K.; Nordiske Jordbruksforskeres Forening. Publications include: Milk Yield & Profit of Milk Production at Different Seasons of Calving, 70th Report from Div. of Animal Production, Royal Agric. College of Norway; Unidentified Chick Growth Factor in Herring Meal & Solubles, Section Papers, 10th World's Poultry Congtess, Edinburgh, 1954; The Potency of Balancing Interactions Between Dietary Proteins, Journal Agric. Science, 1960. Address: Faculty of Veterinary Science, P.O. Kabete, Kenya.

LALANI, Valimahomed Ahmed, born 23rd November 1915. Ophthalmic Surgeon. Education: M.B., B.S., Bombay, India, 1941; D.O.M.S., Vienna, Austria,, 1964.

LAMBO, Awonala Olufunmiḷọla, born 20th October, 1932. Research Parsitologist. Education: Eko Boys' High School, Lagos, Nigeria, 1947-48; Baptist Academy, ibid, 1949-52; Sir John Cass College, London, U.K., 1955-57; London University, 1958-61; University of Nigeria, 1963-66; .B.Sc. Personal details: descended from Oba Olofin of Isheri; married, 1 child. Appointments: Laboratory Assistant, 1953-54; Science Master, 1955; Executive Officer, 1962-63; Research Parasitologist, 1966—. Memberships: Nigeria Institute of International Affairs; Science Association of Nigeria; Society of Health, Nigeria; United Nations Association of Nigeria. Contributor to scientific journals. Honours: St. Botolph Bursary, Sir John Cass College, 1957; Federal Nigerian Government Scholarship, 1964-66; WHO Fellowship, 1967. Address: Malaria Research Institute, Yaba, Lagos State, Nigeria.

LAMBO, Thomas Adeoye, born Abeokuta, Nigeria, 23rd March 1923. University Professor; Physician. Education: St. Paul's Primary Schl., Abeokuta; Baptist Boys' High Schl.; M.B., Ch.B., M.D., Univ of Birmingham, U.K.; D.P.M., Univ. of London Inst. of Psychiatry; M.R.C.P.; F.R.C.P.(Edin.). Married, 3 children. Appointments: House Physician, Mainland Nerve Hosp., Birmingham, U.K., 1950; Med. Officer, Lagos, Zaria & Gusau, Nigeria, 1950-52; Specialist, Western Region Min. of Health Neuro-Psychiatric Ctr., 1957; Cons. Psychiatrist, Univ. Coll. Hosp., Ibadan, 1956; Assoc. Lectr., Univ. of Ibadan, 1956; Sr. Specialist, Western Region Min. of Health Neuro-Psychiatric Ctr., 1960; Prof. of Psychiatry, Hd. of Dept. of Psychiatry, Neurology & Neuro-Surgery, Univ. of Ibadan, 1963; Dean, Med. Faculty, ibid, 1966-68; Vice-Chancellor, 1968—. Memberships include: Assoc. of Psychiatrists in Africa, 1961; Scientific Council for Africa; W.H.O. Advisory Comm. on Medical Research; Vice-Chairman, U.N. Adv. Comm. on Application of Science & Technology to Development; Club of Rome Advisory Comm., for Medical Health, W.H.O.; Royal Medico-Psychological Assoc. of Great Britain; Chmn., U.N. Perm. Advisory Comm. on Prevention of Crime & Treatment of Offenders; Pres., Int. Coll. of Tropical Med., 1968—; Exec. Bd., World Federation for Mental Health. Mbr. of following Bds.: Int. Jrnl. of Psychiatry; Int. Jrnl. of Social Psychiatry; Acta-Socio-Media; Jrnl. of Nigerian Med. Assoc. Contbr. of numerous articles to prof. jrnls. Honours include: O.B.E., 1962; Hon. D.Sc., Ahamadu Bello Univ., Nigeria, 1967; Hon. LL.D., K.S.U; J.P., Western State, 1968. Address: Univ. of Ibadan, Nigeria.

LAMPTEY, Gottfried Cyril Odarlai, born 10th April, 1923. Chartered Librarian. Education: Mfantisipim, 1940-44; Associateship Exams., School of Librarianship, Loughborough Technical College, Leics., U.K., 1955-56; Manchester School of Librarianship, 1962-63; Final Exams of Library Association, 1966. Married, children. Appointments: Civil Servant, Inland Revenue Dept., 1945-50; Chief Library Assistant, University of Science & Technology, Kumasi, Ghana, 1957-60; Librarian, School of Administration, University of Ghana, Legon, 1960—. Memberships: Fellow, Library Association; Councillor, West African Library Association, 1954-55; ibid, Ghana Library Association, 1962-63, 1965-67; Hon. Treasurer, ibid, 1965-67. Address: School of Administration, University of Ghana, P.O. Box 78, Legon, Ghana.

LANDHEER, Jan Engelbert, born 27th June 1939. Physician; Leprolopist. Appointments: Medical Superintendent, Kumi Leprosy Centre, Uganda. Address: P.O. Box 9, Kumi, Uganda.

LANGHAM, Richard Malcolm, born 28th May 1943. Plant Breeder. Education: Warwick School, Warwick, U.K.; Magdalene College, Cambridge University; Ahmadu Bello University, Nigeria, Degrees: M.A.; M.Sc. Appointments: Research Assistant, Ahmadu Bello University; Research Officer, Cotton Research Corporation, Samaru, Nigeria, & Ukiriguru, Tanzania. Memberships: Institute of Biology; British Ecological Society. Publications: Inheritance & Nature of Shoot Fly Resistance in Sorghum, 1968. Address: Research & Training Institute, Ukiriguru, P.O. Box 1433, Mwanza, Tanzania.

LANGLANDS, Bryan Wooleston, born 1928. University Professor Education: London School of Economics & Political Science, U.K., 1949-53. Appointments: Lecturer in Geography, Makerere University, Kampala, Uganda, 1953—; Professor of Geography, ibid, 1968—. Fellowships: Royal Geographical Society; Royal Institute of International Affairs. Memberships: President, Uganada Society, 1970; Honorary Editor, Uganda Journal, 1966—; Chairman, Uganda Geographical Society, 1966—. Publications: Bibliography of the Distribution of Disease in East Africa; Uganada Atlas of Disease Distributions (with S. A. Hall); various articles in Uganda Journal & East African Geographical Review, etc. Address: Makerere University, P.O. Box 7062, Kampala, Uganda.

LANGO, Ephraim, born Kenya, 16th October 1934. Administrator. Education: Rapedhi Primary School, West Nyokal, 1944-48; Kisii School, 1949-53; Diploma in Public Administration, University of Birmingham, U.K., 1970-71. Married, 5 children. Appointments: Assistant Station-master, East African Railways, 1954-59; Tax Officer, East African Community, 1960-64; Executive Officer, ibid, 1964-67; Administrator, 1968—. Honours: Best Pupil in Class, 1945, 1946, 1948, & 1956. Address: East African Institute of Malaria & Vector-borne Diseases, P.O. Amani, Nr. Tanga, Tanzania.

LANIYONU (Chief) Josiah Oladipo, Jagun Olubadan of Ibadan, born Ibadan, Nigeria, 28th December,1908. Licensed Surveyor. Education: Kudeti Primary School, 1915-18; New Class School, Ereko, 1919-20; C.M.S. Grammar School, Lagos, 1921-26; Qualified Government Surveyor, Government Survey School, Ibadan, 1927-30; Licensed Surveyors' Exam., 1947. Personal details: mother, eldest daughter of the Dawodu of Adeniji; installed as Traditional Chief of Ibadan. Appointments: Government Surveyor, Nigeria, 1931-38; Army Service, 1939-46; Civil Service Survey Department, 1946-48; Government Surveyor, 1950; Instructor, Survey School, Kano, 1950-51; Surveyor in Charge, JOS

Township Survey, 1951; ibid, Minesfield Surveys, JOS, 1952; Private Practice as Professional Surveyor, 1952—. Memberships include: Fellow, Royal Geographical Society; ibid, Nigerian Institution of Surveyors; Chairman, West Sports Council, 1963; National Sports Council; Traditional Member & Councillor, Ibadan City Council Management Committee, 1965; Board of Governors, National High School, Aiye Ekiti, 1969; Rehabilitation & Resettlement Commission, Western State Government, 1970. Honours: Star, 1939-45; Africa Star; Burma Star; Defence Medal; War Medal. M.B.E., 1962. Address: P.O. Box 3058, Ibadan, Nigeria.

LARBY, Patricia M., born 18th December 1931. Librarian. Education: Torquay Grammar School for Girls, U.K.; North-Western Polytechnic, London. Married Norman Larby, 1967. Appointments: Librarian, Department of Agriculture, Uganda, 1957-59; ibid, E.A. Literature Bureau, Uganda Branch, 1959-62; Chief Librarian, ibid, 1962-64; Africana Specialist, Juke University Library, U.S.A., 1965-66; Librarian, The Polytechnic, University of Malawi, 1967-69; Deputy Librarian, University of Nairobi, Kenya, 1969—. Memberships: Secretary, Uganda Branch, East African Library Association, 1963-64; ibid, Central Committee, ibid, 1966; Editor, 1962-66, 1970—; Malawi National Libraries Board, 1966-67. Address: University of Nairobi, Box 30197, Nairobi, Kenya.

LAVODRAMA, Prosper, born 24th November 1938. Diplomat. Education: Primary School Finishing Diploma. Married, 9 children. Appointments: Military Service, 1948-52; Civil Servant, French Military Administration, 1952-62; Sub-Prefect, Bimbo, Central African Republic, 1962; Prefect, M'Bomou, 1964; Minister of the Interior, 1968; Secretary of State for Information, 1969; Ambassador Extraordinary & Plenipotentiary to the Democratic Republic of the Congo, Kinshasa, 1970. Memberships: Secretary-General, Union of Civil Personnel of the Army, 1957; Co-Founder, l'Union Panafricaine des Travailleurs Croyants, Brazzaville, 1959; Secretary-General, Confederation Africaine des Travailleurs Croyants de la R.C.A., 1959. Honours: Chevalier de Merite Centrafricain; Officier du Merite Centrafricaine; Commandeur du Merite Centrafricaine. Address: Embassy of the Central African Republic, B.P. 7769, Kinshasa, Democratic Republic of the Congo.

LAW, Eric John Ewan, born Burma, 10th June 1913. Barrister-at-Law; Justice of Appeal, Court of Appeal, East Africa. Education: Wrekin College, 1927-32; St. Catherine's College, Cambridge, 1932-35; B.A.(Hons.), 1935; M.A.(Hons.), 1945; Barrister-at-Law, Middle Temple, 1936. Married to Patricia Seed, 2 sons, 1 daughter. Appointments include: Assistant Judicial Adviser to the Imperial Ethiopian Government, 1942-44; Crown Counsel, Nyasaland, 1944-53; Resident Magistrate & Judge, Zanzibar & Tanganyika, 1953-64; Justice of Appeal, Court of Appeal for East Africa, 1965—. Address: Court of Appeal for East Africa, P.O. Box 30187, Nairobi, Kenya.

LAWAL, Salami Edobor, born Benin City, Nigeria, 22nd April, 1914. General Contractor. Education: Certified Contractor. Married, 3 wives, 11 children. Appointments: served as Food Contractor to various institutions in the country; 1st Contractor, Lafia Hotel, Ibadan & still under service; 1st Contractor, University of Ibadan & University College Hospital; 1st Medical Food Contractor, Ibadan; contracts with Premier Hotel; U.A.C. & John Holt Ltd., 1937-40; Acting Sgt.-Major, Grade 1 Army Nurse, 56th General Hospital, Ibadan, W.W.II; Agent, Davies Tires, 1960-62. Memberships: Ibadan Tennis Club; President, Food Suppliers' Association, Western State, Nigeria; Ibadan Lawn Tennis Club; Treasurer, Benin Welfare Association, Western State Branch, 1967—. Address: P.O. Box 184, Ibadan Western State, Nigeria.

LAWAL, Sikiru Ola, born 2nd April 1944. Teacher. Education: St. Barnabus School, Ilorin; Pitcombe College, Egbe via Ilorin, Gombe Training College, Nigeria. Appointments: Headmaster, Okey Community School, Okey via Igbaja, 1969; ibid, Oke-Aluleo, L.E.A. School, Ilorin. Memberships: former Corporal, Boys' Brigade; Boy Scouts of Nigeria. Publications: Contributor to Ilorin Echo & bi-annual Magazine of Ilorin Descendants Students' Union. Address: c/o Oke-Aluleo L.E.A. School, Ilorin, Nigeria.

LAWS, Sydney Gibson, born 1st December 1902. Medical Laboratory Technologist. Education: Gateshead Secondary School, U.K.; University of Durham, College of Medicine, Newcastle upon Tyne. Married to Beatrice Gale. Appointments: Bacteriological Department, College of Medicine, 1918-23; Research Expedition to British Honduras (organized by London School of Tropical Medicine), 1923-24; Curator, Kitchener School of Medicine, Sudan Medical Service, Khartoum, Sudan, 1924-27; Curator, Uganda Medical School, Uganda Medical Service, 1927-32; Veterinary Department, Uganda, 1932-52; Technical Development Division, Uganda Development Corporation, 1952-58; Personnel Officer, Kampala City Council, 1959-62; Committee Clerk, Town Clerk's Department, Kampala City Council, 1963-71. Fellow, Institute of Medical Laboratory Technology. Publications: various papers on trypanosomiasis, turning sickness, east coast fever, etc. Honours: M.B.E., 1953; Coronation Medal, 1953; Independence Medal, 1964. Address: P.O. Box 210, Kampala, Uganda.

LAWSON, George William, born 18th April 1926. Professor of Botany. Education: various schools; Sunderland Polytechnic, U.K.; King's College, London. Personal details: married to Rowena Mary Lawson, 1 son, 1 daughter. Appointments: Professor, Department of Botany, University of Ghana, Legon. Memberships: Fellow, Linnean Society; International Phycological Society; West African Science Association; Ghana Science Association; British Phycological Society; American Phycological Society; Association for Tropical Biology. Publications: Plant Life in West Africa, 1966; author of approx. 40 scientific articles in e.g., Journal of Ecology & Journal of the West African Science Association. Address: Head, Department of Botany, University of Ghana, Legon, Ghana.

LEAKEY, Colin Louis Avern, born 13th December 1933. Applied Botanist. Education: Gresham's School, Holt; B.A., Natural Science & Botany, King's College, Cambridge, U.K., 1956-59; M.A.(Cantab.); Exeter University, 1959-60; University of West Indies, Trinidad, 1960-61; Diploma in Tropical Agriculture. Personal details: eldest son of Dr. L. S. B. Leakey & Mrs. H. W. Leakey; married to Susan Jane (née Marshall), 3 daughters. Appointments: Plant Pathologist, Colonial Pool (later Commonwealth) of Plant Pathologists, Uganda, 1961-63, 1963-65; Senior Lecturer, Agricultural Botany, Makerere University College, 1965-70; Reader Fellow, Plant Breeding, Makerere University, Kampala, 1970—. Memberships: Fellow, Linnean Society; ibid, Royal Horticultural Society; Founder Member, E.A. Academy; British Mycological Society; Association of Applied Biologists; Federation of British Plant Pathologists; Association for Tropical Biology; Institute of Biology; American Orchid Society; Kenya Orchid Society; President, Uganda Horticultural Society, 1966-67; President, Uganda Orchid Group, 1970. Publications include: Editor, Crop Improvement in East Africa; Scientific Papers include: Problems of introducing new crops in developing countries, 1967; Horticultural Publications include: The Orchids of Uganda 5, 1969. Honours: James Barcroft Prize for Physiology, King's College, Cambridge, 1957; Currie Memorial Prize for Tropical Agriculture, University of the West Indies, 1961. Address: Department of Crop Science & Production, Faculty of Agriculture, Makerere University, Kampala, Uganda.

LEAL, Joseph Lewis Michael, born 1910. Businessman; Government Minister. Education: Royal College, Curepipe, Mauritius; Asst. Pharmacist & Chemist Dip., 1932. Married, 3 children. Appointments: Commandant, Mauritius Branch, Det. No. 7, Rose Hill, British Red Cross, 1942; Director, Pharmacie Nouvelle, Port Louis, 1948-66; Founder & Director, Mauritius Union Assurance, 1948—; Chairman, Rose Hill Cooperative Stores, 1956-64; Director, Rose Hill Transport, 1957—; Founder & Managing Director, Express Newspaper, 1961—; elected Member, Town Council, Beau Bassin-Rose Hill, 1953-63; Vice-Chairman, ibid, 1956, 1960; Chairman, 1958; elected Member, Legislative Assembly, 1963; Parliamentary Secretary, Works & Education Ministeries, 1965; Minister of State (Budget), 1967; Minister of State (Development), 1967-68, & Works, 1969. Memberships: Chairman, Cercle de Rose Hill, 1956-57; Treasurer, Mauritius Labour Party; General Council, Commonwealth Parliamentary Association Conference in Canada, 1966. Honours: Defence Medal. Address: Loreto Convent Street, Curepipe Road, Mauritius.

LEBRET, Antoine Sylvio, born 9th March 1927. Land Surveyor. Education: School Certificate Grade I, 1945; English Scholarship Certificate, 1946. Married, 4 sons. Appointments: Overseer & Clerk of Works, Public Works & Surveys Department; Assistant Surveyor, ibid; Senior Surveyor; Part-time Lecturer, Surveying, University of Mauritius. Memberships: Founder, Mauritius Institute of Surveyors; Society of St. Vincent of Paul. Address: Impasse Trotter, Beau-Bassin, Mauritius.

LE BRETON, Francis Hemery, born Torquay, Devon, U.K., 27th December 1889. British Army Officer, Kenya Farmer. Education: Charterhouse, U.K., 1903-6; Switzerland, 1906-9; Royal Military Academy, Woolwich, U.K., 1909-10; Commissioned to Royal Field Artillery, 1910. Married, 2 sons, 1 daughter. Appointments include: service in France, twice wounded, World War I; retired as Major; became Farmer in Kenya; service in Palestine & Egypt, World War II; retired as Lt.-Colonel; Chairman, Trans Nzoia Farmers' Association, 1934-39; Member, Kenya Legislative Council, 1947-51; Member, Trans Nzoia County Council, 1954; Member, Land Control Board of Kenya, 1948-61; Member, Land Board of Kenya, 1953-61; Director, various private limited liability companies. Memberships include: Vice-President, Kenya Electors: Union, 1952; Executive Council, ibid, many years; President, Trans Nzoia Association, 1953-60; Vice-President, Kenya British Legion, 1963-64; Executive Council, ibid, many years. Publications include: Up-Country Swahili. Honours include: Military Cross, 1918. Address: Kimwondo, Endebess, Kitale, Kenya.

LEEDAM, Elizabeth Janet Dean, born 16th June 1920. Nurse. Education: S.R.N.; S.C.M.; H.V. Cert.; B.S., Nursing, Boston University; M.P.H., University of California, Berkeley, California, U.S.A. Appointments: Area Nursing Officer, Somerset County Council, Public Health Services, U.K., 1956-60; W.H.O. Nurse Educator, Rural Health Services Project, Eastern Nigeria, 1960-65; W.H.O. Nurse Educator, University of Nairobi, Kenya, 1968—. Memberships: East African Academy; International Association of University Women; Kenyan Nurses' Association; Royal College of Nursing, U.K.; American Public Health Association: Sigma Theta Tau. Publications: Public Health Nurse Auxiliary Manual (in preparation). Address: 18 Lucastes Road, Haywards Heath, Sussex, U.K.

LE FLEM, Maurice, born 10th May 1937. Civil Servant. Education: Primary School, Mouila, Gabon; Secondary School, Libreville; Law Studies, Brazzaville, Republic of the Congo. Married, 3 children. Appointments: Assistant to the Chief, Section Apurement aux Finances, Libreville, Gabon, 1955; Chief, Bureau of Accountants & Material, Ministry of Education, 1962; 1st Secretary, Embassy of Gabon, Washington, D.C., U.S.A., 1964; Chief, Division of International Organization, Minister of Foreign Affairs, Gabon, 1966; Chief of Protocol, Presidency of the Republic, 1967; Sub-Prefect, Port-Gentil, 1969; Member of Gabon Delegation to the General Assembly, United Nations, 19th, 20th, & 22nd sessions. Honours: Officier du Merite Centrafricain. Address: Port-Gentil, Gabon.

LEGESSE BEZOU, born 30th January 1930. Government Official. Education: Teferre Makonnen School, Addis Ababa, Ethiopia; University College Extension, Addis Ababa; Certified & Corporate Accountant, Institute of London, U.K. Married, 9 children. Appointments: Inspector-General, Ministry of Finance, 1946-61; Commissioner of Pensions, Ministry of Pensions, 1961-67; Vice-Minister of Interior & General Manager, Election Board, Ministry of Interior, 1967—. Memberships: Youth Advisory Committee, YMCA of Ethiopia; Ethiopian Tennis Association; Walking & Mountaineering Club. Honours: Officer, Star of Honour of Ethiopia, with Rosette Emblem, 1953; Officer, Order of Menelik II, with Rosette Emblem, 1958. Address: Central Election Board, Ministry of Interior, P.O. Box 1375, Addis Ababa, Ethiopia.

LEGG, Frank Stanley, born Bristol, U.K., 7th January 1919. Headmaster. Education: Hardye's School, Dorchester, U.K.; B.A.(Hons.), Exeter University, Exeter; Dip.Ed., ibid. Married to Lilian Trevanion Brockett, 3 sons. Appointments: Deputy Principal, Senga Hill, Agricultural Training College, Senga Hill, Zambia, 1950-54; Acting Principal, Mbereshi Teacher Training College, Kawambwa, Zambia, 1954-58; Headmaster, Mongu Secondary School, 1959-65; Head, Munali School, Lusaka, 1965—. Memberships: Chairman, Zambian Heads of Secondary Schools Association; Lusaka Rotary Club; Committee Member, Lusaka Musical Society. Address: Munali School, P.O. Box 655, Lusaka, Zambia.

LEHAEN (S. E. R. Mgr.) Pierre Frans, born Neerpelt, Belgium, 17th January 1908. Roman Catholic Missionary; Bishop. Education: Primary, Humanities, Greek, Latin, Maastricht, Netherlands, 1919-22; Secondary, ibid, Hechtel, Belgium, 1922-24; Philosophy, Groot-Bijgaarden, 1925, 1926; Licence, Theology, Pontifical Gregorian University, Rome, Italy, 1930-34. Personal details: entered the Novitiate of the Salesiens, Groot-Bijgaarden, 1924. Appointments: Director, Technical School, Kafubu, Belgian Congo, 1936-38; Superior, Salesian Mission Kiniama, 1938-42; Director, College of St. Francis, Lubumbashi, 1942-46; Bishop, Diocese of Sakania, Democratic Republic of the Congo, 1959—. Named, Provincial Superior, Belgium & the Congo, 1946-53; Vice-Provincial, Congo, 1953-59. Honours: Chevalier, Royal Order of the Lion, Belgium, 1951; Pontificale Distinction, 'Benemerenti' from Pius XII, 1951; Gold Medal of Civic Merit, Democratic Republic of the Congo, 1967. Address: Diocese of Kafubu, B.P. 521 Lubumbashi, Democratic Republic of the Congo.

LEISTEN, John Herbert Alain, born 25th January 1970. University Lecturer. Education: B.Sc., University College, London, U.K., 1948; Ph.D., ibid, 1951. Married, 4 children. Appointments: Assistant Scientist, R.A.E. Farnborough, 1945; Chemist, Victoria Margarine Works, 1947; Lecturer, S.E. Essex Technical College, 1951; Assistant Lecturer, Lecturer, Senior Lecturer, University of Sheffield, 1953-65; Professor, Chemistry, University of Malawi, 1965—. Fellowships: Royal Institute of Chemistry; Chemical Society; Member, Climbers' Club. Publications: Studies in Atomic Structure (w. P. J. Hills), 1969; contributor of papers on scientific education to Journal of Chemistry Education, Education in Chemistry, The Science Teacher, & The Malawi Science Teacher; articles on chemical research included in: Journal of the Chemistry Society; Proceedings of the Chemistry Society, Nature, etc. Address: University of Malawi, Box 5200, Limbe, Malawi.

LEMASSON, Lionel-Charles Rene, born St. Louis, Senegal, 4th October 1933. Engineer; Oceanographer. Education: Engineering Agronome, I.N.A.; Chief of Research, Officer of Overseas Scientific & Technical Research; Diploma, Oceanography, ORSTOM. Personal details: married Christiane Falcon, 3 children. Appointments: Oceanographer, ORSTOM Centre, Noumea, Nlle. Caledonie, 1963-66; ibid, Centre of Oceanographic Research, Abidjan, Ivory Coast, 1966—. Memberships: Association Anc. El. INA; Asst. Officers of the Reserve: Seamen's Club of Abidjan. Publications: numerous scientific articles in oceanographic reviews. Honours: Cross of Military Bravery in Commemoration of the Algerian War. Address: Head of Researches, ORSTOM, B.P. V18, Abidjan, Ivory Coast.

LEMON, Richard Michael Laurie, born Chesterfield, U.K. 19th September 1915. Transport Consultant. Education: Malvern College, 1929-33; B.A., M.A., Balliol College, Oxford University, 1933-36. Married, 2 daughters. Appointments include: with Messrs Pickfords Ltd., London; Passenger Transport Board & Great Western Railway, 1936-40; Lt.-Col., Royal Engineers (Transportation), U.K., India & Germany, 1940-46; with Great Western Railway & British Railways, Western Region, 1946-49; with East African Railways & Harbours, Nairobi, Kenya, 1950—; Admin. Assistant, General Manager & Chief Estab. Officer, 1950-54; Chief Assistant to General Manager, 1955-59; Chief Operating Superintendent, 1959-66; Chief Planning Officer (Reorganisation), 1966-68. Chairman of Cricket Section, Nairobi Railway Club. Honours include: C.B.E., 1963. Address: c/o Barclays Bank Ltd., 61 High Street, Pool, Dorset, U.K.

LEOPOLD-THOMAS, Martha Christiana Nene, born 11th May, 1913. Civic Worker; Housewife; Teacher. Education: Primary Government Model School; Secondary, Methodist Girls' High School; attained Last Class, St. Joseph's Convent; passed Junior Cambridge. Personal details: married grandson of late Hon. Mala Mah Thomas, 8 times Mayor of Freetown, Sierra Leone; husband awarded M.B.E.; grandfather, leading educationist in Sierra Leone; 3 sons, 1 daughter. Appointments: Teacher, about 7 years; Note Checker, Bank of West Africa, 1st time the post was Africanized. Memberships: Executive Member, United Christian Council, Sierra Leone; President, United Church Women; Superintendent, St. George's Cathedral Sunday School; Assistant Leader, Bethesda Benevolent Society; Working Committee, Mothers' Union. Honours: Appointed, Justice of the Peace, 1960. Address: 65 Bathurst St., Freetown, Sierra Leone.

LEROY, Paul, born 28th June 1923. Director, National Bank of Paris, Lome, Togo. Address: B.P. 363, Lome, Togo.

LESAMBO, Leon, born 21st June 1929. Bishop. Education: Primary School, Mushie, Lower Seminary, Bokoro; Higher Seminary, Philosophy & Theology, Kabwe; Doctorate, Faculty of Theology, Lovanium, 5 years. Appointments: Ordination, 1956; School Director; Travelling Priest; Secretary to the Bishop, Kutu; Vicar-General, ibid; Bishop, 1967—. B.P. 12 Inongo, Democratic Republic of the Congo.

LESI, Folorunso Ebun Akinboye, born 24th January 1931. Consultant Paediatrician. Education: St. Paul's School, Breadfruit St., Lagos, Nigeria; Reagan Memorial Baptist School, Yaba, 1941-45; C.M.S. Grammar School, Lagos, 1946-51; Royal College of Surgeons, Dublin, Eire, 1953-59; Trinity College, University of Dublin, 1964-68; L.R.C.P.I., L.R.C.S.I., L.M., 1959; D.C.H., 1963; M.R.C.P., 1964; Ph.D., 1969. Married, 3 sons, 1 daughter. Appointments: House Physician & Surgeon, 1959-60; Medical Officer, 1960-63; Senior Medical Officer, 1963-66; Research Fellow, 1961-63, 1966; Lecturer, 1966-70; Senior Lecturer, 1970—. Memberships: Nigerian Medical Association; Paediatric Association of Nigeria; Society of Health, Nigeria; British Medical Association; R.C.S.I. Association of Graduates; Old Grammarian Society, Lagos. Author of original work in fields of nutrition & neo. Honours: Rockefeller Travelling Fellowship, 1963-64; Heinz Fellowship (A) Award, 1970. Address: Department of Paediatrics, College of Medicine of the University of Lagos, P.M.B. 12003, Lagos, Nigeria.

LESI, Frederick Emanuel Afolabi, born Abeokuta, Western State, Nigeria, 24th February 1904. Retired Public Health Inspector. Education: St. Paul's School; Igbore Abeokute & Holy Trinity School, Ebute-Ero, Lagos; Abeokuta District Christ Grammar School; Pupil Teachers' Course, St. Paul's School, Igbore Abeokuta; Training School for Sanitary Inspectors, Public Health Department, Lagos City Council; Certificate of Royal Sanitary Institute for Sanitary Inspector; British West Africa Study Course in the U.K. Married, 2 sons, 2 daughters. Appointments: Pupil Teacher, 1924-25; Sanitary Inspector in Training, Lagos City Council, 1926-27; Second Class Sanitary Inspector, ibid, 1927-32; First Class Sanitary Inspector, 1933-43; Senior Sanitary Inspector, 1944-47; Health Superintendent, 1948-51; Senior Health Superintendent, 1952-59; Retired, 1959. Memberships: General Secretary & President, Young Men's Auxiliary Association, St. Paul's Anglican Church, Igbore Abeokuta; Librarian, General Secretary, & Warden/Treasurer, St. Paul's Anglican Church Choir, Breadfruit, Lagos; Treasurer, DABLAD (Pensioners) Thrift Society; Vice-Chairman, Egbe Omo Igbore (Abeokuta), Lagos; Social Secretary, Warden, General Secretary, & Chairman, Lisabi Club (Nigeria), Lagos. Address: 133 Herbert Macaulay Street, Ebute Metta, Lagos, Nigeria.

LEVAUX, Rene-Alphonse-Andre, born Uccle, Belgium, 16th February 1932. Magistrate. Education: LL.D., Louvain, Belgium, 1954; Bachelor, Commercial & Financial Sciences, ibid, 1955. Married, 5 children. Appointments: Juridical Counseller, Jabena-Belgium World Airlines, Leopoldville, Congo (now Kinshasa, Democratic Republic of the Congo), 1957-60; Sales Promotion, Procter & Gamble Chemicals, Brussels, Belgium, 1960-62; Magistrate, Court of Appeal, Lubumbashi, Democratic Republic of the Congo, 1963—. Memberships: Captain, Reserve, Belgium Army. Author of Analyse Critique du Credit Professionnel en Belgique, 1954. Address: Conseller at the Court of Appeal, Lubumbashi, Katanga, Democratic Republic of the Congo, B.P. 1802Bis.

LEVINSON, Olga May, born South Africa, 8th May. Writer. Education: B.A., Witwatersrand University; A.T.C.L. & L.T.C.L. (Eloc.). Married, 3 sons. Appointments: President, South African Association of Arts, S.W. Africa, 1958-70; Executive Committee, South West Africa Performing Arts Council, 1966. Publications: Call Me Master; The Ageless Land; also numerous articles & short stories in various magazines, newspapers, & books. Regular Broadcaster on South African Broadcasting Corporation. Honours: Winner of 1st Prize, Short Story Competitions, Witwatersrand University, twice. Address: P.O. Box 458, Windhoek, South West Africa.

LEY, Albert, born Burnhaupt-le-Bas, Haut Rhine, France, 17th February 1922. Inspector of Public Property. Education: Diploma of Advanced Studies in Public Law; Doctor of Law, University of Paris. Married, 3 children. Appointments: Head, Office of Registration, Ivory Coast, 1954-56; Head, Officer of Adjoining Land, 1957-61; Head, Office of Public Property, 1961—. Memberships: Institut International de Droit d'Expression Francaise; Treasurer, Association Ivoirienne de Juristes. Publications: Cours de droit dominal et foncier de l'Ecole Nationale d'Administration d'Abidjan; contributor to the review 'Penant'. Address: B.P. 744, Abidjan, Ivory Coast.

LEYS, Colin Temple, born 8th April 1931. Professor of Political Science. Education: B.A., Oxford University, U.K., 1953; M.A., ibid, 1957. Married, 3 children. Appointments: Fellow & Tutor in Politics, Balliol College, Oxford University, 1956-60; Principal, Kwukoni College, Dar es Salaam, Tanzania, 1961-62; Professor of Political Science, Makerere University College, Kampala, Uganda, 1962-65; Professor of Politics, University of Sussex, U.K., 1965-68; Fellow, Institute of Development Studies, ibid, 1967-69; Visiting Professor, University of Nairobi, Kenya, 1969—. Publications: European Politics in Southern Rhodesia (with R. C. Pratt), 1959; A New Deal in Central Africa (ed. with P. Robson), 1960; Federation in East Africa: Problems & Opportunities, 1965; Politicians & Policies; Politics in Acholi, Uganda 1962-65, 1967; Politics & Change in Developing Countries (editor), 1969. Address: P.O. Box 30197, Nairobi, Kenya.

LIBIZANGOMO-JOUMAS, Jacques, born 20th February 1931. Director of Public Works, Gabon. Education: Certificate of Primary Studies, Primary School, Franceville, Gabon,

1944; Secondary Education, Brazzaville, Congo, & Nice, France; Baccalaureat, 1950; Faculty of Science, Poiters & Paris; Diplome d'Ingenieur Mecanicien Electricien, Ecole Sp. de Mecanique et d'Electricite, Paris, 1957; Ecole Nat. Sup. Petrole et Moteurs a Combustion Int., Rueil-Malmaison;. Diplome d'Ingenieur de Recherche et d'Exploitation de Petrole, France, 1962; Dip. Ing. des T.P., Ecole Sp. des Travaux Publics, Paris, France, 1964. Appointments include: Engineer, Societe des Petrole l'Afrique Equatoriale (SPAFE), 1957-63; Engineer des T.P. au Ministry of Public Works, Gabon, 1967—. Memberships: Bureau Politique du Parti Democratique, Gabon; Co-Founder, Engineers' Association, Gabon; Rotary Club, Libreville. Publications: Recueil de Poemes (in preparation). Honours: Chevalier de l'ordre de l'Etoile Equatoriale, 1968; Officer, National Order of Merit, France, 1969. Address: B.P. 49, Libreville, Gabon.

LIMA, William Henry Forcho, born 13th October 1918. Diplomat. Education: Bamenda, West Cameroon; Secondary School, Buea; Teacher Training, Buea & Ibadan, Eastern Nigeria; B.Sc.(Econ.), Central State College, Wilberforce, Ohio, U.S.A., 1950; University of Chicago, Public Administration, University of New York, 1952; Columbia University, New York City; Syracuse University, New York; Clarence Centre, Switzerland. Married, 5 children. Appointments: Instructor, Saint Joseph's College, Sasse, Buea, West Cameroon, Teachers' Training Institute, Basseng, Kumba, & Africa College, Onitcha, Eastern Nigeria; International Civil Servant as Library Assistant, Department of Conference Services, U.N. Secretariat, New York, U.S.A., 1956-59; Assistant Secretary, Ministry of Finance & Secretary of the Economic Development Board, West Cameroon Government, 1960-61; Alternate Representative, Cameroon Mission to the U.N., 1961-62; Counsellor, Cameroon Embassy, Bonn, West Germany, 1963-64; Minister Counsellor, Cameroon Embassy, Washington, D.C., U.S.A., 1964-65; Ambassador of Cameroon to Liberia, 1965-67; Ambassador of Cameroon to U.A.R., Turkey, & Lebanon, 1967—. Honours, Prizes, etc.: U.N. Fellowship & Carnegie Endowment Fellowship for postgraduate study; Das Grosse Verdienstkreuz, National Decoration of the Federal Republic of Germany, 1963; Knight of Order of Valour, Federal Republic of Cameroon, 1967. Address: Embassy of Cameroon, 52 Adbel Moneim Riad Street, Agouza, Cairo, U.A.R.

LIM FAT, Maxime Edouard Limman, born 5th October, 1921; Agricultural & Chemical Engineer. Education: B.Sc., Chemical Engineering, London, U.K.; M.Sc., Agricultural Engineering, Durham. Married, 3 children. Appointments: Principal, Mauritius College of Agriculture, 1963-68; Head, School of Industrial Technology, University of Mauritius, 1968—. Memberships: Fellow, Institution of Agricultural Engine_rs; Institution of Chemical Engineers; Associate, City & Guilds Institute; Provisional Council & Senate, University of Mauritius. Author of various papers in agricultural engineering, education, & industrialization. Address: Reduit Library, University of Mauritius, Mauritius.

LININGTON, Frank, born 12th March 1923. Civil Servant. Education: Elementary; Army Special Corps of Edn. Personal details: married Anna Patricia O'Callaghan of Dublin, 1949. Appointments: Senior Assessor in Charge of Coast Province, Kenya, East African Income Tax Department, 5 years. Memberships: Royal Overseas League; Mombassa Club; Mombassa Sports Club. Address: Senior Assessor in Charge, E.A. Income Tax Department, P.O. Box 525, Mombasa, Kenya.

LIVINGSTONE, Ian, born 11 October 1933. Economist. Education: Sheffield City Grammar School, U.K.; B.A.(Sheffield); M.A.(Yale). Appointments: Lecturer in Economics, Makerere College, Uganda, 1958-61; Lecturer in Economic Statistics, Sheffield University, U.K., 1961-65; Reader in Economics, Makerere College, Uganda, 1965-68; Director, Economic Research Bureau, University College, Dar es Salaam, Tanzania, 1968-70; Research Professor, University of Dar es Salaam, 1970—;. Memberships: English-Speaking Union Fellow, Yale University, 1956-57; Book Review & Country Editor, East African Economic Review; Editorial Board, East African Journal of Rural Development. Publications: Economics for East Africa (with H. W. Ord), 1968; West African Economics (with H. W. Ord), 1969; Economics & Development (with A. S. Goodall), 1970; The Teaching of Economics in African Universities (Editor with R. Routh, J. Riveyemann, K. E. Svendson), 1970; Foreign Aid & Rural Development in Tanzania (Editor with C. Nyitabu); Economic Policy for Development (Editor),· 1971. Address: University of Dar es Salaam, Box 35096, Dar es Salaam, Tanzania.

LLOYD BINNS, Blodwen, born 27th December 1901. Biologist. Education: B.Sc., 1st Class Hons., Botany, University of Wales, U.K., 1922; M.Sc., ibid, 1924; Ph.D., University of Glasgow, 1929. Appointments: Senior Lecturer in Charge, Department of Applied Biology, University of Strathclyde, 1961; Professor, Botany, University of Malawi, 1965—. Fellow, Linnean Society. Publications: Handbook of Botanical Diagrams, 1966; Dictionary of Botanical Terms, 1948; Editor, Science in Films, 1948; Editor, Films For Universities, 1953; first Check-list Herbaceous Flora of Malawi, 1968; Weeds of Malawi; Crop Plants of Malawi, 1969. Address: Chancellor College, University of Malawi, Box 5200, Limbe, Malawi.

LOCK (The Hon. Rev.) Albert Alfred Frank, born 30th June 1917. Minister of Religion, Congregational Church. Education: Congregational Theological Examininations, St. Andrew's College, Birmingham, U.K. Married to Florence Shearman, 3 sons. Appointments: British Civil Service, 1931-45; Congregational Minister, U.K., 1942-55; Missionary of London Missionary Society (now Congregational Council for W.R.L.I.), Mission in Botswana, 1955—; elected Speaker, Botswana National Assembly, 1968; re-elected 1969—. Address National Assembly, P.O. Box 240, Gaborone, Botswana.

LODAM, Benjamin Dusu, born 12th June 1937. Education Officer. Education: S.U.M. Gindiri Secondary School; B.Sc., University

College, Ibadan, Nigeria; M.Sc., University of Ibadan; University of Louvanium, Kinshasa, Democratic Republic of the Congo; University of Aberdeen, U.K. Married, 1 daughter. Appointments: Research Fellow, Ahmadu Bello University, Zaria, Nigeria; Education Officer, Government College, Keffi, Nigeria. Member, Chemical Society, London, U.K. Publications: Metal Complexes Involving Heavier Donor Atoms, Part III (Chemical Society of London). Address: Government College, Keffi, Nigeria.

LOEFLER, Imre J. P., born Budapest, Hungary, 26th March 1929. Professor of Surgery. Education: Schooling, Budapest, Hungary; Medical School, Germany; Graduated, Erlangen, 1954; Postgraduate Training, Surgery, Dusseldorf, Speciality Diploma, 1969; Postgraduate, Cincinnati, Ohio, U.S.A., 1960-64. Appointments: Surgeon, Missionary Hospital, Fort Portal, Uganda, 1964-66; Senior Lecturer, Surgery, Makerere University Medical School, Kampala, Uganda, 1966-69; Professor, ibid, University of Zambia, 1970—; Head, Department of Surgery, The University Teaching Hospital, Lusaka, Zambia, 1970—. Memberships: Association of German Surgeons; Association of East African Surgeons; Exec. Comm., International Society for Research in Medical Education. Publications: Surgical: Portal Hypertension; Malignant Melanoma; Patent Ductus Arteriossus; Colonic Obstruction; Urinary Calculi; & several articles on African medical education & postgraduate training in surgery. Address: The University of Zambia, P.O. Box 2379, Lusaka, Zambia.

LOEWEN, Melvin J., born Steinbach, Canada, December 1925. University Administrator. Education: B.A., Goshen College; B.S., Mankato State; M.A., University of Minnesota, U.S.A.; Ph.D., University of Brussels, Belgium. Appointments include: Director, Congo Polytechnic Institute; President, Universite Libre du Congo; Education Specialist with World Bank. Member of American Scientific Affiliation. Honours include: Chevalier de l'Ordre du Leopard, Congo, 1966. Address: 1818 H. St. N.W., Washington, D.C., 20433, U.S.A.

LOISEAU, Georges Marie Joseph Eugene Martial, born 13th July 1920. Notary. Education: Institution of the Immaculate Conception, Laval; Ecole de Notariat de Paris, France; Diploma of the Chamber of Notaries, Paris. Married, 3 children. Appointments: Notary, Court of Appeal, Abidjan, Ivory Coast, 1953—. Memberships: Founder & Past President, Lions Club of Abidjan, Ivory Coast; Past Vice-Governor, District 403, Lions International Past Vice-President, Centres Internationaux de montagne; Societe d'Etudes et de Preparation du Club des Explorateurs. Honours: Laureate, School of Notaries, Pairs. Address: 6 rue Paris-Village, B.P. 1446, Abidjan, Ivory Coast.

LONG, Peter, born London, U.K., 7th December 1915. Police Officer. Education: St. Bede's Prep. School, Eastbourne, U.K.; Eastbourne College; C.I.D. Course, Hendon, 1949; Security Course, 1950; Bramshill Police College Senior Course, 1954. Married, 1 daughter. Appointments: Metropolitan Police, London, 1936-38; Assistant Superintendent, Superintendent, C.I.D. & Security, Jamaica, 1938-51; Superintendent of C.I.D., Malawi, 1951-53; Senior Superintendent, ibid, 1953-58; Assistant Commissioner of Police, Malawi, 1958-60; Senior Assistant Commissioner of Police, 1960-63; Deputy Commissioner of Police, 1963-64; Commissioner of Police, 1964—. Memberships: Vice-Chairman, Zomba Gymkhana Club, 1953; Founder, Ndirande Sailing Club, & Vice-Commodore, 1959; Rear Commodore, ibid, 1960; Founder Member, Lions International, Malawi. Honours: Colonial Police Medal, Meritorious Service, 1948; Queen's Police Medal, Distinguished Service, 1960; O.B.E., 1964; C.B.E., 1966; Commander, Order of Menelik II, Ethiopia; Commander, Order of Malagasy. Address: Police Headquarters, P.O. Box 41, Zomba, Malawi.

LOUPEKINE, Igor Serge, born Egypt (U.A.R.), 12th September 1920. University Professor; Seismologist. Education: Anseriean University, Cairo, U.A.R., 1935-39; University of Bristol, U.K., 1939-43; B.Sc.; Ph.D.; C.Eng. Appointments: Lecturer in Geology, University of Bristol, 1943-56; Senior Lecturer in Geology, Royal Technical College, Nairobi, Kenya, 1956-60; Professor of Geology & Head of Department of Geology, University College, Nairobi, 1961-70. UNESCO Expert in Earthquakes. Fellowships: Geological Soc. of London; Royal Geographical Soc.; Gemmological Assn. of G.B. Memberships: Institution of Mining & Metallurgy; Mineralogical Society of London; American Mineralogical Society; Geologists' Association; Hon. Sec., Geological Club of Nairobi. Author of many papers in field published in scientific journals. Address: University of Nairobi, P.O. Box 30197, Nairobi, Kenya.

LOVEDAY, Anthony Joseph, born Manchester, U.K., 20th November 1925. University Librarian. Education: M.A.(Cantab.); Dip. Lib.(London); Ampleforth College, Yorks.; Christ's College, Cambridge University; University College, London. Appointments include: Assistant Librarian, University College, London, 1950-57; Assistant Librarian, University of Malaya, Singapore, 1957-59; Assistant Librarian, University of London Library, U.K., 1960-62; Deputy Librarian, Makerere University College, Uganda, 1962-65; University Librarian, University of Zambia, Lusaka, 1965—. Memberships include: Chairman, Professional Board on Library Studies, Zambia; Vice-Chairman (formerly Chairman), Zambia Library Association; former Vice-Chairman, University of Zambia Staff Association. Address: University of Zambia, P.O. Box 2379, Lusaka, Zambia.

LUBALA, Sylvester Doto, born Kwimba District, Tanzania, 30th December 1925. Area Commissioner. Primary Education: Standard 1 to 4 at Sumue Catholic School, 1935-38; Secondary Education: St. 5-9 at Nyegezi Catholic School, 1938-43. Married, 15 children. Appointments include: Nursing Orderly Class II during Second World War; 1943-46; Ward Master, Overseas Food Corporation, Kongwa, Tanganyika; Laboratory Assistant, E.A. Medical Research Institute, Mwanza; Secretary, Transport and General Workers Union, Kwimba; Chairman, Kwimba District Council; Chairman, TANU Kwimba District; ex-Executive Officer, Kwimba District Council; Area Commissioner, Kwimba-Maswa District; Staff Officer, Regional Administration, Morogoro; Area Commissioner, Korogwe. Memberships: Tanganyika African National Union, formerly Chairman and District Secretary; former Member of Trade Union, & Branch Secretary, 1958-60; former Member and Secretary of Catholic Association; Tanganyika Parents' Association. Honours prizes, etc.: Burma Star and War Medal, 1945. Address: P.O. Box 532, Korogwe, Tanga, Tanzania.

LUBANDI, Jether B., born June 1914. Public Administration. Education: Busoga College, Mwiri, Uganda, 1930-36; King's College, Budo, 1937; Makerere University College, 1938-39; U.K., 1954. Appointments: Accounts Clerk, 1940-43; Accountant, 1944-47; Assistant Treasurer, 1948-54; Treasurer, Busoga, 1955-62; Assistant General Manager, Madhvani Group, 1963—; M.P., Busoga West. Memberships: Lions Club, Jinja; Chairman, Madhvani Secondary School; Deputy Chairman, Busoga College, Mwori; Kampala Club; Commonwealth Parliamentary Association. Honours: Independence Medal, 1962; Recognition Award, Uganda Scouts Association, 1970. Address: P.O. Box 3001, Kakira, Uganda.

LUBEGA, Anthony, born 28th September, 1931. Architect. Education: Senior Secondary, St. Mary's College, Ilisubi, Uganda, 1947-52; Engineering School, Ilampola, 1953-57; A.A.Dip., Architectural Association School of Architecture, London, U.K., 1960-65; Post-graduate, Town Planning, Architectural Association; Ph.D., Architecture, University of London, 1970. Married, 6 children. Appointments: Architect, 1965-66; Ph.D. Research Architect, 1967-70; Senior Architect, 1970; Chief Architect, Ministry of Works Communications & Housing, Uganda Government, 1970—. Memberships: Associate, Royal Insitute of British Architects; Uganda Society of Architecture; University College London Old Students' Association; Architectural Association. Author of articles on architecture, planning, & housing in the Africa Features Ltd. Honours: Travel Scholarship Awards, 1962 & 1964; Year Prizes, 1964 & 1965. Address: Ministry of Works Communication & Housing, P.O. Box 10, Entebbe, Uganda.

LUBEGA (Rev.) George William, born 18th March 1933. Clergyman; Provincial Trainer, Church of Uganda, Rwanda & Burondi. Education: Mukono Theological College, 1955-56, 1963-65; Church of England Board of Education Training Programme, U.K., 1970. Appointments: Chaplain to Uganda Police, 1965-67; Chaplain to Mulago Hospital, Kampaga, 1968-69; Provincial Training Officer, 1969—. Patron to Mulago Y.C.A. Address: Church of Uganda, P.O. Box 14123, Kampala, Uganda.

LUBEGA, Matiya, born 26th December 1933. Diplomat. Education: B.A.(London); M.A.(Michigan); Carnegie Fellow in Diplomacy, Columbia University, U.S.A. Appointments: Income Tax Officer, Uganda, 1959; Assistant Secretary, Ministry of Foreign Affairs, 1962; Secretary & Acting High Commissioner of Uganda to Ghana, 1963-65; Uganda's Alternate Representative, U.N. Security Council, 1966-67; Under-Secretary, Ministry of Foreign Affairs, 1967-69; Ambassador of Uganda to the U.S.S.R., 1969—. Contributor to Midwest Journal of Political Science, 1961. Address: Ambassador of Uganda, Pereulok Sadovskikh 5, Moscow, U.S.S.R.

LUBWA, Israel Lachara, born 9th February 1923. Agriculturalist. Education: Gulu C.M.S. Primary School, 1934-37; Gulu High School, 1938-42; Nabumali High School, 1943; King's College, Budo, 1944-45; Diploma in Agriculture, Makerere University, 1945-52. Married, 1 son, 6 daughters. Appointments: Assistant Agricultural Officer, 1953-60; Agricultural Officer, 1961-64; Regional Agricultural Mechanization Officer, Western Region, 1965-66; Regional Agricultural Mechanization Officer, Northern Region, 1967-70. Memberships: Life Member, Uganda Agricultural Society; President, Makerere Agricultural Society; Rehabilitation Committee for ex-prisoners, West Nile, 1958-60; Secretary, Gulu Cultural Society. Publications: A study of resistance of infection of sorghum smut disease (Sphacelothica sorghii); A Chronological History of Establishing Ox Cultivation in Uganda, 1909-1962. Honours: Budo Sports Colour for Athletics, 1945; Makerere University Cross-Country Cup, 1948. Address: Regional Agricultural Mechanization Officer, Northern Region, P.O. Box 163, Gulu, Uganda.

LUCAS, Ajenifuja Ayinla, born Lagos, Nigeria, 25th December 1933. General Trader & Contractor. Education: West African Schl. Cert.; G.C.E. 'A' level. Married, 4 children. Appointments include: Established own business, Ajenifuja Commercial Enterprises, Importer & Exporter, Gen. Trader, Commission Agent, Contractor & Stationery Suppliers. Address: 12 Andrew Street, P.O. Box 3485, Lagos, Nigeria.

LUCAS, Eric, born 22nd May, 1911. Professor of Education: Education: Manchester Grammar School, U.K., 1923-30; B.A., Emmanuel College, Cambridge, 1930-35; M.A., ibid, 1937. Appointments: College & University Teacher, Cambridge, 1933-35; Biology Master, Winchester College, 1935-51; Assistant Master, Alliance High School, Kenya, 1947; Assistant Master & Acting Headmaster, Nyakasura School, Uganda, 1949-50; Professor of Education, Makerere University College, 1951-71; Head, Institute of Education, 1951-64; Research Professor of Education; Part Author, Uganda: Our Homeland; What is a Man?; What is Freedom?; What is Greatness?; (Editor & Part English Traditions in East African Education; Part Author, Uganda: Our Homeland; What is a Man?; What is Freedom?: What is Greatness?; (Editor & Part Author). Recipient, Uganda Independence Medal, 1962. Address: Makerere University, P.O. Box 7062, Kampala, Uganda.

LUCAS, Peter, born 3rd February 1938. Government Commissioner. Education: Rugby School, U.K.; M.A., King's College, Cambridge

University; Solicitor (Hons.) Appointments: Lands Officer, Malawi Government; Senior Lands Officer, ibid; Commissioner for Lands. Memberships: Secretary, Society of Antiquaries of Malawi; Junior Services Club, London. Publications: Land Tenure Amongst the Sena People of the Lower Shire, Journal of Malawi Society; Lugard at Karonga, History Today. Honours: Cook Prizeman, British Law Society, 1962; Order of Lion of Malawi, Class 2, Malawi Government, 1970. Address: P.O. Box 568, Blantyre, Malawi.

LUCK (Rev.) David William, born 3rd September 1926. Teacher; Chaplain. Education: B.A.(Toronto), 1949; L.Th. (Wycliffe College, University of Toronto), 1952; M.A. (McGill University), 1960. Appointments: Lecturer, Panjab University, India, 1953-62; Delhi University, ibid, 1962-63; Agra University, 1963-65; Calcutta University, 1965-67; Tutor, National Teachers' College, Kampala Uganda. Address: National Teachers' College, P.O.B. 20012, Kampala, Uganda.

LUGAKINGIRA, Kamugumya Simon Kahwa, born 15th November 1939. Civil Servant. Education: Kahororo Secondary School; Ilboru Secondary School; Tabora Boys' School; LL.B.(Lond.), University College of Dar es Salaam, Tanzania. Appointments: Assistant Registrar-General; Assistant Administrator-General; Land Officer; Senior Land Officer; Secretary & Legal Adviser, Customary Land Tribunal; Assistant Commissioner for Lands. Vice-President, National Union of Tanzania Students. Address: Ministry of Lands, Housing & Urban Development, P.O. Box 9230, Dar es Salaam, Tanzania.

LUGIRA, Aloysius Muzzanganda, born 19th July, 1931. University Teacher. Primary & Secondary, Masaka, Uganda; Philosophy & Theology, Katigondo Seminary, 1953-58; Ethnology, History of Art & Theology, Fribourg University, Switzerland; S.th.B.; S.Th.L.; S.Th.D.; Postgraduate Diploma, Social Anthropology, Oxford University, U.K., 1966-67. Appointments: Lecturer, Religious Studies & Instructor, Philosophy, Makerere College, University of East Africa, 1965-66; Lecturer, Religious Studies, ibid, 1968-70; Visiting Professor, Religious Studies & Third World Studies, University of California, Santa Cruz, U.S.A., 1970; Fellow, Merrill College; Lecturer, Religious Studies, Makerere University, Kampala, Uganda. Memberships: International Association for the History of Religion; Uganda Society; Founder, Uganda Student Union, Switzerland & Germany; President, Old Seminarians Association, Uganda; Governing Board, Namagunga College. Publications: Ganda Art, 1970; The Concept of Katonda, 1970; Author of articles in international journals; Editor, Dini na Mila; ibid, Uganda Heritage; Editorial Board, Afer. recipient, Inter-University Studentship, 1966-67. Address: Makerere University, P.O. Box 7062, Kampala, Uganda.

LUGOL, Gilbert Marius, born Toulouse, France, 10th May 1920. Chief Mining Engineer. Education: Ecole Polytechnique, Paris; Ecole Nationale Superieure des Mines, Paris; Ecole du Petrole, ibid. Married to Suzanne Michard, 2 sons, 1 daughter. Appointments: Director, Afrique Noire, Madagascar d'ERAP-ELF, 1966; President/Director-General, Society des Petroles de Madagascar, 1965; President/Director-General, ELF-SPAFE, Gabon, 1966; President/Director-General, ELF—SEREPCA, Cameroun, 1966. Honours: Officer, Ordre National Malgache; Commandeur Etoile Equatorial. Address: c/o ERAP—ELF, 7 rue Nelaton, 75 Paris, France.

LUHANGA, Eliuter Kivaula, born 1st January 1914. Administrative Officer. Education: Tosamaganga Secondary School; Medical Training, Sewa Haji Hospital, Dar es Salaam, Tanzania, 1935-37. Married, 4 sons, 2 daughters. Appointments: Medical Assistant, Tanganyika Government, 1938-53; Local Sub-Chief, Uhehe Local Authority, Iringa District, 1953-59; Administrative Officer, Regional Administration of Tanzania, 1970—, posted to various locations in country & capital. Memberships: TANU; Mbozi Club. Address: Mbozi District Office, P.O. Box 45, Mbozi, Tanzania.

LUKE, Thomas Olatunji Josephus Carew, born Lagos, Nigeria, 6th August 1910. Former Civil Servant; Company Director. Education: Sierra Leone Grammar School; Intermediate London; B.A., Private Study, 1932; St. Edmund Hall, Oxford University, U.K., 1946-49; M.A., 1956. Widower, 1 son, 1 daughter. Appointments include: Sierra Leone Clerical Service, 1928-41; Assistant Secretary, Colonial Secretariat, 1941; Clerk to Legislative Council, 1942-46; Chief Estab. Officer, later Estab. Sec., 1950-61; Chairman, Sierra Leone Airways, 1961—; Director, Sierra Leone Development Company Ltd., 1961—; Joint Commnr., advising Uganda Government on acceleration of Africanization in Uganda Civil Service, 1962; Chairman, Localization Commnr., Swaziland, 1965-66; Sole Localization Commnr., Botswana, 1966; Dir., Sierra Leone Diocesan Bookshop Ltd., 1967—. Memberships include: Chairman, Board of Governors, Sierra Leone Grammar School, 1950—; President, Sierra Leone Red Cross Society, 1965—; Sierra Leone Church Synod; former Sierra Leone Pub. Service Commn.; ibid, Fourah Bay Coll. Council; Freetown Dinner Club. Honours include: M.B.E., 1946; J.P., 1949; O.B.E., 1956. Address: P.O. Box 648, Freetown, Sierra Leone.

LUKEERA, Joseph Moses, born 19th February 1938. Lawyer. Education: Primary, Uganda; Cambridge School Certificate, 1st Class, St. John, Kabako, 1957; Barrister-at-Law, Lincoln's Inn, London, U.K., 1963; Teaching Diploma, King's College, London, 1959; LL.B., International University of Comparative Sciences, Luxembourg, 1963. Appointments: Solicitor-General, Uganda, 1964; Commissioner of Customs & Excise, East Africa, 1965-68; Practising Advocate, Kampala, Uganda. Member, Lions Club International. Address: P.O. Box 2346, Kampala, Uganda.

LUKELE, Andrew Manqunte, born 8th August 1929. Attorney-at-Law. Education: B.A., Witwatersrand University, South Africa, 1953; Attorney's Admission Examination,

University of South Africa, 1956; LL.M., Harvard Law School, U.S.A., 1970. Publications: The Agrarian Sector of the Swaziland Economy—Aspects of a Dual Economy; Notes on Custom, Public Accommodations, Corporations & the 14th Amendment. Recipient, Law Society Prize, Transvaal Law Society, 1957. Address: 205 Miller's Mansions, P.O. Box 366, Mbabane, Swaziland.

LUKENGE, Wilson-Kalyaburo, born 19th December 1944. Artist; Art Teacher. Education: Lubiri Senior Secondary School, Uganda; Makerere School of Fine Art; Graduate, Makerere University., Kampala. Personal details: member of Kalyaburo family. Currently, Head, Art Department, Lubiri Senior Secondary School. Held, One-man Exhibition of drawings, paintings, & sculpture, Uganda Museum, 1970. Work represented in University Hall. Member, Nomo Gallery. Recipient, Sculpture Prize, School of Fine Art, Makerere, 1968. Address: Lubiri Senior Secondary School, P.O. Box 14148, Kampala, Uganda.

LUKEY, Frank William, born 17th February 1940. Lecturer in Applied Physics. Education: B.Sc., Physics, Sheffield, U.K., 1964. Married, 1 daughter. Appointments: Assistant Experimental Officer, UKAEA, Harwell, U.K.; Physics Master, Barnsley, Yorks.; Lecturer, Applied Physics, University of Science & Technology, Kumasi, Ghana. Memberships: Grad. Institute of Physics; Methodist Local Preacher, Kumasi. Address: University of Science & Technology, Kumasi, Ghana.

LULUME, Elias, born 18th March 1918. Physician. Education: Buruma Primary School, 1926-29; Nyenga Seminary, 1930-36; Gaba Seminary, 1937-38; Namilyango College, 1939; Makerere University College & Medical School, Kampala, Uganda, 1940-45. Appointments: Medical Officer, Uganda Government, 1946; Medical Superintendent, Kitgum Hospital, Northern Region, 1967; ibid, Kitagata Hospital, Western Region, 1969. Member, Uganda Medical Association. Address: P.O. 959 Masaka, Uganda.

LUSWATA, Frederick James, born 31st December 1926. Agriculturist. Education: B.Sc., Agriculture, University of Wales, Aberystwyth, U.K. Diploma, Agriculture, Makerere University, Kampala, Uganda. Married, 6 children. Appointments: District Agricultural Officer; Senior Agricultural Officer; Assistant Commissioner for Agriculture; General Manager, Agricultural Enterprises Ltd. Address: P.O. Box 7020, Kampala, Uganda.

LUTAYA (Rt. Rev.) Tesito, born 1899, Diocesan Bishop of West Buganda. Education: Mityana Sec. School, 1912-18; Government Scholarship to King's College, Budo, 1918-21. Personal details: family Christian; grandfather, Saza Chief Paul Bakunga; married to Erina Nakibuka, 4 sons, 1 daughter. Appointments: Schoolmaster, Masinsi Secondary School, 1923-29; Headmaster, Masindi Sec. School, 1923; Theological College Bishop Tucker Mukono, 1928-30; Deacon, 1931; Priest, Uganda Diocese, 1932-38; Vicar of St. Paul's Cathedral, Kampala, 1939-41; Chaplain, Theological Bishop Tucker Mukono, 1943-45; Rural Dean, Uganda Diocese, 1946-47; Ridley Hall Cambridge Diocese of Ely, 1947-49; Canon of Uganda & Subdean, The Cathedral, Kampala, 1949-52. Cons. Assistant, Bishop of Uganda, 1952; Diocesan Bishop of West Buganda, 1960—. Memberships: Life Member of Bible Society; C.H.S., England. Honours: 2 Silver Medals, Invested by British Commissioners; Bronze Medal, Invested by H.M. Queen Elizabeth II, 1954. Address: Church of Uganda, P.O. Box 1, Mityana, Uganda.

LUTTERODT, George Daniel, born 15th August 1935. Pharmacologist. Education: Grade I School Certificate, Prempeh College, Ghana, 1956; Higher School Certificate, ibid, 1958; B.Sc.(Gen.), St. Andrew's University, U.K., 1963; B.Sc.(Hons.), ibid, 1964; M.Sc., 1965; Ph.D., Bath University, 1969. Married, 4 children. Appointments: Lecturer, University of Science & Technology, Kumasi, Ghana, 1965 & 1969—; ibid, Bath University, U.K., 1966. Memberships: Medical & Scientific Branch, British Diabetic Association; Secretary, University Academic Staff Association, University of Science & Technology; one-time President, Ghana Students' Union, Dundee & St. Andrews. Author, Retinal & Renal Microangiopathy in Diabetes—An E-M Study, a paper presented at the VIIth International Conference on Diabetes, Buenos Aires, Argentina. Honours: Maths. Prize, 1953; 5th Form Physics Prize, 1956; Senior Art Prize, 1955; Junior Art Prize, 1954. Address: University of Science & Technology, Kumasi, Ghana.

LUYOMBYA, Mbuga Francis Xavier, born 12th December 1933. Agronomist. Education: Primary, Uganda Martyrs' School, Namilango, —1945; Junior, Jinja College, —1950; Senior, St. Henry's College, Kitovu, Masaka, —1954; Graduate, Agriculture, Makerere University, Kampala, —1960; Postgraduate, Soil Science, Rehovot, Israel, —1965; Business Management, I.C.I., London, U.K., 1969. Married, 2 sons, 3 daughters. Currently, Technical Representative, Agriculture & Commercial Assistant, Twiga Chemical Industries Ltd., an I.C.I. Associate Company. Memberships: Uganda Professional Association; Uganda Agricultural Association; Makerere Scientific Society; Makerere Art Society. Address: Twiga Chemical Industries Ltd., P.O. Box 4800, Kampala, Uganda.

LWAMBWA, Crispin, born 7th February 1943. Journalist. Education: Primary, 6 years; Secondary, 5 years; Journalism Course, 1 year. Married, 2 children. Appointments: Broadcaster & Reporter, Radio Nationale, Kinshasa, Democratic Republic of the Congo, 1961-62; Provincial Director, Information Service, Tshikopa, 1963; Editor, Director, 'La Depeche', 1964—; Editor, Radioa Nationale, Katanga, 1965. Memberships: Congolese Press Association; Congolese Newspaper Editors' Association; Regional Committee Member, Youth Party, Katanga, in charge of propaganda, 1968—. Recipient, Certificate, C.V.R. (Corps des Voluntaires de la Republique), 1967. Address: B.P. 884, Lusumbashi, Katanga, Democratic Republic of the Congo.

LWANGA, Stephen Kaggwa, born 21st November 1940. Statistician. Education: King's College, Budo, Uganda; B.A., Makerere University, Kampala; M.Sc., Edinburgh & Aberdeen Universities, U.K.; M.A., Harvard University School of Public Health, U.S.A. Currently, Lecturer, Statistics, Makerere Medical School, Kampala, Uganda, 1967—. Fellow, Royal Statistical Society. Author of various scientific papers in medical journals. Address: Department of Preventive Medicine, Makerere University, P.O. Box 7072, Kampala, Uganda.

LWEBANDIZA, Titus Silas, born 18th October 1918. Veterinary Surgeon; Director of Agriculture. Education: Standard VIII, Primary School, 1938; Standard X, Secondary School, 1939-40; Makerere College, Kampala, Uganda, 1941-45. Married, 2 sons, 7 daughters. Veterinary Practitioner, 1946-62; Acting Director, Training, 1962; Director, Veterinary Services, Ministry of Agriculture, Tanzania, 1962-68; Director of Agriculture, 1969—. Address: Ministry of Agriculture, P.O. Box 9152, Dar es Salaam, Tanzania.

LWEBOGOLA, Laurent Kagoye Kipeche, born Bukoba, Tanzania, 14th August 1934. Teacher; Local Government Officer; Administrative Officer. Education: Primary, Kigarama School, 1950; Secondary, Nyakota School, 1955; G.C.E. O Level, Grammar School, Uganda, 1960; Administrative Law, 1967. Married, 4 sons, 1 daughter. Appointments: Grade A Teacher, 1962-64; Local Government Officer, 1965; Administrative Officer, 1966—. Memberships: Tanganyika African National Union, 1964; Captain, Badminton Club, 1961-62; Chairman, Geographical Society, 1961-62; Choir Master, 1961-62. Recipient, Medal, Royal Society for the Prevention of Cruelty to Animals, Essay Prize, 1954. Address: Administrative Officer, Liwale, Nachingwea, Tanzania.

LWOKYA, Aloysius, born 25th March 1929. Senior Executive Officer. Education: Primary; Junior Secondary; Senior Secondary, Commercial. Married. Appointments: Clerical Officer, General Class, 1950; General Executive Officer, 1956; Superintendent of Typing Pool, 1966; Office Superintendent, Ministry of Education, Uganda, 1960; Higher Executive Officer, 1965; Senior Executive Officer, Establishments, 1968—. Memberships: Secretary, Kisubi Branch, Uganda Martyrs; St. Mary's Old Boys' Association; Blessed Baganda Martyrs' Association. Recipient, Independence Medal, Uganda, 1960. Address: P.O. Box 7063, Kampala, Uganda.

LY, Bocar, born 27th December 1925. Agricultural Engineer. Education: Baccalaureat, Lycée de Daker, Senegal; Engineer, National School of Agriculture, Montpellier, France; Superior School of Tropical Agriculture. Appointments: Past Director, Agriculture, Senegal; Past Technical Adviser, Ministry of Rural Development, ibid; currently with FAO. Memberships: Association of Agricultural Engineers, Senegal; Syndicate of Engineers & Technicians, Senegal. Publications: Le regime foncier des terres inosides dans la vallee du fleuve Senegal, 1954; Le drama de la Vallee du fleuve Senegal, 1958. Honours: laureate, European Congress for Live Products, OECE, 1956. Address: FAO, United Nations, B.P. 466, Ouagadougou, Upper Volta.

LYDALL, John Graham, born 24th January 1920. Coffee Merchant. Education: Preparatory School, 1928-33; Marlborough College, U.K., 1933-38. Married to Blanche L. Wilderspin, née Easdown. Appointments: Director, Naumann Gepp & Co. Ltd., London, 1953-60; Director, Naumann Gepp (E.A.), Ltd., Nairobi, Kenya, 1955-70; Managing Director, Cetco Ltd. (previously known as Tchibo Trading Co. Ltd.), Nairobi, 1960-70. Memberships: President, The Mild Coffee Trade Association of Eastern Africa, 1963-66; Vice-President, presently Acting President, ibid, 1969-70; Vice-President, the Rotary Club of Nairobi (North). Address: Mild Coffee Trade Association, P.O. Box 2732, Nairobi, Kenya.

M

MA'AJI, Solomon Lamarmusa, born Lassa, Adamawa Province, N.E. State, Nigeria, 1938. Teacher, Education: Grade II Teachers' Cert.; Ahmadu Bello University, Zaria, 1969-70. Married, 4 children. Appointments include: Assistant Headmaster, 1956-57; Headmaster, Junior Primary School, 1959-60; Headmaster, Senior Primary School, 1963-69. Memberships: President, Debating Society, Teachers' College, Mubi, 1958-59. Address: Adamawa Local Education Authority, Education Office, Yola, P.O. Yola, Adamawa Province, N.E. State, Nigeria.

MAAZOUN, Ahmed, born 4th January 1942. Professor of Physical Culture; Rehabilitative & Medical Masseur. Education: Diploma in Physiotherapy & 'Medico-Sportive', Institute of Nice, France, 1963; Diploma of Higher Studies in Physical Culture, Institute of Paris, 1962. Married. Memberships: La Federation Tunisienne de Gymnastique, d'halerophilie et de Culturisme; President, Youth Sports Association; Director, Centre for Physical Culture. Publications: Toute la culture physique moderne: Amaiguisante, medical, hygienique, athletique; Gymnestique corrective et medicale; Tous les massages medicaux: orthopedique, sportifs-esthetique, reeducatifs. Honours include: Diploma, Tunisian Federation of Athletics; Diploma, Club of Human Sculpture of Monte Carlo; Diploma, Tunisian Federation of Gymnastics. Address: Centre de Culture Physique de Sfax, 6 rue Remada, Sfax, Tunisia.

MABEYO, Sebastian Mwakami, born 9th August 1924. Chief Accountant. Education: Primary Education, Kauora, Swimba, 1936-40; Secondary Education, Senior Secondary School, Tabora, 1941-47. Married, 8 children. Appointments: Accounts Clerk, Treasury, 1948-51; Cashier, Revenue Offices, 1951-62; Regional Accountant, Treasury, 1963-64; Senior Accountant, 2nd Vice-President's Office, 1964-66; Chief Accountant, ibid, 1966-70; President, East African Currency Board, Tanzania Office, 1969—. Address: c/o Tanzania Office, East African Currency Board, Tanzania.

McCAFFERY, George Bernard, born 29th January 1922. Security Adviser. Education: Plymouth College, U.K., 1930-36; School of Military Engineering, 1936-40. Married to Mignon Reynolds, 1 son. Appointments: joined Colonial Police Force, 1946; served Nigeria, 1946-56; Deputy Commissioner, Mauritius, 1957-64; Commissioner of Police, 1964-69; Security Adviser to Government of Mauritius, 1969—. Honours: Colonial Police Medal, 1957; Queen's Police Medal, 1966. Address: Office of the Prime Minister, Port Louis, Mauritius.

MACARTNEY, W. J. Allan, Born 17th February 1941. Lecturer, Education: M.A. (Edinburgh); B.Litt.(Glasgow), U.K. Married, 3 children. Appointments: Teacher, St. Augustine's Grammar School, Nkwerre-Orlu, Biafra, 1963-64; Lecturer, Department of Government & Administration, University of Botswana, Lesotho, & Swaziland, 1966—. Memberships: African Studies Association, U.S.A.; ibid, U.K.; Political Science Association of the U.K.; American Political Science Association; Royal Commonwealth Society. Publications: The Parliaments of Botswana, Lesotho, & Swaziland, 1969; Botswana Goes to the Polls, 1969; African Westminster? The Parliament of Lesotho, 1970. Address: Department of Government & Administration, University of Botswana, Lesotho, & Swaziland, P.O. Roma, Lesotho.

MACAULAY, Hannah Jan Matilda, born Sierra Leone, 26th December 1901. Missionary. Personal details: daughter & granddaughter of Ministers of Religion; wife of a Canon of the Anglican Church; 45 years a Missionary. Appointments: Mothers' Union Official, 16 years; Justice of the Peace; Mbr., Panel of Radio Prayers. Memberships: Red Cross Society; Associate, Children's Home for Destitute; Associate, Blind School; Associate, Paupers' Home. Address: 60 Wellington Street, Freetown, Sierra Leone.

MACAULEY, Joseph Olatunde, born Porto-Novo, Dahomey, 27th February 1902. Retired Land Officer. Education: Ecole Regionale, Porto-Novo; Ecole Normale, ibid; awarded Scholarship to Dakar Institute of Education; Hope Institute High School, Lagos, Nigeria. Personal details: grandson of Collins Macauley, late of Sierra-Leone, Merchant, Lagos; son of John Oyeyemi Shobo Macauley; married. Appointments: Clerk, Judicial Department; Sub-Inspector of Lands, Land Department, 1927; Land Officer, ibid & 1st Nigerian ever to be so promoted. Memberships: Methodist Church of Nigeria; Church Leader, ibid, 1950; Service on a number of Church Committees; Chairman, Wesley Guild, Ikoyi Church; Freemason; Ikoyi Club Local Association of Nigerian Scout Movement; Vice-Chairman, Political Party (Action Group) Constituency, 1965; Vice President, Lagos City Health Society, 1968-70; Society of Health, Nigeria, 1969. Honours: Coronation Medal, 1953; O.B.E., awarded on retirement from the service of Federation of Nigeria. Address: St. Ceceilia, 10 Obalende Road, Lagos, Nigeria.

McCAULEY (Rt. Rev.) Vincent J., born 8th March 1906. Catholic Bishop. Education: B.A., University of Notre Dame, U.S.A., 1930; Theology, Catholic University, Washington, D.C., 1934; Graduate Studies, English Literature, Boston College, 1934-36. Personal details: father, Chief Test Board Supervisor, Regional Office, Am. Tel. & Tel., Omaha, Nebraska. Appointments: Teacher of English & Greek, U.S.A., 1935 & 1936; Teacher, English & Latin, Bandhura Seminary, East Pakistan, 1936-44; Rector, 1938-44; Rector, Holy Cross Seminary, Washington, D.C., 1946-52. Assistant Director, ibid, 1952-58; Superior of Mission, Fort Portal, Uganda, 1958-61; Bishop of Diocese, 1961-70; Chairman, AMECEA (Association of Bishops of Eastern Africa), 1963-70; Consultor, SECAM (All Africa Symposium of Catholic Bishiops), 1969-70; Vice-Chairman, Uganda Cath. Episcopal Conference, 1966-70; Chairman, Uganda Cath. Medical Bureau, Uganda Cath. Information Bureau, & Uganda Cath. Social Services, 1966-70; Chairman, Uganda Joint Christian Council, 1964-69. Member of Vatican Council II, 1962-65. Publications: Off the Beaten Path, 1950; numerous articles in 'Holy Cross Missions', articles in 'World Mission', N.Y. Address: P.O. Box 214, Fort Portal, Uganda.

McCORKINDALE, Archibald Armour, born 12th July 1923. Consulting Civil Engineer. Education: B.Sc., C.Eng., Glasgow University, U.K. Appointments: training with contractors, U.K.; joined, Sir Alexander Gibb & Partners (Africa), 1950; Partner, 1964; responsible for the design of various projects in East & Central Africa, Mauritius, & Botswana. Memberships: F.I.C.E.; M.ASCE; M.Cons.E.; M.E.A.I.E. Nairobi Club; Muthaiga Club; Past Chairman, Association of Consulting Engineers of Kenya. Address: P.O. Box 30020, Nairobi, Kenya.

McCRAE, Angus Wilson Ritchie, born 14th February 1932. Entomologist. Education: M.A., Jesus College, Cambridge University, U.K., 1953-56. Married, 2 sons. Appointments: Research Assistant, Midge Control Unit, Dept. of Zoology, Edinburgh University, Scotland, 1957-58; Medical Entomologist, Vector Control Division, Ministry of Health, Uganda, 1958-66; Principal Research Officer, Head of Division of Entomology & Vertebrate Ecology, E.A. Virus Research Institute, 1966—. Fellowships: Royal Entomological Society of London; Royal Society of Tropical Medicine & Hygiene. Memberships: Inst. of Biology; Founder Member, E.A. Academy; Committee, E.A. Society for Biological Research, 1962-65; Symposium Organizing Secretary, ibid, 1964; Committee, The Uganda Society, 1964-70; Editorial Board, The Uganda Journal; Organizing Secretary, Natural History Branch, 1964-68; Committee, Mountain Club of Uganda, 1966-70; Hon. Treasurer, 1969-70; Hon. Lecturer, Department of Preventive Medicine, Makerere Medical School, 1967—; Occasional Temporary Consultant, W.H.O. Publications: 24 papers on entomological & epidemiological subjects. Address: East African Virus Research Institute, P.O. Box 49, Entebbe, Uganda.

McCURRY, Patricia, born 7th December 1946. University Lecturer. Education: King Edward VI School for Girls, Camp Hill,

Birmingham, U.K., 1957-65; University of Exeter, Devon, 1965-68; B.Sc.; M.Sc. Appointments: G.V.S.O. Lecturer in Geology, Ahmadu Bello University, Zaria, Nigeria, 1968-70; Assistant Lecturer in Geology, ibid, 1970—. Fellow of the Geological Society of London, U.K. Publications include: Atlantic Fracture Zones and the Guinea Coast (with J. B. Wright), J. Mining & Geology, 1970; First occurrence of manganese ores in Northern Nigeria, Econ. Geol., 1970; Comments on the significance of sandstone inclusions in lavas of the Comores Archipelago (by Flower & Strong), Earth & Plan. Sci. Lett., 1970; Comments on A reappraisal of some aspects of Precambrian shield geology (Anhaeusser, Mason, Viljoen & Viljoen), Geol. Soc. America Bull., 1970; Geological Map of the Zaria area (1:50,000), in Zaria & its region, Dept. of Geog., A.B.U., Acc. Paper, 1970. Address: Geology Dept., Ahmadu Bello University, Zaria, N. Nigeria.

MACDONALD, Andrew Sinclair, born 15th August 1928. Professor of Agriculture. Education: West Ewell Secondary School, U.K., 1939-45; B.Sc., Durham University, 1948; D.T.A, Cambridge University, 1950; Imperial College of Tropical Agriculture, 1949-50. Married to Olive Alexandrina McAndrew, 1 daughter. Appointments: Agricultural Officer, Sierra Leone, 1950-56; Divisional Agric. Officer, Uganda, 1956-60; Lecturer, Senior Lecturer, University of East Africa, 1960-69; Professor of Agriculture, Head of School of Agriculture, University of Mauritius, 1969—. Fellow of the Royal Society of Arts. Member of Military & Naval Gymkhana Club, Mauritius. Publications: various papers on sweet potatoes in scientific journals, also Land use in East Africa & Agricultural Education. Address: School of Agriculture, University of Mauritius, Reduit, Mauritius.

McDONALD, Duncan, born U.K., 29th November 1929. Plant Pathologist. Education: B.Sc, Biology, University of St. Andrews, Scotland, U.K., 1954; B.Sc., Hons., Botany, ibid, 1955; Dip. Agric. Science, University of Cambridge, 1956; D.T.A., Imperial College of Tropical Agriculture, Trinidad, 1957; Ph.D., Ahmadu Bello University, 1968. Appointments: Specialist Agric. Officer, Ministry of Agriculture, Northern Nigeria, 1957-62; Research Fellow, Ahmadu Bello University, 1962-67; Senior Research Fellow, 1967—. Memberships: Science Association of Nigeria; Institute of Biology; Association of Applied Biologists; British Mycological Society. Publications: contbr. to Tropical Science; Food Technology; Nigerian Agric. Journal; Journal of Stored Products Research; Review of Applied Mycology; Transactions of British Mycological Society; Samaru Agric. Newsletter; 4 Samaru miscellaneous papers; papers on diseases & contamination of groundnuts. Address: Institute for Agricultural Research, Ahmadu Bello University, P.M.B. 1044, Samaru, Zaria, Nigeria.

MACDONALD, Robert, born 19th December 1930. Geologist; Educator. Education: Royal Liberty School, Romford, Essex, U.K., 1941-49; B.Sc., King's College, London University, 1949-52; Ph.D., London University, 1963. Married, 1966. Appointments: Geologist, Geological Survey of Uganda, 1952; Principal Geologist, ibid, 1963; Head, Department of Geology, Makerere University, Kampala, 1968—. Fellow, Geological Society of London. Member, Institution of Mining & Metallurgy. Address: Department of Geology, Makerere University, P.O. Box 7062, Kampala, Uganda.

MACHA, Joseph Eugenus, born 1930. Administrative Officer. Education: Kibosho Primary School, Moshi, 1939-44; St. Patrick's School, Singachini, Moshi, 1945-47; St. Mary's School, Tabora, 1948-49; St. Francis College, Pugu, Dar es Salaam, Tanzania, 1950-53; St. Thomas More's Teachers' College, Bukoba, 1954-55; Local Government Course, Tel-Aviv, Israel, 1962-63; Institute of Public Administration, University College, D.S.M., 1964. Married, 7 children. Appointments: Teacher, Umbwe Secondary School & St. Mary's School, Tabora, 1956-59; District Officer, Ukerewe, 1960-61; Staff Officer, Regional Comm.'s Office, Morogoro, 1962-63; Assistant Secretary, Ministry of Education, D.S.M., 1964-65; Area Secretary, Tanga, Tanga Region, 1965-69; Area Secretary, ibid, Kilimanjaro Region, 1969-70. Member of Tanu.

MACHAN, Lorraine, born 31st March 1923. Zoologist. Education: B.Sc., Nursing, Marquette University, U.S.A., 1944; M.S., Zoology, ibid, 1948; Ph.D., Zoology, University of Wisconsin, 1966. Appointments: Science Instructor to Nurses, Marquette University, 1947; Pioneer Member of Science Faculty, Pius XII College, Roma, Lesotho, 1955; Zoology Dept., University of Wisconsin, U.S.A., 1963; Head of Biology Dept., University of Botswana, Lesotho, & Swaziland, 1966—. Memberships: AAAS; Phi Sigma; Sigma Delta Epsilon; Sigma Xi; Lesotho Science Teachers' Assn. Author of papers published in sci. jrnls. Address: Head of Biology Dept., University of Botswana, Lesotho, & Swaziland, Roma, via Maseru, Lesotho.

MACHANGE, Obed Zephania, born 7th July, 1938. Land Surveyor; Mathematician. Education: Mwika Primary School, Moshi, 1946-51; Lutheran Secondary School, Arusha, 1952-55; Government Upper Secondary School, Tabora, Tanzania, 1956-57; Makerere College, Kampala, Uganda, 1958-59; Delhi Polytechnic, India, 1959-60; B.Sc., Maths & Physics, University of Bucharest, Rumania, 1960-65; Parts I & II, Army Survey Diploma, School of Military Survey, Newbury, U.K., 1966-67; Certified Land Surveyor, East Africa; A.R.I.C.S. Appointments: Assistant Surveyor, 1965; Surveyor, Officer in Charge, Computing Office, Department of Surveys & Mapping, Ministry of Lands, Housing & Urgan Development, 1967; Officer in Charge, Mapping Branch, responsible for Topographical Surveys, Aerial Photography & Distribution of Maps, i/c of Drawing Office, Photogrammetric Unit & the Printing & Production Unit. Probationer, Royal Institution of Chartered Surveyors. Publications: X^2 Distribution in Probability Theory, 1965; Preparation of Triangulation Overlays to Overlap the Tanzania 1/50,000 Map Sheets, 1970. Recipient, Prize for Best Overseas Student, Photogrammetry, School of Military Survey, Newbury. Address: East

African Airways Corporation, P.O. Box 1010, Nairobi, Kenya.

MACHUNDA, John Baptist, born 20th February 1931. Director of Administration, Personnel, & Planning. Education: Kagunguli Primary School, 1940-44; Nyegezi Secondary School, 1944-50; St. Mary's, Tabora, 1951-52; Makerere University College, Uganda, 1953-57; Edinburgh University, Scotland, U.K., 1960-61; B.Sc., M.Sc., West Virginia, University, U.S.A., 1962-64; Dip. Agric. (E.A.). Married, 3 sons, 2 daughters. Appointments: Assistant Farm Manager, 1958-59; District Agricultural Officer, 1959-60; Tutor, Agricultural School, 1961-62; Lecturer, ibid, 1964-65; Lecturer, Agricultural College, 1965-68; Deputy Principal, ibid, 1967-68; Publications: pamphlets on calf rearing, pigs, goats, & sheep; ministerial publications. Honours, Prizes, etc.: Muljibhai Madhivan Prize for Best Agricultural Graduate, Makerere University College, Uganda, 1957. Address: P.O. Box 9192, Dar es Salaam, Tanzania.

MacPHERSON, Fergus, born 9th August, 1921. University Dean. Education: Daniel Stewart's College, Edinburgh, U.K.; M.A. (Hons.), History, Edinburgh University; Theology, New College, Edinburgh. Married, 2 sons, 4 daughters. Appointments: Missionary, Mufurira, Mwenzo, Lubwa, Zambia, 1946-56; Principal, Overtown Institution, Livingstonia, Malawi, 1956-59; Parish Minister, Scotland, 1959-63; Teacher, Zambia, 1964-65; Dean, Students, University of Zambia, Lusaka, 1965—. Founder-President, Edinburgh Afro-Scottish Circle, 1942. Publications: Co-translator, Bible in Chibemba; ibid, Amalumbo (Psalms) & Ilayano Kali (Old Testament Selection); One Blood (novel), 1970. Recipient, Brown Downie Prize for Church History, Edinburgh, 1946. Address: P.O. Box 8068, Lusaka, Zambia.

MacPHERSON, Margaret Frances May, born U.K., 10th March 1921. University Lecturer. Education: Talbot Heath School, Bournemouth, U.K.; St. Anne's College, Oxford University. Married, 1942, 1 son, 2 daughters. Appointments: Assistant Mistress, Settrington School & Ribston Hall High School; Headmistress, Makerere College School, Uganda; Lecturer & Senior Lecturer, Department of English (now Literature), Makerere University College (now Makerere University); Senior Tutor, Faculty of Arts, & Director of Drama, ibid. Memberships: Uganda Theatre Guild; Assistant Secretary, Makerere College Union Society; Chairman, Executive Committee, National Cultural Centre, Kampala; Governor, Buloba College & Lubiri School Committee; Uganda Society. Publications: Makerere College Register, 1921-53; They Built for the Future. Honours include: Uganda Independence Medal, 1962. Address: Makerere University, P.O. 7062, Kampala, Uganda.

MADAN, Chunilal, born Nairobi, Kenya, 11th November 1912. High Court Judge. Education: Government Indian School, 1931; Barrister-at-Law, Middle Temple, 1936. Married. Appointments include: Q.C., Kenya, 1957; elected Member, Legislative Council, 1948-61; Parliamentary Secretary, Ministry of Commerce & Industry, 1955-56; Minister without Portfolio, Government of Kenya, 1956-61; President, Law Society of Kenya, 1955, 1957; Puisne Judge, High Court of Kenya, 1961—. Address: P.O. Box 944, Nairobi, Kenya.

MADANI, Bouraoui, born 22nd January 1940. Urban Architect. Personal details: married, 1962, 1 son, 1 daughter; wife has helped in creation of Bureau of Urban Studies, Tunis. Appointments: Principal Engineer; President Director-General, State Society; ibid, Tunisian Society of Engineers & Technicians. Memberships: Socialist Party; Lions Club. Address: 47 Avenue Ferhat Hached, Tunis, Tunisia.

MADARIKAN, Charles Olusoji, born Lagos, Nigeria, 19th February 1922. Barrister-at-Law. Education: St. Paul's Breadfruit School, Lagos; Christian Missionary Society Grammar School, Lagos; Higher College, Yaba; Inns of Court School of Law, London, U.K. Appointments include: Crown Counsel, Nigeria, 1949-56; Senior Crown Counsel, Nigeria, 1956-58; Acting Legal Secretary, Southern Cameroons, 1957-58; Chief Registrar, Federal Supreme Court, Nigeria, 1958-59; Director of Public Prosecutions, Western Region, Nigeria, 1959-60; Judge, High Court of Western Nigeria, 1960-67; Justice, Supreme Court of Nigeria, 1967—. Memberships include: Fellow, Royal Commonwealth Society. Publications include: Selected Judgements of the Federal Supreme Court of Nigeria, 1957, 1958. Address: Supreme Court, Lagos, Nigeria.

MADINA (Rt. Rev.) Yohana, born 3rd February, 1926. Bishop. Education: Mzango Secondary School, Dodoma, Tanzania; Teachers' College, Rungwe; St. Paul's Theological College, Limuru, Kenya. Married, 5 sons, 4 daughters. Appointments: Vicar, Cathedral of Holy Spirit, Dodoma, Tanzania, 1958-64; consecrated Bishop, 1964; Assistant Bishop, Diocese of Central Tanganyika, 1964—; Archdeacon, Dodoma-Mvumi, 1965-69; ibid, Nth District, Diocese of Central Tanganyika, 1970—. Address: P.O. Box 263, Arusha, Tanzania.

MAEDA, Nderingo Kella, born 19th July, 1925. Veterinary Surgeon. Education: Old Moshi Secondary School, Tanzania, 1940-45; Tabora Secondary School, 1946-47; Diploma in Veterinary Science, Makerere University College, Kampala, Uganda, 1948-53; B.V.Sc., Bristol University, U.K., 1960-65. Personal details: member of Chagga Tribe; married, 1 son, 2 daughters. Appointments: Veterinary Officer, Department of Veterinary Services, Ministry of Agriculture, Tanzania, 1954-60; Assistant Director, Veterinary Services, 1965-69; Chief Veterinary Officer, 1969—. Memberships: Royal College of Veterinary Surgeons; President, Tanzania Veterinary Association; Representative of Bristol University Veterinary Society to British Veterinary Students' Union; various local societies. Author, Antibiotics as Dietary Supplements for Poultry (E. African Agric. J.), 1958. Address: Ministry of Agriculture, Food & Cooperatives, P.O. Box 9152, Dar es Salaam, Tanzania.

MAGAGULA, Jonathan Sipho Felizwe, born 2nd February 1932. Permanent Secretary. Education: B.A., U.E.D., Rhodes University; M.P.A., Denver, Colorado, U.S.A. Appointments: Headmaster, Swazi National School, 1965-67; Senior Assistant Secretary, 1967-68; Permanent Secretary, Department of Foreign Affairs, Swaziland, 1968-69; ibid, Department of Establishments & Training, 1969—. Memberships: Teachers' Union, 1957-60; Civil Service Union, 1960-70; President, ibid, 1964-65. Recipient, Governor's Award for Best Student, Denver. Address: Department of Establishments & Training, Mbabare, Swaziland.

MAHAMA, Ibrahim, born Tibung, near Tamale, Ghana, 1936. Member of Parliament, Tamale; Barrister; Solicitor. Education: Savelugu Primary School, 1951-53; Tendi Middle School, 1954-55; Government Secondary School, Tamale, 1956-62; University of Ghana, 1962-66; LL.B., 1965; Bar Examination, 1966. Married, 1 child. Appointments: Commissioner for Secretariats under National Liberation Council; Commissioner for Forestry; Commissioner for Information; General Secretary of National Alliance of Liberals; Member of Parliament for Tamale. Publications: How Britain Governed the Northern Territories of the Gold Coast; Dawn of Colonization in The Northern Territories of the Gold Coast. Address: Parliament House, Accra, Ghana.

MAHAMA, Mahami Saibu, born 3rd March 1929. Farmer. Education: Native Administration School, Yendi, Ghana; Government Middle Boarding School, Tamale; G.C.E. A Level, Private Studies: currently Studying for LL.B. by Correspondence. Married, 10 children. Appointments: Local Court Magistrate, re-named District Court Magistrate, 1961-69. Memberships: Treasurer, Malisung Co-operative Produce Marketing Society Ltd., Yendi. Address: P.O. Box 55, Yendi, Ghana.

MAHAMANE, Abolou Gentil, born 18th September 1918. Deputy to the National Assembly. Education: Diploma of Higher Primary Schooling, Naimey; Diploma de l'Ecole des Missions, A.O.F. Married, 12 children. Appointments: Economic & Social Adviser, Paris, France, 1959-61; Head of Central Subdivision, Takona, 1960-61; Head of Nomade Subdivision, Takona, 1961-64; Deputy, National Assembly, 1965—; Prefect, Nguigui, 1964-65; Deputy Mayor, 1966-70. Memberships: Secretary-General Committee Director of the PPN; RDA, Magaria. Honours: Officer of the National Order, 1962; Commander, National Order of the German Federal Republic. Address: National Deputy, Magaria, Niger.

MAHIMBO, Kristofa Heneri, born 22nd February 1929. Chartered Secretary. Education: Primary School, Iyogwe, Kilosa, 1945-46; Alliance Secondary School, Dodoma, Tanzania, 1946-52; Cambridge School Certificate, St. Andrew's College, Minaki, Dar es Salaam, 1953-54; Grade A Teachers' Certificate, ibid, 1955-56; Intermediate Exam. with Distinction, Accountancy & Economic Theory, Corporation of Secretaries, 1964; Final Exam., Local Government & Public Administration, ibid, 1968. Personal details: officially changed name from Christopher Henry Daud Mahimbo to Kristofa Heneri Daudi Mahimbo, 1969; married, 4 children. Appointments: Headmaster, Mgugu Middle School, 1957-58; Schoolmaster, Housemaster, Alliance Secondary School, Dodoma, 1959-62; Local Government Officer, Ministry of Local Government & Housing, 1962-65; Administrative Officer, Ministry of Regional Administration & Rural Development, 1965-69; Tutor, Mzumbe Local Government Training Centre, 1967-69; Assistant Bursar, University of Dar es Salaam, 1969—. Memberships: Associate, Corporation of Secretaries, 1968—; Chartered Secretary, 1970; Executive Committee, University Branch, T.A.N.U.; Treasurer, University Chapel. Honours: Corporation of Secretaries Prize Certificate; Administration of Nationalized Industries Prize, 1968. Address: University of Dar es Salaam, P.O. Box 35091, Dar es Salaam, Tanzania.

MAHLANGU, Alex, born 16th June 1929. Journalist. Education: Primary Education, Bulawayo, Rhodesia; Cambridge School Certificate, Goromonzi, Salisbury; 'A' Levels, Privately, London, U.K.; Diploma in Journalism. Personal details: father, Police Detective; married to a Nurse, 2 sons, 1 daughter. Appointments: Assistant Editor, Bantu Mirror, 1951-53; Editor, Bantu Mirror, 1953-60; Special Correspondent, Daily News & Parade Magazine, published Salisbury; Editor, Mufulira Mirror, 1967—. Memberships: Gamma Sigma Club, Guild of Journalists; Secretary, Mat. African Football Association; British Association of Industrial Editors; Travel Agents' Correspondent. Publications: Bantu Mirror, Daily News, Parade, & Mufulira Mirror. Address: P.O. Box 67, Mufulira, Zambia.

MAHYER, Jagdish Chandra, born 7th September 1919. District Medical Officer; Medical Officer of Health, Ministry of Health, Uganda. Education: Licentiate, Medical Faculty, Licentiate, Faculty of Tropical Medicine, Calcutta, India, 1941. Personal details: married to Santosh Mahyera, Graduate in Arts, 2 sons, 2 daughters. Appointments: Surgical Office, Chittranjan Hospital, Calcutta, India, 1941; Joint Police Med. Officer, Simla Hill States, 1942-46; Medical Superintendent, District Medical Officer, Medical Officer of Health, Ministry of Health, Uganda. Memberships: Director, Rotary Club, Mbale, Uganda, 1964-65; Charter President, Lions Club, Arua, Uganda, 1967-68; Charter President, Lions Club, Entebbe, Uganda, 1968-69; President, Toro Sports Club, Fort Portal, 1969-70; Director, Mohinder Oil Mills, Sirhind, 1942—; Director, Saw Mills, Sirhind, 1942—. Publications: District Annual Reports. Honours, Prizes, etc: District Governor's Award for Lionism, 1970; Uganda Independence Medal, 1962. Address: District Med. Officer, P.O.B. 217, Fort Portal, Uganda.

MAI, Wolfgang, born Munich, Germany, 9th January 1936. Director, German Volunteer Service in Kenya. Education: Gymnasium (High School), for 7 years; German State Examination; Teacher Training, 2 years; Ph.D., 1962. Married, 2 children. Appointments: Research Assistant, Institute of Geography, University of Munster, 1961-62; Studienoeferendar, Nurnberg &

Munchen, 1963-65; Head of Training Section, German Volunteer Service, Bad Godesburg, Kenya, 1966-67; Director, German Volunteer Service, Kenya, 1967—. Address: P.O. Box 7136, Nairobi, Kenya.

MAIKOSABUNI, Joseph, born Moyo, Madi, 30th March 1931. Deputy Treasurer, Madi District. Education: Ombaci Senior Technical School, 1948-49; Nsamizi Co-operative Development Training, 1954. Personal details: father one of the first Chiefs of Madi to speak Swahili, Langala, & Arabic. Married, 3 sons, 3 daughters. Appointments: Accounts Clerk, Madi District Administration, 1951; Co-operative Supervisor, with Uganda Co-operative Development, 1954; Storekeeper, with Madi District Administration, 1956; Assistant Treasurer, ibid, 1964; Ag. Treasurer, ibid, 1968-69. Memberships: Uganda Club, Kampala; Madi Consumers' Co-op. Society; Moyo Night Club. Address: Madi District Administration, P.O. Box 2, Moyo, Uganda.

MAINI, Ram Saroop, born Nairobi, Kenya, 26th November 1927. Medical Practitioner. Education: Duke of Gloucester School, Nairobi, 1939-45; University of Edinburgh, U.K., 1947-52; M.B., Ch.B., ibid, 1952. Married. Appointments include: Medical Officer, Medical Department, Kenyatta National Hospital, Nairobi, 1953; Medical Practitioner, Nairobi, 1954—. Memberships include: Life Member, Social Service League, Nairobi; Life Member, United Kenya CLub, Nairobi; Kenya Medical Association. Address: P.O. Box 142, Nairobi, Kenya.

MAISSE, Albert Jules Joseph, born 6th June 1928. Judicial Adviser. Education: LL.D., University of Liège, Belgium. Appointments: Advocate, Liège, 1953-57; Inspector of Works, Belgian Congo, 1957-60; Adviser, Ministry of Works, Leopoldville, Dem. Republic of the Congo, 1960-64; Deputy to Attorney, District Court of Kinshasa, 1965-68; Judicial Adviser to Ministry of Social Affaires, Kinshasa, 1968—. Address: B.P. 1841, Kinshasa, Democratic Republic of the Congo.

MAJED, Jaafar, born 27th March 1940. University Professor. Education: Licencié es Lettres; l'Ecole Normal Supérieure, Tunis; Agrégé de l'Université, Sorbonne, Paris, France. Appointments: Professor, Alaoiu College; Professor, Ladiki College; Conseiller Pedagogique; Professor, University of Tunis. Publications: Un Recueil de Poemes, 1968; scientific articles in IBLA, Annual de l'Université de Tunis; Radio & Television. Honours, Prizes, etc: 1st Prize for Poetry, 1969; 1st Prize de Kainouay (Poetry).

MAJEETHIA, Kantilal M., born Songad, India, 5th October 1928. Medical Officer. Education: M.B., B.S., 1954. Married. Appointments: General Practice, 1955—; Industrial Medical Officer, Madhvani Group of Industries, 1967-70; Medical Officer, Jinja Hospital, Jinja, Uganda, 1970. Memberships: Lions Club, Jinja District; Uganda Medical Society; Jinja Medical Association; British Medical Association. Address: P.O. Box 244, Jinja, Uganda.

MAJEKODUNMI, Charles Oladapo Olafimihan, born 11th January 1936. Clinical Pathologist. Education: Lagos Grammar School, Lagos, Nigeria; Eshton School, Skipton, Yorkshire, U.K.; Municipal College, Bournemouth; Trinity College, Dublin, Ireland. Personal details: father, Dr. A. O. Majekodunmi, former Chief Medical Adviser to Western State. Married. Appointments: Medical Registrar, UCH, Ibadan, Nigeria, 1964-65; Medical Officer, Federal Government, Nigeria, 1965-66; Haematology Registrar, North Middlesex Hospital, 1966-67; Morbid Anatomy & History Registrar, ibid, 1967-68. Member of London Playboy Club.

MAJEKODUNMI, Moses Adekoyejo, born 17th August 1916. Medical Doctor. Education: Abeokuta Grammar School; St. Gregory's College, Lagos, Nigeria; Trinity College, Dublin, Ireland; M.A.; M.D.; F.R.C.P.I.; M.A.O.; D.C.H.; L.M.(Rotunda). Married, 7 children. Appointments: House Physician, National Children's Hospital, Dublin, 1941-43; Senior Specialist, i/c Massey Street Maternity Hospital, 1949-59; Senior Specialist Obstetrician, Nigerian Federal Government Medical Services, 1949-60; Senator & Leader of Senate, 1960-66; Minister of State for the Army, 1960—; Federal Minister of Health, 1961-66; Federal Minister of Health & Information, 1965; Administrator, Western Nigeria, 1962; President, 16th World Health Assembly, 1963; International Vice-President, 3rd World Conference on Medical Education, New Delhi, India, 1966; Medical Director & Chairman, Board of Governors, St. Nicholas Hospital, Lagos. Memberships: Royal Society of Medicine, London; Royal Society of Tropical Medicine & Hygiene, London; Lagos Polo Club; Lagos Race Club; Lagos Dining Club; Lagos Island Club; Metropolitan Club. Publications: Premature Infants: Management & Prognosis, 1943; Parial Apresia of the Cervix Complicating Pregnancy, 1946; Sub-Acute Intussusception in Adolescents, 1948; Thiopentone Sodium in Operational Obstetrics, 1954; Rupture of the Uterus Involving the Bladder, 1955; Effects of Malnutrition in Pregnancy & Lactation, 1957; Behold the Key (play), 1944. Honours: C.M.G., 1963; LL.D.(h.c.), Trinity College, Dublin, 1964. Address: St. Nicholas Hospital, 57 Campbell St., P.O. Box 3015, Lagos, Nigeria.

MAJONI, Bettson Brown, born 14th May 1939. Book-keeper & Accountant. Education: Passed, Form 11, Malawi. Married to Era Msodoka, 1 son, 1 daughter. Appointments: Accounts Clerk, Shire Clothing Company, 1965; Assistant Chief Clerk, ibid; Storeman; Planning & Internal Auditor; Foreman, Dispatching Department. Address: Shire Clothing Company, Box 306, Lilongwe, Malawi.

MAKAMBA, Winston, born 27th September 1944. Journalist. Education: B.A., Political Science & Economics, University of East Africa. Currently, Information Officer, Press Section, Ministry of Information & Tourism, Dar es Salaam, Tanzania. Address: P.O. Box 9142, Dar es Salaam, Tanzania.

MAKAMBILA, Pascal, born Brazzaville, Republic of the Congo, 6th August 1944. Museum Director; Deputy Secretary-General,

Association of African Museums. Education: Diploma, Ecole Normale Superieure d'Afrique Centrale, Brazzaville; Section Teacher of English; Diploma of Museum Technicians; Duel Lettres Anglais. Appointments: Curator, National Museum, 1966-69; Director of Museums, 1969—. Member, International Council of Museums. Honours: Knight of the Order of Congolese Merit (Titre Exceptionnel), 1967. Address: National Museum, B.P. 459, Brazzaville, Republic of the Congo.

MAKENETE, Strong Thabo, born 3rd December 1923. Physician. Education: St. Peter's Secondary School, Johannesburg, South Africa; Medical School, University of Witwatersrand, 1949. Married, 2 sons, 2 daughters. Appointments: House Physician/Surgeon, 1950; Government Medical Officer, Lesotho, 1951-63; Senior Medical Officer, Lesotho, 1963-64; Permanent Secretary of Health, Lesotho, 1964—. Memberships: Maseru Club; Lesotho Sporting Club; Judicial Body of Lesotho Sports Association. Author of annual reports, Ministry of Health, 1964-68. Address: P.O. Box 756, Maseru, Lesotho.

MAKOSSO, Gabriel, born Kindamba-Yulu, Congo-Kinshasa, 5th January 1923. Teacher; Journalist. Education: Primary School, Colonie Scolaire, Boma; Teachers' Diploma, Ecole Normale Superieure et Scolasticat, Tumba. Married, 4 children. Appointments: Teacher at Primary, Middle, & Secondary Schools, Tumba, Kinshasa, & Mbandaka, 1945-55; with weekly paper, 'Presence Congolaise', Kinshasa, Congo, 1958; Director, Le Courrier d'Afrique, 1960-70; Director, Administrator, Founder, Publishing Society 'Les Editions Congolaises' (EDICO), 1961—; President, Congolese Press Association, 1960-65; Vice-President for Africa, International Federation of Journalists, 1965-67. Publications: Le Courrier d'Afrique, founded in 1960 & finally closed down in 1970 for political reasons. Honours: recipient of the Golden Pen of Liberty, Italy, 1964; Knight, National Order of the Leopard. Address: B.P. 8312, Kinshasa, Democratic Republic of the Congo.

MAKRAM EBEID, Helmy, born 14th January 1900. Former Judge at the Cairo High Court of Appeal. Education: Primary School, Kena, Upper Egypt, U.A.R.; Secondary School, Victoria College, Alexandria; Graduated in Law, Cambridge University, U.K., 1923; Doctorate, Dijon University, France, 1926. Personal details: family includes Makram Ebeid Pasha, ex-Secretary-General of the Wafd Party; married to Isis, the daughter of Professor Naguib Mahfouz, 2 sons, 1 daughter. Appointments: Private Secretary to the Minister of Justice, substitute of Mixed Parquet in 1930; Chief of Mixed Parquet, 1937; Judge, Mixed Court, 1942; Judge, High Court of Appeal, 1949. Memberships: Gezira Sporting Club, Cairo; Egyptian Automobile Club, Cairo. Publications: Problems Raised by the Egyptian Constitution, 1926. Honours: Collar of the Polar Star, Sweden, 1949; Commander of the Order of Phoenix, Greece, 1949; formerly awarded the title of Bey, now abolished by the 1952 Revolution. Address: 5 Ibrahim Naguib Street, Garden City, Cairo, U.A.R.

MAKWANA, Ramniklal Devji, born 10th May 1941. Medical Officer. Education: attended Government Secondary School, Jinja, Uganda; Cambridge School Certificate, 1958; Pre-medical Examination, Fergusson College, Poona, India; M.B., B.S., B.J. Medical College, Ahmedabad, Gujarat University, India, 1967—. Appointments: Junior House Officer, Jinja Hospital, Uganda, 1968-69; Medical Officer, ibid, 1969—. Address: P.O. Box 85, Jinja, Uganda.

MALABU (Alhaji) Bello, born Yola, Nigeria, 12th May 1913. Diplomat. Education: Yola Provincial School & Katsina Higher College. Appointments include: Schoolteacher, 1933-38; Assistant Lecturer, Fulani Language, School of Oriental & African Studies, London, U.K., 1948-51; Manager of N.A. Schools, Adamawa Province, 1951-52; Member, Nigerian House of Representatives, 1952-59; Member, Nigerian Senate, 1959-60; Ambassador to Cameroun, 1960—. Memberships: Nigerian Ports Authority, 1954-57. Address: Embassy of Nigeria, B.P. 448, Yaoundé, Cameroun.

MALANDA, Edna Faith, born Berega, Kilosa, Tanzania, 20th November 1937. Assistant Superintendent of Police. Education: Primary School, Ibido-Kilosa, 1946-49; Middle School, Mvumi-Dadoma, 1950-53; Secondary School, Tebora, 1954-58. Married, 4 children. Appointments include: Probationary Sub-inspector of Police, 1959; Inspector of Police, 1962; Senior Inspector of Police, 1963; Assistant Superintendent of Police, 1964. Memberships include: Y.W.C.A.; T.A.N.U.; Girl Guides; Regional Executive Committee, U.W.T. Address: P.O. Box 9104, Dar es Salaam, Tanzania.

MALIMA, Kighoma, born 15th December 1938. Lecturer in Economics. Education: B.A., Dartmouth College, Hanover, N.H., U.S.A., 1965; M.A., Yale University, 1966; M.A., Princeton University, 1969. Married to Venantia Fivawo, 2 sons. Appointments: Tanu Official; Lecturer in Economics, University of Dar es Salaam, Tanzania; Member of East African Legislative Assembly. Memberships: Tanzania Economic Society; East African Academy; East African Agricultural Economic Society. Publications: International Trade & Economic Transformation of Tanzania; Subsistence Accounting & Development Planning in Africa; The Economics of Cotton Production in Tanzania. Address: P.O. Box 35024, University Hill, Dar es Salaam, Tanzania.

MALINDA, Thomas Nzioki, born Machakos, Kenya, 19th March 1924. Politician; Businessman. Education: Alliance High School, 1943-44. Married, 5 children. Appointments include: Clerk, Supreme Court; Treasurer, Urban Council; Company Director; Member of Parliament, Kenya; Assistant Minister, Kenya Government. Memberships include: Commonwealth Parliamentary Association; Secretary, Machakos Branch, Kenya African National Union; Agricultural Society of Kenya; Secretary K.A.N.U. Parliamentary Group, until 1968. Address: P.O. Box 147, Machakos, Kenya.

MALOIY, Geoffrey Moriaso Ole, born Kenya, 10th August 1939. Senior Research Officer. Education: B.Sc., University of British

Columbia, Canada, 1964; Ph.D. (Animal Physiology), Aberdeen University, Scotland, U.K., 1968. Appointments: Postgraduate Research Student, Dept. of Physiology, Rowett Research Institute, University of Aberdeen, 1965-68; Senior Research Officer, Head of Animal Physiology Research, East African Veterinary Research Organization, Muguga, Kenya, 1968—; Visiting Research Scientist, Environmental Physiology Dept., The Negev Institute for Arid Zone Research, Beersheva, Israel, 1970. Scientific Fellow, London Zoological Society. Member of Institute of Biology, London. Publications include: African Game Animals as a Source of Protein, Nutr. Abstracts & Reviews, 1965; Grazing Conditions in Kenya Masailand (co-author), Journal Range Management, 1965; Some effects of nitrogen & water intake in sheep & red deer (jt. author), Proc. Nutr. Soc., 1968; Energy Metabolism of the Red Deer, Journal of Physiol., London, 1968; Renal Excretion of Urea & Electrolytes in Sheep & Red Deer, J. Physiol., Lond., 1969; The Water Economy of the Somali Donkey, Am. Journal Physiol., 1970. Address: East African Veterinary Research Organisation, Muguga, P.O. Kabete, Kenya.

MALSCH, Alfred, born 17th April 1918. Director of Societies. Education: Licence en Droit; Diplome, l'Ecole libre des Sciences Politiques. Appointments: Managing Director, Malsch et Cie., d'Alidjou Doushe, Kiushase, Tananarive, Madagascar, Managing Director, de la Societe Malgache de Couvertures, Tananarive; Managing Director, de le Manufacture de Couvertures de Doushe. Address: 23 Rue d' Algerie, Lyon, France.

MAMA, Eli Babajiya, born 4th May, 1931. Medical Pracritioner. Education: St. John's School, Bida, Nigeria; Wusasa Middle School, Zaria; C.M.S. Grammar School, Lagos; London Hospital Medical College, U.K. Married, 2 sons, 1 daughter. Appointments: Medical Officer, Government of Nigeria, 1962; Private Practice, Kaduna, 1963—. Memberships: Chairman, Family Planning Association of Nigeria, Kaduna Branch, 1968, 1969, 1970—; Captain, Kaduna Golf Club, 1970; Rotary Club, Kaduna. Address: P.O. Box 300, Kaduna, N. Central State, Nigeria.

MAMADOU, Joseph-Gilbert, born Kembe, Central African Republic, 16th July, 1932. Diplomat. Married, 5 children. Appointments: Agent, Sanitation, & Hygiene, 1946-48; Chef de Section de l'apurement des Agences Speciales au Centre de Sous-Ordonnanement, Bouar, 1950-54; Assistant to District Chief, Special Agent & Postal Agent, Paoua, 1954-57; Minister, Social Affairs, Public Instruction & Health, 1957-58; District Chief, Bocaranga, 1959-60; Director, Cabinet of the President, 1960; Ambassador Extraordinary & Plenipotentiary, High Representative of the Central African Republic to France, 1960-63; Secretary-General, Ministry of Foreign Affairs, 1964; Ambassador Extraordinary & Plenipotiary to Peking, People's Republic of China, 1965-66; Economic Consellor to the Presidency, 1968-69; Ambassador Extraordinary & Plenipotentiary to the Union of Soviet Socialist Republics, 1970—. Honours: Grand Officier, Ordre du Merite Centrafricaine; Officier, Ordre des Palmes Academiques; Commandeur, Legion d'Honneur; Grand Officier, Ordre de Merite, France; Grand Croix, Ordre de Saint-Gregoire Le Grand, Vatican; Commandeur de Merite Congolais, Democratic Republic of the Congo. Address: Embassy of the Central African Republic, 20 Guilarovsky St., Moscow, U.S.S.R.

MAMAIN, Edgar, born Alger, Algeria, 19th January 1911. Technical Adviser. Education: Doctorate in Engineering; Chemical Engineer, EFT. Appointments: employed in industry until 1967; since then, Technical Adviser, ONU Assistance Technique Française BAD. Publications include: Fabrication Industrielle des Farines et Engrais de Poisson, 1932. Address: 22 Avenue des Etats Unis d'Amerique, Tunis, Tunisia.

MANDU, Joel, born 8th June, 1930. Life Insurance Executive. Education: Bubulo Primary School, 1942-48; Dr. Obote College, 1949-51; Nabumali High. School, 1952; Kyambogo Teachers' Training College, 1955-56; Makerere University College, Uganda, 1965. Personal details: wife, daughter of late Stanley Wanambwa, ex-Secretary-General, Bugisu District & District Commissioner, Uganda who represented Uganda at 1st Constitutional Talks in London before Independence; 3 sons, 3 daughters. Appointments: Teacher Assistant, Nabumali J.S. School, 1957-60; Headteacher, Nabbongo & Nabuyonga Schools, 1961-64; Headmaster, Bubirabi Public School, 1966-67; Agent, British American Insurance Co. Ltd., Mbale, 1968; Assistant Manager, ibid, 1969; Manager, 1970—. Memberships: Secretary, Uganda Teachers' Association, Mbale, 1961-62; Assistant President, ibid, 1963; President, 1964; National Committee, 1964; Mbace Youth Board, Mbale Educational Committee, 1964; Bugisue Football Club, 1964; Makerere College Swimming Club, 1965; Assistant Education Officer, Students' Association, 1966; Fairway Management Committee, 1970; Church Council, 1970; Associate, Uganda Institute of Management, 1970. Address: P.O. Box 1207, Mbale, Uganda.

MANEK, Mansukhlal Dayalji, born Rajkot, India, 16th August 1916. Advocate; Secretary. Education: Qualified as an Advocate while working as a Company Secretary with Muljibhai Madhvani & Co. Ltd.; B.A., LL.B. (Bombay University). Personal details: grandfather & father both lawyers. Appointments: Assistant Secretary, Damodar Jinabhai & Co., Ltd., 1943-47; Secretary, Dayalbhai Madanji & Co. Ltd. & Group, 1947-63; Secretary, Muljibhai Madhvani & Co. Ltd., 1963—. Secretary, Sports Secretary, Indian Recreation Club, Jinja for many years. Recip. of prizes for tennis & billiards, in Uganda. Address: c/o Muljibhai Madhvani & Co. Ltd., Jinja, Uganda.

MANGAT, Daleep Singh, born 1st February 1933. Barrister-at-Law; Advocate of the High Court of Kenya. Education: M.A.(P.P.E.), Exeter College, Oxford University, U.K.; LL.B., University of London; Barrister-at-Law, Lincoln's Inn, London. Personal details: family Sikh, originally from the Punjab, India. Father,

N. S. Mangat, Q.C. Married to Baljeet Neé Uppal, 3 sons. Appointments: Crown Counsel, Attorney-General's Chambers, Nairobi, Kenya, 1960-63; Senior State Counsel, ibid, 1964-67; Legal Draughtsman, East African Community, Arusha, Tanzania, 1968—. Address: c/o Chambers of the Counsel, East African Community, P.O. Box 3172, Arusha, Tanzania.

MANGAT, Harcharan Singh, born Mombasa, Kenya, 22nd March 1932. Chartered Civil & Municipal Engineer. Education: B.E. Civil Engineering; M.I.C.E. (Member of the Institute of Civil Engineers, U.K.). Married. Appointments: Principal Assistant Engineer, Nairobi City Council, 1960-65; Chief Assistant Engineer, ibid, 1965-67; Assistant City Engineer, 1967-69; Consulting Engineer, Partner, I. B. Patel & Partners, 1969—. Fellowships: Institution of Municipal Engineers, U.K.; East African Institute of Engineers. Memberships: Vice-Chairman, Kenya Division, East African Institution of Engineers, 1970-71; President, Lions Club, Nairobi Central, 1969-70. Publications: Urban Traffic Problems in Nairobi, Journal of East African Institution of Engineers. Address: P.O. Box 2629, Nairobi, Kenya.

MANGIDU, Henry, born 1st May 1939. Lawyer. Education: LL.B.(Lond.), University College, Dar es Salaam, Tanzania, 1965. Married. Appointments: Land Officer, 1965-68; City Solicitor, City Council of Dar es Salaam, 1968; Commissioner for Lands, 1968—. Member of The Tanganyika African National Union (TANU). Address: Ministry of Lands, Housing & Urban Development, P.O. Box 9280, Dar es Salaam, Tanzania.

MANGOCHE, Mathurino Valentino Bwirani, born 11th June 1934. Educator. Education: B.A., University of South Africa, 1962; Diploma in Education (Dist. in Theory), University of Durham; Certificate, International Institute of Educational Planning. Appointments: Teacher of English & Maths., Secondary School, 1964-65; Teacher, Teacher Training College, 1965-66; Officer in Charge, Planning Section, Ministry of Education, 1966-68; Senior Assistant Secretary, 1968-70; Commissioner for Training, 1970—. Publications: Visitor's Notebook of Chichewa. Address: P.O.B. 167, Zomba, Malawi.

MANIRAKIZA, Marc, born 22nd December 1936. Administrator. Education: Diploma, School of Administration, Butare, Ruanda; Lic., Commercial Sciences, Brussels. Appointments: Director-General, Technical Assistance Scheme, Burundi, 1963-64; Minister of Foreign Affairs, Commerce & State, 1965-67; Administrator of Societies, 1969—. Publications: Inter-African Commercial Exchanges.

MANONE, Carl J., born Hellertown, Pennsylvania, U.S.A., 17th January, 1924. Educator. Education: Hellertown High School, 1941; Moravian College, Bethlehem, Pa.; Ursinus College, Collegeville; Kent State Universtiy, Ohio; B.A., Lehigh University, Bethlehem, Pa., 1947; M.A., ibid, 1948; D.Ed., Teachers' College, Columbia University, N.Y., 1957; various post-doctral courses. Appointments: Director of Guidance, Souderton Junior-Senior High School, Pa., 1948-52; Co-ordinator, Curriculum & Guidance (Grades K-12), Kennet Public Schools, Kennet Square, Pa., 1953-58; ibid, Abington Senior High School, 1958-60; Assistant to Superintendent, ibid, 1960-62; Assistant Superintendent, Abington Township Public Schools, 1962-66; Acting Superintendent, ibid, 1965-66; Chief of Party, Teacher Education in East Africa Project (Kenya, Tanzania, Uganda, & Zambia), administered by Teachers' College, Columbia University, 1966—. Memberships include: Past President, Soudertown Education Association; Phi Alpha Theta; Pi Gamma Mu; Kappa Delta Pi; Phi Delta Kappa; Pennsylvania Counsellors: Association; Consultant to numerous educational organizations. Member, civic organizations. Publications include: Editor, A Report of the University of East Africa Conference: The Role of the Institute of Education in Curriculum Development, 1967; ibid, New Directions of East Africa Teacher Education: Innovation, Implementation, & Evaluation, 1968; ibid, Staffing Teacher Education Institutions in East Africa: Supply & Demand, Training & Utilization, 1969; Contributor, Proceedings of the 2nd Kenya Conference: New Directions in Teacher Education, 1969. Honours include: Distinguished Flying Cross (with cluster); Air Medal (with 3 clusters); Presidential Citation (with cluster); Asiatic-Pacific Theatre Medal (with 4 battle stars). Address: Box 7062, Kampala, Uganda.

MANSUR, Beatrice Rose (Mrs. David Mansur), born 4th October 1937. Senior Rural Development Officer. Education: Standard 8; Teacher Training Course; Home Economics, University of Minnesota, U.S.A.; Associate in Arts Degree. Married, 3 children. Appointments: with Head Office, Ministry of Regional Administration & Rural Development (Women's Development Schemes, Women's Organizations; Co-ordination of Family & Child Welfare Schemes, Environmental Sanitation, Nutritional Projects); Teacher, Home Economics, Training Centre, Musoma, Tanzania. Memberships: Central Committee of the only Women's Organization in the Country; Y.W.C.A.; TANU. Honours, Prizes, etc.: Certificate of Attendance & Completion, Institute of Community Development, Haifa, Israel. Address: P.O. Box 2248, Dar es Salaam, Tanzania.

MANUWA (Sir) Samuel Layinka Ayodeji, born Ijebu Ode, Nigeria, 4th March 1903. Surgeon; Medical Administrator. Education: Anglican Grammar School, & King's College, Lagos, Nigeria; University of Edinburgh, U.K.; University of Liverpool, U.K.; Royal College of Surgeons, Edinburgh; M.D.; F.R.C.S.; F.R.C.P.; F.A.C.P.; F.R.S.Ed.; F.R.S.A.; D.T.M.&H. Married, 2 sons, 2 daughters. Appointments include: Medical Officer, Senior Surgical Specialist, Inspector-General of Medical Services, British Colonial Medical Service, 1927-54; Chief Medical Adviser to the Government of the Federation of Nigeria, 1954-59; First Federal Public Service Commissioner, 1952—; Member, Western Nigeria House of Assembly, 1948-51; Member, Legislative & Executive Councils of Nigeria, 1951, 1952; Member, Privy Council of Nigeria, 1951-60; Chairman, St. John's Council of Nigeria, 1958-59; Pro-Chancellor, & Chairman of Council, University of Ibadan, 1967—. Memberships include: Fellow, Royal Society of Edinburgh; Fellow, Royal College of Surgeons: Fellow, Royal College of Physicians of Edinburgh; Fellow, Royal Society of Arts; Fellow, Institute of Directors, London; Fellow, American College of Physicians; Fellow, American Public Health Association; Fellow, New York Academy of Sciences; Fellow, American Geographical Society; Past President, World Federation for Mental Health; Past President, Association of Surgeons of West Africa; Past President, Association of Physicians of West Africa; Member, Metropolitan Club, Lagos; Island Club, Lagos; University Union Club, Edinburgh. Contributor to journals, especially in the fields of surgery, tropical diseases, & mental health. Honours & awards include: Knight Bachelor; C.M.G.; O.B.E.; C.St.J.; Hon. LL.D., Edinburgh; Hon. D.Sc., Nigeria; Hon. D.Sc., Ibadan; Hon. D.Litt., Ife. Chieftainship, Iyasere, Itebu-Manuwa; Chieftainship, Obadugba, Ondo; Chieftainship, Olowa Luwagboye, Ijebu Ode; Robert Wilson Memorial Medal & Prize, University of Edinburgh; Wellcome Medal & Prize, University of Edinburgh; John Holt Medal, University of Liverpool. Address: Federal Public Service Commission, Independence Building, Lagos, Nigeria.

MANYENGA, Bonaventure, born 2nd February 1936. Chartered Surveyor. Education: Primary & Central School Education, Kwiro, Malhenge, Tanzania, 1945-53; Secondary Education, St. Mary's Seminary, Nyegezi, Mwanza, 1954-56; Philosophy & Theology, St. Paul's, Kipalapala, Tabora, Tanzania, 1957-63; University College, Nairobi, Kenya, 1963-66; Valuations (Intermediate), Royal Institute of Chartered Surveyors, 1966-68; Finals of Chartered Surveyors & Direct Finals of Chartered Auctioneers & Estate Agents' Institute, 1968; Government Valuer, Tanzanian Government, 1968; Regional Valuer in Charge of Six Regions (Mara, Bukoba, Mwanza, Shinyanga, Tabora, & Kigoma), 1970. Married, 2 daughters. Appointments: President, Editor in Chief, & Founder Philosophico-theological booklet 'Hekima' (Wisdom), 1961; President, Tanzania Students' Union, University College, Nairobi, Kenya, 1965-66; Valuer, 1968; Regional Valuer, 1970. Memberships: World Brotherhood (UN), 1961; TANU, 1964; Secretary-General, St. Vincent de Paul Society, Tanzania, 1969; Superior Council, ibid. Publications: Hekinna (Wisdom), (Founder & First Editor); 'Marcelino' also You & Your Children; (Translated & Printed), both in Swahili & approved by the Swahili Committee. Address: Regional Valuer, P.O. Box 970, Mwanza, Tanzania.

MANZON, Jean-Claude Paul, born 16th June 1941. Lecturer. Education: Ecole Normale Superieure de St. Cloud; Licence d'Anglais— D.E.S. d'Anglais (stylistique). Appointments: Professeur de Français, Institut Français d'Ecosse, Edinburgh, Scotland, U.K., 1964-65; Lecturer in French & Linguistics, University of Dar es Salaam, Tanzania, 1968-71. Vice-President, Affaires Culturelles de l'Union des Grandes Ecoles, Paris, France. Address: The University of Dar es Salaam, P.O. Box 35040, Dar es Salaam, Tanzania.

MARBELL, Edwin, born Accra, Ghana, 1st November 1930. Medical Practitioner. Education: Achimota School, 1945-50; University of Ghana, 1951-53; B.Sc.(London); University of Sheffield, U.K., 1953-58; M.B., Ch.B.; St. George's Hospital Medical School, 1961-65; D.Path. Married, 2 daughters. Appointments include: Medical Officer, Ministry of Health, Ghana, 1960-67; Senior Medical Officer, Pathology, 1967; Senior Medical Officer in charge of Health Laboratory Services. Member: Ghana Medical Association, & Chairman of Ashanti-Brong Ahato Division, ibid., 1968-69. Address: Komfo Anokye Hospital, P.O. Box 1934, Kumasi, Ghana.

MARCO, Sarla V., born 7th July 1939. Gynaecologist; Obstetrician. Education: M.B., B.S., Gujart University, India, 1962; D.G.O., ibid, 1965; D.R.C.O.G., London, 1967; M.R.C.O.G., ibid, 1968. Appointments: Medical Officer (Gynaecologist & Obstetrician), Kenyatta National Hospital, Nairobi, Kenya, —1969 & New Nyanza Provincial General Hospital, Kisumu, Kenya, 1970—. Memberships: Kenya Medical Assn.; British Medical Assn.; Kenya Hospital Assn. Gynaecologists; Medical Defence Union. Address: P.O. Box 22, Nairobi, Kenya.

MARGUERON, Michel Francois, born Lyon, France, 18th August 1931. Chamber of Commerce Official. Education: Licence in Law & Diploma of Science, Institute of Political Studies, Paris. Married. Currently Director of Economic Services & Studies, Chamber of Commerce, Ivory Coast. Memberships: Bureau, Jeune Chambre Economique; Sec., Assn. of Reserve Officers; Secretary-General, Exporters of Cocoa & Coffee Group; Secretary, Armicale des Lyonnais. Honours: Cross of Military Valour; Chevalier, French National Order of Merit. Address: Chamber of Commerce, P.O. B. 1399, Abidjan (RCI), Ivory Coast.

MARIS, Michel Albert Francois, born 22nd February 1920. Company Director. Education: Secondary School, St. Louis College, Le Mans, France; St. Louis Lycée, Paris, France; Naval School. Married, 3 children. Appointments: Naval Officer, 1946; Director-General, Societé Maris & Fils, 1946-61; Deputy Director, Forestry & Maritime Consortium, SNCF, Libreville, Gabon, 1962-63; Director, S.G.C.F.G. (Societeé de Gestion de la Compagnie Française du Gabon), Port-Gentil, 1964; Memberships: Economic & Social Counsel, Gabon; Honours: Legion of Honour, National Order of Merit; Military Honour; Colonial Medal; Equatorial Star; Gabon Honour. Address: B.P. 521, Port-Gentil, Gabon.

MASSOUD, Farid, Born 4th February 1896. Physician; Research Worker. Education: M.D. Faculty of Medicine, Cairo, 1918. Appointments: Director of Researches, Egypt School Medical Service; Member of Board, Representing Egypt, International Association for Research in Ophth. & Allied Sciences; Member of Editorial Board, Excerpta Medica, Oph., Amsterdam,

Netherlands. Rotarian. Publications include: Internal Secretions in Relation to the Eye, Journal of Egypt Medical Association, 1931; Proptosis, Different Diagnoses, British Journal of Ophthalmology, 1946; Differ. Leucoc. Blood Count in relation to the Eye., Bulletin Ophthalmic Soc. of Egypt, 1936; Role of Lymph Cell in Trachoma, Medical Press of Egypt, 1937, etc.

MASSYN, Gert Marais, born 13th October 1927. Company Director. Education: Mkhoma, Malawi; later Humansdorp, Cape Province, South Africa; The University of The Orange Free State, South Africa. Personal details: father, Missionary in the Dutch Reformed Church; married, 4 children. Appointments: Representative, Fur Auction Co., South West Africa; Branch Manager, ibid; General Manager, Fur Auction Co., South Africa; Managing Director, South Africa & South West Africa. Member of Rotary Club. Publications: various articles & bulletins (Fur Industry); Editor of Swakara, two-monthly publication. Address: c/o African Karaku Auctions (Pty.), Ltd., P.O. Box 314, Windhoek, South West Africa.

MATAKA, Johnston Roderick, born 20th November 1933. Teacher. Education: Primary Education until 1949; Teacher Training College, Mkhoma, Central Region, Malawi, 1949-51; Passed Std. 6. National Exams of South Africa, 1958; Junior Certificate, 1964; G.C.E. O Level, 1964, 1968. Appointments: Teacher, 1951-58; Town Councillor, 1965-70; Member of Local Education Board, 1967-70; Town & Country Planning Committee, 1968-70; Housing Allocation Committee, Malawi Housing Corporation, 1970; Headmaster, Zomba Government Primary School, 1968—. Memberships: on School Committee for two schools, 1968; School Committee for a third school, 1970. Publications: in English, Chichewa, Latin & French. Address: Government Primary School, P.O. Box 204, Zomba, Malawi.

MATANO, Robert Stanley, born 28th April 1925. Educator; Government Official. Education: Mazeras Primary School, 1932-36; Katoleni Giriama Primary School, 1937-40; Alliance High School, Kikuyu, 1941-45; Makerere College, Uganda, 1946-48. Married, 3 sons, 3 daughters. Appointments: Headmaster, Ribe Boys' School, 1949-52; Master, Alliance High School, 1953; Assistant Education Officer, Rift Valley, 1954-55; Studied Administration of Education, Cardiff, U.K., 1956; Assistant Minister, Coast Province, 1957-60; Assistant Minister, Foreign Affairs, Health, Home Affairs, 1961—; Assistant Secretary-General, Kanu, 1966—. Memberships: Chairman, Child Welfare Society, 1963; Lions Club, 1964. Recipient, 1st Prize, Swahili Essay, 1945. Address: P.O. Box 30478, Nairobi, Kenya.

MATERU, Mtengie Ephatha Aiyona, born 19th September, 1933. Director, Tropical Pesticides Research Institute. Education: B.Sc., London, U.K., 1959: M.Sc., Michigan State University, U.S.A., 1962; Ph.D., University of East Africa, 1968. Married, 2 children. Appointments: Assistant Entomologist, Tanganyika Coffee Board, 1959-61; Experimental Officer, Tanganyika Government, 1961; Research Officer, Entomologist, East African Community, 1962-66; Principal Scientific Officer, 1966-67; Deputy Director, 1967-69; Director Designate, 1969-70; Director, 1970. Member, International Centre of Insect Physiology & Ecology. Author of 11 publications, mostly on Agricultural Entomology. Address: Director, Tropical Pesticides Research Institute, P.O. Box 3024, Arusha, Tanzania.

MATHEW, Thottacherry Joseph, born India, 15th February 1928. Consultant Surgeon. Education: Kerala, India; B.Sc.(Chemistry), Madras University,; M.B., B.S., ibid; Surgical Training in U.K. Hospitals, 1956-63. Personal details: father Dr. T. M. Joseph. Married, 2 children. Appointments: Surgical Registrar, Whitehaven General Hospital, Cumberland, U.K., 1961-63; Medical Officer, Special Grade, Northern Nigeria, 1963-66; Consultant Surgeon, ibid, 1966-68; Consultant Surgeon, North-western State, Nigeria, 1968-69; Senior Consultant Surgeon, ibid, 1969—; Fellow, Royal College of Surgeons, Edinburgh, U.K.

MATHIAS, Aloysius, born 24th May 1934. Senior Supplies Officer. Education: Dip. B.A., Diploma in Business Administration, Canada; A.C.I.S., Associate of the Chartered Institute of Secretaries; Member of the Institute of Purchasing & Supply; Associate Member, British & Uganda Institutes of Management. Married, 1 son, 1 daughter. Appointments: Stores Administrator, 1961-64; Supplies Officer, 1964-69; Senior Supplies Officer, 1969—. Address: Ministry of Works, Communications & Housing, P.O. Box 7116, Kampala, Uganda.

MATHIESON, Alexander Robinson, born 4th July 1926. University Professor, Head of Department & Deputy Vice-Chancellor. Education: West Hartlepool Grammar School, U.K., 1937-44: University of Durham, 1944-47; University of Nottingham, 1949-52; B.Sc., 1947; M.Sc., 1951; Ph.D., 1952; F.R.I.C., 1960. Married to Sheila Mary Allen, B.Sc., Ph.D., 2 sons. Appointments: Scientific Officer, U.K. Atomic Energy Commission; Lecturer, University of Nottingham; Senior Lecturer, University of Ibadan, Nigeria; Lecturer, University of Leeds, U.K.; Professor of Chemistry & Head of Department of Chemistry, Ahmadu Bello University, Zaria, Nigeria; Deputy Vice-Chancellor, ibid. Fellowships: The Royal Institute of Chemistry; The Chemical Society. Memberships: Science Association of Nigeria; Society for Research into Higher Education: Zaria Club; Ahmadu University Club. Publications: many scientific articles on polymerization, polymer properties, polyelectrolytes, nucleic acid, etc. in Journal of Polymer Science & other periodicals. Address: Department of Chemistry, Ahmadu Bello University, Zaria, Nigeria.

MATOKA (Hon. Minister) Peter Wilfred, Born Nswanakundya Village, Mwinilunga, North Western Province, 8 April 1930. Zambian High Commissioner. Education: Standard IV, Mwinilunga Lower Middle School, 1940-43; Standard VI, Munali Training Centre, 1943-47; Form IV, Munali Secondary School, 1947-50;

B.A., Fort Haire University College, 1952-54; Diploma International Relations, American University, Washington, D.C., 1964. Married, 2 sons, 1 daughter. Appointments: Civil Servant, 1955-63; Minister of Information & Postal Services, 1964-65; Minister of Health, 1965-66; Minister of Works, 1967; Minister of Power, Transport, & Works, 1968; Minister of Luapula Province, 1969; currently, Zambian High Commissioner, U.K. & the Holy See. Honours: Knight of St. Gregory the Great, Pope Paul VI, 1964; Knighthood, U.A.R. President, 1964; ibid, Emperor Hailé Selassié, 1965. Address: Zambia House, 7-11 Cavendish Place, London, W.1, U.K.

MATONDO, Roper Antoine, born 18th December 1939. Magistrate; Councillor to the Court of Appeal. Education: Licenced in Law; Primary Schooling, Protestant Missions, 1945-54; Secondary, L'Athenee, Ngiri-Ngiri, Kinshasa, Democratic Republic of the Congo. Married, 4 children. Appointments: Deputy to the Procurer, Kolnegi State, 1965-66; First Deputy to the Procurer, Kikuit State, 1967-68; Councillor to the Court of Appeal, Kisongain. Address: c/o Court of Appeal, Kisongain, Democratic Republic of the Congo.

MATTENJE, Lewis Frank, born 1st January, 1929. Welfare Supervisor. Education: Malika Primary School of Church of Scholand, Chiradzulu District, 1939-46; Junior Certificate by Correspondence. Appointments: Soil Conservator, Agricultural Department, 1948-50; Stores Clerk, Colonial Development Corporation, 1950-53; Clerk, Nyasaland Railways, now Malawi Railways, 1954; Welfare Supervisor, ibid, 1966—. Memberships: Nyasaland Railways African Workers' Union, 1956; Executive, Nyasaland Railways African Trade Union, 1958; Vice-President & Member, Wages Advisory Board, ibid, 1960; President-General/National Chairman, 1963-66; Union Representative, I.L.O. 49th Session, Geneva, 1965. Address: Personnel Department, P.O. Box 5144, Malawi Railways Ltd., Limbe, Malawi.

MATUPA, Kenneth Clair, born 3rd September 1917. Civil Servant; Chief Executive Officer. Education: Standard VI; Grade III Teacher Certificate. Married, 11 children, 1 grandchild. Appointments: Teacher, 1935-60; Clerical Officer, Civil Service, Malawi, 1940-45; 2nd Grade Clerk, 1945-50; 1st Grade Clerk, 1950-55; Principal Officer Assistant, 1956-60; Assistant Establishment Officer, 1961-62; Divisional Office Manager, 1963-64; Chief Executive Officer, 1965—; Secretary, Government Loans Board. Memberships: Professional Standards Committee; Nyasaland Government Education Advisory Board; Secretary, Works Committee; Treasurer, Road Safety Association, 1958-60; C.C.A.P., Blantyre Synod; Treasurer, Blantyre Church Cong.; ibid, Blantyre Presb.; Chairman, Land, Finance, & Property Committee, Blantyre Synod; ibid, Education Board; Medical Board; Chairman, Stewardship Committee; Transport Committee; Chairman, Urban Court; Treasurer, Night School; Secretary, Civil Service Association; Chairman, ibid, Executive Committee, Nyasaland African Congress; Treasurer, Blantyre Branch, ibid; Representative, Blantyre Synod, St. Andrew's Consultation, Edinburgh, 1965. Recipient, Malawi Independence Medal, 1964. Address: P.O. Box 5095, Limbe, Malawi.

MAULY, Theneyan M. Suleiman, born Pemba, Tanzania, 1st May 1926. Assistant Secretary to the Revolutionary Council. Education: Rural Middle School, Dole, Zanzibar; Teacher Training College, Zanzibar; Course in Public & Social Administration, Torquay, U.K. Married, 2 sons, 3 daughters. Appointments include: Teacher, 1945-47; Assistant Mudir, 1948-49; Mudir, 1950-58; Assistant Private Secretary to British Resident, 1958-60; District Officer, 1961-62; Administrative Secretary, Ministry of Home & Legal Affairs, & Prime Minister's Office, 1962-63; Supernumerary Clerk, National Assembly, 1963-64; Assistant Secretary to the Revolutionary Council, 1964—. Address: P.O. Box 991, Zanzibar, Tanzania.

MAUSO-SAKWA, James William, born Bukhalu, November 1928. Civil Servant. Education:::: Nabumah High School; British Tutorial College; Makerere University College, Uganda. Married, 10 children. Appointments: Interpreter, 1952-63; Executive Officer, 1964-67; Higher Executive Officer; 1967-70. Address: P.O. Box 27, Entebbe, Uganda.

MAWANDA-CHWA (His Highness Prince) George William, born 10th January 1919. Uganda Government Pensioner. Education: Special Tutor, U.K.; Herne Bay College, Kent, 1932; War Office Certificate A; Entrance Examination, Royal Military College, Sandhurst. Personal details: son of Capt. H. H. Sir Daudi Chwa, K.C.M.G., .K.B.E., Kabaka (King) of Buganda; married to Ferikitansi K. Nabisenke, with children. Appointments: commissioned Lieut., King's African Rifles, 1939; served World War II, 1939-45. Appointments: appointed by Uganda Goverment to represent ex-soldiers of Uganda on Civil Reabsorption & Rehabilitation Committee, 1945; Aide-de-Camp to H.H. the Kabaka of Buganda, 1950-55; Representative Uganda Coronation Committee of Her Majesty Queen Elizabeth II, 1953. Memberships: Vice-President, Uganda Branch, British Legion, 1960-70; founder of the African Cricket Club, Uganda, 1947; Captain, A.C.C., 1947-51; represented Uganda v. Kenya, Cricket, 1952. Honours: Queen's Coronation Medal, 1953. Address: Salama Palace, P.O. Box 30014, Kampala, Uganda.

MAWDSLEY, George Henry, born Eiffel Flats, Rhodesia, 25th August, 1927. Personnel Manager. Education: Completed Secondary, Umtali High School, 1943. Personal details: grandparents, Rhodesian pioneers; known as 'Jungle George' in Central Africa for exploration of several rivers by canoe & for big game hunting. Appointments: Personnel Assistant, Rhodesia Railways, 1947-50; ibid, Imperial Tobacco Co., Msasa, 1950-62; Personnel Manager, Chirundu Sugar Estate, 1962-66; ibid, Nchalo Sugar Estate, Malawi; 1966—. Memberships: Executive Member, Agricultural Employers' Association, Malawi; ibid, Employers' Consultative Association. Recipient of cups for shooting & trophies for precision flying. Address: Nchalo Sugar Estate, Box 5598, Limbe, Malawi.

MAWEJJE, Abubaker, born 17th October 1951. Student. Education: completed Primary Education with Grade II Certificate, 1966; Candidate for East African School Certificate, 'O' Level, Kitante Secondary School, Kampala, Uganda, 1970. Member of Kitante Hill School Adventure Club. Address: P.O. Box 1323, Kampala, Uganda.

MAYEGA, Joseph V., born 9th November 1942. Statistician. Education: B.Sc.(Hons., Mathematics), Makerere University, Kampala, Uganda, 1967; M.Sc.(Statistics), Stanford University, California, U.S.A., 1969; Personal details: son of Mr. Valerian Mayega, Deputy Mayor of Mengo Municipal Council, Uganda, 1966-68. Appointments: Statistician, with Statistics Division of East African Community, 1967-68. Memberships: Operations Research Society of America; Institute of Statistics, U.K. Honours, Prizes, etc.: Honours Degree Prize, Makerere University, Kampala, Uganda. Address: P.O. Box 7151, Kampala, Uganda.

MAYENGA, Serard Pascal, born 31st July 1934. Business Executive. Education: Modern Humanities; Administration & Commercial Studies specializing in Social Security. Appointments: with the Government Bureau, Work Direction & Work Inspection, 1952-61; with Economic Affairs Mission, Port Matadi, 1961-62; with International Works Bureau, 1962-63; President, National Institute of Social Security, 1963-66; Delegate Secretary to the Conference on Belgo-Congolese problems, 1966; Proprietor, Hotel du Midi, Kinshasa. Memberships: Honorary President, Cultural Circle of Matadi; Counsellor, Musical Youth of the Congo; General Treasurer, A.C.T. Address: P.O. Box 6271, Kinshasa—6, Congo.

MAYIKO, Ephraim Young, born Aladja-Warri, Nigeria, 12th December 1940. Teacher. Education: Grade III & II Certs., 1967; G.C.E. 'O' Level, 1967. Married, 1 son, 1 daughter. Appointments include: Local Education Authority Headmaster. Memberships: Secretary, Adakporhia Family Meeting; Patron, Aladja Student Union; Publicity Secretary, Adeje-Okuejeba Debating Society. Private Assistant, Accountant, Aladja Town Central Committee. Address: No. 15 Smart St., Warri, Nigeria.

MAYOR, Arthur William, born 8th September 1906. Educator; Missionary. Education: St. Olave's Grammar School, U.K., 1918-25; Oriel College, Oxford University, 1925-30; Diploma of Education, Married, 2 sons, 2 daughters. Appointments: Asst. Classics Master, Sevenoaks School, 1930-33; became Missionary of Church Missionary Society, 1933; Asst. & Vice-Principal to E. Carey Francis, 1 Francis, 1940-51; Principal, Maseno School, Kenya; Supervisor, Anglican Primary Schools, Nyanza Province, 1952; Principal, St. John's Teachers' College, Ngiya, 1953-68; Asst. Master, English & Religious Knowledge, Kisumu Day Secondary School, 1969—. Memberships: Sec., Luo Language Committee, 1940-50; Sec., Luo New Test Revision Committee for the B.F.B.S., 1952-63; Foundation Member, West Kenya Music Society. Lay Reader, Diocese of Maseno South. Address: Box 809, Kisumu, Kenya.

MAZHAR, Mohammed, born 24th August 1938. Physician. Education: Cambridge School Certificate, Eastligh Secondary School, Nairobi, Kenya, 1957; Intermediate Examination, Government College, Lahore, West Pakistan, 1960; M.B., B.S.(Panjab University), Nishtar Medical College, Multan, W. Pakistan, 1965. Personal details: married to Dr. Nusrat, daughter of late Dr. Sardar Ahmed, M.B.E. Appointments: Medical Officer, Kenyatta National Hospital, 1965-66; Resident Medical Officer, Nairobi Hospital, 1966-68; Ophthalmic Registrar, Kenyatta National Hospital, 1968—. Memberships: District Surgeon, Railways, St. John Ambulance Brigade; Automobile Association of East Africa; Ophthalmic Society of East Africa. Honours, Prizes, etc.: Diploma in Ophthalmology Course, Institute of Ophthalmology, London, Scholarship Awarded by the Royal Commonwealth Society for the Blind, London, U.K., 1970. Address: P.O. Box 613, Nairobi, Kenya.

MAZRUI, Ali Al'Amin, born Mombasa, Kenya, 24th February 1933. University Professor.[1] Education: B.A. with Distinction (Manchester); M.A.(Columbia); D.Phil.(Oxon.). Married, 3 sons. Appointments include: Lecturer in Political Science, Makerere University College (now Makerere University), Uganda, 1963-65; Professor & Head of Department of Political Science, ibid, 1965—; Dean, Faculty of Social Sciences, 1967—; Visiting Professorial Scholar, University of Chicago, U.S.A., University of California, Harvard University; University of Singapore, Indian School of International Studies. Memberships: Director & Chairman, The Carnegie Endowment Institute in Diplomacy, Kampala, Uganda; Executive Committee, International Political Science Association; Vice-President, International Congress of Africanization; Associate Editor, Transition. Publications: Towards a Pax Africana, 1967; On Heroes & Uhuru-Worship; The Anglo-African Commonwealth, 1967; Violence & Thought, 1969; Protest & Power in Black Africa (edited jointly with Robert I. Rotberg), 1970; A Crisis of Relevance in East African Universities, 1970-71. Honours, Prizes, etc.: Gladstone Memorial Prize, Huddersfield, U.K., 1957; Wegner Prize for Philosophy, Manchester, 1958; Fleure Prize for International Studies, ibid, 1958, 1960; International Organization Essay Prize, World Peace Council, Boston, U.S.A., 1964. Address: Makerere University, Department of Political Science, P.O. Box 7062, Kampala, Uganda.

MBAKWEM, Onyegbula Benjamin, born 15th August 1927. Specialist Physician. Education: B.Sc., M.D., Ottawa, Canada; L.M.C.C., Canada; D.T.M.&H., Liverpool, U.K.; Postgraduate Studies, Universities of Ottawa & Toronto. Married, 5 children. Appointments: Physician, American Baptist Hospital, Eku via Sapele, Nigeria; Resident Physician, Ottawa General Teaching Hospital, Canada; Resident Surgeon, Royal Children's Hospital, Liverpool, U.K.; Physician, i/c Government Hospital, Okigini Area, Nigeria; ibid, Owerri Area; ibid, Cunetown, Sierra Leone; Joint Hospital, Amaigbo, Orlu. Memberships: Fellow, Royal Society of Tropical Medicine; Independent

Order of Oddfellows; Y.M.C.A.; Branch Secretary, P.G.M.; Aescalepian Club; Board of Directors, Nigerian Scientific & Technical Supplies Ltd. Address: General Hospital, Aba, Nigeria.

MBANEFO, Samuel Ejiofo, born 16th April 1921. Medical Practitioner. Education: St. Mary's Primary School, Onitsha, 1927; Igbobi College (Secondary Grammar), Yaba, Lagos, 1937; M.R.C.S.(Eng.), L.R.C.P.(Lond.), 1954; M.R.C.G.P.(Eng.), 1966. Personal details: son of Chief Isaac Mbanefo, Odu II of Onitsha; grandson of late Chief Mbanefo, Odu I of Onitsha; initiated into the Agbalanze Society of an Ozo Title Holder; married, 2 sons, 1 daughter. Appointments: Founder, Sole Proprietor, & Medical Director, Oshodi Hospital, Ibadan, Nigeria, 1956; part-time Clinical Tutor, Department of Psychiatry, Neurology, & Neuro-Surgery, University of Ibadan, 1963; travelling Rockefeller Foundation Fellow visiting community mental health projects, U.S.A., Canada, & U.K., 1964; Staff, Iyi Enu Hospital, Ogidi, East Central State, Nigeria, 1970. Memberships: Agbalanze Society of Onitsha; Police Officers' Mess, Ibadan; Marriage Guidance Council, Ibadan; Medical Officer, Western Region Boxing Board of Control. Contributor to scientific journals. Address: Oshodi Hospital, P.O. Box 829, Ibadan, Nigeria.

MBAWALA, Leo Paul, born 19th June 1936. Civil Servant; Senior Rural Development Officer. Education: Primary Education at Peramike, 1947-54; Cambridge School Certificate, Pugu College, 1955-58; Cooperative Studies, East African School of Cooperation, Nairobi, Kenya, 1959; Social Leadership Course, London, U.K., 1961-62; Diploma in Social Administration, University of Swansea, S. Wales, 1967-68. Married, 2 sons. Appointments: Cooperative Inspector, 1959-63; Regional Rural Development Officer, 1964-67; Scheduled Officer, Divisional Headquarters, Dar es Salaam, Tanzania, 1968—. Member of TANU. Awards: Diploma in Social Policy & Administration, 1968. Address: P.O. Box 2248, Dar es Salaam, Tanzania.

MBILE (Hon.) Nerius Namaso, born Lipenja, West Cameroon, 4th April 1923. Politician; Journalist; Farmer. Education: Government School, Kumba, 1933-37; Government School, Buea, 1938-39; Government College, Umuahia, 1940; Hope Waddell Training Institute, Calabar, 1940-45. Married, 6 sons, 2 daughters. Appointments include: General Secretary, C.D.C. Workers' Union, 1949-51; President, ibid, 1950-51; Elected Member, House of Assembly, Enugu, 1952-53; Elected Member, House of Representatives, Lagos, 1952-53; Member, Cameroons Development Corporation, 1954-56; Member, Nigeria Cinema Corporation, 1954-56; Elected Member, House of Assembly, Southern Cameroons, 1957—; Minister of Works, 1958, 1965-67; Minister of Lands & Surveys, 1968; Secretary of State for Primary Education, 1969—. Memberships: General Secretary, Cameroon National Union, 1949-51; Deputy Leader, Kamerun People's Party, 1953-59; Deputy Leader, Cameroon People's National Convention, 1960-67; Political Adviser, Ndian Section, Cameroon National Union. Honours, Prizes, etc.: Cameroon Order of Valour. Address: Ministry of Primary Education, Buea, West Cameroon, Federal Republic of Cameroon.

MBILINYI, Simon Michael Mhelema, born Mahante, Tanzania, 20th July 1934. Research Fellow; Lecturer in Economics. Education: Primary Mission Schools, Kigonsera & Ndanda, 1948-54; Pugu Secondary School, Dar es Salaam, Tanzania, 1954-56; B.Sc., Cornell University, Ithaca, New York, U.S.A., 1961-65; M.A. (Economics), Stanford University, 1965-66. Married to Marjorie Jane Power, Psychologist & Lecturer, University of Dar es Salaam, 2 daughters. Appointments: Depot Manager, Urambo, 1957, & Dodoma, 1958; Retail Salesman, Tanzania, 1959-61; Agricultural Officer, Training Division, Ministry of Agriculture, Tanzania Government, 1966-67; Research Fellow, Lecturer in Economics, The University of Dar es Salaam, 1967—; Research Manager & Chief Economic Adviser, with The National Bank of Commerce (1 year secondment), 1967-70. Memberships: Hon. Treasurer, East African Agricultural Economic Society; Executive Committee, ibid; Executive Committee, Tanzania Economic Society; Editorial Board, Uchumi; Tanzania Society; East African Academy; Senator, University of Dar es Salaam. Publications: Estimation of Peasant Farmers Costs of Production, The Case of Bukoba Robusta Coffee; The Economics of Central Coffee Pulperies in Tanzania, a preliminary assessment; Research on Subsidiary Staple Food Marketing in Dar es Salaam; Coffee Salaam Market. Address: Univ. of Dar es Salaam, P.O. Box 35096, Dar es Salaam, Tanzania.

MBITI (Rev.) John, born Kitui, Kenya, 30th November 1931. Anglican Clergyman; University Lecturer. Education: B.A.(Lond.), Makerere Univ. Coll., Uganda; A.B., B.Th., Barrington Coll., U.S.A.; Ph.D., Cambridge Univ., U.K.; Rsch., Hamburg Univ., W. Germany. Married, 1 son, 1 daughter. Appointments include: Teacher, Kangundo Tchr. Training Coll., Kenya, 1957-59; William Paton Lectr., Selly Oak Colls., Birmingham, U.K., 1959-60; Pastoral Work, St. Michael's Church, St. Albans, 1963-64; Lectr., Dept. of Religious Studies, Makerere Univ. Coll., Uganda, 1964—; Visiting Lectr., Theological Fac., Univ. of Hamburg, W. Germany, 1966-67; Actg. Hd., Dept. of Religious Studies, Makerere Univ. Coll., Uganda, 1968. Memberships include: Studiorum Novi Testamenti Societas, 1963—; Commn. of Faith & Order of the World Council of Churches, 1965—; Commn. on the Life of the Church, All-African Conference of Churches, 1965—; Soc. for African Church History. Publications include: Mutunga na Ngowa Yake, 1954; English-Kamba Vocabulary, 1959; Akamba Stories, 1966; Concepts of God in Africa, 1968; Christian Eschatology & the Evangelization of Tribal Africa, 1968; African Love, Marriage, & Family Life, 1968; African Religions & Philosophy, 1969; Poems of Nature & Faith, 1969; Concepts of God in Africa, 1970; New Testament Eschatology in an African Background, 1970; also Author of numerous articles, essays & poems published in int. anthologies, jrnls., & mags. Honours include: Leaderships Award, Barrington Coll., U.S.A., 1957. Address: Makerere Univ. Coll., P.O. Box 7062, Kampala, Uganda.

M'BOW, Amadou-Mahtar, born 20th March 1921. Teacher. Education: Higher Studies, the Sorbonne (Faculty of Letters, University of Paris, France), History & Geography, 1948-51. Married to Raymonde Sylvain, 1951. Appointments: Teacher, College of Rosso, Mauritania, 1951-53; Director of Education, Base of Senegal, 1953-57; Minister of Education & Culture, Senegal, 1957-58; Teacher, Lycée Faidherbe, St. Louis, 1958-64; ibid, Ecole Normale Superieure, 1964-66; Minister of National Education, 1966-68; Minister of Culture, Youth, & Sports, 1968-70; Deputy, National Assembly of Senegal. Memberships: Head, Senegal Delegation to the 14th & 15th General Conferences, UNESCO, 1966-68; President, African Group & the Group of '77', 15th General Conference, UNESCO; Exec. Council, ibid, 1966-70; President, Program Commission & External Relations, ibid, 1968-70; President, 6th Congress, African Prehistory. Publications: Afrique Africaine (joint author), 1963; Le Continent Africain, 1965; L'Afrique, 1968; Co-Director, Collection of History Manuals for Secondary African Education. Honours: Officer, Order of Merit of Senegal; Commander, National Order of the Ivory Coast; Commander, Palmes Academiques de la Republique Française. Address: 45 rue Michel Ange, 75 Paris XVI, France.

MBUAGBAW, Tanyi, born Tali, Mamfé, West Cameroon, 29th September 1929. Lecturer in Education. Education: B.Sc.(Lond.), University College, Ibadan, 1956; M.A.(Educ.), London; Study for Ph.D. at present. Married, 4 sons, 2 daughters. Appointments include: Teacher, Maths. & Physics, Urhobo College, Warri, Nigeria, 1956; Education Officer, Federal Government, Lagos, then posted to Education Department, Buea, W. Cameroon, 1957; Teacher, Maths., Government Teacher Training College, Kumba, 1957; Principal, ibid, 1961; Inspector of Education, Buea, 1961-62; UNESCO Fellowship studying Education & Educational Psychology in France, Switzerland, and U.S.A., 1962; Lecturer, Educational Psychology, Education Institute, Ecole Normale Supérieure, Yaoundé, Cameroon, 1964—; Principal, ibid, 1964; Cultural Delegate, Buea, W. Cameroon, 1965—. Memberships include: Council of Office of International Baccalaureate, Geneva, Switzerland. Author of many articles on education in Cameroon. Honours include: Knight of Order of Valour, 1968. Address: Ecole Normale Supérieure, B.P. 47, Yaoundé, Cameroon.

MBUNTUM, Kwanga Felix, born 25th August 1929. School-teacher. Education: Primary, Shisong-Nso, 1944-51; Qualified as Certificated Teacher, 1952-55; Studied Local Government. Personal details: family Christian; parents, Vincent Kwanga & Elisabeth Bika; married to Natalia Dule, 3 children. Appointments: Chairman (Mayor), NSO Council, 1963; President, N.I.U. (NSO Improvement Union, 1962—); Branch President & Executive Member, Section of the C.N.U. Memberships: N.S.O. (many cultural societies); N.S.O. Community Development Committee. Awards: Holder of the Cameroon Medal of Merit, 1st Class, 1970. Address: c/o NSO Council, Bui Division, West Cameroon.

MCOUAHA, Paul de Dieu, born 21st November 1929. Business Executive. Education: Primary School, Sakbougémé, Edéa, Cameroon, 1942-46. Married, 7 children. Appointments: Assistant Accountant, F.A.O. Co., Douala, 1946-49; With the Triandafillidis Jacordis Society, 1949-56; Business Executive, 1956—. Honours: Recipient of Cameroon Decoration, 3rd class, 1967. Address: B.P. 73, Eséka, Cameroon.

MEBA-SELASSIE ALEMU, born 7th December 1930. Vice-Minister of Press & Information Department, His Imperial Majesty's Private Cabinet. Education: High School, Addis Ababa, Ethiopia; B. Pol. Science, University of Southern California, Los Angeles, U.S.A., 1956; Diploma des Hautes Etudes International, Ecole des Hautes Etudes Internationales, Paris, France, 1958. Married, 3 sons. Appointments: Deputy Head of Press Department, Foreign Office, Addis Ababa, Ethiopia, 1958; Director-General & Head, ibid, 1959—; Acting Minister, Ministry of Information, for 9 months. Member of Tennis Club. Address: Dept., H.I.M.'s Private Cabinet, P.O. Box 389, Addis Ababa, Ethiopia.

MEDE, Moussa Yaya, born 28th December 1931. Educator. Education: Secondary School, Porto-Novo, Dahomey, & Abidjan, Ivory Coast; Baccalaureat, 1952; Higher Education, Dakar, Senegal, & Freetown, Sierra Leone; Licence es Lettres, Toulouse, France, 1958. Appointments: Assistant Teacher, Dover College, U.K., 1959-60; Broadcaster, B.B.C. French Department, 1960-61; Teacher, English, Porto-Novo, Dahomey, 1962-64; Director, Tourist Bureau & Programme Adviser, Educational Broadcasting System, 1964-66; Secretary of State, Education, Youth & Health, Provisional Government, 1966; Headmaster, Lycée Mathieu Bouke, Parakou, 1967—. Associate Member, Nigerian Association of French Teachers. Author of articles in newspapers & educational magazines on cultural topics. Address: Lycée M. Bouke, Parakou, Dahomey.

MEHRL, Martha Mary, born 5th December 1928. Dentist. Education: Primary & Secondary School, Dubuque, Iowa, U.S.A.; B.S. Chemistry, Briar Cliff College, Sioux City, Iowa, 1950; Doctor of Dental Surgery, University of Georgetown, Washington, D.C., 1958. Appointments: Dental Surgeon, Rawalpindi, Pakistan, 1959; Philadelphia, Pa., U.S.A., 1961; Fort Portal, Uganda, 1966; with Uganda Ministry of Health, 1966—. Memberships: Associate Member, American Dental Association; Uganda Dental Association; Society of Catholic Medical Mission Sisters, 1951—. Honours, Prizes, etc.: Valedictorian of Graduating Class, Georgetown University Dental School, 1958; Member of Honour Dental Society, U.S.A., 1958. Address: P.O. Box 233, Fort Portal, Uganda.

MEHTA, Dinesh Bachulal, born Dar es Salaam, Tanzania, 20th March 1939. Physician.

Education: Primary & Secondary Education, City Primary School, & Duke of Gloucester School, Nairobi, Kenya; Premedical Science, Poona, India; Medical Studies, B.J. Medical College, Poona; M.B., B.S. (Poona), 1963; M.D.(Poona), 1965; M.R.C.P.(Edinburgh), 1967; M.R.C.P.(London), 1969. Married to Dr. Shobhana S. Tawde. Appointments include: House Physician & Registrar, Hospitals, Poona, India, 1963-65; Senior House Officer in Neurosurgery, Pinderfields General Hospital, Wakefield, Yorkshire, U.K., 1966; Senior House Officer in Medicine, & subsequently Registrar in Medicine, Wakefield Group of Hospitals, 1967-69; Registrar in Psychogeriatric Medicine, S.W. Regional Board, 1969–. Member, British Medical Association. Address: Pinderfields General Hospital, Wakefield, Yorkshire, U.K.

MEHTA, Hinatlal Jevatlal, born Wan Kaner, India, March 1926. Medical Practitioner. Education: M.B., B.S., University of Bombay, 1952; D.C.H., College of Physicians & Surgeons, Bombay, 1954. Appointments include: Governor, Sacred Heart High School, Mombasa, Kenya, 1966–; Chairman, School Building Committee, ibid, 1966-67; Member, Executive Committee, Indian Association, 1965-66; Member, Executive Committee, Shri D. Jain Sangh & Jain Education Board, 1960–. Memberships include: Kenya Medical Association; Saturday Club. Address: P.O. Box 2228, Mombasa, Kenya.

MEHTA, Jaysukhlal, born 6th June 1939. Businessman. Education: Senior Cambridge Passes, 1957; Royal Society of Arts Examination, Elementary & Intermediate Stage, 1958. Appointments: Clerk, Partner, & Sole Proprietor, Prabhat Trading Co. Address: Prabhat Trading Co., Box 638, Dar es Salaam, Tanzania.

MEHTA, Pravinchandra Ratilal, born Burma, 2nd September 1929. Medical Practitioner. Education: M.B., B.S., F.R.C.S. Memberships: first Vice-President, Lions Club, Nairobi, Kenya; Member of Masonic Lodge; Social Service League.

MEHTA, Premnath, born Dar es Salaam, Tanzania, 30th November 1931. Broker. Education: Fellow of the English Association of Accountants & Auditors. Married, 3 children. Appointments include: Official Broker, National Agricultural Board, Tanzania, 1965-69; currently, Vice-President, Dar es Salaam Produce Exchange. Address: P.O. Box 1000, Dar es Salaam, Tanzania.

MEHTA, Sharad N., born Zanzibar, Tanzania, 21st June 1936. Advocate. Education: High School, Allidina, Mombassa, Kenya; G.C.E., City of London College, London, U.K.; Barrister-at-Law, Middle Temple, London. Married, 2 children. Private Law Practice, Kenya. Memberships include: Kenya Law Society; Mombasa Sports Club; Saturday Club; Mombasa Law Society. Address: P.O. Box 2313, Mombasa, Kenya.

MEISTER, Jean Henri, born Schaffhausen, Switzerland, 3rd March 1909. Missionary Doctor; Surgeon. Education: Swiss Diploma of Medicine, 1933; M.D.(Basel), 1933; Study of the Chinese Language, Examination, 1938; F.M.H., 1949; School of Tropical Medicine, London, U.K., 1951. Married. Appointments include: Medical Missionary, Basel Mission, Hospital Meihsien, Kwantung Province, China, 1937; Medical Superintendent, ibid, 1944; Acting Professor of Surgery, National Sun-Yat-Sen University of China, 1944; Surgeon & Medical Superintendent, Agogo Hospital, Agogo, Ghana, 1952–. Memberships include: 1st Convener, Christian Medical Workers' Fellowship of Ghana, 1960; 1st Chairman, Church Hospital Association of Ghana; Ghana Medical Association. Contributor to journals of medicine. Address: Agogo Hospital (Presbyterian Church of Ghana), P.O. Box 27, Agogo, Ghana.

MEKONNEN MERAWI, Bejirond, born 3rd October 1914. Administrator. Education: Elementary, Alliance Française School, Dire Dawa, Ethiopia; Alliance Française Secondary School, Addis Ababa; Diploma in Leadership Skills & Christian Motiviation, Gabriel Richard Institute. Personal details: Alliance Française Secondary School, Addis Ababa; Diploma in Leadership Skills & CHristian Motivation, Gabriel Richard Institute. Personal details: descended from a family of priests; married, 3 sons, 4 daughters. Appointments: Manager, Bebre Zeit Station, Franco Ethiopian Railway Company, 1937; Clerk, Ministry of Finance, 1942; Secretary-General, Bishoftu District, 1942-43; Secretary-General, Shoa Province (Administrative), 1944; Chief, Shoa Province Treasury, 1952; Representative, Lidetta District, Addis Ababa Municipality Council, 1954, 1958, 1962; Administrator, Quartermaster Corps, Ministry of National Defence, 1963. Memberships: Secretary-General, Patriots Association, 1953; President, Metebaber Association, 1962-70. Honours: Medal from the Emperor, for resistance activity against the Italians; Silver Medal from Pope Paul VI. Address: Rossevelt Street, P.O. 4696, Addis Ababa, Ethiopia.

MEKONNEN ZEWDIE GOBENA, H. E. Ato, born 26th March 1922. Civil Servant. Education: Amharic, Geze, English, & Italian. Married, 7 children. Appointments: Inspector, Ministry of Education, Ethiopia, 1944; General Inspector, ibid, 1948; Director, the 12 Provence, 1956; General Director, Ministry of Pensions, 1958; Commissioner, ibid, 1962; Vice Minister, Ethiopian Orthodox Churches, 1970. Memberships include: General Manager & Founder, Jerusalem Memorial of Ethiopian Believers Association; President, Memorial Coronation Association; ibid, Gondar Development Association; Ethiopian Women's Welfare Association. Author of 6 books. Honours: Medal for authorship, 1955; Menelek Great Star Medal, 1955; Ethiopian Great Cordon with Honours Star, 1970. Address: P.O. Box 3430, Addis Ababa, Ethiopia.

MEKOUAR, Tahar, born 2nd December 1923. Diplomat. Education: Political Science & History. Personal details: son of S.E. Ahmed B. H. T. Mekouar & Fatima Benjelloun; married Aicha Benjelloun, 5 sons. Appointments:

Director of Protocol, Ministry of Foreign Affairs, Rabat, Morocco; Chargé d'Affaires of Morocco in Rome, Italy; Permanent Delegate of Morocco to the F.A.O.; Consul-General of Morocco to Lisbon, Portugal; Director of General Administration to the M.A.E., Rabat; Chargé d'Affaires of Morocco to Lisbon, Portugal. Memberships: Exec. Committee, I.I.S.A.; Club Eca de Queiroz; Diners' Club; Golf Club Estoril; Club Equestre da Marinha. Honours: Decorated by S.M. the King of Morocco with the Order of the Throne, 1967. Address: Avenue das Descobertas, No. 6, Lisbon, Portugal.

MELINDJI, Kacou Benoit, born 23rd May 1924. Head of Service, Provisions, & Stores of the Administration of the Abidjan-Niger Railway. Education: former Pupil, Catholic Primary School, Abidjan Plateau. Married, 6 children. Memberships: Founding Member, Action Catholique des Familles, Ivory Coast; National Bureau, ibid, 1968—; Secretary-General, Young Christian Workers, 1950-56; Permanent Director, 2 associations for the Ivory Coast & the Upper Volta, 1955-56; President of the Council, Youth of the Ivory Coast, 1952-54; several Congresses, World Assembly of Youth & Council of Youth of the French Union; Directing Committee, Union of Railwaymen & the Administration of the Abidjan-Niger Railway, 1960-64. Honours: Medal Bene Merenti, Pope Pius XII, 1957. Address: c/o The Administration of the Abidjan-Niger Railway, B.P. 1394, Abidjan, Niger.

MEMMI, Abdelaziz, born 6th May 1916. Pharmacist. Education: Primary & Secondary Studies, Sousse College, Tunisia; Lycée Mignet, Aix-en-Provence, France; International College, Cannes, France; Aix-Marseille University. Appointments: Laboratory Assistant; Head Pharmacist, Sadiki Hospital, Tunis; Chemistry Inspector, Ministry of Public Health, Tunis; Director of the Central Pharmacy, Tunisia. Memberships: Deputy Treasurer & Vice-President, Promising Sportsmen's Club, Tunis. Author of: De la Nature du Sucre faiblement combiné aux proteines sanguines; Methode d'Extraction de faibles quantités de sucre reducteur dans des solutions. Honours, Prizes, etc: Laureat, Medicine & Pharmacy, Aix-Marseilles University; Diploma, Colonial Pharmacy. Address: Pharmacie Bab-Djedid, 2 H Avenue Bab Djedid, Tunis, Tunisia.

MEMMI, Albert, born Tunis, Tunisia, 15th December 1920. Author; Professor. Education: Philosophy & Sociology Studies. Married, 3 children. Appointments include: Head, Psychology Laboratory, Tunis; Research Assistant, C.N.R.S. (National Centre for Scientific Research), 1956; Professor, Ecole Pratique des Hautes & Etudes, Sorbonne, 1960—; Senior Lecturer, Faculty of Letters, Nanterre. Publications include (narratives): La Statue de Sel, preface by Albert Camus, 1953; Agar, 1955; Portrait du Colonise, precede du Portrait due Colonisateur, preface by J. P. Sartre, 1957; Portrait d'un Juif, 1962; La Liberation du Juif, 1966; L'Homme Domine, 1968; Le Scorpion, 1969. Honours: Prix Carthage, 1953; Prix Feneon, 1954; Commandeur du Nichen Iftikhar; Palmes Academiques. Address: 5 rue Saint Merri, Paris 4o, France.

MENGESHA GEBRE-HIWET, born 11th September 1932. Educator. Education: B.A., University College of Addis Ababa, Ethiopia, 1954; B.Ed., University of Manitoba, Canada, 1955; M.A., Ohio State University, 1956; Ph.D., ibid, 1958. Married, 1 son. Appointments: Director of University Extension & Assistant Professor & Educational Philosophy & Administration, University College of Addis Ababa, Ethiopia, 1958-61; Director-General & Assistant Minister, Ministry of Education & Fine Arts, 1961-66; Head, Conferences & General Services, Economic Commission for Africa, 1966-70; Officer, Manpower Training Section, ibid, 1970. Memberships: Programme Chairman, Rotary Club of Addis Ababa; Board of Directors, Ethiopian Red Cross Society; ibid, Games & Wildlife Conservation; Secretary, International Christian Fellowship; President, Tigrai Development Assistance Organization; Past President, University Alumni Association, H.I.S.U.; Williamsburg International Assembly; Past Chairman, World University Service, Ethiopia. Author of articles on sportsmanship, literacy activities, etc.; Editor of book in Amharic on administration. Honours: Phi Delta Kappa, 1957; Star of Honour, Ethiopia, 1963. Address: Manpower & Training Section, Economic Commission for Africa, Addis Ababa, Ethiopia.

MENOKPOR, Humphrey Kwamla, born 24th November 1933. Physician. Education: Achimota Secondary School, Accra, Ghana; G.C.E. A Levels, West Norwood Technical College, London, U.K., 1956-58; M.B., B.S., Durham University Medical School, Newcastle, 1958-63; D.P.H., Bristol University, 1967-68; Course in Epidemiology, Moscow University Postgraduate School of Medicine, U.S.S.R., 1970-71. Appointments: Medical Officer i/c Sefwi Wiasow Hospital, Ghana, 1965-66: ibid, Yendi Government Hospital, 1966-67; Medical Officer i/c Communicable Diseases, Volta Region, 1968—; ibid, i/c Family Planning Clinic, Ho, 1968-70. Memberships: British Medical Association; Ghana Medical Association; Official Ghana Delegate, International Conference on Leprology, London, 1968; ibid, International Seminar on Tuberculosis, Brazzaville, Congo, 1969. Honours: Ghana Government Scholarship, 1958-63; WHO Fellowship, 1967-68 & 1970-71. Address: Ministry of Health, P.O. Box 72, Ho, Ghana.

MERY, Harry Pierre, born Moule, Guadeloupe, W.I., 4th April 1916. Bank Director. Education: LL.D., English & Philosophy, University of Paris, France; Diploma, University of Atlanta, U.S.A.; Diploma, National School of Economic & Social Organization. Married to Odette Ernie, 1 daughter. Appointments: Assistant Professor, University of Atlanta, U.S.A., 1938-39; Head, Scrap-Iron Organization Service, 1941-43; Head, OCRDI Service, 1943-48; Head Central Bank, 1949-57; Director, Central Bank, Cayenne, French Guiana, S.A., 1957-59; Director, Central Bank, Ivory Coast, 1960-68; Director, Central Bank of Economic Co-operation (Dakar Agency), Senegal. Memberships: Founder-Mbr.,

Rotary Club, Cayenne; Past President, Lions Clubs, Abidjan; Member, Wine Tasters' Association. Honours: Knight, Legion of Honour; Officer, National Order of Lebanon; Commander, Order of the Ivory Coast. Address: 15 Avenue Courbet, Dakar, Senegal.

MESFIN FANTA, born 26th October 1928. Port Administrator. Education: Diploma in Education, Teachers' Training College, Addis Ababa, Ethiopia, 1947; Diploma in Law, Hailé Selassié University, Addis Ababa, 1967. Married to Woizero Berhane Siyoum, 1 son. Appointments: Teacher, Asfa Wossen Elementary School, Addis Ababa, 1947-50; Secretary-General, Ministry of Finance, Tobacco Monopoly Dept., 1950-54; Second Secretary, Ethiopian Embassy, New Delhi, India, 1954-62; Director-General, Marine Dept., 1964; Head of Economic & Budget Division, 1963-64; Assistant Minister, 1967–. Memberships: President, Teachers' Association, 1953-54; Hon. Treasurer, Horticultural Society of Ethiopia, 1968-69; Ethiopian Wild Life Society; Secretary (General), Law Graduates' Association of Ethiopia, 1968-69. Address: Marine Dept. Head Office, P.O. Box 1861, Addis Ababa, Ethiopia.

MESSAYE WONDE-WESSEN KASSA, born Debre-Tabor, 17th October 1935. Farmer. Education: Bible College, Grammar School, 1950-52; Advanced Level Economics & Allied Subjects, Technical College, Bournemouth, U.K., 1952-54; Diploma in Public Administration, Exeter University, 1954-56; External Student, London University, 1956-61. Personal details: father was eldest son of H.R.H. Ras Kassa; imprisoned (with mother) in Naples during Italian occupation; left Europe, 1961. Appointments: Head of Traditional Study, Ministry of the Interior; Governor of Lasta Lalibello, 1964; Resigned, 1966. Honours: Title of Fitawrari bestowed by existing regime, 1964.

MEYER, Hermann W. H., born Wilhelmshaven, Germany, 12th November 1934. Merchant. Education: Nikolaus Cusanus Gymnasium, 1954. Personal details: Collector of Orchids; married, 1 daughter. Appointments include: Raw Cotton Classifier, Prelius Schmidt, Hamburg, Germany, 1954-57; Manager, A. Baumann & Co. (Cotton) Ltd., Kampala, Uganda, 1957-66; Director, East African Cotton Exporters Ltd., Kampala, 1966–. Address: P.O. Box 3980, Kampala, Uganda.

MEYER, Margaret Anne, born 5th October 1938. Medical Officer. Education: Our Lady of Wisdom Academy, New York, U.S.A.; University College, Dublin, Ireland; Medical School. Personal details: member of the Congregation, Medical Missionaries of Mary. Appointments: Medical Officer, Kitovu Hospital, Masaka, Uganda, 1966-70. Address: Kitovu Hospital, P.O. Box 413, Masaka, Uganda.

MFINANGA, Alfred Lucas, born 6th October 1930. Principal Cooperative Officer. Education: Overseas Cambridge School Leaving Certificate, 1951; Tanganyika Government Examination (equivalent to former London Matriculation), 1953; East African School of Co-operation, Kenya, 1953; Loughborough College, U.K., 1957-58. Personal details: eldest brother, Daniel Lucas Mfinanga, now Director & Chief of Protocol & former Tanzania Ambassador to Bonn, Germany; Moscow, U.S.S.R.; married, 3 sons, 3 daughters. Appointments: Assistant Cooperative Inspector, 1952; Cooperative Inspector, 1958; Cooperative Officer, 1961; Senior Cooperative Officer, 1963; Principal Cooperative Officer, 1967; Deputy Secretary-General of C.U.T., 1969. Memberships: Civil Servants' Savings & Credit Society; Vice-Chairman, National Cooperative & Development Bank. Address: P.O. Box 2567, Dar es Salaam, Tanzania.

MGALULA, Kapimpiti Hussein Saidi Lyoba, born Ugombe Village, Tabora District, Tanzania, June, 1937. Teacher. Education: Uyumbu Moravian Primary School, 1947-50; Standard X Certificate, Tabora Government Secondary School, 1951-56; Grade I Teachers' Certificate, Mpwapwa, 1958; Commonwealth Teachers' Certificate, Birmingham University, U.K., 1966-67. Personal details: member of Nyamwezi Tribe, son of former Chief Said Mgalula Lyoba of Ugala Katansonga, Usenga; mother, daughter of last Paramount Chief of Ukengwe Chiefdom, Tabora District; wife, daughter of Sub-Chief of Maswa Chiefdom, south-east shores of Lake Victoria; 4 children. Appointments: Headmaster, Mwisenge Middle School, 1962-66; Assistant Secretary, Unified Teaching Service, Ministry of National Education, 1969–. Memberships: Leader, Nyamwezi Tribal Dance, 1951-56; Presisent & Caretaker, Western Students' Society, 1957-58; Chairman, Photography, 1958; Committee Member, Red Cross Society, Mara Region, 1962-66; Scout Commissioner, Mara Region, 1962-66; ibid, DSM District, 1967–. Recipient, Scout Wood Badge, Birmingham, U.K., 1967. Address: Ministry of National Education, P.O. Box 9121, Dar es Salaam, Tanzania.

MGAMILA, Adineur Stewart, born 4th January 1932. Administrative Officer. Education: Salvation Army School, Chunya, Morovian School, ibid; Standards I & II, 1941; Standard IV, Mchikichini Primary School, 1942-43; Std. V., Old Moshi Secondary School, 1944; Std. X, Dar es Salaam Secondary School, Tanzania; Std. XII, Tabora Upper Secondary School, 1951-52; Cambridge School Certificate, Gade III. Widower, 6 children. Appointments: Assistant District Officer, 1961-62; District Officer, 1962; District Commissioner, Kisakwa, 1962; Area Secretary, 1962-66; Senior Assistant Secretary, Ministry of Lands, Housing & Urban Development, 2nd V.P., Kilimo & Lands Survey, 1966–. Memberships: T.A.N.U.; T.A.P.A. Address: Ministry of Lands, Housing & Urban Development, P.O. Box 9132, Dar es Salaam, Tanzania.

MGAZA (Kihulla), Matthew Andrew, born 29th November 1929. Clerk; Journalist. Education: Standard VIII, 1948. Personal details: Married, 1 son, 4 daughters; wife formerly a nurse. Appointments: Clerk, L.C.S.; Editor of 'Muli', District Newspaper, Handeni; Editor, 'Amboni Yetu', Company's Newspaper; Chief Welfare Officer & Editor, 1968–. Memberships: former Member & Secretary of several social clubs in Dar es Salaam; St. Augustine's Church Council; Tanga Municipal Community Development Management Committee. Publications: 'Muli:, Handeni District Newspaper; Radio News Correspondent, Handeni District, for 6 years; Editor, 'Amboni Yetu'. Honours, Prizes, etc: Certificate of Completion, Course in Journalism, African–American Institute, 1963; Certificate, Course of Personnel Management, 1969. Address: Welfare Department, Amboni Estates Ltd., P.O. Box 117, Tanga, Tanzania.

MGBOJIKWE, Eugene Anyaegbunam, born 11th February 1933. Surgeon. Education: Dennis Memorial Grammar School, Onitsha, Nigeria; University College, Ibadan, Nigeria; King's College Hospital, London, U.K.; Royal College of Surgeons; M.B., B.S., (London); M.R.C.S.; L.R.C.P.(London); F.R.C.S. (Edinburgh). Married. Appointments: Registrar, South London Thoracic Surgical Unit, Brook Hospital, London; Surgeon, Ministry of Health, Lagos, Nigeria; Surgeon, Ministry of Health, Enugu, Medical Director, Emmanuel Clinic; Founder, Private Nursing Home, Enugu. Memberships: Foundation Member, Finchley International Youth League; Association of West African Surgeons. Awards: University Entrance Scholar, University College, Ibadan, Nigeria, 1952-54. Address: Emmanuel Clinic, 28, Ogui Road, Enugu, Nigeria.

MGONJA, Shabani Shimbo, born Pare, Tanzania, 22nd September 1929. Town Clerk. Education: Oldmoshi Secondary School, Tanzania, 1944-49; Medical Training, 1951-53; U.N. Scholarship to the University College of Addis Ababa, Ethiopia; B.A., 1961. Married, 7 children. Appointments include: Laboratory Assistant, Pathological Laboratory, Dar es Salaam, Tanzania, 1954-57; Administrative Officer, Provincial Administration, Tanganyika Government, 1961-62; Town Clerk, Tanga, Tanzania, 1962-68; Chief Executive Officer, East African Community, Central Secretariat, 1968–. Address: Municipal Council of Tanga, P.O. Box 178, Tanga, Tanzania.

MICHEL, Claude, born 16th May 1921. Biologist; Director, Mauritius Institute. Education: Royal College, Mauritius; University of Hull, U.K.; University of London; B.Sc.(Hons.); Postgraduate Certificate in Education. Married, 2 sons. Appointments: Education Officer, 1953-57; Curator, Mauritius Institute, 1957-62; Lecturer, College of Agriculture, 1962-63; Assistant Director, Mauritius Institute, 1963-66, 1966–. Memberships: Associate of the Museums' Association; Science Masters' Association, U.K.; Royal Society of Arts & Sciences, Mauritius; Chairman, Ancient Monuments Board; Chairman, Stamps Advisory Committee; Chairman, Elementary Science Committee. Publications: Notre Fauna, 1966; various papers & articles in technical & popular press. Address: Mauritius Institute, Port Louis, Mauritius.

MIDDLEMISS, Charles Peter, born 13th May 1934. Civil Servant; Agriculturalist. Education: B.Sc.(Agric.), University of Leeds, U.K.; D.T.A., Trinidad. Married. Appointments: Farm Manager, Chitedze Agricultural Research Station, Malawi; Animal Husbandry Officer; Regional Agricultural Officer; Project Manager, Lilongwe Agricultural Development Project; Chief Agricultural Development Officer. Publications: Some observations on the lactation of Blackhead Ewes and the growth of lambs: the composition & yield of milk (with M. H. Butterworth, T. R. Houghton, J. C. Macartney, A. J. Prior, & D. E. Edmond), Journal of Agricultural Science, 1968. Address: Agricultural Development Division, P.O. Box 246, Zomba, Malawi.

MILLAR, James, born Baldernock, Stirlingshire, U.K., 8th January 1909. Broadcaster. Education: Kelvinside Academy, Glasgow, U.K., & Loretto, Musselburgh, 1927-31; St. John's College, Cambridge; B.A.(Hons.), History & Economics. Personal details: father, Thomas Andrew Millar (Architect); married to Margaret Alethea Room. Appointments: in Business as Stockbroker, Glasgow, 1932-39; British Vice-Consul (attached to Foreign Office), Zagreb, Yugoslavia, 1939-42; Major in Intelligence Corps, Army Service in Middle East & Italy, 1942-46; B.B.C. Programme Organizer, East European Service; Assistant Head of Service, Administrative Officer, Overseas Services, 1946-54; Director of Ghana Broadcasting Service, 1954-60; Head of French Service, later Head of Programmes, Scotland, 1960-69; retired from B.B.C., 1969; appointed Director-General of Sierra Leone Radio & T.V., 1969–. Memberships: Glasgow Art Club; Prestwick Golf Club. Publications: Report of the Broadcasting Commission in the Gold Coast (jt. author), 1953; numerous reviews of books on West Africa for 'International Affairs' & other publications. Awarded O.B.E., 1959. Address: Sierra Leone Radio & Television, New England, Freetown, Sierra Leone.

MILLER, Donald Clifford, born 16th September 1915. Professor of Education. Education: B.A.; Dip.Ed.(London); M.Ed. (Hull). Married to Sheila Joan Tobin, 2 daughters. Appointments: various posts with Ministry of Education, Baghdad, Iraq, 1939-51; Senior Inspector, Teaching of English, ibid, 1945-51; Tutor, Institute of Education, University of Hull, U.K., 1953-57; Senior Lecturer, Institute & Department of Education, University of Ibadan, Nigeria, 1957-63; Associate Professor of Education, ibid, 1963-66; Professor of Education, 1966–. Publications: Progressive Writing Books, 1, 2, 3, & 4 (w. S. Hakim), 1949; Oxford English Course for Iraq, 1, 2, & 3 (w. S. Hakim & A. S. Hornby), 1950; Beginning to Teach English, 1963; Choice of Poems (Editor), 1965; Teaching the Reading Passage, 1966; Progressive Oxford English Course, Book 3 (w. S. J. Miller), 1966; Progressive Reading Practice, 1 & 2, 1967; New Oxford English Course (Nigeria), 3rd edn. (w. F. G. French, S. J. Miller), 1967. Address: c/o University of Ibadan, Nigeria.

MILLER, John Roy Mackay, born 26th June 1921. Consultant Surgeon. Education: St. Lawrence College, Ramsgate, U.K.; King's College & King's College Hospital, University of London; M.B., B.S.; F.R.C.S. Appointments: Surgeon, Kenyatta National Hospital, Nairobi,

Kenya; Honorary Clinical Lecturer, University of East Africa. Memberships: Foundation Fellow & Past President, Association of Surgeons of East Africa; Medical Associations of Britain & Kenya; Past President, Kenya Yachting Association; Manager, Kenya Olympic Yachting Team, Rome, 1960. Publications include: The Pattern of General Surgical Diseases in Nairobi, East African Medical Journal, 1964; Duondenal Ulcer in Nairobi, EAMJ, 1966; Portal Hypertension in Nairobi, EAMJ, 1967. Honours, Prizes, etc: Hughes Prize for Anatomy, King's College, 1941. Address: P.O. Box 30024, Nairobi, Kenya.

MILLS, Adjebu-Kojo Osah, born August 1918. Public Service Administrator. Education: Accra Royal School, Ghana, 1923-34; Accra Academy, 1935-38; Cambridge School Certificate (Grade 1 with exemption from London Matriculation), 1938. Personal details: son of late C. O. Mills. Married, 8 children. Appointments: Second Division Clerk, 1949; Administrative Assistant, 1952; Administrative Officer, 1954; Admin. Officer, Class III, 1958; Class II, 1959; Class I, 1961; Principal Secretary, 1961-70; Director of Recruitment, London, U.K., 1961; Member, Governing Council, Institute of Public Administration, 1961-70. Member of Cripples Aid Society. Address: c/o The Postmaster, Kaneshie Post Office, Accra, Ghana.

MILLS, Edward David, born 19th March 1915. Architect & Design Consultant. Education: Ensham School, London, U.K.; Polytechnic School of Architecture, London. Married, 1 son, 1 daughter. Appointments: Senior Partner, Edward D. Mills & Partners; Architect, The Cathedral of St. Andrew, Mbale, Uganda. Fellow of Royal Institute of British Architects. Memberships: R.I.B.A. Council, 1955-62, 1963-69; Chairman, Board of Architectural Education; Faculty of Architecture, British School, Rome; Governor, Canterbury College of Art; Society of Industrial Artists; Uganda Society of Architects. Author of many publications. Honours: C.B.E.; R.I.B.A. Bossom Research Fellow, 1953; Churchill Fellow, 1969. Address: Gate House Farm, Newchapel, Lingfield, Surrey, U.K.

MILONE, born 14th January 1926. Administrator of Building Societies. Engineer of Public Works. Address: 6 Bd. El Hansali, Casablanca, Morocco.

MILOSEVIC, Svetolik, born 12th September 1904. Internist-Cardiologist. Education: Faculty of Medicine, Beograd, Yugoslavia, 1930. Appointments: Assistant, Clinic for Internal Disease, Faculty of Medicine, Beograd; Director & Chief Internist, Miners' Hospital, Beograd; Chief Cardiologist, Central Polyclinic, Beograd; Deputy Chief of Diagnostic Centre, Beograd; Director, & Chief Internist, Ras Desta D. Hospital, Addis Ababa, Ethiopia, 1962–. Memberships: Vice-President & Co-Founder, Yugoslav Association of Cardiologists; Internal Association of Cardiology. Publications: Heart Diseases & Working Capacity; Neuro-Circulatory Distony; Modern Treatment of Arterial Hypertension & many case reports. Address: Ras Desta Damtew Hospital, Addis Ababa, P.O. Box 1032, Ethiopia.

MIMANO, Julius, born 27th September 1935. Mechanical Engineer. Education: Alliance High School, Kikuyu, Kenya, 1952-55; Royal College, Nairobi, Kenya, 1956-61. Appointments: Cadet Mechanical Engineer, with E.A.R.&H., 1961-64; District Mechanical Engineer, at various stations, 1965-67; Senior Mechanical Engineer, Nairobi, Headquarters, 1967-68; Chief Mechanical Engineer, E.A.R. Corporation, 1968–. Address: East African Railway Corp., P.O. Box 30021, Nairobi, Kenya.

MIMBANG, Martin, born Lolodorf, 1924. Education: Government School, Doume, Cameroun; Certificate of Education, Regional School, Batouri; Studied at Professional School, Douala; Diploma, Institute of Crimonology, University of Paris, France; Diploma of Administrative & Financial Studies & Diploma of North-African Judicial Studies, Faculty of Law, Paris; Diploma, French National Overseas School (Administrative Section), Paris. Married, 4 childre. Appointments: with the Prime Minister's Cabinet, Cameroun Government, 1957-58; Head of Cabinet, Secretary of State for Home Affairs, 1958; Director of the Cabinet to the Minister of Home Affairs, 1960; Prefect of Benoue, 1960; Prefect of Bamoun, 1961-63; Technical Counsellor to the Minister of Foreign Affairs, 1963-64; Cabinet Director to the Minister in charge of Territorial Administration and Social Provision, 1964-65; Secretary General ibid, 1965–. Honours: Officer, Cameroun Order of Valour; recipient of Cameroun Decoration, 3rd Class; Commander, National Distinction, Central African Republic. Address: B.P. 993, Yaoundé, Cameroun.

MINAKU, Odon, born 1936. Magistrate. Education: Diploma d'etudes moyennes, L'Ecole Moyennes St. Marie a Idisfa, 4 years, 1959; L'Ecole d'Assistants Agricoles, Yaeseke-Alberta (Equateur); Certifie de cours de formation des Magistrats, Kinshasa, Democratic Republic of the Congo, 1963-64. Married, 4 sons. Appointments: Inspector of Prisons, Kikuit, 1961-63; Magistrate's Course, 1963-64; Deputy to the Tribunal, 1964-66; Head of Tribunal, Kabinda, 1966-69; ibid, Tshikopa, 1969; Luebo, 1969-70; Deputy to the Tribunal of First Appeal, Lubumbashi, 1970–. Address: The Deputy, c/o the Tribunal of First Appeal, B.P. 1123, Lubumbashi, Democratic Republic of the Congo.

MINANI, Raymond, born 12th May, 1940. Director, National Radio of Burundi & the Press. Education: Philosophy & Law, Official University of Bujumbura. Married, 1 child. Appointments: Inspector of Works, 1964; Magistrate, 1966-67; Secretary-General of Youth & Member, Polital Bureau, 1967-68; ibid, Confederation of States, Burundi, 1967-68; Director, 'Voice of the Revolution', National Radio, 1968-70; ibid, the Press, 1970–. Memberships: National Union of Students, Barundi, 1962-66; J.R.R., 1966. Publications: Revolution Borundaise, 1968; Dix d'existance de la Radio-diffusion Nationale du Burundi, 1970; Enquete d'auditaire de la Radiodiffusion Nationale du Burundi, 1970. Address: B.P. 1400, Bujumbura, Burundi.

MINAWA, Ibrahim, born 20th June 1924. Personnel Officer. Education: attended the Military School in Bomba; Training with Bus Company, Newcastle, U.K., 1962. Personal details: father was a Captain, Warrant Officer, King's African Rifles. Married, 11 children. Appointments: Bus Conductor, 1941; Clerk in Charge, 1943; Chief Inspector, 1947; Depot Manager, Mubende, 1947; Depot Manager, Kampala, 1948; Depot Manager, Masindi, 1958; Depot Manager, Masaka, 1959; Depot Manager, Fort Portal, 1959; Depot Manager, Mbarara, 1962; Assistant Traffic Manager, Personnel Officer, Uganda Transport Co., Kampala, Uganda, 1963—. Memberships: Board of Governors of following schools: Lubiri Secondary School; Lady Irene Teacher Training College, Bdesse; Bomba Secondary School; Home Secretary, Social Club, Bomba. Publications: Several articles in local newspapers dealing mainly with transport business as a whole. Awarded Good Service Medal for being the most efficient conductor, 1941. Address: P.O. Box 5342, Kampala, Uganda.

MINCHELL, Robert Alan, born Co. Durham, U.K., 26th January 1927. Land Surveyor; Director of Surveys. Education: B.Sc.(Durham), 1948-51; Diploma in Photogrammetry (London), 1963. Married, 4 children. Appointments: served with Army in Royal Artillery, Middle East, 1945-48; Land Surveyor, Colonial Survey Service, Nyasaland, 1952-64; Senior Surveyor, Mabani, 1964-65; Director of Surveys, Malawi, 1965—. Memberships: A.R.I.C.S.; Photogrammetric Society. Address: P.O. Box 349, Blantyre, Malawi.

MINFORD, Antony Patrick Leslie, born 17th May 1943. Economist. Education: Winchester College, Hants, U.K.; B.A., Balliol College, Oxford University; M.Sc., London School of Economics. Married. Appointments: Economist, Ministry of Overseas Development, London; Economic Adviser, The Treasury, Malawi, 1967-69 & Courtaulds Ltd., London. Address: 18 Hanover Square, London, W.1, U.K.

MINTO, Stanley Derek, born 2nd July, 1919. Agriculturist. Education: Durham School, U.K., 1933-36; B.Sc.(Agric.), Durham University, 1937-39, 1946-47. Appointments: with Scottish Branch, N.I.A.E., 1947; Operational Research Unit, Overseas Food Corp., Tanganyika, 1948-56; i/c E.A. Testing Unit, Overseas Branch of National Institution of Agric. Engineering, 1956-62; Agric. Machinery Co-ordinating Officer, E.A. Community, East African Agric. & Forestry Research Organization, 1962—. Memberships: Fellow, Institution of Agric. Engineers, U.K.; East African Representative, ibid, 1956-62; American Society of Agirc. Engineers. Publications: Developing & Testing a Castor Bean Sheller; The Mechanisation of Groundnut Harvesting; numerous short articles. Recipient, M.B.E., 1945. Address: c/o E.A.A.F.R.O., P.O. Box 30148, Nairobi, Kenya.

MIRIMA, Henry, born 29th April 1938. Journalist. Education: B.A. Journalism, Kent State University, Kent, Ohio, U.S.A. Appointments: Editor Mwebembezi, 1963-64; Editor, Students' Newsletter & Schools' Newsletter, 1966—; Uganda Annual Report. Memberships: Sigma Delta Chi, U.S.A.; Uganda Journalists' Association. Publications: Students' Newsletter; Schools' Newsletter; Uganda Annual Report. Address: P.O. Box 7142, Kampala, Uganda.

MIRUNDI, John Judson Zirimenya, born 19th July, 1936. Teacher. Education: Cambridge School Certificate, 1959; Grade III Teacher. Married, 4 children. Appointments: Games Teacher; Head Teacher, Namirembe Primary School; ibid, Luzira Primary School. Kampala, Uganda. Memberships: Secretary, Kampala Branch, U.T.A.; Chairman, Kampala-Entebbe Schools' Game Association; Secretary, South Kyaddondo Games Association; Secretary, West Mengo District Games Association; Committee Member, Kampala City Head Teachers' Association; U.P.C. Author, Physical Activities for Infants. Address: Luzira Primary School, P.O. Box 4472, Kampala, Uganda.

MISHILI, Joseph Peter, born 9th October 1935. Controller of Supplies, Government Stores, Republic of Tanzania. Education: Secondary Education to London G.C.E. 'A' Level; Graduate Member of Institute of Purchasing & Supply, London, U.K. Personal details: first born of family of 9; married, 3 sons, 2 daughters. Appointments: Stores Clerk, Ministry of Health, Tanzania; Assistant Stock Verifier, Ministry of Finance, ibid; Senior Stock Verifier; Principal Stock Verifier; Superintendent of Stores, Comworks, Tanzania. Address: P.O. Box 9150, Dar es Salaam, Tanzania.

MITCHELL, Francis Harris, born 1st February 1937. Economist. Education: B.A., Victoria University, Victoria, B.C., Canada, 1961; University of California, Los Angeles, Calif., U.S.A. Married to Josephine Leonora Mitchell (née Wrigglesworth), 1 daughter. Appointmets: Research Fellow, Institute for Development Studies, University College, Nairobi, Kenya; Project Expert, York University, Kenya Project. Memberships: Royal Economic Society; American Economic Association; Economics Club of Kenya. Publications: The Value of Tourism in East Africa, Eastern Africa Economic Review, 1970; Macro Aspects of the Plans, East Africa Journal, 1970. Address: York University, Kenya Project, Box 30228, Nairobi, Kenya.

MITCHLEY, Hugh Robert Enrys, born 30th July, 1925. Barrister-at-Law. Education: Malvern College, U.K., 1939-43; M.A., Jurisprudence, Oriel College, Oxford, 1946-48. Personal details: served as Officer, Welsh Guards, 1943-46. Appointments: Member of Parliament, Northern Rhodesia/Zambia, 1962—; Queen's Counsel, 1964. Memberships: Vincent's Club, Oxford; Junior Carlton Club, London; represented Oxford in Athletics & Boxing. Address: P.O. Box 1094, Lusaka, Zambia.

MITHA, Mariam Ibrahim, born 11th June, 1918. Social Worker. Education: Graduate, Bombay University, India; Diploma, Social Science & Administration, London School of Economics, U.K. Personal details: daughter of Khan Bhadur Dr. Haji of Karachi; mother, cousin of late Mahomed Ali Jinnah; husband given title of Vazir by H.H. The Aga Khan. Appointments: Teacher, H.H. The Aga Khan School, Nairobi, Kenya, 1934-45; Government Social Welfare Officer, Nairobi, 1947-51; Member, Uganda Legislative Council, 1955-61; Member, Mbale Municipal Council, Uganda, 1955-59; Alderman, ibid, 1963-69. Recipient, Uganda Independence Medal, 1962. Address: P.O. Box 968, Mbale, Uganda.

MKWIZU, Herman Martin, born 8th April 1940. Educationist. Education: Primary, Pare District, Kilimanjaro Region, Tanzania, 1949-56; Government Secondary Schools, Tanga, Mzumbe-Morogoro, & St. Andrew's College, Minaki, Dar es Salaam, 1957-62; Makerere University College, Kampala, Uganda, 1963-66; Degrees, etc: 1st Class Cambridge Overseas Certificate, 1960; Higher School Certificate (Dist. in History & Geography), 1962; B.Ed.(Hons.), University of East Africa, 1966. Personal details: 4th in family of 7 children; married, 1 child. Appointments: Senior History Master & Career Master, St. Andrew's College, Minaki, Dar es Salaam, 1966; Acting Principal, ibid, 1967-68; Principal Coordinator of History, Geography, & Economics, Headquarters, Ministry of National Education, Dar es Salaam, 1969 —. Memberships: Board of Trustees & Management Committee, National Museum of Tanzania; Treasurer-General, Historical Assn. of Tanzania, 1966-68; Secretary, National History Panel; Secretary, National Economic & Public Affairs Panel; East Africa's History & Geography International Panels; Tanzania Society. Publications: Pictorial Atlas for Tanzanian Primary Schools, Edited for the Ministry of National Education. Address: Ministry of National Education, P.O. Box 9121, Dar es Salaam, Tanzania.

MMIRO, Francis Anthony, born 2nd August 1934. Physician. Education: Namilyango College, Kampala, Uganda; Wilson College, Bombay, India; Grant Medical College, Bombay, 1957; M.B., B.S., 1962; M.R.C.O.G., Queen's College, Belfast, Northern Ireland, U.K., 1968. Married, 2 children. Appointments: Medical Officer, 1964-67; Senior Registrar, 1967-69; Consultant Obstetrician & Gynaecologist, 1969 —. Fellow of Association of Surgeons of East Africa. Memberships: President, Students' Christian Movement, University of Bombay, 1960; Royal College of Obstetricians & Gynaecologists. Publications include: Epedimiology of Anaemia in Uganda. Address: Masaka Hospital, P.O. Box 18, Masaka, Uganda.

MNKANDE, Yohana Samuel, born 1927. Civil Servant. Education: Cambridge School Leaving Certificate, 1950. Married, 6 children. Appointments: Clerk, Secretariat, 1951-60; Communications Assistant, 1960-62; Communications Supervisor, 1963-67; Communications Superintendent, 1968 —. Address: Ministry of Foreign Affairs, United Republic of Tanzania, P.O. Box 900, Dar es Salaam, Tanzania.

MOALLA, Mansour, born Sfax, Morocco, 1st May 1930. Minister Delegate to the Premier Ministre charge du Plan. Education: Secondary Studies, College of Sfax; Higher Studies, University of Paris, France; Licensed in Law, 1951; Licensed in Letters, 1953; LL.D. & Diploma, Institute of Political Studies, 1954; National School of Administration, 1954-56. Married, 4 children. Appointments: Inspector of Finances, General Inspectorate of Finances, 1956; entered Tunisian Administration, 1957; Technical Adviser, Ministry of Finaces; prepared the way for the Central Bank of Tunisia, 1958; First Director-General, ibid; represented Tunisian Secretary of State for Finances in Franco-Tunisian Negotiations, 1959; Representative of Tunisia to the F.M.I., 1961; President Director-General, National Society of Investment; Director of Central Administration; helped establish Council of State & Court of Accounts; helped create African Bank of Development, 1962-63; first Vice-President, ibid, 1964; Director, National School of Administration, 1963; Under-Secretary of State for Industry & Commerce, 1967; Director of Central Administration of the Présidence; Head, State Secretariat of Posts, Telegraphs, & Telephones, 1969; nominated Minister Delegate to the Premier Ministre charge du Plan, 1970—. Memberships: Secretary-General, Paris Section, U.G.E.T., 1953; President, Executive Bureau, 1955. Honours: Commander of the Order of the Republic & Officer of the Order of Independence. Address: 32 Avenue de la Republique, Carthage, Tunisia.

MOANDAT, Jean-Baptiste-Eloi, born Mayumba, Gabon, 1918. Sub-Prefect. Education: former Pupil of the Catholic Mission. Appointments: Government Official since 1946. Honours: Knight of the Equatorial Star & the Central African Medal. Address: Sub-Prefect, Koula-Motou, Gabon.

MOBUTU (His Excellency, Lieutenant-General) Joseph-Desire, President of the Democratic Republic of the Congo, born Lisala, North-West Congo, 14th October 1930. Education: Primary & Secondary Missionary Schools. Appointments: enrolled in the Congolese Army, 1949-56; with daily newspaper, 'L'Avenir'; Editor, 'Actualites Africaines'; Chief of Staff, Congolese Army, 1960; Commander-in-Chief, (promoted from Colonel to Major-General), Congo's Armed Forces, 1961; Lieutenant-General, Congo's Armed Forces, 1965; dismissed his Prime Minister & became Head of State & Head of Government, 1966 —. Address: Kinshasa, Democratic Republic of the Congo.

MODERNE, Frank, born 5th August 1935. Professor of Law. Education: LL.D., 1960; Diploma, Institute of Political Studies, 1955; Certificate of Sociology, 1960; Agreg., Public Law, 1964. Married, 2 children. Appointments: Assistant, Faculty of Law, 1962-63; Senior Lecturer, 1964-67; Professor, Public Law, Faculty of Law & Economic Sciences, University of Madagascar, 1967 —. Memberships include: Association of Overseas University Professors; Rotary Club. Publications include: Droit Public Malgache, 1967; Le Conseil Superieur des Institutions de la Republique Malgache, 1969; La Cooperation agricol en Tanzanie, 1970; La Republique Unie de Tanzanie, 1970. Honours include: Prize for Law Thesis, 1960. Address: Faculty of Law & Economic Sciences, B.P. 905, Tananarive, Malagasy Republic.

MODI, Jitendra R., born 1st February 1938. Economist. Education: M.A., B.Comm., LL.B. (Trinity College, Dublin); Barrister-at-Law, Gray's Inn, London, U.K.; Ph.D., Edinburgh University, Scotland. Married to Hansa J. Modi (Microbiologist). Appointments: Senior Economic Officer, 1964-65; Senior Economist, with Treasury, Tanzania, 1965—. Memberships: Economic Society of Tanzania; Royal Economic Society, U.K. Honours, Prizes, etc.: Commonwealth Scholar, U.K., 1961-64. Address: P.O. Box 1779, Dar es Salaam, Tanzania.

MOFFAT, William Malcolm Unwin, born Kasama, Zambia, 15th December 1932. Physician. Education: Rondebosch Boys' High School; University of Cape Town, South Africa; M.B., Ch.B., University of Edinburgh, Scotland, U.K., 1956; M.R.C.P., ibid, 1966. Appointments: Medical Officer, Ankole Pre-School Protection Programme Uganda, 1967-69; Lecturer, Department of Paediatrics & Child Health, Makerere Medical School, Uganda. Publications: Mobile Young Child Clinics in Rural Uganda, Department of Paediatrics & Child Health, Makerere, 1969. Awards: Heinz Fellowship, British Paediatric Association, 1966. Address: c/o Dept. of Paediatrics & Child Health, P.O. Box 7072, Kampala, Uganda.

MOGWE, Archibald Mooketsa, born Kanye, Botswana, 29th August 1921. Permanent Secretary to the President & Secretary to the Cabinet, Botswana. Education: Molepolole & Kanye, 1928-36; Primary Lower Teachers' Course; Cape Junior & Senior Certificates, 1937-43; Studied privately for Batchelor of Arts (University of South Africa), 1949; Diploma in Educational Administration, University of Reading, U.K., 1962-63; Foreign Service Course, University College, Oxford, 1965-66. Married, 3 children. Appointments: Teacher, Primary & Secondary Schools, 1944-57; Housemaster, Modderpoort Schools (Soc. of the Sacred Mission) O.F.S., South Africa; Education Officer, Bechuanaland Government Service, 1957-64; Principal, Ministry of Local Government, 1964-66; Secretary, External Affairs, 1966-67; Permanent Secretary to the President, 1968; Secretary to the Cabinet, 1969; Secretary for External Affairs & Head of the Civil Service. Memberships: Chairman, Moeng College, Governing Council, 1963-64; Chairman, Maru-a-Pula, Secondary School Council, 1970; President of the Notwani Club, 1964—; Gaborone Branch, Lions International, 1970. Awarded M.B.E., 1966. Address: Office of the President, Private Bag 1, Gaborone, Botswana.

MOHAMED, Adem Ali, born 12th December, 1925. Tailor. Education: Elementary. Married, 10 children. Appointments: first Tailor, Asmara, Ethiopia, 1948—. Address: 21 Wag Street, Asmara, Ethiopia.

MOHAMED, Fouad Salih, born Omdurman, Khartoum Province, 18th November, 1932. Manager, State Bank for Foreign Trade, Khartoum, North Branch. Education: Comtoni College, Khartoum, Sudan; Studied Economics by Correspondence Course; U.K. Managerial Course, D.C.O. Training Centre, Barclays Bank. Appointments: Shorthand Typist, Sudan Mercantile Co. Ltd., 1951; w. Sudan Light & Power, 1951; Book-keeper, Sudan Railways, 1952; various positions with branches of Barclays Bank, 1952—; Accountant, 1957; Head of Ledgers Department, 1961; Manager, 1962-63; Accountant, 1964; Manager, 1965; Administrative Manager, Local Head Office, 1966-67; Assistant Manager, Khartoum, North Branch, 1967—. Address: P.O.B. 261, Khartoum North, Democratic Republic of the Sudan.

MOHAMED, Ismail Jacobus, born 27th July 1930. University Lecturer; Reader in Mathematics. Education: B.Sc., University of Witwatersrand, Johannesburg, South Africa, 1953; B.Sc.(Hons.), ibid, 1954; M.Sc., 1959; Ph.D., University of London, U.K., 1960. Appointments: Assistant Lecturer, University College, Cardiff, Wales, 1959-60; Asst. Lecturer, Queen Mary College, University of London, 1960-61; Lecturer, University of Witwatersrand, Johannesburg, South Africa, 1961-63; Senior Lecturer, ibid, 1964; Lecturer, Birkbeck College, University of London, U.K., 1965; Senior Lecturer, University of Zambia, Lusaka, 1966-68; Senior Lecturer, University of Botswana, Lesotho, Swaziland, 1968-70; Reader, ibid, 1970. Memberships: London Mathematical Society; The South African Mathematical Society. Publications: On series of subgroups related to groups of automorphisms, Proceedings of the London Mathematical Society, 1963; The class of the stability group of a subgroup chain, Journal of London Math. Society, 1964; A group with trivial. centre satisfying the normalizer condition (jt. paper, w. H. Heineken), Journal of Algebra, 1968. Awarded Shell Postgraduate Bursary, 1954. Address: Department of Mathematics, University of Botswana, Lesotho, & Swaziland, P.O. Roma, Lesotho.

MOHAMED OULD, Mohamed Najim, born 1934. Inspector of Administrative Affairs. Education: B.E.P.C.; C.A.P.; Diplome Ecole Nationale de Administration du Mali. Married, 6 children. Appointments: former Schoolteacher, 1951-57; Chef de Cabinet Ministeriel, 1957-59; Commandant de Cercle, 1959-67; Attaché de Cabinet Ministeriel, 1958-70; Inspector of Administrative Affairs, 1958—. Honours: Temoignage de Satisfaction Officielle (for services to the Nation), 1961; Medaille de l'Ordre National (Chevalier), 1967. Address: G.A.A.E.F., Koulouba, Republic of Mali.

MOHINDRA, Baldev Sahai, born Ludhiana, India, 11th April 1910. Business Proprietor. Education: Matriculated D.A.V. High School, Lahore, India, 1927; Government College, Ludhina, India, 1927-29; Punjab University, A.C.P. Diploma, College of Preceptors, 1937, London. Married, 3 sons. Appointments include: Education Officer, Kenya Education Department, 1929-43; Founder Secretary, Boy Scouts Association, Mombasa, 1935-37; Secretary, Civil Servants Association, Mombasa, Treasurer, Arya Samaj, 1934-35; Member Civil Service

Commission, 1956; Member, Board of Commerce & Industry, 1948-57; Member, Legislative Council, 1958-60; Member, Transport Licensing Appeals Tribunal; Member, Immigration Appeals Tribunal; Member, Wages Board; Member, Weights & Measures Board. Memberships: President, Suleman Verjee Gymkhana; President, Indian Chamber of Commerce, 1950-52; President, Federation of Chamber of Commerce & Industry, 1952-54. Publications: published various newspaper articles, 1947-49. Honours: O.B.E., 1957. Address: P.O. Box 1832, Nairobi, Kenya.

MOHIUDDIN, Ahmed, born 19th March 1915. Medical Educator. Education: M.B., B.S., Osmania University, 1937; Ph.D., University of London, U.K., 1947. Member of the Anatomical Society of Great Britain & Northern Ireland. Publications: Handbook of Human Embryology; 40 research papers on anatomy. Honours, Prizes, etc.: Sir Akbar Hydari Gold Medal; Drake Brompton Gold Medal; Life Fellowship, Academy of Zoology, India; Foundation Fellowship in Surgery, Nigeria Medical Council. Address: College of Medicine, University of Lagos, Lagos, Nigeria.

MOI (The Honorable) Daniel Tototich Arap, born Baringo, North-West Kenya, 1924. Vice-President of Kenya & Minister of Home Affairs. Education: Kapsabet Teachers' Training College, Kenya; C.P.A. Course, U.K., 1961. Appointments: Headmaster, Kabarnet Intermediate School, 1948; Assistant Principal, Tambach Teachers' Training College, 1949-54; elected & re-elected, Legislative Council, 1955, 1957, 1961; Minister for Education, 1962; Member for Baringo North, House of Representatives, 1963; first President, Rift Valley Region; Shadow Minister for Agriculture, 1963; Minister for Home Affairs, 1964—; Vice-President, 1967—. Memberships: Board of Governors, Alliance Girls' High School; Chairman, KANU Reorganization Group. Address: P.O. Box 1036, Nakuru, Kenya.

MOKTAR OULD DADDAH (His Excellency), born Boutilimit, 25th December 1924. President of the Islamic Republic of Mauritania. Education: St. Louis, Senegal; LL.D. Paris Law Faculty; Diploma, National School of Oriental Living Languages, 1955. Appointments: Interpreter, 1942-48; Apprentice Lawyer, Dakar, Senegal, 1957; General Secretary, PRM, 1958-61; ibid, 1961—; Member, National Assembly, 1959; Prime Minister & Ministry of the Interior, 1959; President of the Republic, 1961—. Address: Nouakchott, Mauritania.

MOLELEKOA, Moshe, born 18th April 1942. Assistant Lecturer. Education: B.Sc. (Hons.), Applied Mathematics (Dist.), (University of South Africa), 1967; currently studying for M.Sc. Personal details: parents live in Republic of South Africa. Appointments: Assistant Lecturer, part-time, later full-time. Memberships: Academic Staff Association of U.B.L.S.; Staff Club, U.B.L.S. Honours, Prizes, etc.: School Prize, 1956; Mobil Oil Bursary, 1962; Physics & Maths. Prizes, 1963; University of South Africa Awards, 1966, 1968. Address: University of B.L.S., P.O. Roma, Lesotho.

MOLES, George, born 28th February 1923. Medical Practitioner. Education: M.B., B.Ch., B.A.O., Queen's University, Belfast, Northern Ireland, U.K., 1950; D.T.M.&H., Liverpool University, 1952; D.Obst., R.C.O.G., London, 1964. Appointments: Medical Superintendent, Combined (S.U.M.) Hospital, Nguru, Bornu Province, 1953-63; Medical Superintendent, Vom Christian Hospital, Sudan United Mission, via Jos, 1966-70. Address: United Missions, via Jos, Nigeria.

MOLNOS, Angela, born Budapest, Hungary, 2nd July 1923. Psychologist. Education: Universities of Bologna, Padua, & Genoa, Italy, 1942-47; Ph.D., Univ. of Genoa; Diploma in Psychology, Free University of West Berlin, Germany; Univ. of Munich, 1956-57; Diploma, School of Publicity, Hamburg, 1959; Studied with Dr. F. Seifert, Munich, 1956; Dr. Seiler Vogt, Zurich, Switzerland, 1960. Personal details: Uruguayan Citizen, 1955—; married, 1945; divorced, 1955. Appointments include: Lecturer in Psychology, Inst. de Profesores 'Artigas', Montevideo, Uruguay, 1952-55; Consulting Psychologist, Publicity & Public Relations Agency, Dr. R. Farner, Zurich, Switzerland, 1959-60; Head of Motivational Research, Inst. for Applied Psychology, Zurich, 1960-61; Head of Dept. of Sociology & Psychology, Inst. for Social & Market Research, 'Infratest', Munich, Germany, 1961-63; Research in East Africa, Centre of African Studies, Ifo-Institute for Economic Research, Munich, 1963-69; Director, East African Research Information Centre (sponsored by East African Academy, financed by the Ford Foundation), 1967-69; Ford Foundation Project Specialist, 1969-70; Specialist, ibid., conducting a survey on Traditional Attitudes Beliefs & Practices relevant to Family Planning in East Africa, 1970-71. Memberships include: Inter-American Society of Psychology, 1954; Association of German Psychologists, 1957; Founder Member, Social Scientific Study Group of International Problems, Bonn, 1960; Uruguayan Representative, Congress of Psychology, Curitiba, Brazil, 1953; Uruguayan Delegate, XVth Psychological World Congress in Brussels, 1957. Participant in numerous other meetings, conferences, & workshops. Publications include: The Social Scientific Investigation of East Africa, 1954-63, 1965; Attitudes towards Family Planning in East Africa, 1968; Social Science Research on Africa, 1946-69, a guide in the series Africa-Studien, 1971; EARIC, information circulars; many other articles, papers & circulars. Address: c/o The Ford Foundation, P.O. Box 1081, Nairobi, Kenya.

MONNIER, Yves Paul Marie Edouard, born 24th June 1921. Engineer-in-Chief, Rural Engineering, Lakes, & Forests: Head of Service of Reafforestation; Director of Lakes & Forests. Education: Agronomist, 1944; Engineer of Lakes & Forests, 1945; Diploma of Higher Studies in Economic Sciences, 1961. Appointments: Land Restoration Service, Moutagne a Gap, Higher Alps, France, 1946-51; Service des Exploitations en Regie, Germany, 1947-49; Economic Assistant to the Governor of El Jadida, Morocco, 1957-59. Memberships:

Co-founder, Junior Chamber of Commerce, El Jadida, Morocco. Publications include: L'Eucalyptus au Maroc; La Foret Marocaine. Honours: Knight of Agricultural Merit. Address: Office of Lakes & Forests, Rabat, Morocco.

MONTCERISIER, Henri, born 23rd September 1933. Inspector, Groupe Becob Gerant St. Sotref. Married, 2 children. Chevalier, Ordre National Ivoirien, 1967. Address: B.P. 4041, Abidjan, Ivory Coast.

MONTEFIORE, David G., born 28th May 1929. Medical Practitioner. Education: M.A., Clare College, Cambridge, U.K., 1953; M.B., B.Ch., ibid, 1953; M.D., 1960; Dip. Bact., with distinction, Guy's Hospital Medical School, London, 1960. Currently, Professor of Medical Microbiology, University of Ibadan, Nigeria. Memberships: Life Member, New York Academy of Sciences; British Medical Association; Foundation Member, Royal College of Pathology. Author of numerous papers on medical virology & bacteriology. Honours: Scholar, Clare College, Cambridge; 1st Class Hons., Nat. Science, Tripos I, 1949; 1st Class Hons., Moral Science, Tripos II, 1950. Address: Department of Medical Microbiology, University of Ibadan, Nigeria.

MONWELA, Dikgothi Ramakoba, born Maun, 16th January 1931. Member of Parliament; Farmer. Education: J.C. Form II, St. Matthews, Cape. Married, 3 sons, 5 daughters. Memberships: Moremi Wildlife Conservation Society; Batawana Land Board. Address: P.O. Box 45, Maun, Ngamiland, Botswana.

MONZEMU, Frederic-Martin, born 26th October 1936. Journalist; Director-Editor. Education: Humanités Commerciales; Enqueteur, Institut de Recherches Economiques & Sociales, Universite de Lovanium. Married, 5 children. Appointments: Secretaire de Direction; Journalist; Editor; Directeur de Cabinet Ministeriel (Education, Postes et Telecommunications, Information et Jeunesse et Sports); Secretaire General de la Metalkat (filiale de la Gecomin); Editor, later Director-Editor, 'Renouveau'. Memberships: National Press Association; President, Press Club, Kisangani; former President, Local des Journalistes Sportifs du Congo. Publications: 'Le Renouveau', Kisangani daily; L'Etoile, 1963; Présence Congolaire, 1964-65; Horizons, 1959; Contributor to many foreign & Congolese journals. Address: Le Renouveau, Quotidien de Kisangani, B.P. 982, Republic of the Congo.

MOOLLAN (The Hon.) Cassam Ismael, born 26th February 1927. Barrister-at-Law. Education: Royal College, Mauritius; London School of Economics & Political Science, U.K.; Lincoln's Inn, London. Married, 1 son, 2 daughters. Appointments: District Magistrate, 1957; Crown Counsel, 1961; Senior Crown Counsel, 1964; Solicitor-General, 1966; Acting Judge Supreme Court, 1970. Memberships: Past President, The Port Louis Gymkhana; Founder Member, The Mauritius Bar Association; Mauritius Society for Prevention of Cruelty to Animals; Saint John's Council for Mauritius; Old Royals Association. Honours: LL.B.(London), 1951; Queen's Counsel, 1969. Address: Supreme Court, Port Louis, Mauritius.

MORGAN, Ernest Dunstan, born Freetown, Sierra Leone, 17th November 1896. Pharmaceutical Company Director. Education: Zion Day School; Methodist Boys' High School. Married, with children. Appointments include: started business, 1921; elected Member, City Council, 1938; service in numerous Government & Public Committees, including: Chairman, Rent Assessment Committee, Central Ward, 1941-51; Public Service Commission, 1948-52; Hon. Treasurer, Boy Scouts Council, 1948-60; Fourah Bay College Council, 1950-54; West African Examinations Council, 1953—; temporary nominated Member, House of Representatives, 1956; first Nominated Member, ibid, 1957-61; currently, Managing Director, Morgan Pharmacies Ltd., largest distributors of pharmaceuticals in Sierra Leone. Memberships include: President, Sierra Leone African Chamber of Commerce, 1944-60; Chairman, Blind Welfare Association, 1946-62; President, Chamber of Commerce of Sierra Leone, 1961-63. Honours include: M.B.E., 1944; Justice of the Peace, 1952; O.B.E., 1959; Independence Medal, 1961. Address: 64 Westmoreland Street, Freetown, Sierra Leone.

MORIS, Jon Russel, born Tanzania, 19th June 1939. University Lecturer; Rural Sociologist. Education: B.S., Zoology, Seattle Pacific College, U.S.A., 1960; M.A., Anthropology, Northwestern University, 1964; Ph.D., Anthropology, ibid, 1970. Married, 2 children. Appointments: Research Associate, West Virginia University, 1963; Lecturer, Rural Sociology, Makerere University College, Uganda, 1965; Research Fellow, I.D.S., Nairobi, Kenya, 1968; Senior Lecturer in Rural Development, IPA, Dar es Salaam, Tanzania, 1970. Member of East African Agricultural Economics Society. Publications: Rural Development in Kenya (joint author with J. Meyer, D. Ireri), 1970; several articles on rural development. Address: Department of Political Science, The University of Dar es Salaam, Box 35042, Dar es Salaam, Tanzania.

MORROW, Richard Harold, Jr., born Illinois, U.S.A., 13th February 1932. Physician. Education: B.A.(Hons, Economics), Swarthmore College, U.S.A., 1954; M.D., Washington University, St. Louis, 1958; M.P.H., Epidemiology & Tropical Public Health, Harvard School of Public Health, 1965; Medical Internship & 2 years' Medical Residency, Department of Medicine, University of Rochester Medical School, 1958-61. Married, 2 children. Appointments: Research Fellow in Medicine, Navajo-Cornell Field Study Project, Dept. of Public Health, Cornell University Medical College, 1961-62; Medical Officer (United States Public Health Service), National Cancer Institutes of Health, Ghana Project, 1962-64; Board Certified Internal Medicine, 1966; currently, W.H.O. Senior Lecturer in Epidemiology, Dept. of Preventive Medicine, Makerere University Medical College, Kampala, Uganda, 1966-70; Consultant, National Cancer Institute, National Institutes of Health, 1966-70. Fellow of the American College of Physicians. Memberships: Alpha Omega Alpha; American Medical Associaion; American Society of Tropical Medicine & Hygiene; Uganda Medical Association; Council Board, UMA; East African Association of Physicians; American Public Health Association; Society for Epidemiologic Research; American College of Physicians. Publications include: Contributor to: Ghana Medical Journal; Clinical Research; East African Medical Journal; British Medical Journal; Annals of Internal Medicine; The Lancet; Int. Journal of Cancer; Cancer in Africa; British Journal of Prev. & Social Medicine; Companion to Medical Studies in East Africa (chapter in book), 1970, etc. Address: c/o Makerere University Medical College, Kampala, Uganda.

MORTIMER, Charles Edward, born Shipley, Yorkshire, U.K., 1st January 1886. Retired Civil Servant. Education: Hartley College, Manchester. Married, 2 sons. Appointments include: Methodist Minister, U.K., 1910-16; Clerk, Land Department, Kenya, 1917; Land Assistant, 1920-27; Lands Secretary, 1928-38; Commissioner for Local Government, Lands & Settlement, 1938-46; Member for Health, Lands, & Local Government, 1946-45, 1952-54. Memberships include: President, Rotary Club, Nairobi, 1942-43; President, Council for Kenya, Order of St. John, 1953-67; President, Y.M.C.A. for Kenya, 1950-65. Honours include: C.B.E., 1943; Kt. Bachelor, 1950; Kt. of the Order of St. John, 1965. Address: P.O. Box 6890, Nairobi, Kenya.

MORTIMORE, Michael John, born 7th September 1937. Lecturer in Geography. Education: Monkton Combe School, 1948-55; B.A. Geography, University of Leeds, U.K., 1960; M.A. Geography, ibid, 1963. Married to Julia Ann Jackson. Appointments: Lecturer in Geography, Ahmadu Bello University, Zaria, Nigeria, 1962–; Senior Lecturer, ibid, 1970–. Memberships: Institute of British Geographers; International African Institute; Nigerian Geographical Association; African Studies Association of the U.K.; Historical Society of Nigeria. Publications include: Land & population pressure in the Kano close-settled zone, Northern Nigeria, The Advancement of Science, 1967; Zaria & its region: A Nigerian savanna city & its environs (Editor), 1970; Settlement evolution & land use (chapter 10 in Zaria & its Region), 1970; contributor to: The population of tropical Africa, 1968; Collier's Encyclopedia; The Nigerian Geographical Journal, 1970. Address: Department of Geography, Ahmadu Bello University, Zaria, Nigeria.

MORTON, Roger Graham, born 10th March 1937. Agricultural Officer. Education: Certificate in Agriculture (with Credit), Cheshire School of Agriculture, U.K., 1955: National Diploma in Agriculture, College Diploma in Agriculture, Harper Adams Agricultural College, Newport, Shropshire, 1958. Appointments: Field Extension Service, Ministry of Agriculture, Tanzania, 1958-62; Principal, Msinga Farmers' Training Centre, Moshi, 1963-67; in charge of Farmer Training in Tanzania, 1967-69; Adviser on Farmer Training, Ministry of Agriculture, 1970–; Project Coordinator, Research & Training Division, Ministry of Agriculture, Food & Cooperatives, Tanzania, 1970–. Address: Research & Training Division, Ministry of Agriculture, Food & Cooperatives, P.O. Box 2066, Dar es Salaam, Tanzania.

MORZERIA, Jaykrishan, born Kericho, Kenya, 21st January 1938. Advocate. Education: B.A.(Hons.), University of Southampton, U.K.; Barrister-at-Law, Middle Temple. Appointments: Advocate, Kisumu, 1963–. Memberships include: Vice-Chairman, Nyanza Law Society; Hon. Secretary, Kisumu Gymkhana; Chairman, Kisumu Round Table No. 18. Address: P.O. Box 532, Kisumu, Kenya.

MOSDELL, Lionel Patrick, born Berkshire, U.K., August 29th, 1912. Judge. Education: Abingdon School; St. Edmund's Hall, Oxford; M.A.(Oxon.); Solicitor, 1938; Barrister-at-Law, Gray's Inn, 1952. Married, 1 son, 1 daughter Appointments include: Registrar of Lands & Deeds, Rhodesia, 1946; Resident Magistrate, 1950; Senior Resident Magistrate, 1956; Judge of the High Court, Tanganyika, 1960; Judge of the High Court, Kenya, 1966. Memberships include: Special Forces Club; Royal Commonwealth Society; Nairobi Club; Mombasa Club. Address: High Court, P.O. Box 140, Mombasa, Kenya.

MOSHOESHOE II, Constantine Bereng Motlotlehi, Seeiso (King of Lesotho), born Mokhotlong, Lesotho, 2nd May 1938. Education: Roma College, Lesotho; Ampleforth College, U.K.; Corpus Christi College, Oxford University. Personal details: married to Princess Tabitha Masentle, daughter of Chief Lerotholi Mojela; children: Prince Letsie David, Principal Chief-designate of Matsieng Ward & Heir Apparent to the Throne, born 17th July 1963; Prince Seeiso Simeone, born 16th April 1966; Princess Constance Christina Sebueng, born 24th December 1969. Paramount Chief of Basutoland, 1960-65; King of Lesotho, 1965–. Address: Lesotho.

MOTHA, David, born 9th February 1936. Civil Servant. Education: Secondary & High School. Married to a Teacher, 3 children. Appointments: Labour Inspector, 1964-66; Labour Officer, 1966-68; Labour Commissioner, Swaziland Government, 1968–. Address: Commissioner of Labour, c/o Swaziland Government.

MOUHAJU, Mohamed, born 1920. Chef Controleur Autobus, Casablanca. Married, 8 children. Appointments: Controleur, Commune de Marseille, 1948; Moroccan Delegate, 1953; worked in Cite Ojemoia, Casablanca. Memberships: Marocaine de Bienfaisance de Paris, Adherents, 1950. Address: Cite Ojemoia Avenue, A No. 12, Casablanca, Morocco.

MOULINE, Larbi, born 10th November 1934. Mining Engineer. Education: Higher National School of Mines, Saint Etienne, France. Married, 3 children. Appointments: Engineer, Office of Phosphate Research, 1959; Director of Administrative Affaires, 1965; Directeur des Travaux et Marches, 1967; Technical Director, 1970. Member of the Lions Club. Chevalier de l'Ordre du Trone. Address: Villa 'Mouline', Pinede, Souissi, Rabat, Morocco.

MOULIOM, Mfenjou Moise, born 1933. Civil Administrator. Education: Licence in Law & Economic Science, Diploma IHEOM, Paris, France. Married. Appointments: Head of Cabinet, Cameroun Government Service; Head of Department, ibid; Special Agent, ibid; Secretary-General to the Secretary of State for Public Affairs. Honours: Recipient of Cameroun Decoration, 3rd class; Chevalier de l'Ordre de la Valeur. Address: Ministere Delegué à La Fonction Publique Federale, Yaoundé, Cameroun.

MOUMOUNI, Elhadj Amadon, born 8th April 1927. Deputy Directing Head of Services, Posts & Finances of the Office of the PTT, Naimey, Niger. Honours: Knight of the Order of Merit of Niger, 1967. Address: c/o Office of Posts & Finances, PTT, Niamey, Niger.

MOUNTAIN, Derek, born 9th October 1937. Civil Engineer. Education: Rothwell Grammar School, Yorks., U.K.; B.Sc., University College of Swansea. Appointments: Graduate Engineer, County Borough of Swansea, 1962-64; Engineering Assistant, West Suffolk County Council, 1964-68; Acting Regional Engineer, Malawi Government, 1968-69; Project Engineer, Lakeshore Road, Malawi Government, 1969—. Associate Member, Institute of Mechanical Engineers. Address: Ministry of Works & Supplies, Road Construction Unit No. 2, Private Bag, Nkhota Kota, Malawi.

MOURAD, Mohamed Helmi, born 7th July 1919. Former Minister of Education & Information, U.A.R. Education: Lic. in Law, Faculty of Law, University of Cairo, 1939; Higher Diplomas in Public Law & Political Economy, University of Paris, 1947; Doctorate, Political Economy, University of Paris, France, 1949. Appointments: Magistrate, 1942-46; Teacher, Law of Labour, Faculty of Law, University of Alexandria, 1949; Professor, Political Economy, University of Ein-Chams, Cairo, 1956-64; Deputy Rector, ibid, 1964-67; Rector, University of Ein-Chams, Cairo, 1967-68; Minister of Education & Information (accomplished reform of general education), 1968-69. Memberships: President, Union of Arab Economists, 1969-71; Vice-President, Egyptian Society for Political Economy, Statistics, & Legislation, 1968-70, 1970-72. Publications: Droit de travail et Assurances Sociales, 1950; Doctrines et Systemes Economiques, 1951; Principes de Science Economique, 1956-61; Finances Publiques, 1959. Address: 44 rue Farid, Heliopolis, Cairo, U.A.R.

MOURÉ, Emile Florian, born 21st November 1935. Educationalist. Education: African Institute of Planning, Dakar, Senegal; Ecole Normale Superieur, Central Africa. Married, 6 children. Appointments: Director of School, Libreville, Gabon, 1959-61; Head of the Education Planning Service, 1964—. Memberships: International League of Teachers; General Secretary, Gabon League of Teachers; Secretary, Teachers: Union, 1959-61. Author of several papers in his field. Address: B.F. 334, Libreville, Gabon.

MOUSSA, Pierre Louis, born 5th March 1922. President of the Bank of Paris, France. Education: Ecole Normale Superieure, 1940; Agrégé des Lettres, 1943. Appointments: Inspecteur des Finances, 1946-54; Director in Charge of Economic Affairs & Planification for French Overseas Territories, 1954-59; Director of Civil Aviation, 1959-62; Director, Africa Dept., World Bank, Washington, USA, 1962-65; President of the Federation Française des Sociétés d'Assurances. Publications: the Economic Chances of French & African Community, 1957; The Underprivileged Nations, translated into English, Swedish, Norwegian, Danish, Italian, Spanish, Catalan, & Portuguese; The Economy of the Franc Area, 1960; The United States & the Underprivileged Nations, 1965. Honours: Chevalier de la Legion d'Honneur, 1960; Officier de l'Ordre National du Merite, 1966; Officier de l'Ordre de Boyaca, Columbia, 1954; Commandeur de l'Ordre National Mauritanien, 1965; Medaille Aeronautique, 1965. Address: Banque de Paris et des Pays-Bas, 3, rue d'Antin, Paris 2, France.

MOWSCHENSON, Henry, born 13th July 1914. Medical Practitioner. Education: M.D., D.P.H., D.I.H., Universities of Prague, Czechoslovakia, & London, U.K. Appointments: Lieut.-Colonel, R.A.M.C., 1940-46; H.M. Overseas Civil Service. 1946-56; Medical Consultant, Malawi Railways, 1956—; Senior Medical Superintendent, Queen Elizabeth Central Hospital, Blantyre, 1964—. Memberships: Royal Commonwealth Society; British Commonwealth Service League; Rotary International. Publications: Correspondent of: World Medicine, Medical News, & Central African Medical Journal. Awarded O.B.E. Address: P.O. Box 5482, Limbe, Malawi.

MOYES, Ronald William, born 26th April 1929. Medical Practitioner. Education: M.B., B.S., London University, U.K., 1956; D.T.M.&H., University of Liverpool, 1961; D.P.H., ibid, 1963; L.M., Rotunda, Dublin, Ireland, 1966; D.I.H., Dundee Scotland, 1969. Married, 2 children. Fellow of the Royal Society of Tropical Medicine & Hygiene. Memberships: Society of Medical Officers of Health; Mombasa Club, Kenya. Address: P.O. Box 721, Kisumu, Kenya.

MOYO, Petros Hlanzo, born 10th July 1892. Schoolmaster. Education: Loudon Mission Station, 1904-12; Teacher Training, Livingstonia Mission, 1922-26; Govt. Tchrs.' Cert., 1930; 3rd Class Dip. Cert., 1934; 2nd Class Dip. Cert., 1936; 1st Class Hon. Cert., 1938. Married. Appointments: Headmaster, Loudon Schools, 1913-53; Inspector of Schools, 1930-34; Village Headman, 1933—; Mbr., Mombera District Council, 1934-61; Livingstonia Education Comm., 1938-39; Inspector of Schools, 1939-40; Legal Adviser to Chiefs Mzuku, Mzuku II, & Mzikubola, 1939-57. Memberships: Nyasaland Provincial Council (Northern Province), 1950-58; Natural Resources Committee; Land Usage Committee; Sec., Livingstonia Teachers' Council, 1944-46; Elder, Free Church of Scotland, 1930-53. Publications: Early History of Angoni (under print); Translation of Angoni hymns into Chitumbuka Hymn Book. Recipient,

Republic of Malawi Medal, 1966. Address: Emanyaleni South, Swaswa F.P. School, Mzimba South, Malawi.

MPAGI, Paul Ziraye, born 14th March 1927. Librarian. Education: Certificate & Diploma in Librarianship. Married, 8 children. Appointments: Library Asst., 1955-63; Assistant Librarian, 1964-67; Librarian, 1968—. Memberships: East African Library Association; Kabarole Public Library Committee. Address: Kabarole Public Library, P.O. Box 28, Fort Portal, Uganda.

MPOGOLO, Joshua Joseph, born 14th July 1937. Director of Statistics. Education: B.A. Mathematics; Diploma in National Economic Accounting. Married. Appointments: Statistical Officer, 1963-66; Statistician, 1966-69; AG. Director of Statistics, 1969; Director of Statistics, 1969—. Memberships: Association of African Statisticians; Advisory Board, E.A. Statistical Training Centre. Address: Bureau of Statistics, P.O. Box 796, Dar es Salaam, Tanzania.

MSANGI, Francis Kiure, born 11th July 1937. University Lecturer. Education: Primary, Usangi, 1945-51; Secondary, Ilboru School, 1952-55; Teacher Training Course, Mpwapwa, 1956-57; Diploma in Fine Art (1st Class Div.), Makerere College Fine Art School, Uganda, 1959-63; Diploma in Education, Makerere University College, 1964. Married, 1 child. Appointments: Head of Art Dept., Mpwapwa Teacher Training College, Tanzania, 1964; Assistant Headmaster & Head of Art Dept., Iyunga Secondary School, 1967; Art Lecturer, Fine Art Dept., University of Nairôbi, Kenya, 1968. One-man Exhibitions: Chemcheum Cultural Centre, Nairobi (54 works on show), 1964; National Museum, Dar es Salaam, 1967; Nairobi University College, 1968; Group Shows: Union Carbide Building, New York, 1969-70; two-man show, Frankfurt, Dusseldorf, & Hannover, Germany. Publications: Art Handbook for Upper Primary Schools; Ujana na Mapenzi (a sex manual for young men & women in East Africa). Honours, Prizes, etc.: Margaret Trowell Prize for Best All-Round Art Student of the Year, Makerere University College. Address: Department of Fine Art, University of Nairobi, P.O. Box 30197, Nairobi, Kenya.

MSHANA, Eliewaha Elia, born Usangi, Pare, Tanzania, 29th September 1925. Pastor. Education: Marangu Teachers' Training College, 1942-44; Teachers' Certificate Lutheran Theological Seminary, Lwandai, Tanzania, 1950-52; Luther Theological Seminary, St. Paul, Minnesota, U.S.A., 1958-60; B.D. Degree, Union Theological Seminary, New York City, N.Y., Master of Sacred Theology S.T.M., 1965-66. Married, 1 son, 7 daughters. Appointments include: Teacher, Usangi District School, 1945-49; Pastor. Udangi Lutheran Parish, 1953; Pastor, Moshi Town Lutheran Parish, 1954-56; Pastor, Usangi Lutheran Parish, 1956-58; Pare District President, Lutheran Church, 1957-58; Teacher, Lutheran Theological College, Makumira, 1960—; Principal, Lutheran Theological College, Makumira, 1962—. Memberships: Member of the Ecumenical Fellows Program, Union Theological Seminary, New York, 1965—; Honorary Assistant Secretary of the Teachers' League, North Pare Branch and also Branch Secretary, 1948 & 1949; Member of the Usangi Sports & Welfare Club, 1946, later its Honorary Assistant Secretary, 1947; Honorary Secretary, 1949; Member of Tanganyika African Association, later becoming TANU, 1946. Publications (Books): Fidia ya Wengi, a commentary on St. Mark's Gospel in Swahili, 1965; Hotuba Tano, Kanisa na Mabadiliko Ndani ya Mkristo katika Maisha ya Unyumba 1968; Translation work of the New Testament in Chasu, Bible Society in East Africa, 1967. Periodicals: Editor of Africa Theological Journal; Nationalism in Africa as a Challenge and Problem to the Christian Church in Africa; Confessionalism in Risk, of Youth Dept. WCC, Geneva, Vol. II, No. 4 1965. Address: Lutheran Theological College Makumira, P.O. Box 55, Usa River, Tanzania.

MSONDE, Cecil Yakobo Kiondo, born 23rd August 1924. Programmes Officer, Radio Tanzania, Education: Primary School, Mhindulo & Kiwanda; Secondary School, Minaki; Teacher Training, Minaki College; University of Dar es Salaam, Tanzania. Personal details: married 4 sons, 4 daughters. Appointments: Teacher in Primary & Secondary Schools; Teacher, Teachers' College; Educational Assistant; District Education Officer; Inspectorate; Programmes Officer, Radio Tanzania. Member of TANU. Address: Radio Tanzania, P.O. Box 9191, Dar es Salaam, Tanzania.

MSUYA, John Rogers, born Ugweno, 2nd February 1938. Chief Instructor. Education: Secondary Education, 1955; University of Connecticut, U.S.A.; University of Syracuse. Married, 5 children. Appointments: Clerical Officer, 1956; Executive Officer, 1961; Instructor, 1963; Senior Instructor, 1965; Chief Instructor, 1968. Memberships: Tanganyika Young Men's Christian Association; Founder Member, former Secretary & Chairman, Dar es Salaam Branch, ibid.; Committee Member, Tanzania Institute of Management. Publications: Various training materials in management. Address: Management & Office Training Dept., Civil Service Training Centre, Tanzania.

MSUYA, Philemon Maghimbi, born 17th September 1932. University Reader in Biochemistry. Education: B.Sc.; M.Sc.; Ph.D. Married. Appointments: Demonstrator, Medical School, Makerere University College, Kampala, Uganda, 1962; Assistant Lecturer, ibid, 1963; Lecturer, 1964; Senior Lecturer, Faculty of Medicine, University College, Dar es Salaam, Tanzania, 1968; Reader in Biochemistry, University of Dar es Salaam, 1970. Memberships: East African Society for Biological Research; East African Academy of Science. Publications: Contributor to: Biochem. Journal, 1963; Catalyst, 1969; Fed. Proceedings, 1969; Biol. Neonat., 1969; 3 articles in Dsm. Medical Journal. Address: Dept. of Biochemistry, University of Dar es Salaam, Tanzania.

MTAWALI, Alfred Walter, born 3rd January 1923. Administrative Secretary. Education: Blantyre Secondary School, Malawi; Tabora

School, Tanzania. Married, 4 children. Appointments: Clerical Officer, 1945; Assistant District Officer, 1957; District Commissioner, 1960; Administrative Secretary, 1962—. Memberships: Mtwara Social Club, 1964-67; Chairman, ibid, 1966-67; Shinyanga Sports Club, 1968-70; Chairman, ibid, 1969-70; Lions Club of Shinyanga, 1968-70; 2nd Vice-President, ibid, 1969; 1st Vice-President, 1970 Address: Regional Office, P.O. Box 28, Shinyanga, Tanzania.

MTAWALI, Charles Vincent, born Malawi, 4th April, 1919. Medical Practitioner. Education: M.B., Ch.B. (East Africa); D.P.H.(Birmingham); D.T.M.&H.(Liverpool); Medal in Medicine, Surgery, & Midwifery. Appointments: Assistant Medical Officer, 1944-53; Medical Officer, Bukoba, Tanzania, 1954-57; District Medical Officer, Dodoma, ibid, 1958-59; Provincial Medical Officer, ibid, 1960-61; Permanent Secretary, Health, 1962-68; General Practitioner, 1969—. Memberships: Local Secretary, Royal Society of Tropical Medicine & Hygiene; Vice-President, Medical Association, Tanzania; Chairman, Tanzania National Children's Society; Chairman, Tanzania Boy Scouts Association; Life Member, Tanzania Society; President, Tanzania Red Cross Society. Author, A Health Campaign in Tanganyika Territory, 1950. Awarded M.B.E., 1955. Address: P.O. Box 609, Dar es Salaam, Tanzania.

MTEMVU, Zuberi Mwinyisheik Manga, born 20th December, 1928. Civil Servant. Appointments: Civil Servant, Tanzania Government. Memberships: President, African National Congress, 1958-62; Secretary-General, T.A.N.U., 1956; Cell Leader, ibid, 1966-70. Address: P.O. Box 400, Dar es Salaam, Tanzania.

MTIBILI, Frank William, born 19th August, 1921. Administrative Officer. Education: Form IV, Tabora Government Secondary School, Tanzania (Clerical Course), 1943; Institute of Public Administration, University College, Dar es Salaam, 1965-66. Appointments: Secretary, 1944-59; Administrative Officer, Ministry of Regional Administration & Rural Development, Dar es Salaam, 1960-70. Address: Ministry of Regional Administration & Rural Development, P.O. Box 1752, Dar es Salaam, Tanzania.

MUBIRU, Roger Peter, born 9th September 1937. Chartered Secretary. Education: Naluggi Primary School, 1953-58; Rubaga Jun. Secondary School, 1955-56; St. Henry's College, Kitovu, 1957-59; Uganda College of Commerce, 1966-68; South West London College, Tooting, London, U.K., 1969. Appointments: Interpreter, High Court of Uganda, 1960-64; Accounts Clerk, UNT Marketing Board, 1964-66; currently Registrar, Uganda College of Commerce. Associate Member of the Institute of Chartered Secretaries. Address: Uganda College of Commerce, P.O. Box 1337, Kampala, Uganda.

MUCHOPE, Emmanue Mugungu Kyahurwa, born 21st July 1940. Administrative Officer. Education: St. Aloysius Junior Secondary School, Uganda, 1950-57; Certificate of Education; St. Mary's College, Uganda, 1961-63; 1st Class C.S.C. & H.S.C.; B.A., Economics & Geography, Makerere University College, Kampala, Uganda, 1957-64; Cert. in Social Ethics (Oxford), 1963. Married, 1 son. Appointments: Assistant District Commissioner, 1967; Assistant Secretary (Training), 1968—. Memberships: Vice-President-General of the Bunyero Youth Organization; Chairman, Makerere Branch, ibid; Secretary, Kisuli Geographical Society; Treasurer, Higher School History Society; School Debating Society; Assistant, International Conferences in Uganda (Commonwealth Parliamentary Medical Conference & Heads of State Conference), 1967.

MUGALULA-MUKIIBI, Kira, Buganda, Uganda, born 1944. Artist; Art Teacher. Education: Kira Primary School; King's College, Budo; Makerere University School of Fine Art, Kampala; D.F.A.(E.A.); Dip.Ed.(E.A.). One-man Shows: Kampala, 1967; Nairobi, Kenya, 1968; Kampala, 1969; Nairobi, 1970. Currently engaged in constructing an art centre. Member, Uganda Art Club. Author, Clans & Totems of the Baganda. Prizes: Cash Prize, Esso Art Competition, 1964, 1965, 1966; Bronze Medal & Cash Prize, French Embassy & Uganda Art Club, 1968, 1969; Book, Medal & Cash Prize, ibid, 1970. Address: P.O. Box 16195, Wandegeya, Kampala, Uganda.

MUGENYI, Yesero, born Hoima, 21st July 1937. Advocate, High Court of Justice, Uganda. Education: Duhaga Boys' Primary School, Hoima, 1945-50; Nyakasura Secondary School, Fort Portal, 1951-56; B.Sc.(Lond.), Makerere University College, 1962; LL.B.(Hons.), University of London, U.K., 1967. Personal details: married to Andreda Mary Tibakanya (Teacher), 4 sons, 2 daughters. Appointments: Administrative Officer, Uganda Government, 1962-64; Courts Advisor, ibid (study course in law, U.K.), 1964-67; Secretary to the Board, Uganda National Trading Corporation, 1967-69; Legal Private Practice, Uganda, 1970—. Memberships: Uganda Law Society; Uganda Club; Uganda Peoples Congress (the ruling party in Uganda) since 1958—. Author of regular feature & other articles in local press. Honours, Prizes, etc.: Certificate for climbing the Mountains of the Moon, Rwenzori (up to the snow line), 1955. Address: 50 Kampala Road, P.O. Box 5600, Kampala, Uganda.

MUGERA, Gerald Munene, born 21st September 1934. Veterinary Pathologist. Education: Dip. Vet. Sci., Makerere University College, Uganda, 1954-60; Michigan State University, U.S.A., 1961-65; M.Sc., 1962; Ph.D., 1965. Appointments: Vet Sci., Clinicia in Veterinary Medicine, Makerere College, Uganda, 1960-61; Lecturer in Pathology, U.C., Nairobi, Kenya, 1965-67; Senior Lecturer & Head of Department of Veterinary Pathology, 1967-70. Memberships: American Veterinary Medical Association; Kenya Veterinary Association; East Africa Academy. Publications: Author of numerous papers, etc., including: Diagnosis of Poultry Diseases, E.A. Agr. & Forestry Journal, 1967; Respiratory Diseases of Poultry & Their Control, ibid, 1967; Pathology of Coccidiosis in Kenya Goats, Bull. epizoot. Dis. Afr., 1968; Canine & Feline Neoplasms in Kenya, ibid, 1968; A Study of Bovine Neoplasms in Kenya, 1968;

Sarcosporidiosis in Gazelles in Kenya, E. Afr. Wildl. J., 1968. Tumours of the Liver, Kidney, & Lungs in Rats fed Encephalartos Hildebrandtii, Brit. Jour. Cancer, 1968. Address: Dept. of Veterinary Pathology & Microbiology, University College, Nairobi, Kenya.

MUHANNA, L'Adawy Shell, born 25th July 1925. Commercial Officer, Ministry of Commerce & Industries. Education: B.Sc. (Economics), Makerere University, Uganda; World Trade Certificate in Import & Export, California, U.S.A. Personal details: married, 12 children. Appointments: Businessman in Transport Industry; later Farmer, with several acres of coffee trees; Member of Parliament, Tanganyika, 1960-65; Town Councillor. Memberships: International Traders of the World; Tanganyika Library Services. Address: P.O. Box 23140, Dar es Salaam, Tanzania.

MUKABIRE, Paul Hire, born 10th December 1944. Assistant Agricultural Officer. Education: Cambridge School Certificate; Diploma in Agriculture. Appointments: Assistant Agricultural Officer. Address: Department of Agriculture, P.O. Box 911, Mbale, Uganda.

MUKASA, James Benjamin, born Kampala, Uganda, 27th February 1937. Chartered Secretary. Education: Senior Secondary School, Uganda; awarded Uganda Government Scholarship for further studies in U.K., 1961; passed the final examination of the Corporation of Secretaries, 1964. Married, 3 daughters. Appointments include: Auditor, Uganda Government, 1964-65; Assistant Secretary, Uganda Development Corporation Ltd., 1965-67; Acting Secretary, Uganda Development Corporation, Ltd., 1967-68; Secretary, Uganda Development Corporation Ltd., 1968—; Director, Ugadey Holdings Ltd.; ibid, Ugadey Bank Ltd.; Uganda Aviation Ltd. Memberships: Committee Member, Kampala Incorporated Secretaries Society; Y.M.C.A. Address: Uganda Development Corporation Ltd., P.O. Box 7042, Kampala, Uganda.

MUKASA, Sarah. Civic Leader. Education: Gayaza High School, Uganda. Personal details: a daughter of the late Ham Mukasa & Mrs. Sarah Mukasa; married to E. M. K. Mulira, M.P., 4 children. Memberships include: Board of Y.W.C.A., 1953-59; R.S.P.A., 1951-57; Board of Governors, Gayaza High School, 1952-65; Uganda Broadcasting Service Advisory Board, 1952-65; Secretary, Uganda African Women's League (Political), 1953-68; Chairman, Kampala Political Branch, The Progressive Party (1st woman to be elected), 1957-60; Treasurer, Mothers' Union, 1958-61; Joint Secretary, East Buganda & Busoga Diocese, Church of Uganda, 1957-60; Delegate, First All-Africa Church Conference, Ibadan, Nigeria, 1958; Mulago Hospital Advisory Board, General Hospital, 1953—; President, Young Wives' Group, 1954-56; National President, Uganda Council of Women, 1962-63; Board of Governors, Bishop Tucker College, Mukono; Advisory Board, ibid, 1956; Board of Governors, Ndeje Teacher Training College, 1962; Delegate, 12th UNESCO Conference, Paris, France, 1962; Delegate, International Council of Women's Triennial Conference, Washington, D.C., U.S.A., 1963; Delegate: International Conference on Role of Women in the Struggle for Peace & Development in Jerusalem, Israel, 1964; Family Planning Conference, New Delhi, India, 1965; National President, Uganda Family Planning Association, 1967; Seminar on Population Growth, Sussex University, U.K., 1967. Executive Committee, International Council of Women, London, 1967; Councillor, City of Kampala, 1962-66; Councillor, West Mengo District Council, 1966; Executive Committee, Uganda National Cultural Theatre, 1959; Board Member, Kampala & District Water Board, 1968; Director, Housing Finance Committee, 1968. Address: P.O. Box 2530, Kampala, Uganda.

MUKASA, Twaha Abu, born 16th June 1938. Mechanical Engineer. Education: Senior Standard, Aggrey Memorial School, Kampala, Uganda; Higher Secondary Standard, Mombasa Technical School; Engineering Professional Qualifications, Leeds College of Technology, U.K., 1963-67; H.N.C. Mech. Engrng.; A.M.S.E. Mech. Engrng.; Grad., M.I.Plant Engrng.; Grad. E.A.I.E. Married, 1 son. Appointments: Assistant Resident Engineer, Agricultural Enterprises Ltd., Subsidiary of Uganda Development Corporation; Works Mechanical Engineer, Uganda Cement Industries Ltd., ibid. Memberships: Chairman, Agricultural Enterprises Ltd.; Senior Staff Club, Mwenge Tea Co. Honours, Prizes, etc.: Uganda Government Scholarship; Head Student, Mombasa Technical Inst., 1961-62. Address: Uganda Cement Industries, P.O. Box 150, Kasese, Uganda.

MUKASA (Canon) Yokana Balikuddembe, born 13th October 1917. Priest, Anglican Church of Uganda. Education: Duhaga Primary School, Hoima, until 1936; Teacher Training College, Mukono, 1938-40; Special Duty, Makerere College, 1949-50; Theological Training: Bishop Tucker College, Mukono, 1953-54; Ridley Hall, Cambridge, 1956-57; Huron College, London, Ontario, Canada, 1964-66. Personal details: married to Norah Nakacwa, 5 sons, 5 daughters. Appointments: Headmaster, Duhaga Primary School, Hoima, 1942; Assistant Headmaster, Kikoma Junior Secondary School, 1951-52; Warden, Kasawo Catechist Training Centre, 1955-56; Temporary Curacy, Burwell, Cambridgeshire, U.K., 1957; Temporary Curacy, St. Andrews, Plymouth, Devon, 1957; Chaplain-tutor, Namutamba, T.T.C., 1958-60; Tutor, Bishop Tucker Theological College, 1961-64; Deputy Principal, ibid (for 1 year); Tutor, B.T.C., 1966; Dean of St. Pauls Cathedral, 1968—. Memberships: District Scout Commissioner, Asst. Deputy Camp Chief, International Training Team; National H.Q.'s Chaplain, Boy Scouts Assn., Girl Guides Chaplain; Uganda Defence Force. Awarded Medal of Merit. Address: P.O. Box 14297, Kampala, Uganda.

MUKUKA, Cleaver Ernest, born 15th August 1938. Stores Controller. Education: General Certificate of Education, Adult Education Centre, Ndola; International Union of Local Authorities; Certificate of Attendance, Comparative Local Government in Developing Countries, The Hague, Netherlands. Married, 4 children. Appointments: Chairman, Kabushi Branch, U.N.I.P.; Councillor, Ndola City Council; Stores Controller & Buyer, Drake & Gorham (Zambia) Ltd.; Stores Controller & Buyer, Zambia Electricity Supply Corp. Ltd. Memberships: The S.P.S.A., Ndola; Western Planning Committee; Y.M.C.A.; Chairman, Electricity & Work Committee, Ndola City Council. Address: c/o Z.E.S.C. Ltd., P.O. Box 1334, Ndola, Zambia.

MUKWAYA, Francis Xavier Wagwebyasi, born 23rd January 1933. Civil Servant. Education: Bukalasa Seminary; Kabuwoko Secondary School; St. Henry's College Kitovu; St. Joseph's College, Trichinopoly; B.A.(Econs.), Madras University, India. Appointments: Asst. Secretary, Ministry of Finance; Senior Assistant Secretary, ibid; Principle Finance Officer. Memberships: Chairman; Entebbe Consumer Co-operative Society; Treasurer, Nakivubo Settlement, Kampala; Chairman, The Mutual Credit Club, Kampala. Address: P.O. Box 103, Entebbe, Uganda.

MULI, Mattew Guy, born 10th January 1929. Barrister-at-Law. Education: Makerere University College, Kampala, Uganda, 1952-53; Council of Legal Education, U.K., 1956-61; Lincoln's Inn, London. Married, with children. Appointments: Assistant Legal Secretary, East African Community, 1962-63; Deputy Counsel to the East Africa Community, 1964—. Member of Kenya Justice. Publications: Introduction to Kamba (co-author). Awards: Diploma, by Ministry of Overseas Development (for International Law & Legislative Drafting). Address: P.O. Box 30005, Nairobi, Kenya.

MULILO, Chobela Joseph, born 14th May 1939. Education: Diploma in Business Management & Accountancy. Appointments: Youth & Publicity Regional Secretary, Ndola; District Governor, Ndola Urban. Member, United National Independence Party. Address: Office of the District Governor, P.O. Box 210, Ndola Urban, Zambia.

MULLI, Henry Nzioka, born 1925. Politician; Diplomat. Education: G.C.E., Alliance High School, 1945; Makerere College, 1946-47; B.Sc., Fort Hare University College, 1948-50; Analytical Chemists, Govt. Chemists Dept., Dar es Salaam. Tanganyika, 1951-53; Diploma in Education, Oxford, University, U.K., 1960. Married, 4 sons, 2 daughters. Appointments: Analytical Chemist, 1951-53; Political Detainee, 1954-57; Science Master, Machalius High School, 1957-60; Member of Parliament & Assistant Minister for Defence, 1961-63; Ambassador to Peking, 1963-65; Ambassador to U.A.R., 1965-68; Ambassador to Somali Democratic Republic, 1969—.

MULLIGAN, Thomas Osmond, born 6th August, 1935. Surgeon. Education: Royal School, Armagh, Northern Ireland, U.K., 1947-53; M.B., Ch.B., University of Edinburgh Medical School, 1953-59. Married. Appointments: Senior House Surgeon, Royal Hospital for Sick Children, Edinburgh, 1960-61; Medical Superintendant, Annang Joint Hospital, via Abak, S.E. State, Nigeria, 1961-63; Surgical Registrar, Royal Victoria & City Hospitals, Belfast, Northern Ireland, 1963-64; Surgeon, Wesley Guild Hospital, Ilesha, West State, Nigeria, 1964—. Fellow of Royal College of Surgeons, Edinburgh & West African College of Surgeons. Memberships: British Medical Assn.; Christian Medical Fellowship; Executive, Nigerian Cancer Society. Publications include: The Treatment of typhoid perforation of the ileum; Typhoid fever in Ilesha; contbr. to British Journal of Cancer. Address: Wesley Guild Hospital, Ilesha, West State, Nigeria.

MUMBALE, Dimitrios, born 6th February 1927. Specialist in Surgery & Orthopaedics. Education: Diploma in General Education, Egypt, U.A.R., 1954; M.D., University of Athens, Greece, 1962; Diploma in Surgery, after 5-year course in surgery & 1-year course in orthopaedics. Married, 2 children. Member of Christian Medical Society. Publications: various articles in local press. Address: P.O. Box 3970, Kampala, Uganda.

MUMYA, Nehemiah Kamumya, born Uganda, 22nd November 1931. Magistrate. Education: Budaka Primary School, 1944-46; Sipi Primary School, 1947-49; Nabumali High School, 1950-55; Cambridge School Certificate; Co-op. Book-keeping Certificate, 1956; Uganda Law School Diploma, 1962-63. Appointments: Co-operative Assistant, 1956; Uganda Grade 3 Teacher, 1957-59; Inspector of Police, Kenya, 1960-62; Chief Judge, Sebei District Administration, 1962-65; Magistrate, 1965—. Address: Magistrate, Kamuli Court, P.O. Box 11, Kamuli, Uganda.

MUNENE (the Hon.) James F. C., born 28th December 1929. Medical Practitioner; Member of Parliament, Kenya. Education: Kikuyu Primary School; Mangu High School; Makerere University College Uganda; Patna University, India; M.B., B.S. Married, 4 sons. Appointments: Medical Officer, with Kenya Government, 4½ years; Medical Practitioner; Member of Parliament, Kenya. Memberships: Chaian of: National Social Security Fund, Kenya; Kilima Mbogo Teacher Training College; Chania High School; Thika School for the Blind; Prominent member of Thika & Muraya Sports Clubs. Address: P.O. Box 424, Thika, Kenya.

MUNGAI (Professor) Joseph Maina, born Nairobi, Kenya, 4th April 1932. University Teacher. Education: M.S., Ch.B. (E.A.); Ph.D.(Lond.). Married, 3 children. Appointments include: Lecturer in Anatomy, Makerere University College, 1963-67; Senior Lecturer in

Human Anatomy, University College, Nairobi, 1967-68; Professor of Human Anatomy, University College, Nairboi, 1968—; Dean, Faculty of Medicine, ibid. Memberships: President, Kenya Medical Association, 1968; Secretary, East African Academy, 1968; Chairman, World University Service, Kenya, 1968. Address: Faculty of Medicine, University College, Nairobi, P.O. Box 30588, Kenya.

MUNIER, Victor Auguste, born 16th May 1907. Administrative Director. Education: Baccalaureat, Lycée du Puy, 1924; Lic. en Droit, Faculty of Algiers, 1930. Married, 7 children. Appointments: Banque de France, 1925; Chief de Service au Credit Foncier, Algeria & Tunisia, 1928-31; Director, Director, Rabat Agency, C.F.A.T., 1931-46; Director Adjoint, C.F.A.T., Casablanca, 1947; Director des Sieges, Morocco, C.F.A.T., 1957; Administrative Director General, Ste de Banque du Maghreb, C.F.A.T., 1963. Administrator: Credit Immobilier et Hotelier Ste Marocaine de Magasins General Cie North Africa & Intercontinentale D'Assurances; Union Maritime & D'Outre Mer Sofac Credit; Compagnie Immobiliere Franco-Marocaine. Past-President, Rotary Club, Casablanca. Honours: Officier du Ouissam Alaouite, 1948; Chevalier de la Legion d'Honneur, 1957; Chevalier de l'Ordre du Merite de la Republique Italienne, 1963; Grande Medaille d'Or du Travail. Address: 18 rue Pegoud, Casablanca, Morocco.

MUNORU, Gabric Gicia Samson, born 1st January 1938. Lecturer; Advocate. Education: LL.B.(Hons., London); LL.M.(Columbia). Married, 1 son, 4 daughters. Appointments: Lecturer in Law, University of Nairobi, Kenya; Head of the Department of Law & Jurisprudence; Advocate of the High Court of Kenya; Member, Council of Legal Education, Kenya. Honours, Prizes, etc.: Kenya Law Society Prize (awarded to the most improved 2nd year law student), Faculty of Law, Dar es Salaam, 1964. Address: c/o Munoru & Co., Advocates, P.O. Box 7159, Nairobi, Kenya.

MUNTHALI, Charles Vincent Burnett, born 24th March 1935. Civil Servant. Education: Blantyre Secondary School, 1951-55; B.A., Makerere University College, 1956-60; Cambridge University, 1960-61. Married 2 sons. Appointments: Permanent Secretary, Ministry of Education, 1967-68; Permanent Secretary, Ministry of Health, 1968-70; Permanent Secretary, Ministry of Labour. Memberships: Lions Club of Blantyre; Commonwealth Games Association of Malawi. Address: Ministry of Labour, P.O. Box 5594, Limbe, Malawi.

MUOGHALU, Jerome Obi, born Ozubulu, Onitsha Province, 6th June 1920. Chemist & Druggist. Education: School Leaving Certificate, St. Michael's Ozubulu, 1928-36; Cambridge Certificate, Christ the King College, Onitsha, 1939-42; Diploma, School of Pharmacy, Yaba, 1944-47. Married, 8 children. Appointments: Local Councillor, Ozubulu Local Council, 1958-60; County Councillor, Nnewi County Council, 1961-63; Provincial Assemblyman, Onitsha Prov., 1963-65; Director, Nigerian Sugar Company, Bacita, 1962-68; Proprietor & Manager, Central Chemists, Enugu, 1968—.

Memberships: Chairman, Board of Governors, Joint Hospital, Ozubulu, 1964-66; Vice-Chairman, Ozubulu Youths' Organization, 1961-65; Life-Patron, Red Cross Unit, Ozubulu, 1967; National Auditor, Pharmaceutical Society of Nigeria, Eastern Zone, 1963-66; Chairman, Udoka Society; 1965-70; Enugu Recreation Club, 1957—. Honours: Ezechinyelugo, Ozo title taken 1964. Address: c/o Central Chemists, 18 Owerri Road, Enugu, Nigeria.

MURAGE, John Nathan, born Tumutumu, Kenya, November 11th 1922. Agricultural Research Officer. Education: Church of Scotland Mission. Tumutumu; Alliance High School, Kikuyu; University of Kentucky, U.S.A.; Pennsylvania State University; A&M University, Tallahassee; Rio Pedras State University, Puerto Rico. Married. Appointments include: Laboratory Assistant; Assitant Agricultural Officer; Agricultural Officer (Research). Address: Nyandarua Agricultural Research Station, Private Bag, Ol'joro Orok, Kenya.

MURO, Philemon Paul, born 25th September 1924. Diplomat. Education: Studied medicine. Personal details: Peasant Farmer; married, 2 sons, 4 daughters. Appointments: worked as Medical Assistant, Tanzania; National Executive, Tanganyika African National Union (TANU), 1951; Regional Chairman, TANU, 1960-62; Regional Commissioner, 1962-64; appointed to Diplomatic Service as Tanzania Ambassador in Stockholm, Sweden, concurrently accredited also to Norway, Denmark, & Finland, 1964-68; Tanzania High Commissioner in London, U.K., 1968. Address: Tanzania High Commission, 43 Hertford St., London, W.1, U.K.

MURPHY, Gabriel Gilmour, born 8th October 1916. Physician. Education: B.Ph., B.D., Lateran Academy, Rome, Italy; B.A., M.B., B.Ch., B.A.O., National University of Ireland; D.P.H., University of London, U.K. Married, 3 children. Appointments: Medical Officer, Nsambya Mission Hospital, Uganda, 1947; ibid, Providence Hospital, Holyoke, Mass., U.S.A., 1950; District Medical Officer, Kigezi District, Uganda, 1951; Sr. Medical Officer, Ministry of Health, Uganda, 1956; Deputy Med. Adviser, Scottish Council of Health Education, 1963; Sr. Medical Officer of Health, Swaziland, 1966; Member of W.H.O. Expert Advisory Panel on Health Education. Recipient of the Swaziland Independence Medal. Address: Ministry of Health, P.O. Box 5, Mbabane, Swaziland.

MURUWESI, Lewis Edward, born Nkhulambe Village District, Malawi, 22nd December 1925. Tea Grower. Education: Mlanje Mission Church of Scotland Primary. Married, 1 son, 3 daughters. Appointments: Politician, District Chairman, Malawi Congress Party. Memberships: Board Director, Small Holders Tea Authority of Malawi; Advisory Committee Member on Tung & Coffee Experimental Station. Contributor to Malawi Research. Address: Muruwesi Progressive Tea Estate, P.O. Box 35, Cholo, Malawi.

MUSAGA, Isaiah Anaka, born Metta, West Cameroon, 1930. Administrator. Education: First School Leaving Certificate, 1944; Teachers' Grade II Certificate, 1955; B.A.(Hons.), Econ.,

1961. Married, 6 children. Appointments include: Primary School-teacher, 1944-58; West Cameroon Establishment Secretary, 1962-63; Permanent Secretary, Ministry of Education & Social Welfare, & Ministry of Internal Trade, Marketing & Inspection, 1964-65; currently Senior Divisional Officer. Memberships include: President, Nkambe Lawn Tennis Club; President, Nkambe Board of Tourism. Honours include: Cameroon Order of Merit, 1968; Chevalier dans l'Ordre Nationale de la Valeur, 1969. Address: Divisional Office, Nkambe, West Cameroon.

MUSANGI, Richard Sylevester, born 24th April 1934. Senior Lecturer, Department of Animal Production, University of Nairobi, Kenya. Education: Milo Primary School, 1944-49; Kakamega Secondary School, Kenya, 1950-56; B.Sc.(Agric.), Makerere University, Uganda, 1957-62; M.Sc., Wye College, University of London, 1962-64; Ph.D., London University, 1967. Personal details: family farmers in Western Kenya, married, 1 son. Appointments include: Senior Lecturer, Dept. of Animal Production, University of Nairobi, Kenya; Acting Head, Dept. of Animal Science & Production, 1969. Memberships: The Association for the Advancement of Agricultural Science in Africa; The East African Academy; The Kenya Society of Animal Production. Publications: Dairy Husbandry in Eastern Africa, 1969; Pasture Production & Utilization by Cattle in the Tropics, with Special Reference to Uganda (editor), 1969; 15 articles in scientific journals. Awarded, Shell Co. Exhibition Prize. Address: University of Nairobi, P.O. Box 30197, Nairobi, Kenya.

MUSANGO, Francis, born Kampala, Uganda, 6th December 1931. Teacher. Education: St. Mary's College, Kisulu; Mt. St. Theresa Teacher Training College; Makerere Art School, Makerere University: D.F.A., Fine Art; Dip. Ed., C.R.S., Religious Studies; C.D.T., Religious Studies, Mt. St. Theresa Academic Board. Appointments: Deputy Principal, Teacher Training Mt. St. Theresa, 1959; Teacher & Founder, Art Teaching, St. Leo's College, Toro, 1960; Senior Teacher, Art, St. Henry's College, Kitoru, 1961; Career Master, Head, Departments of Art & Music, ibid, 1963-70; Member, Art Panel, Inspectorate, Ministry of Education, 1965-70; currently training to become Art Examiner for Cambridge Exams. in East Africa, 1969-70. Member, Society of East African Artists. Honours: Margret Trowell Art School Prizes for best Performance, 1957-58. Address: P.O. Box 64, Masaka, Uganda.

MUSHANGA, Musa Tibamanya, born 1930. University Lecturer. Education: Kabwohe Primary School; Mbarara High School; Masaka Medical Training School; Makerere University College, University of East Africa; B.A.(Hons.), Sociology & Political Science; currently studying for M.A., Sociology. Appointments: Medical Assistant, Uganda Medical Service, 1955-62; Assistant District Commissioner, Kigezi, 1966; Personnel Officer, Kilembe Mines, 1967; currently Lecturer, Extramural Studies, Makerere University, Kampala, Uganda. Memberships: Past President, Kigezi Branch, Red Cross; Chairman, Kabalore Public Library, Fort Portal; Welfare & Advisory Council, Toro; Africanization Committee for Uganda. Publications: Folk Tales from Ankole; Education & Frustration, East Africa Journal, 1970. Address: Extra Mural Studies Dept., Makerere University, Box 231, Fort Portal, Uganda.

MUSIGA, Luke Odhiambo, born Kenya, 20th December 1926. Civil Servant. Education: B.A.(Hons.), Hull University, U.K; D.P.A.; A.C.I. Appointments include: District Officer, 1957-63; District Commissioner, 1964; Senior Assistant Secretary, 1965; Personal Assistant to Vice-President, 1965; Director, National Social Security Fund, 1966. Awards include: 1st Prize, Uhuru Essay Competition, 'The Kenya We Want', 1964. Address: National Social Security Fund, P.O. Box 30599, Nairobi, Kenya.

MUSOKE, Christopher, born 30th September 1932. Economist/Administrator. Education: completed formal education, 1955; continued study by correspondence course; Fellow, IBRDIEDI. Married, 3 sons & 3 daughters. Appointments: Administrative Officer, 1956-62; Under-Secretary, 1963—; Chairman, Entebbe Town Council, 1965-69; Director, Mengo Hospital, 1966—; Deputy Chairman, Bank of India (U) Ltd., 1970—; Led Uganda Delegations to various economic conferences, international agencies' annual meetings, especially, UNCTAD. Member, S.I.D.A. Honours: Uganda Independence Decoration, 1962. Address: Under-Secretary, Ministry of Commerce & Industry, P.O. Box 7000, Kampala, Uganda.

MUSOKE, John S., born 30th August 1930. Civil Servant. Education: M. Public Administration, University of Pittsburgh, U.S.A.; B.Com., Bombay, India. Married with children. Appointments: Senior Assistant Secretary, Ministry of Commerce & Industry, Uganda, 1968—. Memberships: Lions Club, Kampala; District 411 Lion Tamer, 1969-70; 1st Year Director, 1970-71; Founder Member & Past President, Commerce Graduates' Association. Address: P.O. Box 7000, Kampala, Uganda.

MUSOKE, Swaib Matumbwe, born 18th December 1937. Diplomat. Education: Bishop's School, Mukono, Uganda; Ntare School, Mbarara, ibid; Punjab University, Lahore, Pakistan; Boston University, U.S.A. Appointments: Assistant Secretary, Ministry of Commerce & Industry, 1963-64; Head, Economic Section, Ministry of Foreign Affairs, 1964-69; Commercial Counssellor, Uganda High Commission, London, U.K., 1969—. Address: Counsellor Commercial, Uganda High Commission, 58 Trafalgar Square, London, U.K.

MUSOKE, Theresa, born Uganda, 12th December 1943. Artist. Education: Margaret Trowell School of Fine Art, Makerere University College; Royal College of Art, London, U.K.; Graduate School of Art, University of Pa., U.S.A. Appointments: Teacher of Art in Secondary Schools in Uganda; Lectr. in Fine Art, Margaret Trowell School, Makerere; Producer, several children's art programmes, Uganda Television. Exhibited in London, New York, & Sweden; solo shows in Uganda, Kenya, & Tanzania. In process of organizing a solo exhibition of Etching Lithographs & Paintings in New York. Memberships: Nomo Gallery; Pye-Pye Gallery; Society of East African Artists. Address: School of Fine Art, Makerere University College, P.O. Box 7062, Kampala, Uganda.

MUSTAFA, Ghulam, born 3rd May 1930. Psychiatric Specialist. Education: Duke of Gloucester School, Nairobi, Kenya; Senior Cambridge Certificate; F.Sc.(Medical Group), Government College, Punjab University, W. Pakistan; M.B., B.S., King Edward Medical College, Punjab University, 1957; D.P.M., Institute of Psychiatry, Maudsley Hospital, Denmark Hill, London, 1963. Appointments: Intern, Kenyatta National Hospital, Nairobi, Kenya, 1957-58; Medical Officer in Charge, Lodwar Hospital, Kenya, 1958; Medical Officer, Machakor Hospital, Kenya, 1959; ibid, Mathori Hospital, Nairobi, 1960; Psychiatric Specialist in Charge, ibid, 1966. Memberships: Royal Medico-Psychological Association, U.K.; World Psychiatric Association; Association of Physicians of East Africa; Kenya Branch, East African Academy; Kenya Medical Association. Publications include: Clinical Experiences with Thiothixene (Navane) on 29 hospitalized schizophrenic patients, 1968; Society in Relation to Mental Health in Kenya, 1969; Services for the Mentally Subnormal Children at Mathari Hospital, 1970. Address: c/o Mathari Hospital, Nairobi, Kenya.

MUTAWE, George Willy, born Masaka District, 9th November 1940. Telecommunications Engineer. Education: Nkoni Primary School; St. John's Secondary School, Kabuwoko; St. Henry's College, Kitouu; Central Training School, Nairobi, Kenya; City & Guilds Telecommunications Correspondence Certificates. Married to Emily Mutawe, 2 children. Appointments: Telecommunications Engineer, East African Post & Telecommunications. Member of EAP&T Sports Club. Address: EAP&T, P.O. Box 7171, Kampala, Uganda.

MUTENYO, Solomon Khabakha Molli, born Bugobero, South Bugisu, 31st December 1924. Principal & Proprietor, Elgon Tutorial College. Education: Senior Secondary IV, 1942; Higher Commercial Education Certificate, LCC, 1953. Married, 8 sons, 9 daughters. Appointments: Corporal, Air Formation Signals, Nairobi, 1942-46; Wireless & Teleprinter Operator, Air HQ.EA, 1946-47; Teleprinter Operator, B.O.A.C., Nairobi, 1948; Managing Clerk, F. Graf & Company, Nairobi, 1949; Law Clerk, Parry & Nicoll, Advocates, Nairobi, 1950-55. Memberships: Bugobero Growers' Co-op. Society, Ltd.; President, Bugisi Co-op. Union Ltd., 1958-62; Treasurer, Uganda Co-operative Alliance, 1960-62; Councillor, Bugisu District Council, 1956—; ibid, Mbale Municipal Council, 1964-68; Bugisi Representative Adviser, Uganda Constitutional Conference, London, U.K., 1961; Deputy Secretary-General, Democratic Party (Proscribed 1969); Political Prisoner under Country's Emergency Regulations, 1969. Honours: Army Medal, Her Majesty's Forces, 1946; Certificate of Service, East Africa Forces, 1946; Uganda Independence Medal, 1962.

Address: Elgon Tutorial College, 10 Elgon Avenue, P.O. Box 415, Mbale, Uganda.

MUTHARIKA, Arthur Peter Thom, born 18th July 1940. University Lecturer; Advocate, High Court of Tanzania. Education: LL.B. (Hons.) (London), University College, Dar es Salaam, Tanzania, 1962-65; Princeton University, New Jersey, U.S.A., 1965; LL.M., J.S.D., Yale University, 1965-68. Married to Christophine Griffin, 2 daughters. Appointments: Resident Magistrate, Dar es Salaam, Tanzania, 1965; Visiting Lecturer in International Law, Hailé Selassié I University, Addis Ababa, Ethiopia, 1970; UNITAR Lecturer in International Law, Makerere University, Uganda, 1969; currently Lecturer in International Law, University of Dar es Salaam, Tanzania. Memberships: Associate Editor, Eastern Africa Law Review, 1970; Chairman, Curriculum Revision Committee, Faculty of Law, University of Dar es Salaam; Editor in Chief, Journal of the Denning Law Society, 1963-64; East African Academy; International Law Association. Publications: Thixton's Case, A Brief Comment, Zambia Law Journal, 1969; Deportation of Stateless Persons, Eastern Africa Law Review, 1969; The U.N. & Depriviation of Nationality, Eastern Africa Law Review, 1970; Ethiopian Constitutional Development, A sourcebook (Editor), 1970. Address: Faculty of Law, University of Dar es Salaam, Box 35093, Dar es Salaam, Tanzania.

MUTIBWA, Olivia Mary, Librarian. Education: Gayaza High School, 1948-59; B.A.(Hons., History), Makerere University, Kampala, Uganda, 1960-65; A.L.A., School of Librarianship, Ealing Technical College, 1968-69. Married, 2 children. Appointments: Assistant Administrative Officer, Prime Minister's Office, 1965; Assistant Exchange Control Officer, Bank of Uganda, 1965-67; Assistant Librarian, Education Sub-Library, Makerere University, Kampala, 1969—. Memberships: Committee, Uganda Association of University Women; Committee, Kampala Branch, Uganda Council of Women; East African Library Association. Address: Education Library, Makerere University, P.O. Box 7062, Kampala, Uganda.

MUTIBWA, Phares Mukasa, born 29th July 1936. University Lecturer. Education: King's College, Budo; Graduate in History, Makerere University College, Uganda; Studied French, University of Besançon, France; Research Student, School of African & Asian Studies, University of Sussex, U.K.; Ph.D. in History, ibid. Personal details: father, Musa Mukasa, Coffee Farmer, Bulemezi, Buganda. Appointments: Diplomat, Uganda Ministry of Foreign Affairs, 1963-65;; Lecturer in History, Makerere University, Kampala, Uganda; Board of Directors, The People Newspapers Ltd.; Board of Directors, Uganda Publishing House; Adviser, Milton Obote Foundation Adult Education Centre, Kampala; Secretary, Cultural Research Committee, Uganda National Research Council. Member of Board of Governors, Ndejje Senior Secondary School. Publications: The Malagasy & the Europeans in the Second Half of the 19th Century (in preparation), 1971. Honours: Makerere University College Student Representative, Student Seminar, University of Hawaii, Honolulu, U.S.A., 1960. Address: Dept. of History, Makerere University, Kampala, P.O. Box 7062, Kampala, Uganda.

MUTISO, David Muoka, born 10th July 1932. Architect. Education: Alliance High School; Sheffield University, U.K.; Nottingham University; B.A.(Arch.); Dip. T.P. Appointments: Asst. Architect, Sheffield City Council, 1959-61; Asst. Architect, H. Richard Hughes, 1961-62; Deputy Chief Architect, M.O.W., 1964-66; Chief Architect, M.O.W., 1966—. Corporate Member, Architectural Assn. of Kenya; Associate, R.I.B.A.

MUTTI, Jethro Mukenge, born 3rd May 1934. Minister of State for Rural Development. Married, 1 son, 2 daughters. Appointments: Member of Parliament, 1964—; Parliamentary Secretary, 1965-67; Ambassador of the Republic of Zambia to Ethiopia, 1967-69; Minister of State for Rural Development, 1970—. Memberships (former): Northern Rhodesia African National Congress; United National Independence Party. Address: c/o Ministry of Rural Development, Lusaka, Zambia.

MUTYABA, Mustafa K. L., born 13th September 1937. Manager. Education: Katikamu S.D.A. Primary School; Mengo Junior Secondary School; Nyakasura Secondary School; National Teachers' College, Kyambogo; Institute of Education, Oxford University, U.K. Married, with children. Appointments: Headmaster, Kabukunge Primary, 1959-61; Education Supervisor for Muslim Education, Buganda, 1963; Teacher Trainer, Kibuli T.T.C., 1964; Resident Representative, Longmans of Uganda, 1965-69; Director & Manager, ibid, 1970; Representative of Longmans Group in Somalia, Ruanda, Burundi, & Congo Kinsasa. Treasurer, Nyonza Singing Group, 1970. Address: Longman Uganda, Ltd., P.O. Box 3409, Kampala, Uganda.

MUWANGA, Robert S., born Kako, near Masaka, Uganda, 11th October 1911. Public Administrator. Education: Kako School; King's College, Budo; Makerere College; South Devon Technical College, U.K. Married. Appointments include: Assistant Tutor, Makerere College, 1931-35; Education Department, ibid., 1936-39; Information Department, ibid., 1939-42; Assistant Resident, Buganda, 1943-45; Financial Assistant, & subsequently, Senior Assistant to the Treasurer, Permanent Secretary to the Treasury, Buganda Government, 1946-66; Permanent Secretary to The Katikiro (Prime Minister of Buganda), 1966; Permanent Secretary, Administration, Buganda, 1966; Under-Secretary, Ministry of Labour, Uganda Government, 1967—. Memberships include: President, Lions Club, Kampala, 1967-68; Chairman, St. John Ambulance Association; Chairman, Appeals Committee, Salvation Army, Uganda; Church Warden, Hon. Treasurer, Cathedral Church of St. Paul, Namirembe; Registered Trustee, ibid; Registered Trustee, YMCA, Uganda, 1963, & Mengo Hospital, Kampala. Address: Under-Secretary, Ministry of Labour, P.O. Box 7009, Kampala, Uganda.

MUYANGANA, Christopher Mutemwa, born 30th September 1939. University Senior Assistant Registrar. Education: Standard Certiicate, Barotseland, 1947-54; G.C.E., 1960-61; B.A., Political Science, University of North Carolina, Chapel Hill, U.S.A., 1967. Personal details: father, Fisherman, Farmer, & Cattle Owner; married to Christine Katungu Maboshe (Nurse), 1 son. Appointments: Assistant District Secretary, Civil Service, 1967; Assistant Registrar, University of Zambia, 1968; Senior Assistant Registrar, 1970—. Memberships: University of Zambia Senior Staff Association; Cosmopolitan Club, University of North Carolina. Honours, Prizes, etc.: Best International Student of the Year, University of North Carolina. Address: The University of Zambia, P.O. Box 2379, Lusaka, Zambia.

MVENG, P. Engelbert, born Enam-Ngal, Cameroun, 9th May 1930. Education: Lower Seminary of Akono; Higher Seminary of Otele; Noviciat of Djuma, Congo-Leo; Faculty of Philosophy & Letters, Namur, Belgium; Faculty of Philosophy, Faculty St. Albert, Louvain; Puis de Vals, Chantilly, France; Faculty of Theology, Fourviere, Lyon, France; Faculty of Letters, Paris, Sorbonne & at Lyon; Cand. Philo-Lettres; Lic. en Philosophie scolastique; Lic. en Theologie; Lic. es Lettres; Doctor of Letters. Appointments: Teacher, College Libermann, 1958-60; President, Commission of the Arts of the African Society of Culture; Expert Consultant, UNESCO. Lecturer, Federal University of Yaoundé; Director of Cultural Affairs, Ministry of Education, Culture & Professional Functions. Memberships: Technical Committee for the Preparation of the First World Festival of Negro Arts; International Association of Writers of the French Language, Paris, France; Queen Elizabeth Egyptology Foundation, Belgium. Publications include: Histoire du Cameroun, 1963; Sources de l'Histoire Negro-Africaine, 1966; L'Afrique Noire et le monde antique; Introduction a L'Histoire d'Afrique, 1966-67; Ngoro, Nouveau site archeologique de Cameroun, 1966; Archeologie Camerounaise; Rapport de la mission archeologique en Crete, 1967. Address: B.P. 876, Yaoundé, Cameroun.

MWAJIM, J. M., born 15th November 1940. Teacher. Education: C.B.M. Garkida Primary School; Probationary Teacher; Grade III, Qualified & Certificated Teacher, Teachers' Training College, Waka; Grade II Teachers' Course, ibid, 1967. Personal details: resident of Garkida, Adamawa Province; married to Selina Mwajim, 1 son, 1 daughter. Appointments: Headmaster, various primary schools, 1961-65; Headmaster, Adamawa Local Education Authority, 1968-69. Address: P.A. Garkida via Yola, North Eastern State, Nigeria.

MWAKANGALE, John Benedict Mugogo, born Rungwe District, Tanzania, 13th November 1923. Politician. Education: Malangali Secondary School, 1935-41; Veterinary Assistants' Course, Mpwapwa, 1942-43; Local Government & Public Administration Course, U.K., 1955-56. Married, with children. Appointments include: Veterinary Assistant, Government, 1943-46; Manager, Dairy Farm, Arusha, 1946-48;

Secretary, Rungwe District Council, 1949-58; elected Member, Legislative Council of Tanganyika, 1958; elected Member, Tanganyika National Assembly, 1960; Member, Central Legislative Assembly, 1960; President, Rungwe African Co-operative Union Ltd., Tukuyu, 1959-61; Regional Commissioner, Mbeya, 1962; Secretary, National Housing Corporation of Tanganyika, 1962-63; Junior Minister, Ministry of Local Government & Housing, 1963-64; Regional Secretary, TANU, 1964—; Regional Commissioner, 1964—; Member of Parliament, 1965—; Chairman, Tanzania Tea Authority, 1969—. Memberships include: Tanganyika African National Union; TANU Youth League; Tanganyika African Parents' Association; Tanzania Red Cross Society; Tanzania Society for Prevention of Cruelty to Animals. Address: Regional Commissioner, Private Bag, Iringa, Tanzania.

MWALE, Saidima James, born 12th February 1930. Carpenter; Furniture Shop Owner. Education: passed Standard 6, U.M.C.A., Musoro. Personal details: married to Idas Mwale, Social Worker, 6 children. Memberships: Committee Member, African Mineworkers' Union, 1953-58; UNIP Constituency Chairman, 1959-65; Club Secretary & Board Member, Fisnasa Club; Municipal Councillor, Luanshya; Secretary-General, Zambia Chamber of Commerce & Industry; N.R. Representative, World Council of Churches, Tanzania; Chairman of Labour Council, District Level of U.T.U.C. Address: P.O. Box 146, Luanshya, R. Zambia.

MWALUKO, Eliel Paul, born Dodomo, Tanzania, 20th September 1935. Diplomat. Education: Certificate in Geology, 1956; B.A.(Hons.), London, 1961; Postgraduate Diploma, Economics, Political Science & Philosophy, Oxford, 1963; U.N. Fellowship in Economic Planning, Moscow, 1964. Married. Appointments include: Geological Assistant, Tanzania, 1956; Administrative Officer, Government of Tanzania, 1961; Principal Assistant Secretary, Ministry of Finance, Dar es Salaam, 1963; Counsellor, Permanent Mission to the U.N., 1964; Representative to UNCTAD Trade Board, Alternate Representative to 40th Session of ECOSOC, Head of Delegation to 41st Session of ECOSOC, Vice-Chairman of Ad-Hoc Committee on U.N. Organization for Industrial Development, 1965-66; Ambassador Extraordinary & Plenipotentiary to the People's Republic of China, 1966-69; Deputy Leader to UNCTAD II, New Delhi, 1968. Memberships include: Chief Editor, Tanzania Political Journal, Makerere, 1958; Permanent Secretary to Ministry of Commerce & Industry 1969—. Vice-President for International Affairs, National Union of Makerere Students; Chief Representative to International Conference of Students meeting in Tunis, Nairobi, & Addis Ababa, 1960; Treasurer, African Society, Oxford University, U.K., 1961. Publications include: Role of Colonial Education, 1960. Address: Ministry of Commerce & Industry, P.O. Box 234, Dar es Salaam, Tanzania.

MWAMBA, Emmanuel Mubanga, born Chief Munkonge's Village, Kasama, Zambia, August 12th, 1928. Diplomat. Education: B.A., Political Science & Public Administration, University of South Africa, 1963; Diploma, Diplomacy & International Affairs, American University, 1964. Personal details: grandson of Chief Munkonge Mukaka. Appointments include: 1st Secretary, Zambia High Commission, Accra, Ghana, 1964-65; Zambian Deputy High Commissioner, ibid, 1965-66; Zambian Consul-General, Lubumbashi, Katanga Province, Congo (Kinshasa), 1966-68; Zambian Deputy Ambassador to Cairo, U.A.R., 1968-69; Consul-General, Lubumbashi, Congo (Kinshasa), 1969—. Address: Consulate-General of the Republic of Zambia, P.O. Box 596, Lubumbashi, (Kinshasa), Democratic Republic of the Congo.

MWAMBU, Makai Paph, born 20th May 1933. Veterinarian. Education: Nabumali High School, C. Bugish, 1949-55; Makerere University, Kampala, Uganda, 1956-63; University of Nairobi, Kenya, 1963-64; University of Ibadan, Nigeria, 1966; London School of Tropical Medicine, U.K., 1968-69; B.V.Sc.; M.Sc. Married, 3 children. Appointments: Veterinary Field Officer, Uganda Government; Special Lecturer, Faculty of Veterinary Science, Nairobi University, Kabete, Kenya; Vet. Research Officer, East African Community, EATRO, Tororo, Uganda. Memberships: Uganda Veterinary Assn.; British Society for Parasitology; Lions International; Lions Club, Tororo, Uganda. Author of publs. on trypanosomiasis & T.Vivax infection in cattle. Address: E.A.T.R.O., P.O. Box 96, Tororo, Uganda.

MWANZA, N. Peter, born 13th May 1937. University Lecturer. Education: B.Sc., University of London, U.K.; M.Sc., Ph.D., Ohio State University, U.S.A. Married, 2 children. Appointments: Lecturer in Biology, 1966-70; Senior Lecturer in Biology & Vice-Principal of Chancellor College, University of Malawi, 1970—; Bd. of Directors, Barclays Bank, Malawi. Memberships: Sigma Xi; Chmn., International Biological Programme, Malawi. Publications: Viruses as Predisposing Factors in the Susceptibility of Maize & Wheat Plants to other Pathogens (abstract); Some Characteristics of a Tropical Endorheic Lake in its Drying Phase & Recovery Phase, Lake Chilwa, Malawi, 1970. Address: University of Malawi, Chancellor College, P.O. Box 5200, Limbre, Malawi.

MWASHUMA, V. M., born 16th August 1916. Policeman. Education: Kabera High School, Kenya, until 1935. Married with 7 children. Appointments: Teacher, 1936-37; joined Police as Recruit Constable, 1938; promoted to Superintendent of Police; retiring, February, 1971. Address: Police H.Q.'s, Box 9141, Dar es Salaam, Tanzania.

MWASI, Edward Emmanuel Dunstan, born 18th March, 1926. Teacher; Government Official; Farmer. Education: Private Study for Matriculation, 1948-50; B.Sc., Fort Itare University College, 1950-53; University Education Diploma, ibid, 1955. Married, 2 children. Appointments include: Teacher, Zomba Catholic Secondary School & opened 1st & only night secondary school in Nyasaland, 1954; Schoolmaster, Dedza Government Secondary School, 1958-59; Education Officer, Lilongwe,

1958-59; detained during state of emergency in Nyasaland, 1959-60; Schoolmaster, Mzuzu Government Secondary School, 1960-61, 1963-64; Headmaster, ibid, 1964-65; Nyasaland Students' Liaision Officer, London, U.K., 1962-63; seconded to Ministry of External Affairs as Counsellor, Malawi Embassy, Washington, D.C., 1965-66; Senior Education Officer, i/c Secondary Education, 1967; Participant, UNESCO Biology Pilot Project on new approaches to teaching biology in secondary schools, Cape Coast, Ghana, 1967-68; Organizer, ibid, Malawi, 1968-69; retired from government service, 1970; currently, farming; Participant, various UN & UNESCO conferences. Memberships: Vice-President, Nyasaland Students' Association, 1949-54; Provisional Council, Malawi University, 1964-65; 1st Mzuzu Town Council; Education Consultative Committee, 1967; Committee of Inquiry into Standard 8 Examinations, 1966; Working Party for the Introduction of Agriculture in School., 1968; Secretary, National Biology Study Group, 1968-70; Chairman, Biology Syllabus Committee, 1969-70; Malawi Certificate of Education Examinations Board, 1969—. Joint Author of 12 booklets on investigating living things & a teachers' handbook on microbiology as part of material produced by UNESCO Biology Pilot Project. Address: P.O. Box 82, Mzuzu, Malawi.

MWENBA, Joseph Ben, born 28th July 1917. Teacher; Administrator; Diplomat. Education: S.R., Rusangu Mission School, Solusi Training School; S.A., Matriculation Certificate, Bethel College; B.A., Dip. Ed., Fort Hare University College; Dip. Ed., Ball State Teachers' College, U.S.A.; Diplomatic Affairs, The American University, Washington, D.C., U.S.A. Married, 2 sons, 3 daughters. Appointments: Primary Schoolteacher, 1947-48; Secondary Schoolteacher, 1952-60; Education Officer, 1961-63; Administrative Officer, 1964-65; Permanent Secretary, Ministry of Education, 1965; Permanent Representative at the U.N., 1966-68; Commissioner for Technical Education, & Vocational Training, 1968-69; Deputy Secretary, Z.N.P.F., 1969—. Memberships: President, Northern Rhodesia (now Zambia) Teachers' Association, 1953-60; Vice-Chairman, Lusaka Inter-racial Club, 1957-58; Agricultural Society of Zambia, 1965—. Address: P.O. Box 2144, 11 Ash Road, Woodlands, Lusaka, Zambia.

MWENDWA, Maluki Kitili, born Kitui, Kenya, 24th December 1929. Chief Justice of Kenya. Education: Alliance High School, Kikuyu, Kenya; Diploma in Education, Makerere University College, Kenya, 1948-50; LL.B., University of London, U.K., 1955; Diploma in Public Administration, Exeter University College, 1956; B.A. & M.A. in Philosophy, Politics, & Economics, Oxford, 1956-60; Barrister-at-Law, Lincoln's Inn, London, 1961. Personal details: son of Sr. Chief Mwendwa of Kitui. Married, 1 son, 1 daughter. Appointments include: Lecturer, Kagumo Teacher Training College, Kenya, 1951; Assistant Secretary, Ministry of Commerce & Industry, & Industry, & then Ministry of Works, Communications & Power, 1962; Sr. Assistant Secretary, Ministry of Tourism, Forests & Wildlife, 1962-63; Permanent Secretary, Ministry of Social Services, then Ministry of Home Affairs, 1963-64; Solicitor-General, 1964-68; Chief Justice of Kenya, 1968—; Leader of Kenya Delegation to the following: Commonwealth & Empire Law Conference, Sydney, Australia, 1965; World Through Law Conference, Washington, D.C., U.S.A., 1965; Conference of Plenipotentiaries to Conclude a Convention on the Law of Treaties, Vienna, Austria, 1968; Kenya Representative, 6th Committee, 21st Session, General Assembly, U.N., & on 2nd & 6th Committee, 22nd Session; Vice-Chairman, Kenya Delegation, Special Session & 22nd Session, General Assembly, 1967; Vice-Chairman, 6th Committee, 22nd Session, ibid; Vice-President, Stockholm Conference of Plenipotentiaries on Intellectual Property, 1967. Memberships: Chairman, U.N. Assn., Kenya; Chairman, Bd. of Governors, Parklands School & Ngara Secondary School; former President, Cosmos, Jowett, & St. Catherine's Debating Societies, Oxford University; Executive Council, African Institute of International Law; Agricultural Society of Kenya; Scounts Council, Kenya; Donovan Manie Theatre Club, Nairobi; Westwood Park Country Club, Nairobi. Publications: Constitutional Contrasts in East African States. Honours, prizes, awards: Sir Archibald Bodkin Prize, 1953. Address: Law Courts, P.O. Box 30041, Nairobi, Kenya.

MWESIGA, Bartholomew Gordian (Moto), born Bukoba District, 2nd March 1943. National Promoter of Music. Education: Rubya Seminary, 1955-62; Katigondo Major Seminary, Masaka, 1962-63; Ntungamo Seminary, 1964-66; Diploma Courses in Journalism, Social Anthropology, & Music. Appointments: Editor, Bukoba Co-operative News, 1966-68; Hd. of Music Dept. & Promoter of African Traditional Music, Ministry of National Education, 1968—. Memberships: Church Music Committee, Bukoba, 1967—; Patron, Tanzania Assn. of Musicians & Chmn., Musical Commission, 1969. Address: P.O. Box 9121, Dar es Salaam, Tanzania.

MWIHIA, Francis Mbugua, born Kenya, 11th November 1936. Economist. Education: B.Sc.(Hons., Economics), Moravian College, Bethlehem, Pa., U.S.A., 1962; M.A. Economics, University of Pittsburgh, 1965; Candidate for Ph.D., ibid. Personal details: early life spent in Central Province, Kenya. Appointments: Lecturer in Economics, University College, Nairobi, 1966-68; Head of Economic Division, Ministry of Foreign Affairs, Republic of Kenya, 1969—. Executive Committee Member, Economics Club of Kenya. Honours: Prize for best postgraduate research paper, University of Pittsburgh, U.S.A. 1964-65. Address: P.O. Box 847, Nairobi, Kenya.

MWIINGA, Ditton Chimpati, born 12th February 1930. Trade Unionist; Researcher. Education: Private Academic, Economic & Social Studies; Diploma, Personnel Management. Appointments: Former Minister of State for Commonwealth Affairs, Cabinet Minister of Health & Minister of State for Lands & Mines; Trained by British TUC & ICFTU, London &

Kampala, Uganda. Member, United National Independence Party. Honours: Grand Commander of the Order of Menelik II of Ethiopia, 1967. Address: P.O. Box 76, Mazabuka, Zambia.

MWILA, John Dickson, born 20th December 1940. Banker. Education: Primary Education, Kitwe; Secondary, Chiwala, Ndola, & Munali Secondary Schools, Zambia; B.Com., Dip. Statistics, Universities of Punjab & Aligarh, India, 1968. Appointments: Assistant Accountant, Rhokana Corp. Ltd., Senior Accounting Officer, University of Zambia; Assistant Accountant, Dairy Produce Board; Trainee Executive, National Commercial Bank Ltd. Address: National Commercial Bank Ltd., P.O. Box 2811, Lusaka, Zambia.

MWINGIRA, Augustine Cassian, born 28th August, 1932. Civil Servant. Education: Cambridge School Certificate, 1953; Dip. in Education, 1959. Married, 4 sons, 2 daughters. Appointments: Schoolmaster, 1959-61; Secondary School Headmaster, 1962-64; Education Planner, 1964-67; Chief Education Officer, 1967-68; Principal Secretary, Ministry of Education, 1968—. President of the Tanzania Geographical Assn. Publications: The Process of Education Planning in Tanzania (monograph), UNESCO/IIEP, 1966; The Role of a University in a Developing Nation, article in Journal of East Africa, Institute of Social Studies; The Problems of Implementing Education for Self-Reliance in Tanzania, African Studies Association of U.K. Address: P.O. Box 9121, Dar es Salaam, Tanzania.

MWIRARIA, Daudi Marete, born 3rd September 1938. Statistician. Education: B.A.(Hons.), London University, U.K.; M.A., University of East Africa. Married, 4 children. Appointments: Statistician, East African Common Services Organization, 1962; Deputy Director, East African Statistical Department, 1964; Director, East African Statistics Department, 1965-68; Secretary, Common Market & Economic Affairs, East African Community, 1968—. Memberships: Arusha Gymkhana Club; Mountain Club of Kenya. Author of several articles on statistics & economics. Address: Common Market & Economic Affairs Secretariat, East African Community, P.O. Box 1003, Arusha, Tanzania.

MWITA MARWA, Samson, born Motorio, Bukira Location, South Nyanza District, Kenya, 27th September 1931. Teacher; Member of Parliament; Farmer; Businessman. Education: Ikerege Primary School; The Taranganya Upper Primary School; Itibo Intermediate School; Kisii Teacher Training College. Married, 2 children. Appointments include: Secretary-General, Young Abakuria Association, 1953-55; Vice-Chairman, ibid, 1955-57; Treasurer, Kuria Political Union, 1957-60; Headmaster, Kurutiyange Intermediate School, 1960-63; elected to Nyanza Regional Assembly, 1963; elected Member, South Nyanza County Council; Treasurer, KANU District Branch, South Nyanza, 1964-66; Member of Parliament, 1970—. Memberships: Kenya Agricultural Society; Sports Association of South Nyanza; Kuria Association; KANU. Address: The Kenya National Assembly, Parliament Buildings, P.O. Box 1842, Nairobi, Kenya.

MWITHAGA (The Hon.) Mark Waruiru, born 21st December 1937. Politician. Education: Primary, Kerugoya, Kirinyaga District of Central Province, 1943-50; Secondary, & Priesthood Education, St. Paul's Seminary, Nyeri, 1951-54; privately educated in Public Administration. Personal details: imprisoned under the British. Appointments: Secretary, Transport & Allied Workers' Union, Rift Valley Province, 1959; Organizing Secretary, Nakuru District Congress, 1959; District Chairman & Member of Parliament, KANU, Nakuru, 1960-66. Memberships: Exec. Committee, Rift Valley, Kenya Red Cross; Scouts Master, 1957; Chairman, Finance Committee, Municipal Council, Nakuru, 1965-66; Chairman, Nakuru Local Council of Social Service; Nakuru Athletic Club; Africa Club, Nairobi. To be published: Mistake Me Not (autobiography). Honours: Black Power Law Award, U.S.A., 1969. Address: Nakuru Town Constituency, P.O. Box 821, Nakuru, Kenya.

MYAMBO, Kathleen, born 6th May 1943. Psychologist. Education: B.A., M.S., Pennsylvania State University, University Park, Pa., U.S.A., 1965. Married. Appointments: Lecturer in Psychology, University of Malawi, Limbe, Malawi, 1968—. Member of Phi Beta Kappa. Publications: Co-author; Shape perception for round & elliptically shaped test-objects, 1966 & Effect of stimulus distance and age on shape constancy, 1967; Shape Constancy in Central African Peoples (in preparation). Address: University of Malawi, Chancellor College, P.O. Box 5200, Limbe, Malawi.

MYERS, Alan Arthur, born 2nd March 1942. University Lecturer. Education: Haberdasher's Aske's School, U.K.; The London Polytechnic; Doctorate, The University of Wales, Swansea. Appointments: Lecturer in Zoology, The University of Dar es Salaam, Tanzania, 1968—. Memberships: Marine Biological Assn., U.K.; British Ecological Soc.; East Africa Natural History Society; British Entomological & Natural History Soc. Author of 10 publications in field of zoology; including: Some Aoridae collected by the Hancock Expeditions to the Eastern Pacific, 1931-41, Pacific Sci., 1968; A new genus & two new species of gammaridean Amphipoda from Central America, 1968. Address: Dept. of Zoology, The University of Dar es Salaam, Box 35064, Dar es Salaam, Tanzania.

MZUMARA, Michael J., born 19th June 1934. Administrative Officer. Education: Cambridge School Certificate; Diploma in the Teaching of English as a Second Language, Moray House College of Education, Edinburgh, U.K., 1962-63; Course on Development, Cambridge, U.K., 1967-68. Married, 3 children. Appointments: Schoolmaster; entered Administration as District Commissioner; Course on Development, Cambridge, U.K.; returned as District Commissioner, later Administrative Officer, President's Office. Member of African Society, Cambridge, U.K. Address: President's Office, P.O. Box 53, Zomba, Malawi.

N

NACOULMA, Mamadou, born 25th June 1930. Government Official. Appointments: with the Cabinpt of the High Commissioner of the A.O.F., Dakar, Senegal; Protocol Official with the President's Cabinet, Federation of Mali, at Dakar; Deputy Head of Protocol, ibid. Honours: Officer, Volta Order of Merit; Knight, Islamic Republic of Mauritania.

NAGODE (Alhaji) Salihu Alabi, born 15th September 1928. Administrative Officer. Education: Okesuna Elementary School, 1932-36; Iloring Middle School, 1937-42; Kaduna College, 1942-44. Married, 10 children. Appointments: Clerical Post, 1945-54; Information Officer, Ilorin Local Authority, 1954-55; Council Secretary, ibid, 1955-56; Deputy Development Secretary, 1956-57; Administrative Officer, Northern Nigeria Government, 1956-57; Administrative Officer, Federal Military Government, 1961—; Acting Principal Assistant Secretary, Federal Government Civil Service, 1965—. Memberships: Ansar-Islam Society of Nigeria; Treasurer, Ilorin Progressive Union, Lagos Branch; Federal Civil Service Senior Staff Union. Address: c/o Federal Ministry of Agriculture & Natural Resources, Lagos, Nigeria.

NAGPAL, Om Parkash, born Nairobi, Kenya, 22nd July 1933. Senior State Counsel. Education: LL.B., London, U.K.; Barrister-at-Law, Lincoln's Inn, London. Married. Appointments: Advocate in Private Practice, Kenya, 1955-62; joined Attorney-General's Chambers, Kenya, as State Counsel, 1962; Senior State Counsel, ibid, 1966; acted as Deputy Public Prosecutor, Kenya, 1967-68; Private Practice as Advocate, 1970—. Address: P.O. Box 112, Nairobi, Kenya.

NAJMUDEAN, Kamruddin G., born Surat, India, 7th May 1900. Ophthalmic Surgeon. Education: D.O., Oxford, U.K.; D.O.M.S.; M.B., B.S. Personal details: father-in-law, A. M. Jivanjee was Kenya pioneer & played a major part in development of country. Appointments: Trustee, President, D.B. Education Society; Trustee & Vice-President, Seif Bin Salim Public Library; Trustee, Hatim Sports Club. Address: P.O. Box 430, Mombasa, Kenya.

NAKATINDI (Princess) or Mulena Mukwae, born 30th June 1923. Politician. Education: Luatile Primary School, Lealui, Mongu; Mabumbu Girls' Boarding School, Mongu; Hope Fountain Institution, Bulawayo, N. Rhodesia (now Zambia); Tiger Kloof Institution, Cape Province, South Africa. Personal details: daughter of the late King Yeta III of Barotseland, N. Rhodesia (now Zambia); Ruler of the Sesheke District on the traditional side representing the Litunga of the Barotse people; married to Yuyi Nganga (now called Ishee Malundwelo—Prince Consort). Appointments: first woman to run in the General Election of the Zambian Government; first woman to serve on the United National Independence Party's Central Committee of the Party (U.N.I.P.), 1963; first woman to be elected to Zambian Government; first woman Junior Minister, 1964; first woman District Governor (Seseke District), 1970; first woman to be Traditional Ruler & Member of Parliament, 1966; first woman to serve as Director on 3 Indeco Company, Zambesi River Transport Board of Directors & all Government Statutory Boards. Memberships: Girl Guides of Zambia; Delegation to British Government, 1964; Delegation to Local Government Conference, Accra, Ghana, 1963; Zambian Delegation to the U.N., 1965; Leader, UNESCO Delegation to Tashkent, U.S.S.R., 1966; Zambian Chairman, All-African Women's Conference, Lusaka, Zambia, 1970. Address: P.O. Box 120, Lusaka, Zambia.

NALIKKA, Henry, born 8th October 1932. Electrical Engineer. Education: General Education, Namilyango College, Kampala, Uganda, 1951-53; Electrical Engineering Diploma, Faraday House College, London, U.K., 1957-60; Postgraduate Studies in Power Engineering, University of Aston, Birmingham, 1957-61; Diploma Business Management, Portsmouth College of Technology, 1966-67; Professional Training with General Electric Company Ltd., 1960-62; D.F.H., Dip. Man.; A.M.B.I.M., C.Eng., M.I.E.E. Personal details: married to Sochalastic Cecilia Mulyadzawa (Assistant Nutritionist), 7 children. Appointments: Junior Engineer, Uganda Electricity Board, 1962; Assistant Engineer, U.E.B., 1963-64; Assistant Construction Engineer, ibid, 1964-65; Construction Engineer, 1965-68; Chief Construction Engineer, 1968—. Memberships: Hon. Secretary, Uganda Division & Associate Member, Institute of Engineers, 1969-70; Chairman, Senior Staff Association, Uganda Electricity Board, 1966-68; Associate, British Institute of Management, 1967; Institution of Electrical Engineers, 1969; Registered Engineer in Uganda; Representative, East African Engineering Council, East African University, 1968-70. Address: Uganda Electricity Board, Box 7059, Kampala, Uganda.

NALITOLELA, Stephen Austin, born Masasi, Tanzania, November 1923. Regional Administrative Secretary, Ruvuma Region, Tanzania. Education: Primary, Namalenga, Masasi District, 1933-36; Secondary, St. Joseph's College, Chidya Masasi District, 1937-42; Grade I Teachers' Certificate, St. Andrew's College, Minaki, 1943-44; Teachers' Certificate, University of Reading, U.K., 1960-61. Married with children. Appointments: Teaching Career, Teachers' College & Secondary Schools, 1945-54, 1957; Headmaster, Middle School, 1957-60; District Education Officer, 1961-63; Regional Education Officer, 1963-65; Senior Education Officer, Ministry of National Education Headquarters, Dar es Salaam, 1966-69; Regional Administrative Secretary, Ruvuma Region, Ministry of Rural Administration & Rural Development, Songea, 1969—. Memberships: various committees in official capacities; Chairman, Songea Club. Address: Administrative Secretary, P.O. Box 74, Songea, Tanzania.

NAMBOZE, Josephine Mary. Doctor of Medicine. Education: M.B., Ch.B., Makerere University College Medical School, Kampala,

Uganda; D.C.H., Institute of Child Health, University of London, U.K.; M.P.H., School of Public Health, University of California, Berkeley, U.S.A. Married, 1 daughter. Appointments: Medical Officer, Ministry of Health, Uganda; Medical Officer, Kasomgati Health Centre; Lecturer, Department of Preventive Medicine, Makerere University College Medical School. Memberships: Uganda Medical Association; American Public Health Association; Uganda Association of University Women; Association of Physicians of East Africa. Publications include: Study of Births & Deaths in the Defined Area of Kasomgati Health Centre in 1967. J.Trop.Ped., 1969; The dual role of women at work, Trop.Hlth., 1970; What Buganda men want to know (w. others), Int.J.Hlth.Educ., 1963-64. Address: Medical School, Makerere University, P.O. Box 7072, Kampala, Uganda.

NAMUKULUNGE, Sylvester, born 16th July 1924. Dairy Farmer. Education: Elementary Vernacular School, Buruna Island, 1934-38; Nsamibya Primary School, 1938-41; Nsamibya High School, 1941-44; Diploma in Dairy Farming, Massey University College, New Zealand, 1961-64. Personal details: married, 6 children. Appointments: Army Service as Sergeant, W.W.II., 1939-45; Vetnry. Assistant, Vetnry. School, Entebbe, 1950-61; Animal Husbandry Officer, 1964; Senior Animal Husbandry Officer, 1968; O.C. Dairy Ranch, 1970. Memberships: East African Automobile Association; Shell Driving Club. Address: P.O. Box 7141, Kampala, Uganda.

NAPPER, Charles Geoffrey, born 2nd April 1916. Chartered Electrical Engineer, Telecommunications. Education: Streatham Grammar School, London, U.K.; Colfe's Grammar School, Lewisham, London; Woolwich Polytechnic, University of London; London School of Economics, ibid; School of Oriental & African Studies, ibid. Married. Appointments: Telecommunications Engineer, Standard Telephones & Cables Ltd., North Woolwich, 1935-40; Telecommunications Engineer, H.M. Colonial Postal Service, East African P&T Administration, 1940-61; Telecommunications Engineer, East African Community, East Africa P&T Corporation. Life Member, The Dar es Salaam Club. Address: Office of the Engineer in Charge, East Africa P&T Corporation, P.O. Box 7129, Kampala, Uganda.

NARAN, Parviz Habib Jamal, born 9th October 1943. Marketing Officer. Education: B.A., Economics & Geography. Appointments: Administrative Officer, Ministry of Agriculture, Food & Cooperatives, 1967-70; Marketing Officer, ibid, 1970—. Honours: Secondary School Prize, 1958, 1959; Certificate of Nation Building, 1969. Address: Marketing Officer, Min. of Agriculture, Food, & Cooperatives, P.O. Box 9192, Dar es Salaam, Tanzania.

NASRA, Mohamed, born 21st January 1912. Doctor of Medicine. Education: Diploma, Faculty of Medicine, Montpellier, France. Married, 4 children. Appointments: Resident Doctor, various hospitals in Tunisia; Doctor in charge, Medical District of Gafsa, Tunisia; with Ministry of Public Health, Auxiliary Hospital of En-Fida. Memberships: Associate Mbr., World Medical Association; Lions Club; Vice-President, Red Cross; President, Social Security Committee. Address: Hôpital Auxiliare, En-Fida, Tunisia.

NASSER (His Excellency) Gamal Abdel-Nasser Hussein, born Alexandria, U.A.R., 15th January 1918, deceased 28th September 1970. Former President of the United Arab Republic. Education: El Nahassin Elementary School, Cairo; El Nahda Secondary School, Cairo; Military Academy, Cairo; graduated, ibid, 1938; Staff College, graduated with distinction, 1942. Married, 3 sons, 2 daughters. Appointments include: 3rd Cavalry Battalion, Transferred to Mankabad near Assiut; Alexandria, Alamein, Sudan, 2nd World War; Combat Duty, Palestine War, 1948-49; Lecturer, College of the General Staff; Leader of the Revolution of 23rd July 1952, which forced the abdication & exile of the late King Farouk, the overthrow of the Mohamed Aly dynasty, & on 18th June 1953, the establishment of the Republic of Egypt; Secretary of the Liberation Rally, Deputy Prime Minister, Minister of the Interior, 1953; Prime Minister of Egypt, 1954; negotiation of the agreement for the withdrawal of British troops from the Suez Canal Zone, 1954; elected first President of the Republic of Egypt, 1956; nationalization of the Suez Canal Company, 1956; elected President of the United Arab Republic, 1958; re-elected, 1965; Chairman, Arab Socialist Union; active in forming the Organization of African Unity. Publications include: The Philosophy of the Revolution. Address: The Presidency, Cairo, U.A.R.

NATHOO, Husein, born 12th November 1933. Barrister-at-Law. Education: Wete Indian School, Wete, Pemba, Zanzibar, 1940-45; H.H. Aga Khan Indian School, Wete, 1946; Sir Evan Smith Madressa School, Zanzibar, 1947; Government Secondary School, Zanzibar, 1947; Lincoln's Inn, London, U.K., 1955-57. Married, 2 sons, 1 daughter. Appointments: Clerk to Legislative Council, Zanzibar, 1960; Assistant Secretary, Chief Secretary's Office, Zanzibar, 1958-59; elected Member, Zanzibar Municipal Council, 1962-64; Chairman, Zanzibar Rent Restriction Board, 1964. Memberships: Morogoro People's Club, Tanzania; Tanganyika Law Society, Dar es Salaam. Address: P.O. Box 184, Morogoro, Tanzania.

NAYO, Nicholas Zinzendorf, born Baika-Buem, Volta Region, Ghana, 4th April 1922. Lecturer in Music & Drama. Education: Elementary, to Standard 7, 1928-37; Presbyterian Training College, Akropong, 1938-41; Theological Seminary, 1942; Music Specialist Certificate, Achimota College, 1949-51; Trinity College of Music, London, U.K., 1956-57; Musicological Course, University of Ghana, 1962-64; Boston University, U.S.A., 1968-70; L.R.S.M.(London), 1953; Diploma in African Music (Legon), 1964; Master of Music (Boston), 1970. Personal details: father, Teacher & Choirmaster, brother, M.P. in Ghana. Appointments include: School-teacher, 1943-48; Music Master, Mawuli Secondary School, 1951-62; Assistant Lecturer in Music, College of Technology, Kumasi, Ashanti,

1952-53, 1954-56; Lecturer in Music, School of Music & Drama, University of Ghana, Legon, 1964—; Cultural Tour & Stage Appearances, with University of Ghana Students in Hungary, East Germany, West Germany, Poland, Czechoslovakia, & Russia, 1965; T.V. Appearance, Hungary, 1965. Memberships: Organizer & Chief Adjudicator, Evangelical Presbyterian Church, 1968—; Choir-Union, ibid, Volta Region, Chana; Executive Committee, Ghana Music Society. Publications: Some Suggestions for African Composers, Radio & T.V. Times of Ghana, 1960; Melody & Harmony in African Music, Music Society, 1966; Akpalu & his Songs, thesis, 1964. Musical Compositions include: 12 songs S.A.T.B.; 6 piano & voice songs, 4 cello & piano, 6 violin & piano; 1 trio for strings, 4 orchestral with piano. Address: School of Music & Drama, University of Ghana, Legon, Ghana.

NAZARETH, John Maximian, born Nairobi, Kenya, 21st February 1908. Advocate; Queen's Counsel. Education: St. Mary's High School, Bombay, India, 1916-25; St. Xavier's College, Bombay, 1925-29; B.A., ibid, 1929; Inner Temple, London, U.K., 1930-33. Married, 2 sons, 1 daughter. Appointments: President, East African Indian National Congress, 1950-52; Puisne Judge, High Court of Kenya, 1953; President, Law Society of Kenya, 1954; Queen's Counsel for Kenya, 1955; Member, Kenya Legislative Council, 1956-60; Member, Council of the Royal Technical College of East Africa (now University College, Nairobi), 1956—; Chairman, Ghandi Smarak Nidhi Trustees, 1956—. Awards include: St. Francis Xavier Gold Medal, 1929; Dakshina Fellow, St. Xavier's College, Bombay, 1929-30; Special Prize of the Council of Legal Education in Criminal Law, 1931; Poland Prize of the Inner Temple, 1931; Profumo Prize of the Inner Temple, 1932. Address: P.O. Box 532, Nairobi, Kanya.

NAZARETH, Peter Francis Joseph, born 27th April 1940. Civil Servant. Education: Senior Secondary School, Old Kampala, 1951-56; Senior Secondary School, Kololo, 1954-56; B.A.(Hons.), Makerere University College, 1957-62; Postgraduate Diploma in English Studies, Leeds University, 1965. Married, 2 daughters. Appointments: Teacher, St. Mary's College, Kisubi, 1962; Teacher, Senior Secondary School, Kololo, 1963; Assistant Secretary, Ministry of Finance, 1968—. Memberships: President, Entebbe Institute, 1966 & 1969; Ngoma Players. Publications: 4 literary articles published in English Studies in Africa; 2 literary articles published in Transition; 5 plays broadcast by African Service of B.B.C. Brave New Cosmos, The Hospital, & X; In a Brown Mantie (novel). Address: Ministry of Finance, P.O. Box 103, Entebbe, Uganda.

NCHA (Hon.) Enow Simon, born 22nd November 1922. Politician. Education: Theological College, Nyasoso, Kumba, Western Cameroon; Teacher Training College, Nyasoso, Kumba; Agricultural Colleges at Umuahia & Ibadan, Federal Republic of Nigeria. Appointments. Member of Parliament, West Cameroons, House of Assembly, 1953-61; Cameroon Federal National Assembly, 1962-63; Member of West Cameroon Parliament, 1964; Minister, Secretary of State, West Cameroon Government, 1965-67; Member, West Cameroon Parliament, 1968-70. President, Kesham Elements Progressive Union, 1954-70; Awards: 1st Cameroon Order of Valour, Chevalier; M.H.A. Address: P.O. Box 50, Mamfe, Manyu Division, West Cameroon, Federal Republic of West Cameroon.

NDAHENDEKIRE (Major) William Hark B., born December, 1939. Army Officer. Education: Omunkondo Kashari; Ibanda Primary School; Mbarara High School; Ntare School; K.A.R. Nairobi, Kenya; R.M.A., Sandhurst, U.K.; Hythe & Warminster. Appointments: Adjutant of Unit One BN, Uganda; Staff Officer, Army Headquarters (different posts); O.C. Training Wing, Uganda Army; Co. Commander in the Field; BN Second in Command. Memberships: several local sports organizations: Mountain Club of Uganda; A.A.A.; National Council of Sports, Uganda. Honours: several sports awards; Scout Wood Badge. Address: P.O. Box 10, Moroto, Uganda.

NDEGWA, John, born 13th July 1928. Librarian. Education: Mangu High School, Kenya; Loughborough College, U.K.; North-Western Polytechnic School of Librarianship, London. Married to Lucy Woki. Appointments: Librarian, E.A. Literature Bureau, Nairobi, Kenya; Assistant Librarian, Deputy Librarian & Librarian, University College, Nairobi. Fellow of Library Association, U.K.; Chairman, E.A. Library Association, 1965-66. Address: University of Nairobi, P.O. Box 30197, Nairobi, Kenya.

NDEKANA, Valerian David, born 15th December 1938. Electrical Engineer. Education: Secondary, Cambridge School Certificate, St. Francis College, Pugu, Dar es Salaam, Tanzania, 1957-60; B.Sc. Engineering, University College, Nairobi, Kenya, 1961-64. Married, 1969. Appointments: Assistant Electrical Engineer, Williamson Diamonds Ltd., Mwadui, Tanzania, 1966-68; Electrical Engineer, ibid, 1968—. Memberships: Associate, Institution of Electrical Engineers, U.K.; Graduate Member, East African Institution of Engineers. Address: c/o Williamson Diamonds Ltd., P.O. Box 288, Mwadui, Tanzania.

N'DIA KOFFI, Blaise, born Pakouabo, Ivory Coast, 28th December 1912. Minister of State of the Ivory Republic; Physician. Education: Medical School, Dakar, Senegal. Married, 5 sons, 2 daughters. Appointments: various positions as Physician, Ivory Coast & Upper Volta, 1937-57; Director, Hospital, Treichville & National School of Hospital Attendants, 1957-59; Deputy Legislative Assembly, Ivory Coast, 1959; re-elected, 1960; President, Commission of Public Health, ibid; Minister, Public Health & Population, 1963-70; Minister of State, 1970. Memberships: President, de la Societe d'Equipment de la Côte d'Ivoire; ibid, Society of Ivory Coast Hotels; ibid, Society of Urbanization & Construction; President, Organization de Coordination et de Cooperation pour la Lutte contre les Grandes Endemies, 1966-67; Vice-President, 19th Assembly, Worldwide Organization of Health, 1966; Executive

Council, ibid, 1967-70; President, 19th Session, Regional Committee for Africa, ibid, 1968-70; Executive Council, Ivory Coast Society of Mental Hygiene of the International Union of Mental Health Societies. Honours: Officer, National Order, Ivory Coast; Commander, Public Health, Ivory Coast; ibid, Legion of Honour; ibid, Palmes Academiques Françaises, National Order, Senegal; Grand Officer, Order of Tunisia; Commander, National Order of the Republic of Niger; Officier de l'Etoile Noire du Benin; Medaille des Eipidemies; Medal, Fight against Tuberculosis. Address: B.P. 802, Abidjan, Ivory Coast.

N'DIAYE, Matar, born 2nd September 1929. Gynaecologist. Education: M.D., C.E.S. (Gynaecology), Faculty of Medicine, Bordeaux, France. Married, 5 children. Appointments: former Director of Public Health, Senegal. Author of numerous articles on Gynaecology & Public Health. Honours: Knight, National Order of Senegal; Commander, Sovereign Order of Malta.

N'DJORE, N'djore, born 1936. Inspecteur de Cooperation; Government Deputy. Education: Bachelier en technique et economique; Diploma, National Centre of Cooperation, Paris, France; Diploma, Afro-Asian Institute, Tel Aviv, Israel. Married, 4 children. Appointments: Director, Cooperative Companies; Inspector, ibid, 1961-64; Director of Personnel, Caisse Nationale de eredit Agricole, 1964-65. Address: Deputy, National Assembly, B.P. 8161, Abidjan-Cocody, Ivory Coast.

NDUGWA, Christopher Magala, born 28th October 1939. Medical Practitioner. Education: King's College, Budo, 1947-58; Dover College, U.K., 1958-61; Bristol University Medical School, 1961-66; M.B., Ch.B.; D.C.H. Personal details: father, Medical Practitioner in Private Practice & Government Service for 30 years. Married to Robina Loi Mubish, a Nursing Sister at Mulago Hospital. Appointments: Senior House Officer, Hospital for Sick Children, Great Ormond Street, London, 1967-68; Registrar, Paediatrics Dept., Mulago Hospital Medical School, 1968—. Memberships: Uganda Medical Association; Old Doverian Club. Address: P.O. Box 2184, Kampala, Uganda.

NDUNGURU, Severin, born 20th April 1932. Educator; Administrator. Education: Mango R.C. Mission School, 1939-41; Kigonsera Seminary, 1942-48; Ndanda Secondary School, 1949-50; Teacher Training College, Ihungo, 1951-52; B.A.(Hons.), London, Makerere University College, 1959-64; M.Ed., University of Birmingham, U.K., 1967-68. Married, 7 children. Appointments: Primary Schoolteacher, 1953-59; Secondary School-teacher, 1964; Organizing Tutor, Institute of Education, University College, Dar es Salaam, Tanzania, 1965-67; Lecturer in Education, ibid, 1969—; Warden, Hall V, ibid, 1969—; Associate Dean (Administration), Faculty of Arts & Social Science, 1970—. Memberships: Geographical Society of Tanzania; International Geography Panel (East Africa); Chairman, National Geographical Panel, 1969. Address: Faculty of Arts & Social Science, University College, Dar es Salaam, Tanzania.

NDYAMKAMA, Corneli Theobald, born 1940. Assistant Manager. Education: Secondary, St. Francis College, Pugu, 1956-57; Primary, Kabare & Rubya, Bukaba, Tanganyika, 1949-55. Married, 2 sons, 3 daughters. Appointments: Clerical Officer, 1959-62; Executive Officer, Higher Executive Officer, 1962-65; Administrative Officer, 1965-69; Assistant Manager, 1969—. Memberships: Tanganyika African National Union; TANU Youth League. Courses held: Clerical Course, 1959; Office Management, 1963; Public Administration, 1967-68; Organization & Planning, 1970. Address: East African External Telecommunications Company Ltd., P.O. Box 22, Dar es Salaam, Tanganyika.

NECUS-AGBA, Benedict Ikwebe, born Utukwang, Obudu Division, S.E. State, Nigeria, 19th December 1938. Educator. Education: St. Charles' School, Obudu, 1944-51; P.T.C., Obudu, 1953; Teachers' Certificate Grade III, St. Thomas' E.T.C., Ogoja, 1954-55; Correspondence Student, Wolsey Hall, Oxford, U.K., 1958-59; St. Joseph's Higher Education College, Abakaliki, Nigeria, 1960-61; Rural Science School, Umuahia, 1963; Teachers' Certificate Grade II & G.C.E., Lond., 1962; University of Nigeria, Nsukka, 1964; Ahmadu Bello University, Zaria, 1963-64, 1966-68; B.A. (Hons.), Fine Art, ibid, 1968. Married, 3 children. Appointments include: Headmaster, Sacred Heart School, Ezekwe, 1956-59; Headmaster, St. Patrick's School, Anyugbe-Wonokom, 1958-59; Headmaster, Central School, Sarkwala-Obudu, 1962; Tutor, Teacher Training College, Obudu, 1962; Tutor, St. Thomas' Higher Elementary College, Ogoja, 1968; Principal, Government College, Obudu, 1968—; Divisional Adviser on Festival of the Arts, Obudu, 1968—. Memberships: Publicity Secretary, Catholic Action Group, 1960-61; President, Debating Society, Abakaliki, 1960-61; Councillor, County Council, 1960-66; Member, Obudu Division, Liquor Licensing Bd., 1962-64; Executive Member, Association of Fine Art Students, Ahmadu Bello University, 1964-65; Assistant Secretary, Assoc. of Fine Art Students, Univ. of Nigeria, Nsukka, 1966-67: Assistant Auditor, Utukwang Literates' Association, 1963-64; President, Utugwang Students' Union, 1966-67; Representative, Obudu & Ogoja Divisions, South-Eastern State Scholarship & Loans Board, 1969—. Publications include: Pottery in Obudu (thesis), 1968. Address: Principal, Government College, Obudu, Ogoja, S.E. State, Nigeria.

NEEL, Robert Emile Felix, born 27th January 1910. Director of the Pasteur Institute of Algeria. Education: Doctor of Medicine. Appointments: Deputy to the Director, Pasteur Institute of Madagascar, 1946; Head of Service, State Institute of Serums & Vaccines, Hessarek, Iran, 1950; Director, Pasteur Institute of Tangier, 1955; ibid, Morocco, 1962; ibid, Algeria, 1963—. Memberships: Society of Microbiology; Society of Exotic Pathology. Author of various publications on microbiology, parasitology, epidemiology, & rare diseases. Honours: Officer of the Legion of Honour. Address: Pasteur Institute of Algeria, Algiers, Algeria.

NEGBENEBOR, Frederick Obojie, born 27th September 1930. Gynaecologist-Obstetrician. Education: M.B.B.S., Guy's Hospital, University of London, U.K.; M.R.C.O.G. Married, 5 children. Appointments: Medical Officer, Western Region, Nigeria; Obstetric Registrar, Manchester Hospitals Management Committee; Specialist Obstetrician & Gynaecologist, Midwest Region, Nigeria; Specialist, i/c Iwaye Hospital for Women & Children, Benin City. Memberships: International Federation of Gynaecologists & Obstetricians; Fellow, Association of Surgeons of West Africa. Address: Iwaye Hospital for Women & Children, P.O. Box 15, Benin City, Nigeria.

NEGGA TESSEMA (Ato.), born 26th September 1932. Lawyer. Education: B.A., University College of Addis Ababa, Ethiopia, 1957; B.C.L., McGill University, 1960. Appointments: Assistant in Attorney-General's Office, Ministry of Justice, 1960-61; Chief Public Prosecutor, Supreme Imperial Court, 1961-64; Legal Adviser to Municipality of Addis Ababa, 1964-65; Vice-President (Assistant Mayor), & Legal Adviser, City Council, 1965–. Publications: drafted several pieces of legislation. Address: P.O.B. 356, Addis Ababa, Ethiopia.

NELSON (Right Rev., Major) Aruna Kojo, born 27th April 1908. Anglican Bishop. Education: Elementary, St. Mary's Anglican School, Accra, Ghana; Secondary, St. Nicholas' Grammar School, Cape Coast; St. Augustine Theological College, Kumasi. Married, 3 daughters. Appointments: Parish Priest, 1932-36; Rector, St. Augustine's Theological College, Kumasi, 1936-39; Parish Priest, 1939-58; Senior Chaplain, Ghana Armed Forces, 1st Ghanaian Anglican Chaplain so appointed, Rank—Senior Major, 1958-63; Provost, Holy Trinity Cathedral, Accra, 1963–; consecrated, Bishop, 1966; Canon, Holy Trinity Cathedral, 1958. Gazetted by Ministry of Defence to retain & use the title 'Major'. Address: Provost's Lodge, High Street, P.O. Box 8, Accra, Ghana.

NELSON-COLE, Olakunle John Theodore, born Lagos, Nigeria, 30th November 1913. Physician & Surgeon. Education: C.M.S. Grammar School, Lagos, Nigeria; King's College, Lagos; University of Bristol, U.K.; St. Mungo's College, Royal Infirmary, Glasgow, Scotland; L.R.C.P.(Edin.); L.R.C.S.(Edin.); L.R.F.P.S.(Glasgow), 1947. Personal details: eldest son of late Mr. John Theodore Nelson-Cole, Barrister-at-Law, one of the first 6 Nigerians to qualify & read for Law in U.K.; grandson of the late Consul Jacob Samuel Adelabu Leigh, Consul to Liberia & the first Nigerian to purchase & own steamships. Appointments: House Surgeon, Medical Service, Nigeria, 1947; Medical Officer, in charge of Medical Areas within Nigeria, 1948; currently, Medical Officer on Sessional Duties for the Lagos State Government & Nigerian Railway Corporation. Memberships: British Medical Association; St. Paul's Church (Protestant), Breadfruit, Lagos. Publications: articles in Nigerian Newspapers on non-political subjects including: The Lagos Morning Post (National Paper), 1965. Address: General Hospital, Lagos, P.O. Box 3851, Lagos, Nigeria.

NEOGY, Rajat, born Kampala, Uganda, 17th December 1938. Editor & Publisher. Education: Social Sciences at SOAS, London. Married, 3 children. Appointments include: various journalistic & broadcasting assignments in U.K. & Uganda; founded Transition Magazine, Africa's largest selling magazine of its kind, 1961; Editor-in-Chief & Publisher since that time; Managing Director, Transition Ltd. Memberships include: various local & international cultural organizations. Publications include: poetry & articles. Address: P.O. Box 20026, Kampala, Uganda.

NEUHAUS, Theodore Frederick Charles, born 7th November 1919. Secondary School-teacher. Education: Parramatta High School, 1932-36; B.A.(Hons.), Sydney University, Australia, 1940; Dip.Ed., ibid, 1941; B.D., London University, U.K., 1958; Moore Theological College, 1960. Married, 3 sons, 1 daughter. Appointments: Air Navigator (Flt. Lt.), R.A.F., U.K., Middle East, Aden, 1943-45; Head, English & History, Maclean & Fairfield High Schools, Australia, 1954-59; Head, English Department, Alliance Secondary School, Dodoma, Tanzania, 1963; Acting Principle, Katoke Teachers' College, Bukoba, 1964-65; Head, English & Religion Departments, Mazengo Secondary School, Dodoma, 1967–. Memberships: Missionary, Church Missionary Society in Tanzania, 1960–; Diploma Holder (R.L.S.S.), Examiner & Associate Member, Royal Life Saving Society (Australia). Honours: Star, Atlantic Star, Defence Medals of U.K. & Australia, 1939-45. Address: Mazengo Secondary School, P.O. Box 931, Dodoma, Tanzania.

NEUHAUS, Yvonne Margaret Ellen, born 9th July 1935. State Registered Nurse; State Registered Midwife. Education: Marsden High School, 1947-50; Royal Prince Albert Hospital, 1953-57; Parramatta District Hospital, 1959-60. Married, 3 sons, 1 daughter. Missionary, Church Missionary Society in Tanzania, 1960–. Address: Mazengo Secondary School, P.O. Box 931, Dodoma, Tanzania.

NEVILLE, Patricia Jane, born 15th September 1932. Occupational Therapist. Education: Dorset House School of Occupational Therapy, Oxford, U.K., 1951-54. Appointments: worked at Kumi/Ongeno Leprosy Centre, Uganda, 1959-66; Staff, All-Africa Leprosy & Rehabilitation Training Centre, Addis Ababa, Ethiopia, 1966–; Missionary, Church Missionary Society. Member, Association of Occupational Therapists. Publications: Occupational Therapy in Leprosy (joint author), in Leprosy in Theory & Practice, 1970; Anaesthesia in the Hand & Foot in Leprosy (joint author), in Physiotherapy, 1965. Address: All-Africa Leprosy & Rehabilitation Training Centre, P.O. Box 165, Addis Ababa, Ethiopia.

NEWING (Rev.) Edward George, born 12th July 1930. Anglican Priest; Lecturer, Biblical Studies. Education: A.S.T.C., Civil Engineering, Sydney Technical College, N.S.W. University of

Technology, Australia, 1948-54; Th.L.(Hons.), Moore Theological College, 1958; B.D.(Hons.), London University (External), 1959; M.Th., 1961. Married, 4 children. Appointments: Civil Engineer with various semi-governmental & private enterprises, 1948-56; Rector, Garrison Church, Miller's Point, Sydney, 1959-61; Visiting Lecturer, Hebrew, Moore College, ibid, 1960; Missionary, C.M.S., East Africa, 1961—; Lecturer, St. Paul's United Theological College, Limure, Kenya, 1961-62, 1966-70; Parish Priest, Emmanuel Church, Morogoro, Tanzania, 1962-64; Lecturer, St. Philip's Theological College, Kongwa, 1964-65; Research Student, Old Testament Studies, St. Andrew's University, U.K., 1970-72. Associate Member, American Schools of Oriental Research. Contributor to professional journals. Address: Drumcarrow, Lade Braes, St. Andrew's, Fife, U.K.

NEWMAN, Emmanuel Kofi, born 4th July 1925. Medical Practitioner. Education: Mfantisipim School, Cape Coast, Ghana, 1941-45; Achimota College, Accra, 1946-48; Edinburgh University, Scotland, U.K., 1950-56. Married, 4 children. Appointments: Medical Officer, Ghana, 1957-63; Senior Medical Officer, 1964-66; Lecturer, Ghana Medical School, 1966. Member, Royal College of Obstetricians & Gynaecologists, 1964. Address: Ghana Medical School, Accra, Ghana.

NEWTON, Hilary Skardon, born 8th October 1931. Medical Practitioner. Education: Clifton High School for Girls; Malvern Girls' College; Bristol University, U.K. Married, 1 son, 1 daughter. Appointments: House Surgeon, Bristol Royal Infirmary; House Physician, Southmead General Hospital, Bristol; Casualty Medical Officer, Coast General Hospital, Mombasa, Kenya. Member, British Medical Association. Address: P.O. Box 150, Mombasa, Kenya.

NGAHYOMA, Flora, born Liuli Songea, Tanganyika. Senior Labour Officer. Education: Chiulu Primary School; St. Mary's Girls' School, Liuli; Butimba Teachers' Training College; Trade Unionism Course, U.S.A.; Labour College, Kampala, Uganda; Labour Administration Course, U.K. Married, 2 sons, 2 daughters. Appointments: Teacher, Ministry of Education, 1959-61; Assistant Director of Education, Tanganyika Federation of Labour, 1962-63; Labour Officer, Ministry of Communications, Labour & Works, 1963-68; Senior Labour Officer, ibid, 1968—. Memberships include: TANU; NUTA; Railways Club, Gerezani. Address: The Area Labour Office, P.O. Box 1181, Dar es Salaam, Tanzania.

NGAME NGOMBA, Tite, born 30th July 1928. Civil Administrator. Education: M.P.F., Primary School, Ndoungue, Cameroun, 1938-41; C.E.P.E., 1942; D.M.E.G., Evangelical College of Libamba, 1945-48; B.E., 1952; qualified in Law & Economic Science, 1969. Married, 8 children. Appointments: Teacher, Professor, Evangelical College of Libamba, 1949-60; with the Cabinet, Ministry of National Education, 1960-62; Head, Bureau of Inspection & Control, Ministry of Finance, 1962-64; Head of Bureau, General State Control, 1964-66; Deputy Head of Service of Financial Studies, Financial Secretariat of State, 1969. Memberships: Regional Secretary, Blue Cross, 1950-54; General Treasurer, Cameroun Cultural Association, 1961-68; President, Old Pupils' Association, Libamba, 1964—. Address: Secretariat d'Etat aux Finances, Yaoundé, Cameroun.

NGANKAM, Cyprien, born Fondjomekwet, Bafang, 18th January 1930. Veterinary Nurse. Married, 9 children. Current appointment: Controller, Municipal Abattoirs. Honours include: Mérite Camerounais, 3rd Class, 1960. Address: B.P. 15, Youndé, Cameroun.

NGASSONGWA, Mpandukah Juma Alifa, born 13th August 1942. Agricultural Engineer. Education: Primary, Mpapaba, 1951-54; Middle School, Nawenge, 1955-58; Secondary, Mzumbe, 1959-62; Ing. Agric., University of Prague, Czechoslovakia, 1963-67. Married, July 1970. Appointments: Field Officer, stationed Geita District, 1967-68; National Service, 1968; Agricultural Officer, Headquarters, 1969; Project Officer, Eastern Zone (Coast, Morogoro, & Mtwara Regions); Research Officer, Division of Research & Training. Memberships: TANU; TANU Youth League, 1967—. Publications: Chronic Influence of Gamma Radiation on Rhizobium japonicum in symbiosis with soyabeans (thesis)' Prague, 1967. Address: Research & Training Division, Damba House, Box 2066, Dar es Salaam, Tanzania.

NGENDA-BASAZA, Joseph William-Bizoza, born 30th November 1941. Agricultural Credit Advisory Officer. Education: Gisorora Church School (N.A.C.), 1950-53; Seseme Primary School, 1954-56; Kigezi High School, 1957-59; Busoga College, Mwiri, 1960-64; Arapai Agricultural College, 1965-67. Personal details: brother, Chairman of I.L.O., U.N.; married, wife studied Drama (Diploma from Makerere University). Appointments: Assistant Agricultural Officer, later Agricultural Credit Advisory Officer, Department of Agriculture, Kabale. Memberships: Uganda Agricultural Society; East African Automobile Association; Secretary, Kigezi Agricultural Organization; Western Students' Association: Arapai Alumni Association; Boys' Brigade, Kigezi (B.B.I.). Publications: Agriculture in Schools, Agricultural Journal, 2nd Vol., 1969. Honours include: Uganda Red Cross Certificate, for donating blood in the Blood Transfusion Service, 1964; M. Buscoga College Bursary, 1960. Address: Dept. of Agriculture, Box 6, Kabale, Uganda.

NGOH, Victor Mukwele, born Kumba, Cameroun, 4th April 1942. Solicitor; Barrister. Education: LL.B.(Hons.), 1st Class, University of Biafra; B.L., LL.M., London School of Economics, London University, U.K. Appointments include: Practising Lawyer, West Cameroun; Managing Director, V.I.S. Co.; Executive Director, Creative Arts & Science Institute of Cameroun; Chairman & Legal Adviser, Variety Industrial Services Company Ltd. Memberships include: Secretary, National Union of Cameroun Students; President, Law Students' Association, University of Biafra; Fellow, British Institute of International Company Law, 1967. Publications include: Editor, West Cameroun Year Book; Cross-Love

Tragedy (Novel). Honours include: 1st Prize in English Prose, Biafran Festival of the Arts, 1961; 1st Prize, University of Biafra Short Story Contest, 1963; Runner-up, 'Drum' All-Africa Short Story Contest, 1963; Mbanefo Prize in Law, University of Nigeria, 1966. Address: P.O. Box 79, Kumba Town, West Cameroun, Cameroun.

NGONGANG, Josue-Claude, born 1925. Merchant. Education: Bamena & Bafoussam, West Cameroun; Yaoundé. Personal details: orphaned at the age of 20; responsible for the upbringing of a younger brother & sister. Appointments: entered on a career in commerce, 1946; Licensed Seller, 1947; Aide-Compatable a European, 6 months; since then, a Merchant. Address: B.P. 2003, Yaoundé-Messa, Cameroun.

NGOWELA, Enoch Simeon, born 23rd August 1935. Accounts Clerk. Education: Malawi Government Junior Certificate of Education; 1 year Accounts Training; 2 'O' Levels, Economics & Commerce, London University Board. Appointments: Storekeeper & Tea Leaf Weigher, 1953; Field Office Head Clerk, 1956; Wages Computer, 1961-63; studied Accounts, Universal College of Commerce, Bukoba, Tanzania, 1964; currently, Senior Accounts Assistant Trainee. Memberships: Acting Chairman, Plantation & Agricultural Workers' Union, Malawi; Educational Book Club of South Africa, 1963. Address: Bandanga Tea Estates Ltd., P.O. Box 10, Cholo, Malawi.

N'GUIAMBA N'ZIE, Simon Ernest, born 14th November 1935. Deputy Director-General, Cameroun Society of Cacao, Socacao. Education: Accountancy Studies. Married to Anne-Marie Dhomps, 2 sons, 3 daughters. Appointments: Accounts Inspector, La Direction de la Cooperation et de la Mutualite, 1961-64; Director of Operations, Cameroun Bank of Development, 1965-68; Charge de Mission, National Society of Investment, 1961-68; Administrative Director, CAMEP, 1968—; currently, Deputy Director-General, Socacao. Memberships: Commissioner of Accounts, SFIA; ibid, Cameroun Actualite; SACIA. Address: Deputy Director-General, B.P. 1013, Socacao, Yaoundé, Cameroun.

NGUINI, Marcel, born Yaoundé, 1927. Magistrate. Education: LL.D., University of Aix-Marseille, France. Married, 6 children. Appointments: Inspector, Work Contracts & SOcial Laws, Douala & Yaoundé, Cameroun, 1957-60; Head of Central Services, Ministry of Justice, 1960-62; Counsellor, Supreme Court, Cameroun Oriental, 1962-64; General Assistant, Court of Appeal, Dschang, 1964-65; Advocate-General, Court of Appeal, Douala, 1965-66; Procuror-General, Federal Court of Justice & Supreme Court, Cameroun Oriental, 1966-68; First President, Federal Court of Justice & Supreme Court, Cameroun Oriental, 1968—. Memberships: Yaoundé Section, International Lions Club; International Jurists' Commission, Geneva, Switzerland. Honours: Knight, National Order of Valour, 1961; Officer, ibid, 1967. Address: B.P. 1181, Yaoundé, Cameroun.

NGUMA, Gustave Kunda Peter, born 17th January 1945. Field Officer, Nutrition. Education: R.C. Lower Primary School, Kilema, Moshi, 1952-56; R.C. Upper Primary School, ibid, 1957-60; Secondary Umbwe Kibosho, Moshi, 1961-64; Diploma, U.C.D. Faculty of Agriculture, Moroguro, 1965-67; Course in Applied Human Nutrition, U.C.D. Appointments: Field Officer, Nutrition, Headquarters, Ministry of Agriculture, Food & Cooperatives, Research & Training Division, Dar es Salaam; Agriculture Officer, in charge Food Science Unit, Research & Training Institute, Ilonga, Kilosa. Memberships: Leader, Rover Scouting Crew, Arusha; Secretary, Y.C.S., U.C.D. Fac. of Agriculture, Morogoro; Social Club, ibid. Author of nutritional slogans and a radio broadcast on All Radio Tanzania, Dar es Salaam. Address: F.O. (Nutrition), Research & Training Institute Ilonga, Private Bag, Kilosa, Tanzania.

NG'WANANOGU, John Christopher Petro, born 11th May 1941. Adminstrative Officer. Education: Itabagumba Primary School, Geita District, 1948-52; Kijima Middle School, Kwimba District, 1953-54; Kahororo Secondary School, Bukoba District, 1955-58; Alliance Secondary School, Dodoma; Joint Examination for School Certificate & G.C.E. Division 2, 1960; Qualified Audio-Typist, Grade 2, Dar es Salaam Technical College, 1961; ibid, Grade 1, 1963; Qualified Local Government Officer, Mzumbe Local Government Training Institute, 1964; Tanzania Government Qualifying Law Exam. for Administrative Officers. Personal details: son of a pastor. Appointments: Personal Secretary to the Principal, Butimba Teachers' Training College, 1964-65; Local Government Officer, 1965-70; Area Secretary, Regional Administration, 1970—. Memberships: Ng'wananogu Choir; Utete Members Club. Address: Area Secretary, P.O. Box 28003, Kisarawe, Dar es Salaam, Tanzania.

NHONOLI, Aloysius Mwessa, born 23rd September 1927. Consulting Physician. Education: St. Mary's Secondary School, 1940-46; M.B., Ch.B., D.T.M.&H., M.D., Makerere University College, 1947-54; M.R.C.P. (Ireland). Married. Appointments: Medical Officer, Ministry of Health, 1955-62; Senior Medical Officer, ibid, 1962-64; Specialist Physician, ibid, 1964-65; Consultant Physician, ibid, 1965-68; Senior Lecturer, University of Dar es Salaam, 1968-70; Reader in Medicine, ibid, 1970—; Dean, Faculty of Medicine, 1970—. Memberships: President, The Association of Physicians of East Africa, 1967-68. 1970—; Committee, ibid, 1965—; President, The Medical Association of Tanganyika, 1965-67; Committee, ibid, 1965—; East African Academy; British Medical Association. Author of some 15 publications in medical journals on infant mortality rate, anthrax, malnutrition, anaemia, cardiovascular disease, & duodenal ulcers. Honours: Muljibhai Madhvani Prize for best finalist in Medicine, 1954; First, British Medical Association Essay Competition Prize, 1952, 1953, 1954; Chairman, East African Medical Research Council, 1967-70. Address: Dean, Faculty of Medicine, University of Dar es Salaam, P.O. Box 20693, Dar es Salaam, Tanzania.

NIAT, Njifenji Marcel, born 26th October 1934. Electrical Engineer. Education: Lic. es Sciences; Diploma, Higher School of Electricity, Paris, France; ancien Laureat du Concours General de l'Union Française. Married, 3 children. Appointments: Engineer, Bureau of Studies, ENECLAM, 1962-64; Head of Service, Studies, & Works, EDC, 1964-68; Attaché, Direction Generale EDC, responsible for Studies & Programmes, 1968-70. Memberships: Amicale of Engineers; La Ste Française de Electriciens et Radioelectriciens. Honours: Cameroun Merit, 2nd Class, 1964; Knight of the Cameroun Order of Bravery, 1968. Address: B.P. 4077, Douala, Cameroun.

NICHOLAS, Reginald John, born 14th November 1935. University Lecturer. Education: The Grammar School, Ijebu-Ode, Nigeria, 1948-53; M.B., B.S., King's College, University of Durham, U.K., 1959-64; M.D., University of Newcastle upon Tyne, 1966-69. Appointments: Hon. Senior Research Associate, Univ. of Newcastle upon Tyne, 1966-69; Lecturer in Anatomy, Ghana Medical School, 1969—. Memberships: Anatomical Society of Great Britain & Ireland; Secretary, Eastern Division, Ghana Medical Association. Contributor to professional journals. Address: Department of Anatomy, Ghana Medical School, Accra, Ghana.

NICKEL, John L., born 9th January 1930, Kansas, U.S.A. Agricultural Entomologist; Educator. Education: B.Sc., University of California, Berkeley, 1951; Ph.D., ibid, 1957. Married, 1 son, 1 daughter. Appointments: Entomologist & Production Manager, Maple Leaf Farms, Wasco California, 1951-57; Entomologist, Maple Leaf Foundation, 1955-56; Entomologist, Standard Fruit Co., La Ceita, Honuras, 1959-60; Entomology Adviser, USAID, Phnon Penh, Cambodia, 1961-64; Visiting Entomologist, IRRI, Los Banos, Philippines, 1964; Assistant Entomologist, University of California, Berkeley, U.S.A., 1964-66; Dean, Faculty of Agriculture, Makerere University College, Kampala, Uganda, 1966—. Member, Phi Beta Kappa. Address: Dean, Faculty of Agriculture, Makerere University, P.O. Box 7062, Kampala, Uganda.

NICOL, Davidson Sylvester Hector Willoughby. Permanent Representative & Ambassador of Sierra Leone to the United Nations; Administrator; Physician; Pathologist. Education: Prince of Wales School, Freetown, Sierra Leone; Christ's College, Cambridge, U.K.; London Hospital; M.A., M.D., Ph.D. (Cantab.), Hon. LL.D., Hon. D.Sc. Personal details: African parentage; married, 2 sons, 1 daughter. Appointments: Science Master, Prince of Wales School, Sierra Leone, 1941-43; Foundation Scholar & Prizeman, Cambridge University, U.K., 1943-47; Fellow & Supervisor in Nat. Sciences & Med., Christ's College, 1957-59; Beit Mem. Fellow for Medical Research, 1954; Benn Levy University Studentship, Cambridge, 1956; Universtiy Scholar, House Physician, Medical Unit & Clinical Pathology, Receiving Room Officer & Research Assistant, Physiology, London Hospital, 1947-52; University Lecturer, Medical School, Ibadan, Nigeria, 1952; Visiting Lecturer, Univs. of Toronto, Canada, California at Berkeley, & Mayo Clinic, U.S.A., 1958; Aggrey-Fraser-Guggisberg Mem. Lecturer, University of Ghana, 1963; Danforth Fellowship Lecturer in African Affairs, Assoc. of American Colleges, U.S.A., 1968; Senior Pathologist, Sierra Leone, 1958-60; Principal, Fourah Bay College, Sierra Leone, 1960-68; Vice-Chancellor, University of Sierra Leone, 1966-68; Chairman, Sierra Leone National Library Board, 1959-65; Member, Governing Body, Kumasi University, Ghana; Public Service Commission, Sierra Leone, 1960-68; West African Council for Medical Research, 1959-62; Executive Council, Association of Universities of the British Commonwealth, 1960, 1966; Commission for proposed University of Ghana, 1960; Chairman, University of East Africa Visiting Committee, 1962; Director, Central Bank of Sierra Leone, Sierra Leone Selection Trust Ltd., Consolidated African Selection Trust Ltd. (London); Fellow, Christ's College, Cambridge, U.K.; Fellow, College of Pathologists, London; Perm. Rep. & Ambassador of Sierra Leone to the United Nations, 1969—, & the Security Council, 1970—; Chairman, Committee of 24 (Decolonization), United Nations; Hon. Consultant Pathologist, Sierra Leone Government. Memberships: President, West African Science Association, 1964-69; President, Sierra Leone Red Cross Society, 1962-66; Conference Delegate, WHO Assembly, 1959, 1960; ibid, Commonwealth Prime Ministers' Conference, 1965, 1969; UNESCO Higher Educ. Conf., Tananarive, 1963; Vice-President, CMS London, 1961; President, SCM, Western Nigeria, 1952-54, Sierra Leone, 1959; Chairman, West African Exams. Council, 1964-69; Hon. Fellow, Ghana Acad. of Sciences. Publications: Africa, A Subjective View, 1964; Contbr. to Malnutrition in African Mothers & Children, 1954, H.R.H. the Duke of Edinburgh's Study Conference, vol. 2, 1958, The Mechanism of Action of Insulin, 1960, The Structure of Human Insulin, 1960, Africanus Horton, Black Nationalism 1867, 1969, & to J.Trop.Med./ Biochem.J., Nature, J. of Royal African Soc., etc. Honours: Independence Medal, Sierra Leone, 1961; Margaret Wong Prize and Medal for Literature in Africa, 1952. Address: Suite 608, 30 East 42nd Street, New York, N.Y. 10017, U.S.A.

NICOLAI, Gabriel, born 20th February 1913. Director of CCAP, Centre for Salary & Information. Education: Licenced in Law; Head of Overseas Division. Appointments include: Organizing Head, Planning Bureau, Mauritania; Deputy Director of Finances, Senegal; Technical Adviser, Ministry of Finance. Honours include: War Medal, 1939-45; Knight of the Black Star of Benin; Officer, Agricultural Merit; Knight, French Order of Merit; Commander, Order of Merit of Senegal. Address: Ministry of Finance, Senegal.

NII AMUGI II, Ga Mantse & Paramount Chief of Accra, born 8th June 1940. Education: Sekondi Methodist School, 1946-49; Nsawam Anglican School, 1950-52; African College, 1953-56; Ebenzer Secondary School, Accra, 1957-59. Married, 2 daughters. Appointments: Accounts Clerk, Messrs. C.F.A.O. Ltd., Accra, 1960-65. Enstooled Ga Mantse & Paramount

Chief of Accra, 20th March 1965. Member & Choirmaster/Organist, Saint Andrew's Anglican Church of Accra, 1960-65. Address: P.O. Box 42, Accra, Ghana.

NIMERI (Major-General) Gaafar Mohamed, born Omdurman, 1st January 1930. President of the Revolutionary Council, Prime Minister, & Commander in Chief of the Armed Forces of the Sudan. Education: early schooling, Koranic School & El Hijra Elementary School, Omdurman; attended Medani Government School & Hantoub Secondary School; Graduated 2nd Lieutenant, Military College, 1949-52; Master Degree in Military Science, U.S.A. Appointments: with Air Force Officers, U.A.R., 1952-55; with Northern Command, Shendi, 1957; transferred to many army units owing to his ability to lead men and unify them; Officer in Commad, Troops at Torit, where he lead famous attack on Deto Mountain rebels; Second in Command, Senior Lecturer, Infantry School at Gebeit; Officer in Commad, ibid until May 1969; Promoted to Brigadier during Socialist Revolution, 1969; ibid, Major General, 1969. Address: Khartoum, Sudan.

NJAU, Dunstan Joseph, born Moshi, Tanzania, 23rd May 1930. Agricultural Economist, Dean. Education: Diploma in Agriculture, Makerere College, 1956; B.Sc. (Agriculture), W.Va. University, U.S.A., 1963; M.Sc.(Agriculture Economics), ibid, 1964. Married, 5 children. Appointments include: Assistant Agriculture Officer, 1957-63; Agricultural Officer, 1963; Senior Agricultural Officer, 1964; Principal, Agriculture College, Morogoro, 1965-68; Dean, Faculty of Agriculture, University of Dar es Salaam, 1969—. Memberships: President, East African Agriculture Economics Society; Chairman, Morogoro People's Club; Rehovoth Conferences; East African Council for Agricultural Education. Address: Faculty of Agriculture, University of Dar es Salaam, P.O. Box 643, Morogoro, Tanzania.

NJAU, Hippolitus Pamfili, born Uru-Moshi, Tanzania, 13th August 1938. Chartered Secretary. Education: Private Studies, Cambridge School Certificate Level; Part-time professional studies. Married, with children. Appointments: Junior Stores Clerk, 1955-56; Stores Assistant Trainee, Government, 1956-57; Stores Assistant, ibid, 1957-59; Junior Tax Officer, East African Authority, 1959-63; Treasurer, Local Councils, 1963-64; Income Tax Assessor, East African Authority, 1965-66; Company Secretary, National Development Corporation, 1966-69; Administrative Manager, Corporation Secretary, The State Trading Corporation, Tansania, 1969—. Memberships: Fellow, Chartered Institute of Secretaries; Secretary, Tanganyika Students' Association, Nairobi Royal College; Chairman, Tanganyika Branch, Common Services Organization Trade Union. Address: P.O. Box 2669, Dar es Salaam, Tanzania.

NKATA, Daniel, born Kampala, Uganda, 29th May 1931. Librarian. Education: Mengo Secondary School, Kampala, 1937-44; Makerere College School, 1945-48. Kampala Technical Institute, 1949-51; Sports Training Course, U.K., 1959. Married, 4 children. Appointments include: Manager, Makerere Students' Guild, 1952-55; Businessman, Kampala, 1956-62; Personnel Officer, Kilembe Mines Ltd., 1963; Welfare Officer, B.A.T. (U) Ltd., Jinja, 1964; Personnel Officer, Uganda Garment Industries, 1966; College Warden & Games Tutor, Uganda College of Commerce, 1966-69; Librarian, Aga Khan S.S. School, Kampala, 1970—. Memberships: former Secretary, Uganda Football Referees' Association; Assistant Secretary, Uganda Football Association; Uganda Amateur Athletics Association; Uganda O. A.; Kilembe Miners' Golf Club; Jinja Golf Club; Uganda Golf Club; F.I.F.A. International Referee; All Saints' Church Council, Kampala. Honours, Prizes, etc.: Cup Finals Football Referee Medal; F.I.F.A. Referees' Badge; Benson & Hedges Golf Trophy, Kampala, 1967. Runner-up, CALTEX Open Golf Trophy, Masaka, 1968; Winner, Mountain of the Moon 'B' Golf Trophy, 1970; Runner-up, Bungoro Golf Open Trophy, 1970. Address: Box 16003, Kampala, Uganda.

NKEUNA, Silas, born Bana, 15th March 1926. Business Executive. Education: C.E.P., Protestant School, Ndoungue, 1948. Married, 3 wives, 9 children. Appointments: Assistant Monitor, 1948-49; Commercial employee, 1950-60; Businessman, 1958—. Address: B.P. 206, Nkongsamba, Cameroun.

NKOANE, Johnson Othusitse Moadira, born Moshupa, 1st March, 1907. Teacher; Cattle Rancher; Member of Parliament. Education: Teachers' Course, Tiger Kloof; Secondary, Healdtown; Certificates in Arithmetic & Business Methods, Bennett College, Sheffield. Widower, 1 son, 5 daughters. Appointments: Clerk, Lourenço Marques, 1932-36; Teacher, Maun, Botswana, 1937-40; ibid, Thamaga, 1941-52; Tribal Secretary, Bakwena Administration & Member of Delegation to East Africa to study Local Government, 1952-55; Head, Changate Primary School & Thamaga School, 1956-61; Cattle Marketing Officer, Kweneng District, 1962-64; School Committee Secretary, ibid, 1964; elected to Parliament & served on 2 Parliamentary Committees, 1965; re-elected, 1969; attended African Region Conference, Lusaka, Zambia, 1969; Member, Livestock Industry Advisory Committee, House Committee, Finance Committee, & Commonwealth Parliamentary Association Committee. Memberships: Commonwealth Parliamentary Association; Botswana Red Cross. Address: P.O. Thamaga, via Gaborone, Botswana.

NKOLOMA, Matthew, born Lusaka, 1st May 1933. Trade Unionist and Politician. Studied Law at University. Married with children. Appointments: Civil Servant; General Secretary & Founder Member, Mineworkers' Union of Zambia; General Secretary, N. Rhodesia Trades Union Congress (now Zambia Congress of Trade Unions); Company Personnel & Industrial Relations Manager; Assistant Minister of State, Republic of Zambia; Member of Parliament; First District Governor, Luanshya; currently Governor, Office of the President, Freedom House. Member of the United National

Independence Party. Address: P.O. Box 208, Lusaka, Zambia.

NKULENU-OCLOO, Esther, see OCLOO, Esther Nkulenu-.

NKURRUNA, Livingstone, born 7th March 1938. Administrator. Education: B.A. (Econ.), U.S.A.; Senior Administrative Course, Kenya Institute of Administration; currently studying for LL.B. (External Student, London University) Personal details: father former Teacher, later a Farmer, nr. Nairobi; married 2 sons. Appointments: District Officer & Magistrate, Kenya Government; Ag. District Commissioner, ibid; Secretary, E.A. Community Service Commission; Administrator, E.A. Community, Arusha. Member of Masai Tribe, Ngong, Kajiado, Kenya (first Masai to get a degree in Economics). Address: P.O. Box 3070, Arusha, Tanzania.

NKWABI, Anicet Simba, born 17th April 1935. Senior Economist. Education: G.C.E. 'A' Level, University College, Nairobi, Kenya; B.A.(Econ.), Howard University, U.S.A.; M.A.(Econ.), Wharton School, University of Pennsylvania. Married, 1 son. Appointments: Junior Planning Officer, Ministry of Economic Affairs & Development Planning, Dar es Salaam, Tanzania, 1963-65; Planning Officer, ibid, 1963-68; Economist Grade I, 1968-69; Senior Economist, 1970; General Manager (T), Eastern Africa National Shipping Line Ltd. Memberships: Economic Society of Tanzania; Tanganyika Red Cross Society. Address: Eastern Africa National Shipping Line Ltd., P.O. Box 3335, Dar es Salaam, Tanzania.

NKWETI, Peter Pizizi, born Bafanji, West Cameroon, about July, 1935. Member of Parliament. Education: Bafanji & Mankon, 1940-45; Standard IV Certificate, Mankon, Santa, & Bafut, 1946-52; Certificate, P.T.C., Batibo, 1953; Teachers' Grade III Certificate, E.T.C., Batibo, 1958-59; Teachers' Grade II Certificate, ibid, 1963-64; 4 'O' Level & 2 'A' Level, G.C.E., 1966-70; Teacher, Grade I, 1970. Married, 5 sons, 2 daughters. Appointments: Teacher, 1954; Headmaster, 1955, 1960, 1961; General Prefect. H.E.T.C., Batibo, 1964; Headmaster, Presbyterian School, Bafanji, 1965-67; elected to Regional House of Assembly, West Cameroon, 1968–; Secretary, Bureau of Social Affairs Committee. Memberships: Presbyterian Church, West Cameroon, 1940–; District Chairman, ibid, 1968–. Address: Bafanji Village, Ndop Sub Division, Mezam Division, West Cameroon.

NNAGGENDA, Francis Xavier, born Bukumi, Uganda, 21st May 1936. Sculptor; Painter; Teacher. Education: Namungona Secondary School, Kampala, Uganda; General Certificate in Art & Design, Correspondence Course, Ecole de Dessins de Paris, France; offered Scholarship, Associate, University of Freiburg, Switzerland, 1963; Academy of Fine Art, Munich, West Germany, 1964; Diploma, Mastership in Sculpture with highest Distinction, 1967. Appointments: Art Master, Mutolere Secondary School, Uganda; Art Master Kitante Secondary School, Kampala, 1968; Tutorial Fellowship, University College, Nairobi, Kenya, 1968-69. Exhibitions: State Museum, Munich, West Germany, 1965; City Hall, Nairobi, 1968; Kisumu Art Festival, 1968; Solo Exhibitions: Nommo Gallery, Kampala, Uganda, 1967; Willoughby Hall, University College, Nairobi, 1969; USIS Auditorium, Nairobi, 1970. Publications: African Arts, Vol. III, No. 1, 1969; Welt der Frau, 1966; USIS News in Review; many articles in local newspapers in Germany, Kenya, & Uganda. Honours: 1st Prize, best imaginative sculptural task, 1967; Dip. Meister Bild houer, Munich. Address: P.O. Box 30197, Nairobi, Kenya.

NOEL, Ernest Louis René, born 16th April 1924. Engineer. Education: Lycée Galliénie, Tananarive, Madagascar; College of Agriculture, Mauritius; Royal College of Science & Technology, University of Strathclyde, Glasgow, U.K.; B.Sc.(Hons.) in Mechanical Engrng. Appointments: Sugar Chemist, Terracine Sugar Factory, Mauritius; Technical Adviser, Mon Désert Sugar Factory, Mauritius; Technical Manager, Sté. Sucriere de la Maharay, Madagascar; Factory Manager, St. Antoine Sugar Factory, Mauritius; Manager, St. Antoine Sugar Estate, ibid. Fellow of Institution of Mechanical Engineers. Memberships: Chartered Engineers; British Institution of Management; Societé de Technologie Agricole & Sucriere, Mauritius; Vice-President, Mauritius Chamber of Agriculture. Honours: Honours Diploma & Laureateship, Mtius College of Agriculture, 1944; Associateship in Mech. Engineering, Royal College of Science & Technology, 1949. Address: Compagnie Sucriere de St. Antoine Stee., Goodlands, Mauritius.

NOFAL, Sayed, born 16th March 1910. International Civil Servant. Education: B.A., M.A., Ph.D., University of Cairo, U.A.R. Married. Appointments: Head, Literary Section, Al Siyassa Newspaper, 1935-38; Teacher, Cairo University, 1938; Director of Technical Secr., Ministry of Education & Ministry of Social Affairs, 1939-45; Director, Legislative Dept., Egyptian Senate, 1945; Secretary-General, Draft Constitution Committee, 1952; Director, Political Department, League of Arab States, 1954; Assistant Secretary-General, ibid, 1960. Member, Gezirah Sporting Club. Publications: History of Arabic Rhetoric, 1942; Poetry of Nature in Arabic & Western Literature, 1944; Egypt in the United Nations, 1947; The Egyptian Constitution in a Quarter of a Century, 1951; The Political Status of the Emirates of the Arab Gulf and Southern Arabia, 1959; Arab Policy in Confrontation with Zionism, 1961; Ben Gurion's Version of History, 1962; Arab Action, 1967; The Arab Gulf, 1969. Honours: Prize of Excellence in Higher Studies, Egypt, 1944; Arabic Literature Award, Acad. of Arabic Languages, Cairo, 1946; Syrian Medal of Merit, 1st Degree, 1956. Address: Assistant Secretary-General, League of Arab States, Cairo, U.A.R.

NORMAN, David Wallace, born 5th January 1939. Agricultural Economist. Education: B.Sc.(London); N.D.A.; M.S., Ph.D., Oregon State University, U.S.A. Married, 2 children. Appointments: Head, Rural Economy Research Unit, & Acting Head, Agricultural Economics

Department, Ahmadu Bello University, Zaria, Nigeria. Memberships: AFEA; Nigerian Economic Society; Nigerian Agricultural Society. Contributor of articles & papers to Station Bull., Ore. State Univ.; Jrnl. of Farm Econs.; Bull. of Rural Econs. & Sociol.; Samaru Miscellaneous Papers; Samaru Agricultural Newsletter; Proc. of Agric. Soc. of Nigeria; Nigerian Jrnl. of Econ. & Soc. Studies; Rural Africana; Proc. of Conf. on Livestock Development in the Dry & Intermediate Savanna Zones, etc. Address: Ahmado Bello University, PMB 1044, Zaria, Nigeria.

NORMAN-WILLIAMS (Chief) Charles Modupe, born Lagos, Nigeria, 4th June 1911. Medical Practitioner & Administrator. Education: C.M.S. Grammar School, Lagos; King's College, Lagos & Edinburgh University, U.K., M.B., Ch.B., 1938; D.P.H.(England), 1952. Appointments: Chief Medical Adviser to the Federal Government of Nigeria, 1959-61; Director of Health Services, WHO African Region, 1961-65; Chairman, Lagos State Public Service Commission, 1968—. Memberships: Chairman, Yoruba Tennis Club, Lagos; 1st Vice-Chairman, '400' Club, Lagos. Metropolitan Club, Lagos; Island Club; Lagos Dining CLub; Ex-Chairman, Lagos Race Club; Lions Club of Lagos; Trustee, Lagos Lawn Tennis Club; Parochial Nominee, St. Paul's Church, Breadfruit, Lagos. Honours: Chief Lukotun of Lagos. Address: 14 Maitama Sule Street, P.O. Box 34, Lagos, Nigeria.

NORNYIBE, Anumu Geoffrey, born Ehi-Wheta, 2nd March 1916. Trader. Education: Agbozume A.M.E. Zion Mission School, Personal details: served as Head of Nornyibe's family. Became Regent of the Paramount Stool of Wheta Traditional Area for Torgbi Ashiakpor IV. Married, 8 children. Charman of Local Council, Wheta, 1952-66. Address: P.O. Box 57, Keta, Ghana.

NORTON, Eddy, born 8th November 1925. Assistant Secretary. Education: Cambridge School Certificate (Grade I), 1943; Alliance Française, 1st Division, 1941; Course on Industrial Relations, British Trades Union Congress, 1953. Appointments: Clerical Officer, Civil Service, 1946-50; Executive Officer, ibid, 1950-59; Senior Executive Officer, 1959-61; Assistant Secretary, Ministry of Works, 1961-70; represented Mauritius Civil Servants, International Conference of Civil Servants, Stuttgart, Germany, 1961. Memberships: General Secretary, Government Servants' Association, Mauritius, 1948-59; Secretary, Federation of Civil Service Unions, 1953-61; Adviser, Mauritius Labour Congress, 1968-70. Honours: Silver Medal, League d'Union Latine, 1941; Gold badge, Alliance Française, 1941; Silver Medal, Runner-up, National Weightlifting Competition, 1948; Gold Badge, Government Servants' Association, 1959; Silver Shield, Federation of Civil Service Unions, 1961; Gold Badge, Mauritius Labour Congress, 1970. Address: Ministry of Works, Mauritius.

NOSSEIR, Sami, born 15th August 1925. Research Chemist. Education: B.Sc.(Chem. & Geol.), Cairo University, U.A.R., 1949. Married, 2 daughters, 1 son. Appointments: Assistant Chemist, George Wimpey & Co., 1949-51; Chemist, Chemistry Administration, Min. of Industries, Cairo, 1951-55; Head of Laboratories, Egyptian Iron & Steel Company, 1955-67; Chief Research Officer, Mineral Resources Division, Tanzania, 1967—. Memberships: Syndicate for Scientific Professions in Egypt; Heliolido Club, Heliopolis, Cairo. Address: Mineral Resources Division, Ministry of Commerce & Industries, P.O. Box 903, Dodoma, Tanzania.

NOWACKI, Wlodzimierz Wojciech, born 25th November 1933. Physician. Education: High School Wladyslaw IV The King, Warsaw, Poland, 1951; Diploma in Medicine, Academy of Medicine, Warsaw, 1957. Personal details: married to Anna Nowacki, 2 children. Appointments: A.H.P., III Medical War, Medical Academy, Warsaw; Medical Director, Cooperative Health Centre, Wilga-Warsaw; Senior Medical Officer in Charge of Bechemman Hospital, Bechem, Ghana, 1966—. Memberships: Swimming Pool Club, Sunyani; Automobile Club, Warsaw; Regional Health Planning Committee, Brong Ahafo Region, Ghana. Address: P.O. Box 29, Bechem, Brong, Ahafo, Ghana.

NOYOO, Hastings Ndangwa, born 30th May 1930. Medical Assistant; Politician; Trader. Married, 1 daughter. Appointments: Barotse National Councillor, 1963; Deputy Ngambela Basobe, 1964; Ngambela Basobeland, 1964-66; Member of Parliament (ANC), 1968—. Memberships: U.N.I.P., 1961; resigned, 1966; Vice-Divisional-President, Basobi, 1961-63. Address: Litoya Trading Store, P.O. Box 36, Namushakendi, Zambia.

NQUKU, John June, born Pietermaritzburg, Natal, South Africa, 23rd June 1899. Teacher; Politician; Journalist; Historian. Education: Teachers' Diploma, St. Chad's College, Natal, South Africa, 1919. Married. Appointments: Principal, Siyamu Government School & Impolweni Government School, 1920-30; first African Inspector of African Schools, Swaziland, 1930-40; Superintendent, Tribal Schools, 1934; Founder & Editor, Izwi Lama Swazi, 1934; Founder & Chairman, Msunduza Township Standholders' Association, 1935; appointed Adviser by Swazi King, 1940; Member, Executive, Swazi National Council; Minister of Education & Churches; Finance Committee Member, Swazi National Administration; Member, Board of Governors, Swazi National Schools; 1st man to run a taxi service in Swaziland; Founder & General Secretary, United Christian Church of Africa, 1944—; elected President, Swaziland' Progessive Association, 1945, which became Swaziland Progressive Party, 1966—; Founder & Chairman, African Development Society, Mbabane, 1946; Founder & Superintendent, Msunduza Nursery School, Mbabane, 1953; 1st African to open independent office of his own in Mbabane, 1955; Founder & Editor, Ungwane (The Swazilander), 1955; Founder, The Swaziland Freedom Star, 1961; Chairman, Pan African Solidarity Conference of Basutoland, Bechuanaland, & Swaziland; Member, Advisory Board, Town of Mbabane;

Leader of Delegations to many international conferences, & 5 times leader of SPP delegation to the U.N., New York. Memberships: President, Swaziland African Football Association, 1948; Founder, Joint Council Movement, Swaziland, 1949; Founder, National Council of Swazi Women, 1952. Publications: The Geography of Swaziland, 1936; Amaqhawe ka Ngwane—Swazi Heroes, 1939; Bayethe (Biography of H.M. King Sobhuza II), 1947. Honours: Independence Medal, Swaziland, 1970. Address: P.O. Box 46, Mbabane, Swaziland.

NSIBAMBI, Apolo Robin, born 27th November 1938. Warden & Part-time Lecturer, in Political Science. Education: Njejje Junior Secondary School, King's College, Budo; Makerere University College, Uganda; University of Chicago, U.S.A.; B.Sc.(Hons.), Economics, London, 1964; M.A., Pol. Science, Chicago, 1966. Married. Appointments: Establishment Officer, Former Kabaka's Government, 1964; Lecturer, Centre for Continuing Education, Makerere University College, 1966-68; Warden, New Hall, ibid, & Part-time Lecturer, Department of Political Science, 1968—. Memberships: Secretary, Uganda Branch, East African Academy, 1967-68; Committee Member, ibid, 1968—; Committee, Buloba Board of Governors, 1968—; Chairman, Warden's Meeting, Makerere University; Committee Member, Uganda Social Science Research Committee, Uganda National Research Council; former Chairman, Makerere University College Tender Board. Pulications include: The Rise & Fall of Federalism in Uganda, East African Journal, 1966; The Rhodesian Question, The African Journal, 1966; Some Observations on J. M. Lee's Article, Journal of Commonwealth Political Studies, 1966; Some Problems of Political Integration in Uganda, East Africa Journal, 1969; Increased Central Government's Control of Buganda's Financial Sinews, Journal of Administration Overseas; Some Problems of Linguistic Communication in Uganda, presented to East African Academy Conference, 1969. Address: Makerere University, Kampala, P.O. Box 7062, Uganda.

NSONGAN, Gabriel, born 24th December 1932. Merchant. Primary Schooling, Presbyterian Mission of Kanga, District of Eseka, Department of Nyong & Kele, 1939-45; Catholic Mission of Ngovayane District, 1946-69. Married. Appointments: Skopkeeper, Yaoundé, Cameroun; then Special Trader, 1962—. Memberships: Representative, Chamber of Commerce & Industry, 1967; elected President, Cooperative Section. Honours: Decorated with the Order of Cameroun Merit 3rd Class, 1968. Address: Eseka B.P. 45, Cameroun.

NSUBUGA, Emmanuel Kiwanuka, born 11th February 1914. Archbishop of Kampala. Education: Bukalasa Minor Seminary, 1930-37; Katigondo Major Seminary, 1937-46. Appointments: Parish Priest, Kkonge Parish, 1958; Vicar-General, Rubaga Archdiocese, 1961; Vicar-Capitular, ibid, 1966; Archbishop, Kampala Archdiocese, 1966. Member, Pontificia Academia Mariana Internazionale. Publications: Etabagana n'Abakristu (Ecumenism). Honours: Domestic Prelate, 1962. Address: Archbishop's House, Rubaga, P.O. Box 14125, Mengo, Kampala, Uganda.

NTAMBU, J. Chinenga, born 21st September 1927. District Governor Mufulira; Assistant to Minister of State, Central Province. Education: Chitokoloki Mission, 1944-48; Oxford University Institute of Public Administration, 1963; trained as Agriculturist, Senga Hill Agricultural School & Monze Agricultural School. Personal details: sons of late Chief Ntambu & Nyamanjombo Kamonji Ntambu; married, 3 children. Appointments: w. Kambowa Agricultural Station, Ndola; Provincial President, ANC, North-Western Province, 1958-59; Joined UNIP, 1960; Deputy Divisional Secretary, Central Province, 1960; Deputy Divisional President, UNIP, 1960-62; Administrative Secretary, Regional Secretary, 1963-66; Political Assistant, 1966. Member of Wildlife Organization of Zambia. Address: Office of Minister of State, P.O. Box 691, Mufulira, Nigeria.

NTENDE, Elizaphan Kalange Kawanguz, born 30th August 1931. Company Director. Education: Busoga College, Mwiki, 1939-50; B.A.(London), Makerere University College, 1955. Married. Appointments: Cadet Labour Officer, Uganda Government, 1955; Executive, Shell Oil Company, 1965-63; Deputy Chairman, Uganda Lint Marketing Board, 1963; Chairman, ibid, 1963-67; in Private Business; Member of East African Legislative Assembly, 1968—. Memberships: Uganda Gut Export Promotion Council, 1969—; President, Kampala Rotary Club, 1969-70; President, African Cricket Club, 1968—. Article 'Uganda Cottons' published in the International Cotton Year Book, 1966. Address: P.O. Box 4196, Kampala, Uganda.

NTIMBA, John, born 19th February 1936. Diplomat. Education: St. Led's College, Fort Portal, Uganda, 1953-55; Engineering School, Nakawa, Kampala, 1956-57; B.Sc.(Hons.), Geography, Gauhate University, Assam, India, 1958-61; M.A., Geography, Indiana University, U.S.A., 1963. Married. Appointments: Teacher, Ntare Secondary School, Mbarara, Uganda, 1961; Graduate Teaching Assistant, Indiana University, U.S.A., 1962-63; Teacher, St. Mary's College, Kisubi, Uganda, 1963-64; Assistant Secretary, Ministry of Foreign Affairs, 1964; 3rd Secretary, Uganda High Commission, New Delhi, India, 1964-67; 2nd Secretary, ibid, London, U.K., 1968; 1st Secretary & Head of Chancery, ibid, 1969-70; Principal Assistant Secretary (Administration & Inspectorate), Ministry of Foreign Affairs, Uganda, 1970—. Recipient, Athletics Cups & Trophies, Gauhati University, 1959. Address: High Commission for the Republic of Uganda, Uganda House, Trafalgar Sq., London, W.C.2, U.K.

NTOGOLO, Faustin, born 15th February 1937. Sociologist. Education: Diploma, l'Ecole Pratique des Hauts Etudes; Economic & Social Sciences, the Sorbonne, Paris, France; Diploma, Co-operative College of Paris. Memberships: former Standing Member, J.O.C. Internationale; Federation for Interafrican Development; Anti-Hunger Society. Publications: L'homme et l'okaume; Les religions Anciens de l'Afrique. Address: Commissariat au Plan, B.P. 172 Libreville, Gabon.

NUHU, Shuaibu Ibrahim, born 1933. Pharmacist. Education: Lafia Elementary School, 1940-46; Benue Middle School, Katsina Ala, 1946-51; School of Pharmacy, Zaria, 1951-54; School of Pharmacy, Yaba, 1958-59. Married, 5 sons, 5 daughters. Appointments: Government Pharmacist, 1954-59; Pharmacist, Kano Branch, Majorand Co., 1959-67; Managing Director, United Arewa Chemist, 1967—. Memberships: Pharmaceutical Society; Chairman, North Zonal Branch, ibid; Pharmacists Board of Nigeria; First Chairman, Nasara Club; Le Circle Club. Address: c/o United Arewa Chemists Ltd., P.O. Box 1106, Kano, Nigeria.

NUKUNYA, Godwin Kwaku, born 26th June 1935. University Lecturer; Anthropologist. Education: B.A.(Hons.), Sociology, London, University of Ghana, 1961; Ph.D., London School of Economics, London, U.K., 1964. Married, 4 sons. Appointments: Lecturer, Department of Sociology, University of Ghana, Legon, 1964-67; Visiting Assistant Professor, Department of Anthropology, Michigan State University, East Lansing, Mich., U.S.A., 1967-68; Lecturer, Department of Sociology, Legon, Ghana, 1968—. Memberships: Association of Social Anthropologists of the Commonwealth; Ghana Sociological Association. Publications: Kinship & Marriage among the Auto Ewe, Monographs on Social Anthropology, London School of Economics, 1969; Afa Divination in Anlo: a preliminary report in 'Research Review', Institute of African Studies, Legon, 1969; The Yewe Cult among the Southern Ewe Speaking People of Ghana, Ghana Journal of Sociology, 1969. Address: Department of Sociology, University of Ghana, Legon, Ghana.

NUNOO, John Edward Okoe, born 8th May 1917. Retired Commissioner of Ghana Police Service. Education: St. John's School, Nsawam, Ghana, 1928-36; Metropolitan Police Training School, Hendon, U.K., 1955; Senior Police Officers' Course, Police College, Bramshill House, Hants. Personal details: Scion of the Royal Stool Houses of Abola, Kpatashi & James Town, Accra. Married, 8 children. Appointments: seconded to Tanganyika Police Force as Adviser, 1962-63; Member, National Liberation Council, 1966-69; N.L.C. Member responsible for the Ministries of Agriculture & Forestry, 1966-67; Commissioner of Police, 1966—. Honours: Knight Great Band of the Liberian Humane Order of African Redemption, 1968; Long Service and Efficiency Medal, 1968; Distinguished Service Order, 1968. Address: P.O. 5452, Accra-North, Ghana.

NURSEY-BRAY, Paul Frederick, born 6th December 1940. University Lecturer. Education: B.A.(Hons.), University of Bristol, U.K., 1954-62; M.A., ibid, 1963-65. Married, 1 son, 2 daughters. Appointments: Lecturer, University College of Rhodesia & Nyasaland, 1965-67; Lecturer, Makerere University, Uganda, 1967—. Memberships: Kampala Rugby Club; Chairman, Theatre Group. Author of various papers in field.

Address: Department of Political Science, Makerere University, P.O. Box 7062, Kampala, Uganda.

NUTAN, Ved Parkash, born 14th August 1939. Economist; Statistician. Education: Old Kampala Secondary School; Higher School Certificate, 1963; B.A.(Hons.), Economics, University College, Dar es Salaam, Tanzania, 1967; currently studying for M.Sc. in International Economics, University of Surrey, 1970. Personal details: family live mainly in India. Appointments: Statistician, Ministry of Planning & Economic Development, 1967-70; Senior Research Officer, Economics & Statistics, 1970—. Research Work in problems of balance of payments & statistics of Uganda. Honours & Awards: 1st Prize, debating competition, 1957. Address: Research Dept., Bank of Uganda, Box 7120, Kampala, Uganda.

NWAKAMA OTTIH, P. N., born Aro, Awa Oguta, Eastern Nigeria, 1926. Businessman & Company Director. Education: Primary School, Std. 6, 1940; Secondary School, Class 4, 1943; Business Administration. Personal details: father, late Chief Ottih of Awa, Oguta; married, 2 wives, Grace Ottih & Victoria Ottih, 11 children. Appointments: arrived Victoria, West Cameroon for trading, 1946; Managing Director, Ottih Bros., Victoria, West Cameroon. Memberships: Victoria Club; Victoria S.S. Club. Address: 21 Burnley Street, P.O. Box 38, Victoria, West Cameroon.

NWANKITI (The Right Rev.) Benjamin Chukwuemeka, Second Bishop of Owerri, born 25th April 1928. Education: Denis Memorial Grammar School, 1942-46; B.A.(Hons.), Durham University; Melville Hall Theological College, Ibadan, Nigeria. Appointments: Deacon, 1951; Priest, 1952; Chaplain, All Saints' Cathedral, Onitsha, 1953-55; consecrated Bishop, 1958; Senior Curate, St. Gabriel's, Sunderland, U.K., 1958-59; Vicar, St. Bartholomew's Church, Enugu, 1960-61; in charge of Christian Religious Broadcasting, Eastern Nigeria, 1962-68. Publications: A Short History of the Christian Church. Address: Bishop's House, Egbu, P.O. Box 31, Owerri, Nigeria.

NYAGA, Richard Stanley, born 28th November 1941. Lawyer. Education: Cambridge Higher School Certificate, Strathmore College, Nairobi, Kenya; LL.B.(Hons.), University College, Dar es Salaam, Tanzania; Postgraduate Diploma in Air & Space Law, McGill University, Montreal, Canada. Appointments: State Counsel, Attorney General's Office, Kenya, 1966-67; Assistant Secretary, East African Community, 1967-68; Chief Licencing Officer, Secretary, East African Civil Aviation Board, 1968—; Registrar, C.A.B. Appeals Tribunal. Memberships: Diners Club, Africa Ltd.; International Law Association, Kenya; Gymkana Club, Arusha. Publications: acted as Member & Secretary in production of following reports: Domestic Air Fares & Rates in East Africa, 1970; East African Policy on International Air Charters, 1970. Address: East African Community, P.O. Box 1002, Arusha, Tanzania.

NYAHUNZVI, Timothy Mutero, born Mrewa, Rhodesia, 18th February 1939. Journalist. Education: University Junior Certificate; University of South Africa; at Dadaya Mission, Rhodesia, 1956; Diploma, International Press Institute, Nairobi, Kenya, 1963-64. Married, 1 daughter. Appointments include: Despatch Clerk, Salisbury, Rhodesia, 1957; Typist-Clerk, American Baptist Missionaires, Salisbury, 1958-59; Cub Reporter, African Daily News (since banned), 1959; Reporter, African Mail (predecessor to now government-owned Zambia Mail), Lusaka, Zambia, 1961; News Editor, Zambia Mail, 1964; Lecturer, IPI, Nairobi, 1965; Senior Reporter, Zambia Mail, 1966; Free-lance Correspondent, UPI, 1962—; News Editor, Zambia Mail, 1968-69; Features/Foreign Editor, ibid, 1969; Journalism Lecturer, Communication Department, Evelyn Hone College of Further Education, Lusaka, 1969—. Committee, Lusaka Press Club; Automobile Association, Zambia; Life Member, Lusaka Theatre Club; National Road Safety Council; Cinema Petit. Address: c/o Evelyn Hone College, P.O. Box 29, Lusaka, Zambia.

NYAMWEYA, James, born Kisii, Kenya, 28th December 1927. Politician; Lawyer. Education: Bachelor-of-Law, Honours Degree, King's College, University of London, U.K., 1954-58; Barrister-at-Law, Lincolns Inn, London, 1954-58. Married, 3 sons, 4 daughters. Appointments include: Legal Assistant, Office of the Attorney-General, 1958-59; Advocate, Supreme Court of Kenya, 1959-63; elected to Parliament for Nyaribari Constituency, 1963; Founder Member, & Member of National Executive, KANU, 1960-67; Parlimamentary Secretary, Ministry of Justice & Constitutional Affairs, 1963; Parliamentary Secretary to the Prime Minister Mzee Jomo Kenyatta, 1964; Minister of State, responsible for Provincial Administration, & Leader, Government Business, National Assembly of Kenya, 1965; Minister of State, responsible for Foreign Affairs, & Leader, Government Business, National Assembly of Kenya, 1967; Minister of Power & Communications 1968-69; Minister for Works, 1970—. Honours include: Hon. Doctor of Law Degree, U.S.A., 1967; Elder of the Golden Heart, conferred by the President, Mzee Jomo Kenyatta. Address: Ministry of Works P.O. Box 30260, Nairobi, Kenya.

NYA NGATCHOU, Jean, born 12th September 1939. Agricultural Engineer; Research Scientist. Education: L. es Sc., ORSTOM, Diploma, Paris, France. Married, 1 child. Appointments: Geneticist, French Coffee & Cocoa Institute, 1965-69; Director, Human Resources & Scientific Research, Ministry of Planning & Development, Yaoundé, Cameroun. Memberships: I.T.T.A., Ibadan, Nigeria. Author of several scientific papers. Address: B.P. 501, Yaoundé, Cameroun.

NYASUNU, Alfred Kwao, born Grand-Popo, Dahomey, 16th September 1912. Secretary to Bishop of Accra, Ghana. Education: Accra Wesleyan Schl., Ghana. Married, 9 children. Appointments include: with Lands Dept., 1931; Paymaster, 1936-39; Sec. to Gen. Mgr. & Supvsr. of R.C. Educational Unit; Actg. Gen. Mgr. of Schls., Central Western Regions, 1947; Exec., Officer of Gen. Mgr., R.C. Educ. Unit, Greater Accra & Eastern Ghana, 1956; Fndn. Mbr., All-Ewe Conference; Free-lance Journalist, Editorial Advisory Bd., The Standard (Nat. Catholic Weekly), 1950-54; Sec. to Bishop of Accra, 1964—. Memberships include: Fndr. & Pres., Adabraka Catholic Social & Drama Soc., 1933-49; Comm. Pres., Legion of Mary, Accra & Cape Coast; Exec., Cape Coast Neighbourhood Ctr. Assoc.; Sec., St. Joseph's Ctr. Assoc., Accra; ibid, Ghana Nat. Catholic Independence Celebration Comm., 1957; Sec., Cape Coast Catholic Social Club & Catholic Young Men's Soc.; Nat. Pres., Ghana Educ. Non-Teaching Staff Union, Trades Union Congress, 1954-64; Bd. of Gvnrs., Aquinas Coll., Accra. Contbr. of articles to The Standard. Address: Bishop's House, Catholic Mission, P.O. Box 247, Accra, Ghana.

NYERERE (Mwalimu) Julius Kambarage, President of Tanzania, born Butiama, Lake Victoria, March 1922. Education: Tabora Secondary School; Makerere University College, Uganda, 1942-45; M.A., Edinburgh University, U.K., 1949-52. Appointments: Teacher, Tanganyika, 1952; President, Tanganyika Africa Association, 1953; Founder, Tanganyika African National Union (TANU), 1954; Member, Legislative Council, 1957; Member, Dar es Salaam, 1960; Chief Minister, 1960; Prime Minister, 1961-62; President of the Republic of Tanganyika, 1962-64; President, United Republic of Tanzania, 1964—. Memberships: Fellow, Makerere University College; ibid, University College, Dar es Salaam. Honours: Recipient of Honorary LL.D., Duquesne University, U.S.A.; ibid, University of Edinburgh, U.K. Address: The State House, Dar es Salaam, Tanzania.

NYIMBAE, Joseph Pius, born 12th April 1936. Planning Manager. Education: Nyanza, Kenya, 1946-52, 1953-55; Trainee Manager, Bata Shoe Organization, 1955. Personal details: married, 7 children. Appointments: Manager, Bata Shoe Organization, Entebbe, Tororo & Jinja, Uganda, 1957-59; Sales Manager, ibid, Uganda, 1960-69; Planning Manager, Kenya & East Africa, 1970—. Attended several commercial courses in management & marketing, in U.K., Belgium, France, Holland, Germany, U.S.A., & Canada. Memberships: British Institute of Management; Graduate of American Management Association. Address: P.O. Box 23, Limuru, Kenya.

NYIRENBA (The Hon.) Wesley Pillsbury, born 23rd January 1924. Minister of Education. Education: B.A., History of English; Cand. B.Sc.(Econ.), London, U.K.; Postgraduate Certificate in Education (P.G.C.E.), London. Personal details: father, Teacher (deceased), mother, Teacher (retired). Appointments: Headmaster, Kitwe Main School, 1953; Principal, Ndola Secondary School, 1957; Principal, Monze Secondary School, 1961-62; Education Officer, 1962; Member of Parliament, 1962; Deputy Speaker, 1964; Speaker, 1964-68; Minister of Education, 1968—. Memberships: Vice-President, Commonwealth Parliamentary Association, Zambia Branch; President, ibid,

1964-68; Regional Representative, C.P.A. Africa Region; President, Zambia Olympic, Commonwealth & All-Africa Games Association; President, National Sports Foundation of Zambia; Historical Association; Chairman, Commission on Customary Law, Zambia; Patron, Hockey Association of Zambia. Address: Box RW 93, Ridgeway, Lusaka, Zambia.

NZARO, Esau, born 28th August 1934. Medical Practitioner. Education: Mbarara High School; Nyakasura Government School; M.B., Ch.B., Makerere University College, Uganda, 1960; D.C.P., The Royal Postgraduate Medical School, U.K., 1965; M.R.C.P., London, 1968. Appointments: Resident House Officer, 1961-62; Senior House Officer, 1962-64; Medical Officer, Special Grade, 1968-69; Consultant Clinical Pathologist, Uganda, 1969; Hon. Consultant Haematologist, Mengo Missionary Hospital, Uganda, 1970; Hon. Lecturer in Medicine & Pathology, Makerere Medical School, Uganda. Memberships: British Medical Association; Uganda Medical Association; East African Physicians' Association; Drivers' Club. Address: P.O. Box 7051, Kampala, Uganda.

NZEMBOTE, Jean-Marie, born 5th July 1939. Journalist. Education: Primary School, Makokou, Gabon; Bacc., College-Bessieux, Libreville, 1956-62; Diploma of Journalism, University of Dakar, Senegal; Diploma of Journalism, University of Strasbourg, France. Married, 4 children. Appointments: Secretary-General, Young Christian Students, Gabon, 1961-62; President, Council of Youth, Gabon, 1962; Delegate of the Youth of Gabon to the 4th World Assembly of Youth, Denmark; Attache to the Cabinet of the Ministry of National Economy, Gabon, 1966-67; Director of Cabinet, Ministry of Work, Gabon, 1967-70; currently, Permanent Administrative Secretary, Democratic Party of Gabon. Address: B.P. 268, Libreville, Gabon.

NZE-MINKANG, born 29th December 1937. Inspector of Imports; Head of Estate Returns & Registration. Education: Secondary Studies; Capacitaire en Droit. Married, 1 child. Appointments: Controller of Returns; Principal, Libreville, 1961; Inspector of Returns, 1965—. Address: Estates & Registrations, B.P. 592, Fort Gentil, Gabon.

O

OBASI, Godwin Olu Patrick, born 24th December 1935. Meteorologist; University Lecturer. Education: Government College, Zaria, Nigeria, 1950-53; Nigerian College of Technology, Zaria, 1954-56; B.Sc.(Hons.), Maths. & Physics, McGill University, Montreal, Canada, 1957-59; M.Sc., D.Sc., Massachusetts Institute of Technology, Cambridge, U.S.A., 1959-63. Personal details: great-grandson of Aiyekomeji Baba Okuta, the great Ogorian warrior; fourth generation of Obasi, the Otaro of Okesi. Appointments: various scientific, technical, professional, & administrative posts, Nigerian Meteorological Service, 1963-67; World Meteorological Organization Expert & Senior Lecturer, University of Nairobi, Kenya, 1967—. Memberships: International Commission in Dynamic Meteorology; Associate, Scientific Council for Africa; ibid, Sigma Xi; Fellow, Royal Meteorological Society; American Meteorological Society. Author of several publications in scientific journals. Recipient, Carl Rossby Award for best doctoral thesis, MIT, 1963. Address: Department of Meteorology, University of Nairobi, Nairobi, Kenya.

OBEL-OMIA, Charles C., born 17th March 1937. Lecturer in Administrative Practice. Education: B.A., Pol. Sci., State University of N.Y., Albany, U.S.A., 1966; M.A., Public Policy & Administration, University of Wisconsin, Madison, 1970. Married, 3 sons, 2 daughters. Appointments: Headmaster, Aloi Junior School, Lagos, Nigeria, 1960-62; Assistant District Commissioner, Teso, 1966-68; Assistant Secretary, Ministry of Labour, 1968; Counterpact Lecturer, Institute of Public Administration, 1968-70; Lecturer in Administrative Practice in Institute of Public Administration, Uganda, 1970—. Memberships: American Society of Public Administration; Uganda Club; Comparative Administration Group.

OBENG, Letitia Eva, born Anum, Ghana, 10th January 1925. Research Scientist. Education: Achimota School, 1939-46; B.Sc. Zoology, University of Birmingham, U.K., 1948-52; M.Sc. Parasitology, ibid, 1961; Ph.D., University of Liverpool, 1964. Widow, 2 sons, 1 daughter. Appointments include: Lecturer in Zoology, University of Science & Technology, Ghana, 1952-59; Research Officer, National Research Council, Ghana, 1959-63; Senior Research Officer, Ghana Academy of Science, 1963-65; Director, Freshwater Biology Research Institute of Aquatic Biology, 1965; Co-Manager, Ghana Government, UMDP Volta Lake Research Project, 1968. Memberships include: Fellow, Ghana Academy of Arts & Sciences, 1965. Publications include: Editor, Man-made Lakes (The Accra Symposium). Address: Institute of Aquatic Biology, Council for Scientific & Industrial Research, P.O. Box 38, Achimota, Ghana.

OBERHOFFER, Magdalene Karoline Elisabeth, born Bonn, Germany, 21st October 1923. Physician. Education: Univs. of Innsbruck (Austria) & Düsseldorf; Medical State Examination, University of Bonn, 1947; M.D., 1948; Studies in Tropical Medicine, London School of Tropical Medicine & Hygiene, London, U.K. Appointments: 1st Resident Doctor, Rubaga Hospital, Kampala, Uganda, 1954; in charge, ibid, 1954-61; Medical Officer, 1968—; International President, International Grail Movement, 1961-67. Memberships: The Grail (International Movement for Christian Women); started Grail Movements in East Africa, 1954, bringing the first Catholic lay missionaries to Uganda. Publications: Goethes Krankengeschichte, 1948. Honours: Rubaga Hospital visited by Pope Paul VI, August 1969; Pro Ecclesia et Pontifice, 1969. Address: Rubaga Hospital, P.O. Box 14130, Kampala, Uganda.

OBHRAI, Dalip Singh, born 18th April 1931. Advocate. Education: LL.M.(London);

Barrister-at-Law. Married, 1 daughter. Appointments: Advocate, Municipal Council of Mombasa, 1959—. Memberships: Past President, Lions Club of Mombasa; Member, Board of Trustees, Kenya Young Women's Christian Association. Address: Municipal Council of Mombasa, P.O. Box 440, Mombasa, Kenya.

OBOTE (His Excellency) Milton Apolo, born Akokoro, Maruzi County, Lango District, Northern Region, Uganda, 28th December 1925. President of Uganda. Education: Boroboro Primary School; Gulu High School; Busoga College, Mwiri; Makerere University College, Kampala, 1948-49. Personal details: son of a Chief; married, 3 children. Appointments: Mowlem Construction Company, Uganda & Kenya; Miwani Sugar Works, Kenya; active in Kenya African Union & Kenya African National Union; returned to Uganda, 1957, joined Uganda National Congress; elected to Legislative Council, representing Langa District, 1958; elected President, Uganda People's Congress (formed by merger of Uganda National Congress with Uganda People's Union), 1960—; Leader of the Opposition, Uganda Parliament, 1961-62; Prime Minister, 1962-66; led Uganda to independence, 1962; Leader, Uganda Revolution, 1966, suspending the Constitution and dismissing Sir Edward Mutesa as President of Uganda; President of Uganda, under the Interim Constitution adopted by Parliament, April 1966; 1st Executive President of Uganda under Republican Constitution adopted by National Assembly, 1967—. Publications: Common Man's Charter, 1969 (adopted by Uganda People's Congress as Uganda's blueprint for socialism). Honours: LL.D., University of Long Island, U.S.A., 1963; LL.D., University of New Delhi, India, 1965; LL.D., University of East Africa, 1969; Honoured by His Holiness the Pope, 1969. Address: State House, Kampala, Uganda.

O'CALLAGHAN, Edmond, born 23rd May 1925. Member of H.M. Overseas Civil Service. Education: Chartered Secretary. Appointments: Civil Servant, 1948—; Assistant Commissioner of Taxes, seconded as Secretary & Head of Administration, Malawi Broadcasting Corporation. Address: P.O. Box 453, Blantyre, Malawi.

OCHERO, Louis, born Dokolo, Sombolola, Lango District, 28th June 1930. Senior Health Education Officer. Education: Dokolo Primary School, 1939-44; Soroti College, 1945-47; Tororo College, 1948-49; School of Hygiene, Mbale, 1950-52; E.A. Malaria Institute, Amani, 1959; School of Hygiene, Mbale, 1961-63; Diploma in Health Education, London University, 1964-65. Personal details: son of Paulo Olipa, brought up by an Uncle, Joseph Okelo, now a retired County Chief. Married, with children. Appointments: Assistant Health Inspector (R.S.H. Certificate); Public Health Inspector (R.S.H. Diploma), for general overseas appointments. Memberships: M.R.S.H.; M.A.P.H.I.(U.K.); M.W.H.I.A.; Lions Club. Publications: 'Tape Worm' (under preparation). Address: Ministry of Health H.Q., P.O. Box 8, Entebbe, Uganda.

OCHSNER, Heinz, born 21 August 1922. Medical Doctor. Education: M.D., University of Basel, Switzerland, 1949; Diploma for Eye Specialist, FMH for Ophthalmology of Switzerland, 1955; D.T.M.&H., London, U.K. Appointments: in Ghana, 1956—; opened Eye Clinic, Agogo, 1957—. Memberships: Ophthalmological Society of Switzerland; Medical Society of Basel. Address: Dufourstrasse 5, CH-4000, Basel, Switzerland.

OCLOO, Esther Nkulenu-, born April 1919. Food Technologist. Education: Achimota College, Accra, Ghana; Long Ashton Research Station, Bristol University, U.K.; Good Housekeeping Institute, London. Married, 3 children. Former Assistant General Secretary, Federation of Ghana Women; Past President, Federation of Ghana Industries; Former Chairman, Ghana National Food & Nutrition Board; Vice-President, Ghana Manufacturers' Association; Managing Director, Nkulenu Industries Ltd., Accra. Memberships: Young Women's Christian Association; Ghana Girl Guide Association; many other women's organizations & clubs in Ghana. Recipient, Grand Medal of the Order of The Volta, Ghana, 1968. Address: Nkulenu Industries Ltd., P.O. Box 36, Medina, Accra, Ghana.

ODDOYE, Joseph Kojo Odotei, born 20th December 1920. Dental Surgeon. Education: Achimota College, Ghana, 1927-41; Edinburgh Dental Hospital & School, Edinburgh, U.K., 1944-49; L.D.S.R.C.S.(Edin.). Married, 2 sons, 1 daughter. Appointments: Clerk, Audit Department, Gold Coast Civil Service (Ghana), 1941-44; Dental Surgeon, Ghana Service, 1949-62; Dental Surgeon, Western Nigerian Civil Service, 1962-64; General Dental Practitioner, U.K., 1964—.

ODEGHE, Paul Tebefia, born 30th March 1926. Medical Practitioner. Education: Medical Education: Royal College of Surgeons, Dublin, Ireland, 1953-59; L.R.C.P.; L.R.C.S.; L.M (Ireland); D.T.P.H.(London). Appointments: Medical Officer, Nigeria, 1960-63; Senior Medical Officer, 1964-66; Specialist Leprologist, 1967—. Memberships: Nigerian Medical Association; International Leprosy Association; Benin Club, Nigeria. Address: Ministry of Health, Ossiomo, via Agbor, Nigeria.

ODEI BANING, Edward, born Afosu, 10th October 1910. District Magistrate. Education: Standard 7, Middle School, 1927; Native Tribunal Registrars' Certificate, Cape Coast, Ghana, 1933; Certificate, Clerical Division, Local Government Examination (London), 1957. Married, 2 wives, 10 children. Appointments: Farmer, 1928-30; Registrar, Paramount Chief's Tribunal (Oda) Akim Kotoku, 1931-42; Senior Registrar, ibid (Nyakrom) Agona, 1943-46; Senior Registrar, Denkyira Confederacy Native Courts (Dunkwa), 1946-52; ibid, Akim Kotoku Native Court (Oda), 1952-59; District Magistrate, 1959—. Memberships: District Magistrates' & Circuit Judges' Association; Odd Fellows Society. Address: District Court, P.O. Box 51, Kade, Ghana.

ODERO, Leo Pius, born 19th April 1930. High Commissioner for India. Education: Primary, Rapogi Catholic School; Intermediate, St. Mary's, Yala; Secondary, Tororo College; B.A. (Hons.), History, Delhi University, India; Certificate in Social Administration, Springfield College, Mass., U.S.A. Married. Appointments: School-teacher, Kenya, until 1959; Community Development Officer, Kenya, 1960-61; District Officer, Kenya, 1961-63; Assistant Secretary, 1963-64; Senior Assistant Secretary, Peking, China, 1964-65; Counsellor, Peking, 1965-66; Counsellor, London, U.K., 1967-68; Chargé d'Affaires, Washington, U.S.A., 1968-69; High Commissioner, India, 1969. Address: Kenya High Commission, 18 Jor Bagh, New Delhi, India.

ODEYEMI, Adetunji Olu Victor, born 6th July 1940. Civil Servant. Education: West African School Certificate. Personal details: parents, Mr. Theophilus Odeyemi & Mrs. Esther Odeyemi; married to E. O. Odeyemi. Appointments: Teacher, 1964; Clerk, 1965-68; Machine Tender, 1968-69; Clerical Work, Civil Service, 1969—. Memberships: President, Choral Society; Secretary, Literary & Debating Society; Asst. Choirmaster, Choir C.A.C., Ibadan, Nigeria. Publications: Recorded Church Music. Address: SW8/1111, Oke-Ado Street, Ibadan, Nigeria.

ODHIAMBO, Thomas Risley, born 4th February 1931. Professor of Entomology; Director, International Centre of Insect Physiology & Ecology, Kenya. Education: Makerere University College, Kampala, Uganda, 1950-53; M.A., Ph.D., Cambridge University, U.K., 1959-65. Married, 5 children. Appointments: Assistant Agricultural Officer, Uganda, 1954-61; Entomologist, Uganda, 1962-65; Lecturer, University College, Nairobi, Kenya, 1965-66; Senior Lecturer in Zoology, Nairobi, 1967; Reader in Zoology, ibid, 1968; Professor of Entomology, University of Nairobi, 1970—; Director, International Centre of Insect Physiology & Ecology, Nairobi; Dean, Faculty of Agriculture, Nairobi University, 1970—. Fellow of Royal Entomological Society, London, U.K. Memberships: Founder-Member, East African Academy; former Secretary-General & Treasurer, ibid; Society for Experimental Biology; Biochemical Society; New York Academy of Sciences. Honours: Merit Award by Uganda Govt., for best performance of its scholars abroad, 1963; Tablet of Honour, Maseno Secondary School, Kenya, 1949. Publications include: numerous articles in scientific journals including: Parental care in bugs & non-social insects, New Scientist; The Crisis of Science in East Africa, E.A. Journal; East Africa: Science for Development, Science, 1967; Influence of age & feeding on the success of mating in a tsetse fly species, Nature; The architecture of the accessory reproductive glands of the male desert locust, III—Components of the muscular wall, Tissue & Cell; The architecture of the accessory reproductive glands of the male desert locust, V—Ultrastructure during maturation, Tissue & Cell; Look at Life series (booklets on science for primary schools in Africa); The Science Companion: a manual of reference material for primary & secondary school science teachers. Address: The International Centre of Insect Physiology & Ecology, P.O. Box 30772, Nairobi, Kenya.

ODIASE, Victor Odigie Naiwu, born 25th March 1935. Surgeon. Education: Baptist School, Agbor, 1940; Government School, Benim, 1944; Edo College, Benim, 1947; M.B., B.S., University College, Ibadan, Nigeria, 1961; F.R.C.S.(Edinburgh, U.K.); F.R.C.S.(England), 1966. Personal details: father, Civil Servant; married, 2 sons, 1 daughter. Appointments: Houseman, University College Hospital, Ibadan, 1961-62; Junior Medical Posts in several U.K. hospitals; Surgical Registrar, Addenbrooke's Hospital, Cambridge, 1956-67; Specialist Surgeon, Mid-West State of Nigeria, 1967—. Fellowships: Royal College of Surgeons, Edinburgh; Royal College of Surgeons, England. Memberships: British Medical Association; Nigerian Medical Association; Warri Club, Nigeria. Awards: Commonwealth Scholar, 1963. Address: General Hospital, Warri, Mid-West State, Nigeria.

ODONGA, Alexander Mwa, born 20th September 1922. Medical Practitioner. Education: Gulu Primary School, 1931-34; Gulu High School, 1935-38; Nobumnli High School, 1939; King's College, Budo, 1940-42; L.M.S.(E.A.) & M.B., Ch.B., Makerere University College, 1943-48; F.R.C.S.(Edinburgh), Royal College of Surgeons, England, 1959-62. Appointments: Assistant Medical Officer, 1949-54; Medical Officer, 1954-61; Medical Officer Special Grade, 1962; Consultant Surgeon, 1962-67; Senior Consultant Surgeon, 1967—. Memberships: Fellow, Association of Surgeons of East Africa; Treasurer, ibid; Treasurer, Uganda Medical Association; President, ibid; University Council, University of East Africa. Address: Mulago Hospital, Box 7051, Kampala, Uganda.

ODONGO, John Chrysostom. Police Officer. Education: Gulu High School, Northern Uganda; Police Course, London, U.K., 1961; Detective Training School, Wakefield, 1962; Senior Police Officers' Course, International Police Academy, 1964; Special Course, International Police Services Academy, Washington, D.C., U.S.A.; Diplomas in Police Administration & Criminal Investigation. Married, 13 children. Appointments: Assistant Station Master, E.A.R.&H., 1946; Constable, Uganda Police Force, 1947; Sub-Inspector, 1956; Inspector, 1961; Assistant Superintendent of Police, 1962; Superintendent, 1963; Senior Superintendent, 1964—. Address: P.O. Box 2976, Kampala, Uganda.

ODONKOR, George Tetteh, born 26th May 1931. University Lecturer; Parliamentarian. Education: B.Sc.(Econ.), London School of Economics & Political Science, U.K., 1962; Postgraduate Diploma in Agricultural Economics, Reading University, 1963; M.Sc., Reading University, 1965. Married, 3 daughters. Appointments: Instructor, Universal College, Somanya; Clerk-Secretary, University College, Gold Coast (Ghana); Research Officer, Agricultural Economist, Cocoa Research Institute of Ghana, Tafo; Lecturer in Economics, University of Ghana, Legon, 1967—; Member of Parliament, 1969—. Memberships: Fellow, Royal

Economic Society; British Agricultural Economics Society; International Agricultural Economics Society; Commonwealth Parliamentary Association; Interparliamentary Union. Publications: Organization of Ghana Cocoa Marketing; Agriculture's Contribution Towards Industrial Development in Ghana. Address: National Assembly, Parliament House, Accra, Ghana.

ODULATE, Jacobson Oladele, born 10th August 1930. Consultant Ophthalmic Surgeon. Education: Ibbobi College, Lagos, Nigeria; University of Durham Medical School, U.K.; Moorfields Eye Hospital, London; M.B., B.S.; D.O.; F.M.C.S. Appointments: Ophthalmic Senior House Officer, Royal Victoria Infirmary, Newcastle upon Tyne; Registrar, Nigerian Federal Government, Lagos; Consultant Ophthalmic Surgeon, Lagos State Government; Senior Consultant Ophthalmic Surgeon, ibid. Memberships: Sergeant at Arms, Rotary Club of Lagos; Lagos Motor Boat Club; Ophthalmic Society, U.K.; Editor, Librarian, Ophthalmic Society, Nigeria. Address: P.O. Box 153, Lagos, Nigeria.

ODUMIYI, Julius Oyewole, born Ibokum, Nigeria, 5th May 1939. Teacher. Education: completed Elementary & Primary School; attended D.T.T.C., Ilesha, for Grade III Course & also attended A.T.T.C., Ilesha, for Higher Elementary Course. Personal details: from Royal Family of Ibokum; married, 3 children. Appointments include: Headmaster of a Primary School, Ijeshaland. Memberships: Secretary, Ibokum National Association; ex-Y.M.C.A. Address: 174 Ishokum Str., Ilesha, Nigeria.

ODUNJO (Chief) Joseph Folahan, born Abeokuta, Nigeria, 1904. Teacher. Author of Textbooks. Education: St. Augustine's Catholic Primary School, Abeokuta, 1914-20; Catholic Teachers' Training College, Ibadan, 1920-24; London University Institute of Education, 1946-47. Personal details: son of Chief Odunjo, the Ekerin of Ibara; married, 2 sons, 5 daughters. Appointments: Headmaster, St. Augustine's Catholic School, Abeokuta, 1924-39; Headmaster, St. Paul's Catholic School, Ebute Metta, Lagos, 1940-46; Supervising Teacher, Abeokuta & Colony, 1948-49; Senior Tutor, St. Gregory's College, Lagos, 1949-50; Senior Tutor, St. Leo's Teacher Training College, Abeokuta, 1951; Minister of Lands & Labour, Western Nigeria, 1952-56; Executive Director, Agriculture, Western Nigeria Development Corporation, 1957-62; President, Ibadan Catholic Diocesan Council, 1963-68. Memberships: Assistant Secretary, Nigeria Union of Teachers, 1942-51; Founder & 1st President, Federal Association of Catholic Teachers, Lagos & Yoruba Provinces, 1936-51; Secretary, Egbado Union, Lagos, 1941-51; Member, Knights of Mulumba, 1966. Publications: Alawiye Yoruba Language Series, Books 1-6; Yoruba Novels, Omo Oku Orun, Kuye Kadara ati Egon re; Yoruba Play, Agbalowomeri, Baale, Jontolo; Yoruba Books of Poems: Ijinle Majemu Larin Egba ati Egbado, Akojopo Ewi Aladun; Yoruba Secondary School Course Part 1, 1967; Part 2, 1969. Honours: created Chief Lemo of Ibara, by Head Chief of Ibara, His Highness the Olubara Lalubu II, 1952; Knight of the Order of St. Gregory, Pope Paul, 1966; Oluwe of Ire, 1968; installed, the Asiwaju of Egbas by the Oba Alaiyeluwa Gbadebe II, Alake of Egbaland, 1969. Address: P.O. Box 1297, Ibadan, Nigeria.

ODURO, Kofi Amoa, born Kukuranthumi, Ghana, 30th April 1926. Medical Practitioner. Education: Presbyterian School, Kukurantumi; St. Augustine's College, Cape Coast; University College, Ibadan; University of Glasgow, U.K. Married, 2 sons, 1 daughter. Appointments include: House Officer, Orthopaedics, Highlands General Hospital, London, U.K., 1957; House Officer, Medicine, Victoria Hospital, Accrington, Lancs, 1958; Medical Officer, Medicine, then Obstetrics & Gynaecology, Korle Bu Hospital, Accra, Ghana, 1958-59; Medical Officer i/c, Winneba Hospital, 1959-60; Hon. S.H.O., Anaesthetics, then Hon. Registrar, Western Infirmary of Glasgow, 1960-63; Senior Medical Officer, Anaesthetics, Korle Bu Hospital, Accra, 1963-66; Senior Lecturer & Head, Anaesthetics, Ghana Medical School, Accra. Memberships include: British Medical Association, 1957-64; Fellow, Association of Europeans of West Africa (Member of Council); President, Association of Anaesthetists of Gt. Britain & Ireland; on Board of Trustees of the Education & Relief Foundation of World Federation of Societies of Anaesthesiologists; Past President, Society of Anaesthetists of West Africa. Publications include: Anaesthesia in Ghana—A review with particular reference to indigenous medical conditions; in print, Anaesthesia. Honours include: M.B., Ch.B., University of Glasgow, 1957; D.A., C.R.C.S.&P., 1961; F.F.A.R.C.S. (Ireland), 1963; F.F.A.R.C.S.(England), 1963. Address: Dept. of Anaesthetics, Ghana Medical School, P.O. Box 4236, Accra, Ghana.

ODUWUSI, Edward Olawale, born Lagos, Nigeria, 9th May 1931. Histologist. Education: Primary & Secondary, Hope Waddel Training Institution, Calabu, 1951; University of Ibadan, 1953; B.Tech., Manchester College of Science, 1958-60; Ph.D., Sussex College of Technology, U.K., 1969. Married, 2 sons, 2 daughters. Appointments: Senior Technologist, Professorial Research Unit, College of Medicine, University of Lago, Nigeria; Lecturer, Histology, 1963; established unit which has now expanded into Histology, Hist-Chemistry & Photomicrographic Sections; responsible for administration & management of this unit. Memberships include: Board of Regent, Sussex College of Technology, U.K.; Lagos Lions Club; Chairman, Association of Medical Technologists, College of Medicine & Lagos Teaching Hospital; Publicity Secretary, Lagos Branch, Institute of Science Technology; Fellow, Royal Microscopical Society, U.K., 1962; ibid, Royal Society of Health, U.K., 1965; Ancient Order of Foresters, Lagos, Nigeria. Publications: The Use of Frozen Sections with distortion-free mounting device in dental Histology; Comparative Studies of Jaw Tumour by Photomicrographic Techniques: Photographic Study of Ameloblastoma. Address: Surgical Professorial Research Unit, Department of Surgery, College of Medicine, University of Lagos, P.M.B. 12003, Lagos, Nigeria.

OFFEI, Daniel Nelson, born 7th March 1935. University Lecturer. Education: University College of Ghana, Legon; Queen's College, Dundee, U.K.; B.Sc.; M.Sc. Married, 1 son, 1 daughter. Appointments: Education Officer, Ghana, 1960-62; Assistant Lecturer, University College, Cape Coast, 1963-64; Lecturer, ibid, 1965—; Acting Head, Mathematics Department, 1968—. Memberships: Mathematical Association of Ghana; Edinburgh Mathematical Society; American Association for the Advancement of Science; Subscriber, Mathematical Offprint Service, American Mathematical Society. Publications: Some Asymptotic Expansions of a Third-Order Differential Equation (J. Lond. Math. Soc.); The Use of Boundary Condition Functions for non-self-adjoint Boundary Value Problems (J. Math. Anal. & Applications). Address: Mathematics Department, University College, Cape Coast, Ghana.

OFILI, Veronica Obiamaka, born 30th September 1924. Medical Officer. Education: Teachers' Grade II Certificate; L.R.C.P. & S.I., L.A.H., L.M., Royal College of Surgeons, St. Stephen's Green, Dublin, Ireland, 1947-52. Personal details: first woman Medical Officer in then Eastern Nigeria; married to former Director, Federal Coastal Agent, Lagos, Nigeria; 5 children. Appointments: Headmistress, Convent School, Warri & St. Theresa's School, Sapele; Pre-registration appointments for 18 months in England; Medical Officer, Eastern Nigeria Medical Services, 1954-56; Medical Officer, Federal Medical Services, 1956-66; Medical Officer (on transfer), Eastern Nigeria & East Central State Medical Services. Memberships; Nigeria Medical Association; Nigeria Guides, 1st Sapele Guide Company; Brown Owl, 1st Sapele Brownie Company. Honours: Silver Sports Cup donated in name by former Premier of Eastern Nigeria, Dr. Nnamdi Azikuwe. Address: General Hospital, Enugu, East Central State, Nigeria.

OFOSU, John Benjamin, born 6th February 1944. Educator. Education: Nkawkaw Anglican Primary School, 1950-54; Nkankaw Presbyterian Middle School, 1955-57; Mfantsipim School, Cape Coast, 1958-64; G.C.E. 'O' Level (4 Distinctions), 1962; 'A' Level (3 Distinctions), 1964; B.Sc.(Spec. Maths.), University of Ghana, 1967. Married, 1 child. Appointments: Graduate Teacher in Mathematics & Additional Mathematics; Assistant Lecturer, later Lecturer in Mathematics. Memberships: Ghana Red Cross Society; Y.M.C.A. Publications: currently writing mathematics textbooks for sixth form schools. Honours & Awards: several school prizes in maths.; Sampanthar Prize, University of Ghana, 1964. Address: Department of Mathematics, University College of Cape Coast, Cape Coast, Ghana.

OFSTAD, Jon Egil, born China, 13th October 1918. Radio Programme Director. Education: Matric., Trondheim, 1939; B.Th., Oslo, Norway, 1946; U.E.D., Pietermaritzburg, 1951. Appointments: Principal, Umpumulo Teachers' Training College, Natal, South Africa; Director, Lutheran Production Studios, Roodepoort; Broadcast Editor, Radio Voice of the Gospel, Addis Ababa, Ethiopia; Programme Director, ibid. Publications: 3 travel books in Norwegian; Kloden Paa Langs; Studio St. Ansgar; Via Verdens Ende. Address: Box 654, Addis Ababa, Ethiopia.

OFUSU-ASANTE, Kofi, born 7th August, 1928. Solicitor; Advocate. Education: B.Sc. (Econ.), London, U.K., 1953; LL.B.(Hons.), Birmingham University, 1957; Called to Bar, Middle Temple, London, 1959. Appointments: with Akim Abonakwa Native Authority Treasury, Kibi, Ghana, 1950; Teacher, Abonakwa State College, Kibi, 1950; District Labour Officer, Ministry of Labour, 1954. Member, Honourable Society of the Middle Temple, London. Address: Akyem Chambers, P.O. Box 1522, Accra, Ghana.

OGAN BADA, Barnabe, born Cotonou, Dahomey, 1935. Controller of Taxes. Education: LL.D., 1958; L'Ecole des Impots, Paris, France, 1959-61. Married, 1 son, 1 daughter. Appointments include: Tax Inspector, Bureau of Taxes, working with Director of Taxes, 1961-63; Department Head, Registration & Preservation of Landed Property, 1963-67; Controller of Taxes, 1967-68; Controller of Taxes & Registration, 1968—. Memberships include: Founding Member, Centre for Development & Culture, Contonou, 1962—; Exec. Bureau, ibid; President, ibid, 1967—. Address: B.P. 369, Cotonou, Dahomey.

OGEDENGBE, Samuel Olufisayo, born 24 November 1931. Practising Barrister. Education: St. Mark's School, Iperindo, via Ilesha, 1942-46; St. John's School, Iloro, Ilesha, 1947-48; Ilesha Grammar School, 1949-53; Barrister-at-Law, Gray's Inn, London, U.K., 1959-62. Married, 2 sons, 2 daughters. Appointments: Legal Adviser, Wesley Guild Hospital, Ilesha, Nigeria; Legal Adviser, Ilesha Grammar School; Board of Governors, Methodist High School, Ilesha. Memberships: Methodist Church, Ilesha; Choirmaster, Oke-Eshe Society; Secretary, Ijesha Equire Society. Address: Ilesha, Nigeria.

OGOT, Grace Emily Akinyi, born Asembo, Kenya, 15th May 1930. Business Woman & Author; Nurse. Education: Ngiya Girls' School; Butere High School, Kenya; Mengo Nursing College, Uganda; St. Thomas' Hospital, U.K.; British Hospital for Mothers & Babies, U.K.; Uganda Registered Nurse; State Certified Midwife, U.K. Married, 3 sons, 1 daughter. Appointments: Staff Nurse, Maseno Hospital, 1954-55; Nursing Sister & Midwifery Tutor, ibid, 1958-59; Scriptwriter & Broadcaster, B.B.C., 1960-61; Community Development Officer & Principal, Homecraft Training Centre, Kisumu, 1962-63; Nursing Sister in Charge, Students' Health Service, Makerere University College, 1963-64; Public Relations Officer for East & Central Africa, Air India, 1964-65; Proprietor & Manager, Lindy's Stores, Nairobi, Kenya. Memberships: Dr., Zonta International, Nairobi; Editorial Board, Busara; Board of Governors, Nairobi Girls' Secondary School; Agricultural Society of Kenya; Association of University Women; Executive Committee, National Christian Council of Kenya; Municipal Council Kisumu; Executive Committee, Kenya Council of Women. Publications: The Promised Land,

1966; Land Without Thunder (short stories), 1968; Family Planning & the African Woman, E. African Jrnl., 1967; several other short stories & articles in jrnls., magazines, & anthologies. Honours: Prize, short story competition, East Africa, 1966. Address: University College, Nairobi, Box 30197, Nairobi, Kenya.

OGUAMBA, Andre Francois, born Libreville, 15th June 1922. Government Official. Education: Diploma, Centre of Professional Instruction of Post & Telecommunications, Limoges, France; Diploma, ibid, Outre-Mer, Toulouse, France. Appointments: Assistant Head of Personnel, Equatorial Post & Telecommunications' Office, Brazzaville, Congo, 1959; Deputy Director, ibid, Gabon, 1962-63; Director, ibid, 1963-64; Head of Mission, Ministry of Posts & Telecommunications, ibid, 1965-68; Inspector-General, ibid, 1968—. Honours: Knight, Order of the Equatorial Star; Knight, Central African Republic Postal Decoration. Address: Inspection Générale des Postes et Télécommunications, Libreville, Gabon.

OGUNBIYI, Samuel Aremu (Chief), born Babanloma Town, Share District, Ilorin Province, Nigeria, 1928. Teacher. Education: Elementary Teachers' Certificate, Grade III, 1956; U.K. Vacational Course, 1961; Higher Teachers' Certificate, grade II, 1960; currently studying at College of Education, A.B., U., Zaria. Married with 2 wives, 3sons, 6 daughters. Appointments include: Headmaster, U.M.S. School, Babanloma, 1950; Founder & General Secretary, Share District Progressive Union, 1951 (later converted to Egbo Igbomina Parapo Share Branch); Chief Councillor, Share District Council; Headmaster, Community School, Babanloma, 1957-58; Candidate, Federal House of Parliament, 1964; Free Headmaster, L.E.A. Comm. School, Babanloma, 1961-67; Head, Department of Physical & Health Education; Chairman, Finance Committee, Share District Council. Memberships include: Scout Movement of Nigeria; Vice-President, Babandoma Progressive Union; President, Igbotnina Student Union A.T.C. Branch, Zaria. Author of numerous articles in Nigeria Citizen and News Nigeria appealing for government dispensary for Share Town and water supply for Babandoma; author of memorandum submitted to Minority Commission, 1953, on behalf of Share District Community. Honours include: awarded title of Chief Essa of Babanloma Town, 1967. Address: Advanced Teachers' College, P.M.B. 130, Sokoto, Nigeria.

OGUNDELE, Johnson Adewale, born Okemesi Ekiti, via Elisha, Nigeria, 1941. Teacher. Education: Teachers' Certificate Grade II, Ede Baptist College; General Certificate of Education, Advanced Level; currently studying at University of Ife, Ile-Ife, 1970—. Personal details: son of Chief Legiri Ogundele of Okemesi, & maternal Grandson of Chief Fabunmi, who led the Ekiti Parapo War against Ibadan. Appointments: Headmaster, Boriya Baptist School, 1960-62; Headmaster, Oke Ako Baptist School, 1965; Headmaster, Igbaye Baptist School, 1966-70. Memberships: Nigeria Boy Scouts; Secretary, Okemesi Students' Union, 1964; Secretary, Boy Scouts, Ede Baptist College, 1964; Publicity Secretary, Odo-Otin Rovers Football Club. Address: Oyobi Street, Legiri House, Okemesi Ekiti, via Ilesha, Nigeria.

OGUNDIBO, John Oluremi, born Ijebu-Ode, Nigeria, 20th August 1935. Pharmacist. Education: C.M.S. Girls' School, Lagos, 1940-44; C.M.S. Grammar School, Lagos, 1945-51; B.Pharm.(Hons.), School of Pharmacy, Technical College, Sunderland, U.K., 1955-60; Ph.C., Pharmaceutical Society of Gt. Britain Exam., 1961. Married, 1 son. Appointments include: Accounting Assistant, H.Q., Accounts, Nigerian Railways, EB (now Nigerian Railways Corp.), 1952-55; Dispensing Assistant, General Hospital, Southend-on-Sea, U.K., 1959; Trainee Production Pharmacist, Allen & Hanburys Ltd., Ware, Herts., 1960-61; Production Pharmacist, Tablets Dept., Glaxo Laboratories, Greenford, Middx., 1961-62; Production Pharmacist, Glaxo Laboratories (Nigeria) Ltd., Apapa, Nigeria, 1963; Assistant Factory Manager, ibid, 1964; Factory Manager, 1966-70; Chief Pharmacist, Glaxo-Allenburys (Nigeria) Ltd., 1970. Memberships include: Pharmaceutical Society of Great Britain; Institute of Pharmaceutical Management of Great Britain; Pharmaceutical Society of Nigeria; Parish Society, Anglican Church, Sumbere, Lagos. Address: 41 Creek Rd., Apapa, Nigeria.

OGUNDIPE (Brigadier) Babafemi Olatunde, born 6th September 1924. Diplomatist. Education: Banham Memorial School, Port Harcourt, Nigeria; Staff College, Camberley; Imperial Defence College, London, U.K. Appointments: Brigade Major, Congo, 1960-63; Chief of Staff, U.N. Forces, Congo, 1963; Military Adviser, London, U.K., 1966; Chief of Staff, Nigerian Military Forces, 1966; High Commissioner in U.K., 1966—. Honours: River Bennie Star. Address: 9 Northumberland Avenue, London, U.K.

OGUNLUSI, Samuel Ayodele Afolabi, born 21 May 1927. Medical Practitioner. Education: Government College, Ibadan, Nigeria; University College, Ibadan; London Hospital, U.K. Married. Appointments: Casualty Officer, London Hospital, 1954-55; Medical Officer & Senior Medical Officer, Western Nigeria Medical Service, 1956-66; Chief Medical Officer, Health Services, University of Ife, Ile-Ife, 1966—. Treasurer, Fajuyi Memorial Trust Fund. Address: Chief Medical Officer, Health Centre, University of Ife, Ile-Ife, Nigeria.

OGUNWO (His Highness, Prince) Zaccheaus Adekoya, born Ibido, 18th July 1921. Company Director. Education: Ibido Baptist Day School, Ijebu Province, 1926-32; St. Paul's C.M.S. School, Omu, 1933-34; St. Peter's School, Faji, Lagos, 1936-37; Christchurch Cathedral, Faji School, Lagos, 1938-39; Government Evening Continuation Class, Lagos, 1941-42; Ekoboys High School Evening Class, 1943-44. Personal details: descendant of the Awujale of Ijebuland; father, Prince Ezekiel Ogunwo Mayungbe; married, 2 wives, 13 children. Appointments: Managing Director, Charity Transport Service; Managing Director, Ibido Kajola Stores Nigeria,

Ltd; President, Nigerian Motor Transport Owners' Union, Lagos State; National Vice-President, ibid, Parent Body, ibid. Memberships: Island Club, Lagos; Member & Auditor, Egbe Ifeloju Union Baptist Church, Lagos; Chairman, Ibido Progressive People Union. Address: 53, Odunlamis Street, Lagos, Nigeria.

OGUNYEMI, Daniel Abebayo Akinsanya, born Sagamu, Western State, Nigeria, 22nd May, 1928. Economist; Chemist. Education: Pharmaceutical Chemist; B.Sc.(Hons.), Economics, London University; Associateship of Scottish College of Commerce. Married. Appointments: Manager, West African Drug Co. Ltd., Kano, 1950-54; Managing Director, Industrial Chemists Ltd., Lagos, 1958-60; Head, Industrial Chemicals, Shell Co. of Nigeria Ltd., 1960-64; Chemicals Sales Manager, Shell Chemicals, 1964-66; Marketing Services Manager, ibid, 1966-68; Agricultural Chemicals Manager, ibid, 1968—. Memberships: National Treasurer, Council Member, Pharmaceutical Society of Nigeria; Advanced Lay Reader, Christ Church Cathedral (Anglican), Lagos; Chairman, Shell Clerks, Lagos; Grand United Order of Oddfellows; Pharmacists' Club, Lagos; Sagamu Helpers' Union; Treasurer, Ibadan Grammar School Old Students' Association, Lagos; City Club, Lagos. Correspondent, Pharmaceutical Journal & Journal of Nigeria. Honours include: first African to be awarded Associateship of Scottish College of Commerce, 1958. Address: P.O. Box 131, 35 Church St., Isolo Rd., Mushin, Lagos, Nigeria.

OGUTI, John Ludoviko, born April 1932. Personnel Manager. Education: Tororo Primary School, 1941-46; Tororo College, 1947-49; St. Leo's College, 1952-54; Personnel Management, Oxford University, U.K., 1964. Married, 7 children. Appointments: Administrative Assistant, Sukulu Mines, Tororo, 1957-58; ibid, Technical Department, Development Division, Uganda Development Corporation Ltd., 1959; Junior Executive, ibid, Kampala, 1960-62; Personnel Officer, Agricultural Enterprises Ltd., Bugambe Tea Plantation, 1963; ibid, Salama Estates Ltd., 1964; Assistant Industrial Relations Manager, Head Office, Kampala, 1968; Personnel Manager, 1969—. Memberships: East African Institute of Management; Associate, Uganda Institute of Management. Address: Box 7020, Kampala, Uganda.

OHENE-AMPOFO, Kwadwo, born Mampong-Akwapim, Ghana, 22nd February 1926. Legal Practitioner, Education: Amanase Presbyterian Primary School, 1932-37; Suhum Senior School, 1938; Akropong Presbyterian Senior School, 1939-41; Akropong Presbyterian Training College, 1943-47; Achimota Secondary School, 1948-49; University College of Gold Coast, 1950-52; Gray's Inn, London, U.K., 1955-59. Teachers' Certificate, 1946; Cambridge School Certificate, 1949; London Matriculation, 1950; B.A., London University, 1955; Called to the Bar, Gray's Inn, 1959. Personal Details: last son of Chief H. B. Kwasi Ampogo, Odikro of Amanase. Address: Okasu Chambers, P.O. Box 2338, Accra, Ghana.

OHENE-NYAKO, Seth, born 13th January 1921. Banker; Business Executive. Education: Lareth Presbyterian Primary & Senior Schools; Foundation Member, Presbyterian Secondary School, 1938-42; Studied Banking, Bank of England, Glyn-Mills, London, U.K.; Deutsch Bundesbank, Frankfurt, West Germany & Bank of Israel, Jerusalem. Personal details: Regent to the Stool of Old Akrade in Akwamu. Appointments: Barclays Bank DCO, 1943-53; Founder Member, Bank of the Gold Coast & Ghana Commercial Bank, 1943-57; Founder Member, Bank of Ghana, 1957-68; Executive Director, ibid, 1965-68; 1st Executive Chairman, Capital Investments Board & Organizer, Ghana Investment Centre, Accra & Frankfurt, W. Germany. Directorships: Bank of Ghana; State Electronics Corporation; State Cocoa Products Corporation; National Investment Bank; Fan Milk Ltd.; Capital Investment Board. Served on various Government delegations, commissions, & committees. Memberships: British Institute of Bankers: Life Member, Ghana Red Cross Society; Treasurer, Ghana Olympic & Overseas Games Committee; Founder Member, Ghana International Dining Club; Scouting. Address: P.O. Box 4005, Accra, Ghana.

OJANY, Francis Frederick, born 17th July 1935. University Lecturer in Geomorphology. Education: Alliance High School, Kikuyu, 1951-54; Makerere University College, 1955-60; B.A. (Hons.), Geography, London University, 1960; M.A., Geography, University of Birmingham, U.K., 1963. Married, 4 children. Appointments: Assistant Lecturer in Geography, University of Nairobi, 1963-64; Lecturer in Geography, 1964—. Memberships: Kenya Geographical Association; East African Academy. Publications: The Physique of Kenya, Annals A. American Geographers, 1966; The mound topography of the Thika-Athi Plains, Kenya, Erdkunde, 1968; Inselbergs of Eastern Kenya, Zeitschrift fur Geomorphologie, 1969; Kenya: A Study in Physical & Human Geography (with R. B. Ogendo). Honours: Shell Exhibition Award, Makerere University, 1959; British Commonwealth Scholarship to read Postgraduate Geomorphology, 1960. Address: P.O. Box 30197, Nairobi, Kenya.

OJARA, Austin Laurence, born 12th August 1929. Administrative Officer. Education: Primary School, Gulu, Northern Uganda; Secondary School, Namilyango, Nr. Kampala; Makerere University, Kampala. Married, 6 children. Appointments: Cooperative Officer, later Administrative Secretary with Local Authority; Administrative Officer, Government of Uganda; seconded to Ministry as Senior Assistant Secretary. Memberships: Deputy Chairman, Board of Governors, Kabalega Secondary School; Makerere College Union Society. Honours: 1st Prize in Government Essay Competition, 1960; Independence Medal, 1962. Address: P.O. Box 7096, Kampala, Uganda.

OJO, Olusola Adewole, born 1st February 1927. Obstetrician & Gynaecologist. Education: Cambridge School Certificate with Exemption from London Matriculation; B.A., Dublin, Ireland, 1952; M.B., B.Ch., B.A.O., ibid, 1954;

M.A., M.A.O., 1959; M.R.C.O.G., 1960; M.D., 1964. Married, 2 sons. Appointments: House Appointments in Surgery, Obstetrics, Gynaecology, Medicine, & Paediatrics, 1954-56; Senior House Officer, Obstetrics & Gynaecology, 1956-59; Registrar, ibid, 1959-60; Lecturer, 1962-65; Senior Lecturer, 1965-68; Professor, Obstetrics & Gynaecology, University College Hospital, Ibadan, Nigeria, 1968—. Memberships: Captain, Dublin University Squash Club, 1953; Secretary, Nigeria Union of Students, Dublin, 1951-53; Ikoyi Club, Lagos; Former Member, Ibadan Recreation Club; Secretary, Nigerian Society of Gynaecology & Obstetrics. Author of 23 publications in his field. Recipient, Begley Studentship, Trinity College, Dublin, 1951. Address: University College Hospital, Ibadan, Nigeria.

OKACH, Rowlands Willis, born Kenya, 18th March 1938. Physician. Education: Alliance High School, Kenya, 1954-57; M.B., Ch.B., Makerere University College, 1958-65; D.T.M.&H., M.R.C.P.(Edin.), London & Edinburgh Universities, U.K., 1967-69. Married, 1 son, 1 daughter. Appointments: Intern, 1965-66; Medical Research Officer, 1966-70. Memberships: Fellow, Royal Society of Tropical Medicine & Hygiene; Association of Physicians of East Africa. Publications: The Application of Serological Methods in Mass Diagnosis of African Human Trypanosomiasis; The Use of Berenil in Treatment of Early Cases of African Human Trypanosomiasis; A Case of Congenitally Acquired Human Trypanosomiasis. Honours: Burtt Prize in Bot., Makerere University College, 1957. Address: Box 43, Yala, Kenya.

OKALI, David Uke Ukiwe, born 25th September 1936. University Lecturer. Education: University of Ibadan, Nigeria, 1955-60; University of Sheffield, U.K., 1960-63; University of Oxford, 1966-68; B.Sc.(Lond.); B.A.(Oxon.); Ph.D.(Sheffield). Married, 2 sons. Appointments include: Post-doctoral Research Fellow, University of Ibadan, 1963-65; Lecturer, Department of Forestry, ibid, 1965-68; F.A.O. Fellow, Oxford University, 1966-68; Lecturer in Botany, University of Ghana, 1968—. Memberships: British Ecological Society; Science Association of Nigeria; Ghana Science Association. Articles published in sci. jrnls. Address: Department of Botany, University of Ghana, Legon, Ghana.

OKECH, Mark, born 6th June 1942. Physician. Education: Mbale Junior Secondary School, 1955-56; Tororo College, 1957-60; Mbale Senior Secondary School, 1961-62; M.B., Ch.B. (EA), Makerere University College, 1963-68; currently taking Postgraduate Course in Surgery. Appointments: Medical Officer for 2 years; Honorary Lecturer in Anatomy, Makerere University & Resident Tutor, Northcote Hall. Memberships: President, Debating Society, Tororo College, 1957-60; President, Adhola Students' Association, 1958-60; President, Mbale College Old Boys, 1959-60; President, Soni Educated People's Club, 1959-60. Address: Makerere University, P.O. Box 7062, Kampala, Uganda.

OKECH, Philipo, K., born Gulu, Uganda, 1918. Teacher. Education: Gulu High School, 1926-29; Nabumali High School, 1930-33; Dip. Ed. & Agric, Preliminary Course, Makerere University College, 1934-36. Married, 3 sons, 2 daughters. Appointments: Teacher, Gulu High School, 1937-54; Headmaster, Kitgum High School, 1955-62; ibid, Gulu High School, 1963-64. Memberships: Acholi District Council, 1944-52; Northern Province, Provincial Council, 1948-52; Uganda Legislative Council, under Sir John Harthorn Hall & Sir Andrew Cohen (Governors), 1950-53; Appointments Committee, 1956-58; Appointments Board, 1959-63; Gulu Town Council, 1963-64; Chairman, Town Council Education Committee, 1964; Railways Advisory Board, 1964; Secretary, Acholi Branch, Uganda Teachers' Association, 6 years; Football Captain, Gulu High School Old Boys, 1945-50; Uganda Representative, Festival of Britain, 1951. Honours: H.M. Queen Elizabeth II's Silver Medal, 1964. Address: P.O. Box 1, Moyo, Madi District, Uganda.

OKELLO, Daniel Stephen, born 10th March 1943. Artist; School Teacher. Education: Atede Primary School, 1951-53; Palaro Primary School, 1954-56; House of Study, Alokolum Junior Seminary, 1957; St. Joseph's Junior S.S., 1958-59; D.F.A., School of Fine Art, Makerere University, 1965-69; Dip. Ed., Institute of Education, 1969-70. Married Korima Aceng, 2 children. Appointments: Primary Teacher, 1964; Headmaster, Palenga Primary School, 1965; currently, University of East Africa. Memberships: Old Boys of the Brothers of the Sacred Heart; St. John Ambulance Association & Brigade; Nomo Gallery, City of Kampala. Works exhibited: Art Festival of Gulu, 1965; National Art Festival, National Theatre; University Art Festival, Makerere, 1965-68; University Gallery, Makerere. Honours: 1st Prize, District Level, Bible Knowledge Contest, 1954; Special Award & 2nd Prize, Humane Education Institute of Africa, 1962 & 1963. Address: Fatima Teacher Training College, P.O. Box 94, Lira, Uganda.

OKELO OLONG, Samuel George, born 22nd March 1920. Teacher; Politician; Administrator. Education: Aboke E.V. School, 4 years; Gula High School, 1933-36; King's College, Budo, 1937-39; Makerere College, 1940-42; Diploma in Education, University College of the S.W., Exeter, 1955-56; Praha News Agency School, 1962-63. Personal details: son of Ibrahim Olong (deceased), County Chief of Kole Oyam, Lango District; married to Margaret Joyce Akengo, 4 sons, 5 daughters. Appointments: Headmaster, Lira Junior Secondary School, 1943-59; Member, Lango District Council, 1947-67; President, U.A.T.A. Lango Branch & Secretary Young Lango Assn., 1946-52; Chairman, Lango District Council, 1957-58; Financial Secretary of Lango, 1963-64; Secretary-General of Lango, 1965-67; Administrative Officer, Ministry of Public Service & Cabinet Affairs, 1967-70. Memberships: Young Lango Assn.; Uganda African Teachers' Assn.; Board of Governors, Kabalega Secondary School; Board of Governors, Dr. Obote School, 1961-67; Director: Uganda Electricity Board, 1965-67; Lango Development Company, 1965-68; Lango Ranching Co., 1965-68; Bahama Estates Ltd.,

1970. Publications: Irna me Lango (small book in Luo language); Liveny me Bar Amyem (in preparation). Honours: Prizes in English & Mathematics, King's College, Budo, 1939; U.P.C. Independence Medal, 1965. Address: Uhuru na Kazi Estate, P.O. Box 89, Lira, Uganda.

OKERA, Wazir, born 12th April 1943. Lecturer in Zoology. Education: Primary & Secondary Education in Zanzibar; University College, London, U.K.; currently registered for Ph.D., University of East Africa. Married. Appointments: Tutorial Fellow, Zoology, University of Dar es Salaam, Tanzania, 1967-70; Lecturer, ibid, 1970—. Memberships: Chairman, Marine Biology Section, Tanzania National Committee, International Biological Programme. Publications: Features of Sardinella gibbosa scale with special reference to age determination; A Preliminary Survey of Inshore Plankton of Dar es Salaam Coast; Marine Zoology, in African Encyclopedia (in press). Address: P.O. Box 35064, Department of Zoology, University of Dar es Salaam, Dar es Salaam, Tanzania.

OKIDI, Soloman Basil, born 24th September 1934. Company Secretary. Education: Grad II, Cambridge Overseas School Certificate; Chartered Institute of Secretaries Intermediate Certificate. Married, 7 children. Appointments: Information Officer, Acholi D.A., 1959-60; Treasurer, ibid, 1961-67; Assistant Secretary, Uganda Development Corporation Limited, 1968—. Memberships: Treasurer, Gulu Social Club; Treasurer, Acholi Boy Scouts Association. Address: P.O. Box 7042, Kampala, Uganda.

OKOJIE, Christopher Gbelokoto, born 9th April, 1920. Medical Practitioner. Education: Yaba Higher College, 1941-42; L.S.M., Nigerian School of Medicine, 1942-47; New York University Postgraduate Medical School, U.S.A., 1956-57. Appointments: Chairman, Western Nigeria Development Corporation, 1962-63; Minister of Works & Transport, Midwest, 1963-66; Leader, Midwest House of Assemblies, 1964-66; Founder, Owner, & Medical Director, Zuma Memorial Hospital, Irrua, a 120-bed general hospital with a Grade I school of midwifery. Memberships: Fellow, New York Academy of Science; Treasurer, Nigerian Medical Association (Midwest); Assistant Regional Scout Commissioner, Midwest, 1963—; President, Ugboha Progress Union, 1960—. Author, Ishan Native Laws & Customs, 1960. Honours: Fulbright Scholar, Surgery, 1956-57; Fellow, International College of Surgery, 1957; Certificate of Honour, Boy Scouts of Nigeria, 1960; Order of the Federal Republic of Nigeria, 1964. Address: Zuma Memorial Hospital, Irrua, Midwest, Nigeria.

OKOLO, Paul Timothy Titigbe, born Umuebu, 25th January 1939. Educator. Education: Primary School Leaving Certificate, 1949; Teachers' Grade III cert., 1954; Grade II, 1958; Grade I, 1965; B.A.(Hons.) English, 1967. Appointments include: Headmaster, Catholic School, Ogume, Kwale, 1956; Headmaster, Catholic Secondary Modern School, Ogume, 1959-60; Secretary, Pax Romana University of Ibadan, 1965-66; Financial Secretary, Midwest Students' Union, 1965-66; Chairman, Aboh Division Students' Union, University of Ibadan, 1965-66; Senior Tutor, Mater Dei College, Ashaka, Kwale, 1967-68. Memberships: Secretary, Nigeria Federation of Catholic Students, Pax Romana, 1965-66; Troop Leader, Benin 14th Tropp, Boy Scouts. Address: Mater Dei College, Ashaka, Kwale, Midwest State, Nigeria.

OKONG'O, Owino, born 15th January 1937. Physiologist. Education: B.Sc., Makerere College, 1960; B.A.(Hons.), Brandeis University, U.S.A., 1964; M.A.(Ed.), Antioc-Putney Graduate School, 1964; M.A., Med. Sci., Boston University, 1966. Married, 1970. Appointments: Instructor, Physiology & Biophysics, University of Vermont, U.S.A., 1967; Lecturer, Medical Physiology, Nairobi University, 1969—. Member, Institute of Biology. Publications: Determination of the active state curve of muscle; An electronic switch for massive stimulation of muscle (in press). Honours: Wien International Scholar, 1961-64. Address: Nairobi University, Box 30197, Nairobi, Kenya.

OKONMAH, Philip Ngozi, born 4th May 1937. Physician. Education: Cambridge School Certificate, 1956; Second M.B., B.S., London, U.K., 1962; Final M.B., B.S., Nagpur, India, 1965. Married, 2 children. Appointments: Medical Officer, Children's Hospital, Lagos, Nigeria, 1966-67; ibid, Central Hospital, Tamale, Ghana, 1967-69; Medical Officer in Charge, Government Hospital, Yendi, Ghana, 1969—. Memberships: Patrol Leader, Boy Scouts, Warri, Nigeria, 1954-56; Senior Prefect, Hussey College, Warri, 1956; President, African Students' Association, Nagpur, India, 1966; President, Foreign Students' Association, 1965. Address: Government Hospital, P.O. Box 8, Yendi, Ghana.

OKONO, Jean-Daniel, born 25th December 1930. Civil Administrator. Education: Diploma, Overseas Institute of Higher Studies, Paris, France. Appointments: Head of Cabinet, Minister of Finance, 1958-69; Permanent Representative to the Prime Minister, 1961-62; Cabinet Director to the Prime Minister, 1963-64; Prefect, Department of Haut-Hyong, 1964-66; Head of Administrative & Financial Affairs, 1967—. Memberships: General Secretary, Union of Secretarial Administration, 1954-55. Honours: Recipient of Knighthood for Bravery.

OKORO, Anezionwu Nwankwo, born 17th May 1929. Medical Practitioner. Education: Methodist Schools, Uzuakoli, 1936-40; Methodist College, Uzuakoli, 1941-45; Dennis Memorial Grammar School, Onitsha, 1946-47; University College, Ibadan, Nigeria, 1948-52; University of Bristol, U.K., 1953-56. Married, 4 children. Appointments: Medical Officer, Federal Ministry of Health, Lagos, Nigeria, 1957-64; Specialist Dermatologist, Lagos, 1965-66, & Enugu, 1966—; Senior Lecturer in Medicine, University of Nigeria Medical School, Nsukka, 1967—. Memberships: British Association of Dermatology; Fellow, St. John's Hospital Dermatological Society, London. Publications (novels): The Village School, 1967; New Broom at Amanzu, 196. Address: Department of Dermatology, General Hospital, Enugu, Nigeria.

OKORO, Jerry Ndubuisi, born 27th July 1944. Journalist. Education: Ngwa High School, Aba, Nigeria; International School of Journalism, Budapest, Hungary. Appointments: Assistant Editor, Eastern Nigerian Guardian (daily newspaper); Deputy Editor, Spectator (a monthly Nigerian journal); Assistant Editor, Advance (a socialist weekly published in Lagos); Guest Editor, International Dept., The Hungarian News Agency; Public Relations Officer with a British Company in London; Editor, Tripoli Mirror (an English language Libyan newspaper); Resident Correspondent of The Times, London; Stringer for the News of the World, Gemini News Service & the British monthly African Development. Member of the International Organization of Journalists (I.O.J.). Address: c/o Tripoli Mirror, Box 911, Libya.

OKOT, Longinus James, born October 1939. Principal Assistant Secretary. Education: Cambridge School Certificate, Kisubi, Uganda, 1958; Higher School Certificate, ibid, 1960; B.A.(Hons.), English, Makerere, Uganda, 1964; Law Exams., Administrative Officers (Certificate), 1966. Appointments: Assistant Secretary, Uganda Government, 1964-68; Principal Assistant Secretary, E.A. Community, Arusha, Tanzania, 1968 –. Editor, 'Northern Window' Magazine, Makerere, 1963-64. Publications: A New Passage to Suburbs (in preparation). Honours: Uganda Govt. Scholarship, 1961-64; Play Writing organized by Radio Uganda, 1963. Address: East African Community, Communications & Research Secretariat, Box 1002, Arusha, Tanzania.

OKOTOR KWASI II (Nana) (Omanhene), King of Nkonya, born 1880. Farmer. Personal details: succeeded elder brother Okotor Kwasi I in 1943. Okotor Kwasi I was the grandson of Nana Tedji, who crossed the Volta from Nyanewase Empire. Nana Tedji was the last son of Ntim Gyakari, the last King of the Guan Empire—the Aborigines of the Gold Coast (now Ghana). Address: P.O. Box 16, Nkonya-Ahenkro V.R., Ghana.

OKUNNU, Lateef Olufemi, born Lagos, Nigeria, 19th February 1933. Barrister-at-Law. Education: King's College, Lagos, 1948-53; University College, London University, U.K.; LL.B., ibid, 1958; Gray's Inn, London; Called to the English Bar, 1960. Married, 1 daughter. Appointments include: Federal Commissioner for Works & Housing, Federal Government of Nigeria, 1967 –; Leader of Federal Delegation to Organization of African Unity; Consultative Committee, Nigeria Preliminary Peace Talks, & subsequently, ibid, closing stages, Addis Ababa Peace Talks. Memberships include: Nigeria Bar Council; Executive Committee, Nigeria Bar Association; Legal Adviser, Nigeria Sports Council; ibid, Muslim Students Society of Nigeria; Nigeria Union of Great Britain & Ireland; Secretary, ibid, 1958-59; President, ibid, 1959-60; Vice-Chairman, Socialist Society, University College, London, U.K. Editor, 'African Statesman'; Editor, Nigeria Bar Journal. Author of articles on African & International Affairs in numerous journals. Address: Ministry of Works & Housing, Lagos, Nigeria.

OKUNUGA, Olanuyi Okuyiga, born 24th May 1916. Principal Accountant in the Federal Public Service. Education: St. Saviour's School, Ikenne, Ijebu, 1922-27; St. Paul's School, Sagamu, ibid, 1927-30; St. Saviour's School, Ikenne, 1931-32; St. James' School, Iperu, 1933-34; C.M.S. (now Anglican) Grammar School, Lagos, 1937-38; Nigerian College of Arts & Technology, Ibadan, 1957-58; Personal details: married to Mary Adetayo Ogunsile, 9 children. Appointments: Junior Clerk, Federal Public Service, 1940-59; Executive Officer, Accounts, 1959-62; Accountant, Acting Senior Accountant, 1962-67; Principal Accountant, 1967 –. Memberships: St. John's Church Aroloya, Lagos; Vice-President, Young Men's Auxiliary, ibid, 1955-59; President, 1959-64; District Scoutmaster, Lagos Local Assn., Boy Scouts of Nigeria, 1954; Assistant District Commissioner, ibid, 1956; District Commissioner, 1962; Headquarters Commissioner, Lagos Region, 1967; Deputy State Commissioner, Lagos State, 1970; Deputy National Treasurer, N.H.Q., 1968; attended many international Scout jamborees including: 11th World Jamboree, Marraton, Greece, 1963; 12th Jamboree, Idaho, U.S.A.; 22nd, Seattle, U.S.A. Honours: Scouts Medal of Merit, 1954; Bar to Medal, 1962; Silver Eagle, 1968; Scout Wood Badge, 1959; Cub Wood Badge, 1959. Address: Federal Board of Inland Revenue, Yakubu Gowon Street, Lagos, Nigeria.

OKUWOBI, Babasola, born 1st August 1936. Physician. Education: Ijebu Obe Grammar School, Nigeria; Norwich City College, U.K.; London Hospital Medical College, University of London. Married, 2 sons. Appointments: Receiving Room Officer, London Hospital, 1963; House Physician, Addenbrooke's Hospital, Cambridge, 1964-65; Senior Registrar, Lagos Teaching Hospital, Nigeria, 1965-68; Consultant Physician, ibid, 1968 –; Research Fellow, Cardiovascular Unit, Toronto General Hospital, Canada, 1968-69. Memberships: Royal College of Physicians of London; Academy of Medicine of Toronto; Island Club, Lagos. Publications: Pattern of Heart Disease in Lagos, E. African Med. Jrnl. Honours: Prize in Biochemistry, London Hospital, 1958. Address: Consultant Physician, Lagos University Teaching Hospital, Surulere, Lagos, Nigeria.

OLABISI, Emmanuel Olanrewaju, born Ogbomosho, Nigeria, 16th April 1928. Pharmacist. Education: People's Institute, Ogbomosho, 1933-40; Baptist Day School, Ogbomosho, 1941; Baptist Boys' High School, Abeokuta, 1942-46; School of Pharmacy, Yaba, 1948-51; London University, U.K., 1953-55, 1957-58; Portsmouth College of Technology, 1955-57; Chelsea College of Science & Technology. Personal details: son of Chief Daniel Olabisi, Otun Bale Osupa, Ogbomosho, & Marian Abeni Oyeyiob Alabisi, daughter of Chief Iholaba of Ogboinosho. Appointments include: School-teacher, Baptist Day School, Oshogbo, 1947-48; Government Pharmacist, Superintendent Pharmacist & Pharmaceutical Inspector, 1959-68; Proprietor & Managing Director, Renown Chemists, U.A.C., Ile Itesiwaju, Ibadan, 1968 –. Memberships include: Pharmaceutical Society of Nigeria; Pharmaceutical Society of Gt. Britain & Northern Ireland; past President, Ogbomosho Union of Gt. Britain; Akur Recreation Club; United States Information Service Library, Ibadan; British Council Library, Ibadan. Address: Renown Chemists, U.A.C., Ile Itesiwaju, New Court Road, P.O. Box 664, Ibadan Nigeria.

OLADAPO, Alicemay Oyinwole, born 20th August 1931. Senior Health Educator. Education: Government Class IV Certificate; G.C.E. 'O' Level; S.R.N.; S.C.M.; Dipl. Tropical Diseases; Certificate in Hospital Administration; Diploma in Health Education, London University, U.K. Married, 2 sons, 2 daughters. Appointments: Nursing Sister; Matron; Senior Health Educator, Nigeria. Memberships: Royal Society of Health; Nigerian Council of Women. Address: Health Education Unit, Federal Ministry of Health, Lagos, Nigeria.

OLAGOKE, David Olu, born Nigeria, 22nd January 1930. Lecturer. Education: Methodist Boys' High School, Lagos, 1945-50; University of Ibadan, 1954-57; Institute of Education, University of London, U.K., 1957-58; University of Essex, 1967-68. Married, 3 sons, 1 daughter. Appointments: Education Officer, King's College, Lagos, Nigeria, 1958-60; Principal, Lisabi Grammar School, Abeokuta, 1961-68; Lecturer in English, College of Education, University of Lagos, 1968—. Member, Christian Loving Association, Abeokuta. Publications: The Incorruptible Judge, 1963; The Irokoman and the Woodcarver, 1964. Honours: 1st Prize in Latin, Cambridge School Certificate, 1950. Address: College of Education, University of Lagos, Lagos, Nigeria.

OLALOYE, Olufemi Abimbola, born 2nd October 1939. Medical Practitioner. Education: Igbobi College, Yaba, 1952-56; Trinity College, University of Dublin, Ireland; 1957-63. M.A., M.B.; F.R.C.S. Appointments: Demonstrator, Dept. of Anatomy, Queen's University, Belfast, Northern Ireland, U.K.; Registrar, Dept. of Surgery, Postgraduate Medical School, Hammersmith, Ducane Rd., London. Fellow of the Royal College of Surgeons, Edinburgh. Address: 11 Ikorodu Road, 001-Olowo, Mushin, Nigeria.

OLANG (The Most Rev.) Festo Habakkuk, born November 1914. Archbishop of Kenya. Education: Maseno School, 1928-30; Alliance High School, 1931-35; St. Paul's Theological College, 1944-45; Wycliffe Hall, Oxford, 1948-49. Appointments: School-teacher, 1946-48; consecrated Bishop, 1955 (Asst. Bishop of Mombasa); Bishop of Maseno, 1961; Archbishop of Kenya, 1970. Address: Bishopsbourne, P.O. Box 502, Nairobi, Kenya.

OLANIYAN, Christian Francis Ipoola, born Odeomu, Oshun Division, Western State, Nigeria, 3rd October, 1932. College Principal; School Proprietor. Education: Christ Church School, Ipetumodu, via Ife, 1937-40; Origbo Central School, Ipetumodu, 1941-44; Oduduwa College, Ile Ifé, 1945-49; B.A.(Durham), Fourah Bay College, Freetown, Sierra Leone, 1951-55; Trinity College, Dublin, Ireland, 1956-57; Higher Dip. Ed.; F.R.Econ.Sc. Married, with children. Appointments: Teacher, Sunlight School, Ibadan, 1950; Accounts Clerk, PWD, Abeokuta, 1950-51; Vice-Principal, Anglican Grammer School, Gbongan, 1957-59; 1st Principal, Christ Apostolic Grammar School, Ibadan, 1960-64; ibid, Hope Grammar School, ibid, 1965; Principal, Oriwu College, Ikorodu, 1966—; Manager, Proprietor, Victory High School, Ikeja, Lagos State. Memberships: Western Nigeria Marketing Board; Nigerian Broadcasting Corporation W.R., 1963; Publicity Secretary (West), N.C.N.C., 1963-64; Ibadan Tennis Club, 1963-65; Founder, Concordia Society, Forah Bay College, Freetown; President, ibid, 1955; Chairman, Ikorodu Inner Circle, 1967—. Address: Oriwu College, P.O. Box 92, Ikorodu, Lagos State, Nigeria.

OLAOSEBIKAN, William Aremu, born Oro Ago, Kwara State, Nigeria, 9th May 1938. Teacher. Education: S.I.M. School, Oro Ago, 1944-47; N.A. School, Ogbomosho, 1948; S.I.M. School, Oro Ago, 1949; Keffi Government College, 1950-55; Nigerian College of Technology, 1956-61; Diploma in Fine Art, Art Teachers' Certificate, Goldsmiths' College, London, U.K., 1963-64. Married, 2 sons, 1 daughter. Appointments include: Education Officer, Northern Region of Nigeria, 1961; Head of Department of Art, The Advanced Teachers' College, Zaria, 1962; Vice-Principal, ibid, 1965-67; Inspector of Art & Publicity, Ministry of Education, Kaduna, 1967-68; Principal, Toro Teachers' College, 1968—. Memberships include: President, Nigerian Society of Professional Artists, 1965; Nigerian Society of Artists; Exec., Association of Fine Arts Students, 1958-61; Secretary Assistant Producer, Dramatic Society, 1959-61. Awards include: Sir Sydney Philipson Award, 1960; UNESCO Fellowship in Education Research, 1963-64; History Prize, 1965. Address: Toro Teachers' College, Toro, via Jos, North-Eastern State, Nigeria.

OLATUNDE, Ayoola, born 2nd February, 1935. Clinical Pharmacologist. Education: Primary, Public School, Ido-Ekiti; Secondary, Christ's School, Ado-Ekiti, 1947-52; M.B., B.S. (London), University College, Ibadan, Nigeria, 1954-61; University of Lagos Medical School; Dip. Clin. Pharm., Manchester University, U.K., 1969. Personal details: descendant of the Olu family in Ido-Ekiti; married, 3 children. Appointments: Medical Officer, Adeoyo Hospital, Ibadan, 1962-63; Rural Medical Officer, Ogbomoso, Western Nigeria, 1963-64; Junior Research Fellow, Pharmacology, Medical School, University of Lagos, 1964-66; Lecturer, Pharmacology, College of Medicine, ibid, 1966-68; ibid, University of Ibadan, 1968—. Memberships: Nigeria Medical Association; British Medical Association; Science Association of Nigeria; West African Science Association. Contributor to scientific publications. Address: University of Ibadan, Ibadan, Nigeria.

OLAYEMI, Julius Yinka, born 2nd April, 1942. Teacher. Education: Primary, 1948-55; Secondary, 1956-61; Higher Secondary, 1962-63; B.Sc., Ahmadu Bello University, Zaria, Nigeria, 1963-66. Appointments: Research Student, Chemistry, Ahmadu Bello University, 1966-68; Lecturer, Chemistry, ibid, 1968-70.

Address: Department of Chemistry, Ahmadu Bello University, Zaria, Northern Nigeria.

OLDFIELD, Arthur John, born 19th November, 1915. Bank Manager. Education: St. Bees School, Cumberland, U.K. Married. Appointments: Manager, Barclays Bank DCO, Mombasa, Kenya, 1956; ibid, Seychelles, 1961; Main Branch Manager, Mombasa, 1963—. Captain, Royal Army Pay Corps, 1939-46. Memberships: Fellow, Royal Economics Society, 1942; Associate, Institute of Bankers, 1947; Fellow, ibid, 1961; President, Royal Society of St. George, Mombasa, 1968; Mombasa Club; Mombasa Sports Club; Mombasa Golf Club; Nyali Golf Club. Contributor, Banking Systems of Commonwealth Countries. Address: c/o Barclays Bank D.C.O., P.O. Box 88, Mombasa, Kenya.

OLE LEKEN, Stephen Kapaai, born 20th February 1940. Educator. Education: Kajiado School; Kijabe College; Kikuyu College. Appointments: Headmaster, Kajiado & Ilbissil Boarding Schools, 1960-63; Chief Inspector, Kenya Dairy Board, 1964-66; Publicity Officer, Kenya Meat Commission, 1968; Rancher; Member of Parliament. Memberships: Secretary, Kajiado Branch, Kenya National Union of Teachers, 1960-63; Secretary, Kajiado Farmers' Association, 1967—. Address: P.O. Box 38, Kajiado, Kenya.

OLEMBO, Reuben James, born Kima Mission, Bunyore, Kenya, 28th November 1937. University Lecturer; Research Scientist. Education: C.M.S. Maseno School, 1950-56; The Royal Technical College, 1957-59; B.Sc., Purdue University, Lafayette, Indiana, U.S.A., 1961; M.Sc., 1963; Ph.D., 1965. Married. Appointments include: Graduate Assistant, Purdue University, 1963; Rockefeller Foundation Fellow in Genetics, 1963-65; Lecturer, Genetics, Makerere University College, Uganda, 1965; Academic Warden, University Hall, 1967—; Consultant in Genetics, UNESCO Project in Biology, 1968; Senior Lecturer, Makerere University College, 1968; Senior Lecturer, University College, Nairobi, Kenya, 1969—. Memberships: Genetics Society of America; Member of Exec. & Editor, East African Academy; American Genetics Association; American Association for the Advancement of Science; International Biometrical Society; Board of Governors, Uganda Technical College; President, Kenya Science Teachers' Association. Publications: Author of specialist articles in Genetics & Crop Science; Proceedings of East African Academy & East African Journal. Address: Department of Botany, University of Nairobi, P.O. Box 30197, Nairobi, Kenya.

OLISA, Emeka Geoffrey, born 8th January 1927. Medical Pathologist. Education: St. Gregory's College, Lagos, Nigeria; Rockwell College, Cashel, Ireland; University of Göttingen, Germany; University of Hamburg; University of Cambridge, U.K.; M.B.; M.D.; D.T.M.; M.Sc. Personal details: eldest son of Chief Ezeama Robert Olissa, M.B.E., King designate of Ossomari, Nigeria & late Agnes Idu Olisa (née Okwesa); married to Stella Ifeyinwa Ogo, B.A.(Hons.), University of Nigeria, 3 sons.

Appointments: Medical Officer, Eastern Nigeria Government, 1959-63; Post-doctorate Research Fellow, Pembroke College, Cambridge, U.K., 1960-63; Lecturer in Pathology, University of Ibadan, Nigeria, 1963-66; Senior Lecturer in Pathology, University of Nigeria, 1967—. Memberships: Foundation Member, British Society for Parasitologists; Nigerian Medical Association; Medical Advisory Council for Onitsha Catholic Archdioses. Publications: Experimentalle Untersuchungen uber die Adaptation von Borrelien auf das bebrutete huhnereir, 1959; Observations on Toxoplasma gondii with special reference to morphology & relationship to host cell, 1963; Cytology & Electron microscopy of Toxoplasma gondii, Parasitology, 1963; Diseases in Nigeria. Honours: Fridjof-Nansen Scholar, Göttingen, 1954; Academics-ausland-amt, Scholar, Göttingen, 1955. Address: Dept. of Pathology, University of Nigeria, Enugu Campus, Nigeria.

OLISO-EMOSINGOIT, Francis Xavier, born 2nd February 1929. International Official. Education: Ngora High School, Uganda; Namilyango College; articled to Messrs Gibson & Weldon, Solicitors, London, U.K., 1962-64; admitted to the Inner Temple, 1964. Married. Appointments: Sub-Inspector of Police, Uganda, 1954; Assistant Attaché, Crown Law Office, Crown Counsel, 1956-58; Crown Prosecutor, 1959-62; Deputy Chairman, Representative of Uganda, East African Community, 1967—. Memberships: Secretary-General, Uganda Police Inspectorate Association, 1960-62; Treasurer, UPC, U.K. & Ireland Branch, 1965—; Chairman, ibid, 1966-67; Associate, Law Society, England & Wales; Life Member, Inns of Court Debating Society. Address: E.A. Community Service Commission, P.O. Box 1000, Arusha, Tanzania.

OLIVER, Hugh Walter Latham, born 24th June 1930. Medical Practitioner. Education: Shrewsbury School, U.K., 1944-49; London Hospital Medical College, 1949-54. Married. Appointments: House Surgeon, Harold Wood Hospital, 1954; House Physician, Mile End Hospital, 1955; Medical Officer, R.A.M.C., 1955-57; Sr. House Officer, Paediatrics, St. David's Hospital, Bangor, 1958; House Officer, Obstetrics, City of London Hospital, 1959; Medical Officer, Mengo Hospital, Kampala, Uganda, 1960-70; Medical Superintendent, ibid, 1970—. Member of the Old Salopian Club. Address: Mengo Hospital, P.O. Box 7161, Kampala, Uganda.

OLOYA, Jacobson, born 15th June 1932. Economist. Education: Gulu High School, 1941-48; King's College, Budo, 1949-51; Makerere University, 1952-56; University of Wales, U.K., 1960-66; M.Sc., Ph.D., Dip. Agric., N.C.A. Married, 4 children. Appointments: Assistant Agricultural Officer, Uganda Government, 1957-64; Agricultural Economist, ibid, 1964-67; Lecturer, Makerere University, 1967-70; Acting Head, Department of Agricultural Economics, ibid, 1970—. Memberships: President, East African Agricultural Economics Society, 1969-70; Uganda Economics Association. Publications: Some Aspects of Economic Development; Coffee, Cotton, Sisal, & Tea in the East African

Economies. Address: Acting Head, Dept. of Agricultural Economics, Makerere University, Box 7062, Kampala, Uganda.

OLUFOSOYE (The Right Rev.) Timothy Omotayo, born 31 March 1918. Anglican Bishop. Education: St. Stephen's, Ondo, Nigeria; St. Andrew's College, Oyo; University of British Columbia, Vancouver, B.C., Canada. Married, 1 son, 3 daughters. Appointments: Curate, St. Stephen's, Ondo, Nigeria; Curate, Christ's Church Cathedral, Lagos; Curate, St. Helens, Lancs., U.K.; Curate, Sheffield Cathedral; Vicar, Holy Trinity Church, Lagos, Nigeria; Cannon Residentiary & Provost, Ondo Cathedral; Examining Chaplain; Registrar; Vicar-General; Lord Bishop of Gambia. Memberships: Vice-President, A.A.C.C., U.S.P.G., & W.C.C.E.; President, The Boys' Brigade. Publications: The Problem of Suffering. Honours: Officer of the Order of Nigeria, 1963; Chief Lomofe of Ondo, 1960. Address: Bathurst, The Gambia.

OLUKOYA, Samuel Ayodele (Chief Apebi of Ihoda), born Ibadan, Nigeria, 17th December 1917. Barrister-at-Law; Solicitor; Advocate. Education: Ibadan Grammar School, 1923-32; King's College, Lagos, 1933-37; Called to English Bar, Gray's Inn Law School, London, U.K., 1951. Personal details: father, Adolphus Benjamin Olukoya (deceased), Produce Magnate; mother, Sabaina Idowu Olukoya; married to Patience Olukoya. Appointments: former Trade Unionist & General Secretary, P.W.D. Workers' Union, Nigeria, 1944-47; Hon. Secretary, All-Nigeria Technical & General Workers' Federation, 1945-46. Fellow of Royal Geographical Society. President, Egba Divisional Grade A, Customary Court, Abeokuta, Western Nigeria. Address: SW8, 123A, Ijebu Bye-Pass, Oke-Ado, Ibadan, Western Nigeria.

OLUSOLA, Benedict Olufemi, The Otunba of Ilawe, born Ilawe Ekidi, 12th October. Solicitor & Advocate; Public Notary of Nigeria. Education: Primary 1-5, St. Paul's Catholic, Ebute Metha, 1927-31; Primary VI, Holy Cross Catholic, Lagos, 1932; Grade II, Teachers' Certificate, St. Gregory's College, Lagos, 1934-37; Barrister-at-Law, Lincoln's Inn, London, & Kennington College of Law, London, U.K., 1953-56. Personal details: married, 5 sons, 2 daughters. Appointments: Tutor, St. Paul's Catholic School, 1938-41; Treasury Clerk, Treasury, Lagos, Nigeria, 1942-44; Biology Teacher, St. Gregory's College, Lagos, 1944-47; Biology Master, C.M.S. Grammar School, Lagos, 1948-51; Practising Barrister, Lagos, 1956-57; Executive Director, Western Nigeria Development Corporation, 1957-63; Member of Federal Parliament, Nigeria, Minister of State for Education, 1965-66; Practising Barrister, Ibadan & Lagos, 1966-70. Memberships include: Island Club, Lagos; Ibadan Tennis Club; Commissioner, Boy Scouts, Western State. Honours: Wood Badge; Advanced Scout Training Insignia, 1970. Address: P.O. Box 2073, Ibadan, Nigeria.

OMABOE, Emmanuel Noi, born Amanokrom, Ghana, 29th October 1930. Statistician. Education: Accra Academy, 1946-50; University of Ghana, 1951-54; B.Sc.(Econ.), London School of Economics, University of London, U.K., 1957. Personal details: married, 5 children. Appointments: Economic Research Fellow, University of Ghana, 1957-59; Government Statistician, Central Bureau of Statistics, 1960-66; Chairman, Economic Committee of the NLC, 1966-69; Commissioner for Economic Affairs, 1967-69. Fellow of the Royal Statistical Society. Memberships: American Statistical Assn.; Vice-President, International Statistical Institute; Vice-President, International Union for Scientific Study of the Population; Past-President, Ghana Economic Society. Publications: A Survey of Contemporary Ghana (w. W. B. Birmingham & I. Neustadt), 1966; International Migration Differentials From Conventional Census Questionaire Items in Ghana (w. B. Gil), Isi Session. Recipient of Grand Medal, 1969. Address: E. N. Omaboe Associates, Ltd., P.O. Box 6251, Accra, Ghana.

OMARI, Dunstan Alfred, born Newala, Tanzania, 9th August 1922. Business Consultant; Company Director. Education: Primary & Secondary at various schools in Tanzania, 1929-42; Dip. Ed., Makerere College, Uganda, 1943-45; B.A.(Hons.), Econ., University of Wales, 1949-53. Married, 2 sons, 1 daughter. Appointments include: Teacher, 1946-49; Education Officer with Broadcasting Duties, 1953-54; District Officer, 1955-58; District Commissioner, 1959-61; Tanganyika High Commissioner in U.K., 1961-62; Permanent Secretary, Prime Minister's Office, 1962-63; Secretary-General, East African Common Services Organization, 1964-67; Secretary-General, East African Community, 1967-68; Business Consultant & Company Director, 1968—. Memberships: Member, East African Legislative Assembly, 1964-67; Chairman, East African Currency Board, 1964—; President, Automobile Association of East Africa, 1965-68; Chairman, East African Safari, 1964; Director, African Medical & Research Foundation, 1964—; Trustee, East African Academy, 1964—; President, E.A. Management Foundation, 1966-68. Honours, Prizes, etc.: M.B.E., 1960. Address: P.O. Box 25015, Nairobi, Kenya.

OMITERU, Emman Iyiola, born 7th June 1935. Pharmacist. Education: St. David's Kudeti School, Ibadan, Nigeria, 1942-48; Government College, ibid, 1949-53; Pharmacy School, Yaba, 1955-58. Married. Appointments: worked in Western Government Hospitals, 1959-64; established Crystal Chemists, Ibadan, 1964—. Memberships: Financial Secretary, Pharmaceutical Society of Western Nigeria; Ibadan Tennis Club. Address: Box 3223, Ibadan, Nigeria.

OMITOWOJU, Joshua Olareni, born Ile-Ife, Nigeria, 6th May 1918. Private Medical Practitioner. Education: St. Philip's School, Aiyetoro, Ile-Ife, 1923-30; won Government Scholarship to Government College, Ibadan, 1931-36, & to Higher College, Yaba, 1937-38; L.S.M.(Nigeria), Nigeria Medical School, 1938-43. Married, 8 children. Appointments include: Assistant Medical Officer, 1943-48; Medical Officer, Nigerian Government Medical Services, Lagos, Ibadan, Benin City, Warri,

Agbor, Enugu, Obubra, & Degema, 1948-54; Private Medical Practice, 1954-60; nominated Member, Western Nigeria House of Assembly, 1960; elected Member, ibid, 1960-66; Minister of Chieftaincy Affairs, 1960-62; Regional Minister, Premier's Office, 1963; Minister of Health, 1963-65; Minister of Establishment & Training, 1965-66; Member, Nigerian Senate, 1960. Memberships include: British Medical Association; Fellow, Royal Society of Tropical Medicine & Hygiene; Action Group Party, 1958-62; Nigerian National Democratic Party, 1964-66. Address: P.O. Box 554, Ibadan, Western State, Nigeria.

OMO-DARE, Paul, born June 1931. Professor of Surgery. Education: C.M.S. Grammar School, Lagos, Nigeria, 1946-50; Norwich City College, U.K., 1952-53; Birmingham University Medical School, Birmingham, 1953-59; Edinburgh University, 1961. Appointments: Science Teacher, Victory College, Ikare, Western Nigeria, 1951-52; House Physician, Wolverhampton Royal Hospital, Postgraduate Teaching Hospital of the University of Birmingham, U.K., 1959-60; House Surgeon, Accident Hospital, ibid, 1960; Senior House Officer (Surgery), General Hospital, West Bromwich, Birmingham, 1960; Demonstrator (Temporary Lecturer Grade), Department of Anatomy, University of Birmingham, 1961; Registrar in Surgery, Traumatic Unit, General Hospital, West Bromwich, Birmingham, 1961; Senior House Officer, Registrar in Surgery, Professorial Unit, Department of Surgery, University College Hospital, Ibadan, Nigeria, 1961-64; Senior Registrar in Surgery, Professorial Unit, Department of Surgery, Lagos University Teaching Hospital, Surulere, 1964-65; Lecturer in Surgery, University of Lagos & Consultant Surgeon to Lagos University Teaching Hospital, Surulere, 1965-67; Honorary Clinical Assistant in Urology, St. Paul's Hospital, London, U.K., 1968; Senior Lecturer in Surgery, University of Lagos & Consultant Surgeon to Lagos University Teaching Hospital, Surulere, 1967-69; Associate Professor in Surgery, & Consultant Surgeon, ibid, 1969—. Memberships: Licentiate, Royal College of Physicians, London, U.K.; Fellow, Royal College of Surgeons; ibid, College of Surgeons of West Africa; Paediatrics Association of Nigeria; Council Mbr., St. John's Ambulance, Nigeria; Mbr., Advisory Council on Health to the Kwara State Government, Nigeria. Author of numerous works published in British and African Medical Journals. Honours: Undergraduate Scholarship for performance in the Professional Examination in Anatomy & Physiology, 1956; Research Prize in Surgery, West African College of Surgeons, 1967. Address: Department of Surgery, College of Medicine of the University of Lagos, Lagos, Nigeria.

OMOLOLU, Adewale, born 15th November 1927. Nutritionist; Child Health Specialist; Teacher of Medicine. Education: C.M.S. Grammar School, Lagos, Nigeria; King's College, Lagos; M.R.C.P.I., Royal College of Surgeons of Ireland; D.P.H., School of Hygiene & Tropical Medicine, University of London, U.K.; F.M.C.P.H.(Nigeria); D.C.H.; L.L.M.R.C.P.I.; L.L.M.R.C.S.I. Married. Appointments: Director, Food Science & Applied Nutrition Unit, University of Ibadan, & Consultant in Clinical Nutrition, University College Hospital, Ibadan, Nigeria; Member, Ad-hoc Committee on Feeding the Pre-School Child, WHO/UNICEF/FAO Protein Advisory Group; Secretary, Examining Board, Nigeria Medical Council in Public Health; Expert Advisory Committee on Nutrition, National Health Council of Ministers; WHO Consultant, Government of Mauritius, in Nutrition & Maternal & Child Health, 1966. Memberships: Vice-President, Society of Health of Nigeria; Western State Sports Council; Association of Physicians of West Africa; Executive Council, Nigeria Medical Association (West). Publications include: Child Health in Western Nigeria, WAMJ, 1965; Notes on diets for displaced & needy persons & the treatment of malnutrition, 1968; Dietary Patterns & Nutrition in Nigeria, 8th Int. Congress of Nutrition, 1969; Prevention of Malnutrition, 1970. Honours: Sethi Prizeman, London School of Hygiene & Tropical Medicine, 1962. Address: Food Science & Applied Nutrition Unit, University of Ibadan, Ibadan, Nigeria.

OMORUYI, Bright A., born Benin City, Nigeria, 17th June 1929. Tobacco Company Distributor. Education: Nigerian Baptist Convention School, Benin City, 1940-46; trained as Storekeeper, Accounts Clerk, Messrs John Holt Ltd., Owo, 1950-53; Sales Management Course, Nigerian Tobacco Co. Ltd., Ibadan, 1965. Married, 11 children. Appointments: Teacher, Nigerian Baptist Convention School, 1947-49; Clerk in Charge, John Holt Ltd., Owo, Ikare, 1955-60; Mobil Oil Dealer, Ikare, 1956-68; General Merchant & Registered Distributor for Star Beer, Guiness Stout, Top Beer, Vono Products, & Lever Bros. Products, 1961-65; Distributor, Nigerian Tobacco Co. Ltd., Benin City, 1965—; Director, Bright Omoruyi (Nig.) Ltd., 1969; Dealer, Texaco (Nig.) Ltd., 1970; Proprietor, Bright Omoruyi (Nigeria) Ltd. Rest House. Memberships: Vice-Chairman, Ivbibiwe Nokun Union, Benin City; Akugbe Clan Union; General Secretary, Swimming Pool Fund-raising Committee, Benin City; Rotary Club, Benin City; Chairman, Club 39, ibid; Life Vice-Chairman, 400 Club, Lagos. Address: 49B Ikpoba Rd., Benin City, Nigeria.

OMOTOSO, Akinyemi, born 25th January 1929. Pharmacist. Appointments: Chemist & Druggist, Nigeria, 1951; Pharmaceutical Chemist, U.K., 1957; Managing Director, Omotoso Pharmaceuticals, Lagos, Nigeria. Member of Pharmaceutical Society of U.K., 1958. Address: 13/17, Breadfruit St. P.O. Box 4024, Lagos, Nigeria.

OMWAKWE, Reuben Mbalanya, born 16th June 1937. Librarianship. Education: Maseno High School, 1950-56; North-Western Polytechnic, London, U.K., 1962-63; Columbia University, New York, U.S.A., 1965. Appointments: Librarian, High Court of Kenya, 1964-66; Assistant Librarian, University College, Nairobi, 1967—. Memberships: Library Association of Great Britain; East African Library Association. Address: c/o University College, Nairobi, Kenya.

ONABAMIRO, Sanya Dojo, born Ago-Iwoye, Ijebu Province, Western Nigeria, 24th May 1916. Zoologist; University Dean; Government Official. Education: Teacher Training Course, Wesley College, Ibadan, 1929-32; Science Course, Government Higher College, Yaba, Lagos, 1937-40; B.Sc.(Hons., Zoology), 2nd Class, Upper Division, University of Manchester, U.K., 1944-47; Postgraduate Teacher Education Course, Oxford, 1947-48; Ph.D., University of London, 1951. Appointments: Academic Staff, University of Ibadan, Nigeria, 1949-60; Delegate, Nigerian Constitutional Conference, London, U.K., 1957, 1958; Member, Ashby Commission on Higher Education in Nigeria, 1959, 1960; Cabinet Minister, Government of Western Nigeria, 1960-65; Professor & Head, Department of Zoology, University of Ife, 1962; Head, Department of Biological Sciences & Dean, Faculty of Basic Sciences, Njala University College, Freetown, Sierra Leone, 1969—. Publications: Why Our Children Die, 1949; Food & Health, 1953; several papers in scientific journals. Address: Njala University College, Private Mail Bag, Freetown, Sierra Leone.

ONALAJA, Moronkeji Omotayo, born Ijebu-Ode, Western Nigeria, 24th July 1933. Barrister & Solicitor. Education: Holy Trinity Ebute Ero Lagos Primary School; C.M.S. Grammar School, Lagos; London School of Economics & Political Science, London, U.K. Personal details: married to Folashade Ogunsanya, S.R.N., S.C.M., Q.N. Research Nursing Sister, Institute of Child Health, University of Ibadan, Nigeria, 3 sons, 2 daughters. Appointments: General Assistant Manager, Tekumo Onalaja & Co.; Legal Practitioner; Public Notary; Barrister & Solicitor of the Supreme Court of Nigeria. Memberships: Pastor's Warden, St. Anne's Church, Molete, Ibadan; Youth Christian Circle, St. James Cathedral, Oke Bola, Ibadan; Solidra Circle, Lagos. Publications: Nigerian Monthly Law Reports (Member of Editorial Board). Address: P.O. Box 303, Ibadan, Nigeria.

ONAMBELE, Germain Francois, born 29th January 1935. Inspector of Youth, Sports, & Popular Education. Education: Primary School, Saa; Secondary Studies, College Vogt Yde; Technical Studies, Centre of Physics Education; Higher Studies, l'Ecole Normale Superieure, Yde. Married, 5 children. appointments: Teacher, Physical Education, Technical School, Douda, 1957-60; Head of Service, Civil & School Sports of the Cameroun, 1961-65; Student, Federal University, 1966-68; Inspector, Eastern Region, Cameroun, 1968-70. Membre d'honneur du Club Alucam Edia, 1968-69. Honours: Lauriat au Concours des Inspecteurs, lettres de felicitation du ministre. Address: B.P. 151, Yaoundé, Cameroun.

ONANUGA, Amos Adenuga, born 30th May 1929. Managing Director. Education: St. Matthew's Anglican School, Imodi, Ijebu-Ode, Nigeria. Married. Appointments: Managing Director, Ona Ara Bookshops Nigeria Ltd. Member of United Education Institute Ltd., Nassau, Bahamas. Address: 26, Reclamation Road, P.O. Box 946, Lagos, Nigeria.

ONASANYA, Abiodun, born 29th December 1924. Medical Records Officer. Education: Cambridge School Certificate; School of Medical Records, Royal Infirmary, Bristol, U.K. Married, 1 son, 3 daughters. Appointments: Deputy Medical Records Officer, University College Hospital, Ibadan, Nigeria, 1960-62; Medical Records Officer, Lagos University Teaching Hospital, Lagos, 1962—. Memberships: President, Nigerian Association of Medical Records Officers; Assistant Secretary, Automobile Association of Nigeria. Address: Lagos University Teaching Hospital, P.M.B. 12003, Lagos, Nigeria.

ONGHAIE, Alphonse, born 3rd November 1922. Director of the Hotel Cosmos. Education: Primary School; Edouard Renard High School, Brazzaville, Republic of the Congo. Married, 7 children. Appointments: Director-General, Building Society of the Congo, 1961-63; Director, Annexe ONCPA, Sibiti, Congo, 1965-67; Head of Service, National Construction Funds, 1967-69; Director, Hotel Cosmos, Paruide, 197. Memberships: Representative Counsellsor, Oubangui-Chari, 1946-51; Secretary-Delegate, Standing Commission, ibid; Founding Member, Co-operative of Cotton Producers of Oubangui-Chari, at Bangui, 1950-51. J.O. de l'A.F.F., 1946. Address: Hotel Cosmos, B.P. 2459, Brazzaville, Republic of the Congo.

ONGOM, V. L., born Pakwach, Uganda, 7th June 1933. Physician; Educator. Education: Namilyango College, Uganda, 1953-55; University of Nairobi, Kenya, 1956-58; University of Delhi, India, 1959-60; M.B., B.S., Agra University, Medical College; D.P.H. Married, 5 children. Appointments: Medical Officer, rank of Captain, Uganda Armed Forces, 1966-69; Lecturer, Department of Preventive Medicine, 1969—. Memberships: General Secretary, Students' Council, Nairobi University, 1957; President, Uganda Students' Association of India & Pakistan, 1964; Vice-President, All-African Students' Association of India, 1964. Author of various scientific papers. Address: Department of Preventive Medicine, Makerere University Medical School, P.O. Box 7072, Kampala, Uganda.

ONI-OKPAKU, Benjamin Aigbobasimi, born 25th January 1932. Specialist Surgeon. Education: Christ Church Cathedral School, 1944-46; King's College, Lagos, Nigeria, 1946-51; University of Birmingham, U.K., 1952-58; Royal College of Surgeons, 1960-63; M.B., Ch.B. (Birmingham), 1958; L.R.C.P. (Lond.); M.R.C.S.(Eng.); F.R.C.S.(Edin.); F.R.C.S.(Eng.). Personal details: father, Mr. H. Oni-Okpaku, M.B.E., retired Chief Superintendent of Police, later Chairman, Bendel Development & Town Planning Authority; wife, a Barrister-at-Law, Later Magistrate Grade I, Judicial Dept., Benin City. Appointments: Hallam Hospital, West Bromwich, U.K., 1958-59; Selly Oak Hospital, Birmingham, 1959; St. James's Hospital, Balham, 1960-62, 1963; Gravesend & North Kent Hospital, 1962-63; Lagos University Teaching Hospital, 1963-64; Ministry of Health, Midwest State, serving Sapele, Warri, & Benin, 1964. Memberships:

Island Club, Lagos; Sapele Athletic Club; Vice-President, Warri Club, 1968; Benin Club. Publications include: Administration of Government Hospitals, 1969; Symposium on Health Services in the Midwest State, 1969; Administration of our Hospitals; Private Practice; Financing the Health Scheme. Address: General Hospital, Benin City, Midwest State, Nigeria.

ONOKPASA, Benedict Etedjere, born Adagbrassa, Nigeria, 21st June 1928. Teacher, Poet. Education: R.C. School, Adagbrassa, 1938-45; St. Thomas's College, Ibusa, 1947-49; Forest School, Ibadan, 1951-52; G.C.E. 'A' level, 1953; B.A.(Econ.) Durham, Fourah Bay College, Freetown, Sierra Leone, 1957. Personal details: descended from Evbreke Ruling House, Okpe, Western Urhobo; great-grandparents, Princes Ogoni and Odjokor of Okpe and Agbarho. Married, 6 sons, 2 daughters. Appointments: Forest Assistant, 1952-54; Administrative Officer, Assistant Secretary, Ministry of Finance, Ibadan, 1958; Teacher, Loyola College and City Academy, Ibadan, 1959-62; Senior Economics Master, Urhobo College, Effurun, 1963; Founder, Headmaster, Trinity College, Okwidiemo, 1964—. Memberships include: Founder & President, African Dramatic Society, 1962; Patron, Geographical Society, Trinity College, Okwidiemo; Secretary, Urhobo Orthography Committee, 1963; Founder, Onokpasa-Akemu Scholarship Scheme, Trinity College. Publications include: Modern Urhobe Readers (bks. I-IV; Urhobo Poems; The Hero of Sharpeville (a tragedy). Address: Trinity College, Okwidiemo, Western Urhobo, P.O. Box 27, Adeje, via Warre, Nigeria.

ONUIGBO, Wilson Ikechuku Beniah, born 28th April, 1928. Medical Practitioner. Education: D.M.G.S., Onitsha, Nigeria, 1942-45; Higher College, Yaba, 1946-47; University College, Ibadan, 1951-53; B.Sc.(Lond.), 1954; M.B., Ch.B., Glasgow University, U.K., 1953-57; D.T.M.&H., Liverpool University, 1959; Glasgow University, 1960-62; Ph.D.(Lond.), 1961. Married, 4 children. Appointments: House Physician & Surgeon, General Hospital, Enugu, Nigeria, 1958; Medical Officer, 1959; Research Fellow, Glasgow University, U.K., 1962; Lecturer, Pathology, Lagos University, Nigeria, 1962-63; Specialist Pathologist, Ministry of Health, Enugu, 1964—. Memberships: M.R.C.(Path.), 1963; F.M.C.(Path.), 1970; Royal Society of Medicine; Pathological Society of Great Britain & Ireland; New York Academy of Science; British Academy of Forensic Science; Royal Society of Tropical Medicine & Hygiene. Author of 40 publications in various fields, especially cancer in medical journals. Honours: John Reid Prize for Research in Medical Science & Mary Ure Prize in Child Health, Glasgow University; British Medical Association Prize for medical students, 1957. Address: Pathology Department, General Hospital, Enugu, Nigeria.

ONWU, Simon Ezievno, born 28th December, 1908; deceased, 4th June, 1969. Physician. Education: St. Mary's School, Onitsha; Wesley Boys' High School; King's College, Lagos, Nigeria; London Matriculation; Edinburgh University, U.K., 1932; M.B., Ch.B.; D.T.M.&H. Personal details: son of Late Chief Onwebunta of Affa; wife, daughter of late Chief J. O. Ngemauza; 1st Ibo to qualify as doctor; 8 children, 4 grandchildren. Appointments: Junior Medical Officer; Medical Officer; Senior Medical Officer; Deputy Director, Medical Services; Director, Medical Services & Permanent Secretary, Ministry of Health, Eastern Region, Nigeria; Chairman, Eastern Nigerian Housing Corporation. Memberships: Chairman, Red Cross Society, Eastern Region; Rotary Club; Chairman, Cosmos & Damian, Eastern Region; Vice-President, International Congress, International Union of Building Societies, 1965-67; Dining Club; Vice-Patron, Society for Prevention of Cruelty to Children; Cheshire Home, etc. Honours: Coronation Medal, 1953; M.V.O., 1956; O.B.E., 1954; Knight of St. Sylvester, Papal Award, 1964. Address: c/o Mrs. Ethel Onwu, Eagle Lodge, 74 Ogui Road, Enugo, Nigeria.

ONWUMECHILLI, Cyril Agodi, born 20th January, 1932. University Professor. Education: Scholarship at King's College, Lagos, Nigeria, 1944-49; B.Sc.(Lond.), General, Physics, Pure & Applied Maths., University College, Ibadan, 1953; B.Sc.(Lond.), Special, Physics, ibid, 1954; Ph.D.(Lond.), 1958; Diploma, International Institute of Nuclear Science & Engineering, Argonne National Laboratory, University of Chicago, U.S.A., 1960; F.Inst.P., 1969. Married, 2 sons, 1 daughter. Appointments include: Lecturer Grades, University College, Ibadan, Nigeria, 1958-62; Professor, Physics, ibid, 1962-66; Dean, Faculty of Sciences, 1965-66; Professor & Head, Department, University of Nigeria, Nsukka, 1966-67; Professor & Head, Department, ibid, 1970—; Acting Vice-Chancellor, University of Science of Technology, 1968-69. Director of following observatories in Nigeria: Ibadan Observatory, 1960-66; Zaria Observatory, 1960-63; established, Kontagora Observatory, 1962-66; ibid, Sokoto Observatory, 1963-66. Participant in various international conferences. Gives numerous lectures. Member of many university committees, boards, etc. Memberships include: Chairman, Nigerian Committee for the International Union of Geodesy & Geophysics; Vice-Chairman, Nigerian National Committee for the World Power Conference; Chairman, Nigerian National Committee for the International Years of the Quiet Sun, 1963-67; Nigerian National Committee, UNESCO; Treasurer, West African Science Association, 1961-65; Full Member, Scientific Council for Africa; American Geophysical Union; International Association of Geomagnetism & Aeronomy; Editor in Chief, Nigerian Journal of Science; Nigerian National Committee for Archives; Nigerian National Committee of Africanists; Editorial Board, Journal of West African Science Association. Author of numerous publications in scientific journals. Address: Department of Physics, University of Nigeria, Nsukka, Nigeria.

ONWUMERE, Raphael Egwuonwu, born 4th April 1920. Medical Practitioner. Education: Government School, Ajalhi, 1928-33; Government College, Unumahia, 1934-39; School of Medicine, Yaba, Nigeria, 1940-46; West London Hospital Medical School, U.K., 1952-53;

Institute of Ophthalmology, London, 1953-54, 1959-60. Appointments: Assistant Medical Officer, Medical Department, Nigeria, 1946-51; Medical Officer, 1951-56; Specialist Ophthalmologist, Ministry of Health, Eastern Nigeria, 1956-61; Senior Specialist Ophthalmologist, 1961-70. Publications: Causes of Blindness in Eastern Nigeria (article), 1962; Ocular Complications in Siekel Cell Diseases (article), 1965. Address: 31 Zik Avenue, Enugu, Nigeria.

ONYAC, Onecimo-Oyo, born Koro, 1918. Gazetted Magistrate, Grade II. Education: Gulu High School, 1934-37; Buwalasi T.T.C., 1938-40; Diploma in Law, Nsamizi Law School, 1961-62; Akoli District Administration Bursary, U.K., for 6 months. Married, 10 children. Appointments: Headmaster; School Supervisor; Sub-County Chief; Magistrate Grade III; Magistrate Grade II; Chairman, Acholi Education Committee; Chairman of Laity, Northern Diocese, Uganda. Memberships: Acholi Leprosy Relief Fund; Save the Children Fund; Uganda Boy Scouts Association; Gulu Charity Fund. Honours; Medal of Merit Uganda Scouts Association; Independence Medal of Uganda. Address: P.O. Box 404, Gulu, Uganda.

ONYAII, Stephen Ezekiel, born Uganda 24th September 1933. Veterinary Surgeon. Education: Ongino Primary School, 1941-42; Kumi Primary School, 1943-45; Bukedea Primary School, 1946; Ngora Primary School, 1947; Ngora High School, 1948-50; King's College, Budo, 1951-53; Norwood Technical College, London, U.K., 1955-58; Royal Veterinary College, London University, 1958-64. Personal details: married, 4 children. Appointments: Veterinary Officer, Teso, 1965; District Veterinary Officer, Kigezi, 1965-66; Veterinary Officer, Head Office, 1966-67; Veterinary Officer, Dairy, 1967-68; General Manager, Milk Processing Plant, 1968; Chairman, Managing Director, 1968—. President, Uganda Veterinary Association. Address: Dairy Corporation, P.O. Box 7078, Kampala, Uganda.

ONYANGO, Okudo Ezekiel, born 3rd August 1936. Draughtsman. Education: Ngiya Intermediate School; St. Bernard's College, Masaka; Civil Engineering Course, Diploma in Surveying, British Tutorial College. Married, 4 daughters. Appointments: Trainee District Draughtsman, 1962-64; Acting District Draughtsman, 1963; District Draughtsman, 1964—. Memberships: Founder, Kogwong Abondo, E.A.; Secretary, Kato Union, E.A. Kampala Branch, 1963-65; Secretary, Alego Ragar Union, E.A. Kampala Branch, 1962-65; Assistant Secretary, Gulu Parish Church Council, 1966; Acting Secretary, ibid, 1966-67; Secretary, 1967-68; Team Manager & Member 1st XI U.E.B. Football Club, 1966-68; Committee, Acholi District Football League; U.E.B. Joint Staff Advisory Committee, Lugogo, 1963. Address: Flat 46 Ferranti Amberley Road, P.O. Box 118, Jinja, Uganda.

ONYEMELUKWE, Rufus Nnaeto, born 9th April 1916. Medical Practitioner. Education: Nnewi C.M.S. Central School, Nigeria; D.M.G.S. Grammar School, Onitsha, 1930-32; Teacher Training College, Awka, 1933-35; Achimota College, Ghana, 1937-39; M.B., Ch.B., University of Edinburgh, U.K., 1939-44; D.T.M., D.T.H., University of Liverpool, 1946; D.P.H., Institute of Public Health, London, 1946-47; M.P.H., University of California, Berkeley, U.S.A., 1959-60. Married, 9 children. Appointments: Teacher, Nigeria, 1936; House Surgeon, Royal Infirmary, Sunderland, U.K., 1944-45; Resident Medical Officer, Sherburn Hospital, Durham, 1945-46; Medical Officer, Nigerian Medical Services, 1947-52; Medical Officer of Health, ibid, 1952-57; Specialist Hygienist, Eastern Nigeria Medical Services, 1957-62; Senior Specialist Hygienist, ibid, 1962-66; Chief Health Officer, 1966; WHO short-term Consultant in Health Education, 1966. Memberships: Technical Committee, International Union of Health Education; British Medical Association; Nigerian Medical Association. Publications: Health Education Aspects of Community Development in Eastern Nigeria, I.J.H.E.

ONYEUKWU, Godwin Chibiko, born 17th October 1936. Medical Practitioner. Education: Federal Science School, Lagos, Nigeria; Moscow State University, USSR; Kiev Medical Institute; Friendship University, Moscow. Married, 2 daughters. Appointments: House Surgeon, 1966-67; Senior House Surgeon, 1968-69. Memberships: Soviet Organization of Young Scientists; University Musical Society. Address: General Hospital, Enugu, East Central State, Nigeria.

ONYONKA, Zachary Theodore, born 28th February 1939. Economist; Cabinet Minister, Government of Kenya. Education: Mosocho School, 1947-51; Nyabururu School, 1952-54; St. Mary's School, Yala, 1955-58; B.A.(Econ.), I.A. University, Puerto Rico, 1962; M.A.(Econ.), Syracuse University, Syracuse, N.Y., U.S., 1965; Ph.D., ibid, 1968; Personal details: father, Farmer & Businessman, Kish District of Kenya; married, 1 child. Appointments: Accountant, Gusii County Council, 1959; Research Fellow, University College, Nairobi, Kenya, 1967; Lecturer, Department of Economics, ibid, 1968-69; Minister for Economic Planning & Development, Republic of Kenya, 1970. Fellow, International Bankers' Assn. Member of Economics Club, Kenya. Publications: Air Transportation in East Africa, Industry & Labour in E. Africa; Promoting Economic Development in Kenya, East Africa Journal, 1968. Honours: Winner, Wall Street Journal Student Achievement Award, 1963; Rockefeller Foundation Fellow, 1965-68. Address: Ministry of Economics, Planning & Development, P.O. Box 30651, Nairobi, Kenya.

OOMMEN, Mathilunkal Abraham, born 15th August 1931. Engineer. Education: Diploma in Mechanical & Electrical Engineering, B.Sc. (Marine), University of Durham, U.K.; Corporate Member, Institute of Marine Engineers, London. Appointments: Works Engineer, India; Production Manager, India; Works Manager, India; Executive Engineer, Mechanical, Government of Tanzania; Acting Director, E&M Division, Ministry of Communications, Transport & Labour, Tanzania. Address: Ministry of Communications, Transport & Labour, P.O. Box 9144, Dar es Salaam, Tanzania.

OOZEERALLY, Mohammad Elias, born Mauritius, 17th September 1939. Barrister-at-Law. Education: Higher School Certificate; Barrister-at-Law, Lincoln's Inn, London, U.K.; A.C.I.S. Married, 2 daughters. Appointments include: Clerk of Court, 1959-60; Registrar, Ministry of Housing, 1960-61; Finance Clerk, Government Fire Services, 1961-62; Executive Officer, 1962; Barrister-at-Law, 1965—; Member, Legislative Assembly, 1967, currently Parliamentary Secretary to the Ministry of Economics, Planning & Development; Municipal Council for City of Port Louis, 1969; Company Chairman, 1958-61. Memberships include: Executive Committee, Bar Council; Corporation of Chartered Secretaries. Address: P.O. Box 230, Port Louis, Mauritius.

OPARA, Lambert Osita, born Owerri, Nigeria, 8th October 1936. Educator. Education: B.Sc., Social Science, Indiana State University, U.S.A., 1962; Diploma in Secondary Education, ibid. Personal details: first son of the late Rev. Dr. M. D. Opara, former Member of Eastern Nigeria Parliament; married, 4 children. Appointments: Principal, St. Catherine Teacher Training College, Mbieri Owerri, East Central State, Nigeria, 1963—; President, Zion Methodist Mission (Inc.), 1965—. Zion Mission Representative in the International Council of Christian Churches, Amsterdam. Recipient, Doctor of Divinity, h.c., U.S.A., 1960. Address: St. Catherine Teacher Training College, Box 4, Mbieri Owerri, East Central State, Nigeria.

OPPONG, Christine, born 3rd March 1940. Social Anthropologist. Education: M.A., Social Anthropology, Cambridge; M.A., African Studies, University of Ghana. Married, 2 children. Appointments: Research Fellow, Institute of African Studies, University of Ghana, 1965—; Bye Fellow, Girton College, Cambridge University, U.K., 1968-69. Memberships: British Sociological Association; African Studies Association; Ghana Sociological Association. Author of papers in field published in prof. jrnls.

OPPONG, Emmanuel Nana Waddie, born 2nd April 1927. Veterinary Surgeon; University Lecturer. Education: Veterinary Assistants' Training School, Vom, Nigeria; U.P. College of Veterinary Science & Animal Husbandry, University of Agra, India; School of Veterinary Medicine, University of Cambridge, U.K.; The Royal Dick School of Veterinary Medicine, University of Edinburgh; Veterinary College of Ireland, Trinity College, University of Dublin, Eire, B.V.Sc.&A.H.; Ph.D.; D.T.V.M. Married, 2 children. Appointments: Veterinary Officer, Government of Ghana, 1961-63; Lecturer, University of Ghana, 1963-70; Senior Lecturer, ibid, 1970. Memberships: Royal College of Veterinary Surgeons; Founding Secretary/Treasurer, Ghana Veterinary Medical Association; Pres., ibid, 1967-70; British Mycopathological Soc.; Ghana Science Association; Ghana Agricultural Soc. Author of published papers in field. Address: Faculty of Agriculture, University of Ghana, Legon, Ghana.

ORCHARD, John Richard Sumner, born 11th September 1902. Chartered Engineer. Education: Bradfield, U.K.; M.A.(Hons.), Worcester College, Oxford. Appointments: Controller of Cables Research Department, B.I. Cables, to 1939; Royal Signals, Territorial Army, 1939-47; Assistant Engineer in Chief, East African Ports & Telecommunications, 1948-59; Principal Telecommunications Engineer, Nigerian P&T, 1959-62; Senior Executive Engineer, East African P&T, 1962—. Honours: F.I.E.E., 1945-46; F.I.E.A.A., 1948; Open Mathematics Scholar, Oxford. Address: P.O. Box 30301, Nairobi, Kenya.

OREDEIN (Chief) Samuel Taiwo, born Ogere-Remo, Ijebu Province, Western Nigeria, 1st February 1913. Politician, Businessman, & Company Director. Education: Anglican School, Ogere, Ijebu-Remo; Pupil Teacher, C.M.S. School, Iperu-Remo, Ijebu, 1930-33; C.M.S. Grammar School, Lagos. Appointments: Stenographer, Nigerian Tobacco Company Ltd.; Secretary to the Factory Manager, ibid, 1944-48; Secretary-General, Nigerian Tobacco Workers' Union; Member, Trade Union Congress of Nigeria (now defunct); Executive Member, Trades Union Council of Western Nigeria; Founder-Member, Action Group of Nigeria, 1950; variously, Pro-tem. Secretary of the Party, 1st Administrative Secretary; Organizing Secretary; Principal Organizing Secretary of the Party, directly responsible to the Leader, 1955-66, when the Party was banned by the Federal Military Government of Nigeria; restricted & detained under the Emergency Regulations of Federal Government, 1962; charged (along with Chief Obafemi Awaololo, Leader of Action Group Party) with Treasonable Felony & Conspiracy, 1962; convicted, 1963; acquitted on Appeal, 1964; again charged with crime during troubles of 1965; acquitted, due to intervention of Army Coup, 1966; currently engaged in business generally, wholesale distribution of beer, assorted drinks, etc. Memberships include: Action Group Party, as previously detailed; Chieftaincy Title of Asiwaju of Ogere (Leader), 1961. Publications include: Pamphlet, Party Organization. Address: SW4/689, Oredein Street, Oke-Foko, P.O. Box 1347, Ibadan, Nigeria.

ORRACA-TETTEH, Richard, born 5th March 1932. Nutrition Scientist; Educator. Education: Government Boys' School, 1937-47; Accra Academy Secondary School, Ghana, 1948-51; University of Ghana, 1953-59; London University, UIK., 1960-64. Appointments: Nutrition Officer, Ministry of Health, Ghana; Lecturer, University of Ghana, Legon. Memberships: The Nutrition Society, Britain; Ghana Home Science Association; Ghana Consumers' Association. Publications include: The Need for a Nutrition Policy in National Planning, Interfac. Lectures, Univ. of Ghana, 1969; Higher Living Standards & Improved Diets, 1st Ghana Food Congress, 1970. Honours: Studentship, London School of Hygiene & Tropical Medicine. Address: Dept. of Nutrition & Food Sci., Univ. of Ghana, Legon, Ghana.

ORYEM, Arthur Eture, born 25th May 1924. Education Officer. Education: Police Primary School, Kampala, Uganda; St. Joseph's Primary

School, Gulu; Sacred Heart Lacor Seminary, Gulu; Gulu Primary Teacher Training Centre; Kyambogo Teacher Training Institute; Bristol University, U.K. Personal details: father served in World War II, later joined the Uganda Police Force, now retired. Appointments: Deputy Principal, Teacher Training College; Headmaster, Junior Secondary Schools; District Education Officer. Memberships: Secretary, English Club, Gulu P.T.T.C.; President, Catholic Association, Acholi, Gulu; Vice-President, Gulu Social Club; Member of Acholi District Council; Acholi District Appointments Board; Wild & Munster Constitutions Reports; Uganda National Anthem, Court of Arms, Flag, & Stamps Committee. Recip. of Scout Wood Badge, 1952. Address: Mubende District, P.O. Box 64, Mubende, Uganda.

OSEI-KOFI, Emmanuel, born 28th January 1928. Educator. Education: Adisade College, Cape Coast; Teacher Training, Achimota College; University College of the Gold Coast; University of London Institute of Education; B.A.(Lond.); Diploma in the Teaching of English as a Foreign Language. Married, 3 children. Appointments: Junior Teacher, Grade I, 1951; Education Officer, 1957; Senior Education Officer, 1963; Headmaster, Kumasi Academy, 1964—. Memberships: National Secretary, Conference of Heads of Assisted Secondary Schools of Ghana, 1968—; Lodge Kumasi No. 1472 S.C. Currently working on 'Common Entrance English' for entry into Secondary Schools in West Africa, to be published by Longmans. Address: P.O. Box 3814, Kumasi, Ghana.

OSENI (Alahaji) Muheeb Oloruntele, born 11th January 1918. Legal Practitioner. Education: LL.B.(London), U.K.; Called to the Bar, Middle Temple, 1951. Personal details: made the pilgrimage to Mecca & Medina, 1965 & 1970; married, with children. Appointments: Deputy Chairman, Board of Trustees, Glover Memorial Hall, Lagos, Nigeria, 1965—; Chairman, Lagos City Council Caretaker Committee, 1969—. Memberships: General Secretary, Jama-at-ul Islamijya of Nigeria, 1953-69; President, ibid, 1969—; Island Club, Lagos, 1954—; Treasurer, Nigeria Bar Association, 1957-68; Council of Muslim School Proprietors, 1959—; Board of Governors, Eko Boys' Muslim High School, Lagos, 1960—; Muslim Teacher Training College & Jubril Martin Ahmadijya Grammar School, 1966—. Address: 41 Idoluwo Street, Lagos, Nigeria.

OSHIM, J. Adegoke, born Ondo, Nigeria, 3rd December 1917. Driver. Education: Military. Many wives. Appointments: Full Sergeant, Second World War; Foreman, S. A. Oladapo & Co. Ltd., Ondo. Member, Christian Society. Address: S. A. Oladapo & Co. Ltd., P.O. Box 21, Ondo, Nigeria.

OSHIOKE, Alfred Musa, born Apana-Uzairue, Nigeria, 1922. Teacher. Education: Standard VI, 1943; Teachers' Grade III Cert., 1953; Teachers' Grade II Certificate, 1958. Married, 5 sons, 1 daughter. Appointments: Headmaster, St. Philip's Catholic School, Jattu, 1947-48; St. Patrick's Catholic School, Ewan, 1955; Holy Angel's, Dangbala, 1958-59; Holy Cross, Imoga, 1960-61; St. Bonaventure's Catholic School, Okhashie, 1962-67; St. Vincent's, Auchi, 1968—. Memberships: Nigerian Union of Teachers; Chairman, Okpilla Branch, ibid, 1965-67. Address: St. Vincent's Catholic School, P.O. Box 27, Auchi, Nigeria.

OSHODI, Charles Olayeni, born 3rd September 1920. Medical Practitioner; Psychiatrist. Education: Baptist Academy, Lagos, Nigeria; Igbobi College, Lagos; School of Pharmacy, Lagos; University of Glasgow, U.K.; Institute of Psychiatry, London; M.B., Ch.B. (Glasgow); D.P.M.(England). Personal details: father, a Lagos Chief (deceased). Married. Appointments: Medical Officer, 1951-59; Senior Medical Officer, 1960-63; Specialist Psychiatrist, 1963-65; Senior Specialist Psychiatrist, 1965-67; Lecturer, Ibadan University, 1968-69; Senior Lecturer, Ahmadu Bello University, Zaria, 1969—. Memberships: Association of Psychiatrists of Nigeria; Association of Social Workers of Nigeria; Nigerian Medical Association. Honours: Prize in Ophthalmology, Glasgow University, 1949; 1st Class Certificate in Mental Diseases, 1950; Officer of the Order of the Niger, Nigerian Republic Honours, 1965. Address: A.B.W. Hospital, Kaduna, N. Nigeria.

OSIBOGUN, Adeyemi Adegboyega, born 8th April 1927. Barrister-at-Law; Solicitor. Education: St. Saviour's High School, Lagos, Nigeria, 1932-42; Ijebu-Ode Grammar School, Western Nigeria, 1943-49; Barrister-at-Law, Lincoln's Inn, London, U.K., 1958-62. Married, 3 children. Appointments: Private Legal Practitioner, 1962-66; State Counsel, Malawi Government, 1966-70. Address: Ministry of Justice, P.O. Box 203, Lilongwe, Malawi.

OSMAN, Azad Mahomed, born 21st September 1939. University Educator. Education: Royal College, Port Louis, Mauritius, 1951-52; Royal College, Curepipe, 1953-58; B.Sc.(Agric.), University of Reading, Berkshire, U.K., 1959-62; D.T.A., I.C.T.A., University of the West Indies, St. Augustine, Trinidad. Married, 1 daughter. Appointments: Tea Officer, Department of Agriculture, Mauritius, 1965; Assistant Lecturer, College of Agriculture, ibid, 1966-68; Lecturer, School of Agriculture, University of Mauritius, 1968—. Member, Mauritius Society for the Prevention of Cruelty to Animals. Address: School of Agriculture, University of Mauritius, Reduite, Mauritius.

OSO, Nathaniel Oyenuga, born 6th February 1923. Pharmacist. Education: Methodist School, Ode-Remo, Ijebu, Western State, 1935-38; Ago-Iwoije Methodist School, ibid, 1939-40; Secondary, Government College, Ibadan, 1941-46; School of Pharmacy, Yaba, 1946-49. Married, 3 children. Currently, Managing Proprietor, Amjorim Chemists Ltd., Yaba. Memberships: Methodist Church Leader; Fully Accredited Methodist Local Preacher; Secretary-General, Pharmaceutical Society of Nigeria, 1956-69; Pharmacists Board of Nigeria, 1957-69; Secretary, Pharmacists' Social Club, Lagos, 1965—; Vice-Chairman, Nigeria & Israel Association, known as Bi'dge. Honours: 1st Prize, Sunday School Bible Competition, 1935;

1st Prizes in Primary School. Address: 318 Herbert Macauley St., Yaba, Nigeria.

OSOBA, Olusegun, born 15th July 1941. Journalist. Education: Fellowship Certificate, Commonwealth Press Union; International Press Institute Diploma in Journalism, University of Lagos, Nigeria. Appointments; The Editor, Lagos Weekend. Memberships: The Nigerian Guild of Editors; The Nigerina Union of Journalists. Address: Wsitor, Lagos Weekend, P.O. Box 139, Lagos, Nigeria.

OSOGO, James Charles Nakhwanga, born Bunyala, Kenya, 10th October 1932. Teacher; Politician. Education: St. Mary's High School, Yala; Railway Training School; Kagumo Teachers' College. Married, 4 children. Appointments include: Railway Station-master, 1950-52; Teacher, Sigalame School, 1955; Withur School, 1956; Barding School, 1957; Ndenga School, 1958; Port Victoria, 1959; Headmaster, Kibasanga School, 1960; ibid, Nangina School, 1961-62; Chairman, Kenya Social Guild; Vice-Chairman, Kenya National Union of Teachers; Assistant Minister for Agricultural & Animal Husbandry; Chairman, Kenya Youth Hostels Association; Minister for Information & Broadcasting. Honours, Prizes, etc: Elder of the Golden Heart, 1967; Order of the Star of Africa (Liberia); Grand Cordon of the Star of Ethiopia, 1967; Grand Cross of the Yugoslav Flag (1st Class). Address: Ministry of Commerce & Industry, P.O. Box 30340, Nairobi, Kenya.

OSUAMKPE, Christopher Oforo, born Joinkrama, Ahoada Division, Eastern Nigeria, 14th April 1924. Teacher. Education: Baptist Mission School, Joinkrama; Secondary & Teacher Training Courses, Iwo-Ibadan; Teachers' Higher Elernentary Cert., 1947; B.A., Georgetown College, Ky., U.S.A.; M.A., Columbia University, N.Y. Married, 4 sons, 4 daughters. Education: Headmaster, Primary School, Joinkrama, 1951-53; Principal, Preliminary Teacher Training Centre, 1953-55; Principal, Baptist College, Obinze, Owerri, 1960-68; Acting Principal, St. John's Teachers' College, Rivers State, 1969. Memberships: Phi Delta Kappa. Honours: Australian Visitors Award of Commonwealth Co-operation in Education, 1970. Address: St. John's College, Diobu, P.O. Box 161, Port Harcourt, Nigeria.

OSUIDE, Gabriel Ediale, born 15th March 1935. Pharmacist. Education: Government School, Auchi, Nigeria, 1942-49; Edo Government College, Benin City, 1949-54; Diploma in Pharmacy, Nigerian College of A.S.T., 1956-60; B.Pharm. (1st Class Hons.), London University School of Pharmacy, U.K., 1960-63; Ph.D., ibid, 1963-66. Appointments: Medical Laboratory Technician, General Hospital, Lagos, Nigeria, 1954-56; Lecturer in Pharmacology, University of Ibadan, 1966-68; Lecturer in Pharmacology, Ahmadu Bello University, Zaria, 1968-70; Acting Head, Department of Pharmacology, ibid, 1969—; Examinations Officer, Faculty of Medicine, 1969; Senior Lecturer, 1970—. Memberships: Society of Biological Psychiatry; Secretary, Medical Section, Science Association of Nigeria, 1969—; Representative, Medical Section, Council, ibid, 1969—; Nigerian Society of Neurological Sciences. Author & co-author of various professional papers. Honours: Federal Nigerian Government Scholarship to study Pharmacy in U.K., 1960-63; Sir Sydney Phillipson Prize as best all-round student, Nigerian College of Arts, Science, & Technology, Ibadan, 1960; U.K. Commonwealth Scholarship, 1965-66; U.K. Medical Research Council Award, 1967; Rockefeller Foundation Travel Grant, 1968; WHO Fellowship, Denmark, 1970. Address: Department of Pharmacy & Pharmacology, Faculty of Medicine, Ahmadu Bello University, Zaria, Nigeria.

OSUJI, Samuel Sebastian Ukachi, born 17th November 1917. Administrative Officer, Class I. Education: Cambridge School Certificate (London Matric. Exemption), 1935; B.A. (Durham), 1939; Proficiency Certificate in Public Administration, Washington, D.C., 1960. Personal details: married, 6 sons, 2 daughters. Appointments: Principal, New Bethel College, Onitsha, 1946—; Founder & 1st Principal, Emmanuel College, Owerri, 1947; Education Officer, 1952-59; transferred to Administration, 1959; Principal, Institute of Administration, Eastern Region, Nigeria, 1961-63; Acting Permanent Secretary, Ministries of Information & Health, Enugu, 1963-66; retired Civil Servant. Fellow of Victoria College of Music (Lond.). Member of Enugu Recreation Club, East Central State. Publications: The Fallen Comrade, a short elegy on a foundation scholar of Emmanuel College, Owerri, 1948; Report on Police Prisons & Services in the Federation of Nigeria (joint author), 1966. Address: 22 Chief Ekwuene Street, Uwani, S. Extn., Enugu, East Central State, Nigeria.

OSUNKOYA, Babatunde Olusiji, born 26th October 1934. Pathologist. Education: Methodist Boys' High School, Lagos, Nigeria, 1947-52; University College of Ibadan, 1954-61; M.B., B.S.; Ph.D.; F.M.C.(Path.). Married, 3 children. Appointments: Medical Research Training Fellow, University of Ibadan, 1964-66; Lecturer in Pathology, ibid, 1967-69; Senior Lecturer in Pathology, 1969—; Consultant Pathologist, University College Hospital, Ibadan, 1968—. Fellow of the Nigeria Medical Council, 1970. Memberships: Secretary, Nigerian Cancer Society; Science Assn. of Nigeria; Nigerian Medical Assn.; former Secretary, U.C.H., Ibadan Medical Society; late Vice-President, Argonauts Society of Nigeria. Publications: contributor to: Dokita, 1960, 1963; British J. Cancer, 1965, 1967; West African Medical Journal, 1968, 1969; Cancer Res., 1967; immunology, 1968; Int. J. Cancer, 1969; Afr. J. Med. Sci., 1970; Cancer, 1970; Lancet, 1966; Clin. Chem. Acta., 1967; J. Lab. & Clin. Med., 1968; British Heart Journal, 1969; Short-term tissue culture (in Burkitt's Lymphoma), 1970; Clinical & related evidence of host defence mechanisms (in Burkitt's Lymphoma), 1970. Address: Dept. of Pathology, University College Hospital, Ibadan, Nigeria.

OSUNTOKUN, Benjamin Oluwakayode, born 6th January 1935. Medical Practitioner; Educator. Education: Christ's School, Ado-

Ekiti, Nigeria, 1946-51; M.B., B.S. (Lond.), M.R.P. (Lond.), & Ph.D., University College, Ibadan, 1954-61. Married, 3 sons, 2 daughters. Appointments: House Officer, UCH, Ibadan, 1962-63; Medical Officer of Health, Ijebú-Ode, 1963; Senior House Officer, Welsh School of Medicine, Cardiff, U.K., 1964; Smith & Nephew Fellow in Neurology, Department of Neurology, University of Newcastle upon Tyne & National Hospital for Nervous Diseases, Queen Square, London, 1964-65; Rockefeller Foundation Research Fellowship, Department of Medicine, UCH, Ibadan, Nigeria, 1966; Lecturer & Senior Lecturer in Neurology & Medicine, University of Ibadan & Consultant Physician, UCH, Ibadan, 1966—. Memberships: Ibadan Club; Badan Tennis Club; Lagos Tennis Club; Secretary, Association of Physicians of Nigeria; Nigerian Society of Neurological Sciences. Author of more than 55 publications in several leading journals in neurology, medicine, psychiatry, & nutrition. Address: University of Ibadan, Ibadan, Nigeria.

OSWALD, Ronald William, born 2nd October 1917. Anglican Clergyman. Education: St. Columba's College, Dublin, Ireland; B.A., Dublin University, 1938; M.A., 1955; B.A. (1st Class Hons.) Oriental Languages, 1959; B.D., 1957. Married. Appointments: Curate, St. George's Church, Dublin, 1955-58; St. James' Church, Taunton, Somerset, U.K., 1958-59; Head, CMJ, Tunis, Tunisia, & Embassy Curate, Chaplain, 1960-67; Vicar, St. Nicholas Church, Castle Hedingham, Essex, 1967-70. Address: The Vicarage, Castle Hedingham, Halstead, Essex, U.K.

OTEGBEYE, Olatunji, born 4th June 1929. Medical Practitioner. Education: Primary, Christ Church School, Ilaro, 1934-40; Ibadan Boys' High School, Nigeria, 1941; Government College, Ibadan, 1942-47; University College, ibid, 1948-52; Middlesex Hospital Medical School, London, U.K., 1952-56. Married, 6 children. Currently at Irebi Hospital, Ebute Metta. Memberships: General Secretary, Nigeria Union of Great Britain & Ireland, 1953-54; President, ibid, 1954-55; President, Nigeria Youth Congress, 1960-64; Secretary-General, Socialist Workers & Farmers Party, 1964-66; Central Council, Nigeria Medical Association, 1965-70. Publications: Nigeria & the National Question: Ideological Conflict in Nigerian Politics; One Country, One Destiny for Posterity. Address: Irebi Hospital, 60 Patey Street, Ebute Metta, Nigeria.

OTENG (The Hon. Mr. Justice) Emmanuel Aldo, born 28th November 1928. Lawyer. Education: Ngetta Primary School, Lango, Uganda; Lwala Primary School, Teso; St. Aloysius' College, Nyapea, West Nile; Holborn College of Commerce & Law, London, U.K.; The Honourable Society of Middle Temple, London; The Hebrew University of Jerusalem, Israel. Personal details: married to Pamela Catherine Aiteno, S.R.N., S.C.M. Appointments: Cooperative Assistant, Department of Cooperation, Uganda; State Attorney, Attorney-General's Department, ibid; Assistant Chief Registrar, High Court, Uganda; Magistrate, Grade I; Chief Magistrate, Busoga, Uganda; High Court Judge of Uganda. Memberships: Hon. Society of Middle Temple; Uganda Golf Club, Kampala; Judiciary United Football Club, Kampala. Address: High Court of Uganda, P.O. Box 7085, Kampala, Uganda.

OTENG, Robert, born 2nd June 1925. University Lecturer. Education: Mfantsipim School, Cape Coast, Ghana, 1940-44; B.Sc.(Hons., Physics), University of London, U.K., 1951-55; M.Sc., Ph.D., ibid, 1962-66. Married, 4 children. Appointments: Senior Science Master, Government Sec. School, Tamale, 1958-61; Lecturer in Physics, U.S.T., Kumasi, 1961-68; Senior Lecturer, Ag. Head, Dept. of Physics, Ag. Dean, Faculty of Science, U.C.C.C., 1968—. Fellow of the Royal Microscopic Society. Publications: Molten MF2 complexes in Tin(II) Fluoride (M = Na, K); Environment of the Tin Atom; Mossbauer & other Evidence for the existence of Orthorhumbic Modification of Tin(II) Fluoride; Studies in MF2 compleses in Tin(II) Fluoride (M = Co, Fe, Ni). Address: Department of Physics, University College, Cape Coast, Ghana.

OTOO, Samuel Nii-Amu, born 15th November 1919. Medical Practitioner. Education: Government Boys' School, 1925-33; Mfantsipim School, Ghana, 1934-48; Achimota School, 1939-41; Edinburgh University, U.K., 1944-49; Ross Institute, 1950; Royal Institute of Public Health & Hygiene, 1959. Appointments: Principal Medical Officer, 1960-64; Vice-Dean, Ghana Medical School, 1964-66; Chief Medical Superintendent, 1966-67; Medical Officer of Health, Accra, 1968-70; Member, Panel of Experts in Public Health Administration, WHO. Memberships: Ghana Medical Association; Past President, Christian Medical Workers' Fellowship. Recipient, Ghana Nurses' Association Award for Meritorious Services to Nursing & Health Services, 1970. Address: WHO, P.O. Box 374, Mogadishu, Somalia.

OTTO, Benjamin Nelson, born 25th November 1942. Civil Servant. Education: Sir Samuel Baker School, Gulu, Uganda; B.A. (Hons.), History, Makerere University College, Uganda, 1967. Personal details: son of Mr. P. W. Oola, M.B.E., Major County Chief in Acholi District, Uganda. Appointments: Assistant Secretary for Tourism, Ministry of Information & Tourism, 1967-68; Tourism Attaché, Foreign Ministry, 1968; Tourism Attaché, Bonn, Germany, 1969; Appointed Director, Uganda Tourism Office for Europe, Frankfurt. Address: Uganda Tourist Office, 6 Franfurt am Main I, Luginsland I, West Germany.

OUEDRAOGO, Louis-Dominique, born 21st January 1942. Diplomat. Education: Primary & Secondary Schools, Upper Volta; Diploma, Institute of Political Studies, Paris, France, 1966; Diploma, Overseas Institute of Higher Studies, Paris, 1967. Appointments: Head of Press, Archives, & Documentation Service, Ministry of Foreign Affairs, Ouagadougou, Upper Volta, 1969; First Counsellor, Permanent Mission of Upper Volta to the United Nations, New York, U.S.A., 1969—. Address: 236 East 46th Street, N.Y., N.Y., U.S.A.

OUEDRAOGO, Malick Stanislas, born 3rd February 1940. Public Works Engineer. Education: Technical College; Public Works School, Bamako, Mali; Special School for Public Works, Paris, France; Engineering School for Public Works, Paris. Appointments: Head of Studies Bureau for Public Works; Head, Sub-division of Roads & Buildings, Ouagadougou, Upper Volta; Head of the Eastern Division of TP, Ouagadougou, 1966-67; Director of Public Works & Buildings, 1967—. Address: Direction des Trauvaux Publics et de la Construction, Ouagadougou, Upper Volta.

OULD ABDALLAH, Ahmedou, born 21st November 1940. Director of Industrialization Board. Education: Licensed in Economics, Grenoble, France, !966; Diploma of Political Sciences, Paris, 1968; Diploma of Higher Studies in the Economic Sciences, ibid, 1968. Married. Appointments: Deputy Governor of Nouakchott, 1969; Administrateur du Waif de Nouakchott, 1969; Administrateur de l'Abattoir Frigonfique de Kaedi, 1969; Administrator, Society of Mining of Mauritania, Somima, 1969. Publications: Pourquoi Invester en Mauritanie (Guide to Investments). Address: B.P. 399, Nouakchott, Mauretania.

OULD BAH, Mohamed Sidya, born 1939. Veterinarian. Education: Bacc., Dakar, Senegal, 1959; Veterinary Studies, Toulouse, France, 1960-65; Speciality, Tropical Medicine, Paris, 1966-67. Married, 2 children. Appointments: Directeur de l'Abattoir de Kaedi, 1968; Director, Meat Company, Couima, Mauretania, 1968—; Governor, Kaedi, 1968-69. Publications: La Toxicite du Noyau phenol. Honours: Yugoslav Decoration, 1968; Liberian Decoration, 1969. Address: B.P. 387, Nouakchott, Mauritania.

OUTA, John Nicholas, born 24th March 1936. Assistant Agricultural Officer. Education: Diploma in Agriculture, East African University; Diploma in Agriculture, Arapai College; General Certificate in Agriculture & Animal Management. Personal details: active Choir Member; married, 6 children. Appointments: Agricultural Assistant, Grade II, 1961-66; Agricultural Assistant, Grade I, 1966-68; Assistant Agricultural Officer, Tesso District Farm Institute, Soroti, Uganda, 1969—. Memberships: Technical Officer, Arapai Chapter, Soil Science Club; President, Legion of Mary Tororo College; Vice-President, Iteso Students' Association. Address: Teso District Farm Institute, P.O. Box 136, Soroti, Uganda.

OWEKKER, Sabina, born 21st August, 1945. Midwife; Assistant Health Visitor Trainee. Education: Primary Education, 1950-55; Junior Education, 1956-57; Senior Education, 1958-60; Midwifery Training School. Appointments: Midwife; currently training for Public Health Nursing, Assistant Health Visitor Training School, Entebbe, Uganda. Address: Assistant Health Visitor, Training School, P.O. Box 8, Entebbe, Uganda.

OWIREDU, Peter Augustus, born Cape Coast, 22nd August 1926. Educator. Education: Methodist Senior School, Larteh, 1938-41; Adisadel College, Cape Coast, 1942; Presbyterian Secondary School, Odumasi, 1942-46; Achimota College, 1947-48; University College, Ghana, 1948-52; Postgraduate Institute of Education, 1952-53; B.A.(London); London Postgraduate Certificate in Education. Personal details: direct grandson of King Prempeh I of Ashanti; married to Phyllis Dodoo of Otublohim Royal House, Accra. Appointments: Teacher, Gold Coast (now Ghana) People College, 1947; Teacher, Adisadel College, Cape Coast, 1949-52; Practice Teaching, Accra Academy, 1952 & Achimota School, 1953; Teacher, Form Master, Housemaster, Adisadel College, 1953-58; acted as Head of Latin & Mathematics Departments, ibid; second & last Headmaster, Apam Secondary School (old site), 1959; first Headmaster, Apam Secondary School (new site), 1960—; also many part-time appointments, 1954-64. Memberships: Hon., Hansard Society for Parliamentary Government, U.K., 1958; Associate, Ghana History Society, 1958; Moral Re-armament Group, 1961; Life Mbr., Red Cross Society; Patron, Central Region Arts Council; National Vice-President, Voluntary Work Camp Association. Contributor of articles to newspapers & journals. Address: Apam Secondary School, P.O. Box 29, Apam, Ghana.

OWOR, Raphael, born 7th July 1934. Physician; Educator. Education: Primary, Nagongera, 1943-48; Tororo College, 1949-54; M.B., Ch.B., Makerere University College, Kampala, Uganda, 1955-62; Postgrad. Training in Pathology, Glasgow, U.K., 1965-69. Appointments: Junior House Officer, Mulago Hospital, Uganda, 1962-63; Demonstrator, Department of Pathology, 1963-64; Lecturer, Makerere Medical School, 1964-65; Registrar, Department of Pathology, Glasgow, U.K., 1965-69; Senior Lecturer, Department of Pathology, Makerere Medical School, Uganda, 1969—. Memberships: Royal College of Pathologists; East African Association of Physicians; East African Association of Surgeons. Author of several professional papers in the East African Medical Jrnl. Address: Makerere Medical School, Box 7072, Kampala, Uganda.

OWOSINA, Francis Adedoyin Olusiji, born 17th November 1932. Orthopaedic & Prosthetic Surgeon. Education: Government College, Ibadan, Nigeria, 1948-52; M.B., B.S.(Lond.), University College, Ibadan, 1955-62; F.R.C.S.E., Postgraduate Board in Medicine, Edinburgh, U.K., 1967-69; Cert. Instructor, Prosthetics & Orthotics, United Nations Course, Copenhagen, Denmark, 1969; Dept. of Orthopaedic Surgery, University of Liverpool. Personal details: Son of Chief Owosina of Makun Sagamu; married, 5 children. Appointments: various administrative & professional posts, Civil Service, Western Nigeria, 1962—; Senior Medical Officer, 1966; currently, Locum Medical Assistant, Bootle Hospital as a postgraduate student, Department of Orthopaedic Surgery, University of Liverpool, U.K. Memberships: Associate, International Committee on Prosthetics & Orthotics & International Society for Rehabilitation of the Disabled; Liverpool Medical Institution. Address: Ministry of Health, P. Mail Bag 5027, Ibadan, Nigeria.

OYAKHILOME, Luke James Omogbai, born Ewu Town, Ishan Division, Midwestern Nigeria, 9th June 1908. Teacher. Education: Government School, Ewu, 1927; Standard 6; Bennett College, England, U.K.; Teachers' Higher Elementary Certificate, 1949. Married, 7 sons, 8 daughters. Appointments include: Headmaster, Government School, Auchi, 1957; Headmaster, Irrua Government School, 1958; joined Assemblies of God Mission, 1961; currently Headmaster, A.G.M. Central School, Eko Ewu. Memberships include: Treasurer, Ishan Branch, Mid-West Rubber Farmers' Association; Executive Member, Mid-West Farmers' Union; President, Ewu Progress Union, 1950-56; Political Leader, West Ishan Council; Chairman, Ishan Literature Committee. Publications include: first Ishan Primers I & II in the Ishan Language. Address: Ewu Town, Ishan Division, Midwest State, Nigeria.

OYELEKE, Yunus Abioye, born 16th December 1931. Chartered Accountant. Education: Offa Grammar School, Offa, Nigeria; Trainee Accountant, with Cassleton Elliott & Co., Nigeria; Wright, Stevens & Lloyd, London, U.K.; Price Waterhouse & Co., London; A.A.C.C.A., 1959; A.C.A., 1961. Personal details: member of Anilelerin Royal Family, Offa, Nigeria; married to A. Jibike Soladoye. Appointments: Government Auditor, 1961-62; Principal Accountant, N.N. Marketing Board, 1962-63; Senior Accountant, Auditor, Akintola Williams & Co., Chartered Accountants, 1963-65; Partner, ibid, 1965. Memberships: Treasurer, Kano Rotary Club, Kano, Nigeria, 1969-70; President, Kano State Lawn Tennis Association, 1970—; Nigerian Institute of Management, 1967. Address: c/o Akintola Williams & Co., Bank Road, P.O. Box 179, Kano, Nigeria.

OYENUGA, Victor Adenuga, born Isonyin, Ijebu-Ode, Nigeria, 9th April 1917. University Professor. Education: Immanuel School, Isonyin, 1930; Ado-Ekiti, 1930-32; Ekiti Central School, Ado, 1933; Wasimi African School, 1934; B.Sc.(Agric.), King's College, Durham University, Newcastle upon Tyne, U.K., 1948; B.Sc.(Hons.), Agric. Chemistry, ibid, 1949; Ph.D.(Agric.), ibid, 1951; A.R.I.C., 1953; Course, Agric. Extn. Wageningen, 1953; F.R.I.C., 1959; Cornell University, U.S.A., 1960-61. Personal details: grandson of late Oba Amesofe I, Ajalorun of Ijebu-Ife; brother of Oba Adelbambo Oyenuga, Amesofe II, ibid; married, 3 sons, 3 daughters. Appointments include: Civil Servant, Audit Department & Medical Headquarters, Lagos, 1942-44; Lecturer, Animal Nutrition, University of Ibadan, 1951-52, 1956-57; Senior Lecturer, ibid, 1958-61; Professor & Head, Department of Agric. Chemistry & Soil Science, 1964-67; Professor & Head, Department of Animal Science, 1967—; Dean, Faculty of Agric. Forestry & Veterinary Science, 1966-69; Professor, Agriculture, University of Ife, 1961-64; Dean, Faculty of Agriculture, ibid, 1962-64. Member of numerous scientific committees. Memberships include: President, Interim Executive Committee, Association for the Advancement of Agricultural Sciences in Africa, 1968—; President, Science Association of Nigeria, 1967-70; Council, Agricultural Society of Nigeria, 1968—; Council, International Union of Nutrition Sciences, 1966-69, 1969-72; Committee on Environment & Management, ibid, 1969-72; American Society of Animal Production; American Association for the Advancement of Science; Nutrition Society of Britain. Publications: Nigeria's Foods & Feeding-stuffs: Their Chemical & Nutritive Value, 1955, 1959, 1968; Our Needs & Resources in Food & Agriculture, 1959; Agriculture in Nigeria, 1967; over 50 articles in scientific journals. Address: Department of Animal Science, University of Ibadan, Ibadan, Nigeria.

OYERO, Kunle, born Oyero Village, Abeokuta, Nigeria, 28th October 1927. Legal Practitioner. Education: Primary, Oluke Village, 1930-35; St. Paul's, Zgbore, Abeokuta, 1936; Abeokuta Grammar School, 1937-45; Hull University, U.K., 1951-52; Kennington College of Law & Commerce (external) of London University, 1952-55; Inns of Court, Lincoln's Inn, LL.B.(Hons.), 1952-55. Personal details: son of Chief Emmanuel Oyero, Bale of Oyero; married, 4 children. Appointments include: Teacher, Abeokuta Grammar School, 1945-50; Legal Practitioner, 1956—; Senior Housemaster, Abeokuta Grammar School, 1947-50; Secretary, Debating Society, Hull University Students' Union, 1951; Secretary, Overseas Students' League of Hull University, 1951; Social Secretary, West African Students' Union, London, 1954-55; Legal Adviser, Nigerian Youth Congress, 1961-62; Financial Secretary, Treasurer, etc., Lagos Branch, N.Y.C., a radical youth organization; President, Nigerian Youth Congress, 1963-66; Assistant Secretary, Socialist Workers & Farmers Party of Nigeria; President, Abeokuta Grammar School Old Boys' Association, Lagos Branch, 1967—; Vice-President, Nigeria Bar Association, Lagos Branch; Chairman, Lagos State Amateur Cycling Association, 1968. President, Oyero Progressive Union, 1965—; ibid, Nigerian Bar Association, 1968-69; National Exec. Committee, ibid, 1969-70, 1970-71; Bar Council, 1969-70, 1970-71. Author of pamphlet, The Role of Youth in a Republican Nigeria. Address: 11 Abibu Oki St., Lagos, Nigeria.

OYESINA, Timothy Lajide (The Otunare of Ibadan), born 29th May 1904. School Proprietor & Manager. Education: Senior Certificate, College of Preceptors; Grade II Teachers' Certificate, Nigeria. Married to Comfort Waleola Oyesina, with children. Appointments: Manager & Proprietor, Ibadan Boys' High School Group of Schools, 1938—; Chairman, Board of Directors, Ibadan Traders' Association, 1968—. Memberships: National President, Young Men's Christian Associations of Nigeria; Chairman, Executive Committee, Western State Scout Council; President, Anglican Lay Readers' Association, Ibadan Diocese. Honours: Member of the Order of the Niger, 1960; Justice of the Peace, 1960. Address: Ibadan Boys' High School, P.O. Box 263, Ibadan, Nigeria.

OYIGO, Joshua Oluoch, born Sakwa Ranen, Kenya, 2nd May 1940. Mechanical Engineer. Education: Ranen School; Kissi High School, Kenya; Loughborough Technical College, & later Loughborough University, Upper Second Class

Honours, 1967. Appointments include: Assistant Engineer, East African Oil Refineries Ltd., 1967; 7 Weeks' Course on Oil Processing, Shell Laboratories in Amsterdam; Project Engineer, Kenya, 1969; Delegate, 3rd Technology & Engineering Progress Information Meeting, Batoafse Internationale, The Hague, Netherlands, 1969; Course in Advanced Project Planning, ibid; Office Engineer, E.A.O.R. Ltd., 1970—. Memberships: Graduate Member of the Institution of Mechanical Engineers, London. Address: East African Oil Refineries Ltd., Private Bag, Mombasa, Kenya.

OYINLOLA, Rufus Adeniran Faloni, born 20th February 1929. Mechanical Engineer. Education: Diploma in Mechanical Engineering; Certificate in Management Studies; Certificate in Psychology & Physiology. Personal details: grandson of His Highness Oba Ajilaorun Oyinlola of Erin, Ijesha; first son of Prince G. F. Oyinola; married to Christie Mojisda Omotosho, 3 sons, 3 daughters. Appointments: Senior Civil Servant, Western Nigeria Government; Fellow, Royal Institute of Economics. Memberships: Institute of International Affairs; Society of Nigeria Automobile Association; Automobile Association of Nigeria. Publications: Students' Manual, Britain & Colour Prejudice. Address: 4 Olufemi Olusola St., Ife Road, Ibadan, Nigeria.

OZA, Kantilal Virji, born Zanzibar, 8th July 1926. Medical Practitioner. Education: Senior Cambridge Certificate, Zanzibar, 1946; M.B., B.S., Bombay, India, 1958; Internship, Mulago Hospital, Kampala, Uganda, 1959-60. Married, 1 son, 3 daughters. Appointments: Medical Officer, Hindu Charitable Dispensary Service, 1960; Medical Officer, The Khoja H. N. Noormoh's Dispensary, 1964—. Memberships: Zanzibar Medical Association; Secretary, ibid, 1962-64. Address: P.O. Box 1141, Zanzibar, Tanzania.

OZA, Sureshkumar Rayichandra, born Jamnagar, India, 19th February 1939. Medical Practitioner. Education: Dar es Salaam, Tanzania; Cambridge School Certificate, 1955; 1st & 2nd Year, Jai Hind College, Bombay, India; M.B., B.S., Grant Medical College, Bombay; Intership & Housemanship, J.J. Hospital, Bombay. Personal details: married, wife born in Zanzibar; Graduate B.A. in Philosophy & Psychology, University of Bombay. Appointments: Medical Practitioner, Kilosa, Tanzania. Member of Medical Association of Tanzania. Address: P.O. Box 72, Kilosa, Tanzania.

P

PACHAI, Bridglal, born 30th November 1927. Professor of History. Education: Primary & Secondary, Natal, South Africa; Natal Teachers' Certificates; Natal Teachers' Diploma, 1948, 1949, & 1953; B.A., South Africa, 1954; B.A.(Hons.), ibid, 1956; M.A., 1958; Ph.D., Natal, 1960. Married to Leelawathie Ramnath, 5 children. Appointments: Teacher, Natal Education Department, 1947-60; Lecturer, History, University College of Cape Coast, Ghana, 1961-65; Senior Lecturer, ibid, University of Malawi, 1965-68; Professor, University of Malawi, 1968—. Memberships: Past Chairman, Ladysmith Branch, Natal Indian Teachers' Society; ibid, Ladysmith Indian Child Welfare Society; Central African Historical Association, Rhodesia; Chairman & Trustee, Society for the Blind in Malawi; Chairman, History Syllabus Committee of Malawi, Certificate of Education Board. Publications: History of Indian Opinion, 1961; Memoirs of Lewis Mataka Bandawe, 1970; Editor, Malawi Past & Present, 1970; International Aspects of South African Indian Question. Address: Department of History, University of Malawi, Malawi.

PADERE, Fredrick Paineto, born Kasodo, Pallisa, Bukedi District, 2nd April 1932. Assistant Engineer. Education: Kamuge Primary School, 1941-46; Busoga College, Mwiri, 1946-49; Central Training School, Mbagathi, Nairobi, Kenya, 1949-52. Personal details: married to Loyce Kirya Nairima, 3 sons, 3 daughters. Appointments: District Engineer Officer, Soroti, E.A.P.&T., 1955-58; District Engineer Officer, Tororo, E.A.P.&T., 1963—. Memberships: Mwiri Debating Society; Mbagathi (C.T.S.). Address: Box 72, Tororo, Uganda.

PAGH-BIRK, Ivar, born Hjörring, Denmark, 19th May 1896. Retired. Education: Diploma of Electrical Engineering, A.E.T., Denmark, Section H.&B.T., 1921 (this Diploma is equivalent to the Moroccan Diploma of Engineering). Memberships: Engineers' Association, Copenhagen; Ingénieurs Civils de France, Paris; Groupement des Ingénieurs du Maroc, Casablanca. Honours: Ouissam Alaouite (Chevalier), Morocco, 1947; King Christian de Tiendes Frihedsmedaille (médaille de la libération), Denmark, 1947. Address: 25 rue des Colombes, Casablanca, Morocco.

PAIN, Gabriel Andre Marcel, born 23rd August 1908. Advocate. Education: Lycée Gallieni, Tananarive, Malagasy Republic; Higher Commercial Studies, licensed in law & letters, Paris, France. Married. Appointments: Member, Council of the Order of Advocates; President, Association of Aviation, Sport, & Judo. Memberships: President, Association of the Friends of Jean Laborde; Titular Member, Malagasy Academy. Publications: Histoire de Madagascar (joint author); Publications of the Malagasy Academy. Honours: Croix de Guerre avec palmes; National Order of the Malagasy Republic; Grand Officier de la Grande Comore. Address: B.P. 3, Tananarive, Malagasy Republic.

PAIRAULT, Claude A., born 4th March, 1923. University Lecturer; Director. Education: D. es L. Appointments: Senior Lecturer, School of Arts & Humane Sciences, University of Abidjan, Ivory Coast; Director, Institute of Ethno-Sociology, ibid. Memberships: African Society, Paris, France; International African Institute, London, U.K.; American Anthropological Association, U.S.A.; Current Anthropology, Chicago, U.S.A. Publications: Boum-le-Grand, Village d'Iro, 1966; Documents du parler d'Iro, 1969. Address: INVADES, B.P. 8008, Abidjan, Ivory Coast.

PALMER, William Brian, born 29th April 1924. Mechanical Engineer; Educator. Education: King's College School, Wimbledon,

London, U.K., 1932-42; M.A., Ph.D., C.Eng., Jesus College, Cambridge University, 1942-44, 1947-49. Appointments: Stress Engineer, Rolls-Royce Ltd., Derby; Research Fellow, Department of Textile Industries, Leeds University; Lecturer in Mechanical Engineering, Leeds University; Senior Lecturer, Mechanical Engineering, ibid; Professor of Mechanical Engineering, University College, Nairobi, Kenya; Dean of Engineering, ibid. Memberships: Fellow, Institution of Mechanical Engineers, U.K.; East African Institution of Engineers; Institute of Measurement & Control. Author of various papers on textile drying, metal cutting, metal forming, & engineering education. Address: University College, Nairobi, P.O. Box 30197, Nairobi, Kenya.

PANDIT, Lalit, born 2nd October 1936. Managing Director. Education: A.B.S.; M.K.I.M.; A.M.B.I.M. Married, 2 children. Appointments: Director-Secretary, Kenya Investments Ltd., 1956-59; Managing Director, East African Building Society, 1959–; Director, M/s Jayant Pandit & Bros. (Insurance); Director, M/s Kenya Investments Ltd. (Hire Purchase). Memberships: Associate, Building Societies Institute, The East African Management Foundation, & Institute of Commerce; ex Treasurer & Committee Member, Kenya Institute of Management; Fiscal, General Purposes & Economic Development Committee; Executive Club of Kenya; Nairobi Round Table No. 1; Housing Advisory Committee, Kenya Government. Author of a report for the U.N. Economic Commission for Africa. Address: P.O. Box 8022, Nairobi, Kenya.

PANDYA, Hasmukhlal Devshanker, born 26th March, 1934. Barrister. Education: Government School, Kampala, Uganda; Lincoln's Inn, London, U.K. Appointments: Uganda Public Health Officer, 1952-56; Advocate, High Court of Uganda, Kampala, 1959-62; Senior Assistant Administrator, General Attorney-General's Chambers, 1962-70; Magistrate, Grade I, Judiciary, 1970–. Memberships: Past President, Uganda Professional Civil Servants' Association; Secretary, Uganda Magistrates' Association. Address: P.O. Box 1716, Kampala, Uganda.

PANDYA, Navin, born 22nd August 1931. Medical Practitioner. Education: Bombay University, India; Intermediate Science (1st Class), ibid, 1950; M.B., B.S., 1955; M.D. Part I, 1957. Married, 3 sons. Appointments: House Physician, Medical Unit, Civil Hospital, Ahmedabad, India, 1956-57; T.B. Unit, ibid, 1957; Junior Lecturer in Physiology, B.J. Medical College; Medical Practice in Tanzania, 1958–. Memberships: British Medical Association; Medical Association of Tanganyika; Lions International; Township Authority of Musoma, 1959-63. Honours: J.D. Khambatta Prize, Bombay University, 1952. Address: P.O. Box 162, Musoma, Tanzania.

PANKHANIA, Mohanlal Naran, born 15th January 1943. Mechanical Engineer. Education: Matriculation, 1st Class (Distinction), 1960; Intermediate Science, University of Bombay, India, 1962; Bachelor of Mechanical Engineering, University of Poona, 1966. Married.

Appointments: Assistant Engineer, Production Control, Crude Oil Diesel Engineer Manf. Factory, India, 1966; Assistant Engineer, Production Control M/C Tools Factory, India, 1967; Senior Mechanical Engineer, Madhvani Sugar Works, Ltd., Kakira, Uganda, 1967. Memberships: Graduate Member, East African Institution of Engineers; Professional Centre, Uganda. Address: P.O. Box 3143, Kaira, Uganda.

PANKHURST, Richard Keir Pethick, born 3rd December 1927. Professor; Historian; Educationalist. Education: Bancroft's School, U.K., 1938-46; B.Sc.(Econ.), London School of Economics, University of London, 1946-49; Ph.D., ibid, 1949-54. Personal details: son of Sylvia Pankhurst, Suffragette, Author, & Journalist; married. Appointments: Research Worker, National Institute of Economic & Social Research, & Lecturer, University of London, 1954; Assistant Professor, University College of Addis Ababa, Ethiopia, 1956; Director, Institute of Ethiopian Studies & Professor, Hailé Selassié I University, Addis Ababa, 1963–. Editor: Journal of Ethiopian Studies; Ethiopian Observer. Member, Editorial Board, Abba Salama; Tarik. Publications: Kenya, The History of Two Nations, 1954; An Introduction to the Economic History of Ethiopia, 1961; Travellers in Ethiopia, 1965; State & Land in Ethiopian History, 1966; The Ethiopian Royal Chronicles, 1967; An Introduction to the History of the Ethiopian Army, 1967; Economic History of Ethiopia, 1968. Honours: Medal, International Society of Numismatics, 1969; Cross of St. Mark, 1970. Address: Director, Institute of Ethiopian Studies, Hailé Selassié I University, Addis Ababa, Ethiopia.

PAONASKAR, Ram, born 25th March 1925. Medical Practitioner. Education: M.B., B.S. (Bombay), 1949; D.T.M.&H.(London), 1963. Personal details: son of Doctor; married to Sharea Korgaonkar, M.B., B.S. Appointments: House Surgeon, Sion Hospital, Bombay, India; Assistant Surgeon, Government of Tanzania, 1950-52; Private Medical Practitioner, 1953–; Hon. Officer, Family Planning Association, Moshi. Memberships: President, Rotary Club of Moshi, 1969-70; District Governor, Y's Men's Club, Tanzania; Chairman, Moshi Round Table, 1967; President, Medical Association, 1959-66. Address: P.O. Box 283, Moshi, Tanzania.

PARAISO, Emile Louis, born 4th May 1932. Hydraulic Engineer. Education: Primary & Secondary Studies, Porto-Novo, Dahomey; University Studies, University of Grenoble, France; Technical Studies, Higher School of Hydraulic Engineering, Grenoble, France; Judicial & Economic Studies. Married, 3 sons, 1 daughter. Appointments: Chief Engineer, Hydraulic Studies, 1960-63; Directeur Cabinet President du Conseil Chef du Gouvernement de la Rep. du Dahomey, 1964-65; Director of Hydraulics, 1966-68; Minister of Public Works, Transport, Posts &. Telecommunications, 1968-69; Directeur Hydraulique et Energie, 1970–. Memberships: International Association of Water Distributors; La Houille Blanche de Grenoble. Honours: Commander of the Congolese Order of the Leopard, 1969. Address:

Director of Hydraulics & Energy, B.P. 73, Cotonou, Dahomey.

PARIKH, R. S., born 23 March, 1932. Civil/Structural Consulting Engineer. Education: M.S., Civil Engineering, U.S.A.; M.I.C.E., U.K.; M.ASCE, U.S.A; D.EAIE, East Africa. Appointments: Bridge Engineer, Michigan State Highway Department, U.S.A.; Senior Engineer, M/s Ove Arup & Partners, London, U.K.; Senior Engineer, M/s Roughton & Partners, Uganda; Consulting Engineer in Private Practice, Uganda & Kenya. Memberships: Institution of Civil Engineers, U.K.; America Society of Civil Engineers; East African Institution of Engineers; Rotary Club, Kampala West. Address: P.O. Box 5916, Kampala, Uganda.

PARISH, Dennis Hedley, born 29th January 1926. Soil Scientist. Education: B.Sc.(Hons.), Leeds University, U.K.; M.Agric., Ph.D., Queen's University, Belfast, Appointments: Scientific Officer, Northern Ireland, Queen's University; Chief Chemist, Mauritius Sugar Industry Research Institute; Professor & Head, Soil Science, Makerere University, Kampala, Uganda; Regional Soil Fertility Officer, FAO, Accra, Ghana. Memberships: Royal Institute of Chemistry; British Society of Soil Science; International Soil Science Society; The Fertilizer Society. Address: FAO Regional Office for Africa, P.O. Box 1628, Accra, Ghana.

PARKER, John David, born 2nd July 1934. Research Engineer. Education: King Edward VI School, Stratford-on-Avon; B.Sc.(Hons.), University of Leeds, U.K., 1960. Married, 4 children. Appointments: Technical Adviser, Bath & Portland Stone Firms Ltd.; Liaison Officer, National Institute of Agricultural Engineering, Scotland; Principal Research Officer, Tropical Pesticides Research Institute, Tanzania. Corporate Member, Institution of Agricultural Engineers. Contributor of various papers on technical subjects to professional journals. Address: P.O. Box 3024, Arusha, Tanzania.

PARSON, William, born 19th October 1913. Professor of Medicine. Education: B.A., Columbia College, U.S.A., 1934; M.D., College of Physicians & Surgeons, Columbia University, N.Y., 1937. Married, 4 sons. Appointments: Professor of Medicine, University of Virginia, 1949-66; Professor of Medicine, Makerere University College, Uganda, 1966—. Member of professional societies in the U.S.A. & in East Africa. Author of some 60 Scientific publications. Address: Department of Medicine, Makerere University College Medical School, P.O. Box 7072, Kampala, Uganda.

PASCHAL, Zachary Rwiza, born 17th April 1933. Civil Servant. Education: B.A.(General), London (External Student of Economics, History, & Political Science), 1961. Married, 6 children. Appointments: Establishment Officer, Tanzania Government, 1961-63; Senior Establishment Officer, ibid, 1964-65; Principal Assistant Secretary, 1965-66; Deputy Personnel Manager, E.A.P. & T. Corporation, 1966-68; Director, Administration & Inspectorate, Ministry of Foreign Affairs, 1969—. Member of the Railway Club, D.S.M., 1963—. Address: Ministry of Foreign Affairs, P.O. Box 9000, Tanzania.

PATEL, Anil M., born 27th September 1931. Physician. Education: M.B., B.S., Madras, South India, 1959; M.R.C.P. (speciality qualification in Internal Medicine & Chest Diseases), Edinburgh, 1966; Diploma in Epidemiology & Control of T.B., WHO, CZECK. Personal details: son of Dr. M. M. Patel, O.B.E.; married, 2 children; wife is Editor of Hansard, National Assembly, Parliament, Govt. of Uganda. Appointments: Mediical Officer (T.B.), Uganda; Consultant Physician (T.B.), Uganda, & Chest Physician, Mulago Hospital; Hon. Clinical Lecturer, Clinical Medicine, Makerere University, Kampala, Uganda. Publications: Contributor to Journal Tubercule, London. Sub-Coodinator & Author of many publications in the field of T.B. research, jointly handled by the T.B. Research Organization of the East African Community, with 3 East African Govts. & the British Medical Research Council, Chief Coordinating Centre for Treatment & Control of T.B., Nairobi, Kenya. Address: Box 100, Kampala, Uganda.

PATEL, Arvind U., born 24th November 1931. Medical Practitioner. Education: M.B., B.S., Gujarat University, India; M.D. Married. Appointments: Medical Registrar, Civil Hospital, Ahmedabad, 1958; Medical Officer to Messrs. Sikh Saw Mills & Ginners Ltd., 1961—. Memberships: Uganda Medical Association; President, ibid, Jinja Branch; Lion Tamer, Lions Club of Jinja. Address: P.O. Box 484, Jinja, Uganda.

PATEL, Arvindkumar Chaturbhai, born Mombasa, Kenya, 13th December 1932. General Practitioner. Education: Senior Cambridge & London Matriculation, 1951; M.D., M.G.M. Medical College, Indore, India, 1960. Married. Appointments include: Resident Physician & Surgeon, N.Y. Hospital, Indore, 1960-61; M.G.M. Medical College, Indore; A.V. High School, Mombasa, Kenya. Memberships include: Kenya Medical Association; British Medical Association; World Medical Association; National Geographic Society; Vice-President, Kisii Sports Club, 1966-67, 1967-68. Address: Box 481, Kisii, Kenya.

PATEL, Ashvin Kumar Ishwerbhai, born Kampala, Uganda, 3rd August 1940. Medical Practitioner. Education: M.B., Ch.B., Makerere Medical School, Kampala, Uganda, 1966; M.Med., Makerere Medical School/University of East Africa, 1970. Appointments: Research Fellow in Cardiology & Registrar in Medicine, Makerere Medical School & Mulago Hospital, 1967—. Author of several professional papers, including: Aneurysm of the pulmonary artery: with persistent ductus arteriosus & pulmonary infundibular stenosis. Fatal dissection & rupture in pregnancy, Brit. Heart Jrnl., 1970; The fatty acid composition of serum, breast milk, & foetal brain in Ugandans (w. others), 1970. Address: c/o Dept. of Medicine, Mulago Hosp., P.O. Box 7072, Kampala, Uganda.

PATEL, Babaubhai Chunibhai, born 12th January 1927. Chartered Accountant. Education: B.Com., Bombay University, India; LL.B., ibid. Appointments: Private Practice as an Accountant, Kenya. 1957—. Memberships: Fellow, Institute of Chartered Accountants of India, New Delhi. Address: c/o B. C. Patel & Co., P.O. Box 5931, Nairobi, Kenya.

PATEL, Bachubhai P., born Borsad, India, 16th January 1924. Medical Practitioner; Ophthalmic Surgeon. Education: B.Sc., Bombay, 1944; M.B., B.S., ibid, 1950; D.O.M.S., 1953. Appointments: Medical Practice, Kitale, Kenya, 1953-62; Medical Officer, Kenya Medical Department, 1962-70; Medical Officer, Provincial Hospital, Nakuru, 1962; Medical Officer in Charge, District Hospital, Kapenguria, 1963; Medical Officer of Health, Samburu District, Maralai, 1964; General Practice Service, Kenyatta National Hospital, 1965; Medical Officer in Charge, Kamiti Prison Hospital, 1966, Casualty Department, Coast Hospital, Mombasa, 1967, & District Hospital, Voi, 1968; R.M.O. & Casualty Medical Officer, M.P. Shah Hospital, Nairobi, 1968-70; Private Medical Prac., Racecourse Road, Nairobi. Memberships: Kenya Medical Association; Automobile Association of East Africa. Address: P.O. Box 3546, Nairobi, Kenya.

PATEL, Chandrakant C., born 1st January 1941. Medical Practitioner. Education: M.B., Ch.B., University of East Africa, 1966; M.Med., ibid, 1970. Married. Appointments: S.H.O., Mulago Hospital, Uganda, 1968-70; Physician & Paediatrician, Gulu Hospital. Memberships: Uganda Medical Association; Medical Defence Union, London. Publications: Viral Encephalitis (Uganda Practitioner), 1969; Acute Febiule Encephalopathy at Mulago (W.A.Med.J.), 1970; Gargoylism in African Child (E.A.Med.J.). Address: P.O. Box 160, Gulu, Uganda.

PATEL, Chimanlal A., born India, 11th January 1916. Barrister-at-Law; Advocate. Education: Allidira Visram High School, Mombasa, Kenya; Barrister-at-Law, Lincoln's Inn, London, U.K., 1939. Appointments: Partner, A. B. Patel & Patel, Advocates, Mombasa, Kenya; Chairman, Pan African Insurance Company Ltd.; Director of several companies. Memberships: Saturday Club, Mombasa; Mombasa Sports Club; United Sports Club, Mombasa; President Coast Bridge Association. Honours; Bucanan Prize, Lincoln's Inn, 1939. Address: P.O. Box 274, Mombasa, Kenya.

PATEL, Dahyabhai A., born 3rd April 1920. Barrister-at-Law; Advocate; Commissioner for Oaths; Notary Public. Education: Barrister-at-Law, Lincoln's Inn, London, U.K. Married. Appointments: Member of Parliament, Uganda, 1961—. Memberships: President, Indo Uganda Society; President, Hindu Mandol; President, Art & Literary Circle; President, Mahatma Ghandi Foundation. Author of some 30 books in Gujarati, including novels, poetry, short stories, plays, & essays. Honours: Gold Medal for Literature, 1956. Address: P.O. Box 1602, Kampala, Uganda.

PATEL, G. L., born 25th April 1921. Advocate. Education: Barrister-at-Law, Gray's Inn, London, U.K., 1959. Appointments: Advocate, High Court of Kenya. Address: Box 9 Meru, Kenya.

PATEL, Harihar, Manibhai, born Jinja, Uganda, 19th April, 1944. Agricultural Officer. Education: Prep. (Agric.), 1st Class, Sardar, 1965-66; F.Y.B.Sc.(Agric.), 1st Class, Patel, 1966-67; S.Y.B.Sc.(Agric.), 1st Class, Gujarat University, India, 1967-68; B.Sc.(Agric.), 1st Class, ibid, 1968-69. Currently, Agricultural Officer, Sugar Cane Estate, Jinja, Uganda. Memberships include: Member, Sub High Power Authority, Institute of Agriculture, Anand, 1968-69; Uganda Agricultural Society, 1969-70; Nalubale Ladge, Theosophical Society, 1969-70. Honours include: Merit Scholarship holder from State Government, 1 year; Holder, T. M. Patel Memorial Elocution Shield, 1967-68. Address: P.O. Box 604, Jinja, Uganda.

PATEL, Hiteshchandra Shantilal, born 29th December 1936. Chartered Architect; Student Planner. Education: S.S.C., India, 1953; Diploma in Architecture, Birmingham, U.K., 1962; Associate of R.I.B.A., U.K., 1966; completed Studies in Town Planning, 1965. Personal details: married to Kapila Patel, 2 daughters. Appointments: Architectural Assistant, Clifford Tee & Gale, Birmingham, U.K., 1962-63; Assistant Architect, Birmingham City Corp., 1963-64; Senior Assistant Architect, Hughes & Polkinghorn, Uganda, 1966; Chief Architect, Madhvani Group, 1966—. Memberships: Associate of Royal Institute of British Architects; Architects Registration Council, U.K.; Student Member of Town Planning Institute, U.K.; Uganda Society of Architects; Active Member, Rotary Club of Jinja, Uganda; Lake View Club, Jinja. Designed & supervised buildings of various types including Nursing Home, Shops & Flats; Library for Girls' School; Bulb Factory, all at Jinja. Address: Madhvani Group, P.O. Box 54, Jinja, Uganda.

PATEL, Ishwarlal B., born 9th December 1932. Consulting Civil & Structural Engineer. Education: Bachelor of Engineering (Civil); M.S., University of Illinois, U.S.A. Appointments: Chief Assistant to a Consulting Engineer; Project Engineer, Skidmore, Owings & Merrill, Chicago; Chief Civil Engineer, Gwalior Rayon, India; Chief Structural Engineer, Nairobi City Council, Kenya; Senior Partner, Ishwar B. Patel & Partners, Consulting Engineers, Nairobi. Memberships: Institution of Structural Engineers; Institution of Civil Engineers; East African Institution of Engineers; Council, Association of Consulting Engineers; Council, Architectural Association of Kenya; Chairman, School Committee, Park Road Primary School, Nairobi. Address: P.O. Box 8674, Nairobi, Kenya.

PATEL, Jagdish Maganbhai, born 27th July 1942. Physician. Education: Cambridge Overseas School Certificate, E. Africa; M.B. B.S., India; M.S., University of Baroda, India. Married, 1 Child. Memberships: Lion Tamer, Kabale, Lions Club, 1969-70; Director of the Club, 1970-71. Address: P.O. Box 18, Kabale, Uganda.

PATEL, Jagendra Apabhaj, born 6th September 1938. Physician. Education: 6 years, Primary; 6 years, Secondary; Medical College, 7½ years, India. Married to a doctor. Appointments: Junior Medical Officer, New Mulayo Hospital, 2 years. Address: P.O. Box 6206, Kampala, Uganda.

PATEL, Jamnadas K., born Sojitra, India, 29th August 1920. Advocate. Education: LL.B., Bombay University, India. Married, 3 children. Appointments include: enrolled as Advocate of the High Court of Uganda, 1946—; 2 years' service as Magistrate. Memberships: President, Uganda Law Society, 1962-63. Address: P.O. Box 424, Kampala, Uganda.

PATEL, Jayantilal Chhotabhat, born 17th April 1930. Advocate; Commissioner of Oaths; Notary Public. Education: Barrister-at-Law, Lincoln's Inn, London, U.K., 1956. Married, 1 son, 1 daughter. Appointments: Court Clerk & Interpreter, High Court of Uganda, Kampala, Uganda, 1949-54; Private Practice as Advocate, 1957—. Address: 21 City House, 2/3 Williams Street, P.O. Box 2842, Kampala, Uganda.

PATEL, Jayantilal Khodabhai, born 24th February 1934. Civil Engineer. Education: B.Sc.(Eng.), London University, U.K. Appointments: Executive Engineer, P.W.D. Tanzania, 1960-65; Engineer, Sir Alexander Gibb & Partner, 1965-66; Partner, Patel Associates, 1967. Memberships: M.I.C.E., U.K.; M.E.A.I.E. (E.A.). Address: c/o Patel Associates, Tanzania.

PATEL, Kantibhai Magan, born Kampala, Uganda, 25th March 1931. Educator; Physician; Consultant. Education: Schools in Uganda & India; M.B. B.S.; M.R.C.P.(Edinburgh); M.R.C.P.(G.); D.T.M.&H.; D.C.H.; M.R.C.S.; L.R.C.P. Married, 2 daughters. Appointments include: Senior Lecturer, Medicine, Makerere University College Medical School, Kampala, Uganda; Consultant Physician, Mulago Hospital, Uganda. Memberships: Council, Uganda Medical Association; Association of Physicians of East Africa. Author of some 20 papers on various aspects of medicine. Address: Makerere Medical School, P.O. Box 7072, Kampala, Uganda.

PATEL, Kantilal Dahyabhai, born 14th May 1931. Chartered Electrical Engineer. Education: Government Junior School, Dar es Salaam, Tanzania; Government Secondary School, Dar es Salaam; Faraday House Electrical Engineering College, London, U.K.; D.F.H.; C.Eng. Appointments: Bruce Peebles & Co., Ltd., Engineers, East Pilton, Edinburgh; w. Uganda Electricity Board, 1954—; Junior Engineer, Assistant Engineer, Maintenance Engineer, Assistant Generation Superintendent, Generation Engineer, & currently Chief Generation Engineer, ibid. Memberships: Institution of Electrical Engineers, U.K.; Council, East African Institution of Engineers; Hon. Treasurer, Uganda Division, ibid. Address: Uganda Electricity Board, P.O. Box 1101, Jinja, Uganda.

PATEL, Madhukanta J., born 1st January 1940. Medical Practitioner. Education: 7 yrs. Secondary School; 3 yrs. Higher School; 5½ yrs. Medical School; 2 yrs. Postgrad. Study in Gynaecology & Obstetrics; M.B., B.S.; D.G.O. Married. Appointments: Houseman, Iowrin Hospital Medical College, Jamnuy; Registrar, ibid; Junior Lecturer, Jingu Hospital, Uganda. Address: P.O. Box 6206, Kampala, Uganda.

PATEL, Manjula Arvindbhai. Medical Practitioner. Education: M.B., B.S., Bombay University, India. Member of the Uganda Medical Society and Uganda Medical Association. Address: P.O. Box 484, Jinja, Uganda.

PATEL, Manubhai Ambalal, born 29th August 1923. Legal Assistant. Education: University of Bombay. Appointments: Manager/Accountant, Assam, India, 5 years; Sales Manager (Hardware), Kampala, Uganda, 2 years; Sales Manager (tractor parts), Gailey & Roberts (U) Ltd., Kampala; Storekeeper, Estates Office, Uganda Co. of Africa Ltd.; w. Judicial Department, Uganda; Chief Law Clerk, Messrs Hunter & Greig, Advocates. Address: P.O. Box 2029, Kampala, Uganda.

PATEL, Muljibhai Prabhudas, born Karamsad, India, 8th April 1916. Company Director. Education: Educated in India, Graduating in Course in Dispensing & Compounding Medicines, B.J. Medical School, Ahmedabad, Gujerat, India. Appointments include: Managing Director, Bombay Trading Stores (Uganda) Ltd., Kampala, & Bombay Trading Stores (Textiles) Ltd.; Director, Bomstores (Nairobi) Ltd., Kenya. Memberships: Light of Africa Lodge, Rotary International, Kampala Branch. Address: P.O. Box 65, Kampla, Uganda.

PATEL, Navin H., born 4th October 1940. Medical Practitioner. Education: M.B., B.S., Gujarat, India. Married. Member, Lions Club. Address: Box 707, Kitale, Kenya.

PATEL, Prabhulal Chhotabhai (alias Pravinchandra), born 17th August 1931. Surgeon. Education: Elphinstone College, Bombay, India; M.B., B.S., Grant Medical College, Bombay; D.L.O., Royal College of Surgeons & Physicians, U.K.; Fellow, Royal College of Surgeons of England. Married. Appointments: Houseman, J.J. Group of Hospitals, India; Senior House Surgeon, Whittington Hospital, & Nottingham General Hospital, Royal Surrey County Hospital, Musgrove Park Hospital, U.K.; Registrar, Central Middlesex Hospital, London; Consultant, Ear, Nose, & Throat Surgeon, Kampala, Uganda; Hon. E.N.T. Surgeon, Nsambya Hospital, Kampala. Memberships: British Medical Association; Uganda Medical Association; Association of Surgeons of East Africa; Rotary Club of Kampala, Uganda. Address: P.O. Box 1592, Kampala, Uganda.

PATEL, Prabhulal Ishwerbhai, born 16th April, 1911. Merchant. Education: B.Com., University of Bombay, India. Appointments: Councillor, City Council, Kampala, Uganda, 1948-68; Managing Director, Doshi Hardware (U) Ltd., 1955—; Deputy Mayor, Kampala City Council, 1960-62; Mayor, ibid, 1963. Appointed by Uganda Government to serve on various boards & committees. Memberships: Indian

Merchants Chamber, Kampala, 1942-44; ibid, Central Council, Indian Associations in Uganda, 1946; ibid, Uganda Chamber of Commerce, 1954. Address: P.O. Box 72, Kampala, Uganda.

PATEL, Rajni P., born 21st June 1931. Engineer. Education: B.E.(Mech. & Elec.), Gujarat University; B.Sc.(Hons.), St. Andrews University; M.Eng., McGill University; Ph.D., ibid. Appointments: Assistant Lecturer, 1959-60; Lecturer, 1962-65; Senior Lecturer, 1966—. Memberships: M.I.Mech.E.(London); A.F.R.Ae.S.(London); Hon-Secretary, A.M.I.E.A.E.(East Africa); Hon. Secretary, Academic Staff Association, University College, Nairobi, Kenya. Author of numberous publications including: Complete Specification Rotary Atomiser, N.R.D.C., London.; Note on Turbulent Skin Friction measured with a Preston Tube., 1966; Comparison of Micronair & the New Rotary Atomiser, 1967; Turbulent Jet & Wall Jets in Uniform streaming flow (Aeronautical Quarterly); A study of Two-Dimensional Symmetric & Asymmetric Turbulent Shear Flows, 1970. Recipient of many prizes, bursaries etc. Canadian Commonwealth Scholar, 1960-62; National Science Foundation Fellowship, U.S.A., 1966. Address: P.O. Box 6793, Nairobi, Kenya.

PATEL, Ramlal Bhailalbhai, born India 24th December 1918. Businessman. Education: Pratp High School, Bansda; Fergussion College, Poona; B.Sc., Bombay University, 1941; F.C.C.S., 1966. Married, 5 children. Appointments: Managing Director, General Financiers & Construction Ltd., R.B. Patel & Sons Ltd. & Lwamafa Ltd.; Director, Dastur Ltd., E.A. Theatres (Ug.) Ltd., E.A. Theatres (Jinja) Ltd., E.A. Underwriters (U) Ltd., Sisi Enterprisers Ltd. & General Agencies (Export-Import) Ltd. Memberships: President, Patidar Samaj; Director, Lions Club of Kampala City. Address: P.O. Box 2259, 44 Windsor Crescent Road, Kampala, Uganda.

PATEL, Ramubhai Dahyabhai, born 12th February 1924. Medical Practitioner. Education: M.B. B.S., Bombay University, India, 1949; M.S., ibid, 1953. Married, 3 children. Appointments: Private Medical Practice, Jinja, Uganda. Memberships: Director, Rotary Club of Jinja, 1967; President, ibid, 1968; Y.M.C.A.; President, Uganda Medical Society, Jinja, 1969; Board of Governors, Jinja Public Secondary School. Honours: Best Dissection Prize, 1944; Best Dissectors Prize, 1945; Dr. Shirwdkar Clinical Surgery Gold Medal, 1946; Dr. Desa Gold Medal, Midwifery, 1949; etc. Address: P.O. Box 880, Jinja, Uganda.

PATEL, Rasik, born Mombasa, Kenya, 24th November, 1920. Surgeon. Education: Allidina Visram High School; M.B., B.S., University of Bombay, India, 1950; M.S., ibid, 1962; F.R.C.S., Edinburgh, U.K., 1966. Married. Appointments include: Surgical Registrar, Grant Medical College, Bombay, 1951-52; Surgical Registrar, Southampton Chest Hospital, U.K., 1953-54; Casualty Registrar, Postgraduate Medical School of London, 1955; Registrar, Radiotherapy Department, St. Luke's Hospital, Guildford, 1957; Registrar, Colindale Hospital, London, 1958; Consultant Surgeon, Mombasa, Kenya, 1958; Hon. Consulting Surgeon, Coast Province General Hospital, Mombasa. Memberships: 1st Vice-President, Lions International, Mombasa. Address: P.O. Box 9020, Mombasa, Kenya.

PATEL, Somabhai Shivabhai, born 20th June 1915. Advocate. Education: B.A., Bombay University, India, 1935; LL.B., ibid, 1938; B.T., 1942. Widower, 2 sons. Appointments: Teacher, till 1944; President, Rift Valley Merchants Chamber, Nakuru, 1957-63; National Member, Legislative Council of Kenya, 1961-63; Chairman, School Area Committee, 1960-61; ibid, 1965; President, Nakuru Law Society, 1966—; ibid, Nakuru Brotherhood, 1963—; Life Member, Commonwealth Parliamentary Association. Memberships: Standing Committee, Kenya Indian Congress, Nairobi, 1960-62; Founder Member, Theosophical Society, Nakuru Lodge, 1954—; Indian Association, Nakuru, 1955—; Nakuru Town Celebration Committee & various public institutions of Nakuru. Honours: Silver Medal, for acting in Drama Festival, Poona, 1934. Address: Advocate, P.O. Box 20, Nakuru, Kenya.

PATEL, Suryakant, born 12th May 1930. General Medical Practitioner. Education: Matungo Primary School, Bombay, India; Fergussion College, Poona, 1946-48; Grant Medical College, Bombay, 1948-53; M.B., B.S., University of Bombay, 1954. Married. Address: P.O. Box 290, Bukoba, Tanzania.

PATEL, Suryakant Jashbhai, born 19th April 1925. Surgeon. Education: M.B., B.S., University of Bombay, India, 1952; F.R.C.S., Edinburgh, U.K., 1967. Appointments: General Practice, 1952-60; Medical Officer, 1960-67; General Surgeon, Ministry of Health, 1967—. Memberships: President, Mbale Asian Parents' Association; President, Elgon Rovers; Secretary, Indian Association; Vice-President, Rotary Club of Mbale. Address: P.O. Box 141, Mbale, Uganda.

PATERSON, Adolphus Anang, born Labadi, Accra, Ghana, 19th September 1927. Journalist. Education: Middle School Leaving Certificate, 1947; 2 years Secondary School; 6 months Refresher Course, Indiana University, Bloomington, U.S.A., 1962-63. Married, 4 sons, 1 daughter. Appointments include: Reporter on Spectator Daily (Accra), now defunct, 1955; Deputy Correspondent, Agence France-Presse, 1955-58; Representative in Accra of Ashanti Times, 1958-60; Free-lance Correspondent for Associated Press, Daily Telegraph, London; Time & Life Magazines since 1960; also B.B.C. Correspondent since 1966. Memberships: Ghana Journalists' Association; Indiana Chapter, Sigma Delta Chi, U.S.A., 1963—; Honours: Nominee of Ashanti Times for British Central Office of Information sponsored study tour of Britain, 1959. Address: P.O. Box 2017, Accra, Ghana.

PATERSON, Douglas Monro, born 20th November 1930. Anglican Pastor. Education: Monkton Combe School, Bath, U.K., 1944-48; B.A.(Hons.), Emmanual College, Cambridge, 1950-54; Postgraduate New Testament Studies, ibid, 1954-55; M.A.; Tyndale Hall, Bristol, 1955-57. Appointments: ordained Deacon,

1957, & Priest, 1958; Assistant Minister, Walcot, Bath, 1957-60; Assistant Minister, St. Paul's, Portman Sq., London, & Visiting Lecturer, Oak Hill Theological College, 1960-62; Minister, St. John's, Downshire Hill, Hampstead, London & Visiting Lecturer, All Nations Missionary College, 1962-65; Lecturer, Stanley-Smith Theological College, Gahini, Rwanda, 1967—. Memberships: Latimer House Liturgy Group; Eclectic Society. Address: Stanley-Smith College, E.A.R. Gahini, P.S. Kigali, Rwanda.

PATTISON, Robert, born 15th September 1902. Chartered Engineer; University Lecturer. Education: B.Sc.(Eng.), Imperial College, London University, U.K. Married, 1 son, 1 daughter. Appointments: Lecturer, Industrial Engineering, Birmingham Central Technical College; Lecturer in Industrial Engineering, Lincoln College of Technology; Head, Engineering Department, Burnley Municipal College; Superintendent of Technical Classes, Trinidad & Tobago, West Indies; Head, Engineering & Building Department, South-East Essex Technical College, U.K.; Engineering Department, Kumasi College of Technology, Ghana; Vice-Principal, ibid; Senior Lecturer, Mechanical Engineering, Kings College, University of London, U.K.; Senior Lecturer, Mechanical Engineering, The Polytechnic, University of Malawi; retired. Fellow, Institution of Mechanical Engineers. Honours: Whitworth Senior Scholar, 1925. Address: The Vale Cottage, Cheltenham Road, Cirencester, Glos., U.K.

PATURAU, Joseph Maurice, born 23rd April 1916. Consulting Engineer; Company Director. Education: Royal College, Curepipe, Mauritius; B.Sc.(Eng.) 1st Class Hons., Imperial College, University of London, U.K.; D.I.C. Aeronautics, ibid. Married, 1 son, 2 daughters. Appointments: Squadron Leader, French Air Force & Royal Air Force (342 Squadron); Engineer, then Managing Director, Forges Tardien Partners, Mauritius, 1946-62; Minister of Commerce, Industry & External Communications, Government of Mauritius, 1963-66; Managing Director, Ireland Fraser & Co. Ltd., Mauritius. Memberships: Secretary-General, International Society of Cane Sugar Technologists, 1960-62; President, Mauritius Chamber of Agriculture, 1967; President, Royal Society of Arts & Sciences, Mauritius, 1969; Chairman, Mauritius Sugar Industry Research Institute, 1970. Publications: Pacific Sugar, 1951; By-Products of the Sugar Cane Industry, 1969; Chapter on Steam Economy, in Sugar Technology, ed. by P. Honig, 1963. Honours: D.F.C.; Officer of the Legion of Honour; Companion of the Order of Liberation; C.B.E., 1967. Address: P.O. Box 58, Port Louis, Mauritius.

PAULIAN, Renaud, born 28th May 1913. Educator. Education: Docteur ès Sciences, University of Paris, France, 1941; Docteur ès Lettres (Geography), ibid, 1961. Married, 4 children. Appointments: Assistant Director, Institute of Scientific Research, Madagascar, 1947-61; Director, ORSTOM Centre, Brazzaville, Republic of the Congo, 1961-66; Director, Centre d'Enseignement Supérieur, Brazzaville, 1963-66; Rector, University of Abidjan, Ivory Coast, 1966-69; Rector, Academy of Amiens, France, 1969—. Memberships: Secretary, Entomology Society of France, 1937-39; Life-Secretary, Entomology Society of France, 1937-39; Life-Secretary, Academy of Malagasy, 1955-61; Secretary-General, Scientific Association of the Indian Ocean Countries (PIOSA), 1957-60; President, 4th General Conference of the Scientific Association of West Africa (WASA), 1967; Council, Association of French-speaking Universities (AUPELF), 1967-70; Council, Association of African Universities (AAV), 1967-70; Honorary Member, Royal Society of Mauritius; Non-resident Member, Overseas Academy of Science. Author of numerous publications, concerning mainly tropical biology and biogeography, on the one hand, and education and research in Africa, on the other. Honours: Prix Passet, Entomology Society of France, 1941; Prix Gadeau de Kerville, ibid, 1943; Prix Foulon, Academy of Sciences, Paris, 1948; Commandeur de Mérite Malgache, 1961; Officier due Mérite Congolais, 1966; Officier de la Légion d'Honneur, 1969; Commandeur du Mérite de la République Fédérale Allemande, 1969. Address: 3 Bd. Maignan Larivière, Amiens, France.

PAULOS ASRAT, born 1st June 1931. Assistant Minister, Ministry of Education & Fine Arts, Addis Ababa, Ethiopia. Education: Ethiopian Secondary School Leaving Certificate & London G.C.E., Tafari Makonnen School, Addis Ababa, 1951; B.A., University College, Addis Ababa, 1955; M.A., Education, Michigan State University, U.S.A., 1956; Postgrad. Study, Guidance & Counselling, ibid, 1956-57. Married, 3 children. Appointments: Teacher & Deputy Director, Elementary-Secondary School, 1957-59; Director, Harar Teacher Training Institute, Ethiopia, 1959-63; Dean of Students, Hailé Selassié I University, 1963-65; Assistant Professor; Chief Education Officer, Governorate General of Eritrea, 1965-66; Assistant Minister of Educational Operations, 1966—. Member, Teachers' Association of Ethiopia. Author of various papers & articles on educational & sociological topics. Address: Assistant Minister, Educational Operations, Ministry of Education & Fine Arts, P.O. Box 1367, Addis Ababa, Ethiopia.

PAW, Jayantilal D., born 31st March 1934. Medical Practitioner. Education: Cambridge School Certificate, Jinja, Uganda; London Matriculation, Kampala; N. Wadia College, Poona, India; M.B., B.S., B.J. Medical College, Poona. Married, 2 children. Appointments: Medical Officer, Mulago Hospital, Kampala; Medical Officer, Jinja Hospital, Jinja; Medical Officer, Sordi Hospital; Private Practice, Jinja; Police Surgeon (concurrently), Jinja. Memberships: Past Secretary, Jinja Branch, Uganda Medical Association. Address: 38 A Gabula Road, Jinja, Uganda.

PAYNE, Dorothy Mary, born Liverpool, U.K., 25th August 1920. Teacher. Education: Holly Lodge High School for Girls, Liverpool, 1930-38; St. Gabriel's College, London, 1938-40. Married. Appointments: Headmistress, Fonthill Road C.P. School, Liverpool, 1954-57; Headmistress, Corona School, Ikoyi, Lagos,

Nigeria, 1964-67; Headmistress, St. Saviour's School, Ikoyi, Lagos, 1967—. Address: St. Saviour's School, P.O. Box 413, Lagos, Nigeria.

PEARSON, Charles Andrew, born 10th December 1921. Medical Practitioner. Education: Kingsmoor School, Derbyshire, U.K., 1928-39; M.B., Ch.B., Liverpool University Medical School, 1939-44; D.T.M., Liverpool School of Tropical Medicine, 1945. Married. Appointments: Medical Officer, Methodist General Hospital (& related hospitals), Hankow, Hupeh, China, 1946-51; Medical Superintendent, Wesley Guild Hospital, Ilesha, Nigeria, 1952—. Memberships: Medical Secretary, Methodist Church, Nigeria; Medical Board Secretary, Christian Council of Nigeria; Fellow, Medical Council (General Practice) Nigeria, 1970. Address: Wesley Guild Hospital Ilesha, Nigeria.

PEARSON, Robert E., born 2nd March 1935. University Lecturer. Education: A.B., Carleton College, U.S.A.; Ph.D., University of Illinois. Married. Appointments: Assistant Professor, Earlham College, 1961-63; Lecturer, University of Ghana, 1963-69; Senior Lecturer, ibid, 1969—. Memberships: American Chemical Society; Chemical Society; Ghana Association of Science Teachers; Executive Committee, Ghana Science Association; Alpha Chi Sigma. Contributor to the Journal of the American Chemical Society & Journal of Chemical Education. Address: Department of Chemistry, University of Ghana, Legon, Ghana.

PEDRO, Alfred Omorogba, born 5th March 1914. Business Tycoon. Education: Standard 6. Son of ex-Police Inspector; married 30 wives, 60 children. Appointments: Managing Director, Palm Tree Hotel, Ife, Nigeria; Director, Olufe Mental Disease Hospital, Ife; Chairman of the Directors, General African Medical Herbal Organization of Nigeria. Memberships: Ogboni Iwase Otufe & Apena General of Nigeria; Ife Divisional Council. Address: Apena General of the Federation of Nigeria, 5 Pedro Street, Ile-Ife, Western State, Nigeria.

PEEROO, Abdool Azize, born 16th July 1906. Journalist. Education: English, French, & Urdu. Married, 3 sons, 2 daughters. Appointments: Manager, Universal Printing Service & Editor in Chief, La Voix de l'Islam, 1951—. Memberships: Executive Member, International Year of Human Rights, Mauritius, 1968; General Secretary, Mauritius Muslim League; President, Societe de Nations Unies, Mauritius. Publications: La Voix de l'Islam. Address: Mesnil, Phoenix Mauritius.

PEIRCE, Michael Alan, born 29th March 1942. Veterinary Experimental Officer. Education: A.R.I.P.H.H.; A.I.M.L.T.(Pharmacy). Appointments: Department of Medical Entomology, London School of Hygiene & Tropical Medicine, U.K., 1959-61; M.A.F.F., Central Veterinary Laboratory, Weybridge, Surrey, 1961-68; East African Veterinary Research Organization, Muguga, Kabete, Kenya, 1968-70. Memberships: Wildlife Disease Association; British Society for Parasitology; East African Wildlife Society. Publications include: Two new hosts for Clinostomum Phalacrocoracis from Uganda; The Presence of Grahamella in small mammals from Muguga., Kenya; Observations on the Haematozon found in birds from the Northern Frontier Province of Kenya; African Swine Fever Virus in Ticks (Ornithodoros moubata) collected from Animal Burrows in Tananzia. Address: Muguga, P.O. Kabete, Kenya.

PELLETIER, Fernande, born 8th May 1931. Physician. Education: Fort Kent Primary School, Me., U.S.A.; St. Agatha High School, Me.; Trinity College, Washington, D.C.; Georgetown University, Washington, D.C.; Intern & Resident, St. Francis Hospital, Trenton, N.J. Appointments: Member, Religious Society of Catholic Medical Missionaries, 1948—; Medical Officer, Holy Family Hospital, Berebum Ghana, 1961-67; Medical Director, Sous Secteur Medical de Kiri, Democratic Republic of the Congo, 1968-70; Medical Officer, Berebum Hospital, Ghana, 1970—. Memberships: American Medical Association; Ghana Medical Association; Church Hospital Association of Ghana. Address: Berebum Hospital, Ghana.

PENNY, Catharine Muriel, born Harrogate, U.K., 11th September 1918. State Registered Nurse; Health Visitor; State Certified Midwife. Education: Greenway School, Tiverton; Cheltenham Ladies' College; Harcombe House School of Domestic Science, Uplyme; The Middlesex Hospital, London; Simpson Memorial Maternity Pavilion, Royal Infirmary, Edinburgh. Appointments: Staff Midwife, The Middlesex Hospital, London, 1943-45; Queen's Nursing Sister, 1946-53; Missionary Nurse, Egypt, 1954-56, Malaya, 1957-60, & Egypt, 1961—. Memberships: Missionary, Church Missionary Society. Address: All Saints' Cathedral, 1113, Corniche El Nil, P.O. Box 1427, Cairo, U.A.R.

PERCY, Gerald, born 26th April 1928. Company Director. Education: M.A.(Oxford), U.K., 1950. Married, 4 children. Appointments: Deputy Managing Director, Lonrho Ltd., & Director, various Lonrho Group Companies, Africa and U.K., 1963—. Address: P.O. Box 5498, Limbe, Malawi.

PEREIRA, Herbert Charles, born 12th May 1913. Agricultural Physicist. Education: B.Sc.(Hons.), University of London, U.K., 1934; Ph.D., ibid, 1940; D.Sc., 1961. Married, 3 sons, 1 daughter. Appointments: Army, 1940-46, retiring as Major, Royal Engineers; Soil Scientist, Kenya Coffee Research Station, 1946; Deputy Director, East African Agriculture and Forestry Research Organization, 1955; Director, Agriculture Research Council of Central Africa, 1961; Director, East Malling Research Station, Agricultural Research Council, U.K., 1969. Memberships: Fellow, Royal Society; Companion, Institute of Civil Engineers; Fellow, Institute of Biology; Fellow, Royal Meteorological Society. Author of many research papers and reports. Honours: Hailé Selassié I Award for Agricultural Research in Africa, 1966. Address: East Malling Research Station, Maidstone, Kent, U.K.

PEREIRA, Joseph, born 13th February 1899. Merchant. Married, 2 sons, 3 daughters. Appointments: Merchant, dealing in provisions, fancy goods, etc.; Member of Township Authority, Masindi; Member, Town Council, Masindi. Memberships: Save the Children Fund; Red Cross Society; President, Commercial Community; Lions Club; Trustee, Indian Public Library. Honours: Queen Elizabeth Coronation Medal. Address: P.O. Box 7, Masindi, Uganda.

PERRIER, Joseph Paul, born Mauritius, 29th January 1912. Assistant Commissioner of Police, Mauritius. Education: St. Stanislas College, Rose Hill, Mauritius. Married, 6 sons, 3 daughters. Appointments: joined Mauritius Police Force, 1930; Assistant Commissioner, 1968—. Member, Rose Hill Circle. Honours: Colonial Police Medal, 1957. Address: Line Barracks, Port-Louis, Mauritius.

PERRY, John Walton Beauchamp, born 8th February 1943. Educator. Education: Ellesmere College, Shropshire, U.K., 1952-61; Exeter College, Oxford, 1961-64; University of Sussex, 1966-67. Married, 1 son, 1 daughter. Appointments: Teacher (Graduate V.S.O.), Bishop Cotton Boys' School, Bangalore, India, 1965-66; Lecturer in Geography, University of Botswana, Lesotho, & Swaziland, 1967—. Contributor to professional journals. Address: University of Botswana, Lesotho, & Swaziland, P.O. Roma, Lesotho, Africa.

PETERSIDE, Michael Clement Atowari, born 24th June 1918. Consultant Ophthalmologist; Medical Administrator. Education: Government College, Umualia, Nigeria; Higher College, Yaba; Kings College, London, U.K.; St. George's Hospital Medical School, London. Married, 3 children. Appointments: Medical Officer, Colonial Medical Service, 1950; Senior Medical Officer, Eastern Nigeria Service, 1959; Senior Consultant Ophthalmologist, Eastern Nigeria, 1964; Controller of Medical Services, Rivers State, 1970. Memberships: Ophthalmological Society of the U.K.; Ophthalmological Society of Nigeria; Rotary Club of Port Harcourt. Address: Ministry of Health, Port Harcourt, Nigeria.

PETKANOVA, Salza, born 20th July 1921. Assistant Librarian. Education: M.A., Faculty of History & Philology, Sofia University, Bulgaria; State Librarian, Institut Sofia; M.L.S., Librarianship & Bibliography, Sofia State University. Divorced. Appointments: Head, Reference Department, Sofia University Library, 1951-66; Deputy Librarian, ibid; Assistant Librarian, The Balme Library, University of Ghana, 1966—; Part-time Lecturer, Department of Library Studies, Reference Service, University of Ghana, 1968—. Member, Ghana Library Association. Publications: The Reference Work in Sofia University Library, 1965; Development of Special Bibliography in Sofia University, 1968; contributor of articles to professional journals. Address: University of Ghana, The Balme Library, P.O. Box 24, Legon, Accra, Ghana.

PFALTZGRAFF, Roy Edward, born 13th September 1917. Missionary; Physician. Education: B.S., Elizabethtown College, U.S.A.; M.D., Temple University Medical School, Philadelphia, Pa.; Surgical Resident, Episcopal Hospital, Philadelphia; Diplomate, National Boards. Married, 5 children. Appointments: Medical Officer in Charge, Lassa Hospital, 1945-54; Medical Superintendent, Adamawa Provincial Leprosarium, Nigeria, 1954—; Chief of Rehabilitation, U.S. Public Health Service Hospital, Carville, La., U.S.A., 1964-65. Memberships: American Medical Association; Nigerian Medical Association; Christian Medical Society. Author of several articles on leprosy in professional journals. Address: Church of the Brethren Mission, P.O. Box 626, Jos, Nigeria.

PFISTER, Francois, born 29th March 1932. Architect. Education: Ecole d'Architecture, Switzerland; Diploma, Ecole Polytechnique Federale de Lausanne, 1958. Married, 1 son. Appointments: Collaborator-Designer, Private Architect Offices in Lausanne, 1958-61; Architect, Direction generale de l'Habitat, Ministry of Public Works, Conakry, Guinea, 1961-64; Architect, UNDP team Conakry, 1965-66; Collaborator, Office Cantonal d'Urbanisme, Lausanne, Switzerland, 1966-67; Senior Research Fellow in Urban Design, Department of Housing and Planning Research, Faculty of Architecture, University of Science & Technology, Kumasi, Ghana, 1967—. Member, Societe Suisse des Ingenieurs et Architects. Publications: Habitat et sous-development, in Habitation, 1967; House Types—Family Life, Research Report No. 1, U.S.T. Address: University of Science and Technology, Kumasi, Ghana.

PHILLIPS, Charles George, born Chatham, Kent, U.K., 7th July 1889. Major-General, British Army, Retired. Education: Repton; Sandhurst Royal Military College. Married, 3 daughters. Appointments include: 2nd Lieutenant, The West Yorkshire Regiment, 1909; Lieutenant, 1910; 1st King's African Rifles, 1912; service on Merehan Somali Expedition, Jubaland, Kenya, 1912-14; service in German East Africa (Tanzania), World War I, 1914-17; Captain, 1914; Temp. Lt.-Col., 1916; wounded, 1917; commanded 3rd & 2nd K.A.R. (Nyasa); commanded Column 'Philcol', Portuguese East Africa, 1918; Temp. Lt.-Col., commanded 1st K.A.R. & O.C. Troops, Nyasaland (Malawi), 1919-23; commanded 1st Battalion, The West Yorkshire Regiment, Egypt & India, 1933-37; Brevet Colonel, 1935; commanded 146th Infantry Brigade (West Riding of Yorkshire) T.A., 1938; commanded British Troops, NAMSOS, Norway, 1940; commander, Northern Ireland, 1940-41; ibid, Sierra Leone & Gambia, 1942-44; Temp. Major-General, 1942; Retired, 1944; Kenya Director, Tancot Ltd., 1948-69; Chairman, Horticultural Cooperative Union, 1952-67; Director, Dumez & Co. (East Africa), 1950-70. Memberships include: United Services Club, London, U.K.; Muthaiga Country Club, Kenya; Nairobi Club, Kenya. Honours include: Military Cross, 1915; Crois de Guerre (avec palme), 1917; D.S.O. 1919; Officer, Order of the Aviz, 1919; Brevet Colonel, 1935; Bar to D.S.O., 1940; Commander of the Bath (C.B.), 1944. Address: P.O. Box 2370, Nairobi, Kenya.

PHILLIPS, Charles Malcolm, born Nairobi, Kenya, 5th July 1918. Ophthalmic Surgeon. Education: Sherborne School, 1932-36; Caius College, Cambridge, 1936-39; St. Thomas' Hospital, London, 1939-42; Edinburgh University Tropical School, 1942. Married, 3 children. Appointments: House Surgeon, Senior Surgeon, Casualty Officer, St. Thomas' Hospital, 1943; Medical Officer, Colonial Medical Service, Northern Rhodesia, 1943; Consultant Ophthalmic Surgeon to the Government of Northern Rhodesia, of the Federation of Rhodesia & Nyasaland, & of Zambia, 1949—; Consultant Ophthalmic Surgeon, Panel of Mines, 1949—; Consultant Ophthalmic Surgeon, Rhodesia Railways, 1949—. Memberships: British Medical Association; President, Zambia Medical Association, Branch of BMA; Ophthalmological Society of the United Kingdom; Royal Society of Tropical Medicine & Hygiene; Royal Commonwealth Society; International Wine and Food Society (Secretary, Lusaka Branch). Publications: Blindness in Kawamba District, 1959; Blindness in Africans in Northern Rhodesia, 1961; Problems of Blindness in Central Africa, 1963. Honours: O.B.E., 1963; F.R.C.S., 1953; D.O.M.S., 1948; M.A., 1963; M.B., B.Chir., M.R.C.S., L.R.C.P., 1942; B.A., 1939. Address: P.O. Box RW 46, Ridgeway, Lusaka, Zambia.

PHILLIPS, Pieter Martinus Johannes, born 5th September 1907. Medical Practitioner. Education: Methodist School, Axim, Ghana; Government Boys' School, Cape Coast; S.P.G. Grammar School; University Tutorial College, London, U.K.; University of London, King's College; King's College Hospital Medical School; D.P.H., University of St. Andrews. Married 3 children. Appointments: Junior Medical Officer; Medical Officer; Senior Medical Officer; Principal Medical Officer; Deputy Director of Medical Services. Memberships: Royal College of Surgeons (England); Licentiate, Royal College of Physicians (London). Address: Ministry of Health, P.O. Box M.44, Accra, Ghana.

PHIRI, John Daniel, born Mwase Village, Kasungu District, Malawi, 2nd November 1932. Tobacco Grower. Education: Junior School Certificate, Lyacium Correspondence College, Southern Africa, 1952. Appointments: General Clerk; Motor Car Driver, African Chrome Mine; Primary School Teacher, Roman Catholic Mission, Malawi, 1954; Constable, North Rhodesian Police Force, now Zambia, 1955-56; Labour Officer, Falicon Mines Ltd., Daliney Mine, P.O. Chakari, Gatooma, 1957; Chief Administrative Clerk, ibid, 1963; Flue-cured Tobacco Grower, Kasungu Flue-cured Tobacco Authority, 1963; Growers' Representative, Zomba Malawi Headquarters, Ministry of Agriculture. Memberships: A.N.C. Branch Secretary, African National Congress Party, 1956; Chakari District Secretary, ibid & Malawi Congress Party, 1959-63; Branch Secretary, Malawi Congress Party, 1963; Area Independence Celebration Secretary, Malawi Congress Party for 3 areas, Mziza, Misozi, & Chigodi, 1964-68. Address: Kasungu Flue-cured Tobacco Authority, Private Bag Lilongwe, Malawi.

PHOYA, James Duncan Nkondowaguluka, born 19th March 1907. Accountant. Education: Henry Henderson Institute, 13 Years. Personal details: son of the Rev. James Nthimba Phoya, Moderator of the Church of Central African Presbyterian, Blantyre Mission. Appointments: Accountant, G. F. Ponson Ltd., Blantyre, 31 years; ibid, Malawi Development Corporation, 1969-70; Deputy Mayor, City of Blantyre, 1967-70; Chairman, Finance Committee, ibid, 1967-70; Member, Blantyre Water Board, 1968-70; Deputy Chairman, Farmers' Marketing Board, Limbe, 1970—; Executive Chairman, Malawi Housing Corporation, 1970—; Member, Central Executive, Malawi Congress Party, 1970—. Address: c/o Malawi Housing Corporation, P.O. Box 414, Blantyre, Malawi.

PICKETT, Thomas, born Glossop, U.K., 22nd November 1912. Judge of Appeal. Education: Glossop Grammar School; LL.B., London University; Barrister-at-Law, Lincoln's Inn, London, 1948. Appointments: served with British Army, 1939-50, retiring with permanent rank of Major; Deputy Assistant Director, Army Legal Services, 1948; District Magistrate, Gold Coast, 1950; Resident Magistrate, Northern Rhodesia, 1955; Senior Resident Magistrate, 1956; Puisne Judge, High Court of Northern Rhodesia (later of Zambia), 1961-69; Justice of Appeal, Court of Appeal for Zambia, 1969—; Chairman, Tribunal on Detainees, 1967; Chairman, Electoral Commission (Supervision); Delimitation Commission for Zambia, 1968; Referendum Commission, 1969; Local Governors' Election Commission, 1970. Member, Royal Overseas League, London. Address: Court of Appeal for Zambia, P.O. Box RW 67, Lusaka, Zambia.

PIKE, Patricia Audrey, born 8th March 1921. Physician. Education: St. Margaret's School, Bushey, Herts., U.K.; Slade School of Fine Art; Royal Free School of Medicine; M.R.C.S. & L.R.C.P., Royal Free Hospital, 1951; D.T.M.&H., London School of Hygiene & Tropical Medicine, 1964. Married. Appointments: House Physician, Royal Surrey County Hospital, Guildford, Surrey, 1951; House Physician, German Hospital, London, 1951-52; Senior Hospital Doctor in Pathology, Bethnal Green Hospital, London, 1952-53; Registrar in Pathology, Elizabeth Garrett Anderson Hospital, London, 1954-56; Locum J.H.M.O., Oxford Regional Blood Transfusion Centre, 1956; Registrar in Pathology, London Chest Hospital, 1956-58; Bacteriologist, Pretoria, South Africa, 1958-59; Locum J.H.M.O., Aberdeen Royal Infirmiry, U.K., 1961; J.H.M.O., North London Blood Transfusion Service, Edgware, 1963-64; Scientific Staff, MRC Statistical Research Unit, 1964-65; BECC Research Fellow, Pathology Department, Makerere Medical School, Kampala, Uganda, 1966-67, 1968—; Part-time Assistant, Hospital for Sick Children, London, U.K., 1967. Co-author of following publications: Bone Marrow Involvement in Burkitt's Tumour, in Brit. J. Haemat., 1968; BCG Vaccination against Mycobacterium Ulcerans Infection, in Lancet; Epstein Barr Virus antibody levels in different areas of Uganda and their relation to Burkitt's Lymphoma, in E.Afr.Med.J., 1969; Antibodies to Epstein-Barr virus in Burkitt's Lymphoma and control groups, J.Nat.Canc.

Inst., 1969. Address: 8 Lyngham Court, Holly Park, London, N.4, U.K.

PILLAI, K. N. Chandrasekharan, born 13th September 1927. Statistician. Education: B.Sc., Kerala University, India; M.Sc., ibid. Appointments: Research Officer, then Assistant Director, Department of Statistics, Government of India, New Delhi, 1952-63; United Nations Statistical Adviser to the Governments of Indonesia, Zambia, Sierra Leone, & Kenya, 1963-68; United Nations Adviser, Government of Tanzania, Dar es Salaam, 1968—. Memberships: Indian Association for Research in National Income and Wealth. Publications include: National Accounts of Tanzania, 1966-68; Economic Survey of Central Province, Kenya; National Accounts of Sierra Leone, 1963-64 to 1965-66; National Accounts of Sierra Leone, November, 1966; National Accounts and Balance of Payments of Zambia, 1954-1964. Address: Bureau of Statistics, P.O. Box 796, Government of Tanzania, Dar es Salaam, Tanzania.

PINCH, Henry, born 19th September 1902. Engineer. Education: County Grammar School, St. Austell, Cornwall, U.K.; Imperial College of Science & Technology, London. Married. Appointments: Assistant Experimental Engineer, Petters Ltd., Yeovil, Somerset, 1926-30; Sales Engineer, Petters Ltd., 1931-38; H.M. Forces, R.A.O.C., Workshops & R.E.M.E., 1939-50; retired as Lt.-Col., 1950; Sales Manager, Parry & Co. Ltd., Bombay, 1951-52; Branch Manager, Lehmann's (E.A.) Ltd., Dar es Salaam, Tanzania, 1953-70. Memberships: A.R.C.S.; D.I.C.; C.Eng.; F.I.Prod.E.; M.E.A.I.E.; The Naval & Military Club, Piccadilly, London, U.K. Address: c/o Lehmann's (East Africa) Ltd., P.O. Box 9163, Dar es Salaam, Tanzania.

PINIER, Paul Pierre (His Excellency Monsignor), born 20th October 1899. Former Bishop; Provisionary Apostolic Administrator for the Diocese of Constantine & Hippone, Algeria. Education: Studies for the Priesthood, Seminary of Angers, France; L. es Sc., Catholic University, Angers, France. Appointments: Professor, Catholic University, Angers, 1926-35; General Secretary, ibid, 1935-47; Auxiliary Bishop, Algiers, Algeria, 1948-54; Bishop of Constantine, 1954-70; provisional Apostolic Administrator, Constantine & Hippone, Algeria, 1970—. Honours: Knight, Legion of Honour, 1957. Address: 25 Desmoyen Street, Constantine, Algeria.

PION, Marcel, born 8th January 1911. Director. Appointments: Director, Société Manexor, Sarl, Paris, France. Specialist of the study of markets and exports to French-speaking black Africa. Address: c/o Société Manexor, Sarl, 14 Bd. Montmartre, Paris 9, France.

PIRANI, Badrudin, born Kampala, Uganda, 2nd June 1938. Economist. Education: B.Sc. (Econ.), London. Appointments: Manager, Industrial Promotion Services (Uganda), Ltd. Member, Uganda Institute of Management. Address: P.O. Box 705, Kampala, Uganda.

PIRONE, Michele, born 13th July 1903. Civil Servant. Education: M.D. Humanities (Law), Rome University, Italy. Appointments: District Commissioner, Italian Somaliland, then Provincial Commissioner, Upper Juba, Ogaden, Mudugh; Senior Lecturer, African History, University of Mogadishu. Life Member, British Institute of History and Archaeology in East Africa, 1969. Contributor to various professional journals. Address: P.O. Box 15, Mogadishu, Somalia.

PLESSING, Ove, born Denmark, 29th April 1914. General Manager. Education: Aarhus Kathedralskole; Copenhagen School of Commercial Science; Technical University of Denmark; B.Com.; M.Sc., Chemical Engineering. Married; 1 son, 1 daughter. Appointments: Manager, Addis Ltd., Copenhagen, 1942-48; Managing Director, A/s Petersen & Wraae, ibid, 1948-54; General Manager, A/s Tanganyika Planting Co. Ltd., Moshi, Tanzania, 1954—. Memberships: Chairman, Tanganyika Sugar Manufacturers' Association; Vice-Chairman, National Sugar Board; National Water Resources Council; Director, National Bank of Commerce Ltd.; ibid, Kilombero Sugar Co. Ltd.; Kenya Director, East African Storage Co. Ltd. & Fraternitas Ltd. Honours: Knight of the Dannebrog; Honorary Danish Consul for Northern Tanzania, 1966. Address: Arusha Chini Estate, P.O. Box 93, Moshi, Tanzania.

POGNON, Guy, born 3rd November 1935. Banker; Director. Education: L. es Sc., Faculty of Law, Paris, France. Appointments: Acting Governor to the World Bank & the African Development Bank for Dahomey; Director General, Dahomey Bank of Development. Memberships: Fellow, International Bankers' Association; Administrator of several Societies. Address: B.P. 300, Cotonou, Dahomey.

POLAK, Hanus Egon, born 11th October 1914. Medical Officer. Education: Grammar School Prague, Czechoslovakia, 1925-33; M.D., Medical Faculty, Prague, 1933-38; D.C.H., Institute of Child Health, London, U.K., 1944; D.P.H., London School of Hygiene & Tropical Medicine, 1962-63. Married, 3 children. Appointments: Junior Hospital Medical Officer, U.K. & Czechoslovakia, 1941-47; Senior Assistant Medical Doctor of Health, Middlesex, U.K., 1947-58; Medical Consultant, American Joint Distribution Committee, Iran, 1958-62; WHO Medical Officer, M.C.H., Burundi, 1963-65; Senior Adviser, Maternal & Child Health, WHO Regional Office for Africa, Kenya & Seychelles, 1965-69. Member, British Medical Association. Author of various papers in professional journals. Address: P.O. Box 5335, Nairobi, Kenya.

POLLAK, Rinaldo, born 8th April 1934. Business Executive. Education: Victoria College, Cairo, U.A.R.; Lycée Français, Cairo; D.Pol. Sci., Rome University, Italy; Postgraduate Degrees in International Technical & Economic Assistance & European Economic Studies. Appointments: with AGIP, Rome, 1960; Sales Manager, AGIP Ltd., Uganda Division, 1961-63; Manager, ibid, 1964-66; General Manager, AGIP (Uganda) Ltd., 1966-67; Managing Director, ibid, 1968-69; E.N.I. Delegate for Eastern Africa, Nairobi,

Kenya, 1970. Memberships: Rotary Club, Nairobi; International African Institute. Honours: Knight of the Italian Republic, 1969; Knight of the Order of St. Gregory, Pope Paul, 1969. Address: P.O. Box 5004, Nairobi, Kenya.

POLONYI, Charles Karoly, born 25th May 1928. Architect. Education: Dip. Ing. Arch., Budapest, Hungary, 1950; M.Arch., 1957. Married, 1 daughter. Appointments: Practising Architect & Planner, Hungary, 1950-63; taught at University of Science & Technology, Kumasi, Ghana; Deputy Head of City Planning Dept., Budapest, Hungary; concurrently working on Masterplan for Calabar, Nigeria. Contributor of articles to several architectural reviews and other publications; Calabar—Survey & Development Plan (in book form), 1970. Recipient, Ybl Prize, Budapest, 1961. Address: Városház u 11, Budapest 5, Hungary.

PONTING, David, born 16th April 1936. Education Officer. Education: Devizes Grammar School, Wilts., U.K.; B.Sc.(Hons.), University of Bristol; Postgrad. Cert. in Education, Institute of Education, University of London. Married, 1 son, 2 daughters. Appointments: Head, Maths. Department, Nyakasura School, Fort Portal, Uganda, 1959-65; Tutor in Maths., National Teachers' College, Kampala, Uganda, 1965-67; Lecturer in Maths., Uganda Technical College, Kampala, 1967-70; Inspector of Schools, Educational TV, Ministry of Education, Kampala, Uganda, 1970—. Address: Inspector of Schools, ETV, Ministry of Education, Central Inspectorate, P.O. Box 3568, Kampala, Uganda.

POPAT, Ishwaralal Damodar, born 19th January 1919. Businessman. Married, 1 son, 1 daughter. Appointments: Director & Secretary, Nile Concrete Products Ltd., Magigye Estates Ltd., & Ungu Estates Ltd. Memberships: President, Jinja Rotary Club; Jinja Recreation Club; Jinja Golf Club. Address: P.O. Box 734, Jinja, Uganda.

PORTER, Arthur Thomas, born 26th January 1924. Educator. Education: B.A. (Dunelm), Fourah Bay College, Sierra Leone, 1944; B.A., Cambridge University, U.K., 1950; Postgraduate Certificate in Education, London University, 1951; Ph.D., Boston University, U.S.A., 1959. Married, 2 children. Appointments: Assistant, Department of Social Anthropology, Edinburgh University, U.K., 1951-52; Lecturer, Fourah Bay College, Freetown, Sierra Leone, 1954-56; Research Associate, Boston University, U.S.A., 1956-58; Professor of History, Fourah Bay College, Freetown, Sierra Leone, 1962-64; Head, Department of History, ibid, 1954; Director, Institute of African Studies, 1962-64; Vice-Principal, 1960-64; Principal, University College, Nairobi, Kenya, 1964-70. Memberships: Consultative Director, International African Institute; Board of Trustees, Rural Development College, Holte, Denmark. Publications: Creoledom, 1963; contributions to other publications. Honours: Doctor of Humane Letters (L.H.D.), Boston University, U.S.A., 1969; LL.D., Royal University of Malta, 1969. Address: c/o Ministry of Education, Nairobi, Kenya.

PORTUPHY-LAMPTEY, Victor Emmanuel Odartey, born Dodowa, Ghana, 9th March 1923. Physician & Surgeon. Education: Mfantsipim School, Cape Coast, Ghana, 1940-43; Achimota School, Accra, 1944-46; B.D.S., University of Durham, U.K., 1952; University of Fribourg, Switzerland, 1954-55; M.D., University of Lausanne, 1958. Appointments include: School Dental Officer, County Durham, U.K., 1952-54; Medical Officer, Ministry of Health, Ghana, 1959—. Member, Ghana Medical Association. Address: c/o Ministry of Health, P.O. Box M. 44, Accra, Ghana.

POSKITT, Frederick Richard, born 15th August 1900. Educator. Education: Kilburn Grammar School, 1912-18; B.A., Downing College, Cambridge, 1919-21; M.A., ibid, 1925. Married, 2 sons, 1 daughter. Appointments: Senior History Master, Colchester Royal Grammar School, 1921-25; Head of History Department, Manchester Grammar School, 1926-33; Headmaster, Bolton School, 1933-36; Director, National Teachers' College, Uganda, 1966—. Honours: C.B.E., 1962. Address: National Teachers' College, P.O. Box 20012, Kampala, Uganda.

POTOCKI, Bernard, born 18th November 1932. Physician. Appointments: Head of Study, Diatetics, Faculty of Medicine, Grenoble, France; Professor Agrag., Physiology, Faculty of Medicine, Abidjan, Ivory Coast. Memberships: Association of Physiologists; Biological Society; American Association for the Advancement of Science; Medical Society of the Ivory Coast. Author of numerous memoirs in French scientific reviews. Address: Senior Lecturer, Laboratory of Physiology, Faculty of Medicine, B.P. 20632, Abidjan, Ivory Coast.

POULTER, Sebastian Murray, born 12th August 1942. Senior Lecturer in Law. Education: B.A., Trinity College, Oxford, U.K., 1965; M.A., ibid, 1968; Solicitor of Supreme Court, 1967—. Appointments: Director, School of Social & Economic Studies, University of Botswana, Lesotho, & Swaziland, 1969-70. Memberships: The Law Society; The Dodecadents Club. Publications: The Legal System of Lesotho (w. Vernon V. Palmer); articles on the law of Lesotho. Address: University of Botswana, Lesotho, & Swaziland, Roma, Lesotho.

POWRIE, David Eustace, born 6th September 1931. Civil Engineer. Education: B.Sc.(Hons.), Eng., St. Andrew's University, U.K.; M.I.C.E.; M.I. East African Engineers; School Education, Prince of Wales School, Nairobi, Kenya. Appointments: Maintenance Road Engineer, Ministry of Works, Kenya; Materials Engineer, ibid; Road Design Engineer; Superintending Engineer, Road Development; Chief Engineer, Road Development. Author of Kenya Road Development Plan, 1969-74. Address: P.O. Box 24713, Karen, Kenya.

PRAGNELL, Michael Wykeham, born 2nd April 1918. Company Chairman. Education: Eton College, U.K., 1931-36; B.A. & M.A., Trinity College, Oxford, 1937-39. Married, 3 children. Appointments: international service with Sheli International Petroleum Co. Ltd., 1946—; currently, Chairman, Kenya Shell Ltd., East African Oil Refineries Ltd., & Chief Executive, Shell & B.P. Services Ltd., Nairobi. Member, Cavalry Club. Address: P.O. Box 3561, Nairobi, Kenya.

PRAH, Joseph Henry, born 30th June 1936. Lecturer. Education: Fijai Secondary School & St. Augustine's College, Cape Coast, 1952-59; B.Sc., University of Ghana, 1959-63; M.Sc., University of Essex, U.K., 1965-67. Appointments: Assistant Lecturer, then Lecturer, Cape Coast University, Ghana, 1963—. Secretary, Tennis Club, Hill Club, Cape Coast. Honours: Commonwealth Scholar, 1965-67. Address: Cosmic Ray Group, Imperial College, London, U.K.

PRATT, Charles Alfred, born 29th June 1912. Senior Lecturer; Audio-Visual Aids Specialist. Education: Chartered Physiotherapist; Qualified Teacher, U.K.; Diploma, Health Education, London. Married. Appointments: Lecturer, Teaching Aids, University College, Dar es Salaam, Tanzania; Senior Lecturer, National Institute of Education, Makerere University College, Kampala, Uganda. Publications: '500' A-V. Teacher Training, 1968; Basic Visual Aids Handbook, 1969; Let's Make it Work, 1969; Service Units (Audio-Visual), 1970. Address: Audio-Visual Aids Centre, National Institute of Education, P.O. Box 7062, Kampala, Uganda.

PRENTICE, Michael Ashworth, born 3rd March 1926. Entomologist. Education: Stanley House School, Birmingham, U.K., 1933-39; Leighton Park, Reading, 1939-45; B.Sc., Sheffield University, 1948; B.Sc., Zoology, ibid, 1951. Married, 2 sons, 1 daughter. Appointments: Entomologist (Medical), Uganda, 1951; Senior Entomologist, Ministry of Health, Uganda, & Head, Vector Control Division, 1962—; Honorary Lecturer, Makerere University, 1969—. Memberships: Bilharzia Specialist Committee of East Africa; Commodore, Victoria Nyanza Sailing Club, 1964-65; Sailing Captain, Uganda Kobs, 1968-70; President, Kampala Camera Club, 1961-62; Natural History Section, Uganda Society; East African 505 Class Association. Contributor of papers to professional journals. Address: Vector Control Division, Ministry of Health, P.O. Box 1661, Kampala, Uganda.

PRESTON, Margaret Winifred, born 22nd September 1912. Nurse. Education: General Nurse Training, Goulborn Base Hospital, N.S.W., Australia; Midwifery Training, Royal North Shore Hospital: Infant Welfare, Karatane, Sydney. Appointments: Muumi Hospital, 1943; 2nd Sister, Kilimatinde Hospital, 1944; relieved Sr. i/c, Berega Hospital, 1945 & Kilimatinde, 1946; Muume Hospital, 1948; relieved Sr. i/c, Berega Hospital, 1950; Nursing in North Australia, 1954-55; commenced Leprosy Ward, Makutupora, 1955—; moved whole settlement to Hembolo Leprosy Centre, 1963—. Address: D.C.T. Leprosy Centre, Hembolo, P.O. Box 301, Dodoma, Tanzania.

PRICE, Jean Mary (Wheatley), born 29th March 1934. Missionary; Nurse. Education: Ursuline High School, Brentwood, Essex, U.K., 1947-51; Nuffield Orthopaedic Hospital, Oxford, 1951-53; St. Thomas' Hospital, London, 1954-57; British Hospital for Mothers & Babies, Woolwich, London, 1957. Married, 4 children. Address: P.O. Box 450, Soroti, Uganda.

PRICE, John Wheatley, born 13th August 1931. Missionary Clergyman. Education: Repton School, U.K., 1945-49; Emmanuel College, Cambridge, 1951-54; Ridley Hall, Cambridge, 1954-55; M.A., University of Cambridge. Married, 4 children. Appointments: Missionary, Church Missionary Society; Soroti Diocesan Secretary, Uganda; Warden, St. Peter's Community Centre, Soroti. Address: St. Peter's Community Centre, P.O. Box 450, Soroti, Uganda.

PRIEMS, Cornelius Leo, born 22nd November 1920. Missionary; Educationist. Education: Cadier & Keer, Holland, 1934-40; Aalbeek, 1940-46 (Theological); B.A.(Hons.), double first class, National University of Ireland, 1948-50; M.A., English, first class Hons., ibid, 1954; Postgrad. Diploma in Education, University of London, U.K., 1951. Appointments: First Headmaster, Bishop Herman Secondary School, Ghana, 1952—. Member, Society of African Missions. Address: Bishop Herman Secondary School, P.O. Box 46, Kpando V.R., Ghana.

PROMONTORIO, Victor Charles Antoine, born 29th July 1912. Barrister. Education: Leopoldville, Congo; Diploma, Law, University of Louvain, Belgium, 1935. Appointments: Barrister, Brussels, 1936; joined Belgian Army, 1940; returned to the Bar, Brussels, 1960; Legal Counsel, Round Table, Belgian Congo, 1960; Senator, Parliament, 1960-68; Member of the Bar, Kinshasa, Democratic Republic of the Congo, 1962—; Barrister, Court of Appeal, Kinshasa. Batonnier, Avocats a la Cour d'Appel, Kinshasa. Author, Les Institutions Congolaise. Address: B.P. 1566, Kinshasa, Democratic Republic of the Congo.

PRUDENCIO, Eustache, born 20th September 1926. Inspector of Primary Education. Education: Teachers' Diploma; Diploma for School Principal; Diploma, Inspector of Primary Schools; Diploma, Academy of Elocution. Married, 13 children. Appointments: Teacher, Principal, Dakar, Senegal, 1947-57; Head of Cabinet, Ministry of Interior, Porto Novo, Dahomey, 1957-58; General Secretary to the Republican Party, ibid; School Principal, Diourbel, Senegal, 1958-61; Professor of French, Grammar School, Cotonou, Dahomey, 1961-62; Primary School Inspector, Ouidah, 1962-64; Technical Counsellor, Ministry of Information & Member of the Political Bureau of the Democratic Party, Dahomey, 1964-65; Primary School Inspector, Ouidah, 1965-68; Member of the Constitutional Committee, 1968; Primary School Inspector, Cotonou, Dahomey, 1968—. Memberships: Committee of Afro-Asian Authors; President of the Committee, Scouts Director, Dahomey. Publications: Les Rois d'Abomey (essay); Vade Mecum des Instituteurs;

Pedagogie Vivante; (Poems) Vents du Lac; Ombres et Soleils; Violence de la Race; Foehn sur les Tropiques. Honours: Recipient of First Prize, Academy of Elocution & Dramatic Art, Dakar, Senegal, 1954; Diploma of Honour for Poetry, 1969; Bronze Medal for Education. Address: B.P. 357, Cotonou, Dahomey.

PUJARA, Indulal Shamaldas, born 26th May 1928. Company Executive. Education: B.Commerce, University of Bombay, 1950. Married, 1 son, 3 daughters. Appointments: with Madhvani Group of Companies in Uganda since March 1953; currently, Chief Accountant with Subsidiary Company, Steel Corporation of E.A. Ltd., Jinja, Uganda. Memberships: Uganda Institute of Management, Kampala; British Institute of Management, London; Fellow, Association of Industrial and Commercial Executive Accountants, London. Address: Steel Corporation of E.A. Ltd., P.O. Box 1023, Jinja, Uganda.

PUMPHREY, John Laurence, born Scotland, U.K., 22nd July 1916. Diplomat. Education: 1st Class Hons. Moderations in Greek & Latin Literature, Oxford University, 1936; 1st Class Hons., Literae Humaniores, ibid, 1938. Married, 4 sons, 1 daughter. Appointments include: Deputy British High Commissioner, Nairobi, Kenya, 1965-67; British High Commissioner, Lusaka, Zambia, 1967—. Memberships: Brook's, London; Royal Commonwealth Society, London. Address: c/o D.S.A.O., King Charles St., London, S.W.1, U.K.

PUPLAMPU, Tettey, born Big Ada, Ghana, 25th June 1927. Teacher (Founder & Headmaster, Ada Secondary School). Education: St. Andrew's & Presbyterian Training Colleges, Akropong, 1948, 1949, 1953, 1954; University of Ghana, 1956-61. Married, 7 children. Appointments include: Head Teacher, Ada Local Primary School, 1950-55; Teacher, Big Ada & Ada Presbyterian Middle Schools, 1955-56; Headmaster, Ada Secondary School, 1961—. Address: Ada Secondary School, P.O. Box 47, Ada, Ghana.

PURCELL, John Francis Brownlee, born 11th April 1910. Administrator. Education: St. Mary's College, Dundalk, Co. Louth, Eire; St. John's College, Southsea, Hants, U.K. Married, 3 sons, 1 daughter. Appointments: Clerk, Swaziland Government, 1929; Assistant District Officer, ibid, 1937; District Officer, 1948; Senior District Officer, 1959; Secretary, Swazi Affairs, 1960; war service with Swazi Group, Pioneer Corps, 1942-45. Memberships: Royal Commonwealth Society; Hampshire County Cricket Club. Honours: M.B.E., 1951; O.B.E., 1960; Chevalier of the Papal Order of St. Gregory, 1963. Address: Havelock Mine, P.O. Bulembu, Swaziland.

PURITT, Paul, born 28th July 1938. Social Anthropologist. Education: B.A., University of Toronto, Canada, 1959; M.A., ibid, 1961; Ph.D., University of Illinois, U.S.A., 1970. Married, 2 sons. Appointments: Visiting Lecturer, University of Dar es Salaam, Tanzania. Author of several articles on East African social & political organization & rural development. Address: Department of Sociology, University of Dar es Salaam, P.O. Box 35043, Dar es Salaam, Tanzania.

Q

QUAISON-SACKEY, Alex, born 9th August 1924. Barrister; Solicitor. Education: Mfantsipim School, Cape Coast, Ghana, 1941-45; Achimota College, Accra, 1946-48; Politics, Philosophy & Economics, Exeter College, Oxford, U.K., 1949-52; London School of Economics, 1955. Married, 6 children. Appointments: Labour Officer, 1952-55; Attaché, British Embassy, Rio de Janeiro, 1956; Official Secretary, Ghana High Commission, London, 1957-59; Permanent Secretary to the U.N. & Ambassador to Cuba & Mexico, 1959-65; President, U.N. General Assembly, 1964-65; Foreign Minister, Ghana, 1965-66. Memberships: Oxford Union Society; Achimota Golf Club. Publications: Africa Unbound. Honours: LL.D., University of California, Berkeley, U.S.A., 1965; LL.D., Tuskegee Inst., Albama; Doctor of Letters, Montclaire College, N.Y. Address: Akumbia Lodge, P.O. Box 104, Winneba, Ghana.

QUARCOOPOME, Cornelius Odarquaye, born 6th July 1924. Ophthalmic Surgeon. Education: Accra Academy & Achimota College, 1939-46; M.B., Ch.B., Birmingham University, U.K., 1947-53; Institute of Ophthalmology, London, 1957-58. Married, 4 children. Appointments: Medical Officer, Ministry of Health, Ghana, 1953-59; Specialist Ophthalmologist, ibid, 1960—; Senior Lecturer in Ophthalmology, Ghana Medical School, 1966—. Memberships: Treasurer, Ghana Medical Association; Competitions Secretary, Achimota Golf Club. Contributor of articles to medical journals. Address: Ghana Medical School, P.O. Box 4236, Accra, Ghana.

QUARTEY, Emmanuel Laud, born Accra, Ghana, 22nd June 1920. Chartered Engineer. Education: Bishop Boys' School, 1928-31; Achimota School, 1932-38; Achimota College, 1939-42; B Sc., Queen Mary College, London University, U.K., 1942-43. Personal details: married to Laura Nan Lamiley Lamptey; 2 sons, 2 daughters. Appointments include: Electrical Mechanical Engineer, United Africa Co. Plywood Factory; Electrical Engineer, Nigerian Government Electricity Undertaking; Senior Electrical Engineer, Electricity Department, Government of Ghana, 1956-59; Deputy Chief Electrical Engineer, ibid, 1959; Chief Electrical Engineer, 1960-66; Chief Executive, Volta River Authority, Accra, Ghana, 1966—. Fellowships: Institute of Mechanical Engineers; Institute of Electrical Engineers; Ghana Institute of Engineers; President, Ghana Group of Professional Engineers. Publications: Electricity Development in Ghana (joint author). Honours include: Grand Medal, 1968. Address: Volta River Authority, P.O. Box M.77, Accra, Ghana.

QUARTEY-PAPAFIO, Ruby Lamiley, born 23rd March 1898. Educationist. Education: Accra Grammar School, Ghana, passed College of Preceptors Examination; trained in Southport, U.K.; Refresher Course in Arts, Southampton University; holder of Teachers' Certificate A. Appointments: Headmistress, Accra Government Girls' School; Education Officer, Education Department; retired with rank of Senior Education Officer; Welfare Officer, Department of Social Welfare, retiring as Senior Welfare Officer; Member, NLC Advisory Committee; Chief Commissioner, Girl Guides of Ghana. Memberships: Achimota School Board; Board of Governors, O'Reilly Secondary School; Accra Day Training College; Ghana International School; Chairman, Accra Girls' Secondary School; Adisadel College Board; Young Women's Christian Association; Anglican Church Synod Committee; Council of Women, Ghana. Honours: Certificate of Honour & Badge, 1941; King George V Jubilee Medal, 1935; King George VI Coronation Medal, 1937; Queen Elizabeth Coronation Medal, 1953; M.B.E., 1953; Ghana Grand Medal, 1968. Address: Accra, Ghana.

QUAYE, Charles, born 12th November 1910. Educator. Education: Wesleyan School, Accra, Ghana, 1915-24; Mfantsipim School, Cape Coast, 1926-30; Achimota College, 1932-33; University of London, U.K., 1947-48. Married, 5 sons, 1 daughter. Appointments: Senior History Master, Mfantsipim School, Cape Coast, Ghana, 1934-51; Headmaster, Fijai Secondary School, Sekondi, 1952-65; Lay Magistrate, Juvenile Court, ibid, 1954—; Secretary, School of Education, University College of Cape Coast, 1965—. Memberships: National President, People's Educational Association, 1950-54; West African Examinations Council & Chairman, Ghana National Committee, ibid, 1957-65; Chairman, Conference of Heads of Assisted Secondary Schools, 1958-65; Vice-Chairman, West African Examinations Council, 1964-65; Fellow, Royal Commonwealth Society; International Jurists' Commission. Address: University College, Cape Coast, Ghana.

QUAYE, Hector Tei-Mensah, born 19th August 1931. Bank Manager. Education: Associate, Institute of Book-keepers; Certificate, ibid, 1954; Part I, Institute of Bankers Diploma Examinations, 1966. Personal details: son of retired Bank Official. Appointments: Sub-Accountant, Barclays Bank DCO, Ghana, 1959; Accountant, ibid, 1962; Sub-Manager, 1965; Branch Manager, 1970—. Executive Member of Dunkwa Social Club. Address: Barclays Bank DCO, P.O. Box 77, Dunkwa, Ghana.

QUENUM, Auguste Alfred, born Ouidah, 10th January 1926. Physician; Director, Regional Bureau for Africa, World Organization of Health. Education: Higher Primary School, Victor Ballot, Porto-Novo, Dahomey, 1942-45; Ecole Normale, William Ponty, Sebikhotam, Senegal, 1945-48; Diploma, African School of Medicine & Pharmacy, Dakar, 1948-52; Head Physician, Kaolack Garrison Infirmary, Senegal, 1952-53; Lycée Van Hollen Hoven, Dakar, 1953-54; Bacc., Experimental Sciences, Faculty of Sciences, Bordeaux, 1954-55; Certificates of Higher Studies, M.D., Joint Faculty of Medicine & Pharmacy, Bordeaux, 1954-57. Appointments: President, National Union of Youth, Dahomey, 1960-61; Aggreg., Histology & Embriology, President, Dakar University Club, 1963-65; Member, Committee of Experts for the professional & technical formation of medical & auxiliary personnel, W.H.O., 1964; Regional Director, W.H.O. for Africa, 1965—; Member, Higher Academic Council, University of Lovanium, Democratic Republic of the Congo, 1965; Professor without chair, Joint Faculty of Medicine & Pharmacy, Dakar, 1966—; Member, Honorary Committee of Patronage, Pan-African Secretariat of Pax Romana MIEC & MIIC, 1969. Head of various study courses, scientific missions, & researches. Memberships: West African Biological Society, 1936; Black African French Language Medical Society, 1961; Committee of Patronage, Journees Medicales, Dakar, 1969; Honorary Member, International Society of Researches on Medical Education; World Health Organization; Congress of the International Children's Centre, Conditions of Life for the African Child in an Urban Setting, 1964, & many other conferences. Publications include: over 50 articles of scientific research on medical problems & discussion of socio-medical problems, e.g. Africa's Health Problems, 1969; Pouquoi devons-nous innover en enseignement medical en Afrique?, 1970; Biologie moleculaire et Sante publique, 1970. Honours: Knight, National Order of the Republic of Dahomey; Officer, Order of Merit of Senegal; Officer, Order of Congolese Merit; Commander, The Equatorial Star of the Republic of Gabon; Honorary M.D., University of Abidjan, Ivory Coast, 1970. Address: P.O.B. 6, Brazzaville, Republic of the Congo.

R

RABETALIANA, Charles, born 16th December 1907. Retired Civil Servant. Education: 2nd Class Certificate of Studies; completed Administrative Studies. Married, 6 children. Appointments: Secretary, l'Assistance Médicale Malgache, 1926-29; Interpreter, Malagachian Courts, 1929-33; Assessor, Malagachian Courts of 2nd Instance, 1933-37; Clerk, Service de Législation et Contentieux Malgache, 1937-62; retired, 1962. Memberships: Syndicate of Malagachian Civil Servants; Mutual Aid Society of Malagachian Civil Servants; Football Association. Honours: Chevalier de l'Etoile d'Anjouan, 1948; Chevalier du Mérite de Malagasy, 1952; Chevalier de l'Etoile de la Grande Comore, 1953; Chevalier de l'Ordre du Nichanel Anouar, 1954; Chevalier du Mérite Social, 1956. Address: Lot S.I.A.E. 21, Tananarive, Malagasy.

RADIA, Mansukh Tulshidas, born 3rd June. Merchant. Education: Senior Cambridge; Elementary Accounts, Kay's College, Nairobi, Kenya. Appointments: Junior Staff, New Fabric Stores, 1956-58; Senior Staff, ibid, 1958-61; Partner, 1961-63; Senior Partner, Variety Fabrics, 1963-70. Memberships: Kampala Institute; Lahana Union.

RADO, Emil Richard, born 18th January 1931. Economist; University Lecturer. Education: Berzsenyi D. Gymnazium, Budapest,

Hungary, 1941-47; Ackworth School, Yorks., U.K., 1947-49; University College, London, 1949-52. Married, 1 son, 2 daughters. Appointments: Lecturer & Research Fellow, University of Ghana, 1953-61; Visiting Assistant Professor, Williams College, Mass., U.S.A., 1950-61; Lecturer, Makerere College, Uganda, 1961-65; Senior Lecturer, University of Glasgow, 1965—; Visiting Reader, Econ. Research, University College, Nairobi, 1967-70. Memberships: Fellow, Royal Economic Society; American Economic Association; East African Natural History Society. Publications: Uganda's Medical Manpower (E.A.Med.J.), 1965; Cost-Benefit Analysis of Health & Educational Projects (U.M. Rsch. Inst. for Soc. Dev.), 1965; The Demand for Manpower (J.Dev.Studies), 1965; Manpower Training in East Africa (World Yearbook of Educ.), 1967; Employment & Kenya's Development Plan (E.A.Jrnl.), 1970, etc. Consultant to various governments & international organizations, including Governments of Kenya & Uganda, O.E.C.D., & I.B.R.D. Address: Department of International Economic Studies, University of Glasgow, Glasgow W.2, U.K.

RADOLI, Mark George, born 5th December 1935. Civil Servant. Education: B.A., London University, U.K. Married, 3 children. Appointments: Collector of Customs & Excise, 1962-64; Regional Commissioner of Customs & Excise, Uganda, 1965-66; Assistant Deputy Commissioner of Customs & Excise, East Africa, 1966-67; Deputy Commissioner General of Customs & Excise, East Africa, 1967—. Member, Kenya Red Cross Society. Address: c/o East African Customs & Excise Department, P.O. Box 9061, Mombasa, Kenya.

RAFFRAY, Raymond, born 30th October 1928. Engineer. B.S., Chem. Engrng., Louisiana State University, U.S.A., 1952. Married, 2 sons, 2 daughters. Appointments: Assistant Engineer, Mon Desert Sugar Factory, Mauritius, 1952-58; Technical Adviser, Flacq United Estates Ltd., Mauritius, 1958-68; Factory Manager, Flacq United Estates Ltd., 1968—. Memberships: Societe de Technologie Agricole et Sueriere de l'Ile Maurice; Mauritius Professional Engineers' Association; Dodo Club; Grand Baie Yacht Club; Societe Apicole de l'Ile Maurice. Address: Factory Manager, Union Flacq, Saint Julien, Mauritius.

RAHARISON, Samuel, born 26th September 1928. Physician; Professor Agrege of Medicine. Education: Bacc. Experimental Sciences; State Doctor of Medicine; Certificate of Special Studies in Cardiology; Hospital Doctor; Professor Agrege of Internal Medicine. Married to another doctor, 2 children. Appointments: Head of Medical Service, General Hospital, Tananarive; Professor of Medical Semeiology, Therapeutic & Clinical, Befelatanaue School of Medicine, Tananarive; Head of Studies, Semeiology, National School of Medicine, Tananarive. Memberships: Titular Member, Applied Science Section, Malagasy Academy; Vice-President, Malagasy Society of Medical Science; Associate, French Society of Cardiology; French Society of Aeronautic Medicine. Publications: Author of approximately 20 papers on cardiology & general medicine. Honours: Knight of the National Order of the Malagasy Republic. Address: General Hospital, Tananarive, The Malagasy Republic.

RAHMAN, Abdul Fattah, born 2nd February 1900. Retired Civil Servant. Education: Madrassa Sulaimania School; The Government Model School; St. Edward's School. Married, 2 daughters. Appointments: entered Civil Service in 1918; Chief Clerk & Paymaster, until 1950; Councillor, East Ward, 1951; Alderman, 1957; Chairman, Education Committee; Chairman, Local Education Committee, 1960—; Mayor until 1964; Mayor of Freetown, 1959-64; Justice of the Peace, 1952—; Member, Fourah Bay College Council; Sierra Leone Library Board; Member & Hon. Secretary, Aku Mohamedan Burial Board, Fourah Bay; Director, A. J. Sewards, Sierra Leone Ltd., 1963-67; Director, Guma Valley Water Co., 1961-64; Chairman, Guma Valley Water Co., 1967; Director, Electricity Corporation, 1967. Memberships include: Board of Governors, Methodist Boys' High School, 1966-68; Freetown Teachers' Training College, 1966-68; Chairman, Fourah Bay College Mosque Fund, The University of Sierra Leone; Girl Guide Assn.; Boy Scout Assn.; Nursery Schools Council; Trustee, Jamiul Atig Mosque, Fourah Bay; Brotherhood Assn. Council. Honours: Commander of the Order, Cedar of Lebanon, 1960; O.B.E., 1962. Address: 3 Bungie Street, Freetown, Sierra Leone.

RAHMANI, Kafayatullah, born 12th March 1927. Chartered Engineer. Education: B.A., University of Panjab, Lahore, W. Pakistan; B.Sc., University of Edinburgh, U.K. Married, 4 children. Appointments: Site Engineer, George Wimpey & Co. Ltd., London; Engineer/Designer, ibid; Assistant Engineer, East African Railways & Harbours, Nairobi, Kenya; District Civil Engineer, ibid. Memberships: Institution of Civil Engineers, London; American Society of Civil Engineers, New York; East African Institution of Engineers, Nairobi; Fellow, Permanent Way Institution, U.K.; American Railway Engineering Association, Chicago. Recipient, Merit Certificates in civil engineering design, technical mathematics, & surveying, University of Edinburgh. Address: East African Railways Corporation, P.O. Box 42, Nakuru, Kenya.

RAINGEARD, Michel Joseph Pierre Marie, born Nantes, France, 20th June 1919. President & Director-General. Education: Licensed in Letters; Diploma of Higher Studies in Classical Languages. Appointments: Teacher, Secondary Education, 1940-45; Journaliste, 1945-51; Deputy, National Assembly, 1951-58; Member of Economic & Social Council, 1959-69; President, Technical Cooperation Section of the Council. Memberships include: President & Director-General, SODETAM; President, UDETA; President du Directoire, SORENTENTE; President du Cercle France Outre-Mer. Author of studies, reports, & articles on the development of the 3rd World. Honours: Grand Officer of the National Orders of the Central African Republic, Chad, Upper Volta, Tunisia, & Morocco; Commander of the National Orders of Mauritania, The Ivory Coast, Niger, Dahomey,

Congo, Madagascar, & Gabon; Officer of the National Order of the Cameroon. Address: 60 rue de Maubeuge, Paris IX, France.

RAJI (Alhaji) Lamidi Adegboyega, born Abeokuta, Nigeria, 22nd June 1917. Managing Director. Education: Standard 6; Home Studies, Bennett College International Correspondence College. Married, 13 children. Appointments include: 1st Class Military Nurse, 1945-46; Proprietor & Manager, Akeweje Bros. & Co., 1946-63; Director, Nigeria Red Cross, 1957—, currently active at the War Front caring for wounded & prisoners; Chairman, Board of Directors, Akeweje Bros. & Co. Ltd., 1963—; Managing Director, City Girls Pools, 1963—; Chairman, Board of Directors, City Girls Agencies Ltd., 1964—. Memberships include: Divisional Director, Abeokuta, Nigerian Red Cross Society; ex-Co. Member, Western State Branch, ibid; Secretary, Abeokuta Importers' & Exporters' Association; Treasurer, Abeokuta Patent & Proprietary Medicine Dealers' Association; Chairman, Adire Dyers' Association; ex-Co., Boys' & Girls' Club, Abeokuta. Honours include: World War II Medal; Badge for Loyal Service, World War II; Special Service Cross for saving life of a drowning boy, United Red Cross, 1954. Address: P.O. Box 68, Ikeja Airport, Nigeria.

RAJKOVIC, Alexander D., born 21st February 1920. Physician; Medical Microbiologist; Professor. Education: M.D., University of Zagreb, Yugoslavia, 1949; Cert. Epid., Belgrade, 1950; Dip. Bact., Sarajevo, 1953; D.Sc.(Med.), ibid, 1963. Appointments: Head, Regional Institute of Health, Banja Luka, Yugoslavia; Professor & Head, Department of Microbiology, Faculty of Medicine, Sarajevo; Professor & Head, Department of Microbiology, Ahmadu Bello University, Zaria, Nigeria. Author of some 40 publications in the field of microbiology, including the co-authorship of a textbook of microbiology for medical students, now in its 2nd edition. Address: Department of Microbiology, Ahmadu Bello University, Zaria, Nigeria.

RAJKOVIC-DIMIC, Olivera, born 8th February 1920. Physician; Medical Microbiologist; University Reader. Education: M.D., University of Belgrade, Yugoslavia, 1947; Cert. Bact., University of Belgrade, 1949; Dip. Bact., Sarajevo, 1953. Married. Appointments: Head, Bacteriology Section, Regional Institute of Health, Banja Luka; Head, Division of Bacteriology & Mycology, Institute of Dermatology & Venereology, Sarajevo; College Professor & Head of Chair for Microbiology & Nutrition, University College of Education, Sarajevo; Reader in Microbiology, Department of Microbiology, Ahmadu Bello University, Zaria, Nigeria. Publications include 6 articles in the field of bacteriology, a manual of nutrition and microbiology for students, & co-author of a manual of standard bacteriological laboratory methods. Address: Ahmadu Bello University, Zaria, Nigeria.

RAJWANI, Abdulrahim Alibhai, born Dhank, India, 11th November 1930. Commercial Accountant. Education: Secondary School Certificate Examinations, 1949; Book Keeping, Advanced Level; Royal Society of Arts Examination. Appointments: Accounts Assistant, Bombay, 1949-52; Commercial Accountant, Dar es Salaam, Tanzania, 1952-59; School Accountant, Itinga, Tanzania, 1959-63; Accountant, Agip Petroleum Ltd., 1963—. Memberships: Hon. Treasurer, Ismailia Association for Tanganyika, 1963—; Hon. Treasurer, H.H. Aga Khan High School, Dar es Salaam, Tanzania, 1967-68; Assistant Cub Master, 161st Bombay Pack, 1949-52. Address: P.O. Box 1304, Dar es Salaam, Tanzania.

RAKOTOBE, H. Rene A., born Tananarive, Malagasy Republic, 8th July 1918. Lawyer; Senator. Education: Baccalaureat; LL.B., Faculties of Law, Alger, Algeria, & Paris, France. Married, 4 children. Appointments include: Lawyer, Courts & Tribunals, 1946; Mbr. & Pres., Nat. Constitutional Assembly, 1959; Senator, Vice-Pres. of Senate, 1959-60; Senator, 1960; Keeper of Seals, Ministry of Justice, 1960; Advocate-General, Supreme Court, 1963; Pres., Higher Council for Institutions, 1960—. Memberships include: Corresp., Acad. des Sciences d'Outre-Mer; Pres., Red Cross Soc., Malagasy; ibid, Automobile Club of Madagascar; Pres., Institut International de Droit d'Expression Française; Past Pres., Tananarive Rotary Club; Int. Olympic Comm. Publications: La primaute du Droit dans les Pays en veie de developpement; Les Institutions de la Republique Malgache. Honours include: Grand Officier, Ordre National de la Republique Malgache; Officier, Legion d'Honneur. Address: B.P. 835, Tananarive, Malagasy Republic.

RAKOTOMALALA, Jerome, born 15th July 1914. Archbishop. Education: Primary Studies, Christian Schools, Tananarive, Malagasy Republic; Secondary Studies, Lower Seminary of Tananarive; Higher Studies, Greater Seminary of Tananarive. Appointments: ordained Priest, 1943; Vicar, Cathedral of Tananarive & Professor of Mathematical Sciences, Greater Seminary, 1944-47; Director, District Mission of Ambohimiadane, 1947-53; Director, School of Instructors, 1953-59; Vicar-General of Tananarive, 1959-60; nominated Archbishop, 1960; consecrated Bishop by Pope John XXIII, 1960; elected Cardinal under Pope Paul VI, 1969. Honours: Commander, National Order of the Malagasy Republic, 1960; Officer of the Legion of Honour, 1962; Knight of the Military Order of Saint Sauveur & Saint Brigitte, 1963. Address: The Archbishop of Tananarive, The Malagasy Republic.

RAMADHANE-SAID, Gabriel, born Bouca, Central African Republic, March 1942. Agricultural Engineer. Education: Ecole de Ngatoua, 1951; Ecole, Bouca; Ecole de Ngaragba; CEPE Diploma; 6th Class, College Emile Gentil, Actuel Lycée Boganda; BEPC Diploma; IEAAC, Institut d'Etudes Agronomiques en Afrique Centrale, Wakombo, 1962; Baccalaureat Technique; Iere Candidature Ingenieur Agronome, Faculte de Science, Universite Luvanium, Kinshasa, Congo, 1966. Married, 1 son, 2 daughters. Appointments: Assistant Director, ORDEST, Alindao, 1968; Director, ibid, 1968-70; Director, Haute Sangha

Region, 1970. Memberships: Secretary-General, Students' Association, Institut d'Etudes Agronomiques, Wakombo; General Students' Association, University of Luvanium, Kinshasa. Recipient, numerous scholastic awards. Address: B.P. 112, Berbertati, Central African Republic.

RAMAKRISHNA, Viswanadha, born 28th June 1915. Entomologist. Education: M.A., University of Madras, India. Appointments: Entomologist, Malaria Control Project, U.P. Terai, Bazpur, India, 1951-55; Entomologist, WHO Malaria Control Pilot Project, Birninkebbi, W. Sokoto, Nigeria, 1955-61; Entomologist, West African Inter-Country Malaria Project, Cotonou, Dahomey, 1961-62; Entomologist, Instructor, WHO Malaria Eradication Training Centre, Yaba, Lagos, Nigeria, 1962-65, 1967-69; Entomologist, Basic Health Services Project, Yaba. 1969—; Entomologist, Malaria Project, Manila, Philippines, 1965-67. Memberships: National Society for Malaria & Communicable Diseases, India; Royal Society of Tropical Medicine & Hygiene, London; Royal Entomological Society of London. Publications: Textbook of Malaria Control, 1939, & various articles in professional journals. Address: Basic Health Services Project, Federal Malaria Service, Yaba, Nigeria.

RAMASAWMY, Goinsamy, born Mauritius, 2nd November 1914. Civil Servant. Education: Government Primary School, 1921-28; Royal College, Mauritius, 1929-34. Married, 3 sons, 2 daughters. Appointments: Clerical Service, 1938-41; Traffic Superintendent, Manager of Telecommunications Service, 1942-57; Assistant Secretary, Ministry of Finance, 1957-59; Principal Assistant Secretary, Ministry of Labour, 1959-68; Acting Permanent Secretary, Ministry of Works, 1969—. Memberships: President, Iudo-Mauritian Association, 1960-62; President, Jagriti Hindu Benevolent Association, 1947-60; President, Hundu Samudye Vriddhi Sangam, 1947-48; President, Mauritius Tamil Welfare & Cultural Association, 1959-60. Address: 31 Avenue des Palmiers, Quatre Bornes, Mauritius.

RAMGOOLAM, Seewoosagur, born September 1900. Physician. Education: Royal College, Curepipe, Mauritius; University College, London, U.K. Married, 1 son, 1 daughter. Appointments: Municipal Councillor, Port Louis, 1940-43, 1956—; Deputy Mayor, ibid, 1956; Mayor, 1958; entered Legislative Council, 1940; elected Member, ibid, for Pamplemousses-Riv. du Rempart, 1948, re-elected, 1953; re-elected for Triolet, 1959; Member, Executive Council, 1948, 1953; Liaison Officer for Education, 1951-56; Ministerial Secretary to the Treasury, 1958; Chief Minister & Minister of Finance, 1961; Prime Minister, 1965, 1967—; Minister of Finance, 1960—; Prime Minister, Minister of Defence & Internal Security, & Minister of Information & Broadcasting, 1969—. Memberships: President, Indian Cultural Association; Chairman, Board of Directors, Advance. Editor, Indian Cultural Review. Honours: LL.D., University of New Delhi, India; Knighted, 1965; Grand Croix de l'Ordre National de la Republique Malagasy. Address: Prime Minister's Office, Port Louis, Mauritius.

RAMLALLAH, Beekrumsing, born Mauritius, 2nd September 1915. Journalist, Editor, & Politician. Education: Teachers' Examination, 1934. Married, 3 sons, 3 daughters. Appointments: served in Mauritius Territorial Force, 1937-40; Teacher, 1937-54; Manager, Nalanda Co. Ltd., 1946-69; Editor-Founder, Mauritius Times, 1954—; Member, Legislative Assembly, 1959—; Hon. Director, Mauritius Housing Corporation. Founder-Member, Anglo-Mauritius Society. Address: 30 Bourbon St., Port Louis, Mauritius.

RAMNARAIN (Hon.) Hurry, born 2nd October 1914. Minister of State. Education: Primary & Secondary. Appointments: Hon. Chairman, Plantation Workers' Union; Vice-Chairman, Mauritius Labour Party; Member of Legislative Assembly, Mauritius; Cabinet Member; Minister of State (Agriculture). Memberships: Chairman, Mauritius Workers' Welfare Society. Publications: Mazdur. Honours: O.B.E., 1969. Address: Ministry of Agriculture, Port Louis, Mauritius.

RAMPHUL, Droopnath, born Mauritius, 20th February 1921. Judge. Education: Royal College, Mauritius; London University, U.K. (Economics); Called to the Bar, Lincoln's Inn, 1948. Married, 1 son, 2 daughters. Appointments include: Journalist, London, 1946-48; District Magistrate, Mauritius, 1950-60; Civil Commissioner, Mauritius, 1958; Master & Registrar & Assistant Attorney-General of Mauritius, 1959; Magistrate, Intermediate Criminal Court of Mauritius, 1960-65; President, ibid, 1965; Puisne Judge, Supreme Court of Mauritius, 1967—. Memberships: Chairman, St. John Council for Mauritius; Board of Directors, Mauritius Institute. Publications: India & the Soviet Experiment. Address: Supreme Court, Port Louis, Mauritius.

RAMSDEN, William Arthur, born Leeds, Yorks., U.K., 6th August 1926. Attorney-General of Swaziland. Education: Pretoria Boys' High School, South Africa; University of the Witwatersrand, Johannesburg; Inner Temple, London, U.K.; B.A.; LL.B. Married, 2 sons, 3 daughters. Appointments: Assistant Legal Adviser, Johannesburg Consolidated Investment Co., 1950-54; Professional Assistant, Webber, Wentzel, Hofmeyer, Turnbull & Co., Johannesburg, 1954-55; Registrar, Basutoland, Bechuanaland Protectorate & Swaziland Court of Appeal, Registrar & Master, High Court of Basutoland, Judicial Commissioner & Magistrate, Basutoland, 1955-61; Crown Counsel for High Commission Territories, British Embassy, South Africa, 1962; Crown Counsel & Acting Attorney-General, Swaziland, 1962-67; Attorney-General, Swaziland, ex officio Member, Swaziland Cabinet & Parliament, 1967—. Memberships: Hon. Member, International Society for the Study of Comparative Public Law, Washington, U.S.A.; Executive Committee, Swaziland Branch, University of the Witwatersrand Alumni Association: Mbabane Club; Theatre Club; Freemason. Publications: Editor, Swaziland Law Reports; compiler of Statutes of Swaziland; contributor to legal publications. Honours: Queen's Counsel, 1967. Address: Attorney-

General's Chambers, Embassy House, Mbabane, Swaziland.

RAMYEAD, Devmitra, born 23rd December 1932. Principal Assistant Secretary. Education: Cambridge Higher School Certificate, Royal College, Curepipe, Mauritius, 1945-51; B.Sc. (London) as External Student, 1955. Appointments: Assistant Secretary, Ministry of Agriculture, Mauritius, 1951-59; Principal Assistant Secretary, Ministry of Information, 1959—. Honours: Gold Medal, Chamber of Agriculture, for best work done in science at the Royal College, 1951. Address: Ministry of Information & Broadcasting, Mauritius.

RAMZI, Ahmed, born 9th January 1900. Diplomat; Writer. Education: Cairo, U.A.R.; Lausanne & Zurich, Switzerland; Political Science, Social Science & Military Science. Personal details: son of Brigadier-General Ali Ramzi, Governor General of Sharkieh. Appointments: Barrister-at-Law, Mixed Courts; Consul General, Jerusalem (Israel), Paris (France), Syria, Lebanon: Ambassador to Italy, 1952; Turkey, 1954; Belgium, 1955; Permanent Delegate to the Arab League, 1958; later retired. Memberships: Gezira Sporting Club; Cairo Shooting Club; Egyptian Historical Research Society; Arabic Bayan Society; Vice-President, Turco-Arab Friendship Assn. Publications include: Echoes of the Past; Echoes in War Time. Recipient of Decorations from Syria, Lebanon, Iran etc. Address: Giza Avenue 51, Giza, Cairo, U.A.R.

RANGOOLAM (The Honorable Sir) Seewoosagur, President of Mauritius, born Belle Rive, Mauritius, 1900. Education: Royal College, Curepipe, Mauritius; University College, London, U.K. Appointments: Municipal Councillor, 1940-53; re-elected, ibid, 1956; Deputy Major, Port Louis, 1956; Mayor, ibid, 1958; Member, Legislative Council for Pamplemousses-Riviere du Rempart, 1948; re-elected, ibid, 1953; re-elected for Triolet, 1959; Member, Executive Council, 1948, 1953; Liaison Officer for Education, 1951-56; Ministerial Secretary to Treasury, 1958; Chief Minister & Minister of Finance, 1961; Premier, 1965; Pr]me Minister 1968—. Memberships: Chairman, Board of Directors 'Advance', Daily organ; President, Indian Cultural Association; Editor, 'Indian Cultural Review:; L.R.C.P.; M.R.C.S. Honours: Knighted, 1965. Address: Government House, Port Louis, Mauritius.

RANSOME-KUTI, O. Paediatrician: Educator. Education: Abeokuta Grammar School, Nigeria, 1936-44; Higher College, Yaba, 1946-47; University College, Ibadan, 1948; M.B., Trinity College, Dublin University, Ireland, 1948-54; M.R.C.P.; F.M.C.(Paed). Married. Appointments: House Surgeon, South Shields Hospital, U.K., 1954-55; House Physician, General Hospital, Lagos, Nigeria, 1955; Medical Officer, ibid, 1955-56; Medical Officer, Federal Medical Service, Dept. of Obstetrics & Gynaecology, 1956-57; Senior House Officer, Paediatrics, University College Hospital, Ibadan, 1957-58; Registrar, Paediatrics, ibid, 1958-59; Senior Hospital Officer (A.R.M.O. Tadworth), Hospital for Sick Children, London, U.K., 1960; Registrar (R.M.O. Tadworth), ibid, 1962; Locum House Officer (Neonatal Paediatrics), Postgraduate Medical School, Hammersmith Hospital, London, 1962; Locum House Officer (Medicine—Renal Diseases), ibid, 1962; Senior Registrar, Paediatrics, University College Hospital, Ibadan, Nigeria, 1962-63; Lecturer, Paediatrics, University of Lagos Medical School, Lagos, 1963-66; Senior Lecturer, ibid, 1966-67; Senior Lecturer & Ag. Head, Department of Paediatrics, Lagos University College of Medicine, 1967; Associate Professor & Acting Head, ibid, 1967-70; Professor & Head, 1970—. Memberships: President, Paediatric Association of Nigeria; President, Representative Committee, Nigerian Medical Association; West African Association of Physicians; West African Association of Gastro-enterologists; British Medical Association; Fellow, Royal Society of Medicine; W.H.O. Expert on Maternal & Child Health; Expert Committee, Maternal & Child Health, Federal Government of Nigeria. Contributor of papers to professional journals. Honours: Professor's Prize in Pathology, Trinity College, Dublin, 1952; Kirkpatrick Medal for Outstanding Services to Paediatrics in Nigeria, 1969. Address: College of Medicine of the University of Lagos, P.M.B. 12003, Lagos, Nigeria.

RAO, Sharad Kumar Sadashiv, born 13th October 1935. Advocate. Education: Barrister-at-Law, Lincoln's Inn, London, 1959. Married, 1 daughter. Appointments include: Advocate, A. R. Kapila & Co., Nairobi, Kenya, 1960-69; Senior State Counsel, Office of the Attorney-General, Kenya, 1970—. Memberships: President, Kenya Badminton Association; President, Nairobi Badminton Association; President, Suleman Virjae Gymkhana Club; Chairman, Overseas Tour Committee, & ex-Secretary & President, Kenya Lawn Tennis Association; Council Member, Kenya Olympic & Commonwealth Games Association. Address: P.O. Box 5521, Nairobi, Kenya.

RASEKOAI, Philemon Molefi Jacob, born 1st August 1927. Administrator; Teacher. Education: Roma College; Primary Higher Teachers' Certificate, 1946; Matriculation, 1948; B.A., University of South Africa, 1951; University Education Diploma, ibid, 1956. Personal details: married to Eunice Kefuoe Lequoa, Teacher & Musician. Appointments: Teacher, Mariazell High School, Cape Province, South Africa, 1952-57; Lehana Secondary School, 1957-60; Headmaster, ibid, 1958-60; Teacher, Sacred Heart High School, Lesotho, 1961-66; with Lesotho Civil Service as Assistant Secretary, Ministry of Foreign Affairs, 1966; attached to British Embassy in Ethiopia for 2 months; Assistant Secretary, Cabinet Office, 1967-68; Private Secretary to Hon. Prime Minister of Lesotho, Chief Leabua Jonathan, 1969; Permanent Secretary to the Ministry of the Interior, 1970—. Memberships: Secretary-General, Basutoland African National Teachers' Association, 1962-66. Address: Ministry of the Interior, P.O. Box 174, Maseru, Lesotho.

RASHID, Awadh Makame, born 23rd October 1944. National Service Officer. Education: Secondary. Personal details: married,

3 children. Member of Dar es Salaam Swimming Club. Address: N.S. H.Q., P.O. Box 1694, Dar es Salaam, Tanzania.

RATEFIARISON, born 30th September 1913. Schoolmaster. Education: Docteur es Lettres; Doctor of Commercial Science; Doctor of Philosophy. Married, 8 children. Appointments: Schoolmaster, 1937—; Chronicler of National Broadcasting, Madagascar, 1948—; currently Director, College Moderne et Technique, Tananarive. Memberships: Academie latine des Sciences, Arts et Belles-Lettres; Societe National d'Encouragement au Bien; Society de Medecine et d'Hygiene tropicales. Author of several educational books in the Malagasy language. Honours: Chevalier de l'ordre National Malagasy; Chevalier des Palmes Academiques; Chevalier de l'Ordre Universel du Merite Humain. Address: College Moderne et Technique, Place d'Ambohijatovo, Tananarive, Malagasy.

RATSIMIRAHO, Alfred, born Tanambao, Tamatave, Malagasy Republic, 1911. Physician; Government Official. Education: Ecole Primaire officielle; Ecole Superieure de Flacourt; Ecole de Medicine de Tananarive. Married, 2 sons, 3 daughters. Appointments include: Physician, A.M.I., 1935; Chief Physician, ibid, 1953; Medicine de classe exceptionnelle, 1965; Technical Adviser to Vice-Pres. of Govt., 1960; in charge of Mission of Vice-Pres. of Govt., 1966—. Memberships include: Pres., Tulear Section, Social Democratic Party, 1958-60; Pres., Tananarive Section, ibid, 1962—; Doctors' Club of France; Amis des Eclaireurs; Tantely Kristiana Assoc. of Young Protestants; Malagasy Cultural Ctr.; Friend of the University Library. Author of various articles in Tananarive journals. Honours include: Medaille d'Honneur des Epidemies, 1955; Chevalier de l'Ordre du Nichan el anouar, 1960; Knight, Ordre National Malagasy, 1963; Officer, ibid, 1968. Address: Lot III, R12, Tsarafaritra-Tsimbazaza, Antananarivo, Malagasy Republic.

RAVELOMANANA, Hermann, born Anahimalemy, Malagasy Republic, 28th February 1913. Professor; Senator. Education: Coll. Protestant de Paul Minault, Tananarive; B.A., Sorbonne, Paris, France, 1951. Married, 5 children. Appointments include: Dir. of Schls., French Protestant Missions, Madagascar; Sec. Gen. for Teaching, Protestant Schools, 1958; Mbr., Comm. for compiling Malagasy Republic Constitution, 1959; Senator; attended numerous Int. Conferences on Educ. Memberships include: Assoc. Cretienne des Anciens Etudiants de France; Vice-Pres., Evangelical Church of Madagaskira; Treas., Council of Protestant Churches of Madagaskira. Author of varied articles on educ. & lit. Honours include: Officier des Palmes Academiques. Address: 25 Rue Augey Dufresse, Tananarive, Malagasy Republic.

RAWLINGS, Kenneth, born 25th June 1931. College Librarian. Education: Archbishop Holgate's School, York, U.K.; Culham College; Cert. Ed., Oxford; Rel.T.Cert. Civil Service Law. Married, 2 daughters. Appointments: Librarian, Queen's School, Rheindahlen, Germany, 1960-62; Librarian, Education Officer, Northern Rhodesia, 1962-63; Librarian, Soche Hill College, 1964-66; Librarian, University of Malawi, 1967—. Memberships: Limbe Country Club; Treasurer, Royal Air Forces Association Malawi Branch; former Vice-Chairman, ibid. Licensed Reader, Anglican Church. Publications: A Modified Dewey Decimal Classification for use in Schools & Colleges in Malawi, 1967. Honours: Police Commendation, Northern Rhodesia, 1963. Address: Soche Hill College Library, University of Malawi, P.O. Box 5496, Limbe, Malawi.

RAZAFIMBAHINY, Jules A., born 19th April 1922. Diplomat; Statesman. Education: Institute of Business Law, Law School of the University of Paris; Diploma, Advanced Studies in Economics; Institute of Advanced Political Studies, Paris. Married, 2 children. Appointments: President, Commission of the African and Malagasy countries associated with the economic and social council of the Common Market and Euratom, Brussels, Belgium, 1958-60; Technical Counsellor to Minister of State responsible for the national economy & President, Administrative Board, Society of Energy of Madagascar, 1960-61; General Secretary, African-Malagasy Organization for Economic Cooperation, Yaoundé, Cameroon, 1962-64; Director-General, Ministry of Foreign Affairs, Tananarive, Malagasy, 1964-65; Ambassador Extraordinary & Plenipotentiary of the Malagasy Republic to Great Britain, Italy, Greece, & Israel, residence in London, U.K., 1965; Secretary of State for Foreign Affairs, Malagasy Republic, 1967 (re-appointed to this position in 1969); City Councilman, Tananarive, 1969; Head of Malagasy delegations to several international conferences; Ambassador Extraordinary & Plenipotentiary of Madagascar, Washington, D.C., U.S.A., 1970—. Memberships: Chairman, Charter Mbr. & Mbr., Administrative Board, Pan-African Institute of Development, Douala, Cameroon; Board of the College of Economic & Social Sciences, Paris. Honours: Cmdr., Malagasy National Order; Officer, National Order of Upper Volta; Cmdr., Order of the Moslem Republic of Mauritania; Cmdr., Order of the Republic of Chad; Cmdr., Order of the Leopard, Democratic Republic of the Congo (Kinshasa); Cmdr., Order of the Green Crescent, Comoro Islands; Recipient, Grand Cross, Order of Saint Sylvester & Grand Cross, National Order of the Italian Republic. Address: Embassy of Madagascar, 2374 Massachusetts Avenue, N.W., Washington, D.C. 20008, U.S.A.

RAZAFINDRALAMBO, Edilbert Pierre, born Tananarive, Madagascar (now Malagasy Republic), 3rd October 1921. Chief Justice. Education: Lic. es Lettres, Sorbonne, Paris, France; Certificate of Proficiency in Law; LL.D., Paris; studied at Cambridge University, U.K. Married, 3 children. Appointments: Advocate, Court of Paris, France, 1958-60; Deputy Attorney-General, Appeal Court of Tananarive, Malagasy Republic, 1960-61; Advocate General, Supreme Court of Madagascar, 1961-62; President of the Chamber, Supreme Court, 1962-67; Chief Justice, Supreme Court of Madagascar, 1967—; Professor of Law, Faculty of Law & Institute of Judicial Studies, University of Madagascar, 1962—. Memberships: President, Malagasy society of Judicial Studies; Corresp.,

International Law Journal, Clunet, Paris; Editorial Comm., Revue Juridique & Politique, Independence & Cooperation; Commission of Experts for the Application of Conventions & Recommendations of B.I.T.; American Society of International Law. Publications: Flagrant Infractions in French, English, & Czechoslovak Laws; & contributions to various professional journals. Honours: Knight, National Malagasy Order, 1969; Officer of Comorium Green Crescent, 1969; Officer, French National Order of Merit, 1970. Address: Supreme Court, Tananarive, The Malagasy Republic.

RAZAFINDRATOVO, Henri James, born 29th January 1931. Diplomat. Education: Licencie es Lettres, University of Montpellier, France; Master of Public Affairs, University of Pittsburgh, U.S.A. Married, 4 children. Appointments: Teacher, English, Lycée Gallieni, Tananarive, Malagasy Republic; Chef de Cabinet-Directeur de Cabinet, Ministry of Foreign Affairs, ibid, 1960-61; General Secretary-Director of Studies, National School of Administration, 1961-67; 1st Counsellor, Malagasy Embassy, London, U.K., 1968—. Memberships: General Secretary, English-Speaking Association of Madagascar, 1964-68; President, Cine Club of the Indian Ocean, 1966-68. Publications: Patterns of Leadership in Africa, 1964; Organization & Methods in Malagasy, 1967; The Administrative Organization of Madagascar (New Africa), 1968; Madagascar (New Africa), 1968; Madagascar After Nearly 10 Years of Independence (The Diplomatist), 1969. Honours: Chevalier, Ordre National Malagasy; Officier, Ordre de l'Etoile Noire, France; ibid, Ordre du Merite du Senegal; Commander, Order of the African Redemption, Liberia. Address: Malagasy Embassy, 33 Thurloe Square, London, S.W.7, U.K.

RAZANARPARANY, Marcel Sarirany, born 19th August 1934. Physician. Education: Complementary Studies in Paediatrics. Married, with children. Appointments: former Day Student, Toulouse Hospitals; currently, Head of Services, Paediatrics, Principal Hospital of Tananarive. Memberships: Titular Member, Malagasy Republic; Biological Society; Secretary-General of the Medical Science Society; Municipal Counseller. Author of approximately 30 publications on different branches of paediatrics. Address: Head of Service, Paediatrics, Hospital Befelatanane, Tananarive, The Malagasy Republic.

REED, Norman, born 19th May 1921. Telecommunications Engineer. Education: Cambridge School Certificate; City & Guilds of London Institute in Telecommunications. Appointments: District Engineering Officer, Dodoma, East African Posts & Telecommunications, 1954-56; Personal Assistant to Engineer-in-Chief, Nairobi, ibid, 1957-59; Training Officer, Uganda, 1960-63, 1965-68; Divisional Engineer, Uganda; Officer in Charge of Construction, Kenya Coast, 1963-65; retired from E.A.P.&T., 1968. Memberships: Secretary, Uganda Motor Club, 1962, 1967; Mombassa Club; Institute of Advanced Motorists, Kenya; Assistant Clerk of Course, Uganda, East African Safari, 1962-63. Address: 2 Harlington Road East, Feltham, Middlesex, U.K.

REGNARD, Louis Marcel, born 9th April 1916. Chief Cashier. Education: St. Joseph's College, Curepipe, Mauritius. Married. Appointments: Director, Distributing Station Ltd., 1948-70; Director & Secretary, Mauritius Touring Co. Ltd., 1955-70; Director, Trans-Maurice Ltd., 1970; Chief Cashier, Messrs Rogers & Co. Ltd., Port Louis. Address: Cere Street, Curepipe Road, Mauritius.

REINIS, Stanislav, born Nitra, Czechoslovakia, 22nd December 1931. Neurophysiologist. Education: M.D., Medical Faculty, Charles University, Prague, 1951-57; C.Sc., ibid, Pilsen, 1959-61. Married, 1 son, 1 daughter. Appointments: Part-time Assistant Lecturer, Department of Physiology, Medical Faculty, Charles University, Prague, 1954-57; Intern, Surgery Department, Regional Hospital, Varnsdorf, 1957-58; Research Associate, Department of Pathological Physiology, Medical Faculty, Charles University, Pilsen, 1961-62; Senior Research Associate, ibid, 1962-66; Senior Lecturer, Department of Physiology, Ghana Medical School, Accra, 1966-68; Associate Professor, ibid, 1969-70; Acting Head of Department, 1968-70; Postdoctral Fellow, York University, Ontario, Canada, 1970. Memberships: Czechoslovak Society for the Study of Higher Nervous Activity; Ghana Medical Association; Life Member, American Association for the Advancement of Science. Contributor to textbooks & scientific journals; Author of numerous papers. Address: Department of Psychology, York University, 4700 Keele Street, Downsview, Ont., Canada.

REKIK, Habib-Ali, born 14th October 1909. Physician. Education: Lycée Carnot, Tunis, Tunisia; Faculty of medicine, Paris, France. Married, 2 sons, 4 daughters. Appointments: Physician, Bureau of Hygiene, Sfax; Medecin des Propitaure de Sfax. Author of various medical articles. Honours: Congratulation on Doctoral Thesis of Medicine, 1936. Address: Mouliuville, Sfax, Tunisia.

REOKWAENG (The Hon.) Gaselesika, born 23rd August 1917. Member of Parliament. Education: Molepolole Primary School; St. Francis College, Marian Hill, Natal, South Africa. Appointments: Member of Parliament, Republic of Botswana; Trader, Pastal Agency; Justice of the Peace, 1964. Address: P.O. Lethakeng, via Molepolele, Republic of Botswana.

REY, Joseph Marcel Francis, born 16th October 1925. Chartered Secretary. Education: Royal College, Mauritius. Personal details: married to Marie-Aimee Rey, 3 sons, 1 daughter. Appointments: Secretary, Central Electricity Board, 1952-58, 1962-65; Secretary & Chief Accountant, Scott & Co. Ltd., 1958-62; General Secretary, Mauritius Sugar Producers' Association, 1965—. Fellowships: Chartered Institute of Secretaries; Royal Society of Arts. Member of the Royal Economic Society. Recipient of Defence Medal, 1939-45. Address: Plantation House, Port-Louis, Mauritius.

RHO, Zae Dong, born 19th December 1926. Medical Officer (Ophthalmologist). Education: Medical College of Kyong Book; National University, Tae Gu, Korea. Personal details. married to Kae Wol Kim, 3 sons, 1 daughter. Appointments: Ophthalmologist, Eye Department, Mulago General Hospital, Kampala, Uganda. Address: Eye Department, Mulago Hospital, Box 7051, Kampala, Uganda.

RHODES, John Foster, born 2nd August 1913. Mechanical Engineer. Education: Trent College, Derbyshire, U.K.; Manchester College of Technology. Married, 2 daughters. Appointments: Erection Engineer Trainee, Metropolitan Vickers, Manchester, 1931-51; seconded to Ashanti Goldfields Corporation as Assistant & Acting Chief Engineer, 1939-42; Engineer, i/c Radar Factory, 1942-46; Engineer, Metropolitan Vickers (S.A.), Johannesburg, South Africa, 1946-51; Engineer, Imperial Tobacco Group Ltd., Malawi, 1951-58; Assistant Manager, ibid, 1958-61; Manager, 1961-70; Director, 1964—. Memberships: Fellow, Institution of Mechanical Engineers; Institute of Directors. Awarded, O.B.E. Address: P.O. Box 5050, Limbe, Malawi.

RHODES, R. Allen, born 10th May 1941. Chemist. Education: B.A., Chemistry, Bridgewater College, Bridgewater, Va., U.S.A., 1963; Ph.D., Pharmaceutical Chemistry, University of Maryland, Baltimore, Md., 1968. Married, 1 son. Appointments: Lecturer, Ahmadu Bello University, Zaria, Nigeria, 1968-70. Memberships: American Chemical Society; Sigma Xi; Rho Chi Pharmaceutical Honour Society, 1965. Address: 895 Summit Ave., Harrisonburg, Va., U.S.A.

RIBEIRO-AYRES, Lourenço, born Goa, India, 1st February 1911. Forensic Pathologist; Connoisseur; Traveller. Education: Schools in Nairobi (Kenya), Bangalore & Bombay (India); University College, London, U.K.; Cambridge University, Guy's Hospital, London. Married, 2 sons. Appointments include: Police Surgeon, Nairobi, Kenya, 1958-64; Police Pathologist, Kenya, 1964—. Memberships: Convener, Founder-Member, & 1st President, Medico-Legal Society of Kenya; President, Nairobi Scientific & Philosophical Society; Area Surgeon, St. John Ambulance Association & Brigade; Nairobi Photographic Society; Kenya Medical Association. Publications: A Study of Antiquities in Medicine, Surgery, & Gynaecology; Multi-racial General Practice in Nairobi; Lobster Claw Hands, Fear & Appendicitis, A case of drancuculiasis in Nairobi; Medical Philately; Legal Aspects of Alcoholic Intoxication; Death is My Business; Sudden & Unexpected Deaths; The Cause of Death of Alexander the Great. Honours, Prizes, etc: Hon. Member, St. John Ambulance Association, London, U.K.; Founder-Member, E. African Academy. Address: P.O. Box 2125, Nairobi, Kenya.

RIBET, Evariste Jacques, born 29th August 1911. Commissioner of Police, Mauritius. Education: Cambridge School Certificate, St. Joseph College, Curepipe, 1929; Senior Police Officers' Course, Police College, Ryton-on-Dunsmore, U.K., 1952; Special Branch Course, Scotland Yard, 1955. Married, 1 son, 5 daughters. Appointments: worked up through ranks from Constable to Commissioner of Police, Mauritius Police, 1931—. Memberships: Police Club, Mauritius; International Police Association; Representative of INTERPOL in Mauritius; attended African Territories, Special Branch Conference, Kampala, Uganda, 1957. Honours: Colonial Police Medal for Meritorious Service, 1949; Queen's Police Medal for Distinguished Service, 1969. Address: Police Headquarters, Line Barracks, Port Louis, Mauritius.

RICHARDS, Elizabeth Helen, born 8th May 1945. Physiotherapist. Education: Penrose College, N. Wales, U.K.; Sheffield College of Physiotherapy. Personal details: wife of the Vicar of Mombasa Cathedral, Kenya. Memberships: Chartered Society of Physiotherapists. Address: P.O. Box 1962, Mombasa, Kenya.

RICHARDS, Geraint, born 22nd October 1922. Chartered Civil Engineer. Education: Llandeilo School; Degree, Engineering, Manchester University, U.K.; Cert. Ed., Exeter. Married, 2 sons, 1 daughter. Appointments: Colonial Engineering Service, Messrs Turner & Newall Ltd., 1950-61, 1962-66; Permanent Secretary, Ministry of Works & Supplies, Malawi, Chairman, Capital City Development Corporation, & Member, National Development Council, Malawi, 1967—. Memberships: Associate, Manchester College of Technology; Fellow, Institution of Civil Engineers; Institution of Water Engineers; Regular Army Reserve of Officers, 1947—; Royal Commonwealth Club. Publications: Notes on Simple Buildings, 1956; Interpretation by Engineers of Physical Chemical & Bacteriological Examination of Water Supplies. Address: Private Bag 45, Zomba, Malawi.

RICHARDS, William Neal, born 6th December 1938. Anglican Priest. Education: St. Peter's School, York, U.K.; London College of Divinity. Appointments: Curate, Otley Parish Church, U.K.; Curate, Leamington Spa; Vicar, Mombasa Cathedral. Address: Mombasa Memorial Cathedral, P.O. Box 1962, Mombasa, Kenya.

RICHARDSON, Philip Arthur, born 16th February 1918. Diplomat; Member of the Administrative Service of H.M. Overseas Civil Service. Education: Rugby School, U.K., 1931-36; M.A., Queens' College, Cambridge; Barrister-at-Law, Middle Temple, London. Appointments: Administrative Service, H.M.O.C.S., Nyasaland (now Malawi), 1940-64; Secretary for External Affairs, Malawi, 1964-67; Chargé d'Affaires, Malawi Legation, South Africa, 1967—. Honours: C.B.E., 1967. Address: The Malawi Legation, P.O. Box 11172, Pretoria, Transvaal, S. Africa.

RICKE, Herbert Rudiger, born Hannover, Germany, 27th September 1901. Building Researcher; Egyptologist. Education: Martin Luther Gymnasium, Hannover, 1907-20; Dip. Ing., Technical University, Hannover, 1924; Dr. Ing., ibid, 1931. Married, 2 children. Appointments: Principal, Borchardt Institute, 1939; Scientific Adviser, Swiss Institute for

Research into Egyptian Archaeology, Cairo, U.A.R., 1950; Director, ibid, 1962—. Memberships: Koldeway Society; German Archaeological Institute, 1953; (Hon.) Egyptological Institute of the University of Prague, 1965; Corresponding Mbr., Academy of Science, Göttingen, 1965; Associate, Institute of Egypt, 1968. Publications include: Die Tempel Nektanebos II in Elephantine, 1960; Das Sonnenheiligtum des Königs Userkaf I, 1965 & II, 1969; Ausgrabungen vom Khor-Dehmit bis Bet el Wali, 1967; Der Harmachistempel des Chefren in Giseh, 1970. Address: 13 Sharia el Ma'ahad el Swisri, Cairo-Zamalek, U.A.R.

RICKS, J. Christopher, born 12th July 1932. Foreign Service Officer. Education: Central School, Clay-Ashland, 1940-46; Booker Washington Institute, Kakata, Liberia, 1946-48; College of West Africa, Monrovia, 1949-52; Special Course, Statistics, University of Liberia, 1953; Liberian Foreign Service Training Course, 1960. Appointments: Cadet, Department of State, Monrovia, 1951-53; Statistical Analyst, Bureau of Statistics, 1953-56; Secretary, Department of State, Monrovia, 1956-60; 2nd Secretary & Vice-Consul, Embassy of Liberia, Netherlands, 1960-64; Consul, ibid, Accra, Ghana, 1964—; Chargé d'Affaires, ibid, Lagos, Nigeria, 1970—. Memberships: Past Master, United Brothers of Friendship, Liberia & Nigeria; Master Mason. Honours: Officer, Order of Orange Nassau, Netherlands, 1965. Address: Embassy of Liberia, P.O. Box 3007, Lagos, Nigeria.

RIGBY, Peter J.A., born 27th January 1938. Professor of Sociology. Education: B.A.(Cape Town); Ph.D.(Cantab.). Personal details: married, 1 daughter. Appointments: Research Fellow, Zambian Institute for Social Research, 1959-60; Crawford Student, King's College, Cambridge, U.K., 1960-61, 1963-64; Research Fellow, E.A.I.S.R., Makerere University, Kampala, Uganda, 1961-63; Lecturer in Social Anthropology, Queen's University, Belfast, U.K., 1964-65; Lecturer & Senior Lecturer in Social Anthropology, Makerere University, 1965-68; Visiting Associate Professor, New York University, U.S.A., 1967-68; Professor of Sociology, Makerere University, 1969—. Memberships: Assn. of Social Anthropologists of G.B. & Northern Ireland; African Studies Assn., Columbia University, N.Y. Author of numerous publications including: Dual Symbolic Classification among the Gogo of Central Tanzania (Africa), 1966; Sociological Factors in the Contact of the Gogo of Central Tanzania with Islam (Islam in Tropical Africa), 1966; Political Change in Busoga (Uganda Journal), 1966; Cattle & Kinship among the Gogo: A Semi-Pastoral Society of Central Tanzania, 1969; Aspects of Divination & Symbolism in Peri-Urban Kampala (forthcoming); also many book reviews. Address: Dept. of Sociology, Makerere University, Kampala, Uganda.

RINGADOO, Veerasamy, born 20th October 1920. Barrister-at-Law; Minister of Finance. Education: Port Louis Grammar School, Mauritius; LL.B., London School of Economics, London, U.K., 1948; Called to the Bar, 1949. Married, 2 children. Appointments: 1st Member of the Legislative Assembly for Quartier Militaire & Moka, Mauritius (Labour), 1967; elected Municipal Councillor, 1956; elected Member, Legislative Council for Moka-Flacq, 1951-67; Minister of Labour & Social Security, 1959-64; Minister of Education, 1964-67; Minister of Agriculture & Natural Resources, 1967-68; attended London Constitutional Conference, 1965. Honours: Officier de l'Ordre National Malgache, 1969. Address: Ministry of Finance, Port Louis, Mauritius.

RIORDAN, Edward Brendan, born 6th September 1936. Agricultural Economist. Education: St. Benedict's School, London, U.K., 1948-55; B.Sc., Dip. Agric. Econ., Reading University, 1956-60; M.Sc., Manitoba University, Canada, 1962-64. Appointments: Assistant Economist, International Wheat Council, 1960-62; Lecturer, Makerere University College, Uganda, 1965-69; Senior Research Officer, Agricultural Institute, Ireland, 1969—. Memberships: East African Agricultural Econonics Society; Agricultural Economics Society of England; Irish Agricultural Economics Society. Publications: Agricultural Marketing in East Africa: A Symposium, 1970; author of various prof. papers. Address: The Agricultural Institute, 19 Sandymount Avenue, Dublin 4, Ireland.

RIPLEY, Margaret Jean, born 9th June 1913. Teacher. Education: B.A.(Hons.), Home Science, Toronto University, Canada; Specialist in Home Economics & Supervisors' Certificate, Ontario College of Education. Married, 2 daughters. Appointments: Teacher, Oshawa Collegiate & Vocational Institute, Niagara Falls Collegiate & Vocational Institute, & Ottawa Collegiate Institute Board; Co-ordinator, Home Science, Ottawa Secondary Schools, 1962-67; Lecturer in Home Science, University of Ghana, 1967—. Memberships: Canadian Home Economics Association; President, Ottawa Home Economics Association; Ghana Home Science Association; YWCA; Consumers' Association. Address: P.O. Box M32, Accra, Ghana.

RIZZA, Achille, born Asmara, Ethiopia, 28th September 1939. Building Contractor. Education: Doctor's Degree in Economy & Commerce; Dr. of Political Science. Appointments include: Administrative Manager, Rizza Brothers Pr. Ltd. Co., Building Contractors. Memberships: Ethiopian Red Cross Society; Executive Secretary of Ethiopian Building Contractors' Association; Imperial Ethiopian Aeroclub; Ethiopian Recreational Centre; President of Inter-Ethiopia Sport Club. Address: P.O. Box 2760, Addis Ababa, Ethiopia.

RIZZA, Giuseppe, born Palazzolo Acreide, Siracusa, Italy, 14th January 1934. Building Contractor. Education: Geometer. Married, 1 child. Appointments include: Building Supervisor, Studio A Mezzedimi, Consulting Architect; Building Supervisor, Salini Construttori, Rome; Technical Manager, Rizza Brothers Pr. Ltd. Co., Building Contractors, Ehtiopia. Memberships: Ethiopian Red Cross Society. Address: P.O. Box 2760, Addis Ababa, Ethiopia.

RIZZA, Sebastiano, born Palazzolo Acreide, Siracusa, Italy, 12th January 1938. Building Contractor. Married, 2 children. Appointments include: Building Supervisor, Salini Construttori-Roma, Italy; Assistant to Civil Engineering Contractors, Rome Branch; Technical Manager, Rizza Brothers Pr. Ltd. Co., Building Contractors, 1964—. Member, Ethiopian Red Cross Society. Address: P.O. Box 2760, Addis Ababa, Ethiopia.

ROBANA, Said, born 16th June 1935. Agricultural Engineer; President/Director-General of O.E.P. of Tunisia. Education: Bacc. French & Elementary Maths.; Lycée St. Louis, Paris; Diploma of Agricultural Engineering, National Institute of Agronomy; Certificate of Specialist Economy. Married, 2 children. Appointments: Director of Regional Services, Ministry of Agriculture, Tunisia, 1960; General Director, Office of Estates, Tunisia, 1961-66; Direction of Sections, Offices of the Ministry of Agriculture, 1966-69; P.D.G. de l'Office d'elevage, Tunisia. Honours: Officer of the Order of the Republic of Tunisia. Address: Robana O.E.P., La Rabta, Tunis, Tunisia.

ROBERT, Max Sully Paul, born 30th March 1904. Engineer. Education: former Pupil, Polytechnic School, Paris, France. Appointments: Engineer, 1925; Director, 1935; Deputy General Director, Phosphate Company of Constantine, 1945; Administrateur, Delegue de la Cie Togolaise des Mines du Benin, 1957; President, de la Cie Senegalaise des Phosphates de Taiba, 1966. Honours: Officer of the Legion of Honour, 1962; Commander of the French Order of Military Merit, 1963; Commander of the National Order of Togo, 1964; Officer of the National Order of Senegal, 1969. Address: 8 rue Bellini, Paris, France.

ROBERTS, Bryan Clieve, born 22nd March 1923. Barrister-at-Law. Education: Whitgift School, U.K.; B.A.(Hons.), Magdalen College, Oxford. Appointments: served in World War II, 1941-46, Normandy, Belgium, Holland, Germany. Appointments: Crown Counsel, Northern Rhodesia, 1953-59; Director of Public Prosecutions, ibid, 1959-61; Solicitor-General, Nyasaland, 1961-64; Minister of Justice, ibid, 1962-63; Attorney-General & Permanent Secretary to the President & Cabinet, Malawi, 1964—; Head, Malawi Civil Service, 1965—. Honours: C.M.G., 1964; Officer, Order of Menelek II of Ethiopia, 1965; Commander of the National Order of the Republic of Malagasy, 1969. Address: Office of the President & Cabinet, Zomba, Malawi.

ROBERTS, Frank Rowland, born Freetown, Sierra Leone, 18th June 1906. Education: Wesleyan Boys' High School, Freetown; B.A.(Dunelm), Fourah Bay College, 1926; L.R.C.P., L.R.C.S., University of Edinburgh, U.K.; L.R.F.P.&S., Glasgow; D.T.M.&H., U.K.; F.R.S.H. Appointments include: Teacher, Accra High School, 1926-37; Resident Medical Officer, Otley, West Riding, Yorkshire, U.K.; Government Medical Service, Ghana, 1948—; Principal Medical Officer, all 9 Regions of Ghana; currently, Senior Medical Officer in Charge, Adabraka Polyclinic, Ministry of Health, Accra. Memberships: National Chairman, Ghana Society for the Prevention of TB; Former Director, Community Service, International Rotary Club of Accra; Fellow, Royal Society of Health; Executive, Ghana Society for the Blind; Ghana Society for the Crippled; Past Master, Ancient, Free & Accepted Masons of both England & Scotland; Royal Commonwealth Society; Royal Medical Society of Edinburgh; Fellow, Royal Society of Tropical Medicine & Hygiene; Fellow, German Foundation for Developing Countries; Ghana Medical Association; Chairman, Board of Governors, Accra High School; Delegate, Student Christian Movement, U.K., 1939, World Youth Christian Conference, Amsterdam, 1939, Royal Society of Health Annual Conference, Harrogate, 1960, Health Seminar on Developing Countries, Germany, 1961, W.H.O. Travelling Seminar in the U.S.S.R., 1961, Commonwealth Conference on Health & Chest, Nigeria, 1962, Reunion Conference by the German Foundation on Development & Co-operation, Nigeria, 1965, XVIII International Conference on TB, Germany, 1965, & International TB Conference, New York, 1969. Address: Adabraka Polyclinic, P.O. Box 184, Accra, Ghana.

ROBERTS, George Kayinde Tregson, born Lagos, Nigeria, 23rd Agust 1913. Chief Social Development Officer. Education: Fourah Bay College, 1932-34; 2nd Class Teachers' Certificate, 1934; M.R.S.T., London, 1945; London School of Economics, 1943-45; Certificate in Social Sciences, London, 1945. Married, 1 son, 2 daughters. Appointments include: Welfare Assistant, 1945-46; Headmaster, Approved School, Wellington, Sierra Leone, 1946-61; Social Development Officer, 1955; Principal Social Development Officer, 1962; Chief Social Development Officer, 1965. Memberships: Hon. Secretary, Sierra Leone Teachers' Union, 1938-45; Hon. Sec. People's Educational Association, Sierra Leone, 1954-57; Hon. Sec. Sierra Leone Blind Welfare Society, 1958. Publications: various articles on social welfare matters in the West African Review & local papers. Address: 69D Waterloo Road, Kissy, Freetown, Sierra Leone.

ROBERTS, Lewis Randolph, born Freetown, Sierra Leone, 28th October 1918. Medical Practitioner. Education: Accra High School, 1924-34; Inter-B.A.(Lond.), Achimota College, 1937; private study for B.A.(Hons.), History, London, 1941; M.B., Ch.B.(Edin.), University of Edinburgh, Scotland, 1950; D.T.M.&H.(Eng.), University of London, 1952. Married, 3 children. Appointments include: Senior History Master, Accra High School, 1941-45; Resident Medical Officer, University of Science & Technology, Kumasi, 1955-62; Senior Medical Officer, Ministry of Health, Ghana. Memberships include: Fellow, Royal Medical Society, Edinburgh; Fellow, Royal Society of Tropical Medicine & Hygiene; Fellow, Royal Society of Health; Founding Member, International Society for Tropical Dermatology; Fellow, Academy of Medicine, Toronto. Publications include: Hypochronic Microcytic Anaemia; Malaria—an Environmental Study; Dengue Fever. Honours include: Commonwealth Fellowship in

Medicine. Address: Adum Clinic, P.O. Box 731, Kumasi, Ghana.

ROBERTSHAW, David, born 15th January 1934. Veterinarian. Education: King Edward VI, Stafford, U.K.; Glasgow University. Married. Appointments: Assistant Lecturer, Veterinary Physiology, Glasgow University; Veterinary Research Officer, Physiologist, East African Veterinary Research Organization, Kenya; Senior Scientific Officer, Hannah Dairy Research Institute, Ayr, Scotland, U.K.; Professor & Head of Department of Veterinary Physiology, University of Nairobi, Kenya. Memberships: East African Academy; Physiological Society of Great Britain. Author of Research Papers in various scientific journals, mainly on the subject of Environmental Physiology of both wild & domestic animals. Address: Department of Veterinary Physiology, P.O. Box 30197, Nairobi, Kenya.

ROBERTSON, George Irvine, born Scotland, U.K., 20th May 1919. Physician. Education: M.B., Ch.B., Felles College, Edinburgh, 1943; M.D. with Commendation, 1957. Appointments: House Surgeon & House Physician, Edinburgh Royal Infirmary; R.A.F.V.R. Medical Branch, 1944-47; Medical Department, I.I. Pharmaceutical Division, 1950-56; Private Practice, Nairobi, Kenya, 1957—. Memberships include: Royal College of Physicians of Edinburgh. Address: P.O. Box 20005, Nairobi, Kenya.

ROBINS, Peter Alan, born 27th September 1924. Organic Chemist. Education: A.R.C.S., B.Sc., Royal College of Science, University of London, U.K., 1944; D.I.C., Ph.D., 1947. Married, 1 son, 1 daughter. Appointments: Chemist, Colonial Insecticide Research Unit, Entebbe, Uganda, 1948-50; Research Chemist, Medical Research Council of Great Britain, 1950-57; Lecturer in Chemistry, University College of Rhodesia & Nyasaland, 1957-62; Professor of Chemistry, University College, Nairobi, Kenya, 1962—. Memberships: Fellow, Royal Institute of Chemistry; Chemical Society; Prehistoric Society; East African Academy. Author of many scientific papers in professional journals. Address: Department of Chemistry, University of Nairobi, Box 30197, Nairobi, Kenya.

ROBINSON, Ian Cameron, born Enfield, England, 24th June 1919. Education: Repton School, 1932-37; Emmanuel, Cambridge, 1937-40; B.A., M.A., Dip.Ed., London, 1950. Married, 1 son, 1 daughter. Appointments include: Friends Ambulance Unit, 1940-47; in charge Medical Administration, Tigre Province, Ethiopia, 1942-45; General Secretary, F.A.U. Post-War Service, 1946-47; K.L.V. Camps, British Red Cross, Austria, 1945-46; Assistant Master, Busoga College, Mwiri, Uganda, 1947-57; U.N. Mission to Arab Refugees Gaza Strip, 1949; Headmaster, King's College, Budo, since 1958. Honours, Prizes, etc: Uganda Independence Medal, 1962; M.B.E., 1966. Address: King's College, Budo, Box 7121, Kampala, Uganda.

RODRIGUES, Ferdinand J. E., born 10th December 1933. Civil Servant. Education: Senior Secondary School Certificate, 1949; D.Com., 1950; passed Final Exams. of the Corporation of Secretaries. Married. Appointments: Clerical Grade, Uganda Civil Service, 1950-54; Junior Assistant Secretary, ibid, 1954-59; Establishment Officer, 1959-60; Assistant Secretary, 1961-64; Senior Assistant Secretary, 1964-65; Principal Assistant Secretary, 1965-69; Under-Secretary, 1969—. Memberships: President, Entebbe Institute; Secretary, Uganda Mountain Club; Uganda Outward Bound Trust; Councillor, Entebbe Tennis Council; Chairman, Bugenga Girls' School. Honours: Kt. Commander, Order of St. Gregory the Great, 1969; Uganda Independence Commemoration Medal, 1962. Address: Office of the President, P.O. Box 7168, Kampala, Uganda.

RODRIGUES, Leonido, born Uganda, 28th June 1938. Advocate; Commissioner for Oaths. Education: B.A.(Hons.), History & Political Science, University of Poona, India; LL.B., University of Bombay. Currently, in private practice. Memberships: Bar Council (M), India; Uganda Law Society; Founder-Member, Y.M.C.A., Uganda. Address: P.O. Box 1186, Jinja, Uganda.

RODRIGUES, Nerus Sebastian, born 12th May, 1926. Civil Servant. Education: Matriculation, Bombay University, India. Appointments: Accounts Clerk, Great Indian Peninsular Railway, India; ibid, Uganda Government; Examiner of Accounts, Uganda Audit Department; Distribution Supervisor, Uganda Information Department; Office Superintendent, Ministry of Information, Broadcasting, & Tourism; Senior Executive Officer, ibid; Deputy Chief Censor, Uganda Film Censorship Board. Memberships: President, Kampala Institute, 1966-70; Kampala Lions Club; Uganda Bridge Circle. Honours: Uganda Independence Medal, 1962; Driver of the Year, 3rd Award, Uganda, 1968. Address: P.O. Box 7142, Kampala, Uganda.

ROLAND-GOSSELIN, Jacques, born 21st April 1916. Professor of History & Geography. Education: Doctor of Letters, Sorbonne, University of Paris, France, 1970. Appointments: Lecturer in French, Universities of Wuzzbung & Erlangen, Germany, 1951-56; Professor, Lycée Oumm-el-Bamine, Fez, Morocco, 1956-59. ibid, Lycée Hassan II, Rabat, 1959-70. Publications: Author of articles in educational reviews & doctorate thesis. Address: Vougne d'Auge, Saint Maixent l'Ecole, 2 Sevres, 79, France.

RONSKY (ROSHDESTVENSKY), Rurik Alexis, born St. Petersburg, Russia, 13th September, 1917. Businessman. Education: Degree in Agriculture, Prague University, Czechoslovakia; Art Degree, Prague Academy of Art; Diploma in 5 European Languages. Married, 1 son, 1 daughter. Appointments: Actor & Producer, Czechoslovakia, 1938-45; U.S. Forces in Austria, 1945-48; E.A. Sound Studios, Kenya, 1948-50; E.A. Industries, ibid, 1950-55; Work Manager, Pitt Moore Glassworks, Nairobi, 1955-56; Contracts Manager, Roofing & Flooring Department, C. Dorman Ltd., 1956-66;

Managing Director, R. A. Ronsky Ltd., Roofing & Flooring Specialists, 1966—. Memberships: Host, Lions Club, Nairobi, 1958—; Deputy District Governor, Lions International for Kenya & Tanzania, 1966-68; Governor, District 411 (Kenya, Tanzania, Uganda, & Ethiopia), ibid, 1968-69; Nairobi City Players, 1958—; Founder & Standing Committee, ibid; Executive Committee, Kenya Association of Building & Civil Engineering Contractors; Fellow, Institute of Directors; Chairman, Appeals Committee, Y.M.C.A.; United Kenya Club; Vice-Chairman, Theatre Committee, Kenya Cultural Centre, Kenya National Theatre. Honours include: Numerous awards from Lions International incl. 2 Presidential Awards, Melvin Jones Trophy, 100% Governor. Address: P.O. Box 3542, Nairobi, Kenya.

ROPER, Ronald Frederick, born 5th February 1915. Educational Administrator. Education: Bournemouth School, U.K., 1923-33; London University, 1948. Married, 4 children. Appointments: District Commissioner, Uganda Government, 1950-60; Permanent Secretary, ibid, 1960-65; seconded as Assistant Director, East African Staff College, 1965-69; Director, ibid, 1969—. Honours: O.B.E., 1964. Address: East African Staff College, Nairobi, Kenya.

ROSEVEARE, Martin Pearson, born 24th April 1898. Schoolmaster. Education: Marlborough College, Wilts., U.K., 1911-16; B.A., St. John's College, Cambridge, 1919-21; M.A., ibid, 1924. Married. Appointments: Headmaster, Mzuzu Government Secondary School, Nyasaland/Malawi, 1959-63; Principal, Soche Hill College, Malawi, 1964-67; Teacher, Marymount Secondary School, Mzuzu, Malawi, 1967-70. Honours: Hon. Fellow, St. John's College, Cambridge, 1952; Knight Bachelor, 1946. Address: Box 29, Mzuzu, Malawi.

ROSS, Betty Ada, born 23rd June 1918. Teacher; Missionary. Education: Senior Matriculation, Secondary School, Ontario, Canada; 1st Class Permanent Teachers' Certificate, Ontario; University of Toronto; Diploma in Theology, London, U.K. Married, 1 son, 1 daughter. Appointments: Primary School Teacher, Scarborough, Ontario, Canada, 1937-42; Teacher, St. Monica School, Ogbunike, Eastern Nigeria, 1943-44; Principal, St. Monica's Teacher Training College (Women), Ogbunike, 1944-52; Tutor, Dennis Memorial Grammar School, Onitsha, Eastern Nigeria, 1953; Tutor, St. Mark's Teacher Training College, Nibo-Nise, Awka, 1954-58; Headmistress, Union Primary School, Umuahia, 1959-63; Tutor, Trinity College, Theological College, Umuahia, 1963-67 (evacuated during Civil War); Tutor, Bible Training Institute, Bo, Sierra Leone, 1969—. Memberships: Mothers' Union, Niger Diocese, 1955-59; ibid, Niger Delta Diocese, 1959-69; ibid, Sierra Leone Diocese, 1969—. Address: Church House, Box 124, Bo, Sierra Leone.

ROSS, Philip James, born 10th April 1918. Missionary Clergyman. Education: Merchant Taylors' School, London, U.K.; B.A., St. John's College, Cambridge, 1940; M.A., ibid, 1943; Ridley Hall, Cambridge; Dip. Ed., University of London, Institute of Education, 1948; ordained Deacon, 1941, & Priest, 1942. Married, 1 son, 1 daughter. Appointments: Curate, St. Mary's Church, Islington, 1941-45; C.M.S. Missionary, 1945—; Principal, Dennis Memorial Grammar School, Onitsha, Eastern Nigeria, 1951-53; Principal, St. Mark's College, Nibo-Nise, Awka, 1954-58; Principal, Trinity Theological College, Umuahia, 1960-69; Canon, St. Stephen's Cathedral, Bonny, Niger Delta Diocese, 1967—; Lecturer, Bible Training Institute, Bo, Sierra Leone, 1969—; Canon Missioner, St. George's Cathedral, Bo, 1970—; C.M.S. Representative, Sierra Leone, 1970—; Chaplain to Archbishop of West Africa and Bishop of Sierra Leone, 1970—. Publications: It is Marvellous in our eyes, 1968. Honours; The Pilkington Prize for Public Speaking & Preaching, Diocese of London, 1941; Gospeller, Michaelmas Ordination, St. Paul's Cathedral, London, 1941. Address: Church House, P.O. Box 124, Bo, Sierra Leone.

ROSSIN, Maurice, born 10th August 1942. Engineer; Technical Adviser of the Ministry of Agriculture. Education: Bachelor; Agricultural Engineer of Paris; Rural Engineering, Lakes & Forests. Appointments: Charge de Mission; Technical Adviser to the Ministry of Agriculture. Address: Council of the Ministry of Agriculture, Abidjan, B.P. 1349, The Ivory Coast.

ROTIMI, Olusegun Abayomi, born 16th May 1942. Lecturer; Research Fellow. Education: Emmanuel School, Ado-Ekiti; Christ's School, Ado-Ekiti; Higher School Certificate, Ibadan Grammar School, Nigeria; B.Sc.(Hons.), Biology, Central State University, Ohio, U.S.A.; M.Sc., Crop Physiol., Kansas State University. Personal details: son of Former Education Officer & School Teacher. Married, 1 son. Appointments: Agricultural Officer, Former Northern Ministry of Agriculture, 1964-65; Lecturer, Crop Physiology, Genetics & Crop Botany, Ahmadu Bellow University, Zaria, 1967—. Memberships: Agricultural Society of Nigeria; Local Treasurer, Zaria Conference, ibid, 1968; Nigerian Science Assn.; West African Science Assn.; Agronomy Society of America; Crop Science Society. Publications: Effects of Added N.P.K. on Nodulation & Yield of Clark 63 Soybean (M.Sc. Thesis), 1967; Phosphorus, Zinc Interaction in Two Soyabean Varieties Differing in Sensitivity to Phosphorus Nutrition (Soil Science Soc. of America Proc.), 1968; Effects of Innoculation with Commercial Peat-Base Cowpea Rhizobium Strain on the Development of Cowpea Varieties (The Nigerian Agricultural Journal), 1969. Address: Faculty of Agriculture, Ahmadu Bello University, Zaria, Nigeria.

ROUSSELOT, Pierre Paul Andre, born July 1918. Director of the French Chamber of Commerce & Industry of Morocco. Education: Diploma of Higher Studies in Political Economy; Diploma, Higher School of Journalism. Memberships: Rotary Club; Honorary President, Racer Club. Publications: numerous economic studies; Heloise & Abelard. Honours: Knight of the National Order of Merit; Cross of War, 1939-45; Knight of Palmes Academiques. Address: 15 Avenue Mers Sultana, Casablanca, Morocco.

ROY, Arthur Douglas, born 10th April 1925. Surgeon. Education: Paisley Grammar School, U.K.; University of Glasgow. Appointments: Consultant Surgeon & Hon. Lecturer, Western Infirmary & University of Glasgow; Professor of Surgery, University of Nairobi, Kenya. Memberships: Fellow, Association of Surgeons of Great Britian & Ireland; British Society of Gastro-Enterology; Scottish Society for Experimental Medicine. Author of various publications on gastro-enterology, thyroid disease, educational television, & computers in medicine. Honours: Stockman Medallist, University of Glasgow, 1947. Address: University of Nairobi Medical School, Box 30588, Nairobi, Kenya.

ROYCHOUDHURY, Debnarayon, born 1st April, 1918. Physician. Education: Matriculation Examination, 1st Division with Hons. in Maths., Bagerhat H.E. School; Inter-Science, Presidency College, Culcuttian 1st Division; M.B., R. G. Kar Medical School, Calcutta, India; T.D.D., University of Wales, U.K.; Fellowship, American College of Chest Physicians; Postgraduate Training, Calcutta School of Tropical Medicine; Institute of Chest Disease, London; Pasteur Institute & Lennec Hospital, Paris. Appointments: House Medical Officer, R. G. Kar Medical College, Calcutta, India; Resident Physician, Calcutta School of Tropical Medicine & Hospital; Resident Medical Officer, K.S. Roy T.B. Hospital, Calcutta; House Medical Officer, Peppard Chest Hospital; ibid, Glan Ely T.B. Hospital; ibid, Cheshire Jt. Sanatorium, Salop; Medical Officer, i/c Chest Clinic, Calcutta Municipal Corporation; Hon. Chest Physician, Marwari Relief Society Hospital; Lecturer, Chest & T.B. Institute of Child Health; Lecturer, Chest & T.B., Sevasadan College of Obstetrics & Gynaecology; Senior Consultant, Chest & T.B., Government of Northern Nigeria; Member, Advisory Board, T.B., Federal Government of Nigeria. Memberships: Central Committee, Indian Medical Association, Bengal Branch; Indian Red Cross Society; Indian Tuberculosis Association; Nigerian Medical Association; Nigerian Red Cross Society; Relief Rehabilitation Committee, B/P State, Nigeria; International Union Against Tuberculosis; American College of Chest Physicians; British Medical Association. Contributor to Scientific journals. Address: 70 Main Road, Romford, Essex, U.K.

RUBADIRI, David, born Malawi, 19th July 1930. Poet; Critic, Author, Educator. Education: King's College, Budo, Kampala, Uganda; B.A., Makerere University College; Diploma in Education, Bristol University, U.K.; M.A., King's College, Cambridge. Married, 8 children. Appointments: Ambassador of Malawi to U.S.A. & the United Nations, 1964-65; Lecturer in English Literature, Makerere University College, Uganda, 1965-. Publications: No Bride Price; (articles) The Role of a University in Tropical Africa (E. African Academy); The Chessboard in America (Granta), 1961; Africa: An African Evaluation (Annals of Am. Acad. Pol. & Soc. Sci., vol. 354), 1964; Human Adaption in Tropical Africa (Education for Leisure & Intellectual Development, ed. R. S. Olembo); Why African Literature? (Transition, Kampala), 1964; African Literature (Africa Report, U.S.A.), 1964. Contributor of poetry to numerous anthologies, including: Darkness & Light, London, 1958, African Voices, N.Y., 1958; A Book of African Verse, London, 1964; Modern Poetry from Africa, U.K., 1965; Young Commonwealth Poets '65, London, 1965; New Commonwealth Voices, London, 1968; Zuka I & II, Nairobi, 1968; Pergamon Poets 2: Poetry From Africa, 1970; also to following journals: Transition, Kampala; Penpoint, Makerere; Zuka, Nairobi; East African Journal, Nairobi. Honours: Recipient of the Margaret Graham Poetry Prize, Makerere, 1956. Address: c/o English Department, Makerere University College, Kampala, Uganda.

RUBERTI, Renato Francis, born Bulgaria, 16th July 1927. Neurosurgeon. Education: Medical School, University of Padua, Italy, 1945-46; Institute of Biological Chemistry, University of Padua; Institute of Pathology, University of Padua; M.D., 1952; Ph.D., 1963. Personal details: Italian nationality. Appointments include: Medical Visitor, Neurosurgical Service, Civil Hospital, Padua, 1953-54; Second Assistant Surgeon, ibid, 1954-56; Assistant Surgeon, ibid, 1956-61; Neurosurgical Consultant, Civil Hospital, Udine, 1958-61; Neurosurgical Consultant, Civil Hospital, Palmanova, 1959-63; Chief Resident, Neurosurgical Service, Civil Hospital, Udine, 1961-62; Honorary Assistant Professor, Neurosurgical Clinic, University of Padua, 1962-63; Chief Resident, ibid, 1963-66; Chief Resident, ibid, 1966-; Consultant Neurosurgeon, Kenyatta National Hospital, Nairobi & Aga Khan Hospital, 1968-. Memberships include: Fellow, Italian Association of Neurosurgeons, 1963; Fellow, Internal College of Angiology, 1965; Medico-Chirurgical Order of Province of Padua, 1966: ibid, East African Surgeons Society, 1967. Author of 60 papers on neurophysiology, neuropathology, anaesthesia in neurosurgery, neuroradiology, clinical neurosurgery, surgery in neurological diseases. As a Reader in Neurosurgery, University of Padua, 3 courses of 12 lectures at Medical School on neurosurgery. Participant in many national and international neurological and neurosurgical conferences and visiting surgeon in many neurosurgical services in Europe and U.S. Address: P.O. Box 20406, Nairobi, Kenya.

RUMNEY, Gideon, born Berlin, Germany, 6th September, 1924. Research Biochemist; University Reader. Education: City of Leeds School, U.K.; Ilkley Grammar School, Yorks: Leeds & Edinburgh Universities; B.Sc.(Hons.), Biochemistry; Hebrew University & Hadassah Medical School; Clark University, Worcester, Mass., U.S.; Ph.D. Appointments: Post Doctoral Fellow & Research Associate, McArdle Memorial Laboratory for Cancer Research, University of Wisconsin, Madison, 1954-57; Research Fellow, National Cancer Institute, N.I.H., Worcester Foundation for Experimental Biology, 1957-58; Head, Endocrine Lab,, Beilmson Hospital & Department of Steroid Biochemistry, Tel-Aviv University, Israel, 1958-67; Senior Lecturer, Medical Biochemistry, University of Nairobi, Kenya, 1967-70. Memberships: Biochemical Society, U.K.; Israel Biochemical Society; Foundation Member, Israel Society of

Endocrinology. Author of publications in field of steroid biochemistry & endocrinology. Address: Faculty of Medicine, University of Nairobi, P.O. Box 30197, Nairobi, Kenya.

RUNGS, Henri Martial Gustave, born 23rd August 1915. Physician; Specialist in Digestive Diseases. Education: Bachelor of Philosophy, Rabat, Morocco; Faculty of Bordeaux, France; Certificate of Physics, Chemistry, & Biology, Faculty of Lyon; M.D., Faculty of Algers, Algeria, 1945; Specialist in Digestive Diseases, Faculty of Paris, France. Appointments: Ouverture cabinet medical, Rabat, Morocco, 1946; Chief Consultant Gastro-enterologist, Hospital Avicennes, 1959-70. Memberships: Vice-President, Medical Society of Morocco, 1950; ibid, Union of Physicians of Morocco, 1951-54; Secretary-General, Order of North Moroccan Doctors, 1950-57. Publications include: Amibiase chronique et Proctologie; Influence du traitement chlorhydrique sur les malades atteint de colite Hypochlorhydrique; Etudes des dysproteinies sanguines dans le syndrome colite Hypochlorhydrique; Gastrite chroniques et Amibiases Chroniques; Rectorscopie de l'Amibiase chronique; Vers une simplification du triage et du traitement des malades digestifs en medicine de masse etc. Honours: Knight of the Legion of Honour; Cross of War, 1939-45; Medaille des Epidemies, 1942. Address: 37 rue de Tolitila, Rabat, Morocco.

RUNGTA, Radhe Shyam, born Barakar, India, 10th January 1933. Educator. Education: Matriculation, Patna University, J.H.K. English School, Begusarai, 1949; Intermediate Commerce, Patna University, G.D. College, Begusarai, 1949-51; B.Comm., City College, Evening Session, Calcutta University, 1951-53; LL.B., Calcutta University Law College, 1953-56; M.Com., External, Calcutta University, 1957; Postgraduate Diploma in Business Administration, London School of Economics, U.K., 1957-58; Ph.D., ibid, 1965. Married, 1 son, 1 daughter. Appointments: Management Training, Jaipuria Group of Industries, Calcutta, India, 1951-53; Accountant, Dhubri Oil Mills Ltd., Principal Officer, Bengal Bihar Firebricks & Pottery Works Ltd., & Assistant General Manager, Belgachi Tea Company, Ltd., 1953-57; Part-time Student, London School of Economics, 1958-62 (Leverhulme Research Scholarship for Overseas Students, 1960-61); Lecturer in Finance, University of Nigeria, Nsukka, Nigeria, 1962-64; Temporary Lecturer in Economics, University of Ife, 1965; Lecturer in Business Administration, University of Khartoum, Sudan, 1965-67; Senior Lecturer in Business Administration, ibid, 1967—; Member, Internal Advisory Board, Economic Development Institute, University of Nigeria, 1963-64; Chairman, Confidential Committee to Enquire into Certain Aspects of the Financial Management, ibid; Chairman, Postgraduate Committee, Department of Business Administration, University of Khartoum, 1969-70; Director, Training & Placement of Business Administration Students, ibid, 1967-69; Director of Research, Department of Business Administration, 1967-69; Member, Staff Affairs Committee; Management Consultant, 1967—. Memberships: American Economic Association; American Finance Association; The Institute of Management Sciences; Economic History Society; British Institute of Management; Institute of Marketing; Bar Association, Calcutta High Court; Economic History Society; Association of Asian Studies. Publications: The Rise of Business Corporations in India, 1851-1900, 1970; (articles) Indian Company Law Problems in 1850; The Bengal Gold Craze; Promotion & Finance of Indian Companies before 1850; Relation Between Standard of Living & Production with Reference to the Textile Industry of the Sudan; Some Ideas on How to Make Suq Traders Creditworthy; The Role of Commercial Banks in Developing Countries with Reference to Sudan. Address: Department of Business Administration, Faculty of Economic & Social Studies, University of Khartoum, Khartoum, Sudan.

RUPARELIA, Harish Chakubhai, born 26th June 1928. Medical Practitioner. Education: M.B., B.S., Bombay University, India, 1954; D.C.H., College of Physicians & Surgeons, Bombay, 1957. Appointments: Secretary, Lohana Union, Kampala, Uganda, 1968; Secretary, Uganda Medical Society, Kampala, 1970; President, Lohana Union, Kampala, 1969. Memberships: Royal College of General Practitioners; Uganda Medical Association; Lions Club of Kampala. Address: P.O. Box 224, Kampala, Uganda.

RUSHEDGE, Tumusiime Emmanuel, born 1st March 1941. Doctor of Medicine. Education: Ntare School, Mbarara, Uganda; M.B., Ch.B., Makerere University, Kampala, Uganda. Married to Sister Joyce Sandra Kibuka. Appointments: Internship, Mulago Hospital, Uganda; Senior House Officer, Otorhinolaryngology, ibid; Lecturer in Anatomy, Makerere Medical School, Kampala. Memberships: Uganda Club; Gomba Marina; Uganda Authors' Association; Uganda Christian Medical Fellowship. Publications: Ngoma Series (School English Readers); The Bull's Horn (novel). Honours: Credit, Obstetrics & Gynaecology, 1967. Address: Makerere Medical School, P.O. Box 7072, Kampala, Uganda.

RUSIKE, Abiathat Benjamin Chakuringa, born Marandellas, Rhodesia, 27th June 1926. Journalist; Editor. Education: Primary Education, Rhodesia; Secondary Education, South Africa. Appointments: Primary School-teacher, 1947-52; General News Reporter, Daily News, Salisbury, Rhodesia, 1953-57; Sports Editor, ibid, 1958-61; Assistant News Editor, 1962-63; On-the-job Training in U.K.; News Editor, Zambia News, 1963-64; Editor, ibid, 1964-65; Assistant Editor, Roan Antelope Mine Newspaper, 1965-66; Editor, ibid, 1967—. Memberships: Associate, The British Association of Industrial Editors; Rotary Club of Luanshya; Roan Antelope Dramatic & Operatic Society; Makoma Sailing & Boating Club. Honours: Rhodesian African Soccer XI, 1953-57. Address: Roan Selection Trust Ltd., Luanshya Div., Luanshya, Zambia.

RUSSELL, Robert Neil, born 23rd May 1906. Anglican Bishop. Education: George Watson's College, Edinburgh; M.A., Edinburgh

University, 1928; Cuddesdon Theological College. Appointments: ordained, Old St. Paul's Church, Edinburgh, 1929; Assistant Priest, ibid, 1929-33; Missionery, Southern Rhodesia, 1933-34; Missionery Priest, Diocese of Zanzibar, Tanganyika, 1934-63; Bishop of Zanzibar, 1963-66; Bishop of Korogwe, Tanzania, 1966-68; Member, Fraternity of the Transfiguration, Roslin, Scotland, U.K., & Assistant Bishop of Edinburgh, 1968–. Address: The Fraternity, Roslin, Midlothian, U.K.

RWABUGAHYA, Hosea Garubali Kasomoka, born 1st October 1935. Medical Practitioner. Education: Ikoba Primary School; Kabalega Junior Secondary School; Nyakasura Senior Secondary School; M.B., Ch.B., Makerere University College, 1957-64; M.Med., ibid, 1970. Married, 2 children. Appointments: Medical Superintendent, Hoima Hospital, 1965; Senior House Officer, Mulago Hospital, 1966-67; Registrar (Medicine), ibid, 1968-70; Senior Registrar (Medicine), 1970–. Memberships: Uganda Medical Association; Uganda Pharmacy & Poisons Board. Author of various professional articles. Address: Mulago Hospital, Kampala, Uganda.

RWAKAIKARA, Ausi, born Kijura, Masundi, Uganda, August, 1924. Assistant Secretary-General, Bunyoro. Education: Mohamedan Elementary School, Kihande Masindi, 1937-40; Kabasunela Primary School, Buganda, 1941; Kibuli Secondary School, 1942. Married, 22 children. Appointments include: Bus Conductor, Buganda Bus Service, 1943-49; Bus Conductor, E.A.R.&H., Masindi, 1949-54; Editor, Mugambizi Vernacular Paper, 1954-59; Gombolola Chief, 1960-63; Minister of Works & Natural Resources, Omuliama's Government, 1963; Assistant Secretary-General, Bunyoro. Memberships: National Organizing Secretary, National Association for the Advancement of Moslims; Hoima Sports Club. Honours, Prizes, etc.: Independence Medal, Uganda, 1964. Address: P.O. Box 6, Hoima, Uganda.

RWAKAIKARA, Yonasani Kaijamurubi, born 9th June 1918. Educator and Cleric; Bishop. Education: Primary, 1931-36; Secondary, 1937-39; Teachers' Diploma, Makerere College, Uganda, 1940-42; further studies at Exeter University, U.K., 1953-54, Clifton Theological College, 1963-64, & Bristol University, 1964. Married, 6 sons, 4 daughters. Appointments: Teacher, 1943-46; organizing Teacher, 1947-50; Headmaster, Secondary School, 1951-53; Supervisor of Schools, 1954-63; Clergyman, 1965–; Assistant Bishop, Ruwenzori Diocese, Church of Uganda, 1967–. Address: P.O. Box 20, Hoima, Uganda.

RWAKAIZI, Augustine Barangaire, born 28th August 1945. Agriculturalist. Education: Diploma in Agriculture, Uganda; Diploma in Agriculture, E.A.; Certificate of Agriculture, London. Personal details: married, 1 daughter. Appointments: Farm Manager, Uganda Government Farm, 1969–. Memberships: Dancing & Dramatic Societies; Debating Society; Speech Making Society. Honours: Prizes for Animal Husbandry & Entomology, 1966. Address: Dept. of Agriculture, Box 99, Masindi, Uganda.

RWEGO, Ngenda Byibesho, born 2nd April 1944. Assistant Agricultural Officer. Education: Mutolere Primary School; Mutolere Junior Secondary; Cambridge School Certificate, Kigezi College, Butobere; Diploma in Agriculture, Bukalasa Agricultural College. Married, 1 child. Appointments: Mass Server, 1959; Librarian, 1960; Laboratory Prefect, 1962; Actor, Bukalasa, 1968. Memberships include: St. John Ambulance Brigade; Blood Donor, ibid; First Aider; Uganda Agricultural Society; Bufumbira Youth Club; Young Christian Society. Address: Department of Agriculture, P.O. Box 8, Mbarara, Uganda.

RWERSIBA, William Wycliffe, born 18th April 1922. Educator; Civil Servant. Education: B.Sc., Queen's University, Belfast, U.K.; Teachers' Diploma, Makerere University, Uganda. Appointments: Parliamentary Secretary. Ministry of Natural Resources, Uganda, 1960-61; Executive, Development Division, Uganda Development Corporation, 1961-62; Under-Secretary, Ministry of Education, 1962-63; Permanent Secretary, Ministry of Animal Industry, Game, & Fisheries, 1963-65; Permanent Secretary, Ministry of Education, 1965–. Memberships: Chief Commissioner, Uganda Boy Scouts Association;; President, National Council of Social Service for Uganda. Publications: Primary Science Course for Uganda. Address: Ministry of Education, P.O. Box 7063, Kampala, Uganda.

RWEYEMAMU, Charles Ladislaus, born 2nd December 1926. Administrative Officer. Education: St. More's Secondary, Ihungo, Bukoba, Tanzania, 1949; DSM, Kivukoni College, 1961. Married, 9 children. Appointments: Police Officer, 1949-50; Clerk General Division, Secretariat, Dar es Salaam, 1950-53; Clerk-Interpreter, High Court, 1953-62; Senior Clerk of Court, 1962-63; Local Government Officer, 1963-65; Administrative Officer, 1965–. Memberships: Bahaya Union DSM & Mwanza Committee; Catholic Old Boys' Association, DSM; Secretary, Discussion Group, Social Studies Group & Indoor Game Group. Publications: Regular Contributor to Poetry in Bukyanagandi Vernacular Newspaper. Address: P.O. Box 9011, Dar es Salaam, Tanzania.

RWOMUBITOKE, K. Andrew, born 28th December 1936. Senior Assistant Agricultural Officer. Education: Primary, 6 years; Junior & Senior, 6 years; Bukalas Agricultural College, 3 years; Overseas Training for Diploma, 1 year. Personal details: married, 3 sons, 1 daughter. Member of Uganda Agricultural Society. Address: Farm Institute, P.O. Box 101, Hoima, Uganda.

RYANGARO TAGAMBIRWA, Enosh, born Mrangi Village, Majita Musoma District, 12th March 1933. Area Commissioner. Education: Mrangi Primary School, 1948; Buamangi Middle School, Zanaki, Musoma District, 1952-55; Bwiru Secondary School, Mzanza District, 1956-57. Personal details: married, 6 children. Appointments: District Treasurer, TANU, 1958, 1962; Deputy Regional, TANU Mwanza Region, 1964; Deputy Regional, TANU Coast Region,

1965; Area Commissioner, Iringa District, 1965-67; Karagwe District, W.L. Region, 1967—. Memberships: TANU Youth League; Tanganyika African Parents' Association; Scout Movement. Address: Area Commissioner's Office, P.O. Karagwe, via Bukoba, West Lake Region, Tanzania.

S

SAADI, Moussa, born 13th December 1937. Engineering Geologist. Education: Engineer-geologist Diploma, Higher National School of Applied Geology & Mining Prospection, Nancy, France. Appointments: Deputy Head of Service, Studies of Mining Deposits, 1962-65; Head of Service, ibid, 1966-69; Head of Division of Geology, 1970—. Memberships: Deputy Secretary-General, National Association of Mining Engineers of Morocco, 1967-69; Secretary-General, ibid, 1970. Publications include: Author of several reports on the Copper deposits & the history of the ancient mines of Morocco. Honours: Quissam alaouite (Ordre Rida), 1967. Address: Engineering Geologist, Head, Division of Geology, Direction of Mines & Geology, Rabat, Morocco.

SAAKWA-MANTE, Kwaafo, born Accra, Ghana, 24th February 1924. Physician. Education: M.B., Ch.B., University of Leeds, U.K., 1952; D.T.M.&H., London School of Hygiene, 1954; D.P.H., Royal Institute of Public Health, 1956; M.Sc., University of Aberdeen, 1964. Married, 2 sons, 1 daughter. Appointments: Resident Clinical Pathologist, Booth Hall Hospital, Manchester, 1954-55; Medical Officer of Health, Ghana, 1956-61; Director, Institute of Health & Hygiene, 1965-68; Senior Medical Officer (Statistics), Ministry of Health, 1968—. Memberships: Ghana Medical Association; British Medical Association. Publications: Levels & Patterns of African Infant Mortality (Ghana Med. Jrnl.). Address: Biostatistics & Documentations, Ministry of Health, Accra, Ghana.

SABET, Younis Salem, born 1st January 1898. Retired Educator & Civil Servant. Education: Dipl., High School of Agriculture, Giza, 1921; B.Sc.(Hons.), London, U.K., 1925; M.Sc., Cairo, Egypt, 1934. Married, 4 sons, 1 daughter. Appointments: Plant Breeder, Ministry of Agriculture, 1925; Lecturer, Assistant Professor & Professor of Botany, Cairo University, 1927-46; Dean, Faculty of Agriculture, Alexandria University, 1946-52; Under-Secretary of State for Agriculture, 1953-57; Agricultural Adviser, 1958-59. Memberships: Academy of Science; Botanical Society; Society of Applied Microbiology; Science Union; Agricultural Institute Graduates; Phytopathological Society; Agricultural Club; Heliopolis Sporting Club. Author of research papers on Egyptian soil fungi. Honours: Al Goumkoria Medal, 2nd Order, 1955; Agriculture Medal, 1st Order, 1962. Address: 3 Mostafa El Wakil St., Manchiet Elbakry, Cairo, U.A.R.

SABUM, Michael Ndamandji, born Bali, Bemenda, Cameroun, 17th August 1925. Civil Servant. Education: Cambridge School Certificate; Post-Secondary, B.Sc.(Int.) London, U.K.; LL.B.(Hons.), London University. Married, 2 daughters. Appointments: entered the Administrative Civil Service, Assistant Administrative Officer; Administrative Officer; Senior Administrative Officer, Secretary-General, Federal Inspector's Office, Buea; Permanent Secretary, Ministries of State Development, Public Service, & Interior; Secretary, General Legislative Assembly, West Cameroun; Member, Electricity Corporation of Nigeria for the then Southern Cameroun, 1959-60; appointed Judge, Cameroun Federal Court of Justice, Buea Bench, 1966. Honours: Andrew Marvel Jackson Prize in Law, 1951; Camerounian Order of Merit, 1964. Address: House of Assembly, Buea, West Cameroun, Cameroun Republic.

SABUNI, Jonas Hussein, born 10th October 1926. Accountant; Auditor. Education: Training in U.S. & U.K. Appointments: Chief Clerk, Labour Department, Tanzania, 1947-56; Cashier, I.R.S., 1957-60; Statistical Clerk, Lands, 1960-63; Instructor, Civil Service Training Centre, 1963-64; Senior Instructor, ibid, 1965-67; Chief Instructor, 1967—. Member, National Association of Accountants (U.S.A.). Address: P.O. Box 2574, Dar es Salaam, Tanzania.

SABUR, Akbarali Gulamhussein, born Mbale, Uganda, 3rd June 1921. Civil Servant. Education: Reading Law, Inner Temple, U.K. Married, 2 sons, 4 daughters. Appointments: Clerk, United Africa Co. (U) Ltd.; Court Clerk & Interpreter, Uganda Civil Service, 1949; Higher Executive Officer, Judicial Department, Uganda Government. Memberships: Speaker, Khoja Shia Ithnasheri Jamat, Kampala, Uganda; Councillor, Supreme Council, Federation of Khoja Shia Ithasheri Jamats of Africa, 1958—; Education Board, ibid, 1962—; President, Parent Teacher Association, K.S.I. Primary School, 1966—; Joint Secretary, Parent Teacher Association, Old Kampala Secondary School; Founder & 1st President, Ithna-Ashna-Ashri Primary School; Administrator, Ithra Ashri Secondary School; Uganda Club. Honours: Uganda Independence Medal, 1962. Address: c/o High Court of Uganda, P.O. Box 7085, Kampala, Uganda.

SACHDEVA, Amrit Lall, born 25th January 1938. Civil Engineer. Education: Convent School, Mombasa, Kenya; Allioina Visram High School, Mombasa; Royal College, Nairobi; Dip. Eng. (E.A.); C.Eng. Appointments: Cadet Engineer, East African Railways, 1961-64; Assistant Engineer, ibid, 1964-67; District Civil Engineer, 1967—. Memberships: East African Wildlife Society; Institution of Civil Engineers (East Africa & U.K.); Fellow, Permanent Way Institution; Chairman, Tabora Railway Club. Address: Box 331, Tabora, Tanzania.

SADEK, Fernando, born 10th November 1928. Statistician. Education: 1st Class Hons., Mathematics, Cairo University, U.A.R., 1948; Postgraduate Studies, Imperial College of Science & Technology, London, U.K., 1949-52. Married, 3 children. Appointments: Statistician, Ministry of Health, Cairo; Statistician, World Health Organization, African Region, Ghana,

Nigeria, Togo & Kenya. Address: P.O. Box 6105, Nairobi, Kenya.

SADLEIR, Thomas Randal, born 6th May 1924. Civil Servant. Education: Portora Royal School, Enniskillen, Northern Ireland, U.K., 1938-41; Trinity College, Dublin, Ireland, 1941-42; Wadham College, Oxford, U.K., 1946-47. Married, 1 son, 1 daughter. Appointments: Captain, Royal Inniskilling Fusiliers, British Army, 1942-46; District Officer, Colonial Administrative Service, Tanganyika, 1948; District Commissioner, Kasulu, 1950; District Commissioner, Handeni, 1951-53; Assistant Secretary, Legal Affairs, Dar es Salaam, 1954-55; Senior Public Relations Officer, Dar es Salaam, 1955-60, & Arusha, 1957-58; Chief Training & Publicity Officer, Ministry of Cooperative & Community Development, 1961-64; Principal Assistant Secretary (Admin.), Ministry of Commerce & Cooperatives, 1964-67; Principal Assistant Secretary (Publicity), Ministry of Commerce & Industries, 1967-68; Executive Officer, Tanzanian Pavilion, Expo '70, Japan, 1968-70. Memberships: Director, Dar es Salaam Red Cross, 1958; President, Dar es Salaam Horticultural Society, 1964; Kildare Street Club, Dublin; Vice-President,, Irish Society of Tanganyika, 1956, 1962. Publications: A Note on the Handeni Museum (Tanganyika Notes & Records), 1961; The Cooperative Movement in Tanganyika (booklet), 1961. Address: Ministry of Commerce & Industries, P.O. Box 234, Dar es Salaam, Tanzania.

SAGAR, Thiruveethi Prem, born Salem, India, 18th January 1924. Engineer. Education: B.C.E.(Hons.), University of Madras, 1940-45; M.S.(Highway Engineering), Stanford University & University of Utah, U.S.A., 1946-49; passed Qualifying Exam. for Ph.D. in Highway Engineering, University of Utah, 1949; M.Phil., Civil Engineering, ibid, 1969.. Married, 1 daughter, 1 son. Appointments: Training with LeTourneau-Westinghouse, Barber-Greene, Allis-Chalmers, Cedarapids, Austin-Western International Harvester, La Plant Choate & other manufacturers of earth-moving & construction plant, also with Research Laboratories, Portland Cement Association, Chicago, Asphalt Institute, N.Y., Public Roads Administration, Federal Works Agency, Washington, D.C., Editorial Offices, World Construction & Roads & Streets Jrnls., Gillette Publishing House, Chicago, & Utha State Road Commission, Salt Lake City; Assistapt Engineer (Provincial Engineer), State Highways Department, Madras, India, 1950-51; Operations Engineer, Construction & Maintenance Division, Esso Standard Eastern Inc., Madras, 1951-60; Engineer, Earth-moving & Construction Equipment Division, William Jacks & Co. Ltd., Bombay, 1960-61; Engineer, Roads Division, Ministry of Works, Eastern Nigeria, 1961-67; United Nations Technical Assistance Expert, assigned to Roads & Aerodromes Division, Ministry of Communications, Transport & Labour, United Republic of Tanzania, Dar es Salaam, 1967—. Memberships: Fellow, American Society of Civil Engineers; American Road Builders' Association (Honorary); Institution of Civil Engineers, London; Institution of Engineers, India; Royal Economic Society, London; Association of Professional Engineers (Province of Ontario), Canada. Honours: Merit Scholarship, Government of India, 1945-47; Fellowship, University of Utah, U.S.A., 1947-49. Address: c/o United Nations Development Programme, P.O. Box 9182, Dar es Salaam, Tanzania.

SAGAZ, Angel, born Madrid, Spain, 1st March, 1913. Diplomat. Education: Law Degree. Married, 5 children. Appointments: in Ministry of Foreign Affairs, 1942—; currently Ambassador of Spain to United Arab Republic (i/c U.S.A. Affairs), Sudan, Somalia, Arab Republic of Yeman. Address: 30 Ahmed Hechmat, Zamalek, Cairo, U.A.R.

SAGOE, Aba Segva, born 13th February 1941. Medical Practitioner. Education: Anglican Girls' School, Lagos, Nigeria; Queen's College, ibid; Milton Mount College, Sussex, U.K.; Royal Free Hospital, University of London; M.B., B.S.; L.R.C.P.(Lond.); Dip. Immunol.; M.R.C.S. (Eng.). Currently, Medical Research Fellow, Department of Heamatology, University of Ibadan, Nigeria (3-year research project into the tropical splenomegaly syndrome). Memberships: Commonwealth Society, London; British Medical Association. Contributor to British Medical Journal. Address: Department of Heamatology, University of Ibadan, Nigeria.

SAGOE (Chief) Jumoke Olateju, born 4th January 1911. Educator. Education: Primary, Girls' Seminary, 1916-26; Secondary, Bank House School, Derbyshire, U.K.; Maria Grey Training College, Brondesbury Park, U.K. Personal details: maternal grandfather was a Prince Merchant of Lagos, Jacob Samuel Otolorin Leigh, 1st African to hold post of Consul in Lagos; married. Appointments: Headmistress, Queen's College Junior School; Acting Principal, Queen's College; Education Officer, ibid; Senior Education Officer, Federal Ministry of Education, Lagos, Nigeria. Memberships: Trustee, Past Chief Ranger, Ancient Order of Foresters, Lagos; Trustee, Past Most Noble Governor, Grand United Order of Oddfellows; Representative, Church & State; Leader, Methodist Church. Contributor of articles to education journals. Honours: Chieftancy Title of Honour conferred by the Oba of Lagos. Address: 66 Yaba Road, Yaba, Lagos, Nigeria.

SAGOE, Samuel Quesie, born Lagos, Nigeria, 27th November 1892. Auctioneer; Estate Agent. Education: Methodist Boys' High School, Lagos, 1907-09. Married, 4 children. Appointments include: jointed Municipal Department, Lagos, 1910; retired from the Nigerian Civil Service, 1945; General Superintendent Trinity, Methodist Sunday School, Tinubu, Lagos, for 20 years; Lay Magistrate, Lagos Juvenile Court, 1946-56. Memberships include: President, Methodist High School Old Boys' Association, Lagos, 1930—; Trustee, Member, Board of Governors, Ireti Girls' School, Lagos; Board of Governors, Lagos Anglican Boys' Grammar School; Hostel Committee, Y.M.C.A.; Chairman, Political Party Constituency, Lagos, 1965; Life-President, Lagos Philanthropy Society; President, Cathedral Missionary Society,

Cathedral Church of Christ, Lagos; President & Trustee, Lagos Association of Licensed Auctioneers; Chairman, Lagos Ward Health Society. Honours include: Sunday School Diploma, Methodist Sunday School Department, London, 1921; British Coronation Medal and Certificate, 1937; Govt. Certificate of Honour & Medal, 1939; Long Service Certificate, Methodist Church Sunday School Department, 1946. Address: 61 Odunlami Street, P.O. Box 3111, Lagos, Nigeria.

SAGOE, Taiwo Koffie, born Lagos, Nigeria, 24th June 1927. Barrister. Education: Elizabeth Fowler Memorial School, 1933-38; Eko Boys' High School, Lagos, 1939-40; Methodist, Boys' High School, ibid, 1941-47; 1st Class Diploma, Photographic & Lithographic Reproduction Processes, Leeds College of Technology, U.K., 1949-51; LL.B., University College, London. Married, 1 son, 1 daughter. Appointments: Director, Royal Bunge (Nigeria) Ltd.; ibid, Comexas (Nigeria) Ltd.; Chairman & Director, Group 4 of Nigeria Ltd. Memberships include: Lagos Lawn Tennis Club; Island Club, Lagos. Address: 14 Thorburn Ave., P.O. Box 3111, Lagos, Nigeria.

SAHASRABUDHE, Padmakar W., born 10th February 1933. University Lecturer. Education: M.Sc. Geophysics, Banaras Hindu University, India, 1955; Ph.D., ibid, 1963; A.Inst.P., London, U.K. Married, 1 daughter. Appointments: Full-time Research in Palaeomagnetism, Tata Institute of Fundamental Research, Bombay, India, 1955-66; Teaching Staff, Physics Department, Makerere University, Kampala, Uganda, 1967; Fellow, Indian Geophysical Union. Author of some 30 research papers in palaeomagnetism in various scientific journals. Address: Makerere University, Box 7062, Kampala, Uganda.

SAI, Frederick Torgbor, born Christiansborg, Accra, Ghana, 23rd June 1924. Professor of Medicine; Medical Administrator. Education: Christiansborg Presbyterian Schools, 1930-39; Achimota College, 1940-43; B.Sc., Physiology Special, University College & Hospital, London, U.K., 1947-50; M.B., B.S. (Hons.), ibid, 1950-53; D.T.M.&H., London School of Hygiene & Tropical Medicine, 1956; M.R.C.P. (Edinburgh), Edinburgh University Postgraduate Medical School, 1959; M.P.H., Harvard School of Public Health, U.S.A., 1959-60. Married, 1 son, 3 daughters. Appointments: House Surgeon, Poole General Hospital, U.K., 1954; House Physician, Korle Bu Hospital, Accra, Ghana, 1954-55; Medical Officer, Ghana Government Service, 1955-60; Physician Specialist (Human Nutrition), Ministry of Health, 1960-63; Deputy Chief Medical Officer of Ghana, 1961-62; Regional Nutrition Officer (Africa Region), Food & Agriculture Organization, responsible for nutrition activities in 32 African countries, 1963-66; Professor of Preventive & Social Medicine, Ghana Medical School, 1966—; Director of Medical Services, 1970—; FAO Nutrition Consultant to Somalia, 1961; WHO Consultant Lecturer, Sierra Leone, 1962; WHO Consultant to prepare Report on Communicable Disease Control in the Soviet Union, 1962; External Examiner in Preventive Medicine, Makerere Medical School, Uganda, 1963-68; Consultant to Rockefeller Foundation on Medical Education in Developing Countries, 1962-65; WHO Adviser, Nutrition & Urbanization, 1967-68; Member, Health Committee, National Liberation Council of Ghana, 1966-67. Memberships: Fellow, Royal College of Physicians of Edinburgh; Fellow, Ghana Academy of Sciences; Member, Praesidium or Governing Council, ibid, 1962-65; Hon. Secretary, 1967-69; Secretary, Ghana Medical Association, 1958, 1962-64; Planning Commission of Ghana, 1962-63; WHO Expert Advisory Panel on Nutrition, 1961—; WHO, FAO/UNICEF Protein Advisory Group, 1967—; Christian Medical Commission, World Council of Churches, 1968; Chairman, Medical Committee, Planned Parenthood Association of Ghana, 1967—; Vice-Chairman, Governing Body, International Planned Parenthood Federation, & of its Medical Committee. Active at a number of international conferences, 1960—. Author or co-author of several reports to Governments & International Agencies, 1957—, & also of a number of scientific papers in professional journals. Recipient of a number of study grants & scholarships for education, 1940-59, & WHO fellowship, 1959-60. Address: University of Ghana Medical School, Department of Preventive & Social Medicine, P.O. Box 4236, Accra, Ghana.

SAINA (Honourable) William Morogo Arap, born Kapsabet, Kenya, September 1937. Agriculturalist; Politician; Farmer; Historian. Education: Alliance High School, Nairobi, Kenya; C.D.A., Diploma in Agriculture. Personal details: married; born of famous Talai clan of Kalenjin Tribe, former leaders of Nandi, known as Laibon. Appointments: Agricultural Officer, Kenya Government; Technical Adviser; Windmill Fertilizers (E.A.) Ltd.; Member of Parliament, Eldoret North Kenya. Memberships: East African Wild Life Society; Agricultural Society of Kenya; Kenya National Farmers' Union; Kenya Farmers' Association. Currently researching on the Nandi Tribes, one of the Kalenjin major Tribes. Honours: Perpetual Ellegerini Cup, Agricultural Society of Kenya. Address: Talai Farm, Kipkarren, P.O. Box 292, Eldoret, Kenya.

SAINT-ROSSY, Dan, born 28th November 1921. UNESCO Specialist. Education: A.B., New York University, U.S.A., 1946; M.A., ibid, 1948; Ph.D., Fordham University, N.Y., 1955. Appointments: Associate Professor of Chemistry, Seton Hall University, South Orange, N.J., 1947-58; UNESCO Science Education Expert, Taiwan, Formosa, 1958-66; ibid, India, 1966-69; Deputy Chief, UNESCO Science Office for Africa, Nairobi, Kenya, 1969—. Memberships: American Chemical Society; American Association of University Professors; President, Rotary Club, Taipei, Taiwan, 1963. Contributor to professional journals. Address: UNESCO Field Science Office for Africa, P.O. 30592, Nairobi, Kenya.

SAKRAFO IX, Togbe, Fiaga of Goviefe Traditional Area, born 3rd March 1919. Paramount Chief. Education: General Certificate of Education. Personal details: ancestors founded the present Township of Goviefe; married, 8 children. Appointments: Member, Volta Region House of Chiefs; Member, Dusor/Hokpe Traditional Council; installed as Fiaga, 1942. Address: Goviefe Todzi, P.O. Box 138, Ho, Ghana.

SALAKO, Lateef Akinola, born 5th July 1935. Physician. Education: Methodist Boys' High School, Lagos, Nigeria, 1948-53; M.B., B.S., Hons.(London), University of Ibadan & University College Hospital, Ibadan, 1954-61; Ph.D., Sheffield University, U.K., 1969; M.R.C.P., 1964. Married, 2 children. Appointments: House Appointments in Medicine, 1962-66; Research Fellowship in Pharmacology, 1966-69; Lecturer, then Senior Lecturer, Pharmacology, University of Ibadan, Nigeria, 1970. Memberships: Association of Physicians of Nigeria; Association of Physicians of West Africa; Secretary, Nigerian Society of Neurological Sciences, affil. to World Congress of Neurology. Author of numerous papers in international journals on transepithelial sodium transport and neuromuscular transmission. Honours: University Gold Medallist in Medicine, Ibadan, 1961; Commonwealth Scholar, 1964-65; Smith & Nephew Medical Fellowship, 1967-68; Boots Research Fellowship, University of Sheffield, U.K., 1968-69. Address: Pharmacology Department, University of Ibadan, Ibadan, Nigeria.

SALAKO (Rev.) Nathanael Oduyebo, born Ikenne, Ijebu Remo Division, Western State, Nigeria, 12th December 1903. Methodist Minister. Education: Methodist Schools, Ikenne & Iperu, 1912-22; Sub-Pastor, Wesley College, Ibadan, 1923-27, 1932 & 1934. Married, 1932, 2 daughters; re-married, 1944, 3 sons, 3 daughters. Appointments: Sub-Pastor, i/c Imo & Oyo Churches, 1928-31; Headmaster, Methodist School, Oyo; Circuit Minister, Osu, Ilesha Circuit, 1933; ibid, Imesi-ile Methodist Church, 1935; i/c Oshogbo Methodist Church, 1936-38; Igbo-Ora, Ibadan Circuit, 1939; ordained Minister in Full Connection, 1939; Itesi Methodist Church, Abeokuta Circuit, 1940-46; transferred to Far-Northern Mission affiliated to Tinubu Circuit, 1946-49; Superintendent, Ilesha Circuit, 1949-56; ibid, Ibadan Circuit, 1956-62; Chairman, Ibadan Methodist District, 1962; President, Methodist Church, Nigeria, 1968—. Memberships: Chaplain, Boys' Brigade; ibid, Methodist Youth Club. Publications: Ogbufo Emi Mimo; The So Called Seraphim Movement, 1942. Address: 22 Marina, P.O. Box 2011, Lagos, Nigeria.

SALAU (Alhaji) Halifah O. O., born 23rd February 1931. Medical Practitioner. Education: Ansar-Ud-Deen, Alakoro, Lagos, Nigeria, 1934-36; Ijebu Obe Moslem School, 1937-42; Ijebu Ode Grammar School, 1943-47; C.M.S. Grammar School, Lagos, 1948-49; University Tutorial College, London, U.K., 1955-56; Royal College of Surgeons, Ireland, 1956-62; King's College, University of London, 1969-70. Married. Appointments: Medical Officer, Sierra Leone Government Service, 1963-64; Lecturer, Dispensary School, Connaught Hospital, Sierra Leone, 1963-69. Memberships: Foundation & Executive Member, Medical Practitioner Union, 1964-69; Treasurer, Sierra Leone Medical & Dental Association, 1967-69; President, Nigeria Association of Sierra Leone, 1968-69. Author, The Abuse of Drugs, Medical Practitioner Union Annual Magazine, 1968. Recipient, Junior Hospital Prize in Medicine & Surgery, St. Laurence Hospital (Richmond) Dublin, 1960. Address: 325 Seely Road, London, S.W.17, U.K.

SALE, John Benjamin, born U.K., 29th August 1934. Zoologist. Education: Lutterworth Grammar School; B.Sc.(Hons.), Ph.D., M.I.Biol., University of London. Married, 1 daughter. Appointments: Assistant Lecturer in Biology, Royal Technical College of East Africa, 1957-59; Lecturer, ibid, 1959-61; Lecturer in Zoology, University College, Nairobi, Kenya, 1961-69; Senior Lecturer in Zoology, ibid, 1969—; Editor, East African Wildlife Journal, 1970—. Memberships: Zoological Society of London; Institute of Biology; American Society of Mammalogists; East African Wildlife Society; Chairman, Kenya Christian Graduates' Fellowship, 1967—. Author of numerous papers in scientific journals, mainly on aspects of the biology of the hyrax, including an entry in the Encyclopaedia Britannica. Address: Department of Zoology, University of Nairobi, P.O. Box 30197, Nairobi, Kenya.

SALEH ABDELKADER KEBIRE, born Asmara, Ethiopia, 27th September 1927. Lawyer. Education: completed Secondary School, 1947; Law School, University of Asmara; C.L.-B.A. (LL.B.), American University of Beirut, Lebanon. Appointments: A/District Governor, Tesseney, Eritrea, 1949-50; Vice-President, Tesseney District Court, 1949-50; A/District Governor, Senafe, 1950; ibid, Ghinda, 1950; A/Governor, Asmara District & Municipality Appeal Reviewing Officer, 1950-51; Mayor, Port of Massawa, 1954-56; President, Civil & Commercial Court of Massawa, 1954-56; President, Rent Commission, ibid; Liaison Officer for Implementation of Italian Reparation for former civil & military employees of Italian Administration in Ehtiopia, 1956-58; Director, Legal Affair State Property & Domain Department, 1958-60; A/General Director, Municipality of Addis Ababa for Legal & Personnel Affairs, 1960-62; Legal Adviser, Addis Ababa Bank S.C., 1964; Founder & Senior Partner, Saleh A. Kebire & Associates, Law Firm & Investment Consultants. Memberships: Ethiopian Bar Association; Chamber of Commerce, Addis Ababa; Arbitration Board, ibid; Prince Mekonnen Memorial Club; A.U.B. Alumni Association; Hailé Selassié I Secondary School Alumni Association. Publications: UNRWA Administration, Structure, Organization, Operation, & Problems; The Protection to the Right of the Individual in the Constitution of Lebanon; Comparative Studies of Sharia Law & Ethiopian Civil Law. Address: P.O. Box 3522, Addis Ababa, Ethiopia.

SALI, Barbara Nozipho, born 7th April 1920. Nursing Sister. Education: Primary, St. Peter's School, Rosettenville, South Africa; Secondary, Tigerkloop Instituition, ibid; General Nursing, Lovedale Hospital, 1939; S.C.M., McCurd Hospital, Durban, 1943. Married, 1 son, 2 daughters. Appointments: Staff Nurse, Lovedale Hospital; Nursing Sister, 1945; J.J. Hospital,

Bombay, India; London Chest Hospital & Temperance Hospital, 1962; Nursing Sister, Mengo Hospital, Kampala, Uganda, 1964. Address: Mengo Hospital, P.O. Box 7161, Kampala, Uganda.

SALI, Fred, born Mengo, 16th August 1926. Broadcaster; School Inspector. Education: Kira Primary School, Pl-4, 1936-40; Mengo Junior Secondary School, P5-J3, 1941-44; Mukano Junior Teacher Training College, 1945-47; Mbarara Government Teacher Training College, Uganda, 1953-55; Dip.Phys.Ed., King Alfred's College, Winchester, U.K., 1959-61; Certificate in Instructional T.V., 1965. Married. Appointments: Primary Teacher, 1947-51; Junior Secondary Teacher, 1956-59; Tutor, Namutamba Teachers' Training College, 1961-63; Assistant Education Officer, 1964-66; Inspector of Schools, Uganda, 1967—; Executive Producer, (E.T.V.), 1967—; Acting Programme Organizer, ibid, 1967-70. Memberships: Y.M.C.A.; Language Society; Uganda Referees' Association. Address: c/o Ministry of Education, P.O. Box 3568, Kampala, Uganda.

SALIB, Edward, born 24th June 1924. Petroleum Marketing Executive. Education: B.A. with High Mention, Cairo University, U.A.R., 1945. Appointments: District Manager, Esso, U.A.R., 1960-64; Regional Manager, ibid, 1964-65; President & General Manager, Ivory Coast (responsible for setting up a new Esso Company), 1965-70; Planning Manager, Marine Sales, Europe & Africa, 1970—. Honours: Officier de l'Ordre National, Ivory Coast, 1970. Address: Esso Europe Inc., 50 Stratton St., London, W.1, U.K.

SALIFOU, Illa, born 17th February 1932. Technical Adviser, Ministry of Foreign Affairs of Niger. Education: Secondary Studies, Niamey; Cours' par correspondance d'enseignement general, Stage dans les Assemblees Françaises (Palais, Bourbon, Conseil de la Rep. Union Française, 1957-58; Carnegie Award for International Peace; University Institute for Higher Internal Studies, Geneva, Switzerland, 1966-67. Married, 6 children. Appointments: Secretary of the Courts, 1956; Secretary of the Assembly, 1957-59; Judge of the Peace, 1960; Adviser to the Minister of Justice, 1960; First Secretary, then Adviser to the Embassy at Washington & New York, U.S.A., 1961-66; Director of Cabinet, M.A.E., 1968-70; Technical Adviser, 1970—. Honours: Verdienskreuz 1st Class, Federal Republic of Germany, 1969. Address: c/o Ministry of Foreign Affairs, Niamey, Niger.

SALIRA, Muloni, born 10th December 1942. Lecturer. Education: B.A.(Hons.), East Africa; M.A., Public Policy & Administration, University of Wisconsin, U.S.A. Currently, Lecturer, Management Studies, Uganda Institute of Public Administration, Kampala. Member, American Society for Public Administration. Address: Institute of Public Aministration, P.O. Box 20131, Kampala, Uganda.

SAM, William, born 2nd June 1940. Electrical Engineer. Education: Sekondi Methodist School; Mfantsipim Secondary School; B.Sc., London (External), University of Science & Technology, Kumasi Ghana; M.Phil., Queen Mary College, University of London, U.K.; Ph.D., University of Technology, Loughborough. Personal details: married. Appointments: Projects Engineer, A.E.I., Woolwich, London, 1965-67; Research Engineer & Consultant, University of Technology, Loughborough; Lecturer, Elect. Power Engineering, Kumasi University, 1970; Acting General Manager, Metal Industries Division, Accra, Ghana. Member of Institution of Electrical Engineers. Author of several publications. Address: P.O. Box 2, Komenda, Ghana.

SAMB, Amadou, born 12th December 1927. Director of Primary & Secondary Grade Education, Ministry of National Education, Senegal. Education: Licensed in Letters; Diploma of Higher Studies in Classical Languages; Certificat d'Aptitude au professorat du Second Degre. Appointments: Professeur de Lettres aux lycées, Pothier, Orleans; Pasteur, Neuilly; J. B. Say, Paris; Faidherbe, St. Louis du Senegal; Van Villenhoven, Dakar. Memberships: s: President, Senegal Section, Guillaume Bude Association; Vice-President, Senegal Section of the Pen Club; Permanent Technical Secretary, Conference of Ministers of Education of African Countries & French-Speaking Madagascar. Publications: various articles & conferences on education & culture. Honours: Officer of the Palmes Academiques: Commander of the Order of Merit of Senegal. Address: Bloc Pasteur, Dakar, Senegal.

SANDERS, Allan Cameron Ebblewhite, born 30th July 1934. Headmaster. Education: Peter Symonds' School, Winchester, U.K., 1944-52; M.A., Corpus Christi College, Oxford, 1952-56; Teaching Assistant, Indiana University, U.S.A., 1956-57; M.Ed., East Africa, 1970. Married. Appointments: Teacher, Monkton Combe School, Bath, U.K., 1957-60; Head, Chemistry Department, Alliance High School, Kikuyu, Kenya, 1960-69; Deputy Headmaster, ibid, 1967-70; Headmaster, 1970. Address: Alliance High School, P.O. Box 7, Kikuyu, Kenya.

SANDFORD, Arthur Russell, born 20th August 1916. Medical Practitioner. Education: Breeks School, Ootacamund, India; Kingswood School, Bath, U.K.; St. Mary's Hospital, University of London. Appointments: Colonial Medical Service, Kenya, 1941-52; Private Practice, 1952—. Address: P.O. Box 762, Mombasa, Kenya.

SANGAYA, Jonathan Douglas, born 30th October 1907. Minister of Religion. Education: Primary & Secondary, Henry Henderson Institute, Blantyre Mission, Malawi, 1914-27; Teacher Training, ibid, 1927-29; Theological Training, Mlanje Church of Central African Presbyterian, 1948-51; ordained Minister of Religion, 1951. Appointments: Teacher, Henry Henderson Institute, 1929-43; Sergeant in Charge of Education & later Warrant Officer, Army Education Corps & 14th Battalion, King's African Rifles, 1943-46; Teacher, Henry Henderson Institute, 1948-49; Priest, Bemuy, Blantyre, Katimba, Ngumbe, & Lunzy, 1951-59; Assistant General Secretary, Blantyre Synod,

C.C.A.P., 1959-63; Vice-Moderator, ibid, 1960; General Secretary, Blantyre Synod, 1963–; Moderator of the General Synod, 1965-68. Memberships: Chairman, Board of Governors, Blantyre Secondary School; Chairman, Board of Governors, Kapeni Training College; Chairman, Board of Governors, Henry Henderson Institute; Chairman, Gospel Broadcasting of the Christian Council; former Chairman, Board of Trustees, Museum of Malawi; Chaplain to the Mayor & Council, Blantyre City Council. Honours: War Medal, 1939-45. Address: Blantyre Mission, P.O. Box 413, Blantyre, Malawi.

SANKARNARAYANAN, Thangaraj, born India, 3rd December 1934. Rubber Technologist; Engineer. Education: B.Sc., Chemistry; B.Com.; Rubber Technology & Chartered Engineer (Chemical). Appointments: Shift in Charge, Messrs Fenner Cockill (India) Ltd., 1954-59; Works Manager/Rubber Technologist, Messrs Brahadam Group Rubber Industries, 1959-62; ibid, Messrs Rasmi Cables Pvt. Ltd., 1962-64; ibid, Messrs Radiant Rubber Industries Pvt. Ltd., 1964-65; Messrs Rasmi Cables Group Rubber Industries, 1965-66; Technical Manager, Rubber Technologist, Plastics, & Rubber Industries Ltd., Nairobi, Kenya, 1966–. Technical Adviser to various rubber concerns, India. Memberships: Institution of the Rubber Industry, London; Society of Chemical Industry, London; British Association of Chemists; India Society of Engineers, Calcutta; International Institution of Engineers, Delhi; Associate, East African Institution of Engineers, Kenya; ibid, Institution of Works Managers, London; Affiliate, Division of Rubber Chemistry, Akron; Associate, British Institute of Management; Fellow, Indian Commercial Association, Delhi; A.F.I.C.E.P., Paris, France. Address: Plastics & Rubber Industries Ltd., P.O. Box 6957, Nairobi, Kenya.

SANMARCO, Louis Marius Pascal, born 7th April 1912. French Governor Overseas; President of ASECNA (Agency for the Security of Aeronavigation in Africa, Madagascar); President de SOFREAVIA. Education: Colonial School; Institute of Higher Administrative Studies. Married, 4 children. Appointments: Colonial Administrator, 1935; French Governor Overseas, Gabon, 1952; President, ASECNA, 1960; ibid, SOFREAVIA, 1969. Honours: Officer of the Legion of Honour; Grand Officer of the Central African Republic; Commander of the National Order of Senegal, The Ivory Coast, Upper Volta, Niger, Tchad, Gabon, & The Malagasy Republic. Address: 75 rue la Boetie, Paris 8e, 75, France.

SANON, Salia, born 12th May 1941. Agricultural Engineer. Education: Secondary Studies, Lycées Bobo-Dioulasso & Ougadougou, Upper Volta; Higher studies, Toulouse, France; Diploma of Agricultural Engineering. Appointments: Head of Service of Agricultural Popularization & Direction of Rural Development, Ouagadougou, 1966-67; Director of Regional Organization & Development of the South West, Banfora, 1967–. Memberships: National Association of Agricultural Engineers of France; Philanthropic & Humanist Association. Address: c/o Organization of Regional Development of the South West, B.P. 33, Banfora, Upper Volta.

SANSOM, Hugh Wilfred, born 11th May 1924. Meteorologist. Education: Stowe School, U.K.; M.A., St. John's College, Cambridge; Ph.D., D.I.C., Imperial College of Science & Technology, London. Married, 4 daughters. Appointments: Meteorologist, East African Meteorological Department, 1950; Deputy Director, ibid, 1966–. Memberships: Fellow, Royal Meteorological Society; Chairman, East African Religious Films Library. Author of various scientific papers in Meteorology. Address: Deputy Director-General, P.O. Box 30259, Nairobi, Kenya.

SAPIRO, Marcus Lazarus, born 12th August 1906. Scientist; Educator. Education: B.Sc., Rhodes University College, 1926; M.Sc., ibid, 1927; Ph.D., University of South Africa, 1945. Married, 3 sons, 1 daughter. Appointments: Demonstrator & Assistant Lecturer, South Africa, 1928-39; Officer, Chemical Warfare Unit, 1940-46; Research Officer, South African Department of Veterinary Services, 1946-47; Chemist in Charge, Agriculture Chemistry Laboratories, Overseas Food Corporation, Tanganyika, 1947-51; Biochemist, Kenya Veterinary Department, 1952-65; Officer in Charge, Laboratory Technical Training Unit, Makerere University College, Uganda, 1965-67; Lecturer in Chemistry, Uganda Technical College, Kampala, 1967–. Fellow, Chemical Society. Author of about 12 scientific papers in various journals. Address: Uganda Technical College, P.O. Box 7181, Kampala, Uganda.

SAR, Moustapha, born 7th April 1934. Directeur de l'amenagement du territoire. Education: Licensed in History & Geography; Urban Planning; Dr. of Applied Geography. Married, 1 child. Publications: Louga, La ville et sa region (doctoral thesis). Address: Secretariat of State Planning, Building Administration, Dakar, Senegal.

SAR, Papa Gueye, born 29th March 1908. Journalist. Appointments: Journalist, 1934-38; Agent d'Affaires, 1941-69; Head of Service of Information, 1960-62; Municipal Secretary, 1962-63; Head of Cabinet to the Presidence of the Republic, 1963–. Publications: L'A.O.F.; Le Periscope Africain; Clarte; Le Jeune Senegal (Director & Editor); Le Senegal; Condition Humane. Honours: Officer of the National Order of Senegal; ibid, Order of Senegal Merit; Commander, Ordre du Cedre du Siban. Address: Head of Cabinet, Presidence of the Republic, Dakar, Senegal.

SARDANIS, Andreas Sotiris, born 13th March 1931. Government Officer. Educated privately. Married, 2 sons. Appointments: held managerial posts in trading & transport concerns; Chairman & Managing Director, Industrial Development Corporation, Zambia, 1965-70; Permanent Secretary, Ministry of Commerce, Industry, & Foreign Trade, Ministry of Trade, Industry, & Mines, & Ministry of Development & Finance, 1968-70; Managing Director, Zambia Industrial & Mining Corporation Ltd., Chairman, Indeco Ltd., & Chairman, Mindeco Ltd., 1970-;

Permanent Secretary, Ministry of State Participation, 1970-. Address: Ministry of State Participation, P.O. Box 1969, Lusaka, Zambia.

SARKAR, Dilip Kumar, born 21st May 1929. Specialist in Obstetrics & Gynaecology. Education: M.B., B.S., Calcutta University, India, 1952; D.G.O., ibid, 1955; M.R.C.O.G., London, U.K., 1961; E.C.F.M.G., U.S.A., 1968. Married, 2 daughters. Appointments: Registrar, Obstetrics & Gynaecology, Western Hospital, Doncaster, U.K., 1959-61; Senior Medical Officer in Obstetrics & Gynaecology, Ministry of Health, Ghana, 1962—; Medical Superintendent, Cape Coast Hospital, 1969—. Member, British Medical Association. Publications: Rupture of the Uterus with Special Reference to Difficulties in Diagnosis (Calcutta Med. Jrnl.), 1955. Honours: 1st Certificate of Honours in Anatomy, 1949; Scholarship for General Merit, Medical College, Calcutta, 1948-50. Address: c/o Midland Bank Ltd., 237 Brompton Road, London, S.W.3, U.K.

SARKI, Dominic A. E., born Kutaho, Nigeria, 1948. Teacher. Education: E.C.W.A. School, 1954-57; R.C.M. School, Guni, 1958-59; Sabon Sarki R.C.M. School, 1960-61; St. Ebda's Teacher Training College, Zaria, 1962-66; Zaria Advanced Teachers' College, 1969—. Married, 2 sons. Appointments: Infirmarian, St. Ebda's Teacher Training College, Zaria, 1965-66; Headmaster, St. Clement's School, Aribi, 1967; Headmaster, R.C.M. School, Kurmi Dangana, 1968-69. Memberships: Young Farmers' Club; Secretary, Southern Zaria Students' Union, 1964-66, etc. Honours: N.C.S. Scholarship, 1969; Federal Scholarship, 1970. Address: Advanced Teachers' College, P.M.B. 1041, Zaria, North-Central State, Nigeria.

SASSOON, Hamo, born 22nd February 1920. Archaeologist. Education: Sherborne School, Dorset, U.K., 1934-37; Merton College, Oxford, 1938-39 & 1947-51. Appointments: Deputy Director of Antiquities, Nigeria, 1957-62; Conservator of Antiquities, Tanzania, 1963-68; Conservator of Antiquities, Uganda, 1969—. Memberships: Royal Anthropological Insitute; Museums Association. Author of various articles on iron-smelting & iron age archaeology, & various guide books & annual reports. Address: Ministry of Culture & Community Development, Box 7136, Kampala, Uganda.

SAUNDERSON, Mont Harris, born 12th March 1899. Agricultural Economist. Education: B.Sc., Iowa State University, U.S.A., 1921; M.A., ibid, 1925; University of California, Berkeley, 1921-22. Appointments: Ranch Economist, Montana State University, 1925-38; Rangeland Economist, U.S. Forest Service, 1938-50; Private Consultant, Western Ranch & Lands Development, 1950—. Member, American Society of Agricultural Economists. Publications: Western Stock Ranching; Western Land & Water Use; Economic Aspects of Uganda's Livestock Development, A.S.A.I.D.'s Mission to Uganda; Materials for Study of Land & Water Use. Honours: Member, Beta Gamma Sigma; Flood Fellow, Economics, University of California. Address: P.O. Box 266, Missoula, Mont. 59801, U.S.A.

SAUZIER, Andre Guy, born 20th October 1910. London Representative, Mauritius Chamber of Commerce. Education: Royal College, Mauritius. Married, 3 sons. Appointments: Legal Department, Mauritius Civil Service, 1932-39; Major, British Army, 1939-45; Chief Executive, Mauritius Chamber of Agriculture, 1946-49; London Representative, ibid, U.K., 1959—; Member, Mauritius Legislative Assembly, 1949-59; Minister of Communications, Mauritius, 1957-59; Chairman, Commonwealth Sugar Exporters Price Group, 1961—; Chairman, Executive Committee, International Sugar Organization, 1969—. Official Delegate of Mauritius to Coronation of Queen Elizabeth, 1953, & to political talks, London, 1955. Honours: Defence Medal, War Medal, Efficiency Decoration, Territorials, 1946; C.B.E., 1959. Address: 1306 St. James Court, Buckingham Gate, London, S.W.1, U.K.

SAVAGE, Gabriel Percy Akinfemiwa, born 10th February 1900. Educator. Education: Government School, Cape Coast, Gold Coast; St. Paul's Breadfruit School, Lagos, Nigeria; S.P.C. Grammar School (now Adisadel College), Cape Coast, Gold Coast; B.A.(Dunelm) & M.A. (Dunelm), Fouray Bay College, Sierra Leone. Married, 2 sons. Appointments: Organist, Christ Church, Cape Coast, 1916-19; Organist, St. John's Church, Aroloya, Lagos, Nigeria, 1927-29; Acting Principal, King's College, Lagos, 1948-50, 1955, 1956; Principal, Eilo Boys' High School, Lagos, 1956-62. Memberships: ex-Chaplain, Organist, & Secretary, Court 'Fount of Hope' No. 799, Ancient Order of Foresters; President, ibid, 1953; Founder & President, Triumph Orchestary, Lagos, 1927-49. Honours: Certificate as Incident Officer, Air Raid Precautions Service, Lagos, Nigeria, 1939-45; M.B.E., 1957; Coronation Medal, 1953. Address: Lagos, Nigeria.

SAVANI, Chandulal Bhagwanji, born 29th April 1924. Medical Practitioner. Education: B.Sc.(Chem. & Bot.), University of Bombay, India, 1945; M.B., B.S., University of Bombay, 1950. Married, 2 children. Appointments: General Practitioner, Private Practice, 17 yrs. Memberships: President, Lohana Community, Masaka; Board of Directors, Lions Club of Masaka; Councillor, Masaka Municipal Council. Address: P.O. Box 199, Masaka, Uganda.

SAVORY, Robert, born 22nd September 1938. University Lecturer. Education: B.Sc. (Agric.), London; M.Sc.(Agric.). Current appointment: Lecturer in Soil Science, University of Malawi. Memberships: Soil Science Society of Australia; Australian Institute of Agricultural Science; Grasslands Society of Southern Africa. Address: c/o University of Malawi, Blantyre, Malawi.

SAYLOR, R. Gerald, born Fort Wayne, Ind., U.S.A., 5th March 1940. Economist. Education: B.A., Kalamazoo College, Mich., 1962; Ph.D., Duke University, 1966. Married, 2 sons, 1 daughter. Appointments: Instructor of

Economics, Duke University, 1964-65; Financial Economist, Federal Reserve Bank of Dallas, Tex., 1966; Assistant Professor of Economics, Michigan State University, seconded to the Consortium for the Study of Nigerian Rural Development, Ibadan, Nigeria, 1967; Research Fellow, Economic Research Bureau, University College, Dar es Salaam, 1968-70; Director, ibid, 1970-71. Memberships: Phi Beta Kappa; American Economics Association; Southern Economics Association; Secretary, East African Agricultural Economics Society, 1969-70; Nigeria Economic Association; Tanganyikan Economics Society. Publications: Economic System of Sierra Leone, 1970. Author or co-author of articles in professional journals. Address: P.O. Box 35096, Dar es Salaam, Tanzania.

SCHOEMAN, Johanna Carolina Fransina, born 15th October, 1921. Director of Companies. Education: I.A.C. Diploma. Married, 3 sons. Appointments: Director, Schomans Office Equipment & Service; ibid, Fastkopi (Pty.) Ltd.; Trustee, South Africa Foundation; ibid, University of South Africa. Memberships: Founder President, South West Africa Federation of Business & Professional Women; Committee Member, Windhoek Afrikaanse Sakekamer; Vice-President, Council of Women, S.W.A. Address: P.O. Box 2600, Windhoek, South West Africa.

SCHOPF, Karl Joseph, born Landeck, Tirol, Austria, 12th February 1905. Doctor of Medicine. Education: Mehrerau University, Vienna, Graz, & Innsbruck, 1937; M.D., Innsbruck, 1942; Facharzt für Chirugie, 1951; Surgical training, U.S.A., 1960-51. Married, 4 children. Appointments include: in charge, St. Francis Hospital, Ifakara, Tanzania, 1953—. Publications include: 5 papers on medical problems published in scientific journals. Address: P.O. Box 49, Ifakara, Tanzania.

SCHRAM, Rudolph, born 16th September, 1927. University Reader. Education: King's College School, Wimbledon, U.K.; Downing College, Cambridge, 1946-49; M.A., Chemical Microbiology, St. Thomas' Hospital, London, 1949-54; M.B., B.Ch. (Camb.), 1954; M.D.(Camb.), 1967; D.P.H., London School of Hygiene & Tropical Medicine, 1960; D.I.H. (Lond.), 1961. Married, 4 children. Appointments: Senior Registrar, U.C.H. Ibadan, Nigeria, 1961; Lecturer, Occupational Medicine, St. Andrew's University, Dundee, U.K., 1963; Senior Lecturer, Makerere Medical School, Kampala, Uganda, 1965; Reader, Ahamadu Bello University, Zaria, Nigeria, 1970. Memberships: British Medical Association, 1954—; Society of Occupational Medicine, 1962—; Society of Social Medicine, 1962—; Uganda Medical Association, 1965—; Secretary, ibid, 1967; Nigerian Society of Health, 1966—; Royal Society of Tropical Medicine & Hygiene, 1967—; British Society for the History of Medicine, 1968—; International Society of Medicine, 1970—. Publications: A History of the Nigerian Health Services from 1460-1960, 1970; contributor to medical publications. Honours: Downing College Prize & Exhibition, 1948; Prize of Association of Industrial Medical Officers for D.P.H. Examination, 1960; Proxime accesset to Raymond-Horton Smith Prize for second best M.D. thesis (Camb.), 1967. Address: Ahmadu Bello University Medical School, Zaria, North Central State, Nigeria.

SCOTT, Kenneth Mackenzie, born Sydney, Australia, 1st April 1918. Architect. Education: Sydney Church of England Grammar School; Brighton Grammar School; Brighton School of Art. Married, 2 sons, 2 daughters. Appointments include: commissioned, Worcestershire Regiment, 1940; 7th Battalion, Gold Coast Regiment, 1940-46; Lt.-Col., Campaigns in Burma, 1944-45; Architect, Public Works Department, 1949-51; Partner, James, Cubitt, Scott & Partners, 1951-54; Kenneth Scott Associates, Architects, Accra, Ghana, 1954—. Memberships include: 1st President, Ghana Society of Architects; Council Member, Vice-President, Ghana Institute of Architects; Associate, Royal Institute of British Architects, 1948; Fellow, ibid., 1963. Honours include: Military Cross, 1945. Address: Kenneth Scott Associates, Architects, P.O. Box 1766, Accra, Ghana.

SCOTT, Malcolm Kenneth Merrett, born 22nd June 1930. Clergyman; Chartered Accountant. Education: Berkhamsted School, Herts., U.K., 1939-47; articled to Chartered Accountant, 1947-52; received A.C.A.; Clifton Theological College, 1956-58; ordained, 1958. Married, 1 son. Appointments: Assistant Curate, Highbury, London, 1958-60; Chaplain to Bishop of Rwenzori, 1961-65; Tutor, Bishop Usher Wilson College, 1966; Archdeacon of Toro, Diocese of Rwenzori, 1967—. Memberships: Institute of Chartered Accountants; Graduates' Felloship. Address: P.O. Box 37, Fort Portal, Uganda.

SCOTT, Moses Nathanael Christopher Omoviala, born 18th August 1911. Archbishop of West Africa & Bishop of Sierra Leone. Education: Sierra Leone Grammar School; Fourah Bay College, Freetown; London College of Divinity, U.K. Married, 5 children. Appointments: Teacher/Catechist; Clergyman; Archdeacon; Bishop; Archbishop. Memberships: Freetown Dinner Club; Society for the Deaf of Sierra Leone. Honours: C.B.E., 1970: D.D., Durham University, 1963. Address: Bishopscourt, P.O. Box 128, Freetown, Sierra Leone.

SCOTT, Ralph Roylance, born Riding Mill on Tyne, England, 10th July 1893. Medical Practitioner (retired). Education: Blundell's School, Durham University. Appointments include: House Surgeon, Royal Victoria Infirmary & Fleming Memorial Hospital for Sick Children, Newcastle upon Tyne; Captain, R.A.M.C. (S.R.) 1914-19; Medical Officer of Health, Dar es Salaam 1919-30; Senior Medical Officer of Health, Tanganyika, 1924; Deputy Director of Sanitary Services, Tanganyika, 1932; Director of Medical Services, Tanganyika, 1935-45. Memberships: British Medical Association (1920); Ryl. Soc. Tropical Medicine & Hygiene; Peter Blundell Society; Nairobi Orchestra (founder Member & Patron); E.R. Music Association; Nairobi Club. Publications: Glossary of Scientific Terms (Swahili) 1929;

Introduction: Preventive Medicine, 1935; Annual Medical Reports, Tanganyika 1935-44; Glossary of Musical Terms (Swahili) 1937; Public Health in Dar es Salaam in the 'Twenties' 1963. Honours, prizes, etc.: Medical qualifications M.R.C.S., L.R.C.P., 1916; D.P.H., 1923; M.B., B.S.(Dur.), (1923); Military Cross 1918; Companion of the Order of St. Michael & St. George, 1939; Officer of the Order of St. John, 1943. Address: P.O. Karen, Nairobi, Kenya.

SCOTT, Thelma Ellen, born 14th August 1929. Teacher Education: Teachers' Diploma, Macdonald College, Montreal, Canada; Scholar in Theology, Wycliffe College, Toronto. Married. Appointments: Teacher, Quebec & Montreal Schools; Missionary Teacher, Moose Lake, Manitoba; Member, Staff, Bishop Tucker College, Mukono, Uganda, 1958-65. Address: P.O. Box 37, Fort Portal, Uganda.

SEBAG, Victor-Meyer, born 22nd October 1897. Journalist; Reporter. Education: Secondary studies. Married, 2 children. Appointments: Journalist, 1914—. Memberships: Administrator Delegate of the daily newspaper 'Le Petit Matin'; French & Overseas Press Syndicate; Press Syndicate of North Africa; Founder & Director of Cultural, Educational & Sports Societies; President, Secretary-General & Treasurer. Publications: contributor to several French, Tunisian, & American publications; has represented Tunisia at several international congresses & has participated in political-scientific missions. Honours: Knight of the Legion of Honour; Grand Officer of Nichan Iftikhar; Officer of Academy; Commandeur de l'Ordre Royal Cherifien Ouissam-Alaouite; Officier de l'Ordre Royal du Cambodge; Knight of the Black Order of Benin; Gold Medal for Physical Education; Medaille de Vermeil du Travail, de la Mutualite, du Merite Social, etc. Address: 5 rue Kemal Attaturk, Tunis, Tunisia.

SEBAGEREKA, Samwiri Kato, born Kampala, Uganda, 9th October 1933. Cost Accountant & Chartered Secretary. Education: Ndejje Junior Secondary School, Uganda; King's College, Budo; College of Commerce, Birmingham, U.K.; University of Birmingham. Personal details: son of Chief Simon Kato, former chief of the Buganda Kingdom; Married, 4 daughters. Appointments: Accountant, Uganda Government, 1961-62; Senior Accountant, East African Community, 1962-64; Assistant Accountant-General, ibid, 1964; Accountant-General, ibid, 1965; Commissioner-General of Income Tax, 1965-69; Financial Director, Export & Import Corporation, Uganda, & Chairman, Mackenzie Dalgety Uganda Ltd., 197)—. Memberships: Hon. Treasurer, Uganda Y.M.C.A.; Mbr., Board of Governors, ibid; Hon. Treasurer, Uganda Professional Centre; A.C.W.A.; F.C.I.S.; Nairobi Rotary Club. Address: Kampala, Uganda.

SEBALU, Lawrence, born Buganda, Uganda, 23rd May, 1931. Member of Parliament; Lawyer. Education: Manilyango College, 1950-51; B.A.(Hons.), Economics & Political Science, Calcutta University, India, 1956; LL.B., Delhi University, 1958. Personal details: son of Isaaca Kyompitira, a local chief; married, 8 children. Appointments: Member of Parliament, 1961; Minister of Economic Development, was responsible for Uganda's 1st Five Year Plan, 1961; Minister of Finance, 1962. Member, Democratic Party, Uganda, 1962. Honours: Knight of St. Gregory, Pope Paul IV, 1969. Address: P.O. Box 2980, Kampala, Uganda.

SEBESO, Gaefalele Geolebale, born Shoshong, 4th August, 1908. Teacher; Member of Parliament. Education: Primary Lower Certificate; Junior Certificate by Correspondence, University Correspondence College, South Africa; Lovedale Institution, Cape Province, 1925-30. Personal details: member of family of hereditary chiefs of the Baphaleng Tribe; married, 1939, 2 sons, re-married, 1958, 1 son, 5 daughters. Appointments: Head Teacher, Shoshong Primary School, 1931-36; Supervisor of Schools, 1937-40 & 1947-51; served in W.W.II, Rank, Sergeant-Major, 1942-46; Subordinate Tribal Authority (Chief's Representative), 1953-70; Member of Parliament, Tswapong South Constituency, Botswana, 1965—; Deputy Speaker, 1966—. Memberships: London Missionary Society now United Congregational Church, 1927—; Mahalapye Branch, Red Cross; Chairman, Bamangwato Development Association; Vice-President, Mahalapye Country Club. Honours: Mentioned in a Despatch for distinguished service, 1946; Presidential Order of Honour by President of Botswana, 1969. Address: P.O. Box 4, Mahalapye, Botswana.

SEBULIBA, Paul S. K., born 13th July, 1938. Medical Practitioner. Education: Primary, Nalugi Mission School, 1946-52; Secondary, St. Mary's College, Kisubi, 1953-57; M.B., Ch.B., Makerere University, Kampala, Uganda, 1958-65; D.C.H., U.K., 1968-70. Married. Appointments as Government Medical Officer, Uganda, 1966—. Memberships: British Medical Association; Uganda Medical Association; Royal College of Physicians of the United Kingdom. Author of chapter, The Economy of a Rural Hospital Hospital in Medical Services in Development Countries. Recipient BMA Prize in Anatomy & Physiology, 1960. Address: Mulago Hospital, P.O. Box 7051, Kampala, Uganda.

SEBUWUFU, Peter Hermit, born November, 1933. Medical Doctor. Education: Makerere University, Kampala, Uganda, 1952-58; Ph.D., Cambridge University, U.K., 1967. Married. Appointments: Medical Intern—S.H.O.—Registrar, Mulago Hospital, Makerere Medical School, Uganda; Lecturer—Senior Lecturer—Reader, Makerere University Medical School; Professor of Anatomy, ibid, 1970. Memberships: F.R.C.S., England; F.R.C.S.E., 1963; Associate, M.R.S.M.; Anatomical Society of Great Britain & Ireland; Association of Surgeons of East Africa. Contributor to scientific publications. Honours: Swinnerton Memorial Prize in Biology; Distinctions in Anatomy & Physiology; May & Baker Prize in Pharmacology; Distinctions in Surgery & Obstetrics; Owen & Keene Gold Medals & Mulgibhai Prize for best medical student of the year. Address: Department of Anatomy, Makerere University, Box 7072, Kampala, Uganda.

SEDDON, Stuary Anthony, born 20th January 1939. Education Officer. Education: Highbury Grammar School, U.K., 1950-57; B.Sc.(Hons.) Zoology, University of Wales, 1957-61; Diploma in Education, University of East Africa, 1963-64. Appointments: Assistant Experimental Officer, Scientific Civil Service, 1961-63; Senior Biology Teacher, Senior Science Master, Makerere College School, Uganda, 1964—; Part-time Lecturer, Department of Education, Makerere University, 1964—. Memberships: Fellow, Zoological Society of London; Association for Science Education. Contributor of scientific papers to professional journals. Address: Makerere College School, P.O. Box 7062, Kampala, Uganda.

SEFAKO, Odilon Tlali, born 22nd November 1933. Civil Servant. Education: Senior Certificate (Commercial); Senior Course in Public Administration, Carleton University, Ottawa, Canada, 1968. Personal details: married, 4 children. Appointments: Clerk, Grade 1, 1955-61; Junior Executive Officer, 1962-63; Accounts Assistant, 1963-65; Executive Officer, Accounts, 1965; Higher Executive Officer, 1965-66; Assistant Secretary, Finance, 1966-69; Chief Collector of Revenue, 1969. Memberships: President, Berea N.R.C. Football Club, 1958; Chairman, Maseru Branch, Civil Servants' Association, 1959-61, 1970-71. Honours: Certificate of Merit in Public Administration, Carleton University, 1968. Address: The Treasury, P.O. Box 401, Maseru, Lesotho.

SEIDMAN, Robert B., born 24th February 1920. Professor of Law. Education: B.A., Harvard University, 1941; LL.B., Columbia University, 1948. Personal details: married to Ann Willcox Seidman. Appointments: Private Law Practice, 1948-62; Senior Lecturer in Law, University of Ghana, 1962-64; Senior Lecturer in Law, University of Lagos, Nigeria, 1964-65; Presidential Professor of Law, University of Ghana, 1966; Visiting Professor of Law, University College, Dar es Salaam, Tanzania, 1968-70; Professor of Law, University of Wisconsin, U.S.A., 1966—. Publications: A Sourcebook of the Criminal Law of Africa, 1966; Law, Order & Power (with W. J. Chambliss), 1970; a number of law review articles. Address: University of Wisconsin, Madison, Wisconsin, U.S.A.

SEKABUNGA, J. G., born 2nd September 1929. Medical Practitioner. Education: King's College, Budo, Uganda, 1946-48; M.B., B.S., Makerere University College, 1949-50; Guy's Hospital Medical School, U.K. Appointments: Medical Officer, Special Grade, 1963; Surgeon, Masaka Hospital, Uganda, 1964; Lecturer in Surgery, Makerere University College Medical School, 1964—. Fellow, Royal College of Surgeons of Edinburgh. Contributor of articles to scientific publications. Address: Makerere Medical School, Kampala, Uganda.

SEKONE, Barke Francois, born 1939. Counseller of Foreign Affairs. Education: Primary, France, 1947-55; Secondary, 1955-62; Higher Studies, Political Science. Married. Appointments: Head of Service, Political & Cultural Affairs, 1967; Director of Political Affairs, 1969.

SEMAMBO, Yusufu Balirwana, born 23rd December 1920. Medical Practitioner. Education: Katikamu Primary School; Mengo Boys' School; King's College, Budo; Makerere University College; St. Andrew's University, U.K.; Dip. Med. (E.A.), 1949; L.M.S. (E.A.), 1954; D.P.H. (St. Andrews), 1959; M.B., Ch.B. (E.A.), 1964. Appointments: Resident, Mulego Hospital, Uganda, 1951-53; Medical Officer, West Nile, Uganda; District Medical Officer, Ankole, Uganda; Principal Medical Officer (H), Uganda; Medical Superintendent, Mulago Hospital. Memberships: Past President, Uganda Medical Association; Medical Adviser, Uganda Red Cross Society; Mengo Hospital Board of Governors. Contributor of papers to professional publications. Address: Box 7051, Kampala, Uganda.

SEMMANDA (Rev. Father) John, born 22nd August 1906. Catholic Priest. University-standard Education in Philosophy & Theology. Appointments include: ordained Priest, 1935; Hospital Chaplain, Jinja Parish, 1937; Army Chaplain, 2nd World War, Jinja, 1939, Bududa, 1941; School Supervisor, Naggalma, 1941, & Mulagi, 1942; Priest, Msambya Parish & Chaplain, Mulago Hospital, 1946; Supervisor, Settlement, Mulago Parish, 1956; City Council, Kampala, 1957; Memberships include: Committee of Inquiry into Juvenile Delinquency, 1957; Probation Committee, Uganda. Honours: Independence Medal, Uganda, 1962. Address: P.O. Box 3807, Kampala, Uganda.

SEMPA, Irene, born 13th September 1914. Housewife. Education: Gayciza High School. Personal details: married, 14 children. Memberships: Voluntary Worker, Mothers' Union; Vice-President, ibid, 1958-1960; Mothers' Leader for 12 years; visited, World Conference, Mothers' Union, England, 1968; Uganda Council of Women; Y.W.C.A. Honours: Certificate, Operation Cross Road (Honorary Cross Roader), 1970. Address: P.O. Box 4533, Kla., Uganda.

SEMPANGI, Frederick Kefa, born Kawuna-Kyagwe, Uganda, 8th October 1939. Painter; Sculptor; Art Historian. Education: Mpumu Primary School, until 1956; B.A., Fine Art, School of Fine Art, Makerere University, 1963-67; M.A.(Distinction), Royal College of Art, London, U.K., 1967-70; Free University of Amsterdam, 1970. Personal details: married to Penina Luggya, a Registered Nurse & Midwife. Memberships: President, Makerere Art Club, 1966; Treasurer, Uganda Students' Organization, U.K. & Eire, 1969-70; Executive Member, Gidion Society, Uganda; Lay Preacher, Uganda Full Gospel Churches. Publications: Illustrator of East Africa Series. Exhibitions: Mural Painting, Lee Abbey Chapel, London, U.K.; Mural Painting, Mitchell Hall, Makerere; Statue for the Uganda Teachers' Assn., Kampala. Recipient of prizes for painting & sculpture. Address: P.O. Box 2560, Kampala, Uganda.

SENAPATI, Mihir Kumar, born 30th December 1925. Surgeon. Education: The Doon School, Dehra Dun, India, 1938-43; Prince of Wales' Medical College, Patna, 1943-48; M.B., B.S. (Patna) Hons. in Physiology & Pathology,

1948; F.R.C.S.(England), 1957; F.R.C.S., (Edin.), 1957. Appointments: House Surgeon & Casualty Officer, Hammersmith Hospital, London, U.K., 1951-53; Surgical Registrar, Kent & Canterbury Hospital, Canterbury, 1953-58; Surgeon, H.M. Overseas Civil Service, Northern Nigeria, 1958-70; Senior Consultant Surgeon, Benue Plateau State, 1970—. Fellow, Association of Surgeons of West Africa. Address: P.M.B. 15, Jos, Benue Plateau State, Nigeria.

SENAPATI, Ranganayaki. Medical Practitioner. Education: Loreto Convent, Lucknow, India, 1928-37; Isabella Thoburn College, Lucknow, 1938-49; M.B., B.S., King George's Medical College, Lucknow, 1940-45. Married. Appointments: Medical Officer, Northern Nigeria, 1959-69; Senior Medical Officer, Jos, Benue Plateau State, Nigeria, 1970. Address: P.M.B. 15, Jos, Benue Plateau State, Nigeria.

SENAYAH, Emmanuel Komla Vinyo, born Adina, Kata District, Volta Region, 17th July 1916. Teacher; Radio Broadcaster. Education: Roman Catholic Primary & Middle School, Threctown, Denu, Volta Region; Achimota Teacher Training College, Ghana; General Training Course, Broadcasting Technique, BBC, London, U.K. Appointments: Presentation Manager, i/c Operational & Announcing Staff Radio, Ghana Broadcasting Corporation; Assistant Head, National Service, i/c Broadcasting Programmes & Planning; Head, ibid; Ag. Director, Sound Broadcasting, i/c Policy, National & External Services. Memberships: 1st Vice-President, Board of Trustees, Knights of St. John; Local Branch President, Our Lady of Perpetual Confraternity; General President, ibid, Accra District. Address: P.O. Box 1989, Accra, Ghana.

SENDAGIRE, Rogers Willy George, born Wamala Village, Kyadondo, Uganda, 12th January 1945. Assistant Agricultural Officer. Education: Wamala Nursery School, 1950-51; Mengo Junior School, 1952-60; East African Commercial School, 1961-62; Bugema Missionary College, 1963-65; Diploma in Tropical Agriculture, Bukalasa Agricultural College, 1966-68. Appointments: Assistant Agricultural Officer, East Mengo District, Mukono. Memberships: Uganda Agricultural Society; Uganda Library Service; Bukalasa Mountain Club. Address: Department of Agriculture, East Mengo District, Box 72, Mukono, Uganda.

SENGENDO, Francis, born 20th October 1935. Lawyer; University Administrator. Education: 9 years' Formal Education, later Private Studies leading to University Entrance LL.B., 1968. Personal details: married to a Health Visitor, 1 son, 1 daughter. Appointments: Advocate, High Court of Uganda; Medical Dresser, 1955-56; Trainee Medical Assistant, 1956-59; Medical Assistant, Ministry of Health, 1959-65; Administrative Assistant (Personnel), Makerere University, Kampala, 1968—. Member of Denning Law Society, University College, Dar es Salaam, Tanzania. Publications: Life of Livingstone (book), 1967. Address: P.O. Box 30445, Kampala, Uganda.

SENGHOR, Blaise, born Joal, Senegal, 30th May 1932. Diplomat; Film Producer. Education: Secondary Studies, Lycée Wan Voltenhoven; Bacc., Philosophy & Letters; Lycée de Dakar, Senegal, 1945-51; C.E.L.G., University of Dakar, 1953; Higher Studies, Lycée Louis Le Grand, Paris, France, 1953-54; Licensed in Letters, French, Latin, & Greek, Faculty of Letters & Humanities, Paris, 1954-57; Diploma of Higher Studies in Languages & Classical Literature (Medieval French Philology), 1957-58; Diploma of Production, Institute of Higher Cinematographic Studies, 1958-60. Appointments: Producer of Advertising Films, Films Pierre Remont, Paris, 1960-61; Assistant Producer for Dramatic Transmissions, ORTF; Founder, Film Production Society, Union Cinematographique Africaine, 1961; Technical Adviser, Senegal Ministry of Information on questions of cinematography & television, 1962; Adviser & Permanent Deputy Delegate to Embassy of Senegal in France, responsible for relations with UNESCO, 1965; Permanent Delegate of Senegal to UNESCO, 1968; Minister Plenipotentiary, 1969; elected to the Executive Council of UNESCO, 1970; Delegate to various conferences & international meetings on cinema & television, e.g. Les Moyens d'information en Afrique, UNESCO, Paris, 1962; 2nd Congress of the European Union of Radiodiffusion, Tokyo, Japan; Round Table on African & Arabic Cinema, Rome, Italy, 1965 & 1966; 3rd Congress, ibid, Paris, France, 1967; Representative of Senegal at various cinematographic festivals, e.g. Montreal, Canada, 1961; Berlin, Germany, 1962; Karlovy-Vary, 1963; Moscow, 1964; Leipzig, Germany, 1965; Festival de Cannes, 1962, 1964, 1965, & 1966. Memberships include: Jury cinematographique au ler Festival mondial des Arts Negres, 1966; President, du jury de ler festival du film d'expression française de Dinard, 1969; President, Association for the Promotion of African Cinema; Deputy Head, Senegal Delegation to the 15th Session of the General Conference of UNESCO; Executive Council, 1970; Senegal Delegate to the 30th & 31st Conferences of Public Instruction, Geneva, Switzerland & to the meetings of the International Council of Education, 1966-67, 1968-69; Senegal Representative to the Committee of Governmental Experts for the Prevention of the Import, Export & Transferral of Illegally owned Property of Cultural Wealth, UNESCO, 1970. Honours: Ours d'argent du court metrage au Festival de Berlin, 1962; Grande Medaille d'argent de la Ville de Paris, 1962; Officer of the National Order of French Merit, 1969. Address: Permanent Delegation of Senegal to UNESCO, 32 rue de la Tour, Paris XVIe, France.

SENNOGA, George Wilson, born 23rd March 1936. Teacher. Education: Secondary School until 1954; Science & Mathematics, Makerere University, Kampala, Uganda, 1955-57; Diploma Course in Education, ibid, 1957-59; B.A., Boston University, College of Liberal Arts, U.S.A., 1961-63; Dip. Ed., 1959. Personal details: married, 4 children. Appointments: Teacher, Makerere College Demonstration School, 1959-61; Teacher, ibid, & part-time Lecturer, Faculty of Education, 1963-65; Education

Officer (Planning) in the former Buganda Government, 1965-66; Education Officer, Statistics, Ministry of Education in the Central Government, 1966—. Memberships: Uganda Y.M.C.A.; Uganda Teachers' Assn.; Uganda Science Teachers' Assn., 1963-65. Publications: Educational Statistics (Ministry of Education), 1966, 1967. Address: P.O. Box 7063, Kampala, Uganda.

SENTAMU, John B. K., born Kimbugu, Mawokota County, Uganda, 1909. Teacher. Education: Teacher Training, Makerere. Married, 14 children. Appointments include: Headmaster, Budaka Primary School, 1940; Assistant Headmaster, Rubaga Secondary School, 1946-65; Assistant Head Teacher, 1969. President, Uganda Teachers' Association, 1949-53; Vice-President, ibid, 1955-61; President, 1962-64; Vice-President, 1965-66; currently, General Treasurer; Board of Governors, Uganda Teachers' College, Kyandeogo, 1959-63; ibid, Buloba College, 1963—; Director, Uganda Development Corporation, 1963—; Trustee, Uganda Teachers' Association, 1965—. Address: Kirinnya, P.O. Box 3397, Kampala, Uganda.

SENTONGO, David S. N., born 2nd June 1932. Educator. Education: Nyahascera Secondary School; Makerere University, Uganda; Ohio State University, U.S.A.; University of Pittsburgh; B.A., M.Sc., Dip. Ed. Personal details: married, 4 children. Appointments: Schoolteacher, King's College, Budo; Assistant Secretary, Ministry of Education; Assistant Registrar, Makerere University; Deputy Chief Education Officer. Memberships: Y.M.C.A.; Charter Member, Kampala City Lions Club. Publications: Modern Geographies for Uganda; My First Atlas for Uganda. Address: P.O. Box 7063, Kampala, Uganda.

SENTONGO, Edward Steven, born 15th December 1938. Electrical Engineer. Education: Namirembe Boys' School, 1949-53; Makerere College School, 1954-59; 'A'-Level, Makerere University College, 1960-62; B.Sc.(Eng.), 1962-65; Graduate Training in U.K., 1965-67. Personal details: married, 2 children. Appointments: Junior Engineer, Uganda Electricity Board, 1967; Assistant Engineer, 1968; Operation Engineer, 1969. Memberships: Associate, I.E.E.; Graduate Member, E.A.I.E.E. Address: P.O. Box 7059, Kampala, Uganda.

SERPELL, Robert, born 5th May 1944. Lecturer in Psychology. Education: B.A. (Psychology & Philosophy), Oxford University, U.K., 1965; D.Phil.(Experimental Psychology), University of Sussex, 1969. Appointments: Research Fellow, Human Development Research Unit, Institute for Social Research, University of Zambia, 1965-68; Lecturer, University of Zambia, 1969—. Publications include: The influence of language, education & culture on attentional preference between colour & form (Int.Jrnl.Psychol.), 1969; Attention theory, colour-form preference, second language & copying orientation (African Soc. Rsch.), 1970; Language, tribe, & race in Zambia (Race Today), 1970. Address: University of Zambia, P.O. Box 2379, Lusaka, Zambia.

SERUMAGA, William, born 23rd August 1938. Medical Illustrator. Education: Chadwick Memorial School, Entebbe, Uganda, 1946-51; Cambridge School Certificate, King's College, Budo, 1952-57; Certificate in Fine Art, Makerere University College, 1958-60; Diploma in Fine Art, ibid, 1960-62; Course in Medical Illustration, St. Bartholomew's Medical College & Hospital, U.K., 1962-64; Diploma of Membership, Medical Artists' Association of Great Britain, 1966. Appointments: Medical Illustrator, Medical School, Kampala, Uganda, 1964—; Head of Department, Medical Illustration, 1965—. Memberships: Political Society; Boy Scouts; Secretary, Domus Society, 1957; Secretary & Treasurer, Makerere Association Football Club, 1960-62; Associate, Institute of Medical & Biological Illustration. Contributor of illustrations to scientific books & articles. Honours: Shell Geography Prize, 1957. Address: Medical School, P.O. Box 7072, Kampala, Uganda.

SEWANYANA, Samuel-Musoke, born 24th October 1938. Accountant. Education: Mityana Secondary School; Overseas Cambridge School Certificate, King's College, Buddo, Uganda, 1956; 6 months' training in public accounts & auditing, London, U.K. Married, 1 son, 2 daughters. Appointments: Clerical Officer, 1958-61; Executive Officer, 1962-64; Higher Executive Officer, 1964-67; Senior Executive Officer, 1967—. Address: c/o P.O. Box 7037, Kampala, Uganda.

SEYE, Assane, born 20th February 1915. First President of the Supreme Court of Mali, Bamako. Education: Diploma, Administrative & Judicial Section, Ecole Normale William Ponty, 1937. Married, 9 children. Appointments: Secretary, Bamako, 1938-51; Registrar-in-Chief, Court of Appeal, Bamako, 1952-54; Judge of the Peace of San, Deputy to the Prefect of San, 1958-59; Councillor, Court of Appeal & Member, Constitutional Court, 1960; Technical Adviser, Ministry of Justice, Director of Cabinet, 1961-68; President, Supreme Court, 1969—. Memberships: President of the Red Cross of Mali. Publications: Etudes Juridiques. Honours: Gold Medal, Independence of Mali; Officer of the National Order of Mali; Officer of the National Order of Senegal; Knight of the Black Star of Benin. Address: c/o the Supreme Court of Mali, Bamako, Mali.

SEZI, Charles L., born 6th June, 1936. Consultant Physician. Education: L.M.S.(E.A.), 1962; M.B., Ch.B. (E.A.), 1964; M.R.C.P. (Edinburgh), 1968; D.T.M.&H.(Eng.), 1966. Appointments: Medical Officer, Uganda Government, 1963-68; Medical Officer, Special Grade, 1968-70; Consultant Physician, 1970—. Member, Uganda Medical Association. Recipient, Lehmann Prize, Medicine, 1962. Address: New Mulago Hospital, Box 7051, Kampala, Uganda.

SHAABAN, Mohamed, born 7th December 1928. Physician. Education: M.D., Faculty of Medicine, Lyon, France. Appointments: Doctor, Al Mouassat Hospital, Alexandria, U.A.R., 1960; ibid, Ministry of Public Health, Morocco, 1961. Address: 15 rue d'Erymanthe, Polo, Casablanca, Morocco.

SHAH, Harsuklal Lavji, born 24th March 1934. Chartered Architect. Education: Government Indian Central School, Dar es Salaam, Tanzania; The Polytechnic, Regent Street, London, U.K.; Dip. Arch. Married, 1 daughter. Appointments: Member, Architects & Quantity Surveyors Registration Board, Tanzania; Member, Sub-Committee on Metrication, East African Community. Memberships: Associate, Royal Institute of British Architects; Associate, East African Institute of Architects. Address: 11 City Drive, P.O. Box 1971, Dar es Salaam, Tanzania.

SHAH, Kapoor Jivraj, born 23rd September 1939. Certified Accountant. Education: Senior Cambridge Certificate; B.Com.(Hons.); A.A.C.C.A. Married, 2 children. Appointments: Accounting Assistant; Assistant Accountant. Memberships. Attendance Committee, Lions Club, Nairobi; Examination Sub-Committee, Association of Accountants in East Africa. Address: P.O. Box 1534, Nairobi, Kenya.

SHAH, Narendrakumar, born India, 3rd May 1931. Accountant & Auditor. Education: B.Com.; F.I.C.A.; F.E.A.A.; F.R.E.S.; F.E.A.E.; F.E.A.S.(London). Married. Appointments: came to East Africa, 1951; worked with Chartered Accountants Firm, 1951-64; Chief Accountant with Government, 1964-69; currently Chief Accountant, Impressa Del Benaco S.P.A., Civil Engineering Contractors, Kampala, Uganda. Memberships: Chief Treasurer, Sanatan Dharma Mandal, Kampala; Chief Treasurer, Parent-Teacher Association, Shimani Primary School; Auditor, Parent-Teacher Association, Kalolo Secondary School. Address: P.O. Box 4757, Kampala, Uganda.

SHAH, Syed Mohamedali, born 11th June 1928. Accountancy Assistant. Education: Senior Secondary IV; studied many languages. Personal details: married, 2 sons, 2 daughters. Appointments: Accountancy Assistant, Head Office, Uganda Electricity Board, Kampala. Hon. Secretary, Muslim Sports Club, Kampala for 12 years. Address: P.O. Box 7059, Kampala, Uganda.

SHAH, Vinodray Raishi, born 21st January 1943. Physician. Education: Senior Secondary School, Mbale, Uganda; M.B., Ch.B., Makerere College Medical School, University of East Africa, Kampala. Appointments: Houseman, Medicine & Surgery, Mulago Hospital, Kampala; Senior House Officer, Casualty & Orthopaedics, Crickfield Hospital, Sussex, U.K.; Senior House Officer, General Surgery, Hove General Hospital, Sussex. Address: P.O. Box 156, Mbale, Uganda.

SHAIKH, Ziyauddin Qamaruddin, born 9th January 1924. Physician. Education: Anglo-Urdu High School, Poona, India, 1933-40; Nowrosejeo Wadia College, Poona, 1940-42; M.B., B.S., Grant Medical College, Bombay, 1942-48; D.P.H., Royal Institute of Public Health & Hygiene, London, U.K., 1958; D.I.H., ibid, 1959; D.T.M.&H., School of Tropical Medicine, Liverpool, 1959. Appointments: Assistant Surgeon, Medical Services of Pakistan Western Railways, 1948-60; Assistant Medical Officer, 1961-62; Medical Officer of Health, Government of Northern Nigeria, 1962-63; Acting Principal, Medical Auxiliaries Training School, Kaduna, Nigeria, 1963-65; Senior/Principal Health Officer in Charge, Rural Health Services, Ministry of Health, Government of Northern Nigeria, 1966-68; Principal, Medical Auxiliaries Training School, Kaduna, 1968-69; Chief Medical Officer, Ministry of Health & Social Welfare, North-Central State, Kaduna, 1970—. Fellow, Royal Society of Public Health & Hygiene, London. Publications: Standard Treatment Book for Dispensaries, 1965; Annual reports for Ministry of Health, Northern Nigeria, 1965, 1966. Address: Ministry of Health & Social Welfare, North-Central State, Kaduna, Nigeria.

SHAMSUDDIN, Muhammad, born 1st July 1911. Public Health Administrator. Education: B.Sc., M.B., B.S., B.S.Sc., Madras, India; D.P.H., London, U.K., 1947. Married, 2 sons, 1 daughter. Appointments include: Medical Officer, Madras, India, 1940-42; Assistant Health Officer, ibid, 1942-48; Health Officer, Government Colonies, Karachi, Pakistan, 1948-50; Assistant Director-General, Health, Ministry of Health, Government of Pakistan, 1950-63; Officer on Special Duty—Chief of Health Section, Central Planning Commission, Karachi, 1954-63; WHO Public Health Adviser, Saudi Arabia, 1963-65; ibid, Northern Nigeria, 1966—. Participant in numerous international public health conferences. Member, Rotary Club, Karachi. Publications: Health Conditions in Saudi Arabia—Observations & Recommendations; Health Conditions During Hajj Pilgrimage, 1955. Address: P.O. Box 418, Kaduna, Nigeria.

SHANNON, John Daniel, born 11th March 1927. Telecommunications Engineer. Education: John Watson's School, Edinburgh, U.K., 1936-42; Daniel Stewart's College, Edinburgh, 1942-44; Oxford University, 1944-45; Grad. I.E.E., 1953, A.M. (now M.) I.E.E., 1962; Grad. I.E.R.E., 1954; A.M. (now M.) I.E.R.E., 1958. Appointments: Technical Watchkeeper, Cable & Wireless Ltd., 1950-53; Assistant Superintendent (Radio), Uganda Police, 1954-57; Assistant Engineer, Nigerian Maintenance Service, Marconi Co., 1957-58; Area Engineer, ibid, 1959-60; Assistant Controller, 1960-62; Senior Executive Engineer, East African Posts & Telecommunications, 1963-65; Principal Executive Engineer, ibid, 1965—. Member, Royal Overseas League. Address: c/o Royal Bank of Scotland, 42 St. Andrew's Square, Edinburgh EH2 2YE, U.K.

SHAPER, Andrew Gerald, born 9th August 1927. Physician. Education: M.B., Ch.B.; F.R.C.P.(London); M.R.C.Path.; D.T.M.&H. Appointments: Lecturer, Senior Lecturer, Reader, & Professor, Makerere University College Medical School, Uganda, 1957-59; Member, Scientific Staff, Medical Research Council, London, U.K. Memberships: Chairman, Council on Cardiomyopathics, International Society of Cardiology; WHO Expert, Advisory Panel on Cardiovascular Diseases; British Cardiac Society; International Epidemiological Association. Publications: Introduction to the Cardiomyopathics (ed.), 1969; Blood Pressure &

Hypertension in Africa (E.A.Med.J.), 1969; Companion to Medical Studies in East Africa (ed.) (Brit.Med.J.), 1970. Honours: Milne Medal in Tropical Medicine (Liverpool), 1953. Address: M.R.C. Social Medicine Research Unit, London School of Hygiene & Tropical Medicine, Keppel St., London W.C.1, U.K.

SHARIF SALIM, Dosi, born Bukoba, Tanzania, 1st July 1920. Administrator. Education: Secondary School, Zanzibar, 1930-40; University College, Dar es Salaam, 1965-66. Married, 22 children. Appointments: Clerk, Government Service, 1940; served with Army attaining rank of S./Sergeant, 1940-45; rejoined Civil Service, 1946; Assistant District Officer, 1960. Memberships: Bakwata (Muslim Union of Tanzania); Scouts; Football Association; Tanzania Legion; Lions Club. Honours: Prize, Swahili Competition, Inter-territorial Language Committee of East Africa, 1939; Africa Star, War Medal; Defence Medal; Coronation Medal with Certificate. Address: P.O. Box 320, Shinyanga, Tanzania.

SHARMA, Naresh Kumar, born 13th April 1933. Teacher. Education: Cambridge School Certificate, 1948; Teachers' Certificate, Government Teachers' Training College, Nairobi, Kenya, 1951-52; Teaching of English as a Foreign Language, University of Bristol, 1960-61. Married, 2 children. Currently, Headmaster, Main Street Primary School, Jinja, Uganda. Memberships: Chairman, Nile Round Table, Jinja, 1970-71; Deputy Chief Commissioner, Scouts, Uganda; Founder Member, Board of Directors, Jinja Y.M.C.A.; Executive Committee, Central Council of Y.M.C.A.s, Uganda; Vice-Chairman, Busoga Sports Council; Government Housing Committee, Jinja. Honours: Uganda Independence Medal, 1962; Scout Medal of Merit, 1967; Scout Long Service Award, 1970. Address: Main Street Primary School, P.O. Box 784, Jinja, Uganda.

SHARPE (Rev.) Kenneth Henry, born Sussex, U.K., 29th March 1920. Clerk in Holy Orders. Education: Varndean, Brighton, U.K.; Rochester Theological College. Personal details: married to Mary Swabey, 1 son, 1 daughter. Appointments: Schools Administrator, Eastern Province, Uganda, 1949-54; Diocesan Secretary, Treasurer, Upper Nile Diocese, 1954-60; Mbale Diocese, 1960-64; Chairman, Canon Law Constitution Commission, Church of Uganda, Chairman, Liturgical Committee, 1967; Commissary to the Archbishop of Uganda, Rwanda, & Burundi; Provincial Treasurer, Church of Uganda, 1964-69; Vicar of the Mau, 1969—; Chairman, Uganda Bookshop, 1964-69. Memberships: Uganda Society; Hon. Correspondent for Uganda, Royal Commonwealth Society; Alcuin Club; Anglican Society; Turi Club; Associate Institute of Bankers, 1943. Address: P.O. Box 171, Molo, Kenya.

SHAYO, Anase Geoffrey Isaac, born 13th April 1934. Civil Engineer. Education: Old Moshi Secondary School, Moshi, Tanzania, 1946-51; Tabora Boys' Secondary School, Tabora, 1952-53; B.Sc.(Hons.), London, Makerere University College, Kampala, Uganda, 1954-58; B.Sc.(London), Civil Engineering, Brighton College of Technology, U.K., 1958-61. Personal details: married to Joyceline Nderanosi, a Teacher. Appointments: Engineer with firm of consultants, London, U.K., 1961-65; Civil Servant, Tanzania Government, 1965; Executive Engineer, Senior Executive Engineer, Assistant Director, currently Acting Director of Buildings, Ministry of Communications, Transport, & Labour. Memberships: President, Tanzania Student Assn. of U.K. & Ireland, 1963-65; Institution of Civil Engineers (U.K.); East African Institution of Engineers; Vice-Chairman, Tanzania Division, ibid; Tanzania Engineers' Registration Board. Publications: various papers on engineering. Honours: Archer-Sturrock Prize, Makerere College, 1956; Shell Company Exhibition, ibid, 1957-58; Shell Company Prize, 1958. Address: P.O. Box 104, Ministry of Communications, Transport, & Labour, Dar es Salaam, Tanzania.

SHEFFIELD, Frances Marion Lina, born 3rd February* 1904. Civil Servant; Plant Pathologist. Education: Varndean School, Brighton, U.K.; B.Sc., King's College, University of London, 1925; M.Sc., ibid, 1927; Ph.D., 1929; D.Sc., 1939. Appointments: Research Assistant & Demonstrator, King's College, London, 1927-29; Virus Cytologist, Rothamsted Experimental Station, 1929-49; seconded to Zambia Government to study diseases of cloves, 1947-51; Research Officer, East African Agriculture & Forestry Research Organization, 1949-70; Senior Principal Scientific Officer, 1957-70; Head, Division of Plant Pathology, 1963-68. Memberships: Society for General Microbiology; Association for Applied Biology; Genetical Society; Royal Microscopical Society. Author of numerous scientific papers concerned with plant virology, cytology & anatomy, & quarantine. Address: East African Agriculture & Forestry Research Organization, P.O. Box 30148, Nairobi, Kenya.

SHEHU, Umaru, born 8th December 1930. Doctor of Medicine. Education: Maiduguri, 1935-42; Kaduna College, Kaduna, 1944-47; University College, Ibadan, Nigeria, 1948-53; University of Liverpool, U.K., 1953-56, 1966-67; M.B., B.S.; L.R.C.P.; M.R.C.S.; D.P.H. Appointments: Medical Officer, 1957-63; Senior Medical Officer, 1963-64; Principal Medical Officer, 1964-65; Assistant Chief Medical Officer, 1965-67; Chief Medical Officer, Preventive Services Division, 1967-68; Reader & Head, Dept. of Community Medicine, Ahmadu Bello University, 1968—; Director, Institute of Health, ibid, 1969—; Acting Vice-Chancellor, 1969; Temporary Adviser, W.H.O. Memberships: Nigeria Medical Assn.; Nigeria Medical Council; Expert Committee on Epidemiology, National Council on Health; Committee on Education & Training of Health Post Officers, ibid; Kainji Lake Research Project, Public Health Section; Medical Advisory Committee, Family Planning Council of Nigeria. Publications: The Solution to the Problems of the Medical Assistant in Developing Countries; Contributor to Journal of the Nigeria Medical Assn. Address: Institute of Health, Ahmadu Bello University, Zaria, Nigeria.

SHEPHERD, Joseph Jarvis, born 6th October 1928. Surgeon. Education: Foundation Scholar,

Manchester Grammar School, U.K.; M.B., Ch.B., University of Manchester, 1952; M.D., ibid, 1967; F.R.C.S., Edinburgh, 1959. Appointments: Assistant Lecturer in Anatomy, University of Glasgow; Lecturer & Senior Lecturer in Surgery, Makerere University College, Kampala, Uganda. Fellow, Association of Surgeons of East Africa. Contributor to: Companion of Surgery in Africa, edited by W. W. Davey; Lancet; British Medical Journal; British Journal of Surgery; American Journal of Digestive Disease, etc., mainly on gastroenterology. Address: Dept. of Surgery, P.O. Box 7072, Kampala, Uganda.

SHERIDAN (Sir) Dermot Joseph, born 3rd October 1914. Judge. Education: Downside School, U.K., 1925-33; B.A., 1st Class Hons., Pembroke College, Cambridge, 1935; Barrister-at-Law, Middle Temple, London, 1935. Personal details: son of Sir Joseph Sheridan, Chief Justice of Kenya. Appointments: Resident Magistrate, Uganda, 1942; Crown Counsel, Uganda, 1948; Director of Public Prosecutions, Gold Coast, 1951; Puisne Judge, Uganda, 1955; Chief Justice, Uganda, 1970. Memberships: M.C.C.; East India & Sports Club, London; Kampala Club. Honours: C.M.G. Address: P.O. Box 7085, Kampala, Uganda.

SHERMAN, George Flamma, born Rivercess, Grand Bassa County, Liberia, 28th August 1913. Educationalist, Diplomat, Lawyer. Education: St. Thomas' School, College of West Africa; Liberia College; studied Law & admitted to the Bar, County of Grand Bassa, 1953. Personal details: son of Gleedoh & Joseph Flama Sherman, first Methodist Priest, Rivercess District, Deputy Coastwise Commissioner, Grand Bassa County, Liberia, grandson of King George Flamma of Rivercess; married Miss Victoria Reeves, daughter of Hon. C. A. Reeves, Grand Bassa County, 13th July 1945, 1 son, 5 daughters. Appointments include: Teacher, Bassa High School, 1939-41; Principal, 1942-44; Supervisor of Schools, 1944-52; Governor, Bassa County, 1952-56; Asst. Secretary, Public Works & Utilities, 1956; Consul-General, London, 1956-60; Ambassador to Ghana, 1960—; Chief, Special Mission to the Congo, 1960-61; Member U.N. Conciliation Commission to the Congo, Nov. 1960-61; Dean of Diplomatic Corps, 1963—; Secretary of Education, 1970—; Major, Armed Forces of Liberia, D.S.O. Memberships: St. John's Church, Buchanan; Master Mason, Past Master, United Brothers of Friendship; Bar Association, Grand Bassa; Youngmen Literary Club of Monrovia. Honours, Prizes, etc: Knight Official, Order of African Redemption, 1947; Grand Commander, Star of Africa, 1954; Grand Commander, Venerable Order of the Pioneers, 1955; Knight of the Grand Bath, Order of African Redemption, 1962; Fellow, Institute of Commerce (London), 1959; Grand Medal of Honour (Republic of Ghana), 1968. Address: Secretary of Education, R.L. Department of Education, Monrovia, Liberia.

SHERWOOD, Robyn Lansdowne, born 9th May 1924. Schoolmaster; Education Officer. Education: Swansea Grammar School; B.A.(Hons.), Geography, University College of Wales, Aberystwyth, 1946-49; University College of Swansea; Teaching Diploma, University of Wales, 1950. Personal details: married to Gwyneth Mary Hopkin, 3 sons, 1 daughter. Appointments: War Service; Sergeant Pilot R.A.F.V.R., 1944-46; Sub-Lieutentnat Pilot, R.N.V.R., 1951-54; Lieutenant Pilot, R.N. (Reserve); Assistant Geography & P.E. Master, Abbey Grammar School, Ramsey, Huntingdon, 1950-53, 1957-61; Master, Government Secondary School, Gulu; Head, Geography & Games, Sir Samuel Baker School, Gulu; Acting Headmaster, ibid; Head of Geography & Games, Nyakasura School, Fort Portal; ibid, H.H. Aga Khan School, Kampala, Uganda; Head of Geography & Director of Studies, Kibuli Secondary School, Kampala. Memberships: Committee, Uganda Geographical Association, 1963; Uganda 'Kob', 1956—; Sports Member, Kampala Sports Club, 1970; Ordinary Member, Uganda Golf Club, 1963—. Publications: Physical Education & Some of its Problems in Uganda Secondary Schools, Journal of Uganda Physical Education Teachers' Association, 1969. Address: P.O. Box 4216, Kampala, Uganda.

SHEWAREGED BESHE (Kegnazmach), born 12th May 1909. Governor of Haikoch & Butajira District in Shoa Province, Ethiopia. Education: Church School, Selale District, Shoa Province. Married 1 son, 7 daughters. Appointments: Soldier during Italian occupation; Sub District Governor; Co-ordinator, Hamle 16th Committee; Director, Ministry of Interior; High Court Judge; Governor of Merhabete District, Shoa Province; Governor, Haikoch & Butajira District, ibid. Memberships: Patriotic Association; Adviser, Road Construction from Alemgena to Welamosodo; ibid, Merhabete District; Chairman & Founder, Development Organization of Haikoch & Butajira District. Honours: Patriotic Medals, 1934; Hailé Selassié I Gold Medal with decoration, 1934; Triumphal Star, 1953; Menelek II Officer decoration, 1958. Address: Governor of Haikoch & Butajira District, Shoa Province, Zuway, Ethiopia.

SHIFARRAW BIZUNEH, born Addis Ababa, Ethiopia, 26th February 1930. Engineer. Education: Intermediate Certificate, College of Engineering, Hailé Selassié I University, Ethiopia, 1954; B.SC.E., University of New Mexico, U.S.A., 1956; Structural Design, University of New Mexico Graduate School, 1957; Economic Development Institute, Washington, 1967. Appointments include: Soils & Concrete Inspector, later Draftsman, New Mexico State Highway Dept., 1957; with Imperial Highway Authority of Ethiopia, 1957-58; Construction Division, Imperial Highway Authority, 1959; Construction Engineer, ibid, 1960-65; Deputy Chief Engineer & Dept. Deputy, 1966; participated in IRF Middle East Regional Conference, 1967; General Projects Course, Economic Development Institute, IBRD, Washington, U.S.A., 1967; Study Tours covering Highway Depts., Road Construction Projects in many countries, 1968; organized, from inception, the First African Highway Conference; Organizing Secretary, later Conference Secretary, ibid, 1969; Acting General Manager of Highways, 1969; Chief Engineer, 1969—. Participant in many

International Missions on Highway Engineering. Memberships include: Board Member, Ethiopian Assn. of Engineers & Architects; American Society of Civil Engineers; American Society of Photogrammetry. Publications: Highway Construction in Ethiopia (paper presented at IRF Regional Middle East Conference in Beirut). Honours: Commander of the Order of Menelek II, 1970. Address: P.O. Box 3455, Addis Ababa, Ethiopia.

SHIJA, Lucia, born November 1942. Community & Regional Planner. Education: Tabora Girls' Secondary School, Tanzania, 1954-62; Makerere College, Kampala, Uganda, 1963-66; University of British Columbia, Canada, 1966-68; B.A., 1966; M.A., 1968. Personal details: married to Dr. J. K. Shija, 1 son. Appointments: Assistant Town Planning Officer, 1966; Town Planning Officer, 1968; Assistant Research Fellow, University of Dar es Salaam, 1970. Address: The University of Dar es Salaam, P.O. Box 35097, Dar es Salaam, Tanzania.

SHITTA-BEY, Sikiru Ayodeji, born Lagos, Nigeria, 26th June 1931. Barrister-at-Law; Solicitor of the Supreme Court of Nigeria. Education: LL.B.(Hons.), King's College, London University, U.K.; B.L., Lincoln's Inn, Council of Legal Education, London. Personal details: great-grandson of the late Mohammed Shitta-Bey, Philanthropist & Head of Muslim Community, Lagos. Appointments: Action Group Member of Parliament for Lagos North Central, 1964-66, when Nigerian Parliament was dissolved by the Military Coup; Director, National Insurance Corporation of Nigeria; Member, Federal Public Accounts Committee. Memberships: Executive Member, Action Group; ibid, Island Club of Nigeria; Nigeria Country Club. Address: Jabita Chambers, 208/212 Yakubu Gowon Street, 3rd Floor, Lagos, Nigeria.

SHLIHTER, Seryei B., born 27th February 1931. Transport Economist. Education: M.A., Moscow State University, U.S.S.R.; Dr. of Sci., ibid, 1965. Married, 2 children. Appointments: Scientific Worker, Research Institute for Complex Transport Problems in Moscow; Transport Economist (Adviser), Ministry of Planning & Social Development, Uganda, 1967—. Author of some 19 publications concerning different fields of transport economics & transport geography. Address: P.O. Box 13, Entebbe, Uganda.

SHOLUBI (Chief) Michael Akin, born Abeokuta, Western State, 10th January 1914. Tailor. Education: St. John's School Aroloya, Lagos, Nigeria; Baptist Boys' High School, Ago-Owu Abeokuta, 1934. Personal details: son of Chief Parakoyi of all Egbas; married to Florence Olayinka Sholubi, 1 son, 3 daughters. Appointments: apprenticed to tailor; own business, 1936—. Tenders from the following departments: The Nigerian Railway; Medical Department; Posts & Telegraphs; Inland Revenue; E.C.N.; Importer & Exporter specializing in Carving & Sculpture. Member of Ancient Shepherds Friendly Society, Manchester, U.K. Address: 50 Tejuoso St., Surulere, Lagos, Nigeria.

SHOTE, David Odulaja, born Ijebu-Ode, Nigeria, 4th April 1902. Retired Civil Servant. Education: St. Saviour's Anglican School, Iwade, Ijebu-Ode, 1913-16; Bethel School, 1917-19; St. Jude's School, Ebute-Metta, 1919; Jehovah Salom School, Phoenix Lane, Lagos, 1921; Apprentice Shoemaker, Certified, 1922-23; Ijebu-Ode Grammar School, 1924; School Leaving Certificate, 1925. Married, with children. Appointments: Teacher, St. Jude's School, 1925; Probationer Clerk, Post & Telegraphs Department, 1926-29; 3rd Class Postal Clerk & Telegraphist, 1929; 2nd Class Clerk, 1933; 1st Class, 1947; Supervisor, 1950; retired on pension, 1959; Pay Office, Headquarters, Lagos City Council, 1961-68. Memberships: active in church affairs, including St. Jude's Church, 1919-23; Ethiopian Church, 1925; Cherubim & Seraphim Church, 1959—; Treasurer, ibid, 1959-64; Secretary, Morning Prayer Band, St. Jude's Church, National Church of Xt (Mount Pisga), Ebute-Metta; Aludura, ibid, Deacon & Chairman, Ibukun-Oluwa Society, 1964-68; Life Member, Bible Society of Nigeria, 1969; Ijebu-Ode Grammar School Old Boys' Association, 1925—; Executive Committee, Lagos Branch, ibid, 1962—. Honours: Gift from Western State Government to commemorate the creation of the 12 states in Nigeria, 1968. Address: Victory Lodge, 42 Ondo Street East, Ebute-Metta, Lagos State, Nigeria.

SHUKLA, Himatlal Manishanker, born Borsad, India, 11th December 1908. Legal Practitioner. Education: B.A., Bombay University, 1931; LL.B., ibid, 1933. Appointments: Vice-President, Hindu Union, Mbale, Uganda, 1957-70; President, Theosophical Society, Mbale, 1966-68. Address: P.O. Box 36, Mbale, Uganda.

SHUMBA, Muzi-Pasi Ephron, born 5th May 1940. University Administrator. Education: Swaswa Junior Primary School, 1947-50; Manyamula Senior Primary School, 1951-53; Loudon Senior Primary School, 1954-56; Dedza Secondary School, 1956-62; B.A.(Hons.), English & History, Makerere University College, Uganda, 1965-66. Personal details: married to Nancy Maggie Musopole, 1 child. Appointments: Administrative Assistant, University of Malawi, 1966; Registrar of a Degree College, 1968-69; Assistant Registrar, 1966—. Former Chairman, Kwacha National Theatre Group, 1967-69. Address: University Office, University of Malawi, P.O. Box 5097, Limbe, Malawi.

SHUNDI-KIZENGA, Gerald Frederick, born 23rd May 1928. Chief Compliance Officer. Education: Standard X, Government Secondary School, Tanga, Tanzania, 1943-48. Married, 5 sons. Appointments: Clerk, Overseas Food Corporation, 1949-53; ibid, Labour Department, 1953-60; Senior Labour Inspector, 1960; Labour Officer & Senior Labour Officer, 1960-64; Chief Compliance Officer, National Provident Fund, Dar es Salaam, 1964—. Memberships: TANU (ruling party); NUTA (trade union); Church Council, Church of England. Address: National Provident Fund, P.O. Box 1322, Dar es Salaam, Tanzania.

SICARD, Fernand, born 22nd September 1909. Advocate; Administrator of Societies; Higher Studies of Law. Appointments: Ancien Batounier; former Vice-President, Constitutional Committee of the Malagasy Republic; former Minister, ibid. Memberships include: The Malagasy Academy. Publications: contributor of articles to reviews. Honours include: Legion of Honour; National Order of the Malagasy Republic.

SIDAMBARAM, Mootoosamy, born 3rd November 1926. Bank Manager. Education: Arsenal Church of England Aided School; Bhujoharry College. Personal details: married, 4 children. Appointments: Director, Development Bank of Mauritius; Member, Development Advisory Council; Member, Electoral Boundary Commission; Electoral Supervisory Commission. Fellowships: Chartered Institute of Secretaries; British Society of Commerce. Memberships: Associate, British Institute of Management; Associate, British Institute of Marketing; First Class Sworn & Exchange Broker; Licentiate, Assn. of Commercial Accountants.

SIDAROUSS, Stephanos I (Paul), born Cairo, Egypt, 22nd February 1904. Coptic Catholic Patriarch of Alexandria; Cardinal of the Roman Catholic Church. Education: Jesuits' College, Cairo; Licence en Droit, Paris, France, 1926; Certificate in Political Sciences, Paris, 1926; Novitiate in Philosophy & Theology, Vincentian's Congregation, Paris-Dax, 1933-39. Appointments: Barrister, Mixed Tribunal, Cairo, Egypt, 1926-32; Teacher, Seminaries of Evreux, Dax, & Beauvais, France, 1939-46; Superior in Egypt of Coptic Catholic Seminary of Tahta, transferred to Tanta & Maadi (nr. Cairo), 1946-58; Bishop Auxiliary of the Patriarchate, 1948—; Patriarch of Alexandria, 1958—; Cardinal, Roman Catholic Church, 1966—. Honours: LL.D., St. John's University, N.Y., U.S.A., 1965 & Vincentian's University, Chicago, 1965. Address: Coptic Catholic Patriarchate, 34 Ibn Sander Street, Cairo, U.A.R.

SIFUEL, Sethiel, born Moshi, Tanzania, 7th June 1935. Civil Engineer. Education: Marangu N.A. School, 1944-49; Tabora & Old Moshi Government Schools, 1950-55; Royal Technical College, Nairobi, Kenya, 1956-58; Hailé Selassié University, Ethiopia, & Roorkee University, 1958-61; 1963-64. Personal details: married, 5 children. Appointments: Civil Servant, 1961-68; Assistant Engineer, 1961-63; Executive Engineer, 1965-68; Senior Executive Engineer, City Council, 1968—; Ag. City Engineer, 1968—. Member of M.E.A.I.E. Address: Dar es Salaam City, P.O. Box 9084, Dar es Salaam, Tanzania.

SIKANARTEY, Tetteh, born 9th April 1927. Medical Practitioner; Psychiatrist. Education: Presbyterian Secondary School until 1945; B.S., Biology & Chemistry, Johnson C. Smith University, N.C., U.S.A., 1949-51; University of Minnesota; M.B., Ch.B., University of Glasgow, U.K., 1953-59; D.P.M., University of Edinburgh, 1964. Personal details: Married to Public Health Nurse, 3 sons, 2 daughters. Appointments: Houseman, Surgical, Paisley Royal Infirmary, Scotland, 1959-60; Houseman, Physician, Larkfield Hospital, Greenock, 1960; Medical Officer, Ghana, 1960; Clinical Assistant, Jordanburn Newe Hospital, Edinburgh; Registrar, Psychiatry, Stratheden Hospital, Cupar; Clinical Attachment, Medicine, Glasgow Western Infirmary; Registrar, Psychiatry, Glasgow Gartneval Hospital; Senior Medical Officer, Psychiatry, Ghana, 1968. Memberships: British Medical Assn.; Royal Medico-Psychological Assn. Publications: As Others See Us—Glasgow View from Ghana; Surveys for Ministry of Health, Ghana: Survey Ghana Northern Region for Establishment of Rural Psychiatric Services, 1968; Survey of the Brong-Ahafo Region, Ghana, for the Establishment of a Community Mental Health Service, 1970. Honours: WHO. Fellowship in Psychiatric Nursing, Denmark, 1969. Address: Ankaful Mental Hospital, P.O. Box 412, Cape Coast, Ghana.

SIKUADE, Olaseni, born 30th January 1934. Physician. Education: Pre-medicine, University of Hull, U.K.; M.B., Ch.B., University of Glasgow; D.P.H., University of Bristol. Personal details: son of Chief Kehide Siknade, The Apesin of Kesi, Abeokuta, Nigeria. Appointments: Medical Officer of Health, Western State, Nigeria, 1962-68; Specialist in Preventive Medicine, Western State, 1968—. Memberships: Nigerian Medical Association; Island Club, Lagos; Yoruba Tennis Club, Lagos. Publications: Background to Maternal & Childhealth Problems in Skeja, Western State. Honours: Losimce Prize, Zoology, 1954. Address: State Hospital, Abeokuta, Western State, Nigeria.

SILVA, Marianne Abimbola, born 17th May 1926. Medical Practitioner. Education: C.M.S. Girls' School, 1931-43; Birkenhead High School, U.K.; M.B., Ch.B., Liverpool University, 1951; D.P.H.(Eng.), 1959; M.P.H., University of Michigan, U.S.A., 1966. Married. Appointments: House appointments in Liverpool, U.K., 1952; Medical Officer, Medical Services, Nigerian Government, 1952-57; School Medical Officer, ibid, 1957-59; Medical Superintendent, Health Centre & Maternity Hospital, 1960-62; Public Health Administration, Federal Ministry of Health, 1962-70. Memberships: Nigerian Red Cross; Y.W.C.A.; Nigerian Association of University Women; National Council of Women's Societies; Ladies' Dining Club; International Women's Society. Address: Federal Ministry of Health, Lagos, Nigeria.

SIMBEYE, Eliad Kapigamawe, born 17th April 1932. Sanitarian. Primary & Secondary Education from 1941-52. Married, 1 son, 3 daughters. Appointments: Assistant Health Inspector, 1956-58; Health Inspector (Training Grade), 1959-60; Health Inspector, 1961-65; Chief Health Officer, 1966—. Member, Royal Society of Health. Address: c/o Ministry of Health & Social Welfare, P.O. Box 9083, Dar es Salaam, Tanzania.

SIMMANCE, Alan James Francis, born Kasauli, India, 26th July, 1928. Government Adviser. Education: B.A.(Hons.), Economics, University of Wales, U.K., 1945-49; Research Student, Economics, University of Manchester, 1949-50; Overseas Service Courses, Balliol College, Oxford University, 1952-53, 1956-57;

Barrister-at-Law, Inner Temple, 1957; F.C.C.S., 1963. Married. Flying Officer, Royal Air Force, 1950-52; District Officer, Kenya, 1953-60; Crown Counsel, Kenya, 1960-62; Vice-Principal & Director of Studies, Kenya Institute of Administration, 1962-63; Principal, ibid, 1963-66; Staff Development Adviser, Government of the Republic of Zambia (Ford Foundation appointment), 1966—. Memberships include: Vice-Chairman, Zambian Institute of Management, 1968; British Institute of Management; East African Management Foundation; President, Senior Civil Servants Association of Kenya, 1963-64; Royal African Society; International African Law Association; African Studies Association of U.K.; American Society for Public Administration. Publications include: Articles in Journal of African Law; Journal of Administration Overseas; East Africa Journal. East African Law Journal, etc. Address: Cabinet Office, P.O. Box 208, Lusaka, Zambia.

SIMON-HART, Ezekiel Iyobu, born 25th June, 1931. Medical Practitioner. Education: Government School, Bonny, Nigeria; Government College, Umuahia; University College, Ibadan; Royal College of Surgeons, Ireland; University College, Dublin; L.R.C.P. & L.R.C.S.I., 1959; D.P.H., 1959; D.P.H., 1966. Appointments: Casualty Officer & Orthopaedic House Surgeon, Ashford Hospital, Kent; House Physician, All Saints' Hospital, Chatham, Kent, Casualty & Orthopaedics, Royal Orthopaedic Hospital, Lagos, Nigerian Civil Service; Medical Officer of Health, Kano International Airport; Medical Superintendent, i/c Creek Hospital, Lagos; Deputy Administrative M.O.H., City of Birmingham, U.K.; Staff Member, Malaria Eradication Division, WHO; currently in general practice, Dublin. Author, The Problems of Organizing Basic Health Services in West Africa (in preparation). Address: 49 Cypress Grove Rd., Templeogue, Dublin 6, Ireland.

SIMO NJONOU, Jean Jacques, born Bangou, Mifi, 1932. Civil Servant. Education: Primary Studies, Protestant Mission of Demko, Baham; CEPE, ibid, Mbo, Bandjoun, 1946; Cours de Selection de Dschang; BEPC, College Moderne, Nkongsamba, 1951. Married, 7 children.. Appointments: Secretaire du Conseil du Contentieux Administratif de la Grande Chancellerie, Cabinet du Haut-Commissaire, 1951-54; studies, Lycée Leclerc, 1954-56; Registrar to the Tribunal of Justice of the Peace, Mbalmayo, 1956-58; Special Secretary to the Prime Minister for External Relations, Cabinet du Haut-Commissaire, 1959; Head of Cabinet to the Minister of Health, 1960; passed Professional Examination of Secretary of Administration, 1961; Diplome d'Agent de Developpement, Institute for the Study of Economic & Social Development; Diploma, Institute of Higher Overseas Studies, 1963-65; Head of Service, Administrative Affairs, Ministry of State responsible for Federal Territorial Administration, Cameroun, 1965; First Deputy Prefect, Abong-Mbang, 1966-67; ibid, Mbouda, 1969; Prefect P.I., Department of Nde, 1969—; Prefect, Department of Lekie, Nonatele, 1969—. Memberships: Deputy Secretary-General, Section of Nyong & Sanaga, Cameroun Union, 1959; President, l'Association des Eleves dudit Etablissement, Institute of Higher Overseas Studies, 1963-64. Honours: 3rd, 2nd & 1st Class of Cameroun Merit. Knight of the Order of Bravery. Address: Prefect, Department Lekie, Monatele, Cameroun.

SIMPLICE, Frederick Abiodun, born lagos, Nigeria, 26th December 1910. Civil Servant. Education: Primary, Methodist Girls' High School, Lagos, 1919-22; Preparatory & Secondary Methodist Boys' High School, Lagos, 1923-30. Personal details: eldest son of the late Elkanah Akintunde Simplice & Comfort Simplice; married Oluremi Abati, 1941, 1 son, 3 daughters. Appointments: 3rd Class Clerk, Lagos Executive Development Board, 1933-34; Supervisor, M/S F. B. Mulford Psimadis Gold Mining Syndicate, 1934-36; Salesman & Accounts Clerk, United Africa Company, Kingsway Stores, Lagos, 1937-38; Mercantile Navy, M/S Elder Dempster Lines, 1941; joined Army, Royal West African Frontier Force, 1941-46; Temporary Clerical Assistant, Post & Telegraphs Department, 1947; 3rd Class Clerk, ibid, 1949; 2nd Class Clerk, 1949; 1st Class Clerk, 1952; Assistant Executive Officer, Accounts, 1959; retired, 1961; Accounting Assistant & Pay Officer, 1962-63; Federal Prisons Headquarters, Lagos, Contract Appointment; Accounting Assistant & Pay Officer, Nigerian Ex-Servicemen Welfare Association, Lagos, 1968—. Memberships: Captain, 1st Eleven Cricket Team, Methodist Boys' High School, Lagos, 1930—; Founding Member, Assistant Captain, Lagos African Cricket Club, 1931-35; Auditor, Lagos Royalist, 1963-64; Senior Member, Island Club, 1961-70. Publications: Contributor to the Federal Nigeria Official Gazette, no. 74, 1969 & no. 14, 1961. Honours: Group Photographs & Book, Accounts Branch, Posts & Telegraphs Department, 1961; War Medal, 2nd World War, 1939-45. Address: Nigerian Ex-Servicemen Welfare Association, Private Mail Bag 12545, Block 3 Alagbon Close, Ikoyi, Lagos, Nigeria.

SIMPORE, Mamadu, born 9th May 1936. Administrator. Education: Licensed in Law; Diploma, Higher National School, Paris, France; Diploma, International Studies. Appointments: Director, Office of Postal & Telecommunications, Upper Volta, 1968-70. Lions Club. Address: Office of P.T., Ouagadougou, Upper Volta.

SIMPSON, Dennis, born 30th November 1926. Electrical Engineer. Education: Acton Church School, U.K.; Acton & Nantwich Grammar Schools; 9 'O' Levels, Nantwich Technical School. Married. Appointments: Military Service, 1942-47; Cheshire Regiment & R.A.S.C., U.K.; Middle East, 1943-47. Appointments: Chargehand, Foreman, North Wales Power Co. Ltd., U.K., 1947-55; District Inspector, Lira, Gulu Area, Uganda Electricity Board, 1955-65; District Engineer, Kampala City, 1970—; Deputy District Manager, 1970—. Memberships: Associate Member, East African Institute of Engineers; City & Guilds (Elec.). Publications: Contributor to Journal of East African Institute of Engineers. Address: P.O. Box 7143, U.E.B., Kampala, Uganda.

SIMPSON, Ffreebairn Lidden, born Sydney, N.S.W., Australia, 11th July 1918. Civil Servant. Education: Westminster School, London; B.A.(Hons.), Modern Languages, Trinity College, Cambridge University, U.K., 1938. Married, 1 son. Appointments: British Diplomatic Service, 1939-48; British Treasury, London, 1948-50; Administrative Officer, Gold Coast, 1950-55; Deputy Colonial Secretary, Mauritius, 1955-61; Permanent Secretary, Ministry of Works & Communications, 1961-66; Permanent Secretary, Premier's Office, 1966-67; Secretary to the Cabinet, Mauritius, 1967—. Memberships: Oxford & Cambridge University Club, London; Mauritius Naval & Military Gymkhana Club; Grand' Baie Yacht Club, Mauritius; Founder Member & past Vice-President, Stella Clavisque Club. Honours: Exhibitioner, Trinity College, Cambridge, 1938; C.M.G., 1967. Address: Prime Minister's Office, Port Louis, Mauritius.

SIMPSON, Rowland Justus, born 22nd July 1911. Land Surveyor. Education: Mfantsipim School, Cape Coast, Ghana, 1928-31; Wesley College, Kumasi, 1932-33; Engineering School, Achimota, 1936-40; University College, London, U.K., 1949-51. Appointments: Teacher, Mfantsipim School, 1933-34; Surveyor, 1940-57; Assistant Director, 1958-59; Deputy Director, 1958; Director, 1960-70. Fellow, Ghana Branch, Royal Institution of Chartered Surveyors.

SIMS, Frederick Henry, born Dorset, U.K., 25th November 1924. Barrister-at-Law; Auditor. Education: Queen Elizabeth's Grammar School, Wimborne, Dorset; College of Law, London; Barrister-at-Law, Lincoln's Inn. Married, 1 daughter. Appointments: Auditor, Ghana, 1947; Auditor, Overseas Audit Department, London, U.K., 1950; Senior Auditor, Federal Government of Nigeria, 1953; Principal Auditor, Western Pacific High Commission, 1955; Principal Auditor, Uganda, 1960; Deputy Controller & Auditor-General, Uganda, 1962; Auditor-General, East African Common Services Organization (now East African Community), 1964—; Chairman, British Solomon Islands Trading Corporation, 1956-58; Secretary, Uganda Fiscal Commission, 1962; Chairman, East African Corporation Economy Commission, 1970. Memberships: Reform Club, London; Nairobi Club. Honours: M.B.E., 1957. Address: Office of the Auditor General, P.O. Box 30468, Nairobi, Kenya.

SIMWINGA, Kenneth C. Solomon, born Tunduma, Mbozi, Tanzania, July, 1930. Community Development Officer. Education: Mbozi Primary School, 1942-47; Senior Government School, Broken Hill, Zambia, & privately, 1948-53; Adult Education Course, Mpwapwa, Tanzania, 1955; Certificate in Social Welfare Studies, Social Welfare Training College, Mindolo, Kitwe, Zambia, 1956-58; University College, Swansea, U.K., 1961-62. Senior Diploma, Social Welfare & Administration. Married, 4 sons, 4 daughters. Appointments include: Social Development Assistant, Government of Tanganyika, 1953-56; Assistant Social Welfare Officer, Mufulira Copper Mines Ltd., Zambia, 1958-59; Social Development Organizer, Williamson Diamonds Ltd., Tanzania, 1959-62; Community Development Officer, ibid, 1962—. Memberships include: TANU; Shinyanga Diamond Controlled Area Board; Chairman, Shinyanga Regional Football Association; National Executive Committee, Football Association of Tanzania; Shinyanga Regional Sports Council; Regional Saba-Saba & Republic Anniversary Celebrations Committee; Life Member, Tanzania National Children's Society; Life Member, Old Students' Association, University College, Swansea; Williamson Recreation Club; Twiga Club; Chairman, Nwadui Social & Cultural Association. Publications include: Founder, Past Editor, Habari za Minadui, local magazine. Address: Williamson Diamonds Ltd., P.O. Box 263, Mwadui, Shinyanga, Tanzania.

SINCLAIR, Bruce Alan, born 5th May 1932. Chartered Civil Engineer; Highway & Traffic Engineer. Education: C.Eng., Loughborough College of Technology, Leicestershire, U.K., 1950-55; Postgraduate Highway Engineering Studies, University of Birmingham, 1958-59. Appointments: Government & Local Government Service, Kenya, 1955-65. Memberships: Institution of Civil Engineers, London; Institution of Highway Engineers, London; Fellow, East African Institution of Engineers. Publications: Straight Crossfall Roads for Rural Areas (J.E.A.Inst.Engs.). Address: P.O. Box 6039, Kampala, Uganda.

SINGH, Chanan, born Ikolaha, Punjab, India, 18th January 1908. Judge. Education: B.Sc.(Hons.,Econ.), London, U.K.; Associate Member, Institute of Transport; Barrister-at-Law, Lincoln's Inn, London. Married, 1 son, 4 daughters. Appointments include: came to Kenya, 1923; Locomotive Fitter, East African Railways, 1923-25; Clerk, ibid, 1925-45; Advocate in Private Practice, 1945-64; Judge, High Court of Kenya, 1964—; Member, Legislative Council, Kenya, 1952-56, 1961-63; Member, Kenya Parliament, 1963-64; Parliamentary Secretary for Constitutional Affairs, 1962-63; Parliamentary Secretary, Prime Minister's Office, 1963-64; served on numerous committees & boards in pre-Independence Kenya; Member, Commission on Maize Industry; Member, Commission on Law of Succession; Member, private political mission to U.K., 1961; attended Constitutional Conferences, 1962 & 1963. Memberships include: Kenya Freedom Party; Secretary, Kenya Indian Congress; President, Indian Association, Nairobi; Royal Economic Society; Indian Gymkhana, Nairobi; President, Law Society of Kenya, 1958; Disciplinary Committee, ibid. Publications include: The Indian Case Against the Immigration Bill, 1947; A Short History of Ghandi Memorial Academy Society, 1964; The Republican Constitution of Kenya (I.C.L.Q.), 1955; Some Notes on the Development of Law in East Africa (E.A.Law J.), 1969; also contributed editorials & editorial notes to the Colonial Times, 1947-62. Address: c/o High Court of Kenya, P.O. Box 30041, Nairobi, Kenya.

SINGH, Gurmukh, born 7th August 1913. Businessman. Education: London Matriculation. Appointments: served as Teacher in Government

Schools, Kenya & Uganda; Founder-Secretary, Sikh Union, Kampala; President, Indian Sports Club; Vice-President, Uganda Cricket Association; President, Indian Merchants' Chamber. Memberships: President, Kampala Merchants' Chamber; Vice-President, Tenant Association, Kampala; Vice-President, Indo-Ugandan Society; President, Parent-Teachers' Associations; Indian Association, Kampala; Treasurer, Central Council of Indian Associations in Uganda. Active in educational & social work & voluntary organizations. Address: P.O. Box 942, Kampala, Uganda.

SINGH, Sant Parkash, born 10th October 1931. Oto-laryngologist. Education: B.Sc., Botany & Zoology, Panjab University, Government College, Hoshiapur, India, 1951; M.B., B.S., Agra University, M.G.M. Medical College, Indore, 1956; F.R.C.S. Edinburgh, U.K., 1964. Married, 2 children. Appointments: Resident House-Surgeon, Royal Infirmary, Edinburgh, 1958-59; Senior Lecturer, E.N.T. Department, University of Ibadan, Nigeria, 1965–. Memberships: Nigeria Medical Association; Association of Surgeons of West Africa. Publications: Malignancy of Paranasal Sinuses in Nigeria (J. Laryng. & Oto.), 1969. Address: E.N.T. Department, University College Hospital, Ibadan, Nigeria.

SINGHOTA, Udham Singh, born 15th August 1929. Teacher. Education: B.Sc., B.T., Punjab University, India, 1950; B.T., Agra University, 1952. Personal details: married to Harbans Kaur, Teacher. Appointments: Science Teacher, Old Kampala School, 1953-63; Head of Physics Department, 1962-64; Head of Physics Dept., Mbale, 1964–. Memberships: International Assn. of Lion Club, Mbale, Uganda; Board of Directors, Organizer & Chairman, Leo Club (Under Lions Club); Hon. Sec., Uganda Hockey Assn., 1961-63; Past Member, Uganda Olympic Committee; Uganda Sports Union; Athletic Assn.; Scout Master. Honours: Colonial Service Medal & Certificate. Address: Senior Secondary School, Bou 982, Mbale, Uganda.

SINGINI, Alya Edson, born 22nd May, 1924. Teacher; Social Worker. Education: Livingstonia High School, 1940-41; Teacher Training, 1942-43; Community Dev., World Assembly of Youth, Ceylon, 1957; Diploma in Social Policy & Administration, Swansea University, U.K., 1960-61; Principles & Practices of Community Development, University of California, Berkeley, U.S.A., 1967. Personal details: son of Group Village Headman; Married. Appointments: Teacher, 1943-45; Clerk, 1945-56; Social Development Assistant, 1956-58; Social Development Officer, 1959; Senior Community Development Officer, 1968; Commissioner for Community Development, Limbe, Malawi, 1970. Memberships: General Secretary, Tanganyika African Government Civil Servants Association; Trustee. Tanganyika Federation of Labour. Author, A Guide to Arnantoglu Community Centre. Address: Community Development Headquarters, P.O. Box 5700, Limbe, Malawi.

SIPENDI, Joseph A. born Kilema Moshi, Tanzania, 15th March 1915. Bishop of Moshi. Education: University Course in Philosophy & Theology D.D. Appointments include: Assistant Parish Priest, 1945-49; Teacher Secondary School, 1949-52; Professor Senior Seminary, 1952-58; Assistant Education Secretary-General Tanzania Episcopal Conference, 1958-61; Education Secretary-General, Tanzania Episcopal Conference, 1961-66; Apostolic Administrator of Zanzibar & Pemba, 1966-68; Bishop of Moshi, 1968. Publications: a number of Swahili prayer & devotional booklets, including Misale Ndogo (a popular manual of prayer and devotions). Address: Bishop's House, P.O. Box 3011, Moshi, Tanzania.

SIRANSY, Toure Souleymane, born 17th September 1936. Director of Cabinet, Ministry of Public Works & Transport. Education: Engineer of Public Works, Paris, France, 1963; Sanitary Engineer, Master of Applied Sciences, Polytechnic School. Appointments: Head, Hydraulic Subdivision, 1963-64; Deputy Director, Hydraulic Commission of the Ivory Coast near the River Niger Commission; Secretary-General, Inter-African Hydraulic Studies Committee; Director of Cabinet, 1970; Co-Director of Project PNUD 25, O.M.S. for the Purification & Provision of Water to the Agglomeration of Abidjan. Address: B.P. V. 6, Abidjan, The Ivory Coast.

SITA RAM, Agalik, born 15th January 1933. Accountant. Education: B.Sc., University of Mysore, India; Railway Audit Service Exam.; Cost Accountancy Training, Institute of Cost & Works Accountants, Calcutta. Personal details: married, 2 children. Appointments: Audit Officer, Western Railway Stores, India, 1964-67; Accountant, to the Government of Tanzania, 1968-70; Teacher, Evening Classes in Accountancy, Dar es Salaam Technical College, 1968–. Honours: J.C. Maharaja's College Centenary Prize, University of Mysore, India, 1953. Address: Govt. Stores, P.O. Box 9150, Dar es Salaam, Tanzania.

SKINNER, Neville John, born 28th June 1929. Professor of Physics. Education: Lowestoft Grammar School, U.K., 1940-47; B.Sc. (1st Class Hons.), Nottingham University, 1947-50; Ph.D., London University, 1956. Married. Appointments include: British Army, 1950-52; Lecturer, University of Ibadan, Nigeria, 1952-62; Professor of Physics, Ahmadu Bello University, Zaria, Nigeria, 1962-69; Professor of Physics, University of Nairobi, Kenya, 1969–. Memberships: Fellow, Institute of Physics, London; American Geophysical Union. Author of some 28 scientific papers in field of ionosphere physics. Address: University of Nairobi, P.O. Box 30197, Nairobi, Kenya.

SLADE, Humphrey, born 4th May 1905. Advocate. Education: Eton College, U.K.; B.A.(Hons.), Jurisprudence, Magdalen College, Oxford; English Solicitors' Final Exam. (Hons.). Married, 4 children. Appointments: practised as Advocate, Kenya, 1930-50; Deputy Judge Advocate-General, East African Forces, 1939-41; Farmer & Company Director, 1950-63; Member, Legislative Council of Kenya, 1952-60; Speaker, Legislative Council & National Assembly, 1960-70; Consultant Advocate,

1970–. Memberships: Vice-Patron & Trustee, Agricultural Society of Kenya; Law Society of Kenya; Vice-Chairman, Child Welfare Society of Kenya; Patron, Mountain Club of Kenya; Executive Committee, Kenya National Council of Social Services, etc. Publications: The Parliament of Kenya. Honours: Elder of the Burning Spear, Kenya, 1968. Address: P.O. Box 30333, Nairobi, Kenya.

SMEDEMA, Cornelis Hendrik, born 24th June 1943. Lecturer. Education: M.Sc., Technological University, Eindhoven, Netherlands. Appointments: Philips Research Laboratory, Eindhoven, 1967-69; Lecturer in Control & Computers, Department of Electrical Engineering, Ahmadu Bello University, Zaria, Nigeria. Memberships: Royal Institution of Engineers, Holland. Address: Department of Electrical Engineering, Ahmadu Bello University, Zaria, Nigeria.

SMIT, Albertus Franciscus Johannes, born Amsterdam, The Netherlands, 28th May 1920. Professor of Geology. Education: University of Amsterdam. Married, 1 son, 3 daughters. Appointments include: Assistant, Geological Institute, University of Amsterdam, 1946-53; Lecturer in Geology, University of Ghana, 1954-61; Senior Lecturer, ibid, 1961-67; Acting Head, Department of Geology, 1964-67; Professor of Geology & Head of Department, 1967–; Visiting Professor, University of Bahia, Brazil, summer, 1962. Memberships: Royal Netherlands Geological & Mining Society; Vice-President, Geological Society of Ghana, 1968-69. Author of several articles on Ghanaian Geology. Address: University of Ghana, P.O. Box 58, Legon, Ghana.

SMITH, Abdullahi Henry Frederick Charles, born Westminster, London, 9th May 1920. Historian. Education: Whitgift Middle (Holy Trinity) School, Croydon, & Selwyn College, Cambridge, U.K.; B.A. (Historical Tripos), 1946; Certificate of Education, 1948; M.A., 1951. Personal details: married Adama Sonya Aliyu, Lagos, 1956; adopted Nigerian Citizenship, 1969. Appointments include: Military Service, British & Indian Armies, U.K. & India, 1940-46; Secondary Schoolmaster, Omdurman, Sudan, 1948-55; Lecturer in History, Univ. College, Ibadan, 1955-62; Associate Prof., 1962; Prof. of History, Ahmadu Bello Univ., Zaria, since 1962. Memberships: Foundation Secretary, Sudan Historical Association, 1953-54; Foundation Secretary, Historical Society of Nigeria, 1955-69; Vice-President, ibid, 1969–. Address: Dept. of History, Ahmadu Bello Univ., Zaria, Nigeria.

SMITH, Alan Howard, born 2nd December 1943. Lawyer; University Lecturer. Education: LL.B., Bristol University, U.K., 1961-64; The College of Law, 1964-65; Solicitor of the Supreme Court. Married, 1 son. Appointments: Solicitor, London, 1967; Lecturer in Law, University of East Africa, University College, Nairobi, Kenya, 1968-70; Lecturer, Hong Kong University, 1970–. Associate Editor, East African Law Journal, 1968-69; assisted with the editing of the East African Law Reports, 1969. Memberships: Law Society of England; Kenya Law Society; Hong Kong Law Society. Contributor of articles to legal journals. Address: Department of Law, Hong Kong University, Hong Kong.

SMITH, Alec, born 19th January 1927. Biologist. Education: King Edward VI Grammar School, Birmingham, U.K., 1938-45; B.Sc. (1st Class Hons.) Zoology, University of Birmingham, 1945-48; Ph.D., University of London, 1948-50. Married, 2 children. Appointments: Research Officer, Entomologist, East Africa Filariasis Research Unit, Tanganyika, 1950-53; Research Officer (Entomologist), East African Institute of Malaria & Vector-borne Diseases, 1954-59; Entomologist, Colonial Pesticides Research Unit, 1959-65; Deputy Director, East African Tropical Pesticides Research Institute, 1965-67; Director, ibid, 1967-70; Director (Special Duties), 1970–. Memberships: President, Arusha Gymkhana Club, Tanzania, 1966-67. Author of over 50 publications on research in East Africa in field of medical entomology. Honours: D.Sc., University of Birmingham, 1965; Colonial Medical Research Studentship, 1948-50. Address: East African Tropical Pesticides Research Institute, E.A. Community, P.O. Box 3024, Arusha, Tanzania.

SMITH, Emmanuel Ademola, born 4th April 1932. Physician. Education: Government Standard 6 Leaving Certificate; Cambridge School Leaving Certificate, Grade 1, 1950; Matriculation, Grade II, 1951; Intermediate B.Sc., University of London, 1954; L.R.C.P., 1961; M.R.C.S., 1961; D.P.H., University of London, 1966; Certificate in Epidemiology & Biostatics, National Communicable Disease Centre, Atlanta, U.S.A., 1966; various seminars & conferences. Married. Appointments: House Surgeon, St. Alfege's Hospital, London, U.K., 1961; House Physician, Horton General Hospital, Banbury, Oxford, 1961-62; Locum Casualty Officer, ibid, 1962; Medical Officer, Federal Ministry of Health, Nigeria, 1963; Medical Officer, General Hospital Ikeja Airport & Southern Police College, 1962-64; Medical Officer, John Street Health Centre, 1964-65; Medical Officer Special Grade (Epidemiologist), 1966; Acting Specialist Epidemiologist, 1968; Associate Editor, Your Health Magazine, 1968; current positions: Specialist Epidemiologist, Federal Ministry of Health, Lagos, 1969; Director, Nigeria Smallpox Eradication Measles Control Programme, 1966; Editor-in-Chief, Your Health Magazine, 1969; Secretary, Expert Committee on Epidemiology, National Council on Health, 1969. Memberships include: W.H.O. Fellow; Nigeria Medical Assn.; British Medical Assn.; Royal Society of Health; Lagos Friendly Society; Society of Health, Nigeria. Author of numerous papers including: Control of Communicable Diseases in Nigeria; Epidemiological Enquiries of Cerebrospinal Meningitis in Nigeria. Address: Federal Ministry of Health, Lagos, Nigeria.

SMITH, Ezekiel Olusoji, born 12th September 1921. Medical Practitioner. Education: Igbobi College, Yaba, Nigeria; Charles University, Prague, Czechoslovakia, 1950-57; Academy of Medicine, Warsaw, Poland, 1957-58; Karl-Marx University, Leipzig, German Democratic Republic, 1958-59. Appointments:

Medical Officer, 1959; Senior Medical Officer, 1967; Principal Medical Officer, 1969. Memberships: Social Secretary, Yoruba Tennis Club, 1966; Financial Secretary, ibid, 1968—. Address: Principal Medical Officer, Creek Hospital, Lagos, Nigeria.

SMITH, Leonard Victor, born 16th August 1918. Chartered Muncipal Treasurer. Education: Hastings Grammar School, Sussex, U.K. Married, 2 sons. Appointments: Accountant, Battle R.D.C., Sussex, U.K.; Accountant, Erith Borough Council, Kent; Auditor, South Eastern Electricity Board; Auditor, Nairobi City Council, Kenya; Assistant County Treasurer, Nairobi County Council; Municipal Treasurer, Nakuru Municipal Council. Memberships: Board, Kenya Accountancy & Secretarial National Examinations Board; Clerk of Course & Committee Member, East African Safari Rally; Committee Member & Director, Automobile Association of East Africa. Author of a series of articles on motor rallying in East Africa in Kenya Weekly News, 1967. Honours: Mentioned in Despatches, British Army, 1945. Address: Deputy General Manager (Commercial), Water & Sewerage Department, Nairobi City Council, P.O. Box 30656, Nairobi, Kenya.

SMITH, Raymond Douglas, born 25th March 1931. Anglican Priest, Tutor. Education: Wesley College, Dublin, Ireland; B.A., Trinity College, Dublin, 1953; M.A., B.D., ibid, 1956. Appointments: Curate Assistant, St. Michael's Church, Belfast; Curate Assistant, St. Patrick's Church, Belfast; Vicar, Nyeti, Kenya; Theological Tutor, St. Paul's United Theological College, Limuru, Kenya. Address: St. Paul's United Theological College, P.O. Limuru, Kenya.

SMITH, Robert, born 12th May 1919. Civil Servant. Education: St. John's Grammar School, Hamilton, Scotland, U.K.; Hamilton Academy; Scottish College of Commerce. Personal details: married, 1 son, 1 daughter. Appointments: Accountant, Lanark County Council, 1939-52; 155th (L.Y.) Field Regt. R.A., 1939-45; Internal Auditor, East Kilbride Development, 1952-56; Accounts Mechanization Officer, Central Electricity & Water Administration, Sudan, 1956-64; Auditor, Uganda Government, 1964-68; Chief Accountant, Dairy Industry Corporation, Uganda, 1968—. Memberships include: Institute of Office Management; Market Research Society; Chairman, Uganda Amateur Swimming Assn.; Royal Life Saving Society; Examiner, Amateur Swimming Assn., U.K.; Life Member, Sudan Club. Address: Dairy Industry Corporation, P.O. Box 7078, Kampala, Uganda.

SMITHSON, Jon Barry, born 5th March 1970. Plant Breeder. Education: Arnold School, Blackpool, U.K., 1948-50; B.Sc.(Hon.), King's College, Newcastle, 1956-60; Ph.D., Wye College, University of London. Married, 2 children. Appointments: Research Officer, Cotton Research Corporation, Tanzania, 1963-69, & Nigeria, 1969—. Member, Genetical Society. Author of, or contributor to, various scientific reports. Address: Institute for Agricultural Research, Samaru, P.M.B. 1044, Zaria, Nigeria.

SMITS, Lucas Gerhardus Alfonsus, born 2nd August 1931. Human Geographer. Education: Cand. Soc. Geog., Univ. of Utrecht, Netherlands, 1953; Dr. Soc. Geog., ibid, 1957. Appointments: Senior Lecturer, Human Geography, University of Botswana, Lesotho, & Swaziland. Memberships: Chairman, Commission for preservation of natural & historical monuments, relics & antiques & the protection of fauna & flora; Lesotho Scientific Association; Botswana Society; S. African Association for the Advancement of Science; S. African Archaeological Society; S. African Geographical Society; Fellow, African Studies Association. Address: University of Botswana, Lesotho, & Swaziland, P.O. Roma, Lesotho.

SNOOK, John, born Bridport, Dorset, U.K., 28th October 1921. Headmaster; Author; Broadcaster. Education: Weymouth College. Appointments: Assistant Master, Alfred Colfox Grammar School, Bridport; Victoria Park High School, Port Elizabeth, South Africa; Westerford High School, Rondebosch, Cape; Headmaster, Herbert Stanley School, Emlembe, Swaziland. Member, Havelock Mine Golf Club. Publications: Swaziland Geography Development & General Information, 1968; series of 26 lectures for radio on various aspects of Swaziland geography; articles & essays in field of African education. Honours: Winner, Swaziland Open Golf Championship. Address: P.O. Box 15, Emlembe, Swaziland.

SOBHI, Mohamed Ibrahim, born Alexandria, U.A.R., 28th March 1925. Civil Engineer. Education: B.Sc., Faculty of Engineering, Cairo University; Course in Transport & Administration, U.S.A. Married, 2 sons, 1 daughter. Appointments: Technical Director of the Cabinet of Minister of Transport; Director-General, Maritime Transport; Under-Secretary, Ministry of Transport; ibid, Ministry of Industry; Chairman, Board of Directors, Postal Organization also Acting Secretary-General, African Postal Union & Director-General, U.A.R. Projects in Mali. Memberships: Board of Directors, Egyptian Philatelic Society; ibid, Heliopolis Sporting Club; numerous international philatelic societies. Author, The Role of Planning in the Promotion of Postal Services. Address: The Postal Organization, Cairo, U.A.R.

SOBOYEJO (Chief) Olujimi Akanbi, Sarumi of Igbore, Abeokuta, born 23rd August 1921. Medical Practitioner. Education: C.M.S. Grammar School, Lagos, Nigeria; Birmingham University Medical School, U.K.; T.D.D. National University of Wales, Cardiff, 1955; Institute of Public Health, London; WHO Fellow, 1959; F.M.C.P.H. Nig., 1970. Married. Appointments: House Surgeon, General Hospital, Birmingham, 1951; House Physician, Walsall General Hospital, 1951; Medical Officer, Nigerian Government, 1952; Specialist-Senior Specialist (T.B.), Federal Ministry of Health, Lagos, 1961-68; Associate Lecturer, Medicine, Lagos University Medical School; WHO Expert Advisory Panel on Tuberculosis, 1965; Administrative Officer, Permanent Secretary, Lagos State Ministry of Health & Social Welfare, 1968. Memberships: D. International Commissioner, Boy Scouts of Nigeria; Member of Board, Y.M.C.A.; Past Secretary, Rotary Club of Lagos; Island Club; Yoruba Tennis Club, Lagos; Ikoyi Club; British Tuberculosis Association, Nigeria Medical Association; Treasurer, Nigeria Medical Council. Author of scientific publications. Address: 4 2nd Avenue, Ikoyi, Lagos, Nigeria.

SODZI, Nathaniel Dotse, born 10th July 1935. Lecturer; Electronic & Electrical Engineer. Education: some National School, Ghana, 1948-50; Grade I School Certificate, Mawuli School, Ho, Ghana, 1951-55; Higher School Certificate, Kumasi College of Technology, 1956-57; B.Sc.(Hons.) Engineering (London), ibid, 1958-61; Graduate Apprenticeship in Radio & Communication Engineering, Marconi Company, Chelmsford, U.K., 1961-63; M.Sc., Information Engineering, Birmingham University, 1963-64; Research Experience, ibid, 1964-65; Ph.D., 1967-68. Married, 2 sons, 1 daughter. Appointments: Assistant Lecturer, University of Science & Technology, Kumasi, Ghana, 1962-65; Lecturer in Electrical Engineering, ibid, 1965-67, 1968-69; Senior Lecturer in Electronic & Electrical Engineering, 1969. Memberships: British Institution of Electrical Engineers; Ghana Institution of Engineers; University Council, Kumasi; University Academic Board, Kumasi; Camps Council, Scripture Union of Ghana; Secretary Convenor, Technical Committee, Keta Reclamation Association. Author of papers in field. Address: Faculty of Engineering, University of Science & Technology, Kumasi, Ghana.

SOFOLA, Samuel Adeniyi, born 22nd September 1926. Physician; Surgeon. Education: Patience Modern High School, Lagos, Nigeria, 1944-46; B.Sc., Howerd University; M.D., Howerd University College of Medicine. Appointments: Private Practitioner. Memberships: African Students' Association of the Americas; Parliamentary Secretary, Phi Beta Kappa, 1954. Publications: When a Philosopher Falls in Love (play), 1956. Honours include: 1st Class Honour, Magna Cum Laude, 1954. Address: 318 Herbert Macauley, Yaba, via Lagos, Nigeria.

SOFOLUWE, George Oluwole, born Ilugun, Abeokuta Province, Nigeria, 24th April 1931. Medical Practitioner & University Lecturer. Education: St. Barnabas School, Ilorin, 1936-41; Cambridge School Certificate, Abeokuta Grammar School, Nigeria, 1942-47; Cambridge Higher School Certificate, University College of Ibadan, 1948-49; Inter-B.Sc.(London), 1950; M.B., B.S. (London), 1952; M.B., Ch.B., University of St. Andrews, Scotland, U.K., 1953-57; D.P.H., ibid, 1960-61; D.I.H., 1965; Certificate in Planning for Health, School of Hygiene, Johns Hopkins University, U.S.A., 1966. Appointments: Pre-Registration House Officer, University College Hospital, Ibadan, Nigeria, 1958; Assistant Medical Officer of Health, Lagos City Council, 1959-61; Assistant Maternity & Child Welfare Officer, ibid, 1959-61; Senior Assistant Medical Officer of Health, 1961-63; Acting Deputy Medical Officer of Health, 1961-63; Acting Medical Officer of Health, 1962; Lecturer in Medicine, Igbo-Ora Community Health Project, 1964; Lecturer, Community Health Department, College of Medicine, University of Lagos, 1964-68; Senior Lecturer, ibid, 1968—; Exchange Lecturer, Makerere Medical School, Kampala, Uganda, 1968; Editorial Committee, Journal of the Society of Health, Nigeria; Editorial Committee, Proceedings of the Joint Health Congress, 1967; Nigeria Radio Doctor, 1965-66; Hon. Medical Officer, Amateur Athletic Association of Nigeria; Hon. Director, Society of Health, 1966-67; Lagos State Sports Council, 1963-65; Chairman, ibid, 1967—. Memberships: Fellow, Royal Society of Health, London; Fellow, West African Association of Physicians; Permanent Commission & International Association on Occupational Health; Special Subcommittee for Developing Countries, ibid; American Conference of Governmental Industrial Hygienists; Corresponding Member, American Academy of Occupational Health. Author of a number of scientific papers published in professional journals. Organizer of conferences and seminars. Honours: Hon. Diploma in Sports Medicine, Mexican Olympic Committee; Fellow, Medical Council in Public Health, 1970. Address: Department of Community Health, College of Medicine of the University of Lagos, P.M.B. 12003, Lagos, Nigeria.

SOHI, Baldev Singh, born 5th December 1931. Civil Engineer. Education: B.Sc., Civil Engineering, Edinburgh University, U.K., 1954. Personal details: son of late Dr. U. R. Sohi; married, 2 children. Appointments: Assistant Lecturer, University College, Nairobi, Kenya; Assistant Engineer, Nairobi County Council; Assistant Engineer, Acting County Engineer, County Council of the Central Rife, Nakuru; Assistant Engineer, Assistant Municipal Engineer, Municipal Council of Mombasa. Memberships include: Institution of Municipal Engineers, 1966; E.A. Institution of Engineers, 1968; Life Member: Kenya Red Cross Society; Indian Red Cross Society; St. John's Ambulance Society of India; Social Service League, Kenya; Indian Cancer Society; University of Edinburgh, Graduates' Assn.; Governing Council, Khalsa College, Mahilpur, Punjab, India. Address: Municipal Council of Mombasa, P.O. Box 1861, Mombasa, Kenya.

SOKO (Hon.) Axon Jasper, born 10th June 1930. Accountant; Member of Parliament. Education: Senior Secondary Certificate (Accountancy). Personal details: married, 2 sons, 1 daughter. Appointments: held various positions in Zanc & Unipon Copperbelt; Parliamentary Secretary, Commerce & Industry, 1964; Minister of State, 1964-68; Cabinet Minister, 1968. Member of The Commonwealth Parliamentary Association. Address: P.O. Box 153, Ndola, Zambia.

SOKO, Patrick Harry Brown, born 7th April 1933. Labour Administrator. Education: Blantyre Secondary School, 1948-52; Labour Course, Zambia, 1955 & London 1960; Ruskin College, Oxford, U.K., 1964-66; various seminars & conferences. Personal details: grandson of Rev. Y. M. Nthara. Appointments: Labour Clerk, 1954; Labour Assistant, 1955; Labour Inspector, 1959; Assistant Labour Officer, 1961; Labour

Officer, 1963; Senior Labour Officer, 1967; Principal Labour Officer, 1970. Memberships: Labour Club; African Club, Oxford University; Church Elder, 1963; Chairman, Football League, Mlanje Malawi, 1955; Branch Secretary, Civil Service Assn., Blantyre, 1958. Publications: African Development (Ruskin College Magazine), 1966. Address: c/o Ministry of Labour, Box 5594, Limbe, Malawi.

SOLANKE, Toriola Feisitan, born 9th March 1930. Physician. Education: C.M.S. Grammar School, Lagos, Nigeria, 1940-47; St. Andrews University, Fife, U.K., 1950-56. Appointments: Senior Registrar, University College Hospital, Ibadan, Nigeria, 1964; Associate Professor, Department of Surgery, University of Ibadan. Memberships: Treasurer, Association of Surgeons of West Africa; Secretary, Western Branch, Nigeria Medical Association. Honours: Research Fellowship, Johns Hopkins University, Baltimore, Md., U.S.A., 1964; Travelling Fellowship, Cancer Institute Hospital, Tokyo, Japan, 1968. Address: Department of Surgery, University College Hospital, Ibadan, Nigeria.

SOLANKI, Jaikishen M., born 17th July 1927. Lithographic Printer. Education: Senior Cambridge & Civil Service Examinations. Married, 1 son, 3 daughters. Appointments: Clerk, Hollerith Operator; Chartist; currently Lithography Printer. Member, Suleman Virjee Indian Gymkhana Club. Address: P.O. Box 30022, Nairobi, Kenya.

SOLOMON TEKALIGN, born 29th July 1931. Administrator; Civil Servant. Education: B.A., Public Administration, American University of Beirut, Lebanon, 1955. Personal details: married, 2 sons, 3 daughters. Appointments: entered Government Service, 1955; Section Chief, Director-General, Ministries of Education, Finance & Foreign Affairs; Assistant Minister, Ministry of Justice; with Organization of African Unity, Addis Ababa, 1963-65. Memberships: Commercial Graduates' Association; former Vice-President, ibid. Honours: Officer of the Order of Menelek II, Ethiopia, 1970. Address: P.O. Box 3396, Addis Ababa, Ethiopia.

SOLOMON TSEGAYE, born Addis Ababa, Ethiopia, 15th March 1921. Library Scientist. High School Education. Appointments: Librarian, H.I.M. Hailé Selassié I Private Library, 1951-69; Director-General, National Library of Ethiopia, 1969—. Address: National Library of Ethiopia, P.O. Box 717, Addis Ababa, Ethiopia.

SOMANI, Anilkumar Hasham Merali, born 1st June, 1943. Civil Engineer. Education: Mawinzi Secondary School, Moshi, Tanzania; Loughborough College of Further Education, U.K., 1961-63; Medway College of Technology, Chatham, Kent, 1963-66; B.Sc.(Eng.), London University. Appointments: Assistant Executive Engineer, Water & Drainage Division, Ministry of Lands, Housing & Urban Development, Tanzania, 1966-69; Design Engineer, Norman & Dawban, Architects, Consulting Engineers, Town Planners, Dar es Salaam, 1969—. Memberships: Graduate Member, Institute of Civil Engineers, U.K.; ibid, East African Institute of Engineers; Graduate Representative, Tanzanian Division, ibid, 1968—. Address: P.O. 3217, Dar es Salaam, Tanzania.

SOMERS, Krishna, born 7th October 1926. Educator; Physician. Education: Sastri College, Durban, South Africa, 1939-42; M.B., B.Ch., Witwatersrand University, 1943-49. Appointments: House Officer, McCord Zulu Hospital, Durban; Registrar, Royal Postgraduate Medical School & Hammersmith Hospital, London, U.K.; currently Clinical Professor of Medicine, Makerere University, Uganda; Chief, Division of Cardiology, Mulago Hospital, Kampala. Memberships: British Cardiac Society; Fellow, American College of Cardiology; Fellow, Royal Society of Medicine; Fellow, Royal College of Physicians, London; Association of Physicians of East Africa; British Medical Association; Uganda Medical Association. Author of over 75 publications in scientific and medical journals on cardiology & allied subjects. Honours: Craib Prize, Witwatersrand University, 1949; Government of India Cultural Scholarship, 1952-53; Wellcome Foundation Travelling Fellowship, 1960; World Health Organization Fellowship, 1970. Address: Department of Medicine, Makerere University, P.O. Box 7072, Kampala, Uganda.

SOMJI, Noordin, born 31st December 1929. Merchant; Company Director; Stockbroker. Education: Senior Cambridge Certificate. Appointments: Director, Somji & Co., Kampala, Uganda. Memberships: Treasurer, Kampala Investment Club; Chairman, Uganda Investment Group; Kampala Stock Exchange. Address: Somji & Co., Kampala, Uganda.

SONDHI, Kuldip, born India, 21st March, 1924. Construction Engineer; Writer. Education: Primary & Secondary, India & Kenya; Massachusetts Institute of Technology & Polytechnic Institute of Brooklyn, U.S.A.; M.S., Aero Engineering. Married, 2 children. Currently, Director, 2 engineering companies, Kenya. Memberships: Associate, American Society of Mechanical Engineers; East African Institute of Engineers. Publications: A number of plays & short stories included in the following anthologies: Writing in Africa Today; Short East African Plays in English; Ten One-Act Plays; Ny Afrikans k Prosa; Eleven Short African Plays; Author of 16 plays for radio, stage & television, some of which have been broadcast in East Africa, the BBC, & Germany, & some have been performed by the Kenya National Theatre & televised. Honours: 1st Prize, East African Short Story Competition, 1963; Best Original Play Awards for 'Undesignated' & 'With Strings', Kenya Drama Festivals, 1963, '65. Address: P.O. Box 3058, Mombasa, Kenya.

SONGU, Moses Hinger Francis, born 14th September 1915. Security Officer. Education: Standard VI, 1937. Personal details: grandfather was a Chief in the Town of Sahawa, Bumpa Chiefdom, Bo District; married, 1 son, 4 daughters. Appointments: Battery Sergeant-Major, 1937-46; Produce Inspector, 1946-53; Produce Storekeeper, 1953-61; Chiefdom Police Inspector, 1961-64; Government Diamond Representative, Sierra Leone, 1964-68; Plant Security Officer, Sierra Leone Selection Trust,

1969—. Memberships: Executive Member, Roman Catholic Church, 1928—; Chairman, Sierra Leone Ex-Servicemen's Association; Councillor, Township of Bo; President, Serabu Ex-pupils Association; Tribal Authority, Kakua Chiefdom, Bo; W.V.F.; President, Roman Catholic Parish Centenary Celebrations Committee; Pioneer Total Abstinance Association of the Sacred Heart, Dublin; Catholic Book Club, England; St. Gerard Novena, ibid; President, Christ the King Parish Committee, Yengema; Assessor, Sierra Leone Supreme Court; A Staff Club, S.L.S.T. Ltd., Tongo. Address: c/o Sierra Leone Selection Trust, Yengema, Sierra Leone.

SOPPO PRISO, Paul, born 19th July 1913. Contractor of Public Works & Buildings; Building Society Promoter. Education: General & Technical; self-taught in Economics & Finance. Married, 7 children. Appointments: Administrative Functionary, Tutelle; War Service, 1939-45; Founder, First Movement of Opinion of Cameroun (French Cameroun Youth), 1938; Member, Representative, Assemblies Territorial & Legislative of Cameroun First President, ibid, 1953; Adviser, French Union for Cameroun, 1946-58; Petitioner for the independence of Cameroun before the United Nations Assembly, 1957; Inventer of CAFSO; President Director-General, Enterprise Soppo Priso, 1945; Polyclinique de Douala, 1955, etc. Memberships: General Building Society Union of Cameroun, 1967; President, Union of Contractors of Public Works, Building & Annex Industries of Cameroun; President, Finance Committee, Conference of African Churches, Ecumenical Council of Churches; International Conferences on Economic Development; Administrative Council, Pan-African Institute for Development; l'Organisation Commune Africaine Malgache & Mauricienne. Publications: Author of Numerous communications on economic material & development, the formation of borders & African enterprise to conferences & international meetings. Honours: French Medal of Resistance; Legion of Honour; Black Star of Benin; Cameroun Merit; French Social Merit; Officer of the Order of Bravery, etc. Address: 2 Place de Bagatelle, Neuilly-Sur-Seine, France.

SOSELEJE, Maurice Douglas, born 15th November 1918. Bishop. Education: Primary, 1927-31; St. Joseph's Central School, Chidya, 1932-36; Teacher Training Centre, ibid, 1937-39; Theol. Training, St. Cyprian's Theological College, Namasakata, 1956-57; Diploma in Theology, St. Augustine's College, Canterbury, U.K., 1961-62. Married, 4 sons, 6 daughters. Appointments: Teacher Grade II, St. Joseph's Central School, Chidya, Tanganyika, 1940-41; Second Master, Masasi, 1941-45; Head Teacher, Liloya, 1945-48; Head Teacher, Mbayani Middle School, 1948-52; ordained Deacon, 1954; Deacon, Lulindi, 1954-56; ordained Priest, 1957; Curate, Nakarara, 1957-60; Chaplain, St. Cyprian's Theological College, Namasakata, 1960-61; Curate, St. Giles', Camberwell, London, U.K., 1962; Chaplain, St. Cyprian's College, Ngala (Rondo), Tanzania, 1962-63; Assistant Bishop of Masasi, 1963-69; retired, 1969. Memberships: President, Brotherhood of St. andre, Masasi Diocese, 1963-69; Tanganyika African National Union. Publications: Kusali (To Pray), 1966; Our Calendar—Lives of the Saints, 1966. Address: P.O. Box 82, Masasi, Mtwara Region, Tanzania.

SOYANNWO, Mojisola Akinwumi Oluwole, born 28th December 1934. Medical Practitioner; Lecturer. Education: Ijebu-Ode Grammar School, Nigeria, 1949-54; Abeokuta Grammar School, 1955; M.B., B.S. (London), University College, Ibadan, 1956-62; Ph.D., Queens University, Belfast, U.K., 1966-68; M.R.C.P. (Ireland), 1965; M.R.C.P.(London), 1969. Appointments: House Officer, Paediatrics, Obstetrics, & Gynaecology, University College Hospital, Ibadan, Nigeria, 1962-63; Senior House Officer, Medicine, Belfast City Hospital, U.K., 1964-65; Ibid, Clinical Pathology, 1965-55; Registrar, Medicine (Kidney Unit), 1966-67; Research Fellow, Queen's University, Belfast, 1967-68; Senior Registrar, Medicine, University College Hospital, Ibadan, Nigeria, 1969; Consultant Physician, ibid; Lecturer in Medicine, University of Ibadan, 1969—. Memberships: Nigerian Medical Association; Association of Physicians of West Africa; British Medical Association; European Dialysis & Transplant Association. Address: Department of Medicine, University College Hospital, Ibadan, Western State, Nigeria.

SPEED, Dorothy Elizabeth Maud, born Rabat, Morocco, 28th September, 1928. Medical Practitioner. Education: Lycée de Jaunes Filles, Casablanca, 1939-45; Belvedere School, G.P.D.S.T., Liverpool, U.K., 1946; M.B., Ch.B., University of Liverpool, 1956. Appointments: Medical Registrar, Royal United Hospital, Bath; Research Assistant, Chester Beatty Research Institute, Royal Cancer Hospital, London; Medical Officer, Prison Department, Home Office; Director, Population Control, Ministry of Health, Mauritius, 1967; Medical Consultant, International Planned Parenthood Federation, Regional Office, Nairobi, Kenya, 1968—. Memberships: Royal Society of Medicine, London; British Society of Haematology; Eugenics Society; Medical Association for the Prevention of War. Publications include: Chronic Granulocytic Leukaemia: The Chromosomes & the Disease, 1964; Women in Prison, 1966; Intra Uterine Contraceptive Devices in Mauritius, 1970; Population Crisis in Central Africa (Rwanda & Burundi), 1970. Recipient, Council of Europe Fellowship, leukaemia research, 1960. Address: IPPF Regional Office, P.O. Box 30234, Nairobi, Kenya.

SPENCER, Samuel Lees, born 5th September 1934. Quantity Surveyor; Building Technologist. Education: Liverpool College of Building, U.K. Married, 1 son, 1 daughter. Appointments: Quantity Surveyor, County Borough of Burnley, Lancs., 1957-60; ibid, County Borough of Blackpool, 1960-63; Lecturer, Building Technology, Faculty of Architecture, University of Science & Technology, Kumasi, Ghana, 1963—; Visiting Lecturer, School of Architecture, University of Wisconsin, Milwaukee, U.S.A., 1969. Memberships: Associate, Institute of Quantity Surveyors; ibid, Incorporated Association of Architects & Surveyors; Licentiate, Institute of Building; Royal Society of Health. Publications: Quantity Surveying in Ghana (The

Quantity Surveyor); The Design & Construction of a 60-foot Diameter Dome (Building Technol. & Mgmt); The Bolero Industry—A Clinical Self-Examination; The City Within, detailed account of the world's largest building project. Address: Faculty of Architecture, University of Science & Technology, Kumasi, Ghana.

SPICER, Ivor Dennis, born 2nd April, 1926. Auditor. Education: Archbishop Tennisons & Southgate County G.S. Married, 1 son, 1 daughter. Appointments: Central Office, H.M. Overseas Audit Service, 1949; Assistant Auditor, Nigeria, 1948; Auditor, ibid, 1952; Senior Auditor, Kenya, 1954; Principal Auditor, Eastern Region, Nigeria, 1959; Deputy Director of Audit, ibid, 1961; Director of Audit, Swaziland, 1964—. Address: P.O. Box 98, Mbabane, Swaziland.

SPOERRY, Anne, born Cannes, France, 13th May, 1918. Doctor of Medicine. Education: Baccalaureat, Lycée of Mulhouse, France, 1926-37; Francis Holland School for Girls, London, U.K., 1930-32; Medical Studies, Faculté de Médicine de Paris, France; Diploma of Tropical Medicine, Bale Tropical Institute, 1948; Thesis for M.D., 1950. Appointments include: Externe des Hospitaux de Paris, 1942; Medical Officer, Aden, 1949; General Practitioner, Olkalou, Kenya, 1950-64; Medical Officer of Health, Nyandarua County Council, 1964-65; Flying Doctor (own Piper Cherokee 235 aircraft), African Medical & Research Foundation, 1965, in Charge of Mobile Medicine in Masailand. Memberships include: nominated Member, Naivasha County Council, 1958-62; Past* Chairman, Health & Social Affairs Committee, ibid; Medical Association of Kenya; Life Member, Kenya Branch, British Red Cross Society; Kenya Wild Life Society; East African Aero Club; Hon. Member, Order of St. John, etc. Address: Muringa, P.O. Box 5027, Subukia, Via Nakuru, Kenya.

SPRY, John Farley, born Cambridge, U.K., 11th March 1910. Solicitor of the Supreme Court of England; Judge. Education: Perse School; M.A., Peterhouse, Cambridge. Married, 2 children. Appointments: Assistant Registrar, Titles, & Conveyancer, Uganda, 1936; Chief Inspector of Land Registration, Palestine, 1944; Assistant Director, ibid, 1944; Registrar-General, Tanganyika, 1948; Registrar-General, Kenya; Registrar-General, * Tanganyika, 1952; Legal Draftsman, Tanganyika, 1956; Principal Secretary, Public Service Commission, Tanganyika, 1960; Puisne Judge, Tanganyika, 1961; Justice of Appeal, Court of Appeal for Eastern Africa, 1964; Vice-President, ibid, 1970. Memberships: Chairman, Commission on the Law of Marriage & Divorce, Kenya, 1967-68. Publications: Civil Procedure in East Africa, 1969. Address: Court of Appeal for East Africa, P.O. Box 30187, Nairobi, Kenya.

SPURIN, Patricia, born 24th October 1932. Teacher. Education: B.A.(Hons.) French, Royal Holloway College, University of London, U.K., 1951-54; Postgraduate Certificate in Education, Institute of Education, London, 1954-55. Married. Appointments: Teacher, Gravesend Grammar School, 1955-57; Teacher, Butere Girls' High School, Kenya, 1959-61; Teacher, Maseno Bible School, 1962-65. Memberships: Chairman, Neck Home & Family Life Committee, 1963-64. Address: P.O. Nambale, Kisumu, Kenya.

SPURIN, Richard Mark, born 9th December 1928. Clergyman. Education: M.A., Peterhouse, Cambridge, U.K., 1949-52; Kelham Theological College, 1952-54; Wycliffe Hall, Oxford, 1954-55. Appointments: Chaplain to Bishop of Maseno, Kenya; Rural Dean, Nambale, 1961-65, 1966-69; Coordinator of Village Polytechnics, 1969—. Member, Church Missionary Society. Publications: Village Polytechnics from the Farming Point of View (Annual Review of Selected Devs. in Agric. Educ. & Trng., FAO), 1969-70. Address: P.O. Nambale, Kisumu, Kenya.

SSALI, Gerard Raymond, born Kampala, Uganda, November, 1935. Company Executive. Education: St. Henry's College, Kitovu, Uganda; Diploma in Management Studies, Regent Street Polytechnic, London, U.K.; Associate Member, British Institute of Management. Married, 4 children. Appointments: Executive Officer Trainee, National & Grindlays Bank, Bishopsgate, London; with Uganda Company's Africa Tea Sales Ltd.; Trainee, Tea Tasting & Marketing, Africa Tea Brokers, Nairobi; with various firms of tea brokers & blenders in London, U.K.; Head of Produce & Sales Division, Agricultural Enterprises Ltd. (subsidiary of Uganda Development Corporation); Managing Director, Uganda Tea Export Agency Ltd., 1969—. Address: Uganda Tea Export Agency, P.O. Box 6658, Kampala, Uganda.

SSALI, John Chrysostom, born 24th January 1935. Surgeon. Education: Nkokonjeru Primary School; Nsambye Junior Secondary School; Namilyango College, Makerere University College; Makerere Medical School; F.R.C.S. (Edinburgh); F.R.C.S.(England), Royal College of Surgeons of England, U.K.; St. Thomas' Hospital, London. Appointments: Medical Officer, Ministry of Health, Uganda; Senior Hospital Officer, Emergency Surgery, Pontefract General Infirmary, U.K.; Senior Hospital Officer, Orthopaedics, Batley General Hospital; R.S.O., General Surgery, Dewsbury General Hospital; Surgeon, Ministry of Health, Uganda. Memberships: Uganda Medical Association. Honours: King George VI Scholarship, 1952. Address: Masaka Hospital, P.O. Box 18, Masaka, Uganda.

SSEBUNNYA, Kasule Bellerman Robert, born Lubaga, Uganda, 31st December, 1942. Journalist; Business Executive. Education: Diploma, Journalism, I.P.I., University College, Nairobi, Kenya; Certificate, Mass Communication, Makerere University College, Uganda; Certificate in Economics & Commercial Policy Course U.N.; various seminar, Journalism, Public Relations, & Advertising, locally & in Europe. Appointments include: Editor, Uganda Eyogera Newspaper; Reporter, Uganda Argus, English Newspaper; Public Relations Officer, Madhvani Group of Industries; Director, Secretary, Kiira General Grocers & Traders; Director, Secretary, Manufacturing Stationers & several other companies. Memberships include: British Institute of Public Relations, 1969; Councillor, Jinja Muncipal Council; Chairman, Public Health Committee, ibid; Vice-Chairman; Chairman, Family Welfare Committee; Secretary, Assn. of Uganda Journalists; Executive Member, Uganda Y.M.C.A. Central Council; Ag. Secretary, Jinja Chamber of Commerce & Industry; Advertising Society of Uganda; Jinja Child Welfare Adoption Society; Treasurer, Busoga Joint Welfare Advisory Council; Chairman, General Programme Committee & Vice-Chairman, Board of Directors, Y.M.C.A., Jinja Branch. Honours include: several prizes & certificates of merit from local societies in Uganda. Address: Madhvani Group, P.O. Box 54, Jinja, Uganda.

SSEKANDI, Francis, born 29th September 1940. Lawyer. Education: LL.B.(Hons.), London, U.K.; LL.M., Columbia University, U.S.A. Appointments: Part-time Lecturer, Makerere University, Kampala, Uganda, 1968; Principal State Attorney, Department of Public Prosecutions, Kampala. Member, Uganda Law Society. Publications: Uganda & Kondos (The Capital Punishment Revisited), E.A. Law Review, 1970. Address: P.O. Box 1550, Kampala, Uganda.

SSERULYO, Ignatius, born Masaka District Uganda, 31st July 1937. Artist & Teacher. Education: Villa Maria Mission, Uganda St. Mary's College, Kisubi; Makerere University, 1960-66; 1st class Diploma in Fine Art (East Africa), 1964; Diploma of Education, 1966. Married, with children. Appointments: Art Teacher, 1966—. Work shown at national, Commonwealth and international exhibitions, including the Irving Trust Comp., New York & Expo '70, Japan; murals painted for various departments of Uganda Government, Makerere University, Kampala, & W.H.O. Centre for Africa, Brazzaville, Republic of the Congo. Honours: Painting Prize, Makerere University, 1962; Margaret Travel Prize, ibid, 1964; Honorarium by Mary Stuart Hall, ibid, 1967. Address: Kibuli Secondary School, P.O. Box 4216, Kampala, Uganda.

STAFFORD, Patricia Alice, born 7th November 1924. Teacher. Education: Physical Education Teacher Training, Chelsea, London, U.K. Married, 4 children. Appointments: Teacher, Primary & Secondary Schools, U.K; Teacher Trainer, Buloba Training College, Uganda. Member, Church Missionary Society. Address: c/o Ng'iya Girls' High School, P.O. Ng'iya via Kisumu, Kenya.

STAFFORD, Roy Lawrence, Born 23rd February 1928. Electrical Engineer; Science Teacher; Translator. Education: Sevenoaks School, U.K., 1942-45; B.Sc., A.C.G.I., Imperial College, London University, 1946-49; Postgraduate Certificate in Education, Institute of Education, London, 1957-58. Married, 4 children. Appointments: Research Department, Reyrolle & Co., Hebburn, Co. Durham, 1949-50; Radio Officer, R.A.F., 1950-52; Science Teacher, Maseno Secondary School, Kenya, 1953-64; seconded to Bible Society for Revision of Luo Bible. Member, Church Missionary Society. Publications: Elementary Luo Grammar, 1966. Honours: Duddell Scholar, I.E.E., 1946. Address: c/o Ng'iya Girls' High School, P.O. Ng'iya via Kisumu, Kenya.

STANFIELD, James Paget, born 20th April 1926. Paediatrician. Education: Birkenhead School, U.K.; M.B., Ch.B. (Hons.), Liverpool, 1950; M.D., ibid, 1954; M.R.C.P., London, 1952; D.C.H., London, 1959. Married, 5 children. Appointments: Resident, Medicine & Surgery, Liverpool Royal Infirmary, 1950-51; Research Fellowship, Pathology, University of Liverpool; Deputy Assistant Director, Pathology, R.A.M.C., Malaya, 1954-56; Resident, Paediatrics, Hospital for Sick Children, Great Ormond Street, London, U.K., 1956-58; Research Fellowship, Paediatrics, University of Uppsala, Sweden, 1958; Registrar, Paediatrics, Newcastle upon Tyne, U.K., 1958-59; Registrar, Hospital for Sick Children, London, & Mulago Hospital, Kampala, Uganda, 1959-65; Senior Lecturer, then Reader, Department of Paediatrics, Makerere Medical School, Kampala, Uganda, 1965-69; Paediatrician, M.R.C. Child Nutrition Unit, Kampala, Uganda, 1969—. Memberships: Association of Physicians of East Africa; Uganda Medical Association; Uganda Society. Contributor to professional publications. Address: M.R.C. Child Nutrition Unit, P.O. Box 6717, Kampala, Uganda.

STANLEY-SMITH, Algernon Charles, born 14th February 1890. Medical Practitioner. Education: Chefod School, China, 1896-9; Hurst Court, Ore, Hastings, U.K., 1900-03; Winchester College, 1903-08; B.Sc.(1st Class Hons.), Cambridge University, 1908-11; M.R.C.S., L.R.C.P., St. George's Hospital Medical School, 1913; M.B., B.Ch., Cambridge University, 1914; Dipl. Med. Trop., Belgium, 1930. Married, 2 sons, 2 daughters. Appointments: Lieut., R.A.M.C., 1914-15; Medical Officer, Mengo Hospital, Uganda, 1915-18; Medical Mission, Rwanda Mission (C.M.S.), 1920-52; Translator, Rwanda Bible & Prayer Book, 1952-56, & Ankole Kigezi Bible, Prayer Book, Hymn Book, etc., 1956-70. Honours: Military Cross, 1915; Chevalier de l'Ordre de Léopold II, 1955; Bronze Medal, Royal Africa Society, 1967. Address: P.O. Box 14, Mbarara, Uganda.

STANLEY-SMITH, James, born 22nd March 1929. Teacher. Education: Winchester College, U.K., 1943-47; B.A., Dip.Ed., Durham University, 1950-55; Married, 2 sons, 2 daughters. Appointments: Lecturer, Kigari Teachers' College, Embu, Kenya, 1959-64; Principal, ibid, 1964-66; R.E. Adviser, Diocese of Mt. Kenya, 1967—. Member, Church Missionary Society. Address: Diocese of Mt. Kenya, P.O. Box 21, Muranga, Kenya.

STANLEY-SMITH, Lilian Zoë, born 18th September 1891. Missionary Housewife. Education: Primary; French, one year in Switzerland. Married, 2 sons, 2 daughters. Appointments: Kabale-Kigezi C.M.S. Hospital, 1921-32; Rwanda C.M.S. Hospital, 1933-55; Ankole, for translation of Bible & other books, 1956-70. Address: P.O. Box 14, Mbarara, Uganda.

STANWAY, Alfred, born 9th September 1908. Bishop. Education: Melbourne High School, Australia; Ridley Theological College, Melbourne; Melbourne Teachers' College. Married. Appointments: Curate, St. Albans, Melbourne, 1934-36; Mission of St. James & St. John, 1936-37; C.M.S. Missionary, Kaloleni, Kenya, 1937-44 & Maseno, Kenya, 1944-45; Rural Dean, Nyanza, Tanganyika, 1945-47; Examining Chaplain, Mombasa, Kenya, 1945-51; Bishop of Central Tanganyika, 1951-70; Dean, Province of Tanzania, 1970. Honours: Th.L., Australian College of Theology, 1934; M.A., Lambeth, 1951. Address: P.O. Box 15, Dodoma, Tanzania.

STEVENS, William Noel, born U.K., 23rd December 1920. Hospital Administrator. Appointments: Administrator, Wusasa Hospital, Zaria, Nigeria, 1949—. Member, Church Missionary Society. Honours: M.B.E., 1968. Address: Wusasa, Zaria, Nigeria.

STEVENSON, Anthony John Maxwell, born 28th April 1916. Medical Practitioner. Education: Stonyhurst College; St. Mary's Hospital Medical School. Appointments: R.N.V.R., 1943-46; Medical Officer, Gold Coast, 1946-50; Medical Officer, Nigerian Government, 1951; Principal Medical Officer, Mid-West State, Nigeria. Honours: O.B.E., 1967. Address: General Hospital, Warri, Nigeria.

STEWART, James Ecclestone, born 7th August 1922. University Teacher. Education: B.A., University of Cape Town, South Africa, 1941; LL.B., ibid, 1944; M.A., University of Cambridge, U.K., 1955; Ph.D., ibid, 1968. Married. Appointments: Editor, Cape Standard, 1945; Teacher, University of Botswana, Lesotho, & Swaziland, 1951-62; Lecturer & Senior Lecturer, University of Nairobi, Kenya, 1966-70. Memberships: Cape Bar; Secretary, National Lay Council (Catholic) of Kenya. Honours: Senior Scholar, Trinity College, Cambridge, 1955; African & American Universities Programme, Oppenheimer & Chauncey Stillman grants for further study, 1963-66. Address: University of Nairobi, Kenya.

STICKLEY, Jeffrey Osborne, born 14th January 1936. Civil Servant. Education: London School of Printing, U.K. Appointments: Assistant Manager, British Museum Bindery, H.M.S.O., London, 1961-64; Bookbinding Officer, seconded to Ahmadu Bello University, Nigeria, 1964-66; H.M.S.O., London & Norwich, U.K., 1966-68; Bookbinding Officer, University of Malawi, 1968—. Address: University Library Bindery, P.O. Box 330, Zomba, Malawi.

STICKNEY, Robert Michael, born 29th September 1938. Teacher. Education: Beaumont College, Old Windsor, U.K., 1947-56; West of Scotland Agric. College, 1958-60; Newton Park Teacher Training College, 1964-65. Married, 3 sons. Appointments: Agricultural Supervisor, Malawi, 1961-63; Assistant Agricultural Officer, Uganda, Principal, Ankole District Farm Institute, 1965-67; Agriculture Teacher, Bishops Senior School, Mukono, Uganda, 1968-70. Member, Uganda Agricultural Society. Address: Bishops Senior School, Box 75, Mukono, Uganda.

STIRLING, Leader Dominic, born Finchley, U.K., 19th January 1906. Medical Practitioner. Education: Bishop's Stortford College, 1917-24; M.B., B.S., London Hospital, London University, 1924-29; M.R.C.S.; L.R.C.P. Married. Appointments: Resident House Officer, London Hospital, 1930-32; Outpatient Officer, Miller General Hospital, 1934; Medical Officer, Universities' Mission to Central Africa, 1935-40; came to Tanzania as Missionary Doctor, 1935—; sponsored 1st recognized training school for Tanzanian Nurses, 1936, & continued training Nurses & Rural Medical Aids, 1936-64; Medical Superintendent, Mission Hospitals, 1936-69; Medical Superintendent, Mnero Catholic Hospital, 1949-64, & Kibosho Catholic Hospital, 1964-69; Member, Medical Advisory Committee, 1958—; Member of Parliament (TANU), 1959—; Chairman, Board of Enquiry into Deaths in Sisal Industry, 1963; Member, Presidential Commission on One-Party State, 1964; Chairman, Public Accounts Committee, 1965—; Member, Parliamentary Social Services Committee, 1965—; Medical Secretary, Diocese of Moshi, 1965—; Member, Board of Enquiry into the Failure of the Tanzania National Transport Cooperative, 1968; Visiting Surgeon, Lushoto & other Hospitals, 1969—; Chairman, Board of Governors, Huruma Hospital, Moshi, 1969—. Memberships: TANU National Conference & Regional Executive; Chairman, Tanzania Christian Medical Association; Board, Tanzania Catholic Heart Association; Fellow, Royal Society of Tropical Medicine; Chief Scout of Tanzania; Convocation of University of London. Publications: Ritual Circumcision in Southern Tanganyika (E.A.Med.J.), 1941; Notes on an Ascent of Kilimanjaro (E.A.Med.J.), 1942; Bush Doctor, 1946. Address: P.O. Box 15, Soni, Tanzania.

STOLL, Robert, born 7th September 1921. Agricultural Expert for the Tunisian Government. Education: Lycée Carnot, Tunis, Tunisia; Lycée Hoche, Versailles, France; Diploma of Engineering, Colonial School of Agriculture, Tunis, 1940-42. Married, 4 sons. Appointments: Technical Director, La Ste Agricole L.Stoil, 1945—; Workshop Director, ibid, 1960—; Agricultural Expert to the Tunisian Government, 1969—. Memberships: former Member, Conseil Superieur des Français de l'Etranger, 1968; Vice-President, Tunis Section, l'Union des Français de l'Etranger; Founding Member, Lions Club of Tunis. Honours: Cross of War, France, 1939-45; Knight of the National Order of Merit, France, 1969. Address: Engineer E.C.A.T., 19 rue de Montpellier, Tunis, Tunisia.

STONE, Ian Edwin, born 16th March 1942. Chartered Surveyor. Education: Berkhamsted School, Hertfordshire, U.K., 7 years; R.I.C.S., Brixton College of Building. Appointments: Valuation Surveyor, G.L.C., U.K., 1960-68, & Government of Tanzania, 1968—. Memberships: Dar es Salaam Flying Club. Address: P.O. Box 2795, Dar es Salaam, Tanzania.

STONE, Margaret Mary, born 24th July 1921. Nursing Sister. Education: Milhamford School, Oxford, U.K.; State Registered Nurse, Nottingham General Hospital, 1945; State Certified Midwife, Radcliffe Infirmary, Oxford,

1946; Orthopaedic Certificate, Nuffield Orthopaedic Hospital, Oxford, 1939. Appointments: Matron, Kumi Leprosy Centre, Uganda, 1949-56; Assistant to Dr. K. Brown, Uganda B.C.G. Publications: Trial against Leprosy, 1969-70. Honours: M.B.E., 1969. Address: Kumi Leprosy Centre, P.O. Kumi, Uganda.

STONEMAN, John, born 27th January 1929. Civil Servant; Fisheries Administrator. Education: Heles School, Exeter, U.K., 1935-47; University of Exeter, 1949-54. Married. Appointments: Fisheries Officer, Uganda, 1954-64; Senior Fisheries Officer, Malawi, 1970—. Memberships: Uganda Society; Royal Yachting Association. Publications: New Fishing Industry in Uganda (Fishing News Int.), 1964; Contbr. to Fishing Boats of the World (vol. 3), 1967; Netting More Fish (Financial Times), 1967; Review of Fisheries of Uganda waters of Lake Albert 1928-65 (w. D. Cadwaller) EAFFRO, 1966; The siting & relative importance of the fish landings of Lake Albert (w. D. Cadwaller) The Uganda Jrnl., 1968; Investment in Fishery Industry in Uganda FAO, 1969. Honours: Uganda Independence Medal, 1962. Address: Chief Fisheries Officer, P.O. Box 206, Zomba, Malawi.

STORY, Robin Lewis, born 13th May 1934. Senior Research Fellow. Education: B.A. (Hons.), London, A.K.C. Married, 2 children. Appointments: Soil Survey Officer, Institute for Agricultural Research, Ahmadu Bello University, Zaria, Nigeria, 1958-63; Senior Research Fellow, Publications Secretary, ibid, 1963-70. Memberships: Science Association of Nigeria, 1961-70; Council, Agricultural Society of Nigeria, 1968-70; Deputy Editor-in-Chief, Nigerian Agricultural Journal, 1968-70; Corresponding Member, Presentation of Technical Information Group of U.K.; Editor, Samaru Agricultural Newsletter. Author of 7 soil survey bulletins of the Institute for Agricultural Research, & many general articles & reports on agriculture & its development for Agricultural Research, Samaru, Ahmadu Bello University, P.M.B. 1044, Zaria, Nigeria.

STOVOLD (Venerable) Kenneth Ernest, born Godalming, Surrey, U.K., 8th August, 1909. Archdeacon. Education: Cranleigh School, Surrey, U.K., 1918-28; University College, Oxford, 1928-31; M.A., 1934; Wycliff Hall, ibid, 1939. Married, 1 son, 2 daughters. Appointments: Headmaster, Kaloleni Schoo, Coast, 1932-42; Honorary Chaplain to the Forces, 1941-45; Rural Dean, Nyanza, 1947-53; Canon, Mombasa Cathedral, 1953-55; Archdeacon, Western Kenya, 1953-70; Examining Chaplain to the Bishop, 1959-70. Memberships: Church Missionary Society, 1931—; Life Member, Royal Africa Society; Oxford University Occasionals Hockey Club; Old Crawleighans Club; Inter-Varsity Fellowship. Publications: History of the C.M.S. in Kenya (Coast) 1844-1944; Kuchungulia Maandiko Matakatifu. Recipient, Royal Africa Society Medal, 1966. Address: Box 62, Maseno, Kenya.

STRATFULL, John Frederick, born 22nd July 1929. Auditor. Education: Harrow Weald Secondary Grammar School, U.K., 1940-47; Queen Mary College, University of London, 1949-52. Appointments: H.M. Overseas Audit Service, 1953-68, serving in Tanganyika, Nigeria, Leeward & Windward Islands; Director of Audit, St. Kitts & British Virgin Islands, 1962-68; Director of Audit, Mauritius, 1969—. Memberships: University of London Society; Radio Society of Great Britain; Mauritius Naval & Military Gymkhana Club. Address: Audit Department, Port Louis, Mauritius.

STUBBS, Geoffrey Michael, born 2nd June 1936. University Lecturer. Education: B.A.(Hons.), M.A., D.Phil., University of Oxford, U.K. Married, 1 daughter. Appointments: Social Research Assistant, Manitoba, Canada, 1959-60; District Social Worker, Manitoba, 1960-61; Research Officer, Urban Systems Unit, Ministry of Housing & Local Government, U.K., 1962-68; Senior Lecturer in Regional Planning & Demography, University of Malawi, 1968-70; Visiting Associate Professor, Department of Geography, Northwestern University, U.S.A. Memberships: Institute of British Geographers; Regional Studies Association, U.K.; Fellow, Royal Geographical Society, London; Association, British Computer Society. Publications: Locational References for Administrative & Planning Information Systems (Min. of H.&L.G., London), 1968; Malawi in Maps (co-author), 1971; The Malawian Urban System, spatial, demographic, social & economic characteristics of the population of Malawi, 1966, & The spatial distribution of health services in relation to population distribution and regional spatial systems, Malawi, 1966 (Univ. of Malawi). Address: Department of Geography, Northwestern University, Evanston, Ill. 60201, U.S.A.

STURLEY, Kenneth Reginald, born 19th February 1908. Chartered Electrical Engineer. Education: George Dixon Grammar School, Birmingham, U.K.; B.Sc., Ph.D., Birmingham University. Married, 2 daughters. Appointments: Vice-Principal, Marconi College; Head, B.B.C. Engineer Training Department; Chief Engineer, B.B.C. External Services; Professor of Communications, Ahmadu Bello University, Nigeria. Memberships: Fellow, Institute of Electrical Engineers; Fellow, Institute of Electric & Electronic Engineers; South Midland Centre Chairman, I.E.E.; Chairman, Zaria Branch, West African Professional Engineers Group. Publications: Radio Receiver Design; Frequency Modulated Radio; Sound & Television Broadcasting. Honours: Fleming Premium, I.E.E. (twice), 1940, 1946; Hon. Associate, University of Aston, U.K., 1954. Address: Electrical Engineering Department, Ahmadu Bello University, Zaria, Nigeria.

SUCHAK, Anilkumar Damodar, born 6th May 1934. Barrister-at-Law; Advocate. Education: Senior Cambridge Overseas School Sert., 1952; St. Xavier's College, Bombay, India, 1953; Barrister-at-Law, Lincoln's Inn, London, U.K., 1954-57. Appointments: admitted as Advocate, Kenya, 1959; admitted as Advocate, Uganda, 1960; Resident Magistrate, 1st Grade, Uganda, posted at Mbarara, 1969-70. Memberships: President, Old Allidians' Association, 1966; Vice-President, ibid, Mombasa, 1965. Address: P.O. Box 2135, Mombasa, Kenya.

SUEDI, Abdallah Byalushengo, born 30th June 1930. Foreign Service Officer; Diplomat. Education: Nyakato School, Tanzania; Aggrey Memorial College, Uganda; Management Cooperation Studies, Loughborough Coop. College, U.K. Appointments: Assistant Manager, West Lake Bus Services Ltd.; Area Commissioner, Bukoba District (known as District Commission before Independence); Foreign Service Officer, Headquarters; Counsellor, U.A.R., U.K., N.Y., U.S.A., & Ottawa, Canada. Memberships: Past District Secretary, Tanu; Institute of Marketing, London, U.K. Address: Tanzania High Commission, 124, O'Connor St., Ottawa, Canada.

SULEMAN-HUMAD, Fitawurari, born September 1919. Finance Officer. Education: Alementary Italian School. Married. Appointments: served as a Clerk, Municipality of Asmara; Finance Officer. Memberships: Officers' Club; Football Federation Club. Recipient of Diploma from Football Federation. Address: Municipality of Asmara, 184 Avenue Hailé Selassié 1, P.O. Box 259, Ethiopia.

SUMMERS, Edgar Charles, born 13th January 1931. College Principal. Education: Plymouth, Devon, U.K.; H.M. Dockyard Technical College, Devonport; Plymouth Polytechnic; B.Sc.(Eng.) Hons., London University. 1955; C.Eng. Married, 1 daughter. Appointments: Development Engineer, Bristol Aeroplane Company, 1955; Lecturer, Electrical Engineering, Kaduna Technical Institute, Nigeria, 1957; Head of Department & Principal, ibid, 1961; Training Supervisor & Principal, Williamson Diamonds Ltd., Tanzania, 1962-64; Principal, Mid-Western Technical College, Nigeria, 1965-67; ibid, Uganda Technical College, Kampala, 1968—. Memberships: Institution of Electrical Engineers, U.K.; East African Institution of Engineers; various committees, ibid; University of East Africa Council for Engineering Education. Address: c/o Ministry of Overseas Development, Eland House, Stag Place, London, S.W.1, U.K.

SUMNER, Michael Fairclough, born 22nd September 1936. University Administrator. Education: Mercers' School, Holborn, London, U.K.; M.A., Hertford College, Oxford; Overseas Civil Service 'A' Course, Oxford. Married, 2 children. Appointments: General Duties Commission, Royal Air Force, 1955-57; Government Training Officer, Lesotho, 1961-66; Assistant Registrar, University of Botswana, Lesotho, & Swaziland, Roma, 1966-69; Senior Assistant Registrar, ibid, 1969—. Member, Hertford Society. Address: The University, Roma, Lesotho.

SUNDARAM, Alamelu Shastri, born 28th October 1931. University Professor. Education: B.Sc. Chemistry (1st Class Hons.), Annamalai University, India, 1955; Ph.D., Chemistry, Sydney University, Australia, 1962. Married, 1 son. Appointments: Demonstrator, School of Chemistry, University of Sydney, Australia, 1959-62; Lecturer, University of Ghana, Legon, 1963-69; Senior Lecturer, 1970; Examiner, West African Examinations Council, 1963—. Memberships: University Library Board; Former Tutor, Mensah Sarbah Hall, Legon; Tutor, Volta Hall, ibid. Author of some 17 papers. Address: Department of Chemistry, P.O. Box 56, Legon, Ghana.

SUNDARAM, Kantha Maran Soma, born 27th October 1927. Educator. Education: B.Sc.(Hons.), M.A., M.Sc., Ph.D.(Annam.), Ph.D., Sydney University, Australia. Married. Appointments: Lecturer in Chemistry, Annamalai University, 1952-58; Postdoctoral Fellow, Gritton Scholar, Sydney University, 1959-62; Lecturer in Chemistry, University of Ghana, Legon, 1963-64; Senior Lecturer in Chemistry, ibid, 1965—. Memberships: Fellow, Chemical Society; Associate, Royal Australian Chemical Institute; Associate, Royal Institute of Chemistry. Author of some 42 publications in leading scientific journals of the world. Address: University of Ghana, Legon, Ghana.

SVEDLUND, John Haldan, born Kenya, 8th August 1936. Civil Engineer. Education: Secondary, Duke of York School, Nairobi, 1949-54; Civil Engineering, Loughborough College of Technology, U.K., 1954-58. Married. Appointments: Cadet Engineer, East African Railways Corporation, 1958-60; Assistant Engineer, ibid, 1961-66; District Civil Engineer, 1967—. Memberships: M.I.C.E.; A.M.I.E.A.E.; C.Eng. Recipient, D.L.C.(Hons.), 1958. Address: c/o Chief Civil Engineer, P.O. Box 30079, Nairobi, Kenya.

SWAI, Verankira Ndeonansia, born 17th October 1930. Training Controller. Education: Old Moshi Secondary School; Grade I Teachers' Certificate, Tabora Upper Secondary School; Diploma in English, Moray House College of Education, Edinburgh, U.K.; Diploma in Public Administration, University of Denver, U.S.A. Married, 1 son, 3 daughters. Appointments: Teacher, Grade I, Ministry of Education, Uganda; Education Officer III, ibid; Senior Instructor, Civil Service T. Centre; Vice-Principal, ibid; Acting Principal; Training Controller, East African Posts & Telecommunications. Memberships: Y.M.C.A.; Tanzanian Institute of Institute of Management. Publications: Stories for Easy Reading; Jifunze Kiswahili, Parts I-IV. Address: East African Posts & Telecommunications, P.O. Box 7108, Kampala, Uganda.

SWANK, Wendell George, born 13th September 1917. Wildlife Ecologist. Education: B.Sc., Forestry, West Virginia University, U.S.A., 1941; M.Sc., Wildlife Management, University of Michigan, 1943; Ph.D., Wildlife Management, Agric. & Mec. College of Texas, 1951. Married, 2 sons. Appointments: Wildlife Biologist, West Virginia Conservation Department, 1945-48; Instructor, Texas A & M College, 1948-51; Supervisor, Wildlife Research, Arizona Game & Fish Department, 1951-58; Assistant Director, Arizona Game & Fish Department, 1958-64; Director, Arizona Game & Fish Department, 1964-68; Forestry Officer (Wildlife), Food & Agricultural Organization, 1968—. Memberships: President, The Wildlife Society, 1962-64; Council, ibid, 1955, 1959-61; Executive Committee, International Association of Game & Fish, 1966-68; Wildlife Disease Association;

Society of American Mammalogists. Publications: The Beaver in West Virginia; The Chaparral Mule; Deer; Nesting & Ecology of the Mouring Dove; & many articles & papers in the field of wildlife management. Honours: Fulbright Scholarship for study in East Africa, 1956-57. Address: Wildlife Division, East African Agriculture & Forestry Research Organization, P.O. Box 30148, Nairobi, Kenya.

SWERE, Robert Abwao, born 17th January 1943. Civil Engineer. Education: Primary, 1951-58; Secondary, 1959-62; C.S.C.; H.S.C., Higher School, 1963-64; B.Sc.(Engrng.), University College, Nairobi, Kenya, 1965-68. Appointments: Assistant Executive Engineer, 1968; Engineer in Charge of Design Office, 1969; Water Engineer in Charge of 6 Provinces, 1969-70. Memberships: A.M.I.C.E.; Graduate, E.A.I.E. Address: P.O. Box 1878, Dar es Salaam, Tanzania.

SY, Boubacar, born 1912. Teacher. Personal details: married to a teacher. Appointments: Prefect, M'Backe, 1960-66; Prefect of Department, Bakel, 1966-68; Permanent Deputy Secretary, Conference of Ministers of National Education of the Etats francophones. Memberships: former Member, Executive Committee, Progressive Union of Senegal. Honours: former Municipal Councillor, Diourbel; Knight of the Black Star of Benin; Knight of the Order of Merit; Knight of the National Order; ibid, Palmes Academiques. Address: Cabinet du President, B.P. 1145, Yaoundé, Cameroun.

SY, Seydina Oumar, born 10th October 1937. Diplomat. Education: Licencei en Droit—diplome de l'ENAS major de la section diplomatique; promotion 'Lamine Gueye'. Married, 4 children. Appointments: Chief, United Nations & International Organizations Division, Ministry of Foreign Affairs, Senegal, 1964-65; Director, Political, Cultural, & Social Affairs, ibid, 1965-66; Technical Counsellor, Cabinet of the Minister of Foreign Affairs, 1967; Executive Secretary, Senegal-Gambian Ministerial Inter-State Committee, 1968—. Address: Secretariat Permanent Senegambien, No. 4 Marina, Bathurst, The Gambia.

SY, Yoro Bocar, born 26th November 1928. Magistrate. Education: Baccalaureat, Paris, 1954; Licensed in Law, Grenoble, 1957; LL.D., Dakar, Senegal, 1963. Married, 5 children. Appointments: Advocate, Grenoble, France; Auditor to the Supreme Court of Senegal; Counsellor, then President of the Chamber to the Court of Appeal, Dakar; Assistant, Political Economy, University of Dakar, 1960-62. Member, National Association of Doctors of Law, Paris, France. Address: Court of Appeal, Abidjan, The Ivory Coast.

SYKES, Abbas Kleist, born 3rd September 1929. Foreign Service Officer. Education: King's College, Kampala, Uganda; Dar es Salaam Government School; Tabora Secondary School; Diplomatic Practice Course, Geneva, Switzerland. Personal details: divorced, 2 daughters. Appointments: Executive Member, Tanganyika African National Union Political Party, 1954-65; Privately Employed in Business, 1948-61; First Regional Commissioner, Dar es Salaam, 1962-63; Counsellor, Tanzania Embassy in Paris, France, 1967-68; Counsellor, Tanzania Embassy in Bonn, Germany, for 2 months; High Commissioner, High Commission of Tanzania, Ottawa, Canada, 1968—. Address: High Commission of the United Republic of Tanzania, 124 O'Connor Street, 6th Floor, Ottawa 4, Ontario, Canada.

SYLLA, Sory Ibrahim, born Mourrah, 1932. Army Officer. Married, 6 children. Appointments: Non-commissioned Officer, French Army, 1951-58; Junior Officer, ibid, 1958-60; Officer, 1960-61; transferred to Mali Army, with rank of Sub-Lieutenant, 1961; Captain, 1964—; Governor, 3rd Region, Sikasso. Hon. President, Association of Parents and Pupils of Sikasso, Mali. Honours: Medaillé du merite national du Mali, 1967. Address: Sikasso, Mali.

SZCZYGIEL, Bogdan, born 12th June 1928. Physician. Education: Faculty of Stomatology, Lodz, Poland; Faculty of Medicine, Zabrze; Specialization in Radiology. Appointments: Chief, Medical Equipment, International Civil Service, Algeria, 1964-65; Radiologist, Hospital, Niamey, Niger, 1966—. Memberships: Polish Section, World Union of Medical Writers; Polish Society of Radiology. Publications: Toubib parmis les nomades; Le masque aux niama-niama; Les fleaux noires du continent noir; numerous articles. Address: B.P. 5, Niamey, Niger.

T

TADESSE TERREFE, born 23rd October 1929. Educational Planner. Education: B.A., Health & Economics; Master in Letters & Educational Research; Iowa Wesleyan University, U.S.A.; University of Chicago; University of Pittsburgh. Personal details: married, 1 son. Appointments: Programme Specialist, UNESCO, Paris, France, for over 2 years; currently, Assistant Minister, Programme Planning & Research, Ministry of Education, for 15 years. Memberships: National Education Commission, Ethiopia; Society for International Development. Publications: Progress, Problems & Prospects of Ethiopian Education (article), 1964; several reports in International Education Year Books; Trends & Prospects of African Education (under preparation). Address: Ministry of Education, Addis Ababa, Ethiopia.

TAKYI, Henry Kwabena, born 25th May 1928. Surgical Specialist. Education: Achimota Secondary School, Ghana; Achimota Post Secondary Teacher Training College, Ghana; Bournemouth Municipal College, U.K.; Royal College of Surgeons, Ireland. Personal details: married, 2 children. Appointments: Pre-Reg. House surgeon, Royal City of Dublin Hospital, 1956; Pre-Reg. House Physician, ibid, 1957; Orthopaedic House Surgeon, Bedford General Hospital, 1958-59; Senior House Surgeon in General Surgery, Plastic Surgery, & Orthopaedic Surgery, Leicester General Hospital, 1959-60; Registrar, Casualty Dept., City Hospital, St. Albans, 1961; Senior House Officer in Traumatology, Birmingham Accident Hospital,

1961-62; Registrar, Casualty & Accident Dept., Southend General Hospital, 1963-64; Registrar in General Surgery, Bridgend General Hospital, 1964-65; Senior Medical Officer, Surgery, Ghana Civil Service, 1965-68. Memberships: Fellow, Royal College of Surgeons, Glasgow, U.K. Publications: Adult Hypertrophic Pyloric Stenosis (w. D. R. W. Haddock), 1967; Diverticulum in the Male Urethra, 1968. Address: Korle Bu Teaching Hospital, P.O. Box 77, Accra, Ghana.

TALEB-IBRAHIMI, Ahmed, born 5th January 1932. Minister of National Education, Algeria. Education: M.D., University of Paris, France. Married, 1 son. Appointments: President, Union Generale des Etudiants Musulmans Algeriens, 1955-56; Director, France Federation, Front de Liberation Nationale, 1956-57; imprisoned in France, 1957-62; Physician, Mustapha Hospital, Algiers, Algeria, 1962-65; Minister of National Education, 1965—. Memberships: Executive Board, UNESCO, 1968—; Société de Medecine de Paris. Publications: Lettres de Prison, 1966; also many medical publications. Address: Ministry of National Education, Algiers, Algeria.

TAMALE, Ibrahim Balaba Biri, born 2nd June 1936. Valuation Surveyor; Estate Manager. Education: Associate, Royal Institution of Chartered Surveyors; Associate, Institute of Housing Managers; Diploma, Estates Management. Married, 1 son, 2 daughters. Currently, Valuer, Martin Heymann & Co. Ltd., Kampala, Uganda. Memberships: Uganda Golf Club; Uganda Swimming Club; Uganda Rotary Club. Address: P.O. Box 3203, Kampala, Uganda.

TAMBA, Guillaume, born 10th February 1909. Principal Administrator, Posts & Telecommunications. Education: Diploma, Higher School of Administration. Married, 3 children. Appointments: Federal Director, Posts, Cameroun; Technical Adviser, Ministry of Posts & Telecommunications. Honours: Commander of the Order of Bravery; Knight of the Legion of Honour. Address: Technical Adviser, Ministry of Posts & Telecommunications, Yaoundé, Cameroun.

TAMBLYN, C. David, born 18th March 1943. Doctor of Medicine. Education: M.D., University of Western Ontario, Canada, 1967; Intern & Resident, Montreal General Hospital, 1967-69. Appointments: General Medical Officer, Uganda Government, Entebbe & Jinja, 1969—. Memberships: C.U.S.O. Volunteer. Address: P.O. Box 43, Jinja Uganda.

TAMRAT, Igezu, born 15th January 1916. Governor of Begue-Meoler & Semien. Education: Secondary College of the Brothers of Jerusalem. Appointments: Lt.-Col., Territorial Army; Director-General of the Municipality of Addis Ababa; Commandant en Second, Ethiopian Police; Governor-General of Jimma; Vice-Minister of Justice; ibid, Post, Telegraphs, & Telephones; Minister of Social Community; Governor of Honour. Memberships: President, Federation of Ethiopian Football; ibid, Ethiopian Y.M.C.A.; Vice-President of the Confederation of Sport of Ethiopia. Publications: Le Souvenir de exile a Jerusalem; Un livre de poesie. Honours: Several Ethiopian & English Military medals; Grand Cordons de l'Etoile Ethiopie; ibid, l'Ordre Meneluk; Un Grand Cordan Allemand; ibid, Denmark. Address: c/o Ministry of Social Community, Addis Ababa, Ethiopia.

TAMUSANGE, Shem Lwanga, born 27th November 1938. Medical Practitioner. Education: M.B., Ch.B., Makerere University, Kampala, Uganda, 1966; currently Studying for M.Med. (Obst. & Gyn.). Married, 1 son, 1 daughter. Currently, Medical Officer, Ministry of Health, Uganda Government. Memberships: Uganda Medical Association; Uganda Civil Servants Association. Contributor to Journal of Obstetrics & Gynaecology of the British Commonwealth, 1970. Honours: Nestlé Terminal Prize in Paediatrics, 1964; Nestlé Paediatric Prize, 1965. Address: P.O. Box 1948, Kampala, Uganda.

TAMWO, Soffo Ignace, born February 1940. Director, S.C.E.A. Married, 5 children. Appointments: Merchant, Unionist, Commercial Director of S.C.E.A. Memberships: Secretary, National Financial Syndicate. Author of publications. Address: B.P. 86, M'banga, Cameroun.

TANDIAN, Ibrahima, born 1st November 1935. Civil Administrator. Licensed in Law. Appointments: Technical Adviser; Prefect of the Demen; Prefect of Diourbel; Deputy Governor.

TANDON, Yashpal, born Kaberamaido, Uganda, 21st June 1939. University Lecturer. Education: Cambridge School Certificate, Senior Secondary School, Mbale, 1950-56; G.C.E. A Level, North-Western Polytechnic, London, U.K., 1958; B.Sc.(Econ.), London School of Economics, London University, 1958-61; Ph.D., ibid, 1961-64 (received 1968 in International Relations). Married, 1 child. Appointments: Teacher, Primary School, Mbale, 1957; Lecturer in International Relations, Department of Political Science & Public Administration, Makerere University, Kampala, Uganda, 1964-68; Senior Lecturer, ibid, 1969—; Executive Director & Lecturer, Makerere Institute in Diplomacy, 1966-68; Consultant, Peacemakers' Academy, Oslo, 1968. Author of several papers in International Relations, Africa Quarterly, Minerva, Makerere Political Review, & other scholarly journals & books. Honours: Uganda Government Postgraduate Scholarship, 1961-64; Senior Research Fellowship, School of International Affairs, Columbia University, New York, U.S.A., 1967; Cecil Prize, David Davies Memorial Institute in International Peace, London, U.K. Address: Makerere University College, Department of Political Science, P.O. Box 7062, Kampala, Uganda.

TANIMOWO, Rufus Akinloye, born Modakeke, Ile-Ife, Nigeria, 24th April 1926. Teacher. Education: St. Peter's School, Araromi via Ilesha,1931-34; St. Stephen's School, Modakeke, 1935-36; Oduduwa College, Ile-Ife, 1937-43; Fourah Bay College, Sierra Leone, 1947-51; Higher Dip.Ed., Trinity College,

Dublin, Ireland, 1955-56: B.A., Durham. Married, 2 sons, 3 daughters. Appointments: 3rd Class Clerk, Ife Divisional Council, 1944; Audit Department Lagos, 1945-47; Teacher, Oduduwa College, Ile-Ife, 1952-59; Principal, Modakeke High School, 1960—. Memberships include: British Classical Association; one-time Member, Western Regional Scholarship Board, 1963-65; Chairman, Ife Branch, Nigeria English Studies Association (N.E.S.A.); Secretary, Ife Prison Committee; Anglican Ibadan Diocese. Address: Modakeke High School, P.O. Box 157, Ile-Ife, Nigeria.

TANO-DRAMAN, Michel, born 24th February 1931. Engineer. Education: Primary Studies, Abengouro, CEPE, 1940-46; Secondary Studies, Chateauroux, France, 1946-54; Baccalaureat in Mathematics; MPC & Electricity Certificates, Faculty of Sciences, Poitiers, 1954-59; Engineering Studies, OCORA-ORTF, Paris, France, 1959-63. Married, 2 children. Appointments: Head of Service, Relais Hertzien, 1963-64; Head, Television Production Centre, 1964-68; Inspector of Transmitters & Relais Hertzien, 1968-69; Head of Service, Technical Television, 1969—. Memberships: Treasurer-General, Association of Radio Amateurs of the Ivory Coast. Address: RTI, B.P. 2261, Abidjan, Ivory Coast.

TARANTINO (Rt. Rev.) Angelo, born Italy, 8th April 1908. Bishop of Arua, Uganda. Education: Primary, 6 Years; Secondary, 6 years; Philosophy Course, 3 years; Theology Course, 4 years. Appointments include: School Supervisor for 20 years, Lango District, Uganda; Vicar-General, Diocese of Gulu, 1952-59; Bishop of Arua, 1959—. Publications include: History of the Lango (Luo Language); The Martyrs of Uganda; English Lango Acholi Dictionary; several Primary Readers in Luo Language; The Marriage Amongst Lango (Anthropos). Honours include: M.B.E., 1956; The Uganda Independence Medal, 1962. Address: Bishop's House, P.O. Box 135, Arua, Uganda.

TARAORE, Amidou Noel, born 23rd December 1935. Veterinarian. Education: Lycée Terrassory de Fougere, Bamako, Mali, 1954-56; Lycée National du Parc, Lyon, France, 1956-58; National Veterinary School, Alfort, France, 1958-62; Institute of Breeding & Veterinary Medicine of Tropical Countries, Alfort, 1962-63. Married. Appointments: Director of Services, Breeding & Animal Industries, Upper Volta, 1964; Vice-President, Council of Administration, National Bank of Development, 1967; Member, Administrative Commission, l'Office International des Epizoolies, Paris, 1967-70. Address: 94 Giovanni Branca, Interno 21, Rome, Italy.

TARIMO, Onesphoro Onesmo, born 1st January 1931. Administrative Officer. Education: N.A. Primary School, Marangu; Government Secondary School Old Moshi; Administration Course, Administrative Officers' Training Centre, Mzumbe, 1961; Public Administration Course, Institute of Public Administration, University College, Dar es Salaam, Tanzania, 1964; Labour Administration Course, London, U.K., 1965. Appointments: Clerk, Government Service, 1951; Assistant District Officer, 1961; District Commissioner, 1962; Local Government Officer; Senior Assistant Secretary; Administrative Secretary; Area Secretary. Address: Ministry of Regional Administration, P.O. Box 9011, Dar es Salaam, Tanzania.

TAWIAH, Joseph Kobina Chinto, born 1918. Educator. Education: Standard 7 (Middle Form IV) Certificate, 1933; Certificate A, St. Augustine's Teacher Training College, Cape Coast, Ghana, 1937. Appointments: School Teacher, 1938-42; Army Schoolmaster, Gold Coast Regiment (Ghana), 1942-47; District Education Secretary, 1948-54; Clerk of Council, Sefwi Wiawso, 1954-60; District Court Magistrate, Grade II, 1960—. Recipient, Army Medal, 1939-45. Address: P.O. Box 285, Kumasi, Ghana.

TAY, David Cyril Kwadzo, born 20th May, 1935. Civil (Structural) Engineer. Education: Mawuli Secondary School, Ho, Ghana, 1951-55; 6th Form, College of Technology, Kumasi, 1956-57; B.Sc.(Lond.), Engineering, ibid, 1958-61; M.A.Sc., University of Toronto, Canada, 1963; Ph.D., ibid, 1968. Married, 1 daughter. Appointments: Highway Design Engineer, A. D. Margison & Associates, Consulting Engineers, Toronto, 1962-63; Part-time Instructor, University of Toronto, 1963-67; Design Engineer, Morrison, Hershfield, Millman & Huggins, Toronto, 1968; Lecturer, University of Science & Technology, Kumasi, Ghana, 1968—. Member, American Concrete Institute. Address: Department of Civil Engineering, University of Science & Technology, Kumasi, Ghana.

TAYE MAKURIA, born 5th April 1929. Physician; Surgeon. Education: Hailé Selassié I Secondary School; International College, Beirut, Lebanon; B.A., University of British Columbia, Canada; M.D., American University of Beirut, 1956. Married, 1 son, 3 daughters. Appointments: Surgical Specialization, 1956-62; Surgeon & Assistant Director, St. Paul's Hospital, Addis Ababa, Ethiopia, 1962-64; Medical Director & Chief Surgeon, Armed Forces Hospital, ibid, 1964-67; Study Tour, Britain & U.S.A., 1967-68; Associate Professor, Surgery, Hailé Selassié I University, Ethiopia, 1969—. Memberships: Fellow, Royal College of Surgeons, Ireland & Glasgow; ibid, East African College of Surgeons; ibid, International College of Surgeons; African Federation Secretary & Member, Executive Council, ibid. Author, Ureteral Transplantation. Research on thyroid diseases in Ethiopia & the ulcer problem in Ethiopia. Address: Hailé Selassié I University, P.O. Box 1844, Addis Ababa, Ethiopia.

TAYE TEFERI, born November 1928. Vice-Speaker of the Chamber of Deputies of Ethiopia. Education: Ras Tesemma Nadew Elementary School, Bedelle; Hailé Selassié I Secondary School, Gore; Diploma, Law, Hailé Selassié I University; Certificate in Law. Married, 6 children. Appointments: Governor, Sub-District of Borecha, Illubabor Province; Member, Chamber of Deputies, 12 years; Vice-Speaker, Chamber of Deputies. Member, Inter-parliamentary Union, Ethiopian Group. Address: P.O. Box 1602, Addis Ababa, Ethiopia.

TAYLOR, Barbara Joyce, born 30th December 1931. Teacher. Education: Nelson College for Girls, New Zealand; Christchurch Teachers' College; B.A., Canterbury University College, 1954. Married, 4 daughters. Appointments: Victory School, Nelson, 1951; Infants' Teacher, Beckenham School, Christchurch, 1954-56; Secondary Teacher, Hutt Valley High School, 1957; temporary voluntary relieving positions, Stockley School, Dodema, Tanzania, & Arusha School, 1964-70. Memberships: Christchurch Harmonic Society; Mothers' Union; President, Christ Church Arusha Ladies' Guild; Provincial Secretary, N.Z.C.M.S. League of Youth, 1957-58. Address: P.O. Box 263, Arusha, Tanzania.

TAYLOR, John Barry. Education Officer; Author. Education: B.A.(Hons.), London, U.K.; Dip.Ed., Cambridge; Perugia University. Italy. Appointments: Senior English Master & Second Master, Busoga College, Mwiri, Uganda. Memberships: Uganda Y.M.C.A.; Royal Commonwealth Society, London; Uganda Britain Society; Convocation, London University; Society of Authors; Poetry Society, London. Publications: Dickens (a narrative poem), 1967; Half of the Sun (novel), 1969; The Rhyme of Francis Fall (verse novel), 1970, to be anthologized in East African Poetry, 1971; Midsummer Variations, 1970. Recipient, Uganda Independence Medal, 1963. Address: P.O. Box 20, Jinja, Uganda.

TAYLOR, John Frederic, born 14th March 1935. Surgeon. Education: M.D., Liverpool Medical School, U.K., 1965; F.R.C.S., London, 1966; D.T.M.&H., Liverpool, 1962. Married, 3 children. Appointments: Mission Doctor, Scottish Livingstone Hospital, Molepolde, Bechuanaland, 1960-62; Hon. Lecturer in Surgery, & B.E.C.C. Research Associate, Makerere University Medical School, Kampala, Uganda. Author of various review articles. Address: Makerere Medical School, Box 7072, Kampla, Uganda.

TAYLOR, Ronald John, born 21st September, 1933. Clergyman; Missionary Education: Timaru Boys' High School, New Zealand, 1947-51; B.A., Canterbury University College, 1952-55; M.A., 1960; Th.L.(Hons.), Ridley College, Melbourne, Australia, 1956; currently studying for S.Th. & Ph.D. Married, 4 daughters. Appointments: ordained, Diocese of Wellington, 1957; Curate, St. James' Lower Hutt, 1957; ibid, St. Matthew's, Masterton, 1958-60; Vicar, Martinborough, 1960-63; Chaplain, Cathedral of the Holy Spirit, Dodoma, Tanzania, Education Secretary, Warden of Christian Council Conference Centre, Pastoral Oversight of Great North Road, 1964-67; Vicar, Christ Church, Arusha, 1968—. Memberships: President, Dodoma Club, 1966-67; Secretary, U.M.C.A. Building Fund Campaign, 1969-70; ibid, Rotary Club, Arusha, 1970; Leader, School & University Orchestras. Address: Christ Church, P.O. Box 263, Arusha, Tanzania.

TCHANA, Mesack, born 1943. Agricultural Engineer; Engineer of Waters & Forests responsible for the Animal Life & Hunting in Eastern Cameroon. Education: Secondary Studies, College of Nkmgsamba; Lycée of Yaoundé; Baccalaureat, School of Agriculture, Yaoundé; Diploma, Agricultural Engineering, National School of Rural Engineering, Waters & Forests, France. Address: Head of Service for the Protection of the Animal Life & Hunting, B.P. 194, Yaoundé, Cameroun.

TCHOUTA MOUSSA, born 18th November 1937. Telecommunications Engineer. Education: Lycée Leclerc, Yaoundé; B.E.P.C.; Bacc. Mathematics; Higher Studies, France; Engineering Diploma, Enst, Paris. Personal details: married to Deputy General Magistrate of the Court of Appeal of Yaoundé. Appointments: Engineer, 2nd Class, 3rd Rank; Deputy Director, Posts & Telecommunications of Cameroun; Director of Telecommunications of Cameroun. Address: Director of Telecommunications, Yaoundé, Cameroun.

TEGEGNE YETESHA-WORK, born 15th August 1935. Journalist. Education: B.A., Law, University College, A.A., 1959; M.Sc., Journalism, Boston University, U.S.A., 1961. Appointments: Editor-in-Chief, The Ethiopian Herald (English language daily), 1961-69; General Manager, Press in Ethiopia, 1969—. Member, Lions International. Address: Press Department, P.O. Box 1364, Addis Ababa, Ethiopia.

TEJAN SIE, Banja, born 7th August 1917. Judge, Politician, Acting Governor-General of Sierra Leone. Education: Bo School, Freetown; Prince of Wales School; London School of Economics, University of London, U.K.; Council of Legal Education, 1947-51; Called to the Bar, Lincoln's Inn, 1951. Married. Appointments include: Station Clerk, Sierra Leone Railway, 1938-39; Nurse, Medical Department, 1940-46; Editor, West African Students' Union Magazine & Executive Committee Member, West African Students' Union, 1948-51; National Vice-President, Sierra Leone People's Party, 1953-56; Member, Keith Lucas Commission on Electoral Reform, 1954; Police Magistrate, Northern Province, 1958; Senior Police Magistrate, Provinces, 1961; represented Sierra Leone (with Solicitor-General), Conference on the future of Law in Africa, 1959-60; appointed Speaker of Parliament, 1962; Official Visitor, U.S.A., 1962; led Sierra Leone Delegations to Middle Level Manpower Conference, Puerto Rico, 1962, Commonwealth Parliamentary Association Meeting, Nigeria, 1962, & the Inter-Parliamentary Union, Belgrade, Yugoslavia, 1963; paid Official Visits to Italy & Israel, 1963, & to Germany & Denmark, 1963; Leader, Parliamentary Delegation to U.S.S.R., 1963, Taiwan, Nationalist China, 1965, & U.A.R. & Lebanon, 1965; attended Commonwealth Speakers' Conference, London, U.K., 1965, & 700th anniversary celebration, Simon de Montfort's Parliament, 1965; visited Italy & had private audience with the Pope, 1963; attended Opening Ceremonies, Knesset, Israel, 1966; Chief Justice of Sierra Leone, 1967; Acting Governor-General of Sierra Leone, 1968.

Memberships: Hon. Secretary, Sierra Leone Bar Association, 1957-58; Chairman, Board of Trustees, Cheshire Foundation, Sierra Leone, 1966. Honours, Prizes, etc: C.M.G., 1967. Address: 14B Syke Street, Freetown, Sierra Leone.

TEJUOSO, Adedapo Adewale, born 19th February 1938. Medical Practitioner. Education: Abeokuta Grammar School, Nigeria, 1951-56; Trinity College, Dublin, Ireland, 1958-64; University of Bristol, U.K., 1968-69; Royal Institute of Public Health & Hygiene, 1969-70; M.A.; M.B., Ch.B.; B.A.O.; D.T.M.&H.; D.P.H.; D.I.H. Married. Appointments: House appointments in medicine & surgery & Senior House Officer, Medicine, Lagos University Teaching Hospital, Nigeria, 1964-66. Memberships: General Secretary, Literary & Debating Society, Abeokuta Grammar School, 1956; Senior Prefect, ibid, 1956; President, Nigeria Union of Great Britain & Ireland, Dublin, 1962-63. Author, Schistosomiasis in Nigeria, 1969. Address: 1 Awonaike Crescent, off Tejuoso Street, Surulere, Nigeria.

TEKLE MARIAM ABAYRE (Dejazmach), born 26th June 1926. District Governor. Education: Ecclesiastical, Amharic, Ethiopia; English Language, Kenya; Army Cadet Course; Army Officers' Training Course; Senior Officers' Course (all with diplomas); Diploma, Law (Amharic), Hailé Selassié I University. Appointments: Corporal, Second English Regular Army; Sergeant, Lieutenant & Captain, Body Guard Commander of the Crown Prince in Dessie; Major, Commander of 6th, 17th, & 28th Battalions consecutively; ibid, Head, Department of Law, 2nd Division Headquarters; Lt.-Colonel & Colonel, Head Department of Law, Ministry of Defence; Colonel District Governor, Chebo & Gurage; ibid, Jibat & Mecha. Memberships: Hailé Selassié I Officers' Club; Alemgena to Wollamo Road Construction Firm; Officers' Family Welfare Association; Wolkite to Hosaena Road Construction Firm. Contributor, Voice of Ethiopia & Victory by Law. Honours: 2 medals, British Government; 9 medals, Ethiopian Government. Address: Ambo, Hagere Hiwot, Shoa, Ethiopia.

TEMBO, John Zenus U., born 14th September, 1932. Minister of Trade & Industry of Malawi. Education: B.A.(S.A.); P.C.E. (London). Married, 2 children. Appointments: elected to Parliament of Malawi, 1961; Deputy Minister of Finance, 1962; Minister of Finance, 1964; Minister of Finance, Trade, & Industry & Development & Planning, 1965; Minister of Trade & Industry, 1969—; Governor-Designate, Reserve Bank of Malawi, 1970. Address: P.O. Box 1066, Blantyre, Malawi.

TEMBO, Sylvester Kondwerani, born 2nd March, 1937. Co-operative Officer; Member of National Assembly of Zambia. Education: Form II (N.R.), 1958; Diploma, Co-operative Professional Training, Bonn, Germany, 1964-65. Married, 4 children. Appointments: Supervisor, i/c Export Department & G/Nuts Processing Factory, 1958-61; Constituency Chairman, Katite District, United National Independence Party, 1960; Assistant Manager, Katete Co-operative Marketing Union Ltd. with 44 primary co-ops, 1961-64; Regional Trustee, Katete/Chadiza Re Region, also responsible for youths, 1962-64; Principal Assistant to the Production Director, British American Tobaccos (Zambia) Ltd., 1965-66; Co-operative Officer, Zambian Government, 1966-68; attended Management Course, Staff Training College, now Institute for Public Administration, 1967; elected, Representative, Constituency No. 41, Petauke West on United National Independence Party ticket to the National Assembly, 1968; District Governor, Kalulushi District, 1968; ibid, Ministry of National Guidance, Lusaka, 1969; transferred to the Office of the President. Memberships: Chairman, Katete Youth Organizing Committee; Secretary-General, Welfare Society; ibid, Football Association, 1958-63; Treasurer, Mphangwe Consumers' Co-op.; Chairman & Treasurer, Katete Ohio Brothers' Singing Club. Address: Office of the President, P.O. Box 208, Lusaka, Zambia.

TEMPLE, Paul Harrison, born 1st May 1936. University Teacher. Education: Private school, 1941-46; Bridlington School, U.K., 1946-55; B.A.(Hons.), Liverpool University, 1955-58; Postgraduate Research Studentship & State Scolarship, ibid, 1958; Leverhulme Travelling Scholar, 1959; M.A., 1960; Ph.D., London University, 1966; Visiting Research Fellow, Merton College, Oxford University, 1969. Married. Appointments: Tutor, University of Liverpool, 1958-60; Assistant Lecturer, Makerere University College, Kampala, Uganda, 1960-62; Lecturer, ibid, 1962-67; Senior Lecturer, University College of Dar es Salaam, Tanzania, 1967—; Head, Department of Geography, ibid, 1969-70. Memberships: Fellow, Royal Geographical Society; Fellow, Geological Society of London; Institute of British Geographers; British Geomorphological Research Group; Founder Member, East African Academy. Author of a number of professional papers in scientific publications. Honours: Percy Maude Roxby Memorial Prize, Liverpool University, 1958. Address: Department of Geography, The University, Dar es Salaam, Tanzania.

TENESI, Boniface, born Bukoba District, Tanzania, 15th May, 1936. Senior Agricultural Officer. Education: Ihungo Junior Secondary School; Pugu College; B.Sc.(Lond.), Agriculture, Makerere University College, Kampala, Uganda, 1956-61. Married, 4 children. Appointments: joined Tanzania Civil Service, 1961; District, then Regional Agricultural Officer; with Ministry of Economic Affairs & Development Planning; currently with Planning Division, Ministry of Agriculture Food & Co-operatives. Address: P.O. Box 9192, Dar es Salaam, Tanzania.

TERRY, Philip John, born 29th October 1942. Research Officer; Botanist. Education: B.Tech.(Hons.), Applied Biology, Brunel University (formerly Brunel College of Advanced Technology), U.K., 1961-65. Married. Appointments: Research Officer (Botanist), Tropical Pesticides Research Institute, Arusha, Tanzania, 1966. Memberships: Hon. Treasurer, Arusha Amateur Arts Society, 1967-70. Author of miscellaneous reports. Address: Tropical

Pesticides Research Institute, P.O. Box 3024, Arusha, Tanzania.

TESFAYE ENGUE SELASSIE (Rt. Hon. Deji), born 30th July, 1914. Governor. Education: Church Education; Reading & Writing Amharic. Married, 5 sons, 5 daughters. Appointments: Sub-District Governor with rank of Kangnazmatch; District Governor with rank of Fetawerare; Senator, House of Lords; District Governor with rank of Dadjazmatch. Member, Patriot Association of Ethiopia. Honours: Hailé Selassié I Honorary Medal of Five Leaves; St. George Patriot Medal of Two Leaves; Trinity Medal. Address: Fikre Mariam Abba Techan Street, Addis Ababa, Ethiopia.

TETTEH, Percival Austin, born 16th August, 1929. Community Planner; University Lecturer. Education: Mfantsipim School, Cape Coast, Ghana; University of Ghana, 1949-54; Cornell University, Ithaca, N.Y., 1956-57; Athens Technological Institute, Athens, Greece, 1960-61; University of Pa., 1967-71. Married, 3 children. Appointments: Government Sociologist, Ghana, 1954-60; Census Planner, 1960-61; Assistant Director, Institute for Community Planning, Kumasi, 1961-63; Senior Lecturer, University of Science & Technology, Kumasi. Memberships: Town Planning Institute of Canada; British Sociological Association; International Union for Scientific Study of Population. Publications: Social & Economic Aspects of Urbanization in Ghana (w. B. Gil); Family & Household (chapter in Survey of Contemporary Ghana Vol. 2). Address: University of Science & Technology, Kumasi, Ghana.

THAHANE, Timothy Thahane, born Mpharane, Leribe, Lesotho, 2nd November, 1940. Economist. Education: Moselinyane Primary School, Leribe, 1949-54; Hlotse Higher Primary, ibid, 1955-56; Lesotho High School, Maseru, 1957-60; B.A.(Hons.), Economics, B.Comm., Personnel Administration & Industrial Labour Relations, Memorial University of Newfoundland, St. Johns, Canada, 1962-67; M.A., Economics, University of Toronto, 1967-68. Appointments: Standard Bank Ltd., Meseru, Lesotho, 1961-62; Employment Surveys' Division, Dominion Bureau of Statistics, Ottawa, Canada, 1965; Collective Bargaining Division, Economics & Research Branch, Department of Labour, ibid, 1966; Planning Officer, Government Central Planning Office, Maseru, Lesotho, 1968; Acting Director of Planning, then Principal Assistant Secretary, 1968-70; Director of Planning, 1970—. Member, Regional Science Association, Philadelphia. Publications: Collective Bargaining Provisions in Major Manufacturing Industries in Canada (Labour Gazette), 1967; The Role of Institutions in Manpower Training & Utilization (a report for the Royal Commission on the Economic Prospects of Newfoundland & Labrador), 1967. Address: P.O. Box 656, Maser, Lesotho.

THAIRU, Bernard Kihumbu, born 11th January, 1941. Physician. Education: Cambridge Overseas School Certificate, O Levels, Thika High School, 1956-59; Biology, Physics, Chemistry, Makerere University College, Kampala, Uganda, 1960-62; M.B., Ch.B. (E.A.), Makerere University College Medical School, 1962-67; currently studying for Ph.D., University College, London, U.K. Appointments: Assistant Lecturer, Physiology, University College, Nairobi Medical School, Kenya, 1968. Honours: total of 7 points in School Certificate, Thika High School, 1959; Uganda Medical Association Prize for Anatomy & Alexander Galloway Prize for Physiology & Biochemistry, 1964; One Nestle's Prize in Paediatrics, 1966; Nuffield Travelling Scholarship, 1966; Makerere University College Exhibition Prize, 1966-67; Louis & Mitchell Prize in Medicine & Surgery, 1967. Address: Department of Physiology, University College, Gower St., London, W.C.1, U.K.

THAKKAR, Jayant Ambalal, born India, 13th July 1927. Medical Practitioner. Education: M.B., B.S., Bombay University. Married. Came to Uganda, 1953. Appointments: Trustee, Youth League of Kampala; President, Kampala Kala Kendra; Provost, Uganda Faculty, Royal College of General Practitioners. Memberships: Past President, Youth League of Kampala, Uganda Medical Society, & Uganda Badminton Association; Past Secretary, Kampala Lohana Community & East African Lohana Conference; Past Treasurer, Uganda Medical Society; Uganda Medical Association. Recipient of several swards for actor & producer of drama. Address: P.O. Box 1751, Kampala, Uganda.

THAKKAR, Vadilal Vithaldas, born 9th June 1921. Electrical & Mechanical Engineer. Education: Diploma in Electrical Engineering; Diploma in Mechanical Engineering; Proficiency Second Class Engineer for Steam Engines & Boilers. Married, 4 sons, 2 daughters. Appointments: Assistant Engineer, Alembic Chemical Works Ltd., Baroda, India, 1944-49; Electrical Engineer, Uganda Sisal Estates Ltd., Masindi Port, Uganda, 1949-52; Electrical & Mechanical Engineer, M/S Madhvani Sugar Works Ltd. (oil mill), Kakira-Jinja, Uganda, 1952—. Memberships: Fellow, East African Institution of Engineers; Associate, Institution of Electrical Engineers, London. Address: P.O. Box 3036, Kakira-Jinja, Uganda.

THAKRAR, Narshidas Ranchhoddas, born 20th December 1918. Merchant. Married, 5 children. Appointments: Director, Popat Brothers Ltd.; Director, Y. Karimjee & Co. Ltd.; Director, Seta Coffee Curing Co. Ltd. Address: P.O. Box 588, Kampala, Uganda.

THELEJANE, Thomas Sohl, born 17th October, 1933. Lecturer in Science Education. Education: M.Sc.(Rhodes). Appointments: Head, Zoology Department, Pius XII College, 1959-64; ibid, University of Botswana Lesotho, & Swaziland, 1964-66; Senior Lecturer, Science Methods, School of Education, ibid, 1966—. Memberships: Executive, Science Education Programme for Africa; Chairman, Lesotho Museum Board; Lesotho Science Association; Lesotho Social Studies Programme; Lesotho Science Education Programme. Publications: Pondo Rain Making Ritual: Ukukhonga, (African Studies), 1963; Some Observations on the Activities of Brant's or Basuto Gerbille,

1963; Animals of Lesotho, 1965-66. Address: School of Education, U.B.L.S., Roma, Lesotho.

THIAW, Oumar, born 24th March 1936. Engineer-Statistician. Education: Diploma of Statistics, National School of Statistics & Economic Administration, ENSAE, Paris, France. Appointments: Engineer-Statistician, Statistics Direction, 1962; Director, Planification, 1967—. Author of various publications, e.g. Situation Economique de Senegal. Address: Direction de la Planification, Secretariat of State, Senegal.

THOMAS, Abraham Mannakunnil, born 14 February 1932. University Lecturer. Education: M.Sc., Agra, India; Ph.D., ibid; A.R.I.C. Personal details: married to Grace Thomas, daughter of K. T. Thomas, 1962. Appointments: Lecturer, St. John's College, Agra; ibid, St. Xavier's College, Calcutta; University of Science & Technology, Kumasi, Ghana; Visiting Lecturer, University of California, U.S.A. Author of Research Publications in the Field of Organic Chemistry, Synthetic & Phyto Chemistry. Address: c/o University of California, U.S.A.

THOMAS, Eric Olaniran, born 7th November, 1929. Dental Technologist. Education: St. John's Primary School, Igbein, Abeokuta, Nigeria; Abeokuta Grammar School, 1942-48; 2nd Class Hons., Inter, City & Guilds London Dental Technical Course, 1961; 2nd Class Hons., Final, ibid, 1963. Married. Appointments: Dental Assistant in Training, 1950-54; Dental Technical Assistant, 1956-63; Dental Technologist, 1964. Address: Dental Centre, Abeokuta, Western State, Nigeria.

THOMAS, Ian David, born 7th October 1937. University Lecturer. Education: Hampton Grammar School, U.K.; B.A.(Hons.), University of Wales, 1956-59; M.A.(External), ibid, 1966; Postgraduate Certificate of Education, Institute of Education, University of London, 1959-60. Married, 2 children. Appointments: Overseas Civil Service, Tanganyika, 1960-65; Assistant Lecturer, University College, Swansea, 1965-66; Lecturer, University College of Dar es Salaam, 1966-70. Memberships: Tanzania Society; Royal African Society; Institute of British Geographers; Editor, Journal, Geographical Association of Tanzania, 1967-70. Author of papers in various professional journals. Honours: Population Council Fellowship, 1970-71. Address: University of Dar es Salaam, Tanzania.

THOMPSON, Charles Quarcoo, born 13th March, 1913. Photographer; Civil Servant. Education: Standard 7 (Middle); Secondary Form 4. Married, 5 sons, 4 daughters. Appointments: Dark-room Supervisor, British Information Services under 'Office West African Council', 1943-49; Acting Photographic Superintendent 1949-51 on Scholarship to Britain with Central Office of Information, 1951; Photo Superintendent, 1953; Chief Photographer, Ministry of Information, Accra, Ghana, 1958. Memberships: A.I.B.P., 1954; A.R.P.S., 1957; Accra Hearts of Oak Sporting Club, 1930—; Executive Member, ibid, 1956. Honours: Diploma in Agfa Colour, 1952; Certificate of Honour (World Press Photo), 1963; Diploma, Agfa Black & White & Agfa Colour, 1964. Address: Ministry of Information, Photographic Division, Box 745, Accra, Ghana.

THOMPSON, Olabowale, born 22nd June, 1927. Medical Practitioner. Education: St. Jame's School, Ibadan, Nigeria; St. David's School, Akure; Government College, Ibadan; Higher College, Yaba; University College, Ibadan; West London Hispital, U.K. Personal details: son of Chief James Adegbola Gureje Thompson; wife, daughter of a prince in Ijeshaland. Appointments: Assistant Medical Officer, 1951; Medical Officer, 1954; Senior M.O.H., 1963; Principal Medical Officer, 1965; Epidemiologist, 1966; Chief Health Officer, 1970. Memberships: British Medical Association; Royal Society of Medicine, London; Negerian Medical Association; Nigeria Society of Health; Royal Commonwealth Society, London; Ibadan Tennis Club. Contributor to Nigerian Society of Health Journal. Honours: Provincial Scholarship, 1939; Nigerian Government Scholarship, 194. Address: Ministry of Health, Ibadan, Nigeria.

THOMSON, Kenneth Derek Bousfield, born 16th August 1925. Medical Practitioner. Education: Rugby School; M.B., B.S., D.P.H., & D.T.M.&H., Middlesex Hospital, London, U.K. Married, 1 son, 1 daughter. Appointments: House Physician, Royal Berks. Hospital, Reading, & Rochford General Hospital; Medical Officer, Colonial Medical Service, Nigeria, 1951; Rural Medical Officer, North Nigeria; Senior Medical Officer, ibid; Consultant, Rural Health; Consultant, Sleeping Sickness Service; Consultant, Epidemiological Unit, N.I.T.R., Kaduna. Publications: Rural Health in Northern Nigeria: some recent developments & problems (Trans. Royal Soc. Trop. Med. & Hyg.), 1967; The Present Sleeping Sickness Situation in the Northern States of Nigeria (J. Trop. Med. & Hyg.), 1969. Address: Epidemiological Unit, Nigerian Institute for Trypanosomiasis Research, P.M.B. 2077, Kaduna, Nigeria.

THORNTON, David Dillon, born 16th July 1930. Agricultural Research. Education: Dulwich College, U.K., 1941-48; B.Sc.(Agric.), London University, 1950-53; Dip. Animal Husbandry, Reading University, 1953-54; M.Sc. Animal Husbandry, London University, 1954-55; M.S., Range Management, University of California, U.S.A., 1961. Married, 2 sons, 1 daughter. Appointments: Pasture Agronomist, Department of Veterinary Services & Animal Husbandry, Government of Uganda, 1956-65; Senior Nutritionist, ibid, 1965-66; Chief Research Officer, 1966-68; Agricultural Officer, Range Ecologist, Tanzania, 1969—. Memberships: American Society of Range Management, 1960-69; British Grassland Society. Author of several articles in professional publications. Address: UNDP/SF Livestock Development Project no. 279, c/o Box 9182, Dar es Salaam, Tanzania.

TIBAIJUKA, Philip Bagenda, born 21st November 1923. Teacher; Editor; Literature Secretary & Manager of Bookshop. Education: Teachers' Training College; Writers' Course; Bible Translators' Course; Language Course,

London University. Married with children. Appointments: Teacher, 1942; Headmaster, Primary School, 1948; Assistant Literature Secretary, 1956; Literature Secretary, 1958; Editor, Ija Webonere, 1959; Manager of Bookshop, 1964. Memberships: Chairman, ELCT Publications Boards, 4 years; ibid, C.C.T. Publication Board, 2 years. Publications: Translator, Haya New Testament; Editor of monthly magazine; Tutunze Jamaa; Tuendelee Kusoma; Haya Primers Book I & II; Editor, Swahili Literacy Primer Books 1-9; Editor & Composer of hymnal books, devotional books & history books. Address: c/o Church Bookshop, P.O. Box 277, Bukoba, Tanzania.

TIGRAN KAZANDJIAN, born Addis Ababa, Ethiopia, 31st August 1934. Civil Engineer. Education: American University of Beirut, Lebanon; University College, Hailé Selassié I University, Addis Ababa, Ethiopia. Appointments: R.E. with Imperial Highway Authority, Addis Ababa; Manager, Industrial Department, Seferian & Co. (Ethiopia) Ltd. S.C. Address: P.O. Box 1865, Addis Ababa, Ethiopia.

TIMMIS, William Guy, born 24th April 1910. Medical Missionary. Education: Birkenhead School, U.K.; M.B., Ch.B., D.P.H., D.T.M.&H., Liverpool University, 1928-33. Married. Appointments: M.O., Wrightington Hospital, Lancashire, 1936-38; Captain, R.A.M.C., 1939-45; Uganda Medical Service, 1946-62; Member, Church Missionary Society (Australia), Hombolo Leprosy Centre, Tanzania, 1963—. Member, Royal Society of Tropical Medicine. Address: D.C.T. Hombolo Leprosy Centre, P.O. Box 301, Dodoma, Tanzania.

TOLIA, Jayantilal Narbheram, born 17th August 1922. Physician; Eye Specialist. Education: M.B., B.S., University of Bombay, India, D.O.M.S.; R.C.P.(London); R.C.S. (England). Inventor of Tolia's Discission Needle, a new surgical instrument used in eye surgery. Address: P.O. 10156, Nairobi, Kenya.

TOMBALBAYE (His Excellency) Francois, President of the Republic of Chad, born Bassada, 15th June 1918. Appointments: Teacher, Fort Lamy, Fort-Archambault & various other places; Founder Member, Chad Progressive Party (PPT); President, Secretary-General, ibid, 1960—; Territorial Councillor, Chad, 1952; re-elected, 1957; High Councillor, French Equatorial Africa, 1957; Vice-President, Grand Council, ibid; Member of Parliament for Middle Chari, 1957; Prime Minister, 1959; declared Head of State, 1960-62; President of the Council of Ministers, in charge of National Defence, 1960-62; President of the Republic, 1962—; Minister of the Armed Forces & the Interior, 1966—. Memberships: Organization of African Unity; Common Afro-Malagasy Organization; Central African Customs & Economic Union. Address: Fort Lamy, Chad.

TÖRNKVIST, Leif Sören Erik, born 26th September 1936. Educator. Education: B.Sc., M.Sc., Ph.D., University of Uppsala, Sweden; D.M., Royal Academy of Music, Stockholm. Appointments: Assistant Professor, University of Uppsala; Tutor, Kenya Science Teachers' College; Visiting Reader, University College, Nairobi. Author of a number of papers on nuclear physics in professional journals. Address: Physics Department, University College of Nairobi, P.O. Box 36197, Nairobi, Kenya.

TORTO, Frank Gibbs Tetteh Obaka, born Accra, Ghana, 10th October 1921. Professor of Chemistry. Education: Achimota College, Ghana; B.Sc., 1945, Ph.D., 1947, Queen Mary College, London University. Married, 4 children. Appointments include: Lecturer, University College of the Gold Coast (Ghana) 1948; Professor & Head of Department of Chemistry, University of Ghana, 1962; Scientific Consultant, U.N., 1961-63; Visiting Overseas Fellow, Churchill College, Cambridge, 1968; Dean, Faculty of Science, University of Ghana, 1969—. Memberships: Ghana Academy of Sciences, Member of Praesidium and Chairman of Physical Sciences Section, 1963-68; Past President, Ghana Science Association, 1965-67; Past President, Ghana Association of Science Teachers, 1966; Fellow, Ghana Academy of Arts & Sciences; Member of Council, West African Examination Council; Chemical Society (London), Ghana Representative; Member of Editorial Boards, Ghana Science Journal, West African Journal of Biological Chemistry. Publications: many scientific papers on chemical topics in international scientific journals. Address: Department of Chemistry, University of Ghana, P.O. Box 56, Legon, Ghana.

TOULMIN, George B(owers), born 7th September 1916. Educator; United States Foreign Service Executive. Education: B.A. (Econ.), University of Alabama, U.S.A., 1937; M.A., Political Science, ibid, 1947; University of Minnesota, 1944-45; University of Chicago, 1946-47. Married. Appointments: Staff Member, Legislative Advisory Commission for Jefferson County, Alabama, Survey; Research Director, Commission for Reorganization of Arkansas State Government; Research Assistant, University of Alabama, 1937-39, 1946; U.S. Army, U.S. & Europe, 1943-46; Research Associate, Institute of Public Administration, New York City, 1947-49; Associate Professor, University of Arkansas, 1949-51; U.S. Civil Service, 1939-43, 1951-59; Management Analysis & Planning, New Delhi, India & Paris, France, Foreign Service of U.S.A., 1960-68; Associate Professor of Public Administration, Graduate School of Public & International Affairs, University of Pittsburgh, assigned to Institute of Administration, Ahmadu Bellow University, Zaria, Nigeria, 1968—. Memberships: Nigeria Society for Public Administration; American Association of University Professors; American Association for Advancement of Science; American Society for Public Administration; American Foreign Service Association; American Political Science Association; Zaria Club. Author of various articles & contributor to official reports. Honours: Phi Beta Kappa, 1937. Address: Institute of Administration, P.M.B. 1013, Zaria, North Central State, Nigeria.

TOURE, Mamadou, born 21st November 1932. Technical Adviser. Education: Baccalaureat; Diploma of Higher Commercial, Economic & Financial Studies; Diploma,

Britannic Chamber of Commerce; European Economic Community, Brussels. Married, 3 children. Appointments: Commercial Attaché to the Ivory Coast Embassy in Belgium & the E.E.C., 1962-67; Technical Adviser, Cabinet of the Minister of Agriculture, Abidjan, 1967—. Address: Ministry of Agriculture, B.P. 1.329, Abidjan, Ivory Coast.

TOURE, Oumar, born 13th June 1936. Director of Information, Ministry of Finance, Abidjan, The Ivory Coast. Address: Central Office of Mecanography, B.P. 937, Abidjan, Ivory Coast.

TOURE (His Excellency) Sekou, President of the Republic of Guinea, born Faranah,, 9th January 1922. Education: mainly self-educated. Appointments: started as a Post Office Clerk, 1937, but his great interest lay in Union Organization; Founder Member, African Democratic Rally (RDA), 1946; Secretary-General, General Work Confederation (CGT), 1950; Founder, Secretary-General, General Union of Workers of Black Africa (UGTAN), 1957; Mayor Conakry, Guinea, 1955; Deputy, French National Assembly, 1956-58; Vice-President, Government Council of Guinea, 1957; President & Head of State, 1958—. Address: Conakry, Guinea.

TOUZE, Raphael Leonard, born 8th September 1915. French Ambassador to Mauritius. Education: Licensed in Law; School of Oriental Languages, Paris, France. Married, 3 children. Appointments: Director-General, Development of Senegal; Consul-General of France at Dakar; first Counsellor to the French Embassy at Kinshasa, Democratic Republic of the Congo; French Ambassador to Mauritius. Member, Lions Club. Publications: Lettres a Seydou, 1968; Nouvelles Lettres a Seydou, 1961; Rignona en Casamance, 1963. Honours: Officer of the Legion of Honour; Resistance Medal; Cross of War, 1939-45; Knight of Palmes Academiques & numerous foreign decorations. Address: French Embassy, Port-Louis, Mauritius.

TOWETT, Taita, born Kericho Kenya, 25th May 1925. Board Chairman. Education: Makerere University College; B.A.(Hons.), Philosophy, University of S.A.; M.A., Part I, Philosophy. Married, 15 children. Appointments include: Social Welfare Officer, 1950-57; Community Development Officer, 1957-58; Member of Kenya Parliament, 1958-64; Assistant Minister, Minister, Kenya Government, 2 years; Chairman, Kenya Dairy Board. Memberships include: Founder, Philosophical Society, Makerere College, 1948. Address: Box 15035, Nairobi, Kenya.

TRACEY, Kenneth William Joseph, born 9th December 1929. Dental Surgeon; Medical Administrator; Missionary. Education: Auckland Grammar School, New Zealand, 1943-46; B.D.S., University of Otago, 1947-52; Married, 4 children. Appointments: Instructor, School for Dental Nurses, Auckland, 1954; Dental Officer, S.I.M. Hospital, Egbe, Nigeria, 1956; ibid, Evangel Hospital, Jos, 1961; Medical Secretary i/c S.I.M Medical Work in West Africa, 1964; Supervisor, S.I.M. Rehibilitation Work, Nigeria, 1969. Memberships: Nigerian Medical Association; Chairman, Benue Plateau State Branch, Society of Health; Associate, Nigerian Institute of Management; Secretary, Northern Christian Medical Advisory Committee; Plateau Club, Jos; Honorary Fellow, Medical Council of Nigeria in Dental Surgery, 1970. Address: Sudan Interior Mission, Jos, Nigeria.

TRAILL, Elizabeth Rosemary Janet, born 18th October 1939. Teacher. Education: M.A.(Hons.) Geography & Political Economy, St. Andrews University, U.K., 1962; Cert. Ed. (Cambridge), 1963. Appointments: Teacher, Bilborough Grammar School, Nottingham, U.K., 1963-65; Teacher, Kigezi High School, Kabale, Uganda, on contract as Educqation Officer, Uganda Government, 1967—. Memberships: Missionary, Church Missionary Society, Ruanda Mission, 1966—; Graduates: Fellowship of the Inter-Varsity Fellowship; Geographical Association; Scripture Union; District Commissioner, Girl Guides, Kigezi District, 1968—. Honours: Queen's Guide, 1955. Address: Kigezi High School, P.O. Box 58, Kabale, Uganda.

TRAORE, Abakar Sanya, born 12th October 1932. Inspector-General of Administration with the rank of Minister. Education: Diploma of the Institute of Higher Overseas Studies, Paris, 1959-61. Appointments: Director-General of Foreign Affairs, 1961-62; Inspector of Public Services, 1963; Secretary-General, Council of Ministers, 1964; Director-Genéral of State Control, Presidence of the Republic, 1965; Minister of Finances of Chad, 1966-68; Director-General of State Control, Presidence of the Republic, 1969; Inspector-General of Administration having the rank of Minister, 1970—. Honours: Officer of the National Order of Chad. Address: Inspector-General of Administration, Presidence of the Republic, Fort-Lamy, Chad.

TRIVEDI, Manaharprasad Narayansi, born Nar Gujarat State, India, 6th November 1931. Educator. Education: B.Sc., University of Bombay; B.Ed., Gujarat University, 1962; Married. Appointments: Teacher of Science & Maths., Secondary Schools, Gujarat State, India, 1951—; Administrative & Executive Posts, State Government, 1955-59; Head, Science Department, D.H.T., Secondary School, Kisumu, Kenya, 1967—. Memberships: Cosmopolitan Club of Kisumu. Address: P.O. Box 872, Kisumu, Kenya.

TRIVEDI, Manubhai Chunilal, born Umreth, India, 17th November 1922. Advocate. Education; Baroda College; S.L.D. Arts College, Ahmedabad; LL.B., Sir L. A. Shah Law College, Ahmedabad, 1946. Married, 2 sons, 1 daughter. Appointments include: commenced Legal Practice, 1947; Member, Managing Committee, Umreth Cooperative Store & Umreth Cooperative Bank Ltd., 1948-53; came to Tanganyika, 1953; Hon. Secretary, Hindu Mandal, Moshi, 1955; President, ibid, 1957; appointed Township Authority Member, Moshi, 1955, & Moshi Town Council Member, 1956-59; Member, Indian Education Authority, Tanganyika, 1957-61; Chairman, Fee Remission

Committee, Government Schools, Moshi; Member, Local Education Authority, Moshi Town Council; President, Mawenzi Primary School; President, Moshi Parents' Association; Sponsor & Manager, Kiho Secondary School. Memberships: Kilimanjaro Theosophical Society, Moshi; Tanganyika Law Society, Dar es Salaam. Address: P.O Box 242, Moshi, Tanzania.

TROUGHTON, John Frederick George, born 24th May 1902. Magistrate. Education: B.A. (1st Class Hons.) Trinity College, Dublin, Ireland; LL.B., ibid; Barrister-at-Law. Married, 3 sons, 1 daughter. Appointments: Financial Secretary & Member for Finance, Kenya, 1946-49; Private Legal Practice, Uganda, 1952-61; Magistrate, Swaziland, 1961—. Honours: M.B.E., 1936; C.M.G., 1948. Address: P.O. Box 229, Manzini, Swaziland.

TRUSSELL, Richard Radford, born 10th December 1920. Physician; Obstetrician & Gynaecologist; Educator. Education: M.B., Ch.B., Birmingham University, U.K., 1945; Ch.M., ibid, 1964; F.R.C.O.G., 1963. Married, 3 children. Appointments: Senior Registrar, Birmingham Maternity Hospital & Hospital for Women, 1952-57; Professor of Obstetrics & Gynaecology, Makerere University College, Kampala, Uganda. Memberships: President, Association of Surgeons of East Africa, 1969-70; Uganda Medical Association. Author of several professional papers. Honours: Carnegie Travelling Fellowship, U.S.A. & Canada, 1961; Vis. Professor, Queen's University, Belfast, U.K., 1966; Overseas Examiner, Royal College of Obstetricians & Gynaecologists, 1970. Address: Medical School, P.O. Box 7072, Kampala, Uganda.

TRZEBINSKI, Zbigniew Waclaw, born 28 May 1933. Architect. Education: Stubbington School, Cornwall, U.K.; Mayfield College, Sussex; Dip.Arch., The Polytechnic, Regent Street, London. Appointments: Partner, Trzebinski, Gaal & Associates, Mombasa, Kenya. Memberships: Associate, Royal Institute of British Architects; Corporate Member, Architectural Association of Kenya. Address: P.O. Box 9045, Mombasa, Kenya.

TSIRANANA (His Excellency) Philibert, President of the Republic of Malagasy, born Ambarikorano, 1912. Education: started School at 12 & proving a brilliant pupil, he became a Teacher & later a Professor; qualified as a Technical Teacher, Montpellier, France, 1946-50. Appointments: Councillor, Madagascar Representative Assembly, 1952; Deputy for the West Coast to the French National Assembly, in Paris; Founder & Secretary-General, Social Democratic Party, 1957; Deputy Head, Madagascar Government, 1957-58; President & Head of Government, Malagasy Republic, 1959—. Memberships: OCAM. Honours: Grand Master of the National Order of Malagasy; Grand Cross of the Legion of Honour; recipient of numerous French & foreign decorations. Address: Tananarive, Malagasy.

TUBMAN (His Excellency) William Vacanarat Shadrach, born Harper, Liberia, 29th November 1895. President of the Republic of Liberia. Education: Graduated from Cape Palmas Seminary, 1913; read Law, was called to the Bar & took silk, 1917. Appointments: Recorder, Monthly & Probate Court & Collector of Inland Revenues, 1917-19; County Attorney, Maryland Country, Liberia, 1919; elected to National Legislature, 1923-37; Associate Justice, Supreme Court of Liberia, 1937-44; President, Republic of Liberia, 1944—. Memberships: Phi Beta Sigma; Past Grand Master, Ancient Free & Accepted Masons of Liberia. Honours: Recipient of Honorary Degrees in Law, Liberia College & Wilberforce University; ibid in Civil Law & Ph.D., University of Liberia. Associate Organizer of the Accra Conference, Ghana, 1958; ibid, Sanniquellie, Liberia, 1959; Sponsor & Organizer of the Conference of African Heads of State to promote Unity & Cooperation, Monrovia, Liberia, 1961; attended first conference for the Organization of African Unity, Addis Ababa, Ethiopia, 1963; since then has attended all O.A.U. summit meetings.

TUMBO, Nasson Samuel Kasanga, born 22nd November 1943. Liaison Officer. Education: Primary, Iwensato & Sikonge, 1951-58; Alliance Secondary School, Dodoma, Tanzania, 1959-62; Old Moshi Secondary School, 1963-69; B.A., University of East Africa, Dar es Salaam, 1965-69. Married. Appointments: Assistant Commercial & Industrial Officer, Liaison Officer, Tanzania Petroleum Development Corporation. Memberships: Captain, Swimming, 1965-69; Vice-Captain, Athletics, 1966-69; President, Students' Union, University of East Africa, 1967-68. Author, Towards Nuta: A Search for Permanent Peace in Trade Union Movement of Tanganyike. Address: P.O. Box 234, Dar es Salaam, Tanzania.

TURNER, John Derfel, born 27th February 1928. University Teacher. Education: Manchester Grammar School, U.K., 1939-45; B.A. (1st Class Hons.), Latin & English, Manchester University, 1948; Teachers' Diploma, ibid, 1951; M.A., ibid, 1951. Appointments: Education Officer, Royal Air Force, 1948-50; Master in charge of Latin, Prince Henry's Grammar School, Evesham, Worcs; Lecturer in English, & later, Senior Lecturer in Education, Nigerian College of Arts, Science, & Technology, Zaria, 1953-61; Lecturer in Education, University of Exeter Institute of Education, U.K., 1961-64; Professor of Education & Director of School of Education, University of Botswana, Lesotho, & Swaziland, Roma, Lesotho, 1964-70; Professor of Education & Director of the Colleges of Education Division, University of Manchester Faculty of Education, U.K., 1970—. Publications: Language Laboratories in Great Britain, 1962, 1963, 1965; The Language Laboratory & the Teaching of English in Africa, 1967; Introducing the Language Laboratory, 1968; Programming for the Language Laboratory (ed.), 1968; Using the Language Laboratory (ed.), 1969; Educational Problems of Technological Africa, 1967; Educational Development in Predominantly Rural Countries (co-author), 1969; Poetry for Overseas Students, 1960; also contributor of numerous articles to journals. Address: School of Education, The University, Manchester, M13 9PL, U.K.

TURNER, Peter Herbert, born 13th September 1928. Lecturer. Education: Cambridge High School, U.K., 1940-45; University of Leicester, 1949-54. Married, 4 daughters. Education: Education Officer, Commerce, Kenya Government, 1957-60; Head, Combined Accountant/Auditor Training Unit, Institute of Administration, Ahmadu Bello University, Zaria, Nigeria, 1964-69; various other teaching & administrative posts; currently, Head, Department of Business & Computational Studies, College of Technology, Barnsley, Yorks, U.K. Memberships: Associate, Chartered Institute of Secretaries, 1959; Fellow, Royal Economic Society, 1958. Publications: Accountant: who is thy neighbour (The Commercial Accountant); The Commerce of New Africa, 1969; Introduction to African Economics (w. Dr. L. J. Hunt), 1970. Address: Department of Business & Computational Studies, College of Technology, Barnsley, Yorks, U.K.

TURNER, Rita, born 31st December 1938. Writer; Broadcaster. Education: B.A.(Hons.), Modern Languages, University of Sheffield, U.K.; Sorbonne, Paris, France; University of Aix-en-Provence. Married, 3 sons. Appointments: Studio Manager, External Service of the B.B.C., involving broadcasting to Africa; currently, Editor, Moni, A Malawi monthly magazine for Africans. Address: Editor, Moni, Montfort Press, P.O. Box 592, Limbe, Malawi.

TUT AGYEMAN, Samuel, born 19th March 1903. District Magistrate. Education: Standard VII Certificate, Wesleyan Mission School, 1921; Certificate of Proficiency, Native Court Registrars' Examination, 1948; Certificate, Local Government Training School, 1952. Married, 6 children. Appointments: Pupil Teacher, Wesleyan School, 1921-22; Clerk, Posts & Telegraphs, 1922-27; Cashier, Storekeeper & Produce Factor, Marchantile, 1927-37; Registrar, Native Court, Clerk to Traditional Council, 1937-52; Clerk of Council, Local Government, 1952-59; District Magistrate, Grade II, Ghana, 1959—. Played active part in the Cocoa Dispute, 1937-38, resulting in the creation of the Cocoa Marketing Board. Honours: Book Prize, South Birim Local Council, 1959; ibid, Akim Abuakwa Local Court, 1966. Address: P.O. Box 37, Esiam, Ghana.

TUTUOLA, Amos, born Abeokuta, Nigeria, 1920. Storekeeper; Writer. Education: attended Anglican Central School, Abeokuta, to Class II, Middle. Marrieed, 4 children. Appointments: Senior Storekeeper, Nigerian Broadcasting Corporation. Member, Mbari Club, Ibadan. Publications: The Palm Wine Drunkard, 1952; My Life in the Bush of Ghosts, 1954; Simbi & the Satyr of the Dary Jungle, 1955; The Brave African Huntress, 1958; Feather Woman of the Jungle, 1962; Ajaiyi & His Inherited Poverty, 1967—. Address: Nigerian Broadcasting Corporation, Broadcasting House, Ibadan, Western State, Nigeria.

TYM, Patricia Bridget, born 14th March 1946. Personal Secretary. Education: Cirencester Secondary School for Girls; North Gloucestershire Technical College, Cheltenham. Appointments include: Personal Secretary to the Under-Secretary, Loans Department, Ministry of Finance, Entebbe, Uganda; Personal Secretary, Under-Secretary, Taxation, ibid. Member of the Entebbe Club. Address: 56 rue de Stassart, Brussels 1050, Belgium.

U

UDEH, Uchenna Veronica, born 17th May 1939. Medical Practitioner. Education: Hope Waddell Institute, Calabar; Aggrey Primary School, Arochuku; Aggrey Memorial College, Arochuku; West African Leaving Certificate, 1955; Ibadan Grammar School, Nigeria; Bournemouth Municipal College, U.K.; G.C.E. 'A' Level, Norwood Technical College, London, 1960; M.B., B.S., Royal Free Hospital School of Medicine, University of London, 1966; M.R.C.S.(Eng.); L.R.C.P.(London). Personal details: daughter of Dr. Alvan Ikoku, the 1st Ibo Graduate. Married. Appointments include: Locum House Surgeon, Obstetrics & Gynaecology, Royal Free Hospital, London, 1965; House Surgeon, Royal Free Hospital, 1966; House Physician, Dept. of Pediatrics, University College Hospital, Ibadan, Nigeria, 1966; Medical Officer, Ministry of Health, Eastern Region, Nigeria, 1967; Senior House Officer, Dept. of Medicine, University of Nigeria, Teaching Hospital, 1967; Registrar, Dept. of Medicine, ibid, 1968; Medical Officer, Ministry of Health, East Central State, Nigeria. Memberships: Vice-President, Kawari Club; Treasurer, Africa Society, University of London; British Medical Assn.; Nigerian Medical Assn.; Bible Study Group, Royal Free Hospital. Address: General Hospital Ontisha, East Central State, Nigeria.

UDO, Ime Lot, born 24th October 1937. Medical Practitioner. Education: Ubium N.A. School, Ubium, Eket, Nigeria, 1944-49; Hope Waddell Training Institution, Calabar, Nigeria, 1950-66; Norwich City College, Norwich, U.K., 1958-59; Trinity College, University of Dublin, Ireland, 1959-66; M.A.; M.B., B.Ch.; B.A.O. Appointments: Medical Officer, General Hospital, Port Harcourt, Nigeria, 1966-68; Medical Officer, St. Margaret's Hospital, Calabar, 1968; Medical Officer in Charge, Qua Iboe Hospital, Etinan, 1969 & General Hospital, Opobo, 1969-70. Memberships: Trinity College (Dublin) Association; South Eastern State Branch, Nigerian Medical Assn. Address: St. Margaret's Hospital, Calabar, South Eastern State, Nigeria.

UDO, Reuben Kenrick, born 8th August, 1935. University Lecturer. Education: Ikot Ekpene Methodist Central School, Southeastern State, Nigeria, 1942-49; Uzuakoli Methodist College, East Central State, 1950-54; Nigerian College of Technology, Enugu, 1955-57; B.Sc.(Hons.), Geography, London, University of Ibadan, 1957-62; Ph.D.(Geography), University College, London, U.K., 1962-63. Married, 2 sons, 1 daughter. Appointments: Post-Doctoral Research Fellow, Ibadan University, 1963-64; Lecturer, Geography, ibid, 1964-68; Senior Lecturer, 1968—; Chairman, Southeastern State Agricultural Development Corporation, 1969—. Memberships: Nigerian Geographical Association & Editor, Nigerian Geographical Journal, 1969; Science Association of Nigeria; American Association for the Advancement of Science. Publications: Geographical Regions of Nigeria, 1970; Examination Guidelines for School Certificate Geography, 1970; 20 articles in professional journals. Address: Department of Geography, University of Ibadan, Ibadan, Nigeria.

UPADHYA, Sureshchandra J., born 20th December 1927. Anaesthesiologist. Education: B.B., B.S., University of Gujarat, India, 1955; Diploma in Anaesthesiology, University of Bombay, 1958. Married. Appointments: House Physician, Gulabbai General Hospital, Ahmedabad; House Surgeon, Dabro-Parsee General Hospital, Navsari; Resident Anaesthetist, St. George's Hospital & J.J. Group of Hospitals, Bombay; Senior Resident Anaesthetist, Bombay Hospital; Senior Medical Officer (Anaesthesiology), Effia-Nkwanta Hospital, Sekondi, Ghana, 1963 –. Memberships: Ghana Medical Association. Address: Effia-Nkwanta Hospital, P.O. Box 229, Sekondi, Ghana.

UWALAKA, C. Emmanuel, born Uzunorji, Nigeria, 15th April 1935. Educator. Education: Cambridge School Certificate, Grade Two, 1952; Teachers' Grade II Certificate, 1955; G.C.E. A Level, 1957, 1960; B.A.(Hons.), U.N.N., 1963. Married, 6 children. Appointments: Geography Master, Bishop Shenahan Secondary School, Oelu, 1956-60; History Master, Higher School Section, Stella Maries College, Port Harcourt, 1963; Principal, St. Joseph's Secondary School, Umnatuen-Elche, Port Harcourt, 1964-69; Principal, Ohaji High School, Mgbirichi via Owerri, 1970. Memberships: President, C.I.C. Old Boys' Association, Msukka University, 1960-63; President & Founder, Amator-Amuzu Cooperative Society, 1967-70; Nigeria Red Cross Society. Honours include: Federal Government Scholarship, 1961. Address: Ohaji High School, Mgbisichi, Owerri Box 19, Nigeria.

UZODIKE, Lucius Madubuko, born 15th November 1904. Bishop. Education: Nnewi, 1912-20; Teacher Training, St. Paul's College, Awka, 1926-27; Senior Certificate Course on Agriculture, Rural Education Centre, 1939; Theological Education, Wycliffe Hall, Oxford, U.K., 1944-46. Personal details: married, 5 sons, 2 daughters. Appointments: Headmaster, 1st Grade, Primary Schools, 1931-44; Tutor Chaplain, D.M.G.S., 1946-48; Vicar of Christ Church, Onitsha District, 1950-55; Canon of All Saints' Cathedral, 1952-57; Archdeacon of Jos, Northern Nigeria, 1958-61; Asst. Bishop, 1961-69; Diocesan Bishop, Niger Diocese, 1969 –. Address: Bishopcourt, Box 42, Onitsha, East Central State, Nigeria.

V

VAGHJEE, Harilal Ranchhordas, born 18th January 1912. Barrister-at-Law; Speaker of the Legislative Assembly, Mauritius. Education: Port Louis High School, Mauritius; Middle Temple, U.K. Appointments: Member, Legislative Assembly, Mauritius, 1948-59; Vice-President, Legislative Assembly, 1951-57; Minister of Education, 1958-59; Speaker, Legislative Assembly, 1960 –; Chairman, Provisional Council, University of Mauritius, 1965 –. Honours: Knighted, 1970. Address: Government House, Port Louis, Mauritius.

van BAAR, Antoine, born 22nd March 1924. Executive. Education: France & Morocco. Married. Appointments: Managing Director, Chamber of Commerce, Hollando-Morocaine, 1958 –. Address: 106 rue Abderahmen, Morocco.

VAN DEN REYSEN, Joseph Marcel, born 19th March 1934. Statistician. Education: University of Toulouse, France, 1954-60; Diploma in Statistics, ENSAE, Paris & ISUP, Paris. Appointments: Director of Statistics, Brazzaville, Republic of the Congo, 1962-68; U.N. Economic Commission for Africa, Addis Ababa, Ethiopia, 1968 –. Member, Royal Statistical Society, etc. Author of various statistical publications. Address: U.N. Economic Commission for Africa, Addis Ababa, P.O. Box 3001, Ethiopia.

VANDERLIN, Carl J., Jr., born 28th April 1926. University Lecturer. Education: Ph.D., University of Chicago, U.S.A., 1948; S.B., ibid, 1950; M.S., University of Winsconsin, 1952. Married, 2 sons, 4 daughters. Appointments: Associate Professor, Wisconsin State College, Whitewater, 1956-61; Visiting Associate Professor, Washburn University, Topeka, Kansas, 1961; Lecturer, University Extension, University of Wisconsin, Madison, 1961 –; Visiting Lecturer, Institute of Adult Studies, University College, University of East Africa, Nairobi, Kenya, 1968 –; Chief of Party, USAID/Wisconsin Radio/Correspondence Education Project, 1970 –. Memberships: Pi Mu Epsilon, 1952; Mathematicial Association of America, 1954 –; Chairman, Wisconsin Section, ibid, 1956-57; Member, Board of Governors, 1966-68; Sigma Xi, 1955; Wisconsin Mathematics Council, 1956 –; Vice-President, ibid, 1958-59; Editor, 1961-65; Kenya Mathematical Society, 1968 –. Author, A Review of New Mathematics Curriculum Materials, 1966. Address: Correspondence Course Unit, Institute of Adult Studies, University College, P.O. Box 30197, Nairobi, Kenya.

VAN ECK, Willem Adolph, born 27th July 1928. Senior Lecturer. Education: B.Sc., University of Wageningen, Netherlands; M.Sc., Ph.D., Michigan State University, U.S.A. Appointments: Research Assistant, Plant Ecology, Wageningen, Netherlands, 1949-51; Research Forester, Ghana Government Survey Team, 1952; Research Assistant, Soil Science, Michigan State University, U.S.A., 1952-56; Professor of Soil Science, West Virginia University, 1957-66; Senior Lecturer, Soil & Water Engineering, Makerere University, Uganda, 1966 –. Memberships: Soil Science Society of America; Society of American Foresters; Ecological Society of America; Soil Conservation Society of America; Royal Dutch Agricultural Society; Uganda Society; Uganda Agricultural Society; Uganda Geographical Association. Address: Makerere University, Kampala, Uganda.

VAN LANDEWIJK, Joannes E. J. M., born 10th August 1923. Mineralogist; Geologist. Education: Doctoral Cum Laude, Utrecht, Netherlands, 1954; Dr.Sc., Utrecht, 1957. Married, 2 children. Appointments: Senior Lecturer, Department of Geology, University of Ghana, Legon. Memberships: Royal Dutch Geological & Mining Society; Editing Board, Ghana Science Association; Founder Member, International Association of Engineering Geology. Publications: Introduction to Geological Measurements & Constructions, 1954; Nomograms for Geological Problems, 1957; Integrated Science Teaching, 1970. Co-author: An Occurrence of Corundum in Northern Ghana, 1959; Parallel Slope Retreat, 1962. Address: University of Ghana, P.O. Box 41, Legon, Ghana.

VAN LUNG, Nguyen. Odontologist. Education: Diplomé de Paris, France. Appointments: Head of the Odontology Service, Central Hospital, Abidjan, Ivory Coast; formerly attached to the Stomatology Service, Tenon Hospital, Paris. Honours: Prix et Diplôme d'Honneur de la Ville de Paris, International Dental Congress, 1968. Address: Central Hospital, Abidjan, Ivory Coast.

VARLET, Hubert Valentin Coffie, born 12th November 1915. Medical Practitioner. Married, 9 children. Appointments: Director of the Cabinet, Ministry of Health, Abidjan, Ivory Coast, 1957; Director-General of Public Health, ibid, 1963-70; Inspector-General of Health, 1970—. Memberships: Jury du Prix Littéraire de la Côte d'Ivoire, 1958; President, Football Federation of the Ivory Coast, 1963-67; President, Olympic Committee of the Ivory Coast, 1963-67; President, Tennis Federation of the Ivory Coast, 1964—; President, Sports Union of Bassam Clubs; Administrator, A.B.I. Society (Abidjan Industries); Administrator, Office de Soutien des Habitations Economiques (OSHE); Vice-President, Abidjan Rotary Club. Honours: Officier de Santé de Rérve; Chevalier de l'Ordre Français de la Santé Publique; Chevalier de l'Etoile d'Anjouan; Commandeur de l'Ordre de la Santé Publique de Côte Ivoire; Officier des Palmes Académiques Françaises; Médaille d'Or du Mérite Sportif Ivoirien; Officier du Mérite National Francais. Address: B.P. V.48, Abidjan, Ivory Coast.

VARMA, Ved Kumar, born 22nd April 1936. Architect & Town Planner. Education: B.Arch., Bombay University, India, 1962; Dip. Arch., Bombay; Postgraduate Diploma in Town Planning, Birmingham University, U.K.; Postgraduate Diploma in Tropical Agriculture, Architectural Association, London, 1965. Married. Appointments: Architectural Assistant, Ministry of Works, Dar es Salaam, Tanzania, 1962-63; Town Planning Officer, Ministry of Housing, Dar es Salaam, 1965-67; Architect & Town Planner, own practice, Tanzania. Memberships: Town Planning Institute of U.K.; Associate, Indian Institute of Architects; Uganda Association of Architects; Architectural Association, London. Address: P.O. Box 486, Dar es Salaam, Tanzania.

VARUGHESE, Tachedathu Varughese, born 18th May 1932. Accounts Officer. Education: Senior Intermediate Exam., Travancore University, S. India; Swahili Exams. & Proficiency Exam., Tanzania Government. Personal details: came to Dar es Salaam, 1950; married, 1 son, 3 daughters. Appointments: Executive Grade Clerk, 1950-58; Accounting Assistant, 1958-63; Accounts Officer, East African Community, Arusha, 1963—. Address: c/o East African Community, Accountant-General's Department, P.O. Box 1005, Arusha, Tanzania.

VASSAY, Walter James, born 26th January, 1920. Civil Servant. Education: Rosendale Primary School, London, U.K., —1931; Matriculation, West Norwood Grammar School, ibid. Married, 5 children. Appointments: Insurance Clerk; Private, L/Corp., Corporal, Gordon Highlanders, 1939; Cadet; Officers' College, Dunbar, Scotland, 1940; 2nd Lieutenant, Lieutenant, Captain, Major, Rajputana Rifles, Indian Army, served in India, Iran, Iraq, Palestine, Egypt, & Italy, 1940-46; Finance & Admin. Director, U.N.R.R.A., Italy, 1946-49; Overseas Civil Service, Malaya & Uganda, 1951—; Under-Secretary (Urban), Ministry of Regional Administration. Fellow, Chartered Institute of Secretaries. Address: P.O. Box 7037, Kampala, Uganda.

VAUGHAN, Patrick Handley, born 12th April 1938. Priest; Theological Lecturer. Education: Portora Royal School, Enniskillen, Northern Ireland, U.K., 1950-56; B.A., B.D., Trinity College, Dublin, Ireland, 1956-60; Selwyn College, Cambridge, U.K., 1960-62; Ridley Hall, Cambridge, 1961-63; M.A. (Cantab.). Appointments: Minor Canon of Bradford Cathedral, Yorks; Tutor, Bishop Tucker College, Uganda. Address: Box 4, Mukono, Uganda.

VAUSE, Evelyn Margaret, born 26th August 1932. Nurse. Education: Grammar School for Girls, Southampton, U.K.; Lord Mayor Treloars Orthopaedic Hospital, Alton, Hants; St. Thomas: Hospital, London, S.E.1; Maternity Unit, The General Hospital, Southampton; State Registered Nurse; State Certified Midwife. Member, Church Missionary Society. Address: Mengo Hospital, P.O. Box 7161, Kampala, Uganda.

VAYID, Mohamad Amade, born 24th February 1935. Marketing Manager; Journalist; Company Director. Education: Royal College, Mauritius; Edinburgh University. Married, 1 daughter. Appointments: Administrative Assistant, Ministry of Works, 1960-61; Marketing Manager, British American Tobacco Co. (M) Ltd., 1961—; Chairman, Central Housing Authority, 1967—; ibid, Mauritius Broadcasting Corporation, 1968—; Director, Swan Insurance Co. Ltd., 1969—. Memberships: President, Port Louis Gymkhana; Vice-President, Stella Claviswue Club; President, Lions Club. Author of articles in socio-economic problems & international affairs. Address: Shangri-La, Independence Avenue, Quatre Bornes, Mauritius.

VEIGA-PIRES, Jose Arnaldo, born Oporto on 26th August 1926. Physician; Radiologist. Education: University of Oporto; Royal

Postgraduate Medical School; M.D., C.H.D., D.M.R.D., D.R.D., D.R.&N.M.; Fellow in Radiological Research, James Pickers Foundation, National Academy of Sciences, Washington, D.C., U.S.A., 1959-61. Appointments include: Professor of Radiology, University of Lagos Medical College, Nigeria, —1967. Memberships; Fellow, Royal Society of Medicine; Faculty of Radiologists; Institute of Radiology; British Medical Association; Foundation Mbr., Association of Radiologists of West Africa; Corresponding Mbr., Brazilian College of Angiology; Nigerian Medical Association. Contbr. of articles to prof. journals. Address: Sombreireira, 12 Chestnut Way, Godalming, Surrey, U.K.

VEITCH, Edward, born 26th October 1941. Lecturer in Law. Education: Bell-Baxter High School, Cupar, U.K.; M.A.(Hons.), Edinburgh University, 1963; LL.B., ibid, 1966. Married, 2 children. Appointments: Lecturer & Assistant Dean, Faculty of Law, Ahmadu Bello University, Zaria, Nigeria; Lecturer in Law, Faculty of Law, Makerere University, Kampala, Uganda. Memberships: Society of the Public Teachers of Law, U.K.; Nigerian Law Teachers' Association; East African Law Teachers' Association. Articles published in various U.K. & African journals. Address: Faculty of Law, Makerere University, Kampala, Uganda.

VENEIK, Amar Nath, born Pail, India, 1st April 1931. Chartered Electrical Engineer. Education: B.Sc., Benares; B.Sc., Electrical Engineering, Edinburgh. Married. Appointments include: Design & Development Engineer with M/S Standard Telephone & Cable, London; Senior Sectional Engineer (Planning) with Directorate of Civil Aviation, East Africa; Visiting Lecturer, University College, Nairobi; Kenya Polytechnic: Adult Education Mbeya (University College, Dar es Salaam); Radio Maintenance Instructor with Schools of Aviation, East Africa, run under the UNDP by the ICAO. Memberships: Member of the Institution of Electrical Engineers; Member of the Institution of Electrical & Electronics Engineers; Member of the East African Institution of Engineers; Member of the Institution of Electronics, East Africa. Publications: paper written in 3 parts on Air Ground Communications In East Africa. Address: P.O. Box 142, Nairobi, Kenya.

VERDUGO, Claude, born 4th May 1928. Urban Architect. Education: Diploma, l'École Nationale Supérieure des Beaux Arts, Paris, France; Institut d'Urbanisme, Paris, France. Appointments: Head, Central Office of Studies, Morocco, 1957-59; Consultant Urbanist for the reconstruction of Agadir. Member, Executive Committee, International Union of Architects. Publications: Enquéte Urbaine de Tanger; Les Centres Urbains de la rallée du Zdu Ziz. Honours: 1st Prize, School of Engineers, Rabat, 1959; 3rd Prize, garden at Hambourg, 1963; 1st Prize, plastic sanitary ware, Paris, 1964. Address: 12 Zankat 1bn Aïcha, Rabat, Morocco.

VERIN, Pierre Michel, born Niort, 6th April 1934. University Professor. Education: Baccalaureat, Poitiers, France; Lic. ès Lettres et Droit, Paris, France; Dip. Schl. of Oriental & Living Languages; Brevete Ecole de la F.O.M.; M.A., Anthropology, Yale Univ., U.S.A.; Ph.D., Sorbonne, Paris, France. Married, 4 children. Appointments include: Asst. Master, Fac. of Letters & Humanities, Madagascar; Dir., Archaeology Ctr. of Univ.; Assoc. Prof. in Archaeology. Memberships include: Assoc., Malagasy Acad.; Pres., Malagasy Archaeological Assoc. Author of 80 articles & papers on Ethnology & Archaeology. Address: Centre d'Archaeologie de l'Université, B.P. 907, Tananarive, Malagasy Republic.

VERJEE (Count) Bahadurali Kassam Suleman, born Mombasa, Kenya, 23rd December 1911. Advocate. Education: B.Comm., London School of Economics, U.K.; Barrister-at-Law, Middle Temple, London. Personal details: nephew of Hussein Suleman Verjee, first President, Indian National Congress in Kenya. Appointments: Private Secretary, late Aga Khan, during his Jubilee Tour of East Africa, 1937; appointed Aga Khan's Education Administrator, Uganda, 1937-54; Member, H.H. Aga Khan Federal Council for Africa; Chairman, Supreme Tribunal for All Africa of H.H. Aga Khan, & Member, Supreme Council for All Africa, 1954-62; Advocate, High Court of Kenya & Uganda; Member, Uganda Legislative Assembly, 1954-61; Vice-President, Uganda Law Society, 1965; President, ibid, 1966; Delegate, Lancaster House Conference, London, to negotiate Ugandan independence; Chairman, Mulago Hospital Board, 1964-67; President, Central Council of Muslims for Uganda, 1957. Memberships: Directors' Institute, London; Rotary Club of Kampala, Uganda & Nairobi, Kenya; Secretary, ibid, Kampala, 1964; Commonwealth Parliamentary Association: The Uganda Club; Nairobi Club. Honours: H.M. Coronation Medal, 1952; Title of Count, H.H. the late Aga Khan, 1953; C.B.E., 1960; Uganda Independence Medal, 1962. Address: P.O. Box 6062, Nairobi, Kenya.

VERNISSE, Pierre, 5th February 1914. Industrialist. Appointments: in agriculture & industry; P. Vernisse, Yards & Workshops, house founded in 1898. Honours: Knight of Agricultural Merit. Address: 31 rue Lenine, Tunis, Tunisia.

VERNON, Harold Edmund (Peter), born 27th September 1908, deceased 17th July 1970. Civil Servant; Personnel Officer. Education: Lincoln School, 1916-21; Windsor Secondary School, 1921-26. Married, 2 sons, 1 stepson, 1 stepdaughter. Appointments: General Post Office Engineering Trainee, 1927-30; Metropolitan Police, 1931-47; Chief Security Officer, Williamson Diamond Mine, Tanganyika, 1947-48; Personnel Officer, Nchanga Consolidated Copper Mine, Chingola, Northern Rhodesia, 1949-50; Labour Manager, Owen Falls Construction Company, Jinja, Uganda, 1950-52; Labour Utilization Officer, Labour Department, Uganda, 1952-56; Personnel Officer, Kilembe Copper Mine, ibid, 1956-68; Labour Relations Officer, Aden Port Trust, Aden, 1959-61; Personnel Officer, ibid, 1961-63; Education & Training Officer, 1963-67; Senior Labour Officer, Employment Services Division i/c

Migrant Labour, Labour Department, Malawi, 1968-70. Address: c/o Mrs. C. A. Vernon, 51, Kenau, Hasselaar St., Vlissingen, Netherland.

VEVSTAD, Folkvard, born 11th November 1923. Civil Engineer. Education: Matriculation, 1942; M.Sc.(Civil Eng.), Technical University of Norway, 1948. Appointments: Structural Engineer, E. N. Hylland Consultants, Oslo, Norway, 1948-53; Resident Engineer & Chief Engineer, Ing. Thor Furuholmen Gen. Contr., Oslo, 1953-68; Project Manager, National Construction Corporation Ltd., Nairobi, 1968-69; Project adviser, ibid, 1970—. Fellow of East African Institution of Engineers. Memberships: Norwegian Assn. of Civil Engineers; Norwegian Concrete Assn.; Royal Norwegian Yacht Club. Address: P.O. Box 30201, Nairobi, Kenya.

VIDEGLA, Pamphile, born Cotonou, Dahomey, 21st August 1936. Civil Administrator. Education: Lic. Econ. Seis. & Letters; studied at Ecole d'Administration, Paris, France. Appointments include: Asst. Prefect & Prefect, Dept. of Mono, 1966-68; Govt. Delegate & Head of Urban Admin., Cotonou. Memberships include: former Sec.-Gen. & Vice-Pres., External Affairs, Gen. Union of Students of West Africa; Association of Economists of Dahomey. Honours: Prix de l'Eleve, le Recteur de l'Academie de Dakar, Senegal. Address: Cotonou, B.P. 692, Dahomey.

VINCENT, Olatunde Olabode, born Lagos, Nigeria, 16th May 1925. Economist; Civil Servant, Banker. Education: C.M.S. Grammar School, Lagos; Chartered Institute of Secretaries, London, U.K.; B.A.(Commerce), University of Manchester; Administrative Staff College, Henley, U.K. Married, 4 children. Appointments: Nigerian Army, 1942-46; Budget Division, Exchange Control Office, Government Staff Housing Loan Scheme, Financial Secretary's Office, Nigeria, 1947-56; Assistant Secretary, Banking & Overseas Finance, Federal Ministry of Finance, 1956; Exchange Control Officer, ibid; Secretary, Government Staff Housing Loan Board, 1958; Senior Assistant Secretary, i/c of the Budget, 1959-60; Under-Secretary, Home & Overseas Finance, i/c monetary policy, relations with central bank, banking, including supervision of commercial banks, overseas aid & relations with international financial institutions, 1960-61; Assistant General Manager, Central Bank of Nigeria, 1961; Deputy General Manager, ibid, 1962; General Manager, 1963-66; Vice-President, African Development Bank, 1964-69; re-elected, ibid, 1969—; Lecturer in Economics (part-time), Extramural Department, University College of Ibadan, 1957-60; Member, Lagos Executive Development Board, 1960-61; Director, Nigerian Industrial Development Bank, 1964-66. Memberships: Member of Committee which set up Nigerian Industrial Development Bank; Member, Committee of Nine which set up the African Development Bank; Member, several Nigerian Government Economic & Financial Missions to other countries & International Conferences; Society for International Development. Address: African Development Bank, B.P. 1387, Abidjan, Ivory Coast.

VINCENT, Theophilus, born 17th October 1939. University Lecturer. Education: Primary Mission Schools, Eastern Nigeria; West African School Certificate, Cambridge Higher School Certificate, Methodist Secondary School, Uzuakoli, 1954-60; B.A., Hons., English, University College, Ibadan, Nigeria, 1964; Ph.D., 1969. Personal details: son of Methodist Minister. Married. Appointments: Schoolteacher, Methodist Secondary School, Uzuakoli, 1964; Assistant Lecturer, Dept. of English, University of Ibadan, 1967-69; Post-Doctoral Research Fellow, Dept. of English, ibid, 1969-70; Lecturer, Dept. of English, University of Lagos, 1970—; Editor, The Nigerian Christian, 1968-70. Member of Nigerian English Studies Assn. Publications: Two African Writers of the Eighteenth Century Ignatius Sancho & Offobah Cugoano; Reviews in: Black Orpheus; The West African Journal of Education. Address: Dept. of English, School of Humanities, University of Lagos, Nigeria.

VIRDI, Gurmaze Singh, born 22nd May 1933. Meteorologist. Education: B.A., English, Physics, & Mathematics; Technical Officers' Training Seminar, Nairobi, Kenya, 1964. Married, 4 children. Appointments: Met. Assistant, East African Meteorological Department, 1954; Observer in charge, ibid, Mombasa, Kenya, 1956-57; Junior Technical Officer, 1959; Technical Officer, 1960; Retired, 1967; currently serving department on contract terms as Meteorological Officer. Memberships: Hon. Secretary, Ramgarhia Association, Dar es Salaam; Expatriate & Overseas Educational Association, Dar es Salaam; Automobile Association of East Africa. Address: East African Meteorological Department, P.O. Box 18004, Airport, Dar es Salaam, Tanzania.

VOGEL, Leendert Cornelis, born 1st April 1926. Medical Practitioner. Education: M.B., B.S., State University, Utrecht, Netherlands, 1955; M.D., ibid, 1965; D.P.H., University of Malaya, 1959. Appointments: Medical Officer, West New Guinea, 1956-62; Lecturer, Social Medicine, Utrecht, 1962-65; Associate Professor, Public Health College, Gondar, Ethiopia, 1965-67; Epidemiologist, Medical Research Centre, Nairobi, Kenya, 1967. Address: Nairobi, Kenya.

VON STOKAR, Gerhard, born 3rd October 1922. Sculptor; Potter; University Lecturer. Education: Primary & Secondary, Munich, Germany; Woodcarving Apprentice, Staal. Fachschule fur Holzbildhauerei, Oberammergau, 1946-48; Academy of Fine Art, Munich, 1948-52; Sculpture, Painting, Master Diploma, Ceramics, Staatl. Fachschule fur Keramil, Landshut, 1956. Married, 3 children. Appointments: Owner & Director, Schwabische Mayolika Manufaktur, Krumback, 1952-57; ibid, Private Lehrwerkstatte fur Keramik & Keramische Bildhauerei, 1957-62; Part-time Teacher, Staatliche Berufschule Krumbach; Lecturer, Sculpture, Pottery, & Ceramics, University of Science & Technology, Kumasi, Ghana, 1962-64; Senior Lecturer, Acting Head of Department of Pottery & Ceramics, 1964-68; Part-time Teacher, Sculpture; Senior Lecturer, Ceramics, Ahmadu Bello University, Zaria,

Nigeria, 1969—. Memberships: Subscribing Member, American Craftsman Council; World Crafts Council; Bayrischer Kunsgewerbeverein, Munich; Deutsche Gesellschaft fur Christliche Kunst; Bundesfachgruppe des Deutschen Topferhandwrks. Publications: Kunsthandwerk in Ghana (African Heute); Die Kultur der Ashanti (Unser Werk); Yellow Glaze Stain from Local Stibnite, Ghana Academy of Science. Address: Ahmadu Bello University, Zaria, Nigeria.

VO TOAN, Claude, born 28th April 1929. Artist-Painter. Education: Academie de la Grande Chaumiere, Montparnasse, Paris, France; The Julian Academy, Paris; Ecole du Louvre, Paris. Married to the Architect Cong Vo Toan. Exhibitions at: Rabat, Morocco, 1962-69; Galerie Vendome, Paris, France, 1970. Address: 13 Avenue de Vesoul, Rabat, Morocco.

VO TOAN, Cong, born 5th March 1924. Architect. Education: School of Fine Arts, Paris, France, 1948-54; D.P.L.G.; Architectural Association School of London, 1954. Personal details: married to the Artist Claude Vo Toan, 2 sons. Appointments: Architect, The Republic of Vietnam for the International Exposition & Fairs, 1957-61; Architect, King Hassan II of Morocco for the building of the Mausoleum of the King's Father, Mohammed V, 1961-71. Memberships: Society of Diploma Architects for the Government, Paris; Study Group for the Coordination of Underground Urbanism; Order of Architects of Paris & Morocco. Publications: Garages-Parkings, 1960; Memorandum on the International Architectural Competition for the Central London Mosque, 1969; & several articles in architectural magazines. Honours: Prize Achille Leclerc; Prize Arfridson; Prize Paul Bigot, Institute of France, 1956-58; First Prize, Diploma of Architecture, Paris, 1954; Gold Medal of Higher Studies of Architecture, 1958; 3rd Prize, International Architecture Competition for the Central London Mosque, 1969. Address: 13 Avenue de Vesoul, Rabat, Morocco.

VOULE-FRITZ, Marcel, born 10th July 1934. Technical Adviser; Director of Education, National Institute of Scientific Research. Education: Diploma of Higher Studies in Social Sciences. Married, 4 children. Appointments: Research Assistant, 1964-66; Technical Adviser, Director, 1966-70; Professor of Legislation, C.N.F.S.; National School of Administration. Memberships: Administrator, Centre for Experimental Construction. Publications include: La Fonction Publique Togolaise; Les Origins de l'Administration du Togo. Address: B.P. 493, Lome, Togo.

VOUNDI, Nicolas, born 24th August 1928. Deputy of the National Federal Assembly of Cameroun. Education: Primary Studies, Catholic Mission, Medzek, Akonolinga; Secondary Studies, Lower Seminary Akono, Cameroun; Certificate of Primary Studies; Diplome de Moniteur Indigene. Appointments: School Director, 1946-60; Mayor of the Commune of Akonolinga, 1960-65; Deputy, National Federal Assembly of Cameroun, 1964-70. Honours: Knight of the Order of Bravery of the Cameroun. Address: B.P. 63, Akonolinga, Cameroun.

VUO, Thomas Sedawa, born 30th May 1937. Manpower Officer. Education: Cambridge Overseas School Certificate, 1958; Cambridge Higher School Certificate, 1960; B.A.(Social Science), 1966; International Manpower Seminar, Washington, D.C., U.S.A., 1968. Personal details: son of Canon Ernest S. Vuo, married to Rose Vuo, 2 sons. Appointments: Cooperative Inspector; Labour Inspector; Labour Officer, Employment Officer; Manpower Officer, Manpower Planning & Administration. Member of International Association of Personnel in Employment Security. Publications: Follow-up Study of the Dar es Salaam Engineering Technicans (Official Ministry of Economic Affairs & Development Planning). Address: Uchumi, P.O. Box 9242, Car es Salaam, Tanzania.

VYAS, Bhanushanker Odhavaji, born 5th October 1924. Teacher; Writer. Education: M.A., Bombay, India; M.A., Poona; B.T., Bombay; S.T.C., Bombay; Kovid (Wadha). Married, 3 children. Appointments: Assistant Master, Bombay, 1947; Rationing Inspector, ibid, 1949; Registered Talker, All-India Radio, Bombay, 1954; Uganda Civil Service, 1955-68; Headmaster, Magwa School, 1965-67; ibid, Public School, 1967—. Adviser, 'The Nile', 1958-59; Editor, 'The Mirror', 1960; 'Evolution', 1970. Memberships: President, Gujarati Literary Society, Jinja, 1958 & 1969; Joint Secretary, Sahitya Sammelan for E.A., 1959. Publications: Subhashit Manjoosha, 1952; Parivesh, 1957; Sashikoni Swapnabhoomi, 1959; Melanan Pankhee, 1961; Africani Shreshttha Vartao, 1962; Vishwani Shreshtha Sahaskathao, 1962; Mandarni Parkamma, 1963; Aa Par Pele Par, 1963; The Silent Thunder, 1964; Manav Sanskriti ane Dharma, 1964; Amar Darshaniko, 1966; Sanket, 1966. Honours: Uganda Independence Medal, 1962; Gujarat State Literary Award for Mandarni Parkamma, 1965-66. Address: Jinja Public Secondary School, P.O. Box 454, Jinja, Uganda.

VYAS, Harshadray J., born Devgad Baria, India, 14th November 1916. Commodity Executive. Married, 3 sons. Appointments: Liaison Officer, Lint Marketing Board, Uganda; Sometime Acting Secretary, Kampala Coffee & Produce Exchange. Address: 4 Borup Avenue, P.O. Box 1692, Kampala, Uganda.

VYAS, Prem K., born 13th April 1926. Economist; Statistician. Education: B.A., University of Bombay, India, 1949; R.S.A., Institute of Statistics, London, U.K., 1960. Appointments: Head of Trade & Transport Section, East African Statistical Dept., East African Community, 1961-68; Head of Publication & Documentation Section, 1969—. Member of Nairobi Lodge, Theosophical Society. Publications: Economic & Statistical Review of the East African Statistical Dept. (Editor). Address: The East African Statistical Dept., P.O. Box 30462, Nairobi, Kenya.

WABOMBA-MUTENYO, George Wilson, born 3rd March 1933. Administrator. Education: Bupoto Primary School, 1945-51; Budaka Junior Secondary School, 1952-54; Bosoga College, 1955-57. Appointments: Clerk, Interpreter, D.C.'s Office, Bugisu, 1958-60; Administrative Officer, District Commissioner, 1965-68; Principal Assistant Secretary, 1968. Memberships: Photographic Society & Mountain Club, 1955-57; Resident Gulu Club, 1957-58; President, Lions Club of Gulu, 1958-59; President, Norman Godinho School, Parent Teachers' Association. Address: P.O. Box 7037, Kampala, Uganda.

WABUGE, Wafula, born Kakamega, Kenya, 27th March 1928. Farmer; Politician. Education: Tororo College, Uganda. Married, 10 children. Appointments include: with E.A. Tanning Extract Co. Ltd., 1947-51; Salesman, Gailey Roberts Ltd., 1952-60; Member, Legislative Council, Nakuru Town, 1961-63; President, Western Region Assembly, 1963-64; Chairman, Western Provincial Council, 1964—; Chairman, General Wages Advisory Council, 1965—; Assessor, Business Premises Rent Control, 1965—; Chairman, Board of Governors, Bungoma Secondary School, 1967—; Member, Ergeton College Board of Governors, 1966—; Member, Highlands High School Board of Governors, 1967—; Director, East African Railways Corporation, 1967—; Member of Parliament, Kitale West. Memberships include: Transport Licensing Board; President, Abaluhya Association, Eldoret, 1957-59; President, Eldoret African District Congress, 1958-59; Eldoret African Advisory Council; Assistant Secretary, Eldoret Football Association; Deputy General Secretary, Kadu; National Executive Officer, Kadu; Kenya Seed Growers' Association; Chairman, Kakamega District Branch, Kanu. Address: P.O. Box 341, Kitale, Kenya.

WAKHWEYA, Emmanuel Bwayo, born 25th December 1936. Secretary to the Treasury. Education: B.A.(Hons.), Econs., Delhi, India. Personal details: married with children. Appointments: Principal Assistant, Secretary Treasurer, 1963; Under-Secretary, Treasury, 1964-68; Deputy Governor, Bank of Uganda, 1968; Secretary to the Treasury, 1969. Member of the Uganda Economics Society. Honours: Papal Knight Commander of St. Gregory the Great. Address: P.O. Box 103, Entebbe, Uganda.

WALCOTT-LANDES, Albert Pierre, born Bathurst, The Gambia, 6th September 1909. Retired. Education: Hagan Street Elementary & St. Augustine Secondary Schools (Teacher in the former, January-December, 1930); Cambridge Preliminary Examination, 1930. Married. Appointments: Survey Department, The Gambia Government, 1931; 3rd Grade Surveyor/Draughtsman, 1934; 2nd Grade Surveyor/Draughtsman, 1948; serving at the same time as Calligraphist until retirement; visited U.K. in June 1950 on the invitation of the British Council with the following Programme: attached to the Large & Small Scales Section of the Ordinance Survey, Southampton, in connection with cartography; with the Millbrook Memorial Works in connection with the engraving of epitaphs, etc., on marble, granite, & Portland; with the late M. C. Oliver of the School of Arts in Hampstead, London in connection with calligraphy; appointed Senior Surveyor, 1953; prepared at the request of The Gambia Government, for and on behalf of the people of The Gambia, illuminated loyal addresses to members of the Royal Family as follows: Silver Jubilee of the late King George V; Coronation of the late King George VI; Coronation of Queen Elizabeth II; visit of the Duke of Edinburgh to The Gambia, 1957 (address of welcome). Memberships: Royal Overseas League, London; Committee, National Freedom from Hunger Campaign, Bathurst. Honours: Coronation Medal, 1953; B.E.M., 1957 (list of Honours dated 13th June 1957 refers); Chevalier, Ordre National du Senegal, 1967. Address: 'Wallcottville', P.O. Box 135, 28A Gloucester St., Independence Drive, Bathurst, The Gambia.

WALDRON-RAMSEY, Waldo Emerson, born Barbados, West Indies, 1930. Barrister-at-Law; Economist; Diplomatist. Education: LL.B.(Hons.); B.Sc.(Hons., Econ.); LL.M.; Ph.D., London School of Economics, London, U.K.; The Middle Temple; Hague Academy of International Law; University of Niz. Personal details: married, 1 son, 2 daughters. Appointments: Practice, London Bar & South Western Circuit; Legal Assistant, Colonial Office, London, 1957-60; Marketing Economist, Shell International, 1960-62; Counsellor, Tanzania Mission to U.N., 1962—; U.N. Legal Expert Investigating Middle East Crisis, Human Rights & Political Prisoners in South Africa. Memberships: English Bar; Bar of Trinidad & Tobago; The Tanzania Bar. Honours: Scholar & Prizeman in Public International Law, London School of Economics, 1958; Grand Officer, National Order of Honneur et Mérite, Republic of Haiti, 1968. Address: The Barbados High Commission, Belgravia, London, S.W.1.

WALIGO, Abraham Pellew Nkalubo, born 28th July 1928. Consulting Engineer. Education: King's College, Budo, Uganda, 1935-46; Adams College, Natal, South Africa, 1946-48; Fort Hare University College, 1948-50; Loughborough College of Technology, U.K., 1950-55; D.L.C.(Hons.); B.Sc.(Eng.), London; C.Eng.; F.I.E.E., U.K.; F.E.A.I.E. Appointments: Graduate Trainee, General Electric Company, U.K., 1955-57; Junior Engineer, Chief Engineer, Uganda Electrici y Board, 1957-69; Consulting Engineer, Private Practice, 1969—. Address: P.O. Box 5996, Kampala, Uganda.

WALKER, James Montserrat, born 30 June 1933. Surgeon. Education: Sedbergh School; Queen's University, Belfast, Northern Ireland; F.R.C.S., London & Edinburgh, U.K.; D.T.M.&H., Liverpool. Married. Appointments: House Officer, St. James's Hospital, London, & Bristol Royal Infirmary. Member, British Medical Association. Address: Rwanda Mission C.M.S., St. Marks Church, Kennington Park Road, London, S.E.11., U.K.

WALKER, Shirley Margaret, born 9th July 1938. Physiotherapist. Education: Farringtons School, U.K.; Whyteleafe County Grammar

School; St. Thomas' Hospital School of Physiotherapy, London. Personal details: Presented at Court, 1958; married. Appointments: Physiotherapist, Pembury Hospital, Tunbridge Wells, St. Thomas' Hospital, London, & Luton & Dunstable Hospital, Luton. Address: Rwanda Mission C.M.S., St. Mark's Church, Kennington Park Road, London, S.E.11, U.K.

WALLACE, Brian Anthony, born 14th June 1935. Medical Practitioner. Education: Public School, U.K.; M.B., B.S., London Hospital Medical School; M.R.C.S.; L.R.C.P.; D.Obst., R.C.O.G. Married, 2 children. Appointments: House appointments in surgery, medicine, obstetrics & paediatrics in various London hospitals; Medical Officer, Jinja Hospital, Uganda; District Medical Officer, Busoga; Medical Superintendent, Jinja Hospital, Uganda Ministry of Health. Memberships: Commodore, Jinja Sailing Club, 1969-70. Address: P.O. Box 558, Jinja, Uganda.

WALUSE, Alfred Nyongesa, born January, 1940. Accounts Officer. Education: Intermediate Commerce, Royal Society of Arts. Married, 2 sons. Appointments: Accounting Assistant, 1965-66; Accounts Officer, 1966—. Secretary-General, Tachoni Welfare Association Fund, 1962-66. Address: Lugusi Full Primary School, P.O. Box 14, Broderickfalls, Kenya.

WALUSIMBI, Sam Frank, born 18th January 1918. Physician. Education: Ndejje Primary School; King's College, Budo; M.B., Ch.B., Makerere University College & Mulago Medical School, 1947. Appointments: Practised in Government Hospitals, 1947-57; in Private Practice, 1957—. Address: Rubaga P.O. Box 14147, Kampala, Uganda.

WANDERA, Joshua Geoffrey, born 27th January 1935. Veterinary Surgeon; Veterinary Pathologist. Education: Dip.Vet.Sci., Makerere University, Uganda, 1955-61; M.Sc., Michigan State University, U.S.A., 1961-62; Ph.D., University of East Africa, 1970. Married. Appointments: Veterinary Research Officer, 1963; District Veterinary Officer, 1964; Lecturer, Veterinary Pathology, University of Nairobi, Kenya, 1965—. Memberships: Kenya Veterinary Association; World Association of Veterinary Pathologists. Author of 12 publications in the area of veterinary pathology & microbiology. Honours: Maya Baker Prize as best final-year student, 1960-61; Muljibhai Madhvani Prize as most industrious veterinary student throughout course, 1960-61. Address: University of Nairobi, Kenya.

WANDIRA, Asavia, born February, 1933. University Professor. Education: Busoga College, Mwiri, 1947-52; Makerere University, Kampala, Uganda, 1953-58; London University Institute of Education, U.K., 1959-61. Married. Appointments: Senior History Teacher, Busoga College, Mwiri, 1961-63; Senior Education Officer, Ministry of Education, Uganda, 1963; Secretary & Registrar, Makerere University, 1964-69; Professor of Education, ibid, 1969—. Memberships: Uganda Public Service Commission, 1964—; President, Uganda Education Association, 1969-70. Author of various articles on education. Honours: Hancock Memorial Prize, Makerere University, 1954, 1956; Muejibhai Madhavani Prize in Education, ibid, 1958. Address: Makerere University, P.O. Box 7062, Kampala, Uganda.

WANGATI, Frederick Joshuah, born 12th October 1936. Research Officer. Education: Kagumo High School, 1953-56; B.Sc.(Lond.), Physics & Maths., Makerere University College, Kampala, Uganda, 1957-63; M.Sc., Soil Science & Agro-Met., Rothamsted Experimental Station, U.K. Married, 3 children. Appointments: Research Officer, East African Agriculture & Forestry Research Organization, 1963-68; Senior Research Officer, ibid, 1968—; Head, Physics & Chemistry Division, 1969—. Memberships: Founder Member, East African Academy; Committee, Kenya Branch, ibid, 1967-68; Secretary, Kenya Branch, 1969-70. Author of various professional papers. Address: East African Agriculture & Forestry Research Organization, Muguga, P.O. Box 30148, Nairobi, Kenya.

WANJIGI (Hon.) James Maina, born 7th October 1931. Politician; Businessman; Farmer. Education: Diploma of Agriculture, Makerere University College, Kampala, Uganda, 1955; M.Sc., University of Connecticut, U.S.A.; M.A., University of Stanford, California. Married, 4 children. Appointments: Assistant Director of Agriculture, Kenya, 1964; Deputy Director of Settlement, 1965; Director of Settlement, 1966; Deputy Director of Agriculture, 1967; Executive Director, Industrial & Commercial Development Corporation, 1968-69; Assistant Minister for Agriculture, 1970—. President, Lions Club, Nairobi City. Address: Ministry of Agriculture, Nairobi, Kenya.

WANKULU, Peter, born Kanakamba, Village No. 3, near Kaliro, Uganda, 5th September 1938. Executive Organizer, African Unity Youth Organization; Office Assistant. Education: Primary Schools at Budini, Iganga, Naggalama, Namagunga, Nkokonjeru; Sacred Heart College, Jinja; St. Mary's College, Kisubi; Evidence Guild Instruction Course; Economics, Makerere Extramural Studies. Appointments: Laboratory Assistant, Animal Health Research Centre, Entebbe, 3 years; Staff, the Lebel (E.A.) Ltd., Sole Agents for Nyanza Textiles*Ltd.; Founder Organizer, Director, African Unity Youth Organization (Africa Youth League), 1962—; Office Assistant, Medhvani Sugar Works Ltd., Kakira, 1965—. Memberships: Organizer, Old Entebbe Football Club; Basoga Association; Uganda Youth Organization; one of 1st Members & Secretary, 1 Conference, Uganda Y.M.C.A., 1962; active in the field of African Unity, embracing the whole area of the Black States south of the Sahara, from Dar es Salaam to Dakar, including Southern Sudan, Ethiopia, & Somalia; main aim: 'To encourage & strengthen all the African States to settle problems by cordial negotiations towards achievement of technical & economic independence, find means to keep permanent peace & total change of our great continent'; The seven-point charter of the African Unity Youth Organization is briefly as follows: 1. Complete Union of African States to establish permanent good relations. 2. To stop apartheid policies & fight for equality & human rights throughout Africa. 3. To utilise fully African manpower, minerals, & raw materials for benefit of African people & encourage inter-state economic & scientific research. 4. To prevent war among brother states & discover the principles of African personality, popular democracy, justice, freedom of worship. 5. To facilitate communications between the African States, by transcontinental roads, railways, telephones, air & telegraphic links; to foster a common language, currency, & measuring systems. 6. To bring Africa into the scientific age, with its own trained teachers, pharmacists, mechanics, builders, etc. 7. To fight together against poverty, ignorance, & disease & promote the general welfare. Address: Madwani Sugar Works Ltd., P.O. Box 3001, Kakira, Jinja, Uganda.

WANYAMA-WAMBAALYA, Peter, born 12th November 1937. Economist. Education: Bubirabi Primary School (C.M.S.), 1945-48; African Public School, Mbale, Uganda, 1949-52; Nabumali High School, 1953-55; G.C.E. A Levels, Royal Technical College of East Africa, 1956-58; B.Sc.(Hons., Econ.), University of Hull, U.K., 1959-63. Personal details: father, ex-Chief, Mbale; married. Appointments: Accounts Assistant, Uganda Electricity Board, 1963-65; Senior Auditor, E.A. Community, Posts & Telecommunications, 1965-66; Director of Audit, ibid, 1967-68; ibid, E.A. Community, General Fund Services, 1968-69; Senior Director of Audit, E.A. Community Railways & Harbours, 1969-70. Memberships: East African Automobile Association, 1969-70; Hon. Auditor, St. John's Community Centre, Pumwani, Nairobi, 1965-66; Hon. Treasurer, ibid, 1966-69. Address: P.O. Box 30525, Nairobi, Kenya.

WARD (Lt.-Col.) Alexander John, born 23rd January 1925. British Army Officer, Argyll & Sutherland Highlanders. Education: Falkirk & S.E. London Technical College, U.K. Served with Army as follows: Europe, 1942-45; Palestine & Egypt, 1946-48; Hong Kong, 1951-52; Germany, 1952-53; British Guiana, 1953-54; Uganda, Kenya, & Zanzibar, 1957-63; Singapore & Borneo, 1965-66; Mauritius, 1967—. Memberships: Mauritius Naval & Military Gymkhana Club; Highland Brigade Club. Author, Climbing & Mountain Walking in Mauritius, 1968. Honours: Mauritius Special Mobile Force Merit Award for Gallantry, 1968; O.B.E., 1969. Address: Special Mobile Force, Mauritius.

WARMANN, John St. George, born Obuasi, Ghana, 11th July 1913. Medical Practitioner. Education: King's College, Lagos, Nigeria; L.S.M., School of Medicine, Lagos, 1939; M.R.C.S.(U.K.); L.R.C.P.(Lond.); D.P.H., University of Birmingham, U.K., 1948. Married. Appointments include: Assistant Medical Officer, Nigerian Medical Service, 1939-45; Medical Officer, ibid., 1946-50; Medical Officer of Health & Port Health Officer, 1951-56; Senior Medical Officer, Ministry of Health, Ghana, 1956-57; Principal Medical Officer, ibid., 1957-63; Chief Medical Officer, Volta River Authority, 1963—. Memberships: Ghana Medical Association; British Medical Association; Fellow, Royal Society of Health. Address: Volta River Authority, P.O. Box M77, Accra, Ghana.

WARREN, Sheelagh Ardill, born 23rd November 1927. Teacher. Education: Limum Girls' School, Kenya; St. Margaret's School, Bushey, U.K.; Pease School for Girls, Cambridge; M.A., Girton College, Cambridge; Postgraduate Certificate in Education, Birmingham University. Appointments: Teacher, U.K., 1950-55; Teacher of English, Gauaza High School, Kampala, Uganda, 1957—. Member, Church Missionary Society. Address: P.O. Box 7029, Kampala, Uganda.

WASHINGTON (Lt.-General), G. Toe, born Barclayville, Kru Coast Territory, Maryland County, Liberia, 15th April, 1928. Soldier. Education: African Methodist Episcopal Elementary School, Takoradi, Gold Coast, 1940; English Church Mission Secondary School, 1944; Business College, Kibi, 1948; Officer, Basic Course, Liberia, 1955; Associate Company Officer Course, United States Army Quartermaster School, Fort Lee, Va., U.S.A., 1956; Career Course, U.S. Army Logistic Management School, ibid, 1960-61; U.S. Army Command & General Staff College, 1954. Married, 5 children. Appointments: enlisted, Liberian Army, 1950; promoted 1st Sergeant & assigned to Office of Commanding Officer, Liberian Frontier Force (Regular Army, now Liberian National Guard), 1951; Master Sergeant, assigned Regimental Sergeant-Major, Office of Commanding Officer, ibid, 1952; 2nd Lieutenant, assigned, Office of the Adjutant-General as Personnel Officer, Armed Forces of Liberia, 1953; 1st Lieutenant, 1955; assigned, the Quartermaster, 1956; assigned, Assistant Chief of Staff, G-4 (Logistics), 1959; Major, 1960; Assigned, Assistant Chief of Staff, G1 (Personnel) & Adjutant-General, 1965; Major-General & Chief of Staff, 1965; Lt.-General, 1968; Adviser to the President on Military Affairs, 1970— Memberships: Y.M.C.A.; Liberian Literary Club; Bame Football Club; St. John's Lodge, No. 3, Freemasons; Order of the Eastern Star; United Brothers Fellowship; Oddfellows; Shrine & Porro Society. Honours: Knight Commander, Humane Order of the African Redemption; Grand Band, ibid; Grand Commander, Star of Africa; D.S.C.; D.S.M.; Long Service Medal; Good Conduct Medal; Decorated by Tunisian, Mauritanian, Cameroun & Congo Republic Governments. Address: The Executive Mansion, Monrovia, Liberia.

WASSWA, Augustine Wakiwugulu, born 5th August, 1905. Medical Practitioner. Education: Primary, Mission School, 1916-20; St. Mary's College, Kisubi, 1920-24; qualified in Medicine, Makerere College Medical School. Kampala, Uganda, 1925-28. Widower, 6 children; remarried, 3 children. Appointments: Medical Officer in Government Service & holder of many responsible positions as District Medical Officer in several stations throughout Uganda, 40 years. Memberships: Committee Member, Makerere College University; ibid, Uganda Medical Association. Recipient, Governor's Prize, Makerere College, 1927. Address: Mulago Hospital, P.O. Box 7051, Kampala, Uganda.

WATTS, Edward Ronald, born 15th February 1930. Lecturer in Agricultural Extension. Education: B.Sc.(Agric.), Reading, U.K., 1953; Postgraduate Certificate, Education, London, 1954; Postgraduate Diploma, Agricultural Economics, Oxford, 1959. Married. Appointments: Rural Education Officer, Western Nigeria, 1954-56; Agricultural Officer, ibid, 1956-58; Tribal Agricultural Officer, Botswana, 1959-61; Tutor, Agriculture, Kenya, 1962-65; Principal, Embu Institute of Agriculture, 1965-66; Lecturer, Department of Rural Economy, 1966—. Memberships: Editor, Uganda Agricultural Society; Publicity Secretary, Christian Rural Fellowship of East Africa. Publications: Editor New Hope for Rural Africa, 1969; numerous articles in agricultural journals; weekly column, 'Farm Comment' in 'The People', Kampala, 1967—; Uganda Reporter for farming section in 'The Reporter', Nairobi, 1968-69. Address: Faculty of Agriculture, Makerere University, Box 7602, Kampala, Uganda.

WATTS, Theresa E. E., born 26th December 1930. Medical Practitioner. Education: University College, London, U.K.; London Hospital; M.B., B.S. (Lond.); D.P.H. (East Africa). Married. Appointments: Mulango Hospital, 1955-56; Kaimosi & Embu Hospitals, Kenya, 1962-66; Mulango Hospital, 1966-70. Address: Makerere University, P.O. Box 7062, Kampala, Uganda.

WAUNA, Likwathi Leonard, born 1st June 1937. Cashier. Education: Form II. Married, 4 children. Currently employed by Associated Stores Ltd., Livingstone, Zambia. Address: Associated Stores Ltd., P.O. Box 54, Livingstone, Zambia.

WEBSTER, David Anthony, born Nairobi, Kenya, 18th June 1941. Physician: Medical Missionary of Bible Churchmen's Missionary Society. Education: Nairobi Primary School, 1948-52; Prince of Wales School, Nairobi, 1953-58; M.B., B.S., St. Thomas's Hospital Medical School, London, U.K., 1959-64; Diploma, Obstetrics, Royal College of Obstetricians & Gynaecologists, 1967. Married. Appointments: House Officer, Surgery, Medicine, Gynaecology & Obstetrics, Princess Margaret Hospital, Swindon, 1964-67; Medical Officer in Charge, Amudat Hospital, Karamoja District, Uganda, 1967—. Member, Bible Churchmen's Missionary Society. Address: Amudat Hospital, Private Bag, P.O. Kitale, Kenya.

WEBSTER, Orrin John, born 26th June 1913. Research Director. Education: B.Sc., University of Nebraska, U.S.A., 1934; M.Sc., ibid, 1940; Ph.D., University of Minnesota, 1949. Appointments: Agricultural Engineering Department, University of Nebraska, 1934-35; Trainee, Soil Conservation Service, Albion, Neb., 1935; Agronomist, ibid, Blair & Hartington, Neb., 1935-36; Junior Agronomist, Field Station North Platte, Division of Dry Land Agriculture, U.S. Department of Agriculture, Neb., 1936-43; College of Agriculture, Lincoln, Neb., Forage Crops Division, Cereal Crops Division, U.S. Department of Agriculture, 1943-51; Adviser, British Colonial Service, Nigeria, 1951-52; Researcher, College of Agriculture, Lincoln, Neb., U.S.A., Crops Research Division, U.S. Department of Agriculture, 1951-63 (Sorghum Project Leader for U.S.A. for part of this time); reviewed agricultural projects in India, P.L. 480, & assisted in classification of World Sorghum Collection, 1963; Adviser, Sorghum & Maize Programmes, Nigeria, & major cereal project for West Africa, 1963-64; Director-Coordinator, J.P. 26, 1964-70; Research Director, ibid, 1970—. Memberships: Sigma Xi; American Society of Agronomy; Nigerian Agricultural Society. Author of numerous papers and reports. Address: IAR, PMB 1044, Zaria, Nigeria.

WEEDON, Maxwell Robert, born 26th July 1938. Medical Missionary Doctor. Education: Murrumbena State School, Australia; Gardiner Central School; Melbourne High School; M.B., B.S., Melbourne University, 1961. Married, 2 sons, 1 daughter. Appointments: Resident Medical Officer, Royal Hobart Hospital, 1962-64, St. Andrew's Hall, Melbourne, 1964, & D.C.T. Muumi Hospital, Tanzania, 1964-65; Medical Superintendent, D.C.T. Kilimaginde Hospital, 19l, 1965-70. Member, British Medical Association. Address: D.C.T. Kilimaginde Hospital, P.O. Manyoni, Tanzania.

WEGESA, Philip, born 28th July 1934. Helminthologist. Education: B.Sc., Biology, Makerere University College, Kampala, Uganda, 1958; D.A.P.&E., University of London, U.K., 1965. Appointments: Research Officer, Officer, East African Institute of Malaria & Vector-borne Diseases, 1962-69; Director, ibid, 1970—. Specializes in research of onchocerciasis. Publications: Simulium Vorax Pomeroy a potential vector of Onchocerca volvulus (Ann Trop. Med. & Parasit.), 1967; The comparison of the efficacy of meat meal & Yeast as food material for Anopheles gambiae larvae in the laboratory (WHO/MAL/471), 1964; The resettlement of refugees & onchocerciasis in Tanzania (E.A. Med. J.), 1968; The present status of onchocerciasis in Tanzania: a review of the distribution & prevalence of the disease (Trop. & Geog. Med.), Simulium Nyasalandicum (Amani form), & S. Adersi, two new potential vectors of Onchocerca volvulus in the Eastern Usambara Mountains, North Eastern Tanzania (E.A. Med. J.). Address: E.A. Institute for Malaria & Vector-borne Diseases, P.O. Amani, Tanzania.

WEMAH (Alhaji) Abu, born 21st May 1917. Diplomat. Education: Tamale Government Boarding School, Ghana, 1927-34; Certificate A, Achimota Training College, 1937-40. Appointments: A Pioneer Staff Member, 1st Government 2-year Teacher Training College, Tamale, 1944-53; Assistant Education Officer, Field Work, 1953-57; Local Council Administration, Tamale Urban Council, 1957-58; Administrative Officer, Ghana Civil Service, 1958-60; Government Agent, Bole District, 1959; Foreign Service Officer, 1960; Chargé d'Affairs, Ouagadougou, Ambassador to Upper Volta, 1961-64; Ambassador, Bulgaria, 1964-66; ibid, U.A.R., 1966-68; Mali, 1968, 1970—; Commissioner for Secretariats & Special Departments under the Office of the National

Liberation Council & for State Protocol, 1969. Memberships: Vice-Chairman, Youth Club, Tamale, 1957-59; Director, Red Cross, Northern Region Branch, 1958-60. Honours: National Order, Republic of Upper Volta, 1962; 1st Grade, Order of the United Arab Republic. Address: Embassy of Ghana, B.P. 209, Bamako, Mali.

WERIMO-RUPIA, Alexander, born 4th April 1930. Accountant. Education: Primary Certificate, C.M.S. Meseno School, 1944-46; Secondary Certificate, Kakamega Secondary School, 1947-48; Overseas Cambridge Certificate, British Tutorial College, 1954-56; Accountancy Studies by Correspondence, Rapid Results College, London & Kenya Polytechnic, Nairobi. Married, 4 sons, 3 daughters. Appointments: Stationmaster, East African Railways & Harbours, 1949-54; Accounts Clerk, The Bank of Baroda Ltd., 1954-59; Bank Cashier, First Permanent Building Society, Nairobi, Kenya (1st African Bank Cashier in Kenya), 1959-62; Grade I Accounts Clerk, Nairobi County Council, 1962-63; Accountant, City Council of Nairobi, 1963-68; Senior Accountant, East African Community, 1968—. Memberships: Secretary, Y.M.C.A., 1956; Chairman, ibid, 1957; Church Councillor & Vicar's Warden, St. John's Church, Pumwani, Nairobi, 1968—; Member, Makerere University College Extramural Studies, 1957—. Honours: 1st Prize, Outstanding Student in Class, 1943, 1944; 2nd Prize, ibid, 1947, 1948; named Outstanding Student, Final Exams., Railway Training School, Nairobi, 1949. Address: c/o East African Community, Accountant-General's Department, P.O. Box 30400, Nairobi, Kenya.

WESLEY-HADZIJA, Bozena, born 5th January 1928. Pharmacist; Chemist. Education: B.Sc., Pharmacy; M.Pharm.; Ph.D., Chemistry. Currently, Senior Lecturer, Pharmaceutical Chemistry, University of Science & Technology, Kumasi, Ghana. Memberships: American Association for the Advancement of Science; Pho Chi, Pharm. Honour Society. Author of 12 publications in the field of pharmaceutical chemistry. Address: University of Science & Technology, Kumasi, Ghana.

WHITE, Graham Bruce, born 18th December 1941. Entomologist. Education: G.C.E., Selhurst Grammar School, Croydon, U.K., 1953-60; B.Sc., A.R.C.S., Imperial College, London University, 1960-63; Ph.D., London School of Hygiene & Tropical Medicine, 1963-67; WHO-sponsored course, Vector-Genetics, University of Notre Dame, U.S.A., 1968. Married, 1 son. Appointments: Research Officer, Entomologist, East African Community Institute of Malaria & Vector-borne Diseases, Amani, Tanga, Tanzania, 1967—. Memberships: Royal Society of Tropical Medicine & Hygiene; Fauna Preservation Society; London University Opera Group. Author of review articles & scientific papers. Address: East African Malaria Institute, Amani, Tanga, Tanzania.

WHITEHALL, Harold, born Ramsbottom, Lancs, U.K., 14th May 1905. Educator; Poet; Critic; Radio & Television Performer, Lexicographer. Education: Municipal Technical College, Hull; B.A.(Hons.), University College, Nottingham, 1927; H.Dip.Ed., Cambridge, 1928; Ph.D., University of Iowa, U.S.A., 1931. Married. Appointments: various Instructorships, Lectureships, Assistant & Associate Professorships, U.S. Universities, 1928-49; Professor of English Language & Linguistics, Indiana University, 1949-66; Chairman, Linguistics, ibid, 1949-59; Professor of English Language, University of Ibadan, Western Nigeria, 1966-70; Co-Director, Reading Centre, 1966-70. Memberships: American Dialect Society; Secretary, then Chairman, Middle English Section, Modern Language Association of America, 1941-47; Linguistic Society of America. Publications include: Structural Essentials of English, 1959, & 7 other books & monographs on English language; 31 articles on English language & literary criticism; plays & poems in various journals; translations from French, German, Erse, & Chinese; Linguistic Editor, Webster's New World Dictionary, 1951, 1953, etc. Honours: Senior Fellowship Award, University College, Nottingham, U.K., 1926; Guggenheim Memorial Fellowship, 1940; Rockefeller Fellowship, 1944; Spencer-Trask Lecturer, Princeton University, 1958; Commissioned Hon. Colonel, Commonwealth of Kentucky, U.S.A., 1963; elected Fellow, School of Letters, 1952. Address: c/o Standard Bank of West Africa, London, U.K.

WHITELAW, Brian S., born 28th November 1938. Teacher. Educated in London, U.K. Married, 2 daughters. Memberships: Malawi Government Advisory Council for Sport; former Secretary, National Football League; former Secretary & Founder, Schools Football Association of Malawi. Address: P.O. Box 373, Blantyre, Malawi.

WHITTAKER, Kenneth Charles, born 2nd September 1913. Univesity Professor. Education: Stockport Grammar School, U.K.; B.A., Brasenose College, Oxford, 1935; M.A., ibid, 1939; D.Phil., 1970; B.Sc., London University, 1940; Ph.D., ibid, 1968. Married. Appointments: Master, Achimota College, Ghana, 1936-48; Senior Master, ibid, 1948-50; Assistant Headmaster, 1950-51; Director, Vernacular Literature Bureau, Accra, 1951-55; Lecturer, Kumasi College of Technology, 1956-58; Senior Lecturer, ibid, 1958-61; Senior Lecturer, University of Science & Technology, Kumasi, 1961-62; Professor of Physics, ibid, 1962—. Fellow, Institute of Physics. Various translations into Twi, Fante, & Ga. Address: Department of Physics, University of Science & Technology, Kumasi, Ghana.

WIDDOWS, Michael Hallawell, born 25th February 1924. Chartered Civil Engineer. Education: Merchant Taylors' School, Crosby, U.K.; B.Eng., University of Liverpool. Married, 2 daughters. Appointments: Chief Engineer, Roads, Ministry of Works, Eastern Nigeria; Deputy Controller of Works, ibid; Adviser, Highway Design & Construction, U.N.D.P., Tobago, W.I.; Chief Development Engineer (Opex), Tobago, Government of Trinidad & Tobago; Engineer in Chief, Ministry of Works, Lesotho. Memberships: F.I.C.E.; M.I.H.E.

Honours: O.B.E., 1965. Address: Ministry of Works, P.O. Box 20, Maseru, Lesotho.

WIDMER, Heinz, born 8th June 1937. Electrical Engineer. Education: Diploma, Swiss Federal Institute of Technology, Zurich, Switzerland. Married, 2 daughters. Appointments: Project Engineer, Brown, Boveri & Co. Ltd., Baden, Switzerland, 1963-66; Resident Engineer, East Africa, Brown, Boveri & Co., 1963-69; Technical Assistant to Chief Electrical Engineer, Tanzania Electrical Supply Co., Dar es Salaam. Memberships: Institute of Electrical & Electronics Engineers, U.S.A.; East African Institution of Engineers; The Electronics Institution of East Africa. Publications: A New Power Line Carrier Link in Kenya (Jrnl. E.A. Inst. Engrs.), 1968. Address: c/o Tanesco, Electrical Department, P.O. Box 9024, Dar es Salaam, Tanzania.

WIGGER, Maria Martha, born 3rd June 1925. Specialist Surgeon. Education: Medical Studies in Tubingen, Munich, & Wurzburg, Germany; training for Surgery, Ulm. Appointments: Surgeon, Rubaga Hospital, Kampala, Uganda. Memberships: Deutsche Gesellschaft fur Chirurgie. Address: Rubaga Hospital, Box 14130, Kampala, Uganda.

WIGGINS, Margaret Agnes, born 27th March 1913. Speech Therapist. Education: M.A., University of New Zealand. Married to Bishop Maxwell Wiggins, Bishop of Victoria Nyanza. Address: Mwanza, Tanzania.

WIGGINS, Maxwell Lester, born 5th February 1915. Bishop. Education: Christchurch Boys' High School, New Zealand; B.A., University of New Zealand, 1937; L.Th., New Zealand Board of Theological Studies, 1938. Married. Appointments: Curate, St. Mary's, Nerivale, 1938-41; Vicar, Oxford, N.Z., 1941-45; C.M.S. Missionary, Diocese of Central Tanganyika, 1945; Headmaster, Alliance Secondary School, Dodoma, 1948; Provost & Dean, Dodoma Cathedral, 1949-53; Principal, St. Philips Theological College, 1954-55; Archdeacon, 1956; Assistant Bishop, Central Tanganyika, 1959; first Bishop of Victoria Nyanza, 1963. Address: Box 278, Mwanza, Tanzania.

WIKRAMANAYAKE, George Herbert, born 21st November 1916. Senior Lecturer. Education: B.A., London, U.K.; M.A., Oxford University; Dr.Phil., University of Goettingen, Germany. Appointments: Assistant Lecturer, Classics, University of Ceylon, 1943-47; Lecturer in Classics, ibid, 1947-60; Lecturer in Classics, Fourah Bay College, Freetown, Sierra Leone, 1960-63; Senior Lecturer in Latin, University College, Cape Coast, Ghana, 1963-66; Senior Lecturer in Classics & Head, Department of Classics, ibid, 1966—. Memberships: Classical Association of Cape Coast; Past Hon. Sec., Classical Association of Ceylon; Oxford Union; Sierra Leone; English-Speaking Union. Contributor to professional journals. Honours: Ceylon Government University Scholarship, 1939; Research Fellowship, Alexander von Humboldt-Stiftung, 1956-57. Address: University College, Cape Coast, Ghana.

WILBY, George Lewis, born Yorkshire, England, 30th December 1896. Qualified Mechanical Engineer. Education: St. James's School, New Manston; Leeds Technical College. Married. Appointments: Apprentice Engineer, 1912, 1916-21; Agricultural Engineer, North America, 1921-26; ibid, Victoria Nyanza Sugar Co., Miwani, Kenya, 1927-33; Draftsman & Factory Engineer, ibid, 1933-38; 2nd Engineer, Uganda Sugar Works, Kakira, 1938-39; Chief Engineer, Kenya Sugar Works, Ramisi, 1939-43; ibid, Mor & Kilulu Sisal Estates, Tanganyika, 1944-47; ibid, & Head Office Manager, Ralli Estates Ltd., Tanzania, 1948-69. Memberships: Associate, East African Engineers, 1945; Royal Society of St. George, 1950; Masonic Lodge, Tanga, 1953; British Legion, 1920—. Recipient, 1st Class Artificers' Certificate, Artillery Army. Address: 16 Sackville Road, Hove BN3 3FA, Sussex, U.K.

WILCOCK, Richard Donald Croft, born 5th May 1915. Advocate. Education: Sevenoaks School, U.K. Married, 5 children. Education: admitted as Solicitor, U.K., 1939; Airborne Forces & War Office, British Army, 1939-50; retired from Army with rank of Colonel, 1950; admitted as Advocate, Kenya, 1951; Advocate, Tanzania, 1953. Memberships: Past President, Child Welfare Society of Kenya; President, Kenya Orchid Society. Address: Mutual Building, P.O. Box 10201, Nairobi, Kenya.

WILKINSON, John, born Derby, U.K., 2nd November 1918. Physician & Minister of Religion. Education: Heaton Grammar School, Newcastle upon Tyne; M.B., Ch.B., Edinburgh University, 1941; M.D., ibid, 1956; B.D., 1961; D.T.M.&H., 1956; M.R.C.P.(E.), 1957. Married, 3 children. Appointments include: Captain, R.A.M.C., 1942-45; Missionary, Church of Scotland, Kenya, 1946; Medical Superintendent, Presbyterian Church Hospital, Kikuyu, Kenya; Chairman, Protestant Churches Medical Association, Kenya. Publications: Health & Healing (Editor), 1967; numerous articles in medical & theological journals. Honours, prizes, etc: Hope Prize, New College, Edinburgh, 1946; Mackintosh Prize in Elocution, ibid, 1946; Greig Medal in Tropical Medicine, University of Edinburgh, ibid, 1956. Address: The Presbyterian Church Hospital, P.O. Box 45, Kikuyu, Kenya.

WILKINSON, John Brian, born 31st January 1929. Solicitor; Registrar. Education: Hull Grammar School, U.K.; University College of Hull; LL.B.(London), 1949; Solicitor (England), 1951. Married, 4 sons. Appointments: Assistant Registrar of Titles & Conveyances, Kampala, Uganda, 1965-66; Acting Registrar, ibid, 1966; Acting Deputy Registrar, 1966-67; Deputy Registrar, 1968; Acting Registrar, 1968-70; Registrar, 1970—; Memberships: Law Society, England; Advocate & Solicitor, Supreme Court of Singapore; Advocate & Solicitor, Supreme Court, States of Malaya, Sarawak, & Sabah. Address: c/o Office of Titles, P.O. Box 7061, Kampala, Uganda.

WILLIAMS, Akinwole Olufemi, born Lagos, Nigeria. University Professor. Education: Anglican Girls' School, Lagos, 1940-44; Lagos

Grammar School, 1944-51; King's College, 1952-54; Technical College, Dundee, U.K., 1954-55; B.A., English, Public Administration & Psychology, M.B., B.Ch., B.A.O., Trinity College, Dublin, Ireland, 1955-61; M.A. & M.D., ibid, 1964; M.R.C.P., Ireland & London, 1964; M.C.Path., London, 1966. Married, 3 children. Appointments: House Physician, Cumberland Infirmary, Carlisle, 1961-72; House Surgeon, Musgrave Park Hospital & Belfast City Hospital, 1962; Research Fellow, Tutor, Pathology, Queen's University, Belfast, 1962-64; Lecturer, Pathology, Trinity College, Dublin,964; Examiner, Pathology, ibid, 1964-65; Lecturer, Morbid Anatomy, Department of Pathology, University of Ibadan, Nigeria, 1965; Consultant Pathologist, University College Hospital, ibid, 1965; Senior Lecturer, Pathology, 1966; Acting Head, Department of Pathology, 1966-67; Exchange Professor, Johns Hopkins Medical School, Baltimore, Md., U.S.A., 1967; Visiting Scientist, National Cancer Institute, National Institutes of Health, Bethesda, 1968. Member, several committees, University of Ibadan. Memberships: Pathological Society of Great Britain & Ireland; Association of Physicians of West Africa; Examining Board, Pathology, Nigerian Medical Council; Board for Commonwealth Scholarship Selection, Federal Ministry of Health, Lagos; International Academy of Pathology; Royal Academy of Medicine, Ireland; Science Association of Nigeria; Working Committee on Liver Cancer, International Agency for Research into Cancer. Author of numerous scientific publications. Recipient, several scholastic honours & awards. Address: Department of Pathology, Univesity of Ibadan, Ibadan, Nigeria.

WILLIAMS, David James, born Muswell Hill, London, U.K., 4th July 1929. Missionary Teacher. Education: Barfield Preparatory School, Surrey, 1939-43; Highgate School, London, 1943-48; B.A.(Hons.), English Language & Literature, Christ Church, Oxford, 1949-53; Dip. Ed., 1953. Married, 2 sons, 1 daughter. Appointments: on Staff, Cheltenham Grammar School, 1953-56; Staff, Gindiri Boys' Secondary School, Sudan United Mission, Nigeria, 1956-58; on Staff, Gindiri Teachers' College, ibid, 1959-66; Principal, ibid, 1966—. Memberships: Graduates' Fellowship, I.V.F., London; Association for Teaching of English as a Foreign Language. Publications: English in Africa, Books 1, 2, 3; Faster Reading, A First Course; Articles in Journal of Nigeria English Studies Association; contributions to various publications. Address: Gindiri Teachers' College, Sudan United Mission, P.O. Barakin Ladi, via Jos, Nigeria.

WILLIAMS, Edward Hammond, born 10th November 1915. Missionary and Medical Practitioner. Education: Nairobi School; Reading School, U.K.; M.B., B.S.(Lond.), St. Bartholomew's Hospital, London; M.R.C.S.; L.R.C.P.(Eng.). Married. Appointments: Resident Medical Officer, Mildmay Mission Hospital, London; Medical Officer, Kuluva Hospital, Africa Inland Mission, West Nile District, Uganda. Honours: Coronation Medal, 1953; M.B.E., 1960; Uganda Independence Medal, 1962. Address: Box 28, Arua, Uganda.

WILLIAMS, Gerald Allan, born 5th April 1920. Banker. Education: Monmouth School. Married, 1 son, 1 daughter. Currently, Local Director, Barclays Bank D.C.O., Nairobi, Kenya. Memberships: Honourable Artillery Co.; Nairobi Club; Associate, Institute of Bankers. Hon. Captain, Royal Artillery. Address: c/o Mrs. R. M. E. Williams, 31 Robson Road, Worthing, Sussex, U.K.

WILLIAMS, John Rhys, born 19th March 1925. Entomologist. Education: Bristol University, 1942-45; London University, Imperial College, 1945-46; Cambridge University, Pembroke College, 1946-47; B.Sc., D.I.C., M.Sc. Appointments: Entomologist, Department of Agriculture, Mauritius; Chief Entomologist, Mauritius Sugar Industry Research Institute. Memberships: Fellow, Royal Entomological Society of London; Fellow, Institute of Biology. Author of numerous articles in field. Senior Editor, Pests of Sugar Cane, 1969. Address: Mauritius Sugar Industry Research Institute, Reduit, Mauritius.

WILLIAMS, Laurence Albert Joseph, born Nairobi, Kenya, 23rd April 1929. Geologist. Education: St. Mary's School, Nairobi, 1939-43; Prince of Wales School, Nairobi, 1945-46; B.Sc., 1st Class Hons., Geology, University of Glasgow, U.K., 1947-52. Married. Appointments: Junior Chemist, East African Industrial Research Board, Nairobi, 1946-47; Geologist, Geological Survey of Kenya, 1952-63; Lecturer in Geology, University College, Nairobi, 1963-67; Senior Lecturer, Geology, ibid, 1967—. Memberships: Fellow, Geological Society of London; Founder Member, East African Academy; Secretary, Kenya Branch, ibid, 1965-66; Council, ibid, 1966; Associate, Institution of Mining & Metallurgy, London. Author of numerous professional papers. Address: Department of Geology, University of Nairobi, P.O. Box 30197, Nairobi, Kenya.

WILLIAMS, Prince John Valentine, born 23rd January 1912. Pharmacist; Member of Parliament. Education: St. Edward's Secondary School; Pharmacy Examination, 1941; Studied Local Government, London County Council, U.K., Urban District Council of Enfield & Rural District Council, Cranbrook, Kent, 1954. Appointments: entered Medical Department, now Ministry of Health, 1933; Private Pharmacy, Bo, Sierra Leone, 1949; Member, Sierra Leone People's Party & National Vice-President under late Sir Milton Margai, 1953-58; Representative, Bo Town 11 Constituency, Sierra Leone House of Representatives, 1962-67; Chairman, Bo Town Council, 1959-63; Deputy Speaker & Chairman, Public Accounts Committee, House of Representatives, 1962-63; returned to Parliament as Independent Candidate, 1967; accepted as Member, All-People's Congress, 1969; Resident Minister, Southern Province, 1969-70. Memberships include: Delegacy, National Institute of Education; Chairman, Catholic Teachers' Training College, Bo; ibid, Christ the King College, Bo; Trustee, Sir Milton Cheshire Home; Lady Dorman Nursery School; Bo Club. Honours: J.P., 1959; Commissioner for Oaths, 1960; Sierra Leone Independence Medal, 1961; M.B.E., 1961; Papal Medal, Pro Ecclesia et

Pontifice, 1964; Honorary Citizen, Sioux City, Iowa, U.S.A. Address: Bo via Freetown, Sierra Leone.

WILLMS, Helmuth Bibi F., born 3rd February 1927. Architect. Education: Diploma of Architecture, University of Aachen, West Germany, 1949-54. Appointments: Assistant Professor, Aachen University, 1956-58; Superintendent Architect, Public Works Department, i/c Governmental office buildings design & supervision, Ghana, 1961-66; Project Architect, i/c of design & construction of secondary schools, Uganda, financed by the International Development Association, 1966—. Address: P.O. Box 7063, Kampala, Uganda.

WILLOX, Alan Lowe, born 25th May 1919. Bank Manager. Education: Peterhead Academy, Aberdeenshire, U.K. Appointments: Manager, Chomba, Fort Jameson, Mufulira & President Avenue Branches, Barclays Bank DCO, Zambia. Memberships: Lions International; Rotary; Institute of Bankers in Scotland. Honours: Commissioner of Oaths. Address: P.O. Box 120, Ndola, Zambia.

WILLS, Arthur Samuel, born 13th November 1929. Hospital Administrator. Education: Ashford Middlesex Secondary School. Married, 4 children. Appointments: served in Royal Navy, 1948-55; Missionary, Church Missionary Society, London, 1955—; Hospital Manager, Mengo Hospital, Kampala, Uganda, 1957—. Secretary, Uganda Protestant Medical Bureau, 1964—. Address: Mengo Hospital, P.O. Box 7161, Kampala, Uganda.

WILMOT, Edward Travers, born 22nd July 1924. Agriculturalist. Education: Winchester College, U.K., 1937-42; B.A., Trinity College, Cambridge, 1942-43, 1947-48; Diploma in Agriculture, & M.A., ibid, 1948-50. Married, 2 daughters. Address: Flight Lieutenant, Royal Air Force, 1943-47; Agricultural Officer, Nyasaland, 1950-62; Chief Agricultural Officer, Malawi, 1962-68; Under-Secretary, ibid, 1968-70. Memberships: Royal Commonwealth Society; Royal Air Force Association. Publications: Malawi Agricultural Projections 1965-85 (w. A. W. Lovatt), 1966. Address: Ministry of Agriculture & Natural Resources, P.O. Box 303, Zomba, Malawi.

WILSON, Anthony Emmet, born 20th April 1933. Social Administrator. Education: B.A., University of Oxford, U.K., 1957; Diploma in Social Anthropology, University of Manchester, 1959. Married, 2 sons, 1 daughter. Appointments: Research Officer, Department of Social & Preventive Medicine, University of Manchester, 1959-60; Social Development Officer, Malawi Government, 1960-63; Community Development Officer & Commissioner for Community Development, 1964-69; Administrative Secretary, B. & G. S. Cadbury Trust, Birmingham, U.K., 1969—. Memberships: Chairman, Friends' Service Council (Quakers), Personal Service Committee, & Birmingham Co-ordinating Committee on Overseas Aid & Development; Minister of Overseas Development Advisory Panel on Social Development; Gulbenkian Committee on Community Work, London. Publications: But Few are Chosen (Community Dev. Jrnl.), 1968. Address: B. & G. S. Cadbury Trust, 2 College Walk, Birmingham, B29 6LE, U.K.

WILSON, John Edward Haroun, born 25th December 1922. Company Sales Manager; Evangelist (Church of Uganda). Education: King's College, Budo, 1931-43; Makerere College, Kampala, Uganda, 1944-45; Makerere University College, ibid, 1967-68; various training programmes in management & petroleum marketing, U.S.A. & East Africa, 1956-69. Married, 5 sons, 2 daughters. Appointments: Senior Welfare Assistant, E.A. R. & H., 1948-50; Sand Contractor, Owen Falls Construction, 1950-57; Sales Representative, Motor Mart & Exchange Ltd., 1958-59; Managing Director, Tayani Motors Ltd., 1959-60; Sales Representative, Caltex Oil (Uganda) Ltd., 1961-63; Area Sales Superintendent, ibid, 1964-68; Sales Manager, 1969—. Memberships: Uganda Club; Uganda Institute of Management; Vice-President, Gideons International, Uganda; Executive, Greater Kampala Project, Church of Uganda; Pan African Graduate Christian Fellowship; Scripture Union National Committee; Uganda Keswick Committee; Evangelist, visited U.S.A., Europe, Middle East, & East Africa. Honours: various marketing awards; University Certificate, University of East Africa. Address: Caltex Oil (Uganda) Ltd., P.O. Box 7095, Kampala, Uganda

WILSON, Peter Michael, born 27th June 1931. Civil Servant. Education: Secbergh School, U.K. & in France; Agricultural Diploma, Harper Adams Agricultural College, 1954; Certificate of Education, Moray House, Edinburgh, 1962; Tanzania Higher Swahili, 1962. Married, 3 daughters. Appointments: Farm Manager, U.K., 1953-58; worked in extension, tanzania, 1958-61; Lecturer, Agriculture, 1962-64; Lecturer, Swahili to expatriates, 1964-67; Public Relations, Ministry of Agriculture also Editor, 'Ukubima wa Kisasa', 1968—. Memberships: Deputy Camp Chief, Assistant Akela Leader & Assistant Chief Commissioner (Rover Scouts), Tanzania Boy Scouts Association; Captain, Dar es Salaam Gymkhana Squash Club. Publications: Simplified Swahili (teach yourself course); Classified Vocabulary (English Swahili Technical Dictionary). Address: P.O. Box 2308, Dar es Salaam, Tanzania.

WINFUL, Emmanuel Archibald, born 2nd July 1922. Civil Servant; Management Educationist. Education: Mfantsipim School, Ghana, 1939-42; B.A.(Hons., English), London, University College of the South-West of England, 1947. Married, 1 son. Appointments: Secretary, Public Service Commission, Ghana Civil Service; Director of Training, ibid; Director, Civil Service Academy, 1960; Principal Secretary, Ministry of Education; Principal Secretary, Ministry of Communication; Principal Secretary, Ministry of Health; Chairman, Black Star Line; Director, Ghana Airways, 1967; currently Director, Ghana Institute of Management & Public Administration. Memberships: Royal Institute of Publication; British Institute of Management.

Author of poetry contributed to anthologies & literary magazines, & of teaching & other material commissioned by the Methodist Book Depot. Honours: 2nd Prize, University Labour Federation (Cambridge) Competition, 1944. Address: Ghana Institute of Management & Public Administration, P.O. Box 50, Achimota, Ghana.

WINGFIELD, Ralph Joseph, born 25th May 1926. Specialist in Teaching Language Methodology. Education: M.A.(Hons.); Dip. Ed., London; Dip. Applied Linguistics, Edinburgh. Married, 3 sons. Appointments: Principal, Mubi Training College, Northern Nigeria, 1950-55; Provincial Education Officer, Kabba Province, 1955-57; Principal, Katsina Teachers' College, 1958-60; Inspector, Language Teaching, Ministry of Education, 1960-64; Senior Lecturer, Education Department, University College, Dar es Salaam, 1965-69; Unesco Specialist in English Language Teaching, Papua & New Guinea, 1969—. Memberships: English Language Panel, Ministry of Education, Tanzania; English Syllabus Committee, Papua & New Guinea. Publications: The Story of Ghana; Exercises in Situational Composition; contbr. of various articles to professional journals. Address: P.O. Box 339, Goroka, Papua & New Guinea.

WININGA, Augustin, born 8th August 1935. Professor of Philosophy, Detached to the National Commission for UNESCO. Education: Primary School, Ouagadougou, Koupela; Secondary Studies, Lower Seminary of Pabre, 1949-54; Baccalaureat, 1954-57; Higher Studies, Dakar, Senegal, & Paris, France; Licence & Diploma in Higher Studies of Philosophy. Married, 4 children. Appointments: Teacher, Lycée Ouezzin Coulibaly, Bobo, 1966-67; ibid, Ecole Normale, Ouagadougou, 1967-68; Director, ibid, 1968-69; Secretary-General, National Commission for UNESCO, 1969—. Author of articles in journals. Address: Secretary-General of the National Commission for UNESCO, B.P. 578, Ouagadougou, Upper Volta.

WINSTANLEY, George, born 6th May 1930. Civil Servant. Education: M.A., Selwyn College, Cambridge, U.K. Married, 2 children. Appointments: District Officer, Botswana, 1954-62; Clerk of Legislative Council, 1962-65; Clerk of Executive Council, 1965-66; Clerk to Cabinet, 1966-67; Permanent Secretary, 1967—. Publications: The 1965 General Election, Bechuanaland; Report of the General Election, 1969. Honours: M.B.E., 1966. Address: Private Bag 3, Gaborone, Botswana.

WITSCHAS, Herbert Ernst, born 16th April, 1920. Manager. Education: Matriculation; Food Chemistry, 2 years. Married, 2 sons, 2 daughters. Proprietor, Herings Supermarket Delicatessen, Windhoek, South West Africa, 21 years. Memberships: Representative, Killarney Film Studios, News Department, South West Africa, 1962—; Hon. Member, Modern Merchandising Methods Club, S.A. Address: 8 Casteel Street, P.O. Box 376, Windhoek, South West Africa.

WOLDEHAWARIAT IYOB (Colonel), born 24th January 1919. District Governor. Education: Ethiopian Amharic School; Italian School. Married, 11 children. Appointments: Corporal, Ethiopian Police Force, 1944; Sergeant, 1946; A. Lieutenant, 1947; Lieutenant, 1960; Captain; Major, 1964; A. Colonel, 1968; currently, District Governor. Member, Red Cross. Honours: Silver Medal, 15 years' Service; Gold Medal, 20 years' Service; Gold Star Medal, General Service. Address: King Jorge 6 St., P.O. Box 150, Addis Ababa, Ethiopia.

WONG YOU CHEONG, Yves, born 25th June 1937. Research & Consulting Agricultural Chemist. Education: B.Sc., 1st Class Hons., Chemistry, Queen's University, Belfast, U.K., 1961; B.Agric., 1st Class Hons., Agricultural Chemistry, 1962; Ph.D., Agricultural Chemistry, 1967. Married, 4 children. Appointments: Assistant Registrar & Chief Chemist, Sugar Millers & Planters Central Arbitration & Control Board, Reduit, Mauritius, 1962-63; Chief Chemist, Mauritius Sugar Industry Research Institute, ibid, 1964—; Part-time Lecturer, Soil Science, University of Mauritius. Memberships: International Society of Sugar Cane Technologists; Soil Science Society of America; Royal Institute of Chemistry; American Society of Agronomy; Biochemical Society. Author of 17 publications on various aspects of fertilizer use, soil science & sugarcane nutrition. Address: Mauritius Sugar Industry Research Institute, Reduit, Mauritius.

WOOD, Arthur Michael, born 28th January 1919. Consultant Plastic Surgeon. Education: Winchester College; Middlesex Hospital Medical School, University of London, U.K.; M.R.C.S., L.R.C.P., 1943; M.B., B.S., 1944; F.R.C.S., England, 1946. Married, 2 sons, 2 daughters. Appointments: House Surgeon, Middlesex Hospital, London; Casualty Officer, ibid; Registrar; Senior Registrar, Queen Victoria Hospital, East Grinstead; Consultant Plastic Surgeon, Kenyatta National Hospital, Nairobi, Kenya; ibid, H.H. Aga Khan Hospital; Chairman, East African Medical Research Council incorporating E.A. Flying Doctor Service; Hon. Lecturer, Plastic Surgery, University of Nairobi; Director-General, African Medical & Research Foundation. Fellow, British Association of Plastic Surgeons; President Elect, East African Association of Surgeons; Kenya Medical Association; Aero Club, Nairobi; Muthaiga Country Club. Publications: Principles of the Treatment of Trauma, 1964; articles in professional journals. Honours: Marks Fellow, Plastic Surgery, 1955; Gold Medal, Royal African Society, 1970. Address: African Medical & Research Foundation, P.O. Box 30125, Nairobi, Kenya.

WOOD, Christopher Harald, born 5th June 1924. Medical Practitioner. Education: Middlesex Hospital Medical School, U.K., 1942-47; London School of Hygiene & Tropical Medicine, 1953; Harvard School of Public Health, U.S.A., 1955-56. Appointments: Senior Lecturer in Occupational Health, London School of Hygiene & Tropical Medicine, U.K.; Consultant in Public Health, Tanzania Government; Professor, Social & Preventive Medicine, University of Dar es Salaam.

Memberships: International Epidemiological Association; Society for Social Medicine; Society of Occupational Medicine. Publications: Health Services of Tanganyika (jointly). Honours: Commonwealth Fund Fellowship, 1955-56. Address: Faculty of Medicine, Dar es Salaam University, Dar es Salaam, Tanzania.

WOOD, James Falconer, born 14th December 1935. Medicine. Education: M.B., Ch.B., University of Aberdeen, U.K., 1960; D.P.M., Conjoint Board, London, 1965. Married, 3 children. Appointments: Consultant Psychiatrist, Butabika Hospital for Nervous Diseases, 1966—; Hon. Lecturer in Psychiatry, Department of Psychiatry, Medical School, Makerere University College, Kampala. Memberships: Royal Medico-Psychological Association; British Medical Association. Publications: Psychiatric Section, Uganda Atlas of Disease Distribution, 1968; The Law & Psychiatry (Uganda Practitioner), 1969; The Utilisation of Therapeutic Potential in Psychiatric Hospital Staff (Psychopath. Africaine). Address: Butabika Hospital, P.O. Box 7017, Kampala, Uganda.

WOOD, Kodwo Esem, born Cape Coast, Ghana, 13th November 1922. Chartered Accountant. Education: Axim Methodist School, 1933-39; Adisadel College, Cape Coast, 1939-44; trained as Certified Accountant, North Western & Regent Street Polytechnics, London, U.K., 1950-59. Married, 3 children. Appointments: Area Accountant, Ghana I.D.C., 1959-60; Chief Accountant, National Timber Corporation, Takoradi, 1960-63; ibid, Ghana Academy of Science, 1963-65; Public Practice, 1966—. Memberships: Freemason; Ghana Association for the Advancement of Management (GAAM). Address: P.O. Box 7971, Accra North, Ghana.

WOODLEY, Peter James Frank, born 4th July 1926. Radio Engineer, Manager. Education: Maidenhead County School, U.K.; Cable & Wireless Engineering College. Married, 3 daughters. Appointments: Engineer i/c, Overseas Receiving Station, Cyprus; Engineer i/c, Overseas Transmitting Station, Bahrain; Engineer i/c, Overseas Transmitting Station, Nairobi, Kenya; Manager, East African External Telecommunications Co. Ltd., Kampala, Uganda. Memberships: Associate, E.A. Institution of Engineers. Address: c/o East African External Telecommunications Co. Ltd., P.O. Box 4888, Kampala, Uganda.

WOODMAN, Gordon Roger, born 22nd September 1937. Law Lecturer. Education: Bristol Grammar School, U.K.; Birkenhead School; B.A., LL.B., Ph.D., Gonville & Caius College, Cambridge. Appointments: Research Fellow, Faculty of Law, University of Ghana, 1961-63; Lecturer, ibid, 1963-64; Lecturer, Ahmadu Bello University, Nigeria, 1965-67; Lecturer, Faculty of Law, University of Ghana, 1967-69; Senior Lecturer, Faculty of Law, ibid, 1969—. Memberships: African Law Association; Society of Public Teachers of Law. Author of articles on law in West Africa. Editor, University of Ghana Law Journal, 1968—. Address: Faculty of Law, University of Ghana, Legon, Ghana.

WOOTTON, Alan Eric, born 30th October 1938. Research Chemist. Education: B.S.C. (Hons.), Nottingham University, U.K., 1953. Married. Appointments: Research Chemist, British Sugar Corporation, 1953-58; Research Officer, East African Industrial Research Organization, 1958-68; Chief Chemist, ibid, 1968—. Fellow, Royal Institute of Chemistry. Address: East African Industrial Research Organization, P.O. Box 30650, Nairobi, Kenya.

WOZEI, Muloni Womakuyu, born 16th September 1940. Public Officer. Education: Sipi Primary School; Masaba Junior Secondary School; Mbale Government Senior Secondary School; B.A.(Hons.), Makerere University, Kampala, Uganda; Dip. Dev. Admin., University of Leeds, U.K. Married, 3 children. Appointments: Assistant District Commissioner, 1967-68; Research Officer, 1968—. Member, Eastern African Outward Bound Mountain School, 1965. Publications: The Evolutions of Local Administrations & District Councils in Uganda until 1967, 1967; Karamoja—A Brief Study of Barriers to Development, 1967; Urban Local Government in Uganda, 1968; The Concept of a Nation & the Meaning of Nation Building, 1969; The Role of Elections in the New Political Culture, 1970. Address: Institute of Public Administration, P.O. Box 20131, Kampala, Uganda.

WRIGHT, Francis George de Lonsden, born 30th December 1932. Medical Practitioner. Education: Clifton College, Bristol, U.K.; Emmanual College, Cambridge; St. Mary's Hospital, London. Married, 3 children. Appointments: Uganda Medical Service, 1959-62; in Practice, Jinja, Uganda, 1962—. Memberships: British Medical Association; Uganda Medical Association: Uganda Golf Union & Society. Address: Box 1287, Jinja, Uganda.

WRIGHT, John Bucknall, born Portugal, 19th October 1931. Geologist. Education: Gresham's School, Holt, Norfolk, U.K., 1945-50; B.Sc., M.A., St. Peter's Hall, Oxford, 1951-56; F.G.S. Married. Appointments: Geologist, Geological Survey of Kenya, Nairobi, 1957-60; Lecturer, Department of Geology, Otago University, New Zealand, 1961-66; Head, Geology Department, Ahmadu Bello University, Zaria, Nigeria, 1967-70. Memberships: Innholders Company, London; Geological Society, London; Mineralogical Society, ibid. Author of numerous articles in scientific publications. Address: Department of Earth Sciences, The Open University, Walton Hall, Walton, Bletchley, Bucks., U.K.

WRIGHT, Ronald Hughes, born 9th March 1923. Certified Accountant. Education: Newsham Senior School, Liverpool, U.K.; Clark's College, ibid. Married. Appointments: Senior Auditor, Poulsom & Co., Chartered Accountants, Liverpool; Accountant, Kenya Co-operative Creameries, Naivasha; Divisional Accountant, Provincial Engineer, Western Province; Works Accountant, Central Workshops, Kampala, Uganda; Accountant, Chief Accountant, Ministry of Works, Entebbe. Memberships: Uganda Kobs (Rugby); Uganda Golf Society; Hon. Treasurer, Hon. Secretary, &

Former Golf Captain, Entebbe Club. Address: Entebbe, Uganda.

WURSTER, Richard T., born Riverside, N.J., U.S.A., 5th March 1936. Education: Palmyra High School, N.J., 1953; B.S., General Agriculture, Rutgers, the State University of New Jersey, 1959; M.S., Agriculture, University of California, Davis, 1960; Ph.D., Cornell University, Ithaca, N.Y., 1964. Married, 3 daughters. Appointments include: Graduate Assistant, Department of Vegetable Crops, Cornell University, Ithaca, 1960-64; ibid, University of California, Davis, 1959; Teacher, Ovid Central School, N.Y., 1961; Agricultural Adviser, Near East Foundation, Molla-Sani, Iran, 1964-66; Horticulturist, United States Department of Agriculture, Crops Research Division, Beltville, Md., U.S.A., 1966; Assistant Professor, West Virginia University, Morgantown, 1967–; Senior Lecturer, Makerere University, Kampala, Uganda, 1967–. Memberships: American Society for Horticultural Science; Alpha Gamma Rho; Society for International Development; Vice-Chairman (East Africa), Commission for Tropical & Subtropical Horticulture, International Society for Horticultural Science; Uganda Agricultural Society; Agricultural Society of Kenya. Author of numerous scientific publications. Honours include: Sears & Roebuck Foundation Scholarship, 1955; New Jersey State Scholarship, Rutgers University, 1956-59. Address: Department of Crop Science & Production, Makerere University, Kampala, Uganda.

Y

YAGO, Bernard (Monseigneur), born 1916. Archbishop of Abidjan. Education: Primary & Secondary Studies, Lower Seminary of Bingerville; Philosophy & Theology, Greater Seminary of Koumi, Upper Volta; Licence in Social Sciences, Catholic Institute of Paris, 1957. Appointments: ordained, 1947; successively: Teacher, then Director, l'Ecoles des Petis Clercs, Cure at Treichville, Diocesan Director of Works; elected Archbishop of Abidjan, & consecrated, 1960. Honours: Officer of the Legion of Honour; Officier, l'Ordre Ivoirien. Address: B.P. 1287, Abidjan, The Ivory Coast.

YAHAYA, Adamou, born 1935. Civil Administrator. Education: Cours Normal de Tohoua; Institute of Overseas Higher Studies, Paris, France. Personal details: married, 4 children, 1956; divorced, 1965; second marriage, 2 children. Appointments: Deputy Administrator, 1956-59; I.H.O.M., Paris, 1960-61; Head of Cabinet, Ministry of the Interior, 1961-63; Prefect, Falingue, 1963; ibid, Dorso, 1964-66; State Inspector, 1966-70. Memberships: PPNRDA, 1956; Local Committee Secretary, ibid, 1957-59, 1959-60. Address:

YAHIA, Mohamed Salih, born 20th June 1919. Bank Manager. Education: English Certificate Examination, Sudan School, Sudan. Appointments: Accountant, Sudan Railway; Manager, several Branches, Barclays Bank D.C.O., including Khartoum Branch; Manager, Principal Branch, State Bank for Foreign Trade (formerly Barclays Bank D.C.O.). Memberships: District Governor, Khartoum, Lions Club; Institute of Bankers, London; ex-President, El Nilien Lodge, Khartoum. Address: State Bank for Foreign Trade, Khartoum, Sudan.

YAHYA, O. Menkous, born 1930. Civil Administrator. Education: Diploma of the Institute of Higher Administrative Studies, Paris, France. Married. Appointments: Teacher, 1959-60; Student, Paris, France, 1960-62; Minister, 1962-66; Ambassador to Paris, 1966-67; Prefect & Deputy to the Governor of the Second Region, 1969-70; Prefect of Nema. Memberships: High Committee Director, Mauritanian Youth, 1952-55; Bureau Director of Nahda, Opposition Party, 1957-60. Recipient of Honours. Address: Prefect of Nema, Mauritania.

YAMEOGO, Moussa Edouard, born Yako, Upper Volta, 27th July 1935. Engineer; Company Director; Politician. Education: Lycée Louis Le Grand; Diploma in Engineering, Institut National Agronomique, Paris, France; Diploma in Civil Engineering, Ecole Nationale du Génie Rural; Economic Sciences Faculty, Paris. Married, 1 son. Appointments: Trainee Engineer, Compagnie Nationale du Bas-Rhône, Languedoc, & Tennessee Valley Authority, Knoxville, U.S.A.; Engineer, Génie Rural; Director, Rural Engineering Service, Republic of the Upper Volta, 1962-63; Minister of National Economy, 1963-64; Minister of National Development, 1964-66; Director, Hydraulic & Rural Equipment Services, 1966-69; Director-General, National Water Company, 1970–; Administrator, African Electricity Company, 1964-69; Governor, World Bank, 1963-65; Head, Missions to U.S.A. & to Japan, 1964-65. Memberships: International Commission for Irrigation & Drainage; Regional Association of Hydrometerology. Professor, Inter-States Centre, SARIA, & Inter-States School of Rural Equipment Engineers, Ouagadougou. Honours: Officier de l'Ordre National Voltaïque. Address: B.P. 170, Ouagadougou, Upper Volta.

YAMEOGO, Wiougou Antoine, born 17th January 1928. Economist; Administrator of the F.M.I. Education: Baccalaureat; Licence in Law; DES Political Economy. Married, 3 children. Appointments: Inspector of Finance; Director of the Treasury, Upper Volta; Commissaire au Plan; Minister of National Economy, Upper Volta; Economist, F.M.I.; Administrator, F.M.I. Memberships: Lion's Club. Honours: Medaille d'or elevage; Officer of the National Orders of Upper Volta & the Malagasy Republic; Commander of the National Orders of the Ivory Coast, Niger & the Democratic Republic of the Congo. Address: c/o F.M.I., Upper Volta.

YANGARI, Albert, born 19th July 1943. Journalist; Head of Radiodiffusion Service. Education: Primary Studies, Franceville; Secondary Studies, Lycée Leon, MBA, Libreville, Gabon; Diplome du Studio-Ecole de l'O.R.T.F. Married. Appointments: Journalist; Head, Radio Station Franceville; Head of Radio Programmes, Gabon; Head of Radiodiffusion Service, R.T.G. Honours: Order of Cameroon Merit 1st Class; Knight, National Central African

Order. Address: Radiodiffusion Television Gabonaise, B.P. 150, Libreville, Gabon.

YAO, Kouakou, born 1937. Mechanical Engineer. Education: Public Primary School, Bacanda, 1944-50; Diploma C.E.P.E.; Technical Lycée, Abidjan, 1950-55; B.E.P.C. & B.E.I. Diplomas; Bac. Maths. Tech., Technical Lycée of Dakar, Senegal, 1955-58; National Institute of Applied Sciences, Lyon, France, 1958-62; Diploma, Mechanical Engineering. Appointments: Head, Works Subdivision, Port of Abidjan, 1962-65; Head of Technical Service, Direction of Material of Public Works, 1965; Deputy Director, D.M.T.P., 1966-67; Director of Material of Public Works, 1967—. Address: Director of Material of Public Works, B.P. 2701, Abidjan, The Ivory Coast.

YAW BAAH, Emmanuel, born Larteh-Akwapim, Ghana, 17th March 1930. Town Planner, Landscape Architect. Education: Presbyterian Primary & Middle Schools, Larteh, 1936-45; Adisadel College, 1946-50; Dip. T.P., Dip. L.D., Durham University, Newcastle upon Tyne (now University of Newcastle upon Tyne), U.K., 1960; Associate Member of Town Planning Institute, 1960. Married to Mrs. Julia Baah (née Mary Nyampong), Senior Teacher, 4 children. Appointments include: Assistant Town Planning Officer, Ashanti Regional Town Planning Office, 1960-61; Town Planning Officer in Charge, Northern & Upper Regions, 1961-63; Town Planning Officer in Charge, Eastern & Volta Regions, 1964-67; Assistant Chief Town Planning Officer, 1965; Principal Town Planning Officer in Charge of Ashanti Region including the City of Kumasi; Part-time Lecturer in Planning Administration & Practice, University of Science & Technology, Kumasi; represented Ghana at Conference, Sczecin, Poland, 1963; attended Seminar, Dakar, Senegal, 1969. Memberships: Committees, Koforidua Municipal Council & Kumasi City Council; ex-officio service, numerous Government & Semi-Government Committees, mainly on Physical Planning Matters; Ghana Institute of Planners. Publications: Paper on Planning Law, Administration & Practice in Ghana. Address: Town & Country Planning Dept., P.O. Box 905, Kumasi, Ghana.

YEBOAH, Omane John, born 16th April 1936. Journalist. Education: Middle School Leaving Certificate; West African School Certificate; Diploma in Journalism. Personal details: married, 1 child. Appointments: Managing Editor, Outlook Publications. Member of Journalist's Assn., Ghana. Publications: Lotto & Football. Honours: Top Sports Writer, Ghana Football Assn., 1964; 1st Editor to establish The Sporting News, 1967. Address: Outlook Publications, Ringway Press, P.O. Box 2351, Accra, Ghana.

YEBOAH, Samuel Kofi, born 17th April 1939. Lecturer in Chemistry. Education: B.Sc., M.Sc., Organic Chemistry, University of Ghana, 1960-65; Ph.D., Organic Chemistry, University of Bristol, U.K., 1969. Appointments: Lecturer in Organic Chemistry, University College of Cape Coast, Ghana. Fellow of the Chemical Society, London. Memberships: Ghana Science Assn.; Ghana Assn. of Science Teachers. Publications: Flavonoid Compounds of Citrus Aurantium (University of Ghana), 1965; The Structure of Wortmannin, 1968; The Structure & Chemistry of Wortmannin. Address: University College of Cape Coast, Cape Coast, Ghana.

YIGGA, Yozefu, born 11th September 1914. Agriculturist. Education: Primary School, 1924-26; Junior Seminary, 1927-29; Nandere High School, 1930-31; St. Mary's College, Kisubi, 1932-34; Diploma in Agriculture, Makerere University College, 1939. Personal details: son of Primary School Teacher; Married, 1 son, 5 daughters. Appointments: Extension Staff, Dept. of Agriculture, 1940-67; Acting District Agricultural Officer, Mubende District, 1967-68; Principal, Kigezi District Farm Institute, 1968-69; Principal, Mityana Dist. Farm Institute, 1969—. Memberships: Professional Centre of Uganda; Makerere College Old Boys' Society. Address: P.O. Box 78, Mityana, Uganda.

YOHANNES, Berhane, born 8th September 1928. Judge. Education: Pre-University Education by Correspondence with Wolsey Hall, Oxford, U.K.; J.D., Asmara School of Law, Ethiopia, 1956; M.C.L., George Washington University, U.S.A., 1960; LL.M., Yale Law School, New Haven, 1965; D.C.E., Free University of Brussels, Belgium, 1966. Married, 3 sons, 2 daughters. Appointments: Magistrate, 1955-56; District Judge, 1956-61; Supreme Court Justice, 1961-69; Vice-President, High Court, 1969—. Memberships: President, Eritrean Football League, 1969-70; Vice-President, Y.M.C.A., Eritrea, 1961-70; Director, 'A' Rotary Int., Asmara, 1968-70; American Judicature Society, 1960—; Praesidium Grotius Foundation, 1967. Publications: Delict & Torts: An Introduction to the Sources of the Law of Civil Wrongs in Contemporary Ethiopia, 1969. Address: The High Court of Eritrea-Asmara, Ethiopia.

YOHANNES REDA-EGZY, born 21st October 1910. Senator; Diplomat. Education: American University, Beirut, Lebanon. Personal details: married, 4 children. Appointments: Teacher, Addis Ababa, Ethiopia, 1930-36; Assistant Private Secretary to His Imperial Majesty Hailé Selassié I, 1941-46; First Secretary, Ethiopian Embassy, London, U.K., 1947-50; Director-General, Foreign Office, Addis Ababa, 1951-56; Chargé d'Affaires, Ethiopian Embassy, Mexico, 1957-59; Ambassador to Japan, 1959-65; Minister of State Administration of Antiquities, 1966-67; Ethiopian Chief Delegate to various International Conferences, 1968. Founding Board Member of the Y.M.C.A., Ethiopia. Honours: Grand Officer of the Star of Ethiopia; Mexican Order of the Aztec Eagle 1st Class; Order of Yugoslav Star, IIIrd Class. Address: P.O. Box 2259, Addis Ababa, Ethiopia.

YONKE, Jean-Baptiste, born 2nd January 1935. Director of Agriculture of Eastern Cameroon. Education: Primary Studies, Secondary & University; 5 higher certificates; Agricultural Engineering Diploma, Higher National School of Agronomy, University of Toulouse, France; Expert Diploma in

Development, IRFED, Paris. Married, 5 children. Appointments: Director of Agriculture, Eastern Cameroon, 1961; President, Federal Commission for Agronomy Research, 1962—; African Delegate to the Ad Hoc Committee for the Study of the General Structure of the F.A.O., Rome, 1968; Director, Popular University Nova & Velera, Yaoundé, Cameroon. Memberships: Administrator representing several joint economic societies. Author of numerous publications & articles in the press on Cameroon & African Agriculture. Honours: Officer of the National Order of Agricultural Merit; Knight of the National Order of Bravery. Address: B.P. 1073, Yaoundé, Cameroon.

YORK, Richard Norman, born 27th August 1941. Archaeologist. Education: Worksop College, Notts., U.K.; M.A., St. Catharine's College, Cambridge. Married, 4 children. Current Appointment: Research Fellow, Volta Basin Research Project, University of Ghana, Legon, Accra, Ghana. Address: Holbrook House, Royal Hospital School, Ipswich, Suffolk, U.K.

YOUDS, Edward Ernest, born 21st November 1910. Puisne Judge. Education: Birkenhead School, U.K.; B.A., LL.B.(Hons.), University of Cambridge; Called to the Bar, Gray's Inn, London, 1936. Married, 2 sons, 1 daughter. Appointments: Deputy Chairman, Lancashire County Sessions, 1961-66; County Court Judge, 1966-69; Puisne Judge, High Court, Uganda, 1969—. Honours: M.D., 1945. Address: 38 Prince Charles Drive, Box 5548, Kampala, Uganda.

YOUNES, Adel, born 19th April 1912. Former Chief Justice, United Arab Republic. Education: LL.B., Faculty of Law, Cairo University, 1932; Postgraduate Diploma, Penal Sciences, ibid, 1933. Appointments: Called to the Bar, 1933; Assistant District Attorney, 1933; Parquet-General, Mixed Courts of Egypt, 1943-49; Solicitor-General, 1953; Justice of Court of Cassation, 1958; Deputy Chief Justice, 1964; Chief Justice, 1965-69. Memberships: Scientific Board, International Institute of Juridicial Studies, Rome, Italy; International Association of Penal Law & of Social Defence, Paris, France; Egyptian Association of International Law; Egyptian Association for Legislation & Political Economy, Cairo; International Permanent Court of Arbitration. Author of various studies on criminal researches, social defence problems & legal studies published in various periodicals in U.A.R., France, Algeria, & Germany. Address: 4 Darih Saad Street, Cairo, U.A.R.

YOUNG, Alistair, born 1st November 1944. Research Fellow. Education: Hutchesons' Boys' Grammar School, Glasgow, U.K., 1956-61; M.A.(Hons.), University of Glasgow, 1965. Married, 1 daughter. Appointments: Assistant Lecturer, Department for Social & Economic Research, University of Glasgow, 1965-67; Research Fellow, Economics, Institute for Social Research, University of Zambia, 1967-70; Department of Economics, New University of Ulster, U.K., 1970—. Address: Department of Economics, New University of Ulster, Coleraine, Co. Londonderry, U.K.

YOUNG, Andrew Buchanan, born Falkirk, Scotland, 11th August 1937. Medical Practitioner. Education: Falkirk High School; M.B., Ch.B., Edinburgh University; D.Obst., R.C.O.G.; D.T.M.&H., Liverpool University; M.R.C.P.,, U.K. Married, 1 son, 1 daughter. Appointments: House Surgeon, Falkirk Royal Infirmary; House Surgeon, Artillery Castle Maternity Hospital; House Physician, Royal Infirmary of Edinburgh; House Officer, E.M.M.S. Hospital, Nazareth, Israel; Medical Superintendent, Presbyterian Church of East Africa Hospital, Kenya; currently Medical Officer, ibid. Address: P.C.E.A. Hospital, P.O. Chogoria, Meru, Kenya.

YOUNG, John Richard Dendy, born 4th September 1907. Chief Justice, Republic of Botswana. Education: B.A., LL.B., University of South Africa (External Student). Appointments: Member of Parliament, Southern Rhodesia, 1948-53; Member of Parliament, Federation of Rhodesia & Nyasaland, 1953-56; Judge of the High Court of Rhodesia, 1956-68; Chief Justice, Republic of Botswana, 1968—. Member of Salisbury Club, Southern Rhodesia. Honours: Q.C. Address: Private Bag 1, Lobatse, Botswana.

Z

ZAGAR, Zvonimir, born Vinkovci, Yugoslavia, 15th February 1931. Engineer; Senior Lecturer. Education: Structural Engineering, Faculty of Building Engineering, University of Zagreb, Yugoslavia. Personal details: married, 2 children. Appointments: Structural Engineer, Structural Engineering Section, Directorate of Yugoslav Railways, Zagreb, 1957-61; Structural Engineer, Design Organization of Yugoslav Railways, Zagreb, 1961-63; Lecturer in Structural Engineering, Faculty of Building Engineering, University of Zagreb, 1963-65; Supervising Structural Engineer, Architect's Office, University of Science & Technology, U.S.T., Kumasi, Ghana, 1965-67; Senior Lecturer, Building Technology, Faculty of Architecture, U.S.T., Kumasi, 1967-70. Memberships: S.I.T.J.; S.I.T.H.; D.G.I.T.H. Publications: Glued Timber Trusses (Gradevinar 9) 1959; The Reinforced Crib Retaining Walls, Theory, Design, Prefabrication, & Application, 1959; New Structural Methods, 1968; Introduction to Structures (Mechanics) for 1st Year Students in Architecture, 1969; Research in Lamella Timber Roof Construction, 1970. Address: 4 Brace Durasevic, Zagreb, Yugoslavia.

ZAHORO, S. K. Educator; Local Government Official. Education: Primary, 1918-22; Grade II & Grade I Teachers' Certificate, 1927-33; School Supervision Course, Jeanes School, Kabete, Nairobi, Kenya, 1934. Married, 3 sons, 3 daughters. Appointments: joined Teaching Profession, 1923; 1st School Supervisor, Bukoba, Tanzania, 1935-44; Teacher, Teachers' Training Centre, Mwanza Tanzania, 1945; Treasurer, 3 years, Executive Officer, 14 years, Local Government Service, 1946-64; retired, 1964. Memberships: Customary Land Tribunal, West Lake Region, re-appointed by the Minister for Lands, Housing, & Urban Development; Tanganyika African National Union (TANU); Party Member, Bukoba Town Council; Representative, National Annual Conference, Regional Annual Conference & Regional Working Committee, ibid; Advisory Committee, African Education, Secondary School Board of Governors & District Education Committee; Tanganyika Tea Authority; Farmers' Co-operative. Publications: Editor, Engoma ya Bahaya (The Buhaya Drum), a local government publication; Contributor, Historia ya Wilaya ya Bukoba. Honours: Certificate of Honour & Badge, 1946; M.B.E., 1959; Several prizes on retirement, 1964. Address: P.O. Box 464, Bukoba, Tanzania.

ZAIDAN, George Joseph, born 1st February 1915. Chemical Manufacturer. Education: Chemical Engineer, London, U.K. Married, 3 children. Appointments: Founder, George J. Zaidan & Co., Chemical Manufacturers, Egypt; Member, Board of Directors, Chamber of Chemical Industries, Federation of Industries. Address: 26 Sherif Street, Immobilia Bldg., Cairo, U.A.R.

ZAJACZKOWSKI, Wlodzimierz, born 1st October 1935. Geologist. Education: Institute of Mines, Sverdlovsk, Research Faculty of Geology & Mining, U.S.S.R.; Ingenieur Licencie, D.Sc., Varsovie, Poland. Chief Radioactive Metals Research Section, Institute of Geology, Varsovie; Co-Director, Research Project, Potassium Salts, Onu-Varsovie; Chief, Geological Service, Niger, Niamey. Publications: Methodes de Prospection geochimiques, 1962; Organisation du Service Geologique de Niger et ses activities, 1967; Recherches des gisements d'uranium par les methodes geochimiques sur certaines regions de Sudetes, 1968. Address: B.P. 257, Niamey, Niger.

ZAKI BADAWI, A., born Egypt, 30th April 1910. Educator. Education: Dipl., Institut Superieur du Service Social, Alexandria, 1940; Dipl., Centre des Etudes Economiques, Financieres et Sociales, Paris, France, 1943; Dipl., Ecole des Hautes Etudes Sociales, Paris, 1946; Dr.Soc.Econ., University of Paris, 1946. Appointments: Labour Inspector, Ministry of Labour, Egypt; Director, Management Counselling Centre, Alexandria; Labour Relations Counsellor; Professor, Social Studies, National Institute of Higher Management, Higher Institute of Social Work, Institute of Public Administration, Alexandria; Professor of Social Sciences (Industrial Sociology & Community Development), Faculty of Arts, Alexandria University; Counsellor, Labour & Social Questions, Arab League. Publications (in Arabic): Labour Legislation in Egypt, 1943, 1953; Principles of Social Work, 1947; Welfare Services for Workers, 1958; Labour Legislation in Arab States & the International Norms of Labour, 1968; Labour Relations, 1968; (in French): Legislation du Travail en Egypte, 1942, 1946, 1951; Problems du travail et organisations ouvrieres en Egypte; Legislation du travail au Moyen Orient, 1948; Repertoire du Droit de travail, 1955. Memberships: Past President, Rotary International, Alexandria; Societe Egyptienne d'Economie politique, de statistique et de legislation; Egyptian Institute of Business Administration; Industrial Welfare Society, London; Correspondent, Library, New York State School of Industrial & Labour Relations, Ithaca, N.Y. Recipient of Leadership Award, U.S. Government, 1953. Participant in several national and international conferences concerning social & labour questions during the last 20 years. Address: 59 Avenue Al Horria, Alexandria, U.A.R.

ZALESKA-KWIATKOWSKI, Katherina, born in Poland on 19th February 1918. Ear, Nose, & Throat Surgeon. Education: Agricultural Study, University of Krakow, 1938-39; Diploma, Rockefeller Nursing School, Warsaw, 1943; Medical Diploma, University of Szczecin, 1951; First Degree in ENT Specialization, 1954; Graduated, ENT Surgeon Specialist, University of Szczecin, 1956. Appointments: Assistant, ENT Department, University Teaching Hospital, Szczecin, Poland, 1951-56; ENT Specialist, Clinical Assistant & Locum Registrar, St. James Hospital, Balham, London, 1957-59; ENT Specialist Consultant, General Hospital, Lagos, Nigeria, 1959—. Memberships: Polish Association of Otorhinolaryngologists; 1951-57; Medical Association of Nigeria, 1959—. Author of professional papers. Recipient of two military crosses for action in the underground army in German occupied Poland during the years 1940-44. Address: c/o General Hospital, ENT Department, Lagos, Nigeria.

ZANONE, Livio G., born 29th January 1933. Geologist. Education: Diploma in Geology, Institute of Geology, University of Lausanne, Switzerland; Doctorate, University of Paris, France. Appointments: Geologist, Head of Mission, SODEMI, Abidjan, Ivory Coast; Assistant to the Research Director, ibid; Head, Service de Documentation & d'Informatique Géologiques, ibid. Author of various articles in field of geology. Address: SODEMI, B.P. 2816, Abidjan, Ivory Coast.

ZEREMARIAM AZZAZI, born Mehelab (Keren-Eritrea), Ethiopia, 21st September 1921. Police Officer. Education: High School Level, Amharic, Italian & English; Police Training, U.K. Married, 3 sons, 5 daughters. Appointments: Police Superintendent; Chief Superintendent; D/Commissioner; Commissioner; Senator, Empire of Ethiopia. Memberships: Prince Maconnen Officer's Club, Asmara; Honorary Member, Torary Club, Asmara. Honours: Grand Officer, Star of Honour, Ethiopia, 1964; Ras Grosse Verdienstkreuz mit Stern from H.M. The King of Norway, 1964; C.V.O. from H.M. Queen Elizabeth, 1965; 2nd Grade Homayoun Decoration from H.I.M. the Shah of Iran. Address: Afework Street No. 7, Asmara, Ethiopia.

ZIA-UD-DIN, born 15th October 1925. Doctor of Medicine (Missionary). Education: T.I. High School, Qadian, India; Matriculation, Islamia High School, Gujar Khan, W. Pakistan; Gordon College, Rawalpindi; M.B., B.S., King Edward Medical College, Lahore, 1957; Postgraduate Short Course in Radiology, 1957.

Personal details: family Muslim. Appointments: House Surgeon, Mayo Hospital, Lahore, West Pakistan, 1957-59; Deputy Chief Medical Officer, Fazle Omar Hospital, Rabwah, 1959-61; Medical Officer, Ahmadiyya Mission, Sierra Leone, 1961; Medical Officer, in Charge Ahmadiyya Clinic, Kano, Nigeria, 1962—. Memberships: Pakistan Medical Association; British Medical Assn.; Nigeria Medical Assn.; Registered Medical Practitioner in Pakistan, Sierra Leone & Nigeria; Ahmadiyya Foreign Mission Service; Health Society of Nigeria. Address: P.O. Box 1100, Kano, Nigeria.

ZOA, Jean, born Saa, Yaoundé, Cameroun, 1924. Archbishop. Education: ordained Priest, 1950; Doctorate of Theology, Rome, Italy. Appointments: Archbishop, Yaoundé, 1961. Author of various articles. Memberships: Council of 24 for the Evangelization of the People; Council of Laymen; Permanent Secretariat of the Synod. Address: Archevêché, B.P. 207, Yaoundé, Cameroun.

ZORU, Abba, born 28th October 1933. Broadcaster. Education: Dikwa Elementary School, Nigeria; School Certificate, Bornu Middle School; Senior Cambridge Certificate, Zaria Secondary School & Kaduna College; G.C.E. A Level, Nigerian College of Arts, Science, & Technology. Married. Appointments: Senior Programme Assistant, Nigerian Broadcasting Corporation; Head, Programme Operations, ibid; Deputy Chief Executive, B.C.N.N.; General Manager, ibid. Memberships: Nigerian Red Society; Golf Club.

ZOUNGRANA, Paul, born Onagadongou, Upper Volta, 3rd September 1917. His Eminence, The Cardinal Archbishop of Ouagadougou. Education: Cleric Schl. of Catholic Mission, Ouagadougou; Petit Seminaire de Pabre; Grand Seminaire, Koumi; ordained Priest, 1942; entered Soc. of White Fathers, 1948; Dr. Canon Law, Univ. Gregorienne, 1949; B.Soc.Sci., Catholic Inst., Paris, France. Appointments include: Curate, Cathedral Parish of Ouagadongou, Upper Volta; Prof. of Canon Law, Grand Seminaire, Koumi; Organizer, Rsch. Ctr. for Social Studies, Bobo Dioulasso; named Archbishop of Onagadougou; consecrated ibid, by His Holiness Pope Jean XXIII; created Cardinal, by Pope Paul VI, 1965. Memberships include: Pres., Episcopal Conference of Africa, the French-speaking West; ibid, Symposium of Bishops of Africa. Address: Archeceche, Ougadougou, B.P. 90. Upper Volta.

ZUCCARELLI, Francois, born 3rd January 1927. Technical Adviser to the Ministry of the Interior, Senegal. Education: Dr. of Public Law; Diploma of Higher Studies in Political Science; Brevete, Centre of Higher Administrative Studies on Modern Asia & Africa, University of Paris, France. Publications: Un Parti Politique Africaine Union Progresste Senegalais, 1970; author of different articles on specialized public administration in Senegal. Honours: Knight of the National Order of Senegal. Adress: B.P. 4002, Ministry of the Interior, Dakar, Senegal.

ZUZARTE, Peter Nicholas, born 21st December 1919. Company Secretary; Accountant. Married, 4 sons, 8 daughters. Appointments: Staff Quartermaster, Sergeant, East African Army Service Corps, 1939-49; Chief Accountant, Cooper Motor Corporation (Uganda) Ltd., 1952; Company Secretary, ibid, 1966. Memberships: President, Kampala Institute, 1963-64; President, Kampala Goam Association, 1965; Board of Governors, Norman Godinko School, 1966—. Honours: Africa Star; 1939-45 Star; Defence Medal; Victory Medal. Address: P.O. Box 2169, 3 Makerere Road, Kampala, Uganda.

ZWANA, Ambrose Phesheya, born, Manzini, Swaziland, 30th April, 1924. Political Party President; General Medical Practitioner. Education: Primary, Ngwana School, St. Francis Anglican School, Mbabane; 1935-36; St. Joseph (Mzimpofu) Roman Catholic School, Manzini, 1940-42; Matriculated, 1st Class with Distinction, Physical Science, Inkamana High School, Vryheid, Natal, South Africa, 1943-45; 1st year Medicine, Fort Hare, South African Native College, Cape Provence, Alice; University of Witwatersrand Medical School, 1947-51. Married, 4 sons. Appointments: elected President, Ngwane National Liberatory Congress, leading Panafrican nationalist organization demanding one man, one vote, equal pay for all, & basic human rights under the UN Declaration of Human Rights for the inhabitants of Ngwane & the African people in particular, 1962—. Publications: 2 monthly papers, Kusile Ngwane (Ngwane Arise & Shine) & Ngwane Forum. Awarded, Ngwane Independence Medal by King Sobhuza II of Ngwane, 1970. Address: P.O. Box 326 Mbane, Swaziland.

ADDENDUM

ABALABA, Abson Abraham, born Odi, Nigeria, 1934. Teacher. Education: Primary School, Odi, 1939-44; Primary School, Kaiama, Nigeria, 1945-46; Elementary Teacher Training, Oleh, Nigeria, 1950-51; Higher Teacher Training, Diobu, Nigeria, 1956-57; B.A.(Educ.), University of Nigeria, Nsukka, Nigeria, 1961-64. Appointments include: Postal Prefect, Oleh College, 1951; Food Manager, Diobu College, 1957; Headmaster of Group School, Opokuma, 1958-59; Tutor, Bishop Dimieari Grammar School, Yenagon, 1960-61; History Master, Bishop Dimieari Grammar School, 1965—. Memberships include: President, Odi Patriotic Union, 1952; University Tennis Club, 1962-64; Treasurer, Yenagon Recreation Club, 1966. Address: Bishop Dimieari Grammar School, Yenagon, Rivers State, Nigeria.

ABBA, Abubakar, born 25th December 1932. Bank Manager. Education: Government College, Zaria, North Central State, Nigeria. Appointments: Manager, Barclays Bank of Nigeria Ltd., Bauchi, North-Eastern State, Nigeria. Address: Barclays Bank of Nigeria Ltd., Bauchi, North-Eastern State, Nigeria.

ADEJUNMOBI (Rev.) Theophilus Adedeji, born 15th May 1915. Clergyman; Lecturer; Administrator; Author & Christian Journalist. Education: Secondary & Teacher Training, Baptist College, Ogbomosho, 1934-37; Teacher, High Schools & Training Colleges, 1938-45; Training for Ministry & Serving Pastorates, 1946-51; B.Th., 1950; Postgrad. Studies, B.A., Virginia Union University, Richmond, Va., U.S.A.; M.A., Sociology & History, University of Louisville, Ky.; B.D., Southern Baptist Theological Seminary, Louisville, 1954-58; Protestant Teachers' College, Lagos, Nigeria. Appointments: Lecturer, Theological Seminary & Service as a Clergyman, 1952-54; Pastor, Union Baptist Church, Ibadan, 1958-61; Lecturer, Continuing Education Classes & Seminars; General Secretary, Christian Council, 1962-67; All-Africa Conference of Churches General Commission; Consultant on several W.C.C. Consultations, 1962-69. Memberships: World Leaders of Religion; American Sociological Society; Chairman, Theological Board, A.A.C.C., 1963-67; Joint Negotiation Commission, 1964; Committee, Scout Council, Cheshire Home; General Secretary, Christian Council, Nigeria, 1962-67; Secretary, Yoruba Bible Translation Committee, 1947-54, 1958-64; Bible Revision Comm., 1948-54. Publications: A Survey of Social Change in Nigeria, 1958; Forty-Nine Days in a Teaching Hospital, 1970; Forty Brief Meditations, 1970; A Decade of Stewardship, 1970; The Litmus Life: A Biographical Sketch Reflecting Human Nature, 1971; contributor to Nigerian Baptist. Address: 55 Adeniran Ogunsanya St., Surulere, Lagos, Nigeria.

AFONYA (Rt. Rev.) Hubert Alafuro Ibibama, born 4th August 1916. Education: St. Paul's College, Anka, Nigeria; St. Augustine's College, Canterbury, U.K.; King's College, London. Personal details: married to Angelina Nwanwa Afonya, 4 sons, 3 daughters. Appointments: Vicar, St. Cypriam's Church, Port Harcourt; Archdeacon of Bonny & Assistant Bishop, Diocese of the Niger Delta, Anglican Province of West Africa; Justice of the Peace; Chairman, Port Harcourt Christian Council (Interdenominational) Urban & Industrial Project. Honours: Commander of the Order of the Niger, 1965. Address: Bishop's House, Port Harcourt, Nigeria.

AGGARWAL, Ramesh Lall, born 9th July 1940. Barrister-at-Law. Education: Vasingishu Primary School, Eldoret; Vasingishu Secondary School, ibid; Lincoln's Inn. Appointments: Advocate, High Court of Kenya. Address: P.O. Box 209, Eldoret, Kenya.

AKYEAMPONG, Yaw Appiah-Nuamah, born 28th November 1937. Civil Engineer; University Teacher. Education: Mfantsipim School, Cape Coast, Ghana, 1953-56; Kumasi College of Technology, Ghana, 1957-58; B.S.(Eng.), London, University of Science & Technology, Kumasi, Ghana, 1959-62; M.S. (Tech.), College of Science & Technology, Manchester, U.K., 1962-64; Ph.D., University of Iowa, Iowa City, U.S.A., 1967-70. Married, 1 son, 3 daughters. Appointments: Assistant Projects Engineer, Fuel & Power Secretariat, Accra, Ghana, 1962; Assistant Lecturer, University of Science & Technology, Kumasi, 1962; Senior Lecturer, ibid, 1965—. Memberships: American Society of Civil Engineers; Associate Member, Sigma Xi. Publications: M.Sc. Thesis, Turbulence Stimulation in Open Channels by Water Jets; Ph.D. Thesis, The Local Sediment in Periodically Non-Uniform Flows; Paper to ASA Meeting, Montreal, 1969; Technical Education: A Basic Step in Developing African Economics. Address: P.O. Box 22, Wenchi, B/A, Ghana.

AMIN, Sayid Mohamed, born 14th October 1940. Assistant Minister, Ministry of Land & Settlement; M.P. for Mandera East. Appointments: Member of Parliament for Mandera East; Assistant Minister; worked with Barclays Bank for 2 years. Memberships: Kenya National Library Service Board; Secretary, Mandera Branch, KANU. Address: P.O. Box 30450, Nairobi, Kenya.

ANDRIANANJAINA, Eloi, born Tananarive, Madagascar, 13th December 1906. Trade Unionist; Patriot. Appointments & Memberships: Founding Member, syndicats cegetistes, Madagascar (now the Malagasy Republic); Secretary-General, Metallurgical Union; Deputy Secretary-General, Departmental Union; persecuted & imprisoned for political writings,

1946 for 5 years; elected Provincial Councillor for Tamatave, 1947 (while still in prison); Founding Member, the political organization, 'Fivondronam-pirenena Malagasy', 1964; Deputy Secretary-General, ibid, 1964—; Municipal Councillor, 1964—. Publications: Aretina politika ve ny pesta? Mahafoana ny pesta ve ny tsindrona?; La peste est-elle une maladie politique? La vaccin enraye-t-il la peste?; contributor to Aurore Malagache, Patrie Malagache, Nation Malagache, Proletariat Malagache et Mongo. Address: Horloger-Pavillon 222, Onalakely, Tananarive, Madagascar.

ANIMASHAUN (Alhaji) Anjorin, born 25th May 1927. Physician; Paediatrician. Education: Government College, Ibadan, Nigeria, 1940-45; B.S., Howard University, Washington, D.C., 1949-52; Catholic University of America, 1950; University of the West Indies, Jamaica, 1951; University of Liverpool, 1952-57; Postgrad. Medical School, London, U.K., 1960-61; ibid, Edinburgh, 1961; Glasgow, 1961. Personal details: son of Chief Lamina Sekoni Animashaun, Balogun of Iddo, Gbagura, Abeokuta & Mrs. Jarin Ajike Animashaun, Muslim Religious Leader in Ibadan from the renowned Chief Aminu Egbeyemi Family in Abeokuta. Appointments: Officer of Customs & Excise, Lagos, 1946-48; Medical Officer, General Hospital, Lagos, 1957-60; Paediatrician, Children's Hospital, Lagos, 1962-64; Medical Superintendent in Charge, John Street Health Centre, Lagos, 1965; Deputy Director, Institute of Child Health, Lagos, 1965-68; Lecturer, Paediatrics, College of Medicine, Lagos, 1966—; Honorary Consultant Paediatrician, Lagos University Teaching Hospital, 1966—; Senior Specialist in Charge, Children's Hospital, Massey Street, Lagos, 1966—. Memberships: Hon. Sec., Paediatric Association of Nigeria; Chairman, Society of Health, Lagos; Trustee, Muslim Association of Nigeria; Executive, Boy Scouts of Nigeria, Lagos; Board Member, Atunda Olu School for the Handicapped; British Medical Association; Comm., Island Club, Lagos, 1967-70; Association of Physicians of West Africa. Publications: Infant Feeding Practices of Nigerian Mothers; School Meals; Complication of Small Pox Vaccination; Actiology of Cerebral Palsy (in press); An Outbreak of Blepharo Conjunctivities in Lagos; Editor, Proceedings of Seminar on Child Health in Lagos, 1966; Edit. Board, Journal of Society of Health, Nigeria; Pakistan Paediatric Journal. Honours: Who's Who in American Universities, 1952; Lucie Moten Fellowships, 1951; Nigeria Government Scholar, 1952-57, 1960-62; Swedish International Fellowship, 1965; Commonwealth Foundation Fellowship, 1970; Fellow of the Nigerian Medical Council. Address: Massey Street Children's Hospital, Lagos, Nigeria.

ARTEH, Omer, born Hargeisa, Somali Republic 1930. Politician. Education: Primary, Somali Republic; St. Paul's College, Cheltenham, England (Bristol University). Married, 7 children. Appointments include: Teacher, 1946-49; Headmaster, various elementary schools, 1949-54; Vice-Principal, Intermediate School, Sheikh, Somalia, 1954-56; Principal, Intermediate School, Gabileh, 1958; Officer in Charge of Adult Education, 1959; District Commissioner in Public Administration, 1960-61; First Secretary, Somali Embassy, Moscow, 1961-62; Rapporteur, Special Committee on South-West Africa, U.N., 1962-63; Counsellor to the Somali Permanent Mission to the United Nations, 1964; Ambassador to Addis Ababa, Ethiopia, 1965-68; elected Member of Parliament, Somali National Assembly, 1969; Foreign Secretary, Supreme Revolutionary Council. Memberships include: President, Somali Officials' Union; President, Teachers' Association; President, SOBA (a Somali Youth Organization). Publications include: Back From The Lion Of Judah (in press). Address: c/o Ministry of Foreign Affairs, Mogadishu, Somali Republic.

AYORINDE (Chief) John Adeyemi, born 11th August 1907. Retired Civil Servant; Traditional Chief, The Aare-Egbe-Omo-Olubadan of Ibadan; Member, Western State Cocoa Marketing Board. Education: St. David's Anglican Church School, Kudeti, Ibadan, Nigeria; Ibadan Grammar School, 1920-27; Seminar on Cooperation, Workers' College, Tel Aviv, Israel, 1958-59; Organization of Agricultural Extension & Extension Programme Planning, Wageningen, Holland, 1955; Massey-Harris, Ferguson Tractor Course, Coventry, U.K.; Training in Food Storage, Surrey. Personal details: married, 7 children. Appointments: Cotton Examiner, Former Dept. of Agriculture, 1927-36; Agricultural Assistant, Grade V, 1936; Agricultural Assistant, Grade IV, 1936; Technical Assistant, Grade II, 1937; Assistant Agricultural Officer, Grade II, 1945, Grade I, 1947; Cocoa Survey Officer, 1949; Senior Cocoa Officer, 1954; Senior Agricultural Superintendent, 1957; Officer in Charge of Cocoa, 1958; Principal Agricultural Superintendent, 1959; Principal Cocoa Survey Officer, 1965; retired, 1967. Memberships include: Antiquities Commission of Nigeria; Hon. Research Associate, Yoruba Historical Research Scheme; Hon. Assoc., Inst. of African Studies, University of Ibadan;-Ibadan Progressive Union; Counsellor, Nigeria Psychological Society; Council for Social Work in Nigeria; President, Western Circle, Ibadan; Regional Executive Council, Boy Scout Assn. of Nigeria; Chairman, Management Committee, ibid; Chairman, Western State, Nigeria Arts Council; Western State Resettlement Committee; Board of Governors, many schools & colleges. Publications include: Historical Notes on the Introduction & Development of the Cocoa Industry in Nigeria. African Culture, 1969; various cultural contributions in Odu, Gangan, Lagos Notes, & Records, etc. Honours include: Coronation Medal, 1953; M.B.E., 1961; Member of Federal Republic of Nigeria, 1963; Mogaji Babasanya Koblowu, Koblowu Compound, Oranyan Ibadan, 1965; Jagun Olubadan, 1966; Aare-Onibon Olubadan, 1967; Aare-Egbe-Omo-Olubadan, 1970. Address: NW6/105 Ayorinde St., Ekotedo, Nr. Race Course, Ibadan, Nigeria.

B

BADEJO, Daniel Adebiyi, born Ijebu Igbo, Western State, Nigeria, 13th February 1918. Engineer. Education: Cambridge School

Certificate, Grade 2; Igbobi College, Lagos, 1941; B.Sc., Maths., Virginia Union University, U.S.A., 1951; B.Sc., Civil Engineering, Massachusetts Institute of Technology, 1953; M.Sc., ibid, 1954. Personal details: married to Bernice Ajibade Badejo, 1 son, 4 daughters. Appointments: Engineer, Shell Company of Nigeria Ltd., Lagos, 1954; various positions, Field Organization & Head Office, before becoming Chief Engineer, 1963; Manager, Engineering & Technical Services Dept., 1967; Director, Shell Nigeria Provident Trust Ltd., 1968; Director, Shell Nigeria Ltd., 1970—. Memberships: Representative Member for Shell Co. of Nigeria in the Nigerian Institute of Management; Board of Governors, Molusi College, Ijebu-Igbo; Treasurer, African Church Cathedral (Bethel), Lagos, 1965—. Honours: First Nigerian Government Scholarship Award to study in the U.S.A., 1950. Address: The Shell Company of Nigeria Ltd., P.M.B. 2052, Lagos, Nigeria.

BAKTAVATSALOU, born 20th December 1932. Professor of Mathematics. Education: Doctor of Mathematical Science, Paris, France. Appointments: in Charge of Research, C.N.R.S., Paris, France, 1963-65; Lecturer, 1965-69; Professor of Mathematics, University of Abidjan, Ivory Coast, 1969—. Memberships: Mathematical Society of France; American Mathematical Society; APMEP. Publications: Cahier de Physique, 1963; C.R. Acad. Sciences, Paris, 1964, 1965, 1968. Address: Faculty des Sciences, University of Abidjan, B.P. 4322, Abidjan, Ivory Coast.

BARRISH, Hendrik Francois, born 19th December 1930. Headmaster. Education: B.A., Potchefstroom University, Transvaal, South Africa, 1953; University Education Diploma, 1954. Appointments: History & English Teacher, Transvaal, 1955-57; Proprietor of Grocery Business, 1957-59; Teacher of English & Afrikaans, Evelyn Baring High School, Nhlangano, 1959-69; Deputy Headmaster, Peak Secondary School, Pigg's Peak, 1970. Memberships: Southern Swaziland Country Club; Committee, ibid; Pigg's Peak Country Club. Address: P.O. Box 100, Pigg's Peak, Swaziland.

BASSIR, Olumbe, born Senegal, 20th May 1919. Nutritional Biochemist. Education: Prince of Wales School, Freetown, Sierra Leone; Achimota College, Accra, Ghana; Higher College, Yaba, Nigeria; Liverpool University; London University School of Hygiene & Tropical Medicine, Hon. Degrees in Biochemistry, Physiology, Biology, Chemistry; Doctorate in Hygiene (non-clinical medicine), etc. Appointments include: taught at King's College, Lagos; Prince of Wales School, & Bo School, Sierra Leone, 1940-46; Nuffield Research Fellowship in Human Nutrition at Medical Research Council, London, 1949-52; Senior Clinical Biochemist in Charge, Beverley Hospital, East Riding Group, England, 1952-55; Director, Human Lactation Research Project, West African Council for Medical Research, Lagos, 1955-56; Head of the Dept. of Biochemistry, 1956—; Dean of the Faculty of Science, 1964-65; Member of Council of Ibadan University, 1963—. Memberships include: President, Nigerian Association of University Teachers; President, Nigerian Section, Royal Institute of Chemistry; Member of Executive Committee, Organization for The Collaboration of Scientists of Africa & Asia; member of the Pugwash Movement & of the Executive of the International Peace Research Association and many other international bodies. Publications include: 'Anthology of West African Verse', Ibadan Univ. Press, 1957; 'Biochemical Aspects of Human Malnutrition in The Tropics', 1962; 'Arms Control and The Developing Nations', 1968; 'Handbook of Practical Biochemistry', 1963, and dozens of articles on on Nutrition, Peace & Economics. Honours, Prizes, etc.: Prize for head boy of Prince of Wales School, 1936; award of Nuffield Scholarship, 1946; award of Medal of Merit of Boy Scout Movement, 1962; election to Institute of Patentees, 1957; election to New York Academy of Sciences, 1965. Address: Biochemistry Dept., P.O. Box 4021, University of Ibadan, Ibadan, Nigeria.

BATTA, Benjamin Nyolima, born Metuli, Metu, Uganda, 12th February, 1918. Retired Executive Officer. Education: Senior Secondary School Certificate. Married, 8 children. Appointments include: Clerk-Typist, D.C.'s Office, Moyo, 1944; Chief Clerk, D.C.'s Office, Arua, 1946; Typist, D.C.'s Office, Mbarara, 1946-50; Chief Clerk, D.C.'s Office, Arua, 1950; Cashier, D.C.'s Office, Moyo, 1950-54; Treasurer, Madi Local Administration, 1954-56; Examiner of Accounts, Audit Office, Gulu, 1956-58; Accounts Assistant, Ministry of Local Government (now Ministry of Regional Administration), 1960-63; Finance Officer, Moyo Town Council, 1963—. Memberships include: Treasurer, Marindi Thrift & Loan Society; Committee Member, Moyo Recreation Club. Honours, Prizes, etc.: Independence Medal, 1963. Address: Otse Rd., Moyo Town, P.O. Box 51, Moyo, Uganda.

BOEHRINGER, Gill Hale, born 8th October 1933. Lecturer in Law. Education: Secondary, Philadelphia, Pennsylvania, U.S.A.; B.S. (Industrial Relations), Cornell University, 1955; LL.B., Hastings College of Law, University of California, 1962; LL.M., London School of Economics, University of London, 1967. Personal details: married. Appointments: Lecturer in Law, University of East Africa, Dar es Salaam, Tanzania, 1967-69; Research Officer, Oxford University, Penal Research Unit, U.K., 19., 1970; Visiting Lecturer in Law & Social Studies, Queen's University, Belfast, U.K., 1970-71. Society of Public Teachers of Law; Howard League for Penal Reform; National Assn. for Care & Settlement of Offenders; Institute for the Study & Treatment of Delinquents; National Assn. for Mental Health; Psychiatric Rehabilitation Assn.; University Teachers of Sociology of Law; National Council of Civil Liberties; African Studies Group; British Criminology Society. Publications: Introduction to Criminology in Africa (book); University of East Africa Social Science Conference Papers: Developments in Criminology in Tanzania, 1968; Social Defence Planning in the Context of Development with Special Reference to

Tanzania, 1969; Alternatives to Prison in East Africa (20th International Course in Criminology, Lagos, 1970). Address: Faculty of Law, Queen's University, Belfast, U.K., BTT INN.

C

CHANDE, Jayantilal Keshavji, born Mombasa, Kenya, 27th August 1929. Business Executive; Company Director. Married, 3 sons. Appointments include: Chairman, Dar es Salaam Round Table, Tanzania, 1958; Member, Executive Council, Tanganyika, 1959-61; Member of Parliament, Tanganyika, 1959-61; President, Red Cross Society, Dar es Salaam, Tanzania, 1961-64; President, Dar es Salaam Chamber of Commerce & Agriculture, 1961-62; Association of Chambers of Commerce & Industries in Eastern Africa (Kenya, Uganda, Tanganyika, Ethiopia, & Mauritius), 1966-67; World Council of Young Men's Service Clubs, 1969-70; Hon. Vice-President, 1963-68; General Manager, National Milling Corporation, Tanzania; Chairman, Management Supply Co. Ltd.; Chairman, Tanzania Advisory Committee, Automobile Association of East Africa; Board of Examiners, College of Business Education; Vice-Chairman, Board of Governors, National Museum of Tanzania; Board of Governors, Shaaban Robert Secondary School; Vice-Chairman, The Dar es Salaam Secondary Education Society; Trustee, Gandhi Memorial Academy Society, Nairobi, Kenya; Trustee, Upanga Sports Club, Dar es Salaam; Lohana Education Trust; Director: National Bank of Commerce, Tanzania; East African Harbours Corporation; Tanzania Tourist Corporation; Tanzania Electric Supply Co. Ltd.; International Computers (Tanzania) Ltd.; Tanganyika Instant Coffee Co. Ltd.; Tanzania Shoe Co. Ltd.; National Distributors Ltd.; Tanzania Distilleries Ltd.; Kilimanjaro Breweries Ltd.; Fellow, Institute of Directors; Fellow, Tanzania Institute of Management. Memberships include: Royal Commonwealth Society; Donovan Maule Theatre Club, Nairobi; Dar es Salaam Round Table No. 4. Address: P.O. Box 9251, Dar es Salaam, Tanzania.

CHINERY, William Addo, born 5th April 1934. Scientist. Education: Achimota Secondary School, 1948-52; University College of Ghana, 1954-59; London School of Hygiene & Tropical Medicine, U.K., 1960-63; B.Sc., Ph.D. (London), D.A.P.&E. Personal details: son of John Patrick Clelland Chinery & Effie Maud Chinery; married to Bertha Catherine Chinery, daughter of the late Provost G. E. F. Laing of Holy Trinity Cathedral, Accra, Ghana, 1966. Appointments: Government Entomologist, Ministry of Health, Accra, 1959-64; Research Officer, National Institute of Health & Medical Research, Ghana Academy of Sciences, 1964-68; Lecturer, University of Ghana Medical School, 1968—. Memberships: Fellow, Royal Society of Tropical Medicine & Hygiene; Institute of Biology; International College of Tropical Medicine & Hygiene; Ghana Science Association. Publications include: The Breeding of Culex (Culex) pipiens fatigans Wiedmann & Anopheles (Cellia) gambiae Giles, 1970; The Breeding of Aedes (Stegomyia) aegypti (L.), 1970; The Breeding of Culex (Culex) decens (Theo.), Culex (Culex) thalassius (Theo.) & Culex (Culex) univittatus (Theo.) in Accra, in press. Honours; WHO Fellowship, 1967; British Technical Aid Fellowship, 1967. Address: P.O Box 276, Accra, Ghana.

CHIRCHIR, Isaac Kiprono, born 15th March 1940. Animal Breeder. Education; Kenya African Preliminary Examination, 1958; Cambridge Overseas School Certificate, 1962; Diploma, Animal Husbandry, Egerton College, Njoro, 1965. Personal details: married, 3 children. Appointments: Assistant Livestock Manager, E. A. Tanning Ext. Co. Ltd., 1965-66; Laboratory Technician, Cattle Breeding & Genetics, East African Veterinary Research Organization, Muguga, Kenya. Memberships: Agricultural Society of Kenya; Animal Production Society of East Africa. Recipient of S.C.A.A.P., currently on study tour, National Cattle Breeding Station, C.S.I.R.O., Belmont, Australia. Address: c/o E.A.V.R.O., Muguga, P.O. Kabete, Nairobi, Kenya.

COKER, Ulric William Arthur, born Freetown, Sierra Leone, 21st July 1915. Barrister-at-Law. Education: Cathedral Day School, 1920-27; Sierra Leone Grammar School, 1928-35; Honourable Society of Gray's Inn, London, U.K., 1954; Read Law at the Council of Legal Education, London, 1954-62; Called to the Bar, 1962. Appointments include: Civil Servant, Government of Sierra Leone, 1937-54. Address: 20 Walpole Street, P.O. Box 894, Freetown, Sierra Leone.

D

DAINGUI, Charles, born Ingrakon, Ivory Coast, 1st January 1928. Personal details: son of Chief Monney Daingui; married, 2 children. Appointments: Monitor of Information, Catholic Mission of Andoubatto, Aleppo, 1943-44; ibid, Catholic Mission of Memni, 1944-45; Trainee Telegraphist, Submarine Cables of Grand-Bassam, 1945-46; ibid, BCTR of Abidjan & Grand-Bassam, 1954-55; Receiver, Bongouanou; Receiver, Dabakala, 1955-58; ibid, Anyama, 1958-59; Stagiaire, l'Ecole Superieure des Postes et Telecommunications de Rufisque, Senegal, 1959; ibid, Limoges, France, 1960; Toulouse, 1962; Direction of General Affairs, P. & T., Abidjan, 1962; Gestionnaire-Comptable du Magasin Central des P. & T., Abidjan, 1963-65; President, Ethnic Comm., PDCI-RDA M'BATTO, Treichville, 1963-66; Deputy Secretary, Comm. of Honour, Sect. of PDCI-RDA, ibid; Itinerant Inspector, Ministry of P. & T., Abidjan, 1965; Regional Inspector, ibid, Bouake, 1966; Counsellor-General & Member, Council of Notables, Sub-Prefecture of Aleppo, 1965-70. Memberships: Regional Commission of Development, Departments of the Centre & North, Ivory Coast; Sub-Commission for the Economic Infrastructure, Equipment & Industry; Action Catholique des famillies; National Council, P. & T. Union; Parents' Association of the Central Department. Address: Regional

Inspector, Posts & Telecommunications, Bouake, The Ivory Coast.

DAVEY-HAYFORD, M. Additional information: Membership: First National President, Ghana-Soviet Friendship Society.

DELAITRE, Jean Roland, born Quatre-Bornes, Mauritius, 1st November 1932. Journalist. Education: Royal College, Curepipe. Personal details: Married to Marie Louise Jacqueline Rivet, 4 sons, 1 daughter. Appointments: Mauritius Labour Party Executive, 1953-64; Vice-Chairman, ibid, 1960-62; Director, Mauritius Housing Corporation, 1962-64; Temporary Minister of Health & Reform Institute, later of Labour & Social Security, 1961; Member, Town Council, Quatre-Bornes, 1956—; Vice-Chairman, 1964; Sub-Editor, 'Advance', 1959-63; Editor, L'Express, 1963-64; Head of News, MBC, 1965-67; Programme Controller, Mauritius Broadcasting Corporation, 1967—; Ag. Director-General, 1970—. Memberships include: Chair, Quatre-Bornes Town Council, 1960-61; Rep. of Quatre-Bornes Town Council on Association of Urban Authorities (AUA), 1960-64; Chair, Football Commission, Mauritius Sports Assn., 1968; Executive Committee, Mauritius Sports Assn.; President, ibid, 1970—; Vice-Chairman, Fire Brigade Sports Club; Executive Committee, World Assembly of Youth; Board of Directors, African Youth Institute, World Assembly of Youth, 1968. Honours: Hon. Citizenship of the Township of Quatre-Bornes, 1965—; Chevalier de l'Ordre du Merite de Madagascar, 1969. Address: 14 Stevenson Avenue, Quatre-Bornes, Mauritius.

DELANY, Michael James, born 2nd August 1928. University Lecturer. Education: William Hulme's School, Manchester, U.K., 1940-47; B.Sc., M.Sc., Manchester University, 1947-50; Exeter University, 1950-53; D.Sc., Glasgow, 1967. Appointments: Assistant, Biology, University of Florida, U.S.A., 1953-54; Assistant, Zoology, University of Glasgow, 1954-56; Lecturer, ibid, University of Southampton, 1956-65, 1969—; Professor, Makerere University College, Uganda, 1965-69. Memberships: Fellow, Linnean Society of London; Fellow, Zoological Society, ibid; East African Wildlife Society, Zambian Wildlife Society; Zoological Society of Southern Africa; Uganda Society; British Ecological Society; Mammal Society of the British Isles. Author of numerous scientific papers on ecology & systematics of small mammals in Europe & tropical Africa. Honours: Fulbright Fellow, 1953-54. Address: Department of Zoology, University of Southampton, U.K.

DRAKE (Rev.) Henry Frederick, born 16th September 1917. Minister of Religion. Education: Surbiton County School for Boys, U.K.; Spurgeon's College, London; B.D., London University, 1944; Teachers' Dip., S.T.M., Union Theological Seminary, New York, U.S.A. Personal details: married, 1 daughter. Appointments: Minister, Union Church, Hanwell, London, U.K.; Missionary, w. Baptist Missionary Society, Kinshasa, Congo; Field Secretary, Baptist Missionary Society in the Congo; Associate Overseas Secretary, Baptist Missionary Society, London. Memberships: Youth Secretary, Congo Protestant Council; Radio & Press Officer, ibid. Officer of the British Empire, 1964. Address: Baptist Missionary Society, 93-97 Gloucester Place, London, W1H 4AA, U.K.

DUTTA ROY, Dilip K., born 1st March 1927. Statistician. Education: B.A., Calcutta, India, 1945; M.A., ibid, 1948. Married to Anati Ghosal, 1953, 3 sons. Appointments: Assistant Statistician, Rubber Research Institute, Malaya, 1952-55; Professional Officer, Statistics Division, UN, 1955-57; Head, Statistics Section, Agricultural Research, Sudan, 1957-64; Senior Research Fellow, Institute of Statistics, University of Ghana, 1964-67; Dir., Inst. of Statistical, Social, & Econ. Research, 1967-69; Head, Statistical Unit, National Council of Research, Lusaka, 1969—. Memberships: Fellow, Royal Statistical Society; Chairman, Statistical Reorganization Committee, Government of Ghana, 1969. Publications include: Household Budget Survey; The Eastern Region Household Budget Survey. Address: National Council for Scientific Research, P.O. Box RW166, Ridgeway, Lusaka, Zambia.

E

EDMUNDS, Malcolm, born 24th July 1938. University Lecturer. Education: Leighton Park School, Reading; B.A., Zoology, 1960, Queen's College, Oxford, U.K.; D.Phil., ibid, 1963. Married, 1963, 2 daughters. Appointments: Lecturer, Zoology, University of Ghana, 1963-69; Senior Lecturer, ibid, 1969—. Memberships: Linnean Society; Malacological Society, Institute of Biology; Royal Society for the Protection of Birds; Botanical Society of the British Isles. Publications include: On the European Species of Eubranchus, 1969; Optisthobranchiate Mollusca from Tanzania, 1970. Address: Department of Zoology, University of Ghana, P.O. Box 67, Legon, Ghana.

ENDELEY, Gervasius Mbela (Chief), born Buea Town, Cameroon, 1897. Paramount Chief of Bakweri. Education: German & English Primary Schools. Personal details: married 8 sons, 6 daughters. Appointments include: School-teacher, St. Mary's School, Sasse, 1920-25; President, Customary Court, 1925-58; District Head of Buea District, 1925; Chairman, Bakweri Council, 1925-58; Treasurer, ibid, 1938-48; Supervisor, Bakweri Council Works, 1928-58; Member, House of Chiefs, 1963—. Memberships include: Roman Catholic Mission; Prison Visitor, Prison Committee; Board of Governors, St. Joseph's College, Sasse Buea; Local Committee, Cameroon Red Cross Society. Honours: Coronation Medal, 1953; British Empire Medal; Merite Camerounais, 1st Class Medal, 1964. Address: c/o Bakweri Council Office, Buea, West Cameroon, Federal Republic of Cameroon.

ESEILE, John Sunday, born Eruere, Iuleha, Benin, Nigeria, 10th November 1934. Teacher.

Education: St. John School, Std. VI, 1947; St. David's College, Evboneka, Grade III, 1953; St. John's College, Owo, Grade II, 1958; inter-B.A. Tuition, 1969. Married, 1 son, 3 daughters. Appointments: Headmaster, Secondary Modern School; ibid, St. Peter's School; St. David's School. Memberships: Diocesan Synod, 1963-69; Secretary, Iuleha Welfare Association, 1968-70; ibid, Iuleha-Otuo Road Working Committee, 1968-70; Chairman, Iuleha Elite, 1969-70. Address: St. David's School, Avbiosi New Site, Iuleha, Via Benin City, Nigeria.

EYABU, Christopher Isodo, born 21st November 1941. Electrical Engineer. Education: Ngora Bots Primary School; Soroti Technical School; Uganda Technical College. Appointments: Trainee Electrical Engineer, Kilembe Copper Mines, 1963; Foreman, Kivu Goldmines; Senior Foreman, Kirwa Walfram Mines; Assistant Electrical Engineer, Kilembe Mines; Electrical & Mechanical Officer, East African Community, 1967—. Memberships: Athletics Club; East African Contractors & Engineers Societies. Honours: First Prize, Engineering Drawing, 1963; Best Sportsman of the Year, Athletics, Kilembe Copper Mines, 1964. Address: East African Community, P.O. Box, Kampala, Uganda.

F

FERREIRA (Major) A. A. Jorge. Additional information: Memberships: Chairman, International Affairs Commission.

FRÈRE, Guy, born 22nd January 1924. Director, Senegal Phosphate Company of Thies, & of the African Silicates Company. Education: Civil Engineer; Mining Engineer. Appointments: with Symetain, Kinshasa, Congo; Mines of Bou Azzer, Morocco, Dahomey, St. Johns, Madagascar, & Senegal. Memberships: Lions Club, Dakar; UNISYNDI, Dakar; Union of Senegal Mines; Member of Economic & Social Council. Honours: National Order of Senegal, 1970. Address: B.P. 241, Dakar, Senegal.

G

GINWALA, Frene N., Journalist. Appointments: Managing Editor, Standard & Sunday News, Tanganyika Standard (Newspapers), Ltd., Tanzania. Address: P.O. Box 9033, Dar es Salaam, Tanzania.

GOKANI, Ramnik, born 5th October 1938. Medical Practitioner. Education: Grant Medical College, Bombay, India; M.B., B.S., Bombay University, 1963. Appointments: Intern, Mulago Hospital, Kampala, Uganda; Medical Officer, Kampala City Council; Acting M.O.H., ibid; currently in General Practice. Memberships: Uganda Medical Association; Uganda Medical Society; Medical Protection Society, London; Kampala Sports Club. Honours: Raids Scholarship, 1959. Address: P.O. Box 5466, Kampala, Uganda.

H

HACKENBERG (Lt. Cmdr.) Alan Peter, born 28th June 1927. Electrical & Electronics Engineer. Education: College, Naval Officers' Training School. Appointments: Navy Officer, 1956-64; Factory Planning & Construction, 1964-66. Memberships: Churchill Club, Casablanca, 1966—; N.O. Club, Brussels, Belgium. Address: Villa Alpha, Cil 25, Ain es Sebaa, Morocco.

HARBISON, Frederick H., born 18th December 1912. Professor of Economics & International Affairs. Education: A.B., Princeton University, U.S.A., 1934; Ph.D., ibid, 1940. Appointments: Director, Industrial Relations Section, Princeton University, N.J., U.S.A.; Professor, Economics & International Affairs, ibid. Memberships: President, Industrial Relations Research Association, 1969-70. Publications: Education, Manpower & Economic Growth (w. C. Myers) 1964; Industrialism & Industrial Man (joint author), 1967. Address: Woodrow Wilson School, Princeton University, Princeton, N.J. 08540, U.S.A.

HARTMAN, Cyril Grainger, born 16th February 1935. Physician & Surgeon. Education: B.S., Pacific Union College, Angwin, California, U.S.A., 1957; M.D., Loma Linda University, Calif., 1961. Personal details: married to Charlotte M. Hartman, B.A., M.S., Dietician. Appointments: Missionary Physician, Seventh Day Adventist Church of West Africa, 1962—. Address: Ahoada Hospital, via Port Harcourt, Rivers State, Nigeria.

HENRIES, A. Doris Banks, born U.S.A., 11th February 1919. Educator. Education: Elementary & Secondary Schools, Middletown, Connecticut; Columbia Univ., N.Y.; Connecticut State Teachers' College; Hartford Seminary Foundation; Univ. of Besancon. Major fields of specialization: English, Science, Anthropology, Elementary Education. Married Richard A. Henries, 16th December 1942; husband, a member of the House of Representatives of Liberia. Appointments include: Principal, Fuller Normal School, 1938-40; Education Supervisor, Methodist Schools, Maryland County, Liberia, 1940-42; Prof., Liberia College, 1943-59; Prof., Univ. of Liberia, 1951-55; Director, Teachers' College, U.L., 1951-55; Acting Dean of Univ. of Liberia, 1955-56; Dean of the Univ. 1956-59; Acting President, Univ. of Liberia, 1956-57 (3 months), 1958-59 (4 months); Director of Higher Education & Textbook Research, Dept. of Education, R.L., 1959—. Memberships include: President, National Teachers' Association of Liberia; President National Y.W.C.A. of Liberia; Vice-President, Liberian Historical Society; Vice-President, Society of Liberian Authors; Secretary, Antoinette Tubman Child Welfare Foundation; Board Member, Girl Guides; Board Member, Liberian Red Cross; Member, College Women's Club; Treasurer, Director of Projects, National Federation of Liberian Women, etc.; Executive Committee, WCOTP. Publications include: 20 books, including: The Liberian Nation, 1953, revised, 1966; Civics for Liberian Schools, 1953, Revised, 1966; Liberia the West African Republic (co-author), 1949, Revised, 1955, 1966; Life of Joseph Jenkins Roberts (First President of Liberia), 1963; Presidents of Liberia, 1963; Poems of Liberia, 1836-1963; Heroes & Heroines of Liberia, 1962; Africa Our History, 1968; Folklore, 1966, etc. Honours, Prizes, etc.: Knight Official, Star of Africa, 1950; Grand Band, Humane Order of African Redemption, 1955; Dame Grand Commander, Order of the Knighthood of Pioneers of Liberia, 1959; Doctor of Education, Liberia College, 1949; 'Graduate of the Year', Connecticut State Teachers' College, 1956; Order des Arts et des Lettres (French), 1958; German Order, 1961; Grand Cross, Order of Merit, etc. Address: Dept. of Education, Univ. of Liberia, Monrovia, Liberia.

HUCKSTEP, Ronald Lawrie, born China, 22nd July 1926. Professor of Orthopaedic Surgery. Education: Cambridge University & Middlesex Hospital, London; M.A., M.B., B.Chir. (Cantab.); M.D.(Cantab.); F.R.C.S.(Edin.); F.R.C.S.(Eng.). Married, 3 children. Past Appointments include: various General, Surgical, & Orthopaedic Appointments at the Middlesex, Royal National Orthopaedic, & St. Bartholomew's Hospitals, London. Present Appointments: Hon. Consultant Orthopaedic Surgeon, Mulago & Mengo Hospitals, Kampala, Uganda,& Round Table Polio Clinic, Kampala; Prof. of Orthopaedic Surgery, Makerere Univ. College (now Makerere University), Kampala. Memberships include: Fellow, British Orthopaedic Association; Fellow, Association of Surgeons of East Africa (Members' Council); National Advisory Council for the Rehabilitation of the Cripples in Uganda; Committee for Rehabilitation of the Disabled in Africa; Fellow, Royal Society of Medicine. Publications include: Author of books, chapters in textbooks, booklets, medical films, papers, & communications on typhoid fever, simple appliances for the crippled patient, orthopaedic & traumatic conditions with special reference to developing countries, & rehabilitation of the cripple in economically poor countries. Corresponding Editor for East Africa, 'Journal of Bone and Joint Surgery'. Honours, Prizes, etc: various Medical Prizes; Hunterian Professor, Royal College of Surgeons, England. Address: Dept. of Orthopaedic Surgery, Makerere University Medical School, P.O. Box 7072, Kampala, Uganda.

I

IKENWE, Chukwuma Gideon, born Akwukwu, via Isseleuku, Midwestern State, Nigeria, 12th February 1942. Educationalist. Education: St. Bartholomew's School, Enugu, 1948-54; Okongwu Memorial Grammar School, Nnewi, 1955-59; St. Michael's College (Teacher Training), Oleh, 1960-61; B.A.(Hons.) Ed., University of Nigeria, Nsukka, 1964067. Appointments include: Teacher, Secondary Modern School, Asaba, Midwestern State, 1962; Secondary Modern School, Ubuluku, 1962; Anglican Grammar School, Ubuluku, 1962-64, 1967-68; appointed Headmaster, Anglican Boys' Grammar School, Akwukwu, at request of local people, 1968 –; Education Officer, Ministry of Education, Midwest State, Nigeria; currently attached to Edo Government College, Benin City. Memberships include: elected to Students' Union Parliament, University of Nigeria, 1965; elected to Students' Supreme Council. Author of a thesis on History Teaching in Midwestern Nigeria: A Critical Analysis, 1967. Address: Anglican Boys' Grammar School, Akwukwu, Isseleuku, Midwestern State, Nigeria.

J

JAASUND, Erik, born China, 13th November 1918. Lecturer. Education: Cand. real., Oslo, Norway, 1946; Fil. Lic., Gothenburg, Sweden, 1957; Fil. Dr., ibid, 1965. Personal details: parents Norwegian. Appointments: Meteorologist, Tromso, Norway, 1945-47; Meteorologist, Gothenburg, Sweden, 1947-53; High School Teacher, Katrineholm, Sweden, 1953-66; Lecturer, University College, Dar es Salaam, Tanzania, 1966-70; Amanuensis, University of Tromso, Norway, 1970–. Publications: 2 series of papers: Marine Algae from Northern Norway, 1951, 1957, 1960 a & b, 1961 a & b, 1963, 1964, 1965; Marine Algae from Tanzania 1969, 1970 a, b, c. Contributor to African Encyclopaedia. Address: Tromso Museum, 9000 Tromso, Norway.

JEDRUSZEK, Jerzy, born 12th December 1921. Statistician. Education: B.A., M.Sc., Ph.D., Central School of Planning & Statistics, Warsaw, Poland. Personal details: married, 2 sons. Appointments: Senior Research Fellow, Institute of Nuclear Research, Warsaw; Reader & Head of Department of Statistics, University College, Dar es Salaam, Tanzania. Memberships: Secretary, Warsaw Branch, Polish Economic Society; Assistant Editor, Ekonomista (quarterly); Ghanaian Economic Society; Assistant Editor, Economic Bulletin; Associate Member, Tanzania Branch, East African Academy. Publications include: Longterm Energy Demand in Poland. Address: Dept. of Statistics, University of Dar es Salaam, Tanzania.

JEMBA, Faustine, born 25th February 1934. Auditor. Education: Qualified in Commerce. Personal details: married 3 sons, 2 daughters. Appointments: Secretary, Delbah, 1950-52; Auditor, Douala, Cameroun. Memberships: Former Commissaire aux Comptes de l'Association pour l'Emancipation de la Femme Camerounaise. Recipient of Medals & other honours. Address: Boite Postale 5236, Douala, Cameroun.

JOHNSON, Eldon L., born Putnam County, Indiana, U.S.A., 5th November 1908. University Vice-President. Education: A.B., History & English, Indiana State University, U.S.A., 1929; Ph.M., Political Science, University of Wisconsin, 1933; Ph.D., Pol. Sci. & Econ., ibid, 1939; Postdoctoral Research, London School of Economics, U.K., 1951. Personal details: married, 2 daughters. Appointments: Professor & Chairman, Dept. of Political Science,

University of Oregon, Eugene, Oregon, U.S.A., 1945-48; Acting Director of Summer Session, 1946; Dean, College of Liberal Arts & Graduate School, University of New Hampshire, Durham, 1955-62; President, Great Lakes Colleges Assn., Detroit, Mich., 1962-66; Vice-President, University of Illinois, Urbana, 1966. Memberships: Chairman, International Team Surveying Education in Malawi, 1963-64; Governing Councils of: University of Nigeria, 1959-62; University of Malawi, 1965—; University College, Nairobi, Kenya, 1966—. Publications: Co-author: Study of Comparative Government; Higher Education: Some Newer Developments. Honours: LL.D., University of Rhode Island, 1958; LL.D., University of Maine, 1961: LL.D., Dartmouth College, 1963; LL.D., University of New Hampshire, 1964; Catedratico Honorario, University of San Marcos, Lima, Peru, 1959. Address: University of Illinois, 377, Administration Building, Urbana, Illinois 61801, U.S.A.

K

KALUME (Hon. Rev.), Thomas J., born Bate, Malindi, Kenya, 1926. Member of Parliament, Kenya; Anglican Priest. Education: Primary until 1945; Secondary, Alliance High School, 1946-49; Kagumo College, 1950-51; B.D. (London University), 1962-65; M.R.E., Union & New York Theological Seminary, 1965-67. Personal details: married to Rabeka Kalume, 9 children. Appointments: Tutor, Ribe Teachers' College, 1952-53; Headmaster, Kaloleni Boarding School, 1954-59; Supervisor-Manager of 60 African Schools in Taita District, 1959-62; Priest, Mombasa Cathedral, 1967-69; Member of Parliament, Malindi North Constituency, Kenya. Memberships: Chairman of: Kalolein Hospital; Kalolein Girls' Secondary School; Kanamai Youth Centre & Holiday Camp. Publications: Kenya National Anthem (co-composer, words & Music); composer of African Songs; author of various articles in papers & magazines: Address: P.O. Box 374, Malindi, Kenya.

KASMANI, Nurudeen, born 30th June 1939. Chartered Civil Engineer. Education: B.Sc. (Hons.), Civil Engineering, University of St. Andrew's, U.K., 1963. Married, to Shirin N. Kasmani. Appointments: Assistant Engineer, Country Engineer's Office, Argyllshire, Scotland, U.K., 1963-66; Engineer, Jagdish R. Sondhi, Esq., Mombasa, Kenya, 1966-69; Partner, ibid, 1969—. Memberships: Institution of Civil Engineers; East African Institute of Engineers; Architectural Association of Kenya; Association of Consulting Engineers of Kenya; Mombasa Round Table; Secretary, ibid, 1968-69, 1969-70. Address: P.O. Box 1316, Mombasa, Kenya.

KETTLE, Arnold Charles, born 17th March 1916. University Professor. Education: Merchant Taylors' School, London, U.K.; B.A., Pembroke College, Cambridge University, 1937; M.A., ibid, 1941; Ph.D., 1942. Appointments: Lecturer in English Literature, University of Leeds, 1947-67; Professor of Literature, University College, Dar es Salaam, Tanzania, 1967-70; Professor of Literature, The Open University, U.K., 1970—. Publications: An Introduction to the English Novel, 1951; Shakespeare in a Changing World, 1964; also many critical essays. Address: The Open University, Walton, Bletchley, Bucks, U.K.

KUNGU, Alfred, born 4th March 1935. Medical Practitioner. Education: Cambridge School Certificate, 1st Grade, Alliance High School, Kikwya, 1954; M.B., Ch.B.(E.A.), Makerere University College, 1962. Appointments: District Medical Officer, Muranga, 1963-64; Registrar in Pathology, Medical Research Lab., Nairobi, Kenya, 1964-66; Postgraduate Commonwealth Scholar in Pathology, Western Infirmary, Glasgow, U.K., 1966-68; Senior Registrar in Pathology, Medical Research Lab., 1968—; Lecturer, Pathology Dept., University college, Nairobi, 1968—. Member, Royal College of Physicians, London, 1970. Address: Pathology Dept., Kenyatta National Hospital, P.O. Box 30588, Nairobi, Kenya.

L

LEAKEY (Rev. Canon), Ian Raymond Arundell, born 3rd July 1924. Clergyman. Education: Sherborne School, Dorset, U.K., 1938-42; King's College, Cambridge University, 1942-43, 1946-48; Ridley Hall, Cambridge, 1948-50. Appointments: Lieut., R.N.V.R., 1943-46; Canon, Anglican Diocese of Burundi, 1966. Honours: Choral Scholarship, King's College, Cambridge, 1942. Address: E.A.B. Bulinga, D.S. 127, Bujumibura, Burundi.

LEAKEY, Joyce Mary, born 22nd December 1923. Nurse. Education: St. Aidan's High School, 1932-40; Ridgelands Bible College, 1950-52. Personal details: married. Appointments: with Bank of England, 1940-43; V.A.D. in R.A.M.C., 1943-44; Nurse in Training, Middlesex Hospital, London, U.K., 1945-59; Midwife in Training, Queen Charlotte's Hospital, 1949-50. Honours: Silver Medal, Middlesex Hospital, 1948. Address: E.A.B. Bulinga, D.S. 127, Bujumbura, Burundi.

LEVY, Trevor Hope da Costa, born 23rd April 1931. Barrister-at-Law. Education: with Private tutor; Lincoln's Inn, London, U.K.; Called to the Bar, 1960. Personal details: married, 2 sons, 2 daughters. Appointments: Crown Counsel, Malawi, 1964; Chief Legal Aid Counsel, Malawi, 1965-69. Memberships: Malawi Law Society; Council of Legal Education, Malawi. Address: 82 East St., Kingston, Jamaica, W.I.

LINIECKI, Alina Maria, born Gniezno, Poland, 21st September 1931. Dental Surgeon.

Education: Primary School, City of Gniezno, Poland, 1938-45; Secondary School, ibid, 1945-50; Medical Academy, City of Poznan, 1950-54; Diploma in Dental Surgery(Hons.), ibid; Course on Developmental Psychology & Pedagogical Preparation for Research Workers, 1961-62. Personal details: married to Alexander Liniecki, Professor in Mechanical Engineering. Appointments: Dental Surgeon, Polyclinic, District of Widzew, City of Lodz, 1955-57; Lecturer, Research Fellow, Medical Academy of the City of Lodz, Dept. of Conservative Dentistry, 1958-64; Private Practice, 1955-64; Lecturer in Microbiology, Dept. of Pharmaceutics, Faculty of Pharmacy, University of Science & Technology, Kumasi, Ghana, 1965-67. Memberships: Polish Dental Society; Filipino Dental Society in California, U.S.A., 1969—. Author of 8 publications in the field of Periodontology & Conservative Dentistry in Polish Dental Journals, & others; 5 papers submitted to Conferences in the field of Periodontology & Dental Surgery. Address: 1884 Castro Drive, San Jose, California 95130, U.S.A.

LUCIUS, Jacques, born 7th July 1905. Administrator of Societies. Education: Lic. in Law; Diploma, Free School of Political Sciences. Appointments: Auditor, Council of State, 1932; Master of Requests, 1940; Deputy Secretary-General, Tunisian Government, 1941; Secretary-General, Protectorate of France to Morocco, 1944-49; President, Commission for Overseas Investigation for the Monet Plan. Memberships: Automobile Club of France; President, Industrial & Financial Company of Participations; Administrator, Mokta; ibid; Djebel Djerissa, Chantiers de l'atlantique. Honours: Commander, Legion of Honour, 1960. Address: President, Uranium Mining Co., of Franceville, 191 avenue de Neuilly, 92 Neuilly-sur-Seine, France.

M

MONGORY, Ernest, born 27th March 1907. Businessman. Education: Certificate, 1921; Ecole Normale, Protestant Mission, Ndoungue. Married, 6 sons, 2 daughters. Appointments: Clerk, Board of Directors, Head, Import-Export Service, C.F.A.O., Douala, Cameroun, 1922-35; Head Accountant, S.H.O., ibid, 1936-52; Head, Cost Price Service, 1952-55; Chef Service de Prix Revient, Facturation Interieure, Controle des Holologations de Prix, Statisique Marchandises, 1956-65; Head, Administrative Service, Singer Sewing Machine Co., 1966—; Treasurer, Evangelic Church, Paroisse Bonakou; Auditor, Council, Baptist Evangelic Church. Memberships: Past President & Founder, Christian Union of Young Girls, Cameroun; A Founder & Past President-General, Syndicats Croyants, Cameroun; Social & Economic Council, Cameroun, 1961-66. Honours: Merite Camerounais, 3rd Class, France, 1948; Medaille d'honneur du Travail en Or, France, 1959. Address: B.P. 5094, Akwa, Douala, Cameroun.

MUJUMBA, Rabecca, born 1924. Education: Early Kenya Primary Education Certificate; attended early F.A. Mission School, Kaimosi. Appointments: Schoolmistress; Church Leader; Woman Leader. Memberships: Women Serving Coop. Society; Coffee & Tea Growing Societies. Address: Vihiga High School, P.O. Box 173, Maragoli, Kenya.

MULJIANI, Husseinally Jafferbhai, born Bombay, India, 11th September 1909. Educator. Education: Ephinstone College, Bombay, India: B.A.(Hons.), Bombay University, 1931. Personal details: married, 1 son, 3 daughters; founded school in memory of grandson. Appointments: Teacher, Kenya, for 21 years & India for 1 year; Founder of Mahmud Coaching School (later Mahmud High School), Mengo, Kampala, Uganda; Headmaster, Financier & Administrator, ibid. Memberships: Hon. Secretary, Consumers' Association, Mombasa, Kenya, 1944, 1945; Hon. Secretary, Parents' Association, Aga Khan Schools, Mombasa, 1953, 1954, 1955; Hon. Secretary, Teachers' Assn., Mombasa, 1948, 1949, 1950, 1951, 1952; Teachers' Assn., Jinja, 1963, 1964; Executive Committee, Teachers' Assn., Kampala Private Schools, 1965, 1966, 1967; Director, Kasalina Housing Estate Ltd., Mengo, 1966-70; Director & Hon. Sec., ibid, 1970. Recipient of Sir Ebrahim Rahintula Scholarship, 1927. Address: Mahmud High School, P.O. Box 14054, Mengo, Kampala, Uganda.

MUMBI, Rodgers Maximillian Mulenga, born 12th July 1934. Administrator. Education: Cambridge School Certificate, Muwali Secondary School, 1953-55; Cambridge Higher School Certificate, ibid, 1956-57; University College of Rhodesia & Nyasaland, 1958; Science Politiche, University of Pavia, Italy, 1962-63; B.Soc. Sci., University of Birmingham, U.K., 1963-66; M.A., Sociology Course, University of Zambia, 1969-70. Personal details: married, 3 children. Appointments include: Pay Clerk, Public Works Dept., Northern Rhodesian Government, 1955; Research Assistant, Chartered Exploration Co., 1956; Pasture Research Assistant, Mount Makulu Research Station, 1957-58; Farm Labourer, Petauke Govt. Farm, 1958; Social Research Assistant, Rhodes Livingstone Institute, 1959-60; Social Welfare & Probation Officer, N. Rhodesian Govt., 1960-62; Assistant District Secretary, Govt. of the Republic of Zambia, 1966; Assistant Registrar, University of Zambia, 1966-69; Training Officer, Indeco, Ltd., 1970—; Alternate Director, Indeco Real Estate Group of Companies, 1970; Director: Indeco Board, 1969; Indeco Industrial Finance Co., 1969-70. Address: P.O. Box R.W. 478, Lusaka, Zambia.

MUNDIA, Nalumino, born 21st November 1927. Member of National Assembly of Zambia. Education: Cambridge School Certificate, Munchi Training Centre, Zambia; B.Comm. (Hons.), Shri Ram College of Commerce,

University of Delhi, India; M.B.A., Graduate School of Business Administration, Atlanta University, Georgia, U.S.A., 1967. Personal details: Married to Cecilia Mundia, 1 son, 2 daughters. Appointments: Minister of Local Government (UNIP Government) Zambia, 1964; Minister of Commerce & Industry, ibid, 1965; Minister of Labour & Social Services, 1966—; Member of Parliament for Libonda Constituency, Zambia. Memberships: Chairman, Munchi Debating Society, 1946-49; Secretary, Students' Foreign Association of India, 1954-56; Representative, Central African Students' Union, America; All Africa-American Students' Union, 1956-57. Publications: Grim Peep Into the North (Editor). Address: National Assembly, P.O. Box 1299, Lusaka, Zambia.

MUTYABA, Mark, born Uganda, 1st May 1940. Teacher. Education: 6 years, Primary; 2 years, Junior Secondary; 4 years, Secondary; Diploma, Fine Art, 4 years, Margaret Trowell School of Art; Teaching Diploma. Married, 7 children. Appointments: Teacher, Old Kampala Secondary School, Uganda. Memberships: Vice-President, Uganda Arts Club; Nommo Gallery, Uganda; Association of Professional Artists, Uganda; Y.M.C.A., Uganda. Publications: Patterns In African Art; Dying Architecture of East Africa. Honours: ESSO Calendar Special Prizes, 1964, 1966 & 1967; Uganda Arts Club, 2nd & 3rd Prizes, 1967 & 1968. Address: Old Kampala Senior Secondary School, P.O. Box 330, Kampala, Uganda.

MWAMPONDELE, Abner Simon, born Mwaya Rungwe, 7th October 1938. Administrative Officer. Education: Tosamaganga School; Cooperative Course, Institute of Labour & Cooperative, Tel Aviv, Israel; Professional Course, University College, Dar es Salaam, Tanzania. Personal details: married to a Teacher. Appointments: District Secretary of T.A.N.U., 1959-63; Area Commissioner, 1962-63; Settlement Officer, 1964; Administrative Officer, 1964—. Address: P.O. Box 28, Shinyanga, Tanzania.

N

NAGA, George Angel Vincent, born 23rd April 1929. Teacher. Education: Primary, Mpindinbi, I-LV; ibid, V-VI; Secondary School, X, Chidya Secondary School; Grade I Teachers' Training, St. Andrew's College. Married to Angela Martha Ligunda, 3 children. Appointments: Headmaster, Middle School; Deputy; Liwali Masasi District Council; Administrative Officer, 1961—. Memberships: Boy Scouts; Football Clubs, St. Joseph's College & St. Andrew's College. Honours: Essay Prize, British Council, 1953. Address: Area Secretary, District Office, P.O. Box 1, Singida, Tanzania.

NEWTON, Leonard Eric, born 26th September 1936. Lecturer in Systematic Botany. Education: B.Sc.(Hons.), Botany, University of Wales, U.K., 1959; Dip. Ed., ibid, 1960; M.Sc., University of London, 1965. Appointments: Lecturer, Biology, Erith Technical College, Kent, U.K., 1960-66; ibid, Systematic Botany, University of Science & Technology, Kumasi, Ghana, 1966—; Visiting Research Fellow, Oxford University, U.K., 1970. Memberships: Fellow, Linnean Society, London; International Organization of Succulent Plant Research; International Association for Plant Taxonomists. Author of Repertorium Plantarum Succulentarum (Assistant Editor). Address: Department of Biological Sciences, University of Science & Technology, Kumasi, Ghana.

NYAHOZA, Felix, born 24th November 1936. University Lecturer. Education: B.Sc. (Gen.), London; M.Sc.(Agric.), University of East Africa. Appointments: Special Assistant Lecturer, Agricultural Botany, Makerere College, 1966; Shell Chemicals Sales Representative, 1966-67; Special Lecturer, Botany Department, University of Dar es Salaam, Tanzania, 1967—; currently working for Ph.D., School of Plant Biology, University Coll. of N.Wales, Bangor, Caerns., U.K. Memberships: Scout Movement of Tanganyika (now Tanzania), 1950—; Assistant Scout Master, Tabora, 1960. Climbed highest peak of Mt. Kilimanjaro, 1959. Author of 3 papers on cotton. Honours: May Memorial Scholarship, Cotton Growing Corporation, 1964-66. Address: Botany Department, P.O. Box 35060, Dar es Salaam, Tanzania.

O

OFOSU-AMAAH, Samuel, born 13th January 1931. Physician; Paediatrician. Education: Achimota School; University of Ghana; University of Glasgow, U.K.; University of London; University of Harvard, U.S.A.; B.Sc.; M.B., Ch.B.; D.C.H.; M.R.C.P.; M.P.H. Personal details: married to Virginia Engmann, B.A., 1 son, 1 daughter. Appointments: Medical Officer, Ministry of Health, 1960; Senior Medical Officer, Paediatrics, 1965; Lecturer in Paediatrics & Child Health, Ghana Medical School. Memberships; Ghana Medical Association; British Medical Association; American Public Health Association; Ghana Science Association; Ghana Constituent Assembly, 1969; Medical Association Representative. Author of publications on The Problems of Child Health, Nutrition, Child Development. Address: Ghana Medical School, Korle Bu, Accra, Ghana.

OGU, Andrew Omuta, born Omoku, Eastern Nigeria, 5th May 1940. Teacher. Education: Ase Clan School, Ase, 1945-52; D.M.G.S., Onitsha, 1953-57; St. Mark's College, Awka, 1958-59; University of Nigeria, Nsukka, 1961-65. Personal details: married to Queen Elizabeth Anwoh, 2 children. Appointments include: Senior Geography Master, St. George's College, Obinomba, 1965-67; Principal, St. Vincent College, Okwagbe Warri, since 1968. Memberships: Secretary, Isoko Students' Association, 1961-64; Executive Member, Oyede Improvement Union. Address: St. Vincent's College, c/o P.A. Ganagana, via Warri, Nigeria.

OWEN, John Shirley, born 19th January 1923. Physician. Education: Sebright, Wolverley, Worcs., U.K., 1933-40; University of Birmingham, 1940-45; 1948-49; Institute of Education, University of London, 1955-56. Personal details: married to Jacqueline d'Auban, 2 children. Appointments: House Officer, Birmingham Hospitals, 1945-46; R.A.M.C. Commission; served in B.A.O.R., 1946-48; Senior Assistant M.O.H., County Borough of Smethwick, U.K., 1950-55; Medical Registrar, University College Hospital, Ibadan, Nigeria, 1956-57; Lecturer, Senior Lecturer, Dept. of Soil & Preventive Medicine, University of Ibadan, 1957-67; currently Associate Professor, Social & Preventive Medicine, University of Saskatchewan, Canada, 1967—. Fellow, Society of Medical Officers of Health. Memberships: Hon. Life Member, Society of Health, Nigeria; President, Cheshire Homes of Saskatoon; Vice-President, Co-ordinating Council on Rehabilitation, Saskatchewan; Executive Committee, Sask. Branch, Canadian Public Health Association; Committee, African Studies in Canada. Author of publications on: Health Education; Voluntary Health Organizations; Health Services in Developing Countries; The African Baobab. Address: Dept. of Social & Preventive Medicine, University of Saskatchewan, Saskatoon, Sask., Canada.

P

POSKITT, Frederick Richard, born 15th August 1900. Director of Studies. Education: Kilburn Grammar School, U.K., 1912-18; Downing College, Cambridge, 1919-21. Personal details: married to Margaret Embree Turner, B.A.(Oxon.), M.A.(Manchester). Appointments: Senior History Master, Colchester Royal Grammar School, 1921-25; Head of History Dept., Manchester Grammar School, 1926-33; Headmaster, Bolton School, 1933-66; Director, National Teachers' College, Kampala, Uganda, 1966—. Honours: C.B.E., 1962. Address: National Teachers' College, P.O. Box 20012, Kampala, Uganda.

R

REGNARD, L. Noel, born 29th August 1920. Accountant. Education: St. Joseph College. Married with children. Appointments: Accountant, Caltrex Department, Rogers & Co. Ltd., Port Louis; Manager, Distributing Station Ltd. Memberships: President, Editorial Committee, Dictionary of Mauritian Biography; Comm. Societe de l'Histoire de L'Ile Maurice; Royal Society of Arts & Sciences. Author of La Revue Retrospective de L'Ile Maurice, 6 vols., 1950-55. Address: Pierre de Sornay Street, Curepipe Rd., Mauritius.

RINGELHANN, Bela, born 19th February 1917. Physician. Education: Secondary School, St. Bernard Gymnasium, Eger, Hungary; Medical Faculty, Pazmany Peter University, Budapest. Personal details: came from a patrician family with liberal traditions; father is a mechanical engineer; married in 1949 to Gabriella Horanszky, a former welfare worker; 3 children. Appointments include: Registrar, St. Rokus Hospital, Budapest, 1941-45; Senior Registrar, St. Vincent Hospital, Eger, Hungary, 1945-51; Head of Dept. of Clinical Pathology, County Hospital, Eger, Hungary, 1951-64; Principal Research Officer, National Institute of Health, Ghana Academy of Sciences, Accra, 1964-67; Senior Lecturer, Dept of Pathology, Ghana Medical School, Accra, 1967-68; Associate Professor and Head of Dept. of Chemical Pathology, Ghana Medical School; Principal Investigator of a research project, supported by a grant by the World Health Organization, on the prevalence of haemoglobinopathies and related abnormalities in Ghana and their natural history. Memberships: European Society of Haematology, Basle, Switzerland, 1953—; Hungarian Society of Haematology Governing Body; Biochemical Society of Ghana. Publications: Earlier Scientific publications on various aspects of clinical biochemistry with a special interest in iron metabolism. Publications from Ghana mainly on abnormal haemoglobin diseases/sickle cell anaemia and other forms and on special problems of Chemical Pathology in Ghana. Honours, prizes, etc.: M.D., Budapest, 1941. Cand. Med. Sci., Budapest, 1958. Address: Ghana Medical School, P.O. Box 4236, Accra, Ghana.

ROMBA, Elie Adolphe, born 28th December 1942. Director of Taxes. Education: Lycée Felix Obove; Ecole Nationale des Impots de Paris, France. Appointments: Inspector of Taxes; Director, Registration Services, Lands & Conservator, Landed Property, Chad. Memberships: Rotary Club, Fort Lamy; Past Vice-President, World Student Christian Federation; Association for the Formation of Youth of Chad. Address: B.P. 428, Fort Lamy, Chad.

RUCH, Ernest Albert, born 4th November 1928. Reader in Philosophy. Education: L.Ph. (Licentiate in Philosophy), Gregorian University; Licentiate in Theology, ibid; D.Lit. & Phil., University of South Africa. Appointments: Reader in Philosophy & Head of Dept. of Philosophy, University of Botswana, Lesotho, & Swaziland; Administrator of Pius XII College House; later Superior of same. Member & former President, Society for the Advancement of Philosophy in South Africa. Publications include: Space & Time: A comparative study of the theories of Aristotle & Einstein; The Problem of Christian Philosophy (Philosophy Today), 1961; Philosophy of Science (S.A. Jrnl. of Phil.), 1966; various book reviews & other articles. Address: Dept. of Philosophy, U.B.L.S., Roma, Lesotho.

S

SAGOE, Michael Nun Quesi, born 18th March 1917. Barrister-at-Law; Solicitor of the Supreme Court of Nigeria. Education: St. Peter's School, Lagos, Nigeria; Tinubu Methodist, C.M.S. Grammar School, Lagos, 1927-28; Wesleyan Boys' High School, 1929-31;

Foundation Scholar, Igbobi College, Yaba, 1932-35; Council of Legal Education & Gray's Inn, London, U.K., 1945-48; London School of Economics, 1952; Harvard University Summer School, U.S.A., 1960. Personal details: married, 5 children. Appointments: Meteorological Observer, 1936; Primary School Teacher, 1936-38; Clerical Service, 1938-51; Registrar of Trade Unions, 1952; Deputy Federal Administrator-General of Nigeria, 1955-58; Federal Administrator-General of Nigeria, 1958-69; Acting Solicitor-General of the Federation of Nigeria, 1961; Chairman, Tribunal of Inquiry into Affairs of Lagos Executive Development Board, 1967; Acting Judge of the Lagos State High Court, 1968-69; Chairman, Lagos State Local Government Service Board, 1969–. Memberships include: Island Club, Lagos; Ancient Order of Foresters; Vice-President, Young Men's Christian League, Olowogbowo Church, Lagos; Chairman & Trustee, Lagos YMCA Board of Management, 1962-70; Chairman & Trustee, Nigeria National Council of YMCA, 1970–. Address: 63 Foresythe Street, Lagos, Nigeria.

SAWYERR, George Fashole Akilagpa, born 24th March 1939. Barrister-at-Law; Lecturer in Law. Education: LL.B., University of Durham, U.K., 1962; LL.M., University of London, 1965; LL.M., University of California, Berkeley, U.S.A., 1967. Personal details: married to Judith Sara, 1 daughter. Appointments: Lecturer & Senior Lecturer, Faculty of Law, University College, Dar es Salaam, Tanzania, 1964-70; Associate Dean, Faculty of Law, ibid, 1967-69; Director, Legal. Research Centre, 1969-70; Associate Editor, Eastern Africa Law Review, 1968-70; Lecturer, Faculty of Law, University of Ghana, 1970–; Member of Advisory Council on Vol. XI of the International Encyclopaedia of Comparative Law. Memberships: Hon. Society of Lincoln's Inn; English & Ghanaian Bars; International African Law Association. Publications: East African Law & Social Change, 1967; The Doctrine of Precedent in the Court of Appeal for Eastern Africa (with J. A. Hiller); articles in various legal periodicals. Recipient of many prizes & awards including America Jurisprudence Prize, 1967 & Research fellowships. Address: Faculty of Law, University of Ghana, Legon, Ghana.

SCHICK, Alan S., born U.S.A., 7th April 1937. Educator; Company Executive; Advertising Executive; Editor. Education: Milton Hershey Orphanage; George Junior Republic; J. F. Reynolds Jr. High School; Grove City High School; J. P. McCaskey High School; College of the Ozarks; Utah State University; B.Sc., U.S.A.F.I.; B.Th., Comparative Religion, S.K.S.R.; Diploma in Ceramics, Brooklyn Museum School, N.Y.; University of Chicago Downtown Center; Army Training Courses in CIC, Information Specialist; Penland School of Handicrafts; Richland County Art School; The School, Art Institute of Chicago, III.; University of South Carolina. Appointments include: Fire Control Aid, U.S. National Park Service; Smokejumper, U.S. Forest Service; Mines and Lands Examiner, U.S. Bureau of Land Management; Consulting Forester; Airborne (Paratrooper) Infantryman, U.S. Army, 1968-70; Copywriter, Advertising Layout, Booksellers, Inc.; Special Projects Editor, Education Programmer, Science Editor, Accelerated Instructions Methods Corp.; Education Officer (volunteer under sponsorship of Unitarian-Universalist Service Committee, Boston), Technical Adviser in Programmed Learning, Ministry of Education, H.H. The Kabaka's Government, Kingdom of Buganda, Uganda, 1963; Teacher, seconded to Ndejje Senior Secondary School; Ag/Headmaster, ibid, 1965-66; Research Project (Volunteer), Uganda Game Department, Northern Acholi, 1966; Teacher of Science, Lubiri Senior Secondary School, Ministry of Education, Uganda, 1966-67; Assistant General Manager, General Botanics East Africa Ltd., Sales & Administrative Manager, Copywriter and Design Layout, Skyline Advertising (Uganda) Ltd., 1967–. The Editor, Uganda Publishing House (an organ of the Milton Obote Foundation), 1968. Memberships include: American Civil Liberties Union; Student Non-Violent Coordinating Committee; American Aero-Space Education Foundation; Society of American Foresters; International Parachuting Congress; Utah State Sky-Diving Club; American Motorcycle Association; Alpha Psi Omega; East African Wildlife Society; Uganda Motorcycle Club; Kampala Motorcycle Sports Club. Address: Uganda Publishing House, P.O. Box 2923, Kampala, Uganda, East Africa.

SLATER, Alan Wilfred, born 17th May 1923. Civil Engineer. Education: Primary: Colebrook School, Bognor Regis, U.K.; Secondary: North Vancouver, B.C., Canada; University: U.B.C., Civil, 1951. Appointments: Adviser to Uganda Government; Regional Inspector Engineer, Public Works Engineering; Regional Engineer Dept. of Highways B.C., Kamloops. Memberships: P. Eng., B.C.; Canadian Legion; C.N.A. Publications: Engineering in Uganda (article in P. Eng. Journal), 1968. Address: 1275 East 27th St., North Vancouver, B.C., Canada.

SSENTONGO, Joseph Mugema, born 18th May 1938. Librarian. Education: Cambridge School Certificate; Certificate Library Studies (Makerere); Diploma in Librarianship (University of East Africa); Certificate in Documentation (UNESCO), 1969. Personal details: married, 6 children. Appointments: Library Assistant, Makerere University, Kampala, Uganda & Senior Librarian Assistant, ibid, 1963-70; Librarian, East African Development Bank, 1970–. Memberships: General Secretary, Trade Union; Secretary, Parents' Association. Publications: History & Development of Makerere University College Libraries (University of East Africa). Address: c/o E.A. Development Bank, P.O. Box 7128, Kampala, Uganda.

T

TCHOUA, Isaac, born 15th January 1900. Planter; Manufacturer; Merchant. Personal details: married, 9 children, 5 surviving (1 son, 4 daughters). Appointments: Planter, Milong, 1927; Merchant & Trader, Nsba, 1925-31;

Conveyor, ibid, 1926; Manufacturer, Nsba-Melong, 1936—. Honours: Noir (Medaille), Nsba, 1954. Address: B.P. 91, Nkongsamba, Cameroons.

TENAILLE, Michel, born 22nd June 1907. Petroleum Geologist. Education: Lic. in Sciences; Engineering Diploma, National School of Petrol. Married, 4 children. Appointments: Petroleum Engineer, Petroleum Research Society, Morocco, 1931-38; ibid, French Petroleum Company, Venezuela, 1939; Deputy Director, Exploration, Petroleum Research Society, 1940-41; Head of Petroleum Section, Mining Research Service of Algeria, 1942-45; Director, National Society for Research & Exploitation of Petroleum in Algeria, 1946-55; President/Director-General, African Society for Petroleum, 1956-66; President, African Society for Refining, 1961—; Centre of Studies & Petroleum Information affiliated to the Bureau of Petroleum Research & the National Society of Aquitaine Petroleum, 1962-68; Director for the North Sea, ibid, 1963-65; Director for the Americans, General Direction Exploration-Production, ELF-ERAP, 1966—; President, Elf Oil Canada, d'Elf Petroleum U.S.A., d'Elf Petroleos De Costa Rica, d'Elf Petroleum Surinam, d'Elf Argentina; President/Director-General, Anonymous French Society of Researches for Exploitation of Petroleum, 1966—; President/Director-General, French Society for Research & Exploitation of Petroleum in Algeria, 1966—; Vice-President, SN.REPAL, 1966—. Memberships: R.F.T.P.; A.A.P.G.; Tennis Club of Paris. Honours: Officer of the Legion of Honour; Chevalier du Merite Saharien; Commander of the National Order of Senegal. Address: 23 Avenue Rapp, Paris 7, France.

TESSEMA (H.E. Dejazmach), Kebede, born 24th March 1902. Government Official. Married, 10 children. Appointments: Clerk, Ministry of Pen, 1915; in personal attendance, Imperial Palace, 1917; Chief of the Imperial Household, 1924; Chief of the Imperial Palace Transport, 1930; Director-General of Medals, Decorations, & Imperial Stores, 1931; Director-General of the Imperial Palace, 1935; Governor of Wollega Province w. rank of Fitawrari, 1941; Lord Mayor of Addis Ababa, 1942; Governor-General of Gojam Province w. rank of Dejazmach, 1946; President of the Senate, 1951; Chief Justice, Supreme Imperial Court, 1952; Lord Mayor of Addis Ababa (for 2nd time), 1954; Deputy Governor-General of Shoa Province, 1955; Minister of State, Prime Minister's Office, 1956; Minister, Ministry of Stores & Pensions, 1957; Member of Senate, 1958; Vice-President of Senate, 1959; Minister of State & Chief of Staff of Imperial Territorial Army & Minister of Stores & Pensions, 1962; Chief of Staff of the Imperial Territorial Army w. rank of Minister, 1966; Crown Counsel, 1967. Memberships: Imperial Ethiopian Government Ministerial Council; Ethiopian Patriotic Assn.; Chairman, Menelek II Memorial Assn.; Jerusalem Memorial Assn.; Ethiopian Orthodox Church Board. Honours: Grand Officer of Menelek; Commander of the Trinity; Ethiopian Star of Honour with Cordon; Menelek II with Cordon; Hero of the St. Georges with 2 bars; Patriot's Medal with 2 bars; Medal of Exile with 4 bars; Star of Victory. Address: P.O. Box 602, Addis Ababa, Ethiopia.

THANGARAJ, Sankaranarayanan, born India, 3rd December 1934. Rubber Technologist; Engineer. Education: B.Sc.; B.Comm.; A.M.I.E.T.; A.M.I.C.E.(Chemical). Appointments: with Fenner Cockill (India), Ltd., 1954-59; Works Manager, Rubber Technologist, Brahadam Group, Rubber Industries, 1959-62; Works Manager, Rubber Technologist, Rasmi Cables Pvt., Ltd., 1962-64; Works Manager; Rubber Technologist, Radiant Rubber Industries Pvt., Ltd., 1964-65; Works Manager, Rubber Technologist, Rasmi Cables, Group Rubber Industries, 1965-66; Technical Manager, Rubber Technologist, Plastics & Rubber Industries Ltd., 1966—; Technical Adviser for following: General Latex & Rubber Industries; Star Latex Industries; Sharada Group Latex & Rubber Industries. Fellow of Indian Commercial Assn. Memberships: Institution of the Rubber Industry, London; The Society of Chemical Industry; British Assn. of Chemists; A.F.I.C.E.P., Paris, France; India Society of Engineers; International Institution of Engineers; Associate, East African Institution of Engineers; Affiliate Member, Division of Rubber Chemistry, American Chemical Society; Associate, British Institute of Management & Institution of Works Managers. Address: P.O. Box 6957, Nairobi, Kenya.

TUKEI, Peter Mark, born 23rd November 1936. Medical Research Worker. Education: M.B., Ch.B., University of East Africa, Makerere Medical School, Uganda, 1963; M.Sc.(Virology), University of Birmingham, U.K., 1970. Personal details: married, 3 children. Appointments: Senior House Officer, Ministry of Health, Uganda; Medical Research Officer, East African Community; Principal Medical Research Officer, ibid. Memberships: Uganda Medical Association; Former Editor, Mulago Medical Journal, 1962; Deputy Captain of Tennis, Entebbe Institute. Publications: A Calender for Assessment of the age of Baganda Children (Journal of Trop. Medicine & Hygiene), 1963; Yellow Fever Immunity Surveys in Northern Uganda, Kenya 1966-67 (Bulletin of W.H.O.), 1968; Virus Isolations from Ixodid Ticks (East African Medical Journal), 1970; also contributor to Journal of National Cancer Institute; E.A.V.R.I. Annual Reports. Recipient of Prize for Best Paediatric Student of the Year, 1961-62. Address: E.A.V.R.I., Box 49, Entebbe, Uganda.